34th Annual Edition

GUNS ILLUSTRATED™ 2002

Edited by
Ken Ramage

© 2001
by Krause Publications
Printed in the United States of America.
All rights reserved.

No portion of this publication may be reproduced or transmitted in any form or by any means, electronic or mechanical, including photocopy, recording, or any information storage and retrieval system, without permission in writing from the publisher, except by a reviewer who may quote brief passages in a critical article or review to be printed in a magazine or newspaper, or electronically transmitted on radio or television.

Manuscripts, contributions and inquiries, including first class return postage, should be sent to the GUNS ILLUSTRATED Editorial Offices, Krause Publications, 700 E. State Street, Iola, WI 54990-0001. All materials received will receive reasonable care, but we will not be responsible for their safe return. Material accepted is subject to our requirements for editing and revisions. Author payment covers all rights and title to the accepted material, including photos, drawings and other illustrations. Payment is at our current rates.

CAUTION: Technical data presented here, particularly technical data on the handloading and on firearms adjustment and alteration, inevitably reflects individual experience with particular equipment and components under specific circumstances the reader cannot duplicate exactly. Such data presentations therefore should be used for guidance only and with caution. Krause Publications, Inc., accepts no responsibility for results obtained using this data.

Published by

krause publications

700 E. State Street • Iola, WI 54990-0001
Telephone: 715/445-2214
Web: www.krause.com

Please call or write for our free catalog.

Our toll-free number to place an order or obtain a free catalog is 800-258-0929 or please use our regular business telephone 715-445-2214 for editorial comment and further information.

Library of Congress Catalog Number: 69-11342
ISBN: 0-87349-296-X

—GUNS ILLUSTRATED STAFF—

EDITOR
Ken Ramage

ASSOCIATE EDITOR
Ross Bielema

CONTRIBUTING EDITORS
Holt Bodinson
Doc Carlson
John Haviland
John Malloy
Layne Simpson
Hal Swiggett

Editorial Comments and Suggestions

We're always looking for feedback on our books. Please let us know what you like about this edition. If you have suggestions for articles you'd like to see in future editions, please contact.

Ken Ramage/Guns Illustrated
700 East State St.
Iola, WI 54990
email: ramagek@krause.com

About Our Covers...

Revolvers from Gary Reeder Custom Guns in Flagstaff, Arizona appear on both the front and back covers of this 34th Edition of Guns Illustrated. Today's custom gun business evolved from the Pistol Parlor gun shop founded some 22 years ago – and still operated by Reeder's wife, Colleen.

Initially, Reeder customized only single-shot pistols – the T/C Contender and Remington XP-100 – then expanded into an ever-increasing offering of custom revolvers based predominantly on Ruger single-action and double-action revolver models, plus one from Freedom Arms.

Today Reeder offers over three dozen custom revolver series, including the hunting and cowboy models on our covers, plus custom single-shot pistols based on the Thompson/Center Contender and Encore, custom hunting rifles, one-of-a-kind firearms and restoration services.

The Front Cover
Three hunting handguns from Reeder's extensive line include *(top to bottom)* the **African Hunter**, **Ultimate 41** and the **Alaskan Hunter**.

The Back Cover
Three cowboy guns from Reeder's custom line include *(top to bottom)* the **Trail Rider Classic, Doc Holliday Classic** and the **Tombstone Classic**.

For more information on these, and other Reeder guns and services, contact Gary Reeder Custom Guns at 2710 North Steves Blvd., Ste #22, Flagstaff AZ 86004/520-527-4100; FAX 520-527-0840. Website: www.reedercustomguns.com

Guns Illustrated 2002

The Standard Reference for Today's Firearms
CONTENTS

About Our Covers 3

FEATURES:

Remington's Model 710 Rifle
by Ralph M. Lermayer 6

Gunmaking in the 21st Century
by Robert Hausman 11

Modern Firearms Maintenance
by Robert Hausman 15

NEW PRODUCT REPORTS:

Handgun News: Autoloading Pistols
by John Malloy 21

Handgun News: Revolvers, Single-Shots & Others
by Hal Swiggett 37

Rifle Report!
by Layne Simpson 42

Shotgun Update
by John Haviland 50

Muzzleloader News
by "Doc" Carlson 58

Ammo Update!
by Holt Bodinson 65

Shooter's Marketplace 74

Page 57

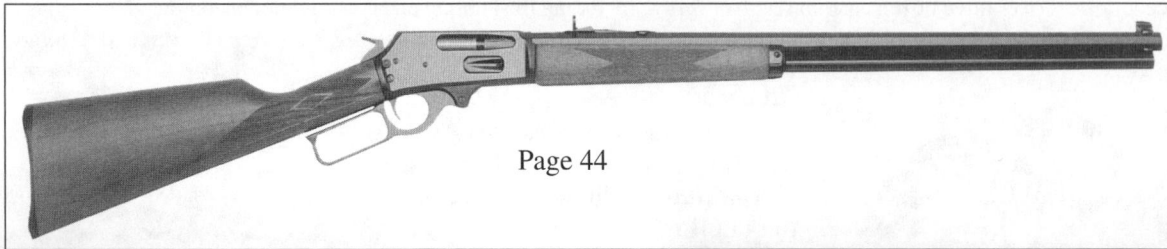

Page 44

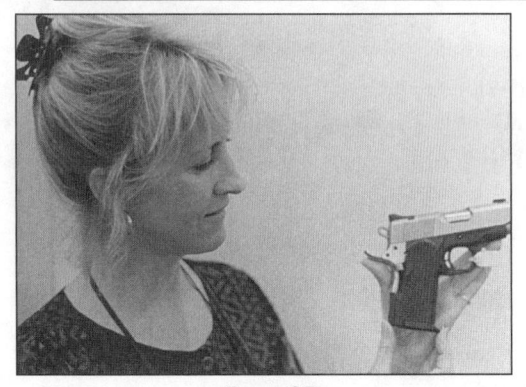

Page 27

Page 73

4 • GUNS ILLUSTRATED

CATALOG OF TODAY'S FIREARMS

GUNDEX® 88

SEMI-CUSTOM ARMS

HANDGUNS
- Autoloaders 102-108
- Revolvers 109-112
- Single-Shot 113

RIFLES
- Bolt-Action Rifles 114-116
- Autoloaders 117-118
- Double Rifles 119
- Single-Shot 120

SHOTGUNS 121

COMMERCIAL ARMS

HANDGUNS
- Autoloaders 130-162
- Competition 163-168
- Double-Action Revolvers 169-178
- Single-Action Revolvers 179-187
- Miscellaneous 188-191

RIFLES
- Centerfire Rifles
  - Autoloaders 192-197
  - Lever & Slide 198-204
  - Bolt Action 205-226
  - Single Shot 227-235
  - Drillings, Combination Guns,
    Double Rifles 236-238
- Rimfire Rifles
  - Autoloaders 239-242
  - Lever & Slide 243-244
  - Bolt Actions & Single Shots ... 245-250
- Competition Rifles
  - Centerfire & Rimfire 251-256

SHOTGUNS
- Autoloaders 257-263
- Slide Actions 264-268
- Over/Unders 269-281
- Side-by-Sides 282-286
- Bolt Actions & Single Shots 287-290
- Military & Police 291-292

BLACKPOWDER
- Single-Shot Pistols 293-294
- Revolvers 295-298
- Muskets & Rifles 299-313
- Shotguns 314

AIRGUNS
- Handguns 315-318
- Long Guns 319-327

REFERENCE
- Directory of the Arms Trade 328

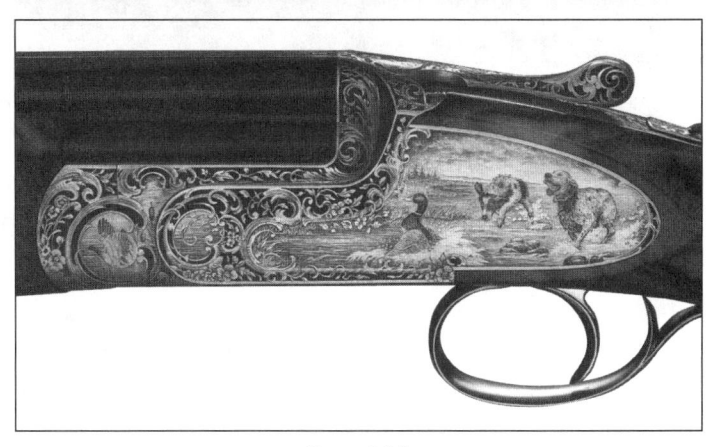

Page 128

Page 152

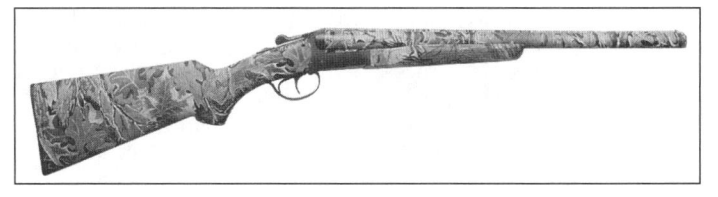

Page 286

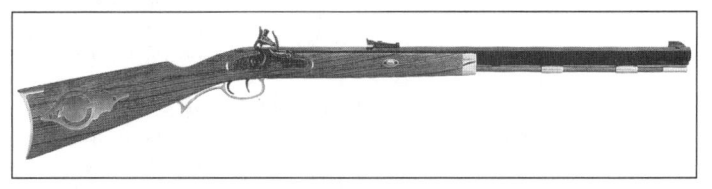

Page 299

34TH EDITION, 2002

The M710 is a rugged rifle that will be at home under any hunting conditions.

Remington's Model 710

A no-frills, hardcore hunting rifle for the new millennium

by Ralph M. Lermayer

RIFLE ENTHUSIASTS HAVE become quite familiar and comfortable with contemporary bolt-action designs. We understand them, because no matter how much we stretch or shorten them, modify or redesign extractors, relocate locking lugs or alter magazines, they are all modifications of the basic Mauser design that's been around for over a hundred years. Not only are they functionally similar, but manufacturing is done pretty much as it was at the turn of the century. A machined and hardened all-steel, flat-sided receiver houses the self-cocking bolt and fire-control mechanism and provides recesses for the bolt lugs to lock into. Barrels thread to the receiver, and the barreled action is secured in a stock. The system is proven and is the foundation for the majority of bolt-action rifles from economy to elegant custom designs, but it's a costly technique, and a changing market may be mandating a new look at how things are done.

Those of us with racks of rifles with a caliber for every application think nothing of dropping five or six hundred dollars every time a new fancy strikes. We don't hesitate to spend the same – or more – on a scope and mounts, but we're the diminishing die-hard core. The future of the shooting sports rests with other shooters, the budget-conscious whose priorities must be home and family before hobby, and the entry-level beginner who gets that first rifle as a gift or buys one to try a hunt with the gang. This vital market is dollar-sensitive, and the availability of an accurate, reliable rifle – complete with scope – at an affordable price is crucial to attracting those shooters to our ranks.

This was the challenge Remington's C.E.O. Tommy Milner gave his team of engineers, *"Build a quality bolt-action rifle, reliable and accurate, that will retail, with a 3-9X scope, mounted and boresighted, for $350.00 complete."* A tall order, but the Remington Model 710 meets that challenge, and does it nicely. Building such a rifle called for a radical departure from tradition, a new approach – and the application of materials and techniques not previously used in building rifles.

A New Kind Of Receiver

Conventional receivers must be extensively machined. Cutouts for trigger installation, lug recesses, bolt guides, barrel threads and a host of other dimensions must be cut, then polished, to create the close tolerance detail for a multi-function receiver. Locking lugs on the bolt, to withstand the pressure generated on firing, lock into recesses cut into the receiver. Receivers must be made of very hard steel to prevent enlargement of those recesses under continual battering. Additionally, a portion of the chamber containing the head of the cartridge is located in the receiver, with the balance of the chamber in the barrel. Conventional receivers are designed for strength, rigidity and to contain high pressures. This is not required in the M710.

In the M710, the receiver starts out as a level 1 3/8- by 6 1/2-inch stainless steel hollow tube. Minimal cutouts for bolt handle, safety, magazine, etc. are machined into that basic tube. Those cuts, as well as the holes for the scope bases, stock screw and bolt release are all made in one pass in an automated CNC machine. There are no barrel threads. The M710 barrel is hydraulically pressed under tremendous pressure into the receiver tube, then a removable polymer insert, with all the finite dimensions pre-molded, is inserted inside the hollow receiver. The insert material is one of those new polymers that is said to be stronger than steel, won't wear or rust, and is slick enough to permanently lubricate the bolt. The use of a polymer takes nothing away from the rifle's strength or performance. The tang, half of the trigger housing, and bolt guide rails are molded into that insert. Most importantly, there are no locking lug cutouts. In the M710, bolt lugs lock into recesses machined directly into the barrel. The entire cartridge chamber is located inside the rear of the barrel, eliminating all but the most basic strength and pressure demands on the receiver. With the strength requirement

6 GUNS ILLUSTRATED

At a recent Remington seminar, author was able to wring out a completed M710. Accuracy ranged from sub-one inch to over two, averaging one and a half inches overall.

removed, M710 receivers serve no purpose other than to guide the bolt and house the trigger assembly. Under that arrangement, the insert makes perfect sense.

The Barrel

Conventional M700 barrels are hammer-forged. A short, twelve-inch blank is installed on a mandrel, which determines final bore size and impresses the rifling. The barrel blank is then hammered repeatedly over the mandrel until it stretches to a twenty-two or twenty-four inch length. The process creates molecular havoc and the finished barrel must be stress-relieved by superheating and cooling four times before it is ready to shoot, a time-consuming and expensive process.

M710 barrels are button-rifled. They start out as a full-length blank with a slightly undersize bore pre-drilled. Then a button is pulled or pushed through the bore to impress the rifling and set final bore dimensions. Debates over which technique makes a better barrel are ongoing, but it's not disputed that button rifling takes half the time, costs half as much and results in a smoother bore. The question is one of hardness. Button rifling calls for somewhat softer steel, perfectly adequate for barrels, but too soft for locking-lug recesses. These recesses must be extremely hard to prevent enlargement under recoil. Remington solved the problem by retempering the chamber area and lug recesses of the finished barrel to proper hardness levels after rifling, then a turn on the lathe to final dimension, a single stress relief, and final polishing. This method creates a quality barrel faster, at half the cost. Barrels are twenty-two inches, drilled and tapped for the provided scope, and finished with a target-style, recessed, protective crown.

A New "*Old*" Trigger

The M710 trigger functions exactly the same as the trigger on the Model 700, but half of its housing is molded as a permanent part of the polymer insert. After the parts are assembled into that half, a metal sideplate is installed to complete the trigger. Remove that plate and a gunsmith can polish, hone, adjust or change springs to custom tune as you would any M700 trigger. Overtravel and sear adjustments are still accessible from the outside. Set from the factory, it's a horrendous four and a half pounds, but my 'smith adjusted it to two pounds. It's crisp and breaks clean – and you can't tell it from the standard M700.

The Bolt

Remington's next departure from the M700 was to use three locking lugs on the bolt instead of the tradi-

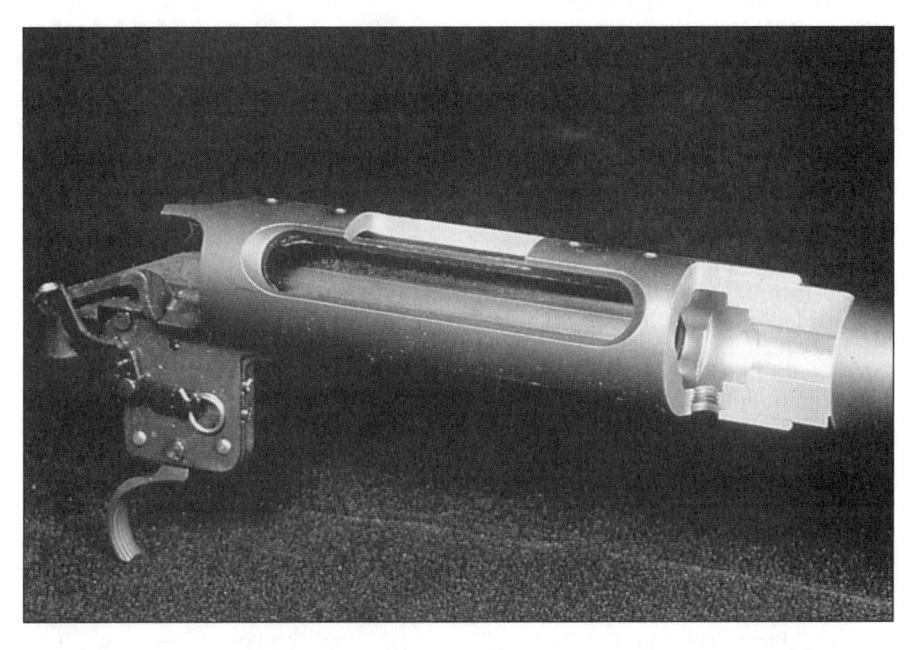

The M710 receiver is a hollow tube, housing an insert made of space-age polymer.

34th EDITION, 2002 **7**

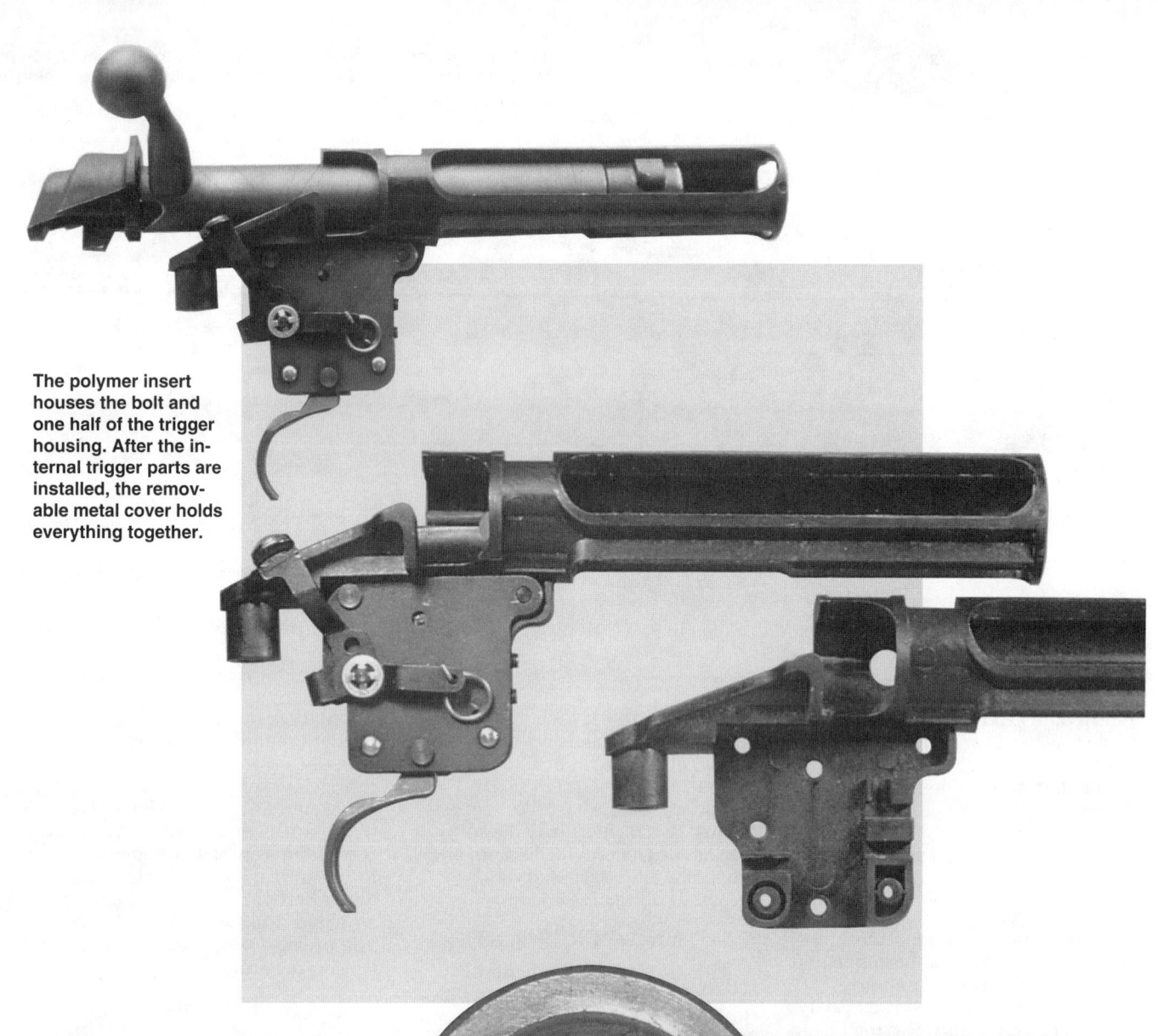

The polymer insert houses the bolt and one half of the trigger housing. After the internal trigger parts are installed, the removable metal cover holds everything together.

◀ **Three locking lugs** *(instead of the usual two)* **lock directly into cutouts in the barrel. The M710 cartridge chamber is located entirely inside the barrel.**

tional two. When milling bolt lug recesses into a narrow, flat receiver, two opposing slots are the most practical, but moving the lug recesses into the barrel removes space constraints. By using three, lockup is stronger, and bolt throw is reduced to a short sixty degrees instead of the ninety-degree throw found on the standard M700. Cycling the bolt to chamber a new round is faster, and the bolt handle need not have a severe bend in it to clear a scope during cycling.

Besides the extra locking lug, the M710 bolt houses another new feature that will soon be standard on all Remington bolt guns – and may even be incorporated into their shotgun line. A key slot, located in a shroud at the rear of the bolt, allows you to lock up the action and disable the rifle. When locked, it can't fire. Two "J"-shaped keys are supplied with each rifle. We don't know yet if all rifles will use the same key. It's an inconvenience but, like it or not, that's where this industry is going.

I'd be sure and have an extra key on hand before I headed for the backcountry. A compartment in the sling would be the perfect place to store one or, as with any lock, you can choose to leave it unlocked if this feature doesn't appeal to you.

The bolt releases via a tab located on the left side of the receiver. Raise the tab and the bolt slides out. Unfortunately, the tab does not return to the locked position automatically. If you forget and leave it up, the first time you cycle the bolt it will come all the way out. That could get cheeky on a hunt. I suspect you would do it only once.

The Stock

Besides providing a functional handle, a rifle stock must contain the recoil generated by high-pressure loads. Recoil drives the rifle's barrel and receiver back against the stock that is held solidly against the shooter's shoulder. To prevent recoil from shifting the action position and battering the stock, a recoil lug, like a washer, is usually placed between the barrel and the receiver. That lug extends down into a matching cutout or recoil lug recess in the stock to

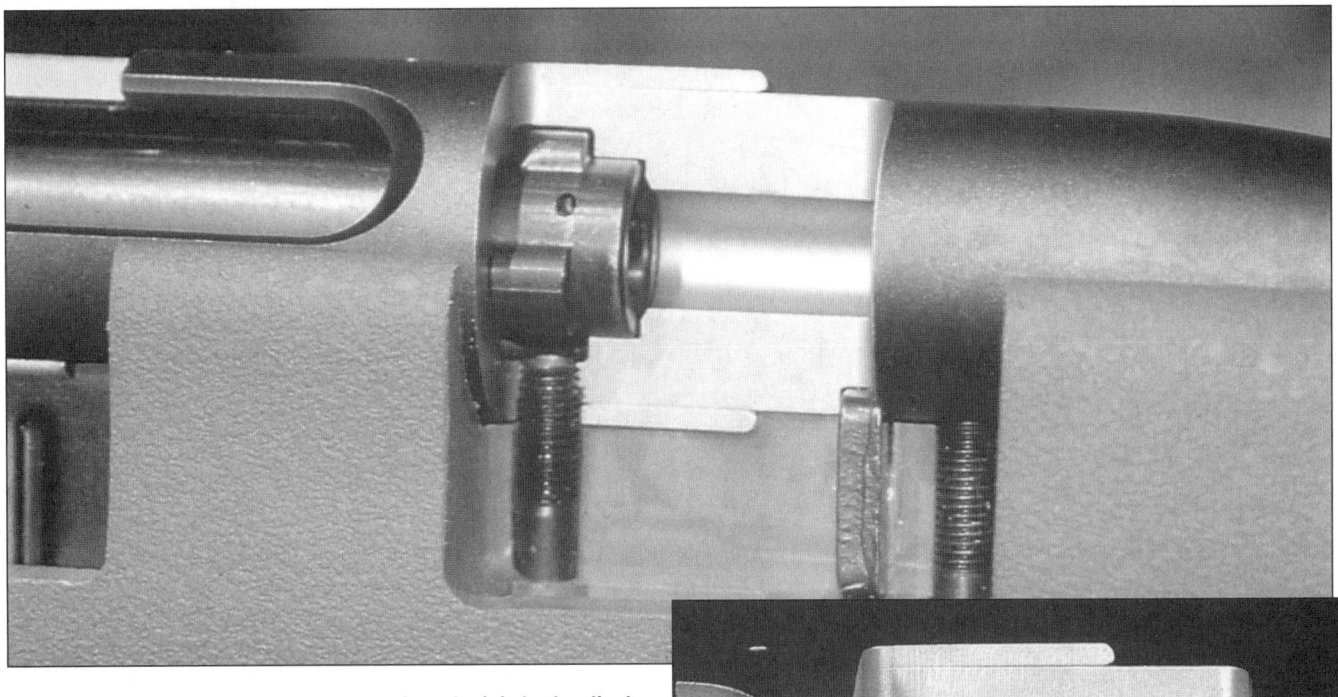

The non-removable M710 barrel has no threads; it is hydraulically pressed into the receiver under tremendous pressure.

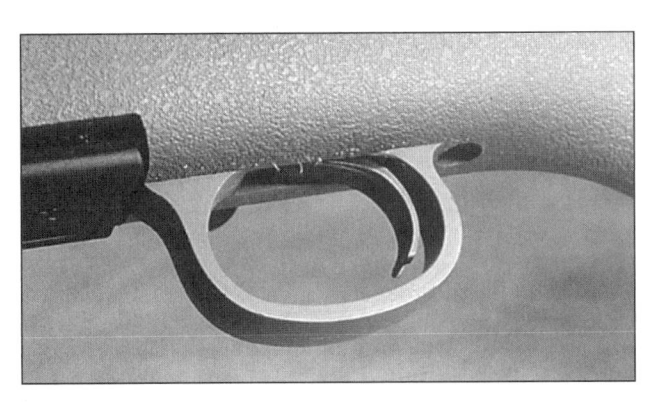

The extremely stout triggerguard is molded as a permanent part of the 710 stock.

keep everything in place. It fits hard against a solid shoulder in the wood or composite and prevents movement.

The M710 doesn't use an integral washer recoil lug. It's not practical with the press fit between barrel and receiver. Instead, a 1/4-inch slot is milled in the bottom of the barrel. A hardened steel lug is then permanently installed in the stock. When you put the barrel and stock together, the lug fits into the cutout in the barrel and the match-up keeps everything together during recoil. Some writers will no doubt wince at this approach, but after shooting the rifle extensively, I can say that it works. There was no shifting of the point of impact after firing several boxes of factory ammo. Time will tell how it will hold up after hundreds or thousands of rounds, but Remington engineers have test-fired the M710 for several thousand rounds and claim no shifting. It's different, but effective. Two screws about two inches apart, one on either side of the integral lug, lock the barreled action to the stock. One concern I do have about the lockup is in the average diameter of the holes these screws go through. It appears as though there is room for shifting here, although I couldn't detect any during testing. If I owned a M710, and I will own one someday, I would insert two steel pillars through these holes, contoured to match the barrel radius, and effectively pillar-bed the action with minimal effort. Remington has no plans to do this, but I predict the after-market accessory suppliers, like Brownells, will jump to fill this need.

The stock is made of a very strong composite built to classic

SPECIFICATIONS: Remington Model 710	
Chamberings:	30-06 Springfield
	270 Winchester
Barrel:	22 inch; blue matte
Sights:	3-9x Bushnell Sharpshooter; Weaver bases & rings
Weight:	Scoped - 8.2 pounds
	Without scope - 7.1 pounds
Stock:	Synthetic, gray, textured
Magazine:	Four round capacity, removable
MSRP:	$359.00 with scope

34th EDITION, 2002

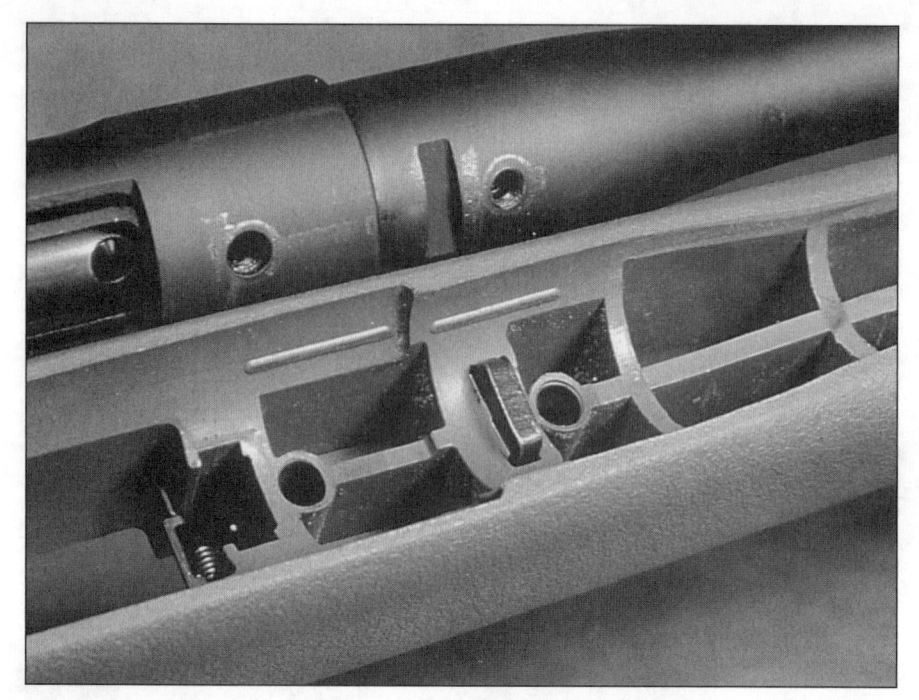

Instead of the usual recoil lug, the M710 uses a milled slot in the barrel that mates to a corresponding lug permanently mounted in the stock. No shifting was detected during the author's initial tests.

lines and proportions, with a low cheekpiece, recoil pad and sling swivel studs attached. It's finished in a dull gray, non-slip surface. It feels good, balances well and gets on target fast. There is no separate metal floorplate or triggerguard as found in standard M700s. Instead, the triggerguard is molded as part of the stock. The guard is extremely stout, and it would take whale of a wallop to break it. The rest of what would be the normal floorplate area is simply a rectangular cutout that accepts a polymer, detachable four-round magazine.

I like the magazine. Cartridges are staggered inside, but feed in a straight line. It fits flush with the stock with no uncomfortable bulge. It never failed to feed even when I tried to jam it with rapid rechambering. One complaint: I was able to slip it in backwards, another thing I suspect you would do only once. A molded-in tab and corresponding cutout in the opening to prevent this would be a nice feature on future designs but, overall, it's a well-designed, perfectly adequate magazine, and spares should be very inexpensive.

At The Range

The M710 will be available in 270 Winchester and 30-06 Springfield. I had two occasions to test fire the 30-06. The first was one of two early prototypes, not even serialized. Tolerances on that rifle were intentionally very loose. The locking lug in the stock was removable for demonstration purposes. Receiver stock screw holes were oversize, as was the lug cutout in the stock. In spite of all of that, that prototype rifle still held to four inches at one hundred yards with a variety of factory ammunition. The second rifle was a finished product brought to the Remington Writers Seminar in Florida earlier this year. While the other writers were testing a variety of products, I took three boxes of 180-grain Remington CoreLokt factory loads, and retired to an end bench to see what it would do. The M710 carried the Bushnell 3-9x that it will come with. When all sixty rounds were gone, I had an assortment of five-shot groups that averaged about an inch and a half. Some were the neat little sub-one inch clusters that you like to cut out and carry in your wallet, while others exceeded two and a half inches depending on what was going on around me. I never cleaned the bore or allowed it to cool. Stellar performance? Not hardly, but predictable and exactly what you can expect from the average hunting rifle anywhere, regardless of make or cost. This is precisely what the M710 was designed for: dependable, reliable hunting performance from a rugged rifle at a very affordable price.

No matter how many rifles are in your rack, it's a safe bet a special one always gets the nod when a serious hunt is planned. Usually not the prettiest or the *"latest & greatest"* loaded with bells and whistles. No, it's that well-used rifle stuck in the corner – the one full of scars and dents, each scratch bringing memories of a great hunt. You don't choose it because it's pretty, but because you know it can be counted on take the abuse of a tough hunt and still get the job done when that hard-earned shot finally presents itself. The definition of a great rifle reads *durable, accurate*, and *reliable*. If it's also one you can buy at a bargain price, so much the better. Such a rifle is the new Remington Model 710.

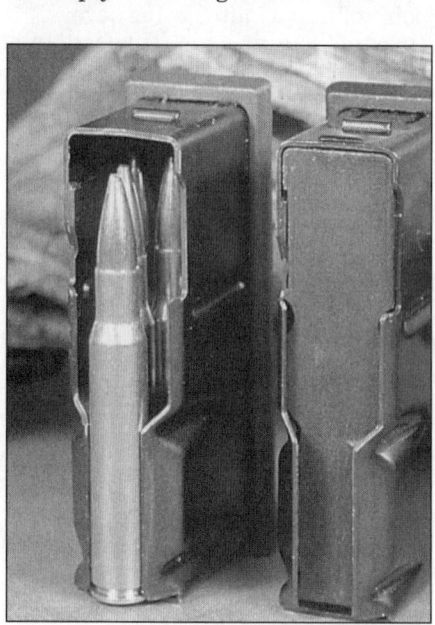

The M710 removable box magazine fits flush with the bottom of the stock. Cartridges are staggered internally, but feed in a straight line.

The Carbon 15 Rifle from Professional Ordnance.

Gunmaking in the 21st Century

*New Materials & Technologies
Show the Future of Firearms Construction*

by Bob Hausman

INNOVATION HAS BEEN the hallmark of the firearms industry throughout its approximately 500-year history. Beginning in the 1200s, when Europeans first learned how to use gunpowder, the first arms using the new substance were cannons. These soon developed into man-portable hand cannons – the first handguns. The earliest rifles were developed in the late 1500s, while smokeless powder was invented some 300 years later. The advent of self-contained cartridges followed shortly thereafter.

With much of the founding work on firearms development completed, manufacturers today focus on improving time-proven designs with changes in firearms construction materials and the methods by which they are manufactured.

Remington Arms Co. recently announced a radical departure in firearm ignition systems with its EtronX™ electronic ignition system. Brass-cased centerfire cartridges are fired by a completely non-mechanical system that ignites primers by means of an electrical pulse – resulting in virtually instantaneous ignition.

Here's how it works. Remington's proven Model 700™ rifle was the platform chosen for the EtronX electronic fire control – which has no moving parts other than the trigger. There is no sear to be released, no firing pin to strike the primer. Instead, an internal electrical circuit sends a charge to a newly developed electrically responsive primer contained within EtronX cartridges. Closing the rifle's bolt establishes contact between the firing pin and the primer. When the trigger is pulled, the electronic circuit sends an electrical pulse through the firing pin directly to the primer.

This all happens nearly instantaneously (actually .0000027 seconds), virtually eliminating the effects of barrel movement while pulling the trigger. In fact, the bullet exits the barrel before a conventional rifle's mechanical firing pin could even hit the primer. The system's trigger pull is exceptionally crisp, with 36% less travel than standard triggers. A single, replaceable nine-volt battery located in the rifle's buttstock powers this advanced system.

A light-emitting diode on top of the grip indicates system status, including whether the rifle is in *"FIRE"* or *"SAFE"* mode, if a cartridge has been chambered and even if the battery is low on power. As an additional safety feature, a key switch located in the bottom of the pistol grip must be turned *"ON"* to enable the electronic system. The EtronX rifle is available in 22-250, 220 Swift and 243 Winchester. For those who reload, EtronX primers are available as components, allowing cartridges to be reloaded with the same amount and type of powder as would be used be used for a rifle with a mechanical firing system.

Lightweight Rifle Barrels

Another area of rifle research and development has focused on rifle barrel design and construction. For example, Magnum Research, the company known for bringing shooters the massive Desert Eagle pistol line, now offers ultra-lightweight graphite rifle barrels for a variety of actions. The uncannily accurate Magnum Lite™ graphite barrel is a Magnum Research exclusive. At 13.04 ounces (in 22 LR and 22 WMR), it's 75% lighter than a conventional bull barrel, yet delivers the

Remington Arms Co. EtronX™ electronic ignition system.

34th EDITION, 2002

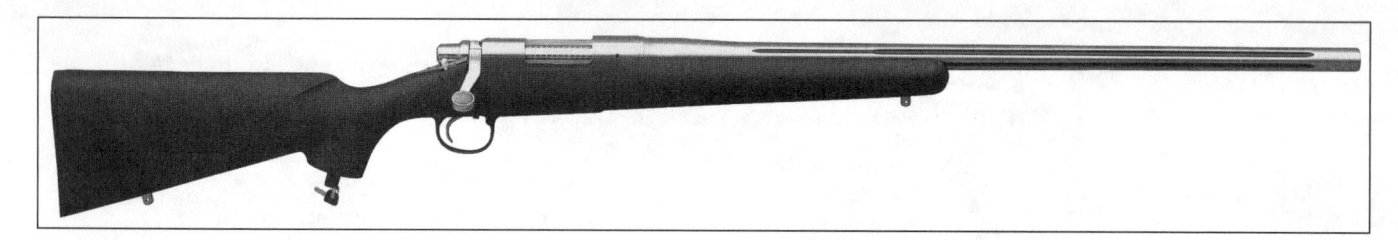

Remington's proven Model 700™ rifle is the platform chosen for the EtronX electronic fire control.

S&W Model 340 Sc.

S&W AirLite Model 340 Sc PD.

S&W AirLite Model 386 Sc PD.

equivalent accuracy of its much-heavier counterpart.

Magnum Lite barrels eliminate many of the shortcomings of steel barrels as they will not twist, walk or whip. The patented uni-directional graphite fiber construction results in an ultra-straight barrel that is six times stiffer than steel, eliminating concerns over barrel harmonics. Unlike steel, graphite dissipates heat, so the barrel stays up to 43% cooler, to eliminate "walking" of shots on the target. The barrels are available as part of a complete rifle, or separately for retrofitting to existing rifles in your battery. Magnum Research offers its Mountain Eagle rifles in 223 Rem., 280 Rem., 7mm Mag., 30-06 Spfld. and 300 Win. Mag. Magnum Lite barrels are also available for the 10/22 action in 22 LR and 22 WMR.

Accessory manufacturer Butler Creek™ is offering new match-grade lightweight steel barrels for the ever-popular Sturm, Ruger 10/22 rifle which are designed to out-perform the heavier "bull barrels" available for this rifle from the Ruger factory. Butler Creek's barrels feature a tensioning system and aluminum sleeves to provide competitive shooters and serious varmint hunters a high degree of accuracy, light weight and cooling capacity.

The 18-inch barrels (.920-inch outside diameter) are available in a black "vented" model with a slotted anodized aluminum outer sleeve and a silver cooling "finned" model with a radially-grooved anodized aluminum sleeve. In addition to the premium tensioning system, each model utilizes the Bentz Match Chamber and a recessed target crown to provide superior accuracy. Designed to be light in weight as well as accurate, each barrel is easier to carry and use over prolonged hunts and shooting sessions than rifles equipped with conventional heavy target barrels.

"These new match-grade barrels are designed to provide precise, consistent accuracy that far exceeds what would be expected of a typical lightweight barrel," said Tom Marx, Butler Creek's director of marketing. *"Our premium tensioning system adds rigidity and straightening pressure to the barrel, thereby adjusting its har-monics and improving its accuracy."*

During Butler Creek's manufacturing process, weight is kept down by actually turning the true barrel surface to a much smaller-than-normal diameter. At the same time, the muzzle end of the barrel tube is threaded. The nut used to retain the outer cooling sleeve fastens to it and, when tightened, it actually stretches – or 'tensions' – the barrel to improve its performance. This tension is pre-set at the factory.

The aluminum sleeves, which bring the outer barrel diameter up to .920 inch, are designed to offer five times the heat dissipation of steel, at one-third the weight. By keeping the barrel from heating as quickly, and shifting its point of aim as a result, accuracy is maintained over a longer period of shooting.

The black vented model has 24 cooling slots that dissipate heat through the flow of air between it and the inner barrel tube. It is fitted with a precision-machined 4150 carbon steel barrel to complement blued receivers.

The silver cooling-finned model features a solid extruded sleeve with ten specially engineered, full-length radial fins to provide 60 percent more cooling surface than a typical one-piece .920-inch barrel. During the manufacturing process, the cooling fins are heated prior to installation. As they cool, the fins actually bond to the inner precision-machined 416 stainless steel barrel to create a 'bi-metal component' for much better performance.

Carbon Fiber

Professional Ordnance, Inc., has built an entire line of rifles and pistols around the use of carbon fiber, a material allowing great reductions in firearm weight. Its top-of-the-line rifle, the Carbon 15 *(Type 97)* in 223 Rem. for example, weighs only 3.9 pounds. Carbon fiber composite is used in the firearm's upper and lower receivers while the barrel is made of fluted stainless steel to further reduce heat and dissipate heat. Other steel components are the extractor and bolt assembly. Not only is carbon fiber lightweight and durable, but also self-lubricating, non-corrosive and offers superior heat dissipation.

Enter Scandium

Nowhere is the trend toward high technology in the field of firearms manufacturing more prominent than at premium handgun manufacturer, Smith & Wesson. The company was the first to produce revolvers with aluminum alloy frames and steel cylinders in its Airweight® series introduced 'way back in 1952. Thirteen years later, Smith & Wesson pro-

▲ S&W AirLite Model 360 Sc.

▲ AirLlite Model 360Sc Kit Gun.

▲ Model 386 Sc "Mountain Lite."

duced another technological advancement - the first stainless steel handgun.

While there have been other advancements made in the ensuing years, such as the introduction of polymer-framed handguns in the gunmaker's Sigma series, one of the most significant was the replacement, in 1998, of the steel cylinders in the Airweight line with cylinders constructed of titanium. This resulted in the launch of the now-familiar Air-Lite Ti™ products that delivered performance in an even lighter revolver.

This technological evolution in handgun manufacturing has now gone one step further with the introduction of firearms using scandium to produce the lightest, yet strongest revolvers available at the present time. Enter the Airlite Sc™ series.

By way of background, scandium is an element located between calcium and titanium in the Periodic Table of the Elements. The possibility of its existence was predicted in 1871 in the scientific community, but it wasn't until 1879 that Swedish chemist, Lars Nilson, discovered this mysterious element after refining it from the mineral Euxenite. The source of this new element was in Scandinavia, so Nilson named it "Scandium."

Pure scandium is extremely difficult to refine, which is one of the reasons it remained unknown for so long. Its overall concentration in the Earth's crust is roughly 5 parts per million. This means that 500 tons of material has to be processed to obtain 5 pounds of scandium. The market price of scandium today is in excess of $7,000 a pound.

Russia discovered a major source of scandium in the Ukraine and started the original investigations of scandium-aluminum alloys in the early 1970s. What soon became apparent to the Russian scientists was that when very small amounts of scandium were combined with some aluminum alloys, major changes took place.

The result was alloys in which there were great increases in tensile strength and enhanced superplastic performance. This translated into far greater fatigue resistance and pressure containment capability. These discoveries rapidly resulted in the use of these new stronger, lightweight alloys in MIG fighters and Russian missiles.

With the fall of the Iron Curtain and the release of countries – such as Ukraine – from communist control, this unique element was made available to the world.

Soon after Smith & Wesson released its first generation of AirLite titanium and aluminum alloy revolvers in the late 1990s, the company's engineers continued searching for stronger, lightweight metal systems to extend the AirLite concept into Magnum chamberings. Company engineers heard about the use of scandium in other industries and the wondrous properties its use brought.

For example, makers of aluminum baseball bats found the addition of a small amount of scandium during manufacturing resulted in a virtually indestructible product that would not wear out. Bats made of aluminum alloy without the addition of scandium wear out after a couple of years of use. It was during this time that the first AirLite Sc™ Magnum revolvers were built.

The startling result of Smith & Wesson's research was a small-frame, under 12-ounce revolver that could safely fire full load 158-grain 357 Magnum rounds, although the heavy recoil experienced in such a lightweight gun is not something all shooters will appreciate. Smith & Wesson's engineers had to do considerable experimenting to determine just the right amount of scandium to add to the aluminum alloy to bring about the desired results. Interestingly, adding too much scandium, it was found, actually made the alloy weaker. Thankfully (due to the element's prohibitive cost), the addition of only a very small amount of scandium was found to be necessary.

The addition of scandium produces a great increase in strength as regular aluminum alloys have a non-uniform coarse grain structure – an undesirable property for yield strength. Even more problematic, this grain structure has a tendency to weaken over time through use. Adding a tiny amount of scandium to the alloy produces several results, the most notable being a new alloy with a much finer grain structure. This means greater strength and reduction or elimination of long-term fatigue effects.

Scandium alloy is a material lighter in weight than titanium or steel, but with tensile strength and fatigue resistance that makes it an ideal candidate for firearms fabrication. While, at present, scandium is used only in revolver production, Smith & Wesson's engineers are studying its application for use in semi-auto pistols.

Smith & Wesson's AirLite Sc revolvers are available in six models. These are built with scandium alloy frames, barrel shroud and yoke. The cylinders are made with titanium and the barrel liner is stainless steel. There are three small J-frame five-shot 1 7/8-inch barreled self-defense revolvers. Models 340 Sc and 340 Sc PD, both in a "Centennial hammerless" configuration are able to handle 357 S&W Magnum and 38 S&W Special +P ammunition, yet weigh only 10.9 ounces. Hogue Bantam grips are included on both models.

The AirLite Model 360 Sc has a traditional exposed hammer, 1 7/8-inch barrel, pinned black serrated ramp front sight and a fixed notch rear sight. A light-gathering Hi-Viz® orange dot front sight and an adjustable V-notch rear sight are standard equipment on the AirLite Model 360 Sc Kit Gun with 3 1/8-inch barrel. Both versions hold five rounds of 357 S&W Magnum or 38 S&W Special +P. The Model 360 Sc comes with Hogue Bantam grips while the Kit Gun has Uncle Mike's combat grips. All small-frame Sc revolvers feature a lanyard pin.

There are also two medium L-frame six-shot revolvers: the Model 386 Sc PD with 2 1/2-inch barrel and the Model 386 Sc "Mountain Lite" with 3 1/8-inch barrel – both chambered for seven rounds of 357 S&W Magnum or 38 S&W Special +P ammo. The Mountain Lite 386 Sc, with a 3 1/8-inch barrel, combines a light-gathering Hi-Viz green dot front sight with an adjustable V-notch rear sight. The 2 1/2-inch barrel Model 386 Sc PD personal defense revolver features a red ramp front and adjustable black rear

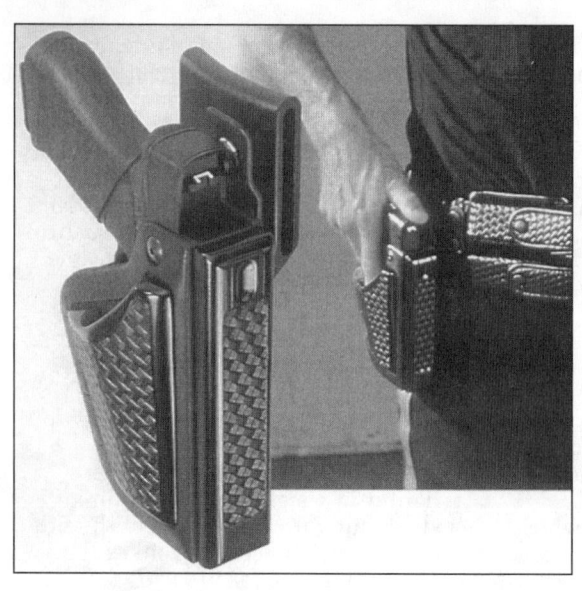

The Pro 4 ID "smart" holster from Michaels of Oregon.

sights. New-style Hogue Bantam grips are included on both models.

The trend to produce politically-correct firearms, that limit manufacturers' potential liability in personal injury suits, has resulted in the development of on-board locking systems for firearms.

Springfield Armory is incorporating its patented Integral Locking System on its entire line of 1911-style pistols. Contained within the mainspring housing, the key locking system (when activated) disables movement of the slide and trigger components. The system is enabled/deactivated by an unobtrusive key-activated control located midway between the grip safety and butt on the rear of the grip. A quick one-quarter turn locks or unlocks the pistol. A kit is available for retrofitting to other non-Springfield Armory-manufactured 1911s. Springfield's pistols are also appearing with a loaded chamber indicator as an added safety enhancement.

Other firearm manufacturers offering, or planning to offer, on-board locking systems with their products include Taurus, Smith & Wesson and Remington.

The "Smart" Holster

Much talk has been heard over the last several years over so-called "smart guns," firearms that contain built-in electronic or other mechanisms to allow operation only by an authorized user. While gunmakers, such as Smith & Wesson, continue development of this concept, one holster maker has produced a product that has turned the whole concept of "smart guns" on its head.

Michaels of Oregon Co., producer of the familiar "Uncle Mike's" brand of firearms accessories, has developed the first "smart holster."

The Pro4 ID holster is a biometric identification retention holster that identifies its owner through his/her fingerprint and allows this individual *(or other pre-determined persons - some 64 separate fingerprint images can be stored in memory)* access to the firearm. The battery-powered holster incorporates a fingerprint reader and circuitry to control a locking device. There is a mechanical over-ride to free the gun if the holster's two power sources fail *(triple-A batteries are the primary power source and a backup cell battery).*

In use, when the trigger finger is placed on the print reader, it activates the circuitry that opens the lock and starts a paging device-type vibrator to alert the wearer that the gun can be removed from the holster. The whole authorization sequence takes less than one second. The window of opportunity allowing the user to withdraw the firearm from the holster can be set to allow removal of the gun anywhere from within one to ten seconds.

Of primary interest to the police market, the holster will be furnished with a Windows-based software program on a CD to allow authorization of department personnel. The technology not only controls access to an officer's sidearm, it also records *(in computer downloadable form)* what access *(if any)* has been made to the firearm during the officer's work shift. Thus, firearm activity by any officers can be determined by downloading information from the holster at the end of a shift. Over time, a transmitter may be added to the holster that would alert a dispatcher if an officer removed a sidearm from the holster, possibly signaling the need for backup assistance.

At the time of this writing, the Pro4 ID holster is expected to sell for about $500, making it a product of interest only to government agencies. In time, as the electronic technology improves, the cost is expected to come down to the point where the holster may be of interest to the average citizen concerned about firearm security.

Lead-Free Primers

Another area of new technological development is that of cartridge primers. Ammunition containing lead-free priming compounds, such as Winchester's "Winclean" and CCI-Speer's "Cleanfire" contain these newer priming compounds. In addition to lessening shooter exposure to the hazards of airborne lead particles *(when fired at an indoor range)* the use of lead-free primers leaves much less fouling residue in fired cases than do conventional lead styphnate primers.

Though an old technology, the makers of firearms have proved themselves highly-innovative in finding ways of "teaching an old dog new tricks." As the industry moves ahead in the 21st century, expect to see even more technological improvements in the near future. •

For more information:

Butler Creek, P.O. Box 1690, Oregon City, OR 97045 Phone: 503-655-7964 Web site: www.michaels-oregon.com

CCI-Speer, 2299 Snake River Ave., Lewiston, ID 83501 Phone: 208-746-2351

Magnum Research, Inc., 7110 University Avenue Northeast, Minneapolis, MN 55432 Phone: 612-574-1868 Web site: www.magnumresearch.com

Michaels of Oregon, PO Box 1690, Oregon City, OR 97045 Phone: 503-655-7964 Web site: www.michaels-oregon.com

Professional Ordnance, 1070 Metric Drive, Lake Havasu City, AZ 86404 Phone: 520-505-2420 Web site: www.professional-ordnance.com

Remington Arms Co., Inc., 870 Remington Drive, P.O. Box 700, Madison, NC 27025-0700 Phone: 800-243-9700 Web site: www.remington.com

Smith & Wesson, 2100 Roosevelt Avenue, Springfield, MA 01104-1698 Phone: 413-781-8300 Web site: www.smith-wesson.com

Winchester Ammunition, 427 North Shamrock Street, East Alton, IL 62024-1174 Phone: 618-258-3692 Web site: www.winchester.com

---

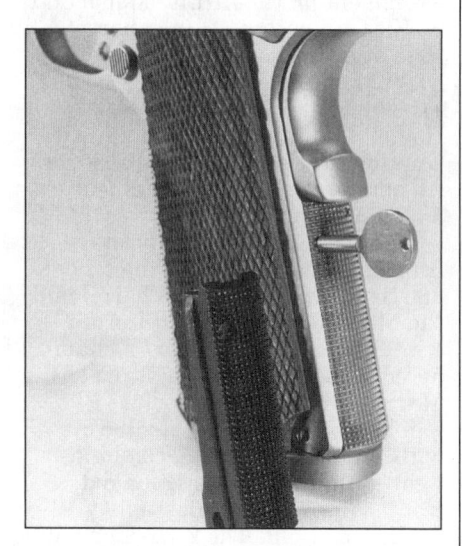

Springfield Armory has made its Integral Locking System a standard feature on its entire line of 1911-style pistols.

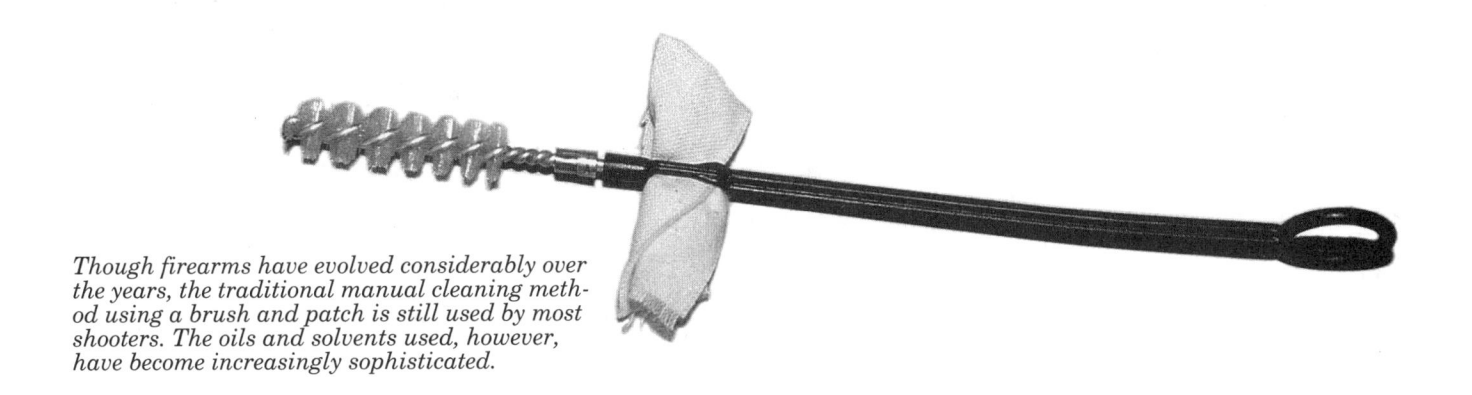

Though firearms have evolved considerably over the years, the traditional manual cleaning method using a brush and patch is still used by most shooters. The oils and solvents used, however, have become increasingly sophisticated.

Modern Firearms Maintenance

As firearms have become increasingly sophisticated in design and construction, so have the solvents and lubricants used to maintain them. Though great strides have been made in firearm technology, it is still necessary to maintain a regular regimen of firearm maintenance to ensure proper functioning. Here's a look at some of the latest and greatest products.

by Robert M. Hausman

IT CAN BE a difficult job for firearms enthusiasts to find the right maintenance products for their needs in what has come to be known as the "*Snake Oil*" business. The development and marketing of such products has acquired this name due to the "miraculous results" claimed by some manufacturers. Some of the gun oils available collect dust and dirt, while becoming gummy and sticky in colder weather. Some products are solely made for lubrication, while offering no rust protection, and vice versa.

The bane of firearms, of course, is rust. A chemical oxidation, rust forms when steel surfaces are exposed to air. Water vapor in the air attacks the iron in the steel. To prevent this from occurring, a chemical coating specifically designed to prevent oxidation must be applied to the metal surface. This protective layer prevents the oxidation reaction from taking place.

In many cases, the first exposure a shooter will have to gun maintenance products is through friends and family. Whatever dear old dad – or a favorite uncle – used to maintain his treasured firearm will usually be the first choice of most shooters. A lot has changed in the basic materials, methods and finishes used in the manufacturing of modern firearms and, as well, the chemicals used to clean and lubricate them.

One of the oldest firms in the firearms maintenance field is **Birchwood Casey**, which has been in business since 1948. New to the line is Stock Restorer and Protectant, a spray-on/ wipe-off formula that revives and protects synthetic and wood stocks - it even adds luster to vinyl gun cases and hunting boots. The formulation is harmless to blued, nickel and stainless metals as well as nearly all plastics. It's non-flammable, odorless, and does not harm camouflage finishes.

Birchwood Casey's Super Strength Bore Scrubber® has been reformulated to provide a "*2 in 1*" bore cleaning action for copper and nitro fouling. It attacks, dissolves and removes all types of barrel fouling including lead, copper, plastic, carbon, and powder fouling, while its rust preventive additives give long-

Birchwood Casey's Deluxe Gun Maintenance Kit contains everything needed to keep firearms in top condition. *Photo by author.*

term protection after cleaning. Though the product is a high strength formulation, it contains no nitrobenzene, butyl cellosolve or other highly toxic ingredients.

A handy item any shooter can buy is Birchwood Casey's SHEATH® Take-Alongs. These are individual 5" x 8" cloths impregnated with SHEATH Rust Preventive and sealed in a foil packet for compact carrying. Take-Alongs are useful for wiping down a gun after firing, as well as serving as a cleaner/protector when run through the gun bore. This is a product the author won't go to the range without.

For convenience and economy, Birchwood Casey has packaged its most essential firearm maintenance products into its Deluxe Gun Maintenance Kit. The kit includes: a lead remover and polishing cloth; 6 oz. of SHEATH Rust Preventive; 9 oz. of GUN SCRUBBER® High Pressure Solvent/Degreaser; 6 oz. of Bore Scrubber cleaner; a Gun & Reel Silicone Cloth; SHEATH Take-Along Gun Wipes; cleaning patches and swabs; and even a supply of self-sticking SHOOT-N-C® targets.

Another firm, **Bore Tech**, makes a cleaning rod case with full-length internal tubes to hold up to six cleaning rods, housed in an outer tube made of high impact styrene. The case keeps cleaning rods organized and ready for use while protecting them from damage.

Bore Tech's "Bore Stix" are among the most advanced design cleaning rods available. Made from tempered spring steel, they are coated with hard epoxy to prevent scratching the bore. The handle core contains stainless ball bearings allowing effortless rotation as brushes and jags follow the rifling to clean the lands and grooves efficiently. Bore Stix are available in sizes from .17 through .50 caliber and in lengths from 24 to 60 inches.

Bore Tech's legendary rod quality is now available for shotgunners. The company's new shotgun cleaning rod is a two-piece 36-inch aluminum design with a non-rotating handle and comes with an adapter to fit the 5/16x27 thread of most popular shotgun brushes and mops. Bore Tech's shotgun jags allow you to clean your shotgun using standard patches instead of using expensive mops that get dirty quickly and are expensive to replace. The jags are available in six sizes to fit .410 bore through 10 gauge guns.

Finally, Bore Tech's Moly Magic is a unique blend of penetrants, surfactants and solvents formulated exclusively to assist in the removal of molybdenum disulfide buildup in rifle bores. Molybdenum disulfide is a "*substantive*" material, meaning it

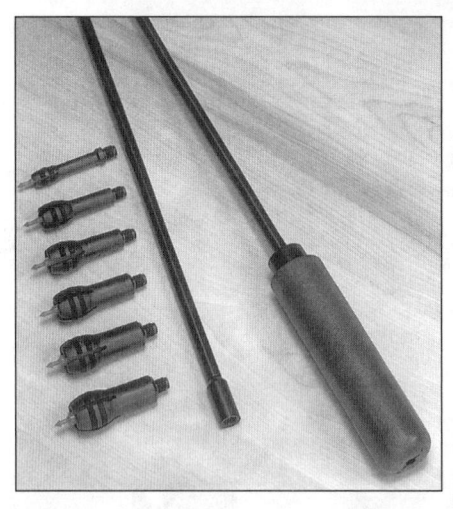

Bore Tech's two-piece, anodized aluminum shotgun cleaning rod brings high-quality cleaning tools to shotgunners.

Iosso Products' case cleaner kit offers a simple and fast way to clean fired cases prior to the reloading process.

clings to metal surfaces readily, and while this is part of the mechanism that allows moly to provide friction reduction, it also makes the material difficult to remove with traditional methods. Bore Tech's Moly Magic penetrates deep into the bore's pores while a specially-formulated surfactant system suspends and then attracts the moly particles to the patch with electrostatic attraction, greatly increasing cleaning efficiency.

Gun Oil Types

Exhaustive research on the various types of firearms maintenance products and their performance has recently been conducted by **Break-Free, Inc.**, maker of the famous triple-action CLP (cleaning, lubrication preservation), a synthetic lubricating oil with extreme pressure and anti-wear additives, rust and corrosion inhibitors.

Gun oils can be broken down into several types. **Mineral oils** are chemically stable, however, the hot,

Hoppe's Cleaner/Degreaser is a must-have item for quickly removing surface oils and grease as a preparatory step in the cleaning process.

wet and dirty environment of firearms operation does not present ideal conditions and mineral oil-based lubricants are subject to aging and decay, Break-Free has found.

Fatty oils are refined from animal tissues or vegetable matter. Although tending to oxidize readily, fatty oils continue to play a role in gun lubrication as their inherent "*oiliness*," or lubricity, makes them an often-used additive where wetting action is desired.

Other products are formulated with **high performance oils** that contain friction-fighting, heat-reducing, load-carrying solid lubricants and an additive package balanced for maximum life and service. While high performance oils are an improvement over mineral oils, they are still subject to aging, decay and irreversible changes in the high temperatures and pressure of firearms use.

Synthetic oils can: *(1)* increase wear protection as they have excellent viscosity, temperature properties and shear stability; *(2)* minimize the formation of deposits since they have good high-temperature oxidation stability; *(3)* yield improved cold weather performance as the typical pour point is extremely low and *(4)* their high stability permits synthetics to last three to five times as long as mineral-based lubricants.

As Break-Free literature points out, the inside of a modern firearm is one hellacious place. When the trigger is pulled on a modern semi-auto firearm, powder explodes, gases expand and temperatures build to searing levels. Steel, copper or lead spins and twists its way down the bore at warp speed, furiously abrading against the inside of the barrel. A piston slams. An extractor drags the shell or cartridge from the chamber. Metal parts slide and push against one another, tossing the spent round aside and shoving another in its place. And with each cycle, everything is coated with the debris of combustion – minute particles of burnt powder, complex gases, tiny flecks of metal and the varnish that forms as superheated gun oils cook and congeal. That's why choosing the proper lubricants and maintenance products for your particular application is critical.

Flitz Products offers its new Rifle/Gun Wax, especially of interest for working hunter's guns. A non-abrasive product, it will protect a firearm's surface from rain up to six months. It produces exceptional results in protecting blued, stainless and nickel surfaces as well as gunstock wood. Containing carnauba and bee's wax, it provides a shield from rust, corrosion caused by handling, water stains, powder residue, tree sap, blood, salt and lime deposits.

To make the job of reloaders easier, Flitz' Tumbler/Media Additive cuts brass tumbling time in half. It is suitable for use with corncob, walnut and other media. To use, add one tablespoon of the product to the tumbling media. With the spoon, mix Flitz well into the media, and then begin the tumbling procedure. Most users report only about half the usual time is needed to tumble their cases clean when Flitz is added to the media.

G96 Products Co., Inc., still offers its aerosol spray G96 Gun Treatment. Not a new product, but one that is hard to beat. It is considered by many to be the single best gun care maintenance product ever designed as it does three tasks – cleans, lubricates and preserves – in a single application. Its unique formulation will not freeze, oxidize or evaporate during use in temperatures from –50 degrees F. to +350 degrees F.

One of the most basic, but often passed-up items needed in a gun fouling warrior's "*arsenal*" is a good degreaser. This product is used to remove surface gunk, oils and grease as one of the first steps in the cleaning process. **Hoppe's**, a name synonymous with firearms maintenance products for generations, has recently come out with a new Cleaner/Degreaser that blasts away fouling deposits, oils, and grease with a powerful cleansing spray. This product can be applied to all gunmetal surfaces and parts. It's particularly good for cleaning the action without having to disassemble the gun, making it ideal for competition shooters who fire a large number of rounds during range sessions. It dries in seconds, leaving metal surfaces clean and dry.

Basic Cleaning Procedure

For those unfamiliar with the process, or as a review for veteran shooters, Hoppe's literature details the basic procedures for cleaning any type of firearm. After ensuring the firearm is not loaded, position the gun on end with the barrel pointing down and away from you. This will allow the cleaning rod to be run through the breech-end, so any deposits or metal fragments come out the muzzle instead of being pushed back into the action. This also guards against damaging the rifling at the muzzle from contact with the metal cleaning rod.

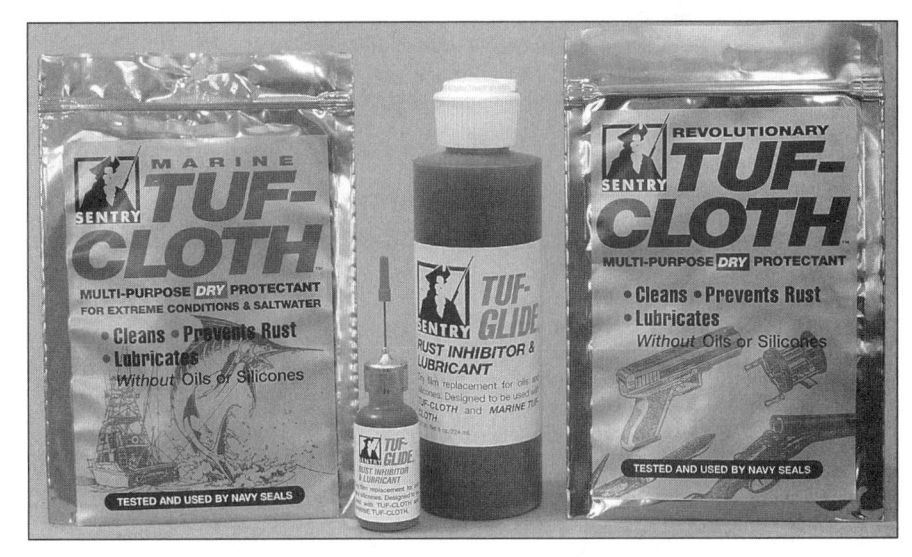

Next, soak a patch or swab in solvent, attach it to the cleaning rod and run it through the bore once or twice. Discard the patch and run a dry patch through the bore several times. Repeat this procedure, alternating between wet and dry patches until the patches stop picking up residue. It is also a good idea to run a bristle brush through the bore a few times to help remove stubborn deposits. It should be noted the most commonly used phosphor bronze and tornado brushes should be run completely through the barrel before pulling either one back out. They can't be reversed inside the barrel without bending, snagging or breaking the bristles. If you have been shooting jacketed bullets, you will also need to use a product such as Hoppe's Bench Rest-9, to remove copper deposits from the bore.

When you've finished cleaning the bore, apply a small amount of lubricant to a clean patch and run it through the bore once. Now you're ready to move on to the action. Moving parts, such as the trigger mechanism and other internal parts, should be scrubbed with a solvent-soaked brush. For hard-to-reach areas use an aerosol spray, such as Hoppe's/Castrol Gun Stripper. Then wipe the parts clean and apply a thin coat of oil. Work the action a few times to ensure good oil penetration.

Finally, wipe the outer surfaces clean. The exposed surfaces should be cleaned last to remove any residual material. Then apply a thin layer of a good metal rust-preventing protectant.

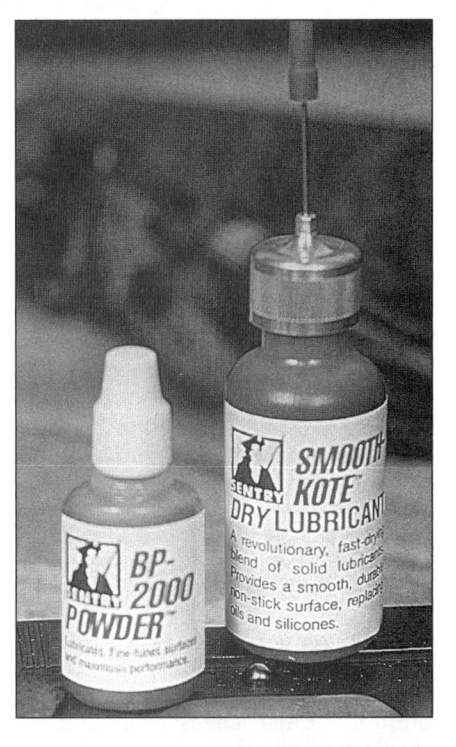

Sentry Solution's Tuf-Cloth and Tuf-Glide are two products that impart a water-displacing micro-bonding crystal barrier to firearms to prevent rust, friction and wear.

When used together, Sentry Solutions' BP-2000 Powder and Smooth-Kote dry lubricant, reduce friction by as much as an additional 20% compared to oil-based products.

Iosso Products' new concentrated paste bore cleaner is ideal for those who want to clean their guns thoroughly, but don't want to spend an undue amount of time doing it. Since it is a paste, it will not drip where you don't want it to go, and it won't spill when transported, making it convenient to bring along to the field or to the range. Used on a patch run through the bore, the cleaner will remove copper, lead, powder fouling and plastic wad residue.

Gun Brite, another Iosso product, safely removes powder fouling, surface rust, tarnish on factory blued,

Black Powder Cleaning Gel from Shooter's Choice is considered a major breakthrough in muzzleloader cleaning.

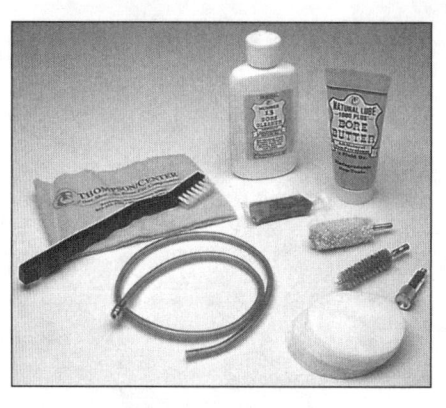

Thompson/Center's In-Line Cleaning System contains everything necessary to clean an in-line muzzleloader the right way.

Shooter's Choice Shotgun & Choke Tube Cleaner quickly removes plastic wad, lead and powder fouling.

stainless steel, chrome and nickel-finished guns. It is particularly good at removing the stubborn powder residue rings that form on the face of revolver cylinders. After application, the polish leaves behind a non-oily protective coating.

A new liquid cleaner for fired cases is available from Iosso Products. The liquid cleaner works particularly well in cleaning the inside of fired cases and the primer pocket area where tumbling media is often ineffective. Furnished as a simple-to-use kit, it includes the liquid cleaner, a pail, lid and strainer bag.

The user pours the solution into the pail, places the casings in the bag and immerses the bag in the solution. Some hand agitation will help loosen the powder residue from the cases that are left in the solution for up to five minutes. The user then removes the bag, rinses the casings and allows them to dry. One quart of cleaning solution will handle 1,000 to 2,500 casings, depending on their size and the degree of fouling.

Kleen-Bore, a well-known name in the gun care field, has improved a couple of its longstanding products to increase their effectiveness. Kleen Brite Gun Polish has been reformulated to create a polish gentle on finishes, yet still powerful enough to remove light rust, tarnish and carbon build-up. It also leaves a thin protective barrier to prevent smudges, powder fouling and other material from adhering to the firearm's finish. Now available in a convenient 2 oz. jar, this polish does not contain ammonia or aggressive abrasives and can be used on factory blued, stainless, chrome and nickel finishes.

Kleen-Bore's No. 10 Copper Cutter has also been enhanced to increase its effectiveness. In tests conducted by Kleen-Bore's research and development department, a 375 H&H-chambered rifle was fired until its barrel was fouled with heavy copper deposits. The copper build-up in the bore was noticeable to the unaided eye and even more apparent with the use of a bore scope. With such severe fouling, several applications of No. 10 Copper Cutter were applied. Much of the copper fouling was removed with just a brass jag and cotton patch saturated in the new formula.

Special indicators contained within No. 10's formula quickly react - turning blue when the slightest trace of copper is detected in the bore. This color change also lets the user know the formula is countering the bond between the copper fouling and the bore. There is no more guesswork; this newly reformulated product lets you know when your barrel is absolutely clean by its color.

Many consider Kleen-Bore's TW25B® to be the ultimate lubricant for all firearms applications. Available in oil, cream, squeeze bottle, tube, pump spray or syringe form, TW25B has been proven to work in temperature ranges of –90 degrees F. to +450 degrees F. The lubricant has been tested and found to protect metal surfaces for over 500 hours, when exposed to salt fog, with no signs of rust or corrosion. This unique formula actually works itself into the microscopic pores of metal to provide lubrication without collecting dust particles. TW25 B is approved for U.S. military use under the National Stock Number System.

Kleen-Bore has a product just for shotgunners – the Multi-Choke Shotgun Cleaning Jag, which can be used on all shotgun bores regardless of the choke variation – even extra-full turkey chokes.

Sentry Solutions, the firm using an image of an American Revolutionary War militiaman in its logo, has taken a revolutionary approach to firearms maintenance – as it was the first company to offer oil-free or dry lubricating products. The benefits of dry lubrication include the absence of liquid that can attract and hold dirt and shooting residue. Being oil-free also means there is nothing to thicken in the cold or thin out from intense heat. Another advantage, particularly to hunters, is that Sentry's products are odor free.

Sentry's product line includes Tuf-Cloth™, a lint-free alternative to oil and silicone wipes. Tuf-Cloth contains a formula of dry-film corrosion inhibitors and lubricants to provide a fast-drying, water-displacing micro-bonding crystal barrier against rust, friction, and wear. Tuf-Glide™ is a dry-film rust inhibitor whose formula bonds to metal and will not wash or wipe off.

Several other Sentry products are worthy of mention. Smooth-Kote™ is a fast-drying lubricant and bore treatment that bonds to metal and eliminates grime with non-stick protection – making guns self-cleaning. The layer of lubricating crystals deposited on the bore's surface by Smooth-Kote provides less resistance to the fired bullet resulting in a limitation of heat transfer. A bore that does not get as hot as it normally would if Smooth-Kote were not used, will tend to last longer and is less apt to spot-weld bullet material to the bore's surface.

Sentry's BP2000 Powder™ is great for trigger jobs, fine-tuning bores, bolts and slides. When used with Smooth-Kote, friction is reduced by as much as 20%, compared to oil. Hi-Slip Grease™ is a synthetic blend that prevents galling of all metals, including titanium, even under extreme conditions and high loads.

For the muzzleloader, **Shooter's Choice** new Black Powder Cleaning Gel is considered a major breakthrough in black powder cleaning. Specially formulated to dissolve, suspend and remove the soft lead and blackpowder fouling that plagues accuracy and barrel life in muzzle-loading firearms, the product eliminates the mess of soap and water cleaning. It also works well on smokeless powder fouling in modern firearms and is excellent for cleaning law enforcement black powder-charged gas guns. Being a gel, it clings and scrubs away at the fouling much faster and more effectively than conventional liquid black powder solvents.

Shooter's Choice Bore Cleaner & Conditioner is unique among firearms cleaning solvents due to the variety of tasks it performs. It is one of the only products on the market capable of totally cleaning a bore of all deposits and fouling in one step. Powder, lead, plastic wad, copper fouling, carbon deposits and corrosion are effectively dissolved and removed, and if used regularly, the product will minimize the accumulation of fouling.

In shotguns, when powder and plastic fouling builds up, it tends to drag on the wad or shotcup of subsequent rounds fired and the fouling can even cause the shotcharge to tilt in the barrel. As a shotgun barrel cools, condensation occurs. Plastic wad and powder fouling attracts moisture and hardens, trapping moisture against the barrel wall resulting in a condition highly susceptible to rust and pitting. Shooter's Choice Shotgun and Choke Tube Cleaner (in a convenient aerosol container) is one option that is designed to quickly remove plastic wad, lead and powder fouling from the barrel, choke tube and barrel ports.

December, 1995 marked a turning point in the chemical industry with the federal government ban on the use of 1-1-1 Trichloroethane, due to environmental concerns. Many firearm solvents contained this chemical, which had a fast-drying feature. Some cleaning products, reformulated since the ban went into effect, now have the negative property of being extremely flammable or are water-based cleaners that evaporate very slowly. Shooter's Choice Quick Scrub III is the result of an exhaustive research project by the company's chemists to develop a product that dissolves dirt, oil, grease, carbon and powder fouling effectively, while being fast-drying, non-flammable and non-water based.

Otis Technology is one of the most innovative and prolific makers of gun cleaning technology products designed to clean firearms from the breech to the muzzle. Cleaning from the muzzle end of a gun can lead to damage of the muzzle crown and, by pushing the cleaning rod or patch in from the muzzle, dirt picked up along the way is carried down into the firearm's action.

Otis' patented all-caliber patches allow six passes through the bore per patch and form a perfectly circular cone-shaped cleaning plug for efficient use. Since the slotted tip containing the patch is pulled through the firearm chamber, the patch is not compressed against the side of the tip or rod. Conventional non-flexible stiff rods often jam in the bore, scraping the rifling in the process. The 750 lb. pull strength of the Otis Memory-Flex rod allows the user to tightly form the patch to the bore, cleaning it rather than just moving the fouling around.

Quick Scrub III Cleaner/Degreaser from Shooter's Choice is an extremely fast-drying, non-flammable product that leaves no residue behind.

Otis' most popular product is its model 750 Tactical Cleaning system. Packaged in a small belt pouch, it contains everything needed and can replace as many as 15 conventional gun cleaning kits. It handles all rifles from .22 through .50 caliber, .410 bore to 10 gauge shotguns and pistols from .22 to .45 caliber. Provided are three memory-flex cleaning rods, three forged brass tips, two obstruction removers, a T-handle, .5 oz. of Otis bore cleaner, a supply of all-caliber patches, a shotgun brush adapter, two patch savers, five bore brushes and a bore reflector.

The top-of-the-line item, and this author's favorite Otis product, is the Model 1000 Elite kit. It includes everything necessary for cleaning all rifles (including those in .17 caliber), shotguns and handguns. Otis' entire line of bronze bore and chamber cleaning brushes, bore cleaning solvent and all-caliber cleaning patches are furnished. All of the components are neatly stored in a supplied lockable black nylon case. The case has a storage area for a handgun with a rust-resistant lining. With over 40 gun-cleaning components, a detailed gun maintenance guide and a lifetime warranty, the "Elite" is Otis' hallmark product for firearms maintenance.

For the black powder shooter, **Thompson/Center Arms Co.**, producer of traditional flintlock,

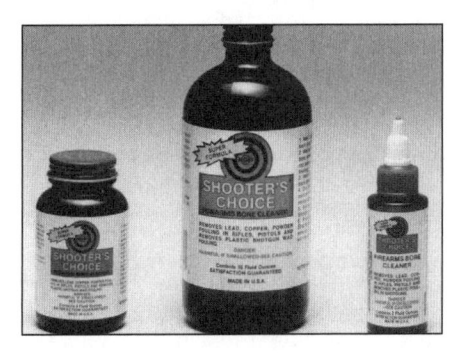

Shooter's Choice Bore Cleaner & Conditioner cleans your gun in one step.

caplock and in-line rifles, now offers two cleaning kits of interest. T/C's Basic Muzzleloading Cleaning Kit gives the muzzleloading hunter everything required for cleaning a .50 caliber rifle in the field. The products chosen for this kit follow the "*all-natural*" approach of maintaining a seasoned bore. Included are: 4 oz. of No. 13™ Bore Cleaner containing no petroleum-based additives; general purpose 2 1/2-inch cotton cleaning patches; a supply of cotton cleaning patches pre-treated with T/C's own Natural Lube 1000 Plus™ Bore Butter; a phosphor bronze bore brush containing 10x32 threads to fit T/C rifle ramrods; and, an extended Super Jag knurled to provide maximum contact between the patch and bore.

Thompson/Center's In-Line Cleaning System contains everything necessary to clean a .50 caliber rifle properly. Included in the kit are: Natural Lube 1000 Plus Bore Butter; Number 13 Bore Cleaner/Powder Solvent; plastic Flush Tube used to flush solvent through the nipple, thereby eliminating the need to disassemble the rifle; bronze bore brush; bore swab; Super Jag; cotton patches; cleaning/utility brush; silicon gun cloth and Gorilla Grease™, an all-natural, anti-seize lubricant formulated for use on the threads of removeable breech plugs and nipples.

Not Glamorous, But Necessary

While it may not be one of the most glamorous aspects of firearms ownership, regular and thorough cleaning of firearms is one of the most important. Like any preventative maintenance program, gun cleaning can greatly extend your firearms' service life.

A thorough cleaning also provides an opportunity to inspect the gun for any apparent defects or patterns of wear which could cause a serious problem in the future. Cleaning can also do a great deal of benefit in terms of accuracy. Each shot causes a slight build-up of fouling inside the barrel and action. Regular cleaning keeps fouling to a minimum and helps to maintain accuracy.

Another occasion when thorough cleaning and inspection is important is after a long period of storage. During storage, oils can become gummy and cause the firearm to malfunction. Congealed oils in a barrel can also elevate pressure upon firing by slowing the bullet's progress down the bore. A safe practice is to fully clean any firearm that has been stored for more than a few months before firing.

Ultrasonics: The Ultimate Firearm Cleaning System

by Robert M. Hausman

The ultimate firearm maintenance products are the Crest Ultrasonics line using sound waves to completely clean a firearm inside and out – within ten minutes. Available in a variety of nine sizes to accommodate handguns and long guns, the system consists of the electrically-powered ultrasonic unit that cleans and lubricates the firearm.

In use, the firearm is fieldstripped and degreased, then placed into a stainless basket and lowered into the heated tank containing a cleaning solution. The machine produces *(barely audible)* high-frequency sound waves that cause alternating high and low pressure resulting in the creation of millions of tiny bubbles that implode on the gun, resulting in a scrubbing action that cleans down to the microscopic level.

The gun is then removed from the cleaning solution, rinsed with clean water and then dried with compressed air. The gun is then placed into a separate basket and tank containing lubricant and set onto the Ultrasonic machine where the firearm is thoroughly lubricated through active bubble action. The gun is removed from the tank and excess oil is then wiped and blown off the gun with compressed air. The firearm is then reassembled and ready for use or storage. The complete process, not including fieldstripping and reassembly, can be performed in less than ten minutes.

The Ultrasonic Cleaning Process

When ultrasonic energy is introduced into the cleaning solution, cavitation, the foundation of ultrasonic cleaning occurs. Ultrasonic energy causes alternating patterns of low and high-pressure phases. During the low-pressure phases, minute bubbles, or vacuum cavities form. During the subsequent high-pressure phases, the bubbles implode violently. This is called cavitation.

Cavitation provides an intense scrubbing action leading to unsurpassed cleaning speed and consistency when compared with simple soaking or immersion with agitation. Additionally, the bubbles are small enough to penetrate even microscopic crevices, cleaning them thoroughly and consistently. As a result, ultrasonic cleaning is one of the most highly effective and efficient methods for cleaning.

Firearms are field-stripped and placed in a basket which is lowered into the Crest Ultrasonics' cleaning solution where they are cleaned through sound wave technology. *Photo by author.*

The cleaning concentrate used, ChemCrest 235, is a mild alkaline-based cleaner with rust inhibitor. When mixed with water for use, it is nearly odorless. Guns are cleaned at approximately 125 degrees F. Approximately 500 firearms can be cleaned with one gallon of CC235 cleaning concentrate, making it one of the most efficient cleaners available. The parts are lubricated with ChemCrest 400L lubricant, an odorless petroleum distillate that lubricates and protects firearms while removing moisture.

The cleaning procedure is safe for both blued and stainless steel firearms, along with night sights, polymer frames and rubber or plastic grips. Wood grips, electronic sights and scopes should be removed from the gun before immersion. On multiple firearm cleaning operations, use of the Crest Ultrasonics system increases actual output many times over hand-cleaning, with the parts restored to a uniform standard of factory-new cleanliness.

Finally, get in the habit of cleaning and visually inspecting any new firearm before its first use. Most are treated with oils to preserve their finish, which should be removed before firing. All of these good habits will add to safe practices and enjoyment of the shooting experience. ●

For more information:

Birchwood Laboratories, Inc, (Birchwood Casey), 7900 Fuller Road, Eden Prairie, MN 55344-2195 Phone: 952-937-7928 FAX: 952-937-7979 Web site: www.birchwoodcasey.com

Bore Tech, Inc., 580 Wyncourtney Drive NE, Atlanta, GA 30328 Phone/FAX: 770-512-7730 Web site: www.boretech.com

Break-Free, Inc., 1035 S. Linwood Ave., Santa Ana, CA 92705 Phone: 714-953-0402 FAX: 714-953-0402 Web site: www.break-free.com

Crest Ultrasonics Corp., Scotch Road, Mercer County Airport, PO Box 7266, Trenton, NJ 08628 Phone: 609-406-7008 FAX: 609-530-0923 Web site: www.policeproductscorp.com or www.guncleaners.com.

Flitz International, Ltd., 821 Mohr Ave., Waterford, WI 53185 Phone: 414-534-5898 FAX: 414-534-2991 Web site: www.flitz.com

G96 Products Co., Inc., 85 Fifth Ave., Bldg. #6, PO Box 1684, Paterson, NJ 07524-1684 Phone: 973-684-4050 FAX: 973-684-3848 Web site: www.G96.com.

Hoppe's, Airport Industrial Mall, Coatesville, PA 19320 Phone: 610-384-6000 FAX: 610-857-5980 Web site: www.hoppes.com

Iosso Products, 1485 Lively Blvd., Elk Grove Village, IL 60007 Phone: 847-437-8400 FAX: 847-437-8478 Web site: www.iosso.com

Kleen-Bore, Inc., 16 Industrial Parkway, Easthampton, MA 01027 Phone: 413-527-0300 FAX: 413-527-0300 Web site: www.kleen-bore.com

Otis Products, Inc., PO Box 582, Lyons Falls, NY 13368 Phone: 315-348-4300 FAX: 315-348-4332 Web site: www.otisgun.com.

Sentry Solutions, Ltd., 111 Sugar Hill Road, PO Box 130, Contoocook, NH 03229 Phone: 603-746-5687 FAX: 603-746-5847 Web site: www.sentrysolutions.com

Thompson/Center Arms Co., Inc., P.O. Box 5002, Rochester, NH 03866 Phone: 603-332-2394 FAX: 603-332-5133 Web site: www.tcarms.com

Ventco, Inc. (Shooter's Choice), 15050 Berkshire Ind. Parkway, Middlefield, OH Phone: 440-834-8888 FAX: 440-834-3388 Web site: www.shooters-choice.com

HANDGUN NEWS

AUTOLOADING PISTOLS

by John Malloy

THE PAST YEAR was one of great uncertainty for both makers and users of autoloading handguns.

There were many aspects. Lawsuits against firearms manufacturers (primarily those making semi-auto pistols), misuse of authority by public officials, media assaults against firearms ownership, and proposed anti-gun legislation at state and federal levels—all of these things played a part.

As the year 2000 went on, the November 7, 2000 elections were seen as a climax that would give an indication as to what the future might hold.

But even the elections added to the uncertainty, and it was over a month later before George W. Bush was finally acknowledged the President-elect. The election of Bush, who is basically pro-gun, should provide needed relief from the anti-gun policies of the Clinton-Gore administration. In the meantime, however, some state legislators and bureaucrats decided they were firearms experts, even when they had no understanding of handgun or ammunition terminology. States such as California, Maryland and Massachusetts initiated differing standards as to what pistols could be sold within their borders. The arbitrary and sometimes conflicting rules baffled many manufacturers. If other states come up with even different criteria, how can any handgun meet them all?

Some manufacturers have held off spending research time or money on new developments due to this uncertainty. Some have suspended certain models from production.

Yet, there is still much going on in the world of autoloading handguns. There are many new offerings. Most of these are variations on the 1911 theme, and the 45 ACP cartridge remains the most popular chambering for new offerings. Polymer frames have not lost their charm, and some interesting polymer/aluminum combinations have been introduced. Small 45s are very popular, but some new full-size variants have been introduced also. However, everything is not 1911 45s. There are also brand-new designs and brand-new cartridges being introduced. The 22-caliber pistol remains popular—both new pistols and conversion units are being introduced in the 22 Long Rifle (22 LR) chambering. New U. S. companies have been set up to market foreign products.

Due to litigation possibilities and state requirements, many manufacturers are offering or designing locking devices that can incapacitate their pistols.

The aftermarket industry is active and creative. Many new accessories for autoloading handguns are being offered.

The industry has become more involved with things electronic. Most companies involved with semiautomatic pistols now have websites or e-mail addresses to provide information about their products. To show that your writer is up with the times, these electronic contacts will be provided here.

Now, let's take a look at what the companies are doing:

Among the new variants of the Alchemy Arms Spectre are the "commander"-size pistols, this one with a lightweight titanium slide.

Beretta offers a nifty new holster for their 9000S pistols—it can be used left or right, straight or tilted, narrow belt or wide.

ALCHEMY ARMS

Alchemy Arms' Spectre pistol was introduced only a year ago, but already variations are being introduced. The original 4.5-inch full-size model has been joined by a 4-inch version. The carbon- and stainless-steel slides in both lengths are now joined by those made of titanium. Titanium reduces the weight of a Spectre to 22 ounces.

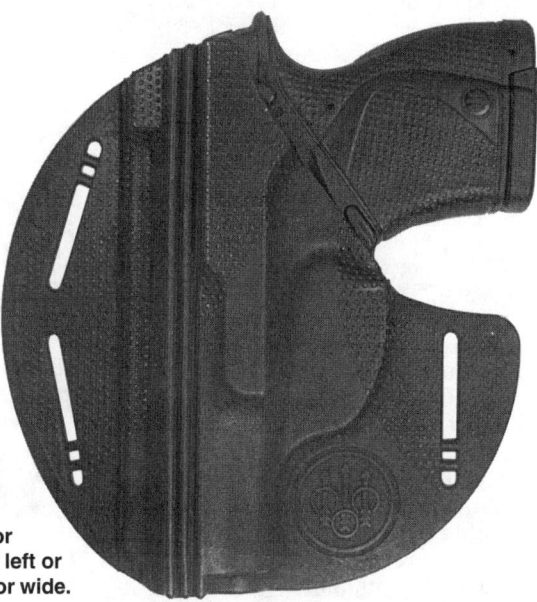

34th EDITION, 2002 **21**

Beretta's Cathy Williams demonstrates the new 9000S pistol, this version a double-action-only (DAO).

Express sights (large bead, shallow notch) are standard now. Alchemy also plans to introduce new wide sights of their own design.

Attentive observers will note that the new full-size Spectres have a more rounded slide contour. Also, the takedown has been simplified and the trigger guard has been reshaped slightly. A notch in the front of the trigger guard serves as what the company calls a "digital safety." When not ready to shoot, the user can place his finger on the notch instead of on the trigger.

www.alchemyltd.com

ARMSCOR

This Philippine manufacturer makes a line of 1911-type pistols. The line consists of full-size (5"), "commander" (4") and compact (3.5") in blue, stainless and dual-tone finishes. Calibers are 45, 40 and 9mm. New for 2001 was a full-size 45-caliber "meltdown" variation, with all the edges rounded off.

www.armscor.com.ph

ARMS MORAVIA

The recently introduced CZ-G 2000 pistol now has a new U. S. importer. Anderson and Richardson Arms Co., of Fort Worth, TX, will handle the Czech-made pistol. The distinctively shaped pistol has a polymer frame and is available in 9mm and 40. It is a conventional Double Action (*DA*) with the decocker recessed into the slide.

arms@arms-moravia.cz

BERETTA

Beretta is celebrating its 475th anniversary in 2001, and rightfully considers itself the oldest firearms company in existence. Records in the company's archives show that in 1526, Bartolomeo Beretta sold 185 arquebus barrels to the Arsenal of Venice. (*He received 296 ducats as payment.*) From that point, the Beretta line has expanded.

The biggest news is the new Model 92 Millennium pistol. Based on the Model 92 design, it is single action, has a steel frame, frame-mounted safety (it can be carried cocked-and-locked), carbon-fiber grips and adjustable rear sight. The slide is the reinforced "Brigadier" type. It is finished in nickel alloy, with special engraving. Production will be limited to 2000 pistols, 1000 of which will be sold in the United States.

The 92/96 series pistols are now available in a Black Inox (black on stainless) variant. Finish is matte black with gray wraparound rubber grips.

On the smaller end, the 3022 Alley Cat variation of its little Tomcat 32 is offered. It has Big Dot tritium express sights, and comes with a special inside-the-pants holster.

The Model 87 22-caliber target pistol has its adjustable sights mounted in a full-length top bar that will accept optical or electronic sights. A nice feature is that the pistol will stand upright when placed on a flat surface.

The 9000S, Beretta's first polymer-frame pistol, is now in full production. The 9000S, the first Beretta with a tilting-barrel locking system, now makes the company the only one to offer all three common locked-breech systems (the 92/96 series has the dropping block, and the Cougar has the rotating barrel system). To retain the traditional Beretta open-top configuration, Beretta engineers moved the locking lugs from the top to the lower side of the 9000S barrel. A clever holster is available for the

Malloy tries out a 40-caliber conventional DA Beretta 9000S in single-action mode. A separate DAO variant is also offered.

22 GUNS ILLUSTRATED

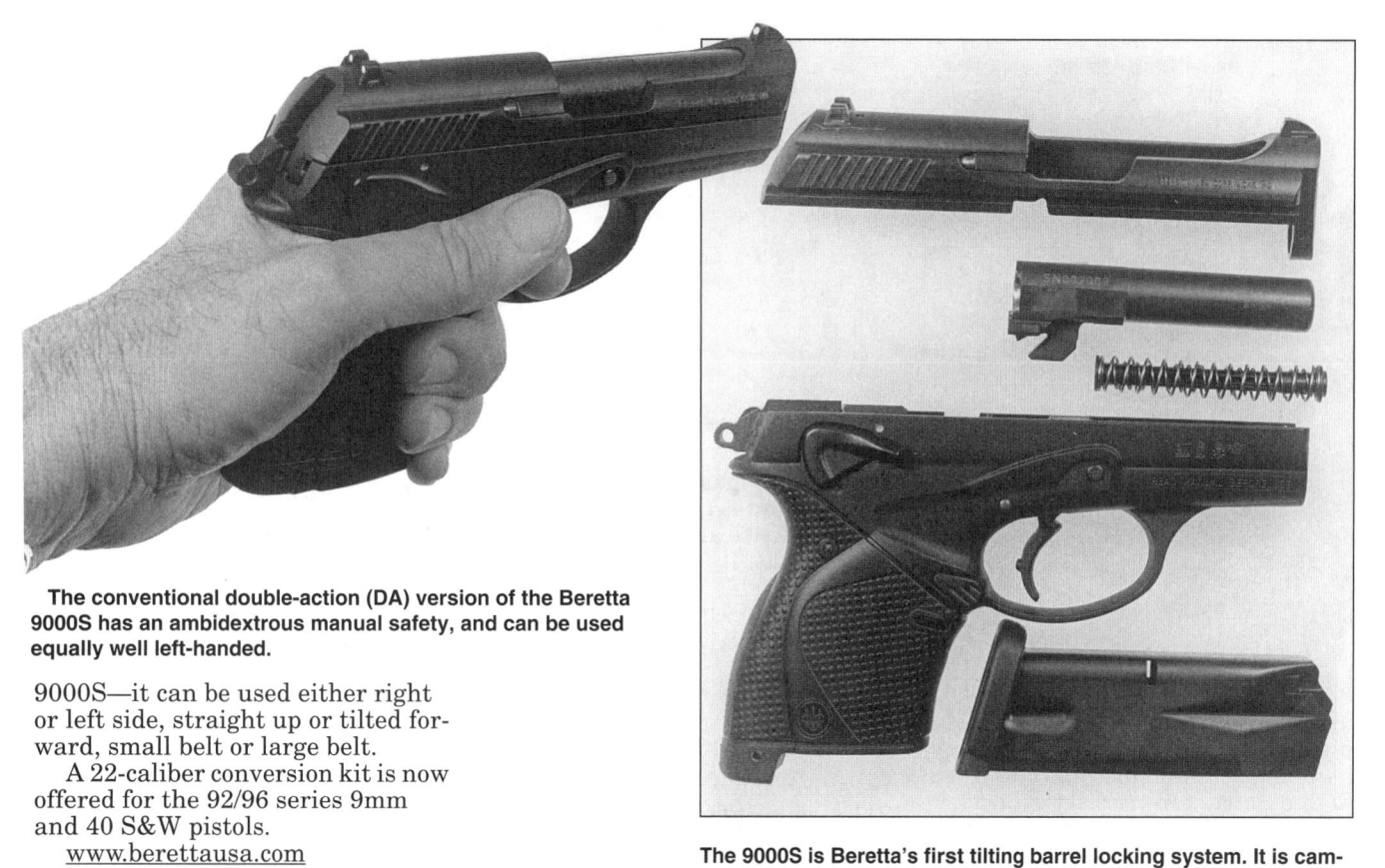

The conventional double-action (DA) version of the Beretta 9000S has an ambidextrous manual safety, and can be used equally well left-handed.

9000S—it can be used either right or left side, straight up or tilted forward, small belt or large belt.

A 22-caliber conversion kit is now offered for the 92/96 series 9mm and 40 S&W pistols.

www.berettausa.com

The 9000S is Beretta's first tilting barrel locking system. It is cam-operated, and the lugs are at the bottom to maintain the traditional Beretta open-top appearance.

BROWNING

Browning is celebrating its 25th year of 22-caliber pistol production in Utah. Accordingly, this year the company is producing a 25th Anniversary Buck Mark pistol with a 6.75-inch barrel and bonded ivory grips with a scrimshaw pattern. 1000 will be made.

Other new items in the pistol line include Buck Mark "Color Camper" pistols. These will be made with red, blue or green frames. A limited run of 1200 pistols will be made in colors.

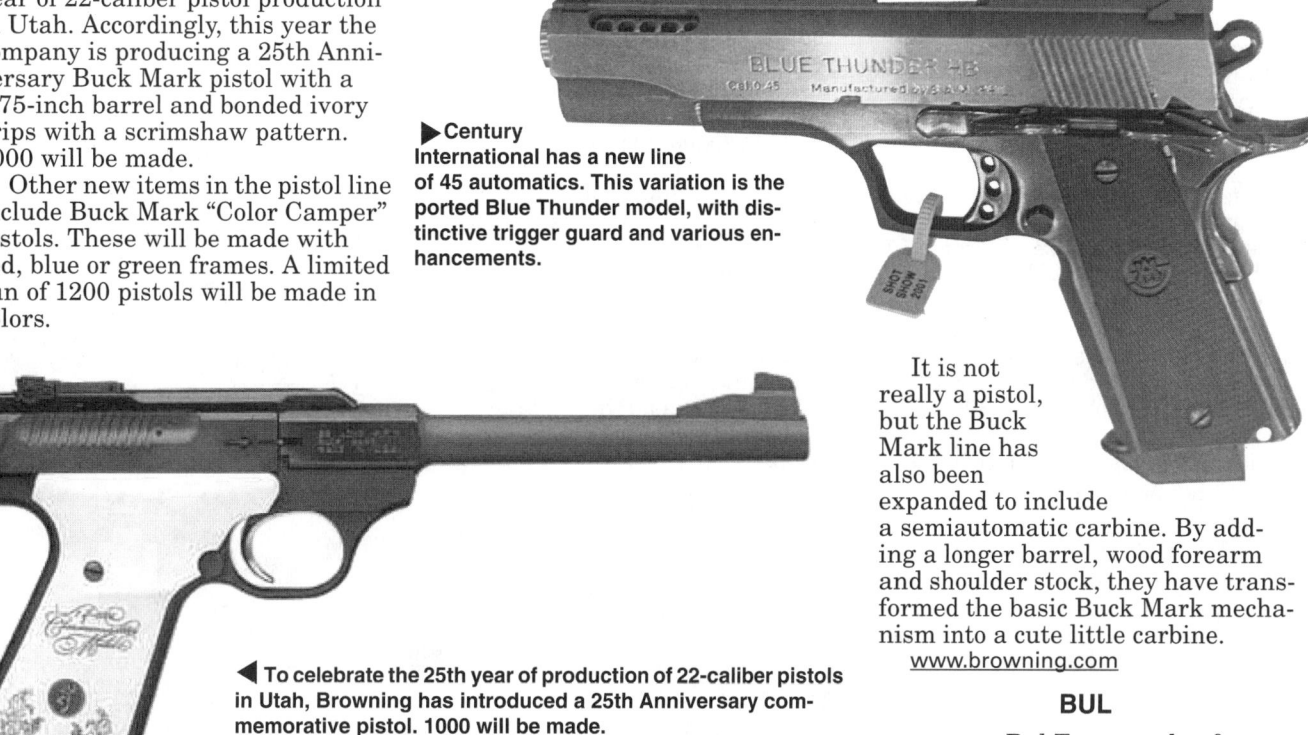

▶**Century International has a new line of 45 automatics. This variation is the ported Blue Thunder model, with distinctive trigger guard and various enhancements.**

It is not really a pistol, but the Buck Mark line has also been expanded to include a semiautomatic carbine. By adding a longer barrel, wood forearm and shoulder stock, they have transformed the basic Buck Mark mechanism into a cute little carbine.

www.browning.com

◀ **To celebrate the 25th year of production of 22-caliber pistols in Utah, Browning has introduced a 25th Anniversary commemorative pistol. 1000 will be made.**

◀ **Browning's Buck Mark pistol is the basis for the new Buck Mark carbine. Not really a pistol, but sort of cute.**

BUL

Bul Transmark, of Israel, introduced a new 10-shot small 45 at the January 2001 SHOT Show. It uses a polymer frame and was so new Bul had not named it yet. It will not be sold in the U. S. under the Bul name. The company is

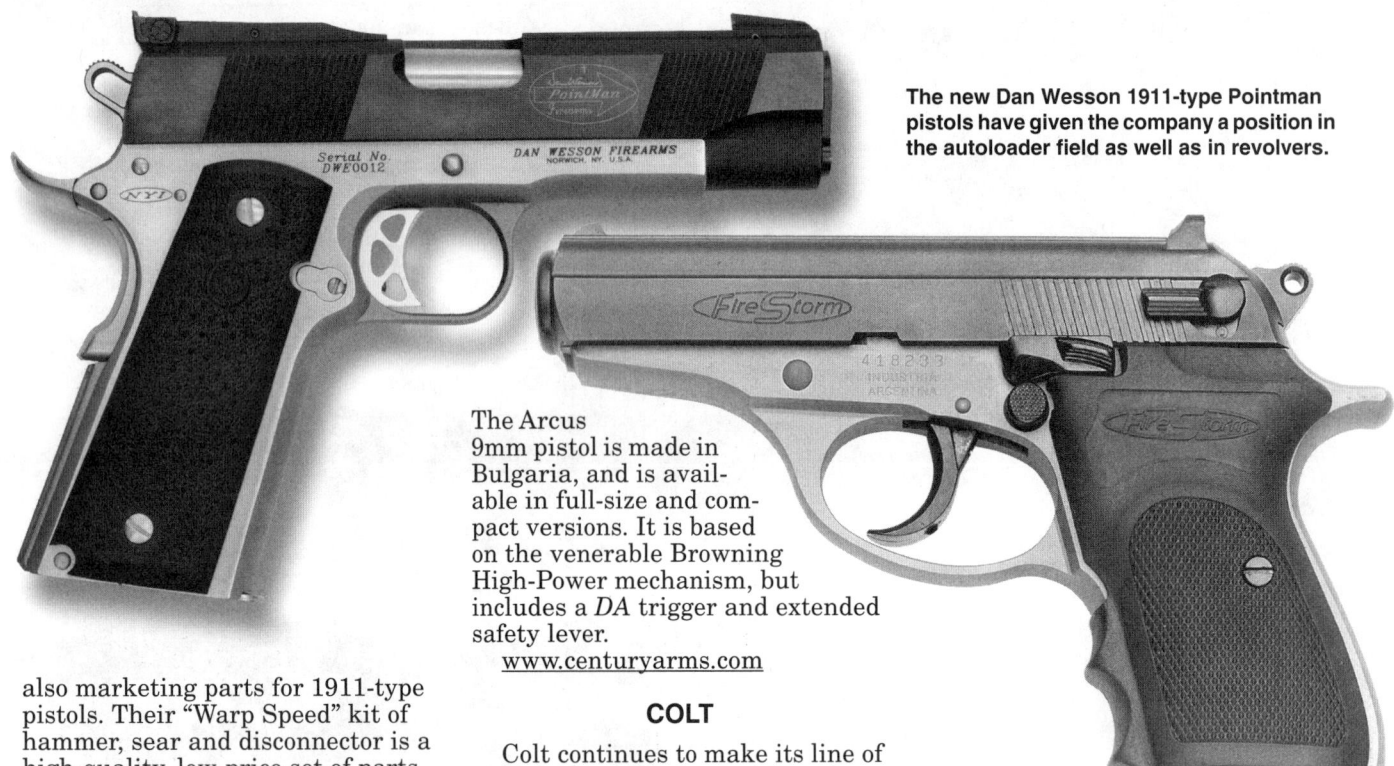

The new Dan Wesson 1911-type Pointman pistols have given the company a position in the autoloader field as well as in revolvers.

also marketing parts for 1911-type pistols. Their "Warp Speed" kit of hammer, sear and disconnector is a high-quality, low-price set of parts that can be installed without fitting.

A "Slideless" pistol attracted considerable attention at the Bul display. The custom 9mm pistol had so much metal removed from the slide it almost seemed a cutaway model. It is claimed to have a very fast action, and the specimen shown was actually used in competition.
www.bultransmark.com

CASULL

Casull Arms, noted for big revolvers and powerful cartridges, has entered the world of semiautomatic pistols. The new Casull autoloader is a 1911-style pistol for, of course, a powerful new cartridge. The new bottleneck round is called the 38 Casull. It reportedly pushes a 124-grain bullet out at about 1800 feet per second (fps), while a 147-grain projectile leaves at about 1650 fps.
www.casullarms.com

CENTURY INTERNATIONAL

Century International's big news is their new line of 45-caliber 1911-style pistols. The guns are available in full-size and "commander" lengths in two styles. The standard model has a beavertail grip safety and extended controls. The Blue Thunder variant adds combat sights, full-length guide rod, a notched front strap, distinctively reshaped trigger guard and (in the full-size versions) an optional ported barrel.

Century also offers the Korean Daewoo "Tri-fire" pistols, in the full-size version, in 9mm and 40 S&W.

The Arcus 9mm pistol is made in Bulgaria, and is available in full-size and compact versions. It is based on the venerable Browning High-Power mechanism, but includes a *DA* trigger and extended safety lever.
www.centuryarms.com

COLT

Colt continues to make its line of 1911-style pistols in 45 ACP only. One special edition model was displayed at the January 2001 SHOT Show, considered by some a reissue. It is a genuine Colt 1911A1 as it was made at the beginning of World War II. It is Parkerized, has the original mechanical construction (no late-model changes), and has the old wide hammer, and—glory be—a lanyard ring. The markings are the same as those of the original Colts of the early WWII period. However, if you look closely, you'll see the serial number has a "WK" prefix. They are the initials of Lt. Gen. William Keyes, Colt's new head man, who supported the project.

It is a little off the subject of autoloading handguns, but many were glad to see a Python 357 revolver back in Colt's display. Plans were to reintroduce the Python during the second quarter of 2001, in a 6-inch stainless-steel version.
www.colt.com

CZ-USA

The CZ 75 and its variants continue to dominate the line for CZ. New at the 2001

The new Firestorm 22 is a Bersa-style pistol handling the popular 22 Long Rifle (22LR) cartridge. Operation is conventional DA and capacity is 10+1.

SHOT Show were the CZ 75 Compact, now in 40 S&W as well as 9mm, and the CZ 75D (decocker) variants. The new decocker model eases the hammer down in two steps; this could be of real interest to those who have never really felt comfortable with the hammer of a loaded pistol slamming forward, no matter what assurances the safety devices provided.

Also available is a CZ 75 Compact "carry" pistol. This is a smooth-

The new FN Forty Nine is a DAO striker-fired pistol sold only by FN of Herstal, Belgium. A new American company has been set up to offer the pistols in the U. S.

24 GUNS ILLUSTRATED

A 380 Comp Gun? Well, why not? Hi-Point's new offering gives a new shooter a low-recoil way to get started. Two magazines are provided—an 8-shot finger-rest version, and a 10-shot extended one.

edged "meltdown" that many shooters seem to like nowadays. A new CZ 75M IPSC pistol has been introduced. In 40 S&W caliber, it is designed to meet MII frame of the 45-caliber CZ 97, and has extended magazine release, compensator, blast deflector and other niceties.

The polymer-frame CZ 100, previously scheduled for United States introduction, will not be imported.

CZ offers a FirePoint sight with a red dot that stays permanently on. The expected life is over five years.

If you have looked at CZ pistols and have wondered why some models have the letter B suffix in the designation, be aware that it indicates that a new firing pin safety is installed. If you see a pin-filled hole in the rear portion of the slide, that also indicates the new safety.

www.cz-usa.com

DAN WESSON

Dan Wesson, a name associated with modern revolvers since 1968, introduced a line of 1911-type pistols in the year 2000. By January 2001, the variety of "Pointman" pistols had grown to eleven different models.

www.danwessonfirearms.com

FIRESTORM

FireStorm is a new name in the shooting world, introduced just last year, which offers new twists in established designs. Its first offering was a line of 1911-styled 45-caliber pistols. A new introduction in early 2001 was a new FireStorm pistol chambered for the 22LR cartridge. Based on the Bersa design, the new pistol has 10+1 capacity and measures about 4.7x6.6 inches. Matte and duo-tone finishes are offered. The FireStorm pistols are available through SGS Importers.

www.firestorm-sgs.com

FN

FN Herstal, of Belgium, sells some handguns in the rest of the world that Browning sells in the United States. The new FN Forty-Nine pistol (*note that the first letters of the company name and the pistol model are the same*), however, is sold only by FN. It is a departure from the traditional pistols based on the Browning 1935 "High Power." The FN is *DAO*, striker-fired – and with a polymer frame, yet.

The pistol feels good in the hand, with a *slantier* grip angle than that of the 1935-type pistols. The slide and barrel are of stainless steel, and a semigloss black finish is available. The polymer frame's forward edge is slotted for whatever accessories the shooter might desire.

The new pistol is offered in 9mm for now. Size is 5.7x7.7 inches, with a 4.25" barrel. Empty weight is about 26 ounces. Magazine capacity is 16 rounds for the rest of the world, 10 for the common folk in America. The Forty-Nine is offered through a new company, FN Manufacturing, Inc. of Columbia, SC.

billf@fnmfg.com

GLOCK

Having filled most of the niches in its autoloading handgun plans, Glock has taken a temporary break from introducing new models this year. However, the company is working on a new internal lock, a prototype of which was present at the 2001 SHOT Show in New Orleans. This prototype device locked with a key through the butt, in the space behind the magazine. When locked, a protrusion at the rear of the grip can be seen or felt.

www.glock.com

HK

Heckler & Koch have introduced a new 40-caliber pistol in their USP Expert series. At present, this pistol is cataloged for law enforcement only. It has a magazine-well extension to funnel the magazine into place rapidly. The magazine is a special 16-round polymer one, which can be used by American law enforcement and the rest of the world. The extension can be removed, and a standard magazine can be used. So, it is possible that a 10-round "civilian" version might be forthcoming if the interest warrants it.

www.hecklerkoch-usa.com

HERITAGE

The nice little Heritage Stealth polymer-frame pistol has taken a sabbatical for now. Cowboy Action shooting has become popular enough that Heritage has expanded its single-action "Rough Rider" revolver line, and temporarily suspended production of the semiautos. A number of shooters have expressed the hope that the Stealth pistols—which have received good

IAI offers new features such as extended controls and large beavertail grip safety on its line of 1911-type pistols. This is a full-size pistol with a 5-inch barrel.

34th EDITION, 2002 **25**

reviews for exceptional accuracy—will soon become available again.
www.heritagemfg.com

HIGH STANDARD

High Standard is offering a "Safety/Fast" shooting kit for its new line of 1911-type pistols. From the full-cock position, the hammer can be pushed forward, a bit like a Daewoo. However, the similarity ends there. The Safety/Fast system automatically engages the thumb safety when the hammer is pushed forward. Now, everything is locked—the hammer cannot be recocked, the trigger cannot be pulled, the slide cannot be moved. At this time a transfer-bar system prevents the hammer from contacting the firing pin. To get the pistol back into action, simply push the thumb safety down. The hammer is automatically recocked, and the pistol is ready to shoot. Pretty nifty.
www.highstandard.com

HI-POINT

Hi-Point Firearms has introduced a new 380 Comp Gun. The new pistol has a 4-inch barrel, adjustable sights and compensator on the muzzle. It comes with two magazines—an 8-round version with a finger rest, and a 10-round extended model. Why a 380? Hi-Point claims it is extremely accurate with very low recoil; perhaps a good way for a new shooter to get started at low cost. Unlike most previous models, the new pistol has a magazine disconnect safety and last-round hold-open. It is also available with a laser mounted to the compensator.
www.high pointFirearms.com

Kahr Arms has expanded its polymer-frame offerings with the new P40, a lightweight pistol cham-

Auto-Ordnance, now operated by Kahr, offers three 1911-style pistols, including this variant with wrap-around grips.

IAI

IAI offers new features on its line of 1911-type pistols such as extended slide stop, safety and magazine release, beavertail grip safety, ambidextrous safety and beveled magazine well. The Houston-based company is now also the sole distributor for the South African RAP 401 (9mm) and RAP 440 (40 S&W) pistols, which are marketed as the IAI M-3000 and IAI M-4000 models, respectively.
www.israelarms.com

HS AMERICA

The HS 2000 pistol, introduced just last year, is now in production in 9mm. 40-caliber versions were scheduled for mid-2001. Recall that the Croatian-designed pistol has a polymer frame, a *"Glock-type"* trigger, and locks by a cam-operated tilting-barrel system. New features such as an accessory rail, front slide serrations, a shorter trigger pull and an outlined stippled grip are now standard. They will be phased in on current production.

Also added is a *"read this"* instruction notice of which American shooters have grown so fond. When bored with shooting, we can just stop and read our guns.
www.hsarms.com

KAHR

Kahr introduced its first polymer-frame 9mm pistol last year, and is filling out its polymer lineup. The new 40 S&W-caliber Kahr P40

Kel-Tec's Renee Goldman holds two of the many options of the company's popular lightweight P-32 pistol.

▶ To help preserve our firearms rights, Kimber offered a special Heritage Fund pistol. The company donated to the Hunting and Shooting Sports Heritage Foundation for each pistol sold.

Wildlife Artist Jocelyn Lillpop Russell takes a break at the 2001 SHOT Show to examine the new Kimber Ultra Ten II pistol.

▲ Kimber believes their new Ultra Ten II is the smallest, lightest 10-shot 45 around. The new pistol is the first to utilize Kimber's new grip-operated safety system.

was introduced at the January 2001 SHOT Show. The P40 weighs in at less than 19 ounces and measures about 4.5x6 inches, with a 3.5-inch barrel. The single-column 6-round magazine keeps the width down to less than an inch. Two magazines come with each pistol.

Recall that Kahr bought Auto-Ordnance two years ago, and with it the right to the 1911-type A-O Thompson pistols. Three versions are now in production: a Parkerized military version, a standard blued version, and a deluxe variant with wrap-around grips and 3-dot sights.
www.kahr.com

KEL-TEC

Kel-Tec has had such good response to the little 6.5-ounce P-32 pistol that they are trying to fill all possible niches of their customers' wants. The P-32 slide may now be had in a hard chrome finish as well as the standard black. The polymer frame is now available in a choice of five colors, in addition to the basic black. Options are silver grey, light blue, dark blue, tan and olive. Mix and match the slides and frames, and it would be possible to have an extensive collection of just P-32s.
www.kel-tec.com

KIMBER

Kimber, reportedly the largest maker of 1911-style pistols, has added a new safety system. The firing pin block is now deactivated by movement of the grip safety, rather than the trigger. This allows the trigger to do the original job of releasing the hammer, without any additional parts going along for the ride that might change the pull. There is no difference in external appearance. The change was scheduled to be phased in during 2001, and the modified pistols will have a "II" designation after the model number.

Kimber designed a special Heritage Fund Edition 45 to help preserve our firearms rights. For each pistol purchased, the company donated $200 to the Hunting and Shooting Sports Heritage Foundation. Each owner also received an individual Heritage Fund membership.

Who offers the smallest, lightest 10-shot 45? Kimber believes their brand-new Ultra Ten II fits that description. At 24 ounces, with its aluminum-insert polymer frame, the new pistol holds a 10-round magazine for 10+1 capacity. Did you notice the "II" in the name? It is the first Kimber produced with the new safety system.
www.kimberamerica.com

KORTH

At its first SHOT Show display in recent years was the elegant German Korth pistol. A new company,

34th EDITION, 2002 **27**

Korth USA, has been formed to market the Korth in the United States. The clever design and beautiful machine work on the Korth variant displayed allows the use of four calibers to be used in a single pistol, with only changes of barrels. Even though they are of different dimensions and shapes, 9x19mm, 9x21mm, 357 SIG and 40 S&W cartridges can be handled in the Korth with the same magazine, slide, extractor, ejector and springs. A lot of thought went into this pistol.
www.korthusa.com

A new company, Korth USA, has been formed to market the elegant German Korth pistol in the United States.

LES BAER

Les Baer Custom is offering a new variation of their 45-caliber Monolith pistol, which was introduced in 2000. Recall that the Monolith frame extends all the way forward to the front of the slide. The new variant is a 4.25-inch barrel pistol called the Comanche. It is available in standard weight and heavyweight styles, and is guaranteed to shoot 3-inch groups at 50 yards. Tritium night sights are included.
www.lesbaer.com

LLAMA

Some years ago, the trend to smaller carry pistols, especially in 45 ACP, became evident. Llama got in on that trend and concentrated on their compact and sub-compact "Minimax" 45s. But there are always those who like the original 1911 size and style. To appeal to them, Llama has reintroduced the government-size 45-caliber MAX-1 pistol, which has a matte black finish.
www.bersa-llama.com

MAGNUM RESEARCH

Polymer is "*in*," and Magnum Research has added a polymer-frame pistol to their Baby Eagle lineup.

Their big boomer, the Desert Eagle, now offers components to switch from one caliber to another almost instantly. Owners of Mark XIX Desert Eagles in 44 Magnum, 440 Cor-Bon, or 50 Action Express (50 AE) can now have the other calibers with just a barrel and magazine change. The 357 Magnum Desert Eagle can also convert to the other calibers, but that swap requires a bolt assembly change also. All chamberings are available with 6- or 10-inch barrels.

Titanium Gold finishes are now available on most of the pistol line, one of eight different finishes the company can provide.

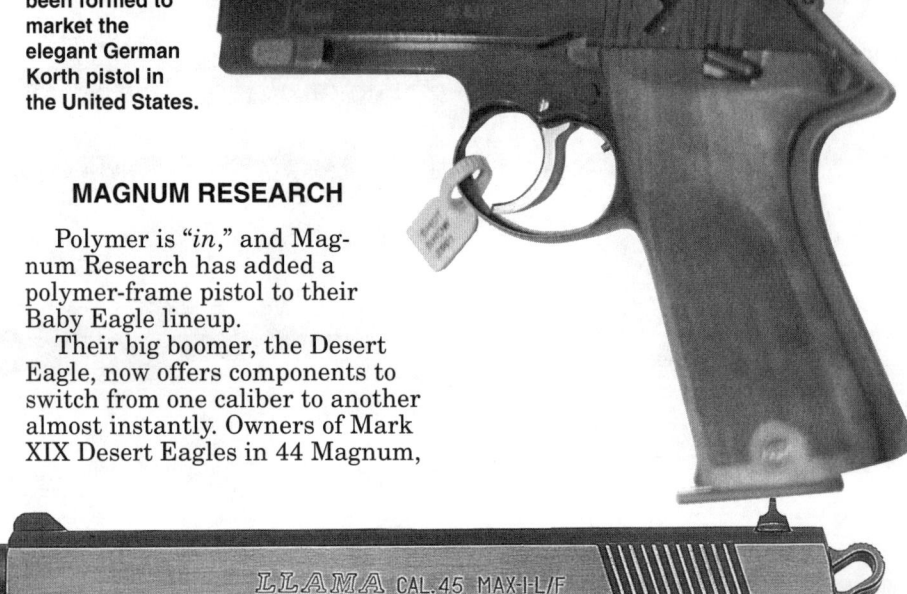

www.magnumresearch.com

Lots of people still like full-size 45s, and Llama has brought its MAX-1 pistol out of temporary retirement and back into the product line.

North American Arms figures that if a small 32 is good, why not a small 380? The new NAA Guardian 380 is only fractions of an inch larger than their 32.

NAA

North American Arms, long a maker of mini-revolvers, was a recent entry into the semi-auto pistol field just a few years ago. Its single offering—the 25-sized 32 Guardian pistol—was well received, so now the company has added another. If a small 32 is good, company officers apparently reasoned, would not a small 380 be better? Their new offering, displayed for the first time at the January 2001 SHOT Show, is the NAA Guardian 380. The new 380 measures 3.5x4.75 inches, with a 2.5-inch barrel. Weight is less than 19 ounces. For comparison, the 32 is 3.3x4.35 inches, so the difference is about .4-inch longer grip and about .2-inch longer slide. Capacity of both pistols is 6+1.

A new version of the 32, the Guttersnipe, was unveiled at the same time. The catchy name comes from a hollow gutter along the top of the slide. At the end of the gutter is a white dot. At the rear of the slide, on the sides of the gutter, are two white dots. Thus, the little pistol offers a 3-

28 GUNS ILLUSTRATED

Introduced during the 1950s, the Whitney Wolverine was considered far ahead of its time. Now, Olympic Arms plans to reintroduce the racy-looking little pistol.

Tom Spithaler of Olympic Arms displays a 22-caliber Whitney Wolverine pistol. The company plans to bring back the neat little pistol, long out of production.

Pacific Armament's Joel Steinberg (*right*) points out features of the company's new line of 1911-type pistols to Gayle Grissett. Long a maker of parts, Pacific Armament now offers a variety of complete pistols.

dot sight system without using any sights. Nothing protrudes and there is nothing to snag.

Also available is an attachable laser that fastens to the front of the pistol and acts as a "*deprinter*," concealing the shape of the pistol when it is carried in a pocket.
www.naaminis.com

NOWLIN

The 40 Super cartridge, introduced last year, has great potential, and Nowlin has brought out a pistol for that recent cartridge. The new Maximum Hunter model was so new, only one sample was available to observe at the SHOT Show. With its 6-inch barrel, velocities are reported to be in the 1800 fps range.

Nowlin also demonstrated other new variations. The company's Compact Carry guns are 6+1 short-grip 1911 variants with 4.25-inch barrels.

A World Cup PPC pistol is available in 9mm, 38 Super, 9x23, 10mm, 40 S&W and 45 ACP. A nice feature is a set of sights that allows preset adjustments for the different PPC ranges.
www.nowlinguns.com

OLYMPIC ARMS

Remember the Whitney Wolverine, the racy-looking 22 pistol made back in the 1950s? Many said it was 50 years ahead of its time. Now that the half-century has passed, Olympic Arms believes it should be offered again. Olympic had actually made most of the parts to begin manufacture, when disaster struck. The factory burned down, and the Wolverine project was dealt a big setback. As of early 2001, a new building was being constructed, and

Kristi McGaha of Professional Ordnance demonstrates the new quick-detachable muzzle brake on the company's big 223-caliber pistol. Using carbon-fiber receivers, the 20-inch pistol weighs only 46 ounces.

the Whitney Wolverine is indeed scheduled to reappear. Minor modifications to the safety will be made, but essentially the pistol will be an exact continuation of the original.
www.olyarms.com

PACIFIC ARMAMENT

A new line of 45-caliber 1911-type pistols has been introduced by Pacific Armament Corp. The company has been making FAL rifle receivers and 1911 parts, and is now offering it own series of complete pistols. Full-size (5") and commander-size (4.25") variants were available in early 2001, with shorter officer-size pistols and versions with 38 Super chambering in the works.
gunparts@att.net

PARA-ORDNANCE

Para-Ordnance, which began with—and gained recognition for—its double-column high-capacity 1911 frames, has introduced its first single-stack pistols. Designed to be slimmer for concealed carry, the first of the new series to be presented are compact, short-barrel *DAO* versions. The L6.45S is a 3.5-inch-barrel version, and the LL6.45S is a 3-incher. They have spurless "snag-free" hammers.

New variants of the LDA (Light Double Action) line, which was introduced two years ago, will be offered with manual safeties.
www.paraord.com

PROFESSIONAL ORDNANCE

Professional Ordnance, makers of the large but relatively light 223-caliber pistols, now offer a quick-detachable compensator for their new pistols. The company uses carbon-fiber upper and lower receivers to make a pistol fully 20 inches long that only weighs 46 ounces. The new compensator reduces muzzle rise, and so makes the pistol easier to shoot. A ball-type lock lets it go on or off the muzzle in seconds.
www.professional-ordnance.com

RUGER

Sturm, Ruger & Co.'s P-series polymer-frame guns have become mainstays in the firm's pistol line. One new variant was introduced at the 2001 SHOT Show. It is a P-95 DA with a conventional manual safety. The safety is ambidextrous and can be operated from either side.
www.ruger-firearms.com

S.A.M.

Shooters Arms Manufacturing, located in the Philippines, is offering a new long-frame 1911 variant. The front of the polymer double-stack frame extends to the front of the slide. The Falcon, as the new series is called, is available in full-size (5" barrel) or compact (4.25" barrel) variants. S.A.M. makes several variations of semiautomatic pistols, all based on the Colt 1911, and all chambered for the 45 ACP cartridge.
www.shootersarms.com.ph

Shooters Arms Manufacturing, located in the Philippines, offers 1911-type pistols. S.A.M.'s Richard Yuson holds the new Falcon, with frame extended to the front of the slide.

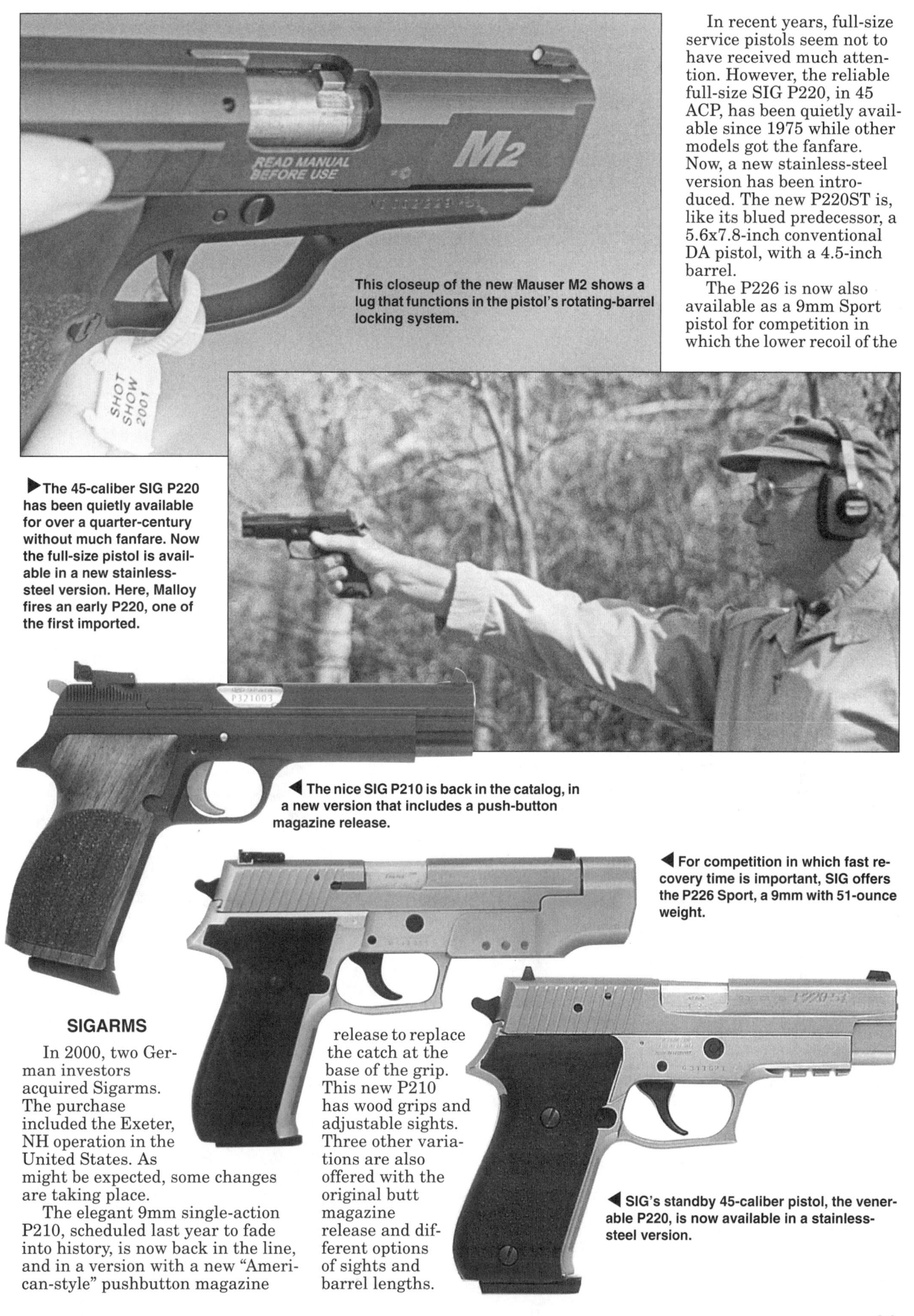

This closeup of the new Mauser M2 shows a lug that functions in the pistol's rotating-barrel locking system.

In recent years, full-size service pistols seem not to have received much attention. However, the reliable full-size SIG P220, in 45 ACP, has been quietly available since 1975 while other models got the fanfare. Now, a new stainless-steel version has been introduced. The new P220ST is, like its blued predecessor, a 5.6x7.8-inch conventional DA pistol, with a 4.5-inch barrel.

The P226 is now also available as a 9mm Sport pistol for competition in which the lower recoil of the

▶ *The 45-caliber SIG P220 has been quietly available for over a quarter-century without much fanfare. Now the full-size pistol is available in a new stainless-steel version. Here, Malloy fires an early P220, one of the first imported.*

◀ *The nice SIG P210 is back in the catalog, in a new version that includes a push-button magazine release.*

◀ *For competition in which fast recovery time is important, SIG offers the P226 Sport, a 9mm with 51-ounce weight.*

SIGARMS

In 2000, two German investors acquired Sigarms. The purchase included the Exeter, NH operation in the United States. As might be expected, some changes are taking place.

The elegant 9mm single-action P210, scheduled last year to fade into history, is now back in the line, and in a version with a new "American-style" pushbutton magazine release to replace the catch at the base of the grip. This new P210 has wood grips and adjustable sights. Three other variations are also offered with the original butt magazine release and different options of sights and barrel lengths.

◀ *SIG's standby 45-caliber pistol, the venerable P220, is now available in a stainless-steel version.*

34th EDITION, 2002 **31**

Sigarm's Laura Burgess displays a Mauser M2 pistol, which is marketed by Sigarms, along with the company's extensive line of SIG pistols.

9mm offers a recovery-time advantage. The new P226 has a heavy 5.6-inch barrel with a weighted frame extension. The weight is upped to over 51 ounces. Capacity is the legal limit of 10+1.

SIG also offers the new rotating-barrel Mauser M2 pistol, a compact 5x6.8-inch size with a 3.5-inch barrel. At about 32 ounces, the M2 comes as a 45, 40S&W or 357 SIG. Capacity is 8+1 in 45, 10+1 in the other calibers.

www.sigarms.com

SMITH & WESSON

Smith & Wesson created considerable discussion in mid-2000 when the company reached an agreement with the Clinton administration. Ostensibly about safety, it actually concerned what they could make, how those products would be marketed and how the company would spend its money. The firearms community apparently did not favor such government control of a private industry. In October 2000, S&W's parent company, the Tomkins group, announced that Ed Schultz had stepped down as president and CEO. He was replaced by George Colclough, a 25-year S&W employee.

By early 2001, the company had dropped a number of items from the line, but had added some new ones, too. Several new semiautomatic pistols were added. The SW9P (9mm) and SW40P (40S&W) are ported pistols in the Sigma series. The new ported guns feature 3-dot sights and an accessory or equipment rail on the forward frame. The sides of the slides are polished bright.

Some models of the S&W 22-caliber pistol line are now offered with "Hi-Viz" sights.

There is now a ported S&W Sigma. The new SW40P and SW9P have barrel porting, three-dot sights and an accessory rail.

For those who want something less bright, S&W has also gone the other way with its unported SW9G and SW40G pistols. Specifications are basically the same, but these are not bright. The polymer frame is NATO green, and a coating of Melonite black hides the stainless slide.

The 22-caliber models 22A and 22S pistols are now offered with

32 GUNS ILLUSTRATED

SIG SAUER
The Science of Accuracy.

SIG Sauer semi-auto pistols are the first choice of elite forces around the world.

P226

- Hammer forged barrel for strength and accuracy

- Interchangeable low profile sights

- Full length rails for strength and accuracy

- Nitron™ finished precision machined stainless steel slide

- Ergonomic design for improved performance

When you pick up a SIG Sauer Classic semi-auto pistol, you are joining thousands of members of the most demanding military and law enforcement organizations in the world – including U.S. Navy SEALs, U.S. Secret Service, and Federal, state and foreign agencies. Whether keeping the peace or upholding the law, they know their SIG Classic will be there when it counts.

SIG Sauer Classics are available in full-size and compact models and in calibers from .380 ACP to .45 ACP, with a wide range of sights, triggers and grips to suit your shooting style. Safety is built in, not added on, with many unique safety features earning Classics an enviable safety record. Quality is built in, too, including hammer-forged barrels, enclosed slide with full-length guide rails, a well-balanced, snag-free, ergonomically-designed frame, and highly durable finishes.

It all adds up to a semi-auto that's easy to use and maintain, gives many years of reliable service, and is in a league by itself when it comes to performance. Like the P220 – rated by experts as one of the most accurate .45s right out of the box – all Classic pistols function with precision and accuracy.

Make a SIG Sauer Classic your first choice. Contact your authorized SIGARMS dealer or SIGARMS, Inc., Corporate Park, Exeter, NH 03833. (603)772-2302. www.sigarms.com

P220 *P229* *P245*

SIGARMS
PRECISION FIREARMS

THE MOST ACCLAIMED REVOLVER IN THE WORLD

FREEDOM ARMS

Freedom Arms Inc.
P.O. Box 150
Freedom, Wyoming 83120
307.883.2468
Website: www.freedomarms.com
E-mail: freedom@freedomarms.com

Model 83 Premier and Field Grade Caliber's available
.50 Action Express
.475 Linebaugh
454 Casull

Optional cylinders in:
.45 Colt
.45 ACP
.45 Win. Mag.
.44 Magnum
.41 Magnum
.357 Magnum
.22 Long Rifle

Optional cylinder in:
.22 Win. Mag.

Model 97 Premier Grade Caliber's available
.45 Colt

Optional cylinder in,
.45 ACP
.41 Magnum
.357 Magnum

Optional cylinder in,
.38 Special

Primary uses are Hunting, Silhouette Shooting, Cowboy Action Shooting and Collecting.

FULLY LOADED
Our most comprehensive line of autoloading shotguns ever.

Gold Camouflage Series Mossy Oak® Shadow Grass™

Gold Stalker Series, Deer (Scope not included)

Gold Upland Special

Waterfowl, turkey, upland game, deer, trap, skeet or sporting clays. Whatever your game, there's a Gold autoloading shotgun for you. With 23 different models, the Gold is the most comprehensive line of autoloading shotguns Browning has ever offered. From specialized target guns to heavy-hitting magnums. Camo, black synthetic and wood finishes. Each model is fully loaded with standard Gold features, such as a self regulating gas system, back-bored barrel and Invector Plus™ chokes that work together to give you the softest-recoiling shotgun on the market. All Golds also have speed loading and a balance point precisely between the shooter's hands.

Always make sure you store your firearms and ammunition separately and make sure you check out the Gold line — It's fully loaded.

The Gold's self-regulating gas system shoots all loads interchangeably, from 1 oz. light target loads to the heaviest magnums.

BROWNING
www.browning.com

MAGNUM*performance*
IS NOW AUTOMATIC

Now you can get high-performance ballistics without sacrificing the tactical edge of a high-capacity autopistol.

GLOCK has taken its proven "Safe Action System" technology and applied it to the sizzling new .357 auto cartridge.

G31
Full Size

G32
Compact

G33
Sub-Compact

GLOCK PERFECTION®

© GLOCK, Inc., 1998

▶ Here is the prototype of the new Sommer & Ockenfuss P21 pistol. The grip safety at the front of the grip allows the gun to fire as a conventional DA pistol. When the grip safety is released, the hammer lowers automatically.

"Hi-Viz" sights. They use light-gathering rods at the front sights that appear to the shooter as a bright orange or bright green dot.
www.smith-wesson.com

SOMMER & OCKENFUSS

The German company is known for its interesting rifle designs. At the January 2001 SHOT Show, SO introduced a new pistol, the P21. The pistol is interesting for both design and ammunition.

At first observation, the pistol reminds one of the HK P7, as it has a long pivoted bar in the front strap of the grip frame. On the HK pistol, this was a cocking lever; on the SO P21, the lever is called a grip safety. When the SO pistol is grasped, it operates as a conventional double-action (*DA*) arm, that is, *DA* for the first shot, SA for succeeding shots. The difference with the P21 is that when the grip safety is released, the hammer is automatically uncocked and drops to the safety position.

As a compact pistol of about 4.7x6.5 inches, the P21 has its 3.1-inch barrel offered in more-or-less standard 9mm and 40 chamberings. However, SO also offers it with a new cartridge, the 224 HV. The new round is essentially an elongated 9mm case necked down to 22 caliber. The overall length is about that of the standard 9mm cartridge. A 40-grain jacketed bullet reportedly goes out at about 2000 feet per second. For comparison, that is faster than the 40-grain 22 Winchester Magnum Rimfire (22 WMR) fired from a rifle. Pretty zippy.
www.sommer-ockenfuss.de

Sommer & Ockenfuss developed the 224 HV cartridge (*left*) for their new P21 pistol. The new SO pistol will also be chambered for the traditional 9mm and 40 S&W cartridges.

Springfield's Donna Rahn displays the armsmaker's new TRP Operator, a 45 with a special frame for accessory attachment. This specimen has a light installed.

34th EDITION, 2002 **33**

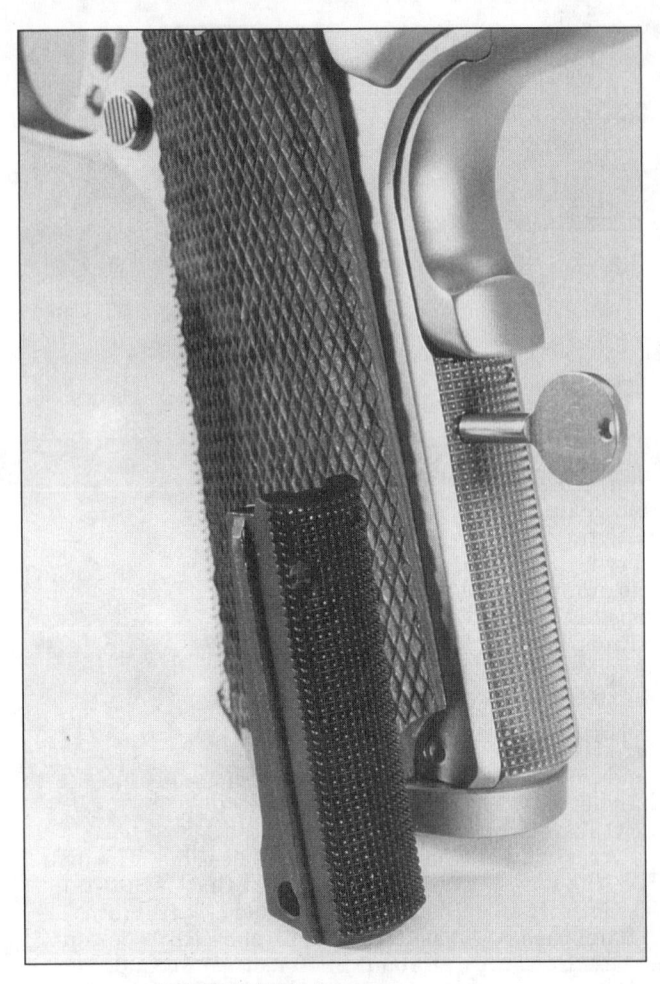

The new Integral Locking System (ILS) from Springfield Armory is a patented locking device that can disable a 1911-type pistol. It is contained entirely within the mainspring housing.

SPRINGFIELD

Springfield has introduced an Internal Locking System (ILS) for their line of 1911-type pistols. The locking device uses a special key to make the pistol inoperable; a reverse turn of the key can put it back into service. The interesting thing about this system is that it is completely contained within the mainspring housing. Springfield began phasing these in on their products in February 2001 and planned to offer a retrofit kit soon afterwards. The installation requires no modification to the pistol.

A new pistol, the TRP Operator, was introduced by Springfield at the January 2001 SHOT Show. The initials stand for Tactical Response Pistol, and the gun is based around the FBI-contract-pistol specifications. The "Operator" portion of the name refers to a special frame with a forged light/accessory rail at the front. The pistol carries most of Springfield's current enhancements, and it has the adjustable rear sight mounted in a forward position on the slide to prevent damage or snagging.

www.springfieldarmory.com

STEYR

The smaller "S" series Steyr pistol, introduced last year, is now in production. The first shipment of 9mms reached the United States in January 2001, with the 40 S&W variant coming soon after.

Steyr's importer, GSI of Trussville, AL, has offered an upgrade of a more consistent trigger assembly for the first group of "M"- series pistols sold. They have the serial numbers of the ones eligible for the upgrade.

The triangular sight system remains standard, but Steyr is considering more sight options for the future.

www.GSIfirearms.com

STI

The V.I.P., a new 45 ACP pistol, was STI's offering for 2001. Based on the 1911, of course, the V.I.P. has an interesting aluminum frame with a double-stack polymer grip. The slide is stainless steel, sized to fit the 3.9-inch barrel. The combination of materials, says STI, makes a potent, lightweight, corrosion-resistant personal-defense firearm. Available in 45 ACP, the capacity is 10+1 and the weight is 25 ounces.

www.stiguns.com

TALON

A new company from Ennis, MT, Talon Industries has introduced pistols in the recent category of inexpensive subcompact polymer-frame carry pistols. Two models, the T-100 (380) and the T-200 (9mm) are offered. Each has a 10-round magazine, with a weight of 17 ounces.

The compact Steyr S-series pistols are now in full production.

Overall size is 4.4x6 inches, and the barrel length is 3.3 inches. Locking is by a tilting-barrel system. Trigger mechanism is DAO.

talonind@3rivers.net

TAURUS

Handy little pistols and more ammunition options have given the 32 ACP a new lease on life in recent years. Now Taurus will have a 32 Automatic in their line. The new Taurus 32 is included in the polymer-frame Millennium series, and is designated PT 132. The little gun was too new to make it into the company's 2001 catalog, so keep an eye peeled for it.

The compact Millenium 45, the PT 145, was introduced last year, but ran into production delays. Quantity delivery of the compact 23-ounce 45 was rescheduled for summer 2001. For those who like a variety of sight options, it may be worth the wait, as night sights will be available when it arrives

www.taurususa.com

VALTRO

Whatever happened to the Valtro 45, the nice Italian-made 1911 design that was introduced several years ago? It had a slow manufacturing start, but is now in production. As of early 2001, the guns were coming out of Italy at the rate of about 100 a month. The pistols are offered in the United States by Valtro USA, of San Rafael, CA.

The subcompact Talon pistol is a new entry in the field of inexpensive polymer-frame carry pistols. It is available in 9mm and 380.

WALTHER USA

Some changes have been taking place at Walther USA since last year. The Hungarian-made PPK/E, announced last year to replace the PPK/S, will not be imported after all. Instead, the PPK/S, which was destined to fade into history, was slightly redesigned and was scheduled to be available by late summer 2001. The remaining stocks of the original-design PPK/S will be sold until they are gone.

Walther realizes that just about everyone can use a 22 pistol. A new offering, a 22-caliber version of the company's P99 pistol, was introduced in January 2001, with availability planned for April 2001. The new P22 is about 25 % smaller than the P99, but retains the same general appearance, although there are mechanical differences. The takedown, ambidextrous magazine release and interchangeable grip backstraps are similar, but the new 22 is hammer-operated, rather than striker-fired. Two versions were announced, a plinker with a 3.4-inch barrel and a more serious version with a weighted 5-inch barrel. The barrels are interchangeable, and the first 1000 will be offered in a kit with both barrels.

www.walther-usa.com

WILSON

Wilson Combat has introduced their KZ-45, a polymer-frame compact carry pistol. A prototype was shown at the January 2001 SHOT Show, and availability was planned for sometime in 2002. A 9+1 45, the new compact Wilson, based on the 1911

Talon's Sharon Edwards points out the features of the Talon 9mm pistol to Sean Gilthorpe at the 2001 SHOT Show.

Pearce Grips offers easily installed 1911 front-strap finger grooves that can be used with the pistol's original grips or with Pearce's big-diamond rubber grips. Here, a combination is used to spruce up the writer's nice old 45 Government Model.

design, sports a 4.1-inch barrel. Although the magazine is of the staggered double-column type, the width is as thin as a standard 1911. The KZ-45 will come with an accuracy guarantee of 1.5 inches at 25 yards.

www.wilsoncombat.com

POSTSCRIPT

Innovative accessories for semi-automatic handguns have been recently introduced. Here are just a few of them:

Pearce Grips offers new items for the ever-popular 1911 pistols. A shooter who likes his present grip panels but would like front-strap finger grooves can get just the rubber front grooves. The Pearce product is a clever way to adapt the finger grooves without modification of the gun. Pearce also offers rubber grip panels, with moulded big-diamond checkering. These can be used by themselves or combined with the finger grooves for a good-feeling grip. www.pearcegrip.com

With the trend to legal-limit magazine capacity in smaller-size pistols, it sometimes becomes harder to load the magazines. There are good magazine loaders available, but generally different ones are required for different magazines. Magloader has introduced a clever new loading aid that will work with all magazines in calibers 32 through 45. The simple loader fits on the shooter's thumb, is easy to carry around, and works great. www.magloader.com

How about a magazine for magazines? The Redi-Clip is a nylon dispenser that holds five loaded magazines and allows them to be withdrawn one at a time. It can clip to a belt or can be otherwise mounted. www.Redi-Clip.com

The Safety Fast shooting kit is available from Numrich Gun Parts for Colt 1911 and Browning High Power pistols. The modified pistol can be safely carried with hammer down on a chambered round. By depressing the manual safety, the hammer is automatically cocked and the pistol is ready to shoot. The kit comes with complete instructions and can be installed without modification to the gun. info@gunpartscorp.com

"Pre-ban" high capacity pistol magazines are treasured items for those with high-capacity pistols. Yet, the magazines can lead a hard life, especially when used in certain types of pistol competition. It is a tragic loss if one is damaged beyond use. Now, the LaPrade Company offers legal replacement magazine bodies for damaged high-capacity Glock magazines. A shooter can put the internal parts of the unusable magazine into the new body and be back in action.

These are just a few of the accessories available for those who enjoy shooting autoloading pistols. A shooter can find an array of metallic sights, optical sights, electronic sights, lasers, grips, holsters, safety devices, specialized parts and magazines, not to mention such staples as ammunition and targets. We should never lose sight of the fact that autoloading handguns and their accessories provide both a creative and an economic boost to our nation.

Among a plethora of new accessories is the Redi-Clip, sort of a magazine for pistol magazines.

HANDGUN NEWS

REVOLVERS, SINGLE SHOTS AND OTHERS

by HAL SWIGGETT

Anschutz

LONG NOTED FOR super-accurate rifles, this German manufacturer does in fact produce bolt-action pistols that equal their rifles: The 64 P is chambered 22 Long Rifle; the 64 P Magnum is chambered for the 22 Winchester Magnum. Magazine capacity for the LR is five; the Magnum, four. Barrel length is 9.8 inches and weight is 3.5 pounds for both. Stocks are black, ergonomic, weatherproof and non-slip synthetic. Both are delivered with sights; both are grooved for scope mounting.

I have been shooting their wood-stocked pistols chambered 22 LR and 22 WMR for many years; both scoped – and they have served well. I look forward to trying the new Anschutz synthetic model.

Anschutz Model G4P Magnum.

Casull Arms

Dick Casull, inventor of the 454 Casull cartridge and builder of the single-action revolver to handle it, has come up with another "winner" – the Casull Arms Model CA 2000. This is a tiny little 5-shot revolver with a fold-up trigger and enclosed hammer that could, very easily, fit in a shirt pocket behind a notebook. It's chambered for the 22 Long Rifle, weighs 8 to 9 ounces and is truly palm-size.

Colt

This Hartford, Connecticut company started manufacturing single-action revolvers in 1836 in Paterson, New Jersey. After two moves they ended up in Hartford in 1848 – and are still in Connecticut.

Their first revolver was the Pocket Model Paterson No. 1, a 28-caliber, 5-shooter. Should you have one in 98-percent original condition it could be worth upwards of $30,000 according to the current edition of *Flayderman's Guide to Antique American Arms and their Values...*

Their current single-action revolver line includes two models – Cowboy Single Action (CSA) and Single Action Army (SAA).

The Cowboy Single Action is blue color-case finished with a 5 1/2-inch barrel, chambered for the 45 Colt.

Charter Arms is offering nothing really new - but continues making their 5-shot stainless steel 44 Special revolver.

... this time with a "Trigger Lock".

Casull Arms' little 22 Long Rifle-chambered 5-shot revolver is, by far, the "cutest" little revolver I've ever seen. With its fold-up trigger it can, easily, fit in a shirt pocket, behind a notebook.

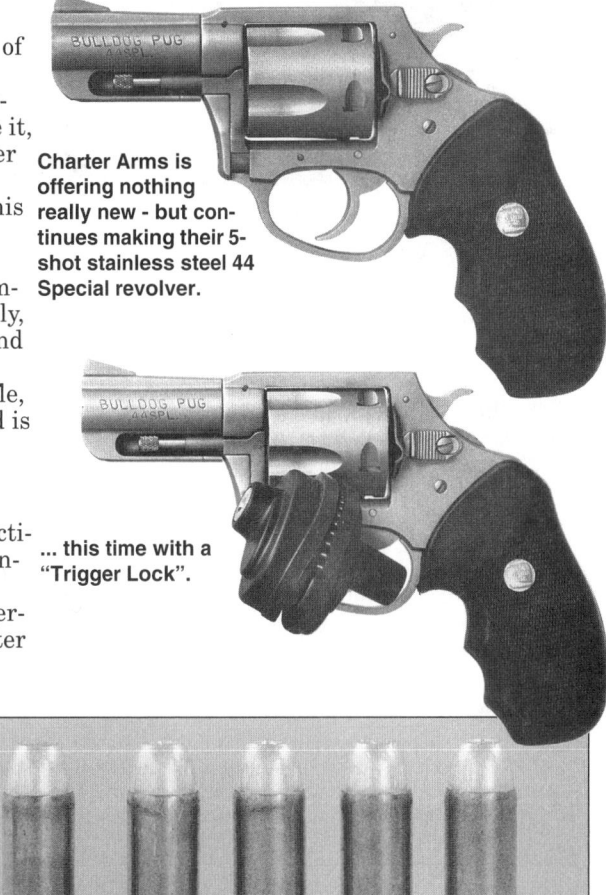

... and it is STILL a 5-shot, double action revolver.

34th EDITION, 2002 **37**

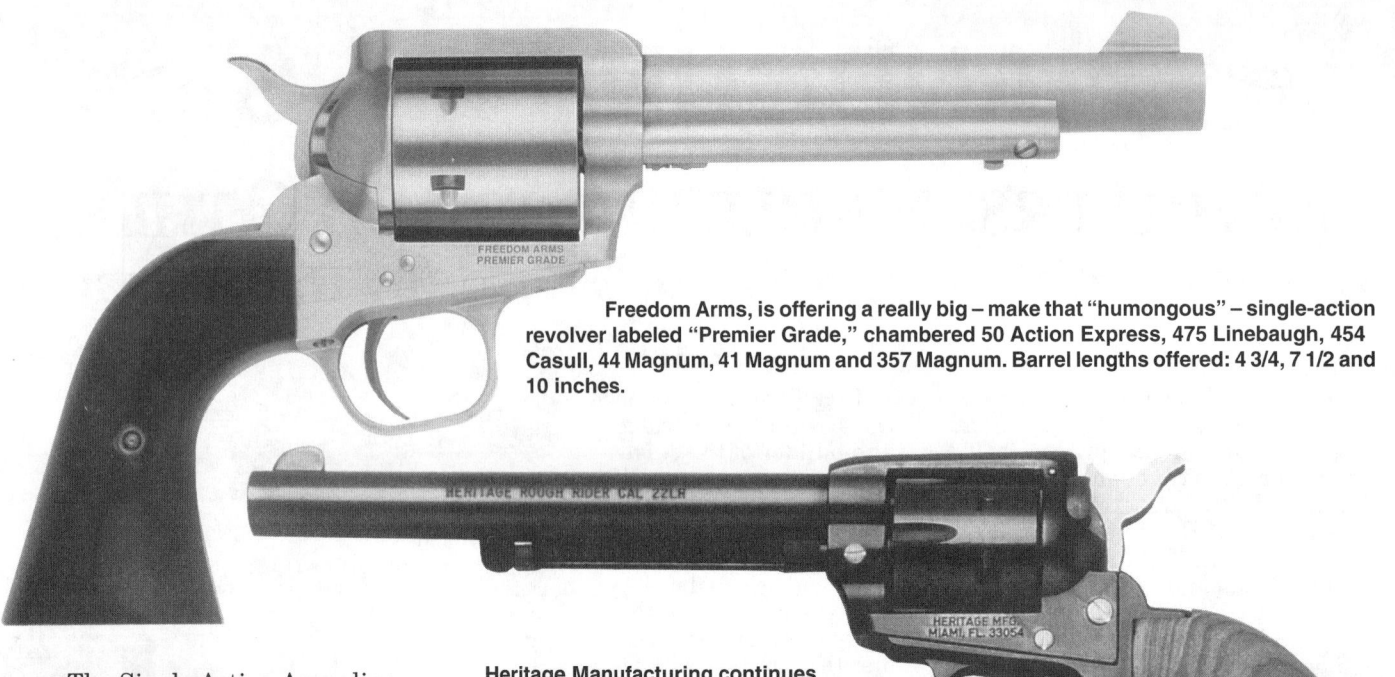

Freedom Arms, is offering a really big – make that "humongous" – single-action revolver labeled "Premier Grade," chambered 50 Action Express, 475 Linebaugh, 454 Casull, 44 Magnum, 41 Magnum and 357 Magnum. Barrel lengths offered: 4 3/4, 7 1/2 and 10 inches.

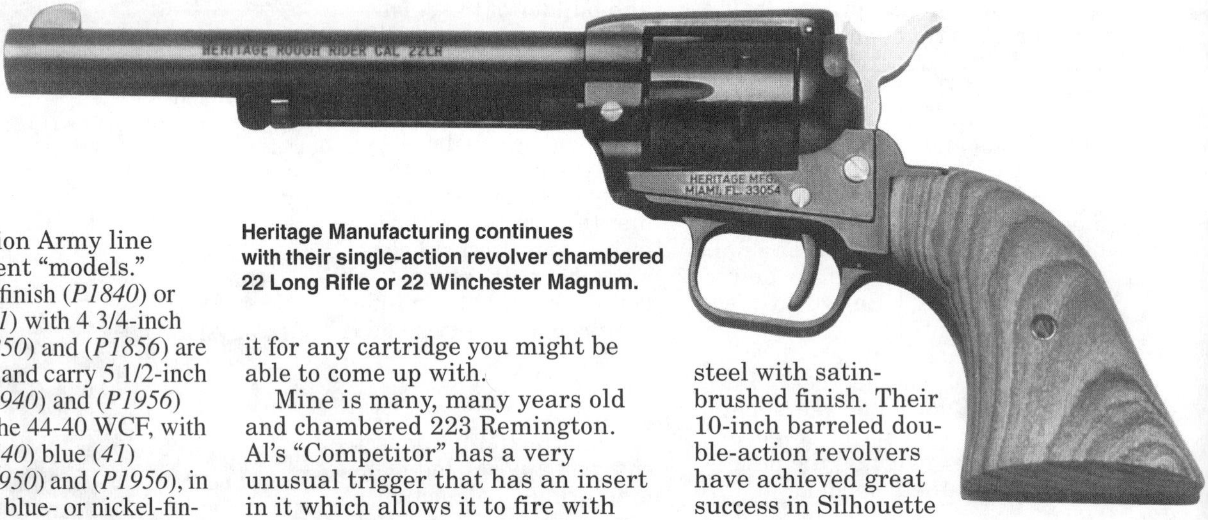

Heritage Manufacturing continues with their single-action revolver chambered 22 Long Rifle or 22 Winchester Magnum.

The Single Action Army line offers eight different "models."

Blue color-case finish (*P1840*) or Nickel finish (*P1841*) with 4 3/4-inch barrels. Model (*P1850*) and (*P1856*) are chambered .45 Colt and carry 5 1/2-inch barrels. Models (*P1940*) and (*P1956*) are chambered for the 44-40 WCF, with 4 3/4-inch barrels [(*40*) blue (*41*) nickel]. Models (*P1950*) and (*P1956*), in that same order, are blue- or nickel-finished with 5 1/2-inch h barrels and also chambered for the 44-40 WCF.

Competitor Corporation, Inc.

Al Straitiff and his wife run this "outfit". They produce a single-shot, cannon-breech pistol and chamber it for any cartridge you might be able to come up with.

Mine is many, many years old and chambered 223 Remington. Al's "Competitor" has a very unusual trigger that has an insert in it which allows it to fire with only 1 1/4 lbs of pressure – not for the casual handgunner.

Dan Wesson Arms

This company has gone through some difficult years but is still turning out their fine Model 360/7360 double-action revolvers. Model 360 is carbon steel with black-oxide bluing. Model 7360 is stainless steel with satin-brushed finish. Their 10-inch barreled double-action revolvers have achieved great success in Silhouette shooting.

Freedom Arms

I have been shooting this company's 454 Casull single-action 5-shot revolvers since their very first production. My lengthy barrel measures 9 1/4 inches (including SSK Industries' ported *"Recoil Reducer"*). This one wears a Simmons 1.5-4x scope in a 4-ring

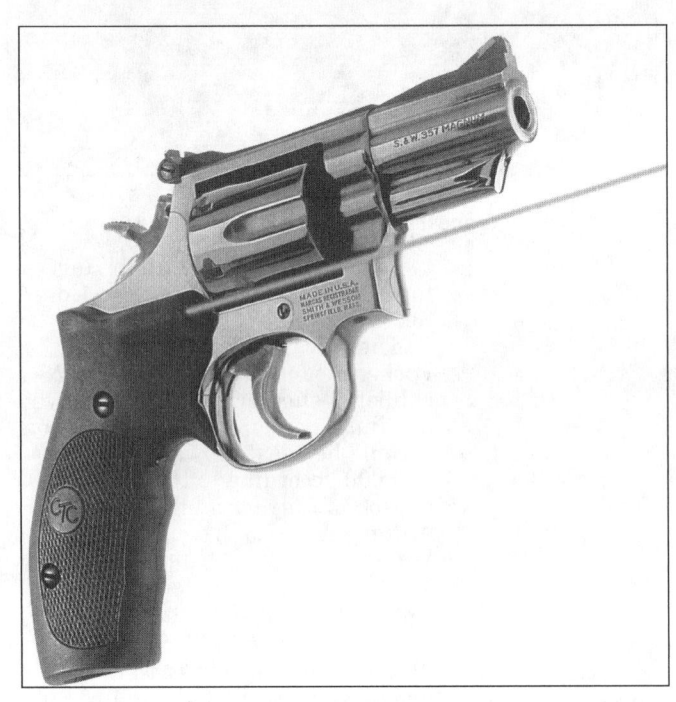

Lasergrips offers a "*beam shooting light*" that lets the shooter know exactly where his bullet will hit.

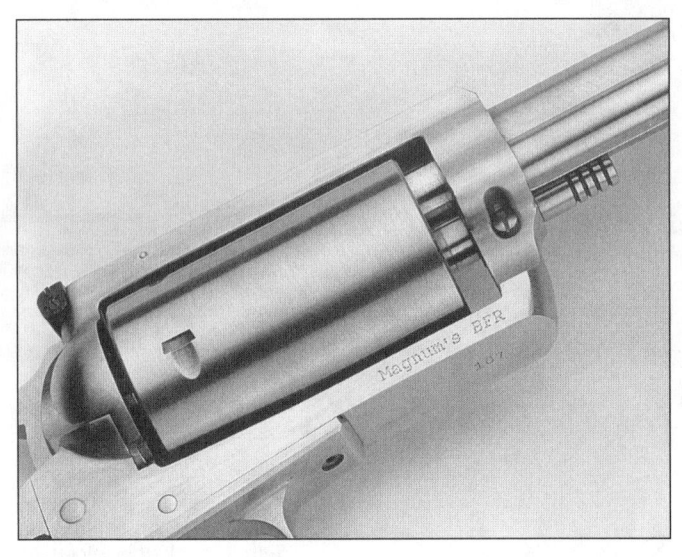

Magnum's BFR boasts a large, rugged frame to accommodate the unusually long cylinder chambered for the 45/70 Government, and others.

38 GUNS ILLUSTRATED

Ruger, this time around, is offering a double action — designed for scope mounting —

6-shot revolver ...

... chambered 480 Ruger (an entirely new cartridge) ...

... manufactured by Hornady.

mount (*yes – you will know when FA's 454 Casull does fire!*).

Freedom Arms has grown! Currently they are offering Premier Grade single actions chambered for the 50 Action Express, 475 Linebaugh, 454 Casull, 44 Magnum, 41 Magnum and 357 Magnum with barrel lengths of 4 3/4, 7 1/2 and 10 inches.

Their Field Grade is available in barrel lengths of 4 3/4, 7 1/2 and 10 inches.

They have not neglected rimfire handgunners. Freedom Arms catalogs a 22 Long Rifle revolver with a 7 1/2-inch barrel.

There are now four Silhouette models: 22 Long Rifle/10 inch; 357 Magnum/9 inch; 41 Magnum/10 inch and 44 Magnum/10 inch.

If you are a handgunner you really do need this manufacturer's catalog.

Heritage Manufacturing, Inc.

This Florida-based manufacturer offers their single-action revolver chambered 22 Long Rifle or 22 Winchester Magnum rimfire. Barrel lengths are 3 3/4, 4 1/2, 6 1/2 or 9 inches. Rough Rider's frame is manufactured from *4140* steel; sights are adjustable. Grips are manufactured from exotic hardwood.

Lasergrips

Crimson Trace Corporation offers grips for revolvers that, when "squeezed," send out a red beam that is easily seen and lets the handgunner know exactly where his bullet will hit.

Though I've never had reason to use it, there is one of my handguns, so rigged, under my pillow every night as I sleep.

Magnum Research

Magnum Research offers their Magnum BFR in two models: Maxine and Little Max – both stainless steel with two cylinder lengths.

Maxine, the larger model, chambers the potent 45/70 Government round, 444 Marlin and 45 Colt/.410.

Little Max is available chambered for the 454 Casull, 45 Colt, 50 A.E. and 22 Hornet. Available barrel lengths are 6 1/2, 7 1/2 or 10 inches.

M.O.A. "Maximum"

Richard R. Mertz, president of this company, has manufactured his "Falling Block Single Shot" pistol for more than a few years. It has won many silhouette titles and taken critters from wild hogs to elk; kudu to moose.

The one I've been shooting is chambered for the 250 Savage Improved and topped with Simmons' 4x32 scope. With its 14-inch long, 3/4-inch diameter barrel it weighs 4 lbs., 15 oz. Trigger pull is

Savage, for 2001, is offering a "Sportsman Model," chambered 22 Long Rifle.

2 1/2 lbs. It has taken antelope in Wyoming – plus deer (both whitetail and mulies), javelina – and many coyotes.

North American Arms

I mention this manufacturer every year for a reason. They are the only manufacturer of a handgun that can be with you totally concealed at all times. All 22s or 22 WMRs with barrel lengths 1 1/8, 1 5/8, 2 and 4 inches. Though I have a concealed carry-license here in Texas, I have – lots of times – had one of these tiny revolvers in my left-side shirt pocket, behind my always-present note book.

Ruger

Their newest, near as I can tell, is a double-action GP100 chambered 357 Magnum offered in blue or stainless steel with barrel lengths of 3, 4 or 6 inches. Plus, your choice of fixed or adjustable sights.

Ruger introduced their Redhawk/Super Redhawk a few years back with the buyer's choice of blue or stainless steel. For 2001 Ruger offers the Super Redhawk chambered for a new cartridge of their design – the 480 Ruger.

Here I quote page 31 in their new catalog: *"The new 480 Ruger cartridge is an exciting new development in handgun hunting cartridges. It offers approximately a third more energy than the powerful 44 Magnum, able to stop big game reliably at typical handgun range."* Ruger's new innovation is offered with the buyer's choice of 7 1/2- or 9 1/2-inch barrels. Finish is SSTG (stainless steel target gray). I will have to have one of these!

Page 36 of the Ruger catalog lists as *NEW*, their Ruger Vaquero with a "Birds Head" grip. Ruger still catalogs their precious little Bearcat.

You need one of their new catalogs.

Savage Arms

I have been shooting one of Savage Arms' Model 516 bolt-action *"short rifles"* (my term because I have found I can do anything with these pistols most riflemen can with their long barrels).

Why am I so fond of it? They made it ever so much easier to shoot because their designer put the bolt on the left side! Plus – its integral muzzle brake allows any shooter to see where the bullets are hitting.

Mine is chambered for the 22-250 Remington. Magazine capacity is 2, making it a 3-shooter. Trigger pull is *"crisp as breaking glass"* at 1 3/4 lbs. A Burris 3x-9x scope is mounted on its 14 1/2-inch barrel (including muzzle brake).

Savage describes Striker's stock as *"dual pillar-bedded ambidextrous mid-grip synthetic"*.

Now, I understand, they are offering a Sportsman model chambered for the 22 Long Rifle. I know I will have to have one of these, too, because it is the only one I would ever consider in any survival situation.

One 500-round carton of 22 Long Rifle cartridges weighs 5-plus pounds. Yet those 500 rounds would feed a family many, many moons.

Rossi /Braztech

For 2001 this Miami company is offering several new revolvers, chambered for the 38 Special or 357 Magnum, depending on the model.

Model 351 is blue steel; Model 352 is stainless. Both with 2-inch barrels, 5-round cylinders chambered for the 38 Special.

Model 461 is blue steel, chambered to accept six 357 Magnum cartridges. Model 462 is stainless steel-constructed; both with 2-inch barrels. Both will accept 38 Special ammunition, along with 357s.

Model 851 is chambered for the 38 Special; blue steel, 6-round capacity with a 4-inch barrel.

Model 971 and Model 972 are chambered for the 357 Magnum. '71 is blue-finished and wears a 4-inch

Smith & Wesson, for 2001, offers their eight-shot Model 317, with a 3-inch barrel, chambered 22 Long Rifle.

40 GUNS ILLUSTRATED

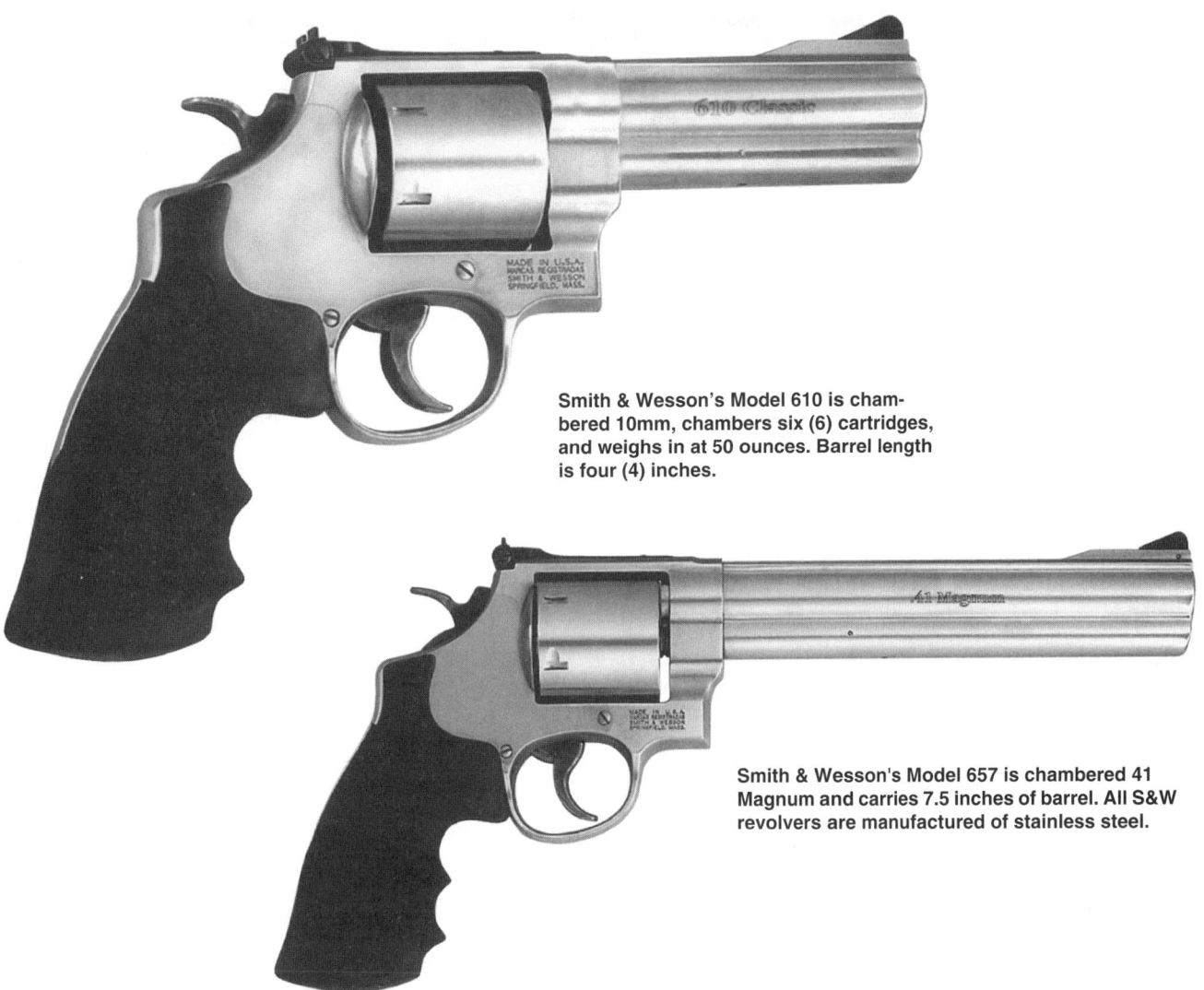

Smith & Wesson's Model 610 is chambered 10mm, chambers six (6) cartridges, and weighs in at 50 ounces. Barrel length is four (4) inches.

Smith & Wesson's Model 657 is chambered 41 Magnum and carries 7.5 inches of barrel. All S&W revolvers are manufactured of stainless steel.

barrel. '72 – of stainless steel – carries a 6-inch barrel.

Models R351 (*blued*) and R352 (*stainless*) are short-barreled, 5-shot, 38 Specials.

Model R461 is also short-barreled, blued – but its cylinder accepts six 357 Magnum cartridges. All are delivered with key locks.

Smith & Wesson

Though this Springfield, Massachusetts, company specializes in *self-shuckers* (autoloaders) they are offering three new revolvers for 2001. Model 317 is chambered 22 Long Rifle, with an 8-shot cylinder. Built on S&W's "J" frame with a 3-inch barrel and target hammer – believe it or not – it weighs only 11.9 ounces. It is manufactured of aluminum alloy and stainless steel to save weight.

S&W's Model 610 is chambered for the 10mm round, chambers six cartridges, and weighs 50 ounces. This revolver has a 4-inch underlug barrel with a ramp front and adjustable rear sight.

Their Model 657 is chambered for the 41 Magnum. This one is fitted with a 7.5-inch barrel, target hammer, smooth trigger – in stainless steel.

Taurus

Up front in their catalog was Titanium Tracker. "*Now available in Total Titanium, the Tracker adds weight and durability benefits of Total Titanium to its list of exclusive features, including rubber grip and extended ejector rod. The Tracker family is available in 41 Magnum and 357 Magnum. All feature adjustable sights.*" Titanium is featured in their Model 85 38 Special, Model 6171 357 Magnum and Model 627 Tracker. They offer a 9-shot 22 rimfire or 8-shot 22 Magnum – their Model 941SS2 – with your choice of 2-, 4- or 5-inch barrel. Taurus' Model 85B2GRC 5-shot is chambered for the 38 Special – another of their short-barreled series.

Taurus' mid-frame service revolver is chambered for the 357 Magnum and is, in their words, "*A Tack Driver*". Their Model 65 is a 6-shot service revolver with fixed sights. Taurus offers another 41 Magnum labeled "Tracker". It, too, is of titanium construction and offered with a 4- or 6-barrel. Cylinder capacity is 5 rounds; weight 24.3 ounces.

Taurus is still cataloging their Raging Bull chambered for the 454 Casull or, if you prefer, 44 Magnum. Barrel lengths offered are: 4, 6 1/2 and 8 3/8 inches. Scope mounts to match barrel lengths and finish (*they offer both blue or stainless*) are also offered for 6 1/2-inch or 8 3/8-inch barrels.

The Raging Hornet wears a 10-inch barrel, carries an 8-shot cylinder and is chambered to accept eight 22 Hornet cartridges.

I've said it before – and I do mean it – you readers really do need catalogs from each of these manufacturers. •

34th EDITION, 2002 **41**

Rifle Report

by Layne Simpson

Beretta

THERE ARE A number of advantages to having the name, Beretta. For one, you appear first in my column – and you always will unless Anschutz has something new or until someone forms the Acme Gun Co., or Albacore Firearms, Inc., or something like that.

Beretta's Mato, a rifle that ranks right up there with the best of 'em in looks, quality and performance is now available in 270 Winchester, 7mm Remington Magnum, 30-06, 300 Winchester Magnum and 375 H&H Magnum. All of those chamberings are available in the synthetic-stocked Mato Synthetic but the 375 H&H Magnum is not available in the wood-stocked Mato Deluxe. The 375-caliber Synthetic rifle comes with a muzzle brake. At the very top of the line is the Mato Deluxe Extra with a steel trapdoor gripcap on its fancy English walnut stock. The bottom edge of the stock has a spare magazine compartment with hinged steel cover. Renaissance-style engraving covers trigger guard, floorplate of the detachable magazine and other parts of the rifle. Sights consist of an express-style folding leaf at the rear and a ramped blade with interchangeable beads up front. This fine rifle comes with its own leather carrying case and it is veeeery expensive.

Browning

The first thought that came to my mind as I reached for Browning's new Buck Mark Sporter was, *"now why would they want to go and do a thing like that?"* The answer came as I handled it. Regardless of how unorthodox this Buck Mark pistol with its 18-inch barrel and nondetachable walnut buttstock might appear to some, it is rather a neat little rig. The Sporter has fiber-optic sights and an integral Weaver-style scope mounting rail on its receiver; the Target is the same except for its heavier barrel and no open sights. Also new from Browning is the BAR Stalker with synthetic forearm and buttstock. Three barrel lengths are available; 20 inches in 243 and 308; 22 inches in 270 and 30-06, and 24 inches in its three magnum chamberings, 7mm Remington, 300 Winchester and 338 Winchester. The Stalker comes with or without open sights, and with or without the BOSS muzzle brake.

Back in September of 2000 I had the opportunity to hunt caribou in Alaska with a A-Bolt Stainless Stalker chambered for the 300 Winchester Short Magnum, a new beltless magnum introduced by Winchester. Think of the 300 Remington Ultra Mag shortened enough to work in short-action rifles and capable of equaling the velocity of the longer 300 Winchester Magnum and you have the new 300 WSM. It is also available in the wood-stocked A-Bolt Hunter. The caribou didn't cooperate but I shot enough Winchester ammo loaded with the 180-grain Fail-Safe bullet on paper to know that I could have hit one a long way off if given the opportunity. Actually, the trip didn't turn out too badly. While everyone else was off looking for caribou that never showed up, I was busy shooting ptarmigan and gadwall with a 28-gauge Model 12 pump gun I had brought along.

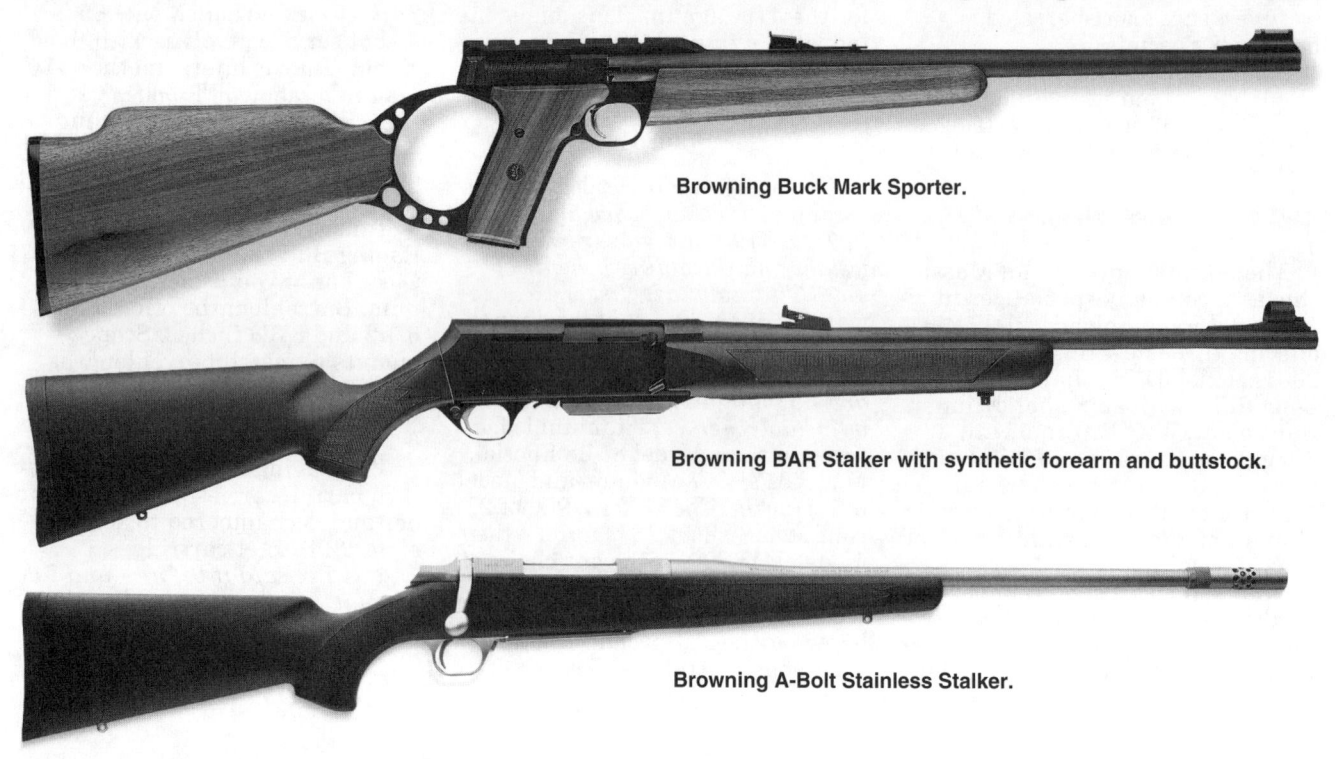

Browning Buck Mark Sporter.

Browning BAR Stalker with synthetic forearm and buttstock.

Browning A-Bolt Stainless Stalker.

Kimber Model 84M Classic Sporter.

Kimber Model 84M Varminter with 26-inch medium-heavy fluted barrel.

Charter 2000

Charter 2000 has introduced a new bolt-action called the Field King. Available in 243, 308, 25-06, 270 and 30-06 Springfield, it has a 22-inch Shaw barrel, M17-type extractor, adjustable trigger, black synthetic stock and a magazine capacity of four rounds. Other features include a one-piece bolt with recessed face and anti-bind groove on one locking lug.

Heckler & Koch

New at Heckler and Koch is an interesting gas-operated autoloading big-game rifle called the SLB 2000. It has interchangeable 22-inch barrels in 7x64mm Brenneke, 30-06 Springfield and 9.3x62mm. Modular in design, the new rifle has a lightweight alloy receiver, a tang-mounted sliding safety button that blocks both hammer and trigger and a premium-grade, oil-finished buttstock and forearm replete with cut checkering. The rifle handles and feels great but I'm not sure American sportsmen will become too excited about the exaggerated curve of its buttstock grip. I failed in my efforts to come up with an official weight but the SLB 2000 felt lighter than any other semiauto I have handled lately.

Kimber

In a previous report I cast my vote for the 22-caliber Kimber Model 82C as the most exciting new rifle of the year. I'm voting in the same direction in 2001 except this time it is for the new Model 84M centerfire. Rated at only 5-3/4 pounds, it should not greatly exceed 6-1/2 pounds when equipped with a light scope such as the Burris Mini or Leupold Compact and George Miller's Conetrol mount. Any sheep hunter who does not lust for one of these hasn't seen how nice it is, nor has he climbed any really steep sheep mountains. My wife doesn't hunt sheep but I am sure she will expect to see her very own Model 84M beneath the tree come Christmas. It will also be ideal for a youngster's first grownup rifle.

Among other dandy things, the Model 84M has a Model 70-type, two-position safety lever on its bolt shroud and a steel trigger guard/floorplate assembly, the latter hinged and with its release at the inside front of the trigger guard. Controlled cartridge feeding is there, compliments of Paul Mauser's nonrotating, claw-type extractor. The blued steel receiver is pillar-bedded into the stock. The Model 84M Classic has a 22-inch chrome-moly barrel with a light-weight contour and is chambered to 243 Winchester, 260 Remington, 7mm-08 and 308 Winchester. Barrels are air-gauged to ensure dimensional integrity of bore and groove diameter to within .001 inch and their chambers are hand-polished to a mirror-smooth finish for ease of spent case extraction. The walnut stock has cut checkering at wrist and forearm, steel gripcap, quick-detach sling swivels and a one-inch Pachmayr Decelerator pad. As far as I know, the Model 84M is the lightest all-steel, wood-stocked big-game rifle available. God willing and the creek doesn't rise above the tops of my hip boots, I will have hunted red stag in New Zealand with a Model 84M in 308 several months before you read this.

Two additional versions of the Sporter are planned for the future, Model 84S with shorter action for the 223 Remington and such, and Model 84L with longer action for

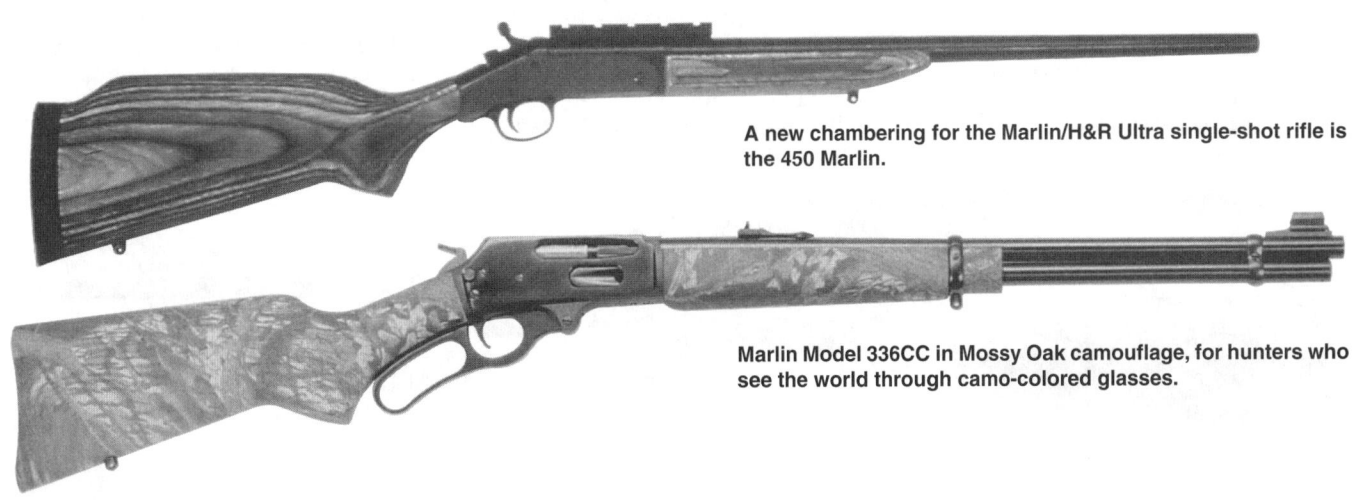

A new chambering for the Marlin/H&R Ultra single-shot rifle is the 450 Marlin.

Marlin Model 336CC in Mossy Oak camouflage, for hunters who see the world through camo-colored glasses.

Marlin Model 1895 Cowboy, with the old square-shaped finger lever, chambered for the 45/70 Government.

the 25-06, 270, 280, 30-06 and others of their breed. Also slated for a 2001 introduction is the Model 84M Varminter with 26-inch medium-heavy fluted barrel in 22-250. Actually, the first 100 will have 24-inch barrels, something Kimber collectors will want to know about.

Kimber's Model 82, the rifle that reintroduced quality and superb accuracy back into the world of small-game rifles, is now available in four versions, Classic for hunting, plinking and target shooting; Hunter Silhouette for NRA metallic silhouette competition; Super America for those who choose to own the world's most handsome standard-production rifle in 22 rimfire, and Short Varmint/Target for everything else.

Lazzeroni

John Lazzeroni is offering Sako TRGS and Savage Model 112 rifles in several of his proprietary chamberings. The Savage has a 24-inch barrel in 308 Patriot and 284 Tomahawk while you can buy the Sako with a 26-inch barrel in 308 Warbird and 284 Firebird.

Les Baer Custom

Les Baer claims half-inch accuracy for five-shot groups at 100 yards from the new Super Custom Varmint version of his 223-chambered AR15 and I can assure you it's no brag. He sent me one along with a supply of Federal Premium ammo loaded with a 52-grain hollow-point bullet and the stuff averaged only a hair over half an inch at 100 long paces. One of my handloads with the 50-grain Nosler Ballistic Tip averaged .482 inch. To be honest, I had to work mighty hard to maintain that level of accuracy because its tubular handguard makes the rifle difficult to stabilize consistently atop a sandbag. I suggested to Les that he offer the option of a detachable, flat, metal plate secured to the bottom of the handguard, and wide enough to snuggle uniformly into a rabbit-ear style bag. He was a step ahead of me because that option was already in the works. An idea he did go for was to build a few rifles in 6x45mm, an extremely accurate little cartridge easily made by necking up the 223 Remington case for 6mm bullets. I still have some Euber match-grade bullets left over from my benchrest shooting days and am looking forward to trying them in one of Les' ARs.

Magnum Research, Inc.

Most of those who own Mountain Eagle rifles made by Magnum Research, Inc. are probably aware of the fact that its action is made by the Finnish company of Sako. Or I should say it was made by Sako because all MRI bolt guns are now built around blueprinted Remington Model 700 actions. I shot the Tactical Rifle version with a 27-inch composite barrel in 308 Winchester and it averaged .702 inch at 100 yards for five-shot groups with Federal 168-grain Gold Match ammo. When fed my handload consisting of a benchrest-prepared Federal case, Federal 210M primer and 42.0 grains of H4895 behind the Nosler 168-grain match bullet, the rifle averaged .510 inch for a 10-group average. Who knows how accurately I might have shot it had it been equipped with the optional Jewell trigger. Comb height and length-of-pull of the synthetic stock are adjustable and after jacking up the comb a bit the stock felt like it was tailor-made for me. The Tactical Rifle in 223 or 22-250 is also not a bad varmint rig and in 300 Winchester Magnum it would not be a bad choice for sitting in one spot all day and occasionally taking a poke at deer on the other side of a bean field.

Marlin

Biggest news from Marlin for 2001 is the company's acquisition of H&R 1871, Inc. which claims to be the world's largest manufacturer of break-action, single-shot rifles and shotguns. They are sold under the brand names of Harrington & Richardson, New England Firearms and Wesson & Harrington. Additional chamberings from H&R in its Ultra rifle line is the 450 Marlin and 22 WMR. It has a 22-inch barrel, cut-checkered stock and forearm of cinnamon laminate, ventilated recoil pad, and sling swivel posts. No open sights are there but the rifle comes with a factory-installed scope mounting base and an offset hammer spur. The 22 WMR is also now available in a rifle from New England Arms. Adult and youth versions of the NEF Sporter are available, both with black synthetic stock and forearm, automatic case ejection, and an exposed hammer replete with a transfer bar-type safety system.

Conservative folks like me winced and groaned loudly when we got our first look at an old classic like the Marlin 336 with its stock and forearm decked out in Mossy Oak camouflage but it will sell like hotcakes to a rapidly growing number of hunters who believe the outcome of a hunt is greatly dependent on how much camo they and their equipment wear. Called the Model 336CC, it has a 20-inch Micro-Grove barrel, six-round magazine and is available only in 30-30 Winchester.

Marlin's new Model 1894CP in 357 Magnum has an American walnut stock with rubber butt pad, semi-buckhorn rear sight, 16 1/4-inch ported barrel and 8-round magazine. It weighs only 5-3/4 pounds.

Remington's all-new Model 710 rifle.

44 GUNS ILLUSTRATED

Remington Model 700 BDL/SS commemorates the Rocky Mountain Elk Foundation.

Remington Model 700T, the first big-game rifle with a titanium receiver to be introduced by a major American manufacturer.

Moving on up to more punch at both ends, the Model 1895GS is the old Model 1895G Guide Gun with a 18 1/2-inch ported, stainless steel barrel with Ballard-style cut rifling and in 45-70 Government. Other features include walnut stock, 4-round magazine and semi-buckhorn, folding rear sight. Then we have the Model 1895 Cowboy, another rifle in 45-70 that should have all those buckaroos and buckarettes out there making quick draws for their wallets. It has a straight-grip stock with the old square-shaped finger lever, black walnut stock with no checkering, 9-round magazine, semi-buckhorn sight and a 26-inch tapered octagon barrel with Ballard-style rifling.

With its economical price, 22-inch barrel, 12-round tubular magazine, screw-adjustable open rear sight and fiberglass-reinforced polycarbonate stock, the new TS version of Marlin's famous Model 84 bolt-action rifle is sure to be a hit among shooters on the lookout for a knockabout rifle in 22 WMR. Add Mossy Oak's Break-Up camo finish to the hardwood stock of the old Model 25MN and you have a new version called the Model 25MNC in 22 WMR. It also has a 7-round detachable magazine, 22-inch Micro-Groove barrel and adjustable rear sight.

One last thing. If you haven't already obtained a copy of the 2001 Marlin catalog you really should because its cover is one of the more handsome seen in recent years. Inside are photos of previous covers dating back to 1899.

Remington

When it comes to introducing new stuff each year, nobody can out-introduce Remington. This is great news to me because I like Remington products and the vast number of new ones unveiled each year go a long way toward filling up this column with things that increase a rifleman's pulse rate.

At the top of this year's introductions is the all-new Model 710 rifle in 270 Winchester and 30-06 for now. For starters, the three-lug bolt with its 60-degree rotation locks up into the barrel rather than the receiver ring and this allows Remington to make the receiver from steel tubing. Rather than being threaded into the receiver, the 22-inch cold-forged, button-rifled barrel is permanently installed by a very large factory worker with a very strong hydraulic press. When engaged, Remington's new key-operated Integrated Security System on the bolt shroud prevents the bolt from closing. Inside the receiver is a fiberglass-reinforced nylon insert within which the bolt travels fro and to. One side of the trigger components housing is injection-molded integrally with the insert.

The Model 710 has a gray-colored synthetic stock replete with recoil pad, quick-detach sling swivel posts and an integral triggerguard. I shot one in 30-06 with Remington's 180-grain Core-Lokt ammo and the first five shots on paper measured 1.68 inches between the least friendly two in the group. Four of those shots went into 0.725 inch and three of them snuggled into 0.312 inch. The fellows in green I talked to said their goal was to make the Model 710 just as accurate as the Model 700 – and looks like they did it. So why did Remington go to all of this trouble when they already had the best-selling Model 700? So they could sell an accurate, seven-pound big-game rifle complete with a factory-installed Bushnell 3-9X Sharpshooter scope for less than $375, that's why.

Just as I said they would last year, Remington has now added 7mm- and 375-caliber members to the Ultra Mag family of cartridges. All told, 12 new Model 700 variations in those two calibers as well as the 300 and 338 Ultra Mags have been added to the list. I shot a couple of 375 Ultra Mag factory loads in a Model 700 LSS with a 26-inch barrel. Three-shot groups fired with the 300-grain A-Frame load averaged 1.87 inches with velocity at 2740 fps, only 20 fps slower than Remington claims. The load with the 300-grain Barnes Super Solid clocked 2792 fps and averaged 1.32 inches on paper. That won't win a benchrest match but it will topple over a African Cape buffalo or Alaskan brown bear in no time flat.

The 7mm Ultra Mag I shot was a Model 77 African Plains Rifle with a 26-inch barrel and laminated wood stock. The 140-grain Core-Lokt factory ammo averaged 2.11 inches at 100 yards and 3377 fps on the chronograph. The 140-grain Nosler Partition averaged 1.32 inches and 3374 fps. This, by the way, is quite comparable to Remington's 140-grain 7mm STW factory ammo as it usually averages just over 3400 fps in a 26-inch barrel. How do you choose between the two? One has a belt, the other doesn't; Remington offers both choices. Before leaving the subject of Ultra Mags, the .338 version is now available in the left-hand Model 700BDL.

Latest from Remington's custom shop is the Model 700 African Big Game Rifle with laminated wood stock, fully-adjustable machined rear sight, ramped and hooded front sight with changeable bead, perch-belly magazine, a barrel band-type detachable sling swivel up front, and a three-shot detachable magazine, all wrapped around the 375 H&H Magnum, 375 Ultra Mag, 416 Remington Magnum or 458 Winchester Magnum. And speaking of commemorative rifles,

34th EDITION, 2002 **45**

Remington hasn't built many through the years so the Model 700 BDL/SS in 300 Ultra Mag cooked up for the Rocky Mountain Elk Foundation might be worth a serious look. It has the RMEF logo laser-etched into the stock and is covered from butt to forearm tip with Realtree Hardwoods camo. Part of the money from each one sold will go to the foundation.

Twenty-first in a series of classic Model 700 classics started with the 7x57mm Mauser back in 1981 is the 2001 edition in a classic deer cartridge, the 7mm-08 Remington. I believe this is the first standard-weight Model 700 hunting rifle to be offered in this chambering with a 24-inch barrel. I keep asking for the 8x57mm Mauser and 35 Remington but they continue to ignore me. Remington's extremely successful family of Model 97 22 rimfire autoloaders has a heavy-barrel addition. The new baby has a 20-inch carbon steel barrel in 22 Long Rifle or 22 WMR, a brown laminated wood stock and it weighs six pounds.

Last but most certainly not least - nor heaviest - is the first big-game rifle with a titanium receiver to be introduced by a major American manufacturer. Barrel and bolt are stainless steel while the trigger-guard/floorplate assembly is made of aluminum. Called the Model 700T, the short-action version weighs 5-1/4 pounds while the long-action version weighs only a quarter-pound more. The titanium receiver is only about 60 percent as heavy as a steel receiver and, in addition to that, a bit more weight disappeared when Remington design engineers decided to go with spiral-cut lightning flutes in the bolt body and to hollow out the bolt handle knob. The rifle got even lighter when they decided to use the lightest Kevlar-reinforced, carbon-fiber, composite stock ever from Remington. Contour of the 22-inch barrel looks to me to be about the same as that of the Model 700 Mountain rifle. Other chamberings are sure to follow but for now there are enough in the 260 Remington, 270 Winchester, 7mm-08 and 30-06 Springfield.

In the things-every-Model 700-rifle-owner-should-have department is an inexpensive new bolt takedown tool made of a synthetic material that won't scratch the bolt. Your friendly neighborhood Remington dealer should have it in stock by now.

Ruger

Not a lot of exciting news from Ruger this year except I noticed quite a bit of wood has been trimmed from the stock of the Model 77 Magnum in 375 H&H and 416 Rigby, a long-awaited modification that greatly improves the handling and feel of the rifle. There is a new version of Ruger's incredibly successful 10/22. It has a stainless steel barreled action in 22 LR only and a thumbhole-style stock of laminated wood and, most unusual for Ruger, Star Wars styling. There is also the rumor of a Model 77 compact with short barrel and stock for shooters with short arms but I have yet to actually see one.

Sako

Now owned by Beretta, the Finnish firm of Sako is introducing a new version of the excellent Model 75 rifle called the Finnlight. Three action sizes are available, No. 3 for the 243, 7mm-08 and 308; No. 4 for the 25-06, 6.5x55mm Swedish, 270, 30-06 and 280 Remington, and No. 5 for the 7mm Remington Magnum and 300 Winchester Magnum. All metal parts of the barreled action are stainless steel with a special coating to prevent wear and oxidation when exposed to the elements. Lengths of the fluted barrels range from 24 to 26 inches, depending on caliber. Weight ranges from six to seven pounds with a few of the missing ounces due to a trigger guard/floorplate assembly made of hard anodized aluminum. The bolt has Sako's latest Key Concept deactivation system which can make the rifle inoperable in unauthorized hands. The magazine is detachable, the single-stage trigger is factory-set at about three pounds and the chamber can be loaded or unloaded while the side-mounted safety switch is engaged. Of all the synthetic stocks I have handled on factory rifles, I'll have to say the one made by Sako is my favorite. Injection-molding the stock in two steps allows the insertion of soft rubber-like inserts in the grip and forearm for a comfortable no-slip grip with hands made slippery by a sudden downpour.

Samco Global Arms

I have been writing this report since 1982 and I don't recall ever covering a military-surplus firearm in it. I have been so impressed by a Model 1898 Persian Mauser I received from Samco, I just had to make it the first exception. Several grades are available ranging from a "collector-quality" rifle in unissued condition (which comes with its original factory target fired when it was built) to the "special select" rifle. I have been shooting the latter grade and with the exception of a few minor storage dings on its stock it was absolutely brand-spanking new when I first received it. If you have ever wanted to go beyond worn-out Mausers with pitted bores and mismatched serial numbers, here is your chance to add something really special to your collection. Accuracy with every factory load I could round up plus handloads with about every bullet available ranged from 1.48 inches to 4.66 inches for five-shot averages at 100 yards, and that with the original barleycorn front sight. I'll leave it that way because it is so much fun to shoot *as-is*, plus I wouldn't dare spoil that untouched Persian lion crest on its receiver by drilling and tapping it for a scope.

Savage

The receiver of the Savage Model 110 rifle has always been long enough to handle full-length magnum cartridges such as the 300 H&H Magnum and 300 Weatherby Magnum but the length of its magazine box restricted it to the use of medium-length magnums such as the 7mm Remington and 300 Winchester. This no longer is true as the latest lineup of Model 116 Weather Warrior rifles have magazine boxes long enough to take the 7mm STW and 300 Remington Ultra Mag, two

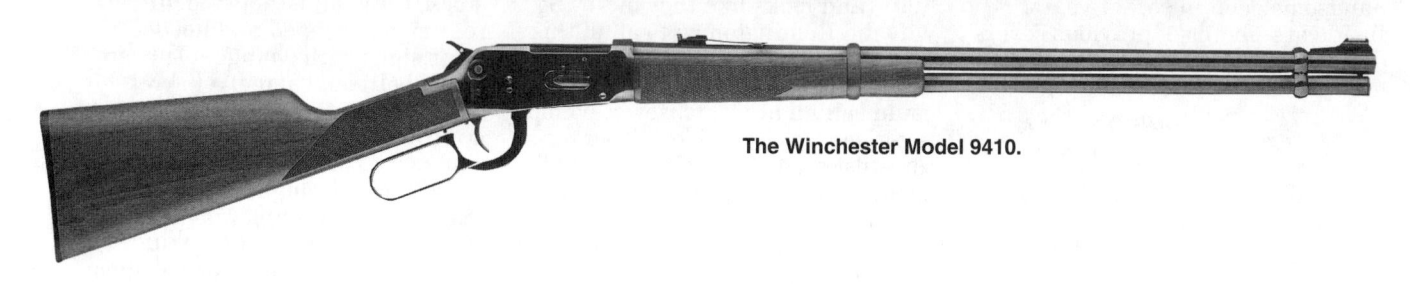

The Winchester Model 9410.

Model 70 Custom Safari Express.

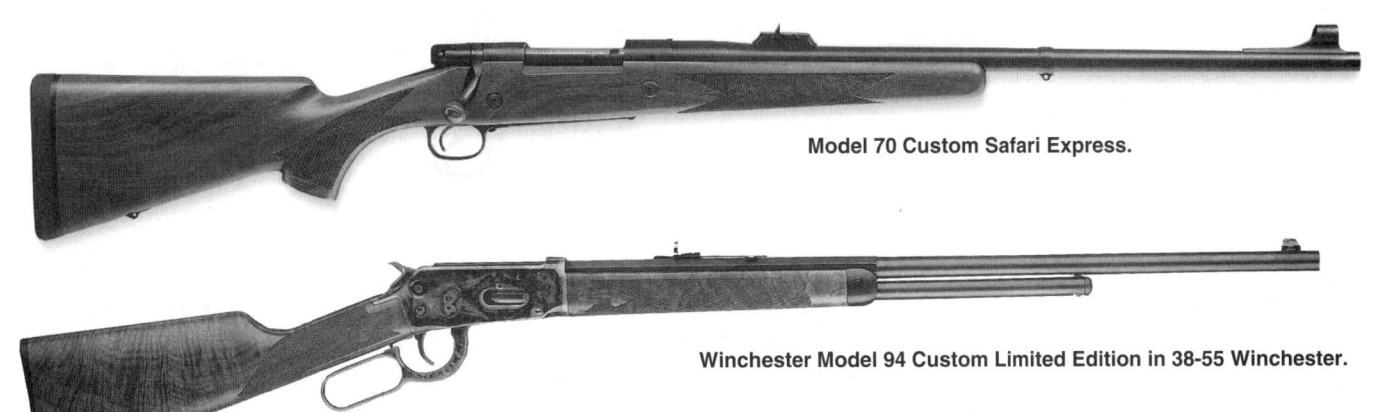

Winchester Model 94 Custom Limited Edition in 38-55 Winchester.

new chamberings for 2001. Rifles in those two chamberings have 26-inch barrels; those in the shorter magnums have 24-inchers while the barrels of those in standard-performance cartridges such as 270 and 30-06 are two inches shorter than that. The 7mm STW is also available in the wood-stocked Model 114 Ultra with a 24-inch barrel. Other news from Savage is the Model 114CE with European-style wood stock and a left-hand version of the Model 93G in 22 rimfire.

Springfield, Inc.

Springfield recently hosted an event during which a few writers, including yours truly, were told there was no way we could shoot up all the ammo on hand in two days. We came very close to proving them wrong and probably would have had the temperature ever made it above freezing and if the wind had dropped below 50 mph. I shot my share of the ammo in 1911-A1 pistols of various calibers and then switched to shooting reactive steel targets at long range with several versions of the 308-caliber M1A rifle. Most incredible of all was the new M32 Tactical Rifle with comb-height adjustable wood stock, folding tripod, Springfield 4-14X mil-dot scope, premium-grade Hart or Krieger barrel and other features too numerous to mention. If you can see it with your naked eyes you can hit it with this rifle! Who would ever have thought such a homely old battle rifle could average half-minute-of-angle with match ammo? I don't know about the other shooters but I really wasn't surprised by such a level of accuracy because I have owned a M1A Super Match with a Hart barrel for several years.

If you haven't read the life story of Marine legend Carlos Hathcock, you owe it to yourself to do so. A recipient of the Silver Star for saving the lives of seven comrades, he spent most of his tour in Vietnam as a sniper which is why the sniper range at Camp Lejeune, NC was named in his honor. The Vietcong who had a $30,000 bounty on his head referred to Hathcock as *"Long Trang"* (The White Feather) because he often wore one in his bush hat. Hathcock passed on in February 2000 and in a special arrangement with his estate and family, Springfield has introduced a special edition of the M1A/M5 with a likeness of his signature and a white feather logo etched on its receiver. Among many other things, the rifle has a heavy Krieger match-grade barrel, Harris folding bipod, National Match operating rod, adjustable match trigger and a McMillan fiberglass stock.

My friends at Springfield keep promising to bring back the M1 carbine with quality equal to that of the M1A they are now building and I keep looking forward to rolling the clock back to my youth while shooting it.

Steyr

The Steyr family of hunting rifles continues to grow and a number of less-than-ordinary features are available. They include a three-position, roller-type tang safety that blocks the firing pin, ice and residue grooves upon the outside of the bolt body, butt spacers that allow length of pull to be adjusted and a steel bushing that supports the spring-loaded extractor when the bolt is closed. Many of the standard chamberings are there, including the 6.5 Swede and 376 Steyr.

Tristar Sporting Arms Ltd.

Previously known mainly for its line of Italian-made over-under and side-by-side shotguns, Tristar is now importing Uberti-built Colt single-action clones in 45 Colt, as well as four different center-fire rifles. Three of the latter are modern reproductions of lever actions of yesteryear, the 1860 Henry, Winchester Model 1866 and Winchester Model 1873 – all available in 44-40 or 45 Colt. Two variations of the Henry are offered, standard rifle with 24 1/4-inch barrel and Trapper with 18 1/2-inch barrel. The Henry also has a brass frame, forged steel tubular magazine and straight-grip walnut buttstock with brass buttplate. The Winchester '66 is available in Sporting and Yellowboy versions and is dressed quite similar to the Henry. The Winchester '73 is available in Sporting makeup only but with a color-case-hardened steel frame, walnut stock with curved steel buttplate and 24 1/4- or 30-inch barrels. The other new rifle is a very nicely done reproduction of the Winchester Model 1885 Hi-Wall. It has a walnut stock with shotgun-style steel buttplate, case-colored frame and underlever, and a 28-inch octagon barrel in 45-70 Government. Weight is 8-3/4 pounds and, at a suggested retail price of $765, it is bound to sell quite well.

Ultra Light Arms

Ultra Light Arms is back and Melvin Forbes is at the wheel. Since his catalog looks the same as it did before he became involved with Colt, I am sure everything will be the same as it used to be, including high quality and superb accuracy wrapped up in a trim little 5-1/4 pound rifle chambered for about any center-fire cartridge you can think of. The Model 22RF in 22 rimfire is also back in production.

U.S. Repeating Arms Co.

There was a time, many years ago, when both Savage and Marlin offered lever-action rifles chambered for the .410 shotshell but with the exception of a few custom rifles built by gunsmiths, the Winchester Model 94 has never been available so chambered. Until now, that is. Chambered only for the 2 1/2-inch cartridge, the Model 9410 (darned neat name) has a smooth-bored barrel with no choke constriction. A repeater, its tubular magazine holds eight or nine rounds depending on the brand of ammo used. Why it has an adjustable rear sight and

One of several chamberings the Weatherby Ultra Lightweight is now available in is the new 338-06 A-Square.

ramped front sight is totally beyond me – but it does.

Several paragraphs back I mentioned hunting caribou in Alaska with a Browning Stainless Stalker in 300 WSM. Since Browning and U.S. Repeating Arms Company (USRAC) are owned by the same parent company, it didn't surprise me to see a Model 70 or two chambered for the 300 WSM on that same trip. That chambering is slated to be available during 2001 in Classic Featherweight, Classic Stainless and Classic Laminated versions of the short-action Model 70. Whereas Browning rifles in this caliber have 23-inch barrels, the Winchesters have 24-inchers. Other additions are the 25-06 and 338 Winchester Magnum in the Classic Super Grade, and 300 Remington Ultra Mag in the Classic Stainless Composite.

I keep seeing more and more interesting projects coming from the Winchester custom shop. One is the Model 70 Custom African Express in 416 Rigby and 470 Capstick. A couple of other nice Model 70s are the Custom Safari Express in 375 Remington Ultra Mag and 416 Rigby and the Custom Ultimate Classic in 7mm Remington Ultra Mag, 338 Remington Ultra Mag and 6.5x55mm Swedish. Then there is the short-action Model 70 Classic Custom, the first factory bolt-action rifle to be offered in 450 Marlin. You can also buy a takedown version of the Model 70 in a variety of calibers.

My favorite Winchester for 2001 is the new Model 94 Custom Limited Edition with fancy cut-checkered walnut, case-colored hammer, receiver and finger lever and 26-inch half-octagon barrel in 38-55 caliber. The good folks in the custom shop, by the way, were first among major rifle builders to offer my 7mm STW and they continue to chamber the Model 70 it and for my 358 STA.

Tom Volquartsen

One of my recent projects was to see how much, if any, the accuracy of 22 WMR ammunition would improve if I sorted it by weight, rim thickness, overall length and a few other things. The autoloading rifle I used in those tests was built by Tom Volquartsen, has a bolt and receiver precision-machined from stainless steel and uses Ruger 10/22 magazines. It also has a match-grade stainless steel barrel and McMillan fiberglass stock. One of Volquartsen's heavier models, it and its Burris 6-24X scope weigh exactly 10 pounds. Reporting on everything in detail about the ammo experiments would fill up an entire article, and it did, so I'll keep it short by saying I ended up with one load that averaged 0.68 inch for 10 five-shot groups at 100 yards. Some groups measured less than half an inch. Only those of us who have seriously worked with the 22 WMR know how fantastic that really is.

Weatherby

Weatherby rifles are now available in two excellent new chamberings. One, called the 338-06 A-Square, is simply the old 338-06 wildcat that was registered with SAAMI by A-Square a few years back. Except for a small difference in bullet diameter between the two, it is also the same cartridge as the old 333 OKH of the 1930s. As its name implies, the 338-06 is the 30-06 case necked down for 338-caliber bullets. It is a great cartridge and not too far behind the 338 Winchester Magnum in everything except recoil. Weatherby is offering ammunition loaded with the 210-grain Nosler Partition at a muzzle velocity of 2750 feet per second. For now, the only rifle to be chambered for it is the Mark V Ultra Lightweight. I just received one of the first rifles built by Weatherby in this caliber but the cartridges are still a few weeks away so I'll wait and report on its performance the next time we meet.

Also headed back to the game fields is another excellent old classic called the 375 Weatherby Mag-

In addition to averaging less than half an inch at 100 yards, the Weatherby Super VarmintMaster was also deadly on California ground squirrels at long range.

48 GUNS ILLUSTRATED

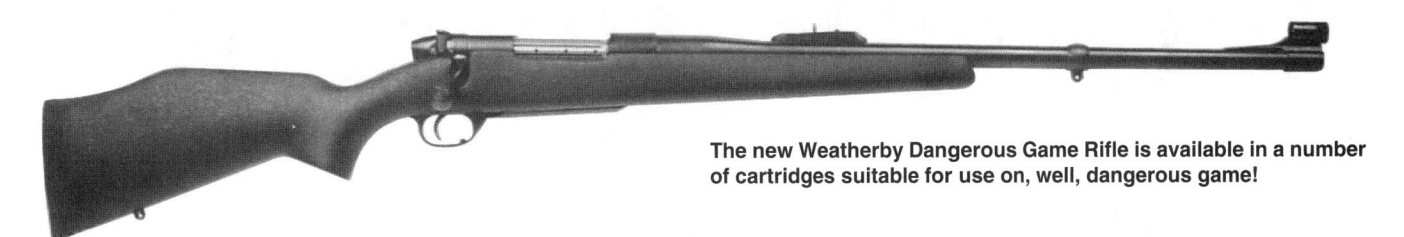

The new Weatherby Dangerous Game Rifle is available in a number of cartridges suitable for use on, well, dangerous game!

num. It was one of the first cartridges designed by Roy Weatherby back in the 1940s and was dropped from production soon after he introduced his bigger 378 Weatherby Magnum in 1953. The 375 Weatherby Magnum case is nothing less than an improved version of the grand old 375 H&H Magnum with less body taper and Weatherby's familiar double-radius shoulder. In a pinch, 375 H&H Magnum ammo can be fired in a rifle chambered for the Weatherby cartridge, something nice to know if you run out of ammo while on safari. Initially to be loaded with the 300-grain Nosler Partition at 2800 fps, I won't be surprised to eventually see this grand old cartridge from Weatherby loaded with at least one other bullet of lighter weight.

The first Mark V to be chambered to 375 Weatherby Magnum is the new Dangerous Game Rifle (*Where have I seen that name before?*). Among other things, this one includes a Bell & Carlson synthetic stock replete with CNC-machined aluminum bedding block and Pachmayr Decelerator pad, 24-inch barrel, pre-'64 Winchester Model 70 Super Grade-style express rear sight and ramped and hooded front sight with a large gold-colored bead. Other chambering options include the 375 H&H Magnum, 416 Remington Magnum, 458 Winchester Magnum and the entire line of Weatherby cartridges of .378, .416 and .460 calibers. Average weight is 8-3/4 pounds except it is increased to 9-1/2 pounds for the 460 Weatherby Magnum. I'll probably be hunting Asian buffalo and other things in Australia this year and may use a Mark V DGR in 375 Weatherby Magnum or the Mark V Ultra Lightweight in 338-06 A-Square.

You might recall that, quite a few years ago, Weatherby beat all of its major-power competition to the punch by being first to offer a big-game rifle with a synthetic stock. It was called the Mark V Fibermark and after being discontinued for several years it is back in 19 different chamberings ranging from the 22-250, 243 Winchester, 270 Winchester and 30-06 on the standard-size Mark V action to the 30-378 Weatherby Magnum, 338 Winchester Magnum, 340 Weatherby Magnum and 375 H&H Magnum on the magnum-size action. Barrel lengths are 26 inches for the Weatherby cartridges and 24 inches for everything else. Barrel contours are No. 4 for the 458 and 460 and No. 3 for the others. Actually, two versions of the Fibermark are available, one with a stainless steel barreled action, the other of blued steel.

Last year, I told you about a Weatherby Super VarmintMaster in 22-250 that had averaged .517-inch for over 50, five-shot groups at 100 yards with a variety of handloads and factory ammo. As it turned out, it was the most accurate off-the-shelf factory rifle I tested during 2000. Well, I just finished testing a Super VarmintMaster in 220 Swift and it averaged .486-inch. A new offspring of that rifle is called Super PredatorMaster and is available in 223, 22-250, 243, 7mm-08 and 308 Winchester. At 6-1/2 pounds it is a couple of pounds lighter than its papa, most of the difference being in their barrels. The Super VarmintMaster has a rather heavy 26-inch barrel while the barrel of PredatorMaster measures 24 inches and is lighter in contour. There you have them, two great varmint rifles from Weatherby, one for shooters who sit a lot and walk very little, the other for those who would rather walk than sit. Other news for 2001 is the 7mm STW and 338-378 Magnum chamberings in the Mark V Synthetic. The 7mm STW is also available in both right- and left-handed versions of the Mark V Accumark.

Wilson Combat

I am not exactly sure if a nifty item Bill Wilson sent to me belongs to me or to our pistol editor because it converts a 45-caliber 1911 pistol into a carbine with a 18-inch barrel – and no modifications are necessary. Simply remove the top assembly from your 1911, slide the frame into the conversion unit, install the slide latch and the job is done. It comes with equipped with a Weaver-style scope mounting rail and works with single-stack pistols made by Kimber, Springfield, Colt and others, as well as double-stackers made by Kimber, Springfield, Para Ordnance and others. I just burned up a variety of factory loads in one attached to a 14-shot Kimber polymer frame and wearing a Tasco red dot sight and everything stayed well inside the palm of your hand, with several groups measuring as small as two inches. Outdoors, it's a fun-gun, maybe even a hog-gun if you like to get close before shooting like I do. Indoors, its compact 33 1/4-inch length and seven-pound heft make it something for someone who cannot shoot a pistol accurately to consider for home defense. ●

Editor's note. Layne is Field Editor for Shooting Times *magazine. Autographed copies of his book "The Custom 1911 Government Model Pistol" are available for $30 from High Country Press, 104 Holly Tree Lane, Simpsonville, SC.*

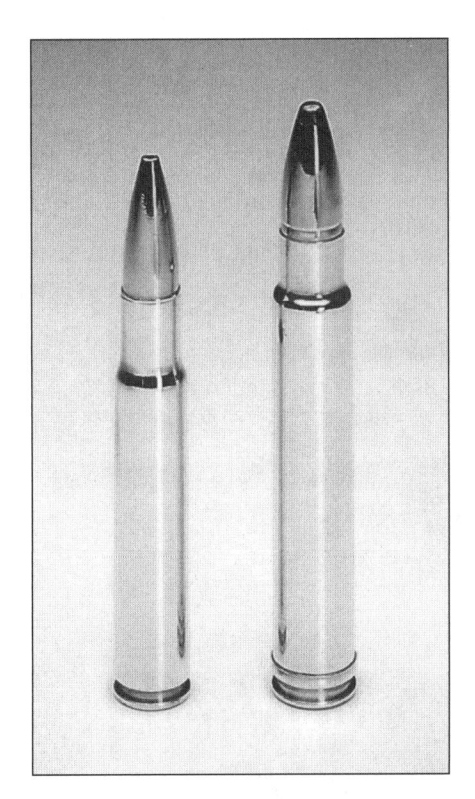

Weatherby 338-06 A-Square (*Left*) and 375 Magnum.

SHOTGUN UPDATE

by John Haviland

NOT MANY YEARS ago the canvas coat was the mantle of upland bird and waterfowl hunters. The coats faded from the days afield to match the tans of frosted alder leaves and cattails. The hunters who wore these coats had lived through the Great Depression or had been told by their parents how tough times had been. They saved their money, made do with what they had and turned off the lights every time they walked out of the room.

Nearly every one of these bird hunters owned one shotgun for all their hunting, from grouse to geese to keeping the eyes tuned up on clay pigeons. The gun was most likely a pump action Winchester Model 12 or Remington 870, or maybe an autoloader like the Browning A-5. The guns were 12 gauge, the 16 and 20 reserved for young shooters in training. The 12 gauge 2 3/4-inch shell held plenty of lead shot to kill any bird that flew. While three-inch guns, like the Winchester Model 12 Heavy Duck gun, were available, most considered the extra shot as superfluous and shells downright expensive.

That was then. Now *'more'* is modern.

Scott Granger, of Browning and Winchester, says he sees two types of shotgunners today. *"There's still a lot of hunters who want one gun to do it all,* Granger says. *"Those hunters want a 12 gauge 3 1/2-inch magnum in a gas-operated autoloader that softens recoil somewhat. They want that 3 1/2- inch magnum for shooting steel shot at geese. Now a lot of guys will never shoot those big shells, but they still want that versatility just in case,"* he says.

"The second type of shotgunner is what I call the technical group," Granger says. "These guys also go with an autoloader in 3 1/2 inch magnum for hunting. But they're also interested in target shooting and you just can't dismiss the influence sporting clays has had on shotguns."

The over/under in 12 gauge is the first choice for sporting clays. *"This is the gun these technical guys have always wanted,"* Granger says. The gun has a somewhat higher rib and a fiber optic front sight to help provide a quicker sight picture.

Eddie Stevens, of Remington Arms, says most hunters these days own at least two shotguns. *"One is a work gun they carry in the boat or in the blind,"* he says. *"The other is a target gun for the trap or sporting clays range".*

Stevens says the working gun is probably a pump or an autoloader. Stock choice is split 50/50 between wood or synthetic – and interchangeable chokes are a necessity. The gun must be chambered for the 12 gauge 3 1/2-inch magnum. *"Sales of the 3 1/2 inch have just skyrocketed,"* Stevens says. *"People want the versatility of being able to shoot all the 12 gauge loads in one gun."*

The second shotgun must be a good-looking gun that can be displayed at the target range. For this show gun, most shotgunners go with an over/under or an autoloader with a checkered stock of figured wood and metal polished bright and deep-blued.

Stevens predicts in the future shotgunners will buy a different shotgun for targets, upland birds, turkeys, waterfowl and deer. *"Of course, we love that,"* he says.

Let's see what manufacturers have new that shotgunners must have this year.

B.C. Outdoors/Verona

B.C. Outdoors is hooked up with PMC Ammunition, Docter Sport Optics and now a line of Verona 12 gauge semiautomatic and competition over/under shotguns imported from Italy.

The over/unders come stocked in dimensions for skeet, trap or sporting. Common features on all three guns include single selective triggers adjustable for length of pull; bores with extended forcing cones, back-boring, porting and four Briley Spectrum chokes.

The Verona semiautomatics are gas-operated and based on the design of the SPAS-12 shotguns. The three Verona semi-auto models are available with a black composite stock or a Turkish walnut stock. All feature aluminum receivers and a chromed bolt assembly. The guns accept 2 3/4- or 3-inch magnum shells and have a magazine cutoff. Barrels are 28 or 26-inches and come equipped with a screw-in choke.

Benelli

Benelli sells 72 different versions of its shotguns for law enforcement, home defense, hunting, target and competition – as well as the largest selection of left-hand semiautomatics in the world.

Benelli engineers started with a clean computer screen when they designed the new Nova, a 3 1/2-inch 12-gauge pump-action shotgun. In place of a conventional steel receiver

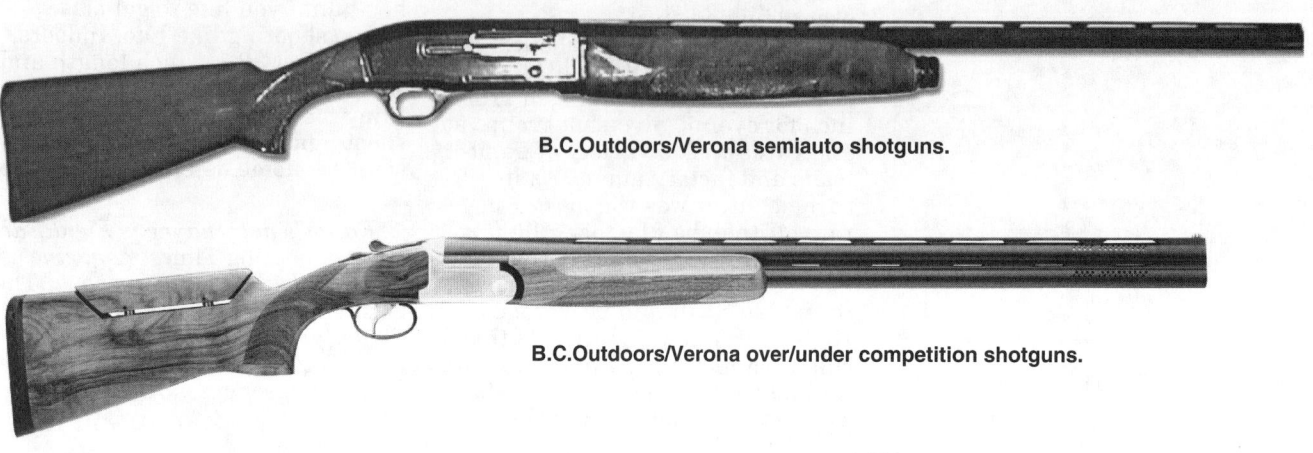

B.C.Outdoors/Verona semiauto shotguns.

B.C.Outdoors/Verona over/under competition shotguns.

and separate buttstock is a single unit that incorporates a light - but rigid - steel liner molded inside a glass-reinforced polymer shell. Molded-in ribs around the grip provide a secure hold. The recoil pad twists off for access to a recess in the buttstock for installation of a recoil reducer to absorb some of the recoil from heavy 3 1/2-inch loads.

Beretta

Beretta has redesigned its S682 Gold E-series of competition over/unders. The four guns include features such as Beretta's Optima-Bore and an adjustable comb. The Optima-Bore consists of chrome-lined bores with lengthened forcing cones, over-boring and extended choke tubes. The comb is adjustable for height and cast – and an indicator scale facilitates easy, accurate adjustments. The triggers are adjustable to vary length of pull 3/8 of an inch from the grip to the trigger. Two trigger shoes are supplied, one with a surface canted for right-hand shooters and the other with a wide, symmetrical face. The guns are the S682 Gold E Trap, Trap Combo, Skeet and Sporting and are shipped in a new ABS hard case.

Engraving is now included on Beretta's 686E Sporting and 687EL Gold Pigeon II over/unders. The Sporting has an ellipsis pattern on its receiver while the Pigeon II is engraved with a game scene. The guns rest in Giugiaro Design cases which include five Beretta Mobilchokes, disassembly tools, interchangeable plastic or rubber recoil pads and oil.

The Beretta ES100 Rifle Slug semiautomatic comes with a 24-inch rifled barrel. This year

Beretta S682 Gold Receiver

Above, from left to right: **Beretta S682 Gold E Sporting, S682 Gold E Skeet, S682 Gold E Trap, and S682 Gold E Trap Combo.**

Beretta 686E Sporting.

Beretta 687EL Gold Pigeon II.

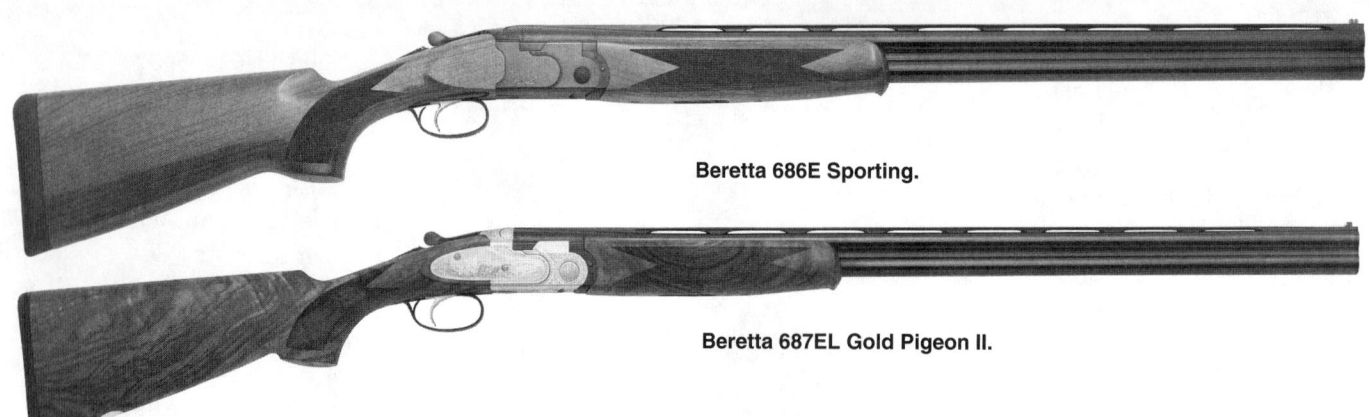

Beretta has added a 28-inch smooth-bored barrel to go along with the Rifle Slug gun to make the ES100 Rifle Slug Combo good for hunters after bucks in the morning and birds in the afternoon.

Ouch! Last week I was patterning several loads from a 12 gauge 3 1/2-inch magnum. The hard rubber recoil pad on the pump gun whacked my shoulder with every ounce of recoil. Immediately after the 15th round a sharp pain shot through my shoulder. After three days I can barely hold my arm straight out. Beretta has created the GEL*TEK recoil pad with people like me in mind. The pad is made with a silicone gel core to soak up recoil. The pad fits the stocks of most Beretta guns and has a clasp that allows easy attachment and removal.

Browning

Browning has brought out a bunch of new guns which are mostly existing models that have been slimmed down or had features added.

Browning teamed with the National Wild Turkey Federation to bring out the NWTF Shotgun Series. The guns are dressed-up Gold autoloading or Browning Pump Shotguns chambered in 10 gauge, 12 gauge 3 1/2-inch or 3-inch. The guns come with a 24-inch barrel with an *Extra-Full* extended choke and Hi-Viz fiber-optic sights atop the muzzle. The NWTF logo is on the side of the buttstock of the guns with the lock, stock and barrels done up in Mossy Oak Breakup Camouflage.

The Browning Gold Upland 12 gauge autoloader shaves 12 ounces from the standard Gold Hunter. That weight savings comes from a straight-grip stock and cutting the barrel back to 24 inches. The 20-gauge Gold Upland is the same weight as the standard Gold in that gauge and is fitted with 26-inch barrels.

The Gold Fusion is a new, trimmed, Gold Hunter 12 gauge. The gun weighs seven pounds four ounces, which is eight ounces lighter than the Gold Hunter. The lighter weight is a result of a slimmer stock and a magazine tube made of aluminum with a steel liner.

The gun is shipped in a hard case containing all sorts of goodies. The accessories include a set of shims that fit between the head of the grip and the receiver to adjust cast and drop of the comb, Hi-Viz fiber-optic sights with different light '*pipes*' and five choke tubes – from *Skeet to Full*.

Early this year I had a chance to shoot a Fusion at a variety of flying targets in Mississippi. I worried the recoil would be a bit much, from such a light gun with a plastic buttplate, shooting Winchester Supreme High Velocity loads of 1 1/4 ounces of steel *BBs* or *2s*. But the gas-operated gun was pleasant to shoot while hunting ducks and geese along the Coldwater River in northern Mississippi.

I also carried the Fusion during a brisk afternoon shooting pen-raised bobwhite quail. The birds kept to the pines and shots were short – at 10 to 15 yards. The Fusion's light weight helped on those quick point-and-fire shots. I really liked the fiber-optic sights. The illuminated dot helped remind me to keep my cheek planted on the comb and served as a reference point on crossing shots.

No fault of the Fusion's, but sporting clays that same outing at The Willows was a humbling experience for me. It's a fun course with targets diving from towers in the timber and springing from tall grass. Again, I liked the fiber-optic sight. If there was one negative, it was that the Fusion was a bit light for a smooth swing on hard crossing shots at fast singles and doubles.

This has little to do with new shotguns, but I'll tell you anyway. Duck Flush is a game at Willows. It is the most fun I've ever had with a shotgun. Three shooters stand abreast, each with 25 cartridges. When the shooting starts five traps

New Browning Fusion in the Mississippi duck blind.

New Browning Fusion and a green-winged teal.

The new Browning Fusion as a saddle gun on a Mississippi bobwhite quail hunt.

Browning Fusion after bobwhite quail.

from different positions in front hurl 75 clay targets toward the shooters in two minutes. All three shooters fire and reload as fast as possible because the targets come quickly in ones or twos, or in a cloud of six or seven. A clay is considered 'lost' when it lands unbroken on the pond in front of the shooters.

Back to Browning shotguns:

Another lightweight is the Gold Ten Gauge Light Camo. The gun's receiver is aluminum alloy, which cuts one pound off the standard model for a weight of 9 pounds 7 ounces. The Ten Gauge Light Camo has a 26- or 28-inch barrel and is covered in Mossy Oak Shadow Grass or Break-Up camouflage patterns.

Browning has five new 20-gauge guns. The development of sabot-type slugs has made the 20 gauge much more effective on big game. With that in mind Browning has introduced the Gold Deer Hunter in 20 gauge. The gun features a three-inch chamber in a rifled 22-inch barrel with a cantilever scope base.

The sideplates of the Citori Privilege 20 gauge are engraved with a ringneck pheasant flushing from under a pointer on the left side and alighting woodcocks on the right. The over/under's barrels are 26- or 28-inches and the stock is hand-oiled walnut with a schnabel forearm.

The Citori Ultra XS Skeet 20 gauge is the little brother to the 12 gauge introduced last year. The Ultra has slim lines, vented side ribs and a high post rib on 28- or 30-inch barrels. Stocks are either fixed or come with an adjustable comb.

The Micro designation has been placed on the 20-gauge autoloading Gold and Browning Pump Shotgun. The Gold has a smaller circumference grip, a shortened 13 7/8-inch length of pull and 26-inch barrels, all wrapped up at 6 pounds 10 ounces. The BPS also has a thinner grip and an easier-to-reach forearm – along with a 22-inch barrel, which is back-bored and threaded for Invector Plus choke tubes.

A final elegant touch is the Browning Side Lock side-by-side. The 12 or 20 gauge gun is made for Browning by Lebeau-Courally. As its name implies, it features sidelocks, double triggers and automatic ejectors. You can choose from grayed or blued metal finish.

Ithaca Gun

For over 50 years my father's Ithaca Model 37 pump-action 12 gauge has been in continual use shooting waterfowl and upland birds. With the idea of having the gun refinished after all that duty, I took the gun to gunsmith Doug Wells to have it checked. Wells said the 37's working parts showed no appreciable wear, although the chipped and oil-soaked butt stock needed replacing. I bought a new walnut butt stock and forearm for the gun. While I finished the wood, Wells went ahead and started work restoring the gun. He polished the screw heads that had been burred by ill-fitting screwdrivers, re-blued the metal and reamed out its full choke to between modified and improved cylinder. (That has proved a good choice for today's tight patterning upland and nontoxic waterfowl loads.) The refinished gun sparkled. My father said the gun looks even better than the day he bought it in 1947. My son shot ruffed grouse and ducks with the 37 this past fall. It never missed a beat. No doubt in another 50 years his grandson will be shooting the Ithaca 37.

The popularity of last year's Ithaca's Model 37 16 gauge has resulted in a 16-gauge deer gun from Ithaca. The Deerslayer II has a fully rifled barrel that is free-floated. The lack of a barrel attachment at the end of the magazine tube removes any stress that might alter alignment between the barrel and receiver. The buttstock has a Monte Carlo comb that positions the eye higher to easily see through a scope mounted on the drilled and tapped receiver.

A good slug load was the only way a 16-gauge slug gun would fly. Lightfield's new 16-gauge sabot ammunition develops energy comparable to a 12-gauge slug, and at a faster velocity.

Ithaca has new 37s stocked to fit women and benefit the NRA Foundation's Women's Programs Endowment. The Ithaca Model 37 Women's Endowment Shotguns in 16 and 20 gauge are straight-stocked with American black walnut with dimensions to fit the average-size woman. An Ithaca stockmaker will make stocks of specific dimensions to order on these or any Model 37. A portion of the money from the sales of these guns will be donated to the NRA Foundation's Women's Programs Endowment.

FABARM

Heckler & Koch is adding four new models to its FABARM shotgun line.

The Classic Lion English is the latest addition to the FABARM Classic Lion shotgun side-by-side family. The Classic Lion English features an English straight-grip stock and dou-

Shooting a round of Duck Flush at the Willow Sporting Clays range.

34th EDITION, 2002   **53**

Above, top to bottom: FABARM Classic Lion English, FABARM Silver Lion Cub, FABARM Field Pump 12 Gauge, FABARM Tactical and FABARM Field Pump 12 Gauge/Camouflage.

ble triggers. The gun is a boxlock with automatic ejectors and safeties and weighs right at seven pounds. Barrels are 26, 28 or 30 inches, complete with *Cylinder, Improved Cylinder, Modified, Improved Modified* and *Full* choke tubes. This 12-gauge gun also has three-inch chambers just in case your upland birds tend toward the huge.

Previously available only in 20 gauge with a 24-inch barrel, the short-stocked FABARM Silver Lion Cub is now also available in 12 and 20 gauge with a standard 26-inch ported barrel and a mid-rib bead.

Joining the FABARM pump-action shotguns is the Field Pump 12 Gauge featuring a 12 gauge three-inch chamber in a 28-inch vent-ribbed barrel or a 24-inch rifled barrel with sights. The Field is based on FABARM police shotguns. The aluminum receiver keeps the gun's weight at seven pounds. The guns come with a black sandblasted matte finish or in Mossy Oak Breakup camouflage – with *Cylinder, Modified* and *Full* choke tubes.

The Tactical semiautomatic is based on their gas-operated sporting shotguns. The Tactical handles all 12-gauge shells, from light 2 3/4-inch to three-inch slugs. The gun weighs 6.6 pounds with a 20-inch barrel. *Picatinny* rails can be screwed to the barrel, receiver and bottom of the forearm to attach accessories like a scope, ghost-ring rear sight, heat shields, lights and other necessities to help initiate tactical movements against weasels and skunks raiding the hen house.

All FABARM shotguns are made with the Tribore Barrel System, which consists of three internal bore profiles. An over-bore region of .7401-inch in 12 gauge begins at the front of the forcing cone to soften recoil. The bore gradually narrows at the middle of the barrel's length to a standard *cylinder* bore of .7244-inch. This leads to a gradual increase in velocity to the shot column. The shot column then passes through a standard choke, followed by a short *cylinder* profile at the muzzle. The *cylinder* dimension between the choke and muzzle acts as a port to bleed off excess powder gas.

Mossberg

Thank goodness for abbreviations, or this section would be taken up spelling out 'Single Shot Interchangeable Rifle/Shotgun.' Last year Mossberg introduced the SSI-One break-action that interchanges rifle cartridge barrels in a matter of minutes.

This year the SSI-One Slug and Turkey guns have been added. The rifled slug barrel is 24 inches long and accepts 12-gauge 2 3/4 or 3-inch slugs. A Weaver-style scope base is provided. Guns average 7.5 pounds in weight. The SSI-One Turkey has a ported 24-inch smoothbore barrel with a 12 gauge 3 1/2-inch chamber. An extended Accu-Mag turkey tube *Extra Full* choke is included with the SSI-One Turkey barrel.

The mandatory use of nontoxic shot (read *steel*) for waterfowl hunting has fairly well removed gauges smaller than the 12 from waterfowl

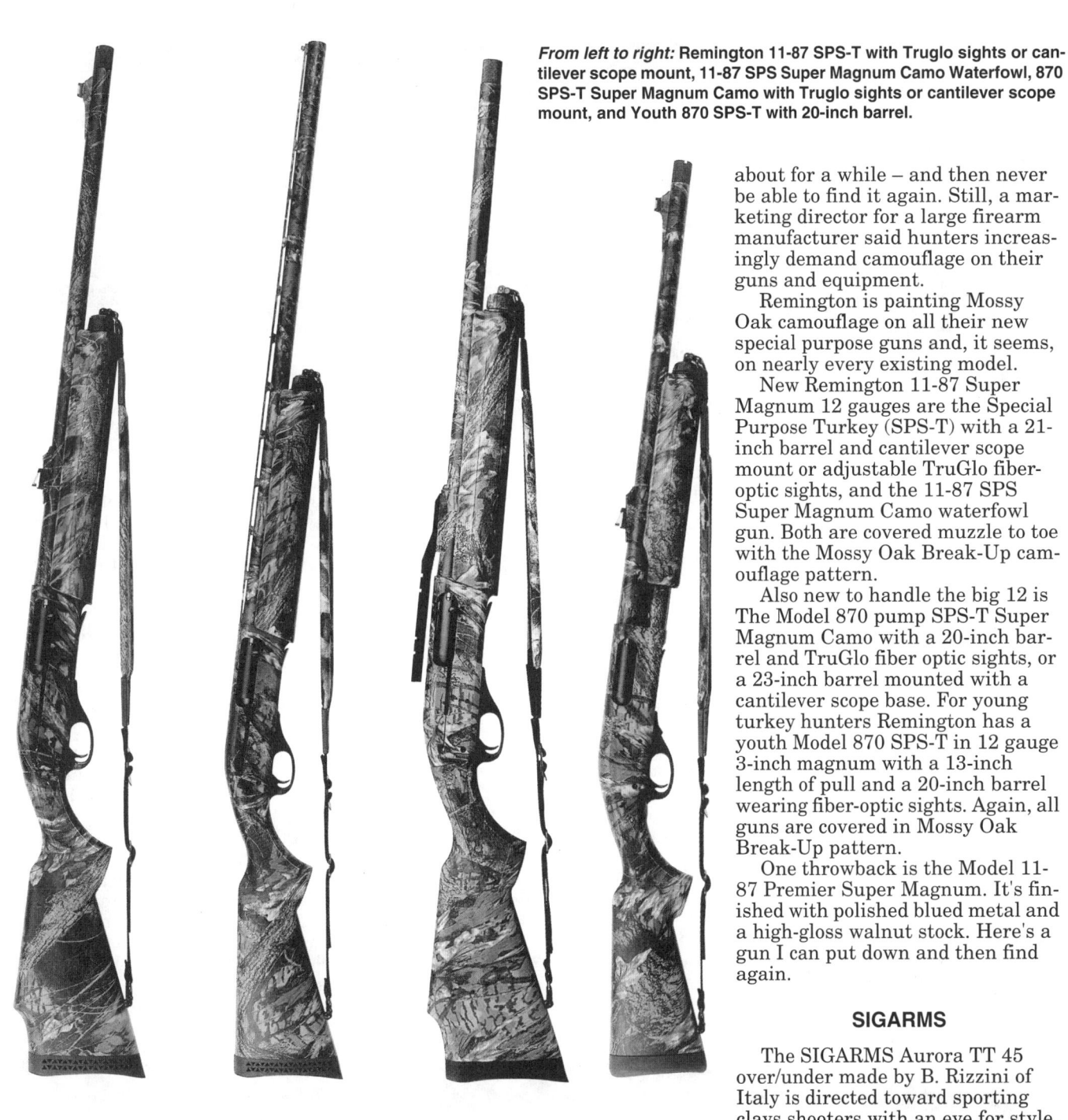

From left to right: Remington 11-87 SPS-T with Truglo sights or cantilever scope mount, 11-87 SPS Super Magnum Camo Waterfowl, 870 SPS-T Super Magnum Camo with Truglo sights or cantilever scope mount, and Youth 870 SPS-T with 20-inch barrel.

hunting. That can be a problem in selecting a gun for smaller-framed shooters. Mossberg has solved that problem with its Model 500 Field 12 gauge Bantam. The Bantam has a shortened buttstock to fit younger shooters, a grip contoured to move the hand closer to the trigger and the forearm moved closer to the rear for an easier reach. The Bantam also comes with a half-price certificate for a full-size buttstock and forearm when the shooter has outgrown the Bantam.

A few final words on Mossberg: The 835 Ulti-Mag has a covering of Realtree Advantage Timber camouflage for hunters after sharp-eyed turkey and waterfowl.

Also, Mossberg now has a stock-drop spacer system. One, or all, of four spacers fit between the rear of the receiver and the head of the stock grip to raise the vertical angle of the stock up to 1/2-inch. This adjustment allows easier eye alignment when shooting with a scope or rifle sights. It also raises the point of pattern impact for shooting rising targets, like pheasants.

Remington

I'm not so sure hunters over 40 (like me) should use guns or gear covered with camouflage unless it is buckled or tied to them. They might put it down somewhere, forget it about for a while – and then never be able to find it again. Still, a marketing director for a large firearm manufacturer said hunters increasingly demand camouflage on their guns and equipment.

Remington is painting Mossy Oak camouflage on all their new special purpose guns and, it seems, on nearly every existing model.

New Remington 11-87 Super Magnum 12 gauges are the Special Purpose Turkey (SPS-T) with a 21-inch barrel and cantilever scope mount or adjustable TruGlo fiber-optic sights, and the 11-87 SPS Super Magnum Camo waterfowl gun. Both are covered muzzle to toe with the Mossy Oak Break-Up camouflage pattern.

Also new to handle the big 12 is The Model 870 pump SPS-T Super Magnum Camo with a 20-inch barrel and TruGlo fiber optic sights, or a 23-inch barrel mounted with a cantilever scope base. For young turkey hunters Remington has a youth Model 870 SPS-T in 12 gauge 3-inch magnum with a 13-inch length of pull and a 20-inch barrel wearing fiber-optic sights. Again, all guns are covered in Mossy Oak Break-Up pattern.

One throwback is the Model 11-87 Premier Super Magnum. It's finished with polished blued metal and a high-gloss walnut stock. Here's a gun I can put down and then find again.

SIGARMS

The SIGARMS Aurora TT 45 over/under made by B. Rizzini of Italy is directed toward sporting clays shooters with an eye for style.

The Aurora's steel receiver is case-colored; with gold overlay game scenes flowing forward to a ventilated rib atop blued barrels. Internally, the boxlock action is machined from chrome-nickel molybdenum steel. Five-inch long forcing cones treat the shot column gently to improve patterns. The gun's walnut stock is finished with satin oil and checkered 20 lines per inch on the palm-swell grip and schnable forearm.

According to a SIGARMS press statement, the Aurora *"stock dimensions have been specifically designed with the American shooter in mind."* The stock has 1 1/2 inches of drop at the head of the comb and only 1/2-inch more drop to the heel and is

SIGARMS Aurora TT 45.

Weatherby Athena III 28 gauge.

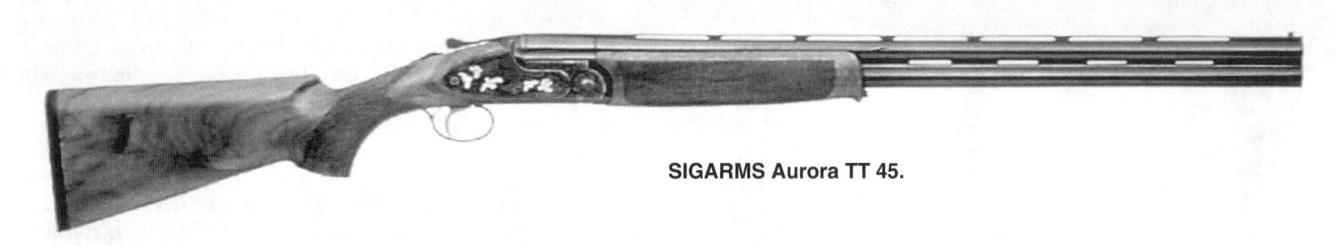

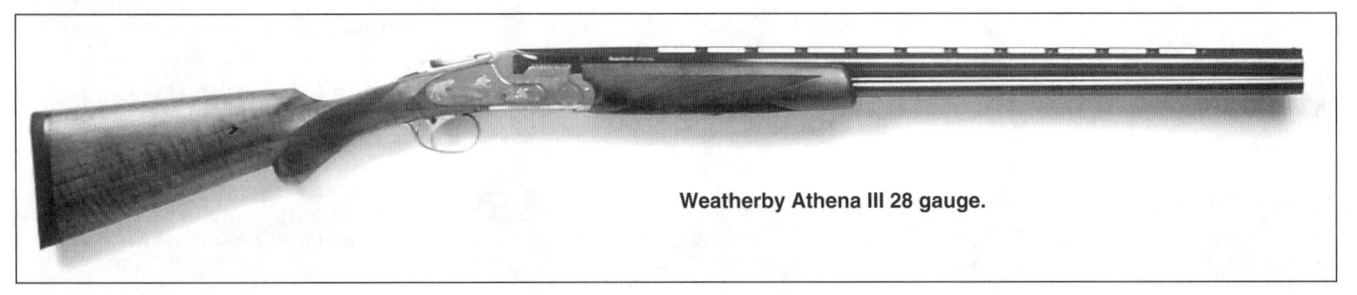

slightly cast off. The length of pull is 14 3/4-inches. That length of pull seems a bit long, until you try it. A SIG SA5 over/under I had came with that length pull. I'm pretty much average size and, for the first few rounds of clay targets, I had to make an extra effort to push the gun well ahead while bringing the stock comb up to my cheek. But after a while I became used to the long pull – and liked it because it helped me keep my cheek planted on the comb.

In 2000 SIGARMS and L.L. Bean introduced the New Englander B. Rizzini over/under shotgun in 12 and 20 gauge. This year the gun will also be chambered in 28 gauge and .410-bore.

The New Englander is a lightweight field gun with a low profile casehardened receiver enclosing a box lock. The barrel bores are chrome lined with three-inch chambers (2 3/4-inches in 28 gauge.) Five screw-in chokes from *Full* to *Skeet* are included. The forearm is beavertail-shaped and stocks are sized proportionately for each gauge. The guns are shipped in an aluminum hard case. They are available through SIGARMS and L.L. Bean in Freeport, Maine.

Weatherby

Weatherby introduced the Athena III in 1999 and this year has added the 28 gauge to its line of Athena Grade III Classic Field over/under shotguns. The 28-gauge model comes with 26- or 28-inch barrels with overall lengths of 43 or 45 inches. The Athena III's stock is oil-finished Claro walnut with hand-cut checkering, a comb with 3/4-inch drop along its length, a rounded grip and slender forearm. The butt is castoff. The Athena III weighs between 6 1/2 and 7 pounds and has a 14 1/4-inch length of pull.

Winchester

A few refinements and one new shotgun from Winchester this year.

A sporting clays model of the Super X2 is now offered. It features a set of shims to adjust the drop and cast of the comb. Two gas pistons are included to ensure cycling of all loads. One is for light target loads and the other for heavy three-inch field loads. In addition to a synthetic stock, the Super X2 Field now has a walnut stock.

Winchester has dressed up its Super X2 3 1/2-inch magnum and Model 1300 pump three-inch magnum 12 gauges to promote the National Wild Turkey Federation. The "Team NWTF" logo is printed on the buttstock of these guns and three-dot TruGlo sights are standard on the Super X2 24-inch barrel and the Model 1300's 22-inch barrel. Each gun comes with a NWTF membership form, a video, hat and six issues of *Turkey Call* magazine.

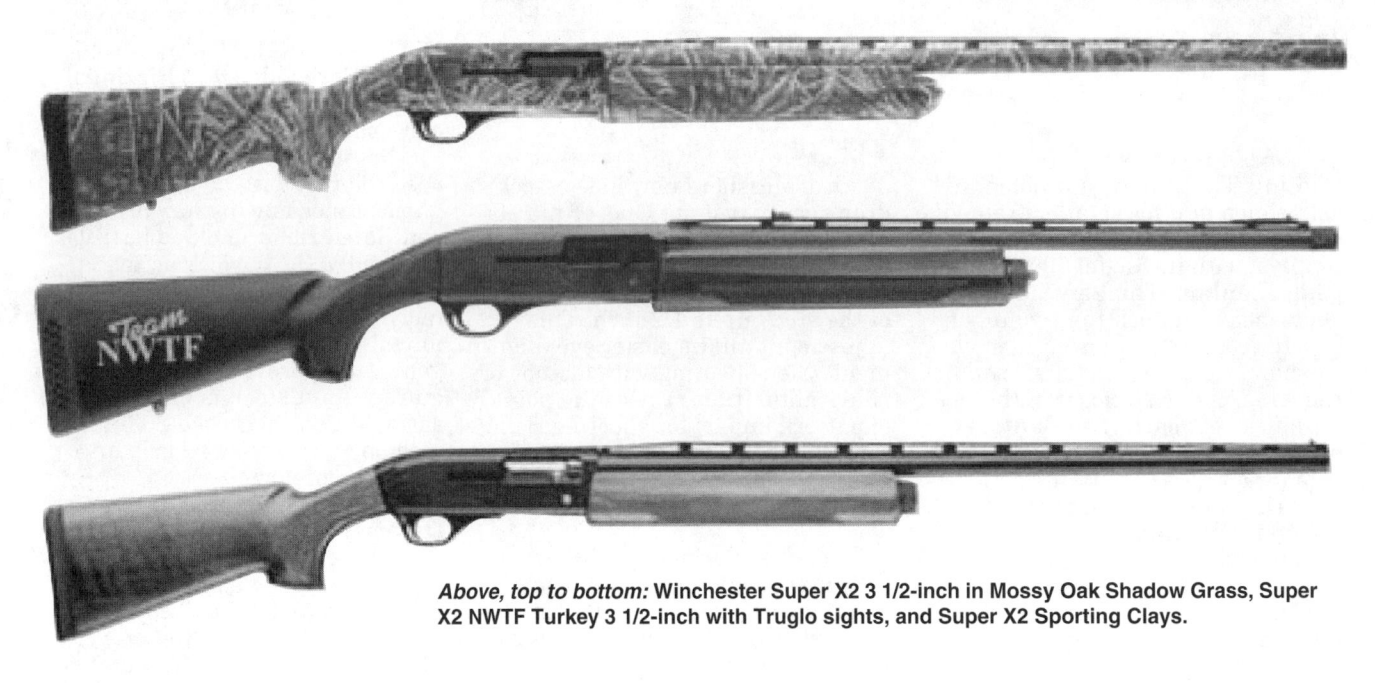

Above, top to bottom: Winchester Super X2 3 1/2-inch in Mossy Oak Shadow Grass, Super X2 NWTF Turkey 3 1/2-inch with Truglo sights, and Super X2 Sporting Clays.

Winchester Model 1300 NWTF Turkey Superflauge Camo.

Winchester Model 9410.

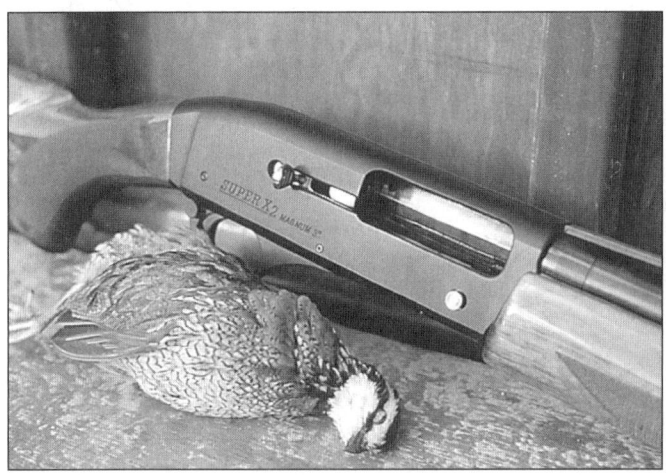

Winchester Super X2 Field gun with new walnut stock and a bobwhite quail.

Winchester Super X2 Field gun.

Winchester's new gun is the Model 9410, which stands for a Model 94 lever action chambered for the .410-bore 2 1/2-inch shell. The 6 3/4 pound rifle – I mean, shotgun – has a smooth bore, *Cylinder*-choked 24-inch barrel. The opening of the rear sight has been enlarged and a TruGlo front sight installed for quick pointing on flying targets. The tube magazine holds nine rounds and will more than take care of any carrot-nibbling rabbits in the garden and grouse along the trail.

34th EDITION, 2002 **57**

Muzzleloader News

by Doc Carlson

BLACKPOWDER SHOOTERS ARE one of the most diverse groups in the shooting sports. Re-enactors and the historical periods they enjoy run the gamut from the French-Indian War, through the Fur Trade Era to the Civil War. Hunters range from the very traditional flintlock/patched round ball shooters to those using the latest in-line technology. The blackpowder cartridge *aficionados* include those involved in Cowboy Action Shooting, Black Powder Cartridge Silhouette, Long Range - and a fair sprinkling of those who hunt with firearms of the black-powder cartridge era. Firearms and accessories for blackpowder shooters show the same wide diversity.

Savage Arms

Probably the biggest news to hit the blackpowder field recently is the introduction by Savage Arms of an in-line type muzzle-loading rifle that is designed for a diet of smokeless powder. For years the watchword of muzzle loading has been *"black powder only."* This new offering by Savage will modify that a bit.

Savage has taken their basic Model 110 bolt-action rifle and adapted it into a 50-caliber muzzle-loading rifle. So far, nothing too innovative; Remington and Ruger have done, basically, the same thing. What makes the Savage different – and has stirred up quite a bit of controversy among muzzleloader shooters and manufacturers – is the use of smokeless powder as a propellant. As stated before, smokeless powder has always been a *"no-no"* in muzzleloaders, so this rifle is certainly a departure from conventional muzzle loading arms and shooting.

The key to the system is a special, heat-treated breech plug that takes a patented "percussion module." The module fits very closely into a chamber in the breech plug and effectively seals against gas leakage when the bolt is closed. The 209 shotgun primer in the module ignites the powder charge through a small orifice when the gun is fired. This system, which restricts the powder gas and pressure to the barrel, sets the Savage Model 10MLSS apart from any other muzzle-loading arm on the market.

The rifle is supplied, at present, in matte blue finish or stainless steel with a synthetic stock. The heavy-contour barrel is 24 inches long with a 1:24-inch twist, intended for conical bullet projectiles, not round ball. Savage recommends the use of 45-caliber bullets and heavy-duty sabots. Many of the sabots on the market will not hold up to the higher pressures of smokeless powders and tend to leak, with the accompanying loss of accuracy. Savage recommends several different smokeless powder and bullet combinations in the brochure supplied with each gun. The rifle comes with two percussion modules, breech plug wrench, ball starter and a de-capper. Extra percussion modules can be purchased for a nominal price.

Reports of shooting tests show the new Savage offering to be very accurate, with proper loads. It easily holds two-minutes-of-angle groups. The weak link seems to be the sabot. If the barrel gets overly hot – or if the weather is extremely hot – the sabots tend to soften, making it easy for gas to 'blow by,' with resulting loss of accuracy. This should be of little consequence under hunting conditions, but is something to keep in mind during load workups. It is also very important to stay with Savage's recommended loads. Smokeless powder is much less forgiving of overloads than black powder and it's replicas.

For those who aren't comfortable with smokeless powder in muzzleloaders – or in those states that don't allow the use of smokeless – the new Savage works just fine with blackpowder or Pyrodex, including the Pyrodex pellets. There will, of course, be a certain amount of fouling buildup with these propellants, something not seen with smokeless.

With the various recommended smokeless powder loads, muzzle velocities of 2200 to 2300 fps are generated with 240-grain 45-caliber bullets and heavy-duty sabots. These loadings deliver energy in the 3000 foot/pounds range, making the rifle a definite "player" for most big game.

Because of the potential of smokeless powder to generate very significant pressures, the recommended loadings should be followed with as much care as reloaders exercise when reloading rifle cartridges. Pre-measured loads, carried in quick-load tubes, will be the most practical for hunting, I imagine.

How hunters and game departments will receive this Savage innovation remains to be seen. I suspect that the total lack of fouling, with the accompanying reduction of cleaning chores, will appeal to many. The higher velocities and somewhat flatter trajectories will also be well received by many muzzle-loading hunters. The introduction of this rifle certainly proves that innovation and invention continues among American firearms makers.

White Rifles

White Rifles has taken their in-line guns into the space age by the addition of a carbon fiber-wrapped stainless steel barrel to their standard in-line action. The advantage of this barrel type is reduced heat buildup during shooting and more barrel stability over wide temperature ranges. Hunters, if your rifle is sighted in during warm weather and then taken to a hunting area that is very cold, there will be very little effect on the point of impact due to

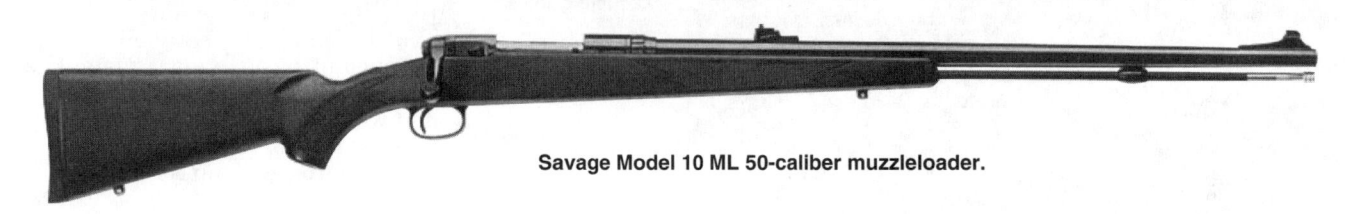

Savage Model 10 ML 50-caliber muzzleloader.

Knight Super Disc Rifle, new in 45 caliber.

the temperature variation. The carbon fiber-wrapped barrel is very stable and ballistically *"quiet."*

This new rifle is bedded in a thumbhole laminated wood stock. The breech plug is equipped with a musket-size nipple for reliable ignition under all conditions. The 50-caliber barrel is set up to use the White System, as are all the White line of firearms. Under this system, under-size bullets are especially designed to load easily down the bore of the rifle and, upon firing, to shorten and upset into the rifling to give a good gas seal and grip the rifling well. This has proven to be a very accurate, hard-hitting and easy-loading system in the hunting field.

Also new this year from White is a series of their bullets sized to load easily in the barrels of Knight, Remington, Ruger, Thompson/Center and other muzzle-loading rifles. Of particular interest to hunters, this product addition allows the use of a full bore-size bullet, of 360 to 430 grains, in most 45, 50 or 54-caliber muzzleloaders.

There seems to be the beginnings of a trend towards the 45-caliber in the in-line rifles. White is making their Whitetail Hunter and Elite Hunter rifles available in this caliber. They join several other manufacturers who are reintroducing this caliber. The 45 fell from favor when most guns on the market were designed to shoot round ball. The smaller ball is short on energy and penetration, beyond 50 yards or so, on deer-size animals. With the increasing use of bullet-type projectiles in hunting muzzleloaders, the 45 caliber is getting a new lease on life. In conical bullet shapes, weighing 350 to 450 grains, this caliber has plenty of long-range energy for the hunting field.

Knight Rifles

Knight Rifles has entered the 45-caliber club also. They are offering the popular D.I.S.C. rifle in 45 caliber, as well as the standard 50 caliber. They are making a sabot-type bullet of 40 caliber to match this new bore diameter. The sabot material is heavy duty to stand up to heavy loads of black powder or Pyrodex. Called the "Red Hot" Barnes bullet, it can be had in 150- or 175-grain weights. A 240-grain "Precision" bullet of lead with a plastic insert in the hollow point to aid expansion is also available, along with a 180-grain pure lead hollow point. The advantage to the 40/45-caliber projectile is, of course, higher velocities and flatter trajectories. The 150-grain Red Hot bullet can be pushed at over 2600 fps (*at the muzzle*) and will deliver in excess of 1700 fps and 1000 ft./lbs. energy at 150 yards, when loaded over 150 grains of Pyrodex pellets and fired by a 209 primer. If zeroed at 100 yards, drop (*below line of sight*) will be 2 1/4 inches at 150 yards and 7 1/4 inches at 200 yards. Pretty darn good ballistics for something that loads from the front with blackpowder – or its substitute.

Called the Knight Super DISC Rifle, this new 45-caliber offering is available in standard composite stock styles, finished in Mossy Oak Break Up, Advantage Timber HD or basic black. If desired, a thumbhole stock can be ordered in black also. The Knight bolt-action DISC system is used, which utilizes a thin plastic disc to hold the 209 shotgun primer. The primed disc is inserted in a slot at the front of the action and, as the bolt is lowered, the bolt body cams ahead to force the disc tightly against an ignition orifice in the rear of the breech plug.

The action is coupled with a fluted Green Mountain barrel in either blued or stainless steel finish. The 1:20-inch twist is matched to the 45-caliber projectiles, producing the exceptional accuracy that Knight rifles are known for. The barrel is topped with fully adjustable TruGlo sights for outstanding sight pictures in all kinds of light conditions. Those fiber-optic sights are a great help to

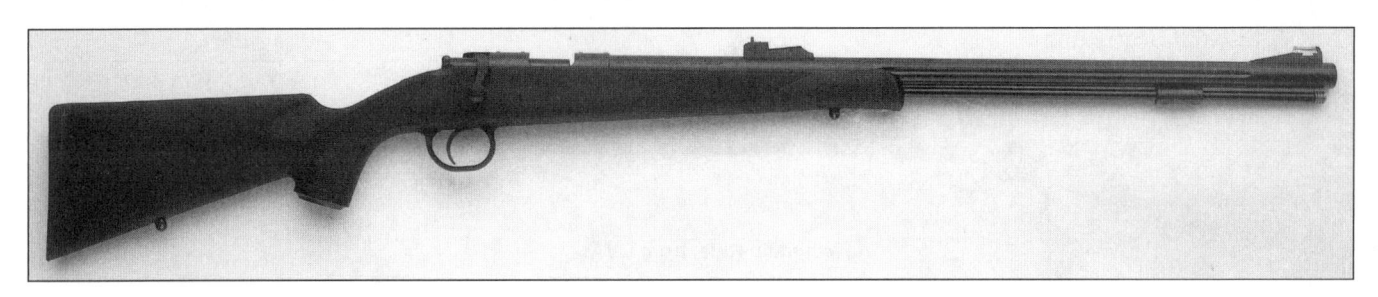

Traditions center-hung hammer pistol.

Traditions 45-caliber Lightning LD Rifle.

Cleland Match Hawken, from T/C.

T/C's Black Mountain Magnum shotgun.

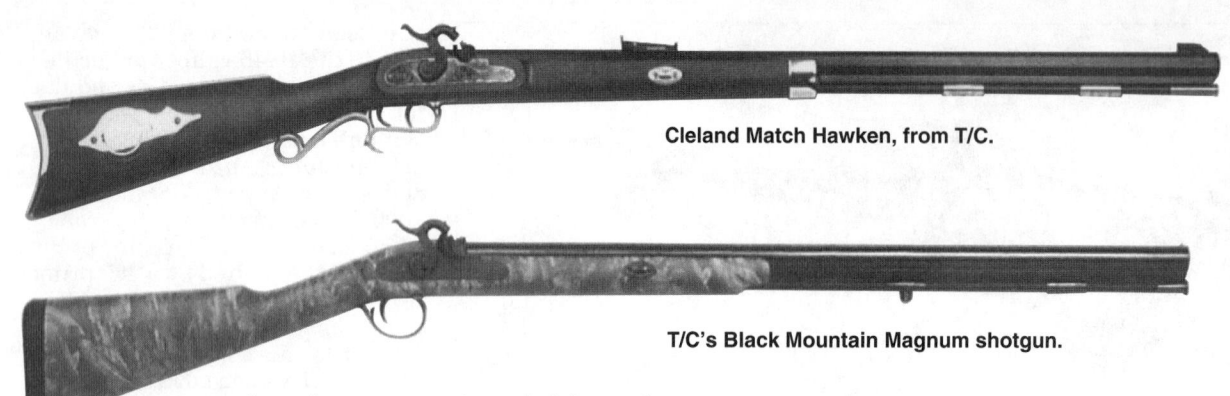

those of us who seem to have lost the ability to see a clear rear sight—some say due to advancing years. *Myself, I think it's due to interference by the guardian angel of deer and other critters.*

Traditions Performance Firearms

Traditions Performance Firearms is another well-known name in the muzzle-loading field that has gotten on the 45-caliber bandwagon. They call their offering the Lightning 45 LD, the 'LD' standing for *long distance*. The bolt-action gun is available with either blue- or C-Nickel-finished fluted barrel, rifled 1:20 inches. The blue version is fitted with a black synthetic stock and the C-Nickel model can be had with either the black - or a High Definition Advantage Timber camouflage pattern - stock. The gun comes with a three-way ignition system using number 11 caps, musket caps or the 209 shotgun primer and is recommended for loads up to 150 grains of black powder or Pyrodex. This rifle also sports the TruGlo fiber-optic sights. This will be a popular addition to Traditions' rather complete line of in-line guns.

True to their name, Traditions also makes a wide range of the traditional side-hammer guns. Their Magnum Plains Percussion Rifle has the look of the half-stock plains rifle of old, but features an ignition system designed to handle the Pyrodex pellets – as well as up to 150 grains of loose black powder or Pyrodex. The gun features double set-triggers, brass butt plate and trigger guard, blued octagon barrel and adjustable fiber-optic sights. The twist of the rifling is 1:32 inches, primarily intended for conical/slug bullets. The barrel is held in the hardwood stock by two barrel keys, typical of Plains-type rifles. The overall style matches the half-stock working gun of the past.

Traditions also make a hybrid-type gun called the Thunder Magnum. This is a Monte Carlo, pistol-grip stock side-hammer gun that also has an ignition system designed for Pyrodex pellets as well as loose powder. The side-hammer lock features a thumb safety. The half-stock rifle has a *"first in the industry"* (according to Traditions) removable stainless steel breech plug so the barrel can be cleaned from the breech end – *ala* in-line action guns. The rifle is available finished in either C-Nickel or blued, with a hardwood stock. The barrel is held in the stock by a easily removable barrel band. This gun is a side-hammer with many of the features of the popular in-line guns to appeal to those who like both styles.

Unique to Traditions is their Crockett rifle. This very traditional-looking half-stock percussion gun is made in 32 caliber—a rarity among the many guns of 45 caliber and up. The trim rifle has a blued octagon barrel, double set triggers and brass fittings. The twist is 1:48 inches, which will handle patched round ball quite well for hunting small game or targets. The Crockett rifle fits well with Traditions' line of flint and percussion full-stock rifles. These other rifles are, almost without exception, equipped with barrels rifled 1:66—obviously intended for round ball.

In the pistol line, Traditions features a group of modernistic muzzle-loaders with center-hung hammers. These guns, in 50-caliber percussion, are available with barrel lengths of 14 3/4 inches to 20 inches, in either C-Nickel or blue finish. The 20-inch model is even available with a muzzle brake to cut down on recoil and muzzle rise. Stocks are either walnut or black-finish hardwood. Equipped with target sights, these pistols are for serious hunters or target shooters. Traditions also have several pistol models in the more traditional designs. Pretty much something for everyone in the Traditions line.

Thompson/Center Arms

For many years, before the proliferation of all the reproductions that we have available today, the standard bore size for most repro muzzleloaders was 40 caliber. It was the caliber most seen on the firing line at the various shoots around the country. A great many of the original guns for target and small game hunting also were of this caliber. The reason was that this is a very accurate caliber for a round-ball gun and recoil is nonexistent. This fine caliber has been pushed into obscurity by the recent trend to 50- and 54-caliber guns.

Thompson/Center has brought back this once-popular caliber in their Cleland Match Hawken rifle. This is a 40-caliber version of the ever-popular Hawken series of T/C rifles. The rifle utilizes an American walnut stock with all brass furniture. The percussion lock and double set triggers are the same as found on the Hawken models. The 1-inch across-the-flats octagon barrel is blued and 31 inches long. The 40-caliber bore is rifled 1:48 inches. This

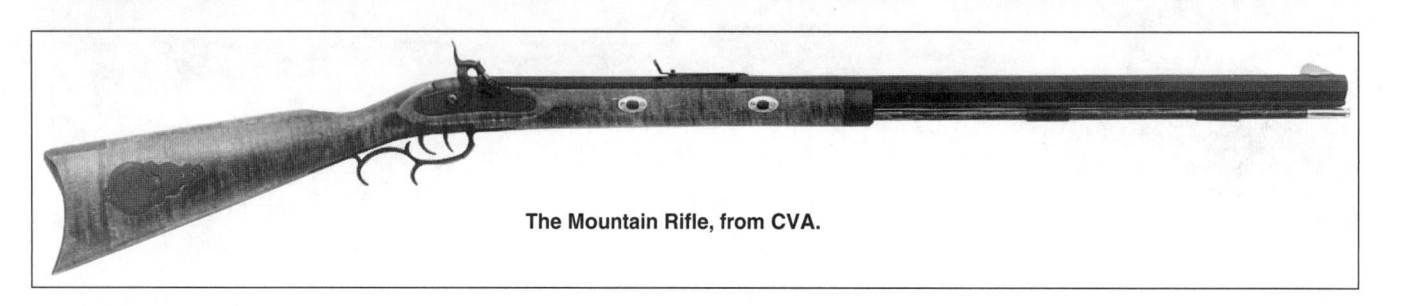

The Mountain Rifle, from CVA.

CVA's Firebolt 209 UltraMag.

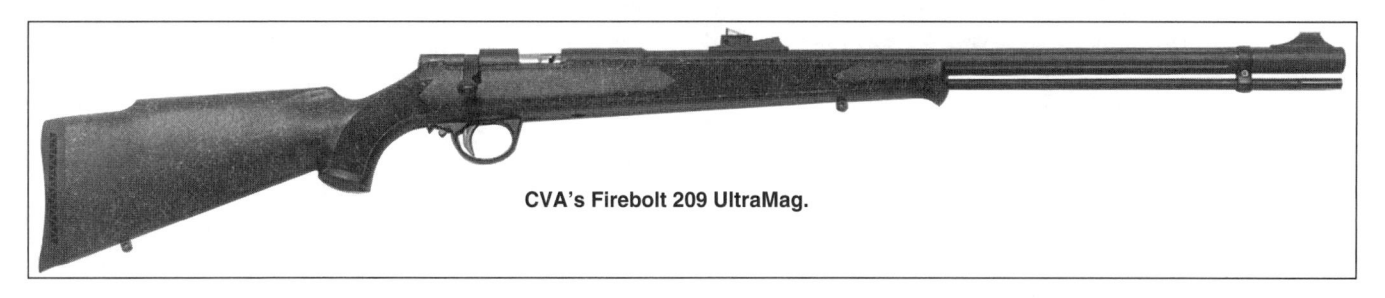

results in a barrel of good weight for steady offhand hold and exceptional accuracy with patched round ball.

Sights are a bead-type front, coupled with an open target rear with knurled windage and elevation screws that are finger-adjustable; no tools are needed to change settings. This target rear sight is also available as an accessory that can be added to any T/C rifle. Advice on design and building this new addition to the T/C line was supplied by Chad Cleland, an NMLRA National Champion, hence the name of the rifle.

Also new this year from the T/C folks is their Black Mountain Magnum in 12 gauge. The blued barrel is 27 inches long, round and comes with a screw-in turkey choke for tight patterns. Loaded with 100 grains of black powder or Pyrodex, behind 1 1/4 oz. of shot, this muzzleloader should be big medicine for the turkey hunter. It should do well on the trap field, also.

The percussion shotgun features a composite stock with Advantage Timber Camo finish and blued hardware with, of course, a single trigger. It is of standard side-hammer lock design with a rubber recoil pad and aluminum ramrod. A no-nonsense shotgun designed with the serious hunter in mind.

Connecticut Valley Arms

CVA has substantially upgraded one of their in-lines and brought back a traditional favorite. The bolt-action Firebolt rifle series now features a 26-inch fluted barrel with 209-primer ignition and loading recommendations up to 150-grain charges. It is made in both 50-, and the newly popular 45-calibers. The action is housed in a heavier, resin-filled stock with rubber recoil pad to cut down on felt recoil. The standard stocks have a soft rubber coating over a FiberGrip cosmetic finish, making them quiet in the woods and easy to grip with cold, wet or gloved hands. The stocks are also available in rubber-coated Break Up camo patterns. The muzzle of the barrel is rebated for ease of loading. The receiver is drilled and tapped for scope mounting, if one wishes, and open sights are of the fiber optic variety.

The updated FireBolt is available in nickel or blued finish with either of the stock finishes previously noted… a good-looking, practical arm for the hunter.

On the traditional side, CVA is reintroducing their Mountain Rifle that was a very popular part of their line some years back. This reasonably priced, traditional half-stock rifle was dropped from the line some years back. It was reinstated a year or so ago as a high-priced, special issue gun and has finally made it back into the line as a middle-priced offering.

The Mountain Rifle starts with a figured hard maple stock showing an oil-type finish. The browned steel barrel is 50 caliber, 32 inches long, with a 1:66-inch twist – definitely a traditional round-ball gun. Browned steel trigger guard, butt plate, forend cap and patchbox add to the traditional look and feel of this rifle. The percussion lock is a Manton style, which was one of the first reproduction locks to come on the market for custom builders back in the 1960s. It was called the Hamm lock after the maker, Russ Hamm. The rifle is made in the USA and will be available in limited quantities.

The sights are a traditional buckhorn rear coupled with a silver blade front, as was typical of the type. This was one of the better-looking reproduction rifles on the market a decade ago and the new offering certainly loses nothing of the look and feel of its predecessor. I think the shooter looking for a gun with the look of an original will find this one to his (or her) liking.

Lyman Products Corporation

Lyman has added a drop-in barrel with a 1:32-inch twist for their Great Plains series of rifles. This will convert the 1:60 round-ball rifles to shoot the slug-type projectiles. The barrels are available to fit both flint and percussion guns in either right or left hand configurations. This will give an added dimension to these popular rifles.

Lyman is also introducing a left-hand version of the Deerstalker rifle in flintlock. This makes this company one of the leaders in catering to

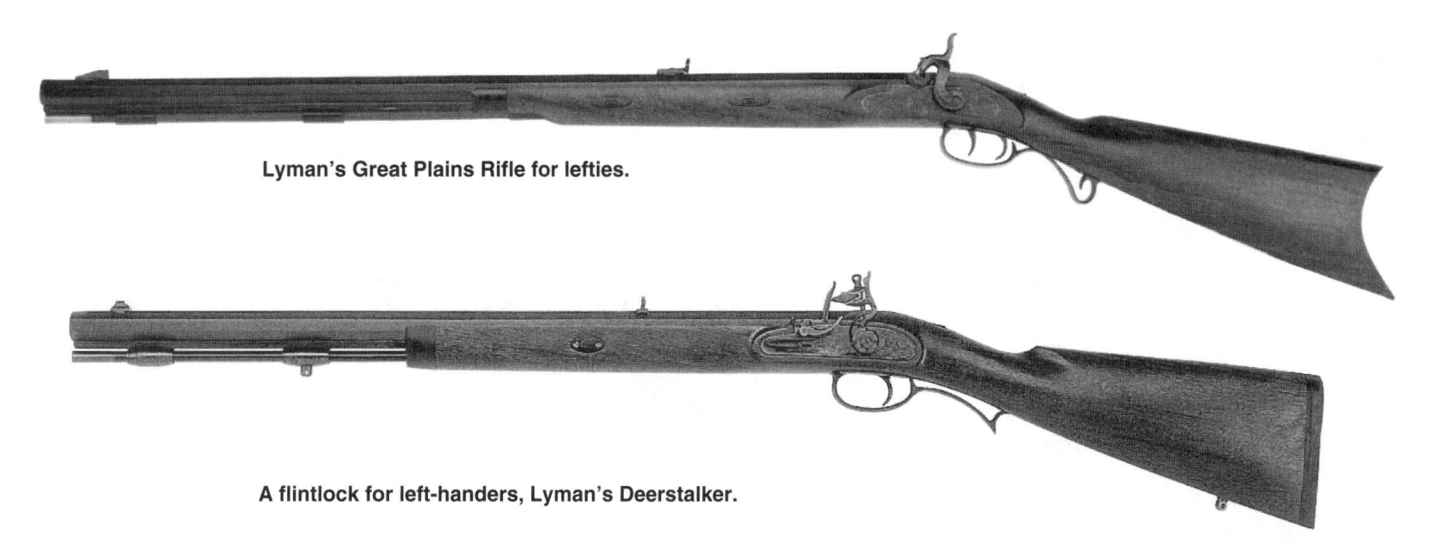

Lyman's Great Plains Rifle for lefties.

A flintlock for left-handers, Lyman's Deerstalker.

Lyman's Black Powder Handbook, Second Edition.

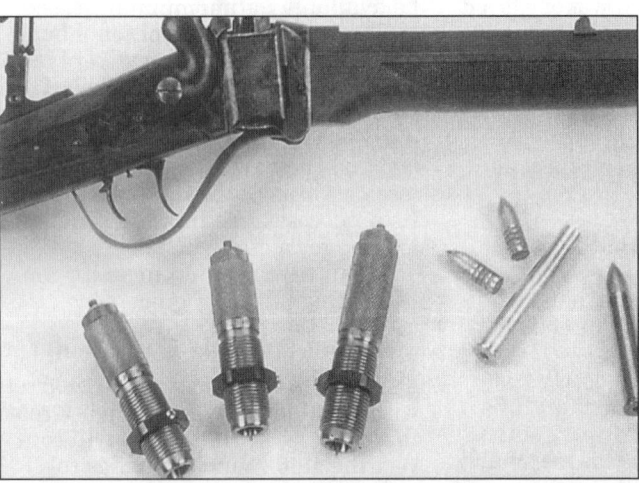

New neck-sizing dies from Lyman.

traditionalists that shoot from the "*wrong*" side. There are a high percentage of shooters out there that handle rifles from the left shoulder and it's good to see a company that works to meet their needs.

Lyman is probably best known for supplying reloading equipment. They can trace their roots in this area well back into the 1800s. Last year they added three-die reloading sets for many of the classic calibers that blackpowder cartridge folks are shooting. These include 40-65, 40-70 Sharps Straight, 45-90, 45-100-2.6, 45-110-2 7/8, 45-120-3 1/4 and 50-90. Now they have added neck-sizer die sets in 40 cal., 45 cal. Short (for up to 45-100), and 45 cal. long (for 45s from 45-110 and longer). These die sets allow the neck of the case to be sized to provide good bullet tension, while maintaining the fire-formed dimensions of the rest of the case. This will extend case life as well as contribute to accuracy. Along with the very complete line of bullet moulds for blackpowder shooters of all stripes, these new dies make Lyman the complete shopping store for the blackpowder cartridge shooter, as well as the muzzleloader.

Also new from Lyman is the new 2nd edition of the *Lyman Black Powder Handbook*. In addition to complete coverage of loads for muzzle-loading firearms – which include Pyrodex pellets, sabotted bullets and conical-type projectiles – the latest *Handbook* contains a section on loads for blackpowder cartridges for both rifles and pistols. Anyone who shoots blackpowder or its substitute, Pyrodex, in any kind of firearm needs a copy of this book. A copy of the annual Lyman catalog will delight the heart of such shooters also.

Tasco

Many states are beginning to allow the use of telescopic sights on muzzleloaders. All of the in-line rifles are drilled and tapped for scopes and most scope mount manufacturers are making mounts to fit the various front loaders on the market. Many states, including my home state of Nebraska, allow the use of scopes only if there is no magnification. Tasco has added a line of scopes specifically designed for muzzleloading guns. Part of their World Class model line, the muzzleloader scopes are made in 1 x 32, 1.75 x 20, 2-7x 32, and 3-9 x 32 – all with 1-inch tubes and 30/30-type reticle. All are finished in blue and have good eye relief, as well as a wide field of view.

Dixie Gun Works

Dixie Gun Works has brought back a great shotgun accessory from days of yore. They are now carrying a double, over-the-shoulder *shot snake* of the type that was a "must have" accessory for the well-equipped muzzle-loading shotgun shooter of years past. The unit consists of two long narrow shot containers made of soft leather and tipped with shutter-type shot measures. The whole works is mounted on a wide shoulder strap and includes a small pouch for wads, capper – or whatever. The wide strap distributes the load evenly and makes carrying shot comfortable and practical. The shutter-type shot dispensers are adjustable for the amount of shot dropped and hang pointing downward for ease of dispensing the shot into the muzzle of the shotgun – a very handy thing for the m/l shotgun shooter to carry in the field.

Tasco's World-Class 1x32mm riflescope for muzzleloaders.

62 GUNS ILLUSTRATED

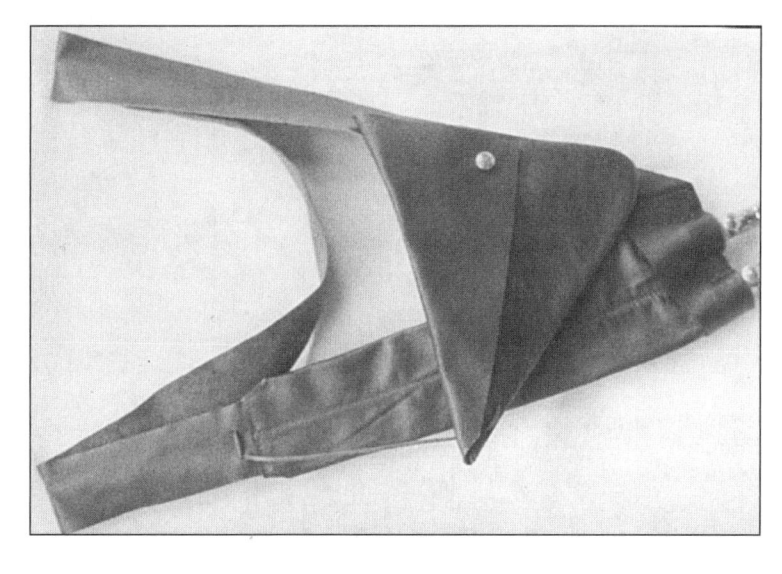

The Shot Snake, from Dixie Gunworks.

If you are into any type of blackpowder shooting and don't have a copy of the Dixie Gun Works catalog, you are missing a real treat. Started by Turner Kirkland in the 1950s, Dixie carries anything the blackpowder shooter could want. The catalog also contains the world's premiere listing of antique gun parts – both original and newly made. Five bucks sent to Dixie for a copy of this 700-plus-page bible for blackpowder shooters is money very well spent.

The blackpowder cartridge shooters and cowboy action aficionados have quite a bit to celebrate this year. There are some great replicas being imported for these folks.

Tristar Sporting Arms, Ltd.

Tristar Sporting Arms, Ltd. is importing a reproduction of the Winchester 1887 12-gauge lever-action shotgun. Made by the Lithgow Small Arms factory in Australia, the shotgun is actually a scaled-down version of the 1901 Winchester 10 gauge lever gun. The 1901 was a much-improved version of the 1887 and incorporated many safety features that are needed for shooting today's smokeless shotshells. The gun is made to shoot only 2 3/4-inch 12 gauge shotshells and will handle either smokeless or blackpowder loadings of same.

The gun will be offered with a 22-inch barrel with *Improved Cylinder* choking. Walnut stocks, oil finished, with steel butt plate and blued metal parts make this shotgun a dead ringer for the original. The guns will be coming into this country starting in February of 2001. They will be imported on a limited basis the first year, with production of around 4000 guns over the next two or three years. I expect we'll see many of these guns on the firing lines of the Cowboy Action shoots around the country.

Interstate Arms Corporation

Another old-timer that is coming back - again a Winchester shotgun - is the venerable Model 1897. Imported by Interstate Arms Corporation, this one is made in China and is a very good replica of this well-known scattergun. Made with a 20-inch *Cylinder-bore* barrel, hardwood stocks finished with a walnut oil color and blued steel; this is another shotgun that should find favor with the Cowboy Action folks. The gun is made with a solid frame, rather than the takedown frame, of the original. This holds the price down to a reasonable level. The only gauge will be 12, at least for the foreseeable future. After an absence of over half a century, it's good to see another of the classic shotguns back on the market.

Navy Arms

The Navy Arms Company is another of those companies that have become a household word among re-enactors, muzzleloading *aficionados* and lovers of reproduction arms. They have one of the more complete lines of reproduction arms – from the very early matchlock to 1900-period guns. Re-enactors portraying nearly all periods of the history of United States use the firearms available from this pioneering company.

The latest addition to this fine line of reproduction guns is the Smith & Wesson Third Model Russian revolver. Smith & Wesson manufactured this gun between 1874 and 1878 for both the Russian military and the civilian commercial market. It is a top-break revolver similar to the famous 1875 Schofield. It is chambered, of course, for the 44 Russian cartridge. It features a blued frame, cylinder and barrel with the hammer and spur trigger guard being casehardened, as original. Walnut grips complete the picture. A lanyard ring is attached to the butt of this very nicely made revolver. Among the well-known shootists of the Old West who reportedly carried this revolver was Pat Garrett, the nemesis of Billy the Kid. I'm sure the Cowboy Action Shooters will welcome this one.

Taylor's & Company, Inc.

One of the more famous guns of the Civil War was *"That damn Yankee rifle you load on Sunday and shoot all week"* – the Spencer. Made in both rifle and carbine versions, the best known is the carbine version that was issued to Union cavalry troops. This was the first really successful cartridge repeater to arrive on

TriStar's new reproduction of the 1887 Winchester 12 gauge. A beauty, made in Australia.

Another beauty, the Spencer carbine from Taylor's, Inc.

The S&W Third Model, in 44 Russian, from Navy Arms.

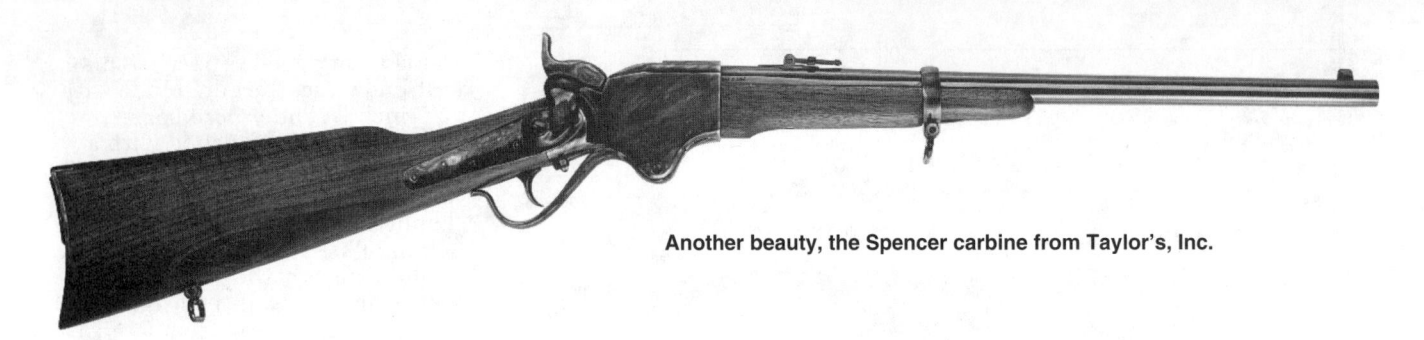

the scene in any numbers and was contemporary with the Henry rifle.

Taylor's & Company, Inc., is now importing a reproduction Spencer carbine that is a real beauty. Made by Armi Sport in Italy, the gun is the Model 1865… which corrected some of the faults of the original 1860 rifle. It holds seven cartridges in a tubular buttstock magazine and feeds them into the chamber by way of a lever action. The hammer must be cocked manually for each shot. This reproduction is very nicely done. I have spent some time with the manufacturer on various occasions and he is very committed to capturing the finest detail of any reproduction guns that he makes.

The carbine features a walnut stock, blued barrel and casehardened lock and action. The barrel length is 20 inches and overall length is 37 inches. The gun will be available chambered for the original 56/50 (*in reloadable centerfire rather than the original rimfire, however*), 44 Russian and 45 Schofield.

Also available will be a very nice reproduction of the original Blakeslee six-tube cartridge carrier that was originally issued with the carbine. This cartridge box was carried under the trooper's left arm and gave a fast reload by use of the tubes, each holding seven cartridges. A shoulder sling with hook to carry the carbine will also be available.

Goex Powder Company

Blackpowder shooting would not amount to much without the powder to shoot. We are lucky to have several suppliers of quality blackpowder and it's replicas.

Goex Powder Co., formerly owned by Du Pont, is probably the oldest American powder company still around. They make Goex black powder in 1Fg, 2Fg, 3Fg, 4 Fg and Cannon grades – as well as Cartridge, which is intended for black-powder cartridge shooting. They have recently brought a reproduction blackpowder, called Clear Shot, on the market that will give black powder pressures without the fouling and clean up requirements associated with the original powder. This is a ball-type powder, which meters nicely through any type of measure. They are also importing a blackpowder from Slovenia called KIK. This will be offered in 2Fg and 3 Fg only, at present.

Luna Tech, Inc.

A company called Luna Tech, Inc. is importing a German powder called Wano. This is available in all the standard grades, with the addition of unglazed 4Fg as an option. This is called '*pan powder*' to be used to prime the pan of flintlock guns—the idea being that unglazed powder will catch the sparks better, giving faster and more reliable ignition.

Petro Explo Co.

Petro Explo Co. brings in Elephant Black Powder in all four Fg grades, and Cannon. They also import Swiss blackpowder that is especially popular with the blackpowder cartridge silhouette shooters. It is available in 1Fg, 1 1/2Fg, 2Fg, 3Fg and 4Fg, with the 1 1/2Fg being the one used in large-capacity black powder cartridges.

Hodgdon Powder Company

Hodgdon Powder Company continues to expand the offerings of their compressed Pyrodex pellets to cover more calibers and charges. Their Pyrodex was the first replica blackpowder on the market and continues to be the one by which all other replica powders are judged.

Clean Shot Technologies, Inc.

Clean Shot Technologies, Inc. makes a replica powder called, of all things, Clean Shot. It is an ascorbic acid-based powder that also duplicates black powder pressures with little or no fouling. This powder is popular with the Cowboy Action crowd due to the lack of clean-up hassle—something that's important when shooting blackpowder loads in a lever gun.

The blackpowder sport continues to prosper. Technology continues to impact the sport also, much to the consternation of some of the traditional shooters. We are free to utilize the advancements or not, as we wish. So, pick the part of the blackpowder sport that appeals to you – and do it. Also recognize that others may like something different. That doesn't make either one wrong – just different. Enjoy your sport—and keep an eye on your back trail.

Frontier Six Shooter

It was said in the Old West that "God created man, but it was the Frontier Six Shooter that made them equal".

.45 Colt, .44 WCF, .38 WCF, 32 WCF, .44 Special, .357 Mag.
3 1/2" 4 3/4", 5 1/2" or 7 1/2" Barrel
Old Model Frame or Pre-War Frame, Old Style Charcoal Blue or Modern Blue

Rough Rider
U.S. Artillery Model

.45 Colt • 5 1/2" Barrel
Old Model Frame
Color Case Hardened

In 1898, the first U.S. Volunteer cavalry is formed under the command of Theodore "Teddy" Roosevelt. This group of gallant young Cowboys from all parts of the American West, recruited in a San Antonio Hotel Bar and trained at Camp Wood, Texas will carry more than 100 of these Artillery Models bravely in the charge up San Juan Hill. These historic American Cowboys will be Known forevermore as the "Rough Riders".

George Armstrong Custer
7th U.S. Cavalry Model

Each authentic firearm is properly marked with "Ainsworth" inspection markings, OWA Cartouch, 2 line patent dates and U.S. on the frame. Stamped into the butt of the backstrap is the Company and 7th Cavalry markings. Production of this model is limited to 2,000 units each of the five companies (C, E, F, I and L) that will perish under Custer's command at the Little Big Horn.

.45 Colt
7 1/2" Barrel
Old Model Frame
Color Case Hardened

CIMARRON F.A. Co.

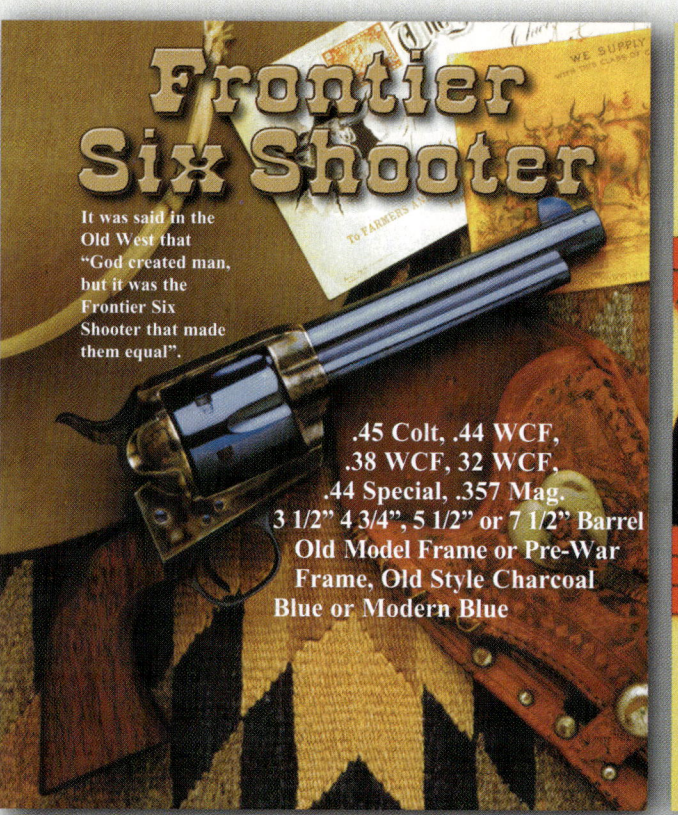

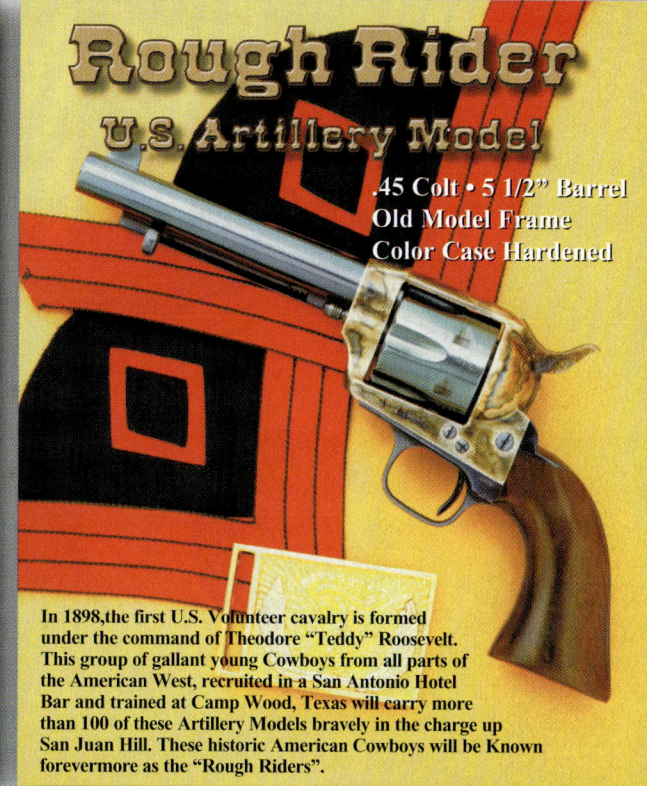

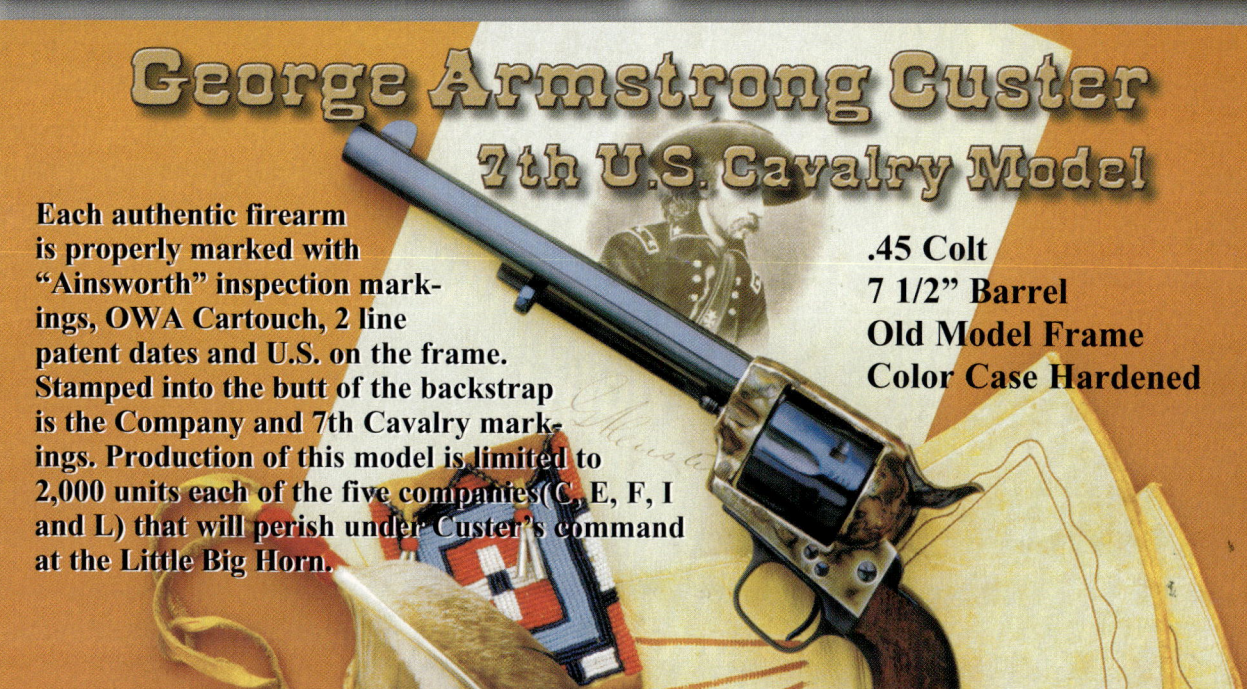

www.cimarron-firearms.com
For Details, Send $5.00
For Our Beautiful
New Color Catalog

P.O. BOX • FREDERICKSBURG, TX 78624 • 830-997-9090 • FAX 830-997-0802

Tired of looking for that certain gun?

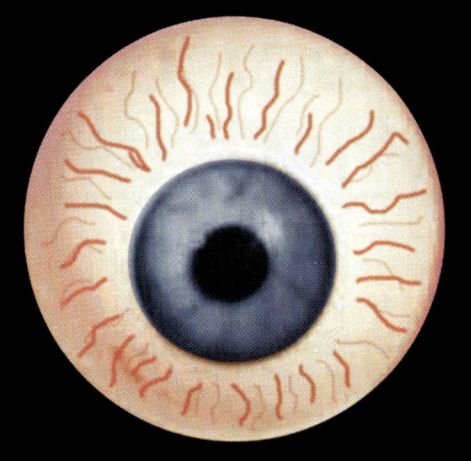

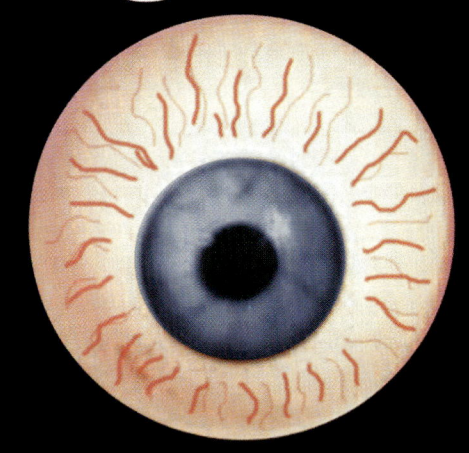

Gun Locator can help!!

"I just wanted to take this time to thank you for making my purchase so easy. This was my first purchase on the internet and you made it an enjoyable experience. I would gladly recommend this site to anyone who is about to purchase a firearm. Again, Thank You."
- C. Herring, Florence, SC

"Found a great deal on a Springfield M1A through gun locator and contacted the dealer directly. Very simple. Very fast. Thanks for your valuable service."
-J. Hicks, Corcoran, CA

"Your website is most thorough and impressive. The link with Shooting Times is a great idea. Keep up the good work."
-R. Evans, Acton, MA

"...Everything went smooth as silk (GunLocator). I picked up the Ruger yesterday afternoon along with a couple boxes of target ammo. I'm quite pleased with my purchase, the service at Dave's and especially your website. I will be telling my friends, and my Dad too who is a major gun nut, NRA life member, competition shooter, etc..."
-G. Church, Denver, CO

Only available at GalleryofGuns.com

Featuring over 32 of today's leading firearms manufacturers

Platinum & Pearl

Fine Quality Handguns Adorned with Gold Accents and Other Unique Features for Discerning Collectors Who Appreciate Craftsmanship and Beauty.

BLACK GOLD

Special Edition Series

TAURUS

www.taurususa.com

Taurus Security System™ included at no additional charge. For information about a FREE trigger lock for your Taurus, or replacing a cable lock previously received from Taurus, phone us at 305-624-1115 or visit us on the internet.

If the gun is special, we make the grips.

Colt .45 Auto Classic Panel Diamond Checkered with Border Super Rosewood

Vacquero/Blackhawk, Fleur-de-lis Checkering Super Rosewood

Sig 230 Ultima Panel Super Rosewood

Smith & Wesson K Frame, with buttcap and checkering, Super Rosewood

Ruger Blackhawk Classic Panel Bonded Ivory Mexican Eagle Carving

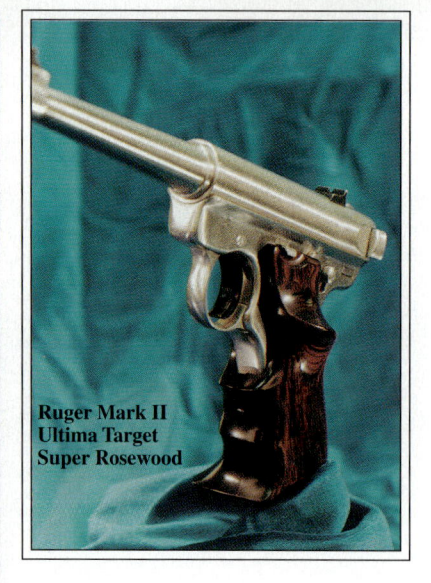

Ruger Mark II Ultima Target Super Rosewood

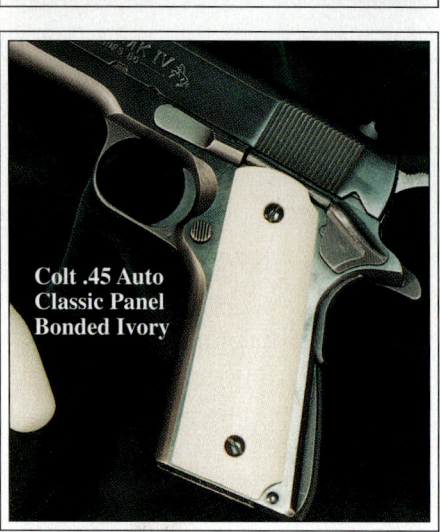

Colt .45 Auto Classic Panel Bonded Ivory

For twenty years we have made grips, from sawing the blocks of wood, to the machining, the sanding, the fitting, and the polishing of the finished grips. We have 42,000 square feet of factory space specializing in making grips, handles, and stocks for the handgun, gunstock, archery, and cutlery industries.

We have available a complete catalog of our handgun grips, which showcases our experience, design ideas, and manufacturing skills. We offer handgun shooters, collectors, and enthusiasts a wide range of distinctive grips for their special guns. Our grips are available direct or at your dealer.

901 N. Church St. • Box 309
Thomasboro, Illinois 61878
800-626-5774 • 217-643-3125
Fax: 217-643-7973

Altamont

Ammo Update

by Holt Bodinson

NOTHING HAS BEEN more exciting lately than the appearance of Winchester's and Lazzeroni's short magnum cartridges. These squat, fat, big-game cartridges seem to do exactly what the makers say they will do: provide the performance levels of the larger magnums with less powder, less recoil and, typically, improved accuracy. Equally intriguing is the appearance of Aguila's 17-caliber rimfire for the small-game enthusiast. Whether your interest runs to rifles, shotguns or handguns, you'll find some interesting new cartridges and components here from the world's leading makers.

Aguila

While it's been whispered about for years, the 17-caliber rimfire is now being commercially produced by Aguila in Mexico. The diminutive small-game round, based on a necked-down 22 LR case, made its debut at this year's SHOT Show – along with drop-in barrels for the Ruger series of rimfire rifles. Ballistics are rather impressive, with a 20-grain soft point or FMJ being launched at 1850 fps. If you've never fussed with a sub-caliber rifle, this might be the one for you. Aguila's "silent" primer-fueled 22 LR Colibri has proven popular indeed for indoor target shooting and backyard pest control, so this year Aguila is introducing the "Super Colibri" with a 20-grain bullet at 500 fps. And two more radical 22 rimfires make their debuts – the "223 RF" featuring a 43-grain FMJ at 1000 fps, and the "22 Goliah" loaded with a 75-grain lead bullet at 1000 fps. This year brings the introduction of Aguila's "smart bullet," the "IQ." The IQ is a dual-purpose, non-lead alloy bullet that breaks into 3 or 4 projectiles when fired directly at a gelatin block while, at the same time, offering cohesion and excellent penetration against hard surfaces such as glass and plastic. The IQ bullet is currently loaded in the 9mm, 45 ACP, and 40 S&W and will soon be released as a 170-grain, 2400 fps loading in the 454 Casull. www.aguilaammo.com

Accurate Arms

No new powders this year-- instead, AA has issued the 2nd Edition of its thoroughly unique "*Loading Guide.*" In it is data for the XMP-5744 reduced load powder and XMR-4064. Both powders were developed after *Guide* Number 1 was published. A whole new section devoted to Cowboy Action Shooting loads has been added – plus loading data for the 300 Whisper, 7.62x25 Tokarev, 357 Sig, 400 CorBon, 44 Russian, 45 S&W Schofield, 460 Rowland, 260 Rem., 300 and 338 Rem. Ultra Mags, 45-90, 45-110, 45-120 and 50-110. Lots of new bullets have been added, including the Remington 30-caliber Sabot! This is a "must have" reloading manual. www.accuratepowder.com

Alliant Powder

Making a major push to improve the clean-burning characteristics of some to its classic powders, Alliant has reduced powder

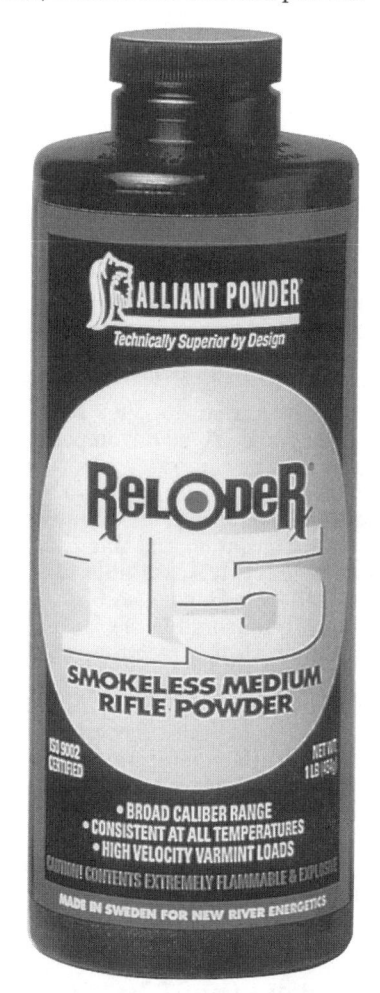

▲Following rigorous testing, Alliant's Reloder-15 was selected as the new propellant for the Army's 7.62mm sniper round.

Alliant's Green Dot is still Green Dot but it burns 50 percent cleaner.

fouling by 50 percent in its Green Dot and Unique canister grades. Significantly, Reloder 15 was selected by the Army as its powder of choice for the 7.62 M118 Special Ball Long-Range Sniper round. In Army trials, canister grade Reloder 15 provided superior performance in the four test categories – accuracy, chamber pressure, ballistic performance and lot-to-lot consistency with temperature ranges from 125°F to -40°F and distances out to 1000 yards. Try some in your 308 Winchester! www.alliantpowder.com

Ballistic Products

This is *THE* one-stop shop for shotshell reloaders. If it's not in their extensive catalog, it probably does not exist for any gauge. New offerings include a plastic X-treme spreader wad that will fit all shells from 20-thru-10 gauge; a 16 gauge Trap Commander wad, and the availability of a wider selection of Fiocchi hulls that can be shipped without additional HAZMAT fees including the 12 gauge 3 1/2 inch and 24, 28 and 32 gauges. The company's line of highly informative and rigorously tested handloading manuals has been updated with new editions this year of "The Sixteen Gauge Manual;" "Statistics & Pellet Ballistics;" "High Performance for Clays;" "The Powder Manual," and "Handloading Steel Shotshells." If you load any shotgun gauges at all, do send for BPI's catalog and don't overlook their terrific handloading manuals and monographs. www.ballisticproducts.com.

Barnes Bullets

Most computer-based ballistic programs seem to be developed by technocrats or computer nerds – not the Barnes program. Here is the easiest to use, most logical ballistics program available, and Barnes has just revised it. It's available as a download from Barnes' web site after one pays a reasonable fee for a user ID number. *Highly recommended*. Barnes X-Bullets are now factory loaded by Lazzeroni, Federal, Sako, PMC and Weatherby, and the new coated X-Bullets being released this year are a 120-grain/6.5mm; 130-grain/308 and a 210-grain/338. Look for the 3rd edition of Barnes reloading manual to make its appearance mid-year – new data will include the XLC and VLC lines. www.barnesbullets.com

Bell Brass (MAST Technology)

Making some of the toughest brass ever produced, Bell is adding the following new cases this year:

Black Hills' 40 S&W load of a 165-grain Gold Dot bullet at 1150 fps is the hottest available within industry pressure standards.

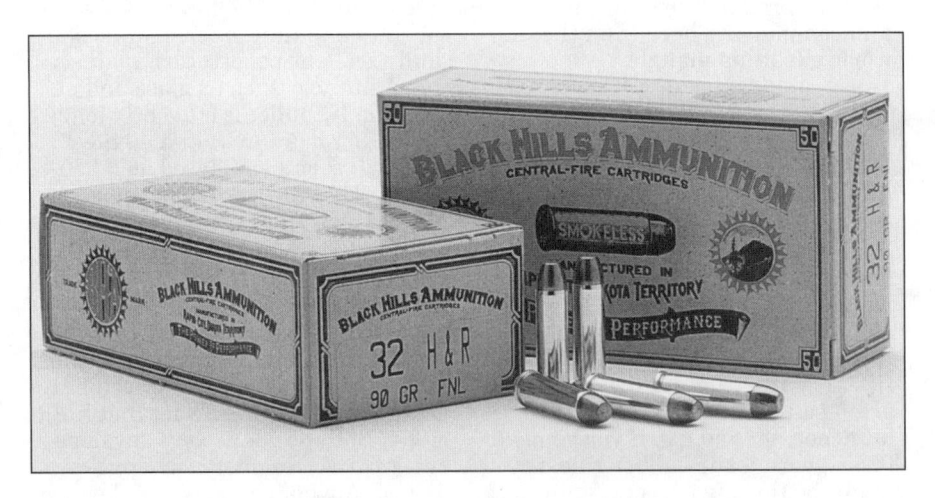

With the return of the 32 H&R to the Ruger Vaquero line, Black Hills offers the perfect cowboy action load – a 90-grain lead bullet at 750 fps.

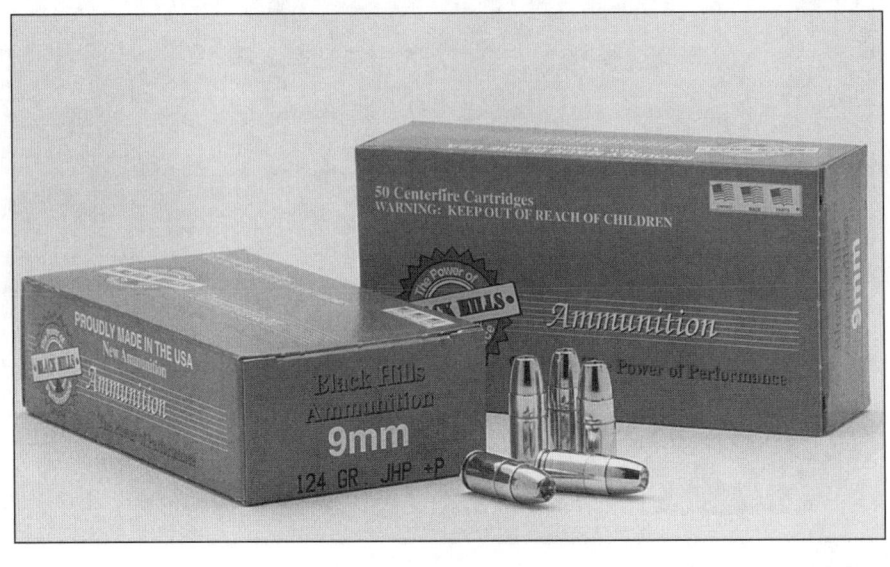

Black Hills' new 9mm+P load features a 124-grain Speer Gold Dot at a sizzling 1250 fps.

66 GUNS ILLUSTRATED

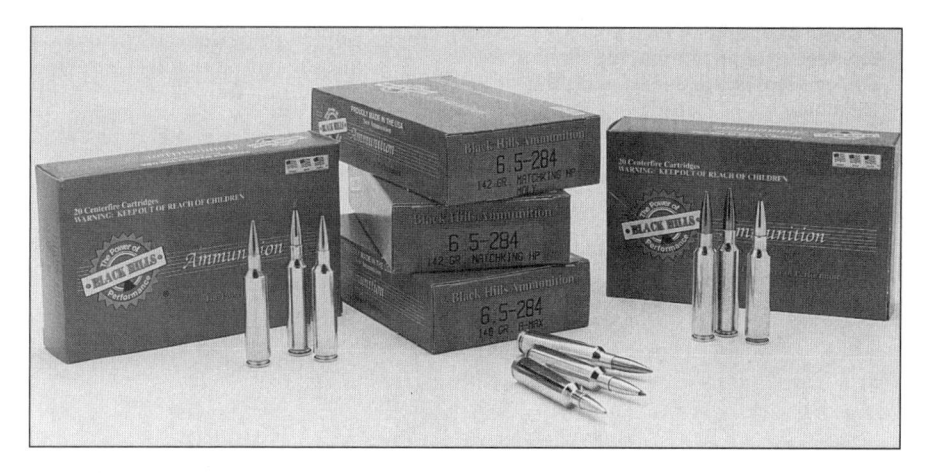

Black Hills, which originally loaded the 6.5-284 for Norma, now offers the ammunition under its own label.

505 Gibbs; 450 NE; 500/465; 475 #2; 450 #2; 577 NE; 405 Win; 7mm Dakota; and 338 Lapua. Keep those boomers booming! www.bellammo.com

Berger Bullets

Founders Walt and Eunice Berger, have sold the business to Spiveco Inc., manufacturer of those jewel-quality J4 bullet jackets. The new owner, J.R. Spivey, is the son of one of the founders of Sierra Bullets, so the fine Berger line is in good hands. During the move of the manufacturing equipment from Phoenix, AZ to Fullerton, CA this past year, Berger bullets have been in short supply. Now, the manufacturing process has been upgraded and automated, so look for Berger benchrest-quality bullets to be back in inventory this year. www.bergerbullets.com

Big Bore Express, Ltd.

Ballistic points for muzzleloading bullets? You bet. Big Bore now has a complete line of saboted, ballistic-pointed bullets for the 45, 50 and 54-caliber muzzle-stuffers. www.bigbore.com

Bismuth

Bismuth has transferred its non-toxic shotgun shell technology to the realm of frangible, non-toxic handgun ammunition. Their new 9mm, 40 S&W and 45 ACP projectiles are created by casting, swaging and then copper-plating a pure Bismuth core, thereby approximating the weight and recoil of lead ammunition. Upon impact, the Bismuth bullets disintegrate into Bismuth dust. Labeled "Bismuth Reduced Hazard Ammunition," the new loads are recommended for high-risk environments – including nuclear, biological, chemical, precious cargo and personal defense situations – where ricochet and over-penetration is to be avoided. www-bismuth-notox.com

Black Hills Ammunition

Loading the 6.5-284 originally for Norma, Black Hills has now released this exceptional target cartridge under its own label. The Black Hill loads feature either a 142-grain Sierra or 140-grain Hornady A-Max match bullet in Norma brass. As an option, either load can be furnished with molycoated bullets. Also new this year, are a 9mm 124-grain JHP+P load at 1250 fps; a 165-grain Gold Dot or FMJ loading for the 40 S&W at maximum velocities; a 45 ACP +P load featuring the 230-grain Hornady XTP bullet at 950 fps; and for the cowboys and cowgirls, a 32 H&R Magnum(!) load featuring a 90-grain lead bullet at 750 fps. Anyway, Black Hills offers superior ammo at great prices. www.black-hills.com

Brenneke

Called the "SuperSabot", Brenneke's latest 12 gauge slug design features a hollow brass cylinder of 63 caliber with an aluminum piston that slides forward during flight to form a pointed nose, increasing the slug's overall aerodynamic qualities. Upon impact, the piston is driven to rear so the brass body forms a 63-caliber *cookie cutter*. The 425-grain slug is loaded to 1,690 fps in the 3-inch hull and 1,542 fps in the 2 3/4-inch case. www.brennekeusa.com

Bull-X Bullets

Renowned for their non-leading CSJ series of cast bullets, Bull-X is fielding three new conventional cast bullets this year – a 245-grain 38-55 bullet sized properly to 0.379 inch; a 300-grain 44-caliber LBT design and a 435-grain 45-70 FP. If you haven't tried the CSJ line of dry film-lubed rifle and pistols bullets, you're missing a technological breakthrough. www.bull-x.com

CCI-Speer

How do you improve the 22 rimfire? Design three new loads for it. CCI is reviving the 22 WRF load with a 45-grain Gold Dot HP at 1300 fps – perfect for those old Winchester 1890 and 1906 models; as well as a reduced load in 22 WMRs. Also added this year are a 50-grain Gold Dot 22 WMR load at 1525 fps and a pre-fragmented 32-grain "QuickShok" 22 RF loading at 1640 fps. The aluminum-cased Blaser line is being expanded with 38 Special, 44 Special and 45 Colt "cowboy" loads. On the Speer side of the shop, the high-performance Gold Dot handgun line has been extended to include the 44 Special, 454 Casull and 50 Action Express, while the 25 and 32 auto cartridges with FMJs now grace the Lawman line. Speer has developed several new bullets this year – a 170-grain Gold Dot SP .357; a 225-grain Grand Slam for the .338; a 300-grain African Grand Slam SP in .375; and a 130-grain FNSP for the 7-30 Waters cartridge. www.cci-ammunition.com

Cfventures

Here's a small mail order operation with a unique product--a *"soft"* gas check that can reduce leading significantly. Actually it's a thin waxy sheet that is pressed cookie-cutter-style into the mouth of the case just before seating the bullet. Worth trying. Reach them at 509 Harvey Drive, Bloomington, IN 47403-1715.

▼ CCI is reviving the 22 WRF load with a 45-grain Gold Dot at 1300 fps.

◀ CCI has added 38 Special, 44 Special and 45 Colt cowboy action loads to its Blaser line.

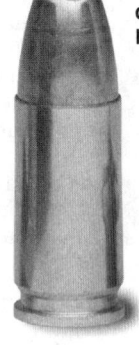

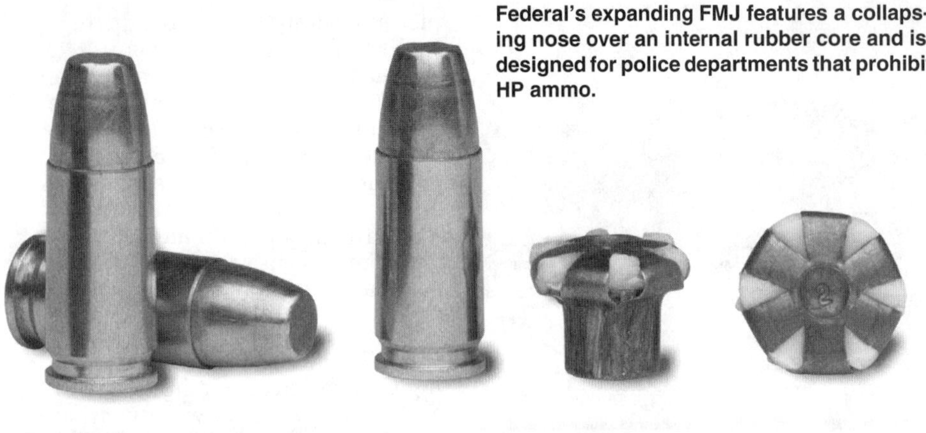

Federal's expanding FMJ features a collapsing nose over an internal rubber core and is designed for police departments that prohibit HP ammo.

Clean Shot Technologies

Clean Shot, the black powder substitute, is now offered in easy-to-handle 30- and 50-grain pellets for muzzleloading, or loading those cowboy action cartridges. Here's the smoke without the mess. www.cleanshot.com

Double Impact

This is a curious new 12 gauge loading invented by Muninord of Italy. The shot column in these loads is packaged within two different wads that project two distinct patterns with each shot – one at close range – the other out to 100 meters! www.newballisticsdoubleimpact.com

Federal

Federal was purchased by Blount recently and will continue to produce fine ammunition under the Federal label. New this year in the rifle ammunition line are a Gold Medal 22 RF load that duplicates the ballistics of their award-winning UltraMatch at amuch less price; a 223 match cartridge featuring Sierra's 77-grain Matchking at 2750 fps; the 338 Rem. UltraMag with a 250-grain Trophy Bonded Bear Claw at 2860 fps; and two new loadings of the Barnes XLC bullet-- the 7mm Rem Mag. with a 160-grain pill at 2940 fps and the 338 Win. Mag. with 225-grains at 2800 fps. The 9mm and 40 S&W have been given a revolutionary bullet that is actually an expanding FMJ featuring a collapsing internal rubber tip just under the nose. Lots of new 12 gauge shotgun loads including a layered tungsten iron and steel loading; a 1 3/8 oz. copper-coated shot load in #s 4,5 and 6 at 1400 fps; a 1 1/8 oz. Handicap load at 1235 fps; and a 3/4 oz. Barnes sabot slug at 1900 fps. New Federal components offered this year are Tungsten-polymer #4 and #6 bulk shot as well as 45- and 50-grain Barnes Expander muzzleloading sabot slugs. www.federalcartridge.com

FNM

This Portuguese maker is loading two hard-to-get cartridges – the 7.5 MAS and 7.5x55 Swiss. Cole Distributing in Bowling Green, KY is importing both loads at very reasonable prices. www.cole-distributing.com

Garrett Cartridges

If you own a 45-70 or 44 Magnum revolver, Garrett delivers all the power you'll ever need for big-game hunting. Garrett loads super-hard cast bullets with broad meplats and of a weight-forward Hammerhead design that leaves adequate room in the case for powder. Want to use your 45-70 for elephant, Cape buffalo or coastal brown bear? Garrett's 540-grain load at 1550 fps will shoot through Cape buffalo lengthwise. Don't quite need that level of power? How about a 420-grain loading at 1850 fps that will provide the same level of performance on elk, moose and heavy bear. Garrett's 44 Magnum handgun loads are equally impressive--a 310-grain bullet at 1325 fps and a 330-grain bullet at 1385 fps. www.garrettcartridges.com

Hevishot

The latest, USFWS-approved non-toxic shot is Hevishot-composed of an alloy of tungsten, nickel and iron. It's heavier than lead, about as hard as steel, produces tight patterns and high pellet energies at long ranges. It was used to win this year's National Wild Turkey Federation's Still Target World Championships. www.hevishot.com

Hodgdon

No new powders this year but lots of new loading data in their "*Basic Reloaders Manual*" including the 376 Steyr, 450 Marlin, 460 Rowland, 'Longshot' pistol loads. and 'Titegroup' shotgun data. www.hodgdon.com

Hornady

As a joint project with Ruger, Hornady released the 480 Ruger cartridge featuring a 325-grain XTP magnum bullet at 1,350 fps. Another impressive joint venture is the 376 Steyr that almost duplicates 375 H&H performance in a standard-length action and non-belted case. A 165- and a 180-grain 30-caliber SST bullet have been added to the component line this year. www.hornady.com

ITD Enterprises

ITD is working with Murom, Russia's largest primer maker, to market a line of non-hygroscopic, lead- and heavy metal-free primers that have at least a 25 year shelf life and which, according to HP White tests, exhibit uniform sensitivity and reliability. Stay tuned. itdprime@aol.com

Lapua

In addition to its new 6.5-284 brass, Lapua is introducing some very unique handgun cartridges this year. There's a rimmed, bottle-necked, 30-357 AeT cartridge sporting a 123-grain bullet at 1992 fps to be chambered in a single-action silhouette revolver made by Fratelli Pietta of Italy. In conjunction with Tanfoglio, Lapua has designed a heavy-walled 9mm case called the 9mm FAR. The purpose of the reinforced case is to permit the manufacture of a high velocity, in-line barrel, blowback action pistol that will offer improved accuracy and performance. Finally, there's a rimless, heavy duty,

Hornady is introducing the new Ruger 480 cartridge, featuring a 325-grain XTP bullet at 1,350 fps.

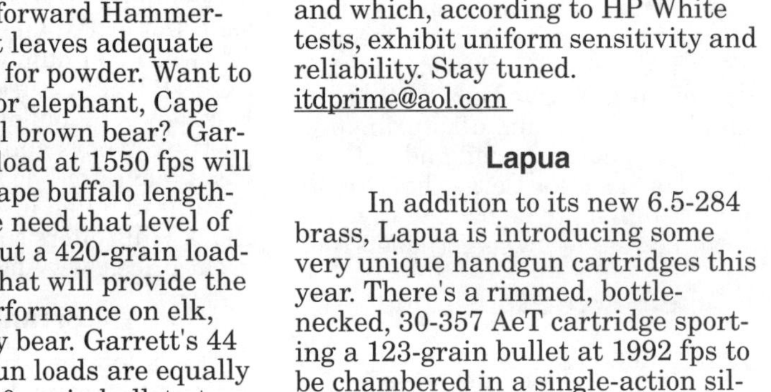

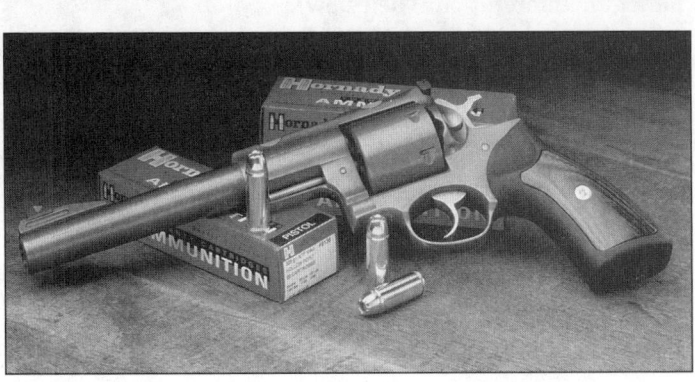

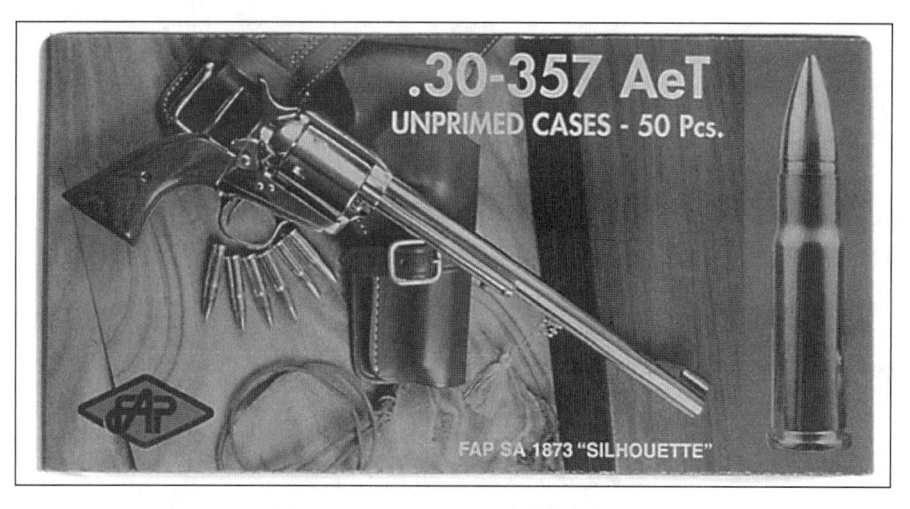

With a 123-grain bullet at 1992 fps, the 30-357 Aet should really perform in Pietta's new silhouette six-shooter.

38 Super Comp version of the 38 Super Auto cartridge that should minimize reloading problems in progressive presses. Speaking about reloading, Lapua and Vihtavuori have released a 38-minute video entitled *Reloading with the Masters* featuring the champs – Leatham, Enos and Hobdell, who do some show-and-tell about reloading for competition. www.lapua.com

Lazzeroni

In this, the year of the short, non-belted magnums, Lazzeroni's 30-caliber Patriot is being factory-loaded with 168-grain moly-coated Sierra Matchkings at 3200 fps from a 24-inch barrel. The compact little Patriot has proven an outstanding 1000-yard target round and surprisingly Sierra's 168-grain MatchKings perform very well on deer-class big game. Watch for the release, mid-year, of Lazzeroni's short 7mm magnum, the Tomahawk, that produces 3,379 fps with a 140-grain bullet. www.lazzeroni.com

Lightfield

Specializing in high-performance shotgun slug designs, Lightfield has developed a complete family of full weight, high-performance slugs for the 12 and 16 gauges. Called the Commander Impact Discarding Sabot, the design features a sabot that stays with the hollowpoint lead slug until impact, thereby stabilizing the slug in flight – and particularly at the critical moment when it becomes subsonic (under 1200 fps). The 16 gauge Commander features a 15/16 oz. slug at 1610 fps. The 12 gauge 3-inch Commander sports a 1-oz. slug at 1800 fps; coming soon is a 3 1/2-inch loading at 2000 fps. Reports coming from municipal deer control programs rate the Lightfield slugs as superior one-shot stoppers. www.lightfield-ammo.com

Lost River Ballistic Technologies

Lost River makes a family of streamlined, high ballistic coefficient, hunting bullets under their "J36" label and a parallel match grade line known as the "J40." Their hollowpoint, boattail bullets are machined on a CNC lathe from a copper/nickel alloy and then fitted with a sharp copper tip. The maker indicates the bullets expand to 1.5-1.75 times their diameter upon impact and do not shed weight. Available in calibers 224 thru 510. www.lostriverballistic.com

Norma

Lots of plentiful new brass this year including the 6.5-284, 404 Jeffery, and 45 Basic – the latter case being drawn slightly oversize so it can be sized properly to sloppy old chambers. In cooperation with Krieghoff, Norma has designed a long, skinny rimmed 6mm case designated the 6x70R. The low-pressure cartridge is loaded with a 90-grain Nosler Ballistic Tip at 2460 fps and is chambered in Krieghoff's combination guns. www.norma.cc

North Fork Technologies

Using CNC-turned jackets and a bonded lead core, North Fork produces a sophisticated line of big-game hunting bullets in calibers 284-416. These are unusual-looking bullets in that the bearing portion of the solid alloy shank is grooved to reduce copper fouling. Reports from African *PH*s indicate the bullet can be driven through a Cape buffalo from stem-to-stern with excellent expansion and weight retention. Tel: (307)436-2726

Northern Precision

Never at a loss for new custom bullet designs, William Noody has developed a 30-caliber "Versatile Benchrest" bullet in 180-230 grain weights. The bullets feature a low-fouling, tapered jacket; a bonded core and can double as a hunting bullet. A similar bonded-core design – but with a heavier jacket for the sizzling veloc-

North Fork Technology's new CNC bullets are designed to expand, hold together, penetrate and minimize fouling. User reports are very positive.

34th EDITION, 2002 **69**

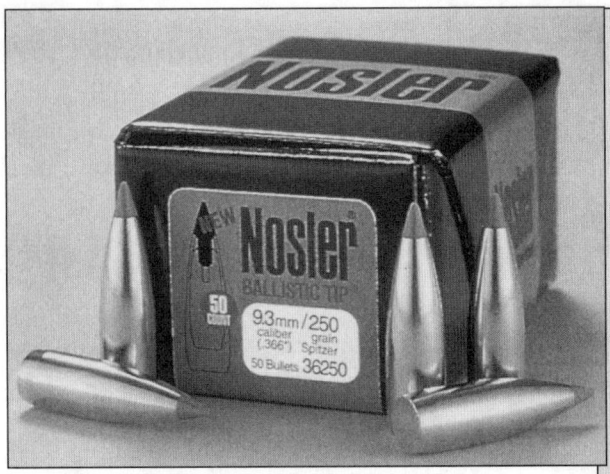

Responding to requests for a streamlined 9.3mm hunting bullet, Nosler is introducing a 250-grain 9.3mm Ballistic Tip.

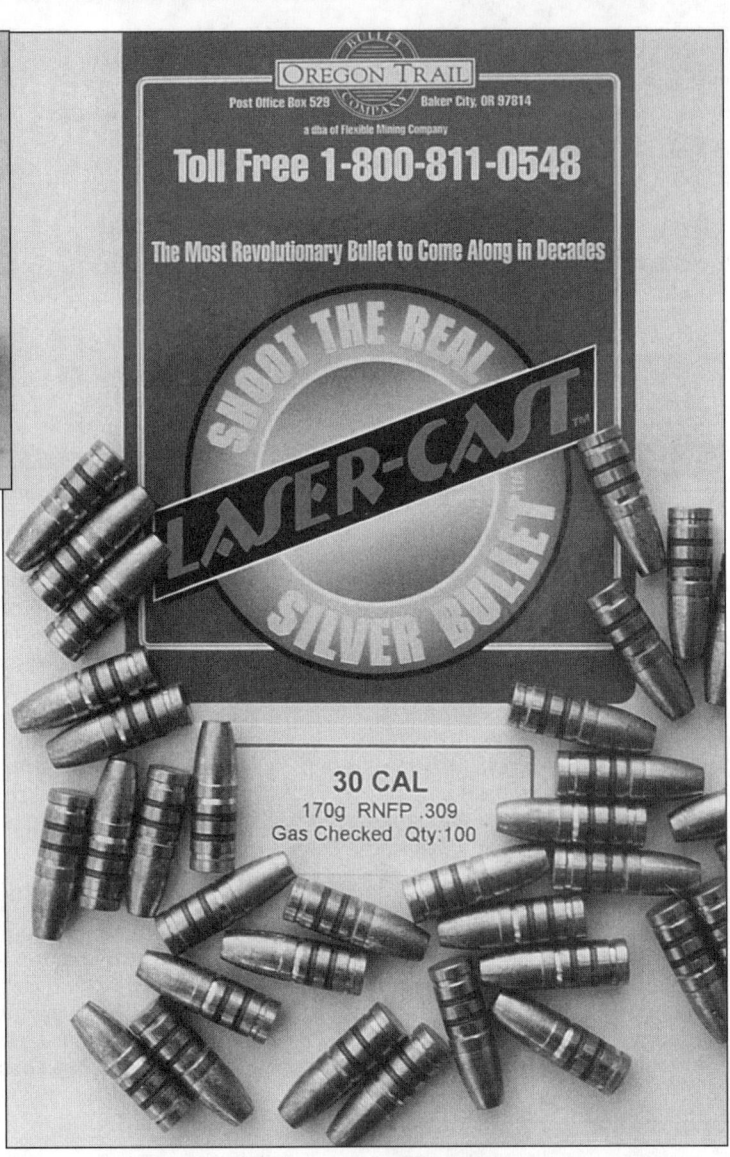

For handgun hunters, Nosler has designed a 90-grain 6mm Ballistic Tip that expands at more moderate velocities.

Laser-Cast's latest 170-grain 30-caliber gas-checked cast bullet is economical and suitable for everything from 30-30s to 300 magnums.

Based on precision J4 jackets, Nosler's new 155-grain 308-caliber match bullet is designed for Palma, service and silhouette competition.

ties of the Lazzeroni Warbird, 300 Ultra Mag and 30-378 Weatherby – is also being offered this year. The company is also offering 50- and 54-caliber muzzleloading sabots featuring spitzer-tipped, bonded-core, 44-caliber bullets in 240 to 350 grain weights. I've been shooting Noody's 150- and 160-grain bonded core, J4-jacketed, "Whitetail" bullets this past year in a 308 Winchester and I've been very pleased with their accuracy, performance and low fouling qualities. Tel: (315)493-1711

Nosler

This is a "Ballistic Tip" year for Nosler with the introduction of some great new calibers and grain weights. In the expanded Ballistic Tip line, there's a 90-grain 243 handgun hunting bullet; a 80-grain 243 varmint bullet; a 180-grain 8mm and a 250-grain 9.3mm. Being added to the competition bullet line is a 30-

Remington continues to expand its UMC Leadless line with the addition of the 40 S&W.

caliber, 155-grain JHP based on the precision J4 jacket. www.nosler.com

Old Western Scrounger

Dangerous Dave now carries the full Kynoch line, so if you need anything from 700 Nitro to 318 Wesley Richards, the *OWS* has it. Several new calibers have been added to the "obsolete" ammunition line – the 7.92x33 *Kurz*; 11mm French Ordnance Revolver and, for you Chicago Palm Pistol owners, the 32 Extra Short Rimfire. OWS is producing loaded ammunition and brass for the 405 Winchester, featuring a 300-grain Woodleigh bullet at 2200 fps. Dave is considering contracting for 1,000,000 round runs of the 5mm Rem. Rimfire Mag. and the 25 Stevens Long Rimfire, so ring him up later. The new catalog's a scream, and filled with rare goodies. www.ows-ammunition.com

Oregon Trail Laser-Cast Bullets

Three sensational new rifle bullets have been added to the Laser Cast lineup. First, there's a gas-check, 170-grain 30-caliber RNFP sized to .309" that is perfect for any 30-caliber. I've been using this bullet in a 30-30 at velocities up to 1970 fps with little or no leading. Its accuracy has been outstanding. Then there are two plain-base bullets – a 170-grain 32-caliber RNFP sized either .321" or .323", making it useful for the 32-40, 32 Special, and 8mms; plus a 165-grain 30-caliber RNFP sized to .310 that is said to be more accurate than the gas-check design at lower velocities(1300 fps). Send for Oregon Trail's latest catalog and loading data. Great bullets-- reasonably priced. www.laser-cast.com

Remington

Big Green has been highly focussed on rounding out their Ultra Mag line with the addition of new premium bullet loads for the 7mm, 300, 338 and 375 Ultra Mags. At the same time, a new Sirocco Bonded bullet line has been added in 270 Win., 7mm Rem. Mag., 308 Win., and 30-06. In the Premier centerfire line, the 22-250 and the 7mm-08 have been added — loaded with Nosler Partitions. With the interest in lead-free ammunition accelerating, Remington has added a UMC Leadless line that includes the 9mm, 380 Auto, 38 Special, 40 S&W and 45 Auto – and developed leadless frangible loads for the 38 Special and 357 Sig. For large volume varmint hunters, inexpensive 223 and 22-250 loadings have been added to the UMC-brand label. Velocity is up in their Premier copper-plated turkey loads with the 3- and 3 1/2-inch shell in #4, 5, and 6 shot at 1300 fps while 2 3/4-inch 12 and 20 gauge loadings in the Upland Express line are now launched at 1400 and 1300 fps, respectively. Finally, a new 1-oz loading of #7 1/2 and #8 at 1290 fps has been added as a 12 gauge Nitro 27 Handicap load. www.remington.com

Sellier & Bellot

Here's a step back in history, S&B has introduced a complete, across-the-gauges line of paper shotshells and a full line of 7/8 and 1 oz. loadings for the 28 gauge. There's also a 174-grain HPBT target load for the 7.62x54mmR and a 196-grain FMJ loading for the 8mm Mauser. www.sb-usa.com

Sierra

The '*Bulletsmiths*' have been playing catch-up ball with their extensive lines. The new product this year is a 250-grain 338 HPBT MatchKing. See their informative catalog and series of technical newsletters at www.sierrabullets.com

Sierra's latest MatchKing offering is a sleek 250-grain .338-caliber bullet with extremely high ballistic coefficients.

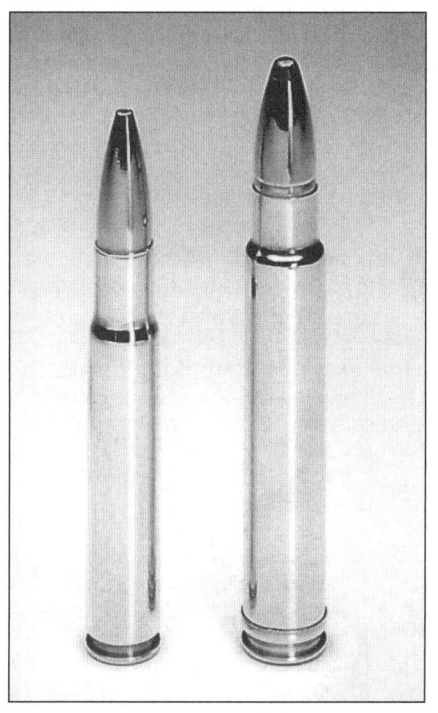

Weatherby is the first major manufacturer to offer the excellent 338-06 A-Square as a standard chambering.

34th EDITION, 2002 **71**

Simunition

Simunition makes and distributes highly refined lines of non-lethal practice ammunition that can be fired in a trainee's personal service weapon. Some of the products are designed for face-to-face combat practice with padded clothing while others are for close-quarter combat target ranges. www.simunition.com

SSK

JD Jones continues to expand his "Whisper" series--this year with a 510 Whisper that is based on the 333 Lapua case. Loaded with only 25 grains of powder and the 750-grain Hornady A-MAX bullet, this subsonic round is reportedly capable of 6-inch groups at 600 yards. SSK's radically *"blown-out"* '06-based single-shot pistol rounds now include the 257, 6.5 and 270 calibers. Finally, Jones reports he's working on a 40mm practice round, using a 30-caliber tracer to duplicate the 40mm's trajectory. www.sskindustries.com

Swift Bullets

Three new Sirocco bullets make their debut this year: 165- and 180-grain 308s and a 130-grain 270 pill. www.swiftbullets.com

Weatherby

Weatherby will be the first major firm to offer the 338-06 A-Square as a factory round. Loaded with a 210-grain Nolser, the legitimized 338 wildcat produces 2750 fps at the muzzle. Returning to the Weatherby line, after being absent for too many years, is the ever-effective 375 Weatherby Magnum, loaded with a 300-grain Nosler Partition at 2800 fps. See these exciting new loads at www.weatherby.com

Winchester

Big news this year has been the introduction of Winchester's new rifle cartridge, the 300 Winchester Short Magnum, dubbed the 300 WSM. Chambered initially in short-action Browning A-Bolts and Winchester Model 70 Featherweights, this highly efficient round features a 35-degree shoulder, rebated rim and a short overall length of 2.8 inches. Initial factory loads feature 180-grain Failsafes and Power-Points at 2970 fps and a 150-grain Ballistic Silvertip at 3300 fps. I'm predicting we may see a 270 WSM in the future.

Winchester has launched a new line of shotshells called Western Target and Field Loads in 12 and 20 gauges and with #7 1/2 and #8 shot

The 270 JDJ#2 is SSK's radically "improved" case that is also available as a 257 or 6.5mm.

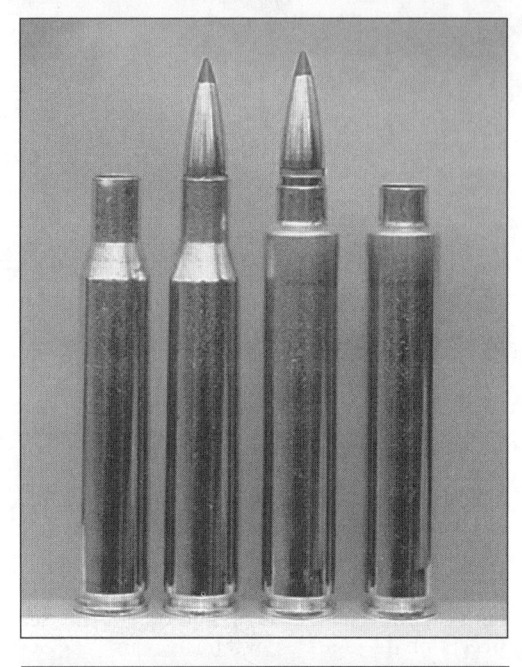

SSK's diminutive 510 Whisper takes 25 grains of powder and generates 1500 fps with a 600-grain bullet.

Winchester's radical 300 Short Magnum delivers 300 Win. Mag. performance in a compact, accurate cartridge – perfect for short-action rifles.

Winchester's new 20 gauge Partition Gold slug, at 1900 fps, offers a flat trajectory – plus excellent penetration of light big game.

for the sporting clays market. For slug hunters, there's an interesting new 20 gauge loading featuring a 260-grain Partition Gold slug at 1900 fps. Some of the most reasonable plinking loads around are Winchester's USA brand 223 with either a 55- or 62-grain FMJ and the 147-grain FMJ in the 30-06. The economical USA Brand line also has been upgraded with the addition of jacketed hollow points for the 38 Special, 9mm, 357 SIG, 40 S&W and 45 Auto. And, to satisfy the demand for leadless loads, the WinClean pistol ammunition line has been expanded to include the 9mm Luger with either a 124- or 147-grain bullet and the 357 SIG loaded with a 125-grain WinClean projectile. www.winchester.com

Wolf

As an importer of ammunition from Russia's Tula Cartridge Works, Wolf continues to expand the line of non-corrosive, steel-cased ammunition. A number of new loads and calibers are being added this year, including the 40 S&W, 223 Rem. HP, 7.62x39mm SP, 7.62x54mmR HP, and match-grade brass-cased 22 rimfire. www.wolfammo.com

It's been a busy year.

Sporting clays shooters should be pleased with Winchester's new Western Target and Field Loads available in #7 1/2 and #8 shot.

34th EDITION, 2002 **73**

SHOOTER'S MARKETPLACE

INTERESTING PRODUCT NEWS FOR THE ACTIVE SHOOTING SPORTSMAN

The companies represented on the following pages will be happy to provide additional information – feel free to contact them.

SWEETSHOOTER™ PREVENTS METAL CORROSION

Sweetshooter's micro-thin film penetrates the pores of barrels and other metal surfaces of firearms, blackpowder arms and knives to prevent corrosion and fouling. Once Sweetshooter™ fills the pores of these metal surfaces, there is no place for copper, lead, carbon and other deposits to collect, except on the film surface. Simply wipe them away! Users have found that Sweetshooter™ smoothes actions, reduces jamming, extends barrel life and improves accuracy. There is no need for immediate cleanup. Soaking of gun parts in solvent is eliminated, too.

While Sweetshooter™ is great for firearms and muzzleloaders, it will also prevent corrosion on knives, fishing tackle and tools, too.

NO MORE FOULING...GUARANTEED!

For information, call 1-800-932-4445 or visit their website at www.tecrolan.com

TECROLAN INC.
P.O. Box 14916, Fort Worth, TX 76117 • Phone: 940-325-6688 • Fax: 940-325-3636

FRIENDLY CLAY TARGET THROWERS

Trius Traps offer shooters superior quality, easy cocking, manual clay target traps. Singles, doubles plus piggy back doubles. Traps are factory-assembled and tested. Attach mount and main spring and you're ready to shoot. All adjustments made without tools. Birdshooter — quality at a budget price. Trius Model 92R — the original "Foot trap." Trapmaster — sit down comfort with pivoting action. The innovative 1-Step (shown) — almost effortless to use. Set arm without tension, place targets on arm and step on pedal to put tension on main spring and release target. High angle target retainer on all traps. Trius, satisfying shooters since 1955.

TRIUS TRAPS, INC.
Attn: Dept. SM'2001, P.O. Box 25, Cleves, OH 45002
Phone: 513-941-5682 • Web: www.triustraps.com

RAZOR SHARP

Finland has a harsh and challenging environment. Long ago, Finns developed a multi-purpose survival knife "the puukko." These basic tools are very sharp, lightweight and durable. Used for many daily tasks, these knives are still being used today. Kellam Knives began to bring these knives into the worldwide marketplace. The "puukko" is an excellent tool that will endure for many decades. This year, one of their makers from the KP Smithy won Best Knifemaker in Finland. His family has been making knives since 1610 and comes from an award-winning tradition.

Kellam Knives offers the largest selection of quality knives made by the most respected knifemakers in Finland.

KELLAM Knives Co.
902 S. Dixie Hwy., Lantana, FL 33462
Phone: 561-588-3185 or 800-390-6918
Fax: 561-588-3186
Web: www.kellamknives.com
Email: info@kellamknives.com

SHOOTER'S MARKETPLACE

CONCEALABLE HOLSTER

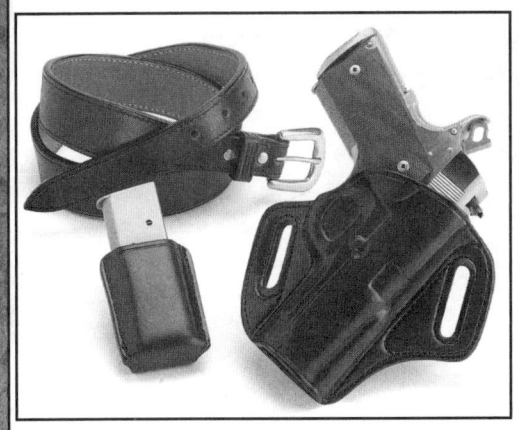

The Concealable™ Holster, Belt and Magazine Carrier provide excellent comfort, style, and workability. The unique two-piece holster construction is contoured on the body side to the natural curve of the hip providing:

- A narrower profile
- Minimizing shifting
- Combat grip
- Comfortable fit
- Deep hand-molding

The 1-1/2" contour belt is fully lined and tapers to 1". The magazine carrier's stitched belt channel fits belts up to 1-1/2".

Available in black or Havana brown premium saddle leather. The holster sells for $85.00 + S&H. The Belt is $107.00 + S&H and the Magazine Carrier is $39.95 + S&H. Color catalog is $8.00.

Galco International "For those who demand the best…and know the difference."

GALCO INTERNATIONAL
2019 W. Quail Ave., Phoenix, AZ 85027
Phone: 623-434-7070 • Fax: 800-737-1725
1-800-US-Galco (874-2526) • www.usgalco.com

CATALOG #23

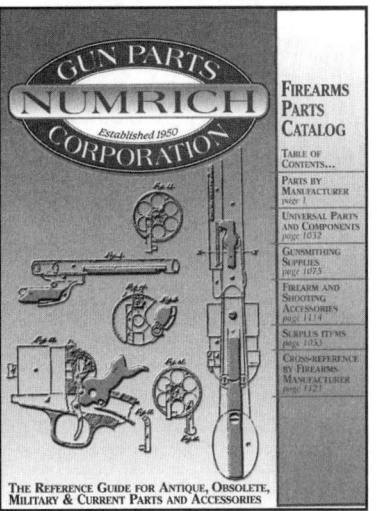

Catalog #23 is Numrich Gun Part Corporation's most recent edition. This 1152-page catalog features more than 450 schematics for use in identifying commercial, military, antique, and foreign guns. Edition #23 contains 180,000 individual items from our inventory of over 650 million parts and accessories, and is a necessity for any true gunsmith or hobbyist. It has been the industry's reference book for firearm parts and identification for over 50 years.

Order Item #RH-23 $12.95
U.S. Orders: Bulk Mail (Shipping charges included)
Foreign Orders: Air Mail-30 day delivery
or Surface-90 day delivery. (Shipping charges additional).

NUMRICH GUN PARTS CORPORATION
226 Williams Lane, West Hurley, NY 12491
Orders: (845) 679-2417 • Customer Service: (845) 679-4867
Toll-Free Fax: (877) Gun Parts
e-GunParts.com • E-mail: info@gunpartscorp.com

CLENZOIL FIELD & RANGE®

This is what museums, collectors, and competitive shooters are switching to in serious numbers.

Clenzoil Field & Range® is a remarkable one-step bore cleaner, lubricant, and long-term protectant that contains absolutely no teflon or silicone, so it never gets gummy or sticky.

A regional favorite for many years, Clenzoil is finally available nationwide. Clenzoil is signing up dealers daily, but your local shop may not carry it yet. If that's the case, you may order 24 hours a day by calling 1-800-OIL-IT-UP. Dealers may join the growing Clenzoil dealer network by calling 440-899-0482.

Clenzoil is a proud supplier to ArmaLite, Inc.

CLENZOIL THE CORPORATION WORLDWIDE
25670 First Street, Westlake, OH 44145
Phone: 440-899-0482 • Fax: 440-899-0483

GLASER SAFETY SLUG

For over 25 years Glaser has provided a state-of-the-art personal defense ammunition used by the law enforcement and civilian communities. Available in two bullet styles, the Glaser Blue is offered in a full range of handgun calibers from 25 ACP to 45 Colt (including the 9mm Makarov and 357 Sig) and four rifle cailbers: 223, 308, 30-06 and 7.62x39. The Glaser Silver is available in all handgun calibers from 380 ACP to 45 Colt.

A complete brochure is available on the internet.

GLASER SAFETY SLUG, INC.
1311 Industry Road, Sturgis, SD 57785
Phone: 605-347-4544 • www.safetyslug.com

SHOOTER'S MARKETPLACE

RIFLE AND PISTOL MAGAZINES

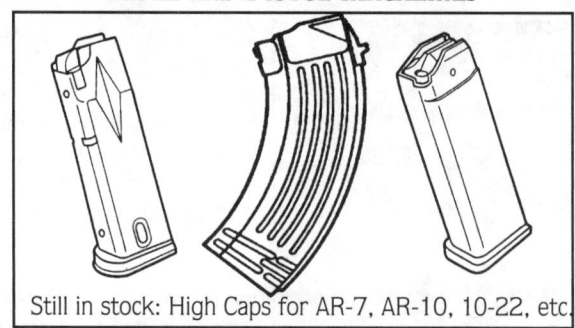

Still in stock: High Caps for AR-7, AR-10, 10-22, etc.

Forrest, Inc. offers shooters one of the largest selections of standard and extended high-capacity magazines in the United States. Whether you're looking for a few spare magazines for that obsolete 22 rifle or pistol, or wish to replace a reduced-capacity ten-shot magazine with the higher-capacity pre-ban original, all are available from this California firm. They offer competitive pricing especially for dealers wanting to buy in quantity. Gun show dealers are our specialty. G.I., O.E.M., factory or aftermarket.

Forrest Inc. also stocks parts and accessories for the Colt 1911 45 Auto pistol, the SKS and MAK-90 rifles as well as many U.S. military rifles. One of their specialty parts is firing pins for obsolete weapons.

Call or write Forrest, Inc. for more information and a free brochure. Be sure and mention *Shooter's Marketplace*.

FORREST, INC.
P.O. Box 326, Dept. #100, Lakeside, CA 92040
Phone: 619-561-5800 • Fax: 888-GUNCLIP
Web: www.gunmags.com

NEW MANUAL AVAILABLE

Accurate Powder's newest manual, Number Two, contains new data on powders XMR 4064 and XMP 5744, as well as a special section on Cowboy Action Shooting. In addition, the 400-page manual has loads for new cartridges, such as the .260 Rem., .300 Rem. Ultra Mag., .338 Rem. Ultra Mag., .357 Sig., .300 Whisper, .400 Corbon and more. It also includes many new bullets for the most popular cartridges as well as data for sabots in selected calibers. The price for the book is $16.95, plus $2.00 for shipping and handling in the continental U.S. To order a copy, call or write to:

ACCURATE ARMS
5891 Hwy. 230 W., McEwen, TN 37101
Phone: 1-800-416-3006 • Web: www.accuratepowder.com

6x18x40 VARMINT/TARGET SCOPE

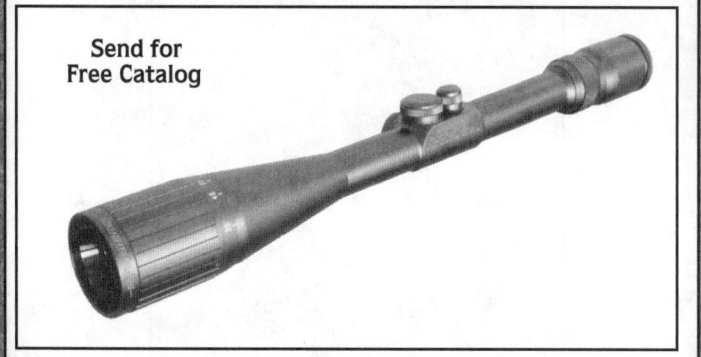

Send for Free Catalog

The Shepherd 6x18x40 Varmint/Target Scope makes long-range varmint and target shooting child's play. Just pick the ranging circle that best fits your target (be it prairie dogs, coyotes or paper varmints) and Shepherd's exclusive, patented Dual Reticle Down Range System does the rest. You won't believe how far you can accurately shoot, even with rimfire rifles.

Shepherd's superior lens coating mean superior light transmission and tack-sharp resolution.

This new shockproof, waterproof scope features 1/4 minute-of-angle clicks on the ranging circles and friction adjustments on the crosshairs that allow fine-tuning to 0.001 MOA. A 40mm adjustable objective provides a 5.5-foot field of view at 100 yards (16x setting). 16.5 FOV @ 6X.

SHEPHERD ENTERPRISES, INC.
Box 189, Waterloo, NE 68069
Phone: 402-779-2424 • Fax: 402-779-4010
E-mail: shepherd@shepherdscopes.com • Web: www.shepherdscopes.com

NYLON COATED GUN CLEANING RODS

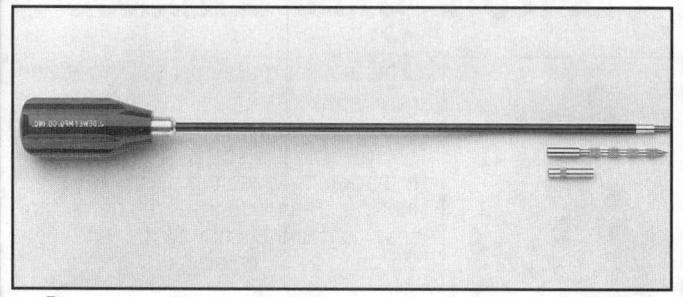

J. Dewey cleaning rods have been used by the U.S. Olympic shooting team and the benchrest community for over 20 years. These one-piece, spring-tempered, steel-base rods will not gall delicate rifling or damage the muzzle area of front-cleaned firearms. The nylon coating elmininates the problem of abrasives adhering to the rod during the cleaning operation. Each rod comes with a hard non-breakable plastic handle supported by ball-bearings, top and bottom, for ease of cleaning.

The brass cleaning jags are designed to pierce the center of the cleaning patch or wrap around the knurled end to keep the patch centered in the bore.

Coated rods are available from 17-caliber to shotgun bore size in several lengths to meet the needs of any shooter. Write for more information.

J. DEWEY MFG. CO., INC.
P.O. Box 2014, Southbury, CT 06488
Phone: 203-264-3064 • Fax: 203-262-6907
Web: www.deweyrods.com

SHOOTER'S MARKETPLACE

CUSTOM COWBOY HANDGUNS

Gary Reeder Custom Guns, builder of full-custom guns, hunting handguns, custom Contenders and Contender barrels and custom Encores and Encore barrels, would be happy to build a custom gun for you. See our Web site at www.reedercustomguns.com, or call Gary Reeder. One of our most popular cowboy guns since 1991 has been our Tombstone Classic. This little beauty has our own birdshead grip, comes in full hi-polished stainless, Black Chromex finish or two-toned. The Tombstone is fully engraved and highly slicked up inside, and is only one of a series of close to 20 custom cowboy guns.

GARY REEDER CUSTOM GUNS
2710 N. Steve's Blvd., #22, Flagstaff, AZ 86004
Phone: 520-526-3313

FINE CAST RIFLE AND HANDGUN BULLETS

The shooters at Oregon Trail Bullet Company set out five years ago with one goal: to make the finest cast rifle and handgun bullets available. Their ongoing R&D program led them to develop their ultra-hard 24BHN 7-element LASER-CAST Silver Alloy, specialized production tooling and quality-control procedures, with the LASER-CAST bullet line now widely recognized as an industry leader. Over 60 advanced designs are now catalogued with more in development, producing a top-performing bullet for any application like IPSC, Cowboy or Silhouette, all backed by their money back guarantee and friendly customer service. Call for a free sample and "Shoot The REAL Silver Bullet."

OREGON TRAIL BULLET COMPANY
Box 529-GD, Baker City, Oregon 97814-0529
Phone: 800-811-0548
Web: www.laser-cast.com

Handguns 2002
14th Edition
Edited by Ken Ramage

A reference for all handgun fans, this completely updated edition has new feature articles and stimulating product reports on today's available handguns and accessories. Includes expanded catalog coverage of handgun grips plus a section on semi-custom and limited production handguns. The pistol catalog listings are completely updated. Articles feature handgun trends, gun tests, handloading, engraved and custom guns, self-defense, concealed carry, vintage and historic arms and handgun hunting.

Softcover • 8-1/2 x 11
320 pages • 500+ b&w photos
Item# H2002 • $22.95

To place a credit card order or for a FREE all-product catalog call
800-258-0929 Offer DTB1
M-F 7am - 8pm • Sat 8am - 2pm, CST

DBI BOOKS
a division of Krause Publications, Inc.

Krause Publications, Offer DTB1
P.O. Box 5009, Iola WI 54945-5009 • www.krausebooks.com

Shipping & Handling: $4.00 first book, $2.00 each additional. Non-US addresses $20.95 first book, $5.95 each additional.
Sales Tax: CA, IA, IL, PA, TN, VA, WI residents please add appropriate sales tax.

VERSATILE GUN REST

Looking for a great value in a shooting rest? Well, here's the one to consider. Introducing MTM Case-Gard's *all new, rifle and shotgun rest* called the Site-N-Clean. A rest so versatile, it makes setting up for shooting and cleaning a breeze. The Site-N-Clean offers easy positioning using Case-Gard's unique (& patented) over-molded shooting forks, along with a rear adjustment leg. Also available is a Site-N-Clean Rest/Case Combo, featuring a roomy 21" x 13" x 9" case. Ask your local retailer, or visit MTM's Web site, for their complete line of practical shooting products. For a full color catalog sent $2 to:

MTM MOLDED PRODUCTS COMPANY
P.O. Box 13117, Dept. GD02
Dayton, OH 45413
Web: www.mtmcase-gard.com

34TH EDITION, 2002 • 77

SHOOTER'S MARKETPLACE

Advanced Multi-function Rifle

DSA offers a complete line of new U.S.-manufactured SA58 rifles. The SA58 rifle is a 21st-century version of the battle proven FAL. DSA is the only U.S. manufacturer of FAL-type rifles with upper and lower receivers machined from solid billets.

Firearm durability, reliability and shooter safety are vital components of the DSA design and manufacturing process. H.P. White Laboratory, Inc. excess pressure tested a SA58 rifle to 101,000 CUP with the receiver remaining undamaged! The SA58 is an incredibly strong and accurate multi-function rifle that can be accessorized to fit the personal needs of each shooter. Available in .308, .243, .260 and 7mm-08 calibers.

DSA carries a huge selection of FAL/SA58 parts and accessories, including two new, DSA exclusive items. The FAL Rail Interface Handguard has a 1913 Picatinny rail on all four sides for attaching accessories where the shooter wants them. The X Series FAL Buttstock gives the shooter a better rifle grip for precision shooting.

For more information, call for a catalog or check out the DSA Web site.

DSA, INC.
P.O. Box 370, Barrington, IL 60011
Phone: 847-277-7258 • Fax: 847-277-7259
Web: www.dsarms.com

Alaskan Hunter

Gary Reeder Custom Guns, builder of full custom guns, including custom cowboy guns, hunting handguns, African hunting rifles, custom Encores and Encore barrels, has a free brochure available or you can check out the large Web site at www.reedercustomguns.com. One of our most popular series is our Alaskan Hunter. This beefy 5-shot 454 Casull is for the serious handgun hunter and joins our 475 Linebaugh and 500 Linebaugh as our most popular hunting handguns. For more information contact:

GARY REEDER CUSTOM GUNS
2710 N Steve's Blvd., Suite 22, Flagstaff, AZ 86004
Phone: 520-526-3313

High Quality Optics

One of the best indicators of quality is a scope's resolution number. The smaller the number, the better. Our scope has a resolution number of 2.8 seconds of angle. This number is about 20% smaller (better) than other well-known scopes costing much more. It means that two .22 caliber bullets can be a hair's breadth apart and edges of each still be clearly seen. With a Shepherd at 800 yards, you will be able to tell a four inch antler from a four inch ear and a burrowing owl from a prairie dog. Bird watchers will be able to distinguish a Tufted Titmouse from a Ticked-Off Field Mouse. Send for free catalog.

SHEPHERD ENTERPRISES, INC.
Box 189, Waterloo, NE 68069
Phone: 402-779-2424 • Fax: 402-779-4010
E-mail: shepherd@shepherdscopes.com • Web: www.shepherdscopes.com

Combination Rifle and Optics Rest

The Magna-Pod weighs less than two pounds, yet firmly supports more than most expensive tripods. It will hold 50 pounds at its low 9-inch height and over 10 pounds extended to 17 inches. It sets up in seconds where there is neither time nor space for a tripod and keeps your expensive equipment safe from knock-overs by kids, pets, pedestrians, or even high winds. It makes a great mono-pod for camcorders, etc., and its carrying box is less than 13" x 13" x 3 1/4" high for easy storage and access.

Attached to its triangle base it becomes an extremely stable table pod or rifle bench rest. The rifle yoke pictured in photo is included.

It's 5 pods in 1: Magna-Pod, Mono-Pod, Table-Pod, Shoulder-Pod and Rifle Rest. Send for free catalog.

SHEPHERD ENTERPRISES, INC.
Box 189, Waterloo, NE 68069
Phone: 402-779-2424 • Fax: 402-779-4010
E-mail: shepherd@shepherdscopes.com • Web: www.shepherdscopes.com

SHOOTER'S MARKETPLACE

FOLDING BIPODS

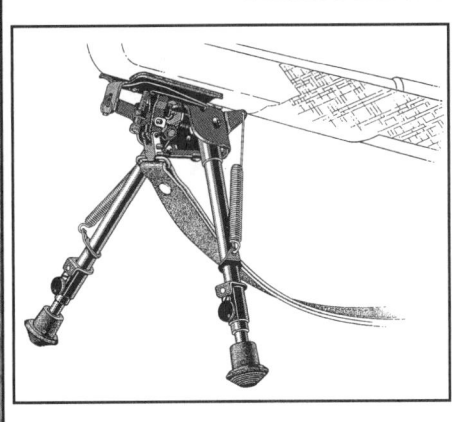

Harris Bipods clamp securely to most stud-equipped bolt-action rifles and are quick-detachable. With adapters, they will fit some other guns. On all models except the Model LM, folding legs have completely adjustable spring-return extensions. The sling swivel attaches to the clamp. This time-proven design is manufactured with heat-treated steel and hard alloys and has a black anodized finish.

Series S Bipods rotate 35° for instant leveling on uneven ground. Hinged base has tension adjustment and buffer springs to eliminate tremor or looseness in crotch area of bipod. They are otherwise similar to non-rotating Series 1A2.

Thirteen models are available from Harris Engineering; literature is free.

HARRIS ENGINEERING INC.
Dept: GD54, Barlow, KY 42024
Phone: 270-334-3633 • Fax: 270-334-3000
Web: www.cyberteklabs.com/harris/main/htm

PRECISION RIFLE REST

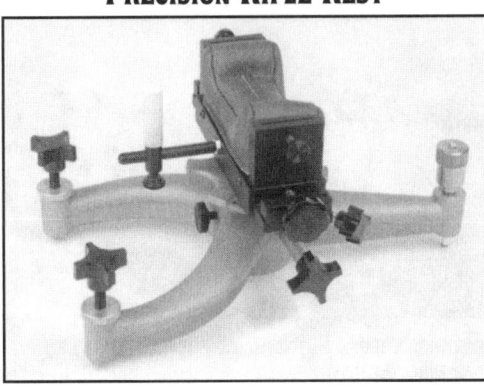

Bald Eagle Precision Machine Co. offers a rifle rest perfect for the serious benchrester or dedicated varminter.

"The Slingshot" or Next Generation has 60° front legs. The rest is constructed of aircraft-quality aluminum or fine-grain cast iron and weighs 12 to 20 lbs. The finish is 3 coats of Imron clear. Primary height adjustments are made with a rack and pinion gear. Secondary adjustment uses a mariner wheel with thrust bearings for smooth operation. A hidden fourth leg allows for lateral movement on the bench.

Bald Eagle offers approximately 150 rest combinations to choose from, including windage adjustable, right or left hand, cast aluminum or cast iron.

Prices: $165.00 to $335.00.

BALD EAGLE PRECISION MACHINE CO.
101-K Allison Street, Lock Haven, PA 17745
Phone: 570-748-6772 • Fax: 570-748-4443
Web: www.baldeaglemachine.com

WORLD CLASS EXHIBITION SHOOTING

Tom Knapp's exhibition shooting videos are now available.

Each video reveals explicit slow motion and unusual camera angles of Tom's unbelievable multi-gun routines.

Video #1: Tom's World Record in the semi-auto class, of shooting *9 hand-thrown* clay targets using no assistance. RT approx. 9 min. **Price $9.95 + $4.55 SH=$14.50 USD**

Video #2: Three segments (including video #1). Also, rare footage of Tom's aerial .22 rifle routines (including shooting aspirins from mid-air!) and a video library of Tom's live show shotgun routines. RT approx. 30 min.
Price $19.95 + $4.55 SH=$24.50 USD

Video #3: Tom Knapp & Bill Dance. As seen on TNN's "*Bill Dance Outdoors*" program. Although Bill knew that Tom was going to demonstrate some of his .22 rifle shooting, he didn't know about the "trick" that Tom had in store for him! RT approx. 35 min.
Price$19.95 + $4.55 SH=$24.50 USD

Mail your check or money order to the address below or you can make a secure credit card order for Tom's Videos & Shooting Accessories from Tom's Web site.

THE SHOOTIST INC.
14618 County Road 35, Elk River, MN 55330
Phone (763) 441-5634, Fax (763) 241-0056
E-mail: tjknapp@qwest.net • Web: www.tomknapp.net

DETACHABLE RINGS & BASES

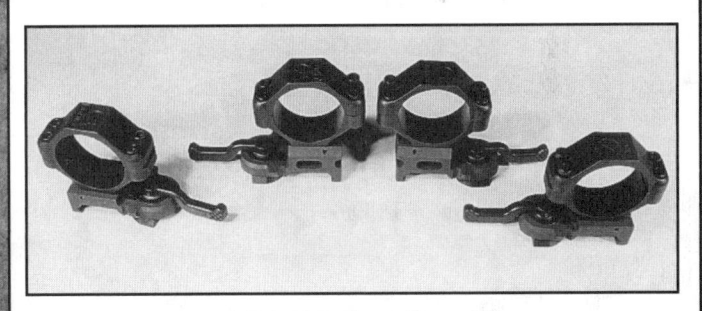

A.R.M.S.® #22 Throw Lever Rings

All steel 30mm ring, secured with A.R.M.S.® dovetail system to an extruded aluminum platform. Built in no-mar patented buffer pads. Available in Low, Medium, and High height. Low height measures .925". Medium height measures 1.150". High height measures 1.450". Height is measured from the center of the optic to the bottom of the base.

Sugg. Retail $99.00
U.S. Patent No. 5,276,988 & 4,845,871
Item #37 to convert 30mm to 1",
   Suggested Retail $29.00

Call for dealer or distributor in your area.

A.R.M.S., INC.
230 W. Center St., West Bridgewater, MA 02379
Phone: (508) 584-7816 • Fax: (508) 588-8045
E-mail: sswan37176@aol.com • Web: www.armsmounts.com

SHOOTER'S MARKETPLACE

AO Pro Express Sights

Uses proven Express Sight Principle with Big Dot Tritium or Standard Dot Tritium Front Sight with a vertical Tritium Bar within the Express Rear Sight. Ideal "flash sight alignment" stressed in defensive handgun courses. The tritium Express Rear enhances low-light sight alignment and acquisition. This improves a handgun for fastest sight picture in both normal and low light. Professional trainers rate it as the fastest acquisition sight under actual stress situations. Improves front sight acquisition for IDPA and IPSC shooting competition. Fits most handguns with factory dovetails; other models require dovetail front cuts. Also available in Adjustable Express Rear for Bomar, LPA, and Kimber.

Price: Pro Express Big Dot Tritium (or Standard Dot Tritium): $120.00

Price: Adjustable Pro Express Big Dot Tritium (or Standard Dot Tritium): $150.00

AO SIGHT SYSTEMS INC.
(Formerly: Ashley Outdoors)
2401 Ludelle, Fort Worth, TX 76105
Phone: 817-536-0136 • Fax: 800-536-3517

Custom Leather

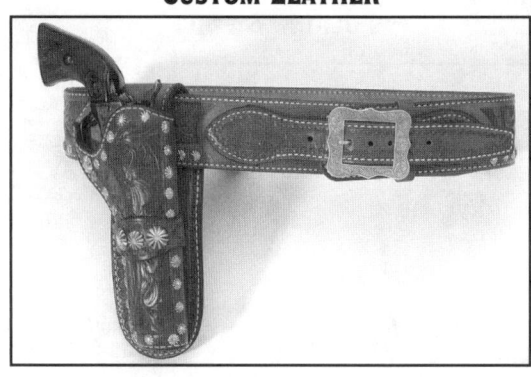

Rod Kibler Saddlery applies 25 years of saddle-making experience to the construction of fine holsters and belts. Kibler has found working on gun leather was a natural extension of saddle work.

Kibler, himself an active cowboy-action shooter, listens to other shooters and incorporates their ideas into his leatherwork for shooters.

Each of his rigs is extensively field-tested to ensure it will perform for the buyer. Several top national competitors have used Rod Kibler rigs for years.

Kibler adheres to old-time methods and quality standards. This commitment assures gun leather that meets the customer's standards, as well as Kibler's.

Only select, oak-tanned skirting leather is used.

The pictured rig is fully hand carved and lined with top-grain leather. The hardware includes solid sterling siver conchos and buckle.

ROD KIBLER SADDLERY
2307 Athens Road, Royston, GA 30662-3231 • Phone: 706-246-0487

e-GunParts.com

GUN PARTS NUMRICH CORPORATION
Established 1950

Numrich Gun Parts Corporation has expanded its website to include full e-commerce purchasing. Our new virtual storefront allows shopping for all your firearms parts and accessories by manufacturer and model. 180,000 items are available to purchase from our secure site, 24 hours a day, from anywhere in the world. You can now browse and buy within four clicks. The updated e-commerce site will also offer specials, new products, and inventory closeouts.

NUMRICH GUN PARTS CORPORATION
226 Williams Lane, West Hurley, NY 12491
Orders: 845-679-2417 • Customer Svc: 845-679-4867
Toll Free Fax: 877-Gun Parts • E-mail: info@gunpartscorp.com

The Gun Digest® Book of Modern Gun Values
11th Edition
Edited by Ken Ramage

Identify, evaluate and price any of the commonly encountered firearms made from 1900 to present. This specialized, heavily illustrated, expanded edition helps you easily identify and value older firearms found in gun shops, auctions, advertisements-or that old family gun you've just inherited. More than 7,500 post-1900 models are gathered by type then listed alphabetically. All prices are fully updated to mid-year. Includes more photos, and new sections covering mechanical inspection and (full-color) condition evaluation. New reference section lists books and associations for collectors.

Softcover • 8-1/2 x 11 • 640 pages
3,000+ b&w photos
Item# MGV11 • $24.95

To place a credit card order or for a FREE all-product catalog call

800-258-0929 Offer DLB1

M-F 7am - 8pm • Sat 8am - 2pm, CST

Krause Publications, Offer DLB1
P.O. Box 5009, Iola WI 54945-5009 • *www.krausebooks.com*

Shipping & Handling: $4.00 first book, $2.00 each additional. Non-US addresses $20.95 first book, $5.95 each additional.
Sales Tax: CA, IA, IL, PA, TN, VA, WI residents please add appropriate sales tax.

SHOOTER'S MARKETPLACE

QUALITY GUNSTOCK BLANKS

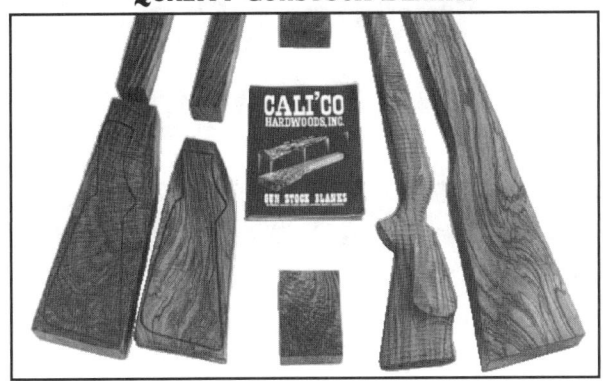

Cali'co Hardwoods has been cutting superior-quality shotgun and rifle blanks for more than 31 years. Cali'co supplies blanks to many of the major manufacturers—Browning, Weatherby, Ruger, Holland & Holland, to name a few—as well as custom gunsmiths the world over.

Profiled rifle blanks are available, ready for inletting and sanding. Cali'co sells superior California hardwoods in Claro walnut, French walnut, Bastogne, maple and myrtle.

Cali'co offers good, serviceable blanks and some of the finest exhibition blanks available. Satisfaction guaranteed.

Color catalog, retail and dealer price list (FFL required) free upon request.

CALI'CO HARDWOODS, INC.
3580 Westwind Blvd., Santa Rosa, CA 95403
Phone: 707-546-4045 • Fax: 707-546-4027

CUSTOM RESTORATION/CASE COLORING

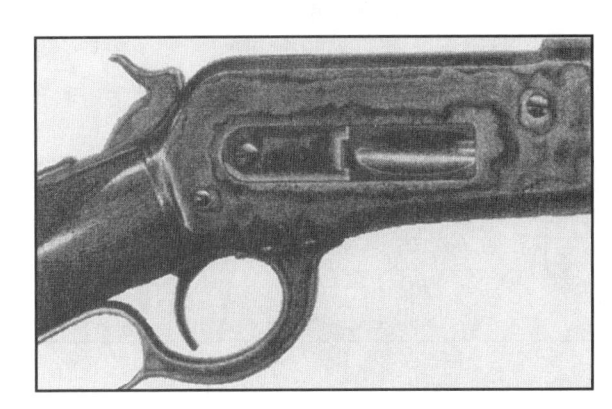

Doug Turnbull Restoration continues to offer bone charcoal case hardening work, matching the original case colors produced by Winchester, Colt, Marlin, Parker, L.C. Smith, Fox and other manufacturers. Also available is charcoal blue, known as Carbona or machine blue, a prewar finish used by most makers. "Specializing in the accurate recreation of historical metal finishes on period firearms, from polishing to final finishing. Including Bone Charcoal Color Case Hardening, Charcoal Bluing, Rust Blue, and Nitre Blue".

DOUG TURNBULL RESTORATION
P.O. Box 471, 6680 Rt 5&20, Dept SM2000
Bloomfield, New York 14469 • Phone/Fax: 716-657-6338
E-mail: turnbullrest@mindspring.com
Web: www.turnbullrestoration.com

FOR THE SERIOUS RELOADER...

Rooster Laboratories® makes two professional quality cannelure lubricants in 1" x 4" hollow or solid sticks, and in 2" x 6" solid. With a 220° F melting point, these lubes won't melt out and kill the powder, nor will they sweat oil. Using a lubrisizer heater, they flow consistently through the dieports, bond securely to the bullet, and harden quickly to a firm, tough finish.

- **ZAMBINI®** is a hard, tough lubricant, primarily for pistols.
- **HVR®** is for high velocity rifles, and is also excellent for pistols.

Contact Rooster Labs for prices, samples, and information on **Rooster Bright®** revolutionary ammonia-free case polish, plus a broad array of specialty bullet and case lubricants.

ROOSTER LABORATORIES®
P.O. Box 414605, Kansas City, MO 64141
Phone: 816-474-1622 • Fax: 816-474-1307
E-mail: roosterlabs@aol.com

WOLF® Performance Ammunition
• 100% Guaranteed • Newly Manufactured • Reliable and Affordable

WOLF, Russia's highest quality ammunition, has expanded its product line to include six additional calibers .223 Rem HP, 7.62x39 SP, 7.62x54R, .22 Rifle (Match Target and Match Gold) and 40 S&W. WOLF's product line of reliable ammunition also includes: 7.62x39, 9mm Luger, .380 Auto, .45 Auto, .223 Rem (55 &62 GR.) and 5.45x39. All products are newly manufactured and non-corrosive. All **WOLF** Performance Ammunition comes with a full performance guarantee.

SSI
Sporting Supplies International, Inc
2201 E. Winston, Suite K,
Anaheim, CA 92806
tel: 714.635.4246 • fax: 714.635.9276
www.wolfammo.com
email: info@wolfammo.com

"Your exclusive representative for WOLF Performance Ammunition and The Tula Cartridge Works and also suppliers of Novosibrirsk LVE Plant, Russia and SK Jagd-und, Germany."

34TH EDITION, 2002 • **81**

SHOOTER'S MARKETPLACE

NEW YOUTH SHOTGUN

The Ithaca Model 37 Ultra Featherlight Youth model is based on the classic Model 37 pump-action shotgun, with bottom ejection and adaptability to either right- or left-handed shooters via a simple safety change. This new model uses a receiver machined from aircraft-grade aluminum to keep the gun's unloaded weight below five pounds, a definite benefit to younger shooters. The Youth model features a 22-inch barrel with interchangeable choke tubes and a vent rib. The American black walnut stock has a 12 3/4-inch length of pull over the ventilated recoil pad. For information, please contact:

ITHACA GUN® CO., LLC
901 Route 34B, King Ferry, NY 13081
Phone: 315-364-7171 • Fax: 315-364-5134
Web: www.ithacagun.com

NEW DEER GUN IN 16-GAUGE

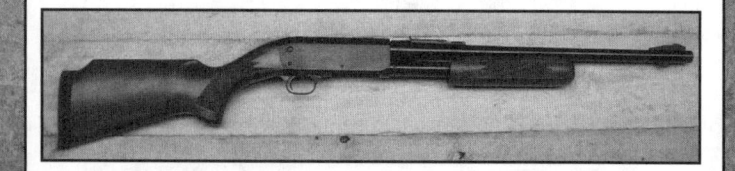

Ithaca Gun is introducing a new 16-gauge fixed-barrel Deerslayer II pump-action shotgun based on the proven Model 37 design.

Like the 12-gauge Deerslayer II, the new 16-gauge version is designed with scope use in mind, featuring a factory drilled and tapped receiver, a Monte Carlo stock and incorporates a free-floated, rifled barrel mated to the all-steel receiver to deliver rifle-like accuracy. The new Ithaca, and Lightfield's 16-gauge impact-discarding sabot ammunition, makes a hard-hitting, flat-shooting combination delivering energy comparable to that of a 12 gauge - from a lighter, easier-to-carry gun.

ITHACA GUN® CO., LLC
901 Route 34B, King Ferry, NY 13081
Phone: 315-364-7171 • Fax: 315-364-5134
Web: www.ithacagun.com

VERSATILE SCOPE
WATERPROOF; MULTI-COATED; SPEED FOCUS

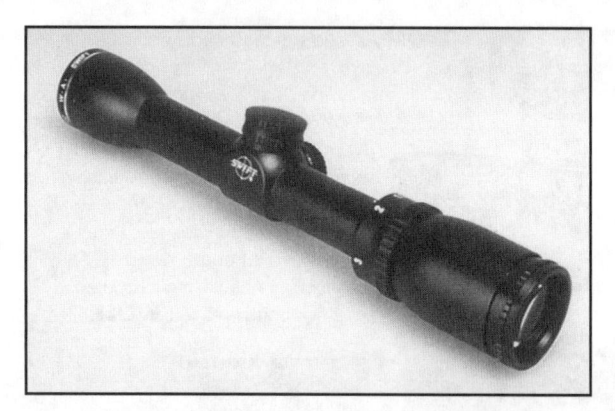

The 1.5-4.5x, 32mm Model 648M Swift *PREMIER*.
Considered by many to be the most versatile scope in our *Premier* line, works well on a shotgun or used as a black powder scope. It is often used in wooded areas for turkeys. It is effective on deer where rifles are permitted. Eye relief from 3.05 to 3.27. Crosshair and circle reticle make this rifle scope easy to focus on target, and ideal for turkey hunting. With black matte finish.

For more information, contact:

SWIFT INSTRUMENTS, INC.
952 Dorchester Avenue, Dept. GD, Boston, MA 02125
Phone: 617-436-2960 • Fax: 617-436-3232
E-mail: info@swiftoptics.com • Web: www.swift-optics.com

MODEL 676S SWIFT PREMIER
4-12X, 40 – WA – WATERPROOF – MULTI-COATED – SPEED FOCUS

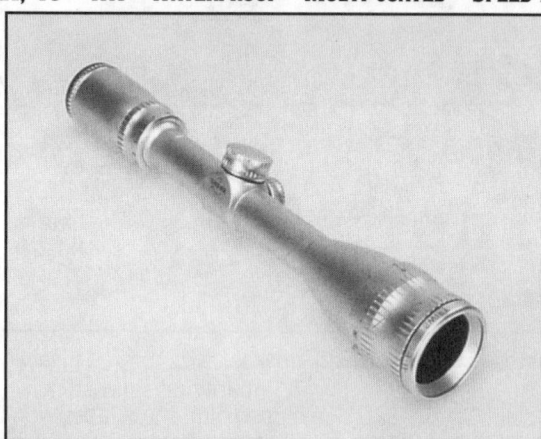

With a parallax adjustment from 10 yards to infinity this scope is highly adaptable and excellent for use as a varminting scope or on gas powered air rifles. Elevation and windage adjustments are full saddle on the hard anodized 1-inch tube. *Speed Focus* adjustment brings you on target easily. The objectives are multi-coated and the self-centering reticle in Quadraplex. Available in regular (676), matte (676M), and silver finish (676S). Gift boxed.

For more information, contact:

SWIFT INSTRUMENTS, INC.
952 Dorchester Avenue, Dept. GD, Boston, MA 02125
Phone: 617-436-2960 • Fax: 617-436-3232
E-mail: info@swiftoptics.com • Web: www.swift-optics.com

SHOOTER'S MARKETPLACE

A New Trend in Gun Collecting: Guns That Can't Shoot!

INTERNATIONAL MILITARY ANTIQUES, INC. of New Jersey, the company that supplied the machine guns used in "*Saving Private Ryan*" and many other World War II block buster movies, has introduced a new trend in gun collecting. Historically significant NON-FIRING machine guns constructed from original G.I. military parts to BATF specifications, making them legally unrestricted by federal law and unconvertible to firing condition. Previously unavailable, these original weapons can complete any 20th century military collection without the extremely high cost, extensive paperwork and security measures that comes with operational machine gun ownership.

Spanning from the WWI water-cooled Maxim and Vickers guns through the myriad of weapons developed by many countries during two World Wars, including the legendary Nazi era MG34 and MG42 series light machine guns, I.M.A. has developed a range of some of the most famous and infamous weapons that forged the modern world we know today.

In addition, I.M.A. offers a vast range of other military-related materials, both original and high quality reproduction. Military holsters, complete with replicated markings together with belts, pouches, swords, helmets, and accoutrements from over 300 years of history cater to the requirements of the collector and reenactor alike.

With its parent company Fire-Power International, Ltd. of England supplying the lion's share of the ex-military equipment, I.M.A.'s offerings are often unique to the U.S. market.

A mail order company operating from a 25,000 sq. ft. facility in New Jersey, the depth and scope of its inventory provides something for everyone. The often humorous but always highly accurate detailed cartoon illustrations by the renowned military artist SCOTT NOVZEN make I.M.A.'s advertisements and catalogs, or a visit to their website an added treat. Take a light hearted look at military history.

For further information contact:

INTERNATIONAL MILITARY ANTIQUES, INC.
Box 256, Millington, New Jersey 07946, U.S.A.
Phone: 908-903-1200 • Fax: 908-903-0106 • www.ima-usa.com

SHOOTER'S MARKETPLACE

COWBOY ACTION

The closest you'll get to the Old West short of a time machine.

Join SASS® and preserve the spirit of the Old West. Members receive a numbered shooter's badge, alias registration, an annual subscription to *The Cowboy Chronicle*, and much more.

SINGLE ACTION SHOOTING SOCIETY™
Phone Toll Free: 1-877-411-SASS
Web: www.sassnet.com

JP ENTERPRISES, INC.

Manufacturer of professional grade semi-auto rifles for competitive shooters and law enforcement. In addition, they offer modifications on bolt rifles, Remington shotguns and Glock pistols using proprietary components and techniques to enhance performance. They also offer their complete line of high performance parts for rifles, pistols and shotguns for sale direct or through several major distributors such as Brownell's. In particular, their recoil eliminators for rifles and the JP precision trigger system for AR-type rifles are known for their outstanding performance and have become the choice for many professional level shooters. Last year, they introduced a new coil reduction system for Remington series shotguns that has received excellent feed back from the action shooting community. Their extensive web site can be seen at www.jpar15.com.

JP ENTERPRISES, INC.
P.O. Box 378, Hugo, MN 55378
Phone: 651-426-9196 • Fax: 651-426-2472

DO-ALL TRAPS

Do-All Traps has a variety of traps and targets for the weekend shooter or commercial range.

The heart of the Do-All Trap is a patented, pivoting adjustable throwing arm. Three simple adjusting bolts allow the arm to be positioned to throw any clay target from a 90-degree vertical springing teal to a ground-bouncing rabbit or standard pair of doubles, and everything in-between.

A sliding, adjustable-tension spring clip on the throwing arm adapts to standard, rabbit, 90mm (midi), 60mm (mini) or battue clays, and allows them to be thrown as singles, stacked doubles or nesting pairs. By varying spring tension, target selection and position of the targets on the throwing arms, the Do-All Trap can create any target presentation desired.

The frame of each Do-All Trap is 3-inch, heavy-duty steel tubing with robotic welds and a durable power-coat paint finish. Each model assembles in seconds and includes an adjusting wrench, protective ring-guard and 15-minute instructional video.

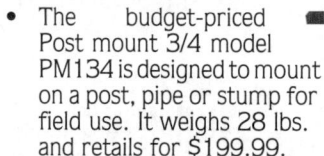

- The budget-priced Post mount 3/4 model PM134 is designed to mount on a post, pipe or stump for field use. It weighs 28 lbs. and retails for $199.99.
- The Single Trap model ST200 includes a fold-down chair, includes legs and also fits a trailer hitch. It weighs 47 lbs. and retails for $139.99.
- The Double Trap 3/4 Trap model DT534 has the same features as the Single Trap, but includes an extra throwing arm for report pairs. It can throw four targets at once. It weighs 94 lbs. and retails for $399.99.

Weekend rifle and airgun shooters will enjoy the fun of swinging targets with The Plinker and Plinker Jr.

- The Plinker, designed to withstand .22 rimfire rounds, has four pendulum targets that swing up when shot. To reset, simply shoot the fifth "reset" target at the top. The 10-lb. steel unit retails for $34.99.
- The Plinker Jr. is similar to The Plinker, but made to withstand airgun pellets. It weighs 1 lb. and retails for $13.99.

DO-ALL TRAPS

8113 Moores Ln., Suite 1900-154, Brentood, TN 37027
Phone: 1-800-252-9247 or 615-269-4889
Fax: 800-633-3172 or 615-269-4434
E-mail: sales@do-alltraps.com • Web: www.do-alltraps.com

SHOOTER'S MARKETPLACE

PERFORMANCE AMMUNITION

For serious enthusiasts who demand quality and accuracy, Black Hills Ammunition offers high quality ammo at a reasonable price with good service. Black Hills Ammunition has been producing high quality rounds for over 20 years. They sell dealer-direct and pay all freight to the continental U.S. Minimum order in only one case. Satisfaction is guaranteed. Black Hills Ammunition specializes in match-quality 223 (both new and remanufactured), .308 Match, cowboy ammo and more. Performance is so good that the U.S. Army, Navy, Air Firce and Marines all use Black Hills.

Ask for it at your dealer, or contact them directly for purchase information.

BLACK HILLS AMMUNITION
P.O. Box 3090, Rapid City, SD 57709
Phone: 1-605-348-5150 • Fax: 1-605-348-9827

ADJUSTABLE APERTURE FOR GLASSES

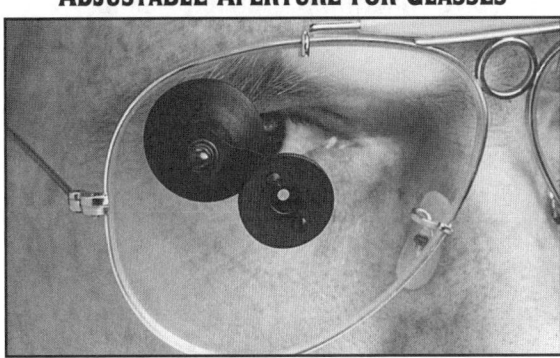

The Merit Optical Attachment is an instantly adjustable iris aperture that allows shooters to see their iron sights and target clearly. The adjustable aperture dramatically increases the eye's depth of focus, eliminating a fuzzy sight picture.

The Optical Attachment works with all types of glasses including bifocals and trifocals. It attaches securely with a small rubber suction cup. The aperture instantly adjusts from .022- to .156-inch in diameter to accommodate different light conditions. It is compact and lightweight.

Merit Corporation makes a full line of adjustable apertures for mounting in peep sights as well. Contact Merit Corporation for information and a free catalog.

MERIT CORPORATION
P.O. Box 9044, Schnectady, NY 12309
Phone: 518-346-1420
Web: www.meritcorporation.com

OBSOLETE AND HARD-TO-FIND AMMO

The Old Western Scrounger has been in the firearms business for 40 years, providing obsolete and hard-to-find ammunition and components, including European and double-rifle calibers. The company now carries the Kynoch line of ammo, ranging from the 318 Westley Richards to the 700 Nitro Express. Old Western Scrounger's own line of ammo covers almost any obsolete rifle or pistol caliber, including a 1 million-round run of the 5mm Remington Mag. (coming soon). The firm also is the exclusive carrier of RWS brass and other reloading components. In addition, Scrounger carries Fiocchi, Norma, Eley and RWS ammunition, as well as some old favorites. Free catalogs and free shipping are provided on orders over $25.00. Call the company if you need help determining which ammo is needed for a particular gun.

OLD WESTERN SCROUNGER, INC.
1540 Lucas Road, Yreka, CA 96097
Phone: 800-UPS-AMMO • Web: www.ows-ammunition.com

QUALITY CUSTOM KNIVES

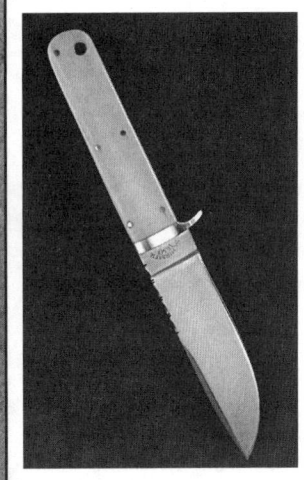

Mike Schirmer's lifelong interest in knives stems from his passion for hunting and since he lives in the heart of Montana's best big-game country, he has had plenty of opportunity to test his blades. Mike has also worked as an elk guide and a "buffalo skinner." (Call him to book a buffalo hunt.) All of Mike's knives, no matter how beautiful, are made to use. D2 is his favorite type of steel, but he will use other steels (including damascus) on special order. All types of handle material are available, as is engraving.

While the majority of his business is hunting knives, Mike also makes camp, fighting, and Old West Period knives. When you purchase a Mike Schirmer knife, you are getting a one-of-a-kind piece of working art that is destined to be a family heirloom. Mike usually has a few knives on hand for immediate delivery, or if you prefer, he will make a custom knife to your design.

For more information, contact Mike at:

RUBY MOUNTAIN KNIVES
P.O. Box 534,
Twin Bridges, MT 59754
Phone: 406-684-5868 • Email: schirmer@3rivers.net

SHOOTER'S MARKETPLACE

CNC MACHINED TRIGGER GUARD

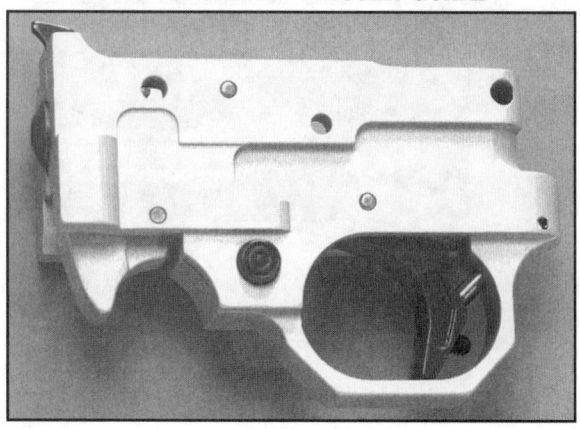

This is a complete CNC machined trigger guard equipped with precision EDM parts. It features an internal pretravel adjustment that is set at the factory in order to greatly reduce pretravel. This new match trigger guard is CNC machined from a solid billet of high strength aircraft aluminum. The hammer is a precision ground 440C stainless steel. The sear and disconnector are EDM manufactured parts. The trigger is black anodized and equipped with an overtravel adjustment screw. The trigger is reset internally. An automatic bolt release and an extended magazine release are also included.

VOLQUARTSEN CUSTOM LTD.
24276 240th Street, P.O. Box 397, Carroll, IA 51401
Phone: 712-792-4238 • Fax: 712-792-2542
E-mail: info@volquartsen.com • Web: www.volquartsen.com

CNC MACHINED STEEL COMPETITION BOLT

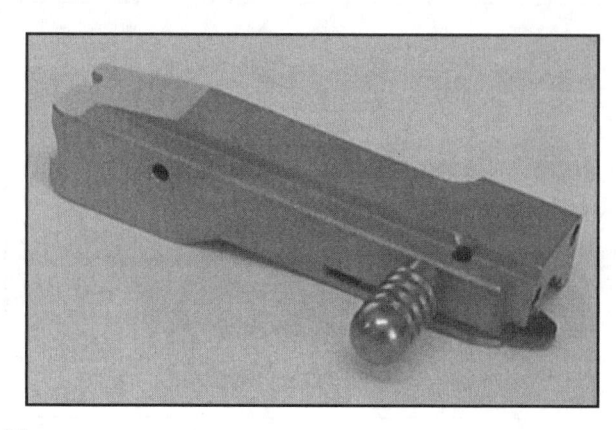

This bolt features hardened (60Rc) and tuned extractor for positive, consistent extraction. It also includes Volquartsen's own unique round titanium firing pin for faster lock time and to assure positive ignition. The new bolt also features interchangeable bolt handles. It is available with their streamline, compact stainless steel handle or a target knob (red or black) for easy cocking control. The bolt comes with Volquartsen's recoil rod and spring for ease of installation in either their stainless steel receiver or for the factory Ruger 10/22® receiver.

VOLQUARTSEN CUSTOM LTD.
24276 240th Street, P.O. Box 397, Carroll, IA 51401
Phone: 712-792-4238 • Fax: 712-792-2542
E-mail: info@volquartsen.com • Web: www.volquartsen.com

BREAK-FREE®
An Armor Holdings Company

Break-Free® is a leading manufacturer of synthetic-based cleaners, lubricants and preservative compounds for military weapon maintenance, law enforcement, civilian firearms, high performance sports equipment and industrial machinery. Break-Free's flagship product Break-Free CLP® was specifically developed to provide reliable weapon lubrication in battlefield conditions and to remove firing residues, carbon deposits and other firing contaminants. Moreover, Break-Free CLP® repels water and dirt and prevents corrosion, and keeps weapons combat ready in any condition – rain, snow, ice, mud, or sand.

Break-Free® has been an approved qualified source and quality supplier to militaries around the globe for over 20 years. To learn more about the Break-Free family of products, visit www.break-free.com or buy online at holsters.com.

BREAK-FREE®, INC.
13386 International Parkway
Jacksonville, FL 32218
Phone: 800-428-0588

M36 PLUSONE™ EXTENSION

Pearce Grip Inc., originators of the popular grip extension line for the Glock® sub-compact auto pistols, introduces the M36 PlusOne™ extension. This unit converts the Glock® model 36 (45 Auto) factory six-round magazine to a seven-round capacity and provides the extra finger groove for shooting comfort and control. The PlusOne™ replaces the factory magazine floor plate and is held securely to the magazine body with an external locking device that doubles as a contour blending feature completing the rear of the grip. This new extension is made from a high-impact polymer and incorporates the same texture and checkering pattern found on the pistol frame for a factory appearance. For more information or for a dealer near you contact:

PEARCE GRIP, INC.
P.O. Box 40367, Fort Worth, TX 76140
Phone: 800-390-9420 • Fax: 817-568-9707

SHOOTER'S MARKETPLACE

1911 MAGAZINE GUIDE

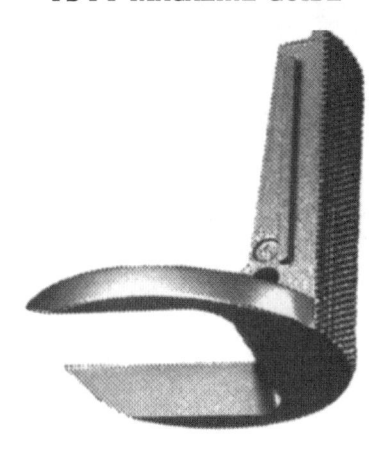

The S&A Mag Guide is the only one-piece magazine guide in the marketplace for 1911 pistols. It's the most popular and practical addition to the 1911 firearm. No frame modification, installs in minutes. Increases magazine opening 100%. 20LPI checkering for maximum grip, adds 1/4" length for extra leverage and recoil control. Will fit most 1911 clones, Colt, Springfield, Kimber, Auto-Ordnance, Norinco and Para Ordnance. Available in stainless steel or blued. Government and officer's models now available in hard anodized aluminum, neutral or black. $74.95 each.

SMITH & ALEXANDER, INC.
P.O. Box 496208, Garland, TX 75049
Phone: 1-800-722-1911 • Fax: 1-972-840-6176
E-mail: sa1911@gte.net • Website: wwwsmithandalexander.com

FINE GUN STOCKS

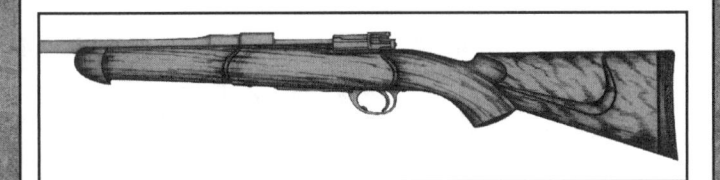

Manufacturing custom and production gunstocks for hundreds of models of rifles and shotguns—made from the finest stock woods and available in all stages of completion.

Visit www.gunstocks.com to view their bargain list of fine custom gunstocks. Each displayed in full color.

GREAT AMERICAN GUNSTOCK COMPANY
3420 Industrial Drive
Yuba City, CA 95993
Phone: 530-671-4570
Fax: 530-671-3906
Gunstock Hotline: 800-784-GUNS (4867)
Web: www.gunstocks.com
E-mail: gunstox@oro.net

BALLARD RIFLE IS BACK!

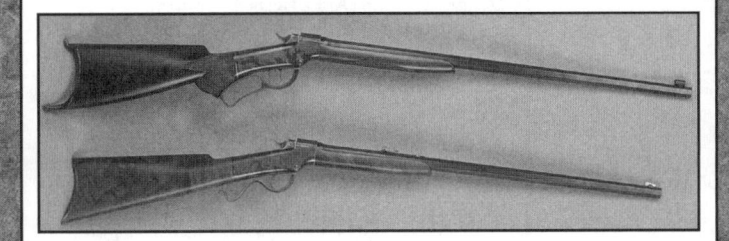

The Ballard rifle is back in production after more than 100 years. At the Cody, Wyoming factory, we have made a firm commitment to honoring the Ballard tradition of superior quality, fit and finish. Our craftsmen focus on that goal every day as they make Ballard rifles from the patent, in all original configurations.

Whether your interest is hunting, target shooting or Schuetzen shooting, there is a Ballard rifle to perfectly fit your needs. Please send for our color catalog of rifles, sights, parts, and bullet molds.

BALLARD RIFLES, LLC
113 W. Yellowstone Ave., Cody, WY 82414
Phone: 307-587-4914 • Fax: 307-527-6097
E-mail: ballard@wyoming.com

PERSONAL PROTECTION

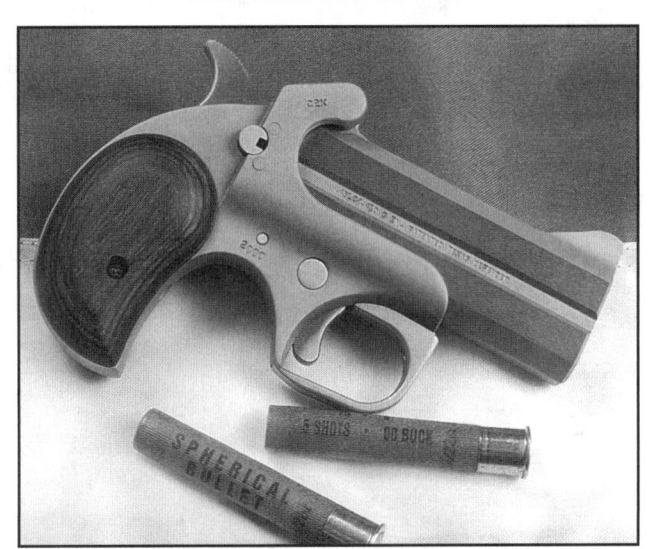

The Century 2000 Defender is designed for self-defense. This Derringer-style pistol has a 3 1/2" double barrel, rebounding hammer, retracting firing pins, crossbolt safety, cammed locking lever, spring-loaded extractor and interchangeable barrels. 3" chambers for .45 Colt or .410 00 buckshot.

For further information, contact:

BOND ARMS, INC.
P.O. Box 1296, Granbury, TX 76048
Phone: 817-573-4445 • Fax: 817-573-5636
E-mail: bondarms@shooters.com • Web: www.bondarms.com

2002 GUNS ILLUSTRATED Complete Compact CATALOG

GUNDEX®	**89**

SEMI-CUSTOM ARMS

HANDGUNS
- Autoloaders 102
- Revolvers 109
- Single Shot 113

RIFLES
- Bolt-Action Rifles 114
- Autoloaders 117
- Double Rifles 119
- Single Shot 120

SHOTGUNS 121

COMMERCIAL ARMS

HANDGUNS
- Autoloaders 130
- Competition 163
- Double-Action Revolvers 169
- Single-Action Revolvers 179
- Miscellaneous Handguns 188

RIFLES
- Centerfire Rifles—
  - Autoloaders 192
  - Lever & Slide 198
  - Bolt Action 205
  - Single Shot 227
- Drillings, Combination Guns, Double Rifles 236
- Rimfire Rifles—Autoloaders .. 239
  - Lever & Slide 243
  - Bolt Actions & Single Shots 245
- Competition Rifles—
  - Centerfire & Rimfire 251

SHOTGUNS
- Autoloaders 257
- Slide Actions 264
- Over/Unders 269
- Side-by-Sides 282
- Bolt Actions & Single Shots. 287
- Military & Police 291

BLACKPOWDER
- Single Shot Pistols 293
- Revolvers 295
- Muskets & Rifles 299
- Shotguns 314

AIRGUNS
- Handguns 315
- Long Guns 319

MANUFACTURERS DIRECTORY 328

A

A.H. Fox Side-By-Side Shotguns, 283
Accu-Tek BL-9 Auto Pistol, 130
Accu-Tek Model AT-32SS Auto Pistol, 130
Accu-Tek Model AT-380 Auto Pistol, 130
Accu-Tek Model HC-380 Auto Pistol, 130
Accu-Tek XL-9 Auto Pistol, 130
Airrow Model A-8S1P Stealth Air Gun, 319
Airrow Model A-8SRB Stealth Air Gun, 319
American Arms Mateba Auto/Revolver, 130
American Derringer DA 38 Model, 188
American Derringer Lady Derringer, 188
American Derringer Model 1, 188
American Derringer Model 10 Lightweight, 188
American Derringer Model 4, 188
American Derringer Model 6, 188
American Derringer Model 7 Ultra Lightweight, 188
American Derringer Texas Commemorative, 188
American Frontier 1851 Navy Conversion, 179
American Frontier 1851 Navy Richards & Mason Conversion, 179
American Frontier 1871-1872 Open-Top Revolvers, 179
American Frontier Richards 1860 Army, 179
AMT 380 DAO Small Frame Backup, 131
AMT 45 ACP Hardballer II, 131
AMT 45 ACP Hardballer Long Slide, 131
AMT Automag II Auto Pistol, 130
AMT Automag III Pistol, 130
AMT Automag IV Pistol, 130
AMT Backup Pistol, 131
Anschutz 1416D/1516D Classic Rifles, 245
Anschutz 1416D/1516D Walnut Luxus Rifles, 245
Anschutz 1451 Target Rifle, 251
Anschutz 1451R Sporter Target Rifle, 251
Anschutz 1518D Luxus Bolt-Action Rifle, 245
Anschutz 1710D Custom Rifle, 245
Anschutz 1733D Rifle, 205
Anschutz 1740 Monte Carlo Rifle, 205
Anschutz 1743d Bolt-Action Rifle, 205
Anschutz 1808D-RT Super Running Target Rifle, 251
Anschutz 1827 Biathlon Rifle, 251
Anschutz 1827BT Fortner Biathlon Rifle, 251
Anschutz 1903 Match Rifle, 251
Anschutz 1907 Standard Match Rifle, 252
Anschutz 1911 Prone Match Rifle, 252
Anschutz 1912 Sport Rifle, 252
Anschutz 1913 Super Match Rifle, 252
Anschutz 1913 Super Match Rifle, 252
Anschutz 2002 Match Air Rifle, 319
Anschutz 2007 Match Rifle, 251
Anschutz 2012 Sport Rifle, 252
Anschutz 2013 Benchrest Rifle, 251
Anschutz 54.18MS REP Deluxe Silhouette Rifle, 252
Anschutz 64-MSR Silhouette Rifle, 251
Anschutz Model 64p Sport/Target Pistol, 188

GUNDEX

Anschutz Super Match Special Model 2013 Rifle, 252
Apollo TR and TT Shotguns, 269
AR-7 Explorer Carbine, 239
Armalite AR-10 (T) Rifle, 252
Armalite AR-10A4 Special Purpose Rifle, 192
Armalite M15A2 Carbine, 192
Armalite M15A4 (T) Eagle Eye Rifle, 253
Armalite M15A4 Action Master Rifle, 253
Armoury R140 Hawken Rifle, 299
Armscor M-1600 Auto Rifle, 239
Armscor M-200DC Revolver, 169
Armscor M-20C Auto Carbine, 239
Armscor M-30F Field Pump Shotgun, 264
Armscor Model AK22 Auto Rifle, 239
Armsport 1866 Sharps Rifle, Carbine, 227
Armsport Model 4540 Revolver, 169
Army 1851 Percussion Revolver, 295
Army 1860 Percussion Revolver, 295
Arnold Arms African Trophy Rifle, 205
Arnold Arms Alaskan Guide Rifle, 205
Arnold Arms Alaskan Rifle, 205
Arnold Arms Alaskan Trophy Rifle, 205
Arnold Arms Grand African Rifle, 205
Arnold Arms Grand Alaskan Rifle, 205
Arnold Arms Safari Rifle, 205
Arrieta Sidelock Double Shotguns, 282
ARS Hunting Master AR6 Air Rifle, 319
ARS/Career 707 Air Rifle, 319
ARS/Farco CO2 Air Shotgun, 319
ARS/Farco CO2 Stainless Steel Air Rifle, 319
ARS/Farco FP Survival Air Rifle, 319
ARS/King Hunting Master Air Rifle, 319
ARS/Magnum 6 Air Rifle, 319
ARS/QB77 Deluxe Air Rifle, 319
Austin & Halleck Model 320 LR In-Line Rifle, 299
Austin & Halleck Model 420 LR In-Line Rifle, 299
Austin & Halleck Mountain Rifle, 299
Autauga 32 Auto Pistol, 131
Auto-Ordnance 1911A1 Automatic Pistol, 131
Auto-Ordnance 1911A1 Custom High Polish Pistol, 131
Auto-Ordnance 1927 A-1 Thompson, 192
Auto-Ordnance 1927A1 Commando, 192
Auto-Ordnance Thompson M1, 192
Auto-Ordnance ZG-51 Pit Bull Auto, 131

B

Baby Dragoon 1848, 1849 Pocket, Wells Fargo, 295
Baer 1911 Bullseye Wadcutter Pistol, 163
Baer 1911 Custom Carry Auto Pistol, 132
Baer 1911 National Match Hardball Pistol, 163
Baer 1911 Premier II Auto Pistol, 132
Baer 1911 S.R.P. Pistol, 132
Baer 1911 Ultimate Master Combat Pistol, 163
Ballard Model 1885 High Wall Single Shot Rifle, 227
Ballard No. 1 3/4 Far West Rifle, 227
Ballard No. 4 Perfection Rifle, 227
Ballard No. 5 Pacific Single-Shot Rifle, 227
Ballard No. 7 Long Range Rifle, 227
Ballard No. 8 Union Hill Rifle, 227
Barrett Model 82A-1 Semi-Automatic Rifle, 192
Barrett Model 95 Bolt-Action Rifle, 206
Barrett Model 99 Single Shot Rifle, 227
Beeman Bearcub Air Rifle, 319
Beeman Crow Magnum Air Rifle, 319
Beeman HW70A Air Pistol, 315
Beeman Kodiak Air Rifle, 320
Beeman Mako Air Rifle, 320
Beeman P1 Magnum Air Pistol, 315
Beeman P2 Match Air Pistol, 315
Beeman P3 Air Pistol, 315
Beeman R1 Air Rifle, 320
Beeman R1 Carbine, 321
Beeman R1 Laser MK II Air Rifle, 320
Beeman R11 Air Rifle, 320
Beeman R6 Air Rifle, 320
Beeman R7 Air Rifle, 320
Beeman R9 Air Rifle, 320
Beeman R9 Deluxe Air Rifle, 320
Beeman RX-1 Gas-Spring Magnum Air Rifle, 321
Beeman S1 Magnum Air Rifle, 321
Beeman Super 12 Air Rifle, 320
Beeman/Feinwerkbau 103 Pistol, 315
Beeman/Feinwerkbau 300-S Mini-Match, 321
Beeman/Feinwerkbau 300-S Series Match Rifle, 321
Beeman/Feinwerkbau 603 Air Rifle, 321
Beeman/Feinwerkbau 65 MKII Air Pistol, 315
Beeman/Feinwerkbau P70 Air Rifle, 321
Beeman/FWB C55 CO2 Rapid Fire Pistol, 315
Beeman/FWB P30 Match Air Pistol, 315
Beeman/HW 97 Air Rifle, 321
Beeman/Webley Hurricane Air Pistol, 315
Beeman/Webley Tempest Air Pistol, 315
Benelli Executive Series Shotguns, 257
Benelli Legacy Shotgun, 257
Benelli Limited Edition Legacy, 257
Benelli M1 Field Auto Shotgun, 257
Benelli M1 Practical, 291
Benelli M1 Tactical Shotgun, 291
Benelli M3 Convertible Shotgun, 291
Benelli M4 Super 90 Joint Service Combat Shotgun, 291
Benelli Montefeltro 20 Gauge Shotgun, 257
Benelli Montefeltro 90 Shotgun, 257
Benelli MP90S World Cup Pistol, 163
Benelli MP95E Atlanta Pistol, 163
Benelli Nova Pump Rifled Slug Gun, 264
Benelli Nova Pump Shotgun, 264
Benelli Nova Pump Slug Gun, 264
Benelli Sport Shotgun, 257
Benelli Super Black Eagle Shotgun, 257
Benelli Super Black Eagle Slug Gun, 257
Benjamin Sheridan CO2 Pellet Pistols, 315

Gundex

Benjamin Sheridan Pneumatic (Pump-Up) Air Rifles, 322
Benjamin Sheridan Pneumatic Pellet Pistols, 316
Benjamin Sheridan W.F. Air Rifle, 322
Beretta 92 FS/CO2 Air Pistols, 316
Beretta AL391 Urika Auto Shotguns, 258
Beretta AL391 Urika Gold and Gold Sporting Auto Shotguns, 258
Beretta AL391 Urika Parallel Target RL and SL Auto Shotguns, 258
Beretta AL391 Urika Sporting Auto Shotguns, 258
Beretta AL391 Urika Trap and Gold Trap Auto Shotguns, 258
Beretta AL391 Urika Youth Shotgun, 258
Beretta DT 10 Trident Shotguns, 269
Beretta DT 10 Trident Trap Top Single Shotgun, 287
Beretta ES 100 Auto Shotguns, 258
Beretta ES100 NWTF Special Auto Shotgun, 258
Beretta Express Double Rifles, 119
Beretta Express SSO O/U Double Rifles, 236
Beretta Mato Deluxe Bolt-Action Rifle, 206
Beretta Mato Synthetic Bolt-Action Rifle, 206
Beretta Model 1201FP Ghost Ring Auto Shotgun, 291
Beretta Model 21 Bobcat Pistol, 133
Beretta Model 3032 Tomcat Pistol, 133
Beretta Model 455 SxS Express Rifle, 236
Beretta Model 470 Silver Hawk Shotgun, 282
Beretta Model 80 Cheetah Series DA Pistols, 133
Beretta Model 8000/8040/8045 Cougar Pistol, 133
Beretta Model 8000/8040/8045 Mini Cougar, 133
Beretta Model 86 Cheetah, 133
Beretta Model 89 Gold Standard Pistol, 163
Beretta Model 9000S Compact Pistol, 133
Beretta Model 92FS 470th Anniversary Limited Edition, 132
Beretta Model 92FS Compact and Compact Type M Pistol, 132
Beretta Model 92FS Pistol, 132
Beretta Model 92FS/96 Brigadier Pistols, 132
Beretta Model 950 Jetfire Auto Pistol, 133
Beretta Model 96 Combat Pistol, 163
Beretta Model 96 Pistol, 132
Beretta Model 96 Stock Pistol, 164
Beretta Model S686 Whitewing O/U, 269
Beretta Model SO5, SO6, SO9 Shotguns, 270
Beretta Over/Under Field Shotguns, 270
Beretta Premium Grade Shotguns, 121
Beretta S682 Gold E Trap O/U, 269
Beretta S686 Onyx Sporting O/U Shotgun, 269
Beretta S687EL Gold Pigeon Sporting O/U, 270

Beretta Series S682 Gold Skeet, Trap Over/Unders, 269
Beretta Sporting Clays Shotguns, 270
Beretta Ultralight Deluxe Over/Under Shotgun, 269
Beretta Ultralight Over/Under, 269
Bersa Thunder 380 Auto Pistols, 133
BF Ultimate Silhouette HB Single Shot Pistol, 164
Bill Hanus Birdgun, 284
Blaser R93 Bolt-Action Rifle, 206
Blaser R93 Long Range Rifle, 253
Blue Thunder/Commodore 1911-Style Auto Pistols, 134
Bond Arms Texas Defender Derringer, 188
Bostonian Percussion Rifle, 299
Briley 1911-Style Auto Pistols, 102
BRNO 500 Combination Guns, 236
BRNO 501.2 Over/Under Shotgun, 270
BRNO 98 Bolt-Action Rifle, 206
BRNO TAU-200 Air Rifle, 322
BRNO TAU-7 CO2 Match Pistol, 316
BRNO ZBK 100 Single Barrel Shotgun, 287
BRNO ZBK 110 Single Shot Rifle, 228
BRNO ZH 300 Combination Gun, 236
BRNO ZH 300 Over/Under Shotgun, 270
BRNO ZH Double Rifles, 236
BRNO ZKM 611 Auto Rifle, 239
Brown Classic Single Shot Pistol, 189
Brown Model 97D Single Shot Rifle, 228
Browning 425 Sporting Clays, 272
Browning A-Bolt Classic Hunter, 207
Browning A-Bolt Composite Stalker, 208
Browning A-Bolt Custom Trophy Rifle, 207
Browning A-Bolt Eclipse Hunter, 207
Browning A-Bolt Eclipse M-1000, 207
Browning A-Bolt Medallion Left-Hand, 207
Browning A-Bolt Medallion, 207
Browning A-Bolt Micro Hunter, 207
Browning A-Bolt Rifles, 207
Browning A-Bolt Stainless Stalker, 207
Browning A-Bolt White Gold Medallion, 207
Browning Acera Straight-Pull Rifle, 207
Browning BAR High-Grade Auto Rifles, 193
Browning BAR Mark II Lightweight Semi-Auto, 193
Browning BAR Mark II Safari Rifle in magnum calibers, 193
Browning BAR Mark II Safari Semi-Auto Rifle, 193
Browning BAR Stalker Auto Rifles, 193
Browning BL-22 Lever-Action Rifle, 243
Browning BPR Pump Rifle, 198
Browning BPS 10 Gauge Camo Pump, 264
Browning BPS 10 Gauge Shotguns, 264
Browning BPS Game Gun Deer Hunter, 265
Browning BPS Game Gun Turkey Special, 265
Browning BPS Micro Pump Shotgun, 265

Browning BPS NWTF Turkey Series Pump Shotgun, 265
Browning BPS Pump Shotgun, 264
Browning BPS Stalker Pump Shotgun, 265
Browning BPS Waterfowl Camo Pump Shotgun, 264
Browning BT-100 Trap Shotgun, 287
Browning BT-99 Trap Shotgun, 287
Browning Buck Mark 5.5, 134
Browning Buck Mark Bullseye, 134
Browning Buck Mark Bullseye, 164
Browning Buck Mark Camper, 134
Browning Buck Mark Challenge, 134
Browning Buck Mark Field 5.5, 164
Browning Buck Mark Micro, 134
Browning Buck Mark Semi-Auto Rifles, 239
Browning Buck Mark Silhouette, 164
Browning Buck Mark Standard 22 Pistol, 134
Browning Buck Mark Target 5.5, 164
Browning Citori Feather XS Shotguns, 271
Browning Citori High Grade Shotguns, 271
Browning Citori Lightning Feather O/U, 271
Browning Citori O/U Shotguns, 270
Browning Citori Sporting Hunter, 271
Browning Citori Ultra XS Skeet, 271
Browning Citori Ultra XS Sporting, 271
Browning Citori Ultra XS Trap, 271
Browning Citori XT Trap Over/Under, 271
Browning Gold 10 Auto Shotgun, 260
Browning Gold 10 Gauge Auto Combo, 260
Browning Gold Classic Hunter Auto Shotgun, 259
Browning Gold Classic Stalker, 259
Browning Gold Deer Stalker, 259
Browning Gold Fusion™ Auto Shotgun, 259
Browning Gold Hunter Auto Shotgun, 258
Browning Gold Ladies/Youth Sporting Clays Auto, 259
Browning Gold Light 10 Gauge Auto Shotgun, 260
Browning Gold Micro Auto Shotgun, 259
Browning Gold Mossy Oak® Break-Up Shotguns, 259
Browning Gold Mossy Oak® Shadow Grass Shotguns, 259
Browning Gold NWTF Turkey Series Camo Shotgun, 260
Browning Gold Rifled Deer Hunter Auto Shotgun, 259
Browning Gold Sporting Clays Auto, 259
Browning Gold Sporting Golden Clays, 259
Browning Gold Stalker Auto Shotguns, 259
Browning Gold Turkey/Waterfowl Camo Shotgun, 259
Browning Gold Upland Special Auto Shotgun, 260

GUNDEX

Browning Hi-Power 9mm Automatic Pistol, 134
Browning Hi-Power Practical Pistol, 134
Browning Light Sporting 802 ES O/U, 271
Browning Lightning BLR Lever-Action Rifle, 198
Browning Lightning BLR Long Action, 198
Browning Lightning Sporting Clays, 271
Browning Micro Citori Lightning, 271
Browning Model 1885 BPCR Rifle, 228
Browning Model 1885 High Wall Single Shot Rifle, 228
Browning Model 1885 Low Wall Rifle, 228
Browning Model 1885 Low Wall Traditional Hunter, 228
Browning Nitra Citori XS Sporting Clays, 271
Browning NWTF Gold Turkey Stalker, 259
Browning Semi-Auto 22 Rifle, 239
Browning Semi-Auto 22, Grade VI, 239
Browning Special Sporting Clays, 271
Browning Superlight Citori Over/Under, 271
BSA 240 Magnum Air Pistol, 316
BSA Magnum Goldstar Magnum Air Rifle, 322
BSA Magnum Supersport™ Air Rifle, 322
BSA Magnum Superstar™ MK2 Magnum Air Rifle, Carbine, 322
BSA Magnum Superten Air Rifle, 322
BSA Meteor MK6 Air Rifle, 322
Buck Mark Commemorative, 134
Bushmaster Auto Rifles, 117
Bushmaster DCM Competition Rifle, 253
Bushmaster M17S Bullpup Rifle, 193
Bushmaster Shorty XM15 E2S Carbine, 193
Bushmaster XM15 E25 AK Shorty Carbine, 194
Bushmaster XM15 E2S Dissipator Carbine, 193
Bushmaster XM15 E2S Target Model Rifle, 253
Bushmaster XM15 E2S V-Match Rifle, 253

C

C. Sharps Arms 1875 Classic Sharps, 234
C. Sharps Arms New Model 1874 Old Reliable, 234
C. Sharps Arms New Model 1875 Old Reliable Rifle, 233
C. Sharps Arms New Model 1875 Target & Long Range, 234
C. Sharps Arms New Model 1885 Highwall Rifle, 234
C. Sharps Arms Rifles, 120
C.S. Richmond 1863 Musket, 309
Cabanas Esproncheda IV Bolt-Action Rifle, 245
Cabanas Laser Rifle, 245
Cabanas Leyre Bolt-Action Rifle, 245
Cabanas Master Bolt-Action Rifle, 245
Cabela's 1858 Henry Replica, 198
Cabela's 1866 Winchester Replica, 198
Cabela's 1873 Winchester Replica, 198
Cabela's Blackpowder Shotguns, 314
Cabela's Blue Ridge Rifle, 299
Cabela's Kodiak Express Double Rifle, 299
Cabela's Millennium Revolver, 179
Cabela's Pine Ridge LR In-Line Rifle, 299
Cabela's Sharps Sporting Rifle, 228
Cabela's Sporterized Hawken Hunter Rifle, 299
Cabela's Starr Percussion Revolvers, 295
Cabela's Traditional Hawken, 299
Calico Liberty 50, 100 Carbines, 194
Calico M-100FS Carbine, 239
Calico M-110 Auto Pistol, 134
Carbon 15 (Type 97) Auto Rifle, 194
Carbon One Bolt-Action Rifle, 208
Carbon-15 (Type 97) Pistol, 134
Century Gun Dist. Model 100 Single-Action, 179
Charles Daly Diamond DL Double Shotgun, 282
Charles Daly Diamond GTX DL Hunter O/U, 273
Charles Daly Diamond GTX Sporting O/U Shotgun, 273
Charles Daly Diamond GTX Trap AE-MC O/U Shotgun, 273
Charles Daly Diamond Regent DL Double Shotgun, 282
Charles Daly Diamond Regent GTX DL Hunter O/U, 272
Charles Daly Empire Combination Gun, 236
Charles Daly Empire EDL Hunter O/U, 273
Charles Daly Empire Grade Auto Rifle, 239
Charles Daly Empire Grade Rifle, 208
Charles Daly Empire Grade Rifle, 246
Charles Daly Empire Hunter Double Shotgun, 282
Charles Daly Empire Magnum Grade Rifle, 245
Charles Daly Empire Sporting O/U, 273
Charles Daly Empire Trap AE MC, 272
Charles Daly Field Grade Auto Rifle, 239
Charles Daly Field Grade Rifle, 245
Charles Daly Field Hunter AE Shotgun, 272
Charles Daly Field Hunter AE-MC, 272
Charles Daly Field Hunter Double Shotgun, 282
Charles Daly Field Hunter Over/Under Shotgun, 272
Charles Daly M-1911-A1P Autoloading Pistol, 135
Charles Daly Superior Bolt-Action Rifle, 208
Charles Daly Superior Bolt-Action Rifle, 245
Charles Daly Superior Combination Gun, 236
Charles Daly Superior Hunter AE Shotgun, 272
Charles Daly Superior Hunter Double Shotgun, 282
Charles Daly Superior Magnum Grade Rifle, 245
Charles Daly Superior Sporting O/U, 272
Charles Daly Superior Trap AE MC, 272
Charles Daly True Youth Bolt-Action Rifle, 246
Chipmunk Single Shot Rifle, 246
Cimarron 1860 Henry Replica, 198
Cimarron 1866 Winchester Replicas, 198
Cimarron 1872 Open Top Revolver, 179
Cimarron 1872 Open-Top Revolver, 180
Cimarron 1873 Frontier Six Shooter, 179
Cimarron 1873 Long Range Rifle, 199
Cimarron 1873 Short Rifle, 199
Cimarron 1873 Sporting Rifle, 199
Cimarron Billy Dixon 1874 Sharps Sporting Rifle, 228
Cimarron Bisley Flat Top Revolver, 180
Cimarron Bisley Model Single-Action Revolvers, 180
Cimarron Creedmoor Rolling Block Rifle, 229
Cimarron Flat Top Single-Action Revolvers, 180
Cimarron Lightning SA, 179
Cimarron Model "P" JR., 179
Cimarron Model 1885 High Wall Rifle, 228
Cimarron Quigley Model 1874 Sharps Sporting Rifle, 228
Cimarron Rough Rider Artillery Model Single-Action, 179
Cimarron Silhouette Model 1874 Sharps Sporting Rifle, 228
Cimarron Thunderer Revolver, 180
Cimarron U.S. Cavalry Model Single-Action, 179
Classic BF Hunting Pistol, 164
Colt 1847 Walker Percussion Revolver, 296
Colt 1848 Baby Dragoon Revolver, 295
Colt 1849 Pocket Dragoon Revolver, 295
Colt 1851 Navy Percussion Revolver, 295
Colt 1860 "Cavalry Model" Percussion Revolver, 295
Colt 1860 Army Percussion Revolver, 295
Colt 1861 Navy Percussion Revolver, 295
Colt 1862 Pocket Police "Trapper Model" Revolver, 295
Colt Accurized Rifle, 253
Colt Cowboy Single-Action Revolver, 180
Colt Defender, 135
Colt Gold Cup Model O Pistol, 164
Colt Government 1911 A1 Air Pistol, 316
Colt Light Rifle Bolt Action, 208
Colt Match Target Competition HBAR II Rifle, 254
Colt Match Target Competition HBAR Rifle, 253
Colt Match Target HBAR Rifle, 253
Colt Match Target Model Rifle, 253
Colt Match Target Rifle, 194
Colt Model 1861 Musket, 299
Colt Model 1991 Model O Auto Pistol, 135
Colt Model 1991 Model O Commander Auto Pistol, 135

34TH EDITION, 2002 • 91

Gundex

Colt Single-Action Army Revolver, 180
Colt Third Model Dragoon, 296
Colt Walker 150th Anniversary Revolver, 296
Colt XSE Lightweight Commander Auto Pistol, 135
Colt XSE Series Model O Auto Pistols, 135
Competitor Single Shot Pistol, 164
Cook & Brother Confederate Carbine, 300
Coonan 357 Magnum, 41 Magnum Pistols, 136
Coonan Compact Cadet 357 Magnum Pistol, 136
Cooper Arms Model 22 Pro Varmint Extreme, 208
Cooper Model 21, 38 Bolt-Action Rifles, 208
Cooper Model 22 Bolt-Action Rifle, 208
Copperhead Black Serpent Rifle, 322
Crosman 2260 Air Rifle, 323
Crosman 2264 X Air Rifle, 323
Crosman Auto Air II Pistol, 316
Crosman Black Fang Pistol, 316
Crosman Black Venom Pistol, 316
Crosman Challenger 2000 Air Rifle, 322
Crosman Model 1008 Repeat Air, 316
Crosman Model 1077 Repeatair Rifle, 323
Crosman Model 1322, 1377 Air Pistols, 316
Crosman Model 2100 Classic Air Rifle, 323
Crosman Model 2200 Magnum Air Rifle, 324
Crosman Model 2289 Rifle, 323
Crosman Model 357 Series Air Pistol, 316
Crosman Model 66 Powermaster, 323
Crosman Model 760 Pumpmaster, 323
Crosman Model 782 Black Diamond Air Rifle, 323
Crosman Model 795 Spring Master Rifle, 323
Crossfire Shotgun/Rifle, 291
Cumberland Mountain Blackpowder Rifle, 300
Cumberland Mountain Plateau Rifle, 229
CVA Bobcat Rifle, 300
CVA Colorado Musket Mag 100 Rifle, 300
CVA Eclipse 209 Magnum In-Line Rifle, 300
CVA Firebolt Musketmag Bolt-Action In-Line Rifles, 300
CVA Hawken Pistol, 293
CVA HunterBolt 209 Magnum Rifle, 300
CVA Mountain Rifle, 300
CVA NWTF Gobbler Series Shotgun, 314
CVA St. Louis Hawken Rifle, 300
CVA Stag Horn 209 Magnum Rifle, 300
CVA Trapper Percussion Shotgun, 314
CVA Youth Hunter Rifle, 300
CZ 100 Auto Pistol, 138
CZ 452 American Classic Bolt-Action Rifle, 246
CZ 452 M 2E Lux Bolt-Action Rifle, 246
CZ 452 M 2E Varmint Rifle, 246
CZ 511 Auto Rifle, 240

CZ 527 American Classic Bolt-Action Rifle, 209
CZ 527 Lux Bolt-Action Rifle, 208
CZ 550 American Classic Bolt-Action Rifle, 209
CZ 550 Lux Bolt-Action Rifle, 209
CZ 550 Magnum Bolt-Action Rifle, 209
CZ 550 Medium Magnum Bolt-Action Rifle, 209
CZ 581 Solo Over/Under Shotgun, 273
CZ 584 Solo Combination Gun, 236
CZ 589 Stopper Over/Under Gun, 236
CZ 700 M1 Sniper Rifle, 209
CZ 75 Champion Competition Pistol, 165
CZ 75 ST IPSC Auto Pistol, 165
CZ 75/85 Kadet Auto Pistol, 138
CZ 75B Auto Pistol, 136
CZ 75B Compact Auto Pistol, 137
CZ 75B Decocker, 136
CZ 75M IPSC Auto Pistol, 137
CZ 83B Double-Action Pistol, 137
CZ 85 Combat, 137
CZ 85B Auto Pistol, 137
CZ 97B Auto Pistol, 137

D

Daisy 1938 Red Ryder 60th Anniversary Classic, 324
Daisy Model 2003 Pellet Pistol, 316
Daisy Model 454 Air Pistol, 316
Daisy Model 840, 324
Daisy Model 990 Dual-Power Air Rifle, 324
Daisy/Powerline 1000 Air Rifle, 324
Daisy/Powerline 1140 Pellet Pistol, 317
Daisy/Powerline 1170 Pellet Rifle, 324
Daisy/Powerline 1270 CO2 Air Pistol, 317
Daisy/Powerline 44 Revolver, 317
Daisy/Powerline 717 Pellet Pistol, 317
Daisy/PowerLine 747 Pistol, 317
Daisy/Powerline 853, 324
Daisy/Powerline 856 Pump-Up Airgun, 324
Daisy/Powerline 880, 324
Daisy/Powerline Eagle 7856 Pump-Up Airgun, 324
Daisy/Youthline Model 105 Air Rifle, 324
Daisy/Youthline Model 95 Air Rifle, 325
Dakota 76 Classic Bolt-Action Rifle, 209
Dakota 76 Safari Bolt-Action Rifle, 210
Dakota 76 Traveler Takedown Rifle, 209
Dakota 97 Lightweight Hunter, 210
Dakota African Grade, 210
Dakota Double Rifle, 237
Dakota Long Range Hunter Rifle, 210
Dakota Longbow Tactical E.R. Rifle, 210
Dakota Model 10 Single Shot Rifle, 229
Dakota Premier Grade Shotguns, 282
Dakota The Dakota Legend Shotguns, 282
Dan Wesson 722M Small Frame Revolver, 177
Dan Wesson Coyote Classic Bolt-Action Rimfire Rifle, 246
Dan Wesson Coyote Target Bolt-Action Rimfire Rifle, 246

Dan Wesson Firearms Model 15/715 and 32/732 Revolvers, 178
Dan Wesson Firearms Model 22/722 Revolvers, 177
Dan Wesson Firearms Model 3220/73220 Target Revolver, 177
Dan Wesson Firearms Model 360/7360 Revolvers, 178
Dan Wesson Firearms Model 40/740 Revolvers, 177
Dan Wesson Firearms Model 41/741, 44/744 and 45/745 Revolvers, 178
Dan Wesson Firearms Model 414/7414 and 445/7445 SuperMag Revolvers, 177
Dan Wesson Firearms Model 460/7460 Revolvers, 178
Dan Wesson Firearms Model 722 Silhouette Revolver, 177
Dan Wesson Firearms Standard Silhouette Revolvers, 178
Dan Wesson Firearms Super Ram Silhouette Revolver, 178
Dan Wesson Pointman Dave Pruitt Signature Series, 162
Dan Wesson Pointman Guardian Auto Pistols, 162
Dan Wesson Pointman Hi-Cap Auto Pistol, 162
Dan Wesson Pointman Major Auto Pistol, 161
Dan Wesson Pointman Minor Auto Pistol, 161
Dan Wesson Pointman Seven Auto Pistols, 162
Davis Big Bore Derringers, 189
Davis D-Series Derringers, 189
Davis Long-Bore Derringers, 189
Davis P-32 Auto Pistol, 138
Davis P-380 Auto Pistol, 138
Desert Eagle Baby Eagle Pistols, 139
Desert Eagle Mark XIX Pistol, 138
Dixie 1863 Springfield Musket, 301
Dixie 1874 Sharps Blackpowder Silhouette Rifle, 229
Dixie 1874 Sharps Lightweight Hunter/Target Rifle, 229
Dixie Deluxe Cub Rifle, 301
Dixie Early American Jaeger Rifle, 301
Dixie English Matchlock Musket, 301
Dixie Engraved 1873 Rifle, 199
Dixie Inline Carbine, 301
Dixie Magnum Percussion Shotgun, 314
Dixie Pedersoli 1766 Charleville Musket, 301
Dixie Pedersoli 1857 Mauser Rifle, 301
Dixie Pennsylvania Pistol, 293
Dixie Sharps New Model 1859 Military Rifle, 301
Dixie U.S. Model 1816 Flintlock Musket, 301
Dixie U.S. Model 1861 Springfield, 301
Dixie Wyatt Earp Revolver, 296
Downsizer WSP Single Shot Pistol, 189
DPMS Panther Arms A-15 Rifles, 194

GUNDEX

E

E.A.A. Bounty Hunter SA Revolvers, 180
E.A.A. European Model Auto Pistols, 139
E.A.A. Standard Grade Revolvers, 169
E.A.A. Witness DA Auto Pistol, 139
E.A.A. Witness Gold Team Auto, 165
E.A.A. Witness Silver Team Auto, 165
E.A.A./HW 660 Match Rifle, 254
E.M.F. 1860 Henry Rifle, 199
E.M.F. 1863 Sharps Military Carbine, 302
E.M.F. 1866 Yellowboy Lever Actions, 199
E.M.F. 1874 Metallic Cartridge Sharps Rifle, 229
E.M.F. Hartford Model 1892 Lever-Action Rifle, 199
E.M.F. Hartford Model Cowboy Shotgun, 283
E.M.F. Model 1873 Lever-Action Rifle, 199
EAA/Baikal Bounty Hunter IZH-43K Shotgun, 283
EAA/Baikal Bounty Hunter MP-213 Coach Gun, 283
EAA/Baikal IZH-18 Single Barrel Shotgun, 287
EAA/Baikal IZH-18Max Single Barrel Shotgun, 287
EAA/Baikal IZH-27 Over/Under Shotgun, 273
EAA/Baikal IZH-32BK Air Rifle, 325
EAA/Baikal IZH35 Auto Pistol, 165
EAA/Baikal IZH-43 Bounty Hunter Shotguns, 283
EAA/Baikal IZH-46 Target Air Pistol, 317
EAA/Baikal IZH-61 Air Rifle, 325
EAA/Baikal IZH-94 Combination Gun, 237
EAA/Baikal MP-133 Pump Shotgun, 265
EAA/Baikal MP-153 Auto Shotgun, 260
EAA/Baikal MP-213 Shotgun, 283
EAA/Baikal MP-233 Over/Under Shotgun, 273
EAA/Baikal MP-512 Air Rifle, 325
EAA/Baikal MP-532 Air Rifle, 325
EAA/Baikal MP-651K Air Pistol/Rifle, 317
EAA/Baikal MP-654K Air Pistol, 317
Ed Brown Classic Custom and Class A Limited 1911-Style Auto Pistols, 102
Ed Brown Custom Bolt-Action Rifles, 114
EMF 1875 Outlaw Revolver, 181
EMF 1890 Police Revolver, 181
EMF 1894 Bisley Revolver, 181
EMF Hartford Express Single-Action Revolver, 181
EMF Hartford Pinkerton Single-Action Revolver, 181
EMF Hartford Single-Action Revolvers, 180
Entréprise Boxer P500 Auto Pistol, 139
Entréprise Elite P500 Auto Pistol, 139
Entréprise Medalist P500 Auto Pistol, 139
Entréprise Tactical P500 Auto Pistol, 140
Entréprise Tournament Shooter Model I, 165

Erma KGP68 Auto Pistol, 140
Euroarms 1861 Springfield Rifle, 302
Euroarms Volunteer Target Rifle, 302
European American Armory Witness Auto Pistols, 102
Excel Industries CP-45 Auto Pistol, 165

F

Fabarm Camo Lion Auto Shotgun, 260
Fabarm Camo Turkey Mag O/U Shotgun, 274
Fabarm Classic Lion Double Shotgun, 283
Fabarm Field Pump Shotgun, 265
Fabarm FP6 Pump Shotgun, 291
Fabarm Gold Lion Mark II Auto Shotgun, 260
Fabarm Max Lion Over/Under Shotguns, 273
Fabarm Monotrap Shotgun, 287
Fabarm Silver Lion Cub Model O/U, 274
Fabarm Silver Lion Over/Under Shotguns, 273
Fabarm Sporting Clays Competition Extra O/U, 274
Fabarm Sporting Clays Extra Auto Shotgun, 260
Fabarm Tactical Semi-Automatic Shotgun, 291
Fabarm Ultra Camo Mag Lion O/U Shotgun, 273
Fabarm Ultra Mag Lion O/U Shotgun, 273
FEG PJK-9HP Auto Pistol, 140
FEG SMC-380 Auto Pistol, 140
Felk MTF 450 Auto Pistol, 140
Franchi AL 48 Deluxe Shotgun, 260
Franchi AL 48 Short Stock Shotgun, 260
Franchi AL 48 Shotgun, 260
Franchi Alcione Field Over/Under Shotgun, 274
Franchi Alcione Light Field (LF) Shotgun, 274
Franchi Alcione Sport O/U Shotgun, 274
Franchi Variopress 612 Defense Shotgun, 261
Franchi Variopress 612 Shotgun, 260
Franchi Variopress 612 Sporting Shotgun, 261
Franchi Variopress 620 Short Stock Shotgun, 261
Freedom Arms Model 252 Varmint Class Revolver, 182
Freedom Arms Model 83 Field Grade Revolver, 181
Freedom Arms Model 83 Field Grade Silhouette Class, 165
Freedom Arms Model 83 Field Grade Varmint Class Revolver, 182
Freedom Arms Model 83 Premier Grade Revolver, 181
Freedom Arms Model 97 Mid-Frame Revolver, 182
French-Style Dueling Pistol, 293

G

Garbi Express Double Rifle, 237

Garbi Model 100 Double, 283
Garbi Model 101 Side-By-Side, 284
Garbi Model 103A, B Side-By-Side, 284
Garbi Model 200 Side-By-Side, 283
Gary Reeder Custom Guns Contender and Encore Pistols, 113
Gary Reeder Custom Guns Revolvers, 109
"Gat" Air Pistol, 317
Gaucher GN1 Silhouette Pistol, 189
Gaucher GP Silhouette Pistol, 165
Glock 17 Auto Pistol, 140
Glock 19 Auto Pistol, 141
Glock 20 10mm Auto Pistol, 141
Glock 21 Auto Pistol, 141
Glock 22 Auto Pistol, 141
Glock 23 Auto Pistol, 141
Glock 26, 27 Auto Pistols, 141
Glock 29, 30 Auto Pistols, 141
Glock 31/31C Auto Pistols, 141
Glock 32/32C Auto Pistols, 142
Glock 33 Auto Pistol, 142
Glock 34, 35 Auto Pistols, 142
Glock 36 Auto Pistol, 142
Gonic Model 93 Deluxe M/L Rifle, 302
Gonic Model 93 M/L Rifle, 302
Gonic Model 93 Mountain Thumbhole M/L Rifles, 302
Griswold & Gunnison Percussion Revolver, 296

H

Hammerli 480 Match Air Pistol, 317
Hammerli 480K2 Match Air Pistol, 317
Hammerli AR 50 Air Rifle, 325
Hammerli Model 450 Match Air Rifle, 325
Hammerli Sp 20 Target Pistol, 165
Hammerli Trailside PL 22 Target Pistol, 142
Harper's Ferry 1803 Flintlock Rifle, 302
Harper's Ferry 1806 Pistol, 293
Harrington & Richardson Model 928 Ultra Slug Hunter Deluxe, 287
Harrington & Richardson NWTF Shotguns, 287
Harrington & Richardson SB2-980 Ultra Slug, 287
Harrington & Richardson Tamer Shotgun, 288
Harrington & Richardson Topper Deluxe Model 098, 288
Harrington & Richardson Topper Deluxe Rifled Slug Gun, 288
Harrington & Richardson Topper Junior Classic Shotgun, 288
Harrington & Richardson Topper Model 098, 288
Harrington & Richardson Ultra Comp Rifle, 230
Harrington & Richardson Ultra Heavy Barrel 22 Mag Rifle, 246
Harrington & Richardson Ultra Hunter Rifle, 229
Harrington & Richardson Ultra Varmint Rifle, 229

34TH EDITION, 2002 • 93

GUNDEX

Harris Gunworks Antietam Sharps Rifle, 230
Harris Gunworks Combo M-87 Series 50-Caliber Rifles, 254
Harris Gunworks Long Range Rifle, 254
Harris Gunworks M-86 Sniper Rifle, 254
Harris Gunworks M-89 Sniper Rifle, 254
Harris Gunworks National Match Rifle, 254
Harris Gunworks Signature Alaskan, 211
Harris Gunworks Signature Classic Sporter, 210
Harris Gunworks Signature Classic Stainless Sporter, 211
Harris Gunworks Signature Jr. Long Range Pistol, 166
Harris Gunworks Signature Titanium Mountain Rifle, 211
Harris Gunworks Signature Varminter, 211
Harris Gunworks Talon Safari Rifle, 211
Harris Gunworks Talon Sporter Rifle, 211
Hawken Rifle, 303
Heckler & Koch Mark 23 Special Operations Pistol, 143
Heckler & Koch P7M8 Auto Pistol, 143
Heckler & Koch SL8-1 Rifle, 195
Heckler & Koch SLB 2000 Rifle, 194
Heckler & Koch USC Carbine, 195
Heckler & Koch USP Auto Pistol, 142
Heckler & Koch USP Compact Auto Pistol, 142
Heckler & Koch USP Expert Pistol, 143
Heckler & Koch USP45 Auto Pistol, 142
Heckler & Koch USP45 Compact, 143
Heckler & Koch USP45 Tactical Pistol, 143
Henry Goldenboy 22 Lever-Action Rifle, 243
Henry Lever-Action 22, 243
Henry Pump-Action 22 Pump Rifle, 243
Henry U.S. Survival Rifle .22, 240
Heritage Rough Rider Revolver, 182
High Standard Trophy Target Pistol, 166
High Standard Victor Target Pistol, 166
Hi-Point 9mm Carbine, 195
Hi-Point Firearms 380 Comp Pistol, 144
Hi-Point Firearms 40 S&W Auto, 143
Hi-Point Firearms 45 Caliber Pistol, 143
Hi-Point Firearms 9mm Comp Pistol, 144
Hi-Point Firearms Model 380 Polymer Pistol, 144
Hi-Point Firearms Model 9mm Compact Pistol, 144
Hoenig Rotary Round Action Double Rifle, 237
Howa Lightning Bolt-Action Rifle, 212
Howa M-1500 Hunter Bolt-Action Rifle, 212
Howa M-1500 PCS Police Counter Sniper Rifle, 212
Howa M-1500 Varmint Rifle, 212
HS America HS 2000 Pistol, 144

I

IAI M-3000 Auto Pistol, 144
IAI M-333 M1 Garand, 195
IAI M-4000 Auto Pistol, 144
IAI M-444 Light Semi-Automatic Rifle, 195
IAI M-5000 Auto Pistol, 144
IAI M-6000 Auto Pistol, 144
IAI M-888 M1 Carbine Semi-Automatic Rifle, 195
IAR Cowboy Shotguns, 284
IAR Model 1872 Derringer, 189
IAR Model 1873 Frontier Marshal, 182
IAR Model 1873 Frontier Revolver, 182
IAR Model 1873 Revolver Carbine, 199
IAR Model 1873 Six Shooter, 182
IAR Model 1888 Double Derringer, 189
Ithaca Classic Doubles Grade 4E Classic SxS Shotgun, 284
Ithaca Classic Doubles Grade 7E Classic SxS Shotgun, 284
Ithaca Classic Doubles Side-By-Side Shotguns, 125
Ithaca Classic Doubles Sousa Special Grade SxS Shotgun, 284
Ithaca Classic Doubles Special Field Grade SxS, 284
Ithaca Model 37 Deerslayer II Pump Shotgun, 265
Ithaca Model 37 Deluxe Pump Shotgun, 265
Ithaca Model 37 Hardwoods 20/2000 Deerslayer, 265
Ithaca Model 37 Hardwoods 20/2000 Turkeyslayer, 265
Ithaca Model 37 Turkeyslayer Pump Shotgun, 265
Ithaca Model 37 Waterfowler, 265

J

J.P. Henry Trade Rifle, 303
J.P. Murray 1862-1864 Cavalry Carbine, 303
John Rigby Custom African Express Rifle, 114
John Rigby Double Rifles, 119
John Rigby Shotguns, 125

K

Kahr K9 9mm Compact Polymer Pistol, 145
Kahr K9, K40 DA Auto Pistols, 144
Kahr MK9/MK40 Micro Pistol, 145
Kel-Tec P-11 Auto Pistol, 145
Kel-Tec P-32 Auto Pistol, 145
Kel-Tec Sub-9 Auto Rifle, 195
Kentuckian Rifle, 303
Kentucky Flintlock Pistol, 293
Kentucky Flintlock Rifle, 303
Kentucky Percussion Pistol, 293
Kentucky Percussion Rifle, 303
Kimber 22 Classic Bolt-Action Rifle, 246
Kimber 22 HS (Hunter Silhouette) Bolt-Action Rifle, 247
Kimber 22 SuperAmerica Bolt-Action Rifle, 247
Kimber 22 SVT Bolt-Action Rilfe, 247
Kimber Compact Auto Pistol, 145
Kimber Custom 1911-Style Auto Pistols, 102
Kimber Custom Auto Pistol, 145
Kimber Gold Combat Auto Pistol, 146
Kimber Gold Match Auto Pistol, 146
Kimber High Capacity Polymer Pistol, 146
Kimber Model 84m Bolt-Action Rifle, 212
Kimber Polymer Gold Match Auto Pistol, 146
Kimber Pro Carry Auto Pistol, 146
Kimber Pro CDP Auto Pistol, 146
Kimber Super Match Auto Pistol, 166
Kimber Ultra Carry Auto Pistol, 146
Kimber Ultra CDP Auto Pistol, 146
Knight 45 Super Disc In-Line Rifle, 303
Knight 50 Caliber Disc In-Line Rifle, 303
Knight American Knight M/L Rifle, 303
Knight Bighorn In-Line Rifle, 303
Knight Master Hunter II Disc In-Line Rifle, 303
Knight TK2000 Muzzleloading Shotgun, 314
Knight Wolverine II Rifle, 304
Kolar AAA Competition Skeet Over/Under Shotgun, 274
Kolar AAA Competition Trap Over/Under Shotgun, 274
Kolar Sporting Clays O/U Shotgun, 274
Krieghoff Classic Big Five Double Rifle, 237
KRieghoff Classic Double Rifle, 237
Krieghoff Hubertus Single-Shot Rifle, 230
Krieghoff K-20 O/U Shotguns, 275
Krieghoff K-80 Four-Barrel Skeet Set, 275
Krieghoff K-80 International Skeet, 275
Krieghoff K-80 O/U Trap Shotgun, 275
Krieghoff K-80 Single Barrel Trap Gun, 288
Krieghoff K-80 Skeet Shotgun, 274
Krieghoff K-80 Sporting Clays O/U, 274
Krieghoff KS-5 Special, 288
Krieghoff KS-5 Trap Gun, 288

L

L.A.R. Grizzly 50 Big Boar Rifle, 212
Le Mat Revolver, 296
Le Page Percussion Dueling Pistol, 293
Lebeau - Courally Boss-Verees O/U, 275
Lebeau - Courally Boxlock SxS Shotgun, 284
Lebeau - Courally Express Rifle SxS, 237
Lebeau - Courally Sidelock SxS Shotgun, 284
Les Baer AR 223 Auto Rifles, 117
Les Baer Custom 1911-Style Auto Pistols, 103
Les Baer Custom Ultimate AR 223 Rifles, 196
Linebaugh Custom Sixguns Revolvers, 109
Ljutic Lm-6 Super Deluxe O/U Shotgun, 275
Ljutic LTX PRO 3 Deluxe Mono Gun, 288
Ljutic Mono Gun Single Barrel, 288
Llama Max-I Auto Pistols, 147
Llama Micromax 380 Auto Pistol, 147

GUNDEX

Llama Minimax Series, 147
Llama Minimax Sub-Compact Auto Pistol, 147
London Armory 1861 Enfield Musketoon, 304
London Armory 2-band 1858 Enfield, 304
London Armory 3-band 1853 Enfield, 304
Lone Star Rolling Block Rifles, 120
LR 300 SR Light Sport Rifle, 196
Luger Classic O/U Shotguns, 275
Luger Ultra Light Semi-Automatic Shotguns, 261
Lyman Cougar In-Line Rifle, 304
Lyman Deerstalker Rifle, 305
Lyman Great Plains Hunter Rifle, 305
Lyman Great Plains Rifle, 305
Lyman Plains Pistol, 293
Lyman Trade Rifle, 304

M

Magnum Research BFR Single-Action Revolver, 182
Magnum Research Little Max Revolver, 183
Magnum Research Lone Eagle Single Shot Pistol, 190
Magnum Research Tactical Rifle, 213
Magtech MT 7022 Auto Rifle, 240
Markesbery KM Black Bear M/L Rifle, 305
Markesbery KM Brown Bear M/L Rifle, 306
Markesbery KM Colorado Rocky Mountain M/L Rifle, 305
Markesbery KM Grizzly Bear M/L Rifle, 306
Markesbery KM Polar Bear M/L Rifle, 306
Marksman 1010 Repeater Pistol, 317
Marksman 1745 BB Repeater Air Rifle, 325
Marksman 1790 Biathlon Trainer, 325
Marksman 1798 Competition Trainer Air Rifle, 325
Marksman 2005 Laserhawk Special Edition Air Pistol, 317
Marksman 2015 Laserhawk™ BB Repeater Air Rifle, 325
Marksman BB Buddy Air Rifle, 325
Marlin 70PSS Papoose Stainless Rifle, 240
Marlin Model 15YN "Little Buckaroo", 247
Marlin Model 1894 Cowboy, Cowboy II, 200
Marlin Model 1894 Lever-Action Carbine, 200
Marlin Model 1894C Carbine, 200
Marlin Model 1894P/1894CP Carbine, 200
Marlin Model 1895 Cowboy Lever-Action Rifle, 201
Marlin Model 1895 Lever-Action Rifle, 201
Marlin Model 1895G Guide Gun Lever-Action Rifle, 201
Marlin Model 1895GS Guide Gun, 201
Marlin Model 1895M Lever-Action Rifle, 201
Marlin Model 1897CB Cowboy Lever Action Rifle, 244
Marlin Model 2000L Target Rifle, 254
Marlin Model 25MG Garden Gun Shotgun, 288
Marlin Model 25MN/25MNC Bolt-Action Rifles, 248
Marlin Model 25N Bolt-Action Repeater, 248
Marlin Model 25NC Bolt-Action Repeater, 248
Marlin Model 336 Cowboy, 200
Marlin Model 336A Lever-Action Carbine, 200
Marlin Model 336C Lever-Action Carbine, 199
Marlin Model 336CC Lever-Action Carbine, 200
Marlin Model 336SS Lever-Action Carbine, 200
Marlin Model 336W Lever-Action Rifle, 200
Marlin Model 39a Golden Lever-Action Rifle, 243
Marlin Model 444 Lever-Action Sporter, 200
Marlin Model 444P Outfitter Lever-Action, 200
Marlin Model 512p Slugmaster Shotgun, 288
Marlin Model 60 Auto Rifle, 240
Marlin Model 60SS Self-Loading Rifle, 240
Marlin Model 7000 Auto Rifle, 241
Marlin Model 7000T Auto Rifle, 255
Marlin Model 795 Auto Rifle, 241
Marlin Model 81TS Bolt-Action Rifle, 247
Marlin Model 83TS Bolt-Action Rifle, 248
Marlin Model 880SQ Squirrel Rifle, 247
Marlin Model 880SS Bolt-Action Rifle, 247
Marlin Model 882 Bolt-Action Rifle, 248
Marlin Model 882SS Bolt-Action Rifle, 248
Marlin Model 882SSV Bolt-Action Rifle, 248
Marlin Model 883 Bolt-Action Rifle, 248
Marlin Model 883SS Bolt-Action Rifle, 248
Marlin Model 922M Auto Rifle, 241
Marocchi Classic Doubles Model 92 Sporting Clays O/U Shotgun, 276
Marocchi Conquista Skeet Over/Under Shotgun, 276
Marocchi Conquista Sporting Clays O/U Shotguns, 275
Marocchi Conquista Trap Over/Under Shotgun, 275
Marocchi Lady Sport O/U Shotgun, 275
Maximum Single Shot Pistol, 190
MDM Buckwacka In-Line Rifles, 306
MDM M2K In-Line Rifle, 306
Medusa Model 47 Revolver, 169
Merkel Boxlock Double Rifles, 238
Merkel Drillings, 237
Merkel Exhibition, Vintagers Expo and Custom Engraved Shotguns, 126
Merkel Model 160 Side-By-Side Double Rifle, 238
Merkel Model 2001EL O/U Shotgun, 276
Merkel Model 2002 EL O/U Shotgun, 276
Merkel Model 280EL and 360EL Shotguns, 284
Merkel Model 280SL and 360SL Shotguns, 285
Merkel Model 303EL O/U Shotgun, 276
Merkel Model 47E, 147E Side-By-Side Shotguns, 284
Merkel Model 47SL, 147SL Side-By-Sides, 284
Merkel Over/Under Double Rifles, 237
Mississippi 1841 Percussion Rifle, 306
Model 1885 High Wall Rifle, 230
Morini 162e Match Air Pistol, 317
Morini Model 84E Free Pistol, 166
Mossberg 590DA Double-Action Pump Shotgun, 292
Mossberg Model 500 Bantam Pump, 266
Mossberg Model 500 Camo Pump, 266
Mossberg Model 500 Persuader Security Shotguns, 291
Mossberg Model 500 Persuader/Cruiser Shotguns, 266
Mossberg Model 500 Slugster, 266
Mossberg Model 500 Sporting Pump, 266
Mossberg Model 500, 590 Ghost-Ring Shotguns, 292
Mossberg Model 500, 590 Mariner Pump, 292
Mossberg Model 590 Shotgun, 292
Mossberg Model 590 Special Purpose Shotguns, 266
Mossberg Model 695 Slugster, 289
Mossberg Model 835 Synthetic Stock, 266
Mossberg Model 835 Ulti-Mag Pump, 265
Mossberg Model HS410 Shotgun, 292
Mossberg SSi-One 12 Gauge Slug Shotgun, 289
Mossberg SSi-One Single Shot Rifle, 230
Mossberg SSi-One Turkey Shotgun, 289
Mountain Eagle Rifle, 213

N

Navy Arms "Pinched Frame" Single-Action Revolver, 183
Navy Arms 1763 Charleville, 306
Navy Arms 1851 Navy Conversion Revolver, 184
Navy Arms 1859 Sharps Cavalry Carbine, 307
Navy Arms 1860 Army Conversion Revolver, 184
Navy Arms 1861 Navy Conversion Revolver, 184
Navy Arms 1861 Springfield Rifle, 307
Navy Arms 1863 C.S. Richmond Rifle, 307
Navy Arms 1863 Springfield, 307
Navy Arms 1866 Yellow Boy Rifle, 201
Navy Arms 1872 Open Top Revolver, 183
Navy Arms 1873 Single-Action Revolver, 183
Navy Arms 1873 Springfield Cavalry Carbine, 231

34TH EDITION, 2002 • 95

Gundex

Navy Arms 1873 Winchester-Style Rifle, 201
Navy Arms 1874 Sharps Buffalo Rifle, 230
Navy Arms 1874 Sharps Cavalry Carbine, 230
Navy Arms 1875 Schofield Revolver, 183
Navy Arms 1885 High Wall Rifle, 231
Navy Arms 1892 Rifle, 202
Navy Arms 1892 Short Rifle, 202
Navy Arms 1892 Stainless Carbine, 202
Navy Arms 1892 Stainless Rifle, 202
Navy Arms Berdan 1859 Sharps Rifle, 307
Navy Arms Bisley Model Single-Action Revolver, 183
Navy Arms Deluxe 1858 Remington-Style Revolver, 296
Navy Arms Flat Top Target Model Revolver, 183
Navy Arms Iron Frame Henry, 201
Navy Arms Military Henry Rifle, 201
Navy Arms New Model Pocket Revolver, 296
Navy Arms New Model Russian Revolver, 184
Navy Arms No. 2 Creedmoor Target Rifle, 231
Navy Arms Parker-Hale Volunteer Rifle, 307
Navy Arms Parker-Hale Whitworth Military Target Rifle, 307
Navy Arms Rolling Block Buffalo Rifle, 231
Navy Arms Sharps No. 3 Long Range Rifle, 231
Navy Arms Sharps Plains Rifle, 230
Navy Arms Sharps Sporting Rifle, 230
Navy Arms Smith Carbine, 307
Navy Arms Starr Double Action Model 1858 Army Revolver, 296
Navy Arms Starr Single Action Model 1863 Army Revolver, 296
Navy Arms Steel Shot Magnum Shotgun, 314
Navy Arms T&T Shotgun, 314
Navy Model 1851 Percussion Revolver, 297
New England Firearms Camo Turkey Shotguns, 289
New England Firearms Handi-Rifle, 231
New England Firearms Special Purpose Shotguns, 289
New England Firearms Sportster™ Single-Shot Rifles, 248
New England Firearms Standard Pardner, 289
New England Firearms Super Light Rifle, 232
New England Firearms Survivor Rifle, 232
New England Firearms Survivor, 289
New England Firearms Tracker Slug Gun, 289
New Model 1858 Army Percussion Revolver, 297
New Ultra Light Arms 20RF Bolt-Action Rifle, 249
New Ultra Light Arms Bolt-Action Rifles, 213
North American Arms Guardian Auto Pistol, 103
North American Arms Guardian Pistol, 147
North American Black Widow Revolver, 184
North American Companion Percussion Revolver, 297
North American Magnum Companion Percussion Revolver, 297
North American Mini-Master, 184
North American Mini-Revolvers, 184

O

October Country Double Rifle, 308
October Country Great American Sporting Rifle, 308
October Country Heavy Rifle, 308
October Country Light American Sporting Rifle, 308
Olympic Arms CAR-97 Rifles, 196
Olympic Arms OA-96 AR Pistol, 147
Olympic Arms OA-98 AR Pistol, 147
Olympic Arms PCR-1 Rifle, 255
Olympic Arms PCR-2, PCR-3 Rifles, 255
Olympic Arms PCR-4 Rifle, 196
Olympic Arms PCR-6 Rifle, 196
Olympic Arms PCR-Servicematch Rifle, 255
One Pro .45 Auto Pistol, 148
One Pro 9 Auto Pistol, 148

P

Pacific Rifle Big Bore, African Rifles, 308
Pacific Rifle Model 1837 Zephyr, 308
Para-Ordnance LDA Auto Pistols, 149
Para-Ordnance LDA Limited Pistols, 149
Para-Ordnance Limited Pistols, 148
Para-Ordnance P-Series Auto Pistols, 148
Pardini GP Rapid Fire Match Pistol, 166
Pardini K22 Free Pistol, 166
Pardini K58 Match Air Pistol, 318
Pardini Model SP, HP Target Pistols, 166
Pedersoli Mang Target Pistol, 293
Peifer Model TS-93 Rifle, 308
Perazzi MX10 Over/Under Shotgun, 276
Perazzi MX12 Hunting Over/Under, 276
Perazzi MX20 Hunting Over/Under, 276
Perazzi MX28, MX410 Game O/U Shotguns, 277
Perazzi MX8 Over/Under Shotguns, 276
Perazzi MX8 Special Skeet Over/Under, 276
Perazzi MX8/20 Over/Under Shotgun, 276
Perazzi MX8/MX8 Special Trap, Skeet, 276
Perazzi SCO, SCO Gold, Extra and Extra Gold Shotguns, 127
Peters Stahl Autoloading Pistols, 149
Phoenix Arms HP22, HP25 Auto Pistols, 149
Piotti Boss Over/Under Shotgun, 277
Piotti King Extra Side-By-Side, 285
Piotti King No. 1 Side-By-Side, 285
Piotti Lunik Side-By-Side, 285
Piotti Piuma Side-By-Side, 285
Pocket Police 1862 Percussion Revolver, 297
Prairie River Arms PRA Bullpup Rifle, 309
Prairie River Arms PRA Classic Rifle, 308
PSA-25 Auto Pocket Pistol, 149

Q

Queen Anne Flintlock Pistol, 294

R

Raptor Bolt-Action Rifle, 213
Remington 40-XB Rangemaster Target Centerfire, 255
Remington 40-XBBR KS, 255
Remington 40-XC Target Rifle, 255
Remington 572 BDL Deluxe Fieldmaster Pump Rifle, 244
Remington 597 Auto Rifle, 241
Remington Custom Shop Auto Shotguns, 129
Remington Custom Shop Pump Shotguns, 129
Remington Custom Shop Rolling Block Rifles, 120
Remington Model 1100 Classic Trap Shotgun, 262
Remington Model 1100 LT-20 Synthetic FR RS Shotgun, 262
Remington Model 1100 Sporting 12 Shotgun, 262
Remington Model 1100 Sporting 20 Shotgun, 262
Remington Model 1100 Sporting 28, 262
Remington Model 1100 Synthetic FR CL Shotgun, 262
Remington Model 1100 Synthetic LT-20, 262
Remington Model 1100 Synthetic, 262
Remington Model 1100 Youth Synthetic Turkey Camo, 262
Remington Model 11-87 Premier Shotgun, 261
Remington Model 11-87 SC NP Shotgun, 262
Remington Model 11-87 SP and SPS Super Magnum Shotguns, 262
Remington Model 11-87 Special Purpose Magnum, 261
Remington Model 11-87 SPS Cantilever Shotgun, 261
Remington Model 11-87 SPS Special Purpose Synthetic Camo, 261
Remington Model 11-87 SPS-Deer Shotgun, 261
Remington Model 11-87 SPS-T Super Magnum Synthetic Camo, 261
Remington Model 11-87 SPS-T Turkey Camo, 261
Remington Model 11-87 Upland Special Shotgun, 262
Remington Model 300 Ideal O/U Shotgun, 277

GUNDEX

Remington Model 40-X Custom Shop Target Rifles, 115
Remington Model 552 BDL Deluxe Speedmaster Rifle, 241
Remington Model 700 ADL Deluxe Rifle, 213
Remington Model 700 ADL Synthetic Youth, 214
Remington Model 700 ADL Synthetic, 213
Remington Model 700 APR African Plains Rifle, 215
Remington Model 700 AWR Alaskan Wilderness Rifle, 215
Remington Model 700 BDL Custom Deluxe Rifle, 214
Remington Model 700 BDL DM Rifle, 214
Remington Model 700 BDL Left Hand Custom Deluxe, 214
Remington Model 700 BDL SS DM Rifle, 214
Remington Model 700 BDL SS DM-B, 214
Remington Model 700 BDL SS Rifle, 214
Remington Model 700 Classic Rifle, 213
Remington Model 700 Custom KS Mountain Rifle, 214
Remington Model 700 Custom Shop Rifles, 115
Remington Model 700 EtronX Electronic Ignition Rifle, 215
Remington Model 700 LSS Mountain Rifle, 214
Remington Model 700 LSS Rifle, 215
Remington Model 700 ML, MLS Rifles, 309
Remington Model 700 MTN DM Rifle, 215
Remington Model 700 Safari Grade, 215
Remington Model 700 Sendero Rifle, 216
Remington Model 700 Sendero SF Rifle, 216
Remington Model 700 Titanium, 215
Remington Model 700 VLS Varmint Laminated Stock, 215
Remington Model 700 VS Composite Rifle, 216
Remington Model 700 VS SF Rifle, 216
Remington Model 700 VS Varmint Synthetic Rifles, 215
Remington Model 710 Bolt-Action Rifle, 216
Remington Model 7400 Auto Rifle, 196
Remington Model 7600 Pump Action, 202
Remington Model 870 50th Anniversary Classic Trap Shotgun, 267
Remington Model 870 Express Rifle-Sighted Deer Gun, 267
Remington Model 870 Express Super Magnum, 267
Remington Model 870 Express Synthetic HD Home Defense, 267
Remington Model 870 Express Turkey, 267
Remington Model 870 Express Youth Gun, 267
Remington Model 870 Express, 267
Remington Model 870 Marine Magnum, 267

Remington Model 870 SPS Super Magnum Camo, 267
Remington Model 870 SPS Super Slug Deer Gun, 267
Remington Model 870 SPS-T Synthetic Camo Shotgun, 267
Remington Model 870 Wingmaster LW 20 ga., 267
Remington Model 870 Wingmaster Super Magnum Shotgun, 267
Remington Model 870 Wingmaster, 266
Remington Model Seven Custom KS, 216
Remington Model Seven Custom MS Rifle, 216
Remington Model Seven Custom Shop Rifles, 115
Remington Model Seven LS, 216
Remington Model Seven LSS Bolt-Action Rifle, 216
Remington Model Seven LSS, 216
Remington Model Seven SS, 216
Remington Model Seven Youth Rifle, 217
Remington Model SP-10 Magnum Camo Shotgun, 263
Remington Model SP-10 Magnum Shotgun, 262
Remington No. 1 Rolling Block Mid-Range Sporter, 232
Republic Patriot Pistol, 150
Rizzini Artemis Over/Under Shotgun, 277
Rizzini Express 90L Double Rifle, 238
Rizzini S782 EMEL Over/Under Shotgun, 277
Rizzini S790 EMEL Over/Under Shotgun, 277
Rizzini S792 EMEL Over/Under Shotgun, 277
Rizzini Sidelock Side-By-Side, 285
Rizzini Upland EL Over/Under Shotgun, 277
Rock River Arms 1911-Style Auto Pistols, 104
Rock River Arms Standard A2 Rifle, 196
Rock River Arms Standard Match Auto Pistol, 150
Rocky Mountain Arms Patriot Pistol, 150
Rogers & Spencer Percussion Revolver, 297
Rossi Matched Pair Single-Shot Rifle/Shotgun, 249
Rossi Matched Pair Single-Shot Shotgun/Rifle, 290
Rossi Model 12-G Shotgun, 290
Rossi Model 351/352 Revolvers, 169
Rossi Model 461/462 Revolvers, 169
Rossi Model 851, 169
Rossi Model 971/972 Revolvers, 169
Rottweil Paragon Over/Under, 277
RPM XL Single Shot Pistol, 190
Ruger 10/22 Autoloading Carbine, 242
Ruger 10/22 Deluxe Sporter, 242
Ruger 10/22 International Carbine, 242
Ruger 10/22 Magnum Autoloading Carbine, 242
Ruger 10/22T Target Rifle, 242
Ruger 22/45 Mark II Pistol, 152
Ruger 77/22 Hornet Bolt-Action Rifle, 217

Ruger 77/22 Rimfire Bolt-Action Rifle, 249
Ruger 77/44 Bolt-Action Rifle, 218
Ruger 77/50 In-Line Percussion Rifle, 309
Ruger Bisley Single-Action Revolver, 186
Ruger Bisley Small Frame Revolver, 186
Ruger Bisley-Vaquero Single-Action Revolver, 185
Ruger Deerfield 99/44 Carbine, 196
Ruger Engraved Red Label O/U Shotguns, 278
Ruger GP-100 Revolvers, 169
Ruger K10/22RP All-Weather Rifle, 242
Ruger K77/22 Varmint Rifle, 249
Ruger KP90 Decocker Autoloading Pistol, 151
Ruger KP94 Autoloading Pistol, 151
Ruger KTS-1234-BRE Trap Model Single-Barrel Shotgun, 290
Ruger M77 Mark II All-Weather Stainless Rifle, 217
Ruger M77 Mark II Compact Rifles, 217
Ruger M77 MARK II Express Rifle, 217
Ruger M77 MARK II Magnum Rifle, 217
Ruger M77 MARK II Rifle, 217
Ruger M77RL Ultra Light, 217
Ruger M77RSI International Carbine, 217
Ruger M77VT Target Rifle, 218
Ruger Mark II Bull Barrel, 166
Ruger Mark II Government Target Model, 166
Ruger Mark II Standard Autoloading Pistol, 152
Ruger Mark II Target Model Autoloading Pistol, 166
Ruger Mini Thirty Rifle, 197
Ruger Mini-14/5 Autoloading Rifle, 197
Ruger Model 96/22 Lever-Action Rifle, 244
Ruger Model 96/44 Lever-Action Rifle, 202
Ruger New Bearcat Single-Action, 185
Ruger New Model Blackhawk Revolver, 184
Ruger New Model Super Blackhawk, 185
Ruger No. 1 RSI International, 233
Ruger No. 1 Stainless Steel Rifles, 233
Ruger No. 1A Light Sporter, 232
Ruger No. 1B Single Shot, 232
Ruger No. 1H Tropical Rifle, 233
Ruger No. 1S Medium Sporter, 233
Ruger No. 1V Varminter, 232
Ruger Old Army Percussion Revolver, 298
Ruger P89 Autoloading Pistol, 150
Ruger P89 Double-Action-Only Autoloading Pistol, 150
Ruger P89D Decocker Autoloading Pistol, 150
Ruger P90 Manual Safety Model Autoloading Pistol, 151
Ruger P93 Compact Autoloading Pistol, 151
Ruger P95 Autoloading Pistol, 151
Ruger P97 Autoloading Pistol, 151
Ruger PC4, PC9 Carbines, 196
Ruger Red Label O/U Shotgun, 278
Ruger Redhawk, 170

GUNDEX

Ruger Single-Six and Super Single-Six Convertible, 186
Ruger SP101 Double-Action-Only Revolver, 170
Ruger SP101 Revolvers, 170
Ruger Sporting Clays O/U Shotgun, 278
Ruger Stainless Competition Model Pistol, 166
Ruger Super Redhawk 454 Casull Revolver, 170
Ruger Super Redhawk Revolver, 170
Ruger Vaquero Single-Action Revolver, 185
Ruger Woodside Over/Under Shotgun, 278
RWS 9B/9N Air Pistols, 318
RWS C-225 Air Pistols, 318
RWS/Diana Model 24 Air Rifle, 326
RWS/Diana Model 34 Air Rifle, 326
RWS/Diana Model 350 Magnum Air Rifle, 326
RWS/Diana Model 36 Air Rifle, 326
RWS/Diana Model 45 Air Rifle, 326
RWS/Diana Model 46 Air Rifle, 326
RWS/Diana Model 52 Air Rifle, 326
RWS/Diana Model 54 Air Rifle, 326
RWS/Diana Model 707/Excalibre Air Rifles, 326
RWS/Diana Model 93/94 Air Rifles, 326

S

Safari Arms Big Deuce Pistol, 167
Safari Arms Carrier Pistol, 152
Safari Arms Carry Comp Pistol, 152
Safari Arms Cohort Pistol, 152
Safari Arms Enforcer Pistol, 152
Safari Arms GI Safari Pistol, 152
Safari Arms Matchmaster Pistol, 152
Sako 75 Deluxe Rifle, 219
Sako 75 Hunter Bolt-Action Rifle, 218
Sako 75 Hunter Stainless Rifle, 219
Sako 75 Stainless Synthetic Rifle, 218
Sako 75 Varmint Rifle, 219
Sako 75 Varmint Stainless Laminated Rifle, 219
Sako Finnfire Hunter Bolt-Action Rifle, 249
Sako Finnfire Sporter Rifle, 249
Sako TRG-22 Bolt-Action Rifle, 255
Sako TRG-42 Bolt-Action Rifle, 218
Sako TRG-S Bolt-Action Rifle, 218
Sarsilmaz Over/Under Shotgun, 278
Sarsilmaz Pump Shotgun, 268
Sarsilmaz Semi-Automatic Shotgun, 263
Sauer 202 Bolt-Action Rifle, 219
Savage 24f Predator O/U Combination Gun, 238
Savage 24F-12/410 Combination Gun, 238
Savage Mark I-G Bolt-Action Rifle, 249
Savage Mark II-FSS Stainless Rifle, 250
Savage Mark II-G Bolt-Action Rifle, 250
Savage Mark II-LV Heavy Barrel Rifle, 250
Savage Model 1000G Air Rifle, 326

Savage Model 10FM Sierra Ultra Light Rifle, 219
Savage Model 10FP Tactical Rifle, 219
Savage Model 10GY, 110GY Rifle, 220
Savage Model 11 Hunter Rifles, 220
Savage Model 110FM Sierra Ultra Light Weight Rifle, 219
Savage Model 110FP Tactical Rifle, 219
Savage Model 110GXP3, 110GCXP3 Package Guns, 219
Savage Model 111 Classic Hunter Rifles, 220
Savage Model 111FXP3, 111FCXP3 Package Guns, 219
Savage Model 112 Long Range Rifles, 221
Savage Model 112BT Competition Grade Rifle, 256
Savage Model 114C Classic Rifle, 220
Savage Model 114CE Classic European, 220
Savage Model 114U Ultra Rifle, 221
Savage Model 116 Weather Warriors, 221
Savage Model 116SE Safari Express Rifle, 221
Savage Model 12 Long Range Rifles, 221
Savage Model 12VSS Varminter Rifle, 221
Savage Model 16FSS Rifle, 221
Savage Model 210F Master Shot Slug Gun, 290
Savage Model 210FT Master Shot Shotgun, 290
Savage Model 560F Air Rifle, 326
Savage Model 600F Air Rifle, 326
Savage Model 64FV Auto Rifle, 242
Savage Model 64G Auto Rifle, 242
Savage Model 900TR Target Rifle, 255
Savage Model 93FSS Magnum Rifle, 250
Savage Model 93FVSS Magnum Rifle, 250
Savage Model 93G Magnum Bolt-Action Rifle, 250
Savage Sport Striker Bolt-Action Hunting Handgun, 191
Savage Striker Bolt-Action Hunting Handgun, 190
Second Model Brown Bess Musket, 309
Seecamp LWS 32 Stainless DA Auto, 152
Sharps 1874 Rifle, 234
Sheriff Model 1851 Percussion Revolver, 298
Shiloh Sharps 1874 Business Rifle, 234
Shiloh Sharps 1874 Long Range Express, 234
Shiloh Sharps 1874 Montana Roughrider, 234
SIG Pro Auto Pistol, 153
SIG Sauer P220 Service Auto Pistol, 152
SIG Sauer P220 Sport Auto Pistol, 153
SIG Sauer P226 Service Pistol, 153
SIG Sauer P229 DA Auto Pistol, 153
SIG Sauer P229 Sport Auto Pistol, 153
SIG Sauer P232 Personal Size Pistol, 153
SIG Sauer P239 Pistol, 154

SIG Sauer P245 Compact Auto Pistol, 153
Sigarms SA5 Over/Under Shotgun, 278
Sigarms SHR 970 Synthetic Rifle, 222
SKB Model 385 Side-By-Side, 285
SKB Model 385 Sporting Clays, 285
SKB Model 485 Side-By-Side, 285
SKB Model 505 Shotguns, 278
SKB Model 585 Gold Package, 279
SKB Model 585 Over/Under Shotgun, 279
SKB Model 785 Over/Under Shotgun, 278
Smith & Wesson 9mm Recon Auto Pistol Model, 154
Smith & Wesson Enhanced Sigma Series Pistols, 156
Smith & Wesson Model 10 M&P HB Revolver, 170
Smith & Wesson Model 14 Full Lug Revolver, 170
Smith & Wesson Model 15 Combat Masterpiece, 171
Smith & Wesson Model 19 Combat Magnum, 171
Smith & Wesson Model 2213, 2214 Sportsman Autos, 154
Smith & Wesson Model 22A Sport Pistol, 154
Smith & Wesson Model 22A Target Pistol, 167
Smith & Wesson Model 22S Sport Pistols, 154
Smith & Wesson Model 22S Target Pistol, 167
Smith & Wesson Model 242 Airlite Ti Revolver, 172
Smith & Wesson Model 296 Airlite Ti Revolver, 172
Smith & Wesson Model 331, 332 Airlite Ti Revolvers, 173
Smith & Wesson Model 337 Chiefs Special Airlite Ti, 173
Smith & Wesson Model 342 Centennial Airlite Ti, 173
Smith & Wesson Model 36, 37 Chief's Special & Airweight, 171
Smith & Wesson Model 36LS, 60LS LadySmith, 171
Smith & Wesson Model 3913 Traditional Double Action, 155
Smith & Wesson Model 3913-LS LadySmith Auto, 155
Smith & Wesson Model 3913TSW/3953TSW Auto Pistols, 155
Smith & Wesson Model 3953 DAO Pistol, 155
Smith & Wesson Model 4006 TDA Auto, 155
Smith & Wesson Model 4013, 4053 TSW Autos, 154
Smith & Wesson Model 4043, 4046 DA Pistols, 155
Smith & Wesson Model 41 Target, 167
Smith & Wesson Model 410 DA Auto Pistol, 154
Smith & Wesson Model 442 Centennial Airweight, 173

98 • GUNS ILLUSTRATED

GUNDEX

Smith & Wesson Model 4500 Series Autos, 155
Smith & Wesson Model 4513TSW/4553TSW Pistols, 155
Smith & Wesson Model 457 TDA Auto Pistol, 154
Smith & Wesson Model 586,686 Distinguished Combat Magnums, 172
Smith & Wesson Model 5900 Series Auto Pistols, 156
Smith & Wesson Model 60 357 Magnum, 171
Smith & Wesson Model 610 Classic Hunter Revolver, 173
Smith & Wesson Model 617 Full Lug Revolver, 173
Smith & Wesson Model 625 Revolver, 172
Smith & Wesson Model 629 Classic DX Revolver, 171
Smith & Wesson Model 629 Classic Revolver, 171
Smith & Wesson Model 629 Revolvers, 171
Smith & Wesson Model 637 Airweight Revolver, 172
Smith & Wesson Model 638 Airweight Bodyguard, 173
Smith & Wesson Model 64 Stainless M&P, 172
Smith & Wesson Model 640 Centennial, 173
Smith & Wesson Model 642 Airweight Revolver, 173
Smith & Wesson Model 642LS LadySmith Revolver, 173
Smith & Wesson Model 649 Bodyguard Revolver, 173
Smith & Wesson Model 65, 171
Smith & Wesson Model 657 Revolver, 173
Smith & Wesson Model 65LS Ladysmith, 172
Smith & Wesson Model 66 Stainless Combat Magnum, 172
Smith & Wesson Model 67 Combat Masterpiece, 172
Smith & Wesson Model 686 Magnum PLUS Revolver, 172
Smith & Wesson Model 6906 Double-Action Auto, 156
Smith & Wesson Model 696 Revolver, 173
Smith & Wesson Model 908 Auto Pistol, 154
Smith & Wesson Model 910 DA Auto Pistol, 155
Smith & Wesson Model CS40 Chiefs Special Auto, 156
Smith & Wesson Model CS45 Chiefs Special Auto, 156
Smith & Wesson Model CS9 Chiefs Special Auto, 156
Smith & Wesson Sigma SW380 Auto, 156
Smith & Wesson Model 317 Airlite, 317 Ladysmith Revolvers, 172
Snake Charmer II Shotgun, 290

Spiller & Burr Revolver, 298
Springfield Armory 1911-Style Auto Pistols, 106
Springfield Inc. Long Slide 1911 A1 Pistol, 157
Springfield Inc. Ultra Compact Pistol, 157
Springfield, Inc. 1911A1 Bullseye Wadcutter Pistol, 167
Springfield, Inc. 1911A1 Champion Pistol, 157
Springfield, Inc. 1911A1 High Capacity Pistol, 157
Springfield, Inc. 1911A1 N.M. Hardball Pistol, 167
Springfield, Inc. 1911A1 Trophy Match Pistol, 167
Springfield, Inc. 1911A1 V-Series Ported Pistols, 157
Springfield, Inc. Basic Competition Pistol, 167
Springfield, Inc. Distinguished Pistol, 167
Springfield, Inc. Expert Pistol, 167
Springfield, Inc. Full-Size 1911A1 Auto Pistol, 156
Springfield, Inc. M1A Rifle, 197
Springfield, Inc. M1A Super Match, 256
Springfield, Inc. M1A/M-21 Tactical Model Rifle, 256
Springfield, Inc. M6 Scout Rifle/Shotgun, 238
Springfield, Inc. TRP Pistols, 157
SSK Industries AR-15 Rifles, 117
SSK Industries Contender and Encore Pistols, 113
Steyr Classic Mannlicher SBS Rifle, 222
Steyr LP 5CP Match Air Pistol, 318
Steyr LP10P Match Pistol, 318
Steyr M & S Series Auto Pistols, 157
Steyr SBS Forester Rifle, 222
Steyr SBS Prohunter Rifle, 222
Steyr Scout Bolt-Action Rifle, 222
Steyr SSG Bolt-Action Rifle, 222
STI 2011 Auto Pistols, 106
STI Compact Auto Pistols, 106
STI Eagle 5.0 Pistol, 168
Stoeger American Eagle Luger, 157
Stoeger/IGA Coach and Deluxe Coach Gun, 286
Stoeger/IGA Condor I Over/Under Shotgun, 279
Stoeger/IGA Condor Waterfowl O/U, 279
Stoeger/IGA Deluxe Uplander Supreme Shotgun, 286
Stoeger/IGA English Stock Side-By-Side, 286
Stoeger/IGA Ladies Side-By-Side, 286
Stoeger/IGA Turkey Model O/U, 279
Stoeger/IGA Turkey Side-By-Side, 286
Stoeger/IGA Uplander Shotgun, 286
Stoeger/IGA Uplander Side-By-Side Shotgun, 285
Stoeger/IGA Youth Side-By-Side, 286
Stoner SR-15 M-5 Rifle, 197
Stoner SR-15 Match Rifle, 256
Stoner SR-25 Carbine, 197
Stoner SR-25 Match Rifle, 256

T

Tactical Response TR-870 Standard Model Shotgun, 292
Tanner 300 Meter Free Rifle, 256
Tanner 50 Meter Free Rifle, 256
Tanner Standard UIT Rifle, 256
Tar-Hunt RSG-12 Professional Rifled Slug Gun, 290
Tar-Hunt RSG-20 Mountaineer Slug Gun, 290
Taurus Model 22H Raging Hornet Revolver, 175
Taurus Model 415 Revolver, 175
Taurus Model 415Ti, 445Ti, 450Ti, 617Ti Revolvers, 176
Taurus Model 425/627 Tracker Revolvers, 175
Taurus Model 44 Revolver, 175
Taurus Model 444/454/480 Raging Bull Revolvers, 176
Taurus Model 445, 445CH Revolvers, 175
Taurus Model 450 Revolver, 176
Taurus Model 605 Revolver, 175
Taurus Model 608 Revolver, 176
Taurus Model 617 Revolver, 176
Taurus Model 617ULT Revolver, 176
Taurus Model 63 Revolver, 173
Taurus Model 650CIA Revolver, 176
Taurus Model 65 Revolver, 174
Taurus Model 66 Revolver, 174
Taurus Model 66 Silhouette Revolver, 174
Taurus Model 72 Pump Rifle, 244
Taurus Model 817 Ultra-Lite Revolver, 176
Taurus Model 82 Heavy Barrel Revolver, 174
Taurus Model 85 Revolver, 174
Taurus Model 850CIA Revolver, 177
Taurus Model 85CH Revolver, 174
Taurus Model 85Ti Revolver, 174
Taurus Model 85UL/Ti Revolver, 174
Taurus Model 94 Revolver, 175
Taurus Model 941 Revolver, 177
Taurus Model 970/971 Tracker Revolvers, 177
Taurus Model 980/981 Silhouette Revolvers, 177
Taurus Model PT 22/PT 25 Auto Pistols, 158
Taurus Model PT-100B Auto Pistol, 158
Taurus Model PT-111 Millennium Auto Pistol, 158
Taurus Model PT-111 Millennium Titanium Pistol, 158
Taurus Model PT-138 Auto Pistol, 158
Taurus Model PT-911 Auto Pistol, 158
Taurus Model PT92B Auto Pistol, 158
Taurus Model PT-938 Auto Pistol, 159
Taurus Model PT-940 Auto Pistol, 159
Taurus Model PT-945 Auto Pistol, 159
Taurus Model PT-957 Auto Pistol, 159
Taurus Model PT99 Auto Pistol, 158
Taurus PT-132 Millenium Auto Pistol, 158

Gundex

Taurus PT-140 Millenium Auto Pistol, 158
Taurus PT-145 Millenium Auto Pistol, 158
Tech Force 25 Air Rifle, 327
Tech Force 35 Air Pistol, 318
Tech Force 36 Air Rifle, 327
Tech Force 51 Air Rifle, 327
Tech Force 6 Air Rifle, 327
Tech Force 8 Air Pistol, 318
Tech Force BS4 Olympic Competition Air Rifle, 327
Tech Force S2-1 Air Pistol, 318
Tech Force SS2 Olympic Competition Air Pistol, 318
Texas Paterson 1836 Revolver, 298
Thompson/Center 22 LR Classic Rifle, 242
Thompson/Center Black Diamond Rifle, 310
Thompson/Center Black Mountain Magnum Rifle, 309
Thompson/Center Black Mountain Magnum Shotgun, 314
Thompson/Center Contender Carbine, 234
Thompson/Center Contender Shooter's Package, 191
Thompson/Center Contender, 191
Thompson/Center Encore 209x50 Magnum Pistol, 294
Thompson/Center Encore 209x50 Magnum, 310
Thompson/Center Encore Pistol, 191
Thompson/Center Encore Rifle, 235
Thompson/Center Encore Rifled Slug Gun, 290
Thompson/Center Fire Storm Rifle, 310
Thompson/Center Hawken Rifle, 311
Thompson/Center Pennsylvania Hunter Carbine, 310
Thompson/Center Pennsylvania Hunter Rifle, 310
Thompson/Center Stainless Contender, 191
Thompson/Center Stainless Encore Pistol, 191
Thompson/Center Stainless Encore Rifle, 235
Thompson/Center Stainless Super 14, 191
Thompson/Center Super 14 Contender, 168
Thompson/Center Super 16 Contender, 168
Thompson/Center System 1 In-Line Rifle, 310
Thompson/Center Thunderhawk Shadow, 310
Tikka Continental Long Range Hunting Rifle, 223
Tikka Continental Varmint Rifle, 223
Tikka Sporter Rifle, 256
Tikka Whitetail Hunter Bolt-Action Rifle, 223
Tikka Whitetail Hunter Deluxe Rifle, 223
Tikka Whitetail Hunter Stainless Synthetic, 223
Tikka Whitetail Hunter Synthetic Rifle, 223
Time Precision Bolt-Action Rifles, 115
Traditions 1860 Henry Rifles, 202
Traditions 1866 Sporting Yellowboy Rifles, 202
Traditions 1866 Yellowboy Carbine, 203
Traditions 1873 Sporting Carbine, 203
Traditions 1873 Sporting Rifles, 203
Traditions 1874 Sharps Deluxe Rifle, 235
Traditions 1874 Sharps Standard Rifle, 235
Traditions ALS 2100 Series Semi-Automatic Shotguns, 263
Traditions ALS 2100 Turkey Semi-Automatic Shotgun, 263
Traditions ALS 2100 Waterfowl Semi-Automatic Shotgun, 263
Traditions Buckhunter In-Line Rifles, 311
Traditions Buckhunter Pro In-Line Pistol, 294
Traditions Buckhunter Pro Magnum In-Line Rifles, 311
Traditions Buckhunter Pro Shotgun, 314
Traditions Buckskinner Carbine, 311
Traditions Classic Series O/U Shotguns, 279
Traditions Deerhunter Rifle Series, 311
Traditions E-Bolt 209 Bolt-Action Rifles, 311
Traditions Elite Series Side-By-Side Shotguns, 286
Traditions Hawken Woodsman Rifle, 311
Traditions Kentucky Pistol, 294
Traditions Kentucky Rifle, 311
Traditions Lightning 45 LD Bolt-Action Rifles, 312
Traditions Lightning Lightweight Magnum Bolt-Action Rifles, 312
Traditions Lightning Mag Bolt-Action Muzzleloader, 312
Traditions Mag 350 Series O/U Shotguns, 279
Traditions Magnum Plains Rifle, 312
Traditions Panther Sidelock Rifle, 312
Traditions Pennsylvania Rifle, 312
Traditions Pioneer Pistol, 294
Traditions Rolling Block Sporting Rifle, 235
Traditions Shenandoah Rifle, 312
Traditions Tennessee Rifle, 313
Traditions Thunder Magnum Rifle, 313
Traditions Tracker 209 In-Line Rifles, 313
Traditions Trapper Pistol, 294
Traditions Vest-Pocket Derringer, 294
Traditions William Parker Pistol, 294
Tristar Phantom Auto Shotguns, 263
Tristar Phantom HP Auto Shotgun, 292
Tristar Rota Model 411 Side-By-Side, 286
Tristar Rota Model 411D Side-By-Side, 286
Tristar Rota Model 411F Side-By-Side, 286
Tristar Rota Model 411R Coach Gun Side-By-Side, 286
Tristar Silver II Shotgun, 279
Tristar Silver Sporting O/U, 279
Tristar TR-Class SL Emilio Rizzini O/U, 280
Tristar TR-Royal Emillio Rizzini Over/Under, 279
Tristar WS/OU 12 Shotgun, 280
Tristar/Uberti 1860 Henry Rifle, 203
Tristar/Uberti 1860 Henry Trapper Carbine, 203
Tristar/Uberti 1866 Sporting Rifle, Carbine, 203
Tristar/Uberti 1873 Sporting Rifle, 203
Tristar/Uberti 1885 Single Shot, 235
Tristar/Uberti Regulator Revolver, 186
Tristar-TR-I, II "Emilio Rizzini" Over/Unders, 280
Tristar-TR-L "Emilio Rizzini" Over/Under, 280
Tristar-TR-MAG "Emilio Rizzini" Over/Under, 280
Tristar-TR-SC "Emilio Rizzini" Over/Under, 279
Tryon Trailblazer Rifle, 313

U

U.S. Fire-Arms "Buntline Special", 187
U.S. Fire-Arms "China Camp" Cowboy Action Revolver, 187
U.S. Fire-Arms Bird Head Model Revolver, 187
U.S. Fire-Arms Bisley Model Revolver, 187
U.S. Fire-Arms Flattop Target Revolver, 187
U.S. Fire-Arms Nettleton Cavalry Revolver, 187
U.S. Fire-Arms Omni-Potent Six Shooter, 187
U.S. Fire-Arms Single Action Army Revolver, 187
U.S. Patent Fire-Arms 1862 Pocket Navy, 298
Uberti 1861 Navy Percussion Revolver, 298
Uberti 1873 Buckhorn Single-Action, 186
Uberti 1873 Cattleman Single-Action, 186
Uberti 1875 SA Army Outlaw Revolver, 186
Uberti 1875 Schofield Revolver, 187
Uberti 1890 Army Outlaw Revolver, 186
Uberti Baby Rolling Block Carbine, 235
Uberti Bisley Model Flat Top Target Revolver, 187
Uberti Bisley Model Single-Action Revolver, 187
Uberti New Model Russian Revolver, 186
Uberti Rolling Block Target Pistol, 191
Unique D.E.S. 32U Target Pistol, 168
Unique D.E.S. 69U Target Pistol, 168
Unique Model 96U Target Pistol, 168
United States Fire-Arms Single-Action Revolvers, 111

V

Vektor Bushveld Bolt-Action Rifle, 223
Vektor CP-1 Compact Pistol, 160
Vektor H5 Slide-Action Rifle, 203

GUNDEX

Vektor Model 98 Bolt-Action Rifle, 223
Vektor SP1 Auto Pistol, 160
Vektor SP1 Sport Pistol, 160
Vektor SP1 Target Pistol, 160
Vektor SP1 Tuned Sport Pistol, 160
Vektor SP1, SP2 Compact General's Model Pistol, 160
Vektor SP1, SP2 Ultra Sport Pistols, 160
Vektor SP1/SP2 Auto Pistols, 106
Verona LX501 Hunting O/U Shotguns, 280
Verona LX680 Skeet/Sporting, Trap O/U Shotguns, 280
Verona LX680 Sporting Over/Under Shotguns, 280
Verona LX692 Gold Hunting Over/Under Shotguns, 280
Verona LX692 Gold Sporting Over/Under Shotguns, 280
Volquartsen Custom 22 Caliber Auto Pistols, 107
Volquartsen Custom 22 Caliber Auto Rifles, 117

W

Walker 1847 Percussion Revolver, 298
Walther CP88 Competition Pellet Pistol, 318
Walther CP88 Pellet Pistol, 318
Walther CP99 Air Pistol, 318
Walther GSP Match Pistol, 168
Walther LP20l Match Pistol, 318
Walther Model TPH Auto Pistol, 161
Walther P-5 Auto Pistol, 161
Walther P88 Compact Pistol, 161
Walther P99 Auto Pistol, 161
Walther P990 Auto Pistol, 161
Walther PP Auto Pistol, 160
Walther PPK American Auto Pistol, 161
Walther PPK/S Air Pistol, 318
Walther PPK/S American Auto Pistol, 160
Weatherby Athena Grade IV O/U Shotguns, 280
Weatherby Athena Grade V Classic Field O/U, 280
Weatherby Athena III Classic Field O/U, 280
Weatherby Custom Shop Bolt-Action Rifles, 116
Weatherby Mark V Accumark CFP Pistol, 191
Weatherby Mark V Accumark Rifle, 225
Weatherby Mark V Accumark Ultra Lightweight Rifles, 225
Weatherby Mark V CFP Pistol, 191
Weatherby Mark V Dangerous Game Rifle, 225
Weatherby Mark V Deluxe Bolt-Action Rifle, 223
Weatherby Mark V Euromark Rifle, 224
Weatherby Mark V Eurosport Rifle, 224

Weatherby Mark V Fibermark Rifles, 225
Weatherby Mark V Lazermark Rifle, 224
Weatherby Mark V SLS Stainless Laminate Sporter, 224
Weatherby Mark V Sporter Rifle, 224
Weatherby Mark V Stainless Rifle, 224
Weatherby Mark V SVM/SPM Rifles, 225
Weatherby Mark V Synthetic, 224
Weatherby Orion Grade I Field O/U, 281
Weatherby Orion Grade II Classic Field O/U, 281
Weatherby Orion Grade II Classic Sporting O/U, 281
Weatherby Orion Grade II Sporting, 281
Weatherby Orion Grade III Classic Field O/U, 281
Weatherby Orion Grade III Field O/U Shotguns, 280
Weatherby Orion III English Field O/U, 281
Weatherby Orion SSC Over/Under Shotgun, 281
Weatherby Orion Upland O/U, 281
Weatherby SAS Auto Shotgun, 263
Wesson & Harrington 38-55 Target Rifle, 235
Wesson & Harrington Buffalo Classic Rifle, 235
Wesson & Harrington Long Tom Classic Shotgun, 290
Whiscombe JW Series Air Rifles, 327
White Barn Workshop 22 Caliber Auto Rifles, 118
White Barn Workshop Mini-14 Auto Rifle, 118
White Model 97 Whitetail Hunter Rifle, 313
White Model 98 Elite Hunter Rifle, 313
Wilderness Explorer Multi-Caliber Carbine, 225
Wilkinson Linda Auto Pistol, 162
Wilkinson Sherry Auto Pistol, 162
Winchester Model 1300 Black Shadow Field Gun, 268
Winchester Model 1300 Camp Defender®, 292
Winchester Model 1300 Deer Black Shadow Gun, 268
Winchester Model 1300 Defender Pump Guns, 292
Winchester Model 1300 NWTF Black Shadow Turkey Gun, 268
Winchester Model 1300 NWTF camouflage guns, 268
Winchester Model 1300 Ranger Pump Gun, 268
Winchester Model 1300 Stainless Marine Pump Gun, 292
Winchester Model 1300 Upland Pump Gun, 268
Winchester Model 1300 Walnut Field Pump, 268

Winchester Model 1885 Low Wall Rimfire, 250
Winchester Model 1886 Extra Light Grade I, 244
Winchester Model 1886 Extra Light Lever-Action Rifle, 204
Winchester Model 1895 Lever-Action Rifle, 204
Winchester Model 52b Bolt-Action Rifle, 250
Winchester Model 63 Auto Rifle, 242
Winchester Model 70 Black Shadow, 226
Winchester Model 70 Classic Compact, 226
Winchester Model 70 Classic Featherweight, 226
Winchester Model 70 Classic Safari Express, 226
Winchester Model 70 Classic Sporter LT, 225
Winchester Model 70 Classic Stainless Rifle, 226
Winchester Model 70 Classic Super Grade, 226
Winchester Model 70 Coyote, 226
Winchester Model 70 Stealth Rifle, 226
Winchester Model 70 WSM Rifles, 226
Winchester Model 94 Legacy, 204
Winchester Model 94 Ranger Compact, 204
Winchester Model 94 Ranger, 204
Winchester Model 94 Traditional Big Bore, 203
Winchester Model 94 Traditional-CW, 203
Winchester Model 94 Trails End™, 204
Winchester Model 94 Trapper™, 203
Winchester Model 9410 Lever-Action ShotgUN, 268
Winchester Model 9422 Lever-Action Rifles, 244
Winchester Super X2 Auto Shotgun, 263
Winchester Super X2 Field 3" Auto Shotgun, 263
Winchester Super X2 Sporting Clays Auto Shotgun, 263
Winchester Supreme O/U Shotguns, 281
Winchester Timber Carbine, 203

Z

Zouave Percussion Rifle, 313

NUMBERS

1861 Navy Percussion Revolver, 298
1862 Pocket Navy Percussion Revolver, 298
1st U.S. Model Dragoon, 298
2nd U.S. Model Dragoon Revolver, 298
3rd U.S. Model Dragoon Revolver, 298

34TH EDITION, 2002 • 101

SEMI-CUSTOM HANDGUNS — AUTOLOADERS

Ed Brown Classic

Ed Brown Classic Class A

Kimber Custom Compact CDP

BRILEY 1911-STYLE AUTO PISTOLS
Caliber: 9mm Para., 38 Super, 40 S&W, 10-shot magazine; 45 ACP, 8-shot magazine. **Barrel:** 3.6" or 5". **Weight:** NA. **Length:** NA. **Grips:** rosewood or rubber. **Sights:** Bo-Mar adjustable rear, Briley dovetail blade front. **Features:** Modular or Caspian alloy, carbon steel or stainless steel frame; match barrel and trigger group; lowered and flared ejection port; front and rear serrations on slide; beavertail grip safety; hot blue, hard chrome or stainless steel finish. Introduced 2000. Made in U.S. From Briley Manufacturing Inc.
Price: Fantom (3.6" bbl., fixed low-mount rear sight, armor coated lower receiver) .... from **$1,795.00**
Price: Fantom with two-port compensator .... from **$2,145.00**
Price: Advantage (5" bbl., adj. low-mount rear sight, checkered mainspring housing) .... from **$1,495.00**
Price: Versatility Plus (5" bbl., adj. low-mount rear sight, modular or Caspian frame) .... from **$1,695.00**
Price: Signature Series (5" bbl., adj. low-mount rear sight, 40 S&W only) .... from **$1,995.00**
Price: Plate Master (5" bbl. with compensator, lightened slide, Briley scope mount) .... from **$1,795.00**
Price: El Presidente (5" bbl. with Briley quad compensator, Briley scope mount) .... from **$2,195.00**

ED BROWN CLASSIC CUSTOM
AND CLASS A LIMITED 1911-STYLE AUTO PISTOLS
Caliber: 45 ACP; 7-shot magazine; 40 S&W, 400 Cor-Bon, 38 Super, 9x23, 9mm Para. **Barrel:** 4.25", 5", 6". **Weight:** NA. **Length:** NA. **Grips:** Hogue exotic checkered wood. **Sights:** Bo-Mar or Novak rear, blade front. **Features:** Blued or stainless steel frame; ambidextrous safety; beavertail grip safety; checkered forestrap and mainspring housing; match-grade barrel; slotted hammer; long lightweight or Videki short steel trigger. Many options offered. Made in U.S. by Ed Brown Products.
Price: Classic Custom (45 ACP, 5" barrel) .... from **$2,750.00**
Price: Class A Limited (all calibers; several bbl. lengths in competition and carry forms) .... from **$2,250.00**

EUROPEAN AMERICAN ARMORY WITNESS AUTO PISTOLS
Caliber: 9mm Para., 9x21, 38 Super, 40 S&W, 45 ACP, 10mm; 10-shot magazine. **Barrel:** 3.55", 3.66", 4.25", 4.5", 4.75", 5.25". **Weight:** 26 to 38 oz. **Length:** 7.25" to 10.5" overall. **Grips:** Black rubber, smooth walnut, checkered walnut, ivory polymer. **Sights:** three-dot, windage-adjustable or fully adjustable rear, blade front. **Features:** Single and double action; polymer or forged steel frame; forged steel slide; field strips without tools; ergonomic grip angle; front and rear serrations on slide; matte blue and stainless steel finish. Frame can be converted to other calibers. Imported from Italy by European American Armory.
Price: Witness Full Size (4.5" bbl., three-dot sights, 8.1" overall) .... from **$399.00**
Price: Witness Compact (3.66" bbl., three-dot sights, 7.25" overall) .... from **$399.00**

Price: Carry-Comp (4.25" bbl. with compensator, three-dot sights, 8.1" overall) .... from **$439.00**
Price: Gold Team (5.25" bbl. with compensator, adjustable sights, 10.5" overall) .... from **$2,195.00**
Price: Silver Team (5.25" bbl. with compensator, adjustable sights, 9.75" overall) .... from **$999.00**
Price: Limited Class (4.75" barrel, adj. sights and trigger, drilled for scope mount) .... from **$999.00**
Price: P-Series (4.55" bbl., polymer frame in four colors, many porting and sight options) .... from **$379.00**

KIMBER CUSTOM 1911-STYLE AUTO PISTOLS
Caliber: 9mm Para., 38 Super, 9-shot magazines; 40 S&W, 8-shot magazine; 45 ACP, 7-shot magazine. **Barrel:** 5". **Weight:** 38 oz. **Length:** 8.7" overall. **Grips:** Black synthetic, smooth or double-diamond checkered rosewood, or double-diamond checkered walnut. **Sights:** McCormick low profile or Kimber adjustable rear, blade front. **Features:** Machined steel slide, frame and barrel; front and rear beveled slide serrations; cut and button-rifled, match-grade barrel; adjustable aluminum trigger; full-length guide rod; Commander-style hammer; high-ride beavertail safety; beveled magazine well. Other models available. Made in U.S. by Kimber Mfg. Inc.
Price: Custom (black matte finish) **$730.00**
Price: Custom Royal (polished blue finish, checkered rosewood grips) **$886.00**
Price: Custom Stainless (satin-finished stainless steel frame and slide) **$832.00**
Price: Custom Target (matte black or stainless finish, Kimber adj. sight) **$837.00**

102 • GUNS ILLUSTRATED

Semi-Custom Handguns — Autoloaders

Kimber Custom Pro CDP

Kimber Ultra CDP

North American Arms Guardian with gold accents

Price: Custom Compact CDP (4" bbl., alum. frame, tritium
three-dot sights, 28 oz.) **$1,142.00**
Price: Custom Pro CDP (4" bbl., alum. frame, tritium sights,
full-length grip, 28 oz.) **$1,142.00**
Price: Ultra CDP (3" bbl., aluminum frame, tritium sights,
25 oz.) **$1,142.00**
Price: Gold Match (polished blue finish, hand-fitted barrel,
ambid. safety) **$1,169.00**
Price: Stainless Gold Match (stainless steel frame and slide,
hand-fitted bbl., amb. safety) **$1,315.00**
Price: Gold Combat (hand-fitted, stainless barrel; KimPro
black finish, tritium sights) **$1,682.00**
Price: Gold Combat Stainless (stainless frame and slide,
satin silver finish, tritium sights) **$1,623.00**
Price: Super Match (satin stainless frame, KimPro black finished,
stainless slide) **$1,927.00**

LES BAER CUSTOM 1911-STYLE AUTO PISTOLS
Caliber: 9mm Para., 38 Super, 40 S&W, 45 ACP, 400 Cor-Bon; 7- or 8-shot magazine. **Barrel:** 4-1/4", 5", 6". **Weight:** 28 to 40 oz. **Length:** NA. **Grips:** Checkered cocobolo. **Sights:** Low-mount combat fixed, combat fixed with tritium inserts or low-mount adjustable rear, dovetail front. **Features:** Forged steel or aluminum frame; slide serrated front and rear; lowered and flared ejection port; beveled magazine well; speed trigger with 4-pound pull; beavertail grip safety; ambidextrous safety. Other models available. Made in U.S. by Les Baer Custom.
Price: Baer 1911 Premier II 5" Model (5" bbl., optional stainless steel frame
and slide) .... from **$1,428.00**
Price: Premier II 6" Model (6" barrel) .... from **$1,595.00**
Price: Premier II LW1 (forged aluminum frame,
steel slide and barrel) .... from **$1,740.00**
Price: Custom Carry (4" or 5" barrel, steel frame) .... from **$1,640.00**
Price: Custom Carry (4" barrel, aluminum frame) .... from **$1,923.00**
Price: Swift Response Pistol (fixed tritium sights,
Bear Coat finish) .... from **$2,495.00**
Price: Monolith (5" barrel and slide with extra-long dust cover)
.... from **$1,599.00**
Price: Stinger (4-1/4" barrel, steel or aluminum frame) ... from **$1,491.00**
Price: Thunder Ranch Special (tritium fixed combat sight,
Thunder Ranch logo) .... from **$1,620.00**
Price: National Match Hardball (low-mount adj. sight;
meets DCM rules) .... from **$1,335.00**
Price: Bullseye Wadcutter Pistol (Bo-Mar rib w/ adj. sight,
guar. 2-1/2" groups) .... from **$1,495.00**
Price: Ultimate Master Combat (5" or 6" bbl., adj. sights,
checkered front strap) .... from **$2,376.00**
Price: Ultimate Master Combat Compensated (four-port
compensator, adj. sights) .... from **$2,476.00**

NORTH AMERICAN ARMS GUARDIAN AUTO PISTOL
Caliber: 32 ACP, 6-shot magazine. **Barrel:** 2.18". **Weight:** 13.57 oz. **Length:** 4.36" overall. **Grips:** Checkered or smooth; cocobolo, kingwood, winewood, goncalo alves, pau ferro, white or black simulated mother of pearl. **Sights:** White dot, fiber optics or tritium (nine models). **Features:** Double action only; stainless steel frame and slide; barrel porting; frame stippling; forward striped or scalloped slide serrations; meltdown (rounded edges) treatment; slide/frame finishes available in combinations that include black titanium, stainless steel, gold titanium and highly polished or matte choices. From North American Arms Custom Shop.
Price: NAA-32 Guardian **$359.00**
Price: Gold or black titanium finish .... add **$120.00**
Price: High-polish finish .... add **$150.00**
Price: Ported barrel .... add **$90.00**

SEMI-CUSTOM HANDGUNS — AUTOLOADERS

North American Arms Guardian with high polish finish

North American Arms Guardian with matte finish

Rock River Arms Elite Commando

Rock River Arms Standard Match

Rock River Arms National Match Hardball

ROCK RIVER ARMS 1911-STYLE AUTO PISTOLS
Caliber: 9mm Para., 38 Super, 40 S&W, 45 ACP. **Barrel:** 4" or 5". **Weight:** NA. **Length:** NA. **Grips:** Double-diamond, checkered cocobolo or black synthetic. **Sights:** Bo-Mar low-mount adjustable, Novak fixed with tritium inserts, Heine fixed or Rock River scope mount; dovetail front blade. **Features:** Chrome-moly, machined steel frame and slide; slide serrated front and rear; aluminum speed trigger with 3.5-4 lb. pull; national match KART barrel; lowered and flared ejection port; tuned and polished extractor; beavertail grip safety; beveled mag. well. Other frames offered. Made in U.S. by Rock River Arms Inc.
Price: Elite Commando (4" barrel, Novak tritium sights) . . from **$1,175.00**
Price: Standard Match (5" barrel, Heine fixed sights) . . . . . from **$1,025.00**
Price: National Match Hardball (5" barrel, Bo-Mar adj. sights)
. . . . from **$1,275.00**
Price: Bullseye Wadcutter (5" barrel, Rock River slide scope
 mount) . . . . from **$1,380.00**
Price: Basic Limited Match (5" barrel, Bo-Mar adj. sights)
. . . . from **$1,395.00**
Price: Limited Match (5" barrel, guaranteed 1-1/2" groups
 at 50 yards) . . . . from **$1,795.00**
Price: Hi-Cap Basic Limited (5" barrel, four frame choices)
. . . . from **$1,895.00**
Price: Ultimate Match Achiever (5" bbl. with compensator,
 mount and Aimpoint) . . . . from **$2,255.00**
Price: Match Master Steel (5" bbl. with compensator,
 mount and Aimpoint) . . . . from **$2,355.00**

SEMI-CUSTOM HANDGUNS — AUTOLOADERS

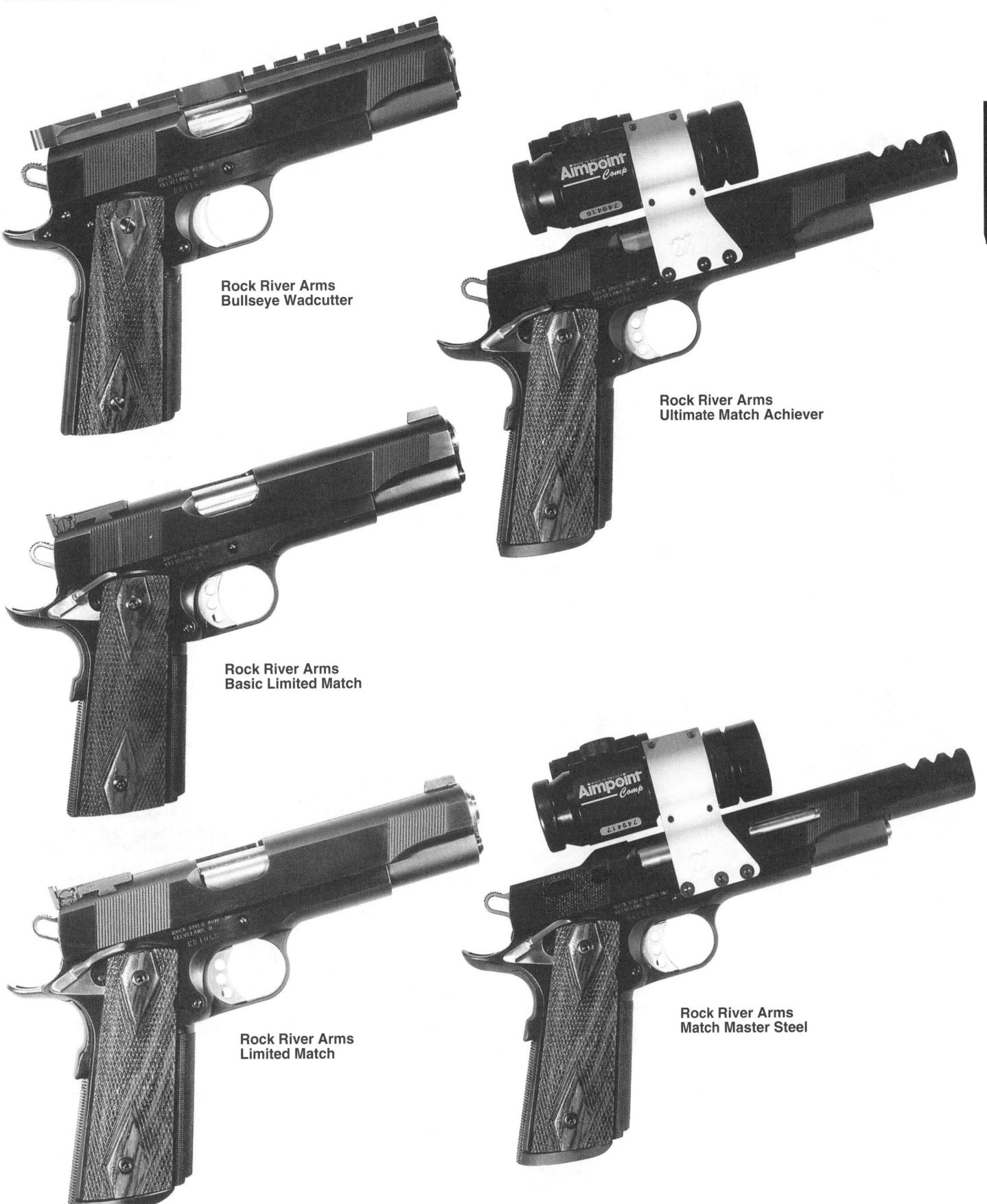

**Rock River Arms
Bullseye Wadcutter**

**Rock River Arms
Ultimate Match Achiever**

**Rock River Arms
Basic Limited Match**

**Rock River Arms
Limited Match**

**Rock River Arms
Match Master Steel**

SEMI-CUSTOM HANDGUNS — AUTOLOADERS

Springfield Pro

Vektor SP1 Target

Vektor SP1 Sport

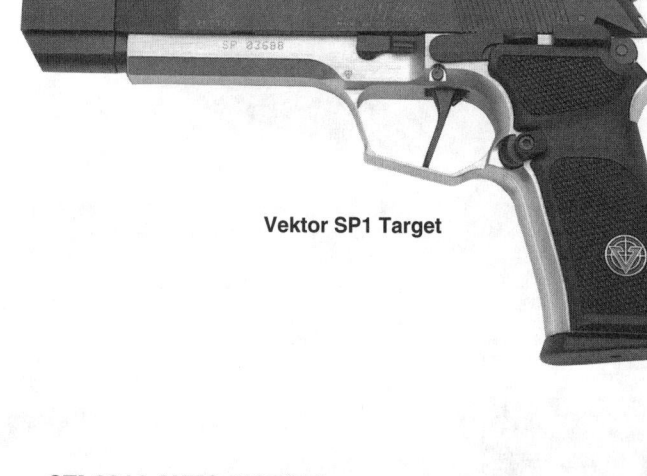

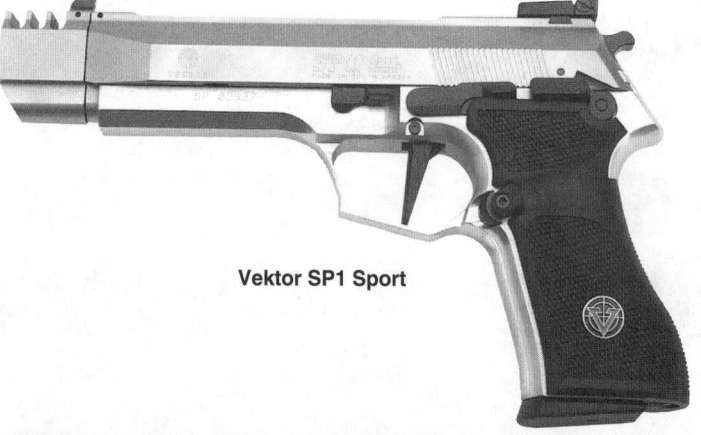

SPRINGFIELD ARMORY 1911-STYLE AUTO PISTOLS
Caliber: 9mm Para., 8- or 9-shot magazine; 45 ACP, 6-, 7-, 8- or 10-shot magazine; 45 Super, 7-shot magazine. **Barrel:** 3.5", 3.9", 5", 6". **Weight:** 25 to 41 oz. **Length:** 7" to 9.5" overall. **Grips:** Checkered cocobolo or synthetic. **Sights:** Novak low-profile, Novak tritium or adjustable target rear; blade front. **Features:** Parkerized, blued, stainless steel or bi-tone frame and slide; lightweight Delta hammer; match trigger; front and rear slide serrations; hammer-forged, air-gauged barrel; beavertail grip safety; extended thumb safety; beveled magazine well. Made in U.S. From Springfield Inc.
Price: Mil-Spec 1911-A1 (5" barrel, fixed three-dot sights,
parkerized finish) $610.00
Price: Full-Size 1911-A1 (5" bbl., Novak fixed or adj. sights,
steel or alum. frame) . . . . from $648.00
Price: Champion 1911-A1 (3.9" bbl., Novak fixed sights,
steel or alum. frame) . . . . from $669.00
Price: Compact 1911-A1 (3.9" bbl., Novak fixed sights,
alum. frame) . . . . from $678.00
Price: Ultra-Compact 1911-A1 (3.5" bbl., Novak fixed sights,
steel or alum. frame) . . . . from $669.00
Price: Trophy Match 1911-A1 (5" or 6" bbl., adj. sights,
blued or stainless) . . . . from $1,089.00
Price: Long Slide 1911-A1 (6" bbl., adj. sights, stainless,
45 ACP or 45 Super) . . . . from $849.00
Price: Full Size High Capacity (5" bbl., Novak fixed sights,
two 10-shot magazines) . . . . from $733.00
Price: Ultra Compact High Capacity (3.5" bbl., Novak fixed sights,
10-shot mag.) . . . . from $759.00
Price: Tactical Response Pistol (3.9" or 5", Novak fixed sights,
Teflon or stain.) . . . . from $1,289.00
Price: Professional Model (5" bbl., Novak three-dot tritium sights,
Black-T finish) . . . . from $2,395.00

STI 2011 AUTO PISTOLS
Caliber: 9mm Para., 9x23, 38 Super, 40 S&W, 40 Super, 10mm, 45 ACP. **Barrel:** 3.4", 5", 5.5", 6". **Weight:** 28 to 44 oz. **Length:** 7" to 9-5/8" overall. **Grips:** Checkered, double-diamond rosewood or glass-filled nylon polymer (six colors). **Sights:** STI, Novak or Heine adjustable rear, blade front. **Features:** Updated version of 1911-style auto pistol; serrated slide, front and rear; STI skeletonized trigger; ambidextrous or single-sided thumb safety; blue or hard-chrome finish; etched logo and model name. From STI International.
Price: Competitor (38 Super, 5.5" barrel, C-More Rail Scope
and mount) . . . . from $2,499.00
Price: Trojan (9mm, 45 ACP, 40 Super, 40 S&W; 5" or 6" barrel)
. . . . from $970.00
Price: Edge 5.0" (40 S&W or 45 ACP; 5" barrel) . . . . from $1,776.00
Price: Eagle 5.0" (9mm, 9x23, 38 Super, 40 S&W, 10mm,
40 Super, 45 ACP; 5" bbl.) . . . . from $1,699.00
Price: Eagle 6.0" (9mm, 38 Super, 40 S&W, 10mm, 40 Super,
45 ACP; 6" bbl.) . . . . from $1,795.40
Price: BLS9/BLS40 (9mm, 40 S&W; 3.4" barrel, full-length grip)
. . . . from $843.70

STI COMPACT AUTO PISTOLS
Caliber: 9mm Para., 40 S&W. **Barrel:** 3.4". **Weight:** 28 oz. **Length:** 7" overall. **Grips:** Checkered double-diamond rosewood. **Sights:** Heine Low Mount fixed rear, slide integral front. **Features:** Similar to STI 2011 models except has compact frame, 7-shot magazine in 9mm (6-shot in 40 cal.), single-sided thumb safety, linkless barrel lockup system, matte blue finish. From STI International.
Price: (9mm Para. or 40 S&W) . . . . from $746.50

VEKTOR SP1/SP2 AUTO PISTOLS
Caliber: 9mm Para., 40 S&W; 10-shot magazine. **Barrel:** 4", 4-5/8", 5", 5-7/8". **Weight:** 31.5 to 42 oz. **Length:** 7-1/2" to 11" overall. **Grips:** Black synthetic. **Sights:** Fixed, three-dot adjustable or scope mount; blade front. **Features:** Cold forged, polygon-rifled barrel; Aluminum alloy frame with machined steel slide; blued, anodized or nickel finish. Imported from South Africa by Vektor USA.
Price: SP1 Service Pistol (9mm Para., 4-5/8" barrel, fixed sights)
. . . . from $619.95
Price: SP2 Service Pistol (40 S&W, 4-5/8" barrel, fixed sights)
. . . . from $649.95
Price: SP1 Sport Pistol (9mm, 5" bbl. with compensator,
combat sight, trigger stop) . . . . from $849.95
Price: SP1 Target Pistol (9mm, 5-7/8" bbl. with compensator,
three-dot sights, adj. trigger) $1,199.95
Price: SP1 Ultra Sport (9mm, 5-7/8" bbl. with comp., integral
Weaver rail, polymer mount) $1,949.95

SEMI-CUSTOM HANDGUNS — AUTOLOADERS

Vektor SP2 Ultra

Price: SP2 Ultra Sport (40 S&W, 5-7/8" bbl. with comp., integral Weaver rail, polymer mount) **$1,949.95**
Price: SP2 Competition (40 S&W, 5-7/8" bbl., combat sights, thickened frame for scope mount) **$999.95**
Price: SP1 General's Model (9mm, 4" barrel, fixed sights) **$659.95**
Price: SP2 General's Model (40 S&W, 4" barrel, fixed sights) ... **$659.95**

VOLQUARTSEN CUSTOM 22 CALIBER AUTO PISTOLS

Caliber: 22 LR; 10-shot magazine. **Barrel:** 3.5" to 10"; stainless steel air gauge. **Weight:** 2-1/2 to 3 lbs. 10 oz. **Length:** NA. **Grips:** Finger-grooved plastic or walnut. **Sights:** Adjustable rear and blade front or Weaver-style scope mount. **Features:** Conversions of Ruger Mk. II Auto pistol. Variety of configurations featuring compensators, underlug barrels, etc. Stainless steel finish; black Teflon finish available for additional $85; target hammer, trigger. Made in U.S. by Volquartsen Custom.

Price: 3.5 Compact (3.5" barrel, T/L adjustable rear sight, scope base optional) **$640.00**
Price: Deluxe (barrel to 10", T/L adjustable rear sight) **$675.00**
Price: Deluxe with compensator **$745.00**
Price: Masters (6.5" barrel, finned underlug, T/L adjustable rear sight, compensator) **$950.00**
Price: Olympic (7" barrel, recoil-reducing gas chamber, T/L adjustable rear sight) **$870.00**
Price: Stingray (7.5" ribbed, ported barrel; red-dot sight) **$995.00**
Price: Terminator (7.5" ported barrel, grooved receiver, scope rings) **$730.00**
Price: Ultra-Light Match (6" tensioned barrel, Weaver mount, weighs 2-1/2 lbs.) **$885.00**
Price: V-6 (6", triangular, ventilated barrel with underlug, T/L adj. sight) **$1,030.00**
Price: V-2000 (6" barrel with finned underlug, T/L adj. sight) ... **$1,095.00**
Price: V-Magic II (7.5" barrel, red-dot sight) **$1,055.00**

Volquartsen 3.5 Compact

Volquartsen Deluxe

Volquartsen Masters

Volquartsen Olympic

Semi-Custom Handguns — Autoloaders

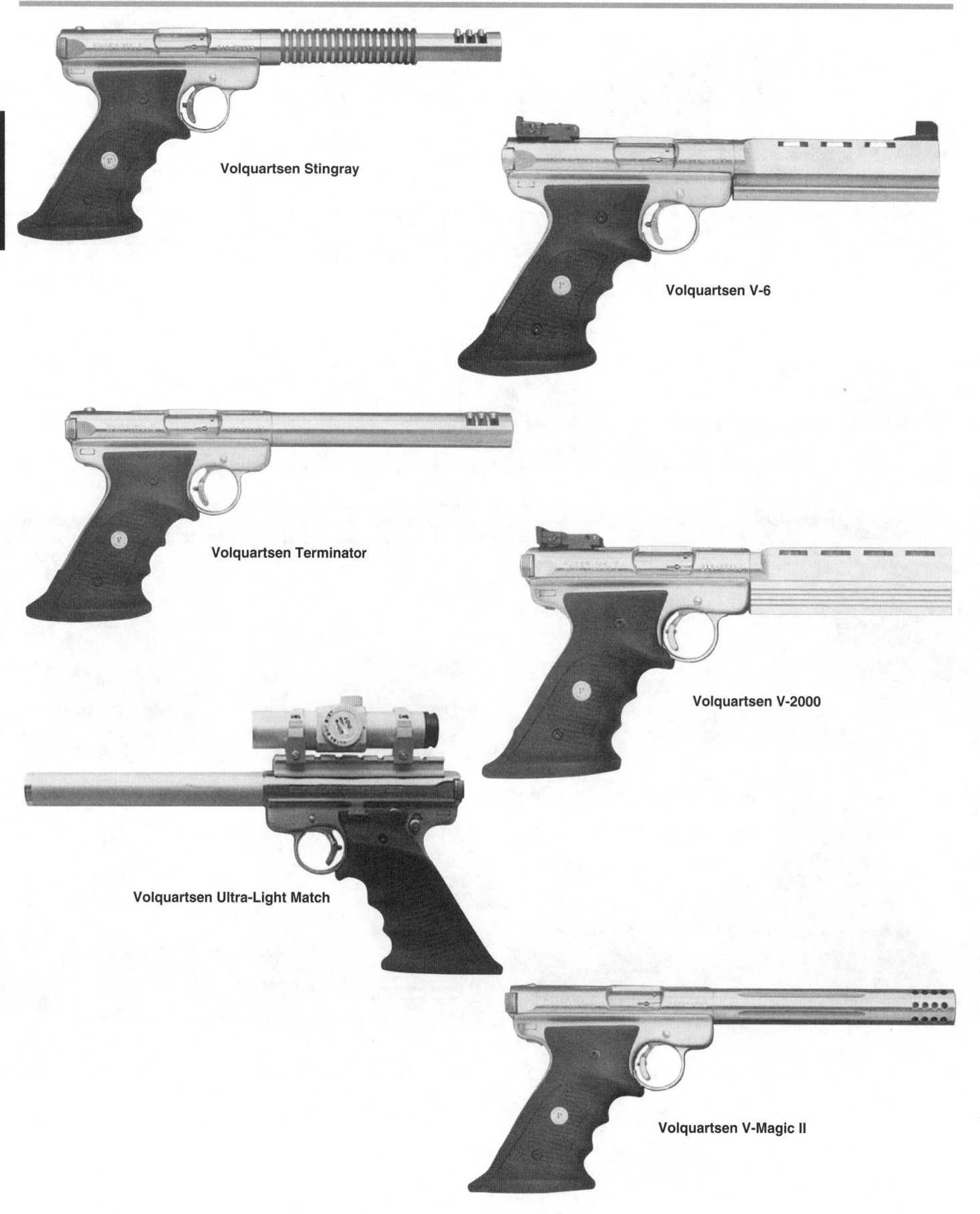

Volquartsen Stingray

Volquartsen V-6

Volquartsen Terminator

Volquartsen V-2000

Volquartsen Ultra-Light Match

Volquartsen V-Magic II

SEMI-CUSTOM HANDGUNS — REVOLVERS

500 Linebaugh

44 Linebaugh Long

500 Linebaugh Long

475 Linebaugh

500 Linebaugh

500 Linebaugh

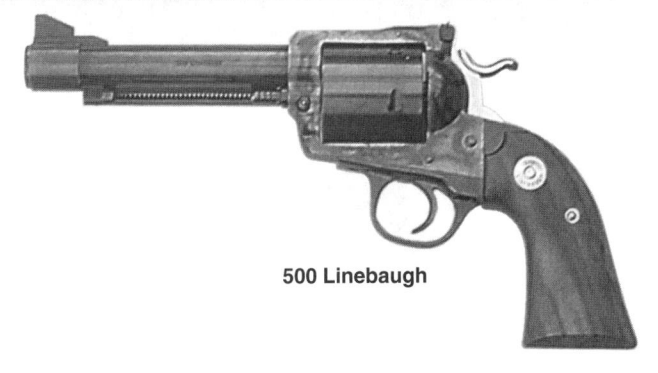

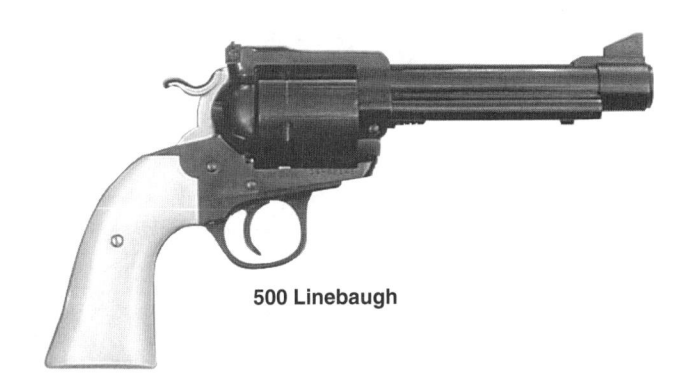

LINEBAUGH CUSTOM SIXGUNS REVOLVERS

Caliber: 45 Colt, 44 Linebaugh Long, 458 Linebaugh, 475 Linebaugh, 500 Linebaugh, 500 Linebaugh Long, 445 Super Mag. **Barrel:** 4-3/4", 5-1/2", 6", 7-1/2"; other lengths available. **Weight:** NA. **Length:** NA. **Grips:** Dustin Linebaugh Custom made to customer's specs. **Sights:** Bowen steel rear or factory Ruger; blade front. **Features:** Conversions using customer's Ruger Blackhawk Bisley and Vaquero Bisley frames. Made in U.S. by Linebaugh Custom Sixguns.

Price: Small 45 Colt conversion (rechambered cyl., new barrel) .... from **$1,000.00**
Price: Large 45 Colt conversion (oversized cyl., new barrel, 5- or 6-shot) .... from **$1,500.00**
Price: 475 Linebaugh, 500 Linebaugh conversions ...... from **$1,500.00**
Price: Linebaugh and 445 Super Mag calibers on 357 Maximum frame .... from **$2,700.00**

GARY REEDER CUSTOM GUNS REVOLVERS

Caliber: 357 Magnum, 45 Colt, 44-40, 41 Magnum, 44 Magnum, 454 Casull, 475 Linebaugh, 500 Linebaugh. **Barrel:** 2-1/2" to 12". **Weight:** Varies by model. **Length:** Varies by model. **Grips:** Black Cape buffalo horn, laminated walnut, simulated pearl, others. **Sights:** Notch fixed or adjustable rear, blade or ramp front. **Features:** Custom conversions of Ruger Vaquero, Blackhawk Bisley and Super Blackhawk frames. Jeweled hammer and trigger, tuned action, model name engraved on barrel, additional engraving on frame and cylinder, integral muzzle brake, finish available in high-polish or satin stainless steel or black Chromex finish. Also available on customer's gun at reduced cost. Other models available. Made in U.S. by Gary Reeder Custom Guns.

Price: Gamblers Classic (2-1/2" bbl., engraved cards and dice, no ejector rod housing) .... from **$995.00**
Price: Tombstone Classic (3-1/2" bbl. with gold bands, notch sight, birdshead grips) .... from **$995.00**
Price: Doc Holliday Classic (3-1/2" bbl., engraved cards and dice, white pearl grips) .... from **$750.00**
Price: Ultimate Vaquero (engraved barrel, frame and cylinder, made to customer specs) .... from **$750.00**
Price: Black Widow (4-5/8" bbl., black Chromex finish, black widow spider engraving) .... from **$995.00**
Price: Cowboy Classic (stainless finish, cattle brand engraved, limited to 100 guns) .... from **$995.00**
Price: African Hunter (6" bbl., with or without muzzle brake, 475 or 500 Linebaugh) .... from **$1,395.00**
Price: Alaskan Survivalist (3" bbl., Redhawk frame, engraved bear, 45 Colt or 44 Magnum) .... from **$995.00**
Price: Ultimate Back-Up (3-1/2" bbl., fixed sights, choice of animal engraving, 475 Linebaugh, 500 Linebaugh) .... from **$1,295.00**

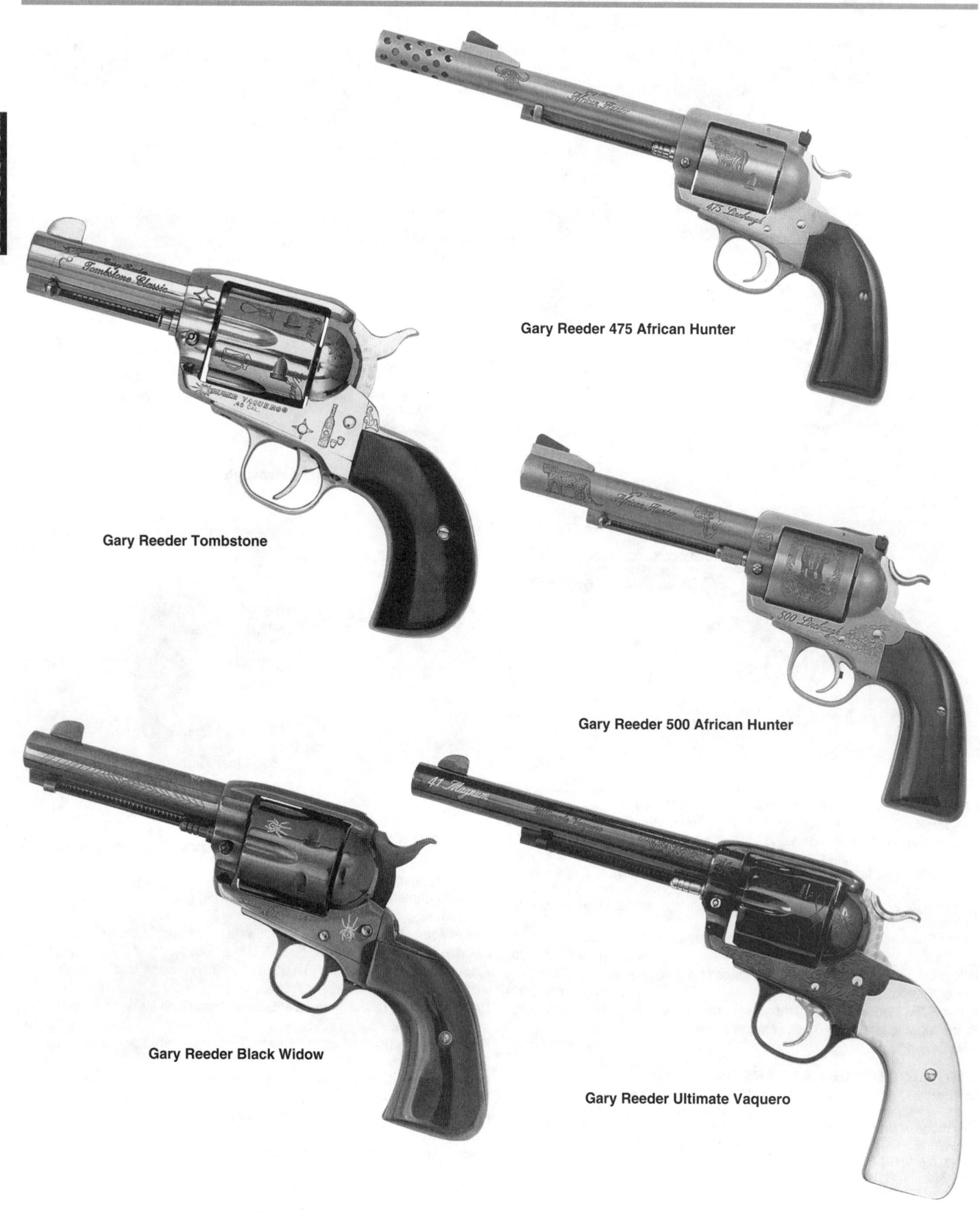

Semi-Custom Handguns — Revolvers

Gary Reeder 475 African Hunter

Gary Reeder Tombstone

Gary Reeder 500 African Hunter

Gary Reeder Black Widow

Gary Reeder Ultimate Vaquero

110 • GUNS ILLUSTRATED

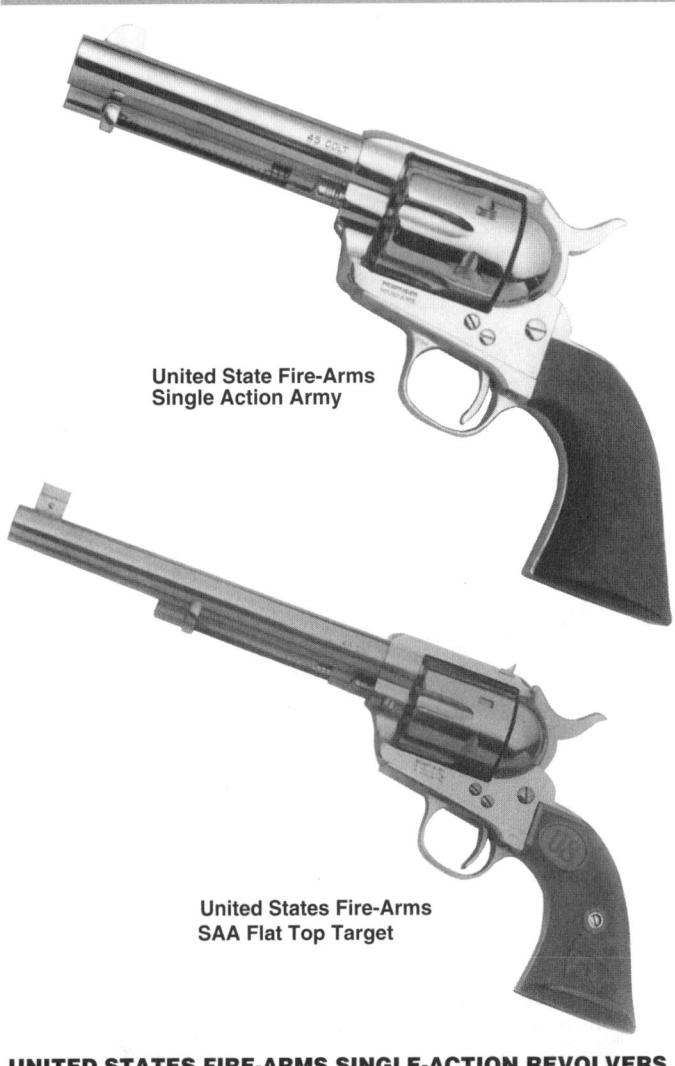

SEMI-CUSTOM HANDGUNS — REVOLVERS

United State Fire-Arms Single Action Army

United States Fire-Arms SAA Bisley

United States Fire-Arms SAA Flat Top Target

United States Fire-Arms Omni-Snubnose

United States Fire-Arms Omni-Potent Six Shooter

UNITED STATES FIRE-ARMS SINGLE-ACTION REVOLVERS
Caliber: 32 WCF, 38 Special, 38 WCF, 41 Colt, 44 WCF, 44 Special, 45 Colt. **Barrel:** 2", 3", 4-3/4", 5-1/2", 7-1/2", 16". **Weight:** NA. **Length:** NA. **Grips:** Hard rubber, rosewood, stag, pearl, ivory, ivory Micarta, smooth walnut, burled walnut and checkered walnut. **Sights:** Notch rear, blade front. **Features:** Hand-fitted replicas of Colt single-action revolvers. Full Dome Blue, Dome Blue, Armory Blue (gray-blue), Old Armory Bone Case (color casehardened) and nickel plate finishes. Carved and scrimshaw grips, engraving and gold inlays offered. Made in U.S. From United States Fire-Arms Mfg. Co.
Price: Single Action Army (32 WCF, 38 Spec., 38 WCF, 41 Colt,
  45 Colt, 44 Spec., 44 WCF) $919.00
Price: SAA Flat Top Target (extended blade front, drift-adj.
  rear sights . . . . from $995.00
Price: SAA Bisley (Bisley grip and hammer) . . . . from $995.00
Price: Omni-Snubnose (2" or 3" barrel, lanyard loop,
  45 Colt only) . . . . from $1,120.00
Price: Omni-Potent Six Shooter (lanyard loop on grip) . . . . from $1,125.00
Price: New Buntline Special (16" bbl., skeleton shoulder stock, case,
  scabbard) . . . . from $2,199.00
Price: China Camp Cowboy Action Gun (4-3/4", 5-1/2" or 7-1/2" bbl.,
  Silver Steel finish) . . . . from $989.00
Price: Henry Nettleton Cavalry Revolver (5-1/2" or 7-1/2" bbl.,
  45 Colt only) . . . . from $1,125.00
Price: U.S. 1851 Navy Conversion (7-1/2" bbl., color casehardened frame,
  38 Spec. only) . . . . from $1,499.00
Price: U.S. Pre-War (SAA, Old Armory Bone Case or
  Armory Blue finish) . . . . from $1,175.00

34TH EDITION, 2002 • 111

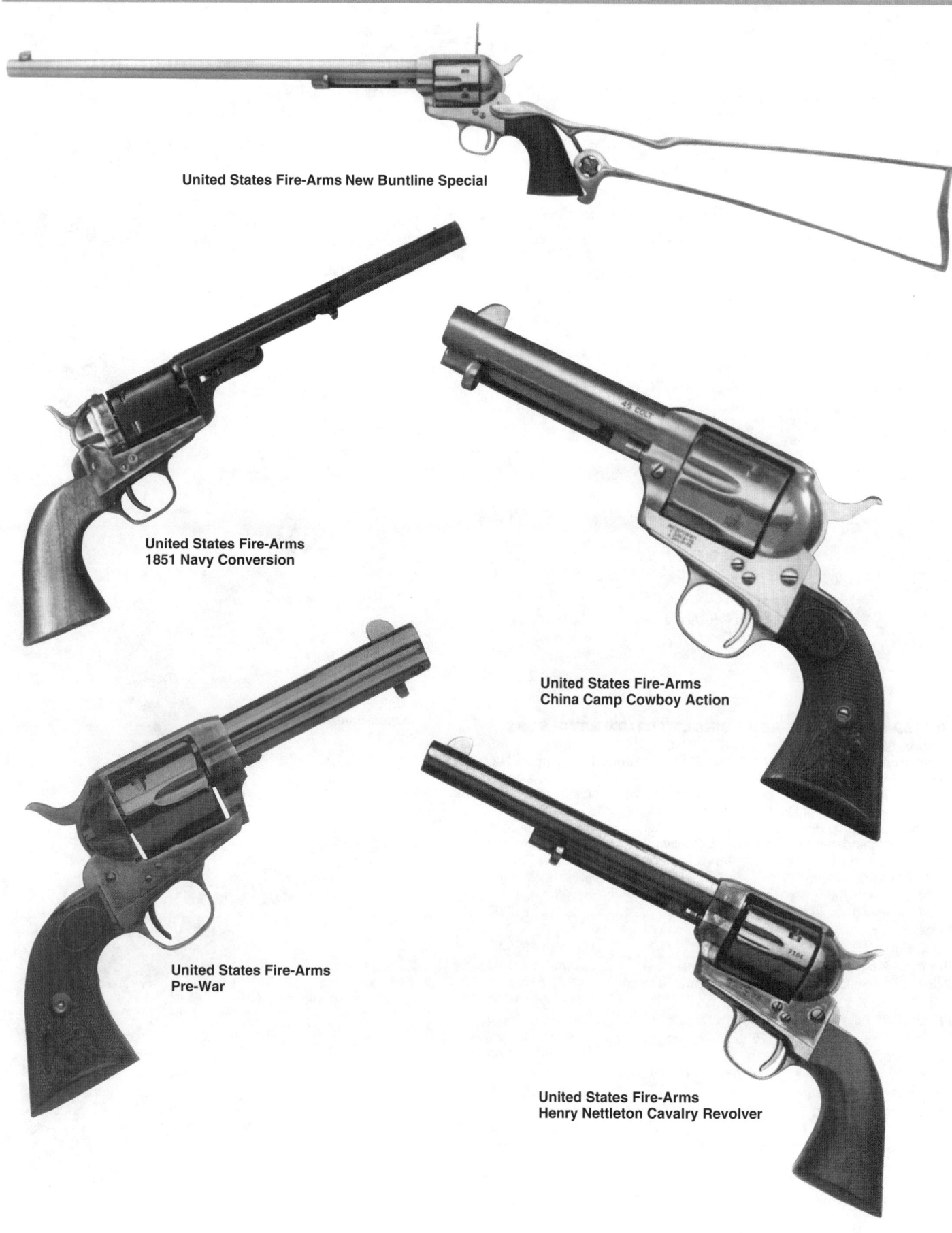

Semi-Custom Handguns — Revolvers

United States Fire-Arms New Buntline Special

United States Fire-Arms
1851 Navy Conversion

United States Fire-Arms
China Camp Cowboy Action

United States Fire-Arms
Pre-War

United States Fire-Arms
Henry Nettleton Cavalry Revolver

SEMI-CUSTOM HANDGUNS — SINGLE SHOT

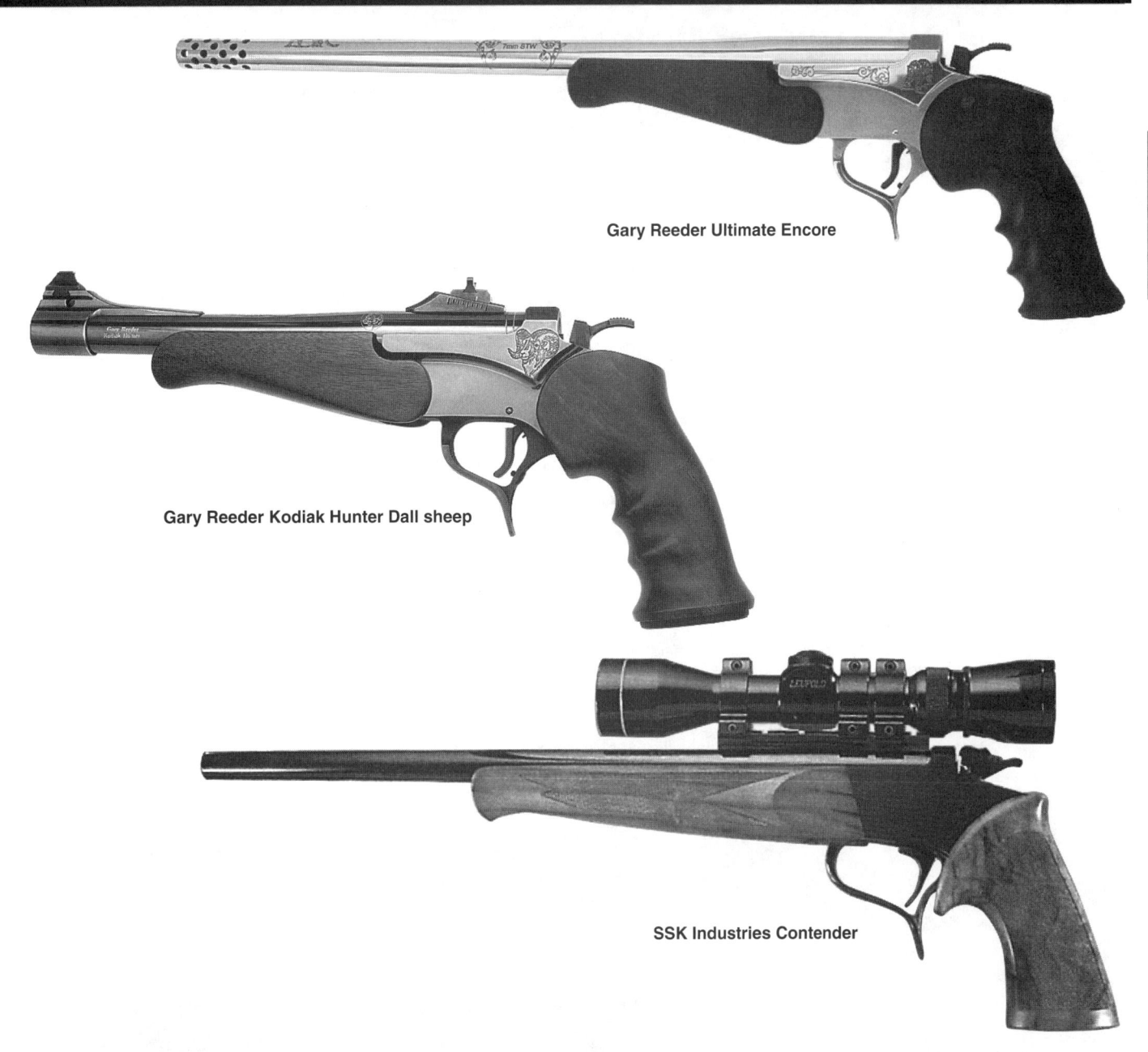

Gary Reeder Ultimate Encore

Gary Reeder Kodiak Hunter Dall sheep

SSK Industries Contender

GARY REEDER CUSTOM GUNS
CONTENDER AND ENCORE PISTOLS

Caliber: 22 Cheetah, 218 Bee, 22 K-Hornet, 22 Hornet, 218 Mashburn Bee, 22-250 Improved, 6mm/284, 7mm STW, 7mm GNR, 30 GNR, 338 GNR, 300 Win. Magnum, 338 Win. Magnum, 350 Rem. Magnum, 358 STA, 375 H&H, 378 GNR, 416 Remington, 416 GNR, 450 GNR, 475 Linebaugh, 500 Linebaugh, 50 Alaskan, 50 AE, 454 Casull; others available. **Barrel:** 8" to 15" (others available). **Weight:** NA. **Length:** Varies with barrel length. **Grips:** Walnut fingergroove. **Sights:** Express-style adjustable rear and barrel band front (Kodiak Hunter); none furnished most models. **Features:** Offers complete guns and barrels in the T/C Contender and Encore. Integral muzzle brake, engraved animals and model name, tuned action, high-polish or satin stainless steel or black Chromex finish. Made in U.S. by Gary Reeder Custom Guns.
Price: Kodiak Hunter (50 AE or 454 Casull, Kodiak bear and Dall sheep engravings)... from **$995.00**
Price: Ultimate Encore (15" bbl. with muzzle brake, grizzly bear engraving)................................. from **$995.00**

SSK INDUSTRIES CONTENDER AND ENCORE PISTOLS

Caliber: More than 200, including most standard pistol and rifle calibers, as well as 226 JDJ, 6mm JDJ, 257 JDJ, 6.5mm JDJ, 7mm JDJ, 6.5mm Mini-Dreadnaught, 30-06 JDJ, 280 JDJ, 375 JDJ, 6mm Whisper, 300 Whisper and 338 Whisper. **Barrel:** 10" to 26"; blued or stainless; variety of configurations. **Weight:** Varies with barrel length and features. **Length:** Varies with barrel length. **Grips:** Pachmayr, wood models available. **Features:** Offers frames, barrels and complete guns in the T/C Contender and Encore. Fluted, diamond, octagon and round barrels; flatside Contender frames; chrome-plating; muzzle brakes; trigger jobs; variety of stocks and forends; sights and optics. Made in U.S. by SSK Industries.
Price: Blued Contender frame .... from **$263.00**
Price: Stainless Contender frame .... from **$290.00**
Price: Blued Encore frame .... from **$290.00**
Price: Stainless Encore frame .... from **$318.00**
Price: Contender barrels .... from **$315.00**
Price: Encore barrels .... from **$340.00**

Semi-Custom Rifles — Bolt-Action

Ed Brown 702 Savanna

Ed Brown 702 Varmint

ED BROWN CUSTOM BOLT-ACTION RIFLES

Caliber: 222, 223, 22-250, 220 Swift, 243, 243 Ackley Imp., 25-06, 270 Win., 280 Rem., 280 Ackley Imp., 6mm, 6.5/284, 7mm/08, 7mm Rem. Mag., 7STW, 30/06, 308, 300 Win. Mag., 338 Win. Mag., 375 H&H, 404 Jeffery, 416 Rem. Mag., 416 Rigby, 458 Win. Mag. **Barrel:** 21", 24", 26". **Weight:** NA. **Length:** NA. **Stock:** Fiberglass synthetic; swivel studs; recoil pad. **Sights:** Optional; Talley scope rings and base furnished; scope mounting included in price (scope extra). **Features:** Machined receiver; hand-fitted bolt with welded handle; M16-type extractor; three-position safety; trigger adjustable for pull and overtravel; match-quality, hand-lapped barrel with deep countersunk crowning. Made in U.S. by Ed Brown Products.
Price: Model 702 Savanna short- or long-action repeater (lightweight 24" or medium-weight 26"barrel) . from **$2,800.00**
Price: Model 702 Tactical long-action repeater (heavy contour 26" barrel) . . . . from **$3,200.00**
Price: Model 702 Ozark short-action repeater (lightweight 21" barrel) . . . . from **$2,500.00**
Price: Model 702 Varmint short-action single shot (med. 26" or hvy. 24") . . . . from **$2,500.00**
Price: Model 702 Light Tactical short-action repeater (med. 21" barrel) . . . . from **$2,800.00**
Price: Model 702 Bushveld dangerous game rifle (24" med. or heavy barrel) . . . . from **$2,900.00**
Price: Model 702 Peacekeeper long-range rifle (26" heavy barrel with muzzle brake) . . . . from **$3,500.00**

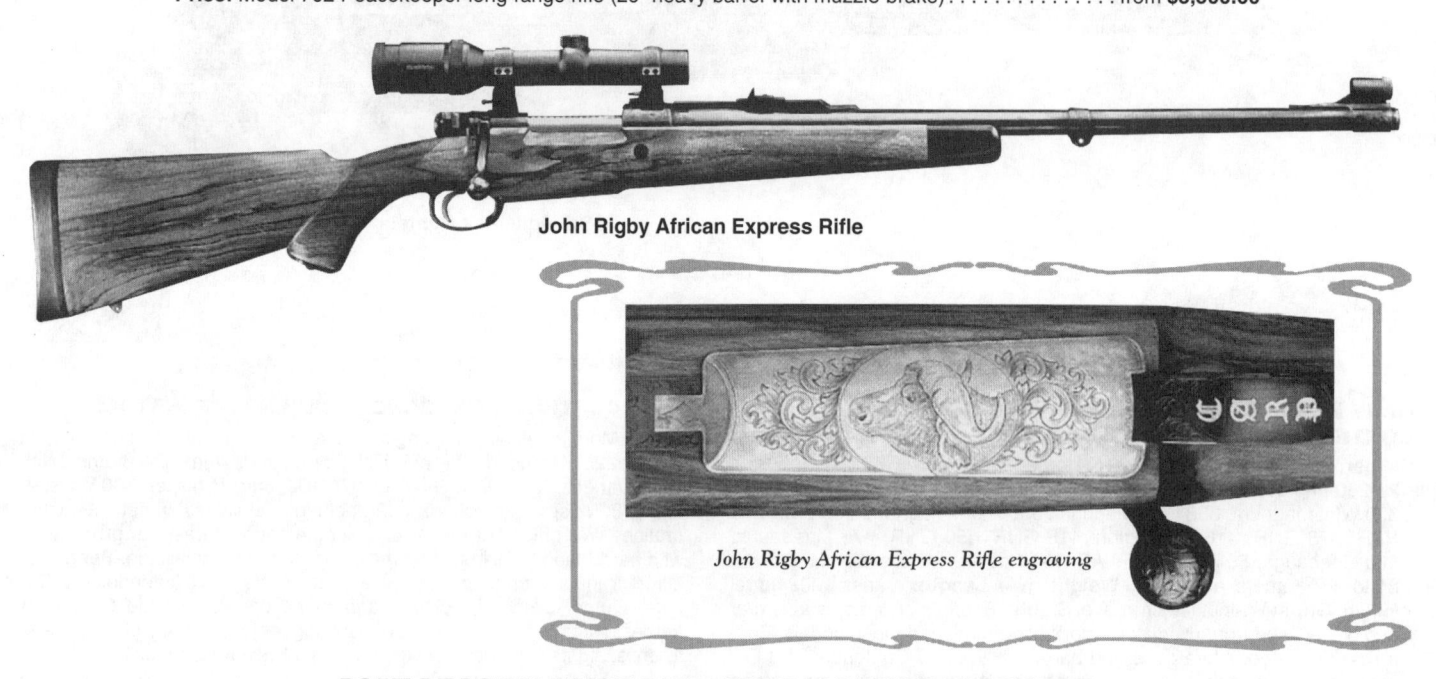

John Rigby African Express Rifle

John Rigby African Express Rifle engraving

JOHN RIGBY CUSTOM AFRICAN EXPRESS RIFLE

Caliber: 375 H&H Magnum, 416 Rigby, 450 Rigby, 458 Winchester, 505 Gibbs. **Barrel:** To customer specs. **Weight:** NA. **Length:** To customer specs. **Stock:** Customer's choice. **Sights:** Express-type rear, hooded ramp front; scope mounts offered. **Features:** Handcrafted bolt-action rifle built to customer specifications. Variety of engraving and stock wood options available. Imported from England by John Rigby & Co.
Price: African Express Rifle . . . . from **$15,500.00**

SEMI-CUSTOM RIFLES — BOLT-ACTION

Remington 700 APR

Remington 700 AWR

REMINGTON MODEL 700 CUSTOM SHOP RIFLES

Caliber: 270 Win., 280 Rem., 30-06, 7mm Rem. Mag., 7mm STW, 300 Win. Mag., 300 Wea. Mag., 338 Win. Mag., 8mm Rem. Mag., 35 Whelen, 375 H&H Mag., 416 Rem. Mag., 458 Win. Mag. **Barrel:** 22", 24", 26". **Weight:** 6 lbs. 6 oz. to 9 lbs. **Length:** 44-1/4" to 46-1/2" overall. **Stock:** Laminated hardwood, walnut or Kevlar-reinforced fiberglass. **Sights:** Adjustable rear (Safari models); all receivers drilled and tapped for scope mounts. **Features:** Black matte, satin blue or uncolored stainless steel finish; hand-fitted action is epoxy-bedded to stock; tuned trigger; bolt-supported extractor for sure extraction; fancy wood and other options available. Made in U.S. by Remington Arms Co.
Price: Custom KS Mountain Rifle (24" barrel, synthetic stock, 6-3/4 lbs. in mag. cals.) . . . . from **$1,221.00**
Price: Custom KS Safari Stainless (22" barrel, synthetic stock, 9 lbs.) . . . . from **$1,410.00**
Price: Safari Classic or Monte Carlo (24" barrel, walnut stock, polished blue finish) . . . . from **$1,225.00**
Price: APR (African Plains Rifle — 26" barrel, laminated stock, satin blue finish) . . . . from **$1,593.00**
Price: AWR (Alaskan Wilderness Rifle — 24" barrel, syn. stock, black matte finish) . . . . from **$1,480.00**

REMINGTON MODEL 40-X CUSTOM SHOP TARGET RIFLES

Caliber: 22 LR, 22 BR Rem., 222 Rem., 223 Rem., 22-250, 220 Swift, 6mm BR Rem., 6mm Rem., 243 Win., 25-06, 260 Rem., 7mm BR Rem., 7mm Rem. Mag., 7mm STW, 308 Win., 30-06, 300 Win. Mag. **Barrel:** 24", 27-1/4"; various twist rates offered. **Weight:** 9-3/4 to 11 lbs. **Length:** 40" to 47" overall. **Stock:** Walnut, laminated wood or Kevlar-reinforced fiberglass. **Sights:** None; receiver drilled and tapped for scope mounts. **Features:** Single shot or 5-shot repeater; carbon steel or stainless steel receiver; externally adjustable trigger (1-1/2 to 3-1/2 lbs.); rubber butt pad. From Remington Arms Co.
Price: 40-XB Rangemaster (27-1/4" bbl., walnut stock, forend rail with hand stop) . . . . from **$1,565.00**
Price: 40-XB Rangemaster with laminated thumbhole stock . . . . from **$1,768.00**
Price: 40-XB KS (27-1/4" bbl., black synthetic stock) . . . . from **$1,768.00**
Price: 40-XBBR KS (24" bbl., Remington green synthetic stock with straight comb) . . . . from **$1,742.00**
Price: 40-XC KS (308, 24" bbl., gray synthetic stock with adj. comb) . . . . from **$1,742.00**

REMINGTON MODEL SEVEN CUSTOM SHOP RIFLES

Caliber: 222 Rem., 223 Rem., 22-250 Rem., 243 Win., 6mm Rem., 250 Savage, 257 Roberts, 260 Rem., 308 Win., 7mm-08 Rem., 35 Rem., 350 Rem. Mag. **Barrel:** 20". **Weight:** 5-3/4 to 6-1/2 lbs. **Length:** 39-1/2" overall. **Stock:** Laminated hardwood or Kevlar-reinforced fiberglass. **Sights:** Adjustable ramp rear, hooded blade front. **Features:** Hand-fitted action; epoxy bedded; deep blue or non-reflective black matte finish; drilled and tapped for scope mounts. From Remington Arms Co.
Price: Model Seven MS (Mannlicher stock, deep blue finish) . . . . from **$1,236.00**
Price: Model Seven Custom KS (synthetic stock, matte finish) . . . . from **$1,221.00**

TIME PRECISION BOLT-ACTION RIFLES

Caliber: 22 LR, 222, 223, 308, 378, 300 Win. Mag., 416 Rigby, others. **Barrel:** NA. **Weight:** 10 lbs. and up. **Length:** NA. **Stock:** Fiberglass. **Sights:** None; receiver drilled and tapped for scope mount. **Features:** Thirty different action types offered, including single shots and repeaters for bench rest, varmint and big-game hunting. Machined chrome-moly action; three-position safety; Shilen match trigger (other triggers available); twin cocking cams; dual firing pin. Built to customer specifications. From Time Precision.
Price: 22 LR Bench Rest Rifle (Shilen match-grade stainless steel bbl., fiberglass stock) . . . . from **$2,202.00**
Price: 22 LR Target Rifle . . . . from **$2,220.00**
Price: 22 LR Sporter . . . . from **$1,980.00**
Price: Hunting Rifle (calibers to 30-06) . . . . from **$2,202.00**
Price: Hunting Rifle (7mm Rem. Mag., 300 Win. Mag., 338 Win. Mag.) . . . . from **$2,322.00**

SEMI-CUSTOM RIFLES — BOLT-ACTION

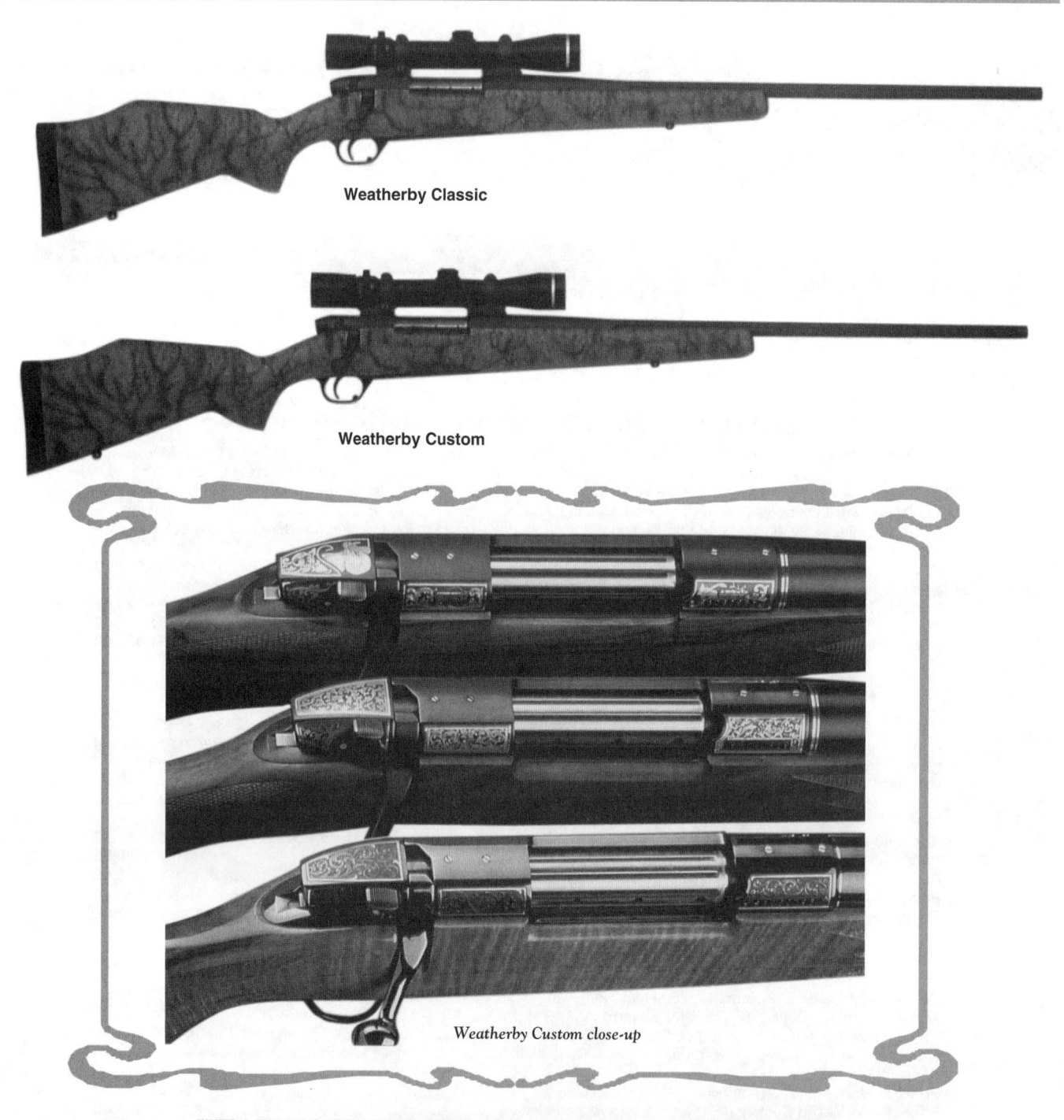

Weatherby Classic

Weatherby Custom

Weatherby Custom close-up

WEATHERBY CUSTOM SHOP BOLT-ACTION RIFLES

Caliber: 257 Wby. Mag., 270 Wby. Mag., 7mm Wby. Mag., 300 Wby. Mag., 340 Wby. Mag., 375 H&H Mag., 378 Wby. Mag., 416 Wby. Mag., 460 Wby. Mag. **Barrel:** 24", 26", 28". **Weight:** NA. **Length:** NA. **Stock:** Monte Carlo, modified Monte Carlo or Classic design in Exhibition- or Exhibition Special Select grades of claro or French walnut; injection-molded synthetic in Snow Camo, Alpine Camo or Dark Timber colors. **Sights:** Quarter-rib rear with one standing and one folding leaf, hooded ramp front (Safari Grade); drilled and tapped for scope mount. **Features:** Rosewood or ebony pistol-grip caps with inlaid diamonds in rosewood, walnut or maple; three grades of engraving patterns for receiver, bolt and handle; gold inlays; wooden inlaid buttstock, forearm and magazine box; three grades of engraved and gold inlaid rings and bases; canvas/leather, solid leather or leather with oak trim case. From the Weatherby Custom Shop.
Price: Classic Custom (bead-blast blue finish, checkered, oil-finished French walnut stock) $5,099.000
Price: Safari Grade (engr. floorplate, oil-finished French wal. stock w/fleur-de-lis checkering.) $5,199.00
Price: Crown (engr., inlaid floorplate, engr. bbl. and receiver, hand-carved walnut stock) $6,599.00
Price: Outfitter Krieger (Krieger stainless steel bbl., Bell and Carlson syn. camo. stock) $3,499.00
Price: Outfitter Custom (standard barrel, Bell and Carlson syn. camo stock) . . . . from $2,149.00

SEMI-CUSTOM RIFLES — AUTOLOADERS

BUSHMASTER AUTO RIFLES

Caliber: 223. **Barrel:** 16" regular or fluted, 20" regular, heavy or fluted, 24" heavy or fluted. **Weight:** 6.9 to 8.37 lbs. **Length:** 34.5" to 38.25" overall. **Stock:** Polymer. **Sights:** Fully adjustable dual flip-up aperture rear, blade front or picatinny rail for scope mount. **Features:** Versions of the AR-15 style rifle. Aircraft-quality aluminum receiver; chrome-lined barrel and chamber; chrome-moly-vanadium steel barrel with 1:9" twist; manganese phosphate matte finish; forged front sight; receiver takes down without tools; serrated, finger groove pistol grip. Made in U.S. by Bushmaster Firearms/Quality Parts Co.
Price: DCM Competition Rifle **$1,525.00**

LES BAER AR 223 AUTO RIFLES

Caliber: 223. **Barrel:** 16-1/4", 20", 22" or 24"; cryo-treated, stainless steel bench-rest grade. **Weight:** NA. **Length:** NA. **Stock:** Polymer. **Sights:** None; picatinny rail for scope mount. **Features:** Forged and machined upper and lower receiver; single- or double-stage adjustable trigger; free-float handguard; Bear Coat protective finish. Made in U.S. by Les Baer Custom.
Price: Ultimate Super Varmint (Jewell two-stage trigger, guar. to shoot 1/2 MOA groups) .... from **$1,989.00**
Price: Ultimate M4 Flattop (16-1/4" bbl., Ultra single-stage trigger, shoots 1 MOA groups) .... from **$2,195.00**
Price: Ultimate IPSC Action (20" bbl., Jewell two-stage trigger, shoots 1 MOA groups) .... from **$2,195.00**

SSK INDUSTRIES AR-15 RIFLES

Caliber: 223, 6mm PPC, 6.5mm PPC, Whisper and other wildcats. **Barrel:** 16-1/2" and longer (to order). **Weight:** NA. **Length:** NA. **Stock:** Black plastic. **Sights:** Blade front, adjustable rear (scopes and red-dot sights available). **Features:** Variety of designs to full match-grade guns offered. Customer's gun can be rebarreled or accurized. From SSK Industries.
Price: Complete AR-15 .... from **$1,500.00**
Price: A2 upper unit (front sight, short handguard **$1,100.00**
Price: Match Grade upper unit (bull barrel, tubular handguard, scope mount) **$1,100.00**

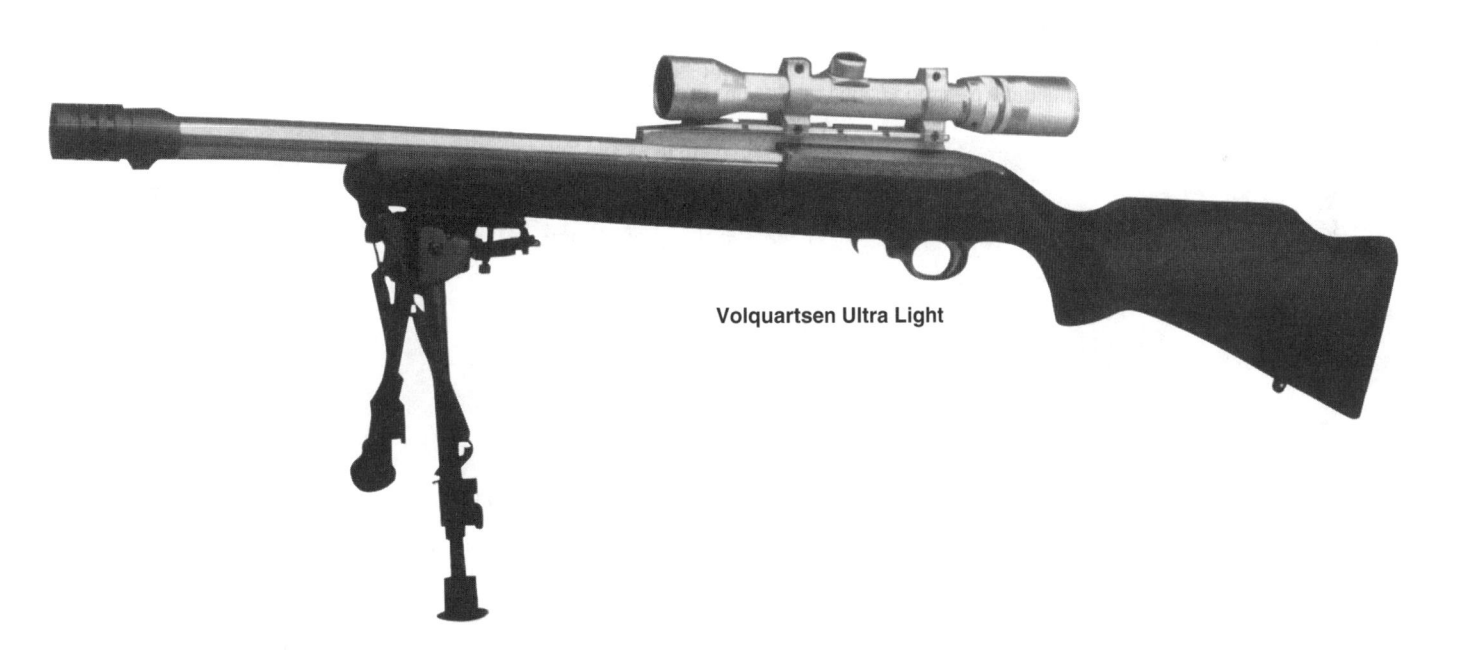

Volquartsen Ultra Light

VOLQUARTSEN CUSTOM 22 CALIBER AUTO RIFLES

Caliber: 22 LR, 22 Magnum. **Barrel:** 16-1/2" to 20"; stainless steel air gauge. **Weight:** 4-3/4 to 5-3/4 lbs. **Length:** NA. **Stock:** Synthetic or laminated. **Sights:** Not furnished; Weaver base provided. **Features:** Conversions of the Ruger 10/22 rifle. Tuned trigger with 2-1/2 to 3-1/2 lb. pull. Variety of configurations and features. From Volquartsen Custom.
Price: Ultra-Light (22 LR, 16-1/2" tensioned barrel, synthetic stock) .... from **$670.00**
Price: Grey Ghost (22 LR, 18-1/2" barrel, laminated wood stock) .... from **$690.00**
Price: Deluxe (22 LR, 20" barrel, laminated wood or fiberglass stock) .... from **$970.00**
Price: Mossad (22 LR, 20" fluted and ported barrel, fiberglass thumbhole stock) .... from **$970.00**
Price: VX-2500 (22 LR, 20" fluted and ported barrel, aluminum/fiberglass stock) .... from **$1,044.00**
Price: Volquartsen 22 LR (stainless steel receiver) .... from **$920.00**
Price: Volquartsen 22 Mag (22 WMR, stainless steel receiver) .... from **$950.00**

SEMI-CUSTOM RIFLES — AUTOLOADERS

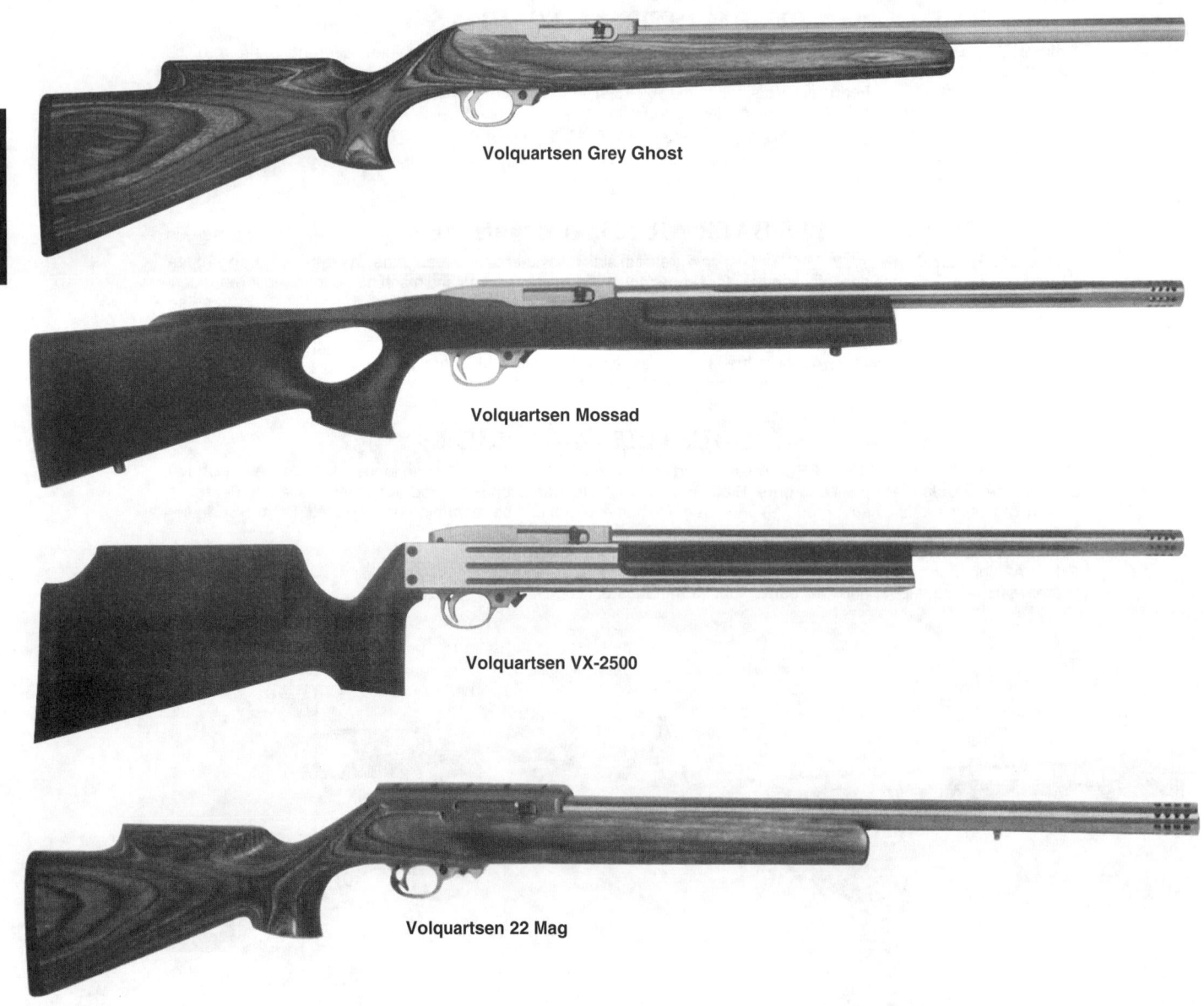

Volquartsen Grey Ghost

Volquartsen Mossad

Volquartsen VX-2500

Volquartsen 22 Mag

WHITE BARN WORKSHOP 22 CALIBER AUTO RIFLES

Caliber: 22 LR, 22 Magnum. **Barrel:** Bull, plain, fluted, tapered or fully compensated. **Weight:** NA. **Length:** NA. **Stock:** Laminated hardwood. **Sights:** None; Trinity Bridge Weaver base and other scope mounts offered. **Features:** Conversions of the Ruger 10/22 rifle. Tuned trigger; extended magazine release; quick bolt release; jeweled bolt; hand-lapped bore; Chief AJ logo. From White Barn Workshop.
Price: Standard Scout 10/22 (Scout barrel mount with Leupold scope, flash hider) .... from **$695.00**
Price: Bull Scout 10/22 (Douglas bull barrel, Scout barrel mount with Leupold scope). .... from **$995.00**
Price: Leader 10/22 (Trinity Bridge scope base and scope, laminated stock) .... from **$1,200.00**
NEW! Price: Millennium 10/22 (laser engraved, laminated stock, limited to 1,000 guns) **$650.00**

WHITE BARN WORKSHOP MINI-14 AUTO RIFLE

NEW! **Caliber:** 223. **Barrel:** Standard with lapped bore. **Weight:** NA. **Length:** NA. **Stock:** Laminated hardwood. **Sights:** None; Leupold scout scope mount and scope furnished. **Features:** Conversions of the Ruger Mini-14 rifle. Tuned trigger, barrel compensator.
Price: Custom Mini-14 Scout Rifle **$1,200.00**

SEMI-CUSTOM RIFLES — DOUBLE RIFLES

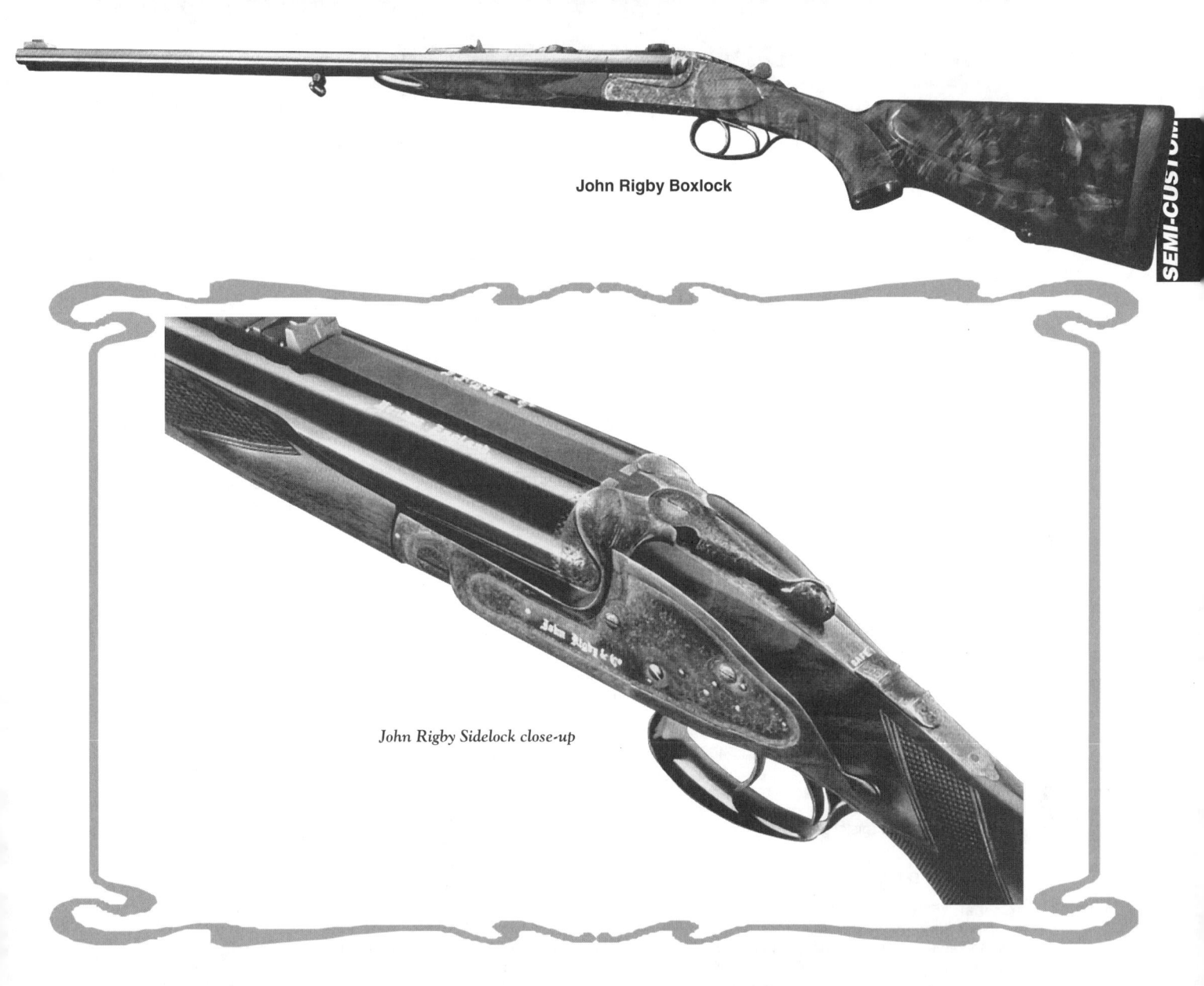

John Rigby Boxlock

John Rigby Sidelock close-up

BERETTA EXPRESS DOUBLE RIFLES

Caliber: 9.3x74R, 375 H&H Mag., 416 Rigby, 458 Win. Mag., 470 Nitro Express, 500 Nitro Express. **Barrel:** 23" to 25". **Weight:** 11 lbs. **Length:** NA. **Stock:** Hand-finished, hand-checkered walnut with cheek rest. **Sights:** Folding-leaf, Express-type rear, blade front. **Features:** High-strength steel action with reinforced receiver sides; top tang extends to stock comb for strength; double triggers (articulated front trigger and automatic blocking device eliminate chance of simultaneous discharge); hand-cut, stepped rib; engraved receiver; trapdoor compartment in stock for extra cartridges; spare front sights stored in pistol-grip cap. Imported from Italy by Beretta USA.
Price: SSO6 o/u (optional claw mounts for scope) . . . . from **$39,500.00**
Price: SSO6 EELL o/u (engraved game scenes or color case-hardened with gold inlays) . . . . from **$42,500.00**
Price: 455 s/s (color case-hardened action) . . . . from **$53,000.00**
Price: 455 EELL s/s (receiver engraved with big-game animals) . . . . from **$72,500.00**

JOHN RIGBY DOUBLE RIFLES

Caliber: 375 H&H, 500/416, 450 Nitro Express, 470 Nitro Express, 500 Nitro Express, 577 Nitro Express. **Barrel:** To customer specs. **Weight:** NA. **Length:** To customer specs. **Stock:** To customer specs. **Sights:** Dovetail, express-type sights; claw-foot scope mount available. **Features:** Handcrafted to customer specifications. Boxlock or sidelock action, hand-fitted; variety of engraving and other options offered. Imported from England by John Rigby & Co.
Price: Rigby 4th Century Boxlock . . . . from **$18,950.00**
Price: Rigby 4th Century Sidelock. . . . . from **$34,950.00**

SEMI-CUSTOM RIFLES — SINGLE SHOT

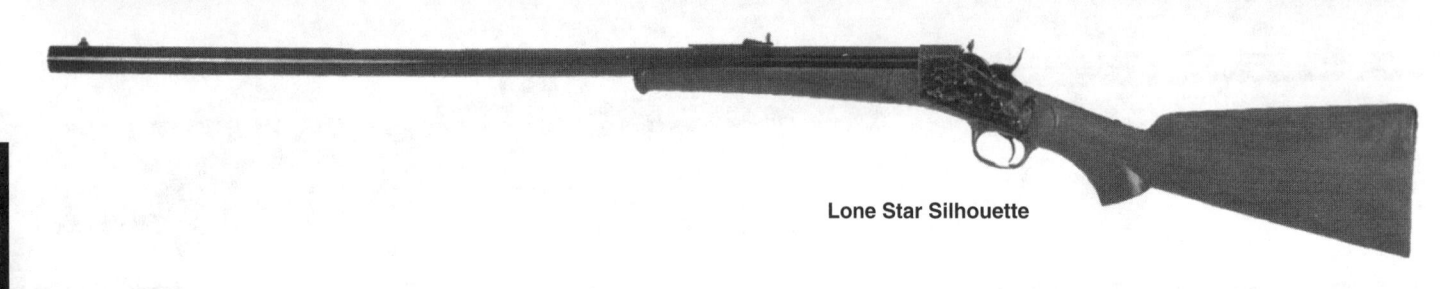

Lone Star Silhouette

C. SHARPS ARMS RIFLES

Caliber: 22 Hornet, 30-40 Krag, 30-30, 348 Win., 40-65, 45-70, 45-90, 50-2-1/2", others. **Barrel:** 22" to 34". **Weight:** NA. **Length:** NA. **Stock:** Extra fancy American walnut. **Sights:** Buckhorn or tang rear, blade or globe with apertures and spirit level front. **Features:** Authentic replicas of Sharps rifles. Octagon or half-octagon hand-polished barrel; German silver nose cap; straight or pistol grip. Made in U.S. by C. Sharps Arms Co. Inc.
Price: New Model 1885 Highwall (machined steel receiver, mid-range tang sight) .... from **$1,999.92**
Price: New Model 1885 Semi-Custom Highwall (silver-inlay pistol grip, single set trigger) .... from **$2,560.12**
Price: New Model 1885 Custom Grade (silver-inlay pistol grip, extra fancy walnut stock) .... from **$2,760.38**
Price: New Model 1875 Sporting Rifle (round barrel, buckhorn rear sight) .... from **$1,309.29**
Price: New Model 1874 Sporting & Long Range Rifle (octagon bbl., long-range tang sight) .... from **$2,542.80**
Price: New Model 1874 Custom Classic (half-octagon bbl., extra fancy walnut stock) .... from **$3,242.09**
Price: New Model 1874 Custom Hartford (oct. bbl. w/Hartford collar, l.range tang sight) .... from **$3,382,82**
Price: New Model 1874 Custom Long Range (oct. bbl. w/Hartford collar, l. range aper. sights) **$3,707.57**

LONE STAR ROLLING BLOCK RIFLES

Caliber: 30-40 Krag, 30-30, 32-40, 38-55, 40-50 SS, 40-50 BN, 40-65, 40-70 SS, 40-70 BN, 40-82, 40-90 SBN, 40-90 SS, 44-90 Rem. Sp., 45 Colt, 45-110 (3-1/4"), 45-110 (2-7/8"), 45-100, 45-90, 45-70, 50-70, 50-90. **Barrel:** 26" to 34". **Weight:** 6 to 11 lbs. **Length:** NA. **Stock:** American walnut. **Sights:** Buckhorn rear, blade or dovetail front. **Features:** Authentic replicas of Remington rolling block rifles. Round, tapered round, octagon, tapered octagon or half-octagon barrel; bone-pack, color case hardened action; drilled and tapped for vernier sight; single, single-set or double-set trigger; variety of sight, finish and engraving options. Fires blackpowder or factory ammo. Made in U.S. by Lone Star Rifle Co. Inc.
Price: No. 5 Sporting Rifle (30-30 or 30-40 Krag, 26" barrel, buckhorn rear sight) **$1,495.00**
Price: Cowboy Action Rifle (28" round barrel, buckhorn rear sight) **$1,495.00**
Price: Silhouette Rifle (32" or 34" round barrel, drilled and tapped for vernier sight) **$1,495.00**
Price: Sporting Rifle (straight grip, semi-crescent butt) .... from **$2,200.00**
Price: Target Rifle (pistol grip, shotgun-type butt) .... from **$2,200.00**

REMINGTON CUSTOM SHOP ROLLING BLOCK RIFLES

Caliber: 45-70. **Barrel:** 30". **Weight:** NA. **Length:** NA. **Stock:** American walnut. **Sights:** Buckhorn rear and blade front (optional tang-mounted vernier rear, globe with spirit level front). **Features:** Satin blue finish with case-colored receiver; single set trigger; steel Schnabel fore end tip; steel butt plate. From Remington Arms Co. Custom Gun Shop.
Price: No. 1 Mid-Range Sporter (round or half-octagon barrel) **$1,348.00**
Price: No. 1 Silhouette (heavy barrel with 1:18" twist; no sights) **$1,448.00**

SEMI-CUSTOM SHOTGUNS

Beretta Jubilee 12-gauge

Beretta Jubilee 20-gauge

Beretta Jubilee 28-gauge

Beretta Jubilee II 12-gauge

Beretta Jubilee II 20-gauge

BERETTA PREMIUM GRADE SHOTGUNS

Gauge: 12, 20, 410, 3" chamber; 28, 2-3/4" chamber. **Barrel:** 26", 28", 30", 32". **Weight:** 5 to 7-1/2 lbs. **Length:** NA. **Stock:** Highly figured English or American walnut; straight or pistol grip; hand-checkered. **Features:** Machined nickel-chrome-moly action, hand-fitted; cross-bolt breech lock; Boehler Antinit steel barrels with fixed chokes or Mobilchoke tubes; single selective or non-selective or double trigger; numerous stock and engraving options. From Beretta USA.
Price: Giubileo (Jubilee) o/u (engraved sideplates, trigger guard, safety and top lever) . . . . from **$13,750.00**
Price: Giubileo II (Jubilee II) s/s (English-style stock, engraved sideplates and fixtures) . . . . from **$13,750.00**
Price: ASE Deluxe o/u (engraved receiver and forend cap) . . . . from **$24,000.00**
Price: SO5 Trap (single, non-selective trigger, heavy beavertail fore end, fixed chokes) . . . . from **$19,500.00**
Price: SO5 Skeet (26" or 28" bbl., heavy beavertail fore end, fixed chokes) . . . . from **$19,500.00**
Price: SO5 Sporting (single, selective trigger, Mobilchoke tubes) . . . . from **$19,500.00**
Price: SO6 EELL o/u (engraved receiver with gold inlays, custom-fit stock) . . . . from **$42,700.00**
Price: SO6 EL o/u (light English scroll engravings on receiver) . . . . from **$25,500.00**
Price: SO6 EESS o/u (enamel-colored receiver in green, red or blue, arabesque engravings) **$51,000.00**
Price: SO9 o/u (single, non-selective trigger, engraved receiver and fixtures) . . . . from **$44,500.00**

Semi-Custom — Shotguns

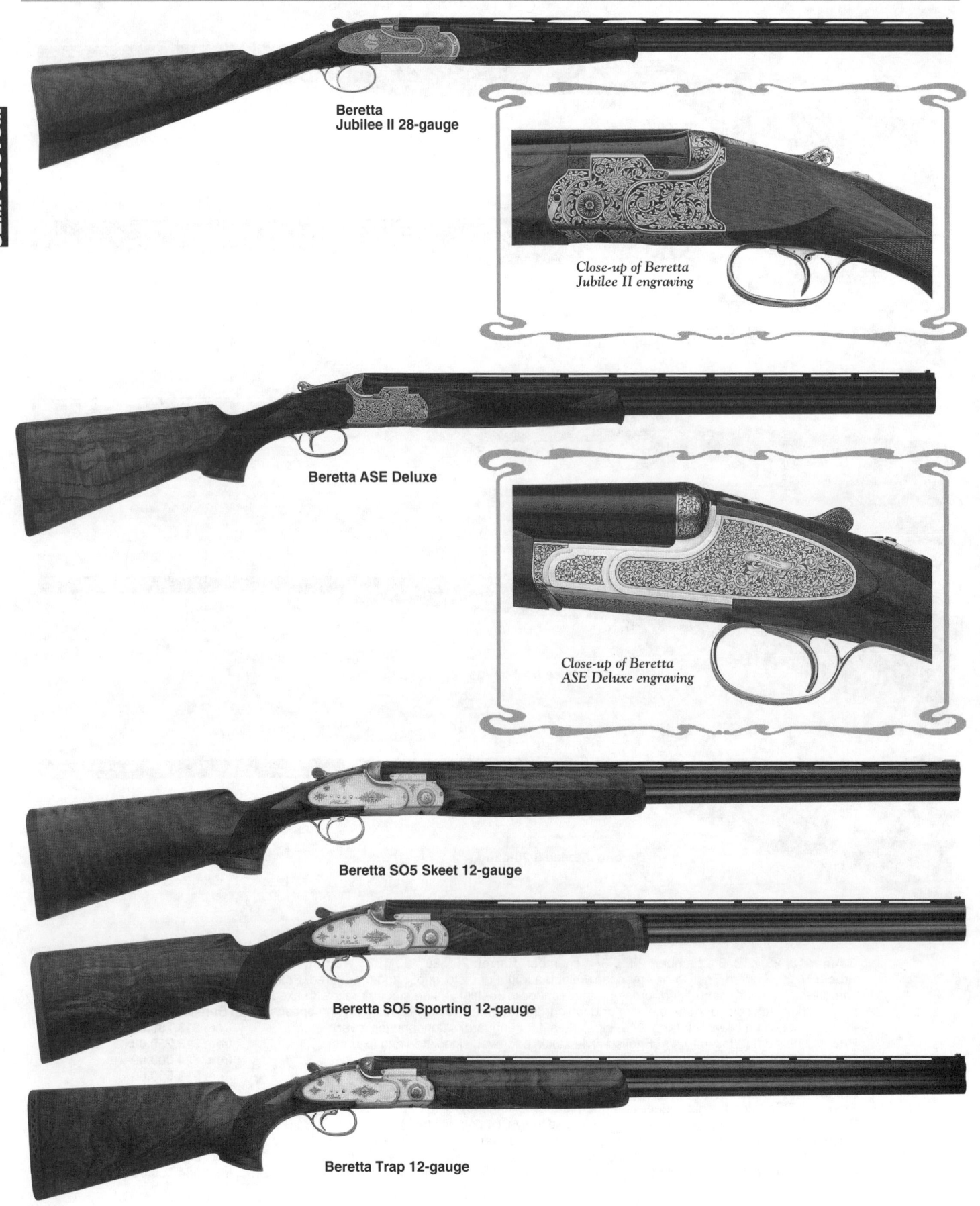

Beretta Jubilee II 28-gauge

Close-up of Beretta Jubilee II engraving

Beretta ASE Deluxe

Close-up of Beretta ASE Deluxe engraving

Beretta SO5 Skeet 12-gauge

Beretta SO5 Sporting 12-gauge

Beretta Trap 12-gauge

Semi-Custom — Shotguns

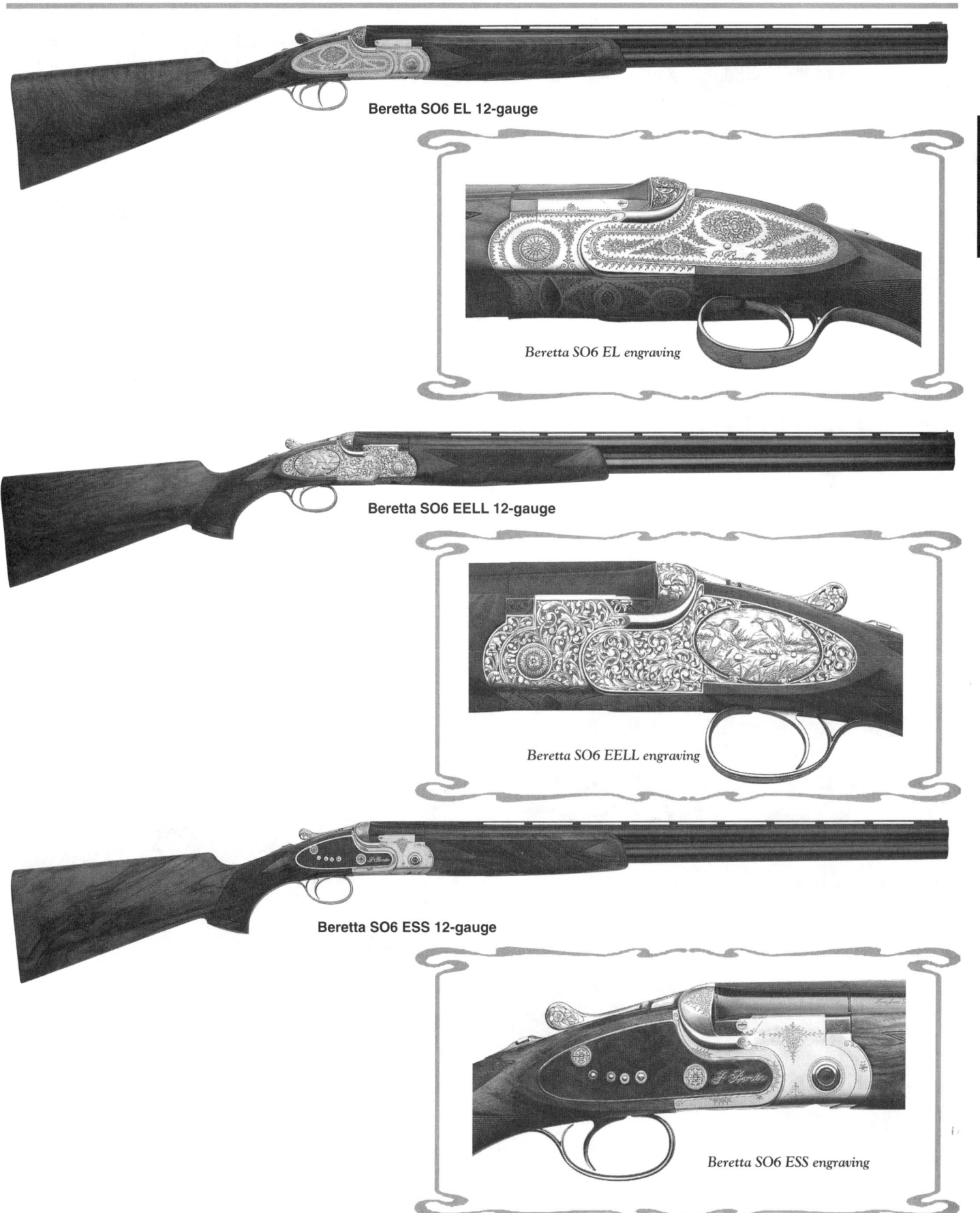

Beretta SO6 EL 12-gauge

Beretta SO6 EL engraving

Beretta SO6 EELL 12-gauge

Beretta SO6 EELL engraving

Beretta SO6 ESS 12-gauge

Beretta SO6 ESS engraving

Semi-Custom — Shotguns

Beretta SO9 12-gauge

Beretta SO9 20-gauge

Beretta SO9 410-gauge

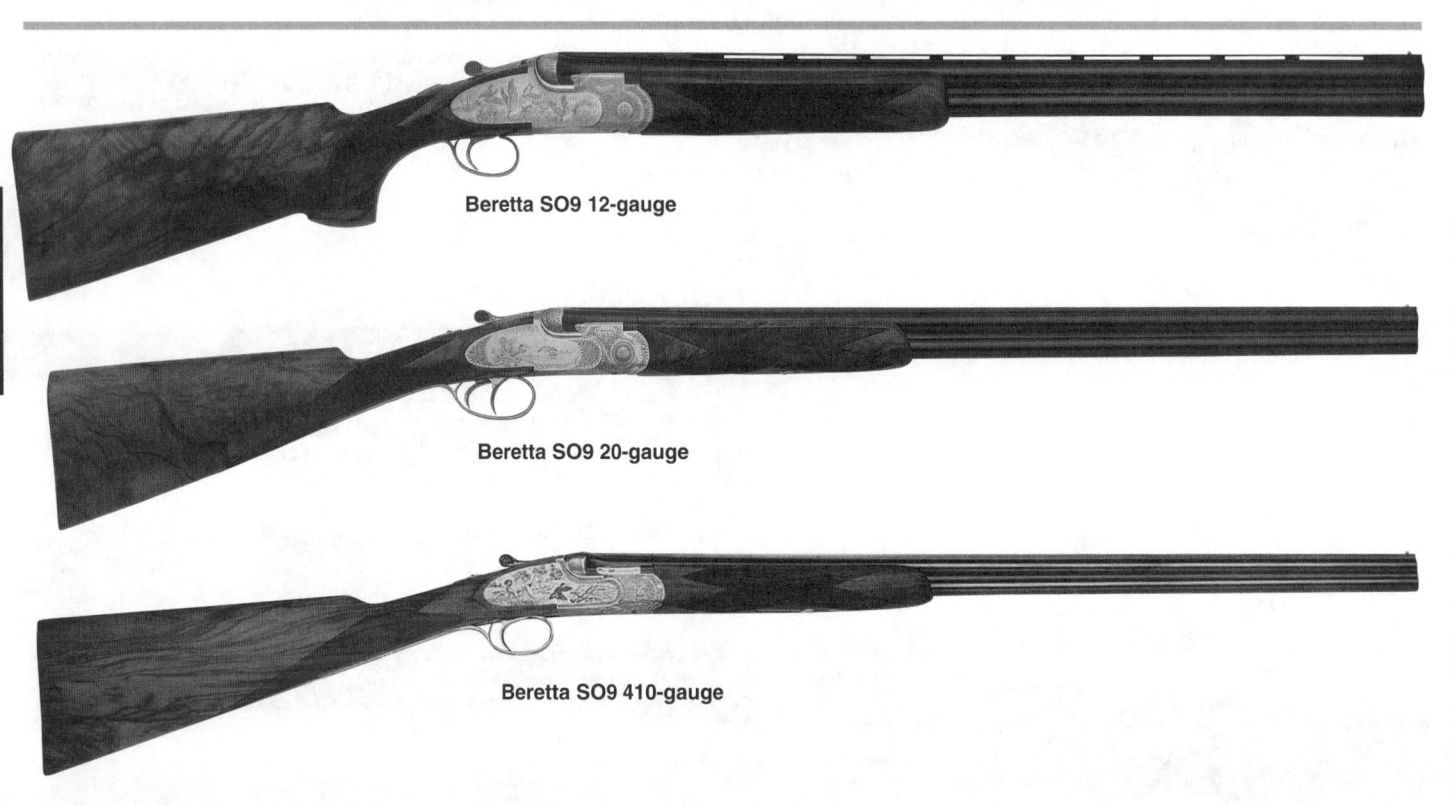

Examples of engraving on Beretta SO9

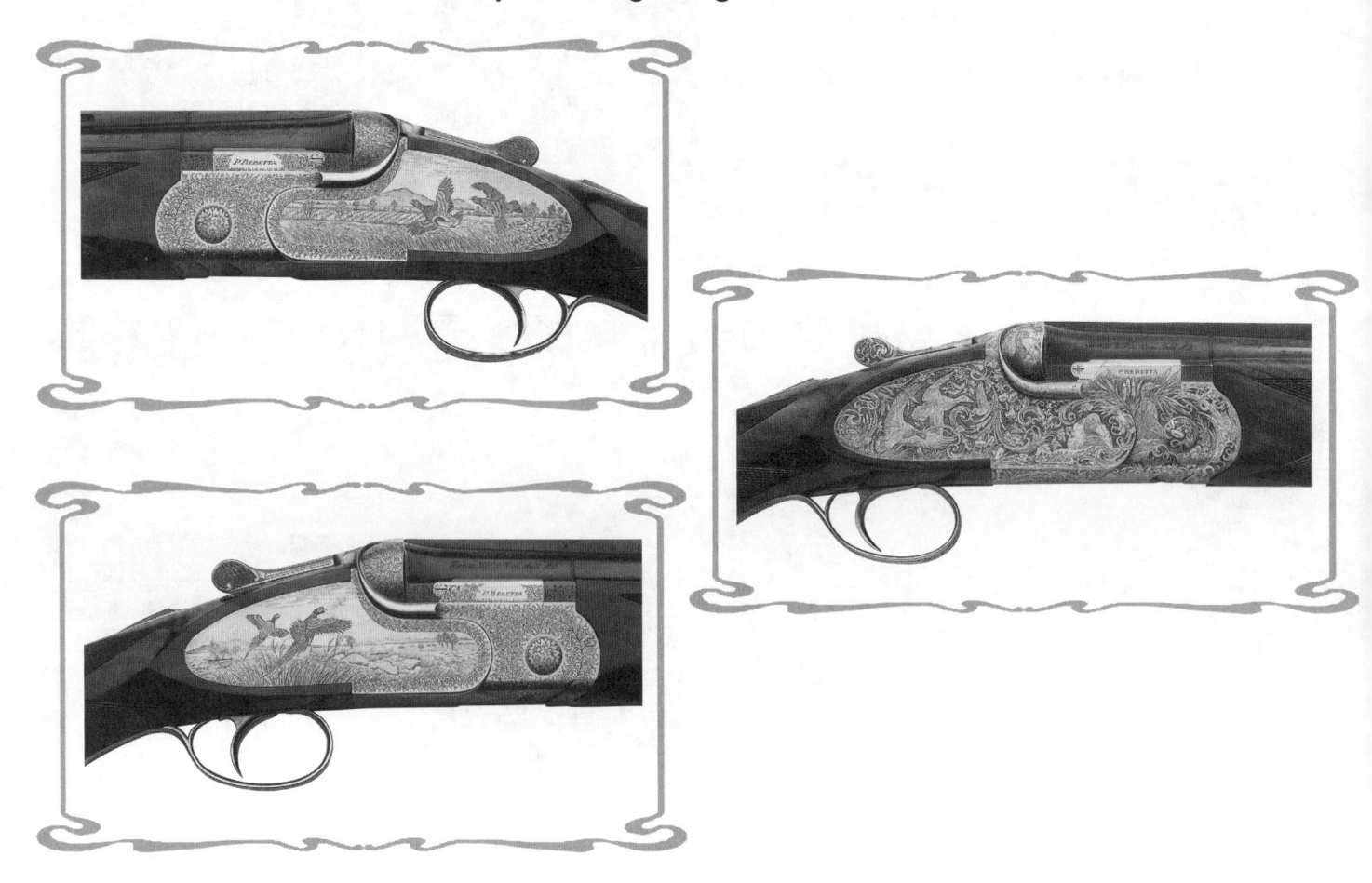

SEMI-CUSTOM — SHOTGUNS

Ithaca Grade 7E

Ithaca Sousa Grade

Ithaca Sousa Grade

ITHACA CLASSIC DOUBLES SIDE-BY-SIDE SHOTGUNS

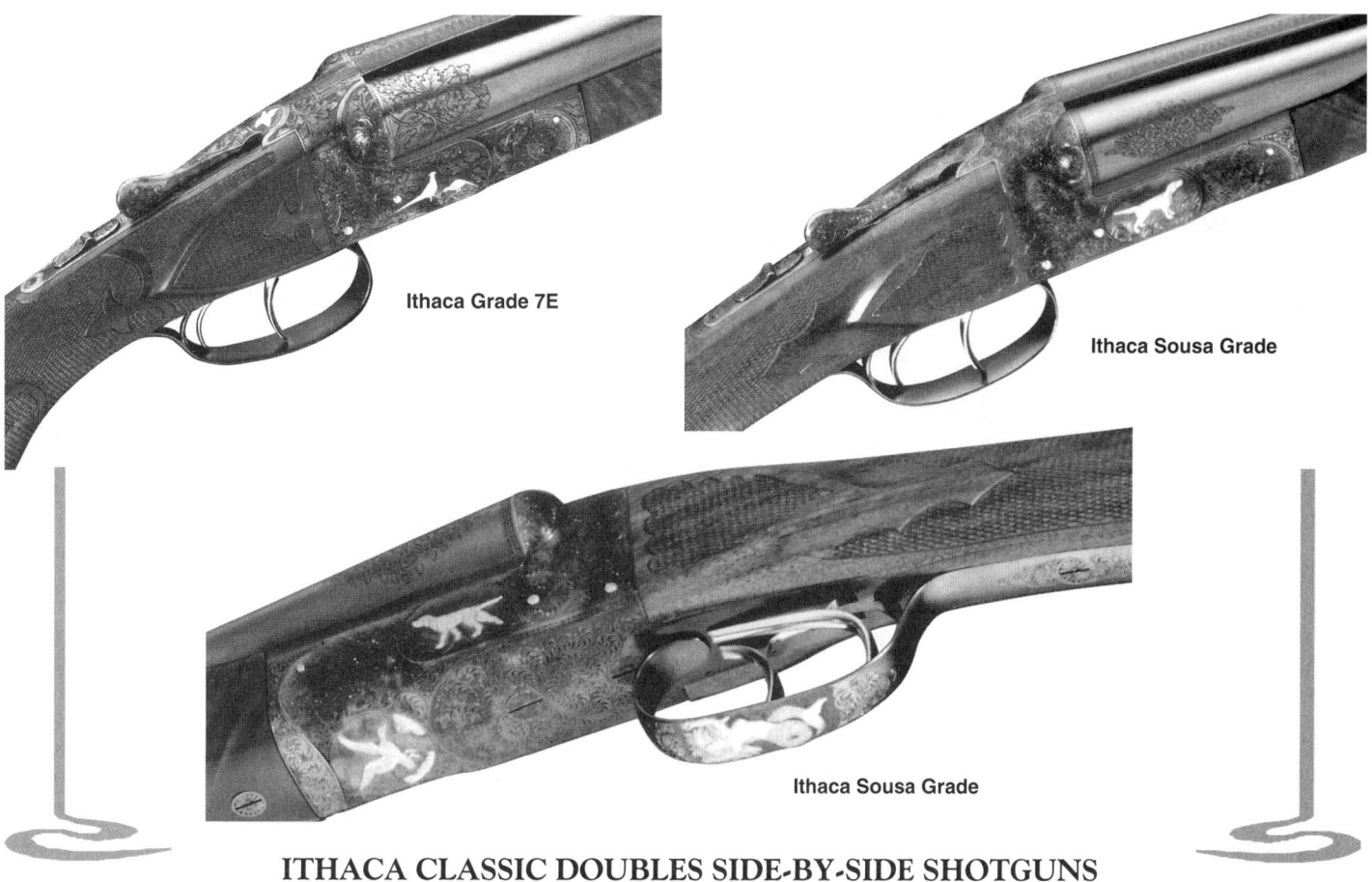

Gauge: 20, 28, 2-3/4" chamber; 410, 3" chamber. **Barrel:** 26", 28", 30". **Weight:** 5 lbs. 5 oz. (410 ga.) to 5 lbs. 14 oz. (20 ga.). **Length:** NA. **Stock:** Exhibition-grade American black walnut, hand-checkered with hand-rubbed oil finish. **Features:** Updated duplicates of original New Ithaca Double double-barrel shotguns. Hand-fitted boxlock action; splinter or beavertail forend; bone-charcoal color case-hardened receiver; chrome-moly steel rust-blued barrels; ejectors; gold double triggers; fixed chokes; hand-engraved game scenes. Made in U.S. by Ithaca Classic Doubles.
Price: Special Skeet Grade (plain color case-hardened receiver, feather crotch walnut stock) $3,465.00
Price: Grade 4E (gold-plated triggers, jeweled barrel flats, engraved game-bird scene) $4,625.00
Price: Grade 7E (gold-inlaid ducks, pheasants and bald eagle on scroll engraving) $9,200.00
Price: Sousa Grade (gold-inlaid setter, pointer, flying ducks and Sousa mermaid) $11,550.00

John Rigby Side-by-Side 12-gauge engraving

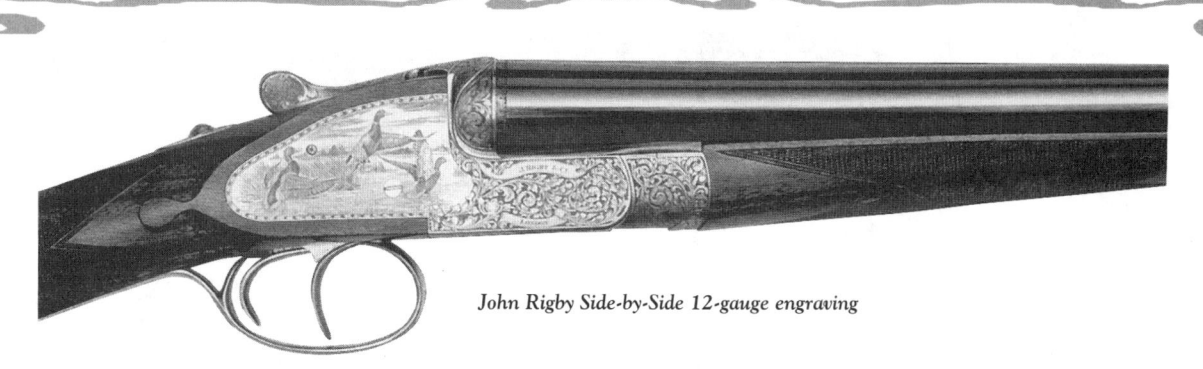

JOHN RIGBY SHOTGUNS

Gauge: 12, 16, 20, 28 and 410. **Barrel:** To customer specs. **Weight:** NA. **Length:** To customer specs. **Stock:** Customer's choice. **Features:** True sidelock side-by-side and over-under shotguns made to customer's specifications. Hand-fitted actions and stocks; engraved receivers embellished with game scenes; over-under includes removable choke tubes. Imported from England by John Rigby & Co.
Price: Sidelock over-under (single selective, non-selective or double triggers, 12 ga. only) . . . . from $28,750.00
Price: Sidelock side-by-side (engraved receiver, choice of stock wood) . . . . from $34,750.00

34TH EDITION, 2002 • 125

SEMI-CUSTOM — SHOTGUNS

Merkel 47E

Merkel 47SL

Merkel 280EL

Merkel 303EL

Merkel 2001EL

MERKEL EXHIBITION, VINTAGERS EXPO AND CUSTOM ENGRAVED SHOTGUNS

Gauge: 12, 16, 20, 28, 410. **Barrel:** 26-3/4", 28"; others optional. **Weight:** NA. **Length:** NA. **Stock:** Highly figured walnut; English (straight) or pistol grip. **Features:** Highly engraved versions of Merkel over-under and side-by-side shotguns. Imported from Germany by GSI Inc.
Price: . . . . NA

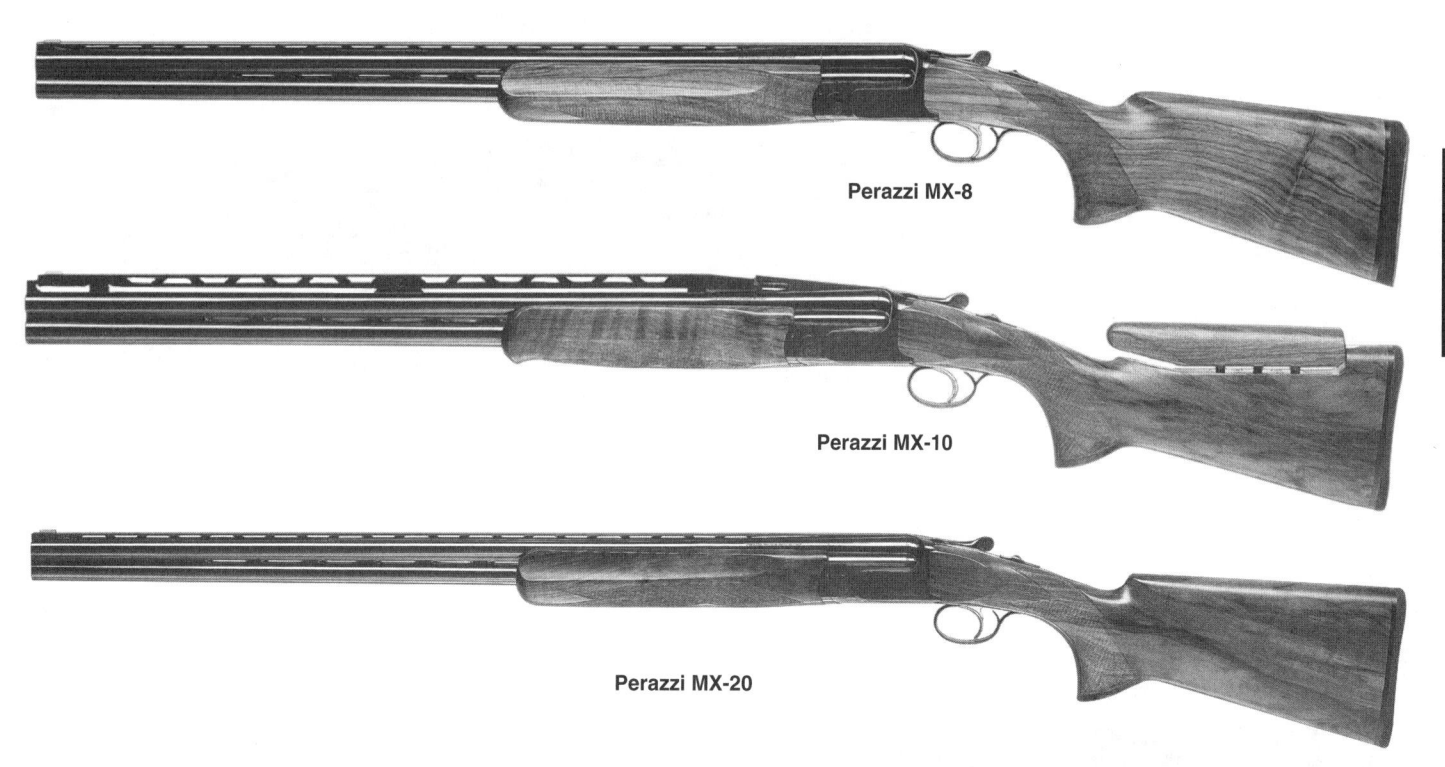

Semi-Custom — Shotguns

Perazzi MX-8

Perazzi MX-10

Perazzi MX-20

PERAZZI SCO, SCO GOLD, EXTRA AND EXTRA GOLD SHOTGUNS
Gauge: 12, 20, 28, 410. **Barrel:** 23-5/8" to 34". **Weight:** 6 lbs. 3 oz. to 8 lb. 13 oz. **Length:** NA. **Stock:** To customer specs. **Features:** Enhanced, engraved models of game and competition over-under shotguns. Customer may choose from many engraved hunting and wildlife scenes. Imported from Italy by Perazzi USA Inc.
Price: SCO Grade in competition and game o/u guns (fully engraved receiver) . . . . from **$25,500.00**
Price: SCO Gold Grade in comp. and game o/u guns (engraved w/gold inlays) . . . . from **$28,800.00**
Price: Extra Grade in competition and game o/u guns (highly detailed engraving) . . . . from **$72,900.00**
Price: Extra Gold Grade in comp. and game o/u guns (detailed engraving w/ gold inlays) . . . . from **$78,500.00**
Price: SCO Grade with engraved sideplates (extends engraved area) . . . . from **$39,100.00**
Price: SCO Gold Grade with engraved sideplates . . . . from **$45,450.00**

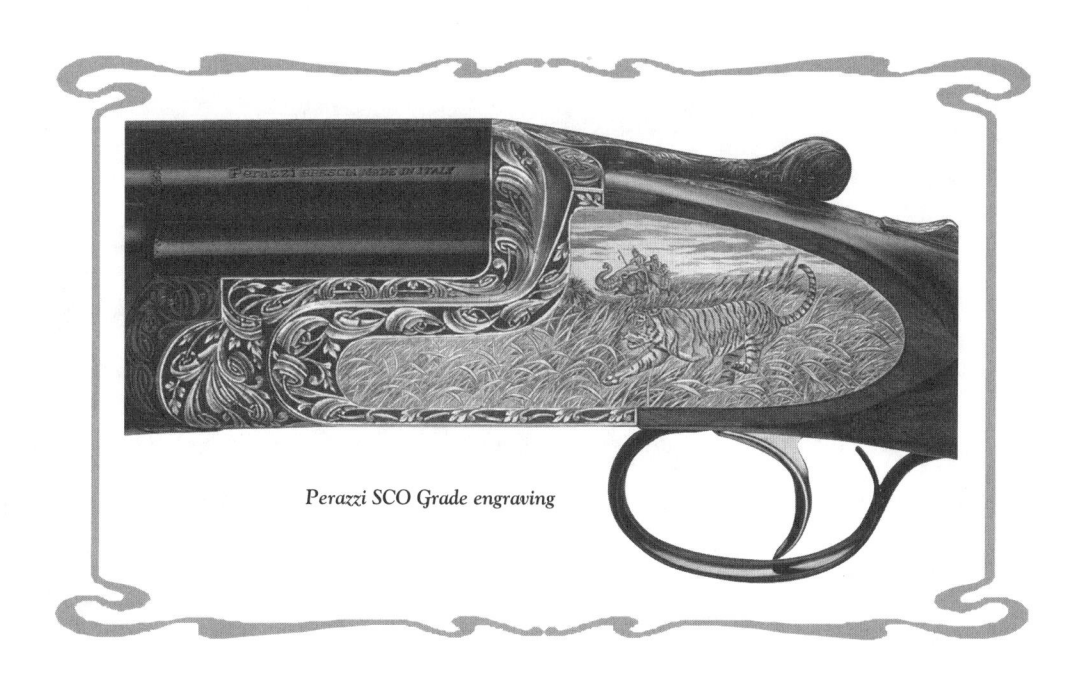

Perazzi SCO Grade engraving

Semi-Custom — Shotguns

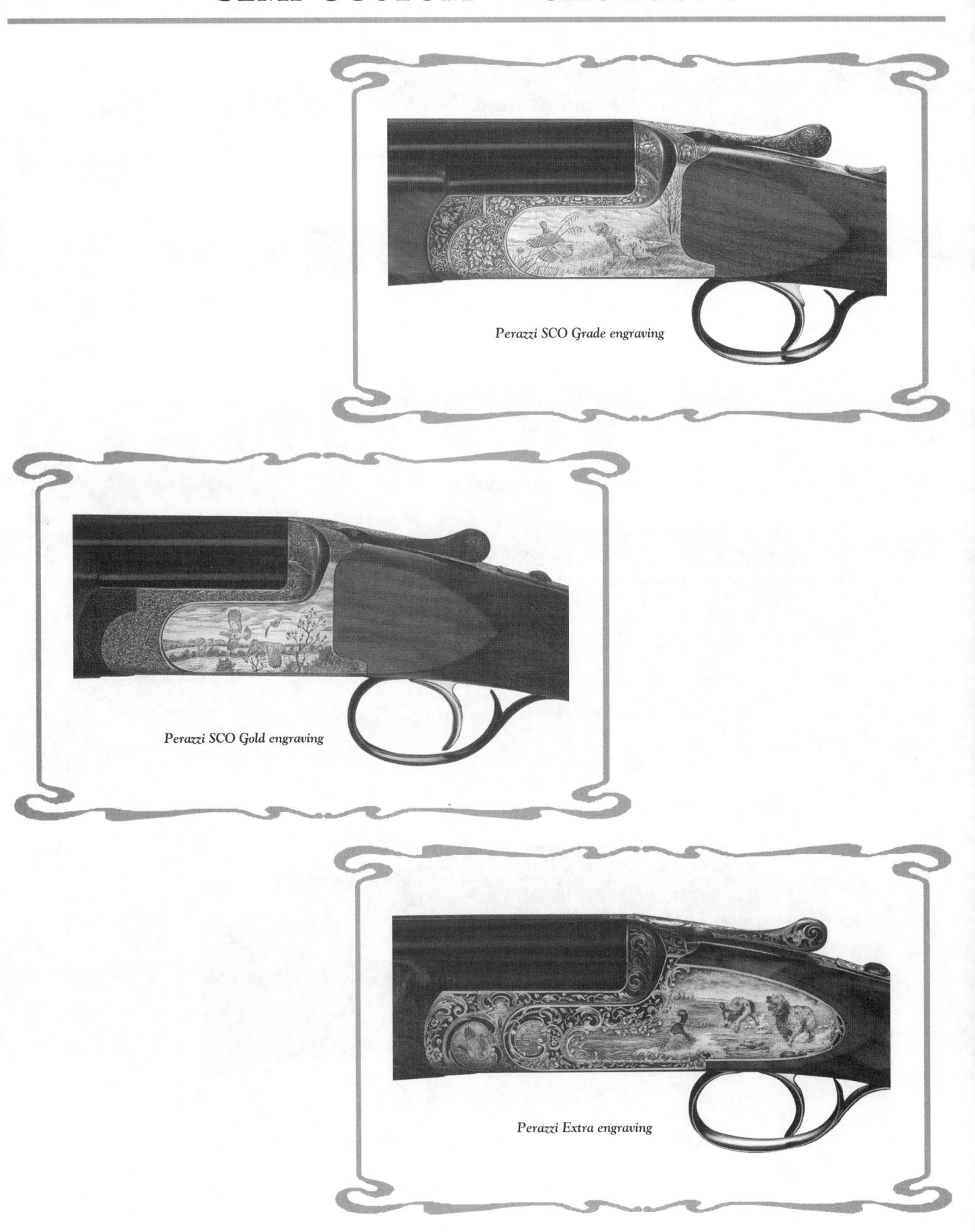

Perazzi SCO Grade engraving

Perazzi SCO Gold engraving

Perazzi Extra engraving

128 • GUNS ILLUSTRATED

SEMI-CUSTOM — SHOTGUNS

Remington 11-87 "F" Grade

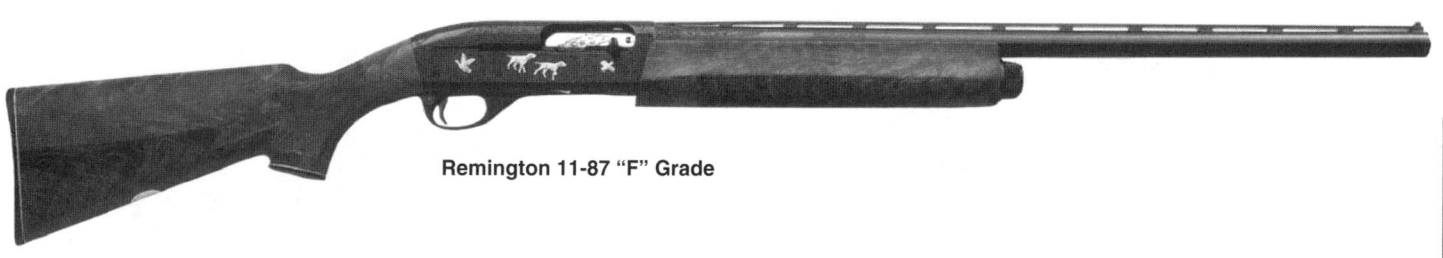

REMINGTON CUSTOM SHOP AUTO SHOTGUNS

Gauge: 10, 12, 20, 28. **Barrel:** 21" to 30". **Weight:** NA. **Length:** NA. **Stock:** Two grades of American walnut. **Features:** Engraved versions of the Model 11-87 and Model 1100 shotgun. "D" or "F" grade fancy walnut, hand-checkered stock; choice of ebony, rosewood, skeleton steel or solid steel grip cap; choice of solid steel, standard, Old English or ventilated recoil pad; optional inletted gold oval with three initials on bottom of stock. From Remington Arms. Co. Custom Gun Shop.
Price: 11-87 and 1100 "D" Grade (English scroll engraving on receiver, breech and trig. guard) $2,806.00
Price: 11-87 and 1100 "F" Grade (engraved game scene, "F" Grade walnut stock) $5,780.00
Price: 11-87 and 1100 "F" Grade with gold inlay (inlaid three-panel engraved game scene) $8,665.00

REMINGTON CUSTOM SHOP PUMP SHOTGUNS

Gauge: 10, 12, 20, 28, 410. **Barrel:** 20" to 30". **Weight:** NA. **Length:** NA. **Stock:** Two grades of American walnut. **Features:** Engraved versions of the Model 870 shotgun. "D" or "F" grade fancy walnut hand-checkered stock; choice of ebony, rosewood, skeleton steel or solid steel grip cap; choice of solid steel, standard, Old English or ventilated recoil pad; optional inletted gold oval with three initials on bottom of stock. From Remington Arms Co. Custom Gun Shop.
Price: 870 "D" Grade (English scroll engraving on receiver, breech and trig. guard) $2,806.00
Price: 870 "F" Grade (engraved game scene, "F" grade walnut stock) $5,780.00
Price: 870 "F" Grade with gold inlay (inlaid three-panel engraved game scene) $8,665.00

HANDGUNS — AUTOLOADERS, SERVICE & SPORT

Includes models suitable for several forms of competition and other sporting purposes.

Accu-Tek BL-9

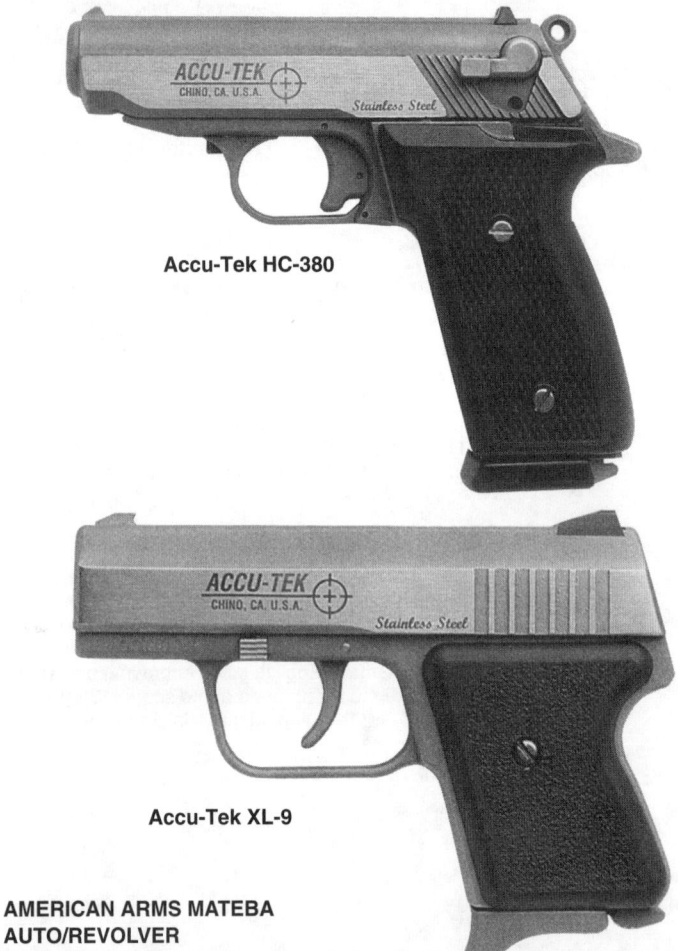

Accu-Tek AT-380

Accu-Tek HC-380

Accu-Tek XL-9

ACCU-TEK BL-9 AUTO PISTOL
Caliber: 9mm Para., 5-shot magazine. **Barrel:** 3". **Weight:** 22 oz. **Length:** 5.6" overall. **Stocks:** Black pebble composition. **Sights:** Fixed. **Features:** Double action only; black finish. Introduced 1997. Price includes cleaning kit and gun lock, two magazines. Made in U.S. by Accu-Tek.
Price: $232.00

Accu-Tek Model AT-32SS Auto Pistol
Same as the AT-380SS except chambered for 32 ACP. Introduced 1991. Price includes cleaning kit and gun lock.
Price: Satin stainless $221.00

ACCU-TEK MODEL AT-380 AUTO PISTOL
Caliber: 380 ACP, 5-shot magazine. **Barrel:** 2.75". **Weight:** 20 oz. **Length:** 5.6" overall. **Stocks:** Grooved black composition. **Sights:** Blade front, rear adjustable for windage. **Features:** Stainless steel frame and slide. External hammer; manual thumb safety; firing pin block, trigger disconnect. Introduced 1991. Price includes cleaning kit and gun lock. Made in U.S. by Accu-Tek.
Price: Satin stainless $221.00

ACCU-TEK MODEL HC-380 AUTO PISTOL
Caliber: 380 ACP, 10-shot magazine. **Barrel:** 2.75". **Weight:** 26 oz. **Length:** 6" overall. **Stocks:** Checkered black composition. **Sights:** Blade front, rear adjustable for windage. **Features:** External hammer; manual thumb safety with firing pin and trigger disconnect; bottom magazine release. Stainless steel construction. Introduced 1993. Price includes cleaning kit and gun lock. Made in U.S. by Accu-Tek.
Price: Satin stainless $231.00

ACCU-TEK XL-9 AUTO PISTOL
Caliber: 9mm Para., 5-shot magazine. **Barrel:** 3". **Weight:** 24 oz. **Length:** 5.6" overall. **Stocks:** Black pebble composition. **Sights:** Three-dot system; rear adjustable for windage. **Features:** Stainless steel construction; double-action-only mechanism. Introduced 1999. Price includes cleaning kit and gun lock, two magazines. Made in U.S. by Accu-Tek.
Price: $248.00

AMERICAN ARMS MATEBA AUTO/REVOLVER
Caliber: 357 Mag., 6-shot. **Barrel:** 4", 6", 8". **Weight:** 2.75 lbs. **Length:** 8.77" overall. **Stocks:** Smooth walnut. **Sights:** Blade on ramp front, adjustable rear. **Features:** Double or single action. Cylinder and slide recoil together upon firing. All-steel construction with polished blue finish. Introduced 1995. Imported from Italy by American Arms, Inc.
Price: $1,295.00
Price: 6" $1,349.00

AMT AUTOMAG II AUTO PISTOL
Caliber: 22 WMR, 9-shot magazine (7-shot with 3-3/8" barrel). **Barrel:** 3-3/8", 4-1/2", 6". **Weight:** About 32 oz. **Length:** 9-3/8" overall. **Stocks:** Grooved carbon fiber. **Sights:** Blade front, adjustable rear. **Features:** Made of stainless steel. Gas-assisted action. Exposed hammer. Slide flats have brushed finish, rest is sandblast. Squared trigger guard. Introduced 1986. From Galena Industries, Inc.
Price: $429.00

AMT AUTOMAG III PISTOL
Caliber: 30 Carbine, 8-shot magazine. **Barrel:** 6-3/8". **Weight:** 43 oz. **Length:** 10-1/2" overall. **Stocks:** Carbon fiber. **Sights:** Blade front, adjustable rear. **Features:** Stainless steel construction. Hammer-drop safety. Slide flats have brushed finish, rest is sandblasted. Introduced 1989. From Galena Industries, Inc.
Price: $529.00

AMT AUTOMAG IV PISTOL
Caliber: 45 Winchester Magnum, 6-shot magazine. **Barrel:** 6.5". **Weight:** 46 oz. **Length:** 10.5" overall. **Stocks:** Carbon fiber. **Sights:** Blade front, adjustable rear. **Features:** Made of stainless st3578eel with brushed finish. Introduced 1990. Made in U.S. by Galena Industries, Inc.
Price: $599.00

HANDGUNS — AUTOLOADERS, SERVICE & SPORT

AMT Backup

Auto-Ordnance Deluxe

Auto-Ordnance 1911A1 Standard

Auto-Ordnance Pit Bull

AMT 45 ACP HARDBALLER II
Caliber: 45 ACP. **Barrel:** 5". **Weight:** 39 oz. **Length:** 8-1/2" overall. **Stocks:** Wrap-around rubber. **Sights:** Adjustable. **Features:** Extended combat safety, serrated matte slide rib, loaded chamber indicator, long grip safety, beveled magazine well, adjustable target trigger. All stainless steel. From Galena Industries, Inc.
Price: $425.00
Price: Government model (as above except no rib, fixed sights) . $399.00
Price: 400 Accelerator (400 Cor-Bon, 7" barrel). $549.00
Price: Commando (40 S&W, Government Model frame) $435.00

AMT 45 ACP HARDBALLER LONG SLIDE
Caliber: 45 ACP. **Barrel:** 7". **Length:** 10-1/2" overall. **Stocks:** Wrap-around rubber. **Sights:** Fully adjustable rear sight. **Features:** Slide and barrel are 2" longer than the standard 45, giving less recoil, added velocity, longer sight radius. Has extended combat safety, serrated matte rib, loaded chamber indicator, wide adjustable trigger. From Galena Industries, Inc.
Price: $529.00

AMT BACKUP PISTOL
Caliber: 357 SIG (5-shot); 38 Super, 9mm Para. (6-shot); 40 S&W, 400 Cor-Bon; 45 ACP (5-shot). **Barrel:** 3". **Weight:** 23 oz. **Length:** 5-3/4" overall. **Stocks:** Checkered black synthetic. **Sights:** None. **Features:** Stainless steel construction; double-action-only trigger; dust cover over the trigger transfer bar; extended magazine; titanium nitride finish. Introduced 1992. Made in U.S. by Galena Industries.
Price: 9mm, 40 S&W, 45 ACP $319.00
Price: 38 Super, 357 SIG, 400 Cor-Bon $369.00

AMT 380 DAO Small Frame Backup
Similar to the DAO Backup except has smaller frame, 2-1/2" barrel, weighs 18 oz., and is 5" overall. Has 5-shot magazine, matte/stainless finish. Made in U.S. by Galena Industries.
Price: $319.00

AUTO-ORDNANCE 1911A1 AUTOMATIC PISTOL
Caliber: 45 ACP, 7-shot magazine. **Barrel:** 5". **Weight:** 39 oz. **Length:** 8-1/2" overall. **Stocks:** Checkered plastic with medallion. **Sights:** Blade front, rear adjustable for windage. **Features:** Same specs as 1911A1 military guns—parts interchangeable. Frame and slide blued; each radius has non-glare finish. Made in U.S. by Auto-Ordnance Corp.
Price: 45 ACP, blue $447.00
Price: 45 ACP, Parkerized $462.00
Price: 45 ACP Deluxe (three-dot sights, textured rubber wraparound grips). $455.00

Auto-Ordnance 1911A1 Custom High Polish Pistol
Similar to the standard 1911A1 except has a Videki speed trigger, extended thumb safety, flat mainspring housing, Acurod recoil spring guide system, rosewood grips, custom combat hammer, beavertail grip safety. High-polish blue finish. Introduced 1998. Made in U.S. by Auto-Ordnance Corp.
Price: $585.00

Auto-Ordnance ZG-51 Pit Bull Auto
Same as the 1911A1 except has 3-1/2" barrel, weighs 36 oz. and has an over-all length of 7-1/4". Available in 45 ACP only; 7-shot magazine. Introduced 1989.
Price: $470.00

AUTAUGA 32 AUTO PISTOL
Caliber: 32 ACP, 6-shot magazine. **Barrel:** 2". **Weight:** 11.3 oz. **Length:** 4.3" overall. **Stocks:** Black polymer. **Sights:** Fixed. **Features:** Double-action-only mechanism. Stainless steel construction. Uses Winchester Silver Tip ammunition.
Price: . . . . NA

HANDGUNS — AUTOLOADERS, SERVICE & SPORT

Baer Custom Carry

Baer Premium II

Beretta 96

BAER 1911 CUSTOM CARRY AUTO PISTOL
Caliber: 45 ACP, 7- or 10-shot magazine. **Barrel:** 5". **Weight:** 37 oz. **Length:** 8.5" overall. **Stocks:** Checkered walnut. **Sights:** Baer improved ramp-style dovetailed front, Novak low-mount rear. **Features:** Baer forged NM frame, slide and barrel with stainless bushing; fitted slide to frame; double serrated slide (full-size only); Baer speed trigger with 4-lb. pull; Baer deluxe hammer and sear, tactical-style extended ambidextrous safety, beveled magazine well; polished feed ramp and throated barrel; tuned extractor; Baer extended ejector, checkered slide stop; lowered and flared ejection port, full-length recoil guide rod; recoil buff. Partial listing shown. Made in U.S. by Les Baer Custom, Inc.

Price: Standard size, blued.	$1,640.00
Price: Standard size, stainless	$1,690.00
Price: Comanche size, blued	$1,640.00
Price: Comanche size, stainless.	$1,690.00
Price: Comanche size, aluminum frame, blued slide	$1,923.00
Price: Comanche size, aluminum frame, stainless slide	$1,995.00

BAER 1911 PREMIER II AUTO PISTOL
Caliber: 9x23, 38 Super, 400 Cor-Bon, 45 ACP, 7- or 10-shot magazine. **Barrel:** 5". **Weight:** 37 oz. **Length:** 8.5" overall. **Stocks:** Checkered rosewood, double diamond pattern. **Sights:** Baer dovetailed front, low-mount Bo-Mar rear with hidden leaf. **Features:** Baer NM forged steel frame and barrel with stainless bushing; slide fitted to frame; double serrated slide; lowered, flared ejection port; tuned, polished extractor; Baer extended ejector, checkered slide stop, aluminum speed trigger with 4-lb. pull, deluxe Commander hammer and sear, beavertail grip safety with pad, beveled magazine well, extended ambidextrous safety; flat mainspring housing; polished feed ramp and throated barrel; 30 lpi checkered front strap. Made in U.S. by Les Baer Custom, Inc.

Price: Blued	$1,428.00
Price: Stainless	$1,558.00
Price: 6" model, blued, from	$1,595.00

BAER 1911 S.R.P. PISTOL
Caliber: 45 ACP. **Barrel:** 5". **Weight:** 37 oz. **Length:** 8.5" overall. **Stocks:** Checkered walnut. **Sights:** Trijicon night sights. **Features:** Similar to the F.B.I. contract gun except uses Baer forged steel frame. Has Baer match barrel with supported chamber, Wolff springs, complete tactical action job. All parts Mag-na-fluxed; deburred for tactical carry. Has Baer Ultra Coat finish. Tuned for reliability. Contact Baer for complete details. Introduced 1996. Made in U.S. by Les Baer Custom, Inc.

Price: Government or Comanche length ... $2,240.00

BERETTA MODEL 92FS PISTOL
Caliber: 9mm Para., 10-shot magazine. **Barrel:** 4.9". **Weight:** 34 oz. **Length:** 8.5" overall. **Stocks:** Checkered black plastic. **Sights:** Blade front, rear adjustable for windage. Tritium night sights available. **Features:** Double action. Extractor acts as chamber loaded indicator, squared trigger guard, grooved front- and backstraps, inertia firing pin. Matte or blued finish. Introduced 1977. Made in U.S. and imported from Italy by Beretta U.S.A.

Price: With plastic grips ... $669.00

Beretta Model 92FS/96 Brigadier Pistols
Similar to the Model 92FS/96 except with a heavier slide to reduce felt recoil and allow mounting removable front sight. Wrap-around rubber grips. Three-dot sights dovetailed to the slide, adjustable for windage. Weighs 35.3 oz. Introduced 1999.

Price: 9mm or 40 S&W, 10-shot	$716.00
Price: Inox models (stainless steel)	$771.00

Beretta Model 92FS 470th Anniversary Limited Edition
Similar to the Model 92FS stainless except has mirror polish finish, smooth walnut grips with inlaid gold-plated medallions. Special and unique gold-filled engraving includes the signature of Beretta's president. The anniversary logo is engraved on the top of the slide and the back of the magazine. Each pistol identified by a "1 of 470" gold-filled number. Special chrome-plated magazine included. Deluxe lockable walnut case with teak inlays and engraving. Only 470 pistols will be sold. Introduced 1999.

Price: ... $2,082.00

Beretta Model 92FS Compact and Compact Type M Pistol
Similar to the Model 92FS except more compact and lighter: overall length 7.8"; 4.3" barrel; weighs 30.9 oz. Has Bruniton finish, chrome-lined bore, combat trigger guard, ambidextrous safety/decock lever. Single column 8-shot magazine (Type M), or double column 10-shot (Compact), 9mm only. Introduced 1998. Imported from Italy by Beretta U.S.A.

Price: Compact (10-shot)	$669.00
Price: Compact Type M (8-shot)	$669.00
Price: Compact Inox (stainless)	$734.00
Price: Compact Type M Inox (stainless)	$721.00

Beretta Model 96 Pistol
Same as the Model 92FS except chambered for 40 S&W. Ambidextrous safety mechanism with passive firing pin catch, slide safety/decocking lever, trigger bar disconnect. Has 10-shot magazine. Available with three-dot sights. Introduced 1992.

Price: Model 96, plastic grips	$669.00
Price: Stainless, rubber grips	$734.00

HANDGUNS — AUTOLOADERS, SERVICE & SPORT

Beretta 950 Jetfire

Beretta M8000/8040 Cougar

Bersa Thunder 380

BERETTA MODEL 80 CHEETAH SERIES DA PISTOLS
Caliber: 380 ACP, 10-shot magazine (M84); 8-shot (M85); 22 LR, 7-shot (M87). **Barrel:** 3.82". **Weight:** About 23 oz. (M84/85); 20.8 oz. (M87). **Length:** 6.8" overall. **Stocks:** Glossy black plastic (wood optional at extra cost). **Sights:** Fixed front, drift-adjustable rear. **Features:** Double action, quick takedown, convenient magazine release. Introduced 1977. Imported from Italy by Beretta U.S.A.
Price: Model 84 Cheetah, plastic grips $576.00
Price: Model 84 Cheetah, wood grips, nickel finish $652.00
Price: Model 85 Cheetah, plastic grips, 8-shot $545.00
Price: Model 85 Cheetah, wood grips, nickel, 8-shot $609.00
Price: Model 87 Cheetah, wood, 22 LR, 7-shot $576.00
Price: Model 87 Target, plastic grips $669.00

Beretta Model 86 Cheetah
Similar to the 380-caliber Model 85 except has tip-up barrel for first-round loading. Barrel length is 4.4", overall length of 7.33". Has 8-shot magazine, walnut grips. Introduced 1989.
Price: $578.00

BERETTA MODEL 950 JETFIRE AUTO PISTOL
Caliber: 25 ACP, 8-shot. **Barrel:** 2.4". **Weight:** 9.9 oz. **Length:** 4.7" overall. **Stocks:** Checkered black plastic or walnut. **Sights:** Fixed. **Features:** Single action, thumb safety; tip-up barrel for direct loading/unloading, cleaning. From Beretta U.S.A.
Price: Jetfire plastic, matte finish $226.00
Price: Jetfire plastic, stainless $267.00

Beretta Model 21 Bobcat Pistol
Similar to the Model 950 BS. Chambered for 22 LR or 25 ACP. Both double action. Has 2.4" barrel, 4.9" overall length; 7-round magazine on 22 cal.; 8 rounds in 25 ACP, 9.9 oz., available in nickel, matte, engraved or blue finish. Plastic grips. Introduced in 1985.
Price: Bobcat, 22 or 25, blue $285.00
Price: Bobcat, 22, stainless $307.00
Price: Bobcat, 22 or 25, matte $252.00

BERETTA MODEL 3032 TOMCAT PISTOL
Caliber: 32 ACP, 7-shot magazine. **Barrel:** 2.45". **Weight:** 14.5 oz. **Length:** 5" overall. **Stocks:** Checkered black plastic. **Sights:** Blade front, drift-adjustable rear. **Features:** Double action with exposed hammer; tip-up barrel for direct loading/unloading; thumb safety; polished or matte blue finish. Imported from Italy by Beretta U.S.A. Introduced 1996.
Price: Blue $370.00
Price: Matte $340.00
Price: Stainless $418.00
Price: Titanium $572.00

BERETTA MODEL 8000/8040/8045 COUGAR PISTOL
Caliber: 9mm Para., 10-shot, 40 S&W, 10-shot magazine; 45 ACP, 8-shot. **Barrel:** 3.6". **Weight:** 33.5 oz. **Length:** 7" overall. **Stocks:** Checkered plastic. **Sights:** Blade front, rear drift adjustable for windage. **Features:** Slide-mounted safety; rotating barrel; exposed hammer. Matte black Bruniton finish. Announced 1994. Imported from Italy by Beretta U.S.A.
Price: $709.00
Price: D model, 9mm, 40 S&W $739.00
Price: D model, 45 ACP $739.00

BERETTA MODEL 9000S COMPACT PISTOL
Caliber: 9mm Para., 40 S&W; 10-shot magazine. **Barrel:** 3.4". **Weight:** 26.8 oz. **Length:** 6.6". **Grips:** Soft polymer. **Sights:** Windage-adjustable white-dot rear, white-dot blade front. **Features:** Glass-reinforced polymer frame; patented tilt-barrel, open-slide locking system; chrome-lined barrel; external serrated hammer; automatic firing pin and manual safeties. Introduced 2000. Imported from Italy by Beretta USA.
Price: 9000S Type F (single and double action, external hammer) $551.00
Price: 9000S Type D (double-action only, no external hammer or safety) $551.00

Beretta Model 8000/8040/8045 Mini Cougar
Similar to the Model 8000/8040 Cougar except has shorter grip frame and weighs 27.6 oz. Introduced 1998. Imported from Italy by Beretta U.S.A.
Price: 9mm or 40 S&W $709.00
Price: 9mm or 40 S&W, DAO $739.00
Price: 45 ACP, 6-shot $739.00
Price: 45 ACP DAO $739.00

BERSA THUNDER 380 AUTO PISTOLS
Caliber: 380 ACP, 7-shot (Thunder 380 Lite), 9-shot magazine (Thunder 380 DLX). **Barrel:** 3.5". **Weight:** 23 oz. **Length:** 6.6" overall. **Stocks:** Black polymer. **Sights:** Blade front, notch rear adjustable for windage; three-dot system. **Features:** Double action; firing pin and magazine safeties. Available in blue or nickel. Introduced 1995. Distributed by Eagle Imports, Inc.
Price: Thunder 380, 7-shot, deep blue finish $248.95
Price: Thunder 380 Deluxe, 9-shot, satin nickel $291.95

34TH EDITION, 2002 • 133

HANDGUNS — AUTOLOADERS, SERVICE & SPORT

Browning Micro Buck Mark Standard

Calico M-110

Browning Buck Mark Challenge

BLUE THUNDER/COMMODORE 1911-STYLE AUTO PISTOLS
Caliber: 45 ACP, 7-shot magazine. **Barrel:** 4-1/4", 5". **Weight:** NA. **Length:** NA. **Grips:** Checkered hardwood. **Sights:** Blade front, drift-adjustable rear. **Features:** Extended slide release and safety, spring guide rod, skeltonized hammer and trigger, magazine bumper, beavertail grip safety. Imported from the Philippines by Century International Arms Inc.
Price: .... $464.80 to $484.80

BROWNING HI-POWER 9mm AUTOMATIC PISTOL
Caliber: 9mm Para.,10-shot magazine. **Barrel:** 4-21/32". **Weight:** 32 oz. **Length:** 7-3/4" overall. **Stocks:** Walnut, hand checkered, or black Polyamide. **Sights:** 1/8" blade front; rear screw-adjustable for windage and elevation. Also available with fixed rear (drift-adjustable for windage). **Features:** External hammer with half-cock and thumb safeties. A blow on the hammer cannot discharge a cartridge; cannot be fired with magazine removed. Fixed rear sight model available. Includes gun lock. Imported from Belgium by Browning.
Price: Fixed sight model, walnut grips $680.00
Price: Fully adjustable rear sight, walnut grips $730.00
Price: Mark III, standard matte black finish, fixed sight, moulded grips, ambidextrous safety $662.00

Browning Hi-Power Practical Pistol
Similar to the standard Hi-Power except has silver-chromed frame with blued slide, wrap-around Pachmayr rubber grips, round-style serrated hammer and removable front sight, fixed rear (drift-adjustable for windage). Available in 9mm Para. Includes gun lock. Introduced 1991.
Price: $717.00

BROWNING BUCK MARK STANDARD 22 PISTOL
Caliber: 22 LR, 10-shot magazine. **Barrel:** 5-1/2". **Weight:** 32 oz. **Length:** 9-1/2" overall. **Stocks:** Black moulded composite with checkering. **Sights:** Ramp front, Browning Pro Target rear adjustable for windage and elevation. **Features:** All steel, matte blue finish or nickel, gold-colored trigger. Buck Mark Plus has laminated wood grips. Includes gun lock. Made in U.S. Introduced 1985. From Browning.
Price: Buck Mark Standard, blue $286.00
Price: Buck Mark Nickel, nickel finish with contoured rubber grips $338.00
Price: Buck Mark Plus, matte blue with laminated wood grips ... $350.00
Price: Buck Mark Plus Nickel, nickel finish, laminated wood grips $383.00

Browning Buck Mark Camper
Similar to the Buck Mark except 5-1/2" bull barrel. Weight is 34 oz. Matte blue finish, molded composite grips. Introduced 1999. From Browning.
Price: $258.00
Price: Camper Nickel, nickel finish, molded composite grips $287.00

Browning Buck Mark Challenge
Similar to the Buck Mark except has a lightweight barrel and smaller grip diameter. Barrel length is 5-1/2", weight is 25 oz. Introduced 1999. From Browning.
Price: $320.00

Browning Buck Mark Micro
Same as the Buck Mark Standard and Buck Mark Plus except has 4" barrel. Available in blue or nickel. Has 16-click Pro Target rear sight. Introduced 1992.
Price: Micro Standard, matte blue finish. $286.00
Price: Micro Nickel, nickel finish $338.00
Price: Buck Mark Micro Plus, matte blue, lam. wood grips $350.00
Price: Buck Mark Micro Plus Nickel $383.00

Browning Buck Mark Bullseye
Same as the Buck Mark Standard except has 7-1/4" fluted barrel, matte blue finish. Weighs 36 oz.
Price: Bullseye Standard, molded composite grips $420.00
Price: Bullseye Target, contoured rosewood grips $541.00

Browning Buck Mark 5.5
Same as the Buck Mark Standard except has a 5-1/2" bull barrel with integral scope mount, matte blue finish.
Price: 5.5 Field, Pro-Target adj. rear sight, contoured walnut grips $459.00
Price: 5.5 Target, hooded adj. target sights, contoured walnut grips $459.00

Buck Mark Commemorative
Same as the Buck Mark Standard except has a 6-3/4" Challenger-style barrel, matte blue finish and scrimshaw-style, bonded ivory grips. Includes pistol rug. Limited to 1,000 guns.
Price: Commemorative $437.00

CALICO M-110 AUTO PISTOL
Caliber: 22 LR. **Barrel:** 6". **Weight:** 3.7 lbs. (loaded). **Length:** 17.9" overall. **Stocks:** Moulded composition. **Sights:** Adjustable post front, notch rear. **Features:** Aluminum alloy frame; compensator; pistol grip compartment; ambidextrous safety. Uses same helical-feed magazine as M-100 Carbine. Introduced 1986. Made in U.S. From Calico.
Price: $570.00

CARBON-15 (Type 97) PISTOL
Caliber: 223, 10-shot magazine. **Barrel:** 7.25". **Weight:** 46 oz. **Length:** 20" overall. **Stock:** Checkered composite. **Sights:** Ghost ring. **Features:** Semi-automatic, gas-operated, rotating bolt action. Carbon fiber upper and lower receiver; chromemoly bolt carrier; fluted stainless match barrel; mil. spec. optics mounting base; uses AR-15-type magazines. Introduced 1992. From Professional Ordnance, Inc.
Price: $1,600.00
Price: Type 20 pistol (light-profile barrel, no compensator, weighs 40 oz.) $1,500.00

HANDGUNS — AUTOLOADERS, SERVICE & SPORT

Carbon-15

Colt 1991 Model O Compact

Charles Daly M-1911-A1P

Colt XS Model O Commander

Colt XS Lightweight Commander

CHARLES DALY M-1911-A1P AUTOLOADING PISTOL
Caliber: 45 ACP, 7- or 10-shot magazine. **Barrel:** 5". **Weight:** 38 oz. **Length:** 8-3/4" overall. **Stocks:** Checkered. **Sights:** Blade front, rear drift adjustable for windage; three-dot system. **Features:** Skeletonized combat hammer and trigger; beavertail grip safety; extended slide release; oversize thumb safety; Parkerized finish. Introduced 1996. Imported from the Philippines by K.B.I., Inc.
Price: $469.95

COLT MODEL 1991 MODEL O AUTO PISTOL
Caliber: 45 ACP, 7-shot magazine. **Barrel:** 5". **Weight:** 38 oz. **Length:** 8.5" overall. **Stocks:** Checkered black composition. **Sights:** Ramped blade front, fixed square notch rear, high profile. **Features:** Matte finish. Continuation of serial number range used on original G.I. 1911 A1 guns. Comes with one magazine and moulded carrying case. Introduced 1991.
Price: $645.00
Price: Stainless.. $800.00

Colt Model 1991 Model O Commander Auto Pistol
Similar to the Model 1991 A1 except has 4-1/4" barrel. Overall length is 7-3/4". Comes with one 7-shot magazine, molded case.
Price: Blue $645.00
Price: Stainless steel $800.00

COLT XSE SERIES MODEL O AUTO PISTOLS
Caliber: 45 ACP, 8-shot magazine. **Barrel:** 4.25", 5". **Weight:** NA. **Length:** NA. **Grips:** Checkered, double diamond rosewood. **Sights:** Drift-adjustable three-dot combat. **Features:** Brushed stainless finish; adjustable, two-cut aluminum trigger; extended ambidextrous thumb safety; upswept beavertail with palm swell; elongated slot hammer; beveled magazine well. Introduced 1999. From Colt's Manufacturing Co., Inc.
Price: XSE Government (5" barrel) $950.00
Price: XSE Commander (4.25" barrel) $950.00

COLT XSE LIGHTWEIGHT COMMANDER AUTO PISTOL
Caliber: 45 ACP, 8-shot. **Barrel:** 4-1/4". **Weight:** 26 oz. **Length:** 7-3/4" overall. **Stocks:** Double diamond checkered rosewood. **Sights:** Fixed, glare-proofed blade front, square notch rear; three-dot system. **Features:** Brushed stainless slide, nickeled aluminum frame; McCormick elongated-slot enhanced hammer, McCormick two-cut adjustable aluminum hammer. Made in U.S. by Colt's Mfg. Co., Inc.
Price: 45, stainless $950.00

COLT DEFENDER
Caliber: 40 S&W, 45 ACP, 7-shot magazine. **Barrel:** 3". **Weight:** 22-1/2 oz. **Length:** 6-3/4" overall. **Stocks:** Pebble-finish rubber wraparound with finger grooves. **Sights:** White dot front, snag-free Colt competition rear. **Features:** Stainless finish; aluminum frame; combat-style hammer; Hi Ride grip safety, extended manual safety, disconnect safety. Introduced 1998. Made in U.S. by Colt's Mfg. Co.
Price: $773.00

HANDGUNS — AUTOLOADERS, SERVICE & SPORT

Colt Lightweight Commander

Colt Defender

Coonan 357 Magnum

CZ 75B 9mm

CZ 75B Decocker

COONAN 357 MAGNUM, 41 MAGNUM PISTOLS
Caliber: 357 Mag., 41 Magnum, 7-shot magazine. **Barrel:** 5". **Weight:** 42 oz. **Length:** 8.3" overall. **Stocks:** Smooth walnut. **Sights:** Interchangeable ramp front, rear adjustable for windage. **Features:** Stainless steel construction. Unique barrel hood improves accuracy and reliability. Link-less barrel. Many parts interchange with Colt autos. Has grip, hammer, half-cock safeties, extended slide latch. Made in U.S. by Coonan Arms, Inc.
Price: 5" barrel, from.................................$735.00
Price: 6" barrel, from.................................$768.00
Price: With 6" compensated barrel................$1,014.00
Price: Classic model (Teflon black two-tone finish, 8-shot magazine, fully adjustable rear sight, integral compensated barrel).....$1,400.00
Price: 41 Magnum Model, from......................$825.00

Coonan Compact Cadet 357 Magnum Pistol
Similar to the 357 Magnum full-size gun except has 3.9" barrel, shorter frame, 6-shot magazine. Weight is 39 oz., overall length 7.8". Linkless bull barrel, full-length recoil spring guide rod, extended slide latch. Introduced 1993. Made in U.S. by Coonan Arms, Inc.
Price:...$855.00

CZ 75B AUTO PISTOL
Caliber: 9mm Para., 40 S&W, 10-shot magazine. **Barrel:** 4.7". **Weight:** 34.3 oz. **Length:** 8.1" overall. **Stocks:** High impact checkered plastic. **Sights:** Square post front, rear adjustable for windage; three-dot system. **Features:** Single action/double action design; firing pin block safety; choice of black polymer, matte or high-polish blue finishes. All-steel frame. Imported from the Czech Republic by CZ-USA.
Price: Black polymer...................................$472.00
Price: Glossy blue.....................................$486.00
Price: Dual tone or satin nickel.......................$486.00
Price: 22 LR conversion unit..........................$279.00

CZ 75B Decocker
Similar to the CZ 75B except has a decocking lever in place of the safety lever. All other specifications are the same. Introduced 1999. Imported from the Czech Republic by CZ-USA.
Price: 9mm, black polymer.............................$467.00
New! Price: 40 S&W...................................$481.00

136 • GUNS ILLUSTRATED

HANDGUNS — AUTOLOADERS, SERVICE & SPORT

CZ 75D Compact

CZ 83B

CZ 85

CZ 97B

CZ 75B Compact Auto Pistol
Similar to the CZ 75 except has 10-shot magazine, 3.9" barrel and weighs 32 oz. Has removable front sight, non-glare ribbed slide top. Trigger guard is squared and serrated; combat hammer. Introduced 1993. Imported from the Czech Republic by CZ-USA.
Price: 9mm, black polymer	$499.00
Price: Dual tone or satin nickel	$513.00
Price: D Compact, black polymer	$526.00

CZ 75M IPSC Auto Pistol
Similar to the CZ 75B except has a longer frame and slide, slightly larger grip to accommodate new heavy-duty magazine. Ambidextrous thumb safety, safety notch on hammer; two-port in-frame compensator; slide racker; frame-mounted Firepoint red dot sight. Introduced 2001. Imported from the Czech Republic by CZ USA.
Price: 40 S&W, 10-shot mag.	$1,498.00
Price: CZ 75 Standard IPSC (40 S&W, adj. sights)	$1,038.00

CZ 85B Auto Pistol
Same gun as the CZ 75 except has ambidextrous slide release and safety-levers; non-glare, ribbed slide top; squared, serrated trigger guard; trigger stop to prevent overtravel. Introduced 1986. Imported from the Czech Republic by CZ-USA.
Price: Black polymer	$483.00
Price: Combat, black polymer	$540.00
Price: Combat, dual tone	$487.00
Price: Combat, glossy blue	$499.00

CZ 85 Combat
Similar to the CZ 85B (9mm only) except has an adjustable rear sight, adjustable trigger for overtravel, free-fall magazine, extended magazine catch. Does not have the firing pin block safety. Introduced 1999. Imported from the Czech Republic by CZ-USA.
Price: 9mm, black polymer	$540.00
Price: 9mm, glossy blue	$561.00
Price: 9mm, dual tone or satin nickel	$561.00

CZ 83B DOUBLE-ACTION PISTOL
Caliber: 9mm Makarov, 32 ACP, 380 ACP, 10-shot magazine. **Barrel:** 3.8". **Weight:** 26.2 oz. **Length:** 6.8" overall. **Stocks:** High impact checkered plastic. **Sights:** Removable square post front, rear adjustable for windage; three-dot system. **Features:** Single action/double action; ambidextrous magazine release and safety. Blue finish; non-glare ribbed slide top. Imported from the Czech Republic by CZ-USA.
Price: Blue	$378.00
Price: Nickel	$378.00

CZ 97B AUTO PISTOL
Caliber: 45 ACP, 10-shot magazine. **Barrel:** 4.85". **Weight:** 40 oz. **Length:** 8.34" overall. **Stocks:** Checkered walnut. **Sights:** Fixed. **Features:** Single action/double action; full-length slide rails; screw-in barrel bushing; linkless barrel; all-steel construction; chamber loaded indicator; dual transfer bars. Introduced 1999. Imported from the Czech Republic by CZ-USA.
Price: Black polymer	$607.00
Price: Glossy blue	$621.00

HANDGUNS — AUTOLOADERS, SERVICE & SPORT

CZ 75/85 Kadet

CZ 100

Davis P-380

Davis P-32

Desert Eagle Mark XIX

CZ 75/85 KADET AUTO PISTOL
Caliber: 22 LR, 10-shot magazine. **Barrel:** 4.88". **Weight:** 36 oz. **Length:** NA. **Stocks:** High impact checkered plastic. **Sights:** Blade front, fully adjustable rear. **Features:** Single action/double action mechanism; all-steel construction. Duplicates weight, balance and function of the CZ 75 pistol. Introduced 1999. Imported from the Czech Republic by CZ-USA.
Price: Black polymer $486.00

CZ 100 AUTO PISTOL
Caliber: 9mm Para., 40 S&W, 10-shot magazine. **Barrel:** 3.7". **Weight:** 24 oz. **Length:** 6.9" overall. **Stocks:** Grooved polymer. **Sights:** Blade front with dot, white outline rear drift adjustable for windage. **Features:** Double action only with firing pin block; polymer frame, steel slide; has laser sight mount. Introduced 1996. Imported from the Czech Republic by CZ-USA.
Price: 9mm Para $405.00
Price: 40 S&W $405.00

DAVIS P-380 AUTO PISTOL
Caliber: 380 ACP, 5-shot magazine. **Barrel:** 2.8". **Weight:** 22 oz. **Length:** 5.4" overall. **Stocks:** Black composition. **Sights:** Fixed. **Features:** Choice of chrome or black Teflon finish. Introduced 1991. Made in U.S. by Davis Industries.
Price: $98.00

DAVIS P-32 AUTO PISTOL
Caliber: 32 ACP, 6-shot magazine. **Barrel:** 2.8". **Weight:** 22 oz. **Length:** 5.4" overall. **Stocks:** Laminated wood. **Sights:** Fixed. **Features:** Choice of black Teflon or chrome finish. Announced 1986. Made in U.S. by Davis Industries.
Price: $107.00

DESERT EAGLE MARK XIX PISTOL
Caliber: 357 Mag., 9-shot; 44 Mag., 8-shot; 50 Magnum, 7-shot. **Barrel:** 6", 10", interchangeable. **Weight:** 357 Mag.—62 oz.; 44 Mag.—69 oz.; 50 Mag.— 72 oz. **Length:** 10-1/4" overall (6" bbl.). **Stocks:** Rubber. **Sights:** Blade on ramp front, combat-style rear. Adjustable available. **Features:** Interchangeable barrels; rotating three-lug bolt; ambidextrous safety; adjustable trigger. Military epoxy finish. Satin, bright nickel, hard chrome, polished and blued finishes available. 10" barrel extra. Imported from Israel by Magnum Research, Inc.
Price: 357, 6" bbl., standard pistol $1,199.00
Price: 44 Mag., 6", standard pistol $1,199.00
Price: 50 Magnum, 6" bbl., standard pistol $1,199.00
Price: 440 Cor-Bon, 6" bbl. $1,389.00

HANDGUNS — AUTOLOADERS, SERVICE & SPORT

Desert Eagle Baby Eagle

Entréprise Elite P500

E.A.A. Witness

Entréprise Boxer P500

DESERT EAGLE BABY EAGLE PISTOLS
Caliber: 9mm Para., 40 S&W, 45 ACP, 10-round magazine. **Barrel:** 3.5", 3.7", 4.72". **Weight:** NA. **Length:** 7.25" to 8.25" overall. **Grips:** Polymer. **Sights:** Drift-adjustable rear, blade front. **Features:** Steel frame and slide; polygonal rifling to reduce barrel wear; slide safety; decocker. Reintroduced in 1999. Imported from Israel by Magnum Research Inc.
Price: Standard (9mm or 40 cal.; 4.72" barrel, 8.25" overall) . . . $499.00
Price: Semi-Compact (9mm, 40 or 45 cal.; 3.7" barrel,
7.75" overall) $499.00
Price: Compact (9mm or 40 cal.; 3.5" barrel, 7.25" overall) $499.00
Price: Polymer (9mm or 40 cal; polymer frame; 3.25" barrel,
7.25" overall) $499.00

E.A.A. WITNESS DA AUTO PISTOL
Caliber: 9mm Para., 10-shot magazine; 38 Super, 40 S&W, 10-shot magazine; 45 ACP, 10-shot magazine. **Barrel:** 4.50". **Weight:** 35.33 oz. **Length:** 8.10" overall. **Stocks:** Checkered rubber. **Sights:** Undercut blade front, open rear adjustable for windage. **Features:** Double-action trigger system; round trigger guard; frame-mounted safety. Introduced 1991. Imported from Italy by European American Armory.
Price: 9mm, blue. $351.00
Price: 9mm, Wonder finish $366.00
Price: 9mm Compact, blue, 10-shot $351.00
Price: As above, Wonder finish $366.60
Price: 40 S&W, blue $366.60
Price: As above, Wonder finish $366.60
Price: 40 S&W Compact, 9-shot, blue $366.60
Price: As above, Wonder finish $366.60
Price: 45 ACP, blue. $351.00
Price: As above, Wonder finish $366.60
Price: 45 ACP Compact, 8-shot, blue $351.00
Price: As above, Wonder finish $366.60

E.A.A. EUROPEAN MODEL AUTO PISTOLS
Caliber: 32 ACP or 380 ACP, 7-shot magazine. **Barrel:** 3.88". **Weight:** 26 oz. **Length:** 7-3/8" overall. **Stocks:** European hardwood. **Sights:** Fixed blade front, rear drift-adjustable for windage. **Features:** Chrome or blue finish; magazine, thumb and firing pin safeties; external hammer; safety-lever takedown. Imported from Italy by European American Armory.
Price: Blue $132.60
Price: Wonder finish $163.80

ENTRÉPRISE ELITE P500 AUTO PISTOL
Caliber: 45 ACP, 10-shot magazine. **Barrel:** 5". **Weight:** 40 oz. **Length:** 8.5" overall. **Stocks:** Black ultra-slim, double diamond, checkered synthetic. **Sights:** Dovetailed blade front, rear adjustable for windage; three-dot system. **Features:** Reinforced dust cover; lowered and flared ejection port; squared trigger guard; adjustable match trigger; bolstered front strap; high grip cut; high ride beavertail grip safety; steel flat mainspring housing; extended thumb lock; skeletonized hammer, match grade sear, disconnector; Wolff springs. Introduced 1998. Made in U.S. by Entréprise Arms.
Price: $739.90

Entréprise Boxer P500 Auto Pistol
Similar to the Medalist model except has adjustable Competizione "melded" rear sight with dovetailed Patridge front; high mass chiseled slide with sweep cut; machined slide parallel rails; polished breech face and barrel channel. Introduced 1998. Made in U.S. by Entréprise Arms.
Price: $1,399.00

Entréprise Medalist P500 Auto Pistol
Similar to the Elite model except has adjustable Competizione "melded" rear sight with dovetailed Patridge front; machined slide parallel rails with polished breech face and barrel channel; front and rear slide serrations; lowered and flared ejection port; full-length one-piece guide rod with plug; National Match barrel and bushing; stainless firing pin; tuned match extractor; oversize firing pin stop; throated barrel and polished ramp; slide lapped to frame. Introduced 1998. Made in U.S. by Entréprise Arms.
Price: 45 ACP. $979.00
Price: 40 S&W $1,099.00

34TH EDITION, 2002 • 139

HANDGUNS — AUTOLOADERS, SERVICE & SPORT

Entréprise Tactical 500

Felk MTF 450

FEG PJK-9HP

Glock 17C

Entréprise Tactical P500 Auto Pistol
Similar to the Elite model except has Tactical2 Ghost Ring sight or Novak lo-mount sight; ambidextrous thumb safety; front and rear slide serrations; full-length guide rod; throated barrel, polished ramp; tuned match extractor; fitted barrel and bushing; stainless firing pin; slide lapped to frame; dehorned. Introduced 1998. Made in U.S. by Entréprise Arms.
Price: $979.90
Price: Tactical Plus (full-size frame, Officer's slide) $1,049.00

ERMA KGP68 AUTO PISTOL
Caliber: 32 ACP, 6-shot, 380 ACP, 5-shot. **Barrel:** 4". **Weight:** 22-1/2 oz. **Length:** 7-3/8" overall. **Stocks:** Checkered plastic. **Sights:** Fixed. **Features:** Toggle action similar to original "Luger" pistol. Action stays open after last shot. Has magazine and sear disconnect safety systems.
Price: $499.95

FEG PJK-9HP AUTO PISTOL
Caliber: 9mm Para., 10-shot magazine. **Barrel:** 4.75". **Weight:** 32 oz. **Length:** 8" overall. **Stocks:** Hand-checkered walnut. **Sights:** Blade front, rear adjustable for windage; three dot system. **Features:** Single action; polished blue or hard chrome finish; rounded combat-style serrated hammer. Comes with two magazines and cleaning rod. Imported from Hungary by K.B.I., Inc.
Price: Blue $259.95
Price: Hard chrome..................................... $259.95

FEG SMC-380 AUTO PISTOL
Caliber: 380 ACP, 6-shot magazine. **Barrel:** 3.5". **Weight:** 18.5 oz. **Length:** 6.1" overall. **Stocks:** Checkered composition with thumbrest. **Sights:** Blade front, rear adjustable for windage. **Features:** Patterned after the PPK pistol. Alloy frame, steel slide; double action. Blue finish. Comes with two magazines, cleaning rod. Imported from Hungary by K.B.I., Inc.
Price: $224.95

FELK MTF 450 AUTO PISTOL
Caliber: 9mm Para. (10-shot); 40 S&W (8-shot); 45 ACP (9-shot magazine). **Barrel:** 3.5". **Weight:** 19.9 oz. **Length:** 6.4" overall. **Stocks:** Checkered. **Sights:** Blade front; adjustable rear. **Features:** Double-action-only trigger, striker fired; polymer frame; trigger safety, firing pin safety, trigger bar safety; adjustable trigger weight; fully interchangeable slide/barrel to change calibers. Introduced 1998. Imported by Felk Inc.
Price: $395.00
Price: 45 ACP pistol with 9mm and 40 S&W slide/barrel assemblies $999.00

GLOCK 17 AUTO PISTOL
Caliber: 9mm Para., 10-shot magazine. **Barrel:** 4.49". **Weight:** 22.04 oz. (without magazine). **Length:** 7.32" overall. **Stocks:** Black polymer. **Sights:** Dot on front blade, white outline rear adjustable for windage. **Features:** Polymer frame, steel slide; double-action trigger with "Safe Action" system; mechanical firing pin safety, drop safety; simple takedown without tools; locked breech, recoil operated action. Adopted by Austrian armed forces 1983. NATO approved 1984. Imported from Austria by Glock, Inc.
Price: Fixed sight, with extra magazine, magazine loader, cleaning kit $641.00
Price: Adjustable sight $671.00
Price: Model 17L (6" barrel) $800.00
Price: Model 17C, ported barrel (compensated) $646.00

HANDGUNS — AUTOLOADERS, SERVICE & SPORT

Glock 22

Glock 26

Glock 30

Glock 31

Glock 19 Auto Pistol
Similar to the Glock 17 except has a 4" barrel, giving an overall length of 6.85" and weight of 20.99 oz. Magazine capacity is 10 rounds. Fixed or adjustable rear sight. Introduced 1988.
Price: Fixed sight $641.00
Price: Adjustable sight $671.00
Price: Model 19C, ported barrel $646.00

Glock 20 10mm Auto Pistol
Similar to the Glock Model 17 except chambered for 10mm Automatic cartridge. Barrel length is 4.60", overall length is 7.59", and weight is 26.3 oz. (without magazine). Magazine capacity is 10 rounds. Fixed or adjustable rear sight. Comes with an extra magazine, magazine loader, cleaning rod and brush. Introduced 1990. Imported from Austria by Glock, Inc.
Price: Fixed sight $700.00
Price: Adjustable sight $730.00

Glock 21 Auto Pistol
Similar to the Glock 17 except chambered for 45 ACP, 10-shot magazine. Overall length is 7.59", weight is 25.2 oz. (without magazine). Fixed or adjustable rear sight. Introduced 1991.
Price: Fixed sight $700.00
Price: Adjustable sight $730.00

Glock 22 Auto Pistol
Similar to the Glock 17 except chambered for 40 S&W, 10-shot magazine. Overall length is 7.28", weight is 22.3 oz. (without magazine). Fixed or adjustable rear sight. Introduced 1990.
Price: Fixed sight $641.00
Price: Adjustable sight $671.00
Price: Model 22C, ported barrel $646.00

Glock 23 Auto Pistol
Similar to the Glock 19 except chambered for 40 S&W, 10-shot magazine. Overall length is 6.85", weight is 20.6 oz. (without magazine). Fixed or adjustable rear sight. Introduced 1990.
Price: Fixed sight $641.00
Price: Model 23C, ported barrel $646.00
Price: Adjustable sight $671.00

GLOCK 26, 27 AUTO PISTOLS
Caliber: 9mm Para. (M26), 10-shot magazine; 40 S&W (M27), 9-shot magazine. **Barrel:** 3.46". **Weight:** 21.75 oz. **Length:** 6.29" overall. **Stocks:** Integral. Stippled polymer. **Sights:** Dot on front blade, fixed or fully adjustable white outline rear. **Features:** Subcompact size. Polymer frame, steel slide; double-action trigger with "Safe Action" system, three safeties. Matte black Tenifer finish. Hammer-forged barrel. Imported from Austria by Glock, Inc. Introduced 1996.
Price: Fixed sight $641.00
Price: Adjustable sight $671.00

GLOCK 29, 30 AUTO PISTOLS
Caliber: 10mm (M29), 45 ACP (M30), 10-shot magazine. **Barrel:** 3.78". **Weight:** 24 oz. **Length:** 6.7" overall. **Stocks:** Integral. Stippled polymer. **Sights:** Dot on front, fixed or fully adjustable white outline rear. **Features:** Compact size. Polymer frame steel slide; double-recoil spring reduces recoil; Safe Action system with three safeties; Tenifer finish. Two magazines supplied. Introduced 1997. Imported from Austria by Glock, Inc.
Price: Fixed sight $700.00
Price: Adjustable sight $730.00

Glock 31/31C Auto Pistols
Similar to the Glock 17 except chambered for 357 Auto cartridge; 10-shot magazine. Overall length is 7.32", weight is 23.28 oz. (without magazine). Fixed or adjustable sight. Imported from Austria by Glock, Inc.
Price: Fixed sight $641.00
Price: Adjustable sight $671.00
Price: Model 31C, ported barrel $646.00

34TH EDITION, 2002 • 141

HANDGUNS — AUTOLOADERS, SERVICE & SPORT

Glock 35

Hammerli Trailside PL 22

Heckler & Koch USP Compact

Heckler & Koch USP45

Glock 32/32C Auto Pistols
Similar to the Glock 19 except chambered for the 357 Auto cartridge; 10-shot magazine. Overall length is 6.85", weight is 21.52 oz. (without magazine). Fixed or adjustable sight. Imported from Austria by Glock, Inc.
Price: Fixed sight	$616.00
Price: Adjustable sight	$644.00
Price: Model 32C, ported barrel	$646.00

Glock 33 Auto Pistol
Similar to the Glock 26 except chambered for the 357 Auto cartridge; 9-shot magazine. Overall length is 6.29", weight is 19.75 oz. (without magazine). Fixed or adjustable sight. Imported from Austria by Glock, Inc.
Price: Fixed sight	$641.00
Price: Adjustable sight	$671.00

GLOCK 34, 35 AUTO PISTOLS
Caliber: 9mm Para. (M34), 40 S&W (M35), 10-shot magazine. **Barrel:** 5.32". **Weight:** 22.9 oz. **Length:** 8.15" overall. **Stocks:** Integral. Stippled polymer. **Sights:** Dot on front, fully adjustable white outline rear. **Features:** Polymer frame, steel slide; double-action trigger with "Safe Action" system; three safeties; Tenifer finish. Imported from Austria by Glock, Inc.
Price: Model 34, 9mm	$770.00
Price: Model 35, 40 S&W	$770.00

GLOCK 36 AUTO PISTOL
Caliber: 45 ACP, 6-shot magazine. **Barrel:** 3.78". **Weight:** 20.11 oz. **Length:** 6.77" overall. **Stocks:** Integral. Stippled polymer. **Sights:** Dot on front, fully adjustable white outline rear. **Features:** Polymer frame, steel slide; double-action trigger with "Safe Action" system; three safeties; Tenifer finish. Imported from Austria by Glock, Inc.
Price: Fixed sight	$700.00
Price: Adj. sight	$730.00

HAMMERLI TRAILSIDE PL 22 TARGET PISTOL
Caliber: 22 LR, 10-shot magazine. **Barrel:** 4.5", 6". **Weight:** 28 oz. (4.5" barrel). **Length:** 7.75" overall. **Stocks:** Wood target-style. **Sights:** Blade front, rear adjustable for windage. **Features:** One-piece barrel/frame unit; two-stage competition-style trigger; dovetail scope mount rail. Introduced 1999. Imported from Switzerland by SIGARMS, Inc.
Price:	NA

HECKLER & KOCH USP AUTO PISTOL
Caliber: 9mm Para., 10-shot magazine, 40 S&W, 10-shot magazine. **Barrel:** 4.25". **Weight:** 28 oz. (USP40). **Length:** 6.9" overall. **Stocks:** Non-slip stippled black polymer. **Sights:** Blade front, rear adjustable for windage. **Features:** New HK design with polymer frame, modified Browning action with recoil reduction system, single control lever. Special "hostile environment" finish on all metal parts. Available in SA/DA, DAO, left- and right-hand versions. Introduced 1993. Imported from Germany by Heckler & Koch, Inc.
Price: Right-hand	$699.00
Price: Left-hand	$714.00
Price: Stainless steel, right-hand	$749.00
Price: Stainless steel, left-hand	$799.00

Heckler & Koch USP Compact Auto Pistol
Similar to the USP except has 3.58" barrel, measures 6.81" overall, and weighs 1.60 lbs. (9mm). Available in 9mm Para. 357 SIG or 40 S&W with 10-shot magazine. Introduced 1996. Imported from Germany by Heckler & Koch, Inc.
Price: Blue	$759.00
Price: Blue with control lever on right	$784.00
Price: Stainless steel	$849.00
Price: Stainless steel with control lever on right	$874.00

Heckler & Koch USP45 Auto Pistol
Similar to the 9mm and 40 S&W USP except chambered for 45 ACP, 10-shot magazine. Has 4.13" barrel, overall length of 7.87" and weighs 30.4 oz. Has adjustable three-dot sight system. Available in SA/DA, DAO, left- and right-hand versions. Introduced 1995. Imported from Germany by Heckler & Koch, Inc.
Price: Right-hand	$799.00
Price: Left-hand	$824.00
Price: Stainless steel right-hand	$859.00
Price: Stainless steel left-hand	$884.00

HANDGUNS — AUTOLOADERS, SERVICE & SPORT

Heckler & Koch USP45 Tactical

Heckler & Koch USP Expert

Heckler & Koch P7M8

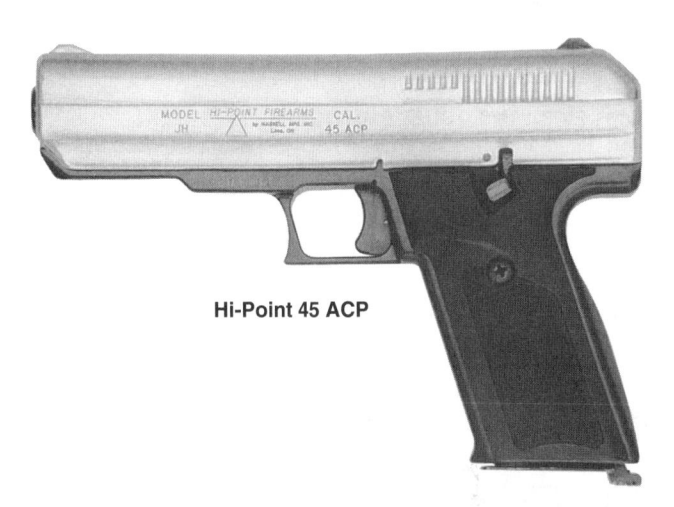

Hi-Point 45 ACP

Heckler & Koch USP45 Compact
Similar to the USP45 except has stainless slide; 8-shot magazine; modified and contoured slide and frame; extended slide release; 3.80" barrel, 7.09" overall length, weighs 1.75 lbs.; adjustable three-dot sights. Introduced 1998. Imported from Germany by Heckler & Koch, Inc.
Price: With control lever on left, stainless. $879.00
Price: As above, blue $879.00
Price: With control lever on right, stainless. $904.00
Price: As above, blue $854.00

HECKLER & KOCH USP45 TACTICAL PISTOL
Caliber: 45 ACP, 10-shot magazine. **Barrel:** 4.92". **Weight:** 2.24 lbs. **Length:** 8.64" overall. **Stocks:** Non-slip stippled polymer. **Sights:** Blade front, fully adjustable target rear. **Features:** Has extended threaded barrel with rubber O-ring; adjustable trigger; extended magazine floorplate; adjustable trigger stop; polymer frame. Introduced 1998. Imported from Germany by Heckler & Koch, Inc.
Price: $1,069.00

HECKLER & KOCH MARK 23 SPECIAL OPERATIONS PISTOL
Caliber: 45 ACP, 10-shot magazine. **Barrel:** 5.87". **Weight:** 43 oz. **Length:** 9.65" overall. **Stocks:** Integral with frame; black polymer. **Sights:** Blade front, rear drift adjustable for windage; three-dot. **Features:** Polymer frame; double action; exposed hammer; short recoil, modified Browning action. Civilian version of the SOCOM pistol. Introduced 1996. Imported from Germany by Heckler & Koch, Inc.
Price: $2,289.00

Heckler & Koch USP Expert Pistol
Combines features of the USP Tactical and HK Mark 23 pistols with a new slide design. Chambered for 45 ACP; 10-shot magazine. Has adjustable target sights, 5.20" barrel, 8.74" overall length, weighs 1.87 lbs. Match-grade single- and double-action trigger pull with adjustable stop; ambidextrous control levers; elongated target slide; barrel O-ring that seals and centers barrel. Suited to IPSC competition. Introduced 1999. Imported from Germany by Heckler & Koch, Inc.
Price: $1,449.00

HECKLER & KOCH P7M8 AUTO PISTOL
Caliber: 9mm Para., 8-shot magazine. **Barrel:** 4.13". **Weight:** 29 oz. **Length:** 6.73" overall. **Stocks:** Stippled black plastic. **Sights:** Blade front, adjustable rear; three dot system. **Features:** Unique "squeeze cocker" in frontstrap cocks the action. Gas-retarded action. Squared combat-type trigger guard. Blue finish. Compact size. Imported from Germany by Heckler & Koch, Inc.
Price: P7M8, blued. $1,369.00

HI-POINT FIREARMS 40 S&W AUTO
Caliber: 40 S&W, 8-shot magazine. **Barrel:** 4.5". **Weight:** 39 oz. **Length:** 7.72" overall. **Stocks:** Checkered acetal resin. **Sights:** Adjustable; low profile. **Features:** Internal drop-safe mechanism; alloy frame. Introduced 1991. From MKS Supply, Inc.
Price: Matte black. $159.00

HI-POINT FIREARMS 45 CALIBER PISTOL
Caliber: 45 ACP, 7-shot magazine. **Barrel:** 4.5". **Weight:** 39 oz. **Length:** 7.95" overall. **Stocks:** Checkered acetal resin. **Sights:** Adjustable; low profile. **Features:** Internal drop-safe mechanism; alloy frame. Introduced 1991. From MKS Supply, Inc.
Price: Matte black. $159.00
Price: Chrome slide, black frame $169.00

HANDGUNS — AUTOLOADERS, SERVICE & SPORT

Hi-Point 9MM Comp

HI-POINT FIREARMS 9MM COMP PISTOL
Caliber: 9mm, Para., 10-shot magazine. **Barrel:** 4". **Weight:** 39 oz. **Length:** 7.72" overall. **Stocks:** Textured acetal plastic. **Sights:** Adjustable; low profile. **Features:** Single-action design. Scratch-resistant, nonglare blue finish, alloy frame. Muzzle brake/compensator. Compensator is slotted for laser or flashlight mounting. Introduced 1998. From MKS Supply, Inc.
Price: Matte black.....................................$159.00

HI-POINT FIREARMS MODEL 9MM COMPACT PISTOL
Caliber: 9mm Para., 8-shot magazine. **Barrel:** 3.5". **Weight:** 29 oz. **Length:** 6.7" overall. **Stocks:** Textured acetal plastic. **Sights:** Combat-style adjustable three-dot system; low profile. **Features:** Single-action design; frame-mounted magazine release; polymer or alloy frame. Scratch-resistant matte finish. Introduced 1993. Made in U.S. by MKS Supply, Inc.
Price: Black, alloy frame...............................$137.00
Price: With polymer frame (29 oz.), non-slip grips..........$137.00
Price: Aluminum with polymer frame....................$137.00

Hi-Point Firearms Model 380 Polymer Pistol
Similar to the 9mm Compact model except chambered for 380 ACP, 8-shot magazine, adjustable three-dot sights. Weighs 29 oz. Polymer frame. Introduced 1998. Made in U.S. by MKS Supply.
Price: $99.95

NEW! Hi-Point Firearms 380 Comp Pistol
Similar to the 380 Polymer Pistol except has a 4" barrel with muzzle compensator; action locks open after last shot. Includes a 10-shot and an 8-shot magazine; trigger lock. Introduced 2001. Made in U.S. by MKS Supply Inc.
Price: $125.00
Price: With laser sight..............................$190.00

HS AMERICA HS 2000 PISTOL
Caliber: 9mm Para., 357 SIG, 40 S&W, 10-shot magazine. **Barrel:** 4.08". **Weight:** 22.88 oz. **Length:** 7.2" overall. **Grips:** Integral black polymer. **Sights:** Drift-adjustable white dot rear, white dot blade front. **Features:** Incorporates trigger, firing pin, grip and out-of-battery safeties; firing-pin status and loaded chamber indicators; ambidextrous magazine release; dual-tension recoil spring with stand-off device; polymer frame; black finish with chrome-plated magazine. Imported from Croatia by HS America.
Price: $419.00

IAI M-3000 AUTO PISTOL
Caliber: 9mm Para., 7-shot magazine. **Barrel:** 3-1/2". **Weight:** 32 oz. **Length:** 6-1/2" overall. **Grips:** Plastic. **Sights:** High-contrast fixed. **Features:** Double-action; all-steel construction; automatic firing-pin safety; field strips without tools; slide stays open after last shot. Imported by IAI Inc.
Price: $373.70

IAI M-4000 AUTO PISTOL
Similar to IAI M-3000 Pistol above, except chambered in 40 S&W. All-steel construction; 7-shot magazine.
Price: $373.70

Kahr K9

Kahr MK40

IAI M-5000 AUTO PISTOL
Caliber: 45 ACP, 8-shot magazine. **Barrel:** 4.25". **Weight:** 36 oz. **Length:** 6" overall. **Grips:** Plastic. **Sights:** Fixed. **Features:** 1911-style; blued steel frame and slide; beavertail grip safety; extended slide stop, safety and magazine release; beveled feed ramp; combat-style hammer; beveled magazine well; ambidexterous safety. Imported from the Philippines by IAI Inc.
Price: $447.40

IAI M-6000 AUTO PISTOL
Caliber: 45 ACP, 8-shot magazine. **Barrel:** 5". **Weight:** 36 oz. **Length:** 8-1/2" overall. **Grips:** Plastic. **Sights:** Fixed. **Features:** 1911-style; blued steel frame and slide; beavertail grip safety; extended slide stop, safety and magazine release; beveled feed ramp and magazine well; combat-style hammer; ambidexterous safety. Imported from the Philippines by IAI Inc.
Price: $447.40

KAHR K9, K40 DA AUTO PISTOLS
Caliber: 9mm Para., 7-shot, 40 S&W, 6-shot magazine. **Barrel:** 3.5". **Weight:** 25 oz. **Length:** 6" overall. **Stocks:** Wrap-around textured soft polymer. **Sights:** Blade front, rear drift adjustable for windage; bar-dot combat style. **Features:** Trigger-cocking double-action mechanism with passive firing pin block. Made of 4140 ordnance steel with matte black finish. Contact maker for complete price list. Introduced 1994. Made in U.S. by Kahr Arms.
Price: E9, black matte finish..........................$399.00
Price: Matte black, night sights 9mm...................$640.00
Price: Matte stainless steel, 9mm......................$580.00
Price: 40 S&W, matte black............................$550.00
Price: 40 S&W, matte black, night sights................$640.00
Price: 40 S&W, matte stainless.........................$580.00
Price: K9 Elite 98 (high-polish stainless slide flats, Kahr combat trigger), from................................$631.00
Price: As above, MK9 Elite 98, from....................$631.00
Price: As above, K40 Elite 98, from.....................$631.00

144 • GUNS ILLUSTRATED

HANDGUNS — AUTOLOADERS, SERVICE & SPORT

Kel-Tec P-11

Kimber Custom 45

Kel-Tec P-32

Kimber Compact Custom

Kahr K9 9mm Compact Polymer Pistol
Similar to K9 steel frame pistol except has polymer frame, matte stainless steel slide. Barrel length 3.5"; overall length 6"; weighs 17.9 oz. Includes two 7-shot magazines, hard polymer case, trigger lock. Introduced 2000. Made in U.S. by Kahr Arms.
Price: $527.00

Kahr MK9/MK40 Micro Pistol
Similar to the K9/K40 except is 5.5" overall, 4" high, has a 3" barrel. Weighs 22 oz. Has snag-free bar-dot sights, polished feed ramp, dual recoil spring system, DA-only trigger. Comes with 6- and 7-shot magazines. Introduced 1998. Made in U.S. by Kahr Arms.
Price: Matte stainless $580.00
Price: Elite 98, polished stainless, tritium night sights $721.00

KEL-TEC P-11 AUTO PISTOL
Caliber: 9mm Para., 10-shot magazine. **Barrel:** 3.1". **Weight:** 14 oz. **Length:** 5.6" overall. **Stocks:** Checkered black polymer. **Sights:** Blade front, rear adjustable for windage. **Features:** Ordnance steel slide, aluminum frame. Double-action-only trigger mechanism. Introduced 1995. Made in U.S. by Kel-Tec CNC Industries, Inc.
Price: Blue $309.00
Price: Hard chrome $363.00
Price: Parkerized $350.00

KEL-TEC P-32 AUTO PISTOL
Caliber: 32 ACP, 7-shot magazine. **Barrel:** 2.68". **Weight:** 6.6 oz. **Length:** 5.07" overall. **Stocks:** Checkered composite. **Sights:** Fixed. **Features:** Double-action-only mechanism with 6-lb. pull; internal slide stop. Textured composite grip/frame. Made in U.S. by Kel-Tec CNC Industries, Inc.
Price: $295.00

KIMBER CUSTOM AUTO PISTOL
Caliber: 45 ACP, 7-shot magazine. **Barrel:** 5", match grade. **Weight:** 38 oz. **Length:** 8.7" overall. **Stocks:** Checkered black rubber (standard), or rosewood. **Sights:** McCormick dovetailed front, low combat rear. **Features:** Slide, frame and barrel machined from steel forgings; match-grade barrel, chamber, trigger; extended thumb safety; beveled magazine well; beveled front and rear slide serrations; high-ride beavertail safety; checkered flat mainspring housing; kidney cut under trigger guard; high cut grip design; match-grade stainless barrel bushing; Commander-style hammer; lowered and flared ejection port; Wolff springs; bead blasted black oxide finish. Made in U.S. by Kimber Mfg., Inc.
Price: Custom $730.00
Price: Custom Walnut (double-diamond walnut grips) $752.00
Price: Custom Stainless $832.00
Price: Custom Stainless 40 S&W $870.00
Price: Custom Stainless Target 45 ACP (stainless, adj. sight) $944.00
Price: Custom Stainless Target 40 S&W $974.00

Kimber Compact Auto Pistol
Similar to the Custom model except has 4" bull barrel fitted directly to the slide without a bushing; full-length guide rod; grip is .400" shorter than full-size gun; no front serrations. Steel frame models weigh 34 oz., aluminum 28 oz. Introduced 1998. Made in U.S. by Kimber Mfg., Inc.
Price: 45 ACP, matte black $764.00
Price: Compact Stainless 45 ACP $871.00
Price: Compact Stainless 40 S&W $902.00
Price: Compact Aluminum Stainless 45 ACP (aluminum frame, stainless slide) $837.00
Price: Compact Aluminum Stainless 40 S&W $873.00

34TH EDITION, 2002 • **145**

HANDGUNS — AUTOLOADERS, SERVICE & SPORT

Kimber Ultra Carry

Kimber High Capacity Polymer

Kimber Pro CDP

Kimber Pro Carry Auto Pistol
Similar to the Compact model except has aluminum frame with full-length grip. Has 4" bull barrel fitted directly to the slide without bushing. Introduced 1998. Made in U.S. by Kimber Mfg., Inc.
Price: 45 ACP... $773.00
Price: 40 S&W.. $808.00
Price: Pro Carry Stainless 45 ACP....................... $845.00
Price: Pro Carry Stainless 40 S&W....................... $881.00

Kimber Ultra Carry Auto Pistol
Similar to the Compact Aluminum model except has 3" balljoint spherical bushingless cone barrel; aluminum frame; beveling at front and rear of ejection port; relieved breech face; tuned ejector; special slide stop; dual captured low-effort spring system. Weighs 25 oz. Introduced 1999. made in U.S. by Kimber Mfg., Inc.
Price: 45 ACP... $808.00
Price: 40 S&W.. $847.00
Price: Stainless, 45 ACP.................................. $886.00
Price: Stainless, 40 S&W.................................. $931.00

KIMBER HIGH CAPACITY POLYMER PISTOL
Caliber: 45 ACP, 10- and 14-shot magazine. **Barrel:** 5". **Weight:** 34 oz. **Length:** 8.7" overall. **Stocks:** Integral; checkered black polymer. **Sights:** McCormick low profile front and rear. **Features:** Polymer frame with steel insert. Comes with 10-shot magazine. Checkered front strap and mainspring housing; polymer trigger; stainless high ride beavertail grip safety; hooked trigger guard. Introduced 1997. Made in U.S. by Kimber Mfg., Inc.
Price: Polymer Custom, matte black finish............... $795.00
Price: Polymer Stainless (satin-finish stainless slide)... $856.00
Price: Polymer Pro Carry (compact slide, 4" bull barrel)... $814.00
Price: Polymer Pro Carry Stainless...................... $874.00
New! **Price:** Polymer Ultra Ten II (polymer/stainless)...... $896.00

Kimber Gold Match Auto Pistol
Similar to the Custom model except has Kimber adjustable sight with rounded and blended edges; stainless steel match-grade barrel hand-fitted to spherical barrel bushing; premium aluminum trigger; extended ambidextrous thumb safety; hand-checkered double diamond rosewood grips. Hand-fitted by Kimber Custom Shop. Made in U.S. by Kimber Mfg., Inc.
Price: Gold Match 45 ACP............................... $1,169.00
Price: Gold Match Stainless 45 ACP (highly polished flats).... $1,315.00
Price: Gold Match Stainless 40 S&W..................... $1,345.00

Kimber Polymer Gold Match Auto Pistol
Similar to the Polymer model except has Kimber adjustable sight with rounded and blended edges; stainless steel match-grade barrel hand-fitted to spherical barrel bushing; premium aluminum trigger; extended ambidextrous thumb safety. Hand-fitted by Kimber Custom Shop. Introduced 1999. Made in U.S. by Kimber Mfg., Inc.
Price:... $1,041.00
Price: Polymer Stainless Gold Match (polished stainless slide). $1,177.00

Kimber Gold Combat Auto Pistol
Similar to the Gold Match except designed for concealed carry. Has two-piece extended and beveled magazine well, tritium night sights; premium aluminum trigger; 30 lpi front strap checkering; special Custom Shop markings; Kim Pro black finish. Introduced 1999. Made in U.S. by Kimber Mfg., Inc.
Price: 45 ACP... $1,682.00
Price: Gold Combat Stainless (satin-finished stainless frame and slide, special Custom Shop markings)............... $1,623.00

KIMBER PRO CDP AUTO PISTOL
Caliber: 45 ACP, 7-shot magazine. **Barrel:** 4". **Weight:** 28 oz. **Length:** 7.7" overall. **Grips:** Hand-checkered. double diamond rosewood. **Sights:** Tritium three-dot. **Features:** Matte black, machined aluminum frame; satin stainless steel slide; match-grade barrel and chamber; beveled magazine well; extended ejector; high-ride beavertail grip safety; match-grade trigger group; ambidextrous safety; checkered frontstrap; meltdown treatment. Introduced 2000. Made in U.S. by Kimber.
Price:... $1,142.00

KIMBER ULTRA CDP AUTO PISTOL
Caliber: 45 ACP, 6-shot magazine. **Barrel:** 3". **Weight:** 25 oz. **Length:** 6.8" overall. **Grips:** Hand-checkered. double diamond rosewood. **Sights:** Tritium three-dot. **Features:** Matte black, machined aluminum frame; satin stainless steel slide; match-grade barrel and chamber; beveled magazine well and ejection port; dual recoil spring system for reliability and ease of manual slide operation; match-grade barrel, chamber and trigger; ambidextrous safety; checkered frontstrap; meltdown treatment. Introduced 2000. Made in U.S. by Kimber.
Price:... $1,142.00

HANDGUNS — AUTOLOADERS, SERVICE & SPORT

Kimber Ultra CDP

Llama Minimax

Llama Micromax

Llama Max-1

LLAMA MICROMAX 380 AUTO PISTOL
Caliber: 32 ACP, 8-shot, 380 ACP, 7-shot magazine. **Barrel:** 3-11/16". **Weight:** 23 oz. **Length:** 6-1/2" overall. **Stocks:** Checkered high impact polymer. **Sights:** 3-dot combat. **Features:** Single-action design. Mini custom extended slide release; mini custom extended beavertail grip safety; combat-style hammer. Introduced 1997. Imported from Spain by Import Sports, Inc.
Price: Matte blue. $281.95
Price: Satin chrome (380 only) $298.95

LLAMA MINIMAX SERIES
Caliber: 9mm Para., 8-shot; 40 S&W, 7-shot; 45 ACP, 6-shot magazine. **Barrel:** 3-1/2". **Weight:** 35 oz. **Length:** 7-1/3" overall. **Stocks:** Checkered rubber. **Sights:** Three-dot combat. **Features:** Single action, skeletonized combat-style hammer, extended slide release, cone-style barrel, flared ejection port. Introduced 1996. Imported from Spain by Import Sports, Inc.
Price: Blue $316.95
Price: Duo-Tone finish (45 only) $324.95
Price: Satin chrome $333.95

Llama Minimax Sub-Compact Auto Pistol
Similar to the Minimax except has 3.14" barrel, weighs 31 oz.; 6.8" overall length; has 10-shot magazine with finger extension; beavertail grip safety. Introduced 1999. Imported from Spain by Import Sports, Inc.
Price: 45 ACP, matte blue. $331.95
Price: As above, satin chrome $349.95
Price: Duo-Tone finish (45 only) $341.95

LLAMA MAX-I AUTO PISTOLS
Caliber: 45 ACP, 7-shot. **Barrel:** 5-1/8". **Weight:** 36 oz. **Length:** 8-1/2" overall. **Stocks:** Black rubber. **Sights:** Blade front, rear adjustable for windage; three-dot system. **Features:** Single-action trigger; skeletonized combat-style hammer; steel frame; extended manual and grip safeties. Introduced 1995. Imported from Spain by Import Sports, Inc.
Price: 45 ACP, 7-shot, Government model. $310.95

NORTH AMERICAN ARMS GUARDIAN PISTOL
Caliber: 32 ACP, 6-shot magazine. **Barrel:** 2.1". **Weight:** 13.5 oz. **Length:** 4.36" overall. **Stocks:** Black polymer. **Sights:** Fixed. **Features:** Double-action-only mechanism. All stainless steel construction; snag-free. Introduced 1998. Made in U.S. by North American Arms.
Price: $359.00

OLYMPIC ARMS OA-96 AR PISTOL
Caliber: 223. **Barrel:** 6", 8", 4140 chrome-moly steel. **Weight:** 5 lbs. **Length:** 15-3/4" overall. **Stocks:** A2 stowaway pistol grip; no buttstock or receiver tube. **Sights:** Flat-top upper receiver, cut-down front sight base. **Features:** AR-15-type receivers with special bolt carrier; short aluminum hand guard; Vortex flash hider. Introduced 1996. Made in U.S. by Olympic Arms, Inc.
Price: $858.00

Olympic Arms OA-98 AR Pistol
Similar to the OA-93 except has removable 7-shot magazine, weighs 3 lbs. Introduced 1999. Made in U.S. by Olympic Arms, Inc.
Price: $990.00

HANDGUNS — AUTOLOADERS, SERVICE & SPORT

North American Arms Guardian

One Pro .45

ONE PRO .45 AUTO PISTOL
Caliber: 45 ACP or 400 Cor-Bon, 10-shot magazine. **Barrel:** 3.75" **Weight:** 31.1 oz. **Length:** 7.04" overall. **Stocks:** Textured composition. **Sights:** Blade front, drift-adjustable rear; three-dot system. **Features:** All-steel construction; decocking lever and automatic firing pin lock; DA or DAO operation. Introduced 1997. Imported from Switzerland by Magnum Research, Inc.
Price: $649.00
Price: Conversion kit, 45 ACP/400, 400/45 ACP $249.00

ONE PRO 9 AUTO PISTOL
Caliber: 9mm Para., 10-shot magazine. **Barrel:** 3.01". **Weight:** 25.1 oz. **Length:** 6.06" overall. **Stocks:** Smooth wood. **Sights:** Blade front, rear adjustable for windage. **Features:** Rotating barrel; short slide; double recoil springs; double-action mechanism; decocking lever. Introduced 1998. Imported from Switzerland by Magnum Research.
Price: $649.00

PARA-ORDNANCE P-SERIES AUTO PISTOLS
Caliber: 9mm Para., 40 S&W, 45 ACP, 10-shot magazine. **Barrel:** 3", 3-1/2", 4-1/4", 5". **Weight:** From 24 oz. (alloy frame). **Length:** 8.5" overall. **Stocks:** Textured composition. **Sights:** Blade front, rear adjustable for windage. High visibility three-dot system. **Features:** Available with alloy, steel or stainless steel frame with black finish (silver or stainless gun). Steel and stainless steel frame guns weigh 40 oz. (P14.45), 36 oz. (P13.45), 34 oz. (P12.45). Grooved match trigger, rounded combat-style hammer. Beveled magazine well. Manual thumb, grip and firing pin lock safeties. Solid barrel bushing. Contact maker for full details. Introduced 1990. Made in Canada by Para-Ordnance.
Price: P14.45ER (steel frame) $750.00
Price: P14.45RR (alloy frame) $740.00
Price: P12.45RR (3-1/2" bbl., 24 oz., alloy) $740.00
Price: P13.45RR (4-1/4" barrel, 28 oz., alloy) $740.00
Price: P12.45ER (steel frame) $750.00
Price: P16.40ER (steel frame) $750.00
Price: P10-9RR (9mm, alloy frame) $740.00
Price: Stainless receiver (40, 45) $799.00
Price: Stainless receiver (9mm) $850.00

Para-Ordnance Limited Pistols
Similar to the P-Series pistols except with full-length recoil guide system; fully adjustable rear sight; tuned trigger with overtravel stop; beavertail grip safety; competition hammer; front and rear slide serrations; ambidextrous safety; lowered ejection port; ramped match-grade barrel; dovetailed front sight. Introduced 1998. Made in Canada by Para-Ordnance.
Price: 9mm, 40 S&W, 45 ACP .... $865.00 to $899.00

Para-Ordnance P12.45

Para-Ordnance LDA

HANDGUNS — AUTOLOADERS, SERVICE & SPORT

Peters Stahl High Capacity

Phoenix Arms HP22

Peters Stahl Trophy Master

Peters Stahl Millenium

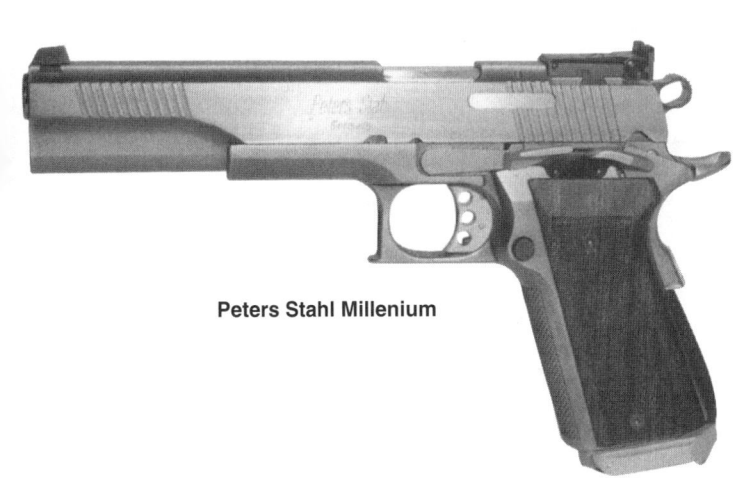

Para-Ordnance LDA Auto Pistols
Similar to the P-series except has double-action trigger mechanism. Steel frame with matte black finish, checkered composition grips. Available in 9mm Para., 40 S&W, 45 ACP. Introduced 1999. Made in Canada by Para-Ordnance.
Price: $775.00

Para-Ordnance LDA Limited Pistols
Similar to the LDA except has ambidextrous safety, adjustable rear sight, front slide serrations and full-length recoil guide system. Made in Canada by Para-Ordnance.
Price: Black finish $899.00
Price: Stainless $929.00

PETERS STAHL AUTOLOADING PISTOLS
Caliber: 9mm Para., 45 ACP. **Barrel:** 5" or 6". **Weight:** NA. **Length:** NA. **Grips:** Walnut or walnut with rubber wrap. **Sights:** Fully adjustable rear, blade front. **Features:** Stainless steel extended slide stop, safety and extended magazine release button; speed trigger with stop and approx. 3-lb. pull; polished ramp. Introduced 2000. Imported from Germany by Phillips & Rogers.
Price: High Capacity (accepts 15-shot magazines in 45 cal.; includes 10-shot magazine) $1,695.00
Price: Trophy Master (blued or stainless, 7-shot in 45, 8-shot in 9mm) $1,995.00
Price: Millenium Model (titanium coating on receiver and slide) $2,195.00

PHOENIX ARMS HP22, HP25 AUTO PISTOLS
Caliber: 22 LR, 10-shot (HP22), 25 ACP, 10-shot (HP25). **Barrel:** 3". **Weight:** 20 oz. **Length:** 5-1/2" overall. **Stocks:** Checkered composition. **Sights:** Blade front, adjustable rear. **Features:** Single action, exposed hammer; manual hold-open; button magazine release. Available in satin nickel, polished blue finish. Introduced 1993. Made in U.S. by Phoenix Arms.
Price: With gun lock and cable lanyard $128.00
Price: HP Rangemaster kit with 5" bbl., locking case and assessories $169.00
Price: HP Deluxe Rangemaster kit with 3" and 5" bbls., 2 mags., case $199.00

PSA-25 AUTO POCKET PISTOL
Caliber: 25 ACP, 6-shot magazine. **Barrel:** 2-1/8". **Weight:** 9.5 oz. **Length:** 4-1/8" overall. **Stocks:** Checkered black polymer, ivory, checkered transparent carbon fiber-filled polymer. **Sights:** Fixed. **Features:** All steel construction; striker fired; single action only; magazine disconnector; cocking indicator. Introduced 1987. Made in U.S. by Precision Small Arms, Inc.
Price: Traditional (polished black oxide) $269.00
Price: Nouveau-Satin (brushed nickel) $269.00
Price: Nouveau-Mirror (highly polished nickel) $309.00
Price: Featherweight (aluminum frame, nickel slide) $405.00
Price: Diplomat (black oxide with gold highlights, ivory grips) . . . $625.00
Price: Montreaux (gold plated, ivory grips) $692.00
Price: Renaissance (hand engraved nickel, ivory grips) $1,115.00
Price: Imperiale (inlaid gold filigree over blue, scrimshawed ivory grips) $3,600.00

HANDGUNS — AUTOLOADERS, SERVICE & SPORT

PSA-25 Auto

Rock River Standard Match

Republic Patriot

Ruger P89

REPUBLIC PATRIOT PISTOL
Caliber: 45 ACP, 6-shot magazine. **Barrel:** 3". **Weight:** 20 oz. **Length:** 6" overall. **Stocks:** Checkered. **Sights:** Blade front, drift-adjustable rear. **Features:** Black polymer frame, stainless steel slide; double-action-only trigger system; squared trigger guard. Introduced 1997. Made in U.S. by Republic Arms, Inc.
Price: About $325.00

ROCK RIVER ARMS STANDARD MATCH AUTO PISTOL
Caliber: 45 ACP. **Barrel:** NA. **Weight:** NA. **Length:** NA. **Grips:** Cocobolo, checkered. **Sights:** Heine fixed rear, blade front. **Features:** Chrome-moly steel frame and slide; beavertail grip safety with raised pad; checkered slide stop; ambidextrous safety; polished feed ramp and extractor; aluminum speed trigger with 3.5 lb. pull. Made in U.S. From Rock River Arms.
Price: $1,025.00

ROCKY MOUNTAIN ARMS PATRIOT PISTOL
Caliber: 223, 10-shot magazine. **Barrel:** 7", with muzzle brake. **Weight:** 5 lbs. **Length:** 20.5" overall. **Stocks:** Black composition. **Sights:** None furnished. **Features:** Milled upper receiver with enhanced Weaver base; milled lower receiver from billet plate; machined aluminum National Match handguard. Finished in DuPont Teflon-S matte black or NATO green. Comes with black nylon case, one magazine. Introduced 1993. From Rocky Mountain Arms, Inc.
Price: With A-2 handle top . . . . $2,500.00 to $2,800.00
Price: Flat top model. . . . . $3,000.00 to $3,500.00

RUGER P89 AUTOLOADING PISTOL
Caliber: 9mm Para., 10-shot magazine. **Barrel:** 4.50". **Weight:** 32 oz. **Length:** 7.84" overall. **Stocks:** Grooved black Xenoy composition.

Sights: Square post front, square notch rear adjustable for windage, both with white dot inserts. **Features:** Double action with ambidextrous slide-mounted safety-levers. Slide is 4140 chrome-moly steel or 400-series stainless steel, frame is a lightweight aluminum alloy. Ambidextrous magazine release. Blue or stainless steel. Introduced 1986; stainless introduced 1990.
Price: P89, blue, with extra magazine and magazine loading tool, plastic case with lock $452.00
Price: KP89, stainless, with extra magazine and magazine loading tool, plastic case with lock $499.00

Ruger P89D Decocker Autoloading Pistol
Similar to the standard P89 except has ambidextrous decocking levers in place of the regular slide-mounted safety. The decocking levers move the firing pin inside the slide where the hammer can not reach it, while simultaneously blocking the firing pin from forward movement—allows shooter to decock a cocked pistol without manipulating the trigger. Conventional thumb decocking procedures are therefore unnecessary. Blue or stainless steel. Introduced 1990.
Price: P89D, blue with extra magazine and loader, plastic case with lock $452.00
Price: KP89D, stainless, with extra magazine, plastic case with lock $499.00

Ruger P89 Double-Action-Only Autoloading Pistol
Same as the KP89 except operates only in the double-action mode. Has a spurless hammer, gripping grooves on each side of the rear of the slide; no external safety or decocking lever. An internal safety prevents forward movement of the firing pin unless the trigger is pulled. Available in 9mm Para., stainless steel only. Introduced 1991.
Price: With lockable case, extra magazine, magazine loading tool $499.00

150 • GUNS ILLUSTRATED

HANDGUNS — AUTOLOADERS, SERVICE & SPORT

Ruger P90

Ruger KP95DAO

Ruger P93D

RUGER P90 MANUAL SAFETY MODEL AUTOLOADING PISTOL
Caliber: 45 ACP, 7-shot magazine. **Barrel:** 4.50". **Weight:** 33.5 oz. **Length:** 7.87" overall. **Stocks:** Grooved black Xenoy composition. **Sights:** Square post front, square notch rear adjustable for windage, both with white dot inserts. **Features:** Double action with ambidextrous slide-mounted safety-levers which move the firing pin inside the slide where the hammer can not reach it, while simultaneously blocking the firing pin from forward movement. Stainless steel only. Introduced 1991.
Price: KP90 with extra magazine, loader, plastic case
with lock $539.00
Price: P90 (blue). $499.00

Ruger KP90 Decocker Autoloading Pistol
Similar to the P90 except has a manual decocking system. The ambidextrous decocking levers move the firing pin inside the slide where the hammer can not reach it, while simultaneously blocking the firing pin from forward movement—allows shooter to decock a cocked pistol without manipulating the trigger. Available only in stainless steel. Overall length 7.87", weighs 34 oz. Introduced 1991.
Price: KP90D with lockable case, extra magazine, and magazine
loading tool $539.00

RUGER P93 COMPACT AUTOLOADING PISTOL
Caliber: 9mm Para., 10-shot magazine. **Barrel:** 3.9". **Weight:** 31 oz. **Length:** 7.3" overall. **Stocks:** Grooved black Xenoy composition. **Sights:** Square post front, square notch rear adjustable for windage. **Features:** Front of slide is crowned with a convex curve; slide has seven finger grooves; trigger guard bow is higher for a better grip; 400-series stainless slide, lightweight alloy frame; also in blue. Decocker-only or DAO-only. Includes hard case with lock. Introduced 1993. Made in U.S. by Sturm, Ruger & Co.
Price: KP93DAO, double-action-only $546.00
Price: KP93D ambidextrous decocker, stainless $546.00
Price: P93D, ambidextrous decocker, blue $467.00

Ruger KP94 Autoloading Pistol
Sized midway between the full-size P-Series and the compact P93. Has 4.25" barrel, 7.5" overall length and weighs about 33 oz. KP94 is manual safety model; KP94DAO is double-action-only (both 9mm Para., 10-shot magazine); KP94D is decocker-only in 40-caliber with 10-shot magazine. Slide gripping grooves roll over top of slide. KP94 has ambidextrous safety-levers; KP94DAO has no external safety, full-cock hammer position or decocking lever; KP94D has ambidextrous decocking levers. Matte finish stainless slide, barrel, alloy frame. Also available in blue. Includes hard case and lock. Introduced 1994. Made in U.S. by Sturm, Ruger & Co.
Price: P94, P944, blue (manual safety) $467.00
Price: KP94 (9mm), KP944 (40-caliber) (manual
safety-stainless) $546.00
Price: KP94DAO (9mm), KP944DAO (40-caliber) $546.00
Price: KP94D (9mm), KP944D (40-caliber)-decock only $546.00

RUGER P95 AUTOLOADING PISTOL
Caliber: 9mm Para., 10-shot magazine. **Barrel:** 3.9". **Weight:** 27 oz. **Length:** 7.3" overall. **Stocks:** Grooved; integral with frame. **Sights:** Blade front, rear drift adjustable for windage; three-dot system. **Features:** Moulded polymer grip frame, stainless steel or chrome-moly slide. Suitable for +P+ ammunition. Safety model, decocker or DAO. Introduced 1996. Made in U.S. by Sturm, Ruger & Co. Comes with lockable plastic case, spare magazine, loading tool.
Price: P95 DAO double-action-only $407.00
Price: P95D decocker only $407.00
Price: KP95 stainless steel. $453.00
Price: KP95DAO double-action only, stainless steel $453.00
Price: KP95 safety model, stainless steel $453.00
Price: P95 safety model, blued finish $407.00

RUGER P97 AUTOLOADING PISTOL
Caliber: 45ACP 8-shot magazine. **Barrel:** 4-1/8". **Weight:** 30-1/2 oz. **Length:** 7-1/4" overall. **Grooved:** Integral with frame. **Sights:** Blade front, rear drift adjustable for windage; three dot system. **Features:** Moulded polymer grip frame, stainless steel slide. Decocker or DAO. Introduced 1997. Made in U.S. by Sturm, Ruger & Co. Comes with lockable plastic case, spare magaline, loading tool. .
Price: (KP97D decock-only) $483.00
Price: (KP97DAO double-action only) $483.00

HANDGUNS — AUTOLOADERS, SERVICE & SPORT

Ruger KMK-4

Ruger KP512

Ruger 22/45-P4

RUGER MARK II STANDARD AUTOLOADING PISTOL
Caliber: 22 LR, 10-shot magazine. **Barrel:** 4-3/4" or 6". **Weight:** 25 oz. (4-3/4" bbl.). **Length:** 8-5/16" (4-3/4" bbl.). **Stocks:** Checkered plastic. **Sights:** Fixed, wide blade front, fixed rear. **Features:** Updated design of the original Standard Auto. Has new bolt hold-open latch. 10-shot magazine, magazine catch, safety, trigger and new receiver contours. Introduced 1982.
Price: Blued (MK 4, MK 6) $278.00
Price: In stainless steel (KMK 4, KMK 6) $364.00

Ruger 22/45 Mark II Pistol
Similar to the other 22 Mark II autos except has grip frame of Zytel that matches the angle and magazine latch of the Model 1911 45 ACP pistol. Available in 4" bull, 4-3/4" standard and 5-1/2" bull barrels. Comes with extra magazine, plastic case, lock. Introduced 1992.
Price: P4, 4" bull barrel, adjustable sights $275.00
Price: KP 4 (4-3/4" barrel), stainless steel, fixed sights $305.00
Price: KP512 (5-1/2" bull barrel), stainless steel, adj. sights ... $359.00
Price: P512 (5-1/2" bull barrel, all blue), adj. sights $275.00

SAFARI ARMS ENFORCER PISTOL
Caliber: 45 ACP, 6-shot magazine. **Barrel:** 3.8", stainless. **Weight:** 36 oz. **Length:** 7.3" overall. **Stocks:** Smooth walnut with etched black widow spider logo. **Sights:** Ramped blade front, LPA adjustable rear. **Features:** Extended safety, extended slide release; Commander-style hammer; beavertail grip safety; throated, polished, tuned. Parkerized matte black or satin stainless steel finishes. Made in U.S. by Safari Arms.
Price: $630.00

SAFARI ARMS GI SAFARI PISTOL
Caliber: 45 ACP, 7-shot magazine. **Barrel:** 5", 416 stainless. **Weight:** 39.9 oz. **Length:** 8.5" overall. **Stocks:** Checkered walnut. **Sights:** G.I.-style blade front, drift-adjustable rear. **Features:** Beavertail grip safety; extended thumb safety and slide release; Commander-style hammer. Parkerized finish. Reintroduced 1996.
Price: $439.00

SAFARI ARMS CARRIER PISTOL
Caliber: 45 ACP, 7-shot magazine. **Barrel:** 6", 416 stainless steel. **Weight:** 30 oz. **Length:** 9.5" overall. **Stocks:** Wood. **Sights:** Ramped blade front, LPA adjustable rear. **Features:** Beavertail grip safety; extended controls; full-length recoil spring guide; Commander-style hammer. Throated, polished and tuned. Satin stainless steel finish. Introduced 1999. Made in U.S. by Safari Arms, Inc.
Price: $714.00

SAFARI ARMS COHORT PISTOL
Caliber: 45 ACP, 7-shot magazine. **Barrel:** 3.8", 416 stainless. **Weight:** 37 oz. **Length:** 8.5" overall. **Stocks:** Smooth walnut with laser-etched black widow logo. **Sights:** Ramped blade front, LPA adjustable rear. **Features:** Combines the Enforcer model, slide and MatchMaster frame. Beavertail grip safety; extended thumb safety and slide release; Commander-style hammer. Throated, polished and tuned. Satin stainless finish. Introduced 1996. Made in U.S. by Safari Arms, Inc.
Price: $654.00

SAFARI ARMS MATCHMASTER PISTOL
Caliber: 45 ACP, 7-shot. **Barrel:** 5" or 6", 416 stainless steel. **Weight:** 38 oz. (5" barrel). **Length:** 8.5" overall. **Stocks:** Smooth walnut. **Sights:** Ramped blade, LPA adjustable rear. **Features:** Beavertail grip safety; extended controls; Commander-style hammer; throated, polished, tuned. Parkerized matte-black or satin stainless steel. Made in U.S. by Olympic Arms, Inc.
Price: 5" barrel $594.00
Price: 6" barrel $654.00

Safari Arms Carry Comp Pistol
Similar to the Matchmaster except has Wil Schueman-designed hybrid compensator system. Made in U.S. by Olympic Arms, Inc.
Price: $1,067.00

SEECAMP LWS 32 STAINLESS DA AUTO
Caliber: 32 ACP Win. Silvertip, 6-shot magazine. **Barrel:** 2", integral with frame. **Weight:** 10.5 oz. **Length:** 4-1/8" overall. **Stocks:** Glass-filled nylon. **Sights:** Smooth, no-snag, contoured slide and barrel top. **Features:** Aircraft quality 17-4 PH stainless steel. Inertia-operated firing pin. Hammer fired double-action-only. Hammer automatically follows slide down to safety rest position after each shot—no manual safety needed. Magazine safety disconnector. Polished stainless. Introduced 1985. From L.W. Seecamp.
Price: $425.00

SIG SAUER P220 SERVICE AUTO PISTOL
Caliber: 45 ACP, (7- or 8-shot magazine). **Barrel:** 4-3/8". **Weight:** 27.8 oz. **Length:** 7.8" overall. **Stocks:** Checkered black plastic. **Sights:** Blade front, drift adjustable rear for windage. Optional Siglite nightsights. **Features:** Double action. Decocking lever permits lowering hammer onto locked firing pin. Squared combat-type trigger guard. Slide stays open after last shot. Imported from Germany by SIGARMS, Inc.
Price: Blue SA/DA or DAO $790.00
Price: Blue, Siglite night sights $880.00
Price: K-Kote or nickel slide $830.00
Price: K-Kote or nickel slide with Siglite night sights $930.00

HANDGUNS — AUTOLOADERS, SERVICE & SPORT

SIG Sauer P220

SIG Arms Pro 2009

SIG Arms P245 Compact

SIG Sauer P229S

SIG Sauer P220 Sport Auto Pistol
Similar to the P220 except has 4.9" barrel, ported compensator, all-stainless steel frame and slide, factory-tuned trigger, adjustable sights, extended competition controls. Overall length is 9.9", weighs 43.5 oz. Introduced 1999. From SIGARMS, Inc.
Price: $1,320.00

SIG Sauer P245 Compact Auto Pistol
Similar to the P220 except has 3.9" barrel, shorter grip, 6-shot magazine, 7.28" overall length, and weighs 27.5 oz. Introduced 1999. From SIGARMS, Inc.
Price: Blue $780.00
Price: Blue, with Siglite sights............................. $850.00
Price: Two-tone.. $830.00
Price: Two-tone with Siglite sights $930.00
Price: With K-Kote finish................................. $830.00
Price: K-Kote with Siglite sights $930.00

SIG Sauer P229 DA Auto Pistol
Similar to the P228 except chambered for 9mm Para., 40 S&W, 357 SIG. Has 3.86" barrel, 7.08" overall length and 3.35" height. Weight is 30.5 oz. Introduced 1991. Frame made in Germany, stainless steel slide assembly made in U.S.; pistol assembled in U.S. From SIGARMS, Inc.
Price: $795.00
Price: With nickel slide $890.00
Price: Nickel slide Siglite night sights $935.00

SIG PRO AUTO PISTOL
Caliber: 9mm Para., 40 S&W, 10-shot magazine. **Barrel:** 3.86". **Weight:** 27.2 oz. **Length:** 7.36" overall. **Stocks:** Composite and rubberized one-piece. **Sights:** Blade front, rear adjustable for windage. Optional Siglite night sights. **Features:** Polymer frame, stainless steel slide; integral frame accessory rail; replaceable steel frame rails; left- or right-handed magazine release. Introduced 1999. From SIGARMS, Inc.

Price: SP2340 (40 S&W) $596.00
Price: SP2009 (9mm Para.) $596.00
Price: As above with Siglite night sights.................. $655.00

SIG Sauer P226 Service Pistol
Similar to the P220 pistol except has 4.4" barrel, and weighs 28.3 oz. 357 SIG or 40 S&W. Imported from Germany by SIGARMS, Inc.
Price: Blue SA/DA or DAO............................... $830.00
Price: With Siglite night sights $930.00
Price: Blue, SA/DA or DAO 357 SIG $830.00
Price: With Siglite night sights $930.00
Price: K-Kote finish, 40 S&W only or nickel slide $830.00
Price: K-Kote or nickel slide Siglite night sights $930.00
Price: Nickel slide 357 SIG............................... $875.00
Price: Nickel slide, Siglite night sights $930.00

SIG Sauer P229 Sport Auto Pistol
Similar to the P229 except available in 357 SIG only; 4.8" heavy barrel; 8.6" overall length; weighs 40.6 oz.; vented compensator; adjustable target sights; rubber grips; extended slide latch and magazine release. Made of stainless steel. Introduced 1998. From SIGARMS, Inc.
Price: $1,320.00

SIG SAUER P232 PERSONAL SIZE PISTOL
Caliber: 380 ACP, 7-shot. **Barrel:** 3-3/4". **Weight:** 16 oz. **Length:** 6-1/2" overall. **Stocks:** Checkered black composite. **Sights:** Blade front, rear adjustable for windage. **Features:** Double action/single action or DAO. Blow-back operation, stationary barrel. Introduced 1997. Imported from Germany by SIGARMS, Inc.
Price: Blue SA/DA or DAO............................... $505.00
Price: In stainless steel.................................. $545.00
Price: With stainless steel slide, blue frame $525.00
Price: Stainless steel, Siglite night sights, Hogue grips $585.00

34TH EDITION, 2002 • 153

HANDGUNS — AUTOLOADERS, SERVICE & SPORT

SIG Sauer P232

Smith & Wesson 4013 TSW

Smith & Wesson 457

SIG SAUER P239 PISTOL
Caliber: 9mm Para., 8-shot, 357 SIG 40 S&W, 7-shot magazine. **Barrel:** 3.6". **Weight:** 25.2 oz. **Length:** 6.6" overall. **Stocks:** Checkered black composite. **Sights:** Blade front, rear adjustable for windage. Optional Siglite night sights. **Features:** SA/DA or DAO; blackened stainless steel slide, aluminum alloy frame. Introduced 1996. Made in U.S. by SIGARMS, Inc.
Price: SA/DA or DAO $620.00
Price: SA/DA or DAO with Siglite night sights $720.00
Price: Two-tone finish $665.00
Price: Two-tone finish, Siglite sights $765.00

SMITH & WESSON MODEL 22A SPORT PISTOL
Caliber: 22 LR, 10-shot magazine. **Barrel:** 4", 5-1/2", 7". **Weight:** 29 oz. **Length:** 8" overall. **Stocks:** Two-piece polymer. **Sights:** Patridge front, fully adjustable rear. **Features:** Comes with a sight bridge with Weaver-style integral optics mount; alloy frame; .312" serrated trigger; stainless steel slide and barrel with matte blue finish. Introduced 1997. Made in U.S. by Smith & Wesson.
Price: 4" $230.00
Price: 5-1/2" $255.00
Price: 7" $289.00

SMITH & WESSON MODEL 457 TDA AUTO PISTOL
Caliber: 45 ACP, 7-shot magazine. **Barrel:** 3-3/4". **Weight:** 29 oz. **Length:** 7-1/4" overall. **Stocks:** One-piece Xenoy, wrap-around with straight backstrap. **Sights:** Post front, fixed rear, three-dot system. **Features:** Aluminum alloy frame, matte blue carbon steel slide; bobbed hammer; smooth trigger. Introduced 1996. Made in U.S. by Smith & Wesson.
Price: $563.00

SMITH & WESSON MODEL 908 AUTO PISTOL
Caliber: 9mm Para., 8-shot magazine. **Barrel:** 3-1/2". **Weight:** 26 oz. **Length:** 6-13/16". **Stocks:** One-piece Xenoy, wrap-around with straight backstrap. **Sights:** Post front, fixed rear, three-dot system. **Features:** Aluminum alloy frame, matte blue carbon steel slide; bobbed hammer; smooth trigger. Introduced 1996. Made in U.S. by Smith & Wesson.
Price: $509.00

SMITH & WESSON 9mm RECON AUTO PISTOL MODEL
Caliber: 9mm Para. **Barrel:** 3-1/2". **Weight:** 27 oz. **Length:** 7" overall. **Stocks:** Hogue wrap-around, finger-groove rubber. **Sights:** Three-dot Novak Low Mount, drift adjustable. **Features:** Traditional double-action mechanism. Tuned action, hand-crowned muzzle, polished feed ramp, hand-lapped slide, spherical barrel bushing. Checkered frontstrap. Introduced 1999. Made by U.S. by Smith & Wesson.
Price: $1,150.00

SMITH & WESSON MODEL 2213, 2214 SPORTSMAN AUTOS
Caliber: 22 LR, 8-shot magazine. **Barrel:** 3". **Weight:** 18 oz. **Length:** 6-1/8" overall. **Stocks:** Checkered black polymer. **Sights:** Patridge front, fixed rear; three-dot system. **Features:** Internal hammer; serrated trigger; single action. Model 2213 is stainless with alloy frame, Model 2214 is blued carbon steel with alloy frame. Introduced 1990. Made in U.S. by Smith & Wesson.
Price: Model 2213 . . . . $340.00
Price: Model 2214 . . . . $292.00

SMITH & WESSON MODEL 4013, 4053 TSW AUTOS
Caliber: 40 S&W, 9-shot magazine. **Barrel:** 3-1/2". **Weight:** 26.4 oz. **Length:** 6-7/8" overall. **Stocks:** Xenoy one-piece wrap-around. **Sights:** Novak three-dot system. **Features:** Traditional double-action system; stainless slide, alloy frame; fixed barrel bushing; ambidextrous decocker; reversible magazine catch. Introduced 1997. Made in U.S. by Smith & Wesson.
Price: Model 4013 TSW $844.00
Price: Model 4053 TSW, double-action-only $844.00

Smith & Wesson Model 22S Sport Pistols
Similar to the Model 22A Sport except with stainless steel frame. Available only with 5-1/2" or 7" barrel. Introduced 1997. Made in U.S. by Smith & Wesson.
Price: 5-1/2" standard barrel $312.00
Price: 5-1/2" bull barrel, wood target stocks with thumbrest $379.00
Price: 7" standard barrel $344.00
Price: 5-1/2" bull barrel, two-piece target stocks with thumbrest . . $353.00

SMITH & WESSON MODEL 410 DA AUTO PISTOL
Caliber: 40 S&W, 10-shot magazine. **Barrel:** 4". **Weight:** 28.5 oz. **Length:** 7.5 oz. **Stocks:** One-piece Xenoy, wrap-around with straight backstrap. **Sights:** Post front, fixed rear; three-dot system. **Features:** Aluminum alloy frame; blued carbon steel slide; traditional double action with left-side slide-mounted decocking lever. Introduced 1996. Made in U.S. by Smith & Wesson.
Price: $563.00

HANDGUNS — AUTOLOADERS, SERVICE & SPORT

Smith & Wesson 3913 TSW

Smith & Wesson 3913 LadySmith

Smith & Wesson 4506

Smith & Wesson Model 3913TSW/3953TSW Auto Pistols
Similar to the Model 3913 and 3953 except TSW guns have tighter tolerances, ambidextrous manual safety/decocking lever, flush-fit magazine, delayed-unlock firing system; magazine disconnector. Compact alloy frame, stainless steel slide. Straight backstrap. Introduced 1998. Made in U.S. by Smith & Wesson.
Price: Single action/double action $724.00
Price: Double action only $724.00

SMITH & WESSON MODEL 4006 TDA AUTO
Caliber: 40 S&W, 10-shot magazine. **Barrel:** 4". **Weight:** 38.5 oz. **Length:** 7-7/8" overall. **Stocks:** Xenoy wrap-around with checkered panels. **Sights:** Replaceable post front with white dot, Novak LoMount Carry fixed rear with two white dots, or micro. click adjustable rear with two white dots. **Features:** Stainless steel construction with non-reflective finish. Straight back-strap. Extra magazine included. Introduced 1990.
Price: With adjustable sights $899.00
Price: With fixed sight. $864.00
Price: With fixed night sights $991.00

Smith & Wesson Model 4043, 4046 DA Pistols
Similar to the Model 4006 except is double-action-only. Has a semi-bobbed hammer, smooth trigger, 4" barrel; Novak LoMount Carry rear sight, post front with white dot. Overall length is 7-1/2", weighs 28 oz. Model 4043 has alloy frame. Extra magazine included. Introduced 1991.
Price: Model 4043 (alloy frame) $844.00
Price: Model 4046 (stainless frame) $864.00
Price: Model 4046 with fixed night sights $991.00

SMITH & WESSON MODEL 4500 SERIES AUTOS
Caliber: 45 ACP, 8-shot magazine. **Barrel:** 5" (M4506). **Weight:** 41 oz. (4506). **Length:** 8-1/2" overall. **Stocks:** Xenoy one-piece wrap-around, arched or straight backstrap. **Sights:** Post front with white dot, adjustable or fixed Novak LoMount Carry on M4506. **Features:** M4506 has serrated hammer spur. All have two magazines. Contact Smith & Wesson for complete data. Introduced 1989.
Price: Model 4506, fixed sight $822.00
Price: Model 4506, adjustable sight $855.00
Price: Model 4566 (stainless, 4-1/4", traditional DA, ambidextrous safety, fixed sight) $897.00
Price: Model 4586 (stainless, 4-1/4", DA only) $897.00

SMITH & WESSON MODEL 4513TSW/4553TSW PISTOLS
Caliber: 45 ACP, 6-shot magazine. **Barrel:** 3-3/4". **Weight:** 28 oz. (M4513TSW). **Length:** 6-7/8 overall. **Stocks:** Checkered Xenoy; straight backstrap. **Sights:** White dot front, Novak Lo Mount Carry 2-Dot rear. **Features:** Model 4513TSW is traditional double action, Model 4553TSW is double action only. TSW series has tighter tolerances, ambidextrous manual safety/decocking lever, flush-fit magazine, delayed-unlock firing system; magazine disconnector. Compact alloy frame, stainless steel slide. Introduced 1998. Made in U.S. by Smith & Wesson.
Price: Model 4513TSW $880.00
Price: Model 4553TSW $837.00

SMITH & WESSON MODEL 910 DA AUTO PISTOL
Caliber: 9mm Para., 10-shot magazine. **Barrel:** 4". **Weight:** 28 oz. **Length:** 7-3/8" overall. **Stocks:** One-piece Xenoy, wrap-around with straight back-strap. **Sights:** Post front with white dot, fixed two-dot rear. **Features:** Alloy frame, blue carbon steel slide. Slide-mounted decocking lever. Introduced 1995.
Price: Model 910. . . . . $509.00

SMITH & WESSON MODEL 3913 TRADITIONAL DOUBLE ACTION
Caliber: 9mm Para., 8-shot magazine. **Barrel:** 3-1/2". **Weight:** 26 oz. **Length:** 6-13/16" overall. **Stocks:** One-piece Delrin wrap-around, textured surface. **Sights:** Post front with white dot, Novak LoMount Carry with two dots, adjustable for windage. **Features:** Aluminum alloy frame, stainless slide (M3913) or blue steel slide (M3914). Bobbed hammer with no half-cock notch; smooth .304" trigger with rounded edges. Straight back-strap. Extra magazine included. Introduced 1989.
Price: $662.00

Smith & Wesson Model 3913-LS LadySmith Auto
Similar to the standard Model 3913 except has frame that is upswept at the front, rounded trigger guard. Comes in frosted stainless steel with matching gray grips. Grips are ergonomically correct for a woman's hand. Novak LoMount Carry rear sight adjustable for windage, smooth edges for snag resistance. Extra magazine included. Introduced 1990.
Price: $744.00

Smith & Wesson Model 3953 DAO Pistol
Same as the Model 3913 except double-action-only. Model 3953 has stainless slide with alloy frame. Overall length 7"; weighs 25.5 oz. Extra magazine included. Introduced 1990.
Price: $724.00

HANDGUNS — AUTOLOADERS, SERVICE & SPORT

Smith & Wesson 4553 TSW

Springfield 1911A1 Standard

Smith & Wesson Sigma SW40V

Springfield Full-Size 1911A1

SMITH & WESSON MODEL 5900 SERIES AUTO PISTOLS

Caliber: 9mm Para., 10-shot magazine. **Barrel:** 4". **Weight:** 28-1/2 to 37-1/2 oz. (fixed sight); 38 oz. (adjustable sight). **Length:** 7-1/2" overall. **Stocks:** Xenoy wrap-around with curved backstrap. **Sights:** Post front with white dot, fixed or fully adjustable with two white dots. **Features:** All stainless, stainless and alloy or carbon steel and alloy construction. Smooth .304" trigger, .260" serrated hammer. Introduced 1989.
Price: Model 5906 (stainless, traditional DA, adjustable sight, ambidextrous safety)................................. $861.00
Price: As above, fixed sight $822.00
Price: With fixed night sights $948.00
Price: Model 5946 DAO (as above, stainless frame and slide) .. $822.00

SMITH & WESSON ENHANCED SIGMA SERIES PISTOLS

Caliber: 9mm Para., 40 S&W, 10-shot magazine. **Barrel:** 4". **Weight:** 26 oz. **Length:** 7.4" overall. **Stocks:** Integral. **Sights:** White dot front, fixed rear; three-dot system. Tritium night sights available. **Features:** Ergonomic polymer frame; low barrel centerline; internal striker firing system; corrosion-resistant slide; Teflon-filled, electroless-nickel coated magazine. Introduced 1994. Made in U.S. by Smith & Wesson.
Price: SW9E, 9mm, 4" barrel, black finish, fixed sights $657.00
Price: SW9V, 9mm, 4" barrel, satin stainless, fixed night sights.. $447.00
Price: SW40E, 40 S&W, 4" barrel, black finish, fixed sights..... $657.00
Price: SW40V, 40 S&W, 4" barrel, black polymer, fixed sights... $447.00

SMITH & WESSON SIGMA SW380 AUTO

Caliber: 380 ACP, 6-shot magazine. **Barrel:** 3". **Weight:** 14 oz. **Length:** 5.8" overall. **Stocks:** Integral. **Sights:** Fixed groove in the slide. **Features:** Polymer frame; double-action-only trigger mechanism; grooved/serrated front and rear straps; two passive safeties. Introduced 1995. Made in U.S. by Smith & Wesson.
Price: $328.00

Smith & Wesson Model 6906 Double-Action Auto

Similar to the Model 5906 except with 3-1/2" barrel, 10-shot magazine, fixed rear sight, .260" bobbed hammer. Extra magazine included. Introduced 1989.
Price: Model 6906, stainless $720.00
Price: Model 6906 with fixed night sights $836.00
Price: Model 6946 (stainless, DA only, fixed sights).......... $720.00

SMITH & WESSON MODEL CS9 CHIEFS SPECIAL AUTO

Caliber: 9mm Para., 7-shot magazine. **Barrel:** 3". **Weight:** 20.8 oz. **Length:** 6-1/4" overall. **Stocks:** Hogue wrap-around rubber. **Sights:** White dot front, fixed two-dot rear. **Features:** Traditional double-action trigger mechanism. Alloy frame, stainless or blued slide. Introduced 1999. Made in U.S. by Smith & Wesson.
Price: Blue or stainless.................................. $648.00

Smith & Wesson Model CS40 Chiefs Special Auto

Similar to the CS9 except chambered for 40 S&W (7-shot magazine), has 3-1/4" barrel, weighs 24.2 oz., and measures 6-1/2" overall. Introduced 1999. Made in U.S. by Smith & Wesson.
Price: Blue or stainless.................................. $683.00

Smith & Wesson Model CS45 Chiefs Special Auto

Similar to the CS40 except chambered for 45 ACP, 6-shot magazine, weighs 23.9 oz. Introduced 1999. Made in U.S. by Smith & Wesson.
Price: Blue or stainless.................................. $683.00

SPRINGFIELD, INC. FULL-SIZE 1911A1 AUTO PISTOL

Caliber: 9mm Para., 9-shot; 38 Super, 9-shot; 40 S&W, 9-shot; 45 ACP, 8-shot. **Barrel:** 5". **Weight:** 35.6 oz. **Length:** 8-5/8" overall. **Stocks:** Checkered plastic or walnut. **Sights:** Fixed three-dot system. **Features:** Beveled magazine well; lowered and flared ejection port. All forged parts, including frame, barrel, slide. All new production. Introduced 1990. From Springfield, Inc.
Price: Mil-Spec 45 ACP, Parkerized $559.00
Price: Standard, 45 ACP, blued $770.00
Price: Standard, 45 ACP, stainless....................... $828.00
Price: Lightweight 45 ACP (28.6 oz., matte finish, night sights).. $832.00
Price: 40 S&W, stainless $812.00
Price: 9mm, stainless $837.00

HANDGUNS — AUTOLOADERS, SERVICE & SPORT

Springfield TRP

Stoeger American Eagle Luger

Springfield V10 Ultra Compact

Springfield, Inc. TRP Pistols
Similar to the 1911A1 except 45 ACP only; has checkered front strap and mainspring housing; Novak Night Sight combat rear sight and matching dovetailed front sight; tuned, polished extractor; oversize barrel link; lightweight speed trigger and combat action job; match barrel and bushing; extended ambidextrous thumb safety and fitted beavertail grip safety; Carry bevel on entire pistol; checkered cocobolo wood grips; comes with two Wilson 8-shot magazines. Frame is engraved "Tactical," both sides of frame with "TRP." Introduced 1998. From Springfield, Inc.
Price: Standard with Armory Kote finish................. $1,395.00
Price: Standard, stainless steel $1,265.00
Price: Champion, Armory Kote, adj. sights.............. $1,407.00

Springfield, Inc. 1911A1 High Capacity Pistol
Similar to the Standard 1911A1 except available in 45 ACP with 10-shot magazine. Has Commander-style hammer, walnut grips, beveled magazine well, plastic carrying case. Introduced 1993. From Springfield, Inc.
Price: Mil-Spec 45 ACP $807.00
Price: 45 ACP Ultra Compact (3-1/2" bbl.) $812.00
Price: As above, stainless steel $884.00

Springfield, Inc. 1911A1 V-Series Ported Pistols
Similar to the standard 1911A1 except comes with scalloped slides with 10, 12 or 16 matching barrel ports to redirect powder gasses and reduce recoil and muzzle flip. Adjustable rear sight, extended thumb safety, Videki speed trigger, and beveled magazine well. Checkered walnut grips standard. Available in 45 ACP, stainless or bi-tone. Introduced 1992.
Price: V-16 Long Slide, stainless $1,080.00
Price: Target V-12, stainless........................... $878.00
Price: V-10 (Ultra-Compact, bi-tone) $853.00
Price: V-10 stainless....................................... NA

Springfield, Inc. 1911A1 Champion Pistol
Similar to the standard 1911A1 except slide is 4.025". Novak Night Sights. Comes with Delta hammer and cocobolo grips. Available in 45 ACP only; Parkerized or stainless. Introduced 1989.
Price: Parkerized $817.00
Price: Stainless... $870.00
Price: Lightweight, matte finish........................ $867.00

Springfield Inc. Ultra Compact Pistol
Similar to the 1911A1 Compact except has shorter slide, 3.5" barrel, beavertail grip safety, beveled magazine well, Novak Low Mount or Novak Night Sights, Videki speed trigger, flared ejection port, stainless steel frame, blued slide, match grade barrel, rubber grips. Introduced 1996. From Springfield, Inc.
Price: Parkerized 45 ACP, Night Sights $817.00
Price: Stainless 45 ACP, Night Sights $884.00
Price: Lightweight, matte finish......................... $867.00
Price: Lightweight, 9mm, stainless...................... $853.00

Springfield Inc. Long Slide 1911 A1 Pistol
Similar to the Full Size model except has a 6" barrel and slide for increased sight radius and higher velocity, fully adjustable sights, muzzle-forward weight distribution for reduced recoil and quicker shot-to-shot recovery. From Springfield Inc.
Price: Target, 45 ACP, stainless with Night Sights $1,002.00
Price: Trophy Match, stainless with adj. sights.......... $1,399.00

STEYR M & S SERIES AUTO PISTOLS
Caliber: 9mm Para., 40 S&W, 357 SIG; 10-shot magazine. **Barrel:** 4" (3.58" for Model S). **Weight:** 28 oz. (22.5 oz. for Model S). **Length:** 7.05" overall (6.53" for Model S). **Grips:** Ultra-rigid polymer. **Sights:** Drift-adjustable, white-outline rear; white-triangle blade front. **Features:** Polymer frame; trigger-drop firing pin, manual and key-lock safeties; loaded chamber indicator; 5.5-lb. trigger pull; 111-degree grip angle enhances natural pointing. Introduced 2000. Imported from Austria by GSI Inc.
Price: Model M (full-sized frame with 4" barrel) $609.95
Price: Model S (compact frame with 3.58" barrel) $609.95
Price: Extra 10-shot magazines (Model M or S) $39.00

STOEGER AMERICAN EAGLE LUGER
Caliber: 9mm Para., 7-shot magazine. **Barrel:** 4", 6". **Weight:** 32 oz. **Length:** 9.6" overall. **Stocks:** Checkered walnut. **Sights:** Blade front, fixed rear. **Features:** Recreation of the American Eagle Luger pistol in stainless steel. Chamber loaded indicator. Introduced 1994. From Stoeger Industries.
Price: 4", or 6" Navy Model $720.00
Price: With matte black finish........................... $798.00

34TH EDITION, 2002

HANDGUNS — AUTOLOADERS, SERVICE & SPORT

Taurus PT 22

Taurus PT92B

TAURUS MODEL PT 22/PT 25 AUTO PISTOLS
Caliber: 22 LR, 8-shot (PT 22); 25 ACP, 9-shot (PT 25). **Barrel:** 2.75". **Weight:** 12.3 oz. **Length:** 5.25" overall. **Stocks:** Smooth rosewood or mother-of-pearl. **Sights:** Blade front, fixed rear. **Features:** Double action. Tip-up barrel for loading, cleaning. Blue, nickel, duotone or blue with gold accents. Introduced 1992. Made in U.S. by Taurus International.
Price: 22 LR or 25 ACP, blue, nickel or with duo-tone finish
with rosewood grips $215.00
Price: 22 LR or 25 ACP, blue with gold trim, rosewood grips $230.00
Price: 22 LR or 25 ACP, blue, nickel or duotone finish with checkered
wood grips. $190.00
Price: 22 LR or 25 ACP, blue with gold trim, mother of pearl grips
. . . . $230.00

TAURUS MODEL PT92B AUTO PISTOL
Caliber: 9mm Para., 15-shot magazine. **Barrel:** 5". **Weight:** 34 oz. **Length:** 8.5" overall. **Stocks:** Black rubber. **Sights:** Fixed notch rear. Three-dot sight system. Also offered with micrometer-click adjustable night sights. **Features:** Double action, exposed hammer, chamber loaded indicator, ambidextrous safety, inertia firing pin. Imported by Taurus International.
Price: Blue $575.00
Price: Stainless steel $595.00
Price: Blue with gold trim, rosewood grips $625.00
Price: Blue with gold trim, mother-of-pearl grips. $645.00
Price: Stainless steel with gold trim, rosewood grips $645.00
Price: Stainless steel with gold trim, mother-of-pearl grips. $655.00
Price: Blue with checkered rubber grips, night sights. $655.00
Price: Stainless steel with checkered rubber grips, night sights. . . $670.00

Taurus Model PT99 Auto Pistol
Similar to the PT92 except has fully adjustable rear sight, smooth Brazilian walnut stocks and is available in stainless steel or polished blue. Introduced 1983.
Price: Blue $595.00
Price: Stainless steel $610.00
Price: 22 Conversion kit for PT 92 and PT99 (includes barrel and slide)
. . . . $266.00

TAURUS MODEL PT-100B AUTO PISTOL
Caliber: 40 S&W, 10-shot magazine. **Barrel:** 5". **Weight:** 34 oz. **Length:** 8-1/2". **Grips:** Checkered rubber, rosewood or mother-of-pearl. **Sights:** 3-dot fixed or adjustable; night sights available. **Features:** Single/double action with three-position safety/decocker. Re-introduced in 2001. Imported by Taurus International.
Price: Blued finish. $575.00
Price: Stainless steel $595.00
Price: Blue with gold accents, rosewood grips $625.00
Price: Blue with gold accents, mother-of-pearl grips $645.00
Price: Stainless w/gold accents, mother-of-pearl grips $655.00

TAURUS MODEL PT-111 MILLENNIUM AUTO PISTOL
Caliber: 9mm Para., 10-shot magazine. **Barrel:** 3.25". **Weight:** 18.7 oz. **Length:** 6.0" overall. **Stocks:** Polymer. **Sights:** 3-dot fixed; night sights available. Low profile, three-dot combat. **Features:** Double action only. Firing pin lock; polymer frame; striker fired; push-button magazine release. Introduced 1998. Imported by Taurus International.
Price: Blue $425.00
Price: Stainless. $435.00
Price: With night sights, blue slide $500.00
Price: With night sights, stainless slide $520.00

Taurus Model PT-111 Millennium Titanium Pistol
Similar to the PT-111 except with titanium slide, night sights.
Price: $585.00

TAURUS PT-132 MILLENIUM AUTO PISTOL
Caliber: 32 ACP, 10-shot magazine. **Barrel:** 3.25". **Weight:** 18.7 oz. **Length:** NA. **Grips:** Polymer. **Sights:** 3-dot fixed; night sights available. **Features:** Double-action only; polymer frame; matte stainless or blue steel slide; manual safety; integral key-lock action. Introduced 2001.
Price: . . . . $422.00 to $438.00

Taurus Model PT-138 Auto Pistol
Similar to the PT-111 except chambered for 380 ACP, with 10-shot magazine. Double-action-only mechanism. Has black polymer frame with blue or stainless slide. Introduced 1999. Imported by Taurus International.
Price: Blue . . . . $425.00 ($500.00 with night sights)
Price: Stainless. . . . . $435.00 ($520.00 with night sights)

TAURUS PT-140 MILLENIUM AUTO PISTOL
Caliber: 40 S&W, 10-shot magazine. **Barrel:** 3.25". **Weight:** 18.7 oz. **Length:** NA. **Grips:** Checkered polymer. **Sights:** 3-dot fixed; night sights available. **Features:** Double-action only; matte stainless or blue steel slide; black polymer frame; manual safety; integral key-lock action. From Taurus International.
Price: . . . . $455.00 to $555.00

TAURUS PT-145 MILLENIUM AUTO PISTOL
Caliber: 45 ACP, 10-shot magazine. **Barrel:** 3.27". **Weight:** 23 oz. **Length:** NA. **Stock:** Checkered polymer. **Sights:** 3-dot fixed; night sights available. **Features:** Double-action only; matte stainless or blue steel slide; black polymer frame; manual safety; integral key-lock action. From Taurus International.
Price: . . . . $490.00 to $575.00

TAURUS MODEL PT-911 AUTO PISTOL
Caliber: 9mm Para., 10-shot magazine. **Barrel:** 4". **Weight:** 28.2 oz. **Length:** 7" overall. **Stocks:** Black rubber. **Sights:** Fixed. Low profile, three-dot combat. **Features:** Double action, exposed hammer; ambidextrous hammer drop; chamber loaded indicator. Introduced 1997. Imported by Taurus International.

HANDGUNS — AUTOLOADERS, SERVICE & SPORT

Taurus PT-911

Taurus PT-940

Taurus PT-938

Taurus PT-945

Price: Blue **$505.00**
Price: Stainless. **$525.00**
Price: Blue with gold accents, rosewood grips **$555.00**
Price: Stainless with gold accents, rosewood grips **$570.00**
Price: Blue/gold accents, mother-of-pearl grips **$570.00**
Price: Stainless/gold accents, mother-of-pearl grips **$585.00**
Price: Blue finish, night sights. **$585.00**
Price: Stainless finish, night sights **$600.00**

TAURUS MODEL PT-938 AUTO PISTOL
Caliber: 380 ACP, 10-shot magazine. **Barrel:** 3.72". **Weight:** 27 oz. **Length:** 6.5" overall. **Grips:** Black rubber. **Sights:** Fixed. Low profile, three-dot combat. **Features:** Double-action only. Chamber loaded indicator; firing pin block; ambidextrous hammer drop. Introduced 1997. Imported by Taurus International.
Price: Blue **$500.00**
Price: Stainless. **$530.00**

TAURUS MODEL PT-940 AUTO PISTOL
Caliber: 40 S&W, 10-shot magazine. **Barrel:** 3.35". **Weight:** 28.2 oz. **Length:** 7.05" overall. **Grips:** Checkered rubber, rosewood or mother-of-pearl. **Sights:** Drift-adjustable front and rear; three-dot combat. **Features:** Single/double action, exposed hammer; manual ambidextrous hammer-drop; inertia firing pin; chamber loaded indicator. Introduced 1996. Imported by Taurus International.
Price: Blue **$525.00**
Price: Stainless steel **$535.00**
Price: Blue with gold accents, rosewood grips **$570.00**
Price: Stainless with gold accents, rosewood grips **$600.00**

TAURUS MODEL PT-945 AUTO PISTOL
Caliber: 45 ACP, 8-shot magazine. **Barrel:** 4.25". **Weight:** 29.5 oz. **Length:** 7.48" overall. **Grips:** Checkered black rubber, rosewood or mother-of-pearl. **Sights:** Drift-adjustable front and rear; three-dot system. **Features:** Single/double-action mechanism. Has manual ambidextrous hammer drop safety, intercept notch, firing pin block, chamber loaded indicator, integral key-lock, last-shot hold-open. Introduced 1995. Imported by Taurus International.

Taurus PT-957

Price: Blue **$560.00**
Price: Stainless. **$580.00**
Price: Blue, ported **$600.00**
Price: Stainless, ported **$620.00**
Price: Blue with gold accents, rosewood grips **$610.00**
Price: Blue with gold accents, mother-of-pearl grips **$625.00**
Price: Stainless w/gold accents, mother-of-pearl grips ... **$645.00**

TAURUS MODEL PT-957 AUTO PISTOL
Caliber: 357 SIG, 10-shot magazine. **Barrel:** 3-5/8". **Weight:** 28 oz. **Length:** 7" overall. **Stocks:** Checkered rubber. **Sights:** Fixed, low profile, three-dot combat; night sights optional. **Features:** Single/double action mechanism; blue, stainless steel, blue with gold accents or stainless with gold accents; exposed hammer; ported barrel/slide; three-position safety with decocking lever and ambidextrous safety. Introduced 1999. Imported by Taurus International.
Price: Blue **$560.00**
Price: Stainless. **$575.00**
Price: Blue with gold accents, rosewood grips **$610.00**
Price: Stainless with gold accents, rosewood grips **$625.00**

HANDGUNS — AUTOLOADERS, SERVICE & SPORT

Vektor SP1

Walther PP

Walther PPK/S

Vektor Ultra with Tasco Scope

VEKTOR SP1 AUTO PISTOL
Caliber: 9mm Para., 40 S&W (SP2), 10-shot magazine. **Barrel:** 4-5/8". **Weight:** 35 oz. **Length:** 8-1/4" overall. **Stocks:** Checkered black composition. **Sights:** Combat-type fixed. **Features:** Alloy frame, steel slide; traditional double-action mechanism; matte black finish. Introduced 1999. Imported from South Africa by Vektor USA.
Price: SP1 (9mm) $599.95
Price: SP1 with nickel finish $629.95
Price: SP2 (40 S&W) $649.95

Vektor SP1, SP2 Compact General's Model Pistol
Similar to the 9mm Para. Vektor SP1 except has 4" barrel, weighs 31-1/2 oz., and is 7-1/2" overall. Recoil operated. Traditional double-action mechanism. SP2 model is chambered for 40 S&W. Introduced 1999. Imported from South Africa by Vektor USA.
Price: SP1 (9mm Para.) $649.95
Price: SP2 (40 S&W) $649.95

VEKTOR CP-1 COMPACT PISTOL
Caliber: 9mm Para., 10-shot magazine. **Barrel:** 4". **Weight:** 25.4 oz. **Length:** 7" overall. **Stocks:** Textured polymer. **Sights:** Blade front adjustable for windage, fixed rear; adjustable sight optional. **Features:** Ergonomic grip frame shape; stainless steel barrel; delayed gas-buffered blowback action. Introduced 1999. Imported from South Africa by Vektor USA.
Price: With black slide $479.95
Price: With nickel slide $499.95
Price: With black slide, adjustable sight $509.95
Price: With nickel slide, adjustable sight $529.95

VEKTOR SP1 SPORT PISTOL
Caliber: 9mm Para., 10-shot magazine. **Barrel:** 5 ".**Weight:** 38 oz. **Length:** 9-3/8" overall. **Stocks:** Checkered black composition. **Sights:** Combat-type blade front, adjustable rear. **Features:** Single action only with adjustable trigger stop; three-chamber compensator; extended magazine release. Introduced 1999. Imported from South Africa by Vektor USA.
Price: $829.95

Vektor SP1 Tuned Sport Pistol
Similar to the Vektor Sport except has fully adjustable straight trigger, LPA three-dot sight system, and hard nickel finish. Introduced 1999. Imported from South Africa by Vektor USA.
Price: $1,199.95

Vektor SP1 Target Pistol
Similar to the Vektor Sport except has 5-7/8" barrel without compensator; weighs 40-1/2 oz.; has fully adjustable straight match trigger; black slide, bright frame. Introduced 1999. Imported from South Africa by Vektor USA.
Price: $1,299.95

Vektor SP1, SP2 Ultra Sport Pistols
Similar to the Vektor Target except has three-chamber compensator with three jet ports; strengthened frame with integral beavertail; lightweight polymer scope mount (Weaver rail). Overall length is 11", weighs 41-1/2 oz. Model SP2 is in 40 S&W. Introduced 1999. Imported from South Africa by Vektor USA.
Price: SP1 (9mm) $2,149.95
Price: SP2 (40 S&W) $2,149.95

WALTHER PP AUTO PISTOL
Caliber: 380 ACP, 7-shot magazine. **Barrel:** 3.86". **Weight:** 23-1/2 oz. **Length:** 6.7" overall. **Stocks:** Checkered plastic. **Sights:** Fixed, white markings. **Features:** Double action; manual safety blocks firing pin and drops hammer; chamber loaded indicator on 32 and 380; extra finger rest magazine provided. Imported from Germany by Carl Walther USA.
Price: 380 . . . . $999.00

Walther PPK/S American Auto Pistol
Similar to Walther PP except made entirely in the United States. Has 3.27" barrel with 6.1" length overall. Introduced 1980.
Price: 380 ACP only, blue $540.00
Price: As above, 32 ACP or 380 ACP, stainless $540.00

HANDGUNS — AUTOLOADERS, SERVICE & SPORT

Walther PPK

Walther P99

Walther TPH

Dan Wesson Pointman Major

Walther PPK American Auto Pistol
Similar to Walther PPK/S except weighs 21 oz., has 6-shot capacity. Made in the U.S. Introduced 1986.
Price: Stainless, 32 ACP or 380 ACP $540.00
Price: Blue, 380 ACP only $540.00

WALTHER MODEL TPH AUTO PISTOL
Caliber: 22 LR, 25 ACP, 6-shot magazine. **Barrel:** 2-1/4". **Weight:** 14 oz. **Length:** 5-3/8" overall. **Stocks:** Checkered black composition. **Sights:** Blade front, rear drift-adjustable for windage. **Features:** Made of stainless steel. Scaled-down version of the Walther PP/PPK series. Made in U.S. Introduced 1987. From Carl Walther USA.
Price: Blue or stainless steel, 22 or 25 . . . . $440.00

WALTHER P88 COMPACT PISTOL
Caliber: 9mm Para., 10-shot magazine. **Barrel:** 3.93". **Weight:** 28 oz. **Length:** NA. **Stocks:** Checkered black polymer. **Sights:** Blade front, drift adjustable rear. **Features:** Double action with ambidextrous decocking lever and magazine release; alloy frame; loaded chamber indicator; matte blue finish. Imported from Germany by Carl Walther USA.
Price: $900.00

WALTHER P99 AUTO PISTOL
Caliber: 9mm Para., 9x21, 40 S&W, 10-shot magazine. **Barrel:** 4". **Weight:** 25 oz. **Length:** 7" overall. **Stocks:** Textured polymer. **Sights:** Blade front (comes with three interchangeable blades for elevation adjustment), micrometer rear adjustable for windage. **Features:** Double-action mechanism with trigger safety, decock safety, internal striker safety; chamber loaded indicator; ambidextrous magazine release levers; polymer frame with interchangeable backstrap inserts. Comes with two magazines. Introduced 1997. Imported from Germany by Carl Walther USA.
Price: $799.00

Walther P990 Auto Pistol
Similar to the P99 except is double action only. Available in blue or silver tenifer finish. Introduced 1999. Imported from Germany by Carl Walther USA.
Price: $749.00

WALTHER P-5 AUTO PISTOL
Caliber: 9mm Para., 8-shot magazine. **Barrel:** 3.62". **Weight:** 28 oz. **Length:** 7.10" overall. **Stocks:** Checkered plastic. **Sights:** Blade front, adjustable rear. **Features:** Uses the basic Walther P-38 double-action mechanism. Blue finish. Imported from Germany by Carl Walther USA.
Price: $900.00

DAN WESSON POINTMAN MAJOR AUTO PISTOL
Caliber: 45 ACP. **Barrel:** 5". **Weight:** NA. **Length:** NA. **Grips:** Rosewood checkered. **Sights: Features:** Blued or stainless steel frame and serrated slide; Chip McCormick match-grade trigger group, sear and disconnect; match-grade barrel; high-ride beavertail safety; checkered slide release; high rib; interchangeable sight system; laser engraved. Introduced 2000. Made in U.S. by Dan Wesson Firearms.
Price: Model PM1-B (blued) $789.00
Price: Model PM1-S (stainless) $799.00

Dan Wesson Pointman Minor Auto Pistol
Similar to Pointman Major except has blued frame and slide with fixed rear sight. Introduced 2000. Made in U.S. by Dan Wesson Firearms.
Price: Model PM2-P $579.00

34TH EDITION, 2002 • 161

HANDGUNS — AUTOLOADERS, SERVICE & SPORT

Dan Wesson Pointman Seven

Dan Wesson Pointman Guardian

Wilkinson Sherry

Dan Wesson Pointman Seven Auto Pistols
Similar to Pointman Major except has dovetail adjustable target rear sight and dovetail target front sight. Available in blued or stainless finish. Introduced 2000. Made in U.S. by Dan Wesson Firearms.
Price: PM7 (blued frame and slide) $999.00
Price: PM7S (stainless finish) $1,099.00

Dan Wesson Pointman Guardian Auto Pistols
Similar to Pointman Major except has a more compact frame with 4.25" barrel. Avaiable in blued or stainless finish with fixed or adjustable sights. Introduced 2000. Made in U.S. by Dan Wesson Firearms.
Price: PMG-FS (blued frame and slide, fixed sights) $769.00
Price: PMG-AS (blued frame and slide, adjustable sights) $779.00
Price: PMGD-FS Guardian Duce (stainless frame and blued slide, fixed sights) $829.00
Price: PMGD-AS Guardian Duce (stainless frame and blued slide, adj. sights) $839.00

NEW! Dan Wesson Pointman Hi-Cap Auto Pistol
Similar to Pointman Minor except has full-size high-capacity (10-shot) magazine with 5" chromed barrel, blued finish and dovetail fixed rear sight. Match adjustable trigger, ambidextrous extended thumb safety, beavertail safety. Introduced 2001. From Dan Wesson Firearms.
Price: PMHC (Pointman High-Cap) $669.00

NEW! Dan Wesson Pointman Dave Pruitt Signature Series
Similar to other full-sized Pointman models except customized by Master Pistolsmith and IDPA Grand Master Dave Pruitt. Alloy carbon-steel from with black oxide bluing and bead-blast matte finish. Front and rear chevron cocking serrations; dovetail-mount fixed Novak style sights; match trigger group, sear and hammer; exotic hardwood grips. Introduced 2001. From Dan Wesson Firearms.
Price: PMDP (Pointman Dave Pruitt) $899.00

WILKINSON SHERRY AUTO PISTOL
Caliber: 22 LR, 8-shot magazine. **Barrel:** 2-1/8". **Weight:** 9-1/4 oz. **Length:** 4-3/8" overall. **Stocks:** Checkered black plastic. **Sights:** Fixed, groove. **Features:** Cross-bolt safety locks the sear into the hammer. Available in all blue finish or blue slide and trigger with gold frame. Introduced 1985.
Price: $195.00

WILKINSON LINDA AUTO PISTOL
Caliber: 9mm Para. **Barrel:** 8-5/16". **Weight:** 4 lbs., 13 oz. **Length:** 12-1/4" overall. **Stocks:** Checkered black plastic pistol grip, walnut forend. **Sights:** Protected blade front, aperture rear. **Features:** Fires from closed bolt. Semi-auto only. Straight blowback action. Cross-bolt safety. Removable barrel. From Wilkinson Arms.
Price: $533.33

HANDGUNS — COMPETITION HANDGUNS

Includes models suitable for several forms of competition and other sporting purposes.

Baer 1911 Ultimate Master

Beretta Model 89

Baer 1911 Bullseye Wadcutter

Beretta Model 96 Combat

BAER 1911 ULTIMATE MASTER COMBAT PISTOL
Caliber: 9x23, 38 Super, 400 Cor-Bon 45 ACP (others available), 10-shot magazine. **Barrel:** 5", 6"; Baer NM. **Weight:** 37 oz. **Length:** 8.5" overall. **Stocks:** Checkered rosewood. **Sights:** Baer dovetail front, low-mount Bo-Mar rear with hidden leaf. **Features:** Full-house competition gun. Baer forged NM blued steel frame and double serrated slide; Baer triple port, tapered cone compensator; fitted slide to frame; lowered, flared ejection port; Baer reverse recoil plug; full-length guide rod; recoil buff; beveled magazine well; Baer Commander hammer, sear; Baer extended ambidextrous safety, extended ejector, checkered slide stop, beavertail grip safety with pad, extended magazine release button; Baer speed trigger. Made in U.S. by Les Baer Custom, Inc.
Price: Compensated, open sights. $2,476.00
Price: 6" Model 400 Cor-Bon $2,541.00

BAER 1911 NATIONAL MATCH HARDBALL PISTOL
Caliber: 45 ACP, 7-shot magazine. **Barrel:** 5". **Weight:** 37 oz. **Length:** 8.5" overall. **Stocks:** Checkered walnut. **Sights:** Baer dovetail front with undercut post, low-mount Bo-Mar rear with hidden leaf. **Features:** Baer NM forged steel frame, double serrated slide and barrel with stainless bushing; slide fitted to frame; Baer match trigger with 4-lb. pull; polished feed ramp, throated barrel; checkered front strap, arched mainspring housing; Baer beveled magazine well; lowered, flared ejection port; tuned extractor; Baer extended ejector, checkered slide stop; recoil buff. Made in U.S. by Les Baer Custom, Inc.
Price: $1,335.00

Baer 1911 Bullseye Wadcutter Pistol
Similar to the National Match Hardball except designed for wadcutter loads only. Has polished feed ramp and barrel throat; Bo-Mar rib on slide; full-length recoil rod; Baer speed trigger with 3-1/2-lb. pull; Baer deluxe hammer and sear; Baer beavertail grip safety with pad; flat mainspring housing checkered 20 lpi. Blue finish; checkered walnut grips. Made in U.S. by Les Baer Custom, Inc.
Price: From. $1,495.00
Price: With 6" barrel, from $1,690.00

BENELLI MP90S WORLD CUP PISTOL
Caliber: 22 Long Rifle, 6- or 9-shot magazine. **Barrel:** 4.4" **Weight:** 2.5 lbs. **Length:** 11.75". **Grip:** Walnut. **Sights:** Blade front, fully adjustable rear. **Features:** Single-action target pistol with fully adjustable trigger and adjustable heel rest; integral scope rail mount; attachment system for optional external weights.
Price: $1,190.00

Benelli MP95E Atlanta Pistol
Similar to MP90S World Cup Pistol, but available in blue finish with walnut grip or chrome finish with laminate grip. Overall length 11.25". Trigger overtravel adjustment only.
Price: (blue finish, walnut grip) $740.00
Price: (chrome finish, laminate grip) $810.00

BERETTA MODEL 89 GOLD STANDARD PISTOL
Caliber: 22 LR, 8-shot magazine. **Barrel:** 6". **Weight:** 41 oz. **Length:** 9.5" overall. **Stocks:** Target-type walnut with thumbrest. **Sights:** Interchangeable blade front, fully adjustable rear. **Features:** Single action target pistol. Matte black, Bruniton finish. Imported from Italy by Beretta U.S.A.
Price: $802.00

BERETTA MODEL 96 COMBAT PISTOL
Caliber: 40 S&W, 10-shot magazine. **Barrel:** 4.9" (5.9" with weight). **Weight:** 34.4 oz. **Length:** 8.5" overall. **Stocks:** Checkered black plastic. **Sights:** Blade front, fully adjustable target rear. **Features:** Uses heavier Brigadier slide with front and rear serrations; extended frame-mounted safety; extended, reversible magazine release; single-action-only with competition-tuned trigger with extra-short let-off and over-travel adjustment. Comes with tool kit. Introduced 1997. Imported from Italy by Beretta U.S.A.
Price: $1,593.00
Price: 4.9" barrel. $1,341.00
Price: 5.9" barrel. $1,634.00
Price: Combo $1,599.00

HANDGUNS — COMPETITION HANDGUNS

BF Ultimate

Browning Buck Mark Bullseye

Browning Buck Mark Target 5.5

Colt Gold Cup Trophy

Beretta Model 96 Stock Pistol
Similar to the Model 96 Combat except is single/double action, with half-cock notch. Has front and rear slide serrations, rubber magazine bumper, replaceable accurizing barrel bushing, ultra-thin fine-checkered grips (aluminum optional), checkered front and back straps, radiused back strap, fitted case. Weighs 35 oz., 8.5" overall. Introduced 1997. Imported from Italy by Beretta U.S.A.
Price: $1,700.00

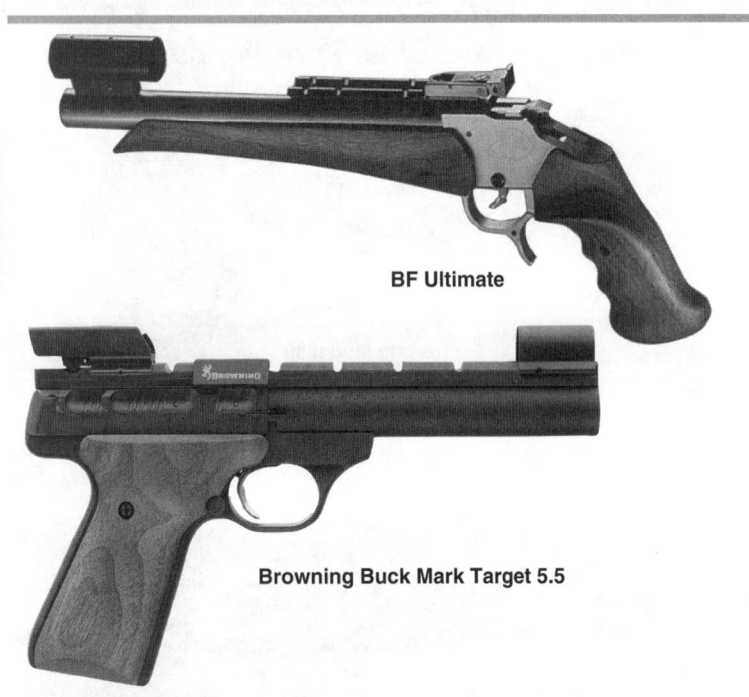

BF ULTIMATE SILHOUETTE HB SINGLE SHOT PISTOL
Caliber: 7mm U.S., 22 LR Match and 100 other chamberings. **Barrel:** 10.75" Heavy Match Grade with 11-degree target crown. **Weight:** 3 lbs., 15 oz. **Length:** 16" overall. **Stocks:** Thumbrest target style. **Sights:** Bo-Mar/Bond ScopeRib I Combo with hooded post front adjustable for height and width, rear notch available in .032", .062", .080" and .100" widths; 1/2-MOA clicks. **Features:** Designed to meet maximum rules for IHMSA Production Gun. Falling block action gives rigid barrel-receiver mating. Hand fitted and headspaced. Etched receiver; gold-colored trigger. Introduced 1988. Made in U.S. by E. Arthur Brown Co. Inc.
Price: $669.00

Classic BF Hunting Pistol
Similar to BF Ultimate Silhouette HB Single Shot Pistol, except no sights; drilled and tapped for scope mount. Barrels from 8 to 15". Variety of options offered. Made in U.S. by E. Arthur Brown Co. Inc.
Price: $599.00

BROWNING BUCK MARK SILHOUETTE
Caliber: 22 LR, 10-shot magazine. **Barrel:** 9-7/8". **Weight:** 53 oz. **Length:** 14" overall. **Stocks:** Smooth walnut stocks and forend, or finger-groove walnut. **Sights:** Post-type hooded front adjustable for blade width and height; Pro Target rear fully adjustable for windage and elevation. **Features:** Heavy barrel with .900" diameter; 12-1/2" sight radius. Special sighting plane forms scope base. Introduced 1987. Made in U.S. From Browning.
Price: $448.00

Browning Buck Mark Target 5.5
Same as the Buck Mark Silhouette except has a 5-1/2" barrel with .900" diameter. Has hooded sights mounted on a scope base that accepts an optical or reflex sight. Rear sight is a Browning fully adjustable Pro Target, front sight is an adjustable post that customizes to different widths, and can be adjusted for height. Contoured walnut grips with thumbrest, or finger-groove walnut. Matte blue finish. Overall length is 9-5/8", weighs 35-1/2 oz. Has 10-shot magazine. Introduced 1990. From Browning.

Price: $425.00
Price: Target 5.5 Gold (as above with gold anodized frame and top rib) $477.00
Price: Target 5.5 Nickel (as above with nickel frame and top rib). $477.00

Browning Buck Mark Field 5.5
Same as the Target 5.5 except has hoodless ramp-style front sight and low profile rear sight. Matte blue finish, contoured or finger-groove walnut stocks. Introduced 1991.
Price: $425.00

Browning Buck Mark Bullseye
Similar to the Buck Mark Silhouette except has 7-1/4" heavy barrel with three flutes per side; trigger is adjustable from 2-1/2 to 5 lbs.; specially designed rosewood target or three-finger-groove stocks with competition-style heel rest, or with contoured rubber grip. Overall length is 11-5/16", weighs 36 oz. Introduced 1996. Made in U.S. From Browning.
Price: With ambidextrous moulded composite stocks $389.00
Price: With rosewood stocks, or wrap-around finger groove $500.00

COLT GOLD CUP MODEL O PISTOL
Caliber: 45 ACP, 8-shot magazine. **Barrel:** 5", with new design bushing. **Weight:** 39 oz. **Length:** 8-1/2". **Stocks:** Checkered rubber composite with silver-plated medallion. **Sights:** Patridge-style front, Bomar-style rear adjustable for windage and elevation, sight radius 6-3/4". **Features:** Arched or flat housing; wide, grooved trigger with adjustable stop; ribbed-top slide, hand fitted, with improved ejection port.
Price: Blue $1,050.00
Price: Stainless... $1,116.00

COMPETITOR SINGLE SHOT PISTOL
Caliber: 22 LR through 50 Action Express, including belted magnums. **Barrel:** 14" standard; 10.5" silhouette; 16" optional. **Weight:** About 59 oz. (14" bbl.). **Length:** 15.12" overall. **Stocks:** Ambidextrous; synthetic (standard) or laminated or natural wood. **Sights:** Ramp front, adjustable rear. **Features:** Rotary canon-type action cocks on opening; cammed ejector; interchangeable barrels, ejectors. Adjustable single stage trigger, sliding thumb safety and trigger safety. Matte blue finish. Introduced 1988. From Competitor Corp., Inc.
Price: 14", standard calibers, synthetic grip $414.95
Price: Extra barrels, from $159.95

164 • GUNS ILLUSTRATED

HANDGUNS — COMPETITION HANDGUNS

Competitor Single Shot

Freedom Arms 252 Silhouette

E.A.A. Witness Gold Team

Hammerli SP 20

CZ 75 CHAMPION COMPETITION PISTOL
Caliber: 9mm Para., 9x21, 40 S&W, 10-shot magazine. **Barrel:** 4.49". **Weight:** 35 oz. **Length:** 9.44" overall. **Stocks:** Black rubber. **Sights:** Blade front, fully adjustable rear. **Features:** Single-action trigger mechanism; three-port compensator (40 S&W, 9mm have two port) full-length guide rod; extended magazine release; ambidextrous safety; flared magazine well; fully adjustable match trigger. Introduced 1999. Imported from the Czech Republic by CZ USA.
Price: 9mm Para., 9x21, 40 S&W, dual-tone finish. $1,484.00

CZ 75 ST IPSC AUTO PISTOL
Caliber: 40 S&W, 10-shot magazine. **Barrel:** 5.12". **Weight:** 2.9 lbs. **Length:** 8.86" overall. **Stocks:** Checkered walnut. **Sights:** Fully adjustable rear. **Features:** Single-action mechanism; extended slide release and ambidextrous safety; full-length slide rail; double slide serrations. Introduced 1999. Imported from the Czech Republic by CZ-USA.
Price: Dual-tone finish $1,038.00

EAA/BAIKAL IZH35 AUTO PISTOL
Caliber: 22 LR, 5-shot magazine. **Barrel:** 6". **Weight:** NA. **Length:** NA. **Grips:** Walnut; fully adjustable right-hand target-style. **Sights:** Fully adjustable rear, blade front; detachable scope mount. **Features:** Hammer-forged target barrel; machined steel receiver; adjustable trigger; manual slide hold back, grip and manual trigger-bar disconnect safeties; cocking indicator. Introduced 2000. Imported from Russia by European American Armory.
Price: Blued finish. $519.00

E.A.A. WITNESS GOLD TEAM AUTO
Caliber: 9mm Para., 9x21, 38 Super, 40 S&W, 45 ACP. **Barrel:** 5.1". **Weight:** 41.6 oz. **Length:** 9.6" overall. **Stocks:** Checkered walnut, competition style. **Sights:** Square post front, fully adjustable rear. **Features:** Triple-chamber cone compensator; competition SA trigger; extended safety and magazine release; competition hammer; beveled magazine well; beavertail grip. Hand-fitted major components. Hard chrome finish. Match-grade barrel. From E.A.A. Custom Shop. Introduced 1992. From European American Armory.
Price: $2,150.00

E.A.A. Witness Silver Team Auto
Similar to the Witness Gold Team except has double-chamber compensator, oval magazine release, black rubber grips, double-dip blue finish. Comes with Super Sight and drilled and tapped for scope mount. Built for the intermediate competition shooter. Introduced 1992. From European American Armory Custom Shop.
Price: 9mm Para., 9x21, 38 Super, 40 S&W, 45 ACP $968.00

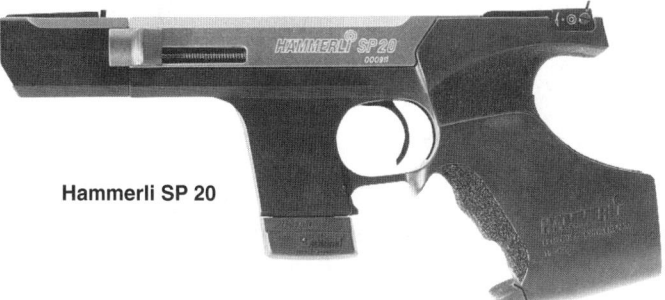

ENTRÉPRISE TOURNAMENT SHOOTER MODEL I
Caliber: 45 ACP, 10-shot magazine. **Barrel:** 6". **Weight:** 40 oz. **Length:** 8.5" overall. **Stocks:** Black ultra-slim double diamond checkered synthetic. **Sights:** Dovetailed Patridge front, adjustable Competizione "melded" rear. **Features:** Oversized magazine release button; flared magazine well; fully machined parallel slide rails; front and rear slide serrations; serrated top of slide; stainless ramped bull barrel with fully supported chamber; full-length guide rod with plug; stainless firing pin; match extractor; polished ramp; tuned match extractor; black oxide. Introduced 1998. Made in U.S. by Entréprise Arms.
Price: $2,300.00
Price: TSMIII (Satin chrome finish, two-piece guide rod) $2,700.00

Excel Industries CP-45 Auto Pistol
Caliber: 45 ACP, 6-shot magazine. **Barrel:** 3-1/4 inches. **Weight:** 31 oz. **Length:** 6-3/8 inches overall. **Grips:** Checkered black nylon. **Sights:** Fully adjustable rear, three-dot; blade front. **Features:** Stainless steel frame and slide; single action with external hammer and firing pin block, manual thumb safety; last-shot hold open. Includes gun lock and cleaning kit. Introduced 2001. Made in U.S. by Excel Industries Inc.
Price: $425.00

FREEDOM ARMS MODEL 83 FIELD GRADE SILHOUETTE CLASS
Caliber: 22 LR, 5-shot cylinder. **Barrel:** 10". **Weight:** 63 oz. **Length:** 15.5" overall. **Stocks:** Black Micarta. **Sights:** Removable patridge front blade; Iron Sight Gun Works silhouette rear, click adjustable for windage and elevation (optional adj. front sight and hood). **Features:** Stainless steel, matte finish, manual sliding-bar safety system; dual firing pins, lightened hammer for fast lock time, pre-set trigger stop. Introduced 1991. Made in U.S. by Freedom Arms.
Price: Silhouette Class $1,765.00
Price: Extra fitted 22 WMR cylinder $264.00

GAUCHER GP SILHOUETTE PISTOL
Caliber: 22 LR, single shot. **Barrel:** 10". **Weight:** 42.3 oz. **Length:** 15.5" overall. **Stocks:** Stained hardwood. **Sights:** Hooded post on ramp front, open rear adjustable for windage and elevation. **Features:** Matte chrome barrel, blued bolt and sights. Other barrel lengths available on special order. Introduced 1991. Imported by Mandall Shooting Supplies.
Price: $425.00

HAMMERLI SP 20 TARGET PISTOL
Caliber: 22 LR, 32 S&W. **Barrel:** 4.6". **Weight:** 34.6-41.8 oz. **Length:** 11.8" overall. **Stocks:** Anatomically shaped synthetic Hi-Grip available in five sizes. **Sights:** Integral front in three widths, adjustable rear with changeable notch widths. **Features:** Extremely low-level sight line; anatomically shaped trigger; adjustable JPS buffer system for different recoil characteristics. Receiver available in red, blue, gold, violet or black. Introduced 1998. Imported from Switzerland by SIGARMS, Inc and Hammerli Pistols USA.
Price: . . . . NA

34TH EDITION, 2002 • 165

HANDGUNS — COMPETITION HANDGUNS

High Standard Trophy

High Standard Victor

HARRIS GUNWORKS SIGNATURE JR. LONG RANGE PISTOL
Caliber: Any suitable caliber. **Barrel:** To customer specs. **Weight:** 5 lbs. **Stock:** Gunworks fiberglass. **Sights:** None furnished; comes with scope rings. **Features:** Right- or left-hand benchrest action of titanium or stainless steel; single shot or repeater. Comes with bipod. Introduced 1992. Made in U.S. by Harris Gunworks, Inc.
Price: $2,700.00

HIGH STANDARD TROPHY TARGET PISTOL
Caliber: 22 LR, 10-shot magazine. **Barrel:** 5-1/2" bull or 7-1/4" fluted. **Weight:** 44 oz. **Length:** 9.5" overall. **Stock:** Checkered hardwood with thumbrest. **Sights:** Undercut ramp front, frame-mounted micro-click rear adjustable for windage and elevation; drilled and tapped for scope mounting. **Features:** Gold-plated trigger, slide lock, safety-lever and magazine release; stippled front grip and backstrap; adjustable trigger and sear. Barrel weights optional. From High Standard Manufacturing Co., Inc.
Price: 5-1/2", scope base $510.00
Price: 7.25" $650.00
Price: 7.25", scope base $591.00

HIGH STANDARD VICTOR TARGET PISTOL
Caliber: 22 LR, 10-shot magazine. **Barrel:** 4-1/2" or 5-1/2"; push-button takedown. **Weight:** 46 oz. **Length:** 9.5" overall. **Stock:** Checkered hardwood with thumbrest. **Sights:** Undercut ramp front, micro-click rear adjustable for windage and elevation. Also available with scope mount, rings, no sights. **Features:** Stainless steel construction. Full-length vent rib. Gold-plated trigger, slide lock, safety-lever and magazine release; stippled front grip and backstrap; polished slide; adjustable trigger and sear. Comes with barrel weight. From High Standard Manufacturing Co., Inc.
Price: $591.00
Price: With Weaver rib $532.00

KIMBER SUPER MATCH AUTO PISTOL
Caliber: 45 ACP, 7-shot magazine. **Barrel:** 5". **Weight:** 38 oz. **Length:** 18.7" overall. **Sights:** Blade front, Kimber fully adjustable rear. **Features:** Guaranteed to have shot 3" group at 50 yards. Stainless steel frame, black KimPro slide; two-piece magazine well; premium aluminum match-grade trigger; 30 lpi front strap checkering; stainless match-grade barrel; ambidextrous safety; special Custom Shop markings. Introduced 1999. Made in U.S. by Kimber Mfg., Inc.
Price: $1,927.00

MORINI MODEL 84E FREE PISTOL
Caliber: 22 LR, single shot. **Barrel:** 11.4". **Weight:** 43.7 oz. **Length:** 19.4" overall. **Stocks:** Adjustable match type with stippled surfaces. **Sights:** Interchangeable blade front, match-type fully adjustable rear. **Features:** Fully adjustable electronic trigger. Introduced 1995. Imported from Switzerland by Nygord Precision Products.
Price: $1,450.00

PARDINI MODEL SP, HP TARGET PISTOLS
Caliber: 22 LR, 32 S&W, 5-shot magazine. **Barrel:** 4.7". **Weight:** 38.9 oz. **Length:** 11.6" overall. **Stocks:** Adjustable; stippled walnut; match type. **Sights:** Interchangeable blade front, interchangeable, fully adjustable rear. **Features:** Fully adjustable match trigger. Introduced 1995. Imported from Italy by Nygord Precision Products.
Price: Model SP (22 LR)............................... $950.00
Price: Model HP (32 S&W)............................ $1,050.00

PARDINI GP RAPID FIRE MATCH PISTOL
Caliber: 22 Short, 5-shot magazine. **Barrel:** 4.6". **Weight:** 43.3 oz. **Length:** 11.6" overall. **Stocks:** Wrap-around stippled walnut. **Sights:** Interchangeable post front, fully adjustable match rear. **Features:** Model GP Schuman has extended rear sight for longer sight radius. Introduced 1995. Imported from Italy by Nygord Precision Products.
Price: Model GP $1,095.00
Price: Model GP Schuman............................ $1,595.00

PARDINI K22 FREE PISTOL
Caliber: 22 LR, single shot. **Barrel:** 9.8". **Weight:** 34.6 oz. **Length:** 18.7" overall. **Stocks:** Wrap-around walnut; adjustable match type. **Sights:** Interchangeable post front, fully adjustable match open rear. **Features:** Removable, adjustable match trigger. Barrel weights mount above the barrel. New model introduced in 1999. Imported from Italy by Nygord Precision Products.
Price: $1,295.00

RUGER MARK II TARGET MODEL AUTOLOADING PISTOL
Caliber: 22 LR, 10-shot magazine. **Barrel:** 6-7/8". **Weight:** 42 oz. **Length:** 11-1/8" overall. **Stocks:** Checkered hard plastic. **Sights:** .125" blade front, micro-click rear, adjustable for windage and elevation. Sight radius 9-3/8". Comes with lockable plastic case with lock.
Features: Introduced 1982.
Price: Blued (MK-678) $336.00
Price: Stainless (KMK-678) $420.00

Ruger Mark II Government Target Model
Same gun as the Mark II Target Model except has 6-7/8" barrel, higher sights and is roll marked "Government Target Model" on the right side of the receiver below the rear sight. Identical in all aspects to the military model used for training U.S. Armed Forces except for markings. Comes with factory test target. Comes with lockable plastic case and lock. Introduced 1987.
Price: Blued (MK-678G) $405.00
Price: Stainless (KMK-678G) $485.00

Ruger Stainless Competition Model Pistol
Similar to the Mark II Government Target Model stainless pistol except has 6-7/8" slab-sided barrel; the receiver top is fitted with a Ruger scope base of blued, chrome moly steel; comes with Ruger 1" stainless scope rings for mounting a variety of optical sights; has checkered laminated grip panels with right-hand thumbrest. Has blued open sights with 9-1/4" radius. Overall length is 11-1/8", weight 45 oz. Comes with lockable plastic case and lock. Introduced 1991.
Price: KMK-678GC..................................... $499.00

Ruger Mark II Bull Barrel
Same gun as the Target Model except has 5-1/2" or 10" heavy barrel (10" meets all IHMSA regulations). Weight with 5-1/2" barrel is 42 oz., with 10" barrel, 51 oz. Comes with lockable plastic case with lock.
Price: Blued (MK-512) $336.00
Price: Blued (MK-10) $340.00
Price: Stainless (KMK-10) $425.00
Price: Stainless (KMK-512) $420.00

HANDGUNS — COMPETITION HANDGUNS

Ruger Mark II Bull Barrel - MK10

Smith & Wesson Model 41

Safari Arms Big Deuce

Springfield 1911A1 Trophy Match

SAFARI ARMS BIG DEUCE PISTOL
Caliber: 45 ACP, 7-shot magazine. **Barrel:** 6", 416 stainless steel. **Weight:** 40.3 oz. **Length:** 9.5" overall. **Stocks:** Smooth walnut. **Sights:** Ramped blade front, LPA adjustable rear. **Features:** Beavertail grip safety; extended thumb safety and slide release; Commander-style hammer. Throated, polished and tuned. Parkerized matte black slide with satin stainless steel frame. Introduced 1995. Made in U.S. by Safari Arms, Inc.
Price: $714.00

SMITH & WESSON MODEL 41 TARGET
Caliber: 22 LR, 10-shot clip. **Barrel:** 5-1/2", 7". **Weight:** 44 oz. (5-1/2" barrel). **Length:** 9" overall (5-1/2" barrel). **Stocks:** Checkered walnut with modified thumbrest, usable with either hand. **Sights:** 1/8" Patridge on ramp base; micro-click rear adjustable for windage and elevation. **Features:** 3/8" wide, grooved trigger; adjustable trigger stop.
Price: S&W Bright Blue, either barrel $801.00

SMITH & WESSON MODEL 22A TARGET PISTOL
Caliber: 22 LR, 10-shot magazine. **Barrel:** 5-1/2" bull. **Weight:** 38.5 oz. **Length:** 9-1/2" overall. **Stocks:** Dymondwood with ambidextrous thumbrests and flared bottom or rubber soft touch with thumbrest. **Sights:** Patridge front, fully adjustable rear. **Features:** Sight bridge with Weaver-style integral optics mount; alloy frame, stainless barrel and slide; matte black finish. Introduced 1997. Made in U.S. by Smith & Wesson.
Price: $320.00

Smith & Wesson Model 22S Target Pistol
Similar to the Model 22A except has stainless steel frame. Introduced 1997. Made in U.S. by Smith & Wesson.
Price: $379.00

Springfield, Inc. 1911A1 Trophy Match Pistol
Similar to the 1911A1 except factory accurized, Videki speed trigger, skeletonized hammer; has 4- to 5-1/2-lb. trigger pull, click adjustable rear sight, match-grade barrel and bushing. Comes with cocobolo grips. Introduced 1994. From Springfield, Inc.
Price: Blue $1,089.00
Price: Stainless steel $1,149.00
Price: High Capacity (stainless steel, 10-shot magazine, front slide serrations, checkered slide serrations) $1,118.00

Springfield, Inc. Expert Pistol
Similar to the Competition Pistol except has triple-chamber tapered cone compensator on match barrel with dovetailed front sight; lowered and flared ejection port; fully tuned for reliability; fitted slide to frame; extended ambidextrous thumb safety, extended magazine release button; beavertail grip safety; Pachmayr wrap-around grips. Comes with two magazines, plastic carrying case. Introduced 1992. From Springfield, Inc.
Price: 45 ACP, Duotone finish $1,724.00
Price: Expert Ltd. (non-compensated) $1,624.00

Springfield, Inc. Distinguished Pistol
Has all the features of the 1911A1 Expert except is full-house pistol with deluxe Bo-Mar low-mounted adjustable rear sight; full-length recoil spring guide rod and recoil spring retainer; checkered frontstrap; S&A magazine well; walnut grips. Hard chrome finish. Comes with two magazines with slam pads, plastic carrying case. From Springfield, Inc.
Price: 45 ACP $2,445.00
Price: Distinguished Limited (non-compensated) $2,345.00

SPRINGFIELD, INC. 1911A1 BULLSEYE WADCUTTER PISTOL
Caliber: 38 Super, 45 ACP. **Barrel:** 5". **Weight:** 45 oz. **Length:** 8.59" overall (5" barrel). **Stocks:** Checkered walnut. **Sights:** Bo-Mar rib with undercut blade front, fully adjustable rear. **Features:** Built for wadcutter loads only. Has full-length recoil spring guide rod, fitted Videki speed trigger with 3.5-lb. pull; match Commander hammer and sear; beavertail grip safety; lowered and flared ejection port; tuned extractor; fitted slide to frame; recoil buffer system; beveled and polished magazine well; checkered front strap and steel mainspring housing (flat housing standard); polished and throated National Match barrel and bushing. Comes with two magazines with slam pads, plastic carrying case, test target. Introduced 1992. From Springfield, Inc.
Price: $1,499.00

Springfield, Inc. Basic Competition Pistol
Has low-mounted Bo-Mar adjustable rear sight, undercut blade front; match throated barrel and bushing; polished feed ramp; lowered and flared ejection port; fitted Videki speed trigger with tuned 3.5-lb. pull; fitted slide to frame; recoil buffer system; checkered walnut grips; serrated, arched mainspring housing. Comes with two magazines with slam pads, plastic carrying case. Introduced 1992. From Springfield, Inc.
Price: 45 ACP, blue, 5" only $1,295.00

Springfield, Inc. 1911A1 N.M. Hardball Pistol
Has Bo-Mar adjustable rear sight with undercut front blade; fitted match Videki trigger with 4-lb. pull; fitted slide to frame; throated National Match barrel and bushing, polished feed ramp; recoil buffer system; tuned extractor; Herrett walnut grips. Comes with two magazines, plastic carrying case, test target. Introduced 1992. From Springfield, Inc.
Price: 45 ACP, blue $1,336.00

34TH EDITION, 2002 • 167

HANDGUNS — COMPETITION HANDGUNS

Thompson/Center Super 14 Contender

Wichita Silhouette

Unique D.E.S. 69U

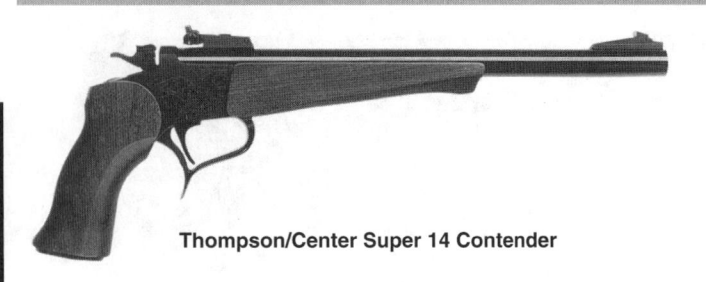

STI EAGLE 5.0 PISTOL
Caliber: 9mm Para., 38 Super, 40 S&W, 45 ACP, 10-ACP, 10-shot magazine. **Barrel:** 5", bull. **Weight:** 34 oz. **Length:** 8.62" overall. **Stocks:** Checkered polymer. **Sights:** Bo-Mar blade front, Bo-Mar fully adjustable rear. **Features:** Modular frame design; adjustable match trigger; skeletonized hammer; extended grip safety with locator pad; match-grade fit of all parts. Many options available. Introduced 1994. Made in U.S. by STI International.
Price: $1,792.00

THOMPSON/CENTER SUPER 14 CONTENDER
Caliber: 22 LR, 222 Rem., 223 Rem., 7-30 Waters, 30-30 Win., 357 Rem. Maximum, 44 Mag., single shot. **Barrel:** 14". **Weight:** 45 oz. **Length:** 17-1/4" overall. **Stocks:** T/C "Competitor Grip" (walnut and rubber). **Sights:** Fully adjustable target-type. **Features:** Break-open action with auto safety. Interchangeable barrels for both rimfire and centerfire calibers. Introduced 1978.
Price: Blued $520.24
Price: Stainless steel $578.40
Price: Extra barrels, blued $251.06
Price: Extra barrels, stainless steel $278.68

Thompson/Center Super 16 Contender
Same as the T/C Super 14 Contender except has 16-1/4" barrel. Rear sight can be mounted at mid-barrel position (10-3/4" radius) or moved to the rear (using scope mount position) for 14-3/4" radius. Overall length is 20-1/4". Comes with T/C Competitor Grip of walnut and rubber. Available in, 223 Rem., 45-70 Gov't. Also available with 16" vent rib barrel with internal choke, caliber 45 Colt/410 shotshell.
Price: Blue $525.95
Price: 45-70 Gov't., blue $531.52
Price: Super 16 Vent Rib, blued $559.70
Price: Extra 16" barrel, blued $245.61
Price: Extra 45-70 barrel, blued $251.08
Price: Extra Super 16 vent rib barrel, blue $278.73

UNIQUE D.E.S. 32U TARGET PISTOL
Caliber: 32 S&W Long wadcutter. **Barrel:** 5.9". **Weight:** 40.2 oz. **Stocks:** Anatomically shaped, adjustable stippled French walnut. **Sights:** Blade front, micrometer click rear. **Features:** Trigger adjustable for weight and position; dry firing mechanism; slide stop catch. Optional sleeve weights. Introduced 1990. Imported from France by Nygord Precision Products.
Price: Right-hand, about $1,350.00
Price: Left-hand, about $1,380.00

UNIQUE D.E.S. 69U TARGET PISTOL
Caliber: 22 LR, 5-shot magazine. **Barrel:** 5.91". **Weight:** 35.3 oz. **Length:** 10.5" overall. **Stocks:** French walnut target-style with thumbrest and adjustable shelf; hand-checkered panels. **Sights:** Ramp front, micro. adjustable rear mounted on frame; 8.66" sight radius. **Features:** Meets U.I.T. standards. Comes with 260-gram barrel weight; 100, 150, 350-gram weights available. Fully adjustable match trigger; dry-firing safety device. Imported from France by Nygord Precision Products.
Price: Right-hand, about $1,250.00
Price: Left-hand, about $1,290.00

UNIQUE MODEL 96U TARGET PISTOL
Caliber: 22 LR, 5- or 6-shot magazine. **Barrel:** 5.9". **Weight:** 40.2 oz. **Length:** 11.2" overall. **Stocks:** French walnut. Target style with thumbrest and adjustable shelf. **Sights:** Blade front, micrometer rear mounted on frame. **Features:** Designed for Sport Pistol and Standard U.I.T. shooting. External hammer; fully adjustable and movable trigger; dry-firing device. Introduced 1997. Imported from France by Nygord Precision Products.
Price: $1,350.00

WALTHER GSP MATCH PISTOL
Caliber: 22 LR, 32 S&W Long (GSP-C), 5-shot magazine. **Barrel:** 4.22". **Weight:** 44.8 oz. (22 LR), 49.4 oz. (32). **Length:** 11.8" overall. **Stocks:** Walnut. **Sights:** Post front, match rear adjustable for windage and elevation. **Features:** Available with either 2.2-lb. (1000 gm) or 3-lb. (1360 gm) trigger. Spare magazine, barrel weight, tools supplied. Imported from Germany by Nygord Precision Products.
Price: GSP, with case $1,495.00
Price: GSP-C, with case $1,595.00

HANDGUNS — DOUBLE ACTION REVOLVERS, SERVICE & SPORT

Includes models suitable for hunting and competitive courses of fire, both police and international.

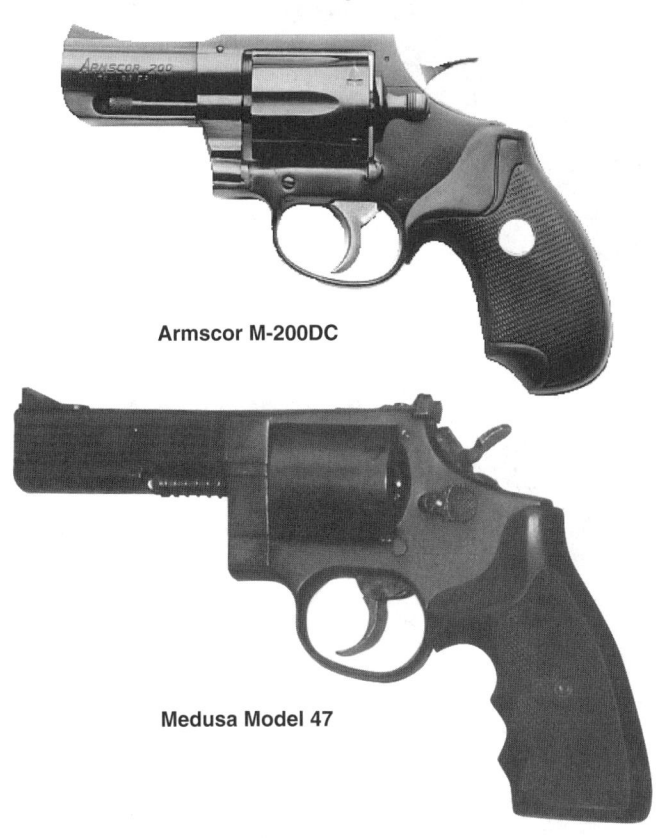

Armscor M-200DC

Ruger GP161

Medusa Model 47

ARMSCOR M-200DC REVOLVER
Caliber: 38 Spec., 6-shot cylinder. **Barrel:** 2-1/2", 4". **Weight:** 22 oz. (2-1/2" barrel). **Length:** 7-3/8" overall (2-1/2" barrel). **Stocks:** Checkered rubber. **Sights:** Blade front, fixed notch rear. **Features:** All-steel construction; floating firing pin, transfer bar ignition; shrouded ejector rod; blue finish. Reintroduced 1996. Imported from the Philippines by K.B.I., Inc.
Price: 2-1/2" $199.99
Price: 4" $205.00

ARMSPORT MODEL 4540 REVOLVER
Caliber: 38 Special. **Barrel:** 4". **Weight:** 32 oz **Length:** 9" overall. **Sights:** Fixed rear, blade front. **Features:** Ventilated rib; blued finish. Imported from Argentina by Armsport Inc.
Price: $140.00

E.A.A. STANDARD GRADE REVOLVERS
Caliber: 38 Spec., 6-shot; 357 magnum, 6-shot. **Barrel:** 2", 4". **Weight:** 38 oz. (22 rimfire, 4"). **Length:** 8.8" overall (4" bbl.). **Stocks:** Rubber with finger grooves. **Sights:** Blade front, fixed or adjustable on rimfires; fixed only on 32, 38. **Features:** Swing-out cylinder; hammer block safety; blue finish. Introduced 1991. Imported from Germany by European American Armory.
Price: 38 Special 2" $180.00
Price: 38 Special, 4" $199.00
Price: 357 Magnum, 2" $199.00
Price: 357 Magnum, 4" $233.00

MEDUSA MODEL 47 REVOLVER
Caliber: Most 9mm, 38 and 357 caliber cartridges; 6-shot cylinder. **Barrel:** 2-1/2", 3", 4", 5", 6"; fluted. **Weight:** 39 oz. **Length:** 10" overall (4" barrel). **Stocks:** Gripper-style rubber. **Sights:** Changeable front blades, fully adjustable rear. **Features:** Patented extractor allows gun to chamber, fire and extract over 25 different cartridges in the .355 to .357 range, without half-moon clips. Steel frame and cylinder; match quality barrel. Matte blue finish. Introduced 1996. Made in U.S. by Phillips & Rogers, Inc.
Price: $899.00

ROSSI MODEL 351/352 REVOLVERS
Caliber: 38 Special, 5-shot. **Barrel:** 2". **Weight:** 24 oz. **Length:** 6-1/2" overall. **Grips:** Rubber. **Sights:** Blade front, fixed rear. **Features:** Patented key-lock Taurus Security System; forged steel frame handles +P ammunition. Introduced 2001. Imported by BrazTech/Taurus.
Price: Model 351 (blued finish) $298.00
Price: Model 352 (stainless finish) $345.00

ROSSI MODEL 461/462 REVOLVERS
Caliber: 357 Magnum, 6-shot. **Barrel:** 2". **Weight:** 26 oz. **Length:** 6-1/2" overall. **Grips:** Rubber. **Sights:** Blade front, low-profile fixed rear. **Features:** Patented key-lock Taurus Security System; forged steel frame handles +P ammunition. Introduced 2001. Imported by BrazTech/Taurus.
Price: Model 461 (blued finish) $298.00
Price: Model 462 (stainless finish) $345.00

ROSSI MODEL 971/972 REVOLVERS
Caliber: 357 Magnum, 6-shot. **Barrel:** 4" or 6". **Weight:** NA. **Length:** 8-1/2" or 10-1/2" overall. **Grips:** Rubber. **Sights:** Red ramp front, adjustable rear. **Features:** Patented key-lock Taurus Security System; forged steel frame handles +P ammunition. Introduced 2001. Imported by BrazTech/Taurus.
Price: Model 971 (blued finish, 4" barrel) $345.00
Price: Model 972 (stainless steel finish, 6" barrel) $391.00

Rossi Model 851
Similar to the Model 971/972 except chambered for 38 Special. Blued finish, 4" barrel. Introduced 2001. From BrazTech/Taurus.
Price: $298.00

RUGER GP-100 REVOLVERS
Caliber: 38 Spec., 357 Mag., 6-shot. **Barrel:** 3", 3" full shroud, 4", 4" full shroud, 6", 6" full shroud. **Weight:** 3" barrel—35 oz., 3" full shroud—36 oz., 4" barrel—37 oz., 4" full shroud—38 oz. **Sights:** Fixed; adjustable on 4" full shroud and all 6" barrels. **Stocks:** Ruger Santoprene Cushioned Grip with Goncalo Alves inserts. **Features:** Uses action and frame incorporating improvements and features of both the Security-Six and Redhawk revolvers. Full length and short ejector shroud. Satin blue and stainless steel.
Price: GP-141 (357, 4" full shroud, adj. sights, blue) $475.00
Price: GP-160 (357, 6", adj. sights, blue) $475.00
Price: GP-161 (357, 6" full shroud, adj. sights, blue), 46 oz. $475.00
Price: GPF-331 (357, 3" full shroud) $465.00
Price: GPF-340 (357, 4") $465.00
Price: GPF-341 (357, 4" full shroud) $465.00
Price: KGP-141 (357, 4" full shroud, adj. sights, stainless) $515.00
Price: KGP-160 (357, 6", adj. sights, stainless), 43 oz. $515.00
Price: KGP-161 (357, 6" full shroud, adj. sights, stainless) 46 oz. $515.00
Price: KGPF-330 (357, 3", stainless) $499.00
Price: KGPF-331 (357, 3" full shroud, stainless) $499.00
Price: KGPF-340 (357, 4", stainless), KGPF-840 (38 Spec.) $499.00
Price: KGPF-341 (357, 4" full shroud, stainless) $499.00

34TH EDITION, 2002 • 169

HANDGUNS — DOUBLE ACTION REVOLVERS, SERVICE & SPORT

Ruger KSP-821

Ruger KSRH-7

Smith & Wesson Model 10

Smith & Wesson Model 14

Ruger SP101 Double-Action-Only Revolver
Similar to the standard SP101 except is double-action-only with no single-action sear notch. Has spurless hammer for snag-free handling, floating firing pin and Ruger's patented transfer bar safety system. Available with 2-1/4" barrel in 357 Magnum. Weighs 25-1/2 oz., overall length 7.06". Natural brushed satin or high-polish stainless steel. Introduced 1993.
Price: KSP321XL (357 Mag.) $458.00

RUGER SP101 REVOLVERS
Caliber: 22 LR, 32 H&R Mag., 6-shot; 38 Spec. +P, 357 Mag., 5-shot. **Barrel:** 2-1/4", 3-1/16", 4". **Weight:** (38 & 357 mag models) 2-1/4"—25 oz.; 3-1/16"—27 oz. **Sights:** Adjustable on 22, 32, fixed on others. **Stocks:** Ruger Santoprene Cushioned Grip with Xenoy inserts. **Features:** Incorporates improvements and features found in the GP-100 revolvers into a compact, small frame, double-action revolver. Full-length ejector shroud. Stainless steel only. Introduced 1988.
Price: KSP-821X (2-1/2", 38 Spec.) $458.00
Price: KSP-831X (3-1/16", 38 Spec.) $458.00
Price: KSP-221X (2-1/4", 22 LR), 32 oz. $458.00
Price: KSP-240X (4", 22 LR), 33 oz. $458.00
Price: KSP-241X (4" heavy bbl., 22 LR), 34 oz. $458.00
Price: KSP-3231X (3-1/16", 32 H&R), 30 oz. $458.00
Price: KSP-321X (2-1/4", 357 Mag.) $458.00
Price: KSP331X (3-1/16", 357 Mag.) $458.00

RUGER REDHAWK
Caliber: 44 Rem. Mag., 45 Colt, 6-shot. **Barrel:** 5-1/2", 7-1/2". **Weight:** About 54 oz. (7-1/2" bbl.). **Length:** 13" overall (7-1/2" barrel). **Stocks:** Square butt Goncalo Alves. **Sights:** Interchangeable Patridge-type front, rear adjustable for windage and elevation. **Features:** Stainless steel, brushed satin finish, or blued ordnance steel. Has a 9-1/2" sight radius. Introduced 1979.
Price: Blued, 44 Mag., 5-1/2" RH-445, 7-1/2" RH-44 .... $560.00
Price: Blued, 44 Mag., 7-1/2" RH44R, with scope mount, rings .. $595.00
Price: Stainless, 44 Mag., 5-1/2", 7-1/2" KRH-445 .... $615.00
Price: Stainless, 44 Mag., 7-1/2", with scope mount, rings KRH-44 .... $615.00
Price: Stainless, 45 Colt, 5-1/2", 7-1/2" KRH-455 .... $615.00
Price: Stainless, 45 Colt, 7-1/2", with scope mount KRH-45 .... $615.00

Ruger Super Redhawk Revolver
Similar to the standard Redhawk except has a heavy extended frame with the Ruger Integral Scope Mounting System on the wide topstrap. Also available in 454 Casull and new 480 Ruger. The wide hammer spur has been lowered for better scope clearance. Incorporates the mechanical design features and improvements of the GP-100. Choice of 7-1/2" or 9-1/2" barrel, both with ramp front sight base with Redhawk-style Interchangeable Insert sight blades, adjustable rear sight. Comes with Ruger "Cushioned Grip" panels of Santoprene with Goncalo Alves wood panels. Satin stainless steel. Introduced 1987.
Price: KSRH-7 (7-1/2"), KSRH-9 (9-1/2") $650.00
Price: KSRH-7454 (7-1/2") 454 Casull $745.00
New! Price: KSRH-7480 (7-1/2") 480 Ruger $745.00
New! Price: KSRH-9480 (9-1/2") 480 Ruger $745.00

Ruger Super Redhawk 454 Casull Revolver
Similar to the Ruger Super Redhawk except chambered for 454 Casull (also accepts 45 Colt cartridges). Unfluted cylinder, 7" barrel, weighs 53 ounces. Comes with 1" stainless scope rings. Introduced 2000.
Price: (Target gray stainless steel finish) $745.00

SMITH & WESSON MODEL 10 M&P HB REVOLVER
Caliber: 38 Spec., 6-shot. **Barrel:** 4". **Weight:** 33.5 oz. **Length:** 9-5/16" overall. **Stocks:** Uncle Mike's Combat soft rubber; square butt. **Sights:** Fixed; ramp front, square notch rear.
Price: Blue $458.00

SMITH & WESSON MODEL 14 FULL LUG REVOLVER
Caliber: 38 Spec., 6-shot. **Barrel:** 6", full lug. **Weight:** 47 oz. **Length:** 11-1/8" overall. **Stocks:** Hogue soft rubber. **Sights:** Pinned Patridge front, adjustable micrometer click rear. **Features:** Has .500" target hammer, .312" smooth combat trigger. Polished blue finish. Reintroduced 1991. Limited production.
Price: $498.00

HANDGUNS — DOUBLE ACTION REVOLVERS, SERVICE & SPORT

Smith & Wesson Model 19

Smith & Wesson Model 36LS

Smith & Wesson Model 629 Classic DX

Smith & Wesson Model 65LS

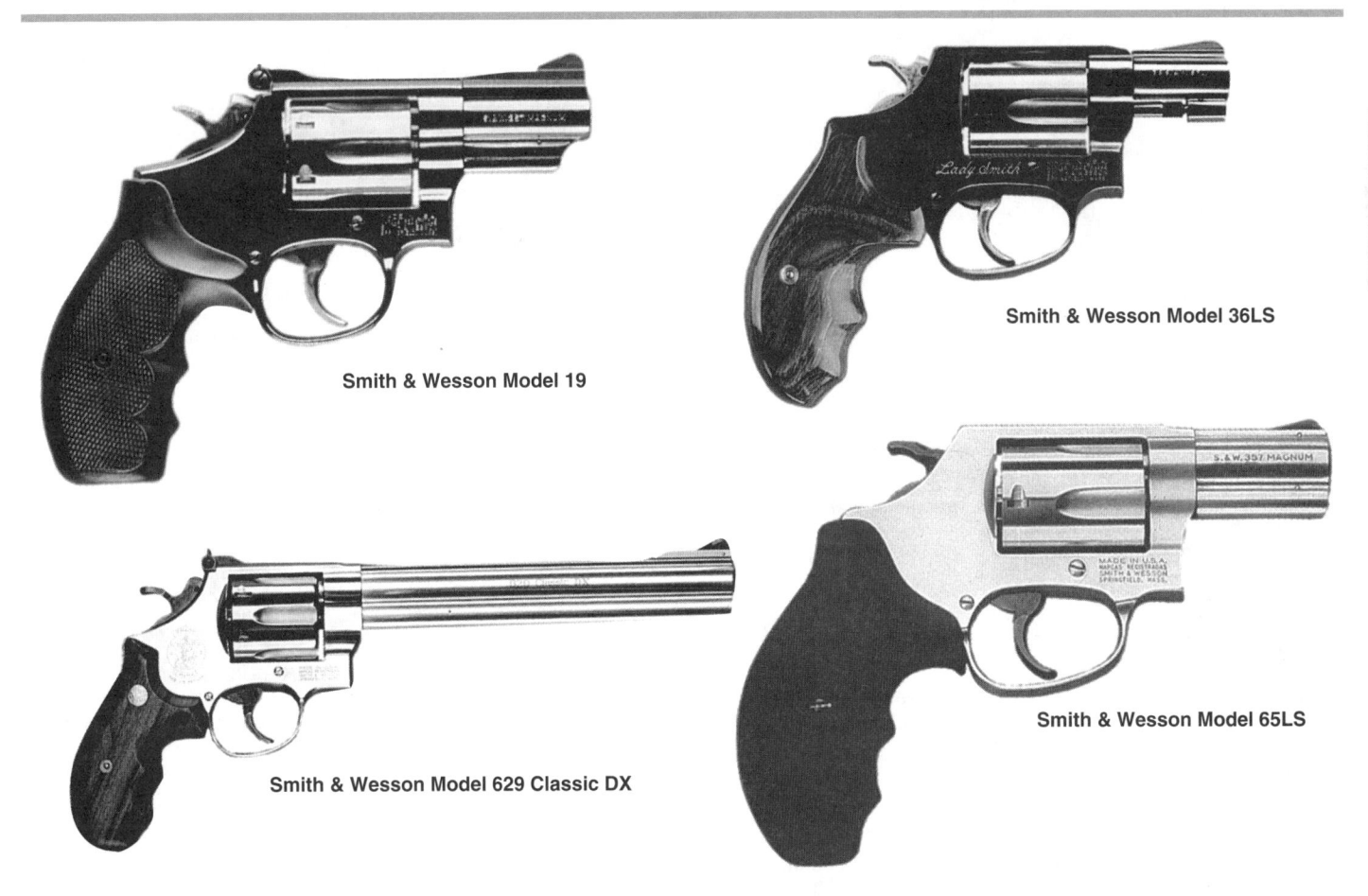

SMITH & WESSON MODEL 15 COMBAT MASTERPIECE
Caliber: 38 Spec., 6-shot. **Barrel:** 4". **Weight:** 32 oz. **Length:** 9-5/16" (4" bbl.). **Stocks:** Uncle Mike's Combat soft rubber. **Sights:** Serrated ramp front, micro-click rear adjustable for windage and elevation.
Price: Blued $450.00

SMITH & WESSON MODEL 19 COMBAT MAGNUM
Caliber: 357 Mag. and 38 Spec., 6-shot. **Barrel:** 4". **Weight:** 36 oz. **Length:** 9-9/16" (4" bbl.). **Stocks:** Uncle Mike's Combat soft rubber; wood optional. **Sights:** Red ramp front, micro-click rear adjustable for windage and elevation.
Price: 4" $457.00

SMITH & WESSON MODEL 629 REVOLVERS
Caliber: 44 Magnum, 6-shot. **Barrel:** 5", 6", 8-3/8". **Weight:** 47 oz. (6" bbl.). **Length:** 11-3/8" overall (6" bbl.). **Stocks:** Soft rubber; wood optional. **Sights:** 1/8" red ramp front, micro-click rear, adjustable for windage and elevation.
Price: Model 629 (stainless steel), 5" $625.00
Price: Model 629, 6" $631.00
Price: Model 629, 8-3/8" barrel......................... $646.00

Smith & Wesson Model 629 Classic Revolver
Similar to the standard Model 629 except has full-lug 5", 6-1/2" or 8-3/8" barrel; chamfered front of cylinder; interchangeable red ramp front sight with adjustable white outline rear; Hogue grips with S&W monogram; the frame is drilled and tapped for scope mounting. Factory accurizing and endurance packages. Overall length with 5" barrel is 10-1/2"; weighs 51 oz. Introduced 1990.
Price: Model 629 Classic (stainless), 5", 6-1/2" $670.00
Price: As above, 8-3/8"................................. $691.00

Smith & Wesson Model 629 Classic DX Revolver
Similar to the Model 629 Classic except offered only with 6-1/2" or 8-3/8" full-lug barrel; comes with five front **sights:** red ramp; black Patridge; black Patridge with gold bead; black ramp; and black Patridge with white dot. Comes with Hogue combat-style and wood round butt grip. Introduced 1991.
Price: Model 629 Classic DX, 6-1/2" $860.00
Price: As above, 8-3/8"................................. $888.00

SMITH & WESSON MODEL 36, 37 CHIEF'S SPECIAL & AIRWEIGHT
Caliber: 38 Spec.+P, 5-shot. **Barrel:** 1-7/8". **Weight:** 19-1/2 oz. (2" bbl.); 13-1/2 oz. (Airweight). **Length:** 6-1/2" (round butt). **Stocks:** Round butt soft rubber. **Sights:** Fixed, serrated ramp front, square notch rear.
Price: Blue, standard Model 36 .... $406.00
Price: Blue, Airweight Model 37 .... $483.00

Smith & Wesson Model 36LS, 60LS LadySmith
Similar to the standard Model 36. Available with 1-7/8" barrel, 38 Special. Comes with smooth, contoured rosewood grips with the S&W monogram. Has a speedloader cutout. Comes in a fitted carry/storage case. Introduced 1989.
Price: Model 36LS $478.00
Price: Model 60LS, as above except in stainless, 357 Magnum . $539.00

SMITH & WESSON MODEL 60 357 MAGNUM
Caliber: 357 Magnum, 5-shot. **Barrel:** 2-1/8" or 3". **Weight:** 24 oz. **Length:** 7-1/2 overall (3" barrel). **Stocks:** Uncle Mike's Combat. **Sights:** Fixed, serrated ramp front, square notch rear. **Features:** Stainless steel construction. Made in U.S. by Smith & Wesson.
Price: 2-1/8" barrel $505.00
Price: 3" barrel $536.00

SMITH & WESSON MODEL 65
Caliber: 357 Mag. and 38 Spec., 6-shot. **Barrel:** 3", 4". **Weight:** 34 oz. **Length:** 9-5/16" overall (4" bbl.). **Stocks:** Uncle Mike's Combat. **Sights:** 1/8" serrated ramp front, fixed square notch rear. **Features:** Heavy barrel. Stainless steel construction.
Price: $501.00

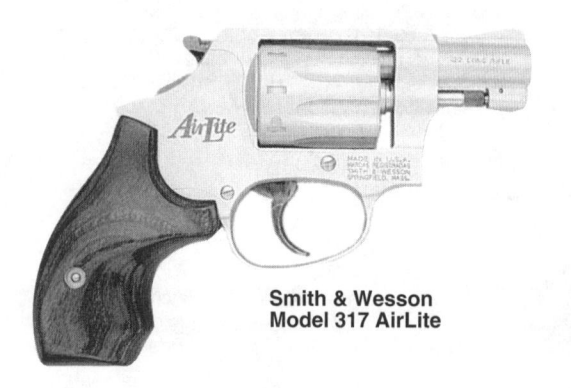

Handguns — Double Action Revolvers, Service & Sport

Smith & Wesson Model 317 AirLite

Smith & Wesson Model 625

Smith & Wesson Model 586, 686 Distinguished Combat

SMITH & WESSON
MODEL 317 AIRLITE, 317 LADYSMITH REVOLVERS
Caliber: 22 LR, 8-shot. **Barrel:** 1-7/8" 3". **Weight:** 9.9 oz. **Length:** 6-3/16" overall. **Stocks:** Dymondwood Boot or Uncle Mike's Boot. **Sights:** Serrated ramp front, fixed notch rear. **Features:** Aluminum alloy, carbon and stainless steels, and titanium construction. Short spur hammer, smooth combat trigger. Clear Cote finish. Introduced 1997. Made in U.S. by Smith & Wesson.
Price: With Uncle Mike's Boot grip $508.00
Price: With DymondWood Boot grip, 3" barrel $537.00
Price: Model 317 LadySmith (DymondWood only, comes with display case) $568.00

Smith & Wesson Model 637 Airweight Revolver
Similar to the Model 37 Airweight except has alloy frame, stainless steel barrel, cylinder and yoke; rated for 38 Spec. +P; Uncle Mike's Boot Grip. Weighs 15 oz. Introduced 1996. Made in U.S. by Smith & Wesson.
Price: $459.00

SMITH & WESSON MODEL 64 STAINLESS M&P
Caliber: 38 Spec., 6-shot. **Barrel:** 2", 3", 4". **Weight:** 34 oz. **Length:** 9-5/16" overall. **Stocks:** Soft rubber. **Sights:** Fixed, 1/8" serrated ramp front, square notch rear. **Features:** Satin finished stainless steel, square butt.
Price: 2" $487.00
Price: 3", 4" $496.00

SMITH & WESSON MODEL 65LS LADYSMITH
Caliber: 357 Magnum, 6-shot. **Barrel:** 3". **Weight:** 31 oz. **Length:** 7.94" overall. **Stocks:** Rosewood, round butt. **Sights:** Serrated ramp front, fixed notch rear. **Features:** Stainless steel with frosted finish. Smooth combat trigger, service hammer, shrouded ejector rod. Comes with case. Introduced 1992.
Price: $539.00

SMITH & WESSON MODEL 66 STAINLESS COMBAT MAGNUM
Caliber: 357 Mag. and 38 Spec., 6-shot. **Barrel:** 2-1/2", 4", 6". **Weight:** 36 oz. (4" barrel). **Length:** 9-9/16" overall. **Stocks:** Soft rubber. **Sights:** Red ramp front, micro-click rear adjustable for windage and elevation. **Features:** Satin finish stainless steel.

Price: 2-1/2" $545.00
Price: 4", 6" $551.00

SMITH & WESSON MODEL 67 COMBAT MASTERPIECE
Caliber: 38 Special, 6-shot. **Barrel:** 4". **Weight:** 32 oz. **Length:** 9-5/16" overall. **Stocks:** Soft rubber. **Sights:** Red ramp front, micro-click rear adjustable for windage and elevation. **Features:** Stainless steel with satin finish. Smooth combat trigger, semi-target hammer. Introduced 1994.
Price: $546.00

SMITH & WESSON MODEL 242 AIRLITE Ti REVOLVER
Caliber: 38 Special, 7-shot. **Barrel:** 2-1/2". **Weight:** 18.9 oz. **Length:** 7-3/8" overall. **Stocks:** Uncle Mike's Boot grip. **Sights:** Serrated ramp front, fixed notch rear. **Features:** Alloy frame, yoke and barrel shroud; titanium cylinder; stainless barrel insert. Medium L-frame size. Introduced 1999. Made in U.S. by Smith & Wesson.
Price: $658.00

SMITH & WESSON MODEL 296 AIRLITE Ti REVOLVER
Caliber: 44 Spec. **Barrel:** 2-1/2". **Weight:** 18.9 oz. **Length:** 7-3/8" overall. **Stocks:** Uncle Mike's Boot grip. **Sights:** Serrated ramp front, fixed notch rear. **Features:** Alloy frame, yoke and barrel shroud; titanium cylinder; stainless steel barrel insert. Medium L-frame size. Introduced 1999. Made in U.S. by Smith & Wesson.
Price: $718.00

SMITH & WESSON MODEL 586, 686 DISTINGUISHED COMBAT MAGNUMS
Caliber: 357 Magnum. **Barrel:** 4", 6" (M 586); 2-1/2", 4", 6", 8-3/8" (M 686). **Weight:** 46 oz. (6"), 41 oz. (4"). **Stocks:** Soft rubber. **Sights:** Red ramp front, S&W micrometer click rear. Drilled and tapped for scope mount. **Features:** Uses L-frame, but takes all K-frame grips. Full-length ejector rod shroud. Smooth combat-type trigger, semi-target type hammer. Also available in stainless as Model 686. Introduced 1981.
Price: Model 586, blue, 4", from $494.00
Price: Model 586, blue, 6" $499.00
Price: Model 686, 6", ported barrel $564.00
Price: Model 686, 8-3/8" $550.00
Price: Model 686, 2-1/2" $514.00

Smith & Wesson Model 686 Magnum PLUS Revolver
Similar to the Model 686 except has 7-shot cylinder, 2-1/2", 4" or 6" barrel. Weighs 34-1/2 oz., overall length 7-1/2" (2-1/2" barrel). Hogue rubber grips. Introduced 1996. Made in U.S. by Smith & Wesson.
Price: 2-1/2" barrel $534.00
Price: 4" barrel $542.00
Price: 6" barrel $550.00

SMITH & WESSON MODEL 625 REVOLVER
Caliber: 45 ACP, 6-shot. **Barrel:** 5". **Weight:** 46 oz. **Length:** 11.375" overall. **Stocks:** Soft rubber; wood optional. **Sights:** Patridge front on ramp, S&W micrometer click rear adjustable for windage and elevation. **Features:** Stainless steel construction with .400" semi-target hammer, .312" smooth combat trigger; full lug barrel. Introduced 1989.
Price: $636.00

HANDGUNS — DOUBLE ACTION REVOLVERS, SERVICE & SPORT

Smith & Wesson Model 442

Smith & Wesson Model 649

SMITH & WESSON MODEL 640 CENTENNIAL
Caliber: 357 Mag., 5-shot. **Barrel:** 2-1/8". **Weight:** 25 oz. **Length:** 6-3/4" overall. **Stocks:** Uncle Mike's Boot Grip. **Sights:** Serrated ramp front, fixed notch rear. **Features:** Stainless steel. Fully concealed hammer, snag-proof smooth edges. Introduced 1995 in 357 Magnum.
Price: $502.00

SMITH & WESSON MODEL 617 FULL LUG REVOLVER
Caliber: 22 LR, 6- or 10-shot. **Barrel:** 4", 6", 8-3/8". **Weight:** 42 oz. (4" barrel). **Length:** NA. **Stocks:** Soft rubber. **Sights:** Patridge front, adjustable rear. Drilled and tapped for scope mount. **Features:** Stainless steel with satin finish; 4" has .312" smooth trigger, .375" semi-target hammer; 6" has either .312" combat or .400" serrated trigger, .375" semi-target or .500" target hammer; 8-3/8" with .400" serrated trigger, .500" target hammer. Introduced 1990.
Price: 4" $534.00
Price: 6", target hammer, target trigger $524.00
Price: 6", 10-shot $566.00
Price: 8-3/8", 10 shot $578.00

SMITH & WESSON MODEL 610 CLASSIC HUNTER REVOLVER
Caliber: 10mm, 6-shot cylinder. **Barrel:** 6-1/2" full lug. **Weight:** 52 oz. **Length:** 12" overall. **Stocks:** Hogue rubber combat. **Sights:** Interchangeable blade front, micro-click rear adjustable for windage and elevation. **Features:** Stainless steel construction; target hammer, target trigger; unfluted cylinder; drilled and tapped for scope mounting. Introduced 1998.
Price: $684.00

SMITH & WESSON MODEL 331, 332 AIRLITE Ti REVOLVERS
Caliber: 32 H&R Mag., 6-shot. **Barrel:** 1-7/8". **Weight:** 11.2 oz. (with wood grip). **Length:** 6-15/16" overall. **Stocks:** Uncle Mike's Boot or Dymondwood Boot. **Sights:** Black serrated ramp front, fixed notch rear. **Features:** Aluminum alloy frame, barrel shroud and yoke; titanium cylinder; stainless steel barrel liner. Matte finish. Introduced 1999. Made in U.S. by Smith & Wesson.
Price: Model 331 Chiefs $682.00
Price: Model 332 .... $699.00

SMITH & WESSON MODEL 337 CHIEFS SPECIAL AIRLITE Ti
Caliber: 38 Spec., 5-shot. **Barrel:** 1-7/8". **Weight:** 11.2 oz. (Dymondwood grips). **Length:** 6-5/16" overall. **Stocks:** Uncle Mike's Boot or Dymondwood Boot. **Sights:** Black serrated front, fixed notch rear. **Features:** Aluminum alloy frame, barrel shroud and yoke; titanium cylinder; stainless steel barrel liner. Matte finish. Introduced 1999. Made in U.S. by Smith & Wesson.
Price: $682.00

SMITH & WESSON MODEL 342 CENTENNIAL AIRLITE Ti
Caliber: 38 Spec., 5-shot. **Barrel:** 1-7/8". **Weight:** 11.3 oz. (Dymondwood stocks). **Length:** 6-15/16" overall. **Stocks:** Uncle Mike's Boot or Dymondwood Boot. **Sights:** Black serrated ramp front, fixed notch rear. **Features:** Aluminum alloy frame, barrel shroud and yoke; titanium cylinder; stainless steel barrel liner. Shrouded hammer. Matte finish. Introduced 1999. Made in U.S. by Smith & Wesson.
Price: $699.00

Smith & Wesson Model 442 Centennial Airweight
Similar to the Model 640 Centennial except has alloy frame giving weight of 15.8 oz. Chambered for 38 Special, 1-7/8" carbon steel barrel; carbon steel cylinder; concealed hammer; Uncle Mike's Boot grip. Fixed square notch rear sight, serrated ramp front. Introduced 1993.
Price: Blue $459.00

SMITH & WESSON MODEL 638 AIRWEIGHT BODYGUARD
Caliber: 38 Spec., 5-shot. **Barrel:** 1-7/8". **Weight:** 15 oz. **Length:** 6-15/16" overall. **Stocks:** Uncle Mike's Boot grip. **Sights:** Serrated ramp front, fixed notch rear. **Features:** Alloy frame, stainless cylinder and barrel; shrouded hammer. Introduced 1997. Made in U.S. by Smith & Wesson.
Price: With Uncle Mike's Boot grip $492.00

Smith & Wesson Model 642 Airweight Revolver
Similar to the Model 442 Centennial Airweight except has stainless steel barrel, cylinder and yoke with matte finish; Uncle Mike's Boot Grip; weighs 15.8 oz. Introduced 1996. Made in U.S. by Smith & Wesson.
Price: $474.00

Smith & Wesson Model 642LS LadySmith Revolver
Same as the Model 642 except has smooth combat wood grips, and comes with case; aluminum alloy frame, stainless cylinder, barrel and yoke; frosted matte finish. Weighs 15.8 oz. Introduced 1996. Made in U.S. by Smith & Wesson.
Price: $505.00

SMITH & WESSON MODEL 649 BODYGUARD REVOLVER
Caliber: 357 Mag., 5-shot. **Barrel:** 2-1/8". **Weight:** 20 oz. **Length:** 6-5/16" overall. **Stocks:** Uncle Mike's Combat. **Sights:** Black pinned ramp front, fixed notch rear. **Features:** Stainless steel construction; shrouded hammer; smooth combat trigger. Made in U.S. by Smith & Wesson.
Price: $502.00

SMITH & WESSON MODEL 657 REVOLVER
Caliber: 41 Mag., 6-shot. **Barrel:** 6". **Weight:** 48 oz. **Length:** 11-3/8" overall. **Stocks:** Soft rubber. **Sights:** Pinned 1/8" red ramp front, micro-click rear adjustable for windage and elevation. **Features:** Stainless steel construction.
Price: $564.00

SMITH & WESSON MODEL 696 REVOLVER
Caliber: 44 Spec., 5-shot. **Barrel:** 3". **Weight:** 35.5 oz. **Length:** 8-1/4" overall. **Stocks:** Uncle Mike's Combat. **Sights:** Red ramp front, click adjustable white outline rear. **Features:** Stainless steel construction; round butt frame; satin finish. Introduced 1997. Made in U.S. by Smith & Wesson.
Price: $525.00

TAURUS MODEL 65 REVOLVER
Caliber: 357 Mag., 6-shot. **Barrel:** 4". **Weight:** 38 oz. **Length:** 10-1/2" overall. **Stocks:** Soft rubber. **Sights:** Serrated front, notch rear. **Features:** Solid rib barrel; +P rated. Integral key-lock action. Imported by Taurus International.
Price: Blue $345.00
Price: Stainless $395.00

34TH EDITION, 2002 • 173

Handguns — Double Action Revolvers, Service & Sport

Smith & Wesson Model 696

Taurus Model 85

Taurus Model 82

Taurus Model 85Ti/731Ti

Taurus Model 85CH

Taurus Model 66 Revolver
Same to the Model 65 except with 4" or 6" barrel, 7-shot cylinder, adjustable rear sight. Integral key-lock action. Imported by Taurus International.
Price: Blue $395.00
Price: Stainless. $435.00

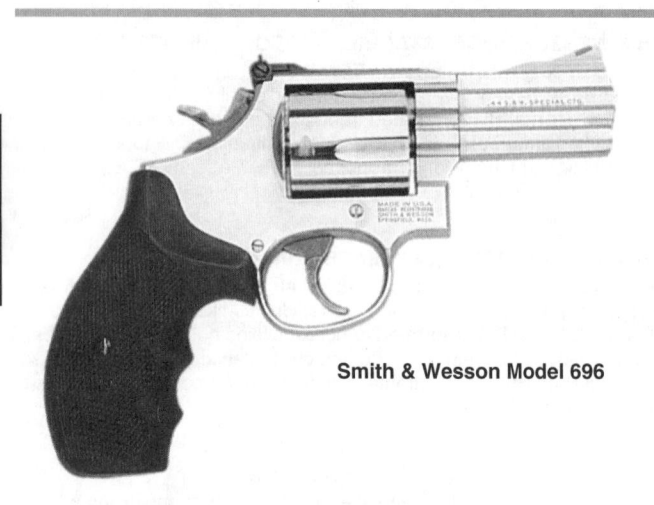

Taurus Model 66 Silhouette Revolver
Similar to the Model 66 except has a 12" barrel with scope mount, 7-shot cylinder, adjustable rear sight. Integral key-lock action, blue or matte stainless steel finish and rubber grips. Introduced 2001. Imported by Taurus International.
Price: . . . . $414.00 to $461.00

TAURUS MODEL 82 HEAVY BARREL REVOLVER
Caliber: 38 Spec., 6-shot. **Barrel:** 4", heavy. **Weight:** 34 oz. (4" bbl.). **Length:** 9-1/4" overall (4" bbl.). **Stocks:** Soft black rubber. **Sights:** Serrated ramp front, square notch rear. **Features:** Imported by Taurus International.
Price: Blue $325.00
Price: Polished, stainless $375.00

TAURUS MODEL 85 REVOLVER
Caliber: 38 Spec., 5-shot. **Barrel:** 2", 3". **Weight:** 21 oz. **Stocks:** Rubber, rosewood or mother-of-pearl. **Sights:** Ramp front, square notch rear. **Features:** Blue, matte, polished stainless steel, blue with gold accents, pearl and blue with gold accents; heavy barrel; rated for +P ammo. Introduced 1980. Imported by Taurus International.
Price: Blue, 2", 3" $345.00
Price: Stainless steel $395.00
Price: Blue, 2", ported barrel $360.00
Price: Stainless, 2", ported barrel. $405.00
Price: Blue, Ultra-Lite (17 oz.), 2" $375.00
Price: Stainless, Ultra-Lite (17 oz.), 2", ported barrel $425.00
Price: Blue with gold trim, ported, rosewood grips $380.00

Taurus Model 85UL/Ti Revolver
Similar to the Model 85 except has titanium cylinder, aluminum alloy frame, and ported aluminum barrel with stainless steel sleeve. Weight is 13.5 oz. International.
Price: $515.00

Taurus Model 85Ti Revolver
Similar to the 2" Model 85 except has titanium frame, cylinder and ported barrel with stainless steel liner; yoke detent and extended ejector rod. Weight is 15.4 oz. Comes with soft, ridged Ribber grips. Available in Bright and Matte Spectrum blue, Matte Spectrum gold, and Shadow Gray colors. Introduced 1999. Imported by Taurus International.
Price: Model 85Ti $530.00

Taurus Model 85CH Revolver
Same as the Model 85 except has 2" barrel only and concealed hammer. Double aciton only. Soft rubber boot grip. Introduced 1991. Imported by Taurus International.
Price: Blue $345.00
Price: Stainless. $395.00
Price: Blue, ported barrel $360.00
Price: Stainless, ported barrel $405.00

HANDGUNS — DOUBLE ACTION REVOLVERS, SERVICE & SPORT

Taurus Model 94UL

Taurus Model 44

Taurus Model 22H Raging Hornet

Taurus Model 415

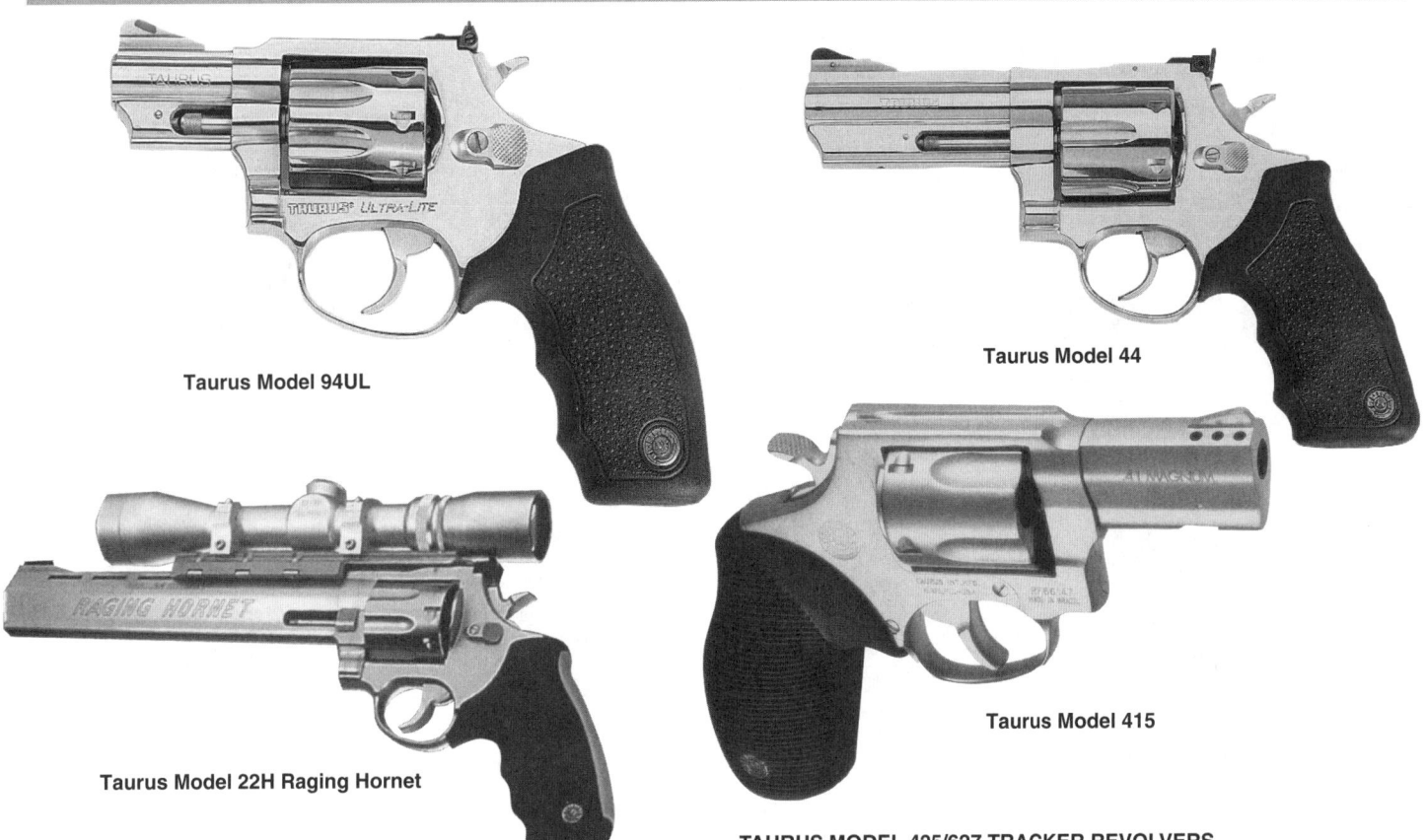

TAURUS MODEL 94 REVOLVER
Caliber: 22 LR, 9-shot cylinder. **Barrel:** 2", 4", 5". **Weight:** 25 oz. **Stocks:** Soft black rubber. **Sights:** Serrated ramp front, click-adjustable rear for windage and elevation. **Features:** Floating firing pin, color case-hardened hammer and trigger. Introduced 1989. Imported by Taurus International.
Price: Blue $325.00
Price: Stainless... $375.00
Price: Model 94 UL, blue, 2", fixed sight, weighs 14 oz. $365.00
Price: As above, stainless $410.00

TAURUS MODEL 22H RAGING HORNET REVOLVER
Caliber: 22 Hornet, 8-shot cylinder. **Barrel:** 10". **Weight:** 50 oz. **Length:** 6.5" overall. **Stocks:** Soft black rubber. **Sights:** Patridge front, micrometer click adjustable rear. **Features:** Ventilated rib; 1:10: twist rifling; comes with scope base; stainless steel construction with matte finish. Introduced 1999. Imported by Taurus International.
Price: $898.00

TAURUS MODEL 44 REVOLVER
Caliber: 44 Mag., 6-shot. **Barrel:** 4", 6-1/2", 8-3/8". **Weight:** 44-3/4 oz. (4" barrel). **Length:** NA. **Stocks:** Soft black rubber. **Sights:** Serrated ramp front, micro-click rear adjustable for windage and elevation. **Features:** Heavy solid rib on 4", vent rib on 6-1/2", 8-3/8". Compensated barrel. Blued model has color case-hardened hammer and trigger, integral key-lock action. Introduced 1994. Imported by Taurus International.
Price: Blue, 4"... $500.00
Price: Blue, 6-1/2", 8-3/8".................................. $525.00
Price: Stainless, 4"....................................... $565.00
Price: Stainless, 6-1/2", 8-3/8"............................ $573.00

TAURUS MODEL 415 REVOLVER
Caliber: 41 Mag., 5-shot. **Barrel:** 2-1/2". **Weight:** 30 oz. **Length:** 7-1/8" overall. **Stocks:** Soft, ridged Ribber. **Sights:** Serrated front, notch rear. **Features:** Stainless steel construction; matte finish; ported barrel. Introduced 1999. Imported by Taurus International.
Price: $475.00

TAURUS MODEL 425/627 TRACKER REVOLVERS
Caliber: 357 Mag., 7-shot; 41 Mag., 5-shot. **Barrel:** 4" and 6". **Weight:** 24.3 oz. (titanium) to 40.0 oz. (6"). **Length:** 8-3/4" and 10-3/4" overall. **Grips:** Soft, ridged Ribber. **Sights:** Blade front, adjustable rear. **Features:** Stainless steel, Shadow Gray or Total Titanium; vent rib (steel models only); integral key-lock action. Imported by Taurus International.
Price: $500.00
Price: (Total Titanium)....................................... $690.00

TAURUS MODEL 445, 445CH REVOLVERS
Caliber: 44 Special, 5-shot. **Barrel:** 2". **Weight:** 28.25 oz. **Length:** 6-3/4" overall. **Stocks:** Soft black rubber. **Sights:** Serrated ramp front, notch rear. **Features:** Blue or stainless steel. Standard or concealed hammer. Introduced 1997. Imported by Taurus International.
Price: Blue $345.00
Price: Blue, ported $360.00
Price: Stainless.. $395.00
Price: Stainless, ported $400.00
Price: M445CH, concealed hammer, blue, DAO $345.00
Price: M445CH, blue, ported $360.00
Price: M445CH, stainless................................. $395.00
Price: M445CH, stainless, ported......................... $400.00
Price: M445CH, Ultra-Lite, stainless, ported $500.00

TAURUS MODEL 605 REVOLVER
Caliber: 357 Mag., 5-shot. **Barrel:** 2-1/4", 3". **Weight:** 24.5 oz. **Length:** NA. **Stocks:** Soft black rubber. **Sights:** Serrated ramp front, fixed notch rear. **Features:** Heavy, solid rib barrel; floating firing pin. Blue or stainless. Introduced 1995. Imported by Taurus International.
Price: Blue $345.00
Price: Stainless.. $395.00
Price: Model 605CH (concealed hammer) 2-1/4", blue, DAO ... $345.00
Price: Model 605CH, stainless, 2-1/4" $395.00
Price: Blue, 2-1/4", ported barrel $360.00
Price: Stainless, 2-1/4", ported barrel.................... $405.00
Price: Blue, 2-1/4", ported barrel, concealed hammer, DAO $360.00
Price: Stainless, 2-1/4", ported barrel, concealed hammer, DAO. $405.00

Handguns — Double Action Revolvers, Service & Sport

Taurus Model 608

Taurus Model 450

Taurus Model 454 Raging Bull

Taurus Model 817

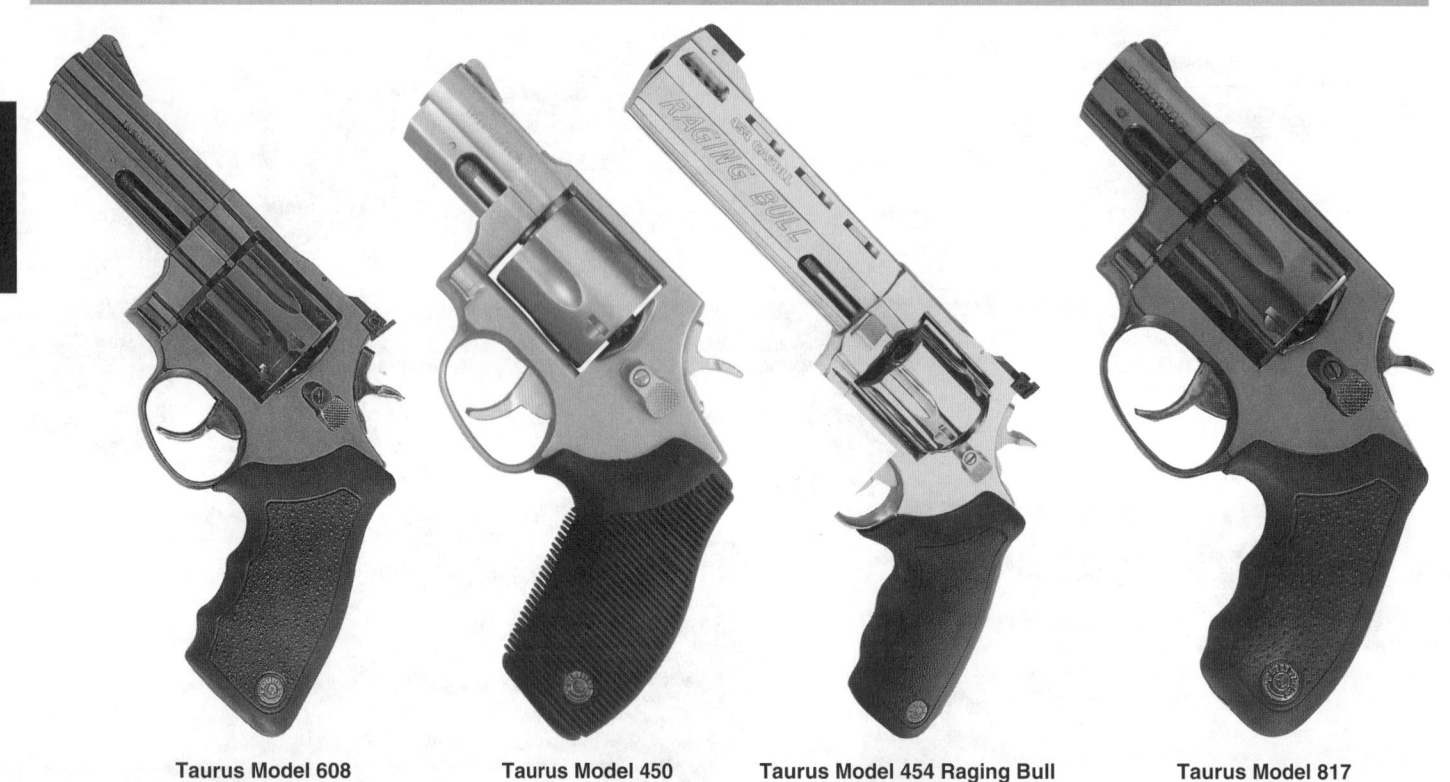

TAURUS MODEL 608 REVOLVER
Caliber: 357 Mag., 8-shot. **Barrel:** 4", 6-1/2", 8-3/8". **Weight:** 44 oz. **Length:** 9-3/8" overall. **Grips:** Soft black rubber. **Sights:** Serrated ramp front, fully adjustable rear. **Features:** Built-in compensator, integral key-lock action. Available in blue or stainless. Introduced 1995. Imported by Taurus International.
Price: Blue, 4", solid rib $445.00
Price: Blue, 6-1/2", 8-3/8", vent rib $465.00
Price: Stainless, 4", solid rib $510.00
Price: Stainless, 6-1/2", 8-3/8", vent rib $525.00

TAURUS MODEL 650CIA REVOLVER
NEW! **Caliber:** 357 Magnum, 5-shot. **Barrel:** 2". **Weight:** NA. **Length:** NA. **Grips:** Rubber. **Sights:** Ramp front, square notch rear. **Features:** Double-action only; blue or matte stainless steel; rated for +P ammo; integral key-lock action. Introduced 2001. From Taurus International.
Price: .... $375.00 to $422.00

TAURUS MODEL 450 REVOLVER
Caliber: 45 Colt, 5-shot cylinder. **Barrel:** 2". **Weight:** 28 oz. **Length:** 6-5/8" overall. **Stocks:** Soft, ridged rubber. **Sights:** Serrated front, notch rear. **Features:** Stainless steel construction; ported barrel. Introduced 1999. Imported by Taurus International.
Price: $470.00
Price: Ultra-Lite (alloy frame) $525.00

TAURUS MODEL 444/454/480 RAGING BULL REVOLVERS
Caliber: 454 Casull, 5-shot (also fires 45 Colt). **Barrel:** 5", 6-1/2", 8-3/8". **Weight:** 53 oz. (6-1/2" barrel). **Length:** 12" overall (6-1/2" barrel). **Stocks:** Soft black rubber. **Sights:** Patridge front, micrometer click adjustable rear. **Features:** Ventilated rib; integral compensating system. Introduced 1997. Imported by Taurus International.
Price: 6-1/2", 8-3/8", blue $785.00
Price: 6-1/2", polished, stainless $855.00
Price: 5", 6-1/2", 8-3/8", matte stainless $855.00
Price: Model 444 (44 Mag.), blue, 6-1/2", 8-3/8", 6-shot $575.00
Price: Model 444, matte, stainless, 6-1/2", 8-3/8" $630.00
New! Price: Model 480 (480 Ruger), 5-shot $855.00

TAURUS MODEL 617 REVOLVER
Caliber: 357 Magnum, 7-shot. **Barrel:** 2". **Weight:** 29 oz. **Length:** 6-3/4" overall. **Stocks:** Soft black rubber. **Sights:** Serrated ramp front, notch rear. **Features:** Heavy, solid barrel rib, ejector shroud. Available with porting, concealed hammer. Introduced 1998. Imported by Taurus International.
Price: Blue, regular or concealed hammer $375.00
Price: Stainless, regular or concealed hammer $420.00
Price: Blue, ported $395.00
Price: Stainless, ported $440.00
Price: Blue, concealed hammer, ported $395.00
Price: Stainless, concealed hammer, ported $440.00

Taurus Model 415Ti, 445Ti, 450Ti, 617Ti Revolvers
Similar to the Model 617 except has titanium frame, cylinder, and ported barrel with stainless steel liner; yoke detent and extended ejector rod; +P rated; ridged Ribber grips. Available in Bright and Matte Spectrum Blue, Matte Spectrum Gold, and Shadow Gray. Introduced 1999. Imported by Taurus International.
Price: Model 617Ti, (357 Mag., 7-shot, 19.9 oz.) $600.00
Price: Model 415Ti (41 Mag., 5-shot, 20.9 oz.) $600.00
Price: Model 450Ti (45 Colt, 5-shot, 19.2 oz.) $600.00
Price: Model 445Ti (44 Spec., 5-shot, 19.8 oz.) $600.00

Taurus Model 617ULT Revolver
Similar to the Model 617 except has aluminum alloy and titanium components, matte stainless finish, integral key-lock action. Rated for +P ammo. Available ported or non-ported. Introduced 2001. Imported by Taurus International.
Price: (5-shot cylinder) .... $530.00 to $545.00

TAURUS MODEL 817 ULTRA-LITE REVOLVER
Caliber: 38 Spec., 7-shot. **Barrel:** 2". **Weight:** 21 oz. **Length:** 6-1/2" overall. **Grips:** Soft rubber. **Sights:** Serrated front, notch rear. **Features:** Compact alloy frame. Introduced 1999. Imported by Taurus International.
Price: Blue $375.00
Price: Blue, ported $395.00
Price: Matte, stainless $420.00
Price: Matte, stainless, ported $440.00

HANDGUNS — DOUBLE ACTION REVOLVERS, SERVICE & SPORT

Taurus Model 941

Dan Wesson Firearms Model 40, compensated

Dan Wesson Firearms Model 445 Supermag

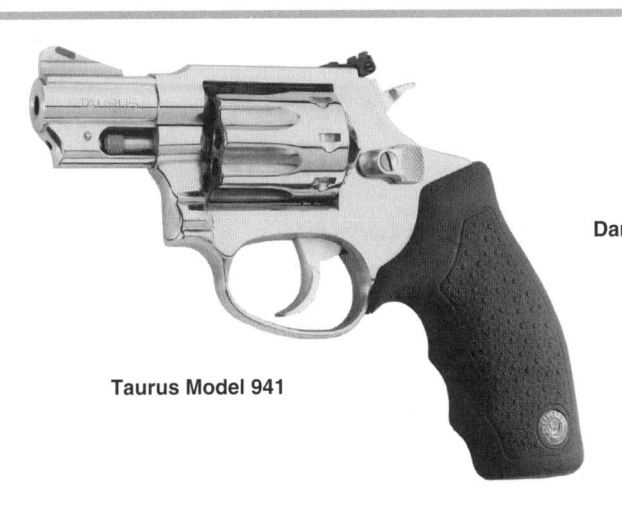

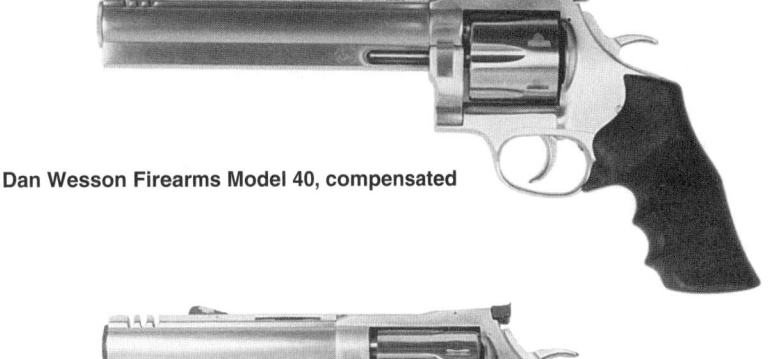

TAURUS MODEL 850CIA REVOLVER
Caliber: 38 Special, 5-shot. **Barrel:** 2". **Weight:** NA. **Length:** NA. **Grips:** Rubber. **Sights:** Ramp front, square notch rear. **Features:** Double-action only; blue or matte stainless steel; rated for +P ammo; integral key-lock action. Introduced 2001. From Taurus International.
Price: .... $375.00 to $422.00
Price: Total Titanium model $563.00

TAURUS MODEL 941 REVOLVER
Caliber: 22 WMR, 8-shot. **Barrel:** 2", 4", 5". **Weight:** 27.5 oz. (4" barrel). **Length:** NA. **Grips:** Soft black rubber. **Sights:** Serrated ramp front, rear adjustable for windage and elevation. **Features:** Solid rib heavy barrel with full-length ejector rod shroud. Blue or stainless steel. Introduced 1992. Imported by Taurus International.
Price: Blue $345.00
Price: Stainless $395.00
Price: Model 941 Ultra Lite, blue, 2", fixed sight, weighs 8.5 oz. . $375.00
Price: As above, stainless $419.00

TAURUS MODEL 970/971 TRACKER REVOLVERS
Caliber: 22 LR (Model 970), 22 WMR (Model 971); 7-shot. **Barrel:** 6". **Weight:** NA. **Length:** NA. **Grips:** Soft, black rubber. **Sights:** Blade front, adjustable rear. **Features:** Heavy barrel with ventilated rib; matte stainless finish. Introduced 2001. From Taurus International.
Price: $855.00

TAURUS MODEL 980/981 SILHOUETTE REVOLVERS
Caliber: 22 LR (Model 980), 22 WMR (Model 981); 7-shot. **Barrel:** 12". **Weight:** NA. **Length:** NA. **Grips:** Soft, black rubber. **Sights:** Blade front, adjustable rear. **Features:** Heavy barrel with ventilated rib and scope mount, matte stainless finish. Introduced 2001. From Taurus International.
Price: (Model 980) $397.00
Price: (Model 981) $414.00

DAN WESSON FIREARMS MODEL 722 SILHOUETTE REVOLVER
Caliber: 22 LR, 6-shot. **Barrel:** 10", vent heavy. **Weight:** 53 oz. **Stocks:** Combat style. **Sights:** Patridge-style front, .080" narrow notch rear. **Features:** Single action only. Satin brushed stainless finish. Reintroduced 1997. Made in U.S. by Dan Wesson Firearms.
Price: 722 VH10 (vent heavy 10" bbl.) $888.00
Price: 722 VH10 SRS1 (Super Ram Silhouette, Bo-Mar sights, front hood, trigger job) $1,164.00

DAN WESSON FIREARMS MODEL 3220/73220 TARGET REVOLVER
Caliber: 32-20, 6-shot. **Barrel:** 2.5", 4", 6", 8", 10" standard vent, vent heavy. **Weight:** 47 oz. (6" VH). **Length:** 11.25" overall. **Stocks:** Hogue Gripper rubber (walnut, exotic hardwoods optional). **Sights:** Red ramp interchangeable front, fully adjustable rear. **Features:** Bright blue (3220) or stainless (73220). Reintroduced 1997. Made in U.S. by Dan Wesson Firearms.
Price: 3220 VH2.5 (blued, 2.5" vent heavy bbl.) $643.00
Price: 73220 VH10 (stainless 10" vent heavy bbl.) $873.00

DAN WESSON FIREARMS MODEL 40/740 REVOLVERS
Caliber: 357 Maximum, 6-shot. **Barrel:** 4", 6", 8", 10". **Weight:** 72 oz. (8" bbl.). **Length:** 14.3" overall (8" bbl.). **Stocks:** Hogue Gripper rubber (walnut or exotic hardwood optional). **Sights:** 1/8" serrated front, fully adjustable rear. **Features:** Blue or stainless steel. Made in U.S. by Dan Wesson Firearms.
Price: Blue, 4" $702.00
Price: Blue, 6" $749.00
Price: Blue, 8" $795.00
Price: Blue, 10" $858.00
Price: Stainless, 4" $834.00
Price: Stainless, 6" $892.00
Price: Stainless, 8" slotted $1,024.00
Price: Stainless, 10" $998.00
Price: 4", 6", 8" Compensated, blue .... $749.00 to $885.00
Price: As above, stainless .... $893.00 to $1,061.00

DAN WESSON FIREARMS MODEL 22/722 REVOLVERS
Caliber: 22 LR, 22 WMR, 6-shot. **Barrel:** 2-1/2", 4", 6", 8" or 10"; interchangeable. **Weight:** 36 oz. (2-1/2"), 44 oz. (6"). **Length:** 9-1/4" overall (4" barrel). **Stocks:** Hogue Gripper rubber (walnut, exotic woods optional). **Sights:** 1/8" serrated, interchangeable front, white outline rear adjustable for windage and elevation. **Features:** Built on the same frame as the Wesson 357; smooth, wide trigger with over-travel adjustment, wide spur hammer, with short double-action travel. Available in blue or stainless steel. Reintroduced 1997. Contact Dan Wesson Firearms for complete price list.
Price: 22 VH2.5/722 VH2.5 (blued or stainless 2-1/2" bbl.) $551.00
Price: 22VH10/722 VH10 (blued or stainless 10" bbl.) $750.00

Dan Wesson 722M Small Frame Revolver
Similar to Model 22/722 except chambered for 22 WMR. Blued or stainless finish, 2-1/2", 4", 6", 8" or 10" barrels.
Price: Blued or stainless finish .... $643.00 to $873.00

Dan Wesson Firearms Model 414/7414 and 445/7445 SuperMag Revolvers
Similar size and weight as the Model 40 revolvers. Chambered for the 414 SuperMag or 445 SuperMag cartridge. Barrel lengths of 4", 6", 8", 10". Contact maker for complete price list. Reintroduced 1997. Made in the U.S. by Dan Wesson Firearms.
Price: 4", vent heavy, blue or stainless $904.00
Price: 8", vent heavy, blue or stainless $1,026.00
Price: 10", vent heavy, blue or stainless $1,103.00
Price: Compensated models .... $965.00 to $1,149.00

34TH EDITION, 2002

HANDGUNS — DOUBLE ACTION REVOLVERS, SERVICE & SPORT

Dan Wesson Firearms Silhouette

Dan Wesson Firearms Super Ram Silhouette

DAN WESSON FIREARMS MODEL 15/715 and 32/732 REVOLVERS
Caliber: 32-20, 32 H&R Mag. (Model 32), 357 Mag. (Model 15). **Barrel:** 2-1/2", 4", 6", 8" (M32), 2-1/2", 4", 6", 8", 10" (M15); vent heavy. **Weight:** 36 oz. (2-1/2" barrel). **Length:** 9-1/4" overall (4" barrel). **Stocks:** Checkered, interchangeable. **Sights:** 1/8" serrated front, fully adjustable rear. **Features:** New Generation Series. Interchangeable barrels; wide, smooth trigger, wide hammer spur; short double-action travel. Available in blue or stainless. Reintroduced 1997. Made in U.S. by Dan Wesson Firearms. Contact maker for full list of models.
Price: Model 15/715, 2-1/2" (blue or stainless) $551.00
Price: Model 15/715, 8" (blue or stainless) $612.00
Price: Model 15/715, compensated . . . . $704.00 to $827.00
Price: Model 32/732, 4" (blue or stainless) $674.00
Price: Model 32/732, 8" (blue or stainless) $766.00

DAN WESSON FIREARMS MODEL 41/741, 44/744 and 45/745 REVOLVERS
Caliber: 41 Mag., 44 Mag., 45 Colt, 6-shot. **Barrel:** 4", 6", 8"; interchangeable; 4", 6", 8" Compensated. **Weight:** 48 oz. (4"). **Length:** 12" overall (6" bbl.) **Stocks:** Smooth. **Sights:** 1/8" serrated front, white outline rear adjustable for windage and elevation. **Features:** Available in blue or stainless steel. Smooth, wide trigger with adjustable over-travel; wide hammer spur. Available in Pistol Pac set also. Reintroduced 1997. Contact Dan Wesson Firearms for complete price list.
Price: 41 Mag., 4", vent heavy (blue or stainless) $643.00
Price: 44 Mag., 6", vent heavy (blue or stainless) $689.00
Price: 45 Colt, 8", vent heavy (blue or stainless) $766.00
Price: Compensated models (all calibers) . . . . $812.00 to $934.00

DAN WESSON FIREARMS MODEL 360/7360 REVOLVERS
Caliber: 357 Mag. **Barrel:** 4", 6", 8", 10"; vent heavy. **Weight:** 64 oz. (8" barrel). **Length:** NA. **Stocks:** Hogue rubber finger groove. **Sights:** Interchangeable ramp or Patridge front, fully adjustable rear. **Features:** New Generation Large Frame Series. Interchangeable barrels and grips; smooth trigger, wide hammer spur. Blue (360) or stainless (7360). Introduced 1999. Made in U.S. by Dan Wesson Firearms.
Price: 4" bbl., blue or stainless $735.00
Price: 10" bbl., blue or stainless $873.00
Price: Compensated models . . . . $858.00 to $980.00

DAN WESSON FIREARMS MODEL 460/7460 REVOLVERS
Caliber: 45 ACP, 45 Auto Rim, 45 Super, 45 Winchester Magnum and 460 Rowland. **Barrel:** 4", 6", 8", 10"; vent heavy. **Weight:** 49 oz. (4" barrel). **Length:** NA. **Stocks:** Hogue rubber finger groove; interchangeable. **Sights:** Interchangeable ramp or Patridge front, fully adjustable rear. **Features:** New Generation Large Frame Series. Shoots five cartridges (45 ACP, 45 Auto Rim, 45 Super, 45 Winchester Magnum and 460 Rowland; six half-moon clips for auto cartridges included). Interchangeable barrels and grips. Available with non-fluted cylinder and Slotted Lightweight barrel shroud. Introduced 1999. Made in U.S. by Dan Wesson Firearms.
Price: 4" bbl., blue or stainless $735.00
Price: 10" bbl., blue or stainless $888.00
Price: Compensated models . . . . $919.00 to $1,042.00

DAN WESSON FIREARMS STANDARD SILHOUETTE REVOLVERS
Caliber: 357 SuperMag/Maxi, 41 Mag., 414 SuperMag, 445 SuperMag. **Barrel:** 8", 10" **Weight:** 64 oz. (8" barrel). **Length:** 14.3" overall (8" barrel). **Stocks:** Hogue rubber finger groove; interchangeable. **Sights:** Patridge front, fully adjustable rear. **Features:** Interchangeable barrels and grips; fluted or non-fluted cylinder; satin brushed stainless finish. Introduced 1999. Made in U.S. by Dan Wesson Firearms.
Price: 357 SuperMag/Maxi, 8" $1,057.00
Price: 41 Mag., 10" $888.00
Price: 414 SuperMag., 8" $1,057.00
Price: 445 SuperMag., 8" $1,057.00

Dan Wesson Firearms Super Ram Silhouette Revolver
Similar to the Standard Silhouette except has 10 land and groove Laser Coat barrel, Bo-Mar target sights with hooded front, and special laser engraving. Fluted or non-fluted cylinder. Introduced 1999. Made in U.S. by Dan Wesson Firearms.
Price: 357 SuperMag/Maxi, 414 SuperMag., 445 SuperMag., 8", blue or stainless $1,364.00
Price: 41 Magnum, 44 Magnum, 8", blue or stainless $1,241.00
Price: 41 Magnum, 44 Magnum, 10", blue or stainless $1,333.00

HANDGUNS — SINGLE ACTION REVOLVERS

Both classic six-shooters and modern adaptations for hunting and sport.

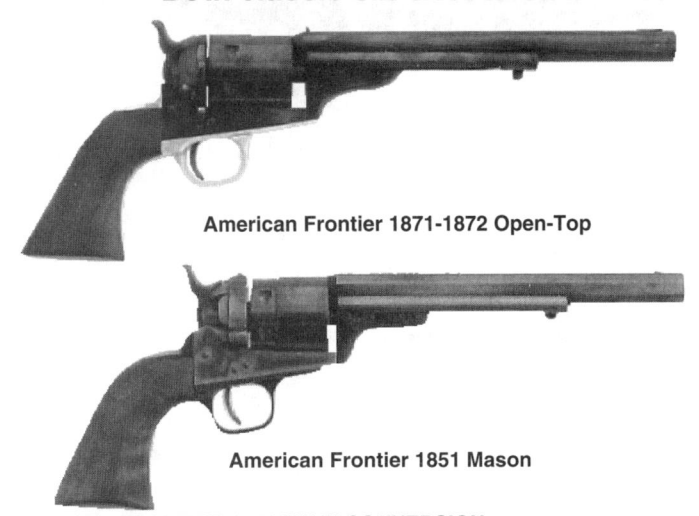

American Frontier 1871-1872 Open-Top

American Frontier 1851 Mason

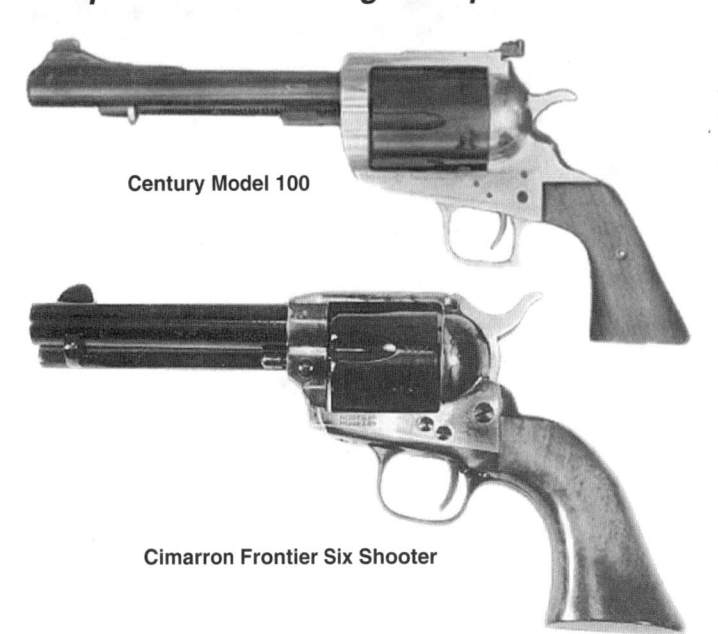

Century Model 100

Cimarron Frontier Six Shooter

AMERICAN FRONTIER 1851 NAVY CONVERSION
Caliber: 38, 44. **Barrel:** 5-1/2", 7-1/2", octagon. **Weight:** NA. **Length:** NA. **Stocks:** Varnished walnut, Navy size. **Sights:** Blade front, fixed rear. **Features:** Shoots metallic cartridge ammunition. Non-rebated cylinder; blued steel backstrap and trigger guard; color case-hardened hammer, trigger, ramrod, plunger; no ejector rod assembly. Introduced 1996.
Price: $795.00

AMERICAN FRONTIER 1871-1872 OPEN-TOP REVOLVERS
Caliber: 38, 44. **Barrel:** 5-1/2", 7-1/2", 8" round. **Weight:** NA. **Length:** NA. **Stocks:** Varnished walnut. **Sights:** Blade front, fixed rear. **Features:** Reproduction of the early cartridge conversions from percussion. Made for metallic cartridges. High polish blued steel, silver-plated brass backstrap and trigger guard, color case-hardened hammer; straight non-rebated cylinder with naval engagement engraving; stamped with original patent dates. Does not have conversion breechplate.
Price: $795.00

AMERICAN FRONTIER RICHARDS 1860 ARMY
Caliber: 38, 44. **Barrel:** 5-1/2", 7-1/2", round. **Weight:** NA. **Length:** NA. **Stocks:** Varnished walnut, Army size. **Sights:** Blade front, fixed rear. **Features:** Shoots metallic cartridge ammunition. Rebated cylinder; available with or without ejector assembly; high-polish blue including backstrap; silver-plated trigger guard; color case-hardened hammer and trigger. Introduced 1996.
Price: $795.00

American Frontier 1851 Navy Richards & Mason Conversion
Similar to the 1851 Navy Conversion except has Mason ejector assembly. Introduced 1996. Imported from Italy by American Frontier Firearms Mfg.
Price: $695.00

CABELA'S MILLENNIUM REVOLVER
Caliber: 45 Colt. **Barrel:** 4-3/4". **Weight:** NA. **Length:** 10" overall. **Grips:** Hardwood. **Sights:** Blade front, hammer notch rear. **Features:** Matte black finish; unpolished brass accents. Introduced 2001. From Cabela's.
Price: $199.99

CENTURY GUN DIST. MODEL 100 SINGLE-ACTION
Caliber: 30-30, 375 Win., 444 Marlin, 45-70, 50-70. **Barrel:** 6-1/2" (standard), 8", 10". **Weight:** 6 lbs. (loaded). **Length:** 15" overall (8" bbl.). **Stocks:** Smooth walnut. **Sights:** Ramp front, Millett adjustable square notch rear. **Features:** Highly polished high tensile strength manganese bronze frame, blue cylinder and barrel; coil spring trigger mechanism. Contact maker for full price information. Introduced 1975. Made in U.S. From Century Gun Dist., Inc.
Price: 6-1/2" barrel, 45-70 .... $2,000.00

CIMARRON LIGHTNING SA
Caliber: 38 Special. **Barrel:** 3-1/2", 4-3/4" or 5-1/2". **Weight:** NA. **Length:** NA. **Grips:** Checkered walnut. **Sights:** Blade front. **Features:** Replica of the Colt 1877 Lightning DA. Similar to Cimarron Thunderer™, except smaller grip frame to fit smaller hands. Blue finish with color-case hardened frame. Introduced 2001. From Cimarron F.A. Co.
Price: $389.00

CIMARRON MODEL "P" JR.
Caliber: 38 Special. **Barrel:** 3-1/2" and 4-1/2". **Weight:** NA. **Length:** NA. **Grips:** Checkered walnut. **Sights:** Blade front. **Features:** Styled after 1873 Colt Peacemaker, except 20 percent smaller. Blue finish with color-case hardened frame; Cowboy Comp® action. Introduced 2001. From Cimarron F.A. Co.
Price: $389.00

CIMARRON U.S. CAVALRY MODEL SINGLE-ACTION
Caliber: 45 Colt. **Barrel:** 7-1/2". **Weight:** 42 oz. **Length:** 13-1/2" overall. **Stocks:** Walnut. **Sights:** Fixed. **Features:** Has "A.P. Casey" markings; "U.S." plus patent dates on frame, serial number on backstrap, trigger guard, frame and cylinder, "APC" cartouche on left grip; color case-hardened frame and hammer, rest charcoal blue. Exact copy of the original. Imported by Cimarron F.A. Co.
Price: $499.00

Cimarron Rough Rider Artillery Model Single-Action
Similar to the U.S. Cavalry model except has 5-1/2" barrel, weighs 39 oz., and is 11-1/2" overall. U.S. markings and cartouche, case-hardened frame and hammer; 45 Colt only.
Price: $499.00

CIMARRON 1872 OPEN TOP REVOLVER
Caliber: 38, 44 Special, 45 S&W Schofield. **Barrel:** 5-1/2" and 7-1/2". **Weight:** NA. **Length:** NA. **Grips:** Walnut. **Sights:** Blade front, fixed rear. **Features:** Replica of first cartridge-firing revolver. Blue, charcoal blue, nickel or Original® finish; Navy-style brass or steel Army-style frame. Introduced 2001 by Cimarron F.A. Co.
Price: $469.00

CIMARRON 1873 FRONTIER SIX SHOOTER
Caliber: 38 WCF, 357 Mag., 44 WCF, 44 Spec., 45 Colt. **Barrel:** 4-3/4", 5-1/2", 7-1/2". **Weight:** 39 oz. **Length:** 10" overall (4" barrel). **Stocks:** Walnut. **Sights:** Blade front, fixed or adjustable rear. **Features:** Uses "old model" blackpowder frame with "Bullseye" ejector or New Model frame. Imported by Cimarron F.A. Co.
Price: 4-3/4" barrel $469.00
Price: 5-1/2" barrel $469.00
Price: 7-1/2" barrel $469.00

34TH EDITION, 2002 • 179

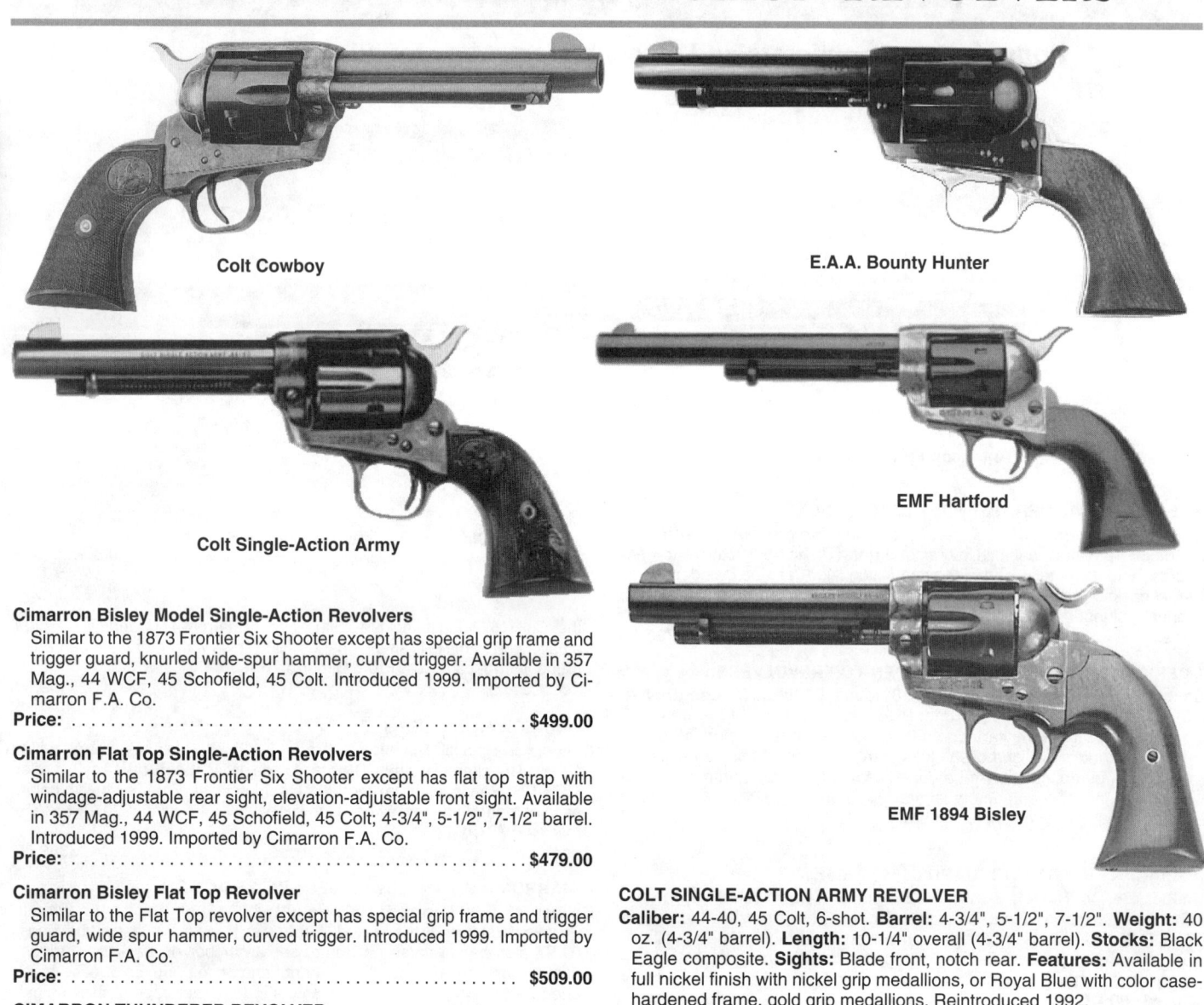

HANDGUNS — SINGLE ACTION REVOLVERS

Colt Cowboy

E.A.A. Bounty Hunter

Colt Single-Action Army

EMF Hartford

EMF 1894 Bisley

Cimarron Bisley Model Single-Action Revolvers
Similar to the 1873 Frontier Six Shooter except has special grip frame and trigger guard, knurled wide-spur hammer, curved trigger. Available in 357 Mag., 44 WCF, 45 Schofield, 45 Colt. Introduced 1999. Imported by Cimarron F.A. Co.
Price: $499.00

Cimarron Flat Top Single-Action Revolvers
Similar to the 1873 Frontier Six Shooter except has flat top strap with windage-adjustable rear sight, elevation-adjustable front sight. Available in 357 Mag., 44 WCF, 45 Schofield, 45 Colt; 4-3/4", 5-1/2", 7-1/2" barrel. Introduced 1999. Imported by Cimarron F.A. Co.
Price: $479.00

Cimarron Bisley Flat Top Revolver
Similar to the Flat Top revolver except has special grip frame and trigger guard, wide spur hammer, curved trigger. Introduced 1999. Imported by Cimarron F.A. Co.
Price: $509.00

CIMARRON THUNDERER REVOLVER
Caliber: 357 Mag., 44 WCF, 44 Spec., 45 Colt, 6-shot. **Barrel:** 3-1/2", 4-3/4", 5-1/2", 7-1/2", with ejector. **Weight:** 38 oz. (3-1/2" barrel). **Length:** NA. **Stocks:** Smooth walnut. **Sights:** Blade front, notch rear. **Features:** Thunderer grip; color case-hardened frame with balance blued. Introduced 1993. Imported by Cimarron F.A. Co.
Price: 3-1/2", 4-3/4", smooth grips $489.00
Price: As above, checkered grips $524.00
Price: 5-1/2", 7-1/2", smooth grips $529.00
Price: As above, checkered grips $564.00

CIMARRON 1872 OPEN-TOP REVOLVER
Caliber: 38 Spec., 38 Colt, 44 Spec., 44 Colt, 44 Russian, 45 Schofield. **Barrel:** 7-1/2". **Weight:** NA. **Length:** NA. **Stocks:** Smooth walnut. **Sights:** Blade front, fixed rear. **Features:** Replica of the original production. Color case-hardened frame, rest blued, including grip frame. Introduced 1999. Imported from Italy by Cimarron F.A. Co.
Price: $579.00

COLT COWBOY SINGLE-ACTION REVOLVER
Caliber: 45 Colt, 6-shot. **Barrel:** 5-1/2". **Weight:** 42 oz. **Stocks:** Black composition, first generation style. **Sights:** Blade front, notch rear. **Features:** Dimensional replica of Colt's original Peacemaker with medium-size color case-hardened frame; transfer bar safety system; half-cock loading. Introduced 1998. Made in U.S. by Colt's Mfg. Co.
Price: About $670.00

COLT SINGLE-ACTION ARMY REVOLVER
Caliber: 44-40, 45 Colt, 6-shot. **Barrel:** 4-3/4", 5-1/2", 7-1/2". **Weight:** 40 oz. (4-3/4" barrel). **Length:** 10-1/4" overall (4-3/4" barrel). **Stocks:** Black Eagle composite. **Sights:** Blade front, notch rear. **Features:** Available in full nickel finish with nickel grip medallions, or Royal Blue with color case-hardened frame, gold grip medallions. Reintroduced 1992.
Price: $1,938.00

E.A.A. BOUNTY HUNTER SA REVOLVERS
Caliber: 22 LR/22 WMR, 357 Mag., 44 Mag., 45 Colt, 6-shot. **Barrel:** 4-1/2", 7-1/2". **Weight:** 2.5 lbs. **Length:** 11" overall (4-5/8" barrel). **Stocks:** Smooth walnut. **Sights:** Blade front, grooved topstrap rear. **Features:** Transfer bar safety; three position hammer; hammer forged barrel. Introduced 1992. Imported by European American Armory.
Price: Blue or case-hardened $280.00
Price: Nickel $298.00
Price: 22LR/22WMR, blue $187.20
Price: As above, nickel $204.36

EMF HARTFORD SINGLE-ACTION REVOLVERS
Caliber: 357 Mag., 32-20, 38-40, 44-40, 44 Spec., 45 Colt. **Barrel:** 4-3/4", 5-1/2", 7-1/2". **Weight:** 45 oz. **Length:** 13" overall (7-1/2" barrel). **Stocks:** Smooth walnut. **Sights:** Blade front, fixed rear. **Features:** Identical to the original Colts with inspector cartouche on left grip, original patent dates and U.S. markings. All major parts serial numbered using original Colt-style lettering, numbering. Bullseye ejector head and color case-hardening on frame and hammer. Introduced 1990. From E.M.F.
Price: $500.00
Price: Cavalry or Artillery $390.00
Price: Nickel plated, add $125.00
Price: Casehardened New Model frame $365.00

180 • GUNS ILLUSTRATED

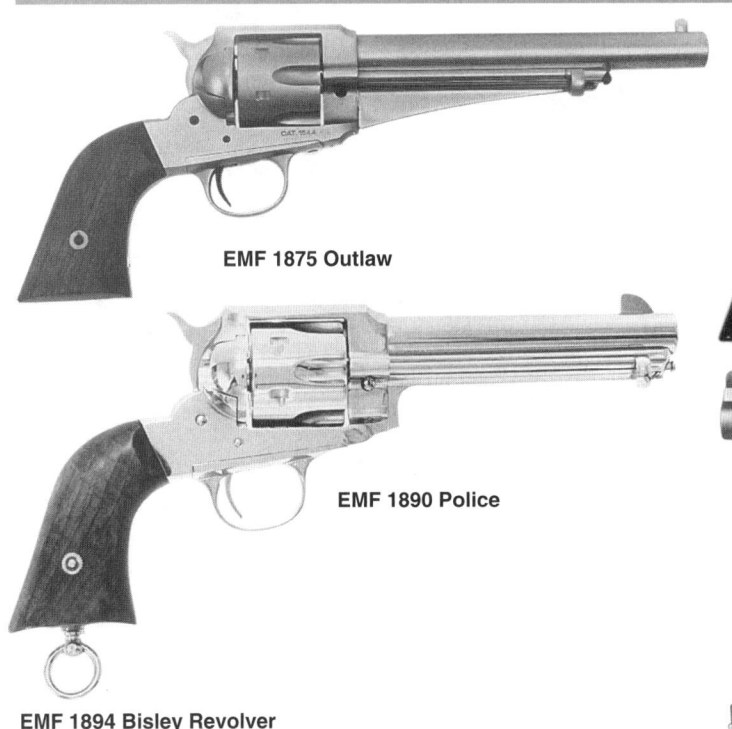

HANDGUNS — SINGLE ACTION REVOLVERS

EMF 1875 Outlaw

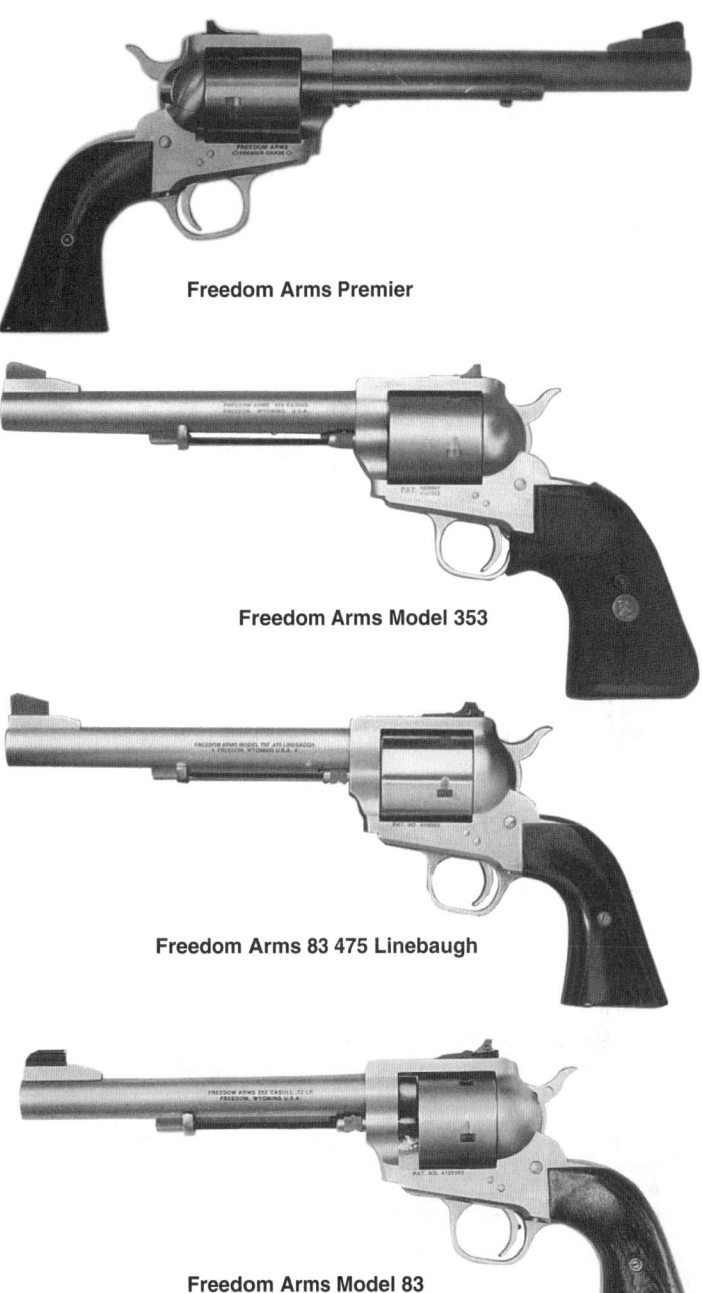

EMF 1890 Police

Freedom Arms Premier

Freedom Arms Model 353

Freedom Arms 83 475 Linebaugh

Freedom Arms Model 83

EMF 1894 Bisley Revolver
Similar to the Hartford single-action revolver except has special grip frame and trigger guard, wide spur hammer; available in 38-40 or 45 Colt, 4-3/4", 5-1/2" or 7-1/2" barrel. Introduced 1995. Imported by E.M.F.
Price: Casehardened/blue $400.00
Price: Nickel $525.00

EMF Hartford Pinkerton Single-Action Revolver
Same as the regular Hartford except has 4" barrel with ejector tube and birds head grip. Calibers: 357 Mag., 45 Colt. Introduced 1997. Imported by E.M.F.
Price: $375.00

EMF Hartford Express Single-Action Revolver
Same as the regular Hartford model except uses grip of the Colt Lightning revolver. Barrel lengths of 4", 4-3/4", 5-1/2". Introduced 1997. Imported by E.M.F.
Price: $375.00

EMF 1875 OUTLAW REVOLVER
Caliber: 357 Mag., 44-40, 45 Colt. **Barrel:** 7-1/2". **Weight:** 46 oz. **Length:** 13-1/2" overall. **Stocks:** Smooth walnut. **Sights:** Blade front, fixed groove rear. **Features:** Authentic copy of 1875 Remington with firing pin in hammer; color case-hardened frame, blue cylinder, barrel, steel backstrap and brass trigger guard. Also available in nickel, factory engraved. Imported by E.M.F.
Price: All calibers $575.00
Price: Nickel $735.00

EMF 1890 Police Revolver
Similar to the 1875 Outlaw except has 5-1/2" barrel, weighs 40 oz., with 12-1/2" overall length. Has lanyard ring in butt. No web under barrel. Calibers 357, 44-40, 45 Colt. Imported by E.M.F.
Price: All calibers $590.00
Price: Nickel $750.00

FREEDOM ARMS MODEL 83 PREMIER GRADE REVOLVER
Caliber: 357 Mag., 41 Rem. Mag., 44 Rem. Mag., 454 Casull, 475 Linebaugh, 50 AE, 5-shot. **Barrel:** 4-3/4", 6", 7-1/2", 9" (357 Mag. only), 10" (except 475 Linebaugh). **Weight:** 52 oz. **Length:** 14" overall (7-1/2" bbl.). **Stocks:** Impregnated hardwood (Premier grade), or Pachmayr (Field Grade). **Sights:** Blade front, notch or adjustable rear. **Features:** All stainless steel construction; sliding bar safety system. Lifetime warranty. Made in U.S. by Freedom Arms, Inc.

Price: 454 Casull, 475 Linebaugh, 50 AE, adj. sights $1,958.00
Price: 454 Casull, fixed sight $1,894.00
Price: 357 Mag., 41 Rem. Mag., 44 Rem. Mag., adj. sights.... $1,519.00
Price: 44 Rem. Mag., fixed sight $1,816.00
Price: Extra cylinder $264.00

Freedom Arms Model 83 Field Grade Revolver
Made on the Model 83 frame. Weighs 52 oz. Field grade model has adjustable rear sight with replaceable front blade, matte finish, Pachmayr grips. All stainless steel. Introduced 1992. Made in U.S. by Freedom Arms Inc.
Price: 454 Casull, 475 Linebaugh, 50 AE, adj. sights $1,519.00
Price: 454 Casull, fixed sights $1,484.00
Price: 357 Mag., 41 Rem. Mag., 44 Rem. Mag., adj. sights.... $1,442.00
Price: Extra cylinder $264.00

HANDGUNS — SINGLE ACTION REVOLVERS

Freedom Arms 97

Heritage Rough Rider

IAR Model 1873 Six Shooter

IAR Model 1873 Frontier

IAR Model 1873 Frontier Marshal

Freedom Arms Model 83 Field Grade Varmint Class Revolver
Made on the Model 83 frame. Chambered for 22 LR with 5-shot cylinder; 5-1/8" or 7-1/2" barrel. Weighs 58 oz. (7-1/2" barrel). Brass bead front, adjustable rear express with shallow "V." All-stainless construction with matte finish, manual sliding-bar safety system, dual firing pins, lightened hammer, pre-set trigger stop. Made in U.S. by Freedom Arms.
Price: Varmint Class $1,714.00
Price: Extra fitted 22 WMR cylinder $264.00

FREEDOM ARMS MODEL 97 MID-FRAME REVOLVER
Caliber: 357 Mag., 6-shot cylinder; 45 Colt, 41 Rem. Mag., 5-shot. Barrel: 4-1/4", 5-1/2", 7-1/2". Weight: 41 oz. (5-1/2" barrel). Length: 10-3/4"overall (5-1/2" barrel). Grips: Impregnated hardwood or black Micarta optional. Sights: Blade on ramp front, fixed or fully adjustable rear. Features: Made of stainless steel; brushed finish; automatic transfer bar safety system. Introduced 1997. Made in U.S. by Freedom Arms.
Price: Adjustable sight $1,576.00
Price: 357 Mag., 45 Colt, fixed sight $1,500.00
Price: Extra cylinder $264.00

FREEDOM ARMS MODEL 252 VARMINT CLASS REVOLVER
Caliber: 22 LR, 5-shot. Barrel: 5.125", 7.5". Weight: 58 oz. (7.5" barrel). Length: NA. Stocks: Black and green laminated hardwood. Sights: Brass bead express front, express rear with shallow V-notch. Features: All stainless steel construction. Dual firing pins; lightened hammer; pre-set trigger stop. Built on Model 83 frame and accepts Model 83 Freedom Arms sights and/or scope mounts. Introduced 1991. Made in U.S. by Freedom Arms.
Price: $1,527.00
Price: Extra fitted 22 WMR cylinder $264.00

HERITAGE ROUGH RIDER REVOLVER
Caliber: 22 LR, 22 LR/22 WMR combo, 6-shot. Barrel: 2-3/4", 3-1/2", 4-3/4", 6-1/2", 9". Weight: 31 to 38 oz. Length: NA. Grips: Exotic hardwood, laminated wood or mother of pearl; bird's head models offered. Sights: Blade front, fixed rear. Adjustable sight on 6-1/2" only. Features: Hammer block safety. High polish blue or nickel finish. Introduced 1993. Made in U.S. by Heritage Mfg., Inc.
Price: . . . . $184.95 to $239.95

IAR MODEL 1873 SIX SHOOTER
Caliber: 22 LR/22 WMR combo. Barrel: 5-1/2". Weight: 36-1/2" oz. Length: 11-3/8" overall. Stocks: One-piece walnut. Sights: Blade front, notch rear. Features: A 3/4-scale reproduction. Color case-hardened frame, blued barrel. All-steel construction. Made by Uberti. Imported from Italy by IAR, Inc.
Price: $360.00

IAR MODEL 1873 FRONTIER REVOLVER
Caliber: 22 RL, 22 LR/22 WMR. Barrel: 4-3/4". Weight: 45 oz. Length: 10-1/2" overall. Stocks: One-piece walnut with inspector's cartouche. Sights: Blade front, notch rear. Features: Color case-hardened frame, blued barrel, black nickel-plated brass trigger guard and backstrap. Bright nickel and engraved versions available. Introduced 1997. Imported from Italy by IAR, Inc.
Price: $395.00
Price: Nickel-plated $485.00
Price: 22 LR/22WMR combo $425.00

IAR MODEL 1873 FRONTIER MARSHAL
Caliber: 357 Mag., 45 Colt. Barrel: 4-3/4", 5-1/2, 7-1/2". Weight: 39 oz. Length: 10-1/2" overall. Stocks: One-piece walnut. Sights: Blade front, notch rear. Features: Bright brass trigger guard and backstrap, color case-hardened frame, blued barrel and cylinder. Introduced 1998. Imported from Italy by IAR, Inc.
Price: $395.00

MAGNUM RESEARCH BFR SINGLE-ACTION REVOLVER
Caliber: 22 Hornet, 45 Colt +P, 454 Casull (Little Max, standard cylinder). Barrel: 7-1/2", 10". Weight: 4 lbs. Length: 11" overall with 7-1/2" barrel. Stocks: Checkered rubber. Sights: Orange blade on ramp front, fully adjustable rear. Features: Stainless steel construction. Optional exotic wood finger-groove grips available. Introduced 1997. Made in U.S. From Magnum Research, Inc.
Price: $999.00

HANDGUNS — SINGLE ACTION REVOLVERS

Navy Arms Flat Top

Navy Arms 1873

Navy Arms Pinched Frame

Navy Arms Schofield

Navy Arms Bisley

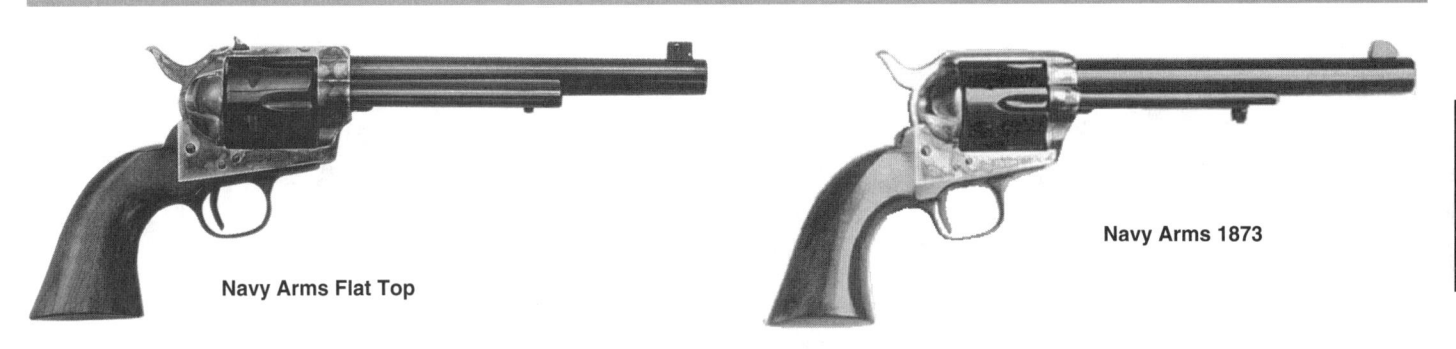

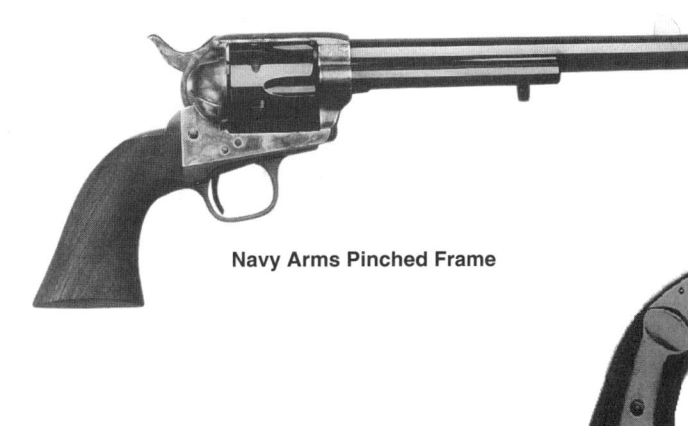

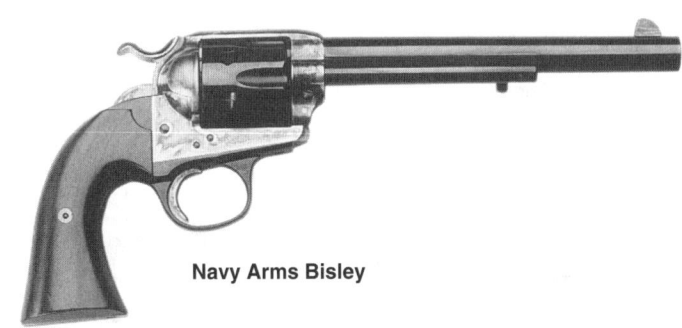

MAGNUM RESEARCH LITTLE MAX REVOLVER
Caliber: 22 Hornet, 45 Colt, 454 Casull, 50 A.E. **Barrel:** 6-1/2", 7-1/2", 10". **Weight:** 45 oz. **Length:** 13" overall (7-1/2" barrel). **Stocks:** Rubber. **Sights:** Ramp front, adjustable rear. **Features:** Single action; stainless steel construction. Announced 1998. Made in U.S. From Magnum Research.
Price: $999.00
Price: Maxine model (7-1/2", 10", 45 Colt/410, 45-70, 444 Marlin) $999.00

NAVY ARMS FLAT TOP TARGET MODEL REVOLVER
Caliber: 45 Colt, 6-shot cylinder. **Barrel:** 7-1/2". **Weight:** 40 oz. **Length:** 13-1/4" overall. **Stocks:** Smooth walnut. **Sights:** Spring-loaded German silver front, rear adjustable for windage. **Features:** Replica of Colt's Flat Top Frontier target revolver made from 1888 to 1896. Blue with color case-hardened frame. Introduced 1997. Imported by Navy Arms.
Price: $435.00

NAVY ARMS "PINCHED FRAME" SINGLE-ACTION REVOLVER
Caliber: 45 Colt, 6-shot. **Barrel:** 7-1/2". **Weight:** 37 oz. **Length:** 13" overall. **Stocks:** Smooth walnut **Sights:** German silver blade, notch rear. **Features:** Replica of Colt's original Peacemaker. Color case-hardened frame, hammer, rest charcoal blued. Introduced 1997. Imported by Navy Arms.
Price: $415.00

NAVY ARMS BISLEY MODEL SINGLE-ACTION REVOLVER
Caliber: 44-40 or 45 Colt, 6-shot cylinder. **Barrel:** 4-3/4", 5-1/2", 7-1/2". **Weight:** 40 oz. **Length:** 12-1/2" overall (7-1/2" barrel). **Stocks:** Smooth walnut. **Sights:** Blade front, notch rear. **Features:** Replica of Colt's Bisley Model. Polished blue finish, color case-hardened frame. Introduced 1997. Imported by Navy Arms.
Price: $415.00

NAVY ARMS 1872 OPEN TOP REVOLVER
Caliber: 38 Spec., 6-shot. **Barrel:** 5-1/2" or 7-1/2". **Weight:** 2 lbs., 12 oz. **Length:** 11" or 13". **Stocks:** Smooth walnut. **Sights:** Blade front, notch rear. **Features:** Replica of Colt's first production cartridge "six shooter." Polished blue finish with color case hardened frame, silver plated trigger guard and backstrap Introduced 2000. Imported by Navy Arms.
Price: $390.00

NAVY ARMS 1873 SINGLE-ACTION REVOLVER
Caliber: 357 Mag., 44-40, 45 Colt, 6-shot cylinder. **Barrel:** 4-3/4", 5-1/2", 7-1/2". **Weight:** 36 oz. **Length:** 10-3/4" overall (5-1/2" barrel). **Stocks:** Smooth walnut. **Sights:** Blade front, notch rear. **Features:** Blue with color case-hardened frame. Introduced 1991. Imported by Navy Arms.
Price: $395.00
Price: 1873 U.S. Cavalry Model (7-1/2", 45 Colt, arsenal markings) $465.00
Price: 1895 U.S. Artillery Model (as above, 5-1/2" barrel) $465.00

NAVY ARMS 1875 SCHOFIELD REVOLVER
Caliber: 44-40, 45 Colt, 6-shot cylinder. **Barrel:** 3-1/2", 5", 7". **Weight:** 39 oz. **Length:** 10-3/4" overall (5" barrel). **Stocks:** Smooth walnut. **Sights:** Blade front, notch rear. **Features:** Replica of Smith & Wesson Model 3 Schofield. Single-action, top-break with automatic ejection. Polished blue finish. Introduced 1994. Imported by Navy Arms.
Price: Hideout Model, 3-1/2" barrel $695.00
Price: Wells Fargo, 5" barrel........................... $695.00
Price: U.S. Cavalry model, 7" barrel, military markings $695.00

HANDGUNS — SINGLE ACTION REVOLVERS

Navy Arms New Model Russian

North American Black Widow

North American Mini

Ruger Blackhawk

North American Mini-Master

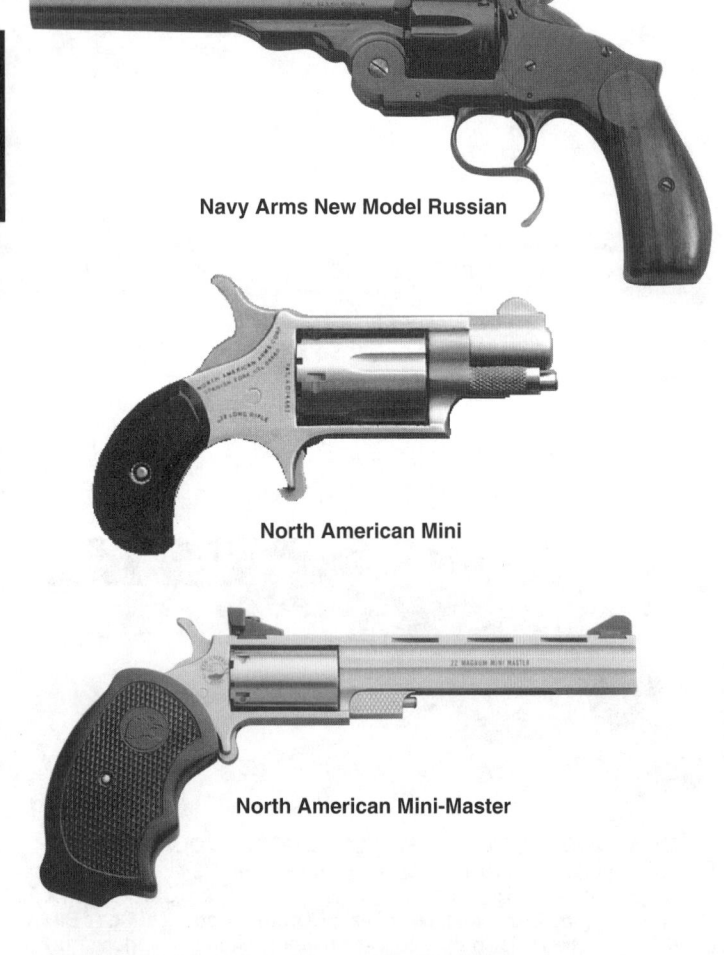

NAVY ARMS NEW MODEL RUSSIAN REVOLVER
Caliber: 44 Russian, 6-shot cylinder. **Barrel:** 6-1/2". **Weight:** 40 oz. **Length:** 12" overall. **Stocks:** Smooth walnut. **Sights:** Blade front, notch rear. **Features:** Replica of the S&W Model 3 Russian Third Model revolver. Spur trigger guard, polished blue finish. Introduced 1999. Imported by Navy Arms.
Price: $745.00

NAVY ARMS 1851 NAVY CONVERSION REVOLVER
Caliber: 38 Spec., 38 Long Colt. **Barrel:** 5-1/2", 7-1/2". **Weight:** 44 oz. **Length:** 14" overall (7-1/2" barrel). **Stocks:** Smooth walnut. **Sights:** Bead front, notch rear. **Features:** Replica of Colt's cartridge conversion revolver. Polished blue finish with color case-hardened frame, silver plated trigger guard and backstrap. Introduced 1999. Imported by Navy Arms.
Price: $365.00

NAVY ARMS 1860 ARMY CONVERSION REVOLVER
Caliber: 38 Spec., 38 Long Colt. **Barrel:** 5-1/2", 7-1/2". **Weight:** 44 oz. **Length:** 13-1/2" overall (7-1/2" barrel). **Stocks:** Smooth walnut. **Sights:** Blade front, notch rear. **Features:** Replica of Colt's conversion revolver. Polished blue finish with color case-hardened frame, full-size 1860 Army grip with blued steel backstrap. Introduced 1999. Imported by Navy Arms.
Price: $365.00

NAVY ARMS 1861 NAVY CONVERSION REVOLVER
Caliber: 38 Spec., 38 Long Colt. **Barrel:** 5-1/2", 7-1/2". **Weight:** 44 oz. **Length:** 13-1/2" overall (7-1/2" barrel). **Stocks:** Smooth walnut. **Sights:** Blade front, notch rear. **Features:** Replica of Colt's cartridge conversion. Polished blue finish with color case-hardened frame, silver plated trigger guard and backstrap. Introduced 1999. Imported by Navy Arms.
Price: $365.00

NORTH AMERICAN MINI-REVOLVERS
Caliber: 22 Short, 22 LR, 22 WMR, 5-shot. **Barrel:** 1-1/8", 1-5/8". **Weight:** 4 to 6.6 oz. **Length:** 3-5/8" to 6-1/8" overall. **Stocks:** Laminated wood. **Sights:** Blade front, notch fixed rear. **Features:** All stainless steel construction. Polished satin and matte finish. Engraved models available. From North American Arms.
Price: 22 Short, 22 LR $176.00
Price: 22 WMR, 1-5/8" bbl. $194.00
Price: 22 WMR, 1-1/8" or 1-5/8" bbl. with extra 22 LR cylinder .. $231.00

NORTH AMERICAN MINI-MASTER
Caliber: 22 LR, 22 WMR, 5-shot cylinder. **Barrel:** 4". **Weight:** 10.7 oz. **Length:** 7.75" overall. **Stocks:** Checkered hard black rubber. **Sights:** Blade front, white outline rear adjustable for elevation, or fixed. **Features:** Heavy vent barrel; full-size grips. Non-fluted cylinder. Introduced 1989.
Price: Adjustable sight, 22 WMR or 22 LR $299.00
Price: As above with extra WMR/LR cylinder $336.00
Price: Fixed sight, 22 WMR or 22 LR $281.00
Price: As above with extra WMR/LR cylinder $318.00

North American Black Widow Revolver
Similar to the Mini-Master except has 2" heavy vent barrel. Built on the 22 WMR frame. Non-fluted cylinder, black rubber grips. Available with either Millett Low Profile fixed sights or Millett sight adjustable for elevation only. Overall length 5-7/8", weighs 8.8 oz. From North American Arms.
Price: Adjustable sight, 22 LR or 22 WMR $269.00
Price: As above with extra WMR/LR cylinder $306.00
Price: Fixed sight, 22 LR or 22 WMR $251.00
Price: As above with extra WMR/LR cylinder $288.00

RUGER NEW MODEL BLACKHAWK REVOLVER
Caliber: 30 Carbine, 357 Mag./38 Spec., 41 Mag., 45 Colt, 6-shot. **Barrel:** 4-5/8" or 5-1/2", either caliber; 7-1/2" (30 Carbine and 45 Colt). **Weight:** 42 oz. (6-1/2" bbl.). **Length:** 12-1/4" overall (5-1/2" bbl.). **Stocks:** American walnut. **Sights:** 1/8" ramp front, micro-click rear adjustable for windage and elevation. **Features:** Ruger transfer bar safety system, independent firing pin, hardened chrome-moly steel frame, music wire springs throughout. Comes with plastic lockable case and lock.

184 • GUNS ILLUSTRATED

HANDGUNS — SINGLE ACTION REVOLVERS

Ruger Bisley Vaquero

Ruger Bisley Single-Action

Ruger New Bearcat

Ruger Super Single-Six

Price: Blue 30 Carbine, 7-1/2" (BN31) $415.00
Price: Blue, 357 Mag., 4-5/8", 6-1/2" (BN34, BN36) $415.00
Price: As above, stainless (KBN34, KBN36) $505.00
Price: Blue, 357 Mag./9mm Convertible, 4-5/8", 6-1/2" (BN34X, BN36X) $465.00
Price: Blue, 41 Mag., 4-5/8", 6-1/2" (BN41, BN42) $415.00
Price: Blue, 45 Colt, 4-5/8", 5-1/2", 7-1/2" (BN44, BN455, BN45) $415.00
Price: Stainless, 45 Colt, 4-5/8", 7-1/2" (KBN44, KBN45) $505.00
Price: Blue, 45 Colt/45 ACP Convertible, 4-5/8", 5-1/2" (BN44X, BN455X) $465.00

RUGER NEW MODEL SUPER BLACKHAWK

Caliber: 44 Mag., 6-shot. Also fires 44 Spec. **Barrel:** 4-5/8", 5-1/2", 7-1/2", 10-1/2" bull. **Weight:** 48 oz. (7-1/2" bbl.), 51 oz. (10-1/2" bbl.). **Length:** 13-3/8" overall (7-1/2" bbl.). **Stocks:** American walnut. **Sights:** 1/8" ramp front, micro-click rear adjustable for windage and elevation. **Features:** Ruger transfer bar safety system, fluted or un-fluted cylinder, steel grip and cylinder frame, round or square back trigger guard, wide serrated trigger and wide spur hammer. Comes with plastic lockable case and lock.
Price: Blue, 4-5/8", 5-1/2", 7-1/2" (S458N, S45N, S47N) $489.00
Price: Blue, 10-1/2" bull barrel (S411N) $499.00
Price: Stainless, 4-5/8", 5-1/2", 7-1/2" (KS458N, KS45N, KS47N) $510.00
Price: Stainless, 10-1/2" bull barrel (KS411N) $519.00

RUGER VAQUERO SINGLE-ACTION REVOLVER

Caliber: 357 Mag., 44-40, 44 Mag., 45 Colt, 6-shot. **Barrel:** 4-5/8", 5-1/2", 7-1/2". **Weight:** 41 oz. **Length:** 13-1/8" overall (7-1/2" barrel). **Stocks:** Smooth rosewood with Ruger medallion. **Sights:** Blade front, fixed notch rear. **Features:** Uses Ruger's patented transfer bar safety system and loading gate interlock with classic styling. Blued model has color case-hardened finish on the frame, the rest polished and blued. Stainless model has high-gloss polish. Introduced 1993. From Sturm, Ruger & Co.
Price: 357 Mag. BNV34 (4-5/8"), BNV35 (5-1/2"). $510.00
Price: 357 Mag. KBNV34 (4-5/8"), KBNV35 (5-1/2") stainless. . . $510.00
Price: BNV44 (4-5/8"), BNV445 (5-1/2"), BNV45 (7-1/2"), blue . . $510.00
Price: KBNV44 (4-5/8"), KBNV455 (5-1/2"), KBNV45 (7-1/2"), stainless $510.00
Price: 45 Colt BNV455, all blue finish, 4-5/8" or 5-1/2" $510.00
Price: 45 Colt KBNV455, stainless, 5-1/2" $510.00

Ruger Bisley-Vaquero Single-Action Revolver

Similar to the Vaquero except has Bisley-style hammer, grip and trigger and is available in 357 Magnum, 44 Magnum and 45 Colt only, with 4-5/8" or 5-1/2" barrel. Has smooth rosewood grips with Ruger medallion. Roll-engraved, unfluted cylinder. Introduced 1997. From Sturm, Ruger & Co.
Price: Color case-hardened frame, blue grip frame, barrel and cylinder, RBNV-475, RBNV-455 . . . . $510.00
Price: High-gloss stainless steel, KRBNV-475, KRBNV-455 . . . . . $529.00
Price: For simulated ivory grips add $36.00
Price: 44-40 BNV40 (4-5/8"), BNV405 (5-1/2"), BNV407 (7-1/2") . $510.00
Price: 44-40 KBNV40 (4-5/8"), KBNV405 (5-1/2"), KBNV407 (7-1/2") stainless $510.00

RUGER NEW BEARCAT SINGLE-ACTION

Caliber: 22 LR, 6-shot. **Barrel:** 4". **Weight:** 24 oz. **Length:** 8-7/8" overall. **Stocks:** Smooth rosewood with Ruger medallion. **Sights:** Blade front, fixed notch rear. **Features:** Reintroduction of the Ruger Bearcat with slightly lengthened frame, Ruger patented transfer bar safety system. Available in blue only. Introduced 1993. Comes with plastic lockable case and lock. From Sturm, Ruger & Co.
Price: SBC4, blue $359.00

34TH EDITION, 2002 • **185**

HANDGUNS — SINGLE ACTION REVOLVERS

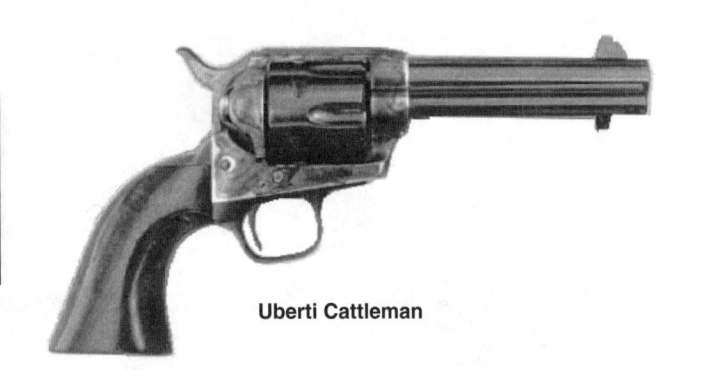

Uberti Cattleman

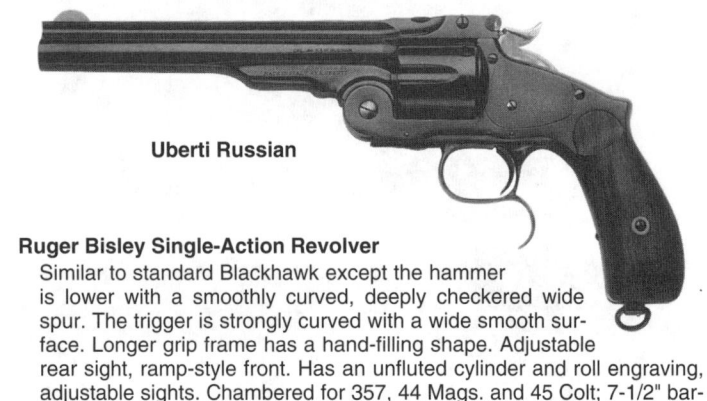

Uberti 1875 Army

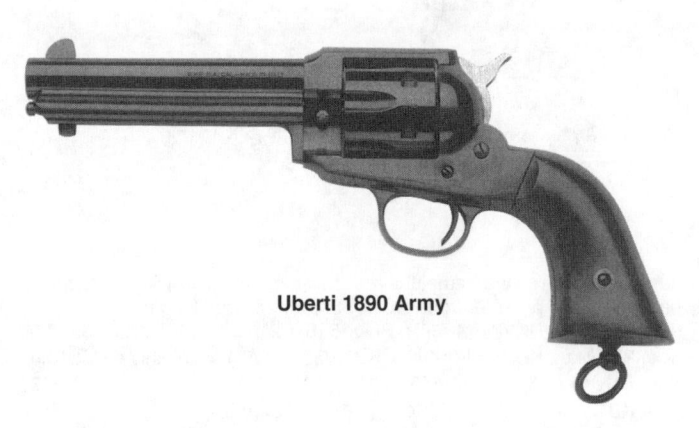

Uberti 1890 Army

Uberti Russian

Ruger Bisley Single-Action Revolver
Similar to standard Blackhawk except the hammer is lower with a smoothly curved, deeply checkered wide spur. The trigger is strongly curved with a wide smooth surface. Longer grip frame has a hand-filling shape. Adjustable rear sight, ramp-style front. Has an unfluted cylinder and roll engraving, adjustable sights. Chambered for 357, 44 Mags. and 45 Colt; 7-1/2" barrel; overall length of 13"; weighs 48 oz. Comes with plastic lockable case and lock. Introduced 1985.
Price: RB-35W, 357Mag, R3-44W, 44Mag, RB-45W, 45 Colt ... **$510.00**

TRISTAR/UBERTI REGULATOR REVOLVER
Caliber: 45 Colt. **Barrel:** 4-3/4", 5-1/2", 7-1/2". **Weight:** 32-38 oz. **Length:** 8-1/4" overall (4-3/4" bbl.) **Grips:** One-piece walnut. **Sights:** Blade front, notch rear. **Features:** Uberti replica of 1873 Colt Model "P" revolver. Color-case hardened steel frame, brass backstrap and trigger guard, hammer-block safety. Imported from Italy by Tristar Sporting Arms.
Price: Regulator **$335.00**
Price: Regulator Deluxe (blued backstrap, trigger guard) **$367.00**

UBERTI 1873 CATTLEMAN SINGLE-ACTION
Caliber: 22 LR/22 WMR, 38 Spec., 357 Mag., 44 Spec., 44-40, 45 Colt/45 ACP, 6-shot. **Barrel:** 4-3/4", 5-1/2", 7-1/2"; 44-40, 45 Colt also with 3", 3-1/2", 4". **Weight:** 38 oz. (5-1/2" bbl.). **Length:** 10-3/4" overall (5-1/2" bbl.). **Stocks:** One-piece smooth walnut. **Sights:** Blade front, groove rear; fully adjustable rear available. **Features:** Steel or brass backstrap, trigger guard; color case-hardened frame, blued barrel, cylinder. Imported from Italy by Uberti U.S.A.
Price: Steel backstrap, trigger guard, fixed sights **$435.00**
Price: Brass backstrap, trigger guard, fixed sights **$365.00**
Price: Bisley model **$435.00**

Uberti 1873 Buckhorn Single-Action
A slightly larger version of the Cattleman revolver. Available in 44 Magnum or 44 Magnum/44-40 convertible, otherwise has same specs.
Price: Steel backstrap, trigger guard, fixed sights **$410.00**
Price: Convertible (two cylinders) **$475.00**

RUGER SINGLE-SIX AND SUPER SINGLE-SIX CONVERTIBLE
Caliber: 22 LR, 6-shot; 22 WMR in extra cylinder. **Barrel:** 4-5/8", 5-1/2", 6-1/2", 9-1/2" (6-groove). **Weight:** 35 oz. (6-1/2" bbl.). **Length:** 11-13/16" overall (6-1/2" bbl.). **Stocks:** Smooth American walnut. **Sights:** Improved Patridge front on ramp, fully adjustable rear protected by integral frame ribs (super single-six); or fixed sight single six). **Features:** Ruger transfer bar safety system, loading gate interlock, hardened chrome-moly steel frame, wide trigger, music wire springs throughout, independent firing pin.
Price: 4-5/8", 5-1/2", 6-1/2", 9-1/2" barrel, blue, adjustable sight NR4, NR6, NR9, NR5 .... **$369.00**
Price: 5-1/2", 6-1/2" bbl. only, stainless steel, adjustable sight KNR5, KNR6 .... **$449.00**
Price: 5-1/2", 6-1/2" barrel, blue fixed sights **$369.00**

UBERTI 1875 SA ARMY OUTLAW REVOLVER
Caliber: 357 Mag., 44-40, 45 Colt, 45 Colt/45 ACP convertible, 6-shot. **Barrel:** 5-1/2", 7-1/2". **Weight:** 44 oz. **Length:** 13-3/4" overall. **Stocks:** Smooth walnut. **Sights:** Blade front, notch rear. **Features:** Replica of the 1875 Remington S.A. Army revolver. Brass trigger guard, color case-hardened frame, rest blued. Imported by Uberti U.S.A.
Price: **$435.00**
Price: 45 Colt/45 ACP convertible **$475.00**

UBERTI 1890 ARMY OUTLAW REVOLVER
Caliber: 357 Mag., 44-40, 45 Colt, 45 Colt/45 ACP convertible, 6-shot. **Barrel:** 5-1/2", 7-1/2". **Weight:** 37 oz. **Length:** 12-1/2" overall. **Stocks:** American walnut. **Sights:** Blade front, groove rear. **Features:** Replica of the 1890 Remington single-action. Brass trigger guard, rest is blued. Imported by Uberti U.S.A.
Price: **$435.00**
Price: 45 Colt/45 ACP convertible **$475.00**

UBERTI NEW MODEL RUSSIAN REVOLVER
Caliber: 44 Russian, 6-shot cylinder. **Barrel:** 6-1/2". **Weight:** 40 oz. **Length:** 12" overall. **Stocks:** Smooth walnut. **Sights:** Blade front, notch rear. **Features:** Repica of the S&W Model 3 Russian Third Model revolver. Spur trigger guard, polished blue finish. Introduced 1999. Imported by Uberti USA.
Price: **$775.00**

Ruger Bisley Small Frame Revolver
Similar to the Single-Six except frame is styled after the classic Bisley "flat-top." Most mechanical parts are unchanged. Hammer is lower and smoothly curved with a deeply checkered spur. Trigger is strongly curved with a wide smooth surface. Longer grip frame designed with a hand-filling shape, and the trigger guard is a large oval. Adjustable dovetail rear sight; front sight base accepts interchangeable square blades of various heights and styles. Has an unfluted cylinder and roll engraving. Weighs 41 oz. Chambered for 22 LR, 6-1/2" barrel only. Comes with plastic lockable case and lock. Introduced 1985.
Price: RB-22AW **$402.00**

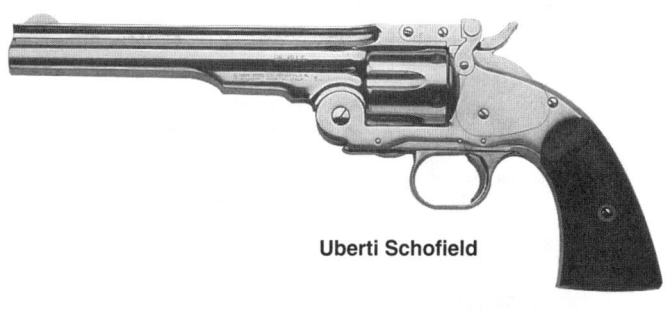

HANDGUNS — SINGLE ACTION REVOLVERS

Uberti Schofield

Uberti Bisley

Uberti Bisley Flat Top

UBERTI 1875 SCHOFIELD REVOLVER
Caliber: 44-40, 45 Colt, 6-shot cylinder. **Barrel:** 5", 7". **Weight:** 39 oz. **Length:** 10-3/4" overall (5" barrel). **Stocks:** Smooth walnut. **Sights:** Blade front, notch rear. **Features:** Replica of Smith & Wesson Model 3 Schofield. Single-action, top-break with automatic ejection. Polished blue finish. Introduced 1994. Imported by Uberti USA.
Price: $700.00

UBERTI BISLEY MODEL SINGLE-ACTION REVOLVER
Caliber: 38-40, 357 Mag., 44 Spec., 44-40 or 45 Colt, 6-shot cylinder. **Barrel:** 4-3/4", 5-1/2", 7-1/2". **Weight:** 40 oz. **Length:** 12-1/2" overall (7-1/2" barrel). **Stocks:** Smooth walnut. **Sights:** Blade front, notch rear. **Features:** Replica of Colt's Bisley Model. Polished blue finish, color case-hardened frame. Introduced 1997. Imported by Uberti USA.
Price: $435.00

Uberti Bisley Model Flat Top Target Revolver
Similar to the standard Bisley model except with flat top strap, 7-1/2" barrel only, and a spring-loaded German silver front sight blade, standing leaf rear sight adjustable for windage. Polished blue finish, color case-hardened frame. Introduced 1998. Imported by Uberti USA.
Price: $455.00

U.S. FIRE-ARMS SINGLE ACTION ARMY REVOLVER
Caliber: 44 Russian, 38-40, 44-40, 45 Colt, 6-shot cylinder. **Barrel:** 4", 4-3/4", 5-1/2", 7-1/2", 10". **Weight:** 37 oz. **Length:** NA. **Grips:** Hard rubber. **Sights:** Blade front, notch rear. **Features:** Recreation of original guns; 3" and 4" have no ejector. Available with all-blue, blue with color case-hardening, or full nickel-plate finish. Made in U.S. by United States Fire-Arms Mfg. Co.
Price: 4" blue $1,099.00
Price: 4-3/4", blue/cased-colors $1,199.00
Price: 7-1/2", carbonal blue/case-colors $1,425.00
Price: 7-1/2" nickel $1,349.00

U.S. Fire-Arms Nettleton Cavalry Revolver
Similar to the Single Action Army, except in 45 Colt only, with 7-1/2" barrel, color case-hardened/blue finish, and has old-style hand numbering, exact cartouche branding and correct inspector hand-stamp markings. Made in U.S. by United States Fire-Arms Mfg. Co.
Price: $1,225.00
Price: Artillery Model, 5-1/2" barrel $1,225.00

U.S. Fire-Arms Bird Head Model Revolver
Similar to the Single Action Army except has bird's-head grip and comes with 3-1/2", 4" or 4-3/4" barrel. Made in U.S. by United States Fire-Arms Mfg. Co.
Price: 3-1/2" or 4" blue/color-case hardening $1,199.00
Price: 4-3/4", nickel-plated $1,299.00

U.S. Fire-Arms Flattop Target Revolver
Similar to the Single Action Army except 4-3/4", 5-1/2" or 7-1/2" barrel, two-piece hard rubber stocks, flat top frame, adjustable rear sight. Made in U.S. by United States Fire-Arms Mfg. Co.
Price: 4-3/4", blue, polished hammer $1,150.00
Price: 4-3/4", blue, case-colored hammer $1,150.00
Price: 5-1/2", blue, case-colored hammer $1,150.00
Price: 5-1/2", nickel-plated $1,299.00
Price: 7-1/2", blue, polished hammer $1,150.00
Price: 7-1/2", blue, case-colored hammer $1,150.00

U.S. FIRE-ARMS BISLEY MODEL REVOLVER
Caliber: 4 Colt, 6-shot cylinder. **Barrel:** 4-3/4", 5-1/2", 7-1/2", 10". **Weight:** 38 oz. (5-1/2" barrel). **Length:** NA. **Grips:** Two-piece hard rubber. **Sights:** Blade front, notch rear. **Features:** Available in all-blue, blue with color case-hardening, or full nickel plate finish. Made in U.S. by United States Patent Fire-Arms Mfg. Co.
Price: 5-1/2", blue/case-colors $1,350.00
Price: 7-1/2", blue/case-colors $1,350.00
Price: 10", nickel $1,435.00

U.S. Fire-Arms "China Camp" Cowboy Action Revolver
Similar to Single Action Army revolver except available in Silver Steel finish only. Offered in 4-3/4", 5-1/2", 7-1/2" and 10" barrels. Made in U.S. by United States Fire-Arms Mfg. Co.
Price: $995.00

U.S. Fire-Arms "Buntline Special"
Similar to Single Action Army revolver except has 16" barrel, flip-up rear peep sight, 45 Colt only. Bone case frame, armory blue or nickel finish. Made in U.S. by United States Fire-Arms Mfg. Co.
Price: $2,199.00

U.S. Fire-Arms Omni-Potent Six Shooter
Similar to Single Action Army revolver except has bird's head grip with lanyard ring and hump in backstrap. Offered in 4-3/4", 5-1/2" and 7-1/2" barrels. Made in U.S. by United States Fire-Arms Mfg. Co.
Price: 3-1/2", 4" blue/color case hardening $1,340.00
Price: 4-3/4", nickel plated $1,439.00

34TH EDITION, 2002

HANDGUNS — MISCELLANEOUS

Specially adapted single-shot and multi-barrel arms.

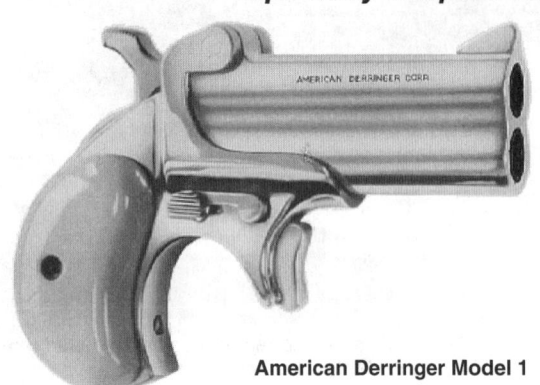

American Derringer Model 1

Bond Arms C2K Defender

AMERICAN DERRINGER MODEL 1
Caliber: 22 LR, 22 WMR, 30 Carbine, 30 Luger, 30-30 Win., 32 H&R Mag., 32-20, 380 ACP, 38 Super, 38 Spec., 38 Spec. shotshell, 38 Spec. +P, 9mm Para., 357 Mag., 357 Mag./45/410, 357 Maximum, 10mm, 40 S&W, 41 Mag., 38-40, 44-40 Win., 44 Spec., 44 Mag., 45 Colt, 45 Win. Mag., 45 ACP, 45 Colt/410, 45-70 single shot. **Barrel:** 3". **Weight:** 15-1/2 oz. (38 Spec.). **Length:** 4.82" overall. **Stocks:** Rosewood, Zebra wood. **Sights:** Blade front. **Features:** Made of stainless steel with high-polish or satin finish. Two-shot capacity. Manual hammer block safety. Introduced 1980. Available in almost any pistol caliber. Contact the factory for complete list of available calibers and prices. From American Derringer Corp.
Price: 22 LR $320.00
Price: 38 Spec. $320.00
Price: 357 Maximum. $345.00
Price: 357 Mag. $335.00
Price: 9mm, 380 .... $320.00
Price: 40 S&W $335.00
Price: 44 Spec. $398.00
Price: 44-40 Win. $398.00
Price: 45 Colt $385.00
Price: 30-30, 45 Win. Mag. $460.00
Price: 41, 44 Mags. $470.00
Price: 45-70, single shot. $387.00
Price: 45 Colt, 410, 2-1/2" $385.00
Price: 45 ACP, 10mm Auto $340.00

American Derringer Model 4
Similar to the Model 1 except has 4.1" barrel, overall length of 6", and weighs 16-1/2 oz.; chambered for 357 Mag., 357 Maximum, 45-70, 3" 410-bore shotshells or 45 Colt or 44 Mag. Made of stainless steel. Manual hammer block safety. Introduced 1985.
Price: 3" 410/45 Colt. $425.00
Price: 45-70 .... $560.00
Price: 44 Mag. with oversize grips $515.00
Price: Alaskan Survival model (45-70 upper barrel, 410 or 45 Colt lower). $475.00

American Derringer Model 6
Similar to the Model 1 except has 6" barrel chambered for 3" 410 shotshells or 22 WMR, 357 Mag., 45 ACP, 45 Colt; rosewood stocks; 8.2" o.a.l. and weighs 21 oz. Shoots either round for each barrel. Manual hammer block safety. Introduced 1986.
Price: 22 WMR $440.00
Price: 357 Mag. $440.00
Price: 45 Colt/410 .... $450.00
Price: 45 ACP $440.00

American Derringer Model 7 Ultra Lightweight
Similar to Model 1 except made of high strength aircraft aluminum. Weighs 7-1/2 oz., 4.82" o.a.l., rosewood stocks. Available in 22 LR, 22 WMR, 32 H&R Mag., 380 ACP, 38 Spec., 44 Spec. Introduced 1986.
Price: 22 LR, WMR. $325.00
Price: 38 Spec. $325.00

Price: 380 ACP $325.00
Price: 32 H&R Mag/32 S&W Long $325.00
Price: 44 Spec. $565.00

American Derringer Model 10 Lightweight
Similar to the Model 1 except frame is of aluminum, giving weight of 10 oz. Stainless barrels. Available in 38 Spec., 45 Colt or 45 ACP only. Matte gray finish. Introduced 1989.
Price: 45 Colt $385.00
Price: 45 ACP $330.00
Price: 38 Spec. $305.00

American Derringer Lady Derringer
Same as the Model 1 except has tuned action, is fitted with scrimshawed synthetic ivory grips; chambered for 32 H&R Mag. and 38 Spec.; 357 Mag., 45 Colt, 45/410. Deluxe Grade is highly polished; Deluxe Engraved is engraved in a pattern similar to that used on 1880s derringers. All come in a French fitted jewelry box. Introduced 1991.
Price: 32 H&R Mag. $375.00
Price: 357 Mag. $405.00
Price: 38 Spec. $360.00
Price: 45 Colt, 45/410 .... $435.00

American Derringer Texas Commemorative
A Model 1 Derringer with solid brass frame, stainless steel barrel and rosewood grips. Available in 38 Spec., 44-40 Win., or 45 Colt. Introduced 1987.
Price: 38 Spec. $365.00
Price: 44-40 .... $420.00
Price: Brass frame, 45 Colt $450.00

AMERICAN DERRINGER DA 38 MODEL
Caliber: 22 LR, 9mm Para., 38 Spec., 357 Mag., 40 S&W. **Barrel:** 3". **Weight:** 14.5 oz. **Length:** 4.8" overall. **Stocks:** Rosewood, walnut or other hardwoods. **Sights:** Fixed. **Features:** Double-action only; two-shots. Manual safety. Made of satin-finished stainless steel and aluminum. Introduced 1989. From American Derringer Corp.
Price: 22 LR $435.00
Price: 38 Spec. $460.00
Price: 9mm Para. $445.00
Price: 357 Mag. $450.00
Price: 40 S&W $475.00

ANSCHUTZ MODEL 64P SPORT/TARGET PISTOL
Caliber: 22 LR, 22 WMR, 5-shot magazine. **Barrel:** 10". **Weight:** 3 lbs, 8 oz. **Length:** 18-1/2" overall. **Stock:** Choate Rynite. **Sights:** None furnished; grooved for scope mounting. **Features:** Right-hand bolt; polished blue finish. Introduced 1998. Imported from Germany by AcuSport.
Price: 22 LR $455.95
Price: 22 WMR $479.95

BOND ARMS TEXAS DEFENDER DERRINGER
Caliber: 9mm Para, 38 Spec./357 Mag., 40 S&W, 44 Spec./44 Mag., 45 Colt/410 shotshell. **Barrel:** 3", 3-1/2". **Weight:** 21 oz. **Length:** 5" overall. **Stocks:** Laminated black ash or rosewood. **Sights:** Blade front, fixed rear.

HANDGUNS — MISCELLANEOUS

Davis Big Bore

Downsizer Single Shot

Davis Long-Bore

Gaucher GN1 Silhouette

IAR Model 1872 Derringer

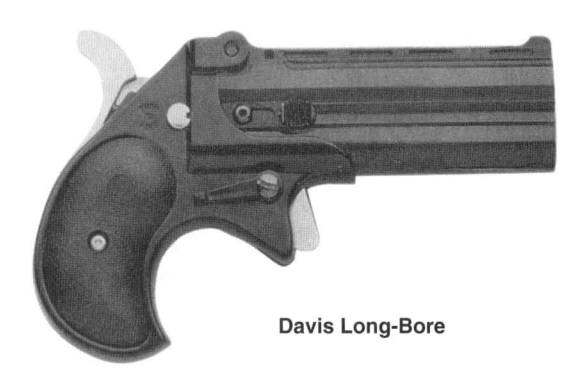

Features: Interchangeable barrels; retracting firing pins; rebounding firing pins; cross-bolt safety; removable trigger guard; automatic extractor for rimmed calibers. Stainless steel construction with blasted/polished and ground combination finish. Introduced 1997. Made in U.S. by Bond Arms, Inc.
Price: $349.00
Price: Century 2000 Defender (410-bore, 3-1/2" barrels). $369.00

BROWN CLASSIC SINGLE SHOT PISTOL
Caliber: 17 Ackley Hornet through 45-70 Govt. **Barrel:** 15" airgauged match grade. **Weight:** About 3 lbs., 7 oz. **Stocks:** Walnut; thumbrest target style. **Sights:** None furnished; drilled and tapped for scope mounting. **Features:** Falling block action gives rigid barrel-receiver mating; hand-fitted and headspaced. Introduced 1998. Made in U.S. by E.A. Brown Mfg.
Price: $499.00

DAVIS BIG BORE DERRINGERS
Caliber: 22 WMR, 38 Spec., 9mm Para. **Barrel:** 2.75". **Weight:** 11.5 oz. **Length:** 4.65" overall. **Stocks:** Textured black synthetic. **Sights:** Blade front, fixed notch rear. **Features:** Alloy frame, steel-lined barrels, steel breech block. Plunger-type safety with integral hammer block. Chrome or black Teflon finish. Introduced 1992. Made in U.S. by Davis Industries.
Price: $98.00
Price: 9mm Para. $104.00

DAVIS LONG-BORE DERRINGERS
Caliber: 22 WMR, 38 Spec., 9mm Para. **Barrel:** 3.5". **Weight:** 13 oz. **Length:** 5.65" overall. **Stocks:** Textured black synthetic. **Sights:** Fixed. **Features:** Chrome or black Teflon finish. Larger than Davis D-Series models. Introduced 1995. Made in U.S. by Davis Industries.
Price: $104.00
Price: 9mm Para. $110.00
Price: Big-Bore models (same calibers, 3/4" shorter barrels). $98.00

DAVIS D-SERIES DERRINGERS
Caliber: 22 LR, 22 WMR, 25 ACP, 32 ACP. **Barrel:** 2.4". **Weight:** 9.5 oz. **Length:** 4" overall. **Stocks:** Laminated wood or pearl. **Sights:** Blade front, fixed notch rear. **Features:** Choice of black Teflon or chrome finish; spur trigger. Introduced 1986. Made in U.S. by Davis Industries.
Price: $99.50

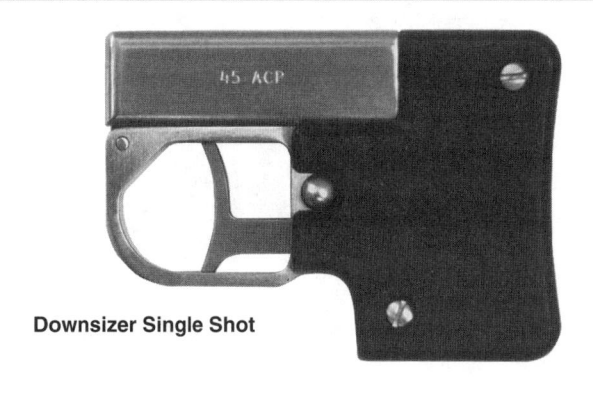

DOWNSIZER WSP SINGLE SHOT PISTOL
Caliber: 357 Magnum, 45 ACP. **Barrel:** 2.10". **Weight:** 11 oz. **Length:** 3.25" overall. **Stocks:** Black polymer. **Sights:** None. **Features:** Single shot, tip-up barrel. Double action only. Stainless steel construction. Measures .900" thick. Introduced 1997. From Downsizer Corp.
Price: $459.00

GAUCHER GN1 SILHOUETTE PISTOL
Caliber: 22 LR, single shot. **Barrel:** 10". **Weight:** 2.4 lbs. **Length:** 15.5" overall. **Stocks:** European hardwood. **Sights:** Blade front, open adjustable rear. **Features:** Bolt action, adjustable trigger. Introduced 1990. Imported from France by Mandall Shooting Supplies.
Price: About $525.00
Price: Model GP Silhouette $425.00

IAR MODEL 1872 DERRINGER
Caliber: 22 Short. **Barrel:** 2-3/8". **Weight:** 7 oz. **Length:** 5-1/8" overall. **Stocks:** Smooth walnut. **Sights:** Blade front, notch rear. **Features:** Gold or nickel frame with blue barrel. Reintroduced 1996 using original Colt designs and tooling for the Colt Model 4 Derringer. Made in U.S. by IAR, Inc.
Price: $99.00
Price: Single cased gun $125.00
Price: Double cased set $215.00

IAR MODEL 1888 DOUBLE DERRINGER
Caliber: 38 Special. **Barrel:** 2-3/4". **Weight:** 16 oz. **Length:** NA. **Stocks:** Smooth walnut. **Sights:** Blade front, notch rear. **Features:** All steel construction. Blue barrel, color case-hardened frame. Uses original designs and tooling for the Uberti New Maverick Derringer. Introduced 1999. Made in U.S. by IAR, Inc.
Price: $395.00

34TH EDITION, 2002 • 189

HANDGUNS — MISCELLANEOUS

IAR Model 1888 Derringer

Maximum Single Shot

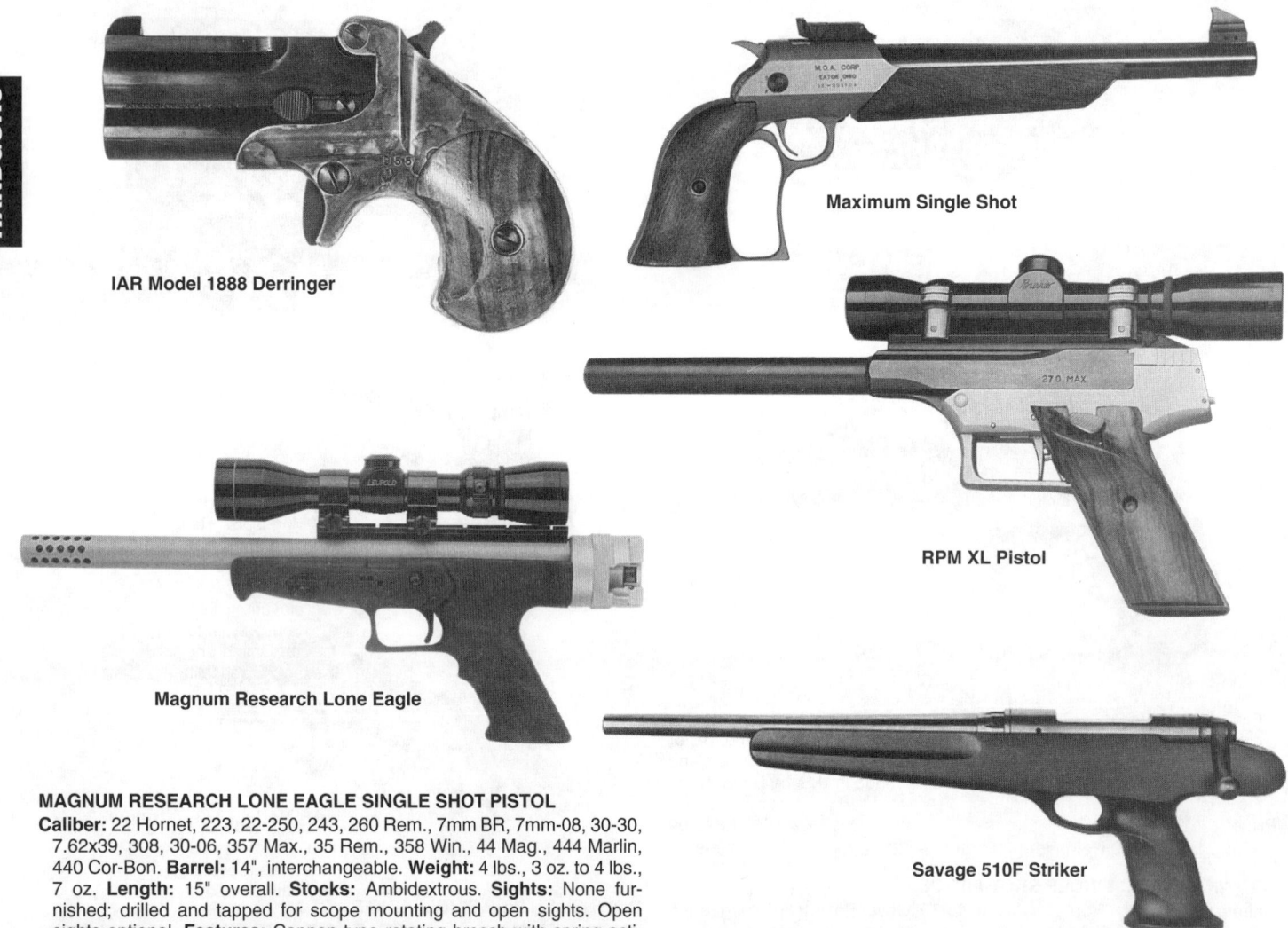

RPM XL Pistol

Magnum Research Lone Eagle

Savage 510F Striker

MAGNUM RESEARCH LONE EAGLE SINGLE SHOT PISTOL
Caliber: 22 Hornet, 223, 22-250, 243, 260 Rem., 7mm BR, 7mm-08, 30-30, 7.62x39, 308, 30-06, 357 Max., 35 Rem., 358 Win., 44 Mag., 444 Marlin, 440 Cor-Bon. **Barrel:** 14", interchangeable. **Weight:** 4 lbs., 3 oz. to 4 lbs., 7 oz. **Length:** 15" overall. **Stocks:** Ambidextrous. **Sights:** None furnished; drilled and tapped for scope mounting and open sights. Open sights optional. **Features:** Cannon-type rotating breech with spring-activated ejector. Ordnance steel with matte blue finish. Cross-bolt safety. External cocking lever on left side of gun. Muzzle brake optional. Introduced 1991. Available from Magnum Research, Inc.

Price: Complete pistol, black	$438.00
Price: Barreled action only, black	$319.00
Price: Complete pistol, chrome	$478.00
Price: Barreled action, chrome	$359.00
Price: Scope base	$14.00
Price: Adjustable open sights	$35.00

MAXIMUM SINGLE SHOT PISTOL
Caliber: 22 LR, 22 Hornet, 22 BR, 22 PPC, 223 Rem., 22-250, 6mm BR, 6mm PPC, 243, 250 Savage, 6.5mm-35M, 270 MAX, 270 Win., 7mm TCU, 7mm BR, 7mm-35, 7mm INT-R, 7mm-08, 7mm Rocket, 7mm Super-Mag., 30 Herrett, 30 Carbine, 30-30, 308 Win., 30x39, 32-20, 350 Rem. Mag., 357 Mag., 357 Maximum, 358 Win., 375 H&H, 44 Mag., 454 Casull. **Barrel:** 8-3/4", 10-1/2", 14". **Weight:** 61 oz. (10-1/2" bbl.); 78 oz. (14" bbl.). **Length:** 15", 18-1/2" overall (with 10-1/2" and 14" bbl., respectively). **Stocks:** Smooth walnut stocks and forend. Also available with 17" finger groove grip. **Sights:** Ramp front, fully adjustable open rear. **Features:** Falling block action; drilled and tapped for M.O.A. scope mounts; integral grip frame/receiver; adjustable trigger; Douglas barrel (interchangeable). Introduced 1983. Made in U.S. by M.O.A. Corp.

Price: Stainless receiver, blue barrel	$799.00
Price: Stainless receiver, stainless barrel	$883.00
Price: Extra blued barrel	$254.00
Price: Extra stainless barrel	$317.00
Price: Scope mount	$60.00

RPM XL SINGLE SHOT PISTOL
Caliber: 22 LR through 45-70. **Barrel:** 8", 10-3/4", 12", 14". **Weight:** About 60 oz. **Length:** NA. **Stocks:** Smooth Goncalo Alves with thumb and heel rests. **Sights:** Hooded front with interchangeable post, or Patridge; ISGW rear adjustable for windage and elevation. **Features:** Barrel drilled and tapped for scope mount. Visible cocking indicator. Spring-loaded barrel lock, positive hammer-block safety. Trigger adjustable for weight of pull and over-travel. Contact maker for complete price list. Made in U.S. by RPM.

Price: Hunter model (stainless frame, 5/16" underlug, latch lever and positive extractor)	$1,295.00
Price: Extra barrel, 8" through 10-3/4"	$387.50
Price: Extra barrel with positive extractor, add	$100.00
Price: Muzzle brake	$100.00

SAVAGE STRIKER BOLT-ACTION HUNTING HANDGUN
Caliber: 223, 22-250, 243, 206, 7mm-08, 308, 2-shot magazine. **Barrel:** 14". **Weight:** About 5 lbs. **Length:** 22-1/2" overall. **Stock:** Black composite ambidextrous mid-grip; grooved forend; "Dual Pillar" bedding. **Sights:** None furnished; drilled and tapped for scope mounting. **Features:** Short left-hand bolt with right-hand ejection; free-floated barrel; uses Savage Model 110 rifle scope rings/bases. Introduced 1998. Made in U.S. by Savage Arms, Inc.

Price: Model 510F (blued barrel and action)	$425.00
Price: Model 516FSS (stainless barrel and action)	$462.00
Price: Model 516FSAK (stainless, adjustable muzzle brake)	$512.00
Price: Super Striker	$512.00

GUNS ILLUSTRATED

HANDGUNS — MISCELLANEOUS

T/C Encore

T/C Stainless Contender

Weatherby Mark V CFP

Savage Sport Striker Bolt-Action Hunting Handgun
Similar to the Striker, but chambered in 22 LR and 22 WMR. Detachable, 10-shot magazine (5-shot magazine for 22 WMR). Overall length 19", weighs 4 lbs. Ambidextrous fiberglass/graphite composite rear grip. Drilled and tapped, scope mount installed. Introduced 2000. Made in U.S. by Savage Arms Inc.
Price: Model 501F (blue finish, 22LR) $201.00
Price: Model 502F (blue finish, 22 WMR). $221.00

THOMPSON/CENTER ENCORE PISTOL
Caliber: 22-250, 223, 260 Rem., 7mm-08, 243, 308, 270, 30-06, 44 Mag., 454 Casull, 444 Marlin single shot. **Barrel:** 12", 15", tapered round. **Weight:** NA. **Length:** 21" overall with 12" barrel. **Stocks:** American walnut with finger grooves, walnut forend. **Sights:** Blade on ramp front, adjustable rear, or none. **Features:** Interchangeable barrels; action opens by squeezing the trigger guard; drilled and tapped for scope mounting; blue finish. Announced 1996. Made in U.S. by Thompson/Center Arms.
Price: $554.06
Price: Extra 12" barrels. $240.68
Price: Extra 15" barrels. $248.14
Price: 45 Colt/410 barrel, 12" $263.24
Price: 45 Colt/410 barrel, 15" $280.39

Thompson/Center Stainless Encore Pistol
Similar to the blued Encore except made of stainless steel and available with 15" barrel in 223, 22-250 7mm-08, 308. Comes with black rubber grip and forend. Made in U.S. by Thompson/Center Arms.
Price: $620.99

Thompson/Center Stainless Super 14
Same as the standard Super 14 and Super 16 except they are made of stainless steel with blued sights. Both models have black Rynite forend and finger-groove, ambidextrous grip with a built-in rubber recoil cushion that has a sealed-in air pocket. Receiver has a different cougar etching. Available in 22 LR Match, .223 Rem., 30-30 Win., 35 Rem. (Super 14), 45 Colt/410. Introduced 1993.
Price: $578.40
Price: 45 Colt/410, 14" $613.94

Thompson/Center Contender Shooter's Package
Package contains a 14" barrel without iron sights (10" for the 22 LR Match); Weaver-style base and rings; 2.5x-7x Recoil Proof pistol scope; and a soft carrying case. Calibers 22 LR, 223, 7-30 Waters, 30-30. Frame and barrel are blued; grip and forend are black composite. Introduced 1998. Made in U.S. by Thompson/Center Arms.
Price $735.00

THOMPSON/CENTER CONTENDER
Caliber: 7mm TCU, 30-30 Win., 22 LR, 22 WMR, 22 Hornet, 223 Rem., 270 Rem., 7-30 Waters, 32-20 Win., 357 Mag., 357 Rem. Max., 44 Mag., 10mm Auto, 445 SuperMag., 45/410, single shot. **Barrel:** 10", bull barrel and vent. rib. **Weight:** 43 oz. (10" bbl.). **Length:** 13-1/4" (10" bbl.). **Stock:** T/C "Competitor Grip." Right or left hand. **Sights:** Under-cut blade ramp front, rear adjustable for windage and elevation. **Features:** Break-open action with automatic safety. Single-action only. Interchangeable bbls., both caliber (rim & centerfire), and length. Drilled and tapped for scope. Engraved frame. See T/C catalog for exact barrel/caliber availability.
Price: Blued (rimfire cals.) $509.03
Price: Blued (centerfire cals.) $509.03
Price: Extra bbls. $229.02
Price: 45/410, internal choke bbl. $235.11

Thompson/Center Stainless Contender
Same as the standard Contender except made of stainless steel with blued sights, black Rynite forend and ambidextrous finger-groove grip with a built-in rubber recoil cushion that has a sealed-in air pocket. Receiver has a different cougar etching. Available with 10" bull barrel in 22 LR, 22 LR Match, 22 Hornet, 223 Rem., 30-30 Win., 357 Mag., 44 Mag., 45 Colt/410. Introduced 1993.
Price: $566.59
Price: 45 Colt/410. . . . . $590.44
Price: With 22 LR match chamber $578.40

UBERTI ROLLING BLOCK TARGET PISTOL
Caliber: 22 LR, 22 WMR, 22 Hornet, 357 Mag., 45 Colt, single shot. **Barrel:** 9-7/8", half-round, half-octagon. **Weight:** 44 oz. **Length:** 14" overall. **Stock:** Walnut grip and forend. **Sights:** Blade front, fully adjustable rear. **Features:** Replica of the 1871 rolling block target pistol. Brass trigger guard, color case-hardened frame, blue barrel. Imported by Uberti U.S.A.
Price: $410.00

WEATHERBY MARK V CFP PISTOL
Caliber: 22-250, 243, 7mm-08, 308. **Barrel:** 15" fluted stainless. **Weight:** NA. **Length:** NA. **Stock:** Brown laminate with ambidextrous rear grip. **Sights:** None furnished; drilled and tapped for scope mounting. **Features:** Uses Mark V lightweight receiver of chrome-moly steel, matte blue finish. Introduced 1998. Made in U.S. From Weatherby.
Price: $1,049.00

WEATHERBY MARK V ACCUMARK CFP PISTOL
Caliber: 223, 22-250, 243, 7mm-08, 308; 3-shot magazine. **Barrel:** 15"; 1:12" twist (223). **Weight:** 5 lbs. **Length:** 26-1/2" overall. **Stock:** Kevlar-fiberglass composite. **Sights:** None; drilled and tapped for scope mounting. **Features:** Molded-in aluminum bedding plate; fluted stainless steel barrel; fully adjustable trigger. Introduced 2000. From Weatherby.
Price: . . . . NA

CENTERFIRE RIFLES — AUTOLOADERS

Both classic arms and recent designs in American-style repeaters for sport and field shooting.

Armalite M15A2

Armalite AR-10A4

Auto-Ordnance 1927 A-1 Thompson

Barrett Model 82A-1

ARMALITE M15A2 CARBINE
Caliber: 223, 7-shot magazine. **Barrel:** 16" heavy chrome lined; 1:9" twist. **Weight:** 7 lbs. **Length:** 35-11/16" overall. **Stock:** Green or black composition. **Sights:** Standard A2. **Features:** Upper and lower receivers have push-type pivot pin; hard coat anodized; A2-style forward assist; M16A2-type raised fence around magazine release button. Made in U.S. by ArmaLite, Inc.
Price: Green $930.00
Price: Black $945.00

ARMALITE AR-10A4 SPECIAL PURPOSE RIFLE
Caliber: 308 Win., 10-shot magazine. **Barrel:** 20" chrome-lined, 1:12" twist. **Weight:** 9.6 lbs. **Length:** 41" overall **Stock:** Green or black composition. **Sights:** Detachable handle, front sight, or scope mount available; comes with international style flattop receiver with Picatinny rail. **Features:** Proprietary recoil check. Forged upper receiver with case deflector. Receivers are hard-coat anodized. Introduced 1995. Made in U.S. by ArmaLite, Inc.
Price: Green $1,378.00
Price: Black $1,393.00

AUTO-ORDNANCE 1927 A-1 THOMPSON
Caliber: 45 ACP. **Barrel:** 16-1/2". **Weight:** 13 lbs. **Length:** About 41" overall (Deluxe). **Stock:** Walnut stock and vertical forend. **Sights:** Blade front, open rear adjustable for windage. **Features:** Recreation of Thompson Model 1927. Semi-auto only. Deluxe model has finned barrel, adjustable rear sight and compensator; Standard model has plain barrel and military sight. From Auto-Ordnance Corp.
Price: Deluxe $950.00
Price: 1927A1C Lightweight model (9-1/2 lbs.) $950.00

Auto-Ordnance Thompson M1
Similar to the 1927 A-1 except is in the M-1 configuration with side cocking knob, horizontal forend, smooth unfinned barrel, sling swivels on butt and forend. Matte black finish. Introduced 1985.
Price: $950.00

Auto-Ordnance 1927A1 Commando
Similar to the 1927A1 except has Parkerized finish, black-finish wood butt, pistol grip, horizontal forend. Comes with black nylon sling. Introduced 1998. Made in U.S. by Auto-Ordnance Corp.
Price: $950.00

BARRETT MODEL 82A-1 SEMI-AUTOMATIC RIFLE
Caliber: 50 BMG, 10-shot detachable box magazine. **Barrel:** 29". **Weight:** 28.5 lbs. **Length:** 57" overall. **Stock:** Composition with energy-absorbing recoil pad. **Sights:** Scope optional. **Features:** Semi-automatic, recoil operated with recoiling barrel. Three-lug locking bolt; muzzle brake. Adjustable bipod. Introduced 1985. Made in U.S. by Barrett Firearms.
Price: From $7,200.00

CENTERFIRE RIFLES — AUTOLOADERS

Browning Mark II Safari

Bushmaster M17S

Bushmaster XM15 E2S

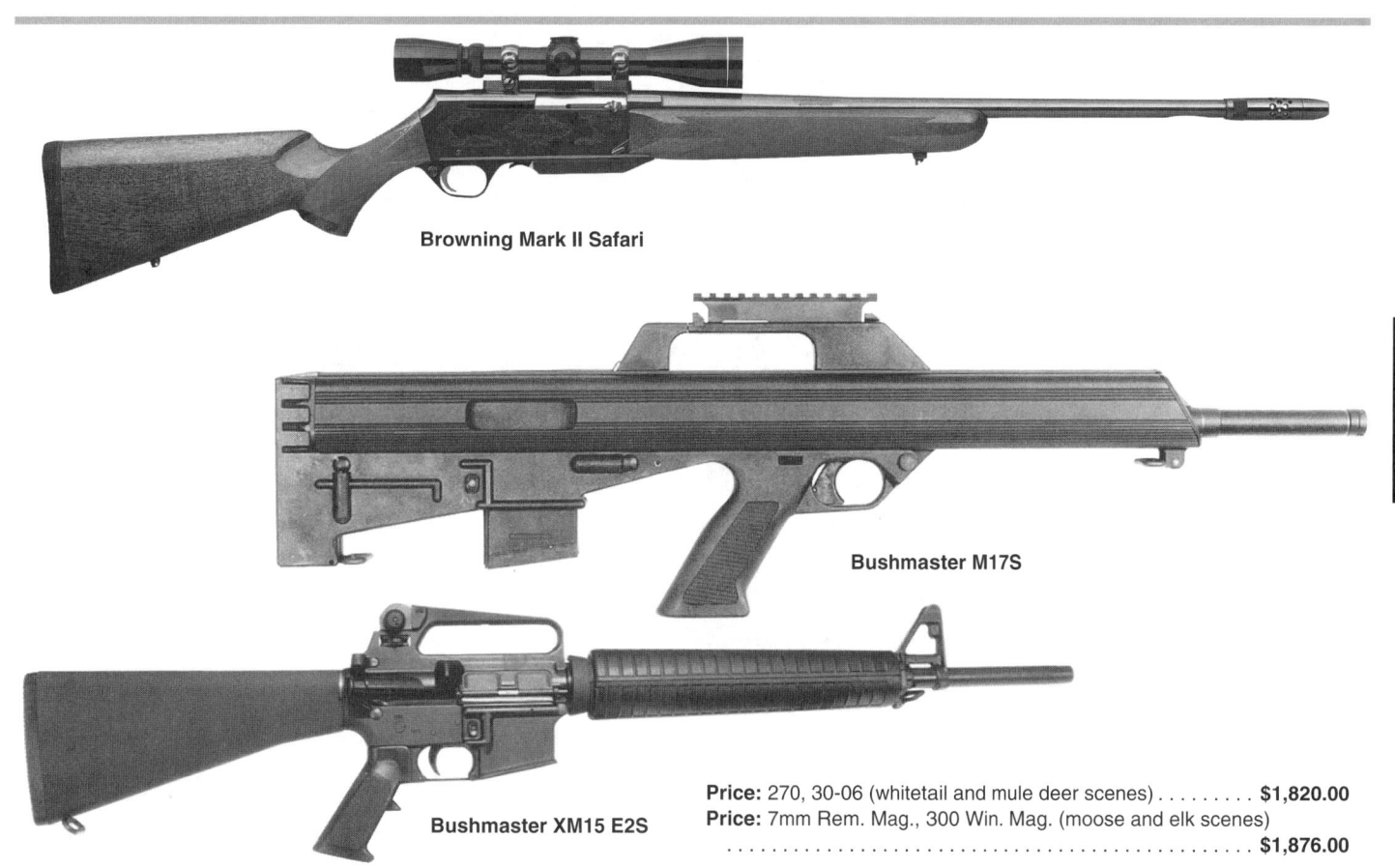

BROWNING BAR MARK II SAFARI SEMI-AUTO RIFLE
Caliber: 243, 25-06, 270, 30-06, 308. **Barrel:** 22" round tapered. **Weight:** 7-3/8 lbs. **Length:** 43" overall. **Stock:** French walnut pistol grip stock and forend, hand checkered. **Sights:** Gold bead on hooded ramp front, click adjustable rear, or no sights. **Features:** Has new bolt release lever; removable trigger assembly with larger trigger guard; redesigned gas and buffer systems. Detachable 4-round box magazine. Scroll-engraved receiver is tapped for scope mounting. BOSS barrel vibration modulator and muzzle brake system available only on models without sights. Mark II Safari introduced 1993. Imported from Belgium by Browning.
Price: Safari, with sights $833.00
Price: Safari, no sights $815.00
Price: Safari, 270 and 30-06, no sights, BOSS $891.00

Browning BAR MARK II Lightweight Semi-Auto
Similar to the Mark II Safari except has lighter alloy receiver and 20" barrel. Available in 243, 308, 270, 30-06, 7mm Rem. Mag., 300 Win. Mag., 338 Win. Mag. Weighs 7 lbs., 2 oz.; overall length 41". Has dovetailed, gold bead front sight on hooded ramp, open rear click adjustable for windage and elevation. Introduced 1997. Imported from Belgium by Browning.
Price: 243, 308, 270, 30-06 .... $833.00
Price: 7mm Rem. Mag., 300 Win. Mag., 338 Win. Mag $909.00

Browning BAR Mark II Safari Rifle in magnum calibers
Same as the standard caliber model, except weighs 8-3/8 lbs., 45" overall, 24" bbl., 3-round mag. Cals. 7mm Mag., 300 Win. Mag., 338 Win. Mag. BOSS barrel vibration modulator and muzzle brake system available only on models without sights. Introduced 1993.
Price: Safari, with sights $909.00
Price: Safari, no sights $890.00
Price: Safari, no sights, BOSS $967.00

Browning BAR High-Grade Auto Rifles
Similar to BAR Mark II Safari model except has grayed receiver with big-game scenes framed in gold with select walnut stock and forearm. Furnished with no sights. Introduced 2001.

Price: 270, 30-06 (whitetail and mule deer scenes) $1,820.00
Price: 7mm Rem. Mag., 300 Win. Mag. (moose and elk scenes)
.... $1,876.00

BROWNING BAR STALKER AUTO RIFLES
Caliber: 243, 308, 270, 30-06, 7mm Rem. Mag., 300 Win. Mag., 338 Win. Mag. **Barrel:** 20", 22" and 24". **Weight:** 6 lbs., 12 oz. (243) to 8 lbs., 2 oz. (magnum cals.) **Length:** 41" to 45" overall. **Stock:** Black composite stock and forearm. **Sights:** Hooded front and adjustable rear or none. **Features:** Optional BOSS (no sights); gas-operated action with seven-lug rotary bolt; dual action bars; 3- or 4-shot magazine (depending on caliber). Introduced 2001. Imported by Browning.
Price: BAR Stalker, open sights (243, 308, 270, 30-06)..... $809.00
Price: BAR Stalker, open sights (7mm, 300 Win. Mag.,
338 Win. Mag.) $883.00
Price: BAR Stalker, BOSS (7mm, 300 Win. Mag., 338 Win. Mag.) $941.00

BUSHMASTER M17S BULLPUP RIFLE
Caliber: 223, 10-shot magazine. **Barrel:** 21.5", chrome lined;1:9" twist. **Weight:** 8.2 lbs. **Length:** 30" overall. **Stock:** Fiberglass-filled nylon. **Sights:** Designed for optics—carrying handle incorporates scope mount rail for Weaver-type rings; also includes 25-meter open iron sights. **Features:** Gas-operated, short-stroke piston system; ambidextrous magazine release. Introduced 1993. Made in U.S. by Bushmaster Firearms, Inc./Quality Parts Co.
Price: $625.00

BUSHMASTER SHORTY XM15 E2S CARBINE
Caliber: 223,10-shot magazine. **Barrel:** 16", heavy; 1:9" twist. **Weight:** 7.2 lbs. **Length:** 34.75" overall. **Stock:** A2 type; fixed black composition. **Sights:** Fully adjustable M16A2 sight system. **Features:** Patterned after Colt M-16A2. Chrome-lined barrel with manganese phosphate finish. "Shorty" handguards. Has forged aluminum receivers with push-pin. Made in U.S. by Bushmaster Firearms Inc.
Price: $780.00

Bushmaster XM15 E2S Dissipator Carbine
Similar to the XM15 E2S Shorty carbine except has full-length "Dissipator" handguards. Weighs 7.6 lbs.; 34.75" overall; forged aluminum receivers with push-pin style takedown. Made in U.S. by Bushmaster Firearms, Inc.
Price $790.00

CENTERFIRE RIFLES — AUTOLOADERS

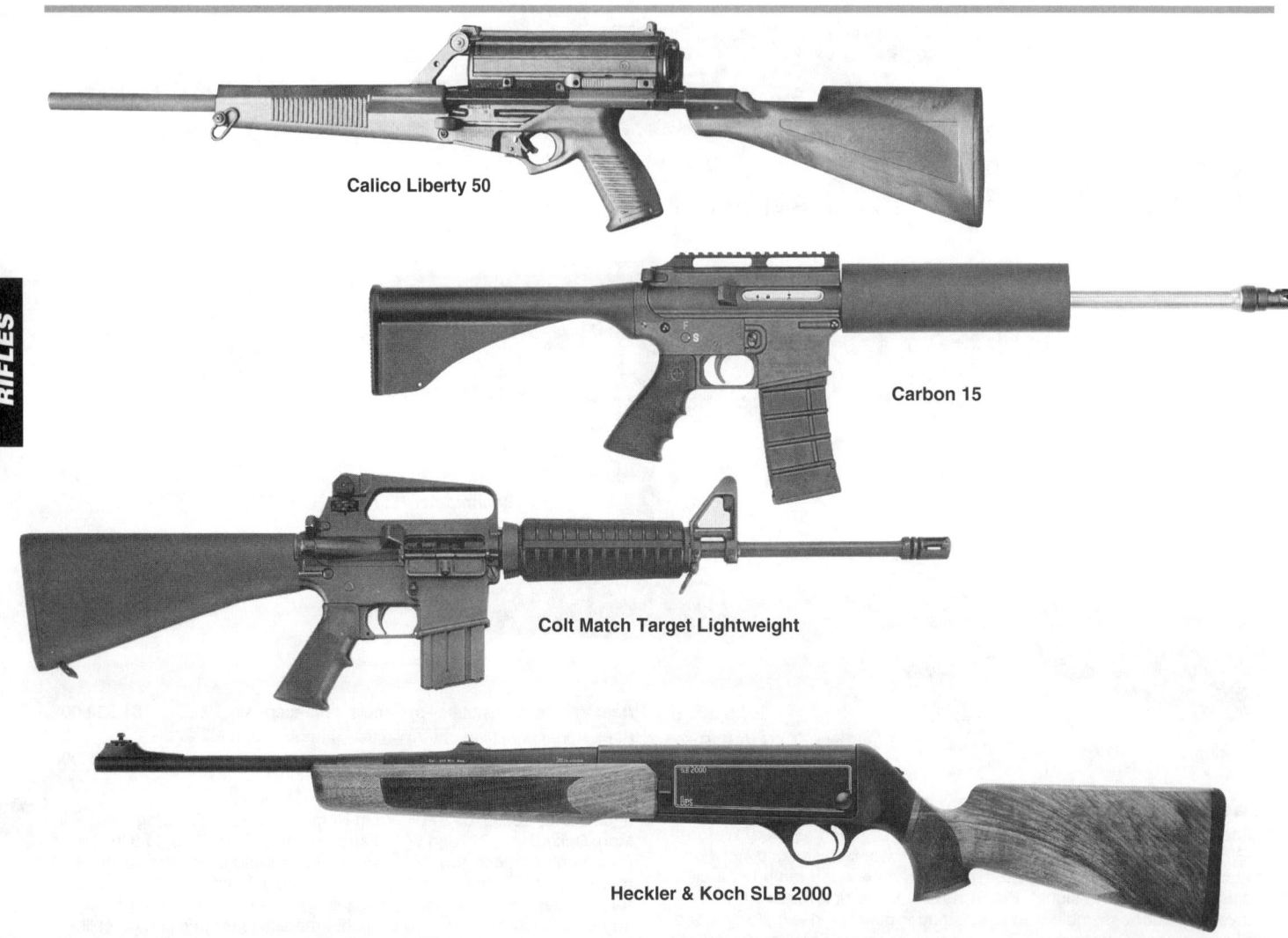

Calico Liberty 50

Carbon 15

Colt Match Target Lightweight

Heckler & Koch SLB 2000

Bushmaster XM15 E25 AK Shorty Carbine
Similar to the XM15 E2S Shorty except has 14.5" barrel with an AK muzzle brake permanently attached giving 16" barrel length. Weighs 7.3 lbs. Introduced 1999. Made in U.S. by Bushmaster Firearms, Inc.
Price: $800.00

CALICO LIBERTY 50, 100 CARBINES
Caliber: 9mm Para. **Barrel:** 16.1". **Weight:** 7 lbs. **Length:** 34.5" overall. **Stock:** Glass-filled, impact resistant polymer. **Sights:** Adjustable front post, fixed notch and aperture flip rear. **Features:** Helical feed magazine; ambidextrous, rotating sear/striker block safety; static cocking handle; retarded blowback action; aluminum alloy receiver. Introduced 1995. Made in U.S. by Calico.
Price: Liberty 50 .... $860.00
Price: Liberty 100 .... $925.00

CARBON 15 (TYPE 97) AUTO RIFLE
Caliber: 223. **Barrel:** 16". **Weight:** 3.9 lbs. **Length:** 35" overall. **Stock:** Carbon fiber butt and forend, rubberized pistol grip. **Sights:** None furnished; optics base. **Features:** Carbon fiber upper and lower receivers; stainless steel match-grade barrel; hard-chromed bolt and carrier; quick-detachable compensator. Made in U.S. by Professional Ordnance Inc.
Price: .... $1,120.00 to $1,285.00
Price: Type 20 (light-profile stainless barrel, compensator optional) $1,550.00

COLT MATCH TARGET RIFLE
Caliber: 223 Rem., 5-shot magazine. **Barrel:** 16.1" or 20". **Weight:** 7.1 to 8-1/2 lbs. **Length:** 34-1/2" to 39" overall. **Stock:** Composition stock, grip, forend. **Sights:** Post front, rear adjustable for windage and elevation. **Features:** 5-round detachable box magazine, flash suppressor, sling swivels. Forward bolt assist included. Introduced 1991. Made in U.S. by Colt's Manufacturing Co. Inc.
Price: Colt Light Rifle $779.00
Price: Match Target HBAR, from $1,194.00

DPMS PANTHER ARMS A-15 RIFLES
Caliber: 223 Rem., 7.62x39. **Barrel:** 16" to 24". **Weight:** 7-3/4 to 11-3/4 lbs. **Length:** 34-1/2 to 42-1/4" overall. **Stock:** Black Zytel® composite. **Sights:** Square front post, adjustable A2 rear. **Features:** Steel or stainless steel heavy or bull barrel; hard-coat anodized receiver; aluminum free-float tube handguard; many options. From DPMS Panther Arms.
Price: Panther Bull A-15 (20" stainless bull barrel) $915.00
Price: Panther Bull Twenty-Four (24" stainless bull barrel) $945.00
Price: Bulldog (20" stainless fluted barrel, flat top receiver) $1,219.00
Price: Panther Bull Sweet Sixteen (16" stainless bull barrel) $885.00
Price: DCM Panther (20" stainless heavy bbl., n.m. sights) $1,099.00
Price: Panther 7.62x39 (20" steel heavy barrel) $849.00

HECKLER & KOCH SLB 2000 RIFLE
Caliber: 30-06; 2-, 5- and 10-shot magazines. **Barrel:** 19.7". **Weight:** 8 lb. **Length:** 41.3". **Stock:** Oil-finished, checkered walnut. **Sights:** Ramp front, patridge rear. **Features:** Short-stroke, piston-actuated gas operation; modular steel and polymer construction; free-floating barrel; pistol grip angled for natural feel; interchangeable barrels in other calibers (available soon). Introduced 2001. From H&K.
Price: .... NA

194 • GUNS ILLUSTRATED

CENTERFIRE RIFLES — AUTOLOADERS

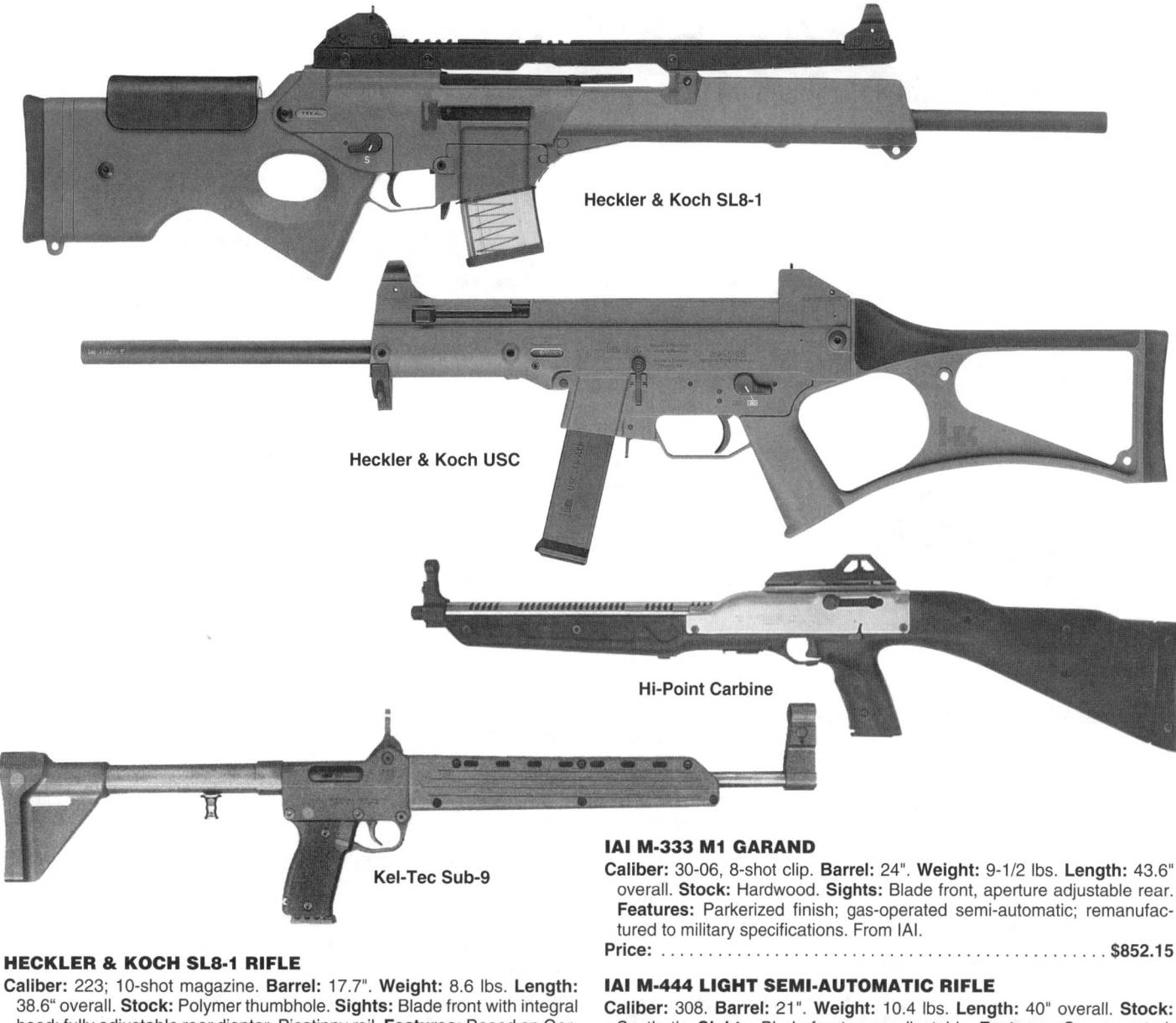

Heckler & Koch SL8-1

Heckler & Koch USC

Hi-Point Carbine

Kel-Tec Sub-9

HECKLER & KOCH SL8-1 RIFLE
Caliber: 223; 10-shot magazine. **Barrel:** 17.7". **Weight:** 8.6 lbs. **Length:** 38.6" overall. **Stock:** Polymer thumbhole. **Sights:** Blade front with integral hood; fully adjustable rear diopter. Picatinny rail. **Features:** Based on German military G36 rifle. Uses short-stroke piston-actuated gas operation; almost entirely constructed of carbon fiber-reinforced polymer. Free-floating heavy target barrel. Introduced 2000. From H&K.
Price: $1,599.00

HECKLER & KOCH USC CARBINE
Caliber: 45 ACP, 10-shot magazine. **Barrel:** 16". **Weight:** 8.6 lb. **Length:** 35.4" overall. **Stock:** Skeletonized polymer thumbhole. **Sights:** Blade front with integral hood, fully adjustable diopter. **Features:** Based on German UMP submachine gun. Blowback operation; almost entirely constructed of carbon fiber-reinforced polymer. Free-floating heavy target barrel. Introduced 2000. From H&K.
Price: $1,199.00

HI-POINT 9MM CARBINE
Caliber: 9mm Para., 40 S&W, 10-shot magazine. **Barrel:** 16-1/2" (17-1/2" for 40 S&W). **Weight:** 4-1/2 lbs. **Length:** 31-1/2" overall. **Stock:** Black polymer. **Sights:** Protected post front, aperture rear. Integral scope mount. **Features:** Grip-mounted magazine release. Black or chrome finish. Sling swivels. Introduced 1996. Made in U.S. by MKS Supply, Inc.
Price: Black or chrome, 9mm $199.00
Price: 40 S&W $225.00

IAI M-333 M1 GARAND
Caliber: 30-06, 8-shot clip. **Barrel:** 24". **Weight:** 9-1/2 lbs. **Length:** 43.6" overall. **Stock:** Hardwood. **Sights:** Blade front, aperture adjustable rear. **Features:** Parkerized finish; gas-operated semi-automatic; remanufactured to military specifications. From IAI.
Price: $852.15

IAI M-444 LIGHT SEMI-AUTOMATIC RIFLE
Caliber: 308. **Barrel:** 21". **Weight:** 10.4 lbs. **Length:** 40" overall. **Stock:** Synthetic. **Sights:** Blade front, rear adjustable. **Features:** Gas-operated; receiver machined from forged steel; muzzle brake; pistol grip. Imported from Imbel of Brazil by IAI.
Price: $896.95

IAI M-888 M1 CARBINE SEMI-AUTOMATIC RIFLE
Caliber: 30 Carbine. **Barrel:** 18". **Weight:** 5-1/2 lbs. **Length:** 35" overall. **Stock:** Walnut or birch. **Sights:** Blade front, adjustable rear. **Features:** Gas-operated; parkerized finish; manufactured to military specifications. From IAI.
Price: (birch stock, metal handguard) $541.45
Price: (walnut stock, metal handguard) $572.95
.... ($588.65 for wooden handguard)

KEL-TEC SUB-9 AUTO RIFLE
Caliber: 9mm Para or 40 S&W. **Barrel:** 16.1". **Weight:** 4.6 lbs. **Length:** 30" overall (extended), 15.9" (closed). **Stock:** Metal tube; grooved rubber butt pad. **Sights:** Hooded post front, flip-up rear. Interchangeable grip assemblies allow use of most double-column high capacity pistol magazines. **Features:** Barrel folds back over the butt for transport and storage. Introduced 1997. Made in U.S. by Kel-Tec CNC Industries, Inc.
Price: 9mm $700.00
Price: 40 S&W $725.00

34TH EDITION, 2002 • 195

CENTERFIRE RIFLES — AUTOLOADERS

Remington Model 7400

Ruger Deerfield 99/44 Carbine

Ruger PC4 Carbine

LES BAER CUSTOM ULTIMATE AR 223 RIFLES
Caliber: 223. **Barrel:** 18", 20", 22", 24". **Weight:** 7-3/4 to 9-3/4 lb. **Length:** NA. **Stock:** Black synthetic. **Sights:** None furnished; Picatinny-style flat top rail for scope mounting. **Features:** Forged receiver; Ultra single-stage trigger (Jewell two-stage trigger optional); titanium firing pin; Versa-Pod bipod; chromed National Match carrier; stainless steel, hand-lapped and cryo-treated barrel; guaranteed to shoot 1/2 or 3/4 MOA, depending on model. Made in U.S. by Les Bear Custom Inc.
Price: Super Varmint Model $1,989.00
Price: M4 Flattop Model $2,195.00
Price: IPSC Action Model $2,195.00

LR 300 SR LIGHT SPORT RIFLE
Caliber: 223. **Barrel:** 16-1/4"; 1:9" twist. **Weight:** 7.2 lbs. **Length:** 36" overall (extended stock), 26-1/4" (stock folded). **Stock:** Folding, tubular steel, with thumbhold-type grip. **Sights:** Trijicon post front, Trijicon rear. **Features:** Uses AR-15 type upper and lower receivers; flattop receiver with weaver base. Accepts all AR-15/M-16 magazines. Introduced 1996. Made in U.S. from Z-M Weapons.
Price: $2,550.00

OLYMPIC ARMS CAR-97 RIFLES
Caliber: 223, 7-shot; 9mm Para., 45 ACP, 40 S&W, 10mm, 10-shot. **Barrel:** 16". **Weight:** 7 lbs. **Length:** 34.75" overall. **Stock:** A2 stowaway grip, telescoping-look butt. **Sights:** Post front, fully adjustable aperture rear. **Features:** Based on AR-15 rifle. Post-ban version of the CAR-15. Made in U.S. by Olympic Arms, Inc.
Price: 223 . . . . $780.00
Price: 9mm Para., 45 ACP, 40 S&W, 10mm $840.00
Price: PCR Eliminator (223, full-length handguards) $803.00

OLYMPIC ARMS PCR-4 RIFLE
Caliber: 223, 10-shot magazine. **Barrel:** 20". **Weight:** 8 lbs., 5 oz. **Length:** 38.25" overall. **Stock:** A2 stowaway grip, trapdoor buttstock. **Sights:** Post front, A1 rear adjustable for windage. **Features:** Based on the AR-15 rifle. Barrel is button rifled with 1:9" twist. No bayonet lug. Introduced 1994. Made in U.S. by Olympic Arms, Inc.
Price: $792.00

OLYMPIC ARMS PCR-6 RIFLE
Caliber: 7.62x39mm (PCR-6), 10-shot magazine. **Barrel:** 16". **Weight:** 7 lbs. **Length:** 34" overall. **Stock:** A2 stowaway grip, trapdoor buttstock. **Sights:** Post front, A1 rear adjustable for windage. **Features:** Based on the CAR-15. No bayonet lug. Button-cut rifling. Introduced 1994. Made in U.S. by Olympic Arms, Inc.
Price: $845.00

REMINGTON MODEL 7400 AUTO RIFLE
Caliber: 243 Win., 270 Win., 280 Rem., 308 Win., 30-06, 4-shot magazine. **Barrel:** 22" round tapered. **Weight:** 7-1/2 lbs. **Length:** 42-5/8" overall. **Stock:** Walnut, deluxe cut checkered pistol grip and forend. Satin or high-gloss finish. **Sights:** Gold bead front sight on ramp; step rear sight with windage adjustable. **Features:** Redesigned and improved version of the Model 742. Positive cross-bolt safety. Receiver tapped for scope mount. Introduced 1981.
Price: About $612.00
Price: Carbine (18-1/2" bbl., 30-06 only) $612.00
Price: With black synthetic stock, matte black metal, rifle or carbine $509.00

ROCK RIVER ARMS STANDARD A2 RIFLE
Caliber: 45 ACP. **Barrel:** NA. **Weight:** 8.2 lbs. **Length:** NA. **Stock:** Thermoplastic. **Sights:** Standard AR-15 style sights. **Features:** Two-stage, national match trigger; optional muzzle brake. Made in U.S. From River Rock Arms.
Price: $925.00

RUGER DEERFIELD 99/44 CARBINE
Caliber: 44 Mag., 4-shot rotary magazine. **Barrel:** 18-1/2". **Weight:** 6-1/4 lbs. **Length:** 36-7/8" overall. **Stock:** Hardwood. **Sights:** Gold bead front, folding adjustable aperture rear. **Features:** Semi-automatic action; dual front-locking lugs lock directly into receiver; integral scope mount; push-button safety; includes 1" rings and gun lock. Introduced 2000. Made in U.S. by Sturm, Ruger & Co.
Price: $649.00

RUGER PC4, PC9 CARBINES
Caliber: 9mm Para., 40 cal., 10-shot magazine. **Barrel:** 16.25". **Weight:** 6 lbs., 4 oz. **Length:** 34.75" overall. **Stock:** Black DuPont (Zytel) with checkered grip and forend. **Sights:** Blade front, open adjustable rear; integral Ruger scope mounts. **Features:** Delayed blowback action; manual push-button cross bolt safety and internal firing pin block safety automatic slide lock. Introduced 1997. Made in U.S. by Sturm, Ruger & Co.
Price: PC9, PC4, (9mm, 40 cal.) $575.00

CENTERFIRE RIFLES — AUTOLOADERS

Ruger Mini 14/5R

Springfield M1A

Springfield National Match M1A

Springfield Super Match with Camo M1A

RUGER MINI-14/5 AUTOLOADING RIFLE
Caliber: 223 Rem., 5-shot detachable box magazine. **Barrel:** 18-1/2". Rifling twist 1:9". **Weight:** 6.4 lbs. **Length:** 37-1/4" overall. **Stock:** American hardwood, steel reinforced. **Sights:** Ramp front, fully adjustable rear. **Features:** Fixed piston gas-operated, positive primary extraction. New buffer system, redesigned ejector system. Ruger S100RH scope rings included.
Price: Mini-14/5R, Ranch Rifle, blued, scope rings $649.00
Price: K-Mini-14/5R, Ranch Rifle, stainless, scope rings $710.00
Price: Mini-14/5, blued, no scope rings $606.00
Price: K-Mini-14/5, stainless, no scope rings $664.00
Price: K-Mini-14/5P, stainless, synthetic stock............... $664.00
Price: K-Mini-14/5RP, Ranch Rifle, stainless, synthetic stock $710.00

Ruger Mini Thirty Rifle
Similar to the Mini-14 Ranch Rifle except modified to chamber the 7.62x39 Russian service round. Weight is about 6-7/8 lbs. Has 6-groove barrel with 1:10" twist, Ruger Integral Scope Mount bases and folding peep rear sight. Detachable 5-shot staggered box magazine. Blued finish. Introduced 1987.
Price: Blue, scope rings $649.00
Price: Stainless, scope rings $710.00

SPRINGFIELD, INC. M1A RIFLE
Caliber: 7.62mm NATO (308), 5- or 10-shot box magazine. **Barrel:** 25-1/16" with flash suppressor, 22" without suppressor. **Weight:** 8-3/4 lbs. **Length:** 44-1/4" overall. **Stock:** American walnut with walnut-colored heat-resistant fiberglass handguard. Matching walnut handguard available. Also available with fiberglass stock. **Sights:** Military, square blade front, full click-adjustable aperture rear. **Features:** Commercial equivalent of the U.S. M-14 service rifle with no provision for automatic firing. From Springfield, Inc.
Price: Standard M1A, black fiberglass stock $1,569.00
Price: Standard M1A, black fiberglass stock, stainless $1,629.00
Price: National Match, about $1,995.00
Price: Super Match (heavy premium barrel), about $2,449.00
Price: M21 Tactical Rifle (adj. cheekpiece), about........... $2,975.00

STONER SR-15 M-5 RIFLE
Caliber: 223. **Barrel:** 20". **Weight:** 7.6 lbs. **Length:** 38" overall. **Stock:** Black synthetic. **Sights:** Post front, fully adjustable rear (300-meter sight). **Features:** Modular weapon system; two-stage trigger. Black finish. Introduced 1998. Made in U.S. by Knight's Mfg.
Price: $1,595.00
Price: M-4 Carbine (16" barrel, 6.8 lbs) $1,495.00

STONER SR-25 CARBINE
Caliber: 7.62 NATO, 10-shot steel magazine. **Barrel:** 16" free-floating **Weight:** 7-3/4 lbs. **Length:** 35.75" overall. **Stock:** Black synthetic. **Sights:** Integral Weaver-style rail. Scope rings, iron sights optional. **Features:** Shortened, non-slip handguard; removable carrying handle. Matte black finish. Introduced 1995. Made in U.S. by Knight's Mfg. Co.
Price: $2,995.00

CENTERFIRE RIFLES — LEVER AND SLIDE

Both classic arms and recent designs in American-style repeaters for sport and field shooting.

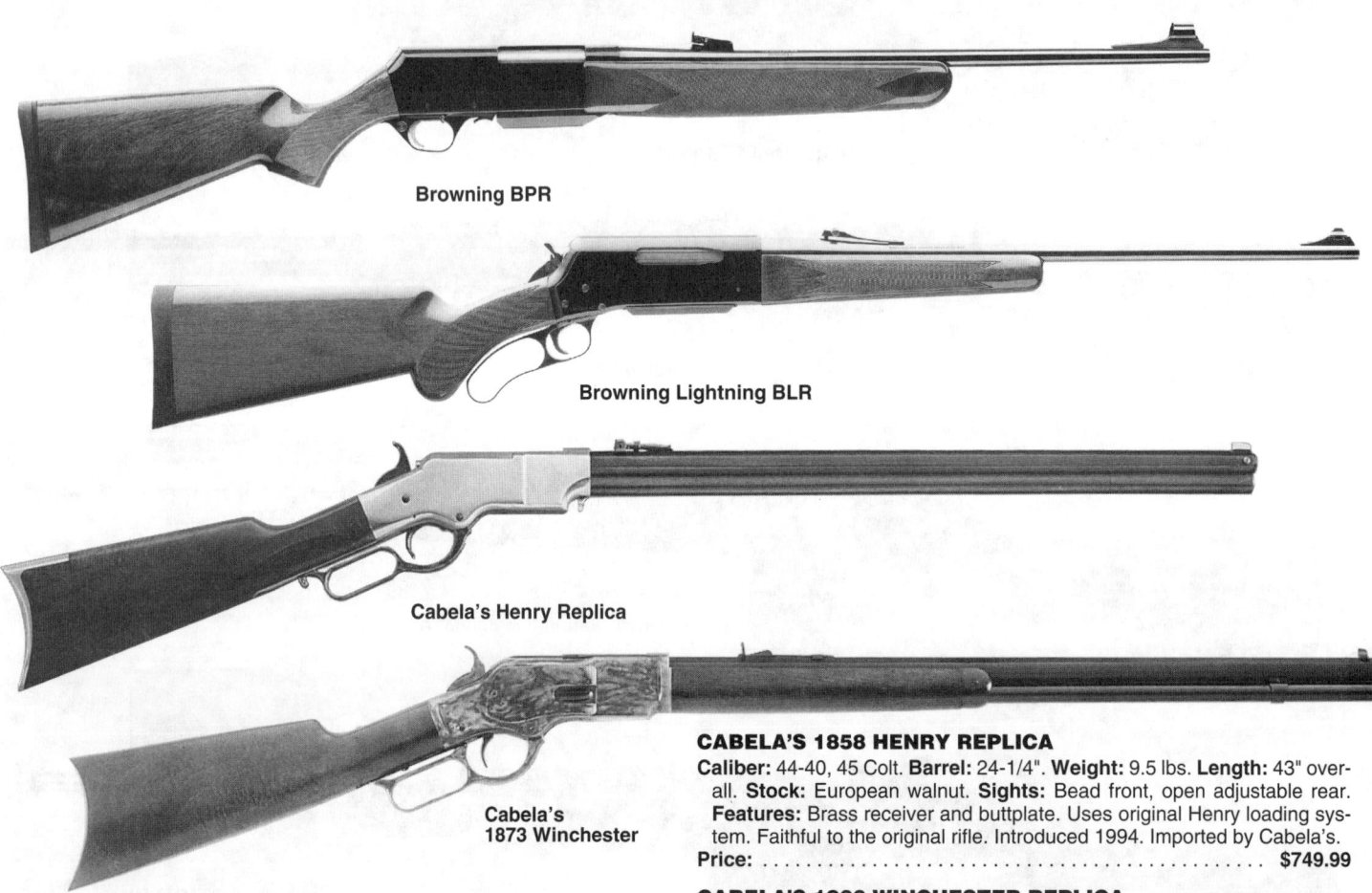

Browning BPR

Browning Lightning BLR

Cabela's Henry Replica

Cabela's 1873 Winchester

BROWNING BPR PUMP RIFLE
Caliber: 243, 308 (short action); 270, 30-06, 7mm Rem. Mag., 300 Win. Mag., 4-shot magazine (3 for magnums). **Barrel:** 22"; 24" for magnum calibers. **Weight:** 7 lbs., 3 oz. **Length:** 43" overall (22" barrel). **Stock:** Select walnut with full pistol grip, high gloss finish. **Sights:** Gold bead on hooded ramp front, open click adjustable rear. **Features:** Slide-action mechanism cams forend down away from the barrel. Seven-lug rotary bolt; cross-bolt safety behind trigger; removable magazine; alloy receiver. Introduced 1997. Imported from Belgium by Browning.
Price: Standard calibers $718.00
Price: Magnum calibers $772.00

BROWNING LIGHTNING BLR LEVER-ACTION RIFLE
Caliber: 22-250, 243, 7mm-08, 308 Win., 4-shot detachable magazine. **Barrel:** 20" round tapered. **Weight:** 6 lbs., 8 oz. **Length:** 39-1/2" overall. **Stock:** Walnut. Checkered grip and forend, high-gloss finish. **Sights:** Gold bead on ramp front; low profile square notch adjustable rear. **Features:** Wide, grooved trigger; half-cock hammer safety; fold-down hammer. Receiver tapped for scope mount. Recoil pad installed. Introduced 1996. Imported from Japan by Browning.
Price: $649.00

Browning Lightning BLR Long Action
Similar to the standard Lightning BLR except has long action to accept 30-06, 270, 7mm Rem. Mag. and 300 Win. Mag. Barrel lengths are 22" for 30-06 and 270, 24" for 7mm Rem. Mag. and 300 Win. Mag. Has six-lug rotary bolt; bolt and receiver are full-length fluted. Fold-down hammer at half-cock. Weighs about 7 lbs., overall length 42-7/8" (22" barrel). Introduced 1996.
Price: $686.00

CABELA'S 1858 HENRY REPLICA
Caliber: 44-40, 45 Colt. **Barrel:** 24-1/4". **Weight:** 9.5 lbs. **Length:** 43" overall. **Stock:** European walnut. **Sights:** Bead front, open adjustable rear. **Features:** Brass receiver and buttplate. Uses original Henry loading system. Faithful to the original rifle. Introduced 1994. Imported by Cabela's.
Price: $749.99

CABELA'S 1866 WINCHESTER REPLICA
Caliber: 44-40, 45 Colt. **Barrel:** 24-1/4". **Weight:** 9 lbs. **Length:** 43" overall. **Stock:** European walnut. **Sights:** Bead front, open adjustable rear. **Features:** Solid brass receiver, buttplate, forend cap. Octagonal barrel. Faithful to the original Winchester '66 rifle. Introduced 1994. Imported by Cabela's.
Price: $619.99

CABELA'S 1873 WINCHESTER REPLICA
Caliber: 44-40, 45 Colt. **Barrel:** 24-1/4", 30". **Weight:** 8.5 lbs. **Length:** 43-1/4" overall. **Stock:** European walnut. **Sights:** Bead front, open adjustable rear; globe front, tang rear. **Features:** Color case-hardened steel receiver. Faithful to the original Model 1873 rifle. Introduced 1994. Imported by Cabela's.
Price: Sporting model, 30" barrel, 44-40, 45 Colt. $749.99
Price: Sporting model, 24" or 25" barrel. $729.99

CIMARRON 1860 HENRY REPLICA
Caliber: 44 WCF, 13-shot magazine. **Barrel:** 24-1/4" (rifle), 22" (carbine). **Weight:** 9-1/2 lbs. **Length:** 43" overall (rifle). **Stock:** European walnut. **Sights:** Bead front, open adjustable rear. **Features:** Brass receiver and buttplate. Uses original Henry loading system. Faithful to the original rifle. Introduced 1991. Imported by Cimarron F.A. Co.
Price: $1,029.00

CIMARRON 1866 WINCHESTER REPLICAS
Caliber: 22 LR, 22 WMR, 38 Spec., 44 WCF. **Barrel:** 24-1/4" (rifle), 19" (carbine). **Weight:** 9 lbs. **Length:** 43" overall (rifle). **Stock:** European walnut. **Sights:** Bead front, open adjustable rear. **Features:** Solid brass receiver, buttplate, forend cap. Octagonal barrel. Faithful to the original Winchester '66 rifle. Introduced 1991. Imported by Cimarron F.A. Co.
Price: Rifle $839.00
Price: Carbine... $829.00

CENTERFIRE RIFLES — LEVER AND SLIDE

Cimarron 1866 Winchester Replica

Cimarron Long Range 30"

Dixie 1873

IAR 1873 Revolver Carbine

CIMARRON 1873 SHORT RIFLE
Caliber: 22 LR, 22 WMR, 357 Mag., 44-40, 45 Colt. **Barrel:** 20" tapered octagon. **Weight:** 7.5 lbs. **Length:** 39" overall. **Stock:** Walnut. **Sights:** Bead front, adjustable semi-buckhorn rear. **Features:** Has half "button" magazine. Original-type markings, including caliber, on barrel and elevator and "Kings" patent. From Cimarron F.A. Co.
Price: $799.00

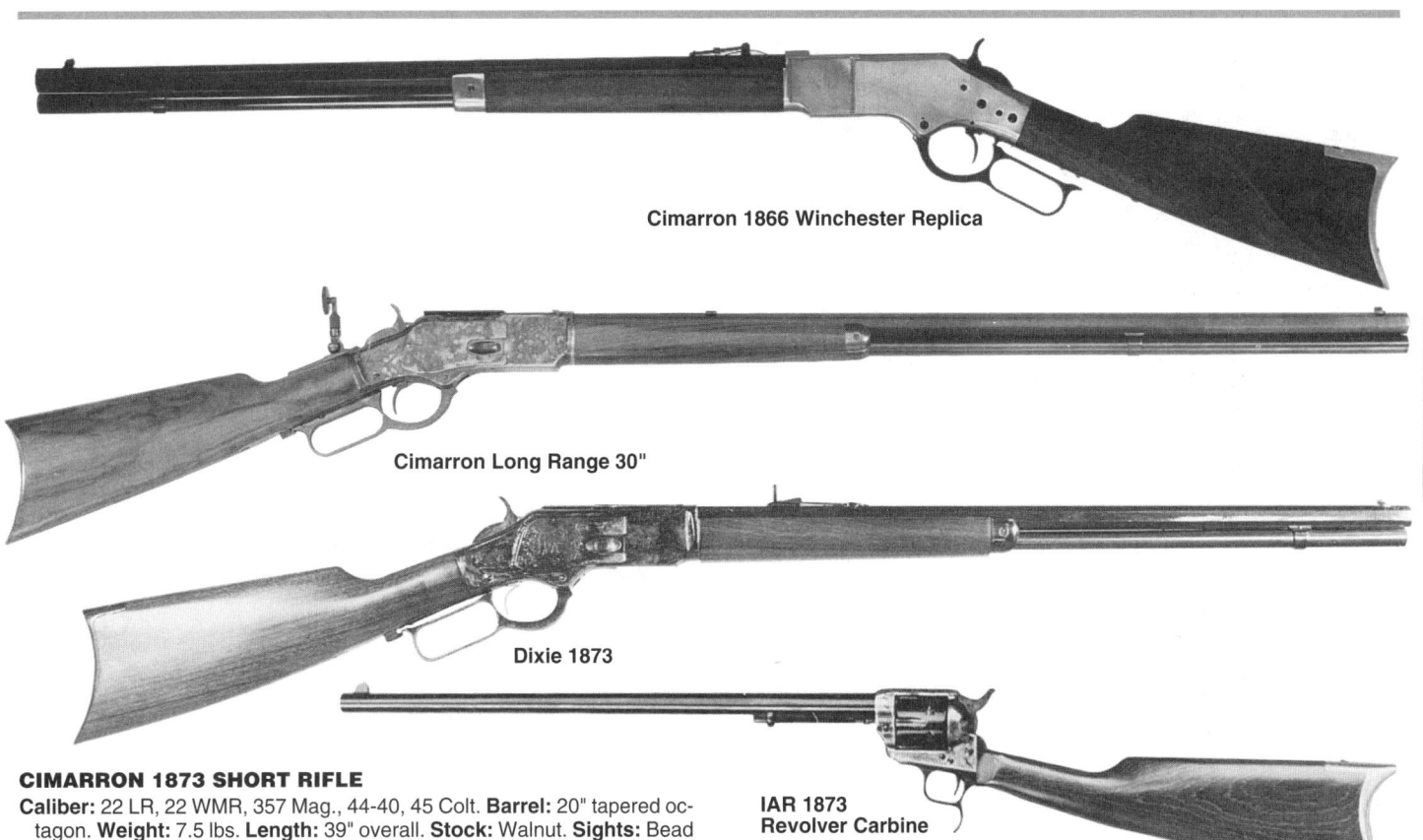

CIMARRON 1873 LONG RANGE RIFLE
Caliber: 22 LR, 22 WMR, 357 Mag., 38-40, 44-40, 45 Colt. **Barrel:** 30", octagonal. **Weight:** 8-1/2 lbs. **Length:** 48" overall. **Stock:** Walnut. **Sights:** Blade front, semi-buckhorn ramp rear. Tang sight optional. **Features:** Color case-hardened frame; choice of modern blue-black or charcoal blue for other parts. Barrel marked "Kings Improvement." From Cimarron F.A. Co.
Price: $999.00

Cimarron 1873 Sporting Rifle
Similar to the 1873 Long Range except has 24" barrel with half-magazine.
Price: $949.00
Price: 1873 Saddle Ring Carbine, 19" barrel $949.00

DIXIE ENGRAVED 1873 RIFLE
Caliber: 44-40, 11-shot magazine. **Barrel:** 20", round. **Weight:** 7-3/4 lbs. **Length:** 39" overall. **Stock:** Walnut. **Sights:** Blade front, adjustable rear. **Features:** Engraved and case-hardened frame. Duplicate of Winchester 1873. Made in Italy. From 21 Gun Works.
Price: $1,295.00
Price: Plain, blued carbine $850.00

E.M.F. 1860 HENRY RIFLE
Caliber: 44-40 or 45 Colt. **Barrel:** 24.25". **Weight:** About 9 lbs. **Length:** About 43.75" overall. **Stock:** Oil-stained American walnut. **Sights:** Blade front, rear adjustable for elevation. **Features:** Reproduction of the original Henry rifle with brass frame and buttplate, rest blued. From E.M.F.
Price: Brass frame $850.00
Price: Steel frame $950.00

E.M.F. 1866 YELLOWBOY LEVER ACTIONS
Caliber: 38 Spec., 44-40. **Barrel:** 19" (carbine), 24" (rifle). **Weight:** 9 lbs. **Length:** 43" overall (rifle). **Stock:** European walnut. **Sights:** Bead front, open adjustable rear. **Features:** Solid brass frame, blued barrel, lever, hammer, buttplate. Imported from Italy by E.M.F.
Price: Rifle $690.00
Price: Carbine.. $675.00

E.M.F. HARTFORD MODEL 1892 LEVER-ACTION RIFLE
Caliber: 45 Colt. **Barrel:** 24", octagonal. **Weight:** 7-1/2 lbs. **Length:** 43" overall. **Stock:** European walnut. **Sights:** Blade front, open adjustable rear. **Features:** Color case-hardened frame, lever, trigger and hammer with blued barrel, or overall blue finish. Introduced 1998. Imported by E.M.F.
Price: Standard... $590.00

E.M.F. MODEL 1873 LEVER-ACTION RIFLE
Caliber: 32/20, 357 Mag., 38/40, 44-40, 44 Spec., 45 Colt. **Barrel:** 24". **Weight:** 8 lbs. **Length:** 43-1/4" overall. **Stock:** European walnut. **Sights:** Bead front, rear adjustable for windage and elevation. **Features:** Color case-hardened frame (blue on carbine). Imported by E.M.F.
Price: Rifle $865.00
Price: Carbine, 19" barrel.............................. $865.00

IAR MODEL 1873 REVOLVER CARBINE
Caliber: 357 Mag., 45 Colt. **Barrel:** 18". **Weight:** 4 lbs., 8 oz. **Length:** 34" overall. **Stock:** One-piece walnut. **Sights:** Blade front, notch rear. **Features:** Color case-hardened frame, blue barrel, backstrap and triggerguard. Introduced 1998. Imported from Italy by IAR, Inc.
Price: Standard... $490.00

MARLIN MODEL 336C LEVER-ACTION CARBINE
Caliber: 30-30 or 35 Rem., 6-shot tubular magazine. **Barrel:** 20" Micro-Groove®. **Weight:** 7 lbs. **Length:** 38-1/2" overall. **Stock:** Checkered American black walnut, capped pistol grip with white line spacers. Mar-Shield® finish; rubber butt pad; swivel studs. **Sights:** Ramp front with Wide-Scan hood, semi-buckhorn folding rear adjustable for windage and elevation. **Features:** Hammer-block safety. Receiver tapped for scope mount, offset hammer spur; top of receiver sandblasted to prevent glare. Includes safety lock.
Price: $502.00

CENTERFIRE RIFLES — LEVER AND SLIDE

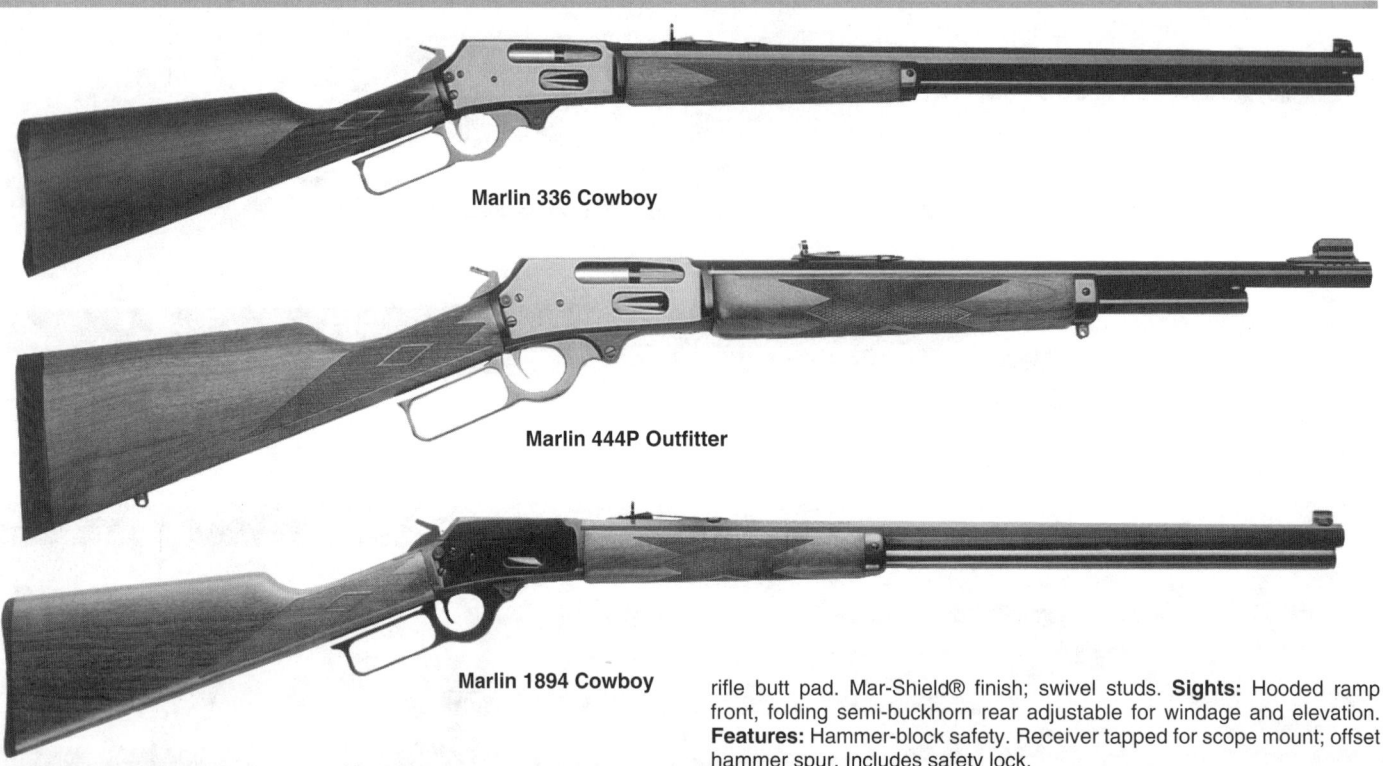

Marlin 336 Cowboy

Marlin 444P Outfitter

Marlin 1894 Cowboy

Marlin Model 336 Cowboy
Similar to the Model 336CS except chambered for 30-30 and 38-55 Win., 24" tapered octagon barrel with deep-cut Ballard-type rifling; straight-grip walnut stock with hard rubber buttplate; blued steel forend cap; weighs 7-1/2 lbs.; 42-1/2" overall. Introduced 1999. Includes safety lock. Made in U.S. by Marlin.
Price: $697.00

Marlin Model 336A Lever-Action Carbine
Same as the Marlin 336CS except has cut-checkered, walnut-finished Maine birch pistol grip stock with swivel studs, 30-30 only, 6-shot. Hammer-block safety. Adjustable rear sight, brass bead front. Includes safety lock.
Price: $429.00
Price: With 4x scope and mount. $474.00

Marlin Model 336CC Lever-Action Carbine
NEW! Same as the Marlin 336A except has Mossy Oak® Break-Up camouflage stock and forearm. 30-30 only, 6-shot; receiver tapped for scope mount or receiver sight. Introduced 2001. Includes safety lock. Made in U.S. by Marlin.
Price: $478.00

Marlin Model 336SS Lever-Action Carbine
Same as the 336C except receiver, barrel and other major parts are machined from stainless steel. 30-30 only, 6-shot; receiver tapped for scope. Includes safety lock.
Price: $608.00

Marlin Model 336W Lever-Action Rifle
Similar to the Model 336CS except has walnut-finished, cut-checkered Maine birch stock; blued steel barrel band has integral sling swivel; no front sight hood; comes with padded nylon sling; hard rubber butt plate. Introduced 1998. Includes safety lock. Made in U.S. by Marlin.
Price: $434.00
Price: With 4x scope and mount. $481.00

MARLIN MODEL 444 LEVER-ACTION SPORTER
Caliber: 444 Marlin, 5-shot tubular magazine. **Barrel:** 22" deep cut Ballard rifling. **Weight:** 7-1/2 lbs. **Length:** 40-1/2" overall. **Stock:** Checkered American black walnut, capped pistol grip with white line spacers, rubber rifle butt pad. Mar-Shield® finish; swivel studs. **Sights:** Hooded ramp front, folding semi-buckhorn rear adjustable for windage and elevation. **Features:** Hammer-block safety. Receiver tapped for scope mount; offset hammer spur. Includes safety lock.
Price: $599.00

Marlin Model 444P Outfitter Lever-Action
Similar to the 444SS except has a ported 18-1/2" barrel with deep-cut Ballard-type rifling; weighs 6-3/4 lbs.; overall length 37". Available only in 444 Marlin. Introduced 1999. Includes safety lock. Made in U.S. by Marlin.
Price: $612.00

MARLIN MODEL 1894 LEVER-ACTION CARBINE
Caliber: 44 Spec./44 Mag., 10-shot tubular magazine. **Barrel:** 20" Ballard-type rifling. **Weight:** 6 lbs. **Length:** 37-1/2" overall. **Stock:** Checkered American black walnut, straight grip and forend. Mar-Shield® finish. Rubber rifle butt pad; swivel studs. **Sights:** Wide-Scan hooded ramp front, semi-buckhorn folding rear adjustable for windage and elevation. **Features:** Hammer-block safety. Receiver tapped for scope mount, offset hammer spur, solid top receiver sand blasted to prevent glare. Includes safety lock.
Price: $526.00

Marlin Model 1894C Carbine
Similar to the standard Model 1894S except chambered for 38 Spec./357 Mag. with full-length 9-shot magazine, 18-1/2" barrel, hammer-block safety, hooded front sight. Introduced 1983. Includes safety lock.
Price: $526.00

Marlin Model 1894P/1894CP Carbine
Similar to the Model 1894 except has ported 16-1/4" barrel with 8-shot magazine. Overal length 33-1/4", weighs 5-3/4 lbs. Includes safety lock. Made in U.S. by Marlin.
Price: Model 1894P (44 Spec./44 Mag.) $546.00
New! Price: Model 1894CP (38 Spec./357 Mag.). $546.00

MARLIN MODEL 1894 COWBOY, COWBOY II
Caliber: 357 Mag., 44 Mag., 45 Colt, 10-shot magazine. **Barrel:** 24" tapered octagon, deep cut rifling. **Weight:** 7-1/2 lbs. **Length:** 41-1/2" overall. **Stock:** Straight grip American black walnut with cut checkering, hard rubber buttplate, Mar-Shield® finish. **Sights:** Marble carbine front, adjustable Marble semi-buckhorn rear. **Features:** Squared finger lever; straight grip stock; blued steel forend tip. Designed for Cowboy Shooting events. Introduced 1996. Includes safety lock. Made in U.S. by Marlin.
Price: Cowboy I, 45 Colt. $775.00
Price: Cowboy II, 357 Mag., 44 Mag. $775.00

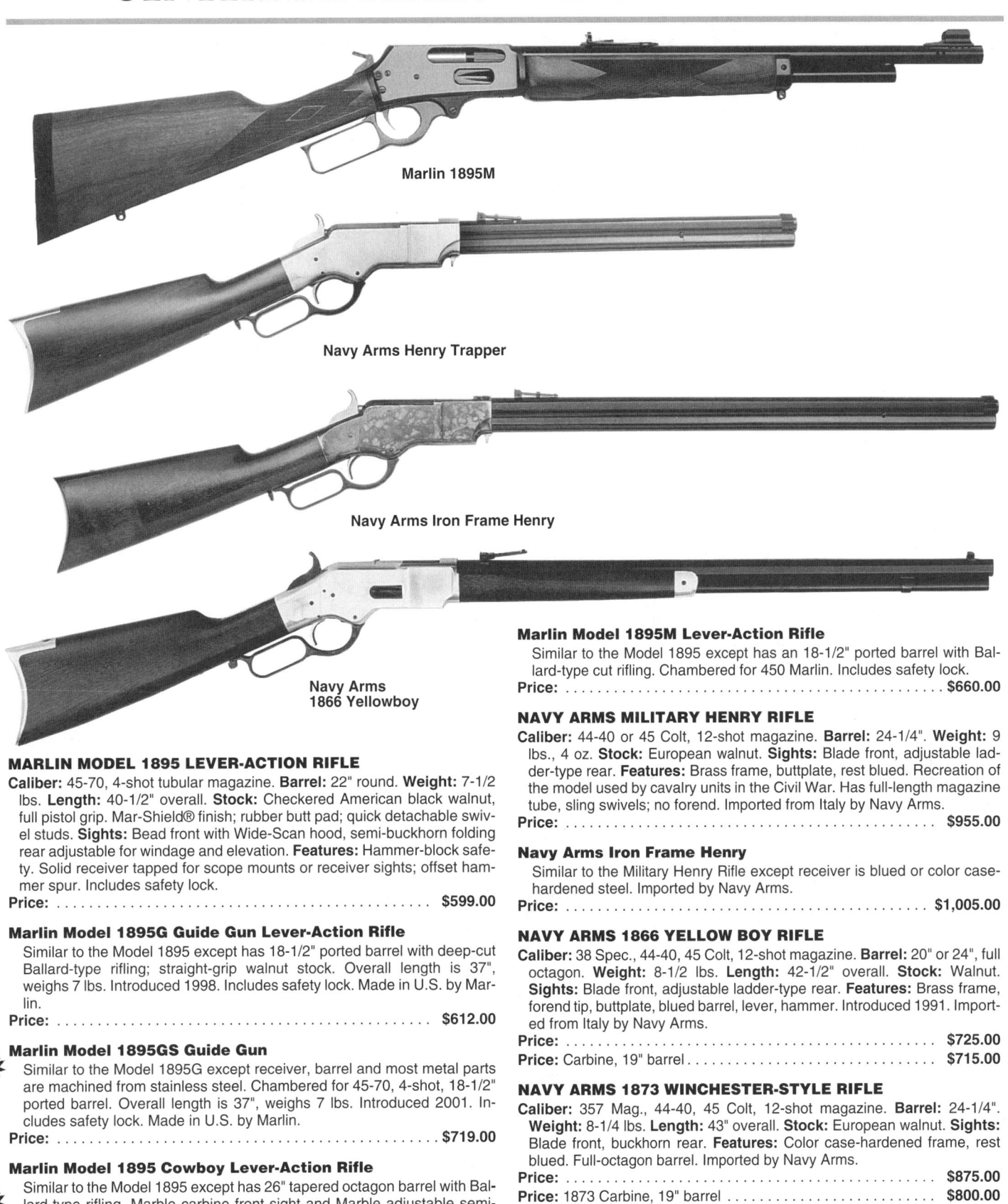

CENTERFIRE RIFLES — LEVER AND SLIDE

Marlin 1895M

Navy Arms Henry Trapper

Navy Arms Iron Frame Henry

Navy Arms 1866 Yellowboy

MARLIN MODEL 1895 LEVER-ACTION RIFLE
Caliber: 45-70, 4-shot tubular magazine. **Barrel:** 22" round. **Weight:** 7-1/2 lbs. **Length:** 40-1/2" overall. **Stock:** Checkered American black walnut, full pistol grip. Mar-Shield® finish; rubber butt pad; quick detachable swivel studs. **Sights:** Bead front with Wide-Scan hood, semi-buckhorn folding rear adjustable for windage and elevation. **Features:** Hammer-block safety. Solid receiver tapped for scope mounts or receiver sights; offset hammer spur. Includes safety lock.
Price: $599.00

Marlin Model 1895G Guide Gun Lever-Action Rifle
Similar to the Model 1895 except has 18-1/2" ported barrel with deep-cut Ballard-type rifling; straight-grip walnut stock. Overall length is 37", weighs 7 lbs. Introduced 1998. Includes safety lock. Made in U.S. by Marlin.
Price: $612.00

Marlin Model 1895GS Guide Gun
Similar to the Model 1895G except receiver, barrel and most metal parts are machined from stainless steel. Chambered for 45-70, 4-shot, 18-1/2" ported barrel. Overall length is 37", weighs 7 lbs. Introduced 2001. Includes safety lock. Made in U.S. by Marlin.
Price: $719.00

Marlin Model 1895 Cowboy Lever-Action Rifle
Similar to the Model 1895 except has 26" tapered octagon barrel with Ballard-type rifling, Marble carbine front sight and Marble adjustable semi-buckhorn rear sight. Receiver tapped for scope or receiver sight. Overall length is 44-1/2", weighs about 8 lbs. Introduced 2001. Includes safety lock. Made in U.S. by Marlin.
Price: $775.00

Marlin Model 1895M Lever-Action Rifle
Similar to the Model 1895 except has an 18-1/2" ported barrel with Ballard-type cut rifling. Chambered for 450 Marlin. Includes safety lock.
Price: $660.00

NAVY ARMS MILITARY HENRY RIFLE
Caliber: 44-40 or 45 Colt, 12-shot magazine. **Barrel:** 24-1/4". **Weight:** 9 lbs., 4 oz. **Stock:** European walnut. **Sights:** Blade front, adjustable ladder-type rear. **Features:** Brass frame, buttplate, rest blued. Recreation of the model used by cavalry units in the Civil War. Has full-length magazine tube, sling swivels; no forend. Imported from Italy by Navy Arms.
Price: $955.00

Navy Arms Iron Frame Henry
Similar to the Military Henry Rifle except receiver is blued or color case-hardened steel. Imported by Navy Arms.
Price: $1,005.00

NAVY ARMS 1866 YELLOW BOY RIFLE
Caliber: 38 Spec., 44-40, 45 Colt, 12-shot magazine. **Barrel:** 20" or 24", full octagon. **Weight:** 8-1/2 lbs. **Length:** 42-1/2" overall. **Stock:** Walnut. **Sights:** Blade front, adjustable ladder-type rear. **Features:** Brass frame, forend tip, buttplate, blued barrel, lever, hammer. Introduced 1991. Imported from Italy by Navy Arms.
Price: $725.00
Price: Carbine, 19" barrel $715.00

NAVY ARMS 1873 WINCHESTER-STYLE RIFLE
Caliber: 357 Mag., 44-40, 45 Colt, 12-shot magazine. **Barrel:** 24-1/4". **Weight:** 8-1/4 lbs. **Length:** 43" overall. **Stock:** European walnut. **Sights:** Blade front, buckhorn rear. **Features:** Color case-hardened frame, rest blued. Full-octagon barrel. Imported by Navy Arms.
Price: $875.00
Price: 1873 Carbine, 19" barrel $800.00
Price: 1873 Sporting Rifle (full oct. bbl., checkered walnut stock and forend) $995.00
Price: 1873 Border Model, 20" octagon barrel $875.00
Price: 1873 Deluxe Border Model $995.00

CENTERFIRE RIFLES — LEVER AND SLIDE

Navy Arms 1873 Winchester Style

Navy Arms 1892 Rifle

Navy Arms 1892 Short Rifle

Remington 7600 Rifle

Ruger Model 96/44

NAVY ARMS 1892 RIFLE
Caliber: 357 Mag., 44-40, 45 Colt. Barrel: 24-1/4" octagonal. Weight: 7 lbs. Length: 42" overall. Stock: American walnut. Sights: Blade front, semi-buckhorn rear. Features: Replica of Winchester's early Model 1892 with octagonal barrel, forend cap and crescent buttplate. Blued or color case-hardened receiver. Introduced 1998. Imported by Navy Arms.
Price: $525.00

Navy Arms 1892 Stainless Carbine
Similar to the 1892 Rifle except stainless steel, has 20" round barrel, weighs 5-3/4 lbs., and is 37-1/2" overall. Introduced 1998. Imported by Navy Arms.
Price: $500.00

Navy Arms 1892 Short Rifle
Similar to the 1892 Rifle except has 20" octagonal barrel, weighs 6-1/4 lbs., and is 37-3/4" overall. Replica of the rare, special order 1892 Winchester nicknamed the "Texas Special." Blued or color case-hardened receiver and furniture. Introduced 1998. Imported by Navy Arms.
Price: $525.00
Price: (stainless steel, 20" octagon barrel) $565.00

NAVY ARMS 1892 STAINLESS RIFLE
Caliber: 357 Mag., 44-40, 45 Colt. Barrel: 24-1/4" octagonal. Weight: 7 lbs. Length: 42". Stock: American walnut. Sights: Brass bead front, semi-buckhorn rear. Features: Designed for the Cowboy Action Shooter. Stainless steel barrel, receiver and furniture. Introduced 2000. Imported by Navy Arms.
Price: $565.00

REMINGTON MODEL 7600 PUMP ACTION
Caliber: 243, 270, 280, 30-06, 308. Barrel: 22" round tapered. Weight: 7-1/2 lbs. Length: 42-5/8" overall. Stock: Cut-checkered walnut pistol grip and forend, Monte Carlo with full cheekpiece. Satin or high-gloss finish. Sights: Gold bead front sight on matted ramp, open step adjustable sporting rear. Features: Redesigned and improved version of the Model 760. Detachable 4-shot clip. Cross-bolt safety. Receiver tapped for scope mount. Introduced 1981.
Price: $576.00
Price: Carbine (18-1/2" bbl., 30-06 only) $576.00
Price: With black synthetic stock, matte black metal, rifle or carbine $473.00

RUGER MODEL 96/44 LEVER-ACTION RIFLE
Caliber: 44 Mag., 4-shot rotary magazine. Barrel: 18-1/2". Weight: 5-7/8 lbs. Length: 37-5/16" overall. Stock: American hardwood. Sights: Gold bead front, folding leaf rear. Features: Solid chrome-moly steel receiver. Manual cross-bolt safety, visible cocking indicator; short-throw lever action; integral scope mount; blued finish; color case-hardened lever. Introduced 1996. Made In U.S. by Sturm, Ruger & Co.
Price: 96/44M, 44 Mag $499.00

TRADITIONS 1860 HENRY RIFLES
Caliber: 45 Colt. Barrel: 24-1/4" octagonal; 1:16" twist. Weight: 9.26 lbs. Length: 43-3/4" overall. Stock: Walnut. Sights: Blade front, adjustable folding rear. Features: Steel color-case hardened or brass receiver; 13-shot magazine. Introduced 2001. Imported from Uberti by Traditions.
Price: (steel color-case hardened receiver) $869.00
Price: (brass receiver) $819.00

TRADITIONS 1866 SPORTING YELLOWBOY RIFLES
Caliber: 45 Colt. Barrel: 24-1/4" octagonal; 1:16" twist. Weight: 8.16 lbs. Length: 43-3/4" overall. Stock: Walnut. Sights: Blade front, adjustable folding rear. Features: Brass receiver; blued or white barrel; 13-shot magazine. Introduced 2001. Imported from Uberti by Traditions.
Price: (blued barrel) $669.00
Price: (white barrel) $749.00

CENTERFIRE RIFLES — LEVER AND SLIDE

Winchester Model 94 Big Bore

Winchester 94 Traditional

Winchester Model 94 Trapper

TRADITIONS 1866 YELLOWBOY CARBINE
Similar to 1866 Sporting Yellowboy, except has 19" round, blued barrel with adjustable rear sight, 10-shot magazine. Weighs 7.35 lbs.; overall length 38-1/4". Introduced 2001. Imported from Uberti by Traditions.
Price: $669.00

TRADITIONS 1873 SPORTING RIFLES
Caliber: 45 Colt. **Barrel:** 24-1/4" octagonal; 1:16" twist. **Weight:** 8.16 lbs. **Length:** 43-3/4" overall. **Stock:** Walnut. **Sights:** Blade front, adjustable rear. **Features:** Blued barrel with color-case hardened receiver or white barrel and receiver; 13-shot magazine. Introduced 2001. Imported from Uberti by Traditions.
Price: (color-case hardened receiver and blued barrel) $819.00
Price: (white receiver and barrel) $899.00
Price: (Deluxe Sporting Rifle with checkered, high-grade walnut stock; adj. folding rear sight) $969.00

TRADITIONS 1873 SPORTING CARBINE
Similar to 1873 Sporting Rifle, except has 19" round, blued barrel with adjustable rear sight, 10-shot magazine. Weighs 7.38 lbs. Overall length 38-1/4". Introduced 2001. Imported from Uberti by Traditions.
Price: $819.00

TRISTAR/UBERTI 1873 SPORTING RIFLE
Caliber: 44-40, 45 Colt. **Barrel:** 24-1/4", 30", octagonal. **Weight:** 8.1 lbs. **Length:** 43-1/4" overall. **Stock:** Walnut. **Sights:** Blade front adjustable for windage, open rear adjustable for elevation. **Features:** Color case-hardened frame, blued barrel, hammer, lever, buttplate, brass elevator. Imported from Italy by Tristar Sporting Arms Ltd.
Price: 24-1/4" barrel $919.00
Price: 30" barrel $964.00

TRISTAR/UBERTI 1866 SPORTING RIFLE, CARBINE
Caliber: 22 LR, 22 WMR, 38 Spec., 44-40, 45 Colt. **Barrel:** 24-1/4", octagonal. **Weight:** 8.1 lbs. **Length:** 43-1/4" overall. **Stock:** Walnut. **Sights:** Blade front adjustable for windage, rear adjustable for elevation. **Features:** Frame, buttplate, forend cap of polished brass, balance charcoal blued. Imported by Tristar Sporting Arms Ltd.
Price: $775.00
Price: Yellowboy Carbine (19" round bbl.) $735.00

TRISTAR/UBERTI 1860 HENRY RIFLE
Caliber: 44-40, 45 Colt. **Barrel:** 24-1/4", half-octagon. **Weight:** 9.2 lbs. **Length:** 43-3/4" overall. **Stock:** American walnut. **Sights:** Blade front, rear adjustable for elevation. **Features:** Frame, elevator, magazine follower, buttplate are brass, balance blue. Imported by Tristar Sporting Arms Ltd. Arms, Inc.
Price: $982.00
Price: 1860 Henry White (polished steel finish) $1,040.00

TRISTAR/UBERTI 1860 HENRY TRAPPER CARBINE
Similar to the 1860 Henry Rifle except has 18-1/2" barrel, measures 37-3/4" overall, and weighs 8 lbs. Introduced 1999. Imported from Italy by Tristar Sporting Arms Ltd.
Price: Brass frame, blued barrel......................... $982.00
Price: Henry Trapper White (brass frame, polished steel barrel) $1,040.00

VEKTOR H5 SLIDE-ACTION RIFLE
Caliber: 223 Rem., 5-shot magazine. **Barrel:** 18", 22". **Weight:** 9 lbs., 15 oz. **Length:** 42-1/2" overall (22" barrel). **Stock:** Walnut thumbhole. **Sights:** Comes with 1" 4x32 scope with low-light reticle. **Features:** Rotating bolt mechanism. Matte black finish. Introduced 1999. Imported from South Africa by Vektor USA.
Price: $849.95

WINCHESTER MODEL 94 TRADITIONAL BIG BORE
Caliber: 444 Marlin, 6-shot magazine. **Barrel:** 20". **Weight:** 6-1/2 lbs. **Length:** 38-5/8" overall. **Stock:** American walnut. Satin finish. **Sights:** Hooded ramp front, semi-buckhorn rear adjustable for windage and elevation. **Features:** All external metal parts have Winchester's deep blue finish. Rifling twist 1:12". Rubber recoil pad fitted to buttstock. Introduced 1983. From U.S. Repeating Arms Co., Inc.
Price: $465.00

Winchester Timber Carbine
Similar to the Model 94 Big Bore. Chambered for 444 Marlin; 18" barrel is ported; half-pistol grip stock with butt pad; checkered grip and forend. Introduced 1999. Made in U.S. by U.S. Repeating Arms Co., Inc.
Price: $573.00

WINCHESTER MODEL 94 TRADITIONAL-CW
Caliber: 30-30 Win., 6-shot; 44 Mag., 11-shot tubular magazine. **Barrel:** 20". **Weight:** 6-1/2 lbs. **Length:** 37-3/4" overall. **Stock:** Straight grip checkered walnut stock and forend. **Sights:** Hooded blade front, semi-buckhorn rear. Drilled and tapped for scope mount. Post front sight on Trapper model. **Features:** Solid frame, forged steel receiver; side ejection, exposed rebounding hammer with automatic trigger-activated transfer bar. Introduced 1984.
Price: 30-30 .... $440.00
Price: 44 Mag. $463.00
Price: Traditional (no checkering, 30-30 only) $407.00

Winchester Model 94 Trapper™
Similar to Model 94 Traditional except has 16" barrel, 5-shot magazine in 30-30, 9-shot in 357 Mag., 44 Magnum/44 Special, 45 Colt. Has stainless steel claw extractor, saddle ring, hammer spur extension, smooth walnut wood.
Price: 30-30 .... $407.00
Price: 44 Mag., 357 Mag., 45 Colt $431.00

CENTERFIRE RIFLES — LEVER AND SLIDE

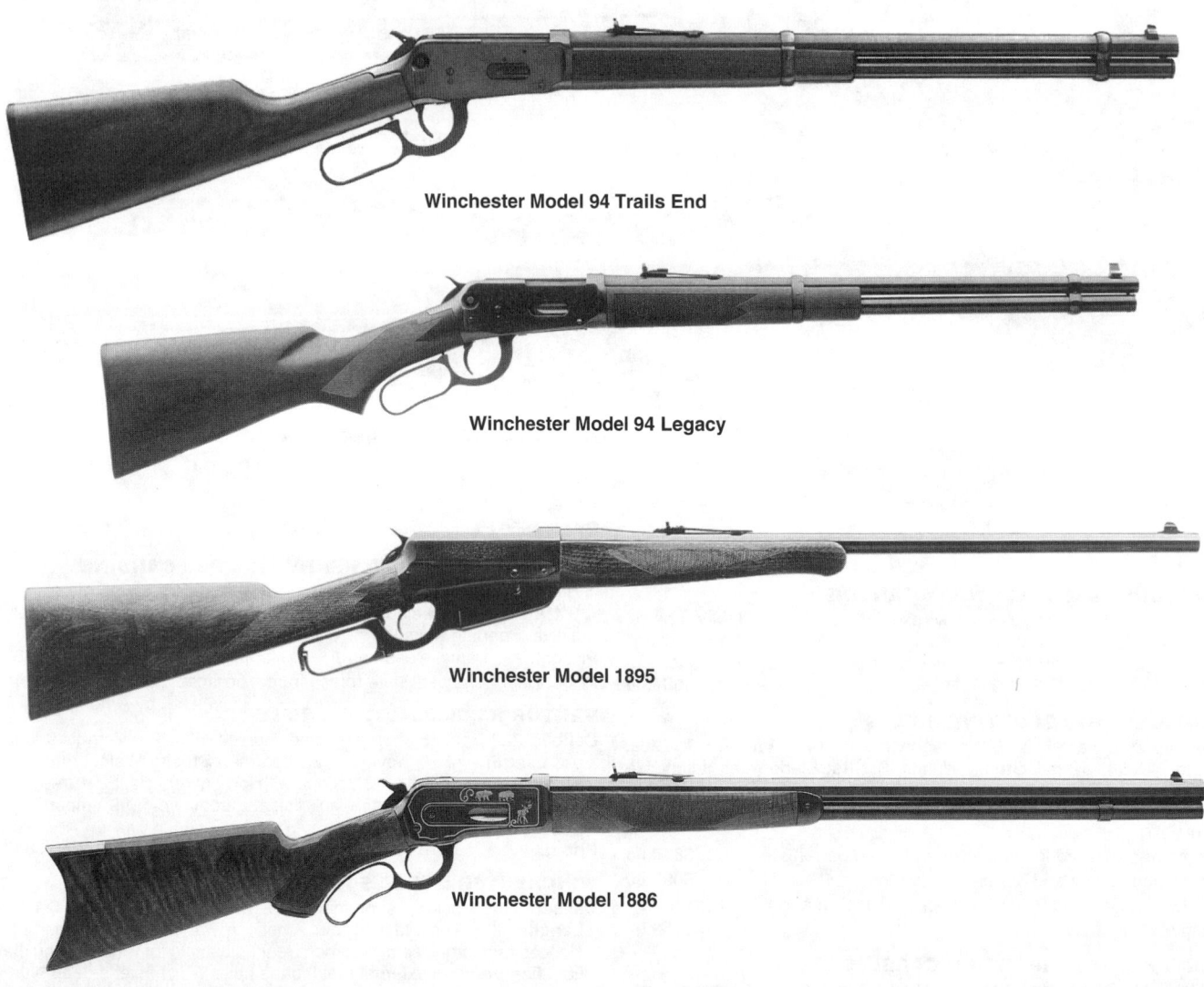

Winchester Model 94 Trails End

Winchester Model 94 Legacy

Winchester Model 1895

Winchester Model 1886

Winchester Model 94 Trails End™
Similar to the Model 94 Walnut except chambered only for 357 Mag., 44-40, 44 Mag., 45 Colt; 11-shot magazine. Available with standard lever loop. Introduced 1997. From U.S. Repeating Arms Co., Inc.
Price: With standard lever loop. $445.00

Winchester Model 94 Legacy
Similar to the Model 94 Traditional-CW except has half-pistol grip walnut stock, checkered grip and forend. Chambered for 30-30, 357 Mag., 44 Mag., 45 Colt; 24" barrel. Introduced 1995. Made in U.S. by U.S. Repeating Arms Co., Inc.
Price: With 24" barrel $457.00

Winchester Model 94 Ranger
Similar to the Model 94 Traditional except has a hardwood stock, post-style front sight and hammer-spur extension.
Price: (20" barrel) $355.00

Winchester Model 94 Ranger Compact
Similar to the Model 94 Ranger except has 16" barrel and 12-1/2" length of pull, rubber recoil pad, post front sight. Introduced 1998. Made in U.S. by U.S. Repeating Arms Co., Inc.
Price: 357 Mag. $378.00
Price: 30-30 . . . . $355.00

WINCHESTER MODEL 1895 LEVER-ACTION RIFLE
Caliber: 405 Win, 4-shot magazine. **Barrel:** 24", round. **Weight:** 8 lbs. **Length:** 42" overall. **Stock:** American walnut. **Sights:** Gold bead front, buckhorn rear adjustable for elevation. **Features:** Recreation of the original Model 1895. Polished blue finish with Nimschke-style scroll engraving on receiver. Scalloped receiver, two-piece cocking lever, Schnabel forend, straight-grip stock. Introduced 1995. From U.S. Repeating Arms Co., Inc.
Price: Grade I $1,045.00
Price: High Grade $1,532.00

WINCHESTER MODEL 1886
EXTRA LIGHT LEVER-ACTION RIFLE
Caliber: 45-70, 4-shot magazine. **Barrel:** 22", round tapered. **Weight:** 7-1/4 lbs. **Length:** 40-1/2" overall. **Stock:** Smooth walnut. **Sights:** Bead front, ramp-adjustable buckhorn-style rear. **Features:** Recreation of the Model 1886. Polished blue finish; crescent metal butt plate; metal forend cap; pistol grip stock. Reintroduced 1998. From U.S. Repeating Arms Co., Inc.
Price: Grade I $1,152.00
Price: High Grade $1,440.00

CENTERFIRE RIFLES — BOLT ACTION

Includes models for a wide variety of sporting and competitive purposes and uses.

Anschutz 1733D

Arnold Arms Alaskan

Arnold Arms Safari

ANSCHUTZ 1743D BOLT-ACTION RIFLE
Caliber: 222 Rem., 3-shot magazine. **Barrel:** 19.7". **Weight:** 6.4 lbs. **Length:** 39" overall. **Stock:** European walnut. **Sights:** Hooded blade front, folding leaf rear. **Features:** Receiver grooved for scope mounting; single stage trigger; claw extractor; sling safety; sling swivels. Imported from Germany by AcuSport Corp.
Price: $1,588.95

ANSCHUTZ 1740 MONTE CARLO RIFLE
Caliber: 22 Hornet, 5-shot clip; 222 Rem., 3-shot clip. **Barrel:** 24". **Weight:** 6-1/2 lbs. **Length:** 43.25" overall. **Stock:** Select European walnut. **Sights:** Hooded ramp front, folding leaf rear; drilled and tapped for scope mounting. **Features:** Uses match 54 action. Adjustable single stage trigger. Stock has roll-over Monte Carlo cheekpiece, slim forend with Schnabel tip, Wundhammer palm swell on grip, rosewood gripcap with white diamond insert. Skip-line checkering on grip and forend. Introduced 1997. Imported from Germany by AcuSport Corp.
Price: From... $1,439.00
Price: Model 1730 Monte Carlo, as above except in 22 Hornet $1,439.00

Anschutz 1733D Rifle
Similar to the 1740 Monte Carlo except has full-length, walnut, Mannlicher-style stock with skip-line checkering, rosewood Schnabel tip, and is chambered for 22 Hornet. Weighs 6.4 lbs., overall length 39", barrel length 19.7". Imported from Germany by AcuSport Corp.
Price: $1,588.95

ARNOLD ARMS ALASKAN RIFLE
Caliber: 243 to 338 Magnum. **Barrel:** 22" to 26". **Weight:** NA. **Length:** NA. **Stock:** Synthetic; black, woodland or arctic camouflage. **Sights:** Optional; drilled and tapped for scope mounting. **Features:** Uses Apollo, Remington or Winchester action with controlled round feed or push feed; chrome-moly steel or stainless; one-piece bolt, handle, knob; cone head bolt and breech; three-position safety; fully adjustable trigger. Introduced 1996. Made in U.S. by Arnold Arms Co.
Price: From... $2,695.00

Arnold Arms Alaskan Guide Rifle
Similar to the Alaskan rifle except chambered for 257 to 338 Magnum; choice of A-grade English walnut or synthetic stock; three-position safety; scope mount only. Introduced 1996. Made in U.S. by Arnold Arms Co.
Price: From... $3,249.00

Arnold Arms Grand Alaskan Rifle
Similar to the Alaskan rifle except has AAA fancy select or exhibition-grade English walnut; barrel band swivel; comes with iron sights and scope mount; 24" to 26" barrel; 300 Magnum to 458 Win. Mag. Introduced 1996. Made in U.S. by Arnold Arms Co.
Price: From... $7,570.00

Arnold Arms Alaskan Trophy Rifle
Similar to the Alaskan rifle except chambered for 300 Magnum to 458 Win. Mag.; 24" to 26" barrel; black synthetic or laminated stock; comes with barrel band on 375 H&H and larger; scope mount; iron sights. Introduced 1996. Made in U.S. by Arnold Arms Co.
Price: From... $3,249.00

ARNOLD ARMS SAFARI RIFLE
Caliber: 243 to 458 Win. Mag. **Barrel:** 22" to 26". **Weight:** NA. **Length:** NA. **Stock:** Grade A and AA Fancy English walnut. **Sights:** Optional; drilled and tapped for scope mounting. **Features:** Uses Apollo, Remington or Winchester action with controlled or push round feed; one-piece bolt, handle, knob; cone head bolt and breech; three-position safety; fully adjustable trigger; chrome-moly steel in matte blue, polished, or bead blasted stainless. Introduced 1996. Made in U.S. by Arnold Arms Co.
Price: From... $6,495.00

Arnold Arms African Trophy Rifle
Similar to the Safari rifle except has AAA Extra Fancy English walnut stock with wrap-around checkering; matte blue chrome-moly or polished or bead blasted stainless steel; scope mount standard or optional Express sights. Introduced 1996. Made in U.S. by Arnold Arms Co.
Price: Blued chrome-moly steel $6,921.00
Price: Stainless steel $6,971.00

Arnold Arms Grand African Rifle
Similar to the Safari rifle except has Exhibition Grade stock; polished blue chrome-moly steel or bead-blasted or Teflon-coated stainless; barrel band; scope mount, express sights; calibers 338 Magnum to 458 Win. Mag.; 24" to 26" barrel. Introduced 1996. Made in U.S. by Arnold Arms Co.
Price: Chrome-moly steel............................... $8,172.00
Price: Stainless steel $8,022.00

CENTERFIRE RIFLES — BOLT ACTION

Beretta Mato Deluxe

Barrett Model 95

Beretta Mato Synthetic

Blaser R93 Classic

BARRETT MODEL 95 BOLT-ACTION RIFLE
Caliber: 50 BMG, 5-shot magazine. **Barrel:** 29". **Weight:** 22 lbs. **Length:** 45" overall. **Stock:** Energy-absorbing recoil pad. **Sights:** Scope optional. **Features:** Bolt-action, bullpup design. Disassembles without tools; extendable bipod legs; match-grade barrel; high efficiency muzzle brake. Introduced 1995. Made in U.S. by Barrett Firearms Mfg., Inc.
Price: From $4,950.00

BERETTA MATO DELUXE BOLT-ACTION RIFLE
Caliber: 270, 280 Rem., 30-06, 7mm Rem. Mag., 300 Win. Mag., 338 Win. Mag., 375 H&H. **Barrel:** 23.6". **Weight:** 7.9 lbs. **Length:** 44.5" overall. **Stock:** XXX claro walnut with ebony forend tip, hand-rubbed oil finish. **Sights:** Bead on ramp front, open fully adjustable rear; drilled and tapped for scope mounting. **Features:** Mauser-style action with claw extractor; three-position safety; removable box magazine; 375 H&H has muzzle brake. Introduced 1998. From Beretta U.S.A.
Price: $2,470.00
Price: 375 H&H. $2,795.00

Beretta Mato Synthetic Bolt-Action Rifle
Similar to the Mato except has fiberglass/Kevlar/carbon fiber stock in classic American style with shadow line cheekpiece, aluminum bedding block and checkering. Introduced 1998. From Beretta U.S.A.
Price: $1,117.00
Price: 375 H&H. $1,474.00

BLASER R93 BOLT-ACTION RIFLE
Caliber: 22-250, 243, 6.5x55, 270, 7x57, 7mm-08, 308, 30-06, 257 Wea. Mag., 7mm Rem. Mag., 300 Win. Mag., 300 Wea. Mag., 338 Win Mag., 375 H&H, 416 Rem. Mag. **Barrel:** 22" (standard calibers), 26" (magnum). **Weight:** 7 lbs. **Length:** 40" overall (22" barrel). **Stock:** Two-piece European walnut. **Sights:** None furnished; drilled and tapped for scope mounting. **Features:** Straight pull-back bolt action with thumb-activated safety slide/cocking mechanism; interchangeable barrels and bolt heads. Introduced 1994. Imported from Germany by SIGARMS.
Price: R93 Classic $3,680.00
Price: R93 LX $1,895.00
Price: R93 Synthetic (black synthetic stock) $1,595.00
Price: R93 Safari Synthetic (416 Rem. Mag. only) $1,855.00
Price: R93 Grand Lux $4,915.00
Price: R93 Attaché $5,390.00

BRNO 98 BOLT-ACTION RIFLE
Caliber: 7x64, 243, 270, 308, 30-06, 300 Win. Mag., 9.3x62. **Barrrel:** 23.6". **Weight:** 7.2 lbs. **Length:** 40.9" overall. **Stock:** European walnut. **Sights:** Blade on ramp front, open adjustable rear. **Features:** Uses Mauser 98-type action; polished blue. Announced 1998. Imported from the Czech Republic by Euro-Imports.
Price: Standard calibers $507.00
Price: Magnum calibers $547.00
Price: With set trigger, standard calibers $615.00
Price: As above, magnum calibers $655.00
Price: With full stock, set trigger, standard calibers $703.00
Price: As above, magnum calibers $743.00

CENTERFIRE RIFLES — BOLT ACTION

Browning A-Bolt II Medallion

Browning A-Bolt II Eclipse M-1000

Browning A-Bolt II Micro

BROWNING ACERA STRAIGHT-PULL RIFLE
Caliber: 30-06, 300 Win. Mag. **Barrel:** 22"; 24" for magnums. **Weight:** 6 lbs., 9 oz. **Length:** 41-1/4" overall. **Stock:** American walnut with high gloss finish. **Sights:** Blade on ramp front, open adjustable rear. **Features:** Straight-pull action; detachable box magazine; Teflon coated breechblock; drilled and tapped for scope mounting. Introduced 1999. Imported by Browning.
Price: 30-06, no sights $845.00
Price: 300 Win. Mag., no sights $877.00
Price: 30-06 with sights $869.00
Price: 300 Win. Mag., with sights $901.00
Price: 30-06, with BOSS $901.00
Price: 300 Win. Mag., with BOSS $933.00

BROWNING A-BOLT RIFLES
Caliber: 223, 22-250, 243, 7mm-08, 308, 25-06, 260, 270, 30-06, 260 Rem., 7mm Rem. Mag., 300 Win. Mag., 300 Win. Short Mag., 300 Win. Mag., 338 Win. Mag., 375 H&H Mag. **Barrel:** 22" medium sporter weight with recessed muzzle; 26" on mag. cals. **Weight:** 6-1/2 to 7-1/2 lbs. **Length:** 44-3/4" overall (magnum and standard); 41-3/4" (short action). **Stock:** Classic style American walnut; recoil pad standard on magnum calibers. **Features:** Short-throw (60°) fluted bolt, three locking lugs, plunger-type ejector; adjustable trigger is grooved and gold-plated. Hinged floorplate, detachable box magazine (4 rounds std. cals., 3 for magnums). Slide tang safety. BOSS barrel vibration modulator and muzzle brake system not available in 375 H&H. Introduced 1985. Imported from Japan by Browning.
Price: Hunter, no sights $620.00
Price: Hunter, no sights, magnum calibers $646.00
Price: For BOSS add $80.00

Browning A-Bolt Medallion
Similar to standard A-Bolt except has glossy stock finish, rosewood grip and forend caps, engraved receiver, high-polish blue, no sights.
Price: Short-action calibers $730.00
Price: Long-action calibers $756.00
Price: Medallion, 375 H&H Mag., open sights $767.00
New! **Price:** 300 Win. Short Magnum $756.00
New! **Price:** 300 Rem. Ultra Mag., 338 Rem. Ultra Mag. $756.00
Price: For BOSS, add $80.00

Browning A-Bolt Medallion Left-Hand
Same as the Medallion model A-Bolt except has left-hand action and is available in 270, 30-06, 7mm Rem. Mag., 300 Win. Mag. Introduced 1987.
Price: 270, 30-06 (no sights) $758.00
Price: 7mm Mag., 300 Win. Mag. (no sights) $784.00
Price: For BOSS, add $80.00

Browning A-Bolt White Gold Medallion
Similar to the standard A-Bolt except has select walnut stock with brass spacers between rubber recoil pad and between the rosewood gripcap and forend tip; gold-filled barrel inscription; palm-swell pistol grip, Monte Carlo comb, 22 lpi checkering with double borders; engraved receiver flats. In 270, 30-06, 7mm Rem. Mag. and 300 Win. Mag. Introduced 1988.
Price: 270, 30-06 .... $1,046.00
Price: 7mm Rem. Mag., 300 Win. Mag. $1,072.00
Price: For BOSS, add $76.00

Browning A-Bolt Custom Trophy Rifle
Similar to the A-Bolt Medallion except has select American walnut stock with recessed swivel studs, octagon barrel, skeleton pistol gripcap, gold highlights, shadowline cheekpiece. Calibers 270, 30-06, 7mm Rem. Mag., 300 Win. Mag. Introduced 1998. Imported from Japan by Browning.
Price: $1,360.00

Browning A-Bolt Eclipse Hunter
Similar to the A-Bolt II except has gray/black laminated, thumbhole stock, BOSS barrel vibration modulator and muzzle brake. Available in long and short action with heavy barrel. In 270 Win., 30-06, 7mm Rem. Mag. Introduced 1996. Imported from Japan by Browning.
Price: 270, 30-06, with BOSS $1,017.00
Price: 7mm Rem. Mag, with BOSS $1,043.00

Browning A-Bolt Eclipse M-1000
Similar to the A-Bolt II Eclipse except has long action and heavy target barrel. Chambered only for 300 Win. Mag. Adjustable trigger, bench-style forend, 3-shot magazine; laminated thumbhold stock; BOSS system standard. Introduced 1997. Imported for Japan by Browning.
Price: $1,048.00

Browning A-Bolt Micro Hunter
Similar to the A-Bolt II Hunter except has 13-5/16" length of pull, 20" barrel, and comes in 260 Rem., 243, 308, 7mm-08, 223, 22-250, 22 Hornet. Weighs 6 lbs., 1 oz. Introduced 1999. Imported by Browning.
Price: (no sights) $614.00

Browning A-Bolt Classic Hunter
Similar to the A-Bolt unter except has low-luster bluing and walnut stock with Monte Carlo comb, pistol grip palm swell, double-border checkering. Available in 270, 30-06, 7mm Rem. Mag., 300 Win. Mag. Introduced 1999. Imported by Browning.
Price: 270, 30-06 .... $698.00
Price: 7mm Mag., 300 Mag. $724.00

Browning A-Bolt Stainless Stalker
Similar to the Hunter model A-Bolt except receiver and barrel are made of stainless steel; the rest of the exposed metal surfaces are finished with a durable matte silver-gray. Graphite-fiberglass composite textured stock. No sights are furnished. Available in 260, 243, 308, 7mm-08, 270, 280, 30-06, 7mm Rem. Mag., 300 WSM, 300 Rem. Ultra Mag., 338 Win. Mag., 338 Rem. Ultra Mag., 375 H&H. Introduced 1987.

34TH EDITION, 2002 • 207

CENTERFIRE RIFLES — BOLT ACTION

Charles Daly Superior

CZ 527

Price: Short-action calibers. $813.00
Price: Magnum calibers $839.00
New! Price: 300 Win. Short Magnum $839.00
New! Price: 300 Rem. Ultra Mag., 338 Rem. Ultra Mag. $839.00
Price: For BOSS, add $80.00
Price: Left-hand, 270, 30-06 .... $838.00
Price: Left-hand, 7mm, 300 Win. Mag., 338 Win. Mag. $864.00
Price: Left-hand, 375 H&H, with sights. $864.00
Price: Left-hand, for BOSS, add $80.00
Price: Carbon-fiber barrel, 22-250 .... $1,750.00
Price: Carbon-fiber barrel, 300 Win. Mag. $1,776.00

Browning A-Bolt Composite Stalker
Similar to the A-Bolt Hunter except has black graphite-fiberglass stock with textured finish. Matte blue finish on all exposed metal surfaces. Available in 223, 22-250, 243, 7mm-08, 308, 30-06, 270, 280, 25-06, 7mm Rem. Mag., 300 WSM, 300 Win. Mag., 338 Win. Mag. BOSS barrel vibration modulator and muzzle brake system offered in all calibers. Introduced 1994.
Price: Standard calibers, no sights. $639.00
Price: Magnum calibers, no sights $665.00
Price: For BOSS, add $77.00

CARBON ONE BOLT-ACTION RIFLE
Caliber: 22-250 to 375 H&H. **Barrel:** Up to 28". **Weight:** 5-1/2 to 7-1/4 lbs. **Length:** Varies. **Stock:** Synthetic or wood. **Sights:** None furnished. **Features:** Choice of Remington, Browning or Winchester action with free-floated Christensen graphite/epoxy/steel barrel, trigger pull tuned to 3 - 3-1/2 lbs. Made in U.S. by Christensen Arms.
Price: Carbon One Hunter Rifle, 6-1/2 to 7 lbs. $1,499.00
Price: Carbon One Custom, 5-1/2 to 6-1/2 lbs., Shilen trigger . $2,750.00
Price: Carbon Ranger, 50 BMG, 5-shot repeater $4,750.00
Price: Carbon Ranger, 50 BMG, single shot $3,950.00

CHARLES DALY SUPERIOR BOLT-ACTION RIFLE
Caliber: 22 Hornet, 5-shot magazine. **Barrel:** 22.6". **Weight:** 6.6 lbs. **Length:** 41.25" overall. **Stock:** Walnut-finished hardwood with Monte Carlo comb and cheekpiece. **Sights:** Ramped blade front, fully adjustable open rear. **Features:** Receiver dovetailed for tip-off scope mount. Introduced 1996. Imported by K.B.I., Inc.
Price: $364.95

Charles Daly Empire Grade Rifle
Similar to the Superior except has oil-finished American walnut stock with 18 lpi hand checkering; black hardwood gripcap and forend tip; highly polished barreled action; jewelled bolt; recoil pad; swivel studs. Imported by K.B.I., Inc.
Price: $469.95

COLT LIGHT RIFLE BOLT ACTION
Caliber: 243, 7x57, 7mm-08, 308 (short action); 25-06, 270, 280, 7mm Rem., Mag., 30-06, 300 Win. Mag. **Barrel:** 24" **Weight:** 5.4 to 6 lbs.

Length: NA. **Stock:** Black synthetic. **Sights:** None furnished; low, medium, high scope mounts. **Features:** Matte black finish; three-position safety. Introduced 1999. Made in U.S. From Colt's Mfg., Inc.
Price: $779.00

COOPER MODEL 22 BOLT-ACTION RIFLE
Caliber: 22 BR, 22-250 Rem., 22-250 Ackley Imp., 243, 25-06, 25-06 Ackley Imp., 220 Swift, 257 Roberts, 257 Roberts Ackley Imp., 6mm Rem., 6mm PPC, 6mm BR, 7mm-08, single shot. **Barrel:** 24" stainless match grade. **Weight:** 7-3/4 to 8 lbs. **Stock:** AA Claro walnut, 20 lpi checkering. **Sights:** None furnished. **Features:** Uses three front locking lug system. Fully adjustable trigger. Many options available. Made in U.S. by Cooper Firearms.
Price: Classic $1,295.00
Price: Varminter $1,199.00
Price: Varmint Extreme $1,895.00
Price: Custom Classic $2,195.00
Price: Western Classic $2,495.00

COOPER MODEL 21, 38 BOLT-ACTION RIFLES
Caliber: 17 Rem., 17 Mach IV, 17 Javelina, 19-223 Calhoon, 20 VarTag, 22 PPC, Model 21, 6mm PPC, 221 Fireball, 222 Rem., 222 Rem. Mag., 223 Rem., 223 Ackley Imp., 6x45, 6x47, single shot; Model 38—17 Squirrel, 17 HeBee, 17 Ackley Hornet, 22 Hornet, 22 K Hornet, 218 Mashburn Bee, 218 Bee, 22 Squirrel, single shot. **Barrel:** 24" stainless match grade. **Weight:** 6-1/2 to 7-1/4 lbs. **Stock:** AA Claro walnut; 20 l.p.i. checkering. **Sights:** None furnished. **Features:** Uses three front locking lug system. Fully adjustable trigger. Many options available. Contact maker for details. Made in U.S. by Cooper Firearms.
Price: Classic $1,050.00
Price: Varminter $995.00
Price: Varmint Extreme $1,795.00
Price: Custom Classic $1,995.00
Price: Western Classic $2,295.00

COOPER ARMS MODEL 22 PRO VARMINT EXTREME
Caliber: 22-250, 220 Swift, 243, 25-06, 6mm PPC, 308, single shot. **Barrel:** 26"; stainless steel match grade, straight taper; free-floated. **Weight:** NA. **Length:** NA. **Stock:** AAA Claro walnut, oil finish, 22 lpi wrap-around borderless ribbon checkering, beaded cheekpiece, steel gripcap, flared varminter forend, Pachmayr pad. **Sights:** None furnished; drilled and tapped for scope mounting. **Features:** Uses a three front locking lug system. Available with sterling silver inlaid medallion, skeleton gripcap, and French walnut. Introduced 1995. Made in U.S. by Cooper Arms.
Price: $1,795.00
Price: Benchrest model with Jewell trigger. $2,195.00
Price: Black Jack model (McMillan synthetic stock) $1,795.00

CZ 527 LUX BOLT-ACTION RIFLE
Caliber: 22 Hornet, 222 Rem., 223 Rem., detachable 5-shot magazine. **Barrel:** 23-1/2"; standard or heavy barrel. **Weight:** 6 lbs, 1 oz. **Length:** 42-1/2" overall. **Stock:** European walnut with Monte Carlo. **Sights:** Hooded front, open adjustable rear. **Features:** Improved mini-Mauser action with non-rotating claw extractor; single set trigger; grooved receiver. Imported from the Czech Republic by CZ-USA.
Price: $540.00
Price: Model FS, full-length stock, cheekpiece. $607.00

208 • GUNS ILLUSTRATED

CENTERFIRE RIFLES — BOLT ACTION

CZ 550 Lux

CZ 550 American Classic

CZ 550 Magnum

Dakota 76 Classic

Price: 375 H&H. $756.00
Price: 416 Rigby $796.00
Price: 458 Win. Mag. $744.00

CZ 527 American Classic Bolt-Action Rifle
Similar to the CZ 527 Lux except has classic-style stock with 18 l.p.i. checkering; free-floating barrel; recessed target crown on barrel. No sights furnished. Introduced 1999. Imported from the Czech Republic by CZ-USA.
Price: 22 Hornet, 222 Rem., 223 Rem. $540.00

CZ 550 LUX BOLT-ACTION RIFLE
Caliber: 22-250, 243, 6.5x55, 7x57, 7x64, 308 Win., 9.3x62, 270 Win., 30-06. **Barrel:** 20.47". **Weight:** 7.5 lbs. **Length:** 44.68" overall. **Stock:** Turkish walnut in Bavarian style or FS (Mannlicher). **Sights:** Hooded front, adjustable rear. **Features:** Improved Mauser-style action with claw extractor, fixed ejector, square bridge dovetailed receiver; single set trigger. Imported from the Czech Republic by CZ-USA.
Price: Lux . . . . $561.00 to $609.00
Price: FS (full stock) $645.00

CZ 550 American Classic Bolt-Action Rifle
Similar to the CZ 550 Lux except has American classic-style stock with 18 l.p.i. checkering; free-floating barrel; recessed target crown. Has 25.6" barrel; weighs 7.48 lbs. No sights furnished. Introduced 1999. Imported from the Czech Republic by CZ-USA.
Price: . . . . $576.00 to $609.00

CZ 550 Medium Magnum Bolt-Action Rifle
Similar to the CZ 550 Lux except chambered for the 300 Win. Mag. and 7mm Rem. Mag.; 5-shot magazine. Adjustable iron sights, hammer-forged barrel, single-set trigger, Turkish walnut stock. Weighs 7.5 lbs. Introduced 2001. Imported from the Czech Republic by CZ USA.
Price: $621.00

CZ 550 Magnum Bolt-Action Rifle
Similar to the CZ 550 Lux except has long action for 300 Win. Mag., 375 H&H, 416 Rigby, 458 Win. Mag. Overall length is 46.45"; barrel length 25"; weighs 9.24 lbs. Comes with hooded front sight, express rear with one standing, two folding leaves. Imported from the Czech Republic by CZ-USA.
Price: 300 Win. Mag. $717.00

CZ 700 M1 SNIPER RIFLE
Caliber: 308 Winchester, 10-shot magazine. **Barrel:** 25.6". **Weight:** 11.9 lbs. **Length:** 45" overall. **Stock:** Laminated wood thumbhole with adjustable buttplate and cheekpiece. **Sights:** None furnished; permanently attached Weaver rail for scope mounting. **Features:** 60-degree bolt throw; oversized trigger guard and bolt handle for use with gloves; full-length equipment rail on forend; fully adjustable trigger. Introduced 2001. Imported from the Czech Republic by CZ USA.
Price: $2,097.00

DAKOTA 76 TRAVELER TAKEDOWN RIFLE
Caliber: 257 Roberts, 25-06, 7x57, 270, 280, 30-06, 338-06, 35 Whelen (standard length); 7mm Rem. Mag., 300 Win. Mag., 338 Win. Mag., 416 Taylor, 458 Win. Mag. (short magnums); 7mm, 300, 330, 375 Dakota Magnums. **Barrel:** 23". **Weight:** 7-1/2 lbs. **Length:** 43-1/2" overall. **Stock:** Medium fancy-grade walnut in classic style. Checkered grip and forend; solid butt pad. **Sights:** None furnished; drilled and tapped for scope mounts. **Features:** Threadless disassembly—no threads to wear or stretch, no interrupted cuts, and headspace remains constant. Uses modified Model 76 design with many features of the Model 70 Winchester. Left-hand model also available. Introduced 1989. Made in U.S. by Dakota Arms, Inc.
Price: Classic $4,495.00
Price: Safari $5,495.00
Price: Extra barrels . . . . $1,650.00 to $1,950.00

DAKOTA 76 CLASSIC BOLT-ACTION RIFLE
Caliber: 257 Roberts, 270, 280, 30-06, 7mm Rem. Mag., 338 Win. Mag., 300 Win. Mag., 375 H&H, 458 Win. Mag. **Barrel:** 23". **Weight:** 7-1/2 lbs. **Length:** 43-1/2" overall. **Stock:** Medium fancy grade walnut in classic style. Checkered pistol grip and forend; solid butt pad. **Sights:** None furnished; drilled and tapped for scope mounts. **Features:** Has many features of the original Model 70 Winchester. One-piece rail trigger guard assembly; steel gripcap. Model 70-style trigger. Many options available. Left-hand rifle available at same price. Introduced 1988. From Dakota Arms, Inc.
Price: $3,595.00

CENTERFIRE RIFLES — BOLT ACTION

Dakota 76 Safari

Dakota Longbow

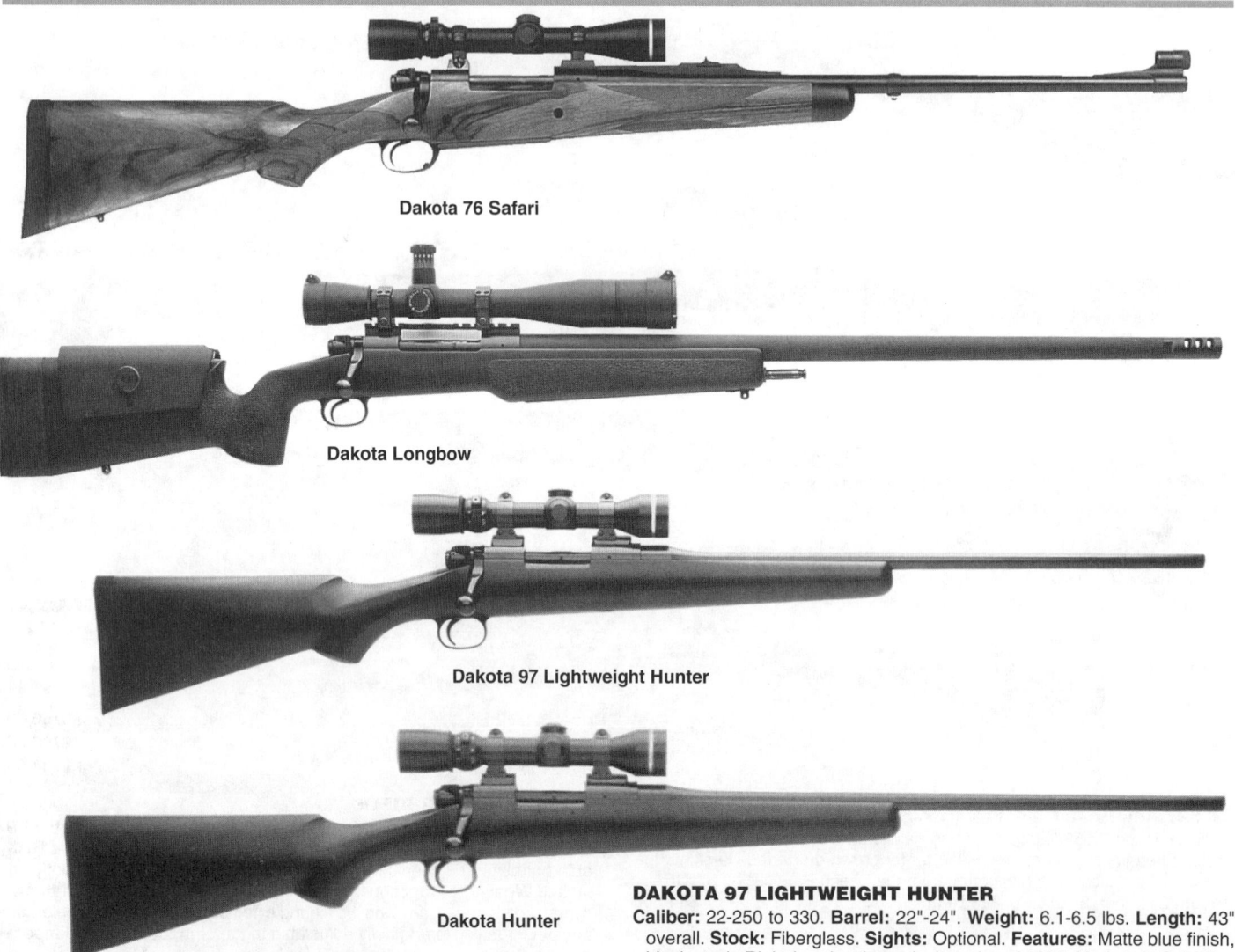

Dakota 97 Lightweight Hunter

Dakota Hunter

DAKOTA 76 SAFARI BOLT-ACTION RIFLE
Caliber: 270 Win., 7x57, 280, 30-06, 7mm Dakota, 7mm Rem. Mag., 300 Dakota, 300 Win. Mag., 330 Dakota, 338 Win. Mag., 375 Dakota, 458 Win. Mag., 300 H&H, 375 H&H, 416 Rem. **Barrel:** 23". **Weight:** 8-1/2 lbs. **Length:** 43-1/2" overall. **Stock:** XXX fancy walnut with ebony forend tip; point-pattern with wrap-around forend checkering. **Sights:** Ramp front, standing leaf rear. **Features:** Has many features of the original Model 70 Winchester. Barrel band front swivel, inletted rear. Cheekpiece with shadow line. Steel gripcap. Introduced 1988. From Dakota Arms, Inc.
Price: Wood stock. $4,595.00

Dakota African Grade
Similar to the 76 Safari except chambered for 338 Lapua Mag., 404 Jeffery, 416 Rigby, 416 Dakota, 450 Dakota, 4-round magazine, select wood, two stock cross-bolts. Has 24" barrel, weight of 9-10 lbs. Ramp front sight, standing leaf rear. Introduced 1989.
Price: $4,995.00

DAKOTA LONGBOW TACTICAL E.R. RIFLE
Caliber: 300 Dakota Magnum, 330 Dakota Magnum, 338 Lapua Magnum. **Barrel:** 28", .950" at muzzle **Weight:** 13.7 lbs. **Length:** 50" to 52" overall. **Stock:** Ambidextrous McMillan A-2 fiberglass, black or olive green color; adjustable cheekpiece and buttplate. **Sights:** None furnished. Comes with Picatinny one-piece optical rail. **Features:** Uses the Dakota 76 action with controlled-round feed; three-position firing pin block safety, claw extractor; Model 70-style trigger. Comes with bipod, case tool kit. Introduced 1997. Made in U.S. by Dakota Arms, Inc.
Price: $4,250.00

DAKOTA 97 LIGHTWEIGHT HUNTER
Caliber: 22-250 to 330. **Barrel:** 22"-24". **Weight:** 6.1-6.5 lbs. **Length:** 43" overall. **Stock:** Fiberglass. **Sights:** Optional. **Features:** Matte blue finish, black stock. Right-hand action only. Introduced 1998. Made in U.S. by Dakota Arms, Inc.
Price: $1,995.00

DAKOTA LONG RANGE HUNTER RIFLE
Caliber: 25-06, 257 Roberts, 270 Win., 280 Rem., 7mm Rem. Mag., 7mm Dakota Mag., 30-06, 300 Win. Mag., 300 Dakota Mag., 338 Win. Mag., 330 Dakota Mag., 375 H&H Mag., 375 Dakota Mag. **Barrel:** 24", 26", match-quality; free-floating. **Weight:** 7.7 lbs. **Length:** 45" to 47" overall. **Stock:** H-S Precision black synthetic, with one-piece bedding block system. **Sights:** None furnished. Drilled and tapped for scope mounting. **Features:** Cylindrical machined receiver controlled round feed; Mauser-style extractor; three-position striker blocking safety; fully adjustable match trigger. Right-hand action only. Introduced 1997. Made in U.S. by Dakota Arms, Inc.
Price: $1,995.00

HARRIS GUNWORKS SIGNATURE CLASSIC SPORTER
Caliber: 22-250, 243, 6mm Rem., 7mm-08, 284, 308 (short action); 25-06, 270, 280 Rem., 30-06, 7mm Rem. Mag., 300 Win. Mag., 300 Wea. (long action); 338 Win. Mag., 340 Wea., 375 H&H (magnum action). **Barrel:** 22", 24", 26". **Weight:** 7 lbs. (short action). **Stock:** Fiberglass in green, beige, brown or black. Recoil pad and 1" swivels installed. Length of pull up to 14-1/4". **Sights:** None furnished. Comes with 1" rings and bases. **Features:** Uses right- or left-hand action with matte black finish. Trigger pull set at 3 lbs. Four-round magazine for standard calibers; three for magnums. Aluminum floorplate. Wood stock optional. Introduced 1987. From Harris Gunworks, Inc.
Price: $2,700.00

CENTERFIRE RIFLES — BOLT ACTION

Harris Gunworks Alaskan

Harris Gunworks Signature Titanium Mountain

Harris Gunworks Signature Super Varminter

Harris Gunworks Talon Safari

Harris Gunworks Signature Classic Stainless Sporter
Similar to the Signature Classic Sporter except action is made of stainless steel. Same calibers, in addition to 416 Rem. Mag. Comes with fiberglass stock, right- or left-hand action in natural stainless, glass bead or black chrome sulfide finishes. Introduced 1990. From Harris Gunworks, Inc.
Price: $2,900.00

Harris Gunworks Signature Alaskan
Similar to the Classic Sporter except has match-grade barrel with single leaf rear sight, barrel band front, 1" detachable rings and mounts, steel floorplate, electroless nickel finish. Has wood Monte Carlo stock with cheekpiece, palm-swell grip, solid butt pad. Chambered for 270, 280 Rem., 30-06, 7mm Rem. Mag., 300 Win. Mag., 300 Wea. Mag., 358 Win., 340 Wea., 375 H&H. Introduced 1989.
Price: $3,800.00

Harris Gunworks Signature Titanium Mountain Rifle
Similar to the Classic Sporter except action made of titanium alloy, barrel of chrome-moly steel. Stock is of graphite reinforced fiberglass. Weight is 5-1/2 lbs. Chambered for 270, 280 Rem., 30-06, 7mm Rem. Mag., 300 Win. Mag. Fiberglass stock optional. Introduced 1989.
Price: $3,300.00
Price: With graphite-steel composite light weight barrel. $3,700.00

Harris Gunworks Signature Varminter
Similar to the Signature Classic Sporter except has heavy contoured barrel, adjustable trigger, field bipod and special hand-bedded fiberglass stock. Chambered for 223, 22-250, 220 Swift, 243, 6mm Rem., 25-06, 7mm-08, 7mm BR, 308, 350 Rem. Mag. Comes with 1" rings and bases. Introduced 1989.
Price: $2,700.00

HARRIS GUNWORKS TALON SAFARI RIFLE
Caliber: 300 Win. Mag., 300 Wea. Mag., 300 Phoenix, 338 Win. Mag., 30/378, 338 Lapua, 300 H&H, 340 Wea. Mag., 375 H&H, 404 Jeffery, 416 Rem. Mag., 458 Win. Mag. (Safari Magnum); 378 Wea. Mag., 416 Rigby, 416 Wea. Mag., 460 Wea. Mag. (Safari Super Magnum). **Barrel:** 24". **Weight:** About 9-10 lbs. **Length:** 43" overall. **Stock:** Gunworks fiberglass Safari. **Sights:** Barrel band front ramp, multi-leaf express rear. **Features:** Uses Harris Gunworks Safari action. Has quick detachable 1" scope mounts, positive locking steel floorplate, barrel band sling swivel. Match-grade barrel. Matte black finish standard. Introduced 1989. From Harris Gunworks, Inc.
Price: Talon Safari Magnum. $3,900.00
Price: Talon Safari Super Magnum $4,200.00

HARRIS GUNWORKS TALON SPORTER RIFLE
Caliber: 22-250, 243, 6mm Rem., 6mm BR, 7mm BR, 7mm-08, 25-06, 270, 280 Rem., 284, 308, 30-06, 350 Rem. Mag. (long action); 7mm Rem. Mag., 7mm STW, 300 Win. Mag., 300 Wea. Mag., 300 H&H, 338 Win. Mag., 340 Wea. Mag., 375 H&H, 416 Rem. Mag. **Barrel:** 24" (standard). **Weight:** About 7-1/2 lbs. **Length:** NA. **Stock:** Choice of walnut or fiberglass. **Sights:** None furnished; comes with rings and bases. Open sights optional. **Features:** Uses pre-'64 Model 70-type action with cone breech, controlled feed, claw extractor and three-position safety. Barrel and action are of stainless steel; chrome-moly optional. Introduced 1991. From Harris Gunworks, Inc.
Price: $2,900.00

CENTERFIRE RIFLES — BOLT ACTION

Howa Lightning

Howa M-1500 Hunter

Howa M-1500 PCS Police Counter Sniper

Howa M-1500 Varmint

L.A.R. Grizzly

HOWA LIGHTNING BOLT-ACTION RIFLE
Caliber: 223, 22-250, 243, 270, 308, 30-06, 7mm Rem. Mag., 300 Win. Mag., 338 Win. Mag. **Barrel:** 22", 24" magnum calibers. **Weight:** 7-1/2 lbs. **Length:** 42" overall (22" barrel). **Stock:** Black Bell & Carlson Carbelite composite with Monte Carlo comb; checkered grip and forend. **Sights:** None furnished. Drilled and tapped for scope mounting. **Features:** Sliding thumb safety; hinged floorplate; polished blue/black finish. Introduced 1993. From Legacy Sports International.
Price: Blue, standard calibers $435.00
Price: Blue, magnum calibers $455.00
Price: Stainless, standard calibers $485.00
Price: Stainless, magnum calibers $505.00

Howa M-1500 Hunter Bolt-Action Rifle
Similar to the Lightning model except has walnut-finished hardwood stock. Polished blue finish or stainless steel. Introduced 1999. From Legacy Sports International.
Price: Blue, standard calibers $455.00
Price: Stainless, standard calibers $505.00
Price: Blue, magnum calibers $475.00
Price: Stainless, magnum calibers $525.00

Howa M-1500 PCS Police Counter Sniper Rifle
Similar to the M-1500 Lightning except chambered only for 308 Win., 24" hammer-forged heavy barrel. Trigger is factory set at 4 lbs. Available in blue or stainless steel, polymer or hardwood stock. Introduced 1999. Imported from Japan by Legacy Sports International.
Price: Blue, polymer stock $465.00
Price: Stainless, polymer stock $525.00
Price: Blue, wood stock $485.00
Price: Stainless, wood stock $545.00

Howa M-1500 Varmint Rifle
Similar to the M-1500 Lightning except has heavy 24" hammer-forged barrel. Chambered for 223 and 22-250. Weighs 9.3 lbs.; overall length 44.5". Introduced 1999. Imported from Japan by Interarms/Howa.
Price: Blue, polymer stock $465.00
Price: Stainless, polymer stock $525.00
Price: Blue, wood stock $485.00
Price: Stainless, wood stock $545.00

KIMBER MODEL 84M BOLT-ACTION RIFLE
Caliber: 22-250, 243, 260 Rem., 7mm-08, 308, 5-shot magazine. **Barrel:** 22", 26". **Weight:** 5 lbs., 10 oz. to 7 lbs., 5 oz. **Length:** 41.25" overall (22" bbl.). **Stock:** Claro walnut, checkered with steel grip cap. **Sights:** None furnished; drilled and tapped for scope mount. **Features:** Mauser claw extractor; two-position wing safety; action bedded on aluminum pillars; free-floated barrel; match-grade trigger set at 3-1/2 - 4 lbs.; matte blue finish. Includes cable lock. Introduced 2001. Made in U.S. by Kimber Mfg. Inc.
Price: Classic (243, 260, 7mm-08, 308; 22" light sporter bbl.) $895.00
Price: Varmint (22-250; 26" stainless heavy sporter bbl.) $978.00

L.A.R. GRIZZLY 50 BIG BOAR RIFLE
Caliber: 50 BMG, single shot. **Barrel:** 36". **Weight:** 28.4 lbs. **Length:** 45.5" overall. **Stock:** Integral. Ventilated rubber recoil pad. **Sights:** None furnished; scope mount. **Features:** Bolt-action bullpup design; thumb safety. All-steel construction. Introduced 1994. Made in U.S. by L.A.R. Mfg., Inc.
Price: $2,570.00

CENTERFIRE RIFLES — BOLT ACTION

Magnum Research Tactical

Mountain Eagle Varmint

Raptor Bolt-Action

Remington 700 ADL Synthetic

MAGNUM RESEARCH TACTICAL RIFLE
Caliber: 223 Rem., 22-250, 308 Win., 300 Win. Mag. **Barrel:** 26" Magnum Lite™ graphite. **Weight:** 8.3 lbs. **Length:** NA. **Stock:** H-S Precision™ tactical black synthetic. **Sights:** None furnished; drilled and tapped for scope mount. **Features:** Accurized Remington 700 action; adjustable trigger; adjustable comb height. Tuned to shoot 1/2" MOA or better. Introduced 2001. From Magnum Research Inc.
Price: $2,400.00

MOUNTAIN EAGLE RIFLE
Caliber: 222 Rem., 223 Rem. (Varmint); 270, 280, 30-06 (long action); 7mm Rem. Mag., 7mm STW, 300 Win. Mag., 338 Win. Mag., 300 Wea. Mag., 375 H&H, 416 Rem. Mag. (magnum action). **Barrel:** 24", 26" (Varmint); match-grade; fluted stainless on Varmint. Free floating. **Weight:** 7 lbs., 13 oz. **Length:** 44" overall (24" barrel). **Stock:** Kevlar-graphite with aluminum bedding block, high comb, recoil pad, swivel studs; made by H-S Precision. **Sights:** None furnished; accepts any Remington 700-type base. **Features:** Special Sako action with one-piece forged bolt, hinged steel floorplate, lengthened receiver ring; adjustable trigger. Krieger cut-rifled benchrest barrel. Introduced 1996. From Magnum Research, Inc.
Price: Right-hand $1,499.00
Price: Left-hand $1,549.00
Price: Varmint Edition $1,629.00
Price: 375 H&H, 416 Rem., add $300.00
Price: Magnum Lite (graphite barrel) $2,295.00

NEW ULTRA LIGHT ARMS BOLT-ACTION RIFLES
Caliber: 17 Rem. to 416 Rigby (numerous calibers available). **Barrel:** Douglas, length to order. **Weight:** 4-3/4 to 7-1/2 lbs. **Length:** Varies. **Stock:** Kevlar®/graphite composite, variety of finishes. **Sights:** None furnished; drilled and tapped for scope mount. **Features:** Timney trigger, hand-lapped action, button-rifled barrel, hand-bedded action, recoil pad, sling-swivel studs, optional Jewell Trigger. Made in U.S. by New Ultra Light Arms.
Price: Model 20 (short action) $2,500.00
Price: Model 24 (long action) $2,600.00
Price: Model 28 (magnum action) $2,900.00
Price: Model 40 (300 Wea. Mag., 416 Rigby) $2,900.00
Price: Left-hand models, add $100.00

RAPTOR BOLT-ACTION RIFLE
Caliber: 270, 30-06, 243, 25-06, 308; 4-shot magazine. **Barrel:** 22". **Weight:** 7 lbs., 6 oz. **Length:** 42.5" overall. **Stock:** Black synthetic, fiberglass reinforced; checkered grip and forend; vented recoil pad; Monte Carlo cheekpiece. **Sights:** None furnished; drilled and tapped for scope mounts. **Features:** Rust-resistant "Taloncote" treated barreled action; pillar bedded; stainless bolt with three locking lugs; adjustable trigger. Announced 1997. Made in U.S. by Raptor Arms Co., Inc.
Price: $249.00

REMINGTON MODEL 700 CLASSIC RIFLE
Caliber: 7mm-08. **Barrel:** 24". **Weight:** About 7-1/4 lbs. **Length:** 44-1/2" overall. **Stock:** American walnut, 20 lpi checkering on pistol grip and forend. Classic styling. Satin finish. **Sights:** None furnished. Receiver drilled and tapped for scope mounting. **Features:** A "classic" version of the BDL with straight comb stock. Fitted with rubber recoil pad. Sling swivel studs installed. Hinged floorplate. Limited production in 2001 only.
Price: $633.00

REMINGTON MODEL 700 ADL DELUXE RIFLE
Caliber: 270, 308, 30-06 and 7mm Rem. Mag. **Barrel:** 22" or 24" round tapered. **Weight:** 7-1/4 to 7-1/2 lbs. **Length:** 41-5/8" to 44-1/2" overall. **Stock:** Walnut. Satin-finished pistol grip stock with fine-line cut checkering, Monte Carlo. **Sights:** Gold bead ramp front; removable, step-adjustable rear with windage screw. **Features:** Side safety, receiver tapped for scope mounts.
Price: From $531.00

Remington Model 700 ADL Synthetic
Similar to the 700 ADL except has a fiberglass-reinforced synthetic stock with straight comb, raised cheekpiece, positive checkering, and black rubber butt pad. Metal has matte finish. Available in 22-250, 223, 243, 270, 308, 30-06 with 22" barrel, 300 Win. Mag., 7mm Rem. Mag. with 24" barrel. Introduced 1996.
Price: From $457.00

34TH EDITION, 2002 • 213

Centerfire Rifles — Bolt Action

Remington 700 BDL

Remington 700 BDL Left Hand

Remington 700 BDL SS DM

Remington 700 BDL SS DM-B

Remington Model 700 ADL Synthetic Youth
Similar to the Model 700 ADL Synthetic except has 1" shorter stock, 20" barrel. Chambered for 243, 308. Introduced 1998.
Price: $484.00

Remington Model 700 BDL Custom Deluxe Rifle
Same as the 700 ADL except chambered for 222, 223 (short action, 24" barrel), 22-250, 25-06. (short action, 22" barrel), 243, 270, 30-06; skip-line checkering; black forend tip and gripcap with white line spacers. Matted receiver top, fine-line engraving, quick-release floorplate. Hooded ramp front sight; quick detachable swivels. 7mm-08, .280.
Price: $633.00
Also available in 17 Rem., 7mm Rem. Mag., 7mm Rem. Ultra Mag., 7mm-08, 280, 300 Win. Mag. (long action, 24" barrel); 338 Win. Mag., (long action, 22" barrel); 300 Rem. Ultra Mag. 338 Rem. Ultra Mag. (26" barrel), 375 Rem. Ultra Mag. Overall length 44-1/2", weight about 7-1/2 lbs. 338 Rem Ultra Mag.
Price: $660.00

Remington Model 700 BDL Left Hand Custom Deluxe
Same as 700 BDL except mirror-image left-hand action, stock. Available in 270, 30-06, 7mm Rem. Mag., 300 Rem. Ultra Mag.
Price: $660.00
Price: 7mm Rem. Mag., 300 Rem. Ultra Mag. $687.00

Remington Model 700 BDL DM Rifle
Same as the 700 BDL except has detachable box magazine (4-shot, standard calibers, 3-shot for magnums). Has glossy stock finish, fine-line engraving, open sights, recoil pad, sling swivels. Available in 270, 30-06, 7mm Rem. Mag., 300 Win. Mag. Introduced 1995.
Price: From $681.00

Remington Model 700 BDL SS Rifle
Similar to the 700 BDL rifle except has hinged floorplate, 24" standard weight barrel in all calibers; magnum calibers have magnum-contour barrel. No sights supplied, but comes drilled and tapped. Has corrosion-resistant follower and fire control, stainless BDL-style barreled action with fine matte finish. Synthetic stock has straight comb and cheekpiece, textured finish, positive checkering, plated swivel studs. Calibers—270, 30-06; magnums—7mm Rem. Mag., 300 Rem. Ultra Mag. (26" barrel) 300 Win. Mag., 338 Win. Mag., 338 Rem. Ultra Mag., 375 H&H. Weighs 7-3/8 - 7-1/2 lbs. Introduced 1993.
Price: From $681.00

Remington Model 700 BDL SS DM Rifle
Same as the 700 BDL SS except has detachable box magazine. Barrel, receiver and bolt made of #416 stainless steel; black synthetic stock, fine-line engraving. Available in 25-06, 260 Rem., 270, 280, 30-06, 7mm Rem. Mag., 7mm-08, 300 Win. Mag., 300 Wea. Mag. Introduced 1995.
Price: From $756.00

Remington Model 700 BDL SS DM-B
Same as the 700 BDL SS DM except has muzzle brake, fine-line engraving. Available only in 7mm STW, 300 Win. Mag. Introduced 1996.
Price: $845.00

Remington Model 700 Custom KS Mountain Rifle
Similar to the 700 BDL except custom finished with Kevlar reinforced resin synthetic stock. Available in both left- and right-hand versions. Chambered for 270 Win., 280 Rem., 30-06, 7mm Rem. Mag., 7mm STW, 300 Win. Mag., 338 Rem. Ultra Mag., 300 Win. Mag., 300 Wea. Mag., 35 Whelen, 338 Win. Mag., 8mm Rem. Mag., 375 H&H, with 24" barrel (except 300 Rem. Ultra Mag., 26"). Weighs 6 lbs., 6 oz. Introduced 1986.
Price: .338 Ultra $1,221.00

Remington Model 700 LSS Mountain Rifle
Similar to Model 700 Custom KS Mountain Rifle except has stainless steel 22" barrel and two-tone laminated stock. Chambered in 260 Rem., 7mm-08, 270 Winchester and 30-06. Overall length 42-1/2", weighs 6-5/8 oz. Introduced 1999. From Remington Arms Co.
Price: $744.00

CENTERFIRE RIFLES — BOLT ACTION

Remington 700 Safari KS

Remington 700 APR African Plains

Remington 700 VLS

Remington 700 Varmint Synthetic

Remington Model 700 Safari Grade
Similar to the 700 BDL except custom finished and tuned. In 8mm Rem. Mag., 375 H&H, 416 Rem. Mag. or 458 Win. Mag. calibers only with heavy barrel. Hand checkered, oil-finished stock in classic or Monte Carlo style with recoil pad installed. Classic available in right- and left-hand versions.
Price: From $1,225.00
Price: Safari KS (Kevlar stock), from $1,410.00

Remington Model 700 AWR Alaskan Wilderness Rifle
Similar to the Model 700 BDL except has stainless barreled action with satin blue finish; special 24" Custom Shop barrel profile; matte gray stock of fiberglass and graphite, reinforced with DuPont Kevlar, straight comb with raised cheekpiece, magnum-grade black rubber recoil pad. Chambered for 7mm Rem. Mag., 7mm STW, 300 Rem. Ultra Mag., 300 Win. Mag., 300 Wea. Mag., 338 Rem. Ultra Mag., 338 Win. Mag., 375 H&H. Introduced 1994.
Price: From $1,480.00

Remington Model 700 APR African Plains Rifle
Similar to the Model 700 BDL except has magnum receiver and specially contoured 26" Custom Shop barrel with satin finish, laminated wood stock with raised cheekpiece, satin finish, black butt pad, 20 lpi cut checkering. Chambered for 7mm Rem. Mag., 300 Rem. Ultra Mag., 300 Win. Mag., 300 Wea. Mag., 338 Win. Mag., 338 Rem. Ultra Mag., 375 H&H. Introduced 1994.
Price: $1,593.00

Remington Model 700 EtronX Electronic Ignition Rifle
Similar to Model 700 VS SF except features battery-powered ignition system for near-zero lock time and electronic trigger mechanism. Requires ammunition with EtronX electrically fired primers. Aluminum-bedded 26" heavy, stainless steel, fluted barrel; overall length 45-7/8"; weight 8 lbs. 14 oz. Black, Kevlar-reinforced composite stock. Light-emitting diode display on grip top indicates fire or safe mode, loaded or unloaded chamber, battery condition. Introduced 2000. From Remington Arms Co.
Price: 220 Swift, 22-250 or 243 Win. $1,999.00

Remington Model 700 LSS Rifle
Similar to the 700 BDL except has stainless steel barreled action, gray laminated wood stock with Monte Carlo comb and cheekpiece. No sights furnished. Available in 7mm Rem. Mag., 300 Rem. Ultra Mag., 300 Win. Mag., and 338 Rem. Ultra Mag. in right-hand, and 270, 7mm Rem. Mag., 30-06, 300 Rem. Ultra Mag., 300 Win. Mag., 338 Rem. Ultra Mag. in left-hand model. Introduced 1996.
Price: From $771.00

Remington Model 700 MTN DM Rifle
Similar to the 700 BDL except weighs 6-1/2 to 6-5/8 lbs., has a 22" tapered barrel. Redesigned pistol grip, straight comb, contoured cheekpiece, hand-rubbed oil stock finish, deep cut checkering, hinged floorplate and magazine follower, two-position thumb safety. Chambered for 260 Rem., 270 Win., 7mm-08, 25-06, 280 Rem., 30-06, 4-shot detachable box magazine. Overall length is 41-5/8"-42-1/2". Introduced 1995.
Price: About $681.00

Remington Model 700 Titanium
Similar to 700 BDL except has titanium receiver, spiral-cut fluted bolt, skeletonized bolt handle and carbon-fiber and Kevlar® stock with sling swivel studs. Barrel 22"; weighs 5-1/4 lbs. (short action) or 5-1/2 lbs. (long action). Satin stainless finish. Introduced 2001. From Remington Arms Co.
Price: $1,199.00

Remington Model 700 VLS Varmint Laminated Stock
Similar to the 700 BDL except has 26" heavy barrel without sights, brown laminated stock with beavertail forend, gripcap, rubber butt pad. Available in 223 Rem., 22-250, 6mm, 243, 308. Polished blue finish. Introduced 1995.
Price: From $675.00

Remington Model 700 VS Varmint Synthetic Rifles
Similar to the 700 BDL Varmint Laminated except has composite stock reinforced with DuPont Kevlar, fiberglass and graphite. Has aluminum bedding block that runs the full length of the receiver. Free-floating 26" barrel. Metal has black matte finish; stock has textured black and gray finish and swivel studs. Available in 223, 22-250, 308. Right- and left-hand. Introduced 1992.
Price: From $759.00

34TH EDITION, 2002 • 215

CENTERFIRE RIFLES — BOLT ACTION

Remington 700 VS Composite

Remington 700 VF SF

Remington 700 Sendero SF

Remington Model Seven

Remington Model 700 VS Composite Rifle
Similar to the Model 700 VS Varmint Synthetic except has a composite varmint-weight barrel, weighs 7-1/8 lbs., and is available in right-hand in 22-250, 223, 308 Win. Introduced 1999.
Price: $1,912.00

Remington Model 700 VS SF Rifle
Similar to the Model 700 Varmint Synthetic except has satin-finish stainless barreled action with 26" fluted barrel, spherical concave muzzle crown. Chambered for 223, 220 Swift, 22-250. Introduced 1994.
Price: From... $916.00

Remington Model 700 Sendero Rifle
Similar to the Model 700 Varmint Synthetic except has long action for magnum calibers. Has 26" heavy varmint barrel with spherical concave crown. Chambered for 25-06, 270, 7mm Rem. Mag., 300 Win. Mag. Introduced 1994.
Price: From... $759.00

Remington Model 700 Sendero SF Rifle
Similar to the 700 Sendero except has stainless steel action and 26" fluted stainless barrel. Weighs 8-1/2 lbs. Chambered for 25-06, 7mm Rem. Mag., 300 Wea. Mag., 7mm STW, 300 Rem. Ultra Mag., 338 Rem. Ultra Mag., 300 Win. Mag. Introduced 1996.
Price: From... $943.00

NEW! REMINGTON MODEL 710 BOLT-ACTION RIFLE
Caliber: 270 Win., 30-06. **Barrel:** 22". **Weight:** 7-1/8 lbs. **Length:** 42-1/2" overall. **Stock:** Gray synthetic. **Sights:** Bushnell Sharpshooter 3-9x scope mounted and bore-sighted. **Features:** Unique action locks bolt directly into barrel; 60-degree bolt throw; 4-shot dual-stack magazine; key-operated Integrated Security System locks bolt open. Introduced 2001. Made in U.S. by Remington Arms Co.
Price: $425.00

REMINGTON MODEL SEVEN LSS BOLT-ACTION RIFLE
Caliber: 22-250, 243, 7mm-08. **Barrel:** 20". **Weight:** 6-1/2 lbs. **Length:** 39-1/4" overall. **Stock:** Brown laminated. Cut checkering. **Sights:** Ramp front, adjustable open rear. **Features:** Short-action design; silent side safety; free-floated barrel except for single pressure point at forend tip. Introduced 1983.
Price: $727.00

Remington Model Seven Custom KS
Similar to the Model Seven except has gray Kevlar reinforced stock with 1" black rubber recoil pad and swivel studs. Metal has black matte finish. No sights on 223, 260 Rem., 7mm-08, 308; 35 Rem. and 350 Rem. have iron sights.
Price: $1,221.00

Remington Model Seven LSS
Similar to Model Seven except has satin-finished, brown laminated stock, stainless steel 20" barrel and receiver. Overall length, 39-1/4", weighs 6-1/2 lbs. Chambered for 22-250, 243, 7mm-08 Rem. Introduced 2000.
Price: $633.00

Remington Model Seven LS
Similar to Model Seven except has satin-finished, brown laminated stock with 20" carbon steel barrel. Introduced 2000.
Price: $633.00

Remington Model Seven SS
Similar to the Model Seven except has stainless steel barreled action and black synthetic stock, 20" barrel. Chambered for 223, 243, 260 Rem., 7mm-08, 308. Introduced 1994.
Price: $681.00

Remington Model Seven Custom MS Rifle
Similar to the Model Seven except has full-length Mannlicher-style stock of laminated wood with straight comb, solid black recoil pad, black steel forend tip, cut checkering, gloss finish. Barrel length 20", weighs 6-3/4 lbs. Available in 222 Rem., 223, 22-250, 243, 6mm Rem., 260 Rem., 7mm-08 Rem., 308, 350 Rem. Mag. Calibers 250 Savage, 257 Roberts, 35 Rem. Polished blue finish. Introduced 1993. From Remington Custom Shop.
Price: From... $1,236.00

CENTERFIRE RIFLES — BOLT ACTION

Ruger 77/22 Hornet Varmint

Ruger M77 Mark II All-Weather

Ruger 77/44

Remington Model Seven Youth Rifle
Similar to the Model Seven except has hardwood stock with 12-3/16" length of pull and chambered for 223, 243, 260 Rem., 7mm-08. Introduced 1993.
Price: $519.00

Ruger M77RSI International Carbine
Same as the standard Model 77 except has 18" barrel, full-length International-style stock, with steel forend cap, loop-type steel sling swivels. Integral-base receiver, open sights, Ruger 1" steel rings. Improved front sight. Available in 243, 270, 308, 30-06. Weighs 7 lbs. Length overall is 38-3/8".
Price: M77RSIMKII $735.00

RUGER M77 MARK II EXPRESS RIFLE
Caliber: 270, 30-06, 7mm Rem. Mag., 300 Win. Mag., 338 Win. Mag., 4-shot magazine (3-shot Magnum calibers). **Barrel:** 22" (std. calibers) or 24" (Magnum calibers), with integral steel rib; barrel-mounted front swivel stud; hammer forged. **Weight:** 7.5 lbs. **Length:** 42.125" overall. **Stock:** Hand-checkered circassian walnut with steel gripcap, black rubber butt pad, swivel studs. **Sights:** Ramp front, V-notch two-leaf express rear adjustable for windage mounted on rib. **Features:** Mark II action with three-position safety, stainless steel bolt, steel trigger guard, hinged steel floorplate. Introduced 1991.
Price: M77RSEXPMKII $1,695.00

RUGER 77/22 HORNET BOLT-ACTION RIFLE
Caliber: 22 Hornet, 6-shot rotary magazine. **Barrel:** 20". **Weight:** About 6 lbs. **Length:** 39-3/4" overall. **Stock:** Checkered American walnut, black rubber butt pad. **Sights:** Brass bead front, open adjustable rear; also available without sights. **Features:** Same basic features as the rimfire model except has slightly lengthened receiver. Uses Ruger rotary magazine. Three-position safety. Comes with 1" Ruger scope rings. Introduced 1994.
Price: 77/22RH (rings only) $555.00
Price: 77/22RSH (with sights) $575.00
Price: K77/22VHZ Varmint, laminated stock, no sights $599.00

RUGER M77 MARK II RIFLE
Caliber: 223, 220 Swift, 22-250, 243, 6mm Rem., 257 Roberts, 25-06, 6.5x55 Swedish, 270, 7x57mm, 260 Rem., 280 Rem., 308, 30-06, 7mm Rem. Mag., 300 Win. Mag., 338 Win. Mag., 4-shot magazine. **Barrel:** 20", 22"; 24" (magnums). **Weight:** About 7 lbs. **Length:** 39-3/4" overall. **Stock:** Hand-checkered American walnut; swivel studs, rubber butt pad. **Sights:** None furnished. Receiver has Ruger integral scope mount base, comes with Ruger 1" rings. Some models have iron sights. **Features:** Short action with new trigger and three-position safety. New trigger guard with redesigned floorplate latch. Left-hand model available. Introduced 1989.
Price: M77RMKII (no sights) $649.00
Price: M77RSMKII (open sights) $725.00
Price: M77LRMKII (left-hand, 270, 30-06, 7mm Rem. Mag., 300 Win. Mag.)
.... $649.00

Ruger M77 Mark II All-Weather Stainless Rifle
Similar to the wood-stock M77 Mark II except all metal parts are of stainless steel, and has an injection-moulded, glass-fiber-reinforced Du Pont Zytel stock. Also offered with laminated wood stock. Chambered for 223, 243, 270, 308, 30-06, 7mm Rem. Mag., 300 Win. Mag., 338 Win. Mag. Has the fixed-blade-type ejector, three-position safety, and new trigger guard with patented floorplate latch. Comes with integral Scope Base Receiver and 1" Ruger scope rings, built-in sling swivel loops. Introduced 1990.
Price: K77RFPMKII $649.00
Price: K77RLFPMKII Ultra-Light, synthetic stock, rings, no sights. $649.00
Price: K77LRBBZMKII, left-hand bolt, rings, no sights, laminated stock $699.00
Price: K77RSFPMKII, synthetic stock, open sights $725.00
Price: K77RBZMKII, no sights, laminated wood stock, 223, 22/250, 243, 270, 280 Rem., 7mm Rem. Mag., 30-06, 308, 300 Win. Mag., 338 Win. Mag. $699.00
Price: K77RSBZMKII, open sights, laminated wood stock, 243, 270, 7mm Rem. Mag., 30-06, 300 Win. Mag., 338 Win. Mag. ... $765.00

Ruger M77RL Ultra Light
Similar to the standard M77 except weighs only 6 lbs., chambered for 223, 243, 308, 270, 30-06, 257 Roberts; barrel tapped for target scope blocks; has 20" Ultra Light barrel. Overall length 40". Ruger's steel 1" scope rings supplied. Introduced 1983.
Price: M77RLMKII $699.00

Ruger M77 Mark II Compact Rifles
Similar to the standard M77 except reduced in size with 16-1/2" barrel; weighs 5-3/4 lbs. Chambered for 223, 243, 260 Rem. and 308.
Price: M77CR MKII (blued finish, walnut stock) $649.00
Price: KM77CRBBZ MkII (stainless finish, black laminated stock). $699.00

RUGER M77 MARK II MAGNUM RIFLE
Caliber: 375 H&H, 4-shot magazine; 416 Rigby, 3-shot magazine. **Barrel:** 23", with integral steel rib; hammer forged. **Weight:** 9.25 lbs. (375); 9-3/4 lbs. (416, Rigby). **Length:** 40.5" overall. **Stock:** Circassian walnut with hand-cut checkering, swivel studs, steel gripcap, rubber butt pad. **Sights:** Ramp front, two leaf express on serrated integral steel rib. Rib also serves as base for front scope ring. **Features:** Uses an enlarged Mark II action with three-position safety, stainless bolt, steel trigger guard and hinged steel floorplate. Controlled feed. Introduced 1989.
Price: M77RSMMKII $1,695.00

34TH EDITION, 2002 • 217

CENTERFIRE RIFLES — BOLT ACTION

Ruger M77VT Target

Sako TRG-S

Sako 75 Hunter

Sako 75 Deluxe

Sako 75 Stainless Hunter

RUGER 77/44 BOLT-ACTION RIFLE
Caliber: 44 Magnum, 4-shot magazine. **Barrel:** 18-1/2". **Weight:** 6 lbs. **Length:** 38-1/4" overall. **Stock:** American walnut with rubber butt pad and swivel studs or black polymer (stainless only). **Sights:** Gold bead front, folding leaf rear. Comes with Ruger 1" scope rings. **Features:** Uses same action as the Ruger 77/22. Short bolt stroke; rotary magazine; three-position safety. Introduced 1997. Made in U.S. by Sturm, Ruger & Co.
Price: Blue, walnut, 77/44RS $580.00
Price: Stainless, polymer, stock, K77/44RS $580.00

RUGER M77VT TARGET RIFLE
Caliber: 22-250, 220 Swift, 223, 243, 25-06, 308. **Barrel:** 26" heavy stainless steel with target gray finish. **Weight:** 9-3/4 lbs. **Length:** Approx. 44" overall. **Stock:** Laminated American hardwood with beavertail forend, steel swivel studs; no checkering or gripcap. **Sights:** Integral scope mount bases in receiver. **Features:** Ruger diagonal bedding system. Ruger steel 1" scope rings supplied. Fully adjustable trigger. Steel floorplate and trigger guard. New version introduced 1992.
Price: K77VTMKII $779.00

SAKO TRG-S BOLT-ACTION RIFLE
Caliber: 338 Lapua Mag., 30-378 Weatherby, 3-shot magazine. **Barrel:** 26". **Weight:** 7.75 lbs. **Length:** 45.5" overall. **Stock:** Reinforced polyurethane with Monte Carlo comb. **Sights:** None furnished. **Features:** Resistance-free bolt with 60-degree lift. Recoil pad adjustable for length. Free-floating barrel, detachable magazine, fully adjustable trigger. Matte blue metal. Introduced 1993. Imported from Finland by Beretta USA.
Price: $875.00

Sako TRG-42 BOLT-ACTION RIFLE
Similar to TRG-S except has 5-shot magazine, fully adjustable stock and competition trigger. Offered in 338 Lapua Mag. and 300 Win. Mag. Imported from Finland by Beretta USA.
Price: $2,760.00

SAKO 75 HUNTER BOLT-ACTION RIFLE
Caliber: 17 Rem., 222, 223, 22-250, 243, 7mm-08, 308 Win., 25-06, 270, 280, 30-06; 270 Wea. Mag., 7mm Rem. Mag., 7mm STW, 7mm Wea. Mag., 300 Win. Mag., 300 Wea. Mag., 338 Win. Mag., 340 Wea. Mag., 375 H&H, 416 Rem. Mag. **Barrel:** 22", standard calibers; 24", 26" magnum calibers. **Weight:** About 6 lbs. **Length:** NA. **Stock:** European walnut with matte lacquer finish. **Sights:** None furnished; dovetail scope mount rails. **Features:** New design with three locking lugs and a mechanical ejector; key locks firing pin and bolt; cold hammer-forged barrel is free-floating; two-position safety; hinged floorplate or detachable magazine that can be loaded from the top; short 70 degree bolt lift. Available in five action lengths. Introduced 1997. Imported from Finland by Beretta USA.
Price: Standard calibers $1,115.00
Price: Magnum Calibers $1,145.00

Sako 75 Stainless Synthetic Rifle
Similar to the 75 Hunter except all metal is of stainless steel, and the synthetic stock has soft composite panels moulded into the forend and pistol grip. Available in 22-250, 243, 308 Win., 25-06, 270, 30-06 with 22" barrel, 7mm Rem. Mag., 7mm STW, 300 Win. Mag., 338 Win. Mag. and 375 H&H Mag. with 24" barrel and 300 Wea. Mag., 300 Rem.Ultra Mag. with 26" barrel. Introduced 1997. Imported from Finland by Beretta USA.
Price: Standard calibers $1,205.00
Price: Magnum calibers $1,235.00

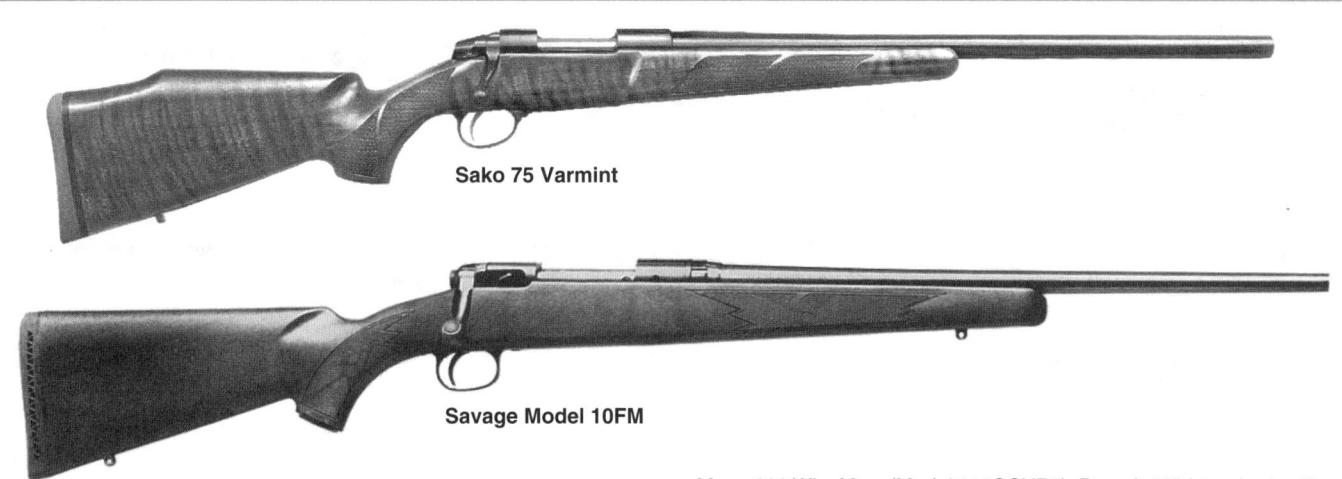

CENTERFIRE RIFLES — BOLT ACTION

Sako 75 Varmint

Savage Model 10FM

Sako 75 Deluxe Rifle
Similar to the 75 Hunter except has select wood rosewood gripcap and forend tip. Available in 17 Rem., 222, 223, 25-06, 243, 7mm-08, 308, 25-06, 270, 280, 30-06; 270 Wea. Mag., 7mm Rem. Mag., 7mm STW, 7mm Wea. Mag., 300 Win. Mag., 300 Wea. Mag., 338 Win. Mag., 340 Wea. Mag., 375 H&H, 416 Rem. Mag. Introduced 1997. Imported from Finland by Beretta USA.
Price: Standard calibers $1,615.00
Price: Magnum calibers $1,645.00

Sako 75 Hunter Stainless Rifle
Similar to the Sako 75 Hunter except all metal is of stainless steel. Comes with walnut stock with matte lacquer finish, rubber butt pad. Introduced 1999. Imported from Finland by Beretta USA.
Price: 270, 30-06 . . . . $1,205.00
Price: 7mm Rem. Mag., 7mm STW, 300 Win. Mag.,
300 Wea. Mag., 338 Win. Mag. $1,235.00

Sako 75 Varmint Stainless Laminated Rifle
Similar to the Sako 75 Hunter except chambered only for 222, 223, 22-250, 22 PPC USA, 6mm PPC; has heavy 24" barrel with recessed crown; all metal is of stainless steel; has laminated wood stock with beavertail forend. Introduced 1999. Imported from Finland by Beretta USA.
Price: $1,375.00

Sako 75 Varmint Rifle
Similar to the Model 75 Hunter except chambered only for 17 Rem., 222 Rem., 223 Rem., 22-250 Rem., 22 PPC and 6mm PPC; 24" heavy barrel with recessed crown; beavertail forend. Introduced 1998. Imported from Finland by Beretta USA.
Price: $1,280.00

SAUER 202 BOLT-ACTION RIFLE
Caliber: Standard—243, 6.5x55, 270 Win., 308 Win., 30-06; magnum—7mm Rem. Mag., 300 Win. Mag., 300 Wea. Mag., 375 H&H. **Barrel:** 23.6" (standard), 26" (magnum). **Weight:** 7.7 lbs. (standard). **Length:** 44.3" overall (23.6" barrel). **Stock:** Select American Claro walnut with high-gloss epoxy finish, rosewood grip and forend caps; 22 lpi checkering. Synthetic also available. **Sights:** None furnished; drilled and tapped for scope mounting. **Features:** Short 60" bolt throw; detachable box magazine; six-lug bolt; quick-change barrel; tapered bore; adjustable two-stage trigger; firing pin cocking indicator. Introduced 1994. Imported from Germany by Sigarms, Inc.
Price: Standard calibers, right-hand $1,035.00
Price: Magnum calibers, right-hand $1,106.00
Price: Standard calibers, synthetic stock $985.00
Price: Magnum calibers, synthetic stock $1,056.00

SAVAGE MODEL 110GXP3, 110GCXP3 PACKAGE GUNS
Caliber: 223, 22-250, 243, 25-06, 270, 300 Sav., 30-06, 308, 7mm Rem. Mag., 7mm-08, 300 Win. Mag. (Model 110GXP3); 270, 30-06, 7mm Rem. Mag., 300 Win. Mag. (Model 110GCXP3). **Barrel:** 22" (standard calibers), 24" (magnum calibers). **Weight:** 7.25-7.5 lbs. **Length:** 43.5" overall (22" barrel). **Stock:** Monte Carlo-style hardwood with walnut finish, rubber butt pad, swivel studs. **Sights:** None furnished. **Features:** Model 110GXP3 has fixed, top-loading magazine, Model 110GCXP3 has detachable box magazine. Rifles come with a factory-mounted and bore-sighted 3-9x32 scope, rings and bases, quick-detachable swivels, sling. Left-hand models available in all calibers. Introduced 1991 (GXP3); 1994 (GCXP3). Made in U.S. by Savage Arms, Inc.
Price: Model 110GXP3, right- or left-hand $513.00
Price: Model 110GCXP3, right- or left-hand $513.00

Savage Model 111FXP3, 111FCXP3 Package Guns
Similar to the Model 110 Series Package Guns except with lightweight, black graphite/fiberglass composite stock with non-glare finish, positive checkering. Same calibers as Model 110 rifles, plus 338 Win. Mag. Model 111FXP3 has fixed top-loading magazine; Model 111FCXP3 has detachable box. Both come with mounted 3-9x32 scope, quick-detachable swivels, sling. Introduced 1994. Made in U.S. by Savage Arms, Inc.
Price: Model 111FXP3, right- or left-hand $476.00
Price: Model 111FCXP3, right- or left-hand $525.00

SAVAGE MODEL 110FM SIERRA ULTRA LIGHT WEIGHT RIFLE
Caliber: 243, 270, 308, 30-06. **Barrel:** 20". **Weight:** 6-1/4 lbs. **Length:** 41-1/2" overall. **Stock:** Graphite/fiberglass-filled composite. **Sights:** None furnished; drilled and tapped for scope mounting. **Features:** Comes with black nylon sling and quick-detachable swivels. Introduced 1996. Made in U.S. by Savage Arms, Inc.
Price: $449.00

Savage Model 10FM Sierra Ultra Light Rifle
Similar to the Model 110FM Sierra except has a true short action, chambered for 223, 243, 308; weighs 6 lbs. "Dual Pillar" bedding in black synthetic stock with silver medallion in gripcap. Comes with sling and quick-detachable swivels. Introduced 1998. Made in U.S. by Savage Arms, Inc.
Price: $449.00

SAVAGE MODEL 110FP TACTICAL RIFLE
Caliber: 223, 25-06, 308, 30-06, 300 Win. Mag., 7mm Rem. Mag., 4-shot magazine. **Barrel:** 24", heavy; recessed target muzzle. **Weight:** 8-1/2 lbs. **Length:** 45.5" overall. **Stock:** Black graphite/fiberglass composition; positive checkering. **Sights:** None furnished. Receiver drilled and tapped for scope mounting. **Features:** Pillar-bedded stock. Black matte finish on all metal parts. Double swivel studs on the forend for sling and/or bipod mount. Right or left-hand. Introduced 1990. From Savage Arms, Inc.
Price: Right- or left-hand $476.00

Savage Model 10FP Tactical Rifle
Similar to the Model 110FP except has true short action, chambered for 223, 308; black synthetic stock with "Dual Pillar" bedding. Introduced 1998. Made in U.S. by Savage Arms, Inc.
Price: $476.00
Price: Model 10FLP (left-hand) $476.00

CENTERFIRE RIFLES — BOLT ACTION

Savage Model 10FP

Savage Model 11F

Savage Model 11G

Savage Model 10GY

Savage Model 114CE

SAVAGE MODEL 111 CLASSIC HUNTER RIFLES
Caliber: 223, 22-250, 243, 250 Sav., 25-06, 270, 300 Sav., 30-06, 308, 7mm Rem. Mag., 7mm-08, 300 Win. Mag., 338 Win. Mag. (Models 111G, GL, GNS, F, FL, FNS); 270, 30-06, 7mm Rem. Mag., 300 Win. Mag. (Models 111GC, GLC, FAK, FC, FLC). **Barrel:** 22", 24" (magnum calibers). **Weight:** 6.3 to 7 lbs. **Length:** 43.5" overall (22" barrel). **Stock:** Walnut-finished hardwood (M111G, GC); graphite/fiberglass filled composite. **Sights:** Ramp front, open fully adjustable rear; drilled and tapped for scope mounting. **Features:** Three-position top tang safety, double front locking lugs, free-floated button-rifled barrel. Comes with trigger lock, target, ear puffs. Introduced 1994. Made in U.S. by Savage Arms, Inc.
Price: Model 111FC (detachable magazine, composite stock, right- or left-hand) $445.00
Price: Model 111F (top-loading magazine, composite stock, right- or left-hand) $419.00
Price: Model 111FNS (as above, no sights, right-hand only) $411.00
Price: Model 111G (wood stock, top-loading magazine, right- or left-hand) $395.00
Price: Model 111GC (as above, detachable magazine), right- or left-hand $433.00
Price: Model 111GNS (wood stock, top-loading magzine, no sights, right-hand only) $389.00
Price: Model 111FAK Express (blued, composite stock, top loading magazine, Adjustable muzzle brake) .... NA

Savage Model 11 Hunter Rifles
Similar to the Model 111F except has true short action, chambered for 223, 22-250, 243, 308; black synthetic stock with "Dual Pillar" bedding, positive checkering. Introduced 1998. Made in U.S. by Savage Arms, Inc.
Price: Model 11F $419.00
Price: Model 11FL (left-hand) $419.00
Price: Model 11FNS (right-hand, no sights) $411.00
Price: Model 11G (wood stock) $395.00
Price: Model 11GL (as above, left-hand) $395.00
Price: Model 11GNS (wood stock, no sights) $389.00

Savage Model 10GY, 110GY Rifle
Similar to the Model 111G except weighs 6.3 lbs., is 42-1/2" overall, and the stock is scaled for ladies, small-framed adults and youths. Chambered for 223, 243, 270, 308. Ramp front sight, open adjustable rear; drilled and tapped for scope mounts. Made in U.S. by Savage Arms, Inc.
Price: Model 110GY $395.00
Price: Model 10GY (short action, calibers 223, 243, 308) $395.00

SAVAGE MODEL 114C CLASSIC RIFLE
Caliber: 270, 30-06, 7mm Rem. Mag., 300 Win. Mag.; 4-shot detachable box magazine in standard calibers, 3-shot for magnums. **Barrel:** 22" for standard calibers, 24" for magnums. **Weight:** 7-1/8 lbs. **Length:** 45-1/2" overall. **Stock:** Oil-finished American walnut; checkered grip and forend. **Sights:** None furnished; drilled and tapped for scope mounting. **Features:** High polish blue on barrel, receiver and bolt handle; Savage logo laser-etched on bolt body; push-button magazine release. Introduced 1996. Made in U.S. by Savage Arms, Inc.
Price: $556.00

Savage Model 114CE Classic European
Similar to the Model 114C except the oil-finished walnut stock has a Schnabel forend tip, cheekpiece and skip-line checkering; bead on blade front sight, fully adjustable open rear; solid red butt pad. Chambered for 270, 30-06, 7mm Rem. Mag., 300 Win. Mag. Introduced 1996. Made in U.S. by Savage Arms, Inc.
Price: $635.00

CENTERFIRE RIFLES — BOLT ACTION

Savage Model 12FV

Savage Model 16FSS

Savage Model 116FCSAK

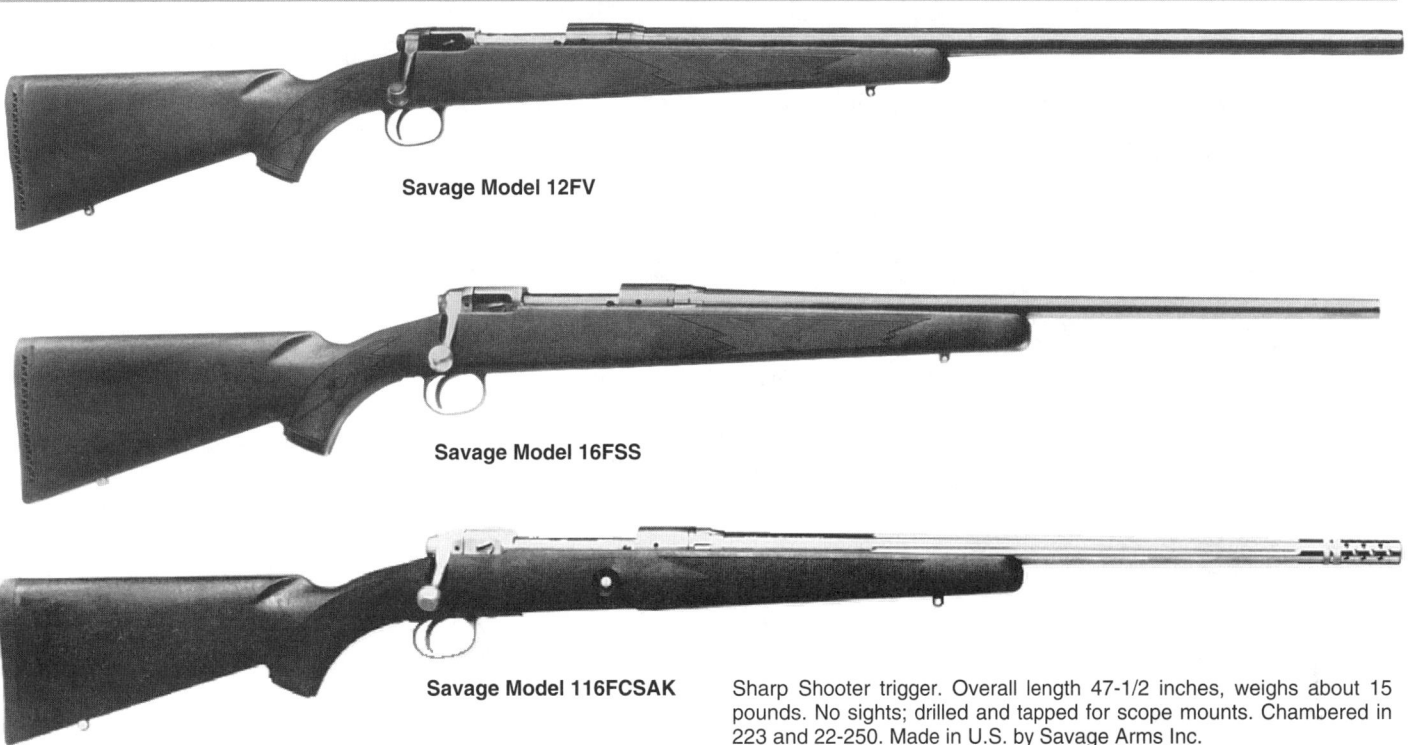

Savage Model 114U Ultra Rifle
Similar to the Model 114C except has high-luster blued finish, high-gloss walnut stock with custom cut checkering, ebony tip. No sights; drilled and tapped for scope. Chambered for 270, 30-06, 7mm Rem. Mag., 7mm STW and 300 Win.
Price: $504.00

SAVAGE MODEL 112 LONG RANGE RIFLES
Caliber: 22-250, 223, 5-shot magazine. **Barrel:** 26" heavy. **Weight:** 8.8 lbs. **Length:** 47.5" overall. **Stock:** Black graphite/fiberglass filled composite with positive checkering. **Sights:** None furnished; drilled and tapped for scope mounting. **Features:** Pillar-bedded stock. Blued barrel with recessed target-style muzzle. Double front swivel studs for attaching bipod. Introduced 1991. Made in U.S. by Savage Arms, Inc.
Price: Model 112FVSS (cals. 223, 22-250, 25-06, 7mm Rem. Mag., 300 Win. Mag., stainless barrel, bolt handle, trigger guard), right- or left-hand $549.00
Price: Model 112FVSS-S (as above, single shot) $549.00
Price: Model 112BVSS (heavy-prone laminated stock with high comb, Wundhammer swell, fluted stainless barrel, bolt handle, trigger guard) $575.00
Price: Model 112BVSS-S (as above, single shot) $575.00

Savage Model 12 Long Range Rifles
Similar to the Model 112 Long Range except with true short action, chambered for 223, 22-250, 308. Models 12FV, 12FVSS have black synthetic stocks with "Dual Pillar" bedding, positive checkering, swivel studs; model 12BVSS has brown laminated stock with beavertail forend, fluted stainless barrel. Introduced 1998. Made in U.S. by Savage Arms, Inc.
Price: Model 12FV (223, 22-250 only, blue) $455.00
Price: Model 12FVSS (blue action, fluted stainless barrel) $549.00
Price: Model 12FLVSS (as above, left-hand) $549.00
Price: Model 12FVSS-S (blue action, fluted stainless barrel, single shot) $549.00
Price: Model 12BVSS (laminated stock) $575.00
Price: Model 12BVSS-S (as above, single shot) $575.00

Savage Model 12VSS Varminter Rifle
Similar to other Model 12s except has blue/stainless steel action, fluted stainless barrel, Choate full pistol-grip, adjustable synthetic stock and Sharp Shooter trigger. Overall length 47-1/2 inches, weighs about 15 pounds. No sights; drilled and tapped for scope mounts. Chambered in 223 and 22-250. Made in U.S. by Savage Arms Inc.
Price: $852.00

SAVAGE MODEL 116SE SAFARI EXPRESS RIFLE
Caliber: 300 Win. Mag., 338 Win. Mag., 375 H&H, 458 Win. Mag. **Barrel:** 24". **Weight:** 8.5 lbs. **Length:** 45.5" overall. **Stock:** Classic-style select walnut with ebony forend tip, deluxe cut checkering. Two cross bolts; internally vented recoil pad. **Sights:** Bead on ramp front, three-leaf express rear. **Features:** Controlled-round feed design; adjustable muzzle brake; one-piece barrel band stud. Satin-finished stainless steel barreled action. Introduced 1994. Made in U.S. by Savage Arms, Inc.
Price: $925.00

SAVAGE MODEL 116 WEATHER WARRIORS
Caliber: 223, 243, 270, 30-06, 7mm Rem. Mag., 300 Win. Mag., 338 Win. Mag. (Model 116FSS); 270, 30-06, 7mm Rem. Mag., 300 Win. Mag. (Models 116FCSAK, 116FCS); 270, 30-06, 7mm Rem. Mag., 300 Win. Mag., 338 Win. Mag. (Models 116FSAK, 116FSK). **Barrel:** 22", 24" for 7mm Rem. Mag., 300 Win. Mag., 338 Win. Mag. (M116FSS only). **Weight:** 6.25 to 6.5 lbs. **Length:** 43.5" overall (22" barrel). **Stock:** Graphite/fiberglass filled composite. **Sights:** None furnished; drilled and tapped for scope mounting. **Features:** Stainless steel with matte finish; free-floated barrel; quick-detachable swivel studs; laser-etched bolt; scope bases and rings. Left-hand models available in all models, calibers at same price. Models 116FCS, 116FSS introduced 1991; Model 116FSK introduced 1993; Model 116FCSAK, 116FSAK introduced 1994. Made in U.S. by Savage Arms, Inc.
Price: Model 116FSS (top-loading magazine) $528.00
Price: Model 116FCS (detachable box magazine) . . . . NA
Price: Model 116FCSAK (as above with Savage Adjustable Muzzle Brake system) $668.00
Price: Model 116FSAK (top-loading magazine, Savage Adjustable Muzzle Brake system) $602.00
Price: Model 116FSK Kodiak (as above with 22" Shock-Suppressor barrel) $569.00

Savage Model 16FSS Rifle
Similar to the Model 116FSS except has true short action, chambered for 223, 243, 308; 22" free-floated barrel; black graphite/fiberglass stock with "Dual Pillar" bedding. Introduced 1998. Made in U.S. by Savage Arms, Inc.
Price: $528.00
Price: Model 16FLSS (left-hand) $528.00

CENTERFIRE RIFLES — BOLT ACTION

Sigarms SHR 970

Steyr Mannlicher SBS

Steyr SBS Forester

Steyr SBS Prohunter

Steyr Scout Rifle

SIGARMS SHR 970 SYNTHETIC RIFLE
Caliber: 270, 30-06. **Barrel:** 22". **Weight:** 7.2 lbs. **Length:** 41.9" overall. **Stock:** Textured black fiberglass or walnut. **Sights:** None furnished; drilled and tapped for scope mounting. **Features:** Quick takedown; interchangeable barrels; removable box magazine; cocking indicator; three-position safety. Introduced 1998. Imported by Sigarms, Inc.
Price: Synthetic stock...$499.00
Price: Walnut stock..$550.00

STEYR CLASSIC MANNLICHER SBS RIFLE
Caliber: 243, 25-06, 308, 6.5x55, 6.5x57, 270, 7x64 Brenneke, 7mm-08, 7.5x55, 30-06, 9.3x62, 6.5x68, 7mm Rem. Mag., 300 Win. Mag., 8x685, 4-shot magazine. **Barrel:** 23.6" standard; 26" magnum; 20" full stock standard calibers. **Weight:** 7 lbs. **Length:** 40.1" overall. **Stock:** Hand-checkered fancy European oiled walnut with standard forend. **Sights:** Ramp front adjustable for elevation, V-notch rear adjustable for windage. **Features:** Single adjustable trigger; 3-position roller safety with "safe-bolt" setting; drilled and tapped for Steyr factory scope mounts. Introduced 1997. Imported from Austria by GSI, Inc.
Price: Full-stock, standard calibers........................$1,749.00

STEYR SBS FORESTER RIFLE
Caliber: 243, 25-06, 270, 7mm-08, 308 Win., 30-06, 7mm Rem. Mag., 300 Win. Mag. Detachable 4-shot magazine. **Barrel:** 23.6", standard calibers; 25.6", magnum calibers. **Weight:** 7.5 lbs. **Length:** 44.5" overall (23.6" barrel). **Stock:** Oil-finished American walnut with Monte Carlo cheekpiece. Pachmayr 1" swivels. **Sights:** None furnished. Drilled and tapped for Browning A-Bolt mounts. **Features:** Steyr Safe Bolt systems, three-position ambidextrous roller tang safety, for Safe, Loading Fire. Matte finish on barrel and receiver; adjustable trigger. Rotary cold-hammer forged barrel. Introduced 1997. Imported by GSI, Inc.
Price: Standard calibers..$799.00
Price: Magnum calibers...$829.00

Steyr SBS Prohunter Rifle
Similar to the SBS Forester except has ABS synthetic stock with adjustable butt spacers, straight comb without cheekpiece, palm swell, Pachmayr 1" swivels. Special 10-round magazine conversion kit available. Introduced 1997. Imported by GSI.
Price Standard calibers..$769.00
Price Magnum calibers...$799.00

STEYR SCOUT BOLT-ACTION RIFLE
Caliber: 308 Win., 5-shot magazine. **Barrel:** 19", fluted. **Weight:** NA. **Length:** NA. **Stock:** Gray Zytel. **Sights:** None furnished; comes with Leupold M8 2.5x28 IER scope on Picatinny optic rail with Steyr mounts. **Features:** Comes with luggage case, scout sling, two stock spacers, two magazines. Introduced 1998. From GSI.
Price: From..$1,969.00

STEYR SSG BOLT-ACTION RIFLE
Caliber: 308 Win., detachable 5-shot rotary magazine. **Barrel:** 26" **Weight:** 8.5 lbs. **Length:** 44.5" overall. **Stock:** Black ABS Cycolac with spacers for length of pull adjustment. **Sights:** Hooded ramp front adjustable for elevation, V-notch rear adjustable for windage. **Features:** Sliding safety; NATO rail for bipod; 1" swivels; Parkerized finish; single or double-set triggers. Imported from Austria by GSI, Inc.
Price: SSG-PI, iron sights.....................................$1,699.00
Price: SSG-PII, heavy barrel, no sights.......................$1,699.00
Price: SSG-PIIK, 20" heavy barrel, no sights..................$1,699.00
Price: SSG-PIV, 16.75" threaded heavy barrel with flash hider.$2,659.00

CENTERFIRE RIFLES — BOLT ACTION

Tikka Whitetail Hunter

Tikka Whitetail Hunter Stainless Synthetic

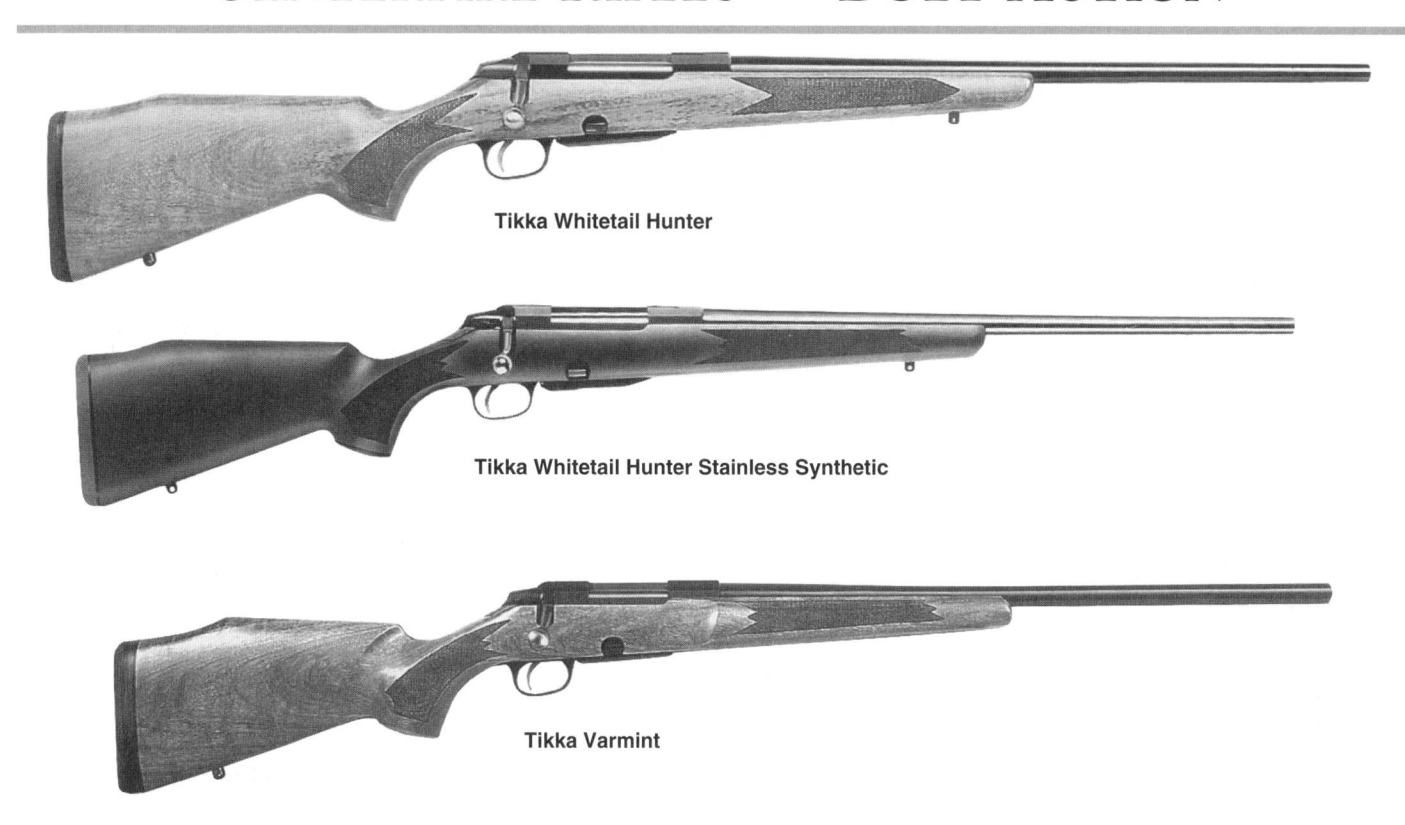

Tikka Varmint

TIKKA WHITETAIL HUNTER BOLT-ACTION RIFLE
Caliber: 22-250, 223, 243, 7mm-08, 25-06, 270, 308, 30-06, 7mm Rem. Mag., 300 Win. Mag., 338 Win. Mag. **Barrel:** 22-1/2" (std. cals.), 24-1/2" (magnum cals.). **Weight:** 7-1/8 lbs. **Length:** 43" overall (std. cals.). **Stock:** European walnut with Monte Carlo comb, rubber butt pad, checkered grip and forend. **Sights:** None furnished. **Features:** Detachable four-shot magazine (standard calibers), three-shot in magnums. Receiver dovetailed for scope mounting. Reintroduced 1996. Imported from Finland by Beretta USA.
Price: Standard calibers $615.00
Price: Magnum calibers $645.00

Tikka Continental Varmint Rifle
Similar to the standard Tikka rifle except has 26" heavy barrel, extra-wide forend. Chambered for 17 Rem., 22-250, 223, 308. Reintroduced 1996. Made in Finland by Sako. Imported by Beretta USA.
Price: $720.00

Tikka Whitetail Hunter Deluxe Rifle
Similar to the Whitetail Hunter except has select walnut stock with rollover Monte Carlo comb, rosewood grip cap and forend tip. Has adjustable trigger, detachable magazine, free-floating barrel. Same calibers as the Hunter. Introduced 1999. Imported from Finland by Beretta USA.
Price: Standard calibers $745.00
Price: Magnum calibers $775.00

Tikka Whitetail Hunter Synthetic Rifle
Similar to the Whitetail Hunter except has black synthetic stock; calibers 223, 22-250, 243, 7mm-08, 25-06, 270 Win., 30-06, 7mm Rem. Mag., 300 Win. Mag., 338 Win. Mag. Introduced 1996. Imported from Finland by Beretta USA.
Price: Standard calibers $615.00
Price: Magnum calibers $645.00

Tikka Continental Long Range Hunting Rifle
Similar to the Whitetail Hunter except has 26" heavy barrel. Available in 25-06, 270 Win., 7mm Rem. Mag., 300 Win. Mag. Introduced 1996. Imported from Finland by Beretta USA.
Price: 25-06, 270 Win. $720.00
Price: 7mm Rem. Mag., 300 Win. Mag. $750.00

Tikka Whitetail Hunter Stainless Synthetic
Similar to the Whitetail Hunter except all metal is of stainless steel, and it has a black synthetic stock. Available in 22-250, 223, 243, 7mm-08, 25-06, 270, 308, 30-06, 7mm Rem. Mag., 300 Win. Mag., 338 Win. Mag. Introduced 1997. Imported from Finland by Beretta USA.
Price: Standard calibers $680.00
Price: Magnum calibers $710.00

VEKTOR BUSHVELD BOLT-ACTION RIFLE
Caliber: 243, 308, 7x57, 7x64 Brenneke, 270 Win., 30-06, 300 Win. Mag., 300 H&H, 9.3x62. **Barrel:** 22"-26". **Weight:** NA. **Length:** NA. **Stock:** Turkish walnut with wrap-around hand checkering. **Sights:** Blade on ramp front, fixed standing leaf rear. **Features:** Combines the best features of the Mauser 98 and Winchester 70 actions. Controlled-round feed; Mauser-type extractor; no cut-away through the bolt locking lug; M70-type three-position safety; Timney-type adjustable trigger. Introduced 1999. Imported from South Africa by Vektor USA.
Price: . . . . $1,595.00 to $1,695.00

VEKTOR MODEL 98 BOLT-ACTION RIFLE
Caliber: 243, 308, 7x57, 7x64 Brenneke, 270 Win., 30-06, 300 Win. Mag., 300 H&H, 375 H&H, 9.3x62. **Barrel:** 22"-26". **Weight:** NA. **Length:** NA. **Stock:** Turkish walnut with hand-checkered grip and forend. **Sights:** None furnished; drilled and tapped for scope mounting. **Features:** Bolt has guide rib; non-rotating, long extractor enhances positive feeding; polished blue finish. Updated Mauser 98 action. Introduced 1999. Imported from South Africa by Vektor USA.
Price: . . . . $1,149.00 to $1,249.00

WEATHERBY MARK V DELUXE BOLT-ACTION RIFLE
Caliber: All Weatherby calibers plus 22-250, 243, 25-06, 270 Win., 280 Rem., 7mm-08, 308 Win. **Barrel:** 26" round tapered. **Weight:** 8-1/2 to 10-1/2 lbs. **Length:** 46-5/8" to 46-3/4" overall. **Stock:** Walnut, Monte Carlo with cheekpiece; high luster finish; checkered pistol grip and forend; recoil pad. **Sights:** None furnished. **Features:** Cocking indicator; adjustable trigger; hinged floorplate, thumb safety; quick detachable sling swivels. Made in U.S. From Weatherby.
Price: 257, 270, 7mm. 300, 340 Wea. Mags., 26" barrel $1,649.00
Price: 416 Wea. Mag. with Accubrake, 26" barrel $1,999.00
Price: 460 Wea. Mag. with Accubrake, 26" barrel $2,349.00

34TH EDITION, 2002 • 223

CENTERFIRE RIFLES — BOLT ACTION

Weatherby Mark V Lazermark

Weatherby Mark V Euromark

Weatherby Mark V Stainless

Weatherby Mark V Synthetic

Weatherby Mark V Lazermark Rifle
Same as Mark V Deluxe except stock has extensive oak leaf pattern laser carving on pistol grip and forend. Introduced 1981.
Price: 257, 270, 7mm Wea. Mag., 300, 340, 26" $1,849.00
Price: 378 Wea. Mag., 26" $2,179.00
Price: 416 Wea. Mag., 26", Accubrake $2,179.00
Price: 460 Wea. Mag., 26", Accubrake $2,559.00

Weatherby Mark V Sporter Rifle
Same as the Mark V Deluxe without the embellishments. Metal has low-luster blue, stock is Claro walnut with high-gloss epoxy finish, Monte Carlo comb, recoil pad. Introduced 1993.
Price: 257, 270, 280, 7mm-08, 30-06, 308, 300, 340 Wea. Mags., 26" $1,049.00
Price: 375 H&H, 24" $1,099.00
Price: 7mm Rem. Mag., 270 Wea. Mag., 7 mm Wea. Mag., 300 Wea. Mag., 300 Win. Mag., 338 Win. Mag., 24" $1,099.00

Weatherby Mark V Euromark Rifle
Similar to the Mark V Deluxe except has raised-comb Monte Carlo stock with hand-rubbed oil finish, fine-line hand-cut checkering, ebony grip and forend tips. All metal has low-luster blue. Right-hand only. Uses Mark V action. Introduced 1995. Made in U.S. From Weatherby.
Price: 257, 270, 7mm, 300, 340 Wea. Mags., 26" barrel $1,749.00
Price: 7mm Rem. Mag., 300 Win. Mag., 338 Win. Mag., 375 H&H, 24" barrel $1,749.00
Price: 378 Wea. Mag., 416 Wea. Mag., 28" barrel $2,049.00

Weatherby Mark V Stainless Rifle
Similar to the Mark V Deluxe except made of 410-series stainless steel. Also available in 30-378 Wea. Mag. Has lightweight injection-moulded synthetic stock with raised Monte Carlo comb, checkered grip and forend, custom floorplate release. Right-hand only. Introduced 1995. Made in U.S. From Weatherby.
Price: 22-250, 243, 240 Wea. Mag., 25-06, 270, 280, 7mm-08, 30-06, 308, 7mm Rem. Mag., 300, 338 Win. Mags., 24" barrel $979.00
Price: Wea. Mags (257, 270, 7mm, 300, 340); 26" barrel $1,029.00
Wea. Mag.Price: 7mm Rem. Mag., 375 H&H, 24" barrel $1,029.00
Price: 30-378 Wea. Mag., 28" barrel $1,189.00
Price: Stainless Carbine (as above with 20" barrel, 243 Win., 7mm-08 Rem., 308 Win.), weighs 6 lbs. $979.00

Weatherby Mark V SLS Stainless Laminate Sporter
Similar to the Mark V Stainless except all metalwork is 400 series stainless with a corrosion-resistant black oxide bead-blast matte finish. Action is hand-bedded in a laminated stock with a 1" recoil pad. Weighs 8-1/2 lbs. Introduced 1997. Made in U.S. From Weatherby.
Price: 257, 270, 7mm, 300, 340 Wea. Mags., 26" barrel $1,339.00
Price: 7mm Rem. Mag., 300 Win. Mag., 338 Win. Mag., 24" barrel $1,339.00

Weatherby Mark V Eurosport Rifle
Similar to the Mark V Deluxe except has raised-comb Monte Carlo stock with hand-rubbed satin oil finish, low-luster blue metal. No gripcap or forend tip. Right-hand only. Introduced 1995. Made in U.S. From Weatherby.
Price: 257, 270, 7mm, 300, 340 Wea. Mags., 26" barrel $1,099.00
Price: 7mm Rem. Mag., 300, 338 Win. Mags., 24" barrel $1,099.00
Price: 375 H&H, 24" barrel $1,099.00

Weatherby Mark V Synthetic
Similar to the Mark V Stainless except made of matte finished blued steel. Injection moulded synthetic stock. Weighs 6-1/2 lbs., 24" barrel. Available in 22-250, 240 Wea. Mag., 243, 25-06, 270, 7mm-08, 280, 30-06, 308. Introduced 1997. Made in U.S. From Weatherby.
Price: $779.00
Price: 257, 270, 7mm, 300, 340 Wea. Mags., 26" barrel $829.00
Price: 7mm STW, 7mm Rem. Mag., 300, 338 Win. Mags $829.00
Price: 375 H&H, 24" barrel $829.00
Price: 30-378 Wea. Mag., 338-378 Wea. $979.00

CENTERFIRE RIFLES — BOLT ACTION

Weatherby Accumark

Wilderness Explorer

Winchester Model 70 Classic

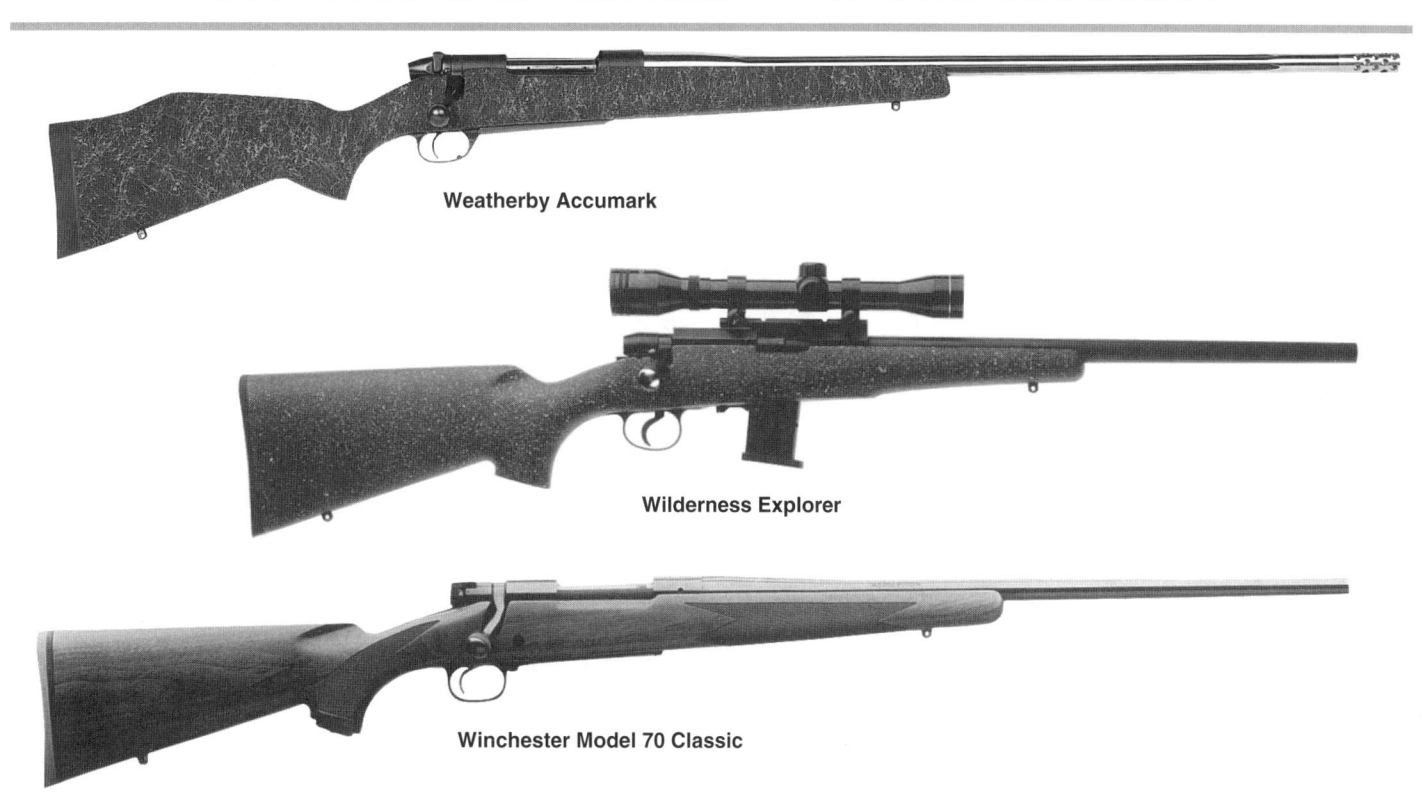

WEATHERBY MARK V ACCUMARK RIFLE
Caliber: 257, 270, 7mm, 300, 340 Wea. Mags., 338-378 Wea. Mag., 30-378 Wea. Mag., 7mm STW, 7mm Rem. Mag., 300 Win. Mag. **Barrel:** 26". **Weight:** 8-1/2 lbs. **Length:** 46-5/8" overall. **Stock:** H-S Precision Pro-Series synthetic with aluminum bedding plate. **Sights:** None furnished. Drilled and tapped for scope mounting. **Features:** Uses Mark V action with heavy-contour stainless barrel with black oxidized flutes, muzzle diameter of .705". Introduced 1996. Made in U.S. From Weatherby.
Price: $1,459.00
Price: 30-378 Wea. Mag., 338-378 Wea. Mag., 28",
Accubrake. $1,669.00
Price: 223, 22-250, 243, 240 Wea. Mag., 25-06, 270,
280 Rem., 7mm-08, 30-06, 308; 24" $1,399.00
Price: Accumark Left-Hand 257, 270, 7mm, 300, 340 Wea.
Mag., 7mm Rem. Mag., 7mm STW, 300 Win. Mag. $1,499.00
Price: Accumark Left-Hand 30-378, 333-378 Wea. Mags. $1,719.00

Weatherby Mark V Accumark Ultra Lightweight Rifles
Similar to the Mark V Accumark except weighs 5-3/4 lbs.; free-floated 24" fluted barrel with recessed target crown; hand-laminated stock with CNC-machined aluminum bedding plate and faint gray "spider web" finish. Available in 257, 270, 7mm, 300 Wea. Mags., 243, 240 Wea. Mag., 25-06, 270 Win., 280 Rem., 7mm-08, 7mm Rem. Mag., 30-06, 338-06 A-Square, 308, 300 Win. Mag. Introduced 1998. Made in U.S. by Weatherby.
Price: .... $1,349.00 to $1,399.00
Price: Left-hand models $1,459.00

Weatherby Mark V SVM/SPM Rifles
Similar to the Mark V Accumark except has 26" fluted (SVM) or 24" fluted Krieger barrel, spiderweb-pattern tan laminated synthetic stock. SVM has a fully adjustable trigger. Chambered for 223, 22-250, 220 Swift (SVM only), 243, 7mm-08 and 308. Made in U.S. by Weatherby.
Price: SVM (Super VarmintMaster), repeater or single-shot ... $1,459.00
New! Price: SPM (Super PredatorMaster) $1,459.00

Weatherby Mark V Fibermark Rifles
Similar to other Mark V models except has black Kevlar® and fiberglass composite stock and bead-blast blue or stainless finish. Chambered for 19 standard and magnum calibers. Introduced 1983; reintroduced 2001. Made in U.S. by Weatherby.
Price: Fibermark .... $849.00 to $1,079.00
Price: Fibermark Stainless .... $1,079.00 to $1,289.00

WEATHERBY MARK V DANGEROUS GAME RIFLE
Caliber: 375 H&H, 375 Wea. Mag., 378 Wea. Mag., 416 Rem. Mag., 416 Wea. Mag., 458 Win. Mag. and 460 Wea. Mag. **Barrel:** 24" or 26". **Weight:** 8-3/4 to 9-1/2 lbs. **Length:** 44-5/8" to 46-5/8" overall. **Stock:** Kevlar® and fiberglass composite. **Sights:** Barrel-band hooded front with large gold bead, adjustable ramp/shallow "V" rear. **Features:** Designed for dangerous-game hunting. Black oxide matte finish on all metalwork; Pachmayr Decelerator™ recoil pad, short-throw Mark V action. Introduced 2001. Made in U.S. by Weatherby.
Price: .... $2,599.00 to $2,659.00

WILDERNESS EXPLORER MULTI-CALIBER CARBINE
Caliber: 22 Hornet, 218 Bee, 44 Magnum, 50 A.E. (interchangeable). **Barrel:** 18", match grade. **Weight:** 5.5 lbs **Length:** 38-1/2" overall. **Stock:** Synthetic or wood. **Sights:** None furnished; comes with Weaver-style mount on barrel. **Features:** Quick-change barrel and bolt face for caliber switch. Removable box magazine; adjustable trigger with side safety; detachable swivel studs. Introduced 1997. Made in U.S. by Phillips & Rogers, Inc.
Price: $995.00

WINCHESTER MODEL 70 CLASSIC SPORTER LT
Caliber: 25-06, 270 Win., 30-06, 7mm STW, 7mm Rem. Mag., 300 Win. Mag., 338 Win. Mag., 3-shot magazine; 5-shot for 25-06, 270 Win., 30-06. **Barrel:** 24", 26" for magnums. **Weight:** 7-3/4 to 8 lbs. **Length:** 46-3/4" overall (26" bbl.). **Stock:** American walnut with cut checkering and satin finish. Classic style with straight comb. **Sights:** None furnished. Drilled and tapped for scope mounting. **Features:** Uses pre-64-type action with controlled round feeding. Three-position safety, stainless steel magazine follower; rubber butt pad; epoxy bedded receiver recoil lug. From U.S. Repeating Arms Co.
Price: 25-06, 270, 30-06 .... $699.00
Price: Other calibers $727.00
Price: Left-hand, 270 or 30-06 .... $733.00
Price: Left-hand, 7mm Rem. Mag or 300 Win. Mag. $761.00

34TH EDITION, 2002

CENTERFIRE RIFLES — BOLT ACTION

Winchester Model 70 Classic Stainless

Winchester Model 70 Classic Featherweight

Winchester Model 70 Classic Compact

Winchester Model 70 Classic Super Grade

Winchester Model 70 Classic Stainless Rifle
Same as the Model 70 Classic Sporter except has stainless steel barrel and pre-64-style action with controlled round feeding and matte gray finish, black composite stock impregnated with fiberglass and graphite, contoured rubber recoil pad. No sights (except 375 H&H). Available in 270 Win., 30-06, 7mm STW, 7mm Rem. Mag., 300 Win. Mag., 300 Ultra Mag., 338 Win. Mag., 375 H&H Mag. (24" barrel), 3- or 5-shot magazine. Weighs 7-1/2 lbs. Introduced 1994.
Price: 270, 30-06 .... $768.00
Price: 375 H&H Mag., with sights $889.00
Price: Other calibers $798.00

Winchester Model 70 Classic Featherweight
Same as the Model 70 Classic except has action bedded in a standard-grade walnut stock. Available in 22-250, 243, 6.5x55, 308, 7mm-08, 270 Win., 30-06. Drilled and tapped for scope mounts. Weighs 7 lbs. Introduced 1992.
Price: $712.00

Winchester Model 70 Classic Compact
Similar to the Classic Featherweight except scaled down for smaller shooters. Has 20" barrel, 12-1/2" length of pull. Pre-'64-type action. Available in 243, 308 or 7mm-08. Introduced 1998. Made in U.S. by U. S. Repeating Arms Co.
Price: $712.00

Winchester Model 70 Black Shadow
Similar to the Ranger except has black composite stock, matte blue barrel and action. Push-feed bolt design; hinged floorplate. Available in 270, 30-06, 7mm Rem. Mag., 300 Win. Mag. Made in U.S. by U.S. Repeating Arms Co.
Price: 270, 30-06 .... $512.00
Price: 7mm Rem. Mag., 300 Win. Mag. $542.00

Winchester Model 70 Coyote
Similar to the Model 70 Black Shadow except has laminated wood stock, 24" medium-heavy stainless steel barrel.
Price: Coyote (223, 22-250 or 243) $679.00

WINCHESTER MODEL 70 STEALTH RIFLE
Caliber: 223, 22-250, 308 Win. **Barrel:** 26". **Weight:** 10-3/4 lbs. **Length:** 46" overall. **Stock:** Kevlar/fiberglass/graphite Pillar Plus Accu-Block with full-length aluminum bedding block. **Sights:** None furnished. **Features:** Push-feed bolt design; matte finish. Introduced 1999. Made in U.S. by U.S. Repeating Arms Co.
Price: $768.00

WINCHESTER MODEL 70 CLASSIC SUPER GRADE
Caliber: 25-06, 270, 30-06, 5-shot magazine; 7mm Rem. Mag., 300 Win. Mag., 338 Win. Mag., 3-shot magazine. **Barrel:** 24", 26" for magnums. **Weight:** 7-3/4 lbs. to 8 lbs. **Length:** 44-1/2" overall (24" bbl.) **Stock:** Walnut with straight comb, sculptured cheekpiece, wrap-around cut checkering, tapered forend, solid rubber butt pad. **Sights:** None furnished; comes with scope bases and rings. **Features:** Controlled round feeding with stainless steel claw extractor, bolt guide rail, three-position safety; all steel bottom metal, hinged floorplate, stainless magazine follower. Introduced 1994. From U.S. Repeating Arms Co.
Price: 25-06, 270, 30-06 .... $975.00
Price: Other calibers $1,003.00

WINCHESTER MODEL 70 CLASSIC SAFARI EXPRESS
Caliber: 375 H&H Mag., 416 Rem. Mag., 458 Win. Mag., 3-shot magazine. **Barrel:** 24". **Weight:** 8-1/4 to 8-1/2 lbs. **Stock:** American walnut with Monte Carlo cheekpiece. Wrap-around checkering and finish. **Sights:** Hooded ramp front, open rear. **Features:** Controlled round feeding. Two steel cross bolts in stock for added strength. Front sling swivel stud mounted on barrel. Contoured rubber butt pad. From U.S. Repeating Arms Co.
Price: $1,081.00
Price: Left-hand, 375 H&H only $1,117.00

WINCHESTER MODEL 70 WSM RIFLES
Caliber: 300 WSM, 3-shot magazine. **Barrel:** 24". **Weight:** 7-1/4 to 7-3/4 lbs. **Length:** 44" overall. **Stock:** Checkered walnut, black synthetic or laminated wood. **Sights:** None. **Features:** Model 70 designed for the new 300 Winchester Short Magnum cartridge. Short-action receiver, three-position safety, knurled bolt handle. Introduced 2001. From U.S. Repeating Arms Co.
Price: Classic Featherweight WSM (checkered walnut stock and forearm) $740.00
Price: Classic Stainless WSM (black syn. stock, stainless steel bbl.) $798.00
Price: Classic Laminated WSM (laminated wood stock) $761.00

CENTERFIRE RIFLES — SINGLE SHOT

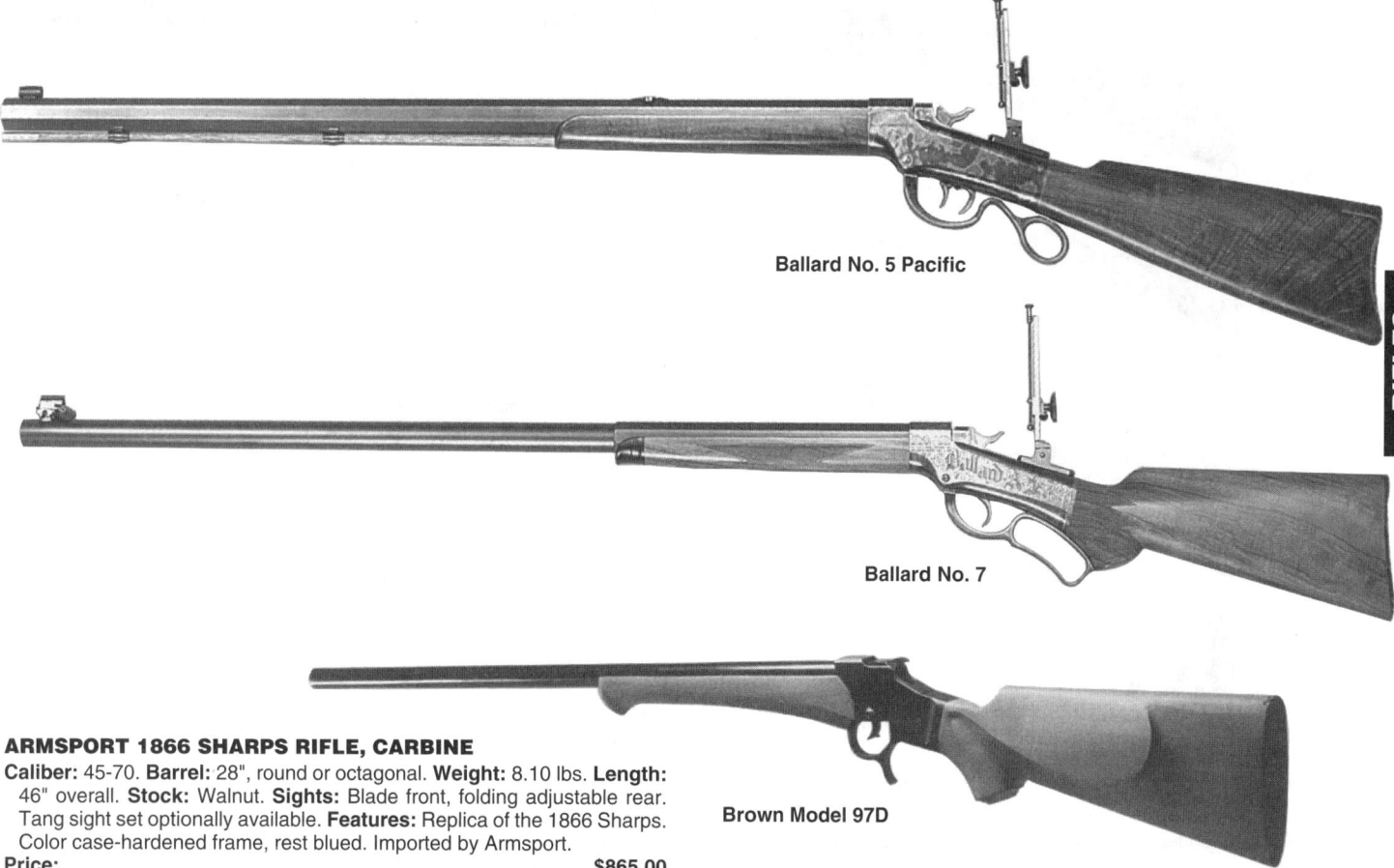

Ballard No. 5 Pacific

Ballard No. 7

Brown Model 97D

ARMSPORT 1866 SHARPS RIFLE, CARBINE
Caliber: 45-70. **Barrel:** 28", round or octagonal. **Weight:** 8.10 lbs. **Length:** 46" overall. **Stock:** Walnut. **Sights:** Blade front, folding adjustable rear. Tang sight set optionally available. **Features:** Replica of the 1866 Sharps. Color case-hardened frame, rest blued. Imported by Armsport.
Price: $865.00
Price: With octagonal barrel $900.00
Price: Carbine, 22" round barrel $850.00

BALLARD NO. 1 3/4 FAR WEST RIFLE
Caliber: 22 LR, 32-40, 38-55, 40-65, 40-70, 45-70, 45-110, 50-70, 50-90. **Barrel:** 30" std. or heavyweight. **Weight:** 10-1/2 lbs. (std.) or 11-3/4 lbs. (heavyweight bbl.) **Length:** NA. **Stock:** Walnut. **Sights:** Blade front, Rocky Mountain rear. **Features:** Single or double-set triggers, S-lever or ring-style lever; color case-hardened finish; hand polished and lapped Badger barrel. Made in U.S. by Ballard Rifle & Cartridge Co.
Price: $2,050.00

BALLARD NO. 4 PERFECTION RIFLE
Caliber: 22 LR, 32-40, 38-55, 40-65, 40-70, 45-70, 45-90, 45-110, 50-70, 50-90. **Barrel:** 30" or 32" octagon, standard or heavyweight. **Weight:** 10-1/2 lbs. (standard) or 11-3/4 lbs. (heavyweight bbl.). **Length:** NA. **Stock:** Smooth walnut. **Sights:** Blade front, Rocky Mountain rear. **Features:** Rifle or shotgun-style buttstock, straight grip action, single or double-set trigger, "S" or right lever, hand polished and lapped Badger barrel. Made in U.S. by Ballard Rifle & Cartridge Co.
Price: $2,050.00

BALLARD NO. 5 PACIFIC SINGLE-SHOT RIFLE
Caliber: 32-40, 38-55, 40-65, 40-90, 40-70 SS, 45-70 Govt., 45-110 SS, 50-70 Govt., 50-90 SS. **Barrel:** 30", or 32" octagonal. **Weight:** 10-1/2 lbs. **Length:** NA. **Stock:** High-grade walnut; rifle or shotgun style. **Sights:** Blade front, Rocky Mountain rear. **Features:** Standard or heavy barrel; double-set triggers; under-barrel wiping rod; ring lever. Introduced 1999. Made in U.S. by Ballard Rifle & Cartridge Co.
Price: $2,575.00

BALLARD NO. 7 LONG RANGE RIFLE
Caliber: 32-40, 38-55, 40-65, 40-70 SS, 45-70 Govt., 45-90, 45-110. **Barrel:** 32", 34" half-octagon. **Weight:** 11-3/4 lbs. **Length:** NA. **Stock:** Fancy walnut; checkered pistol grip shotgun butt, ebony forend cap. **Sights:** Globe front. **Features:** Designed for shooting up to 1000 yards. Standard or heavy barrel; single or double-set trigger; hard rubber or steel buttplate. Introduced 1999. Made in U.S. by Ballard Rifle & Cartridge Co.
Price: From $2,950.00

BALLARD NO. 8 UNION HILL RIFLE
Caliber: 22 LR, 32-40, 38-55, 40-65 Win., 40-70 SS. **Barrel:** 30" half-octagon. **Weight:** About 10-1/2 lbs. **Length:** NA. **Stock:** Fancy walnut; pistol grip butt with cheekpiece. **Sights:** Globe front. **Features:** Designed for 200-yard offhand shooting. Standard or heavy barrel; double-set triggers; full loop lever; hook Schuetzen buttplate. Introduced 1999. Made in U.S. by Ballard Rifle & Cartridge Co.
Price: From $2,850.00

BALLARD MODEL 1885 HIGH WALL SINGLE SHOT RIFLE
Caliber: 17 Bee, 22 Hornet, 218 Bee, 219 Don Wasp, 219 Zipper, 22 Hi-Power, 225 Win., 25-20 WCF, 25-35 WCF, 25 Krag, 7mmx57R, 30-30, 30-40 Krag, 303 British, 33 WCF, 348 WCF, 35 WCF, 35-30/30, 9.3x74R, 405 WCF, 50-110 WCF, 500 Express, 577 Express. **Barrel:** Lengths to 34". **Weight:** NA. **Length:** NA. **Stock:** Straight-grain American walnut. **Sights:** buckhorn or flat top rear, blade front. **Features:** Faithful copy of original Model 1885 High Wall; parts interchange with original rifles; variety of options available. Introduced 2000. Made in U.S. by Ballard Rifle & Cartridge LLC.
Price: From $1,850.00
Price: With single set trigger from $2,050.00

BARRETT MODEL 99 SINGLE SHOT RIFLE
Caliber: 50 BMG. **Barrel:** 33". **Weight:** 25 lbs. **Length:** 50.4" overall. **Stock:** Anodized aluminum with energy-absorbing recoil pad. **Sights:** None furnished; integral M1913 scope rail. **Features:** Bolt action; detachable bipod; match-grade barrel with high-efficiency muzzle brake. Introduced 1999. Made in U.S. by Barrett Firearms.
Price: From $3,000.00

34TH EDITION, 2002 • **227**

CENTERFIRE RIFLES — SINGLE SHOT

Browning Model 1885 Traditional Hunter

Browning Model 1885 Low Wall

Cabela's Sharps

BROWN MODEL 97D SINGLE SHOT RIFLE
Caliber: 17 Ackley Hornet through 45-70 Govt. **Barrel:** Up to 26", air gauged match grade. **Weight:** About 5 lbs., 11 oz. **Stock:** Sporter style with pistol grip, cheekpiece and Schnabel forend. **Sights:** None furnished; drilled and tapped for scope mounting. **Features:** Falling block action gives rigid barrel-receiver matting; polished blue/black finish. Hand-fitted action. Many options. Made in U.S. by E. A.rthur Brown Co. Inc.
Price: From $699.00

BROWNING MODEL 1885 HIGH WALL SINGLE SHOT RIFLE
Caliber: 22-250, 30-06, 270, 7mm Rem. Mag., 454 Casull, 45-70. **Barrel:** 28". **Weight:** 8 lbs., 12 oz. **Length:** 43-1/2" overall. **Stock:** Walnut with straight grip, Schnabel forend. **Sights:** None furnished; drilled and tapped for scope mounting. **Features:** Replica of J.M. Browning's high-wall falling block rifle. Octagon barrel with recessed muzzle. Imported from Japan by Browning. Introduced 1985.
Price: $1,027.00

Browning Model 1885 BPCR Rifle
Similar to the 1885 High Wall rifle except the ejector system and shell deflector have been removed; chambered only for 40-65 and 45-70; color case-hardened full-tang receiver, lever, buttplate and gripcap; matte blue 30" part octagon, part round barrel. The Vernier tang sight has indexed elevation, is screw adjustable windage, and has three peep diameters. The hooded front sight has a built-in spirit level and comes with sight interchangeable inserts. Adjustable trigger. Overall length 46-1/8", weighs about 11 lbs. Introduced 1996. Imported from Japan by Browning.
Price: $1,766.00

Browning Model 1885 Low Wall Traditional Hunter
Similar to the Model 1885 Low Wall except chambered for 357 Mag., 44 Mag. and 45 Colt; steel crescent buttplate; 1/16" gold bead front sight, adjustable buckhorn rear, and tang-mounted peep sight with barrel-type elevation adjuster and knob-type windage adjustments. Barrel is drilled and tapped for a Browning scope base. Oil-finished select walnut stock with swivel studs. Introduced 1997. Imported for Japan by Browning.
Price: $1,289.00

Browning Model 1885 Low Wall Rifle
Similar to the Model 1885 High Wall except has trimmer receiver, thinner 24" octagonal barrel. Forend is mounted to the receiver. Adjustable trigger. Walnut pistol grip stock, trim Schnabel forend with high-gloss finish. Available in 22 Hornet and 260 Rem. Overall length 39-1/2", weighs 6 lbs., 11 oz. Rifling twist rates: 1:16" (22 Hornet); 1:9" (260). Polished blue finish. Introduced 1995. Imported from Japan by Browning.
Price: $997.00

BRNO ZBK 110 SINGLE SHOT RIFLE
Caliber: 222 Rem., 5.6x52R, 22 Hornet, 5.6x50 Mag., 6.5x57R, 7x57R, 8x57JRS. **Barrel:** 23.6". **Weight:** 5.9 lbs. **Length:** 40.1" overall. **Stock:** European walnut. **Sights:** None furnished; drilled and tapped for scope mounting. **Features:** Top tang opening lever; cross-bolt safety; polished blue finish. Announced 1998. Imported from The Czech Republic by Euro-Imports.
Price: Standard calibers $223.00
Price: 7x57R, 8x57JRS $245.00
Price: Lux model, standard calibers $311.00
Price: Lux model, 7x57R, 8x57JRS $333.00

CABELA'S SHARPS SPORTING RIFLE
Caliber: 45-70 or 45-120. **Barrel:** 32", tapered octagon. **Weight:** 9 lbs. **Length:** 47-1/4" overall. **Stock:** Checkered walnut. **Sights:** Blade front, open adjustable rear. **Features:** Color case-hardened receiver and hammer, rest blued. Introduced 1995. Imported by Cabela's.
Price: $849.99
Price: (Deluxe engraved Sharps) $1,429.99
Price: (Heavy target Sharps, 45-70 or 45-120) $999.99
Price: (Quigley Sharps, 45-70 or 45-120) $1,299.99

CIMARRON BILLY DIXON 1874 SHARPS SPORTING RIFLE
Caliber: 40-65, 45-70. **Barrel:** 32" tapered octagonal. **Weight:** NA. **Length:** NA. **Stock:** European walnut. **Sights:** Blade front, Creedmoor rear. **Features:** Color case-hardened frame, blued barrel. Hand-checkered grip and forend; hand-rubbed oil finish. Introduced 1999. Imported by Cimarron F.A. Co.
Price: $1,295.00

CIMARRON QUIGLEY MODEL 1874 SHARPS SPORTING RIFLE
Caliber: 45-70, 45-120. **Barrel:** 34" octagonal. **Weight:** NA. **Length:** NA. **Stock:** Checkered walnut. **Sights:** Blade front, adjustable rear. **Features:** Blued finish; double set triggers. From Cimarron F.A. Co.
Price: $1,495.00

CIMARRON SILHOUETTE MODEL 1874 SHARPS SPORTING RIFLE
Caliber: 45-70. **Barrel:** 32" octagonal. **Weight:** NA. **Length:** NA. **Stock:** Walnut. **Sights:** Blade front, adjustable rear. **Features:** Pistol-grip stock with shotgun-style butt plate; cut-rifled barrel. From Cimarron F.A. Co.
Price: $1,095.00

CIMARRON MODEL 1885 HIGH WALL RIFLE
Caliber: 38-55, 40-65, 45-70, 45-90. **Barrel:** 30" octagonal. **Weight:** NA. **Length:** NA. **Stock:** European walnut. **Sights:** Bead front, semi-buckhorn rear. **Features:** Replica of the Winchester 1885 High Wall rifle. Color case-hardened receiver and lever, blued barrel. Curved buttplate. Optional double set triggers. Introduced 1999. Imported by Cimarron F.A. Co.
Price: $995.00

CENTERFIRE RIFLES — SINGLE SHOT

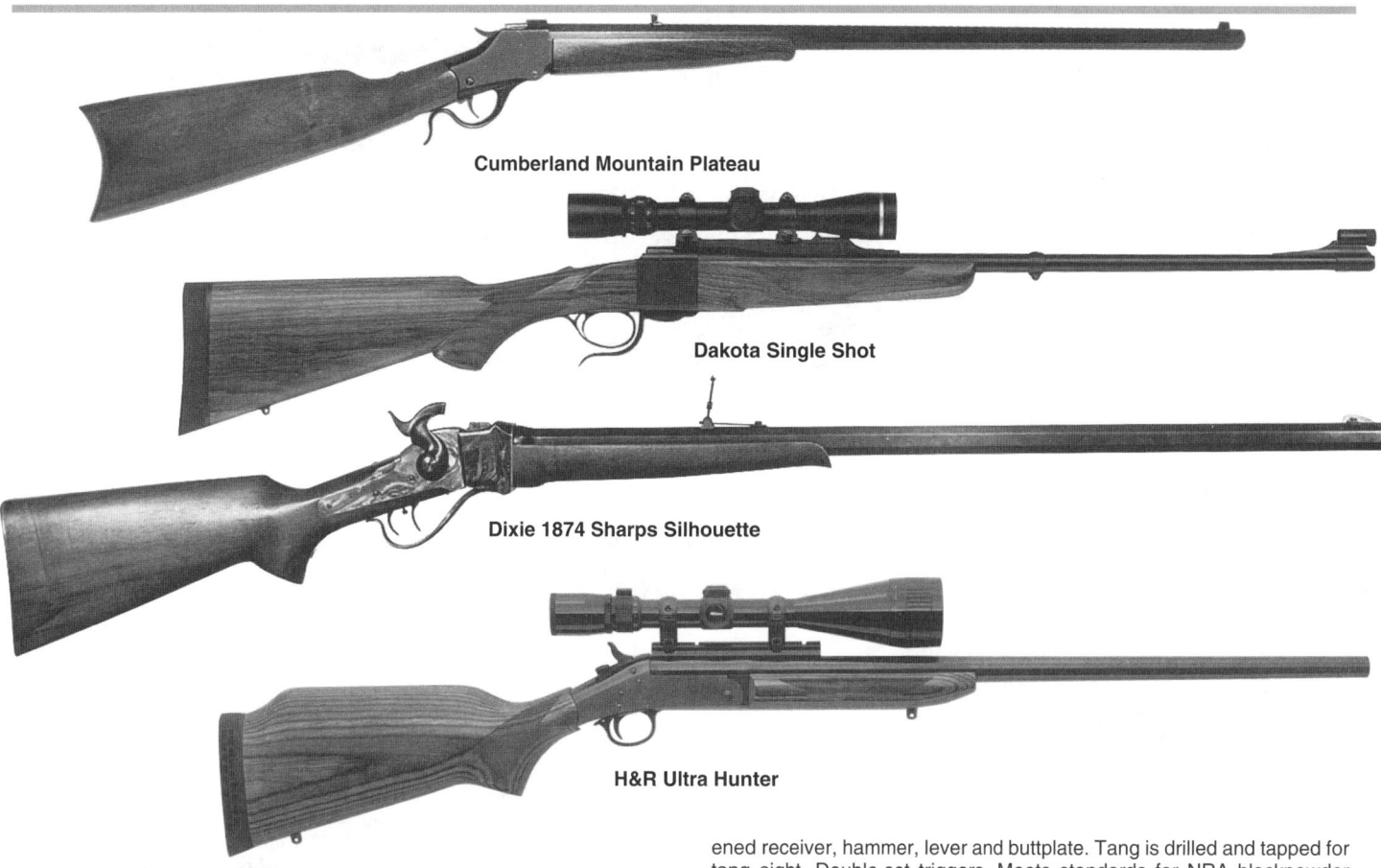

Cumberland Mountain Plateau

Dakota Single Shot

Dixie 1874 Sharps Silhouette

H&R Ultra Hunter

CIMARRON CREEDMOOR ROLLING BLOCK RIFLE
Caliber: 40-65, 45-70. **Barrel:** 30" tapered octagon. **Weight:** NA. **Length:** NA. **Stock:** European walnut. **Sights:** Globe front, fully adjustable rear. **Features:** Color case-hardened receiver, blued barrel. Hand-checkered pistol grip and forend; hand-rubbed oil finish. Introduced 1999. Imported by Cimarron F.A. Co.
Price: $1,295.00

CUMBERLAND MOUNTAIN PLATEAU RIFLE
Caliber: 40-65, 45-70. **Barrel:** Up to 32"; round. **Weight:** About 10-1/2 lbs. (32" barrel). **Length:** 48" overall (32" barrel). **Stock:** American walnut. **Sights:** Marble's bead front, Marble's open rear. **Features:** Falling block action with underlever. Blued barrel and receiver. Stock has lacquer finish, crescent buttplate. Introduced 1995. Made in U.S. by Cumberland Mountain Arms, Inc.
Price: $1,085.00

DAKOTA MODEL 10 SINGLE SHOT RIFLE
Caliber: Most rimmed and rimless commercial calibers. **Barrel:** 23". **Weight:** 6 lbs. **Length:** 39-1/2" overall. **Stock:** Medium fancy grade walnut in classic style. Checkered grip and forend. **Sights:** None furnished. Drilled and tapped for scope mounting. **Features:** Falling block action with under-lever. Top tang safety. Removable trigger plate for conversion to single set trigger. Introduced 1990. Made in U.S. by Dakota Arms.
Price: $3,595.00
Price: Barreled action $2,095.00
Price: Action only $1,850.00
Price: Magnum calibers $3,595.00
Price: Magnum barreled action $2,050.00
Price: Magnum action only $1,675.00

DIXIE 1874 SHARPS BLACKPOWDER SILHOUETTE RIFLE
Caliber: 45-70. **Barrel:** 30"; tapered octagon; blued; 1:18" twist. **Weight:** 10 lbs., 3 oz. **Length:** 47-1/2" overall. **Stock:** Oiled walnut. **Sights:** Blade front, ladder-type hunting rear. **Features:** Replica of the Sharps #1 Sporter. Shotgun-style butt with checkered metal buttplate; color case-hardened receiver, hammer, lever and buttplate. Tang is drilled and tapped for tang sight. Double-set triggers. Meets standards for NRA blackpowder cartridge matches. Introduced 1995. Imported from Italy by Dixie Gun Works.
Price: $995.00

Dixie 1874 Sharps Lightweight Hunter/Target Rifle
Same as the Dixie 1874 Sharps Blackpowder Silhouette model except has a straight-grip buttstock with military-style buttplate. Based on the 1874 military model. Introduced 1995. Imported from Italy by Dixie Gun Works.
Price: $995.00

E.M.F. 1874 METALLIC CARTRIDGE SHARPS RIFLE
Caliber: 45-70, 45/120. **Barrel:** 28", octagon. **Weight:** 10-3/4 lbs. **Length:** NA. **Stock:** Oiled walnut. **Sights:** Blade front, flip-up open rear. **Features:** Replica of the 1874 Sharps Sporting rifle. Color case-hardened lock; double-set trigger; blue finish. Imported by E.M.F.
Price: From $700.00
Price: With browned finish $1,000.00
Price: Military Carbine $650.00

HARRINGTON & RICHARDSON ULTRA VARMINT RIFLE
Caliber: 223, 243. **Barrel:** 24", heavy. **Weight:** About 7.5 lbs. **Length:** NA. **Stock:** Hand-checkered laminated birch with Monte Carlo comb. **Sights:** None furnished. Drilled and tapped for scope mounting. **Features:** Break-open action with side-lever release, positive ejection. Comes with scope mount. Blued receiver and barrel. Swivel studs. Introduced 1993. From H&R 1871, Inc.
Price: $254.95

Harrington & Richardson Ultra Hunter Rifle
Similar to the Ultra Varmint rifle except chambered for 25-06 with 26" barrel, or 308 Win. with 22" barrel. Stock and forend are of cinnamon-colored laminate; hand-checkered grip and forend. Introduced 1995. Made in U.S. by H&R 1871, LLC.
Price: $268.95
New! Price: 450 Marlin, 22" barrel $268.95

34TH EDITION, 2002 • 229

CENTERFIRE RIFLES — SINGLE SHOT

Model 1885 High Wall

Mossberg SSi-One Sporter

Navy Arms 1874 Sharps

Harrington & Richardson Ultra Comp Rifle
Similar to the Ultra Varmint except chambered for 270 or 30-06; has compensator to reduce recoil; camo-laminate stock and forend; blued, highly polished frame; scope mount. Made in U.S. by H&R 1871, LLC.
Price: $303.95

HARRIS GUNWORKS ANTIETAM SHARPS RIFLE
Caliber: 40-65, 45-75. **Barrel:** 30", 32", octagon or round, hand-lapped stainless or chrome-moly. **Weight:** 11.25 lbs. **Length:** 47" overall. **Stock:** Choice of straight grip, pistol grip or Creedmoor with Schnabel forend; pewter tip optional. Standard wood is A Fancy; higher grades available. **Sights:** Montana Vintage Arms #111 Low Profile Spirit Level front, #108 mid-range tang rear with windage adjustments. **Features:** Recreation of the 1874 Sharps sidehammer. Action is color case-hardened, barrel satin black. Chrome-moly barrel optionally blued. Optional sights include #112 Spirit Level Globe front with windage, #107 Long Range rear with windage. Introduced 1994. Made in U.S. by Harris Gunworks.
Price: $2,400.00

KRIEGHOFF HUBERTUS SINGLE-SHOT RIFLE
Caliber: 222, 243, 270, 308, 30-06, 5.6x50R Mag., 5.6x52R, 6x62R Freres, 6.5x57, 6.5x57R, 6.5x65R, 7x57, 7x57R, 7x64, 7x65R, 8x57JRS, 8x75RS, 270 Wea. Mag., 7mm Rem. Mag., 300 Win. Mag. **Barrel:** 23-1/2". **Weight:** 6-1/2 lbs. **Length:** NA. **Stock:** High-grade walnut. **Sights:** Blade front, open rear. **Features:** Break-loading with manual cocking lever on top tang; take-down; extractor; Schnabel forearm; many options. Imported from Germany by Krieghoff International Inc.
Price: Hubertus single shot, from $5,850.00
Price: Hubertus, magnum calibers $6,850.00

MODEL 1885 HIGH WALL RIFLE
Caliber: 30-40 Krag, 32-40, 38-55, 40-65 WCF, 45-70. **Barrel:** 26" (30-40), 28" all others. Douglas Premium #3 tapered octagon. **Weight:** NA. **Length:** NA. **Stock:** Premium American black walnut. **Sights:** Marble's standard ivory bead front, #66 long blade top rear with reversible notch and elevator. **Features:** Recreation of early octagon top, thick-wall High Wall with Coil spring action. Tang drilled, tapped for High Wall tang sight. Receiver, lever, hammer and breechblock color case-hardened. Introduced 1991. Available from Montana Armory, Inc.
Price: $1,095.00

MOSSBERG SSi-ONE SINGLE SHOT RIFLE
Caliber: 223 Rem., 22-250 Rem., 243 Win., 270 Win., 308 Rem., 30-06. **Barrel:** 24". **Weight:** 8 lbs. **Length:** 40". **Stock:** Satin-finished walnut, fluted and checkered; sling-swivel studs. **Sights:** None (scope base furnished). **Features:** Frame accepts interchangeable barrels, including 12-gauge, fully rifled slug barrel and 12 ga., 3-1/2" chambered barrel with Ulti-Full Turkey choke tube. Lever-opening, break-action design; single-stage trigger; ambidextrous, top-tang safety; internal eject/extract selector. Introduced 2000. From Mossberg.
Price: SSi-One Sporter (standard barrel) or 12 ga.,
3-1/2" chamber $459.00
Price: SSi-One Varmint (bull barrel, 22-250 Rem. only;
weighs 10 lbs.) $480.00
Price: SSi-One 12-gauge Slug (fully rifled barrel, no sights,
scope base) $480.00

NAVY ARMS 1874 SHARPS CAVALRY CARBINE
Caliber: 45-70. **Barrel:** 22". **Weight:** 7 lbs., 12 oz. **Length:** 39" overall. **Stock:** Walnut. **Sights:** Blade front, military ladder-type rear. **Features:** Replica of the 1874 Sharps military carbine. Color case-hardened receiver and furniture. Imported by Navy Arms.
Price: $1,000.00

NAVY ARMS 1874 SHARPS BUFFALO RIFLE
Caliber: 45-70, 45-90. **Barrel:** 28" heavy octagon. **Weight:** 10 lbs., 10 oz. **Length:** 46" overall. **Stock:** Walnut; checkered grip and forend. **Sights:** Blade front, ladder rear; tang sight optional. **Features:** Color case-hardened receiver, blued barrel; double-set triggers. Imported by Navy Arms.
Price: $1,160.00

Navy Arms Sharps Plains Rifle
Similar to the Sharps Buffalo rifle except 45-70 only, has 32" medium-weight barrel, weighs 9 lbs., 8 oz., and is 49" overall. Imported by Navy Arms.
Price: $1,125.00

Navy Arms Sharps Sporting Rifle
Same as the Navy Arms Sharps Plains Rifle except has pistol grip stock. Introduced 1997. Imported by Navy Arms.
Price: 45-70 only $1,160.00

CENTERFIRE RIFLES — SINGLE SHOT

Navy Arms 1885 High Wall

Navy Arms 1873 Springfield

Navy Arms #2 Creedmoor

Navy Arms No. 3 Long Range

New England Firearms Handi-Rifle

NAVY ARMS 1885 HIGH WALL RIFLE
Caliber: 45-70; others available on special order. **Barrel:** 28" round, 30" octagonal. **Weight:** 9.5 lbs. **Length:** 45-1/2" overall (30" barrel). **Stock:** Walnut. **Sights:** Blade front, vernier tang-mounted peep rear. **Features:** Replica of Winchester's High Wall designed by Browning. Color case-hardened receiver, blued barrel. Introduced 1998. Imported by Navy Arms.
Price: 28", round barrel, target sights $900.00
Price: 30" octagonal barrel, target sights $975.00

NAVY ARMS 1873 SPRINGFIELD CAVALRY CARBINE
Caliber: 45-70. **Barrel:** 22". **Weight:** 7 lbs. **Length:** 40-1/2" overall. **Stock:** Walnut. **Sights:** Blade front, military ladder rear. **Features:** Blued lockplate and barrel; color case-hardened breechblock; saddle ring with bar. Replica of 7th Cavalry gun. Imported by Navy Arms.
Price: $930.00

NAVY ARMS ROLLING BLOCK BUFFALO RIFLE
Caliber: 45-70. **Barrel:** 26", 30". **Stock:** Walnut. **Sights:** Blade front, adjustable rear. **Features:** Reproduction of classic rolling block action. Available with full-octagon or half-octagon-half-round barrel. Color case-hardened action, steel fittings. From Navy Arms.
Price: $815.00

Navy Arms No. 2 Creedmoor Target Rifle
Similar to the Navy Arms Rolling Block Buffalo Rifle except has 30" tapered octagon barrel, checkered full-pistol grip stock, blade front sight, open adjustable rear sight and Creedmoor tang sight. Imported by Navy Arms.
Price: $995.00

NAVY ARMS SHARPS NO. 3 LONG RANGE RIFLE
Caliber: 45-70, 45-90. **Barrel:** 34" octagon. **Weight:** 10 lbs., 12 oz. **Length:** 51-1/2". **Stock:** Deluxe walnut. **Sights:** Globe target front and match grade rear tang. **Features:** Shotgun buttplate, German silver forend cap, color case hardenend receiver. Imported by Navy Arms.
Price: $1,860.00

NEW ENGLAND FIREARMS HANDI-RIFLE
Caliber: 22 Hornet, 223, 243, 7x57, 7x64 Brenneke, 30-30, 270, 280 Rem., 308, 30-06, 357 Mag., 44 Mag., 45-70. **Barrel:** 22", 24"; 26" for 280 Rem. **Weight:** 7 lbs. **Stock:** Walnut-finished hardwood; black rubber recoil pad. **Sights:** Ramp front, folding rear (22 Hornet, 30-30, 45-70). Drilled and tapped for scope mount; 223, 243, 270, 280, 30-06 have no open sights, come with scope mounts. **Features:** Break-open action with side-lever release. The 223, 243, 270 and 30-06 have recoil pad and Monte Carlo stock for shooting with scope. Swivel studs on all models. Blue finish. Introduced 1989. From New England Firearms.
Price: $219.95
Price: 7x57, 7x64 Brenneke, 24" barrel $219.95
Price: 280 Rem., 26" barrel $219.95
Price: Synthetic Handi-Rifle (black polymer stock and forend, swivels, recoil pad) $228.95
Price: Handi-Rifle Youth (223, 243) $219.95

CENTERFIRE RIFLES — SINGLE SHOT

New England Firearms Super Light

New England Firearms Survivor

Remington No. 1 Mid-Range

Ruger No. 1B

New England Firearms Super Light Rifle
Similar to the Handi-Rifle except has new barrel taper, shorter 20" barrel with recessed muzzle and special lightweight synthetic stock and forend. No sights are furnished on the 223 and 243 versions, but have a factory-mounted scope base and offset hammer spur; Monte Carlo stock; 22 Hornet has ramp front, fully adjustable open rear. Overall length is 36", weight is 5.5 lbs. Introduced 1997. Made in U.S. by New England Firearms.
Price: 22 Hornet, 223 Rem. or 243 Win.. $228.95

NEW ENGLAND FIREARMS SURVIVOR RIFLE
Caliber: 223, 308 Win., single shot. **Barrel:** 22". **Weight:** 6 lbs. **Length:** 36" overall. **Stock:** Black polymer, thumbhole design. **Sights:** None furnished; scope mount provided. **Features:** Receiver drilled and tapped for scope mounting. Stock and forend have storage compartments for ammo, etc.; comes with integral swivels and black nylon sling. Introduced 1996. Made in U.S. by New England Firearms.
Price: Blue finish. $227.95

REMINGTON NO. 1 ROLLING BLOCK MID-RANGE SPORTER
Caliber: 45-70. **Barrel:** 30" round. **Weight:** 8-3/4 lbs. **Length:** 46-1/2" overall. **Stock:** American walnut with checkered pistol grip and forend. **Sights:** Beaded blade front, adjustable center-notch buckhorn rear. **Features:** Recreation of the original. Polished blue metal finish. Many options available. Introduced 1998. Made in U.S. by Remington.
Price: $1,348.00

RUGER NO. 1B SINGLE SHOT
Caliber: 218 Bee, 22 Hornet, 220 Swift, 22-250, 223, 243, 6mm Rem., 25-06, 257 Roberts, 270, 280, 30-06, 7mm Rem. Mag., 300 Win. Mag., 338 Win. Mag., 270 Wea., 300 Wea. **Barrel:** 26" round tapered with quarter-rib; with Ruger 1" rings. **Weight:** 8 lbs. **Length:** 43-3/8" overall. **Stock:** Walnut, two-piece, checkered pistol grip and semi-beavertail forend. **Sights:** None, 1" scope rings supplied for integral mounts. **Features:** Under-lever, hammerless falling block design has auto ejector, top tang safety.
Price: 1B. $797.00
Price: Barreled action $575.00
Price: K1-B-BBZ Stainless steel, laminated stock 25-06, 7MM mag, 7MM STW, 300 Win Mag. $845.00

Ruger No. 1A Light Sporter
Similar to the No. 1B Standard Rifle except has lightweight 22" barrel, Alexander Henry-style forend, adjustable folding leaf rear sight on quarter-rib, dovetailed ramp front with gold bead. Calibers 243, 30-06, 270 and 7x57. Weighs about 7-1/4 lbs.
Price: No. 1A $797.00
Price: Barreled action $575.00

Ruger No. 1V Varminter
Similar to the No. 1B Standard Rifle except has 24" heavy barrel. Semi-beavertail forend, barrel ribbed for target scope block, with 1" Ruger scope rings. Calibers 22-250, 220 Swift, 223, 25-06. Weight about 9 lbs.
Price: No. 1V $797.00
Price: Barreled action $575.00
Price: K1-V-BBZ stainless steel, laminated stock 22-250 . . . . . . $845.00

CENTERFIRE RIFLES — SINGLE SHOT

Ruger K1-B-BBZ

Ruger No. 1V Varminter

Ruger No. 1 RSI

Ruger No. 1H Tropical

C. Sharps New Model 1875 Old Reliable

Ruger No. 1 RSI International
Similar to the No. 1B Standard Rifle except has lightweight 20" barrel, full-length International-style forend with loop sling swivel, adjustable folding leaf rear sight on quarter-rib, ramp front with gold bead. Calibers 243, 30-06, 270 and 7x57. Weight is about 7-1/4 lbs.
Price: No. 1 RSI $818.00
Price: Barreled action $575.00

Ruger No. 1H Tropical Rifle
Similar to the No. 1B Standard Rifle except has Alexander Henry forend, adjustable folding leaf rear sight on quarter-rib, ramp front with dovetail gold bead, 24" heavy barrel. Calibers 375 H&H, 416 Rem. Mag. (weighs about 8-1/4 lbs.), 416 Rigby, and 458 Win. Mag. (weighs about 9 lbs.).
Price: No. 1H $797.00
Price: Barreled action $575.00

Ruger No. 1S Medium Sporter
Similar to the No. 1B Standard Rifle except has Alexander Henry-style forend, adjustable folding leaf rear sight on quarter-rib, ramp front sight base and dovetail-type gold bead front sight. Calibers 218 Bee, 7mm Rem. Mag., 338 Win. Mag., 300 Win. Mag. with 26" barrel, 45-70 with 22" barrel. Weighs about 7-1/2 lbs. In 45-70.
Price: No. 1S $797.00
Price: Barreled action $575.00

Ruger No. 1 Stainless Steel Rifles
Similar to No. 1 Standard except has stainless steel receiver and barrel, laminated hardwood stock. Calibers 25-06, 7mm Rem. Mag., 7mm STW, 300 Win. Mag. (Standard) or 22-250 (Varminter). Introduced 2000.
Price: No. 1 Stainless Standard (26" barrel, 8 lbs.) $845.00
Price: No. 1 Stainless Varminter (24" heavy barrel, 9 lbs.) $845.00

C. SHARPS ARMS NEW MODEL 1875 OLD RELIABLE RIFLE
Caliber: 22LR, 32-40 & 38-55 Ballard, 38-56 WCF, 40-65 WCF, 40-90 3-1/4", 40-90 2-5/8", 40-70 2-1/10", 40-70 2-1/4", 40-70 2-1/2", 40-50 1-11/16", 40-50 1-7/8", 45-90, 45-70, 45-100, 45-110, 45-120. Also available on special order only in 50-70, 50-90, 50-140. **Barrel:** 24", 26", 30" (standard), 32", 34" optional. **Weight:** 8-12 lbs. **Stock:** Walnut, straight grip, shotgun butt with checkered steel buttplate. **Sights:** Silver blade front, Rocky Mountain buckhorn rear. **Features:** Recreation of the 1875 Sharps rifle. Production guns will have case colored receiver. Available in Custom Sporting and Target versions upon request. Announced 1986. From C. Sharps Arms Co. and Montana Armory, Inc.
Price: 1875 Carbine (24" tapered round bbl.) $810.00
Price: 1875 Saddle Rifle (26" tapered oct. bbl.) $910.00
Price: 1875 Sporting Rifle (30" tapered oct. bbl.) $975.00
Price: 1875 Business Rifle (28" tapered round bbl.) $860.00

CENTERFIRE RIFLES — SINGLE SHOT

C. Sharps New Model 1874

C. Sharps New Model 1885

Thompson/Center Contender

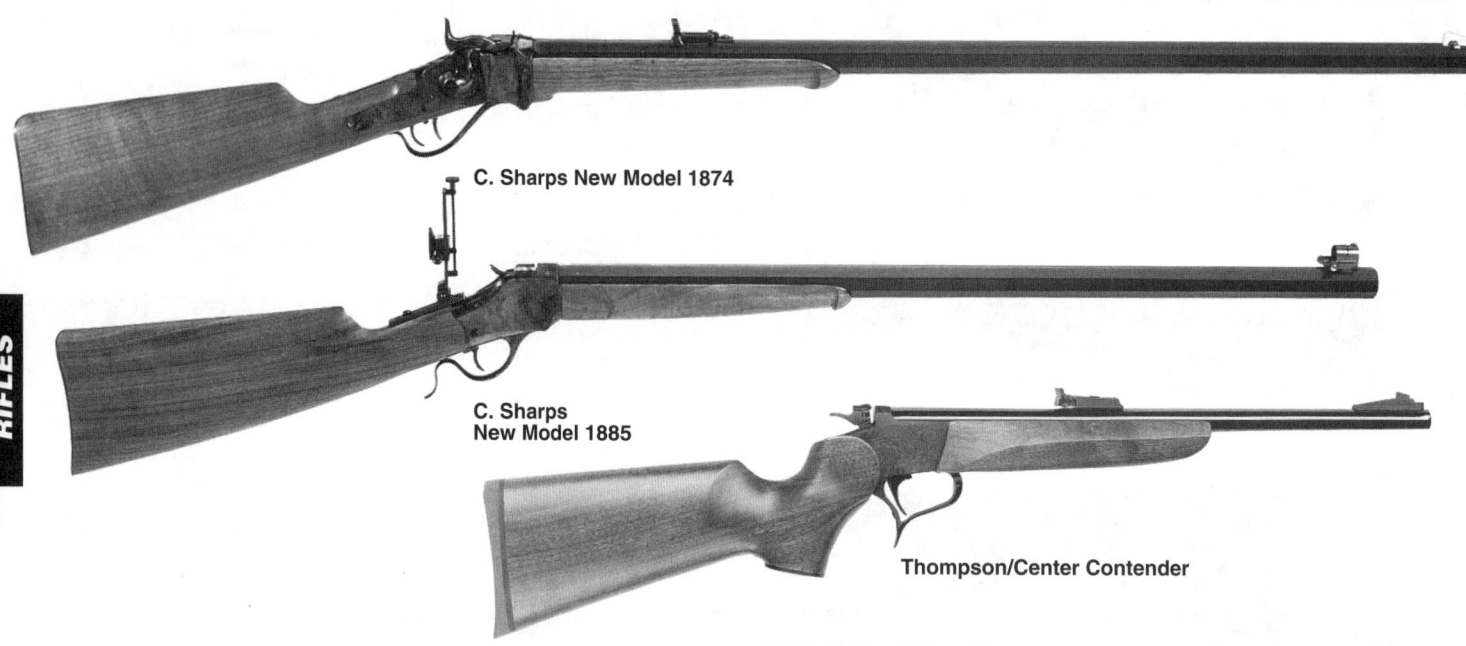

C. Sharps Arms 1875 Classic Sharps
Similar to the New Model 1875 Sporting Rifle except has 26", 28" or 30" full octagon barrel, crescent buttplate with toe plate, Hartford-style forend with cast German silver nose cap. Blade front sight, Rocky Mountain buckhorn rear. Weighs 10 lbs. Introduced 1987. From C. Sharps Arms Co. and Montana Armory, Inc.
Price: $1,185.00

C. Sharps Arms New Model 1875 Target & Long Range
Similar to the New Model 1875 except available in all listed calibers except 22 LR; 34" tapered octagon barrel; globe with post front sight, Long Range Vernier tang sight with windage adjustments. Pistol grip stock with cheek rest; checkered steel buttplate. Introduced 1991. From C. Sharps Arms Co. and Montana Armory, Inc.
Price: $1,535.00

C. SHARPS ARMS NEW MODEL 1874 OLD RELIABLE
Caliber: 40-50, 40-70, 40-90, 45-70, 45-90, 45-100, 45-110, 45-120, 50-70, 50-90, 50-140. **Barrel:** 26", 28", 30" tapered octagon. **Weight:** About 10 lbs. **Length:** NA. **Stock:** American black walnut; shotgun butt with checkered steel buttplate; straight grip, heavy forend with Schnabel tip. **Sights:** Blade front, buckhorn rear. Drilled and tapped for tang sight. **Features:** Recreation of the Model 1874 Old Reliable Sharps Sporting Rifle. Double set triggers. Reintroduced 1991. Made in U.S. by C. Sharps Arms. Available from Montana Armory, Inc.
Price: $1,175.00

C. SHARPS ARMS NEW MODEL 1885 HIGHWALL RIFLE
Caliber: 22 LR, 22 Hornet, 219 Zipper, 25-35 WCF, 32-40 WCF, 38-55 WCF, 40-65, 30-40-Krag, 40-50 ST or BN, 40-70 ST or BN, 40-90 ST or BN, 45-70 2-1/10" ST, 45-90 2-4/10" ST, 45-100 2-6/10" ST, 45-110 2-7/8" ST, 45-120 3-1/4" ST. **Barrel:** 26", 28", 30", tapered full octagon. **Weight:** About 9 lbs., 4 oz. **Length:** 47" overall. **Stock:** Oil-finished American walnut; Schnabel-style forend. **Sights:** Blade front, buckhorn rear. Drilled and tapped for optional tang sight. **Features:** Single trigger; octagonal receiver top; checkered steel buttplate; color case-hardened receiver and buttplate, blued barrel. Many options available. Made in U.S. by C. Sharps Arms Co. Available from Montana Armory, Inc.
Price: From $1,195.00

SHARPS 1874 RIFLE
Caliber: 45-70. **Barrel:** 28", octagonal. **Weight:** 9-1/4 lbs. **Length:** 46" overall. **Stock:** Checkered walnut. **Sights:** Blade front, adjustable rear. **Features:** Double set triggers on rifle. Color case-hardened receiver and buttplate, blued barrel. Imported from Italy by E.M.F.
Price: Rifle or carbine $950.00

Price: Military rifle, carbine $860.00
Price: Sporting rifle $860.00

SHILOH SHARPS 1874 LONG RANGE EXPRESS
Caliber: 40-50 BN, 40-70 BN, 40-90 BN, 45-70 ST, 45-90 ST, 45-110 ST, 50-70 ST, 50-90 ST, 50-110 ST, 32-40, 38-55, 40-70 ST, 40-90 ST. **Barrel:** 34" tapered octagon. **Weight:** 10-1/2 lbs. **Length:** 51" overall. **Stock:** Oil-finished semi-fancy walnut with pistol grip, shotgun-style butt, traditional cheek rest, Schnabel forend. **Sights:** Globe front, sporting tang rear. **Features:** Recreation of the Model 1874 Sharps rifle. Double set triggers. Made in U.S. by Shiloh Rifle Mfg. Co.
Price: $1,796.00
Price: Sporting Rifle No. 1 (similar to above except with 30" bbl., blade front, buckhorn rear sight) $1,706.00
Price: Sporting Rifle No. 3 (similar to No. 1 except straight-grip stock, standard wood) $1,504.00
Price: 1874 Hartford model $1,702.00

Shiloh Sharps 1874 Montana Roughrider
Similar to the No. 1 Sporting Rifle except available with half-octagon or full-octagon barrel in 24", 26", 28", 30", 34" lengths; standard supreme or semi-fancy wood, shotgun, pistol grip or military-style butt. Weight about 8-1/2 lbs. Calibers 30-40, 30-30, 40-50x1-11/16"BN, 40-70x2-1/10" BN, 45-70x2-1/10"ST. Globe front and tang sight optional.
Price: Standard supreme $1,504.00
Price: Semi-fancy $1,704.00

Shiloh Sharps 1874 Business Rifle
Similar to No. 3 Rifle except has 28" heavy round barrel, military-style buttstock and steel buttplate. Weight about 9-1/2 lbs. Calibers 40-50 BN, 40-70 BN, 40-90 BN, 45-70 ST, 45-90 ST, 50-70 ST, 50-100 ST, 32-40, 38-55, 40-70 ST, 40-90 ST.
Price: $1,604.00
Price: 1874 Saddle Rifle (similar to Carbine except has 26" octagon barrel, semi-fancy shotgun butt) $1,706.00

THOMPSON/CENTER CONTENDER CARBINE
Caliber: 22 LR, 22 Hornet, 223 Rem., 7x30 Waters, 30-30 Win. **Barrel:** 21". **Weight:** 5 lbs., 2 oz. **Length:** 35" overall. **Stock:** Checkered American walnut with rubber butt pad. Also with Rynite stock and forend. **Sights:** Blade front, open adjustable rear. **Features:** Uses the T/C Contender action. Eleven interchangeable barrels available, all with sights, drilled and tapped for scope mounting. Introduced 1985. Offered as a complete Carbine only.
Price: Rifle calibers $571.38
Price: Extra barrels, rifle calibers, each $251.08

234 • GUNS ILLUSTRATED

CENTERFIRE RIFLES — SINGLE SHOT

Thompson/Center Encore

THOMPSON/CENTER ENCORE RIFLE
Caliber: 22-250, 223, 243, 25-06, 270, 7mm-08, 308, 30-06, 7mm Rem. Mag., 300 Win. Mag. **Barrel:** 24", 26". **Weight:** 6 lbs., 12 oz. (24" barrel). **Length:** 38-1/2" (24" barrel). **Stock:** American walnut. Monte Carlo style; Schnabel forend or black composite. **Sights:** Ramp-style white bead front, fully adjustable leaf-type rear. **Features:** Interchangeable barrels; action opens by squeezing trigger guard; drilled and tapped for T/C scope mounts; polished blue finish. Introduced 1996. Made in U.S. by Thompson/Center Arms.
Price: $582.29
Price: Extra barrels $249.10
Price: With black composite stock and forend $582.29

Thompson/Center Stainless Encore Rifle
Similar to the blued Encore except made of stainless steel with blued sights, and has black composite stock and forend. Available in 22-250, 223, 7mm-08, 30-06, 308. Introduced 1999. Made in U.S. by Thompson/Center Arms.
Price: $650.42

TRADITIONS 1874 SHARPS DELUXE RIFLE
Caliber: 45-70. **Barrel:** 32" octagonal; 1:18" twist. **Weight:** 11.67 lbs. **Length:** 48.8" overall. **Stock:** Checkered walnut with German silver nose cap and steel butt plate. **Sights:** Globe front, adjustable creedmore rear with 12 inserts. **Features:** Color-case hardened receiver; double-set triggers. Introduced 2001. Imported from Pedersoli by Traditions.
Price: $969.00

TRADITIONS 1874 SHARPS STANDARD RIFLE
Similar to 1874 Sharps Deluxe Rifle, except has blade front and adjustable buckhorn-style rear sight. Weighs 10.67 pounds. Introduced 2001. Imported from Pedersoli by Traditions.
Price: $749.00

TRADITIONS ROLLING BLOCK SPORTING RIFLE
Caliber: 45-70. **Barrel:** 30" octagonal; 1:18" twist. **Weight:** 11.67 lbs. **Length:** 46.7" overall. **Stock:** Walnut. **Sights:** Blade front, adjustable rear. **Features:** Antique silver, color-case hardened receiver, drilled and tapped for tang/globe sights; brass butt plate and trigger guard. Introduced 2001. Imported from Pedersoli by Traditions.
Price: $749.00

TRISTAR/UBERTI 1885 SINGLE SHOT
Caliber: 45-70. **Barrel:** 28". **Weight:** 8.75 lbs. **Length:** 44.5" overall. **Stock:** European walnut. **Sights:** Bead on blade front, open step-adjustable rear. **Features:** Recreation of the 1885 Winchester. Color case-hardened receiver and lever, blued barrel. Introduced 1998. Imported from Italy by Tristar Sporting Arms Ltd.
Price: $765.00

UBERTI BABY ROLLING BLOCK CARBINE
Caliber: 22 LR, 22 WMR, 22 Hornet, 357 Mag., single shot. **Barrel:** 22". **Weight:** 4.8 lbs. **Length:** 35-1/2" overall. **Stock:** Walnut stock and forend. **Sights:** Blade front, fully adjustable open rear. **Features:** Resembles Remington New Model No. 4 carbine. Brass trigger guard and buttplate; color case-hardened frame, blued barrel. Imported by Uberti USA Inc.
Price: $490.00
Price: Baby Rolling Block Rifle, 26" bbl. $590.00

WESSON & HARRINGTON BUFFALO CLASSIC RIFLE
Caliber: 45-70. **Barrel:** 32" heavy. **Weight:** 9 lbs. **Length:** 52" overall. **Stock:** American black walnut. **Sights:** None furnished; drilled and tapped for peep sight; barrel dovetailed for front sight. **Features:** Color case-hardened Handi-Rifle action with exposed hammer; color case-hardened crescent buttplate; 19th century checkering pattern. Introduced 1995. Made in U.S. by H&R 1871, Inc.
Price: About $349.95

Wesson & Harrington 38-55 Target Rifle
Similar to the Buffalo Classic rifle except chambered for 38-55 Win., has 28" barrel. The barrel and steel furniture, including steel trigger guard and forend spacer, are highly polished and blued. Color case-hardened receiver and buttplate. Barrel is dovetailed for a front sight, and drilled and tapped for receiver sight or scope mount. Introduced 1998. Made in U.S. by H&R 1871, Inc.
Price: $389.95

DRILLINGS, COMBINATION GUNS, DOUBLE GUNS

Designs for sporting and utility purposes worldwide.

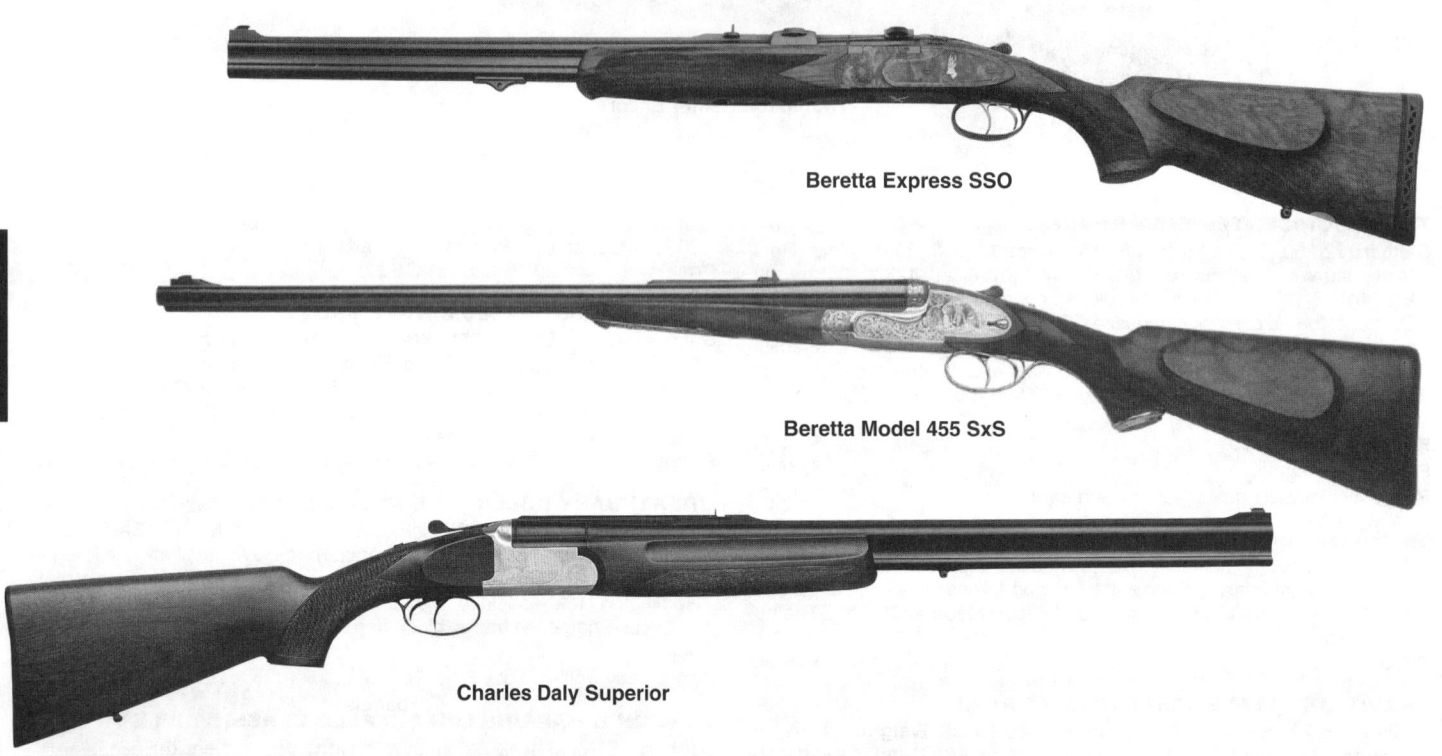

Beretta Express SSO

Beretta Model 455 SxS

Charles Daly Superior

BERETTA EXPRESS SSO O/U DOUBLE RIFLES
Caliber: 375 H&H, 458 Win. Mag., 9.3x74R. **Barrel:** 25.5". **Weight:** 11 lbs. **Stock:** European walnut with hand-checkered grip and forend. **Sights:** Blade front on ramp, open V-notch rear. **Features:** Sidelock action with color case-hardened receiver (gold inlays on SSO6 Gold). Ejectors, double triggers, recoil pad. Introduced 1990. Imported from Italy by Beretta U.S.A.
Price: SSO6 . . . . $21,000.00
Price: SSO6 Gold $23,500.00

BERETTA MODEL 455 SxS EXPRESS RIFLE
Caliber: 375 H&H, 458 Win. Mag., 470 NE, 500 NE 3", 416 Rigby. **Barrel:** 23-1/2" or 25-1/2". **Weight:** 11 lbs. **Stock:** European walnut with hand-checkered grip and forend. **Sights:** Blade front, folding leaf V-notch rear. **Features:** Sidelock action with easily removable sideplates; color case-hardened finish (455), custom big game or floral motif engraving (455EELL). Double triggers, recoil pad. Introduced 1990. Imported from Italy by Beretta U.S.A.
Price: Model 455. . . . . $36,000.00
Price: Model 455EELL $47,000.00

BRNO 500 COMBINATION GUNS
Caliber/Gauge: 12 (2-3/4" chamber) over 5.6x52R, 5.6x50R, 222 Rem., 243, 6.x55, 308, 7x57R, 7x65R, 30-06. **Barrel:** 23.6". **Weight:** 7.6 lbs. **Length:** 40.5" overall. **Stock:** European walnut. **Sights:** Bead front, V-notch rear; grooved for scope mounting. **Features:** Boxlock action; double set trigger; blue finish with etched engraving. Announced 1998. Imported from The Czech Republic by Euro-Imports.
Price: $1,023.00
Price: O/U double rifle, 7x57R, 7x65R, 8x57JRS $1,125.00

BRNO ZH 300 COMBINATION GUN
Caliber/Gauge: 22 Hornet, 5.6x50R Mag., 5.6x52R, 7x57R, 7x65R, 8x57JRS over 12, 16 (2-3/4" chamber). **Barrel:** 23.6". **Weight:** 7.9 lbs. **Length:** 40.5" overall. **Stock:** European walnut. **Sights:** Blade front, open adjustable rear. **Features:** Boxlock action; double triggers; automatic safety. Announced 1998. Imported from The Czech Republic by Euro-Imports.
Price: $724.00

BRNO ZH Double Rifles
Similar to the ZH 300 combination guns except with double rifle barrels. Available in 7x65R, 7x57R and 8x57JRS. Announced 1998. Imported from The Czech Republic by Euro-Imports.
Price: $1,125.00

CHARLES DALY SUPERIOR COMBINATION GUN
Caliber/Gauge: 12 ga. over 22 Hornet, 223 Rem., 22-250, 243 Win., 270 Win., 308 Win., 30-06. **Barrel:** 23.5", shotgun choked Imp. Cyl. **Weight:** About 7.5 lbs. **Stock:** Checkered walnut pistol grip buttstock and semi-beavertail forend. **Features:** Silvered, engraved receiver; chrome-moly steel barrels; double triggers; extractors; sling swivels; gold bead front sight. Introduced 1997. Imported from Italy by K.B.I. Inc.
Price: $1,249.95

Charles Daly Empire Combination Gun
Same as the Superior grade except has deluxe wood with European-style comb and cheekpiece; slim forend. Introduced 1997. Imported from Italy by K.B.I., Inc.
Price: $1,789.95

CZ 584 SOLO COMBINATION GUN
Caliber/Gauge: 7x57R; 12, 2-3/4" chamber. **Barrel:** 24.4". **Weight:** 7.37 lbs. **Length:** 45.25" overall. **Stock:** Circassian walnut. **Sights:** Blade front, open rear adjustable for windage. **Features:** Kersten-style double lump locking system; double-trigger Blitz-type mechanism with drop safety and adjustable set trigger for the rifle barrel; auto safety, dual extractors; receiver dovetailed for scope mounting. Imported from the Czech Republic by CZ-USA.
Price: $850.00

CZ 589 STOPPER OVER/UNDER GUN
Caliber: 458 Win. Magnum. **Barrels:** 21.7". **Weight:** 9.3 lbs. **Length:** 37.7" overall. **Stock:** Turkish walnut with sling swivels. **Sights:** Blade front, fixed rear. **Features:** Kersten-style action; Blitz-type double trigger; hammer-forged, blued barrels; satin-nickel, engraved receiver. Introduced 2001. Imported from the Czech Republic by CZ USA.
Price: $2,999.00
Price: Fully engraved model $3,999.00

DRILLINGS, COMBINATION GUNS, DOUBLE GUNS

Hoenig Round Action

Krieghoff Classic Double Rifle

DAKOTA DOUBLE RIFLE
Caliber: 470 Nitro Express, 500 Nitro Express. **Barrel:** 25". **Weight:** NA. **Length:** NA. **Stock:** Exhibition-grade walnut. **Sights:** Express. **Features:** Round action; selective ejectors; recoil pad; Americase. From Dakota Arms Inc.
Price: $25,000.00

EAA/BAIKAL IZH-94 COMBINATION GUN
Caliber/Gauge: 12, 3" chamber; 222 Rem., 223, 5.6x50R, 5.6x55E, 7x57R, 7x65R, 7.62x39, 7.62x51, 308, 7.62x53R, 7.62x54R, 30-06. **Barrel:** 24", 26"; imp., mod. and full choke tubes. **Weight:** 7.28 lbs. **Stock:** Walnut; rubber butt pad. **Sights:** Express style. **Features:** Hammer-forged barrels with chrome-lined bores; machined receiver; single-selective or double triggers. Imported by European American Armory.
Price: Blued finish... $499.00

GARBI EXPRESS DOUBLE RIFLE
Caliber: 7x65R, 9.3x74R, 375 H&H. **Barrel:** 24-3/4". **Weight:** 7-3/4 to 8-1/2 lbs. **Length:** 41-1/2" overall. **Stock:** Turkish walnut. **Sights:** Quarter-rib with express sight. **Features:** Side-by-side double; H&H-pattern sidelock ejector with reinforced action, chopper lump barrels of Boehler steel; double triggers; fine scroll and rosette engraving, or full coverage ornamental; coin-finished action. Introduced 1997. Imported from Spain by Wm. Larkin Moore.
Price: $16,900.00

HOENIG ROTARY ROUND ACTION DOUBLE RIFLE
Caliber: Most popular calibers from 225 Win. to 9.3x74R. **Barrel:** 22"-26". **Weight:** NA. **Length:** NA. **Stock:** English Walnut; to customer specs. **Sights:** Swivel hood front with button release (extra bead stored in trap door gripcap), express-style rear on quarter-rib adjustable for windage and elevation; scope mount. **Features:** Round action opens by rotating barrels, pulling forward. Has inertia extractor system; rotary safety blocks the strikers; single lever quick-detachable scope mount. Simple takedown without removing forend. Introduced 1997. Made in U.S. by George Hoenig.
Price: $19,980.00

KRIEGHOFF CLASSIC DOUBLE RIFLE
Caliber: 7x65R, 308 Win., 30-06, 30R Blaser, 8x57 JRS, 8x75RS, 9.3x74R. **Barrel:** 23.5". **Weight:** 7.3 to 8 lbs. **Length:** NA. **Stock:** High grade European walnut. Standard has conventional rounded cheekpiece, Bavaria has Bavarian-style cheekpiece. **Sights:** Bead front with removable, adjustable wedge (375 H&H and below), standing leaf rear on quarter-rib. **Features:** Boxlock action; double triggers; short opening angle for fast loading; quiet extractors; sliding, self-adjusting wedge for secure bolting; Purdey-style barrel extension; horizontal firing pin placement. Many options available. Introduced 1997. Imported from Germany by Krieghoff International.

Price: With small Arabesque engraving $7,850.00
Price: With engraved sideplates........................ $9,800.00
Price: For extra barrels................................ $4,500.00
Price: Extra 20-ga., 28" shotshell barrels $3,200.00

Krieghoff Classic Big Five Double Rifle
Similar to the standard Classic excpet available in 375 Flanged Mag. N.E., 500/416 N.E., 470 N.E., 500 N.E. 3". Has hinged front trigger, non-removable muzzle wedge (larger than 375-caliber), Universal Trigger System, Combi Cocking Device, steel trigger guard, specially weighted stock bolt for weight and balance. Many options available. Introduced 1997. Imported from Germany by Krieghoff International.
Price: $9,450.00
Price: With engraved sideplates....................... $11,400.00

LEBEAU - COURALLY EXPRESS RIFLE SxS
Caliber: 7x65R, 8x57JRS, 9.3x74R, 375 H&H, 470 N.E. **Barrel:** 24" to 26". **Weight:** 7-3/4 to 10-1/2 lbs. **Stock:** Fancy French walnut with cheekpiece. **Sights:** Bead on ramp front, standing left express rear on quarter-rib. **Features:** Holland & Holland-type sidelock with automatic ejectors; double triggers. Built to order only. Imported from Belgium by Wm. Larkin Moore.
Price: $41,000.00

MERKEL DRILLINGS
Caliber/Gauge: 12, 20, 3" chambers; 16, 2-3/4" chambers; 22 Hornet, 5.6x50R Mag., 5.6x52R, 222 Rem., 243 Win., 6.5x55, 6.5x57R, 7x57R, 7x65R, 308, 30-06, 8x57JRS, 9.3x74R, 375 H&H. **Barrel:** 25.6". **Weight:** 7.9 to 8.4 lbs. depending upon caliber. **Length:** NA. **Stock:** Oil-finished walnut with pistol grip; cheekpiece on 12-, 16-gauge. **Sights:** Blade front, fixed rear. **Features:** Double barrel locking lug with Greener cross-bolt; scroll-engraved, case-hardened receiver; automatic trigger safety; Blitz action; double triggers. Imported from Germany by GSI.
Price: Model 96K (manually cocked rifle system), from $6,495.00
Price: Model 96K Engraved (hunting series on receiver) $7,995.00

MERKEL OVER/UNDER DOUBLE RIFLES
Caliber: 22 Hornet, 5.6x50R Mag., 5.6x52R, 222 Rem., 243 Win., 6.5x55, 6.5x57R, 7x57R, 7x65R, 308, 30-06, 8x57JRS, 9.3x74R. **Barrel:** 25.6". **Weight:** About 7.7 lbs. depending upon caliber. **Length:** NA. **Stock:** Oil-finished walnut with pistol grip, cheekpiece. **Sights:** Blade front, fixed rear. **Features:** Kersten double cross-bolt lock; scroll-engraved, case-hardened receiver; Blitz action with double triggers. Imported from Germany by GSI.
Price: Model 221 E (silver-grayed receiver finish, hunting scene engraving)..................................... $10,895.00

34TH EDITION, 2002 • **237**

DRILLINGS, COMBINATION GUNS, DOUBLE GUNS

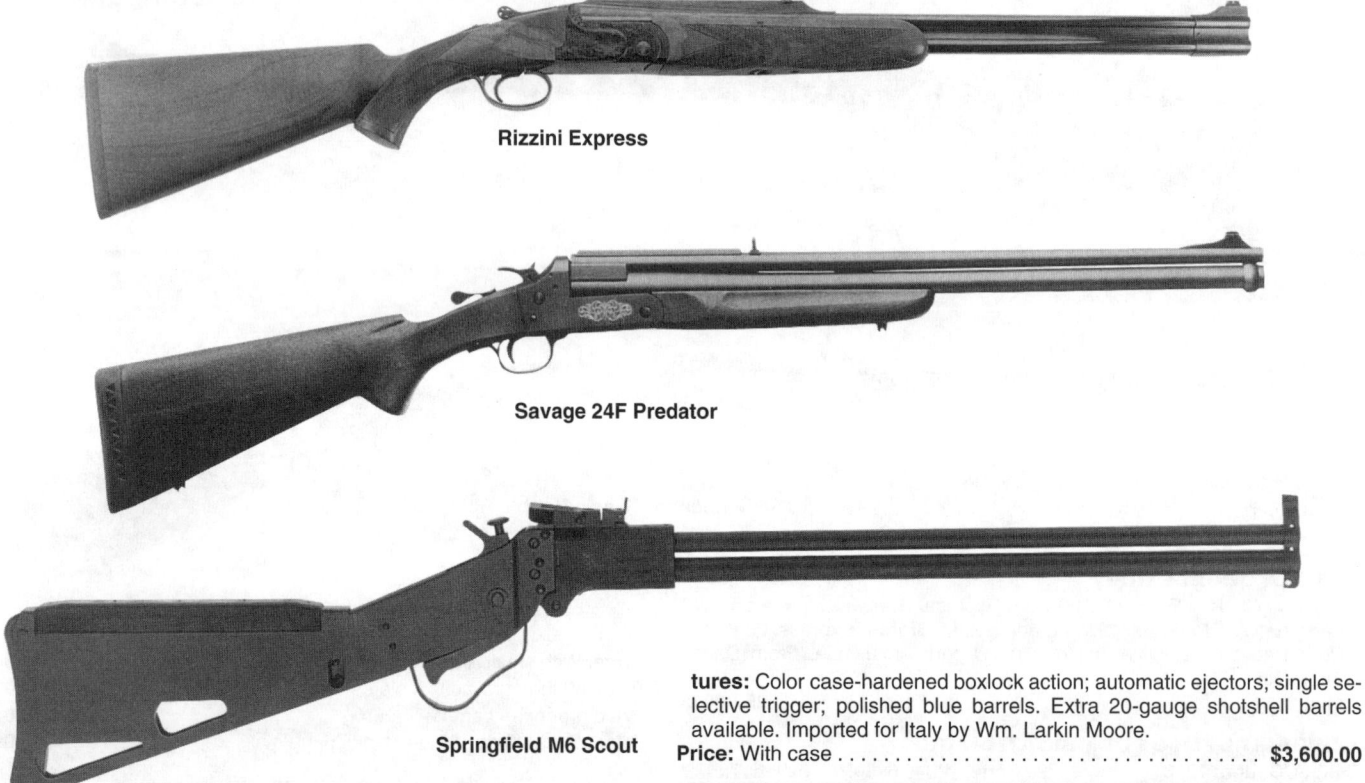

Rizzini Express

Savage 24F Predator

Springfield M6 Scout

MERKEL MODEL 160 SIDE-BY-SIDE DOUBLE RIFLE
Caliber: 22 Hornet, 5.6x50R Mag., 5.6x52R, 222 Rem., 243 Win., 6.5x55, 6.5x57R, 7x57R, 7x65R, 308, 30-06, 8x57JRS, 9.3x74R, 375 H&H. **Barrel:** 25.6". **Weight:** About 7.7 lbs, depending upon caliber. **Length:** NA. **Stock:** Oil-finished walnut with pistol grip, cheekpiece. **Sights:** Blade front on ramp, fixed rear. **Features:** Sidelock action. Double barrel locking lug with Greener cross-bolt; fine engraved hunting scenes on sideplates; Holland & Holland ejectors; double triggers. Imported from Germany by GSI.
Price: From $13,295.00

Merkel Boxlock Double Rifles
Similar to the Model 160 double rifle except with Anson & Deely boxlock action with cocking indicators, double triggers, engraved color case-hardened receiver. Introduced 1995. Imported from Germany by GSI.
Price: Model 140-1, from $5,995.00
Price: Model 140-1.1 (engraved silver-gray receiver), from $6,995.00
Price: Model 150-1 (false sideplates, silver-gray receiver, Arabesque engraving), from $7,495.00
Price: Model 150-1.1 (as above with English Arabesque engraving), from $8,995.00

RIZZINI EXPRESS 90L DOUBLE RIFLE
Caliber: 30-06, 7x65R, 9.3x74R. **Barrel:** 24". **Weight:** 7-1/2 lbs. **Length:** 40" overall. **Stock:** Select European walnut with satin oil finish; English-style cheekpiece. **Sights:** Ramp front, quarter-rib with express sight. **Features:** Color case-hardened boxlock action; automatic ejectors; single selective trigger; polished blue barrels. Extra 20-gauge shotshell barrels available. Imported for Italy by Wm. Larkin Moore.
Price: With case $3,600.00

SAVAGE 24F PREDATOR O/U COMBINATION GUN
Caliber/Gauge: 22 Hornet, 223, 30-30 over 12 (24F-12) or 22 LR, 22 Hornet, 223, 30-30 over 20-ga. (24F-20); 3" chambers. **Action:** Takedown, low rebounding visible hammer. Single trigger, barrel selector spur on hammer. **Barrel:** 24" separated barrels; 12-ga. has Full, Mod., Imp. Cyl. choke tubes, 20-ga. has fixed Mod. choke. **Weight:** 8 lbs. **Length:** 40-1/2" overall. **Stock:** Black Rynite composition. **Sights:** Ramp front, rear open adjustable for elevation. Grooved for tip-off scope mount. **Features:** Removable butt cap for storage and accessories. Introduced 1989.
Price: 24F-12 . . . . $476.00
Price: 24F-20 . . . . $449.00

Savage 24F-12/410 Combination Gun
Similar to the 24F-12 except comes with "Four-Tenner" adaptor for shooting 410-bore shotshells. Rifle barrel chambered for 22 Hornet, 223 Rem., 30-30 Win. Introduced 1998. Made in U.S. by Savage Arms, Inc.
Price: $504.00

SPRINGFIELD, INC. M6 SCOUT RIFLE/SHOTGUN
Caliber/Gauge: 22 LR or 22 Hornet over 410-bore. **Barrel:** 18.25". **Weight:** 4 lbs. **Length:** 32" overall. **Stock:** Folding detachable with storage for 15 22 LR, four 410 shells. **Sights:** Blade front, military aperture for 22; V-notch for 410. **Features:** All-metal construction. Designed for quick disassembly and minimum maintenance. Folds for compact storage. Introduced 1982; reintroduced 1996. Imported from the Czech Republic by Springfield, Inc.
Price: Parkerized $185.00
Price: Stainless steel $219.00

RIMFIRE RIFLES — AUTOLOADERS

Designs for hunting, utility and sporting purposes, including training for competition

Armscor M-20C Carbine

Browning Auto 22

Calico M-100FS

AR-7 EXPLORER CARBINE
Caliber: 22 LR, 8-shot magazine. **Barrel:** 16". **Weight:** 2-1/2 lbs. **Length:** 34-1/2" / 16-1/2" stowed. **Stock:** Moulded Cycolac; snap-on rubber butt pad. **Sights:** Square blade front, aperture rear. **Features:** Takedown design stores barrel and action in hollow stock. Light enough to float. Reintroduced 1999. From AR-7 Industries, LLC.
Price: Black matte finish $150.00
Price: AR-20 Sporter (tubular stock, barrel shroud) $200.00
New! **Price:** AR-7 camo- or walnut-finish stock $164.95

ARMSCOR MODEL AK22 AUTO RIFLE
Caliber: 22 LR, 10-shot magazine. **Barrel:** 18.5". **Weight:** 7.5 lbs. **Length:** 38" overall. **Stock:** Plain mahogany. **Sights:** Adjustable post front, leaf rear adjustable for elevation. **Features:** Resembles the AK-47. Matte black finish. Introduced 1987. Imported from the Philippines by K.B.I., Inc.
Price: About $219.95

ARMSCOR M-1600 AUTO RIFLE
Caliber: 22 LR, 10-shot magazine. **Barrel:** 18.25". **Weight:** 6.2 lbs. **Length:** 38.5" overall. **Stock:** Black finished mahogany. **Sights:** Post front, aperture rear. **Features:** Resembles Colt AR-15. Matte black finish. Introduced 1987. Imported from the Philippines by K.B.I., Inc.
Price: About $199.95

ARMSCOR M-20C AUTO CARBINE
Caliber: 22 LR, 10-shot magazine. **Barrel:** 18.25". **Weight:** 6.5 lbs. **Length:** 38" overall. **Stock:** Walnut-finished mahogany. **Sights:** Hooded front, rear adjustable for elevation. **Features:** Receiver grooved for scope mounting. Blued finish. Introduced 1990. Imported from the Philippines by K.B.I., Inc.
Price: $154.95

BROWNING BUCK MARK SEMI-AUTO RIFLES
Caliber: 22 LR, 10-shot magazine. **Barrel:** 18" tapered (Sporter) or heavy bull (Target). **Weight:** 4 lbs., 2 oz. (Sporter) or 5 lbs., 4 oz. (Target). **Length:** 34" overall. **Stock:** Walnut stock and forearm with full pistol grip. **Sights:** Hi-Viz adjustable (Sporter). **Features:** A rifle version of the Buck Mark Pistol; straight blowback action; machined aluminum receiver with integral rail scope mount; recessed muzzle crown; manual thumb safety. Introduced 2001. From Browning.
Price: Sporter (adj. sights) $518.00
Price: Target (heavy bbl., no sights) $518.00

BROWNING SEMI-AUTO 22 RIFLE
Caliber: 22 LR, 11-shot. **Barrel:** 19-1/4". **Weight:** 5 lbs., 3 oz. **Length:** 37" overall. **Stock:** Checkered select walnut with pistol grip and semi-beavertail forend. **Sights:** Gold bead front, folding leaf rear. **Features:** Engraved receiver with polished blue finish; cross-bolt safety; tubular magazine in buttstock; easy takedown for carrying or storage. Imported from Japan by Browning.
Price: Grade I $479.00

Browning Semi-Auto 22, Grade VI
Same as the Grade I Auto-22 except available with either grayed or blued receiver with extensive engraving with gold-plated animals: right side pictures a fox and squirrel in a woodland scene; left side shows a beagle chasing a rabbit. On top is a portrait of the beagle. Stock and forend are of high-grade walnut with a double-bordered cut checkering design. Introduced 1987.
Price: Grade VI, blue or gray receiver $1,028.00

BRNO ZKM 611 AUTO RIFLE
Caliber: 22 WMR, 6- or 10-shot magazine. **Barrel:** 20.4". **Weight:** 5.9 lbs. **Length:** 38.9" overall. **Stock:** European walnut. **Sights:** Hooded blade front, open adjustable rear. **Features:** Removable box magazine; polished blue finish; cross-bolt safety; grooved receiver for scope mounting; easy takedown for storage. Imported from The Czech Republic by Euro-Imports.
Price: $475.00

CALICO M-100FS CARBINE
Caliber: 22 LR. **Barrel:** 16.25". **Weight:** 5 lbs. **Length:** 36" overall. **Stock:** Glass-filled, impact-resistant polymer. **Sights:** Adjustable post front, notch rear. **Features:** Has helical-feed magazine; aluminum receiver; ambidextrous safety. Made in U.S. by Calico.
Price: $650.00

CHARLES DALY FIELD GRADE AUTO RIFLE
Caliber: 22 LR, 10-shot magazine. **Barrel:** 20-3/4". **Weight:** 6.5 lbs. **Length:** 40-1/2" overall. **Stock:** Walnut-finished hardwood with Monte Carlo. **Sights:** Hooded front, adjustable open rear. **Features:** Receiver grooved for scope mounting; blue finish; shell deflector. Introduced 1998. Imported by K.B.I.
Price: $124.00
Price: Superior Grade (cut checkered stock, fully adjustable sight) $199.00

Charles Daly Empire Grade Auto Rifle
Similar to the Field Grade except has select California walnut stock with 24 l.p.i. hand checkering, contrasting forend and gripcaps, damascened bolt, high-polish blue. Introduced 1998. Imported by K.B.I.
Price: $369.00

34TH EDITION, 2002 • 239

RIMFIRE RIFLES — AUTOLOADERS

Charles Daly Superior Grade

CZ 511 Auto

Henry U.S. Survival

Marlin Model 60

Marlin Model 60 SSK

Marlin Model 70PSS

CZ 511 AUTO RIFLE
Caliber: 22 LR, 8-shot magazine. **Barrel:** 22.2". **Weight:** 5.39 lbs. **Length:** 38.6" overall. **Stock:** Walnut with checkered pistol grip. **Sights:** Hooded front, adjustable rear. **Features:** Polished blue finish; detachable magazine; sling swivel studs. Imported from the Czech Republic by CZ-USA.
Price: $351.00

HENRY U.S. SURVIVAL RIFLE .22
Caliber: 22 LR, 8-shot magazine. **Barrel:** 16" steel lined. **Weight:** 2.5 lbs. **Stock:** ABS plastic. **Sights:** Blade front on ramp, aperture rear. **Features:** Takedown design stores barrel and action in hollow stock. Light enough to float. Silver, black or camo finish. Comes with two magazines. Introduced 1998. From Henry Repeating Arms Co.
Price: $165.00

MAGTECH MT 7022 AUTO RIFLE
Caliber: 22 LR, 10-shot magazine. **Barrel:** 18". **Weight:** 4.8 lbs. **Length:** 37" overall. **Stock:** Brazilian hardwood. **Sights:** Hooded blade front, fully adjustable open rear. **Features:** Cross-bolt safety; last-shot bolt hold-open; alloy receiver is drilled and tapped for scope mounting. Introduced 1998. Imported from Brazil by Magtech Ammunition Co.
Price: $100.00

MARLIN MODEL 60 AUTO RIFLE
Caliber: 22 LR, 14-shot tubular magazine. **Barrel:** 22" round tapered. **Weight:** About 5-1/2 lbs. **Length:** 40-1/2" overall. **Stock:** Press-checkered, walnut-finished Maine birch with Monte Carlo, full pistol grip; Mar-Shield® finish. **Sights:** Ramp front, open adjustable rear. **Features:** Matted receiver is grooved for scope mount. Manual bolt hold-open; automatic last-shot bolt hold-open.
Price: $176.00
Price: With 4x scope. $183.00

Marlin Model 60SS Self-Loading Rifle
Same as the Model 60 except breech bolt, barrel and outer magazine tube are made of stainless steel; most other parts are either nickel-plated or coated to match the stainless finish. Monte Carlo stock is of black/gray Maine birch laminate, and has nickel-plated swivel studs, rubber butt pad. Introduced 1993.
Price: $281.00
Price: Model 60SSK (black fiberglass-filled stock). $244.00
Price: Model 60SB (walnut-finished birch stock) $223.00
Price: Model 60SB with 4x scope. $237.00

MARLIN 70PSS PAPOOSE STAINLESS RIFLE
Caliber: 22 LR, 7-shot magazine. **Barrel:** 16-1/4" stainless steel, Micro-Groove® rifling. **Weight:** 3-1/4 lbs. **Length:** 35-1/4" overall. **Stock:** Black fiberglass-filled synthetic with abbreviated forend, nickel-plated swivel studs, moulded-in checkering. **Sights:** Ramp front with orange post, cutaway Wide Scan® hood; adjustable open rear. Receiver grooved for scope mounting. **Features:** Takedown barrel; cross-bolt safety; manual bolt hold-open; last shot bolt hold-open; comes with padded carrying case. Introduced 1986. Made in U.S. by Marlin.
Price: $288.00

RIMFIRE RIFLES — AUTOLOADERS

Marlin Model 922

Marlin 7000

Marlin 795

Remington 597

MARLIN MODEL 922M AUTO RIFLE
Caliber: 22 WMR, 5-shot magazine. **Barrel:** 20.5". **Weight:** 6.5 lbs. **Length:** 39.75" overall. **Stock:** Now walnut finished hardwood, swivel studs, rubber butt pad. **Sights:** Ramp front with bead and removable Wide-Scan® hood, adjustable folding semi-buckhorn rear. **Features:** Action based on the centerfire Model 9 Carbine. Receiver drilled and tapped for scope mounting. Automatic last-shot bolt hold-open; magazine safety. Introduced 1993.
Price: $454.00

MARLIN MODEL 7000 AUTO RIFLE
Caliber: 22 LR, 10-shot magazine **Barrel:** 18" heavy target with 12-groove Micro-Groove® rifling, recessed muzzle. **Weight:** 5-1/2 lbs. **Length:** 37" overall. **Stock:** Black fiberglass-filled synthetic with Monte Carlo combo, swivel studs, moulded-in checkering. **Sights:** None furnished; comes with ring mounts. **Features:** Automatic last-shot bolt hold-open, manual bolt hold-open; cross-bolt safety; steel charging handle; blue finish, nickel-plated magazine. Introduced 1997. Made in U.S. by Marlin Firearms Co.
Price: $236.00

Marlin Model 795 Auto Rifle
Similar to the Model 7000 except has standard-weight 18" barrel with 16-groove Micro-Groove rifling. Comes with ramp front sight with brass bead, screw adjustable open rear. Receiver grooved for scope mount. Introduced 1997. Made in U.S. by Marlin Firearms Co.
Price: $167.00

REMINGTON MODEL 552 BDL DELUXE SPEEDMASTER RIFLE
Caliber: 22 S (20), L (17) or LR (15) tubular mag. **Barrel:** 21" round tapered. **Weight:** 5-3/4 lbs. **Length:** 40" overall. **Stock:** Walnut. Checkered grip and forend. **Sights:** Bead front, step open rear adjustable for windage and elevation. **Features:** Positive cross-bolt safety, receiver grooved for tip-off mount.
Price: $365.00

REMINGTON 597 AUTO RIFLE
Caliber: 22 LR, 10-shot clip. **Barrel:** 20". **Weight:** 5-1/2 lbs. **Length:** 40" overall. **Stock:** Gray synthetic. **Sights:** Bead front, fully adjustable rear. **Features:** Matte black finish, nickel-plated bolt. Receiver is grooved and drilled and tapped for scope mounts. Introduced 1997. Made in U.S. by Remington.
Price: $163.00
Price: Model 597 Magnum, 22 WMR, 8-shot clip $321.00
Price: Model 597 LSS (laminated stock, stainless) $272.00
Price: Model 597 Magnum LS (laminated stock) $377.00
Price: Model 597 SS (22 LR, stainless steel, black synthetic stock) $217.00
New! Price: Model 597 LS Heavy Barrel (22 LR, laminated stock) $265.00
New! Price: Model 597 Magnum LS Heavy Barrel (22 WMR, lam. stock) $399.00

34TH EDITION, 2002

RIMFIRE RIFLES — AUTOLOADERS

Ruger 10/22 International

Savage Model 64FV

RUGER 10/22 AUTOLOADING CARBINE
Caliber: 22 LR, 10-shot rotary magazine. **Barrel:** 18-1/2" round tapered. **Weight:** 5 lbs. **Length:** 37-1/4" overall. **Stock:** American hardwood with pistol grip and barrel. band. **Sights:** Brass bead front, folding leaf rear adjustable for elevation. **Features:** Detachable rotary magazine fits flush into stock, cross-bolt safety, receiver tapped and grooved for scope blocks or tip-off mount. Scope base adaptor furnished with each rifle.
Price: Model 10/22 RB (blue) $235.00
Price: Model K10/22RB (bright finish stainless barrel) $273.00
Price: Model 10/22RP (blue, synthetic stock) $235.00

Ruger 10/22 International Carbine
Similar to the Ruger 10/22 Carbine except has full-length International stock of American hardwood, checkered grip and forend; comes with rubber butt pad, sling swivels. Reintroduced 1994.
Price: Blue (10/22RBI) $275.00
Price: Stainless (K10/22RBI) $299.00

Ruger 10/22 Deluxe Sporter
Same as 10/22 Carbine except walnut stock with hand checkered pistol grip and forend; straight buttplate, no barrel band, has sling swivels.
Price: Model 10/22 DSP $299.00

Ruger 10/22T Target Rifle
Similar to the 10/22 except has 20" heavy, hammer-forged barrel with tight chamber dimensions, improved trigger pull, laminated hardwood stock dimensioned for optical sights. No iron sights supplied. Introduced 1996. Made in U.S. by Sturm, Ruger & Co.
Price: 10/22T $415.00
Price: K10/22T, stainless steel $465.00
New! Price: K10/22TNZ, stainless steel 20" bbl. with cut-out pistol-grip laminated stock. $649.00

Ruger K10/22RP All-Weather Rifle
Similar to the stainless K10/22/RP except has black composite stock of thermoplastic polyester resin reinforced with fiberglass; checkered grip and forend. Brushed satin, natural metal finish with clear hardcoat finish. Weighs 5 lbs., measures 36-3/4" overall. Introduced 1997. From Sturm, Ruger & Co.
Price: $273.00

RUGER 10/22 MAGNUM AUTOLOADING CARBINE
Caliber: 22 WMR, 9-shot rotary magazine. **Barrel:** 18-1/2". **Weight:** 6 lbs. **Length:** 37-1/4" overall. **Stock:** Birch. **Sights:** Gold bead front, folding rear. **Features:** All-steel receiver has integral Ruger scope bases for the included 1" rings. Introduced 1999. Made in U.S. by Sturm, Ruger & Co.
Price: $450.00

SAVAGE MODEL 64G AUTO RIFLE
Caliber: 22 LR, 10-shot magazine. **Barrel:** 20". **Weight:** 5-1/2 lbs. **Length:** 40" overall. **Stock:** Walnut-finished hardwood with Monte Carlo-type comb, checkered grip and forend. **Sights:** Bead front, open adjustable rear. Receiver grooved for scope mounting. **Features:** Thumb-operated rotating safety. Blue finish. Side ejection, bolt hold-open device. Introduced 1990. Made in Canada, from Savage Arms.
Price: $134.00
Price: Model 64F, black synthetic stock $124.00
Price: Model 64GXP Package Gun includes 4x15 scope and mounts $140.00
Price: Model 64FXP (black stock, 4x15 scope) $128.00

Savage Model 64FV Auto Rifle
Similar to the Model 64F except has heavy 21" barrel with recessed crown; no sights provided—comes with Weaver-style bases. Introduced 1998. Imported from Canada by Savage Arms, Inc.
Price: $164.00

THOMPSON/CENTER 22 LR CLASSIC RIFLE
Caliber: 22 LR, 8-shot magazine. **Barrel:** 22" match-grade. **Weight:** 5-1/2 pounds. **Length:** 39-1/2" overall. **Stock:** Satin-finished American walnut with Monte Carlo-type comb and pistol grip cap, swivel studs. **Sights:** Ramp-style front and fully adjustable rear, both with fiber optics. **Features:** All-steel receiver drilled and tapped for scope mounting; barrel threaded to receiver; thumb-operated safety; trigger-guard safety lock included.
Price: T/C 22 LR Classic (blue) $335.55

WINCHESTER MODEL 63 AUTO RIFLE
Caliber: 22 LR, 10-shot magazine. **Barrel:** 23". **Weight:** 6-1/4 lbs. **Length:** 39" overall. **Stock:** Walnut. **Sights:** Bead front, open adjustable rear. **Features:** Recreation of the original Model 63. Magazine tube loads through a port in the buttstock; forward cocking knob at front of forend; easy takedown for cleaning, storage; engraved receiver. Reintroduced 1997. From U.S. Repeating Arms Co.
Price: Grade I $678.00
Price: High grade, select walnut, cut checkering, engraved scenes with gold accents on receiver (made in 1997 only) $1,083.00

RIMFIRE RIFLES — LEVER & SLIDE ACTION

Classic and modern models for sport and utility, including training.

Browning BL-22

Henry Lever-Action 22

Henry Goldenboy 22

Henry Pump-Action 22

Marlin Model 39AS

BROWNING BL-22 LEVER-ACTION RIFLE
Caliber: 22 S (22), L (17) or LR (15), tubular magazine. **Barrel:** 20" round tapered. **Weight:** 5 lbs. **Length:** 36-3/4" overall. **Stock:** Walnut, two-piece straight grip Western style. **Sights:** Bead post front, folding-leaf rear. **Features:** Short throw lever, half-cock safety, receiver grooved for tip-off scope mounts, gold-colored trigger. Imported from Japan by Browning.
Price: Grade I $415.00
Price: Grade II (engraved receiver, checkered grip and forend) . $471.00
Price: Classic, Grade I (blued trigger, no checkering) $415.00
Price: Classic, Grade II (cut checkering, satin wood finish,
  polished blueing) $471.00

HENRY LEVER-ACTION 22
Caliber: 22 Long Rifle (15-shot). **Barrel:** 18-1/4" round. **Weight:** 5-1/2 lbs. **Length:** 34" overall. **Stock:** Walnut. **Sights:** Hooded blade front, open adjustable rear. **Features:** Polished blue finish; full-length tubular magazine; side ejection; receiver grooved for scope mounting. Introduced 1997. Made in U.S. by Henry Repeating Arms Co.
Price: $239.95
Price: Youth model (33" overall, 11-rounds 22 LR) $229.95

HENRY GOLDENBOY 22 LEVER-ACTION RIFLE
Caliber: 22 LR, 16-shot. **Barrel:** 20" octagonal. **Weight:** 6.25 lbs. **Length:** 38" overall. **Stock:** American walnut. **Sights:** Blade front, open rear. **Features:** Brasslite receiver, brass buttplate, blued barrel and lever. Introduced 1998. Made in U.S. from Henry Repeating Arms Co.
Price: $379.95

HENRY PUMP-ACTION 22 PUMP RIFLE
Caliber: 22 LR, 15-shot. **Barrel:** 18.25". **Weight:** 5.5 lbs. **Length:** NA. **Stock:** American walnut. **Sights:** Bead on ramp front, open adjustable rear. **Features:** Polished blue finish; receiver groved for scope mount; grooved slide handle; two barrel bands. Introduced 1998. Made in U.S. from Henry Repeating Arms Co.
Price: $249.95

MARLIN MODEL 39A GOLDEN LEVER-ACTION RIFLE
Caliber: 22 S (26), L (21), LR (19), tubular magazine. **Barrel:** 24" Micro-Groove®. **Weight:** 6-1/2 lbs. **Length:** 40" overall. **Stock:** Checkered American black walnut with white line spacers at pistol gripcap and buttplate; Mar-Shield® finish. Swivel studs; rubber butt pad. **Sights:** Bead ramp front with detachable Wide-Scan™ hood, folding rear semi-buckhorn adjustable for windage and elevation. **Features:** Hammer-block safety; rebounding hammer. Takedown action, receiver tapped for scope mount (supplied), offset hammer spur; gold-plated steel trigger.
Price: $525.00

RIMFIRE RIFLES — LEVER & SLIDE ACTION

Marlin Model 1897CB Cowboy

Remington Model 572

Ruger Model 96/22

Winchester 9422 Large Loop

Marlin Model 1897CB Cowboy Lever Action Rifle
Similar to the Model 39A except it has straight-grip stock with hard rubber buttplate; blued steel forend cap; 24" tapered octagon barrel with Micro-Groove® rifling; adjustable Marble semi-buckhorn rear sight, Marble carbine front with brass bead; overall length 40". Introduced 1999. Made in U.S. by Marlin.
Price: $708.00

REMINGTON 572 BDL DELUXE FIELDMASTER PUMP RIFLE
Caliber: 22 S (20), L (17) or LR (14), tubular magazine. **Barrel:** 21" round tapered. **Weight:** 5-1/2 lbs. **Length:** 40" overall. **Stock:** Walnut with checkered pistol grip and slide handle. **Sights:** Blade ramp front; sliding ramp rear adjustable for windage and elevation. **Features:** Cross-bolt safety; removing inner magazine tube converts rifle to single shot; receiver grooved for tip-off scope mount.
Price: $379.00

RUGER MODEL 96/22 LEVER-ACTION RIFLE
Caliber: 22 LR, 10-shot rotary magazine; 22 WMR, 9-shot rotary magazine. **Barrel:** 18-1/2". **Weight:** 5-1/4 lbs. **Length:** 37-1/4" overall. **Stock:** American hardwood. **Sights:** Gold bead front, folding leaf rear. **Features:** Cross-bolt safety, visible cocking indicator; short-throw lever action. Screw-on dovetail scope base. Introduced 1996. Made in U.S. by Sturm, Ruger & Co.
Price: 96/22 (22 LR) $349.50
Price: 96/22M (22 WMR) $375.00

TAURUS MODEL 62 PUMP RIFLE
Caliber: 22 LR, 12- or 13-shot. **Barrel:** 16-1/2" or 23" round. **Weight:** 4.6 to 5 lbs. **Length:** 39" overall. **Stock:** Walnut-finished hardwood, straight grip, grooved forend. **Sights:** Fixed front, adjustable rear. **Features:** Blue or stainless steel finish; bolt-mounted safety; tubular magzine; quick takedown; integral security lock system. Imported from Brazil by Taurus International.
Price: (blued finish) $280.00
Price: (stainless steel finish) $295.00

Taurus Model 72 Pump Rifle
Same as Model 62 except chambered in 22 WMR; 16-1/2" bbl. holds 10 shots, 23" bbl. holds 11 shots. Introduced 2001. Imported from Brazil by Taurus International.
Price: (blued finish) $295.00
Price: (stainless steel finish) $310.00

WINCHESTER MODEL 9422 LEVER-ACTION RIFLES
Caliber: 22 LR, 22 WMR, tubular magazine. **Barrel:** 20-1/2". **Weight:** 6-1/4 lbs. **Length:** 37-1/8" overall. **Stock:** American walnut, two-piece, straight grip (Traditional) or semi-pistol grip (Legacy). **Sights:** Hooded ramp front, adjustable semi-buckhorn rear. **Features:** Side ejection, receiver grooved for scope mounting, takedown action. From U.S. Repeating Arms Co.
Price: Traditional, 22 LR 15-shot $444.00
Price: Traditional, 22WMR, 11-shot $464.00
Price: Legacy, 22 LR 15-shot $473.00
Price: Legacy 22 WMR, 11-shot $496.00

WINCHESTER MODEL 1886 EXTRA LIGHT GRADE I
Caliber: 45-70, 4-shot magazine. **Barrel:** 22". **Weight:** 7-1.4 lbs. **Length:** 40-1/2" overall. **Sights:** Blade front, buckhorn-style ramp-adjustable rear. **Features:** Round, tapered barrel; shotgun-style steel buttplate; half-magazine. Limited production. Introduced 2000. From U.S. Repeating Arms Co., Inc.
Price: $1,152.00
Price: High Grade (extra-fancy, checkered walnut stock, engraved elk and deer scenes) $1,440.00

RIMFIRE RIFLES — BOLT ACTIONS & SINGLE SHOTS

Includes models for a variety of sports, utility and competitive shooting.

Anschutz 1518D Luxus

Anschutz 1710D

Charles Daly Field Grade

ANSCHUTZ 1416D/1516D CLASSIC RIFLES
Caliber: 22 LR (1416D), 5-shot clip; 22 WMR (1516D), 4-shot clip. **Barrel:** 22-1/2". **Weight:** 6 lbs. **Length:** 41" overall. **Stock:** European hardwood with walnut finish; classic style with straight comb, checkered pistol grip and forend. **Sights:** Hooded ramp front, folding leaf rear. **Features:** Uses Match 64 action. Adjustable single stage trigger. Receiver grooved for scope mounting. Imported from Germany by AcuSport Corp.
Price: 1416D, 22 LR $755.95
Price: 1516D, 22 WMR $779.95
Price: 1416D Classic left-hand $679.95

Anschutz 1416D/1516D Walnut Luxus Rifles
Similar to the Classic models except have European walnut stocks with Monte Carlo cheekpiece, slim forend with Schnabel tip, cut checkering on grip and forend. Introduced 1997. Imported from Germany by AcuSport Corp.
Price: 1416D (22 LR) $755.95
Price: 1516D (22 WMR) $779.95

ANSCHUTZ 1518D LUXUS BOLT-ACTION RIFLE
Caliber: 22 WMR, 4-shot magazine. **Barrel:** 19-3/4". **Weight:** 5-1/2 lbs. **Length:** 37-1/2" overall. **Stock:** European walnut. **Sights:** Blade on ramp front, folding leaf rear. **Features:** Receiver grooved for scope mounting; single stage trigger; skip-line checkering; rosewood forend tip; sling swivels. Imported from Germany by AcuSport Corp.
Price: $1,186.95

ANSCHUTZ 1710D CUSTOM RIFLE
Caliber: 22 LR, 5-shot clip. **Barrel:** 24-1/4". **Weight:** 7-3/8 lbs. **Length:** 42-1/2" overall. **Stock:** Select European walnut. **Sights:** Hooded ramp front, folding leaf rear; drilled and tapped for scope mounting. **Features:** Match 54 action with adjustable single-stage trigger; roll-over Monte Carlo cheekpiece, slim forend with Schnabel tip, Wundhammer palm swell on pistol grip, rosewood gripcap with white diamond insert; skip-line checkering on grip and forend. Introduced 1988. Imported from Germany by AcuSport Corp.
Price: $1,289.95

CABANAS MASTER BOLT-ACTION RIFLE
Caliber: 177, round ball or pellet; single shot. **Barrel:** 19-1/2". **Weight:** 8 lbs. **Length:** 45-1/2" overall. **Stocks:** Walnut target-type with Monte Carlo. **Sights:** Blade front, fully adjustable rear. **Features:** Fires round ball or pellet with 22-cal. blank cartridge. Bolt action. Imported from Mexico by Mandall Shooting Supplies. Introduced 1984.
Price: $189.95
Price: Varmint model (has 21-1/2" barrel, 4-1/2 lbs., 41" overall length, varmint-type stock) $119.95

Cabanas Leyre Bolt-Action Rifle
Similar to Master model except 44" overall, has sport/target stock.
Price: $149.95
Price: Model R83 (17" barrel, hardwood stock, 40" o.a.l.) $79.95
Price: Mini 82 Youth (16-1/2" barrel, 33" overall length, 3-1/2 lbs.) . $69.95
Price: Pony Youth (16" barrel, 34" overall length, 3.2 lbs.) $69.95

Cabanas Espronceda IV Bolt-Action Rifle
Similar to the Leyre model except has full sporter stock, 18-3/4" barrel, 40" overall length, weighs 5-1/2 lbs.
Price: $134.95

CABANAS LASER RIFLE
Caliber: 177. **Barrel:** 19". **Weight:** 6 lbs., 12 oz. **Length:** 42" overall. **Stock:** Target-type thumbhole. **Sights:** Blade front, open fully adjustable rear. **Features:** Fires round ball or pellets with 22 blank cartridge. Imported from Mexico by Mandall Shooting Supplies.
Price: $159.95

CHARLES DALY SUPERIOR BOLT-ACTION RIFLE
Caliber: 22 LR, 10-shot magazine. **Barrel:** 22-5/8". **Weight:** 6.7 lbs. **Length:** 41.25" overall. **Stock:** Walnut-finished mahogany. **Sights:** Bead front, rear adjustable for elevation. **Features:** Receiver grooved for scope mounting. Blued finish. Introduced 1998. Imported by K.B.I., Inc.
Price: $189.95

Charles Daly Field Grade Rifle
Similar to the Superior except has short walnut-finished hardwood stock for small shooters. Introduced 1998. Imported by K.B.I., Inc.
Price: $134.95
Price: Field Youth (17.5" barrel) $144.95

Charles Daly Superior Magnum Grade Rifle
Similar to the Superior except chambered for 22 WMR. Has 22.6" barrel, double lug bolt, checkered stock, weighs 6.5 lbs. Introduced 1987.
Price: About $204.95

Charles Daly Empire Magnum Grade Rifle
Similar to the Superior Magnum except has oil-finished American walnut stock with 18 lpi hand checkering; black hardwood gripcap and forend tip; highly polished barreled action; jewelled bolt; recoil pad; swivel studs. Imported from the Philippines by K.B.I., Inc.
Price: $364.95

34TH EDITION, 2002 • 245

RIMFIRE RIFLES — BOLT ACTIONS & SINGLE SHOT

Chipmunk Deluxe

CZ 452 American Classic

Kimber 22 Classic

Charles Daly Empire Grade Rifle
Similar to the Superior except has oil-finished American walnut stock with 18 lpi hand checkering; black hardwood gripcap and forend tip; highly polished barreled action; jewelled bolt; recoil pad; swivel studs. Imported by K.B.I., Inc.
Price: $329.00

CHARLES DALY TRUE YOUTH BOLT-ACTION RIFLE
Caliber: 22 LR, single shot. **Barrel:** 16-1/4". **Weight:** About 3 lbs. **Length:** 32" overall. **Stock:** Walnut-finished hardwood. **Sights:** Blade front, adjustable rear. **Features:** Scaled-down stock for small shooters. Blue finish. Introduced 1998. Imported by K.B.I., Inc.
Price: $154.95

CHIPMUNK SINGLE SHOT RIFLE
Caliber: 22 LR, 22 WMR, single shot. **Barrel:** 16-1/8". **Weight:** About 2-1/2 lbs. **Length:** 30" overall. **Stocks:** American walnut. **Sights:** Post on ramp front, peep rear adjustable for windage and elevation. **Features:** Drilled and tapped for scope mounting using special Chipmunk base ($13.95). Engraved model also available. Made in U.S. Introduced 1982. From Rogue Rifle Co., Inc.
Price: Standard.. $194.25
Price: Standard 22 WMR $209.95
Price: Deluxe (better wood, checkering)......................... $246.95
Price: Deluxe 22 WMR $262.95
Price: Laminated stock $209.95
Price: Laminated stock, 22 WMR $225.95
Price: Black-coated stock $183.95
Price: Black-coated stock, 22 WMR $199.95
Price: Bull barrel models of above, add $16.00

CZ 452 M 2E LUX BOLT-ACTION RIFLE
Caliber: 22 LR, 22 WMR, 5-shot detachable magazine. **Barrel:** 24.8". **Weight:** 6.6 lbs. **Length:** 42.63" overall. **Stock:** Walnut with checkered pistol grip. **Sights:** Hooded front, fully adjustable tangent rear. **Features:** All-steel construction; adjustable trigger; polished blue finish. Imported from the Czech Republic by CZ-USA.
Price: 22 LR $351.00
Price: 22 WMR $378.00
Price: Synthetic stock, nickel finish, 22 LR $344.00

CZ 452 M 2E Varmint Rifle
Similar to the Lux model except has heavy 20.8" barrel; stock has beavertail forend; weighs 7 lbs.; no sights furnished. Available only in 22 LR. Imported from the Czech Republic by CZ-USA.
Price: $369.00

CZ 452 American Classic Bolt-Action Rifle
Similar to the CZ 452 M 2E Lux except has classic-style stock of Circassian walnut; 22.5" free-floating barrel with recessed target crown; receiver dovetail for scope mounting. No open sights furnished. Introduced 1999. Imported from the Czech Republic by CZ-USA.
Price: 22 LR $351.00
Price: 22 WMR $378.00

DAN WESSON COYOTE CLASSIC BOLT-ACTION RIMFIRE RIFLE
Caliber: 22 LR or 22 WMR. 5-shot magazine (10-shot optional magazine). **Barrel:** 22-3/4". **Weight:** NA. **Length:** NA. **Stock:** Laminated wood or exotic hardwood. **Sights:** Fully adjustable V-notch rear, brass bead ramp front. **Features:** Receiver drilled and tapped for scope mount; checkered pistol grip and fore end with DW medallion end cap; recessed target crown; sling swivel studs. Introduced 2001. From Dan Wesson Firearms.
Price: Coyote Classic, 22 LR or 22 WMR $219.00

DAN WESSON COYOTE TARGET BOLT-ACTION RIMFIRE RIFLE
Caliber: 22 LR or 22 WMR, 5-shot magazine (10-shot optional magazine). **Barrel:** 18-3/8" heavy. **Weight:** NA. **Length:** NA. **Stock:** Laminated wood or exotic hardwood. **Sights:** None furnished. **Features:** Receiver drilled and tapped for scope mount; target-crowned muzzle; high comb, smooth pistol grip and rubber butt plate. Introduced 2001. From Dan Wesson Firearms.
Price: Coyote Target, 22 LR or 22 WMR $259.00

HARRINGTON & RICHARDSON ULTRA HEAVY BARREL 22 MAG RIFLE
Caliber: 22 WMR, single shot. **Barrel:** 22" bull. **Weight:** NA. **Length:** NA. **Stock:** Cinnamon laminated wood with Monte Carlo cheekpiece. **Sights:** None furnished; scope mount rail included. **Features:** Hand-checkered stock and forend; deep-crown rifling; tuned trigger; trigger locking system; hammer extension. Introduced 2001. From H&R 1871 LLC.
Price: $135.95

KIMBER 22 CLASSIC BOLT-ACTION RIFLE
Caliber: 22 LR, 5-shot magazine. **Barrel:** 22" Kimber match grade; 11-degree target crown. **Weight:** About 6.5 lbs. **Length:** 40.5" overall. **Stock:** Classic style in Claro walnut with 18 l.p.i. hand-cut checkering; satin finish; steel gripcap; swivel studs. **Sights:** None furnished; Kimber sculpted bases available that accept all rotary dovetail rings. **Features:** All-new action with Mauser-style full-length claw extractor; two-position in M70-type safety; fully adjustable trigger set at 2 lbs.; pillar-bedded action with recoil lug, free-floated barrel. Introduced 1999. Made in U.S. by Kimber Mfg., Inc.
Price: $950.00

246 • GUNS ILLUSTRATED

RIMFIRE RIFLES — BOLT ACTIONS & SINGLE SHOT

Kimber 22 SVT

Kimber 22 HS

Marlin Model 15YN

Marlin Model 880SS

Marlin 880SQ Squirrel

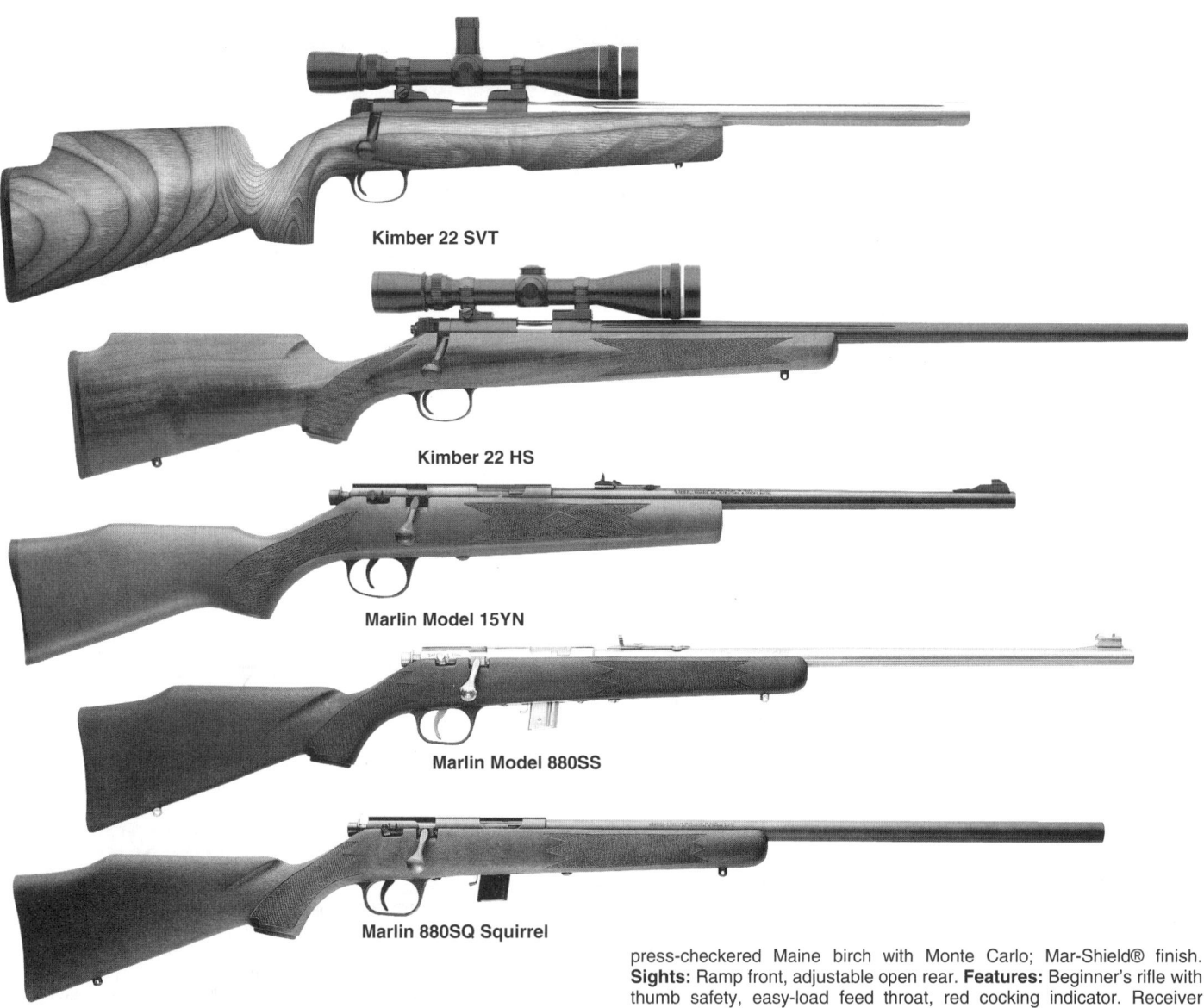

Kimber 22 SuperAmerica Bolt-Action Rifle
Similar to the 22 Classic except has AAA Claro walnut stock with wraparound 22 l.p.i. hand-cut checkering, ebony forened tip, beaded cheekpiece. Introduced 1999. Made in U.S. by Kimber Mfg., Inc.
Price: $1,560.00

Kimber 22 SVT Bolt-Action Rilfe
Similar to the 22 Classic except has 18" stainless steel, fluted bull barrel, gray laminated, high-comb target-style stock with deep pistol grip, high comb, and beavertail forend with bipod stud. Weighs 7.5 lbs., overall length 36.5". Matte finish on action. Introduced 1999. Made in U.S. by Kimber Mfg., Inc.
Price: $950.00

Kimber 22 HS (Hunter Silhouette) Bolt-Action Rifle
Similar to the 22 Classic except has 24" medium sporter match-grade barrel with half-fluting; high comb, walnut, Monte Carlo target stock with 18 l.p.i. checkering; matte blue metal finish. Introduced 1999. Made in U.S. by Kimber Mfg., Inc.
Price: $814.00

MARLIN MODEL 15YN "LITTLE BUCKAROO"
Caliber: 22 S, L, LR, single shot. **Barrel:** 16-1/4" Micro-Groove®. **Weight:** 4-1/4 lbs. **Length:** 33-1/4" overall. **Stock:** One-piece walnut-finished, press-checkered Maine birch with Monte Carlo; Mar-Shield® finish. **Sights:** Ramp front, adjustable open rear. **Features:** Beginner's rifle with thumb safety, easy-load feed throat, red cocking indicator. Receiver grooved for scope mounting. Introduced 1989.
Price: $197.00

MARLIN MODEL 880SS BOLT-ACTION RIFLE
Caliber: 22 LR, 7-shot clip magazine. **Barrel:** 22" Micro-Groove®. **Weight:** 6 lbs. **Length:** 41" overall. **Stock:** Black fiberglass-filled synthetic with nickel-plated swivel studs and moulded-in checkering. **Sights:** Ramp front with orange post and cutaway Wide-Scan™ hood, adjustable semi-buckhorn folding rear. **Features:** Stainless steel barrel, receiver, front breech bolt and striker; receiver grooved for scope mounting. Introduced 1994. Made in U.S. by Marlin.
Price: $297.00

Marlin Model 81TS Bolt-Action Rifle
Same as the Marlin 880SS except blued steel, tubular magazine, holds 17 Long Rifle cartridges. Weighs 6 lbs.
Price: $200.00

Marlin Model 880SQ Squirrel Rifle
Similar to the Model 880SS except uses the heavy target barrel of Marlin's Model 2000L target rifle. Black synthetic stock with moulded-in checkering; double bedding screws; matte blue finish. Comes without sights, no dovetail or filler screws; receiver grooved for scope mount. Weighs 7 lbs. Introduced 1996. Made in U.S. by Marlin.
Price: $312.00

34TH EDITION, 2002 • 247

RIMFIRE RIFLES — BOLT ACTIONS & SINGLE SHOT

Marlin 25NC

Marlin 25MNC

Marlin 883SS

Marlin 83TS

Marlin Model 25N Bolt-Action Repeater
Similar to Marlin 880, except walnut-finished hardwood stock, adjustable open rear sight, ramp front.
Price: $199.00
Price: With 4x scope and mount. $205.00

Marlin Model 25NC Bolt-Action Repeater
Same as the Model 25N except has a Mossy Oak® Break-Up camouflage stock. Made in U.S. by Marlin.
Price: $233.00

Marlin Model 25MN/25MNC Bolt-Action Rifles
Similar to the Model 25N except chambered for 22 WMR. Has 7-shot clip magazine, 22" Micro-Groove® barrel, checkered walnut-finished Maine birch stock. Introduced 1989.
Price: 25MN $227.00
New! Price: 25MNC (Mossy Oak® Break-Up camouflage stock).. $263.00

Marlin Model 882 Bolt-Action Rifle
Same as the Marlin 880 except 22 WMR cal. only with 7-shot clip magazine; weight about 6 lbs. Comes with swivel studs.
Price: $304.00
Price: Model 882L (laminated hardwood stock; weighs 6-1/4 lbs.) $322.00

Marlin Model 882SS Bolt-Action Rifle
Same as the Marlin Model 882 except has stainless steel front breech bolt, barrel, receiver and bolt knob. All other parts are either stainless steel or nickel-plated. Has black Monte Carlo stock of fiberglass-filled polycarbonate with moulded-in checkering, nickel-plated swivel studs. Introduced 1995. Made in U.S. by Marlin Firearms Co.
Price: $314.00

Marlin Model 882SSV Bolt-Action Rifle
Similar to the Model 882SS except has selected heavy 22" stainless steel barrel with recessed muzzle, and comes without sights; receiver is grooved for scope mount and 1" ring mounts are included. Weighs 7 lbs. Introduced 1997. Made in U.S. by Marlin Firearms Co.
Price: $309.00

MARLIN MODEL 883 BOLT-ACTION RIFLE
Caliber: 22 WMR. **Barrel:** 22"; 1:16" twist. **Weight:** 6 lbs. **Length:** 41" overall. **Stock:** Walnut Monte Carlo with sling swivel studs, rubber butt pad. **Sights:** Ramp front with brass bead, removable hood; adjustable semi-buckhorn folding rear. **Features:** Thumb safety; red cocking indicator; receiver grooved for scope mount. Made in U.S. by Marlin Firearms Co.
Price: $317.00

Marlin Model 883SS Bolt-Action Rifle
Same as the Model 883 except front breech bolt, striker knob, trigger stud, cartridge lifter stud and outer magazine tube are of stainless steel; other parts are nickel-plated. Has two-tone brown laminated Monte Carlo stock with swivel studs, rubber butt pad. Introduced 1993.
Price: $337.00

Marlin Model 83TS Bolt-Action Rifle
Same as the Model 883 except has a black Monte Carlo fiberglass-filled synthetic stock with sling swivel studs. Weighs 6 lbs., length 41" overall. Introduced 2001. Made in U.S. by Marlin Firearms Co.
Price: $244.00

NEW ENGLAND FIREARMS SPORTSTER™ SINGLE-SHOT RIFLES
Caliber: 22 LR, 22 WMR, single-shot. **Barrel:** 20". **Weight:** 5-1/2 lbs. **Length:** 36-1/4" overall. **Stock:** Black polymer. **Sights:** None furnished; scope mount included. **Features:** Break open, side-lever release; automatic ejection; recoil pad; sling swivel studs; trigger locking system. Introduced 2001. Made in U.S. by New England Firearms.
Price: $121.95
Price: Youth model (20" bbl., 33" overall, weighs 5-1/3 lbs.) $121.95

RIMFIRE RIFLES — BOLT ACTIONS & SINGLE SHOT

Ruger K77/22 Varmint

Ruger 77/22R

Sako Finnfire

NEW ULTRA LIGHT ARMS 20RF BOLT-ACTION RIFLE

Caliber: 22 LR, single shot or repeater. **Barrel:** Douglas, length to order. **Weight:** 5-1/4 lbs. **Length:** Varies. **Stock:** Kevlar®/graphite composite, variety of finishes. **Sights:** None furnished; drilled and tapped for scope mount. **Features:** Timney trigger, hand-lapped action, button-rifled barrel, hand-bedded action, recoil pad, sling-swivel studs, optional Jewell Trigger. Made in U.S. by New Ultra Light Arms.
Price: 20 RF single shot $800.00
Price: 20 RF repeater $850.00

ROSSI MATCHED PAIR SINGLE-SHOT RIFLE/SHOTGUN

Caliber: 22 LR or 22 WMR. **Barrel:** 18-1/2" or 23". **Weight:** NA. **Length:** NA. **Stock:** Hardwood (brown or black finish). **Sights:** Ramp front, fully adjustable rear. **Features:** Break-open breech with external hammer; transfer-bar manual safety; blued or stainless steel finish; sling-swivel studs; includes matched 410-, 20- or 12-gauge shotgun barrel with bead front sight. Introduced 2001. Imported by BrazTech/Taurus.
Price: 22 LR/410-, 20- or 12-gauge, blued finish,
 brown hardwood stock $140.00
Price: 22 LR/410-gauge, stainless finish, black hardwood stock . . $170.00
Price: 22 WMR/12-gauge, blued finish, brown hardwood stock . . . $140.00

RUGER K77/22 VARMINT RIFLE

Caliber: 22 LR, 10-shot, 22 WMR, 9-shot detachable rotary magazine. **Barrel:** 24", heavy. **Weight:** 7.25 lbs. **Length:** 43.25" overall. **Stock:** Laminated hardwood with rubber butt pad, quick-detachable swivel studs. No checkering or gripcap. **Sights:** None furnished. Comes with Ruger 1" scope rings. **Features:** Made of stainless steel with target gray finish. Three-position safety, dual extractors. Stock has wide, flat forend. Introduced 1993.
Price: K77/22VBZ, 22 LR $565.00
Price: K77/22VMBZ, 22 WMR $565.00

RUGER 77/22 RIMFIRE BOLT-ACTION RIFLE

Caliber: 22 LR, 10-shot rotary magazine; 22 WMR, 9-shot rotary magazine. **Barrel:** 20". **Weight:** About 5-3/4 lbs. **Length:** 39-3/4" overall. **Stock:** Checkered American walnut or injection-moulded fiberglass-reinforced DuPont Zytel with Xenoy inserts in forend and grip, stainless sling swivels. **Sights:** Brass bead front, adjustable folding leaf rear or plain barrel with 1" Ruger rings. **Features:** Mauser-type action uses Ruger's 10-shot rotary magazine. Three-position safety, simplified bolt stop, patented bolt locking system. Uses the dual-screw barrel attachment system of the 10/22 rifle. Integral scope mounting system with 1" Ruger rings. Blued model introduced in 1983. Stainless steel model and blued model with the synthetic stock introduced in 1989.
Price: 77/22R (no sights, rings, walnut stock) $525.00
Price: 77/22RS (open sights, rings, walnut stock) $535.00
Price: K77/22RP (stainless, no sights, rings, synthetic stock) . . . $525.00
Price: K77/22RSP (stainless, open sights, rings, synthetic stock) . $535.00
Price: 77/22RM (22 WMR, blue, walnut stock) $525.00
Price: K77/22RSMP (22 WMR, stainless, open sights, rings,
 synthetic stock) $535.00
Price: K77/22RMP (22 WMR, stainless, synthetic stock) $525.00
Price: 77/22RSM (22 WMR, blue, open sights, rings,
 walnut stock) $535.00

SAKO FINNFIRE HUNTER BOLT-ACTION RIFLE

Caliber: 22 LR, 5-shot magazine. **Barrel:** 22". **Weight:** 5.75 lbs. **Length:** 39-1/2" overall. **Stock:** European walnut with checkered grip and forend. **Sights:** Hooded blade front, open adjustable rear. **Features:** Adjustable single-stage trigger; has 50-degree bolt lift. Introduced 1994. Imported from Finland by Beretta USA.
Price: $874.00
Price: Varmint (heavy barrel) $924.00

SAKO FINNFIRE SPORTER RIFLE

Caliber: 22 LR. **Barrel:** 22"; heavy, free-floating. **Weight:** NA. **Length:** NA. **Stock:** Match style of European walnut; adjustable cheekpiece and buttplate; stippled pistol grip and forend. **Sights:** None furnished; has 11mm integral dovetail scope mount. **Features:** Based on the Sako P94S action with two bolt locking lugs, 50-degree bolt lift and 30mm throw; adjustable trigger. Introduced 1999. Imported from Finland by Beretta USA.
Price: $984.00

SAVAGE MARK I-G BOLT-ACTION RIFLE

Caliber: 22 LR, single shot. **Barrel:** 20-3/4". **Weight:** 5-1/2 lbs. **Length:** 39-1/2" overall. **Stock:** Walnut-finished hardwood with Monte Carlo-type comb, checkered grip and forend. **Sights:** Bead front, open adjustable rear. **Features:** Thumb-operated rotating safety. Blue finish. Rifled or smooth bore. Introduced 1990. Made in Canada, from Savage Arms Inc.
Price: Mark I, rifled or smooth bore, right- or left-handed $119.00
Price: Mark I-GY (Youth), 19" barrel, 37" overall, 5 lbs. $127.00

34TH EDITION, 2002 • 249

RIMFIRE RIFLES — BOLT ACTIONS & SINGLE SHOT

Savage Mark II-FXP

Savage Model 93G

Winchester Model 52B

SAVAGE MARK II-G BOLT-ACTION RIFLE
Caliber: 22 LR, 10-shot magazine. **Barrel:** 20-1/2". **Weight:** 5-1/2 lbs. **Length:** 39-1/2" overall. **Stock:** Walnut-finished hardwood with Monte Carlo-type comb, checkered grip and forend. **Sights:** Bead front, open adjustable rear. Receiver grooved for scope mounting. **Features:** Thumb-operated rotating safety. Blue finish. Introduced 1990. Made in Canada, from Savage Arms, Inc.
Price: $140.00
Price: Mark II-GY (youth), 19" barrel, 37" overall, 5 lbs. $140.00
Price: Mark II-GL, left-hand $140.00
Price: Mark II-GLY (youth) left-hand $140.00
Price: Mark II-GXP Package Gun (comes with 4x15 scope),
right- or left-handed $147.00
Price: Mark II-FXP (as above except with black synthetic
stock) $133.00
Price: Mark II-F (as above, no scope) $127.00

Savage Mark II-LV Heavy Barrel Rifle
Similar to the Mark II-G except has heavy 21" barrel with recessed target-style crown; gray, laminated hardwood stock with cut checkering. No sights furnished, but has dovetailed receiver for scope mounting. Overall length is 39-3/4", weight is 6-1/2 lbs. Comes with 10-shot clip magazine. Introduced 1997. Imported from Canada by Savage Arms, Inc.
Price: $222.00
Price: Mark II-FV, with black graphite/polymer stock $194.00

Savage Mark II-FSS Stainless Rifle
Similar to the Mark II-G except has stainless steel barreled action and graphite/polymer filled stock; free-floated barrel. Weighs 5 lbs. Introduced 1997. Imported from Canada by Savage Arms, Inc.
Price: $169.00

Savage Model 93FVSS Magnum Rifle
Similar to the Model 93FSS Magnum except has 21" heavy barrel with recessed target-style crown; satin-finished stainless barreled action; black graphite/fiberglass stock. Drilled and tapped for scope mounting; comes with Weaver-style bases. Introduced 1998. Imported from Canada by Savage Arms, Inc.
Price: $222.00

SAVAGE MODEL 93G MAGNUM BOLT-ACTION RIFLE
Caliber: 22 WMR, 5-shot magazine. **Barrel:** 20-3/4". **Weight:** 5-3/4 lbs. **Length:** 39-1/2" overall. **Stock:** Walnut-finished hardwood with Monte Carlo-type comb, checkered grip and forend. **Sights:** Bead front, adjustable open rear. Receiver grooved for scope mount. **Features:** Thumb-operated rotary safety. Blue finish. Introduced 1994. Made in Canada, from Savage Arms.
Price: About $160.00
Price: Model 93F (as above with black graphite/fiberglass
stock) $154.00

Savage Model 93FSS Magnum Rifle
Similar to the Model 93G except has stainless steel barreled action and black synthetic stock with positive checkering. Weighs 5-1/2 lbs. Introduced 1997. Imported from Canada by Savage Arms, Inc.
Price: $194.00

WINCHESTER MODEL 52B BOLT-ACTION RIFLE
Caliber: 22 Long Rifle, 5-shot magazine. **Barrel:** 24". **Weight:** 7 lbs. **Length:** 41-3/4" overall. **Stock:** Walnut with checkered grip and forend. **Sights:** None furnished; grooved receiver and drilled and tapped for scope mounting. **Features:** Has Micro Motion trigger adjustable for pull and over-travel; match chamber; detachable magazine. Reintroduced 1997. From U.S. Repeating Arms Co.
Price: $662.00

WINCHESTER MODEL 1885 LOW WALL RIMFIRE
Caliber: 22 LR, single-shot. **Barrel:** 24-1/2"; half-octagon. **Weight:** 8 lbs. **Length:** 41" overall. **Stock:** Walnut. **Sights:** Blade front, semi-buckhorn rear. **Features:** Drilled and tapped for scope mount or tang sight; target chamber. Limited production. From U.S. Repeating Arms Co.
Price: Grade I (2,400 made) $828.00
Price: High Grade (1,100 made; engraved/gold inlaid
squirrel and rabbit) $1,180.00

COMPETITION RIFLES — CENTERFIRE & RIMFIRE

Includes models for classic American and ISU target competition and other sporting and competitive shooting.

Anschutz 1451 Target

Anschutz 2013

ANSCHUTZ 1451R SPORTER TARGET RIFLE
Caliber: 22 LR, 5-shot magazine. **Barrel:** 22" heavy match. **Weight:** 6.4 lbs. **Length:** 39.75" overall. **Stock:** European hardwood with walnut finish. **Sights:** None furnished. Grooved receiver for scope mounting or Anschutz micrometer rear sight. **Features:** Sliding safety, two-stage trigger. Adjustable buttplate; forend slide rail to accept Anschutz accessories. Imported from Germany by AcuSport Corp.
Price: $549.00

ANSCHUTZ 1451 TARGET RIFLE
Caliber: 22 LR. **Barrel:** 22". **Weight:** About 6.5 lbs. **Length:** 40". **Sights:** Optional. Receiver grooved for scope mounting. **Features:** Designed for the beginning junior shooter with adjustable length of pull from 13.25" to 14.25" via removable butt spacers. Two-stage trigger factory set at 2.6 lbs. Introduced 1999. Imported from Germany by Gunsmithing, Inc.
Price: $347.00
Price: #6834 Match Sight Set............................. $227.10

ANSCHUTZ 1808D-RT SUPER RUNNING TARGET RIFLE
Caliber: 22 LR, single shot. **Barrel:** 32-1/2". **Weight:** 9 lbs. **Length:** 50" overall. **Stock:** European walnut. Heavy beavertail forend; adjustable cheekpiece and buttplate. Stippled grip and forend. **Sights:** None furnished. Grooved for scope mounting. **Features:** Designed for Running Target competition. Nine-way adjustable single-stage trigger, slide safety. Introduced 1991. Imported from Germany by Accuracy International, Gunsmithing, Inc.
Price: Right-hand $1,364.10

ANSCHUTZ 1903 MATCH RIFLE
Caliber: 22 LR, single shot. **Barrel:** 25.5", .75" diameter. **Weight:** 10.1 lbs. **Length:** 43.75" overall. **Stock:** Walnut-finished hardwood with adjustable cheekpiece; stippled grip and forend. **Sights:** None furnished. **Features:** Uses Anschutz Match 64 action and #5098 two-stage trigger. A medium weight rifle for intermediate and advanced Junior Match competition. Introduced 1987. Imported from Germany by Accuracy International, Gunsmithing, Inc.
Price: Right-hand $720.40
Price: Left-hand $757.90

ANSCHUTZ 64-MSR SILHOUETTE RIFLE
Caliber: 22 LR, 5-shot magazine. **Barrel:** 21-1/2", medium heavy; 7/8" diameter. **Weight:** 8 lbs. **Length:** 39.5" overall. **Stock:** Walnut-finished hardwood, silhouette-type. **Sights:** None furnished. **Features:** Uses Match 64 action. Designed for metallic silhouette competition. Stock has stippled checkering, contoured thumb groove with Wundhammer swell. Two-stage #5098 trigger. Slide safety locks sear and bolt. Introduced 1980. Imported from Germany by AcuSport Corp., Accuracy International, Gunsmithing, Inc.
Price: 64-MSR $704.30

ANSCHUTZ 2013 BENCHREST RIFLE
Caliber: 22 LR, single shot. **Barrel:** 19.6". **Weight:** About 10.3 lbs. **Length:** 37.75" to 42.5" overall. **Stock:** Benchrest style of European hardwood. Stock length adjustable via spacers and buttplate. **Sights:** None furnished. Receiver grooved for mounts. **Features:** Uses the Anschutz 2013 target action, #5018 two-stage adjustable target trigger factory set at 3.9 oz. Introduced 1994. Imported from Germany by Accuracy International, Gunsmithing, Inc.
Price: $1,757.20

Anschutz 2007 Match Rifle
Uses same action as the Model 2013, but has a lighter barrel. European walnut stock in right-hand, true left-hand or extra-short models. Sights optional. Available with 19.6" barrel with extension tube, or 26", both in stainless or blue. Introduced 1998. Imported from Germany by Gunsmithing, Inc., Accuracy International.
Price: Right-hand, blue, no sights $1,766.60
Price: Right-hand, blue, no sights, extra-short stock $1,756.60
Price: Left-hand, blue, no sights........................ $1,856.80

ANSCHUTZ 1827 BIATHLON RIFLE
Caliber: 22 LR, 5-shot magazine. **Barrel:** 21-1/2". **Weight:** 8-1/2 lbs. with sights. **Length:** 42-1/2" overall. **Stock:** European walnut with cheekpiece, stippled pistol grip and forend. **Sights:** Optional globe front specially designed for Biathlon shooting, micrometer rear with hinged snow cap. **Features:** Uses Super Match 54 action and nine-way adjustable trigger; adjustable wooden buttplate, Biathlon butthook, adjustable hand-stop rail. Introduced 1982. Imported from Germany by Accuracy International, Gunsmithing, Inc.
Price: Right-hand, with sights, about .... $1,500.50 to $1,555.00

Anschutz 1827BT Fortner Biathlon Rifle
Similar to the Anschutz 1827 Biathlon rifle except uses Anschutz/Fortner system straight-pull bolt action, blued or stainless steel barrel. Introduced 1982. Imported from Germany by Accuracy International, Gunsmithing, Inc.
Price: Right-hand, with sights.................. $1,908.00 to $2,210.00
Price: Left-hand, with sights................... $2,099.20 to $2,395.00
Price: Right-hand, sights, stainless barrel (Gunsmithing, Inc.).. $2,045.20

34TH EDITION, 2002

COMPETITION RIFLES — CENTERFIRE & RIMFIRE

Anschutz 54.18MS REP

Armalite AR-10 (T)

ANSCHUTZ SUPER MATCH SPECIAL MODEL 2013 RIFLE
Caliber: 22 LR, single shot. **Barrel:** 25.9". **Weight:** 13 lbs. **Length:** 41.7-42.9". **Stock:** A thumbhole version made of European walnut, both the cheekpiece and buttplate are highly adjustable. **Sights:** None furnished. **Features:** Developed by Anschütz for women to shoot in the sport rifle category. Stainless or blue. This top of the line rifle was introduced in 1997.
Price: Right-hand, blue, no sights, walnut $2,219.30
Price: Right-hand, stainless, no sights, walnut $2,345.30
Price: Left-hand, blue, no sights, walnut $2,319.50

ANSCHUTZ 2012 SPORT RIFLE
Caliber: 22 LR, 5-shot magazine. **Barrel:** 22.4" match; detachable muzzle tube. **Weight:** 7.9 lbs. **Length:** 40.9" overall. **Stock:** European walnut, thumbhole design. **Sights:** None furnished. **Features:** Uses Anschutz 54.18 barreled action with two-stage match trigger. Introduced 1997. Imported from Germany by Accuracy International, AcuSport Corp.
Price: .... $1,425.00 to $2,219.95

ANSCHUTZ 1911 PRONE MATCH RIFLE
Caliber: 22 LR, single shot. **Barrel:** 27-1/4". **Weight:** 11 lbs. **Length:** 46" overall. **Stock:** Walnut-finished European hardwood; American prone-style with adjustable cheekpiece, textured pistol grip, forend with swivel rail and adjustable rubber buttplate. **Sights:** None furnished. Receiver grooved for Anschutz sights (extra). **Features:** Two-stage #5018 trigger adjustable from 2.1 to 8.6 oz. Extremely fast lock time. Stainless or blue barrel. Imported from Germany by Accuracy International, Gunsmithing, Inc.
Price: Right-hand, no sights $1,714.20

ANSCHUTZ 1912 SPORT RIFLE
Caliber: 22 LR, single shot. **Barrel:** 25.9". **Weight:** About 11.4 lbs. **Length:** 41.7-42.9". **Stock:** European walnut or aluminum. **Sights:** None furnished. **Features:** Light weight sport rifle version. Still uses the 54 match action like the 1913 but weighs 1.5 pounds less. Stainless or blue barrel. Introduced 1997.
Price: Right-hand, blue, no sights, walnut $1,789.50
Price: Right-hand, blue, no sights, aluminum $2,129.80
Price: Right-hand, stainless, no sights, walnut $1,910.30
Price: Left-hand, blue, no sights, walnut $1,879.00

ANSCHUTZ 1913 SUPER MATCH RIFLE
Caliber: 22 LR, single shot. **Barrel:** 27.1". **Weight:** About 14.3 lbs. **Length:** 44.8-46". **Stock:** European walnut, color laminate, or aluminum. **Sights:** None furnished. **Features:** Two-stage #5018 trigger. Extremely fast lock time. Stainless or blue barrel.
Price: Right-hand, blue, no sights, walnut stock $2,262.90
Price: Right-hand, blue, no sights, color laminate stock $2,275.10
Price: Right-hand, blue, no sights, aluminum stock $2,262.90
Price: Left-hand, blue, no sights, walnut stock $2,382.20

Anschutz 1913 Super Match Rifle
Same as the Model 1911 except European walnut International-type stock with adjustable cheekpiece, or color laminate, both available with straight or lowered forend, adjustable aluminum hook buttplate, adjustable hand stop, weighs 15.5 lbs., 46" overall. Stainless or blue barrel. Imported from Germany by Accuracy International, Gunsmithing, Inc.
Price: Right-hand, blue, no sights, walnut stock.. $2,139.00 to $2,175.00
Price: Right-hand, blue, no sights, color laminate stock....... $2,199.40
Price: Right-hand, blue, no sights, walnut, lowered forend $2,181.80
Price: Right-hand, blue, no sights, color laminate, lowered forend $2,242.20
Price: Left-hand, blue, no sights, walnut stock... $2,233.10 to $2,275.00

Anschutz 54.18MS REP Deluxe Silhouette Rifle
Same basic action and trigger specifications as the Anschutz 1913 Super Match but with removable 5-shot clip magazine, 22.4" barrel extendable to 30" using optional extension and weight set. Weight id 8.1 lbs. Receiver drilled and tapped for scope mounting. Stock is Thumbhole silhouette version or standard silhouette version, both are European walnut. Introduced 1990. Imported from Germany by Accuracy International, Gunsmithing, Inc.
Price: Thumbhole stock $1,461.40
Price: Standard stock $1,212.10

Anschutz 1907 Standard Match Rifle
Same action as Model 1913 but with 7/8" diameter 26" barrel (stainless or blue). Length is 44.5" overall, weighs 10.5 lbs. Choice of stock configurations. Vented forend. Designed for prone and position shooting ISU requirements; suitable for NRA matches. Also available with walnut flat-forend stock for benchrest shooting. Imported from Germany by Accuracy International, Gunsmithing, Inc.
Price: Right-hand, blue, no sights, hardwood stock $1,253.40 to $1,299.00
Price: Right-hand, blue, no sights, colored laminated stock .... $1,316.10 to $1,375.00
Price: Right-hand, blue, no sights, walnut stock............. $1,521.10
Price: Left-hand, blue barrel, no sights, walnut stock......... $1,584.60

ARMALITE AR-10 (T) RIFLE
Caliber: 308, 10-shot magazine. **Barrel:** 24" target-weight Rock 5R custom. **Weight:** 10.4 lbs. **Length:** 43.5" overall. **Stock:** Green or black compostion; N.M. fiberglass handguard tube. **Sights:** Detachable handle, front sight, or scope mount available. Comes with international-style flat-top receiver with Picatinny rail. **Features:** National Match two-stage trigger. Forged upper receiver. Receivers hard-coat anodized. Introduced 1995. Made in U.S. by ArmaLite, Inc.
Price: Green $2,075.00
Price: Black $2,090.00
Price: AR-10 (T) Carbine, lighter 16" barrel, single stage trigger, weighs 8.8 lbs. Green $1,970.00
Price: Black $1,985.00

252 • GUNS ILLUSTRATED

COMPETITION RIFLES — CENTERFIRE & RIMFIRE

Bushmaster XM15 E2S Target

Bushmaster DCM

Colt Match Target HBAR

ARMALITE M15A4 (T) EAGLE EYE RIFLE
Caliber: 223, 7-shot magazine. **Barrel:** 24" heavy stainless; 1:8" twist. **Weight:** 9.2 lbs. **Length:** 42-3/8" overall. **Stock:** Green or black butt, N.M. fiberglass handguard tube. **Sights:** One-piece international-style flattop receiver with Weaver-type rail, including case deflector. **Features:** Detachable carry handle, front sight and scope mount (30mm or 1") available. Upper and lower receivers have push-type pivot pin, hard coat anodized. Made in U.S. by ArmaLite, Inc.
Price: Green $1,378.00
Price: Black $1,393.00

ARMALITE M15A4 ACTION MASTER RIFLE
Caliber: 223, 7-shot magazine. **Barrel:** 20" heavy stainless; 1:9" twist. **Weight:** 9 lbs. **Length:** 40-1/2" overall. **Stock:** Green or black plastic; N.M. fiberglass handguard tube. **Sights:** One-piece international-style flattop receiver with Weaver-type rail. **Features:** Detachable carry handle, front sight and scope mount available. National Match two-stage trigger group; Picatinny rail; upper and lower receivers have push-type pivot pin; hard coat anodized finish. Made in U.S. by ArmaLite, Inc.
Price: $1,175.00

BLASER R93 LONG RANGE RIFLE
Caliber: 308 Win., 10-shot detachable box magazine. **Barrel:** 24". **Weight:** 10.4 lbs. **Length:** 44" overall. **Stock:** Aluminum with synthetic lining. **Sights:** None furnished; accepts detachable scope mount. **Features:** Straight-pull bolt action with adjustable trigger; fully adjustable stock; quick takedown; corrosion resistant finish. Introduced 1998. Imported from Germany by Sigarms.
Price: $2,360.00

BUSHMASTER XM15 E2S TARGET MODEL RIFLE
Caliber: 223. **Barrel:** 20", 24", 26"; 1:9" twist; heavy. **Weight:** 8.3 lbs. **Length:** 38.25" overall (20" barrel). **Stock:** Black composition; A2 type. **Sights:** Adjustable post front, adjustable aperture rear. **Features:** Patterned after Colt M-16A2. Chrome-lined barrel with manganese phosphate exterior. Forged aluminum receivers with push-pin takedown. Made in U.S. by Bushmaster Firearms Co./Quality Parts Co.
Price: 20" match heavy barrel $960.00

Bushmaster DCM Competition Rifle
Similar to the XM15 E2S Target Model except has 20" extra-heavy (1" diameter) barrel with 1.8" twist for heavier competition bullets. Weighs about 12 lbs. with balance weights. Has special competition rear sight with interchangeable apertures, extra-fine 1/2- or 1/4-MOA windage and elevation adjustments; specially ground front sight post in choice of three widths. Full-length handguards over free-floater barrel tube. Introduced 1998. Made in U.S. by Bushmaster Firearms, Inc.
Price: $1,525.00

BUSHMASTER XM15 E2S V-MATCH RIFLE
Caliber: 223. **Barrel:** 20", 24", 26"; 1:9" twist; heavy. **Weight:** 8.1 lbs. **Length:** 38.25" overall (20" barrel). **Stock:** Black composition. A2 type. **Sights:** None furnished; upper receiver has integral scope mount base. **Features:** Chrome-lined .950" heavy barrel with counter-bored crown, manganese phosphate finish; free-floating aluminum handguard; forged aluminum receivers with push-pin takedown, hard anodized mil-spec finish. Competition trigger optional. Made in U.S. by Bushmaster Firearms, Inc.
Price: 20" Match heavy barrel $1,025.00
Price: 24" Match heavy barrel $1,040.00
Price: V-Match Carbine (16" barrel) $1,015.00

COLT MATCH TARGET MODEL RIFLE
Caliber: 223 Rem., 8-shot magazine. **Barrel:** 20". **Weight:** 7.5 lbs. **Length:** 39" overall. **Stock:** Composition stock, grip, forend. **Sights:** Post front, aperture rear adjustable for windage and elevation. **Features:** Five-round detachable box magazine, standard-weight barrel, sling swivels. Has forward bolt assist. Military matte black finish. Model introduced 1991.
Price: $1,144.00
Price: With compensator $1,150.00

Colt Accurized Rifle
Similar to the Colt Match Target Model except has 24" stainless steel heavy barrel with 1.9" rifling, flattop receiver with scope mount and 1" rings, weighs 9.25 lbs. Introduced 1998. Made in U.S. by Colt's Mfg. Co., Inc.
Price: $1,424.00

Colt Match Target HBAR Rifle
Similar to the Target Model except has heavy barrel, 800-meter rear sight adjustable for windage and elevation. Introduced 1991.
Price: $1,194.00

Colt Match Target Competition HBAR Rifle
Similar to the Sporter Target except has flat-top receiver with integral Weaver-type base for scope mounting. Counter-bored muzzle, 1:9" rifling twist. Introduced 1991.
Price: Model R6700 .... $1,199.00

COMPETITION RIFLES — CENTERFIRE & RIMFIRE

Harris Gunworks Long Range

Harris Gunworks M-86

Marlin Model 2000L

Colt Match Target Competition HBAR II Rifle
Similar to the Match Target Competition HBAR except has 16:1" barrel, weighs 7.1 lbs., overall length 34.5"; 1:9" twist barrel. Introduced 1995.
Price: $1,172.00

E.A.A./HW 660 MATCH RIFLE
Caliber: 22 LR. Barrel: 26". Weight: 10.7 lbs. Length: 45.3" overall. Stock: Match-type walnut with adjustable cheekpiece and buttplate. Sights: Globe front, match aperture rear. Features: Adjustable match trigger; stippled pistol grip and forend; forend accessory rail. Introduced 1991. Imported from Germany by European American Armory.
Price: About $999.00
Price: With laminate stock $1,159.00

HARRIS GUNWORKS NATIONAL MATCH RIFLE
Caliber: 7mm-08, 308, 5-shot magazine. Barrel: 24", stainless steel. Weight: About 11 lbs. (std. bbl.). Length: 43" overall. Stock: Fiberglass with adjustable buttplate. Sights: Barrel band and Tompkins front; no rear sight furnished. Features: Gunworks repeating action with clip slot, Canjar trigger. Match-grade barrel. Available in right-hand only. Fiberglass stock, sight installation, special machining and triggers optional. Introduced 1989. From Harris Gunworks, Inc.
Price: $3,500.00

HARRIS GUNWORKS LONG RANGE RIFLE
Caliber: 300 Win. Mag., 7mm Rem. Mag., 300 Phoenix, 338 Lapua, single shot. Barrel: 26", stainless steel, match-grade. Weight: 14 lbs. Length: 46-1/2" overall. Stock: Fiberglass with adjustable buttplate and cheekpiece. Adjustable for length of pull, drop, cant and cast-off. Sights: Barrel band and Tompkins front; no rear sight furnished. Features: Uses Gunworks solid bottom single shot action and Canjar trigger. Barrel twist 1:12". Introduced 1989. From Harris Gunworks, Inc.
Price: $3,620.00

HARRIS GUNWORKS M-86 SNIPER RIFLE
Caliber: 308, 30-06, 4-shot magazine; 300 Win. Mag., 3-shot magazine. Barrel: 24", Gunworks match-grade in heavy contour. Weight: 11-1/4 lbs. (308), 11-1/2 lbs. (30-06, 300). Length: 43-1/2" overall. Stock: Specially designed McHale fiberglass stock with textured grip and forend, recoil pad. Sights: None furnished. Features: Uses Gunworks repeating action. Comes with bipod. Matte black finish. Sling swivels. Introduced 1989. From Harris Gunworks, Inc.
Price: $2,700.00

HARRIS GUNWORKS M-89 SNIPER RIFLE
Caliber: 308 Win., 5-shot magazine. Barrel: 28" (with suppressor). Weight: 15 lbs., 4 oz. Stock: Fiberglass; adjustable for length; recoil pad. Sights: None furnished. Drilled and tapped for scope mounting. Features: Uses Gunworks repeating action. Comes with bipod. Introduced 1990. From Harris Gunworks, Inc.
Price: Standard (non-suppressed) $3,200.00

HARRIS GUNWORKS
COMBO M-87 SERIES 50-CALIBER RIFLES
Caliber: 50 BMG, single shot. Barrel: 29, with muzzle brake. Weight: About 21-1/2 lbs. Length: 53" overall. Stock: Gunworks fiberglass. Sights: None furnished. Features: Right-handed Gunworks stainless steel receiver, chrome-moly barrel with 1:15" twist. Introduced 1987. From Harris Gunworks, Inc.
Price: $3,885.00
Price: M87R 5-shot repeater $4,000.00
Price: M-87 (5-shot repeater) "Combo" $4,300.00
Price: M-92 Bullpup (shortened M-87 single shot with bullpup stock) $4,770.00
Price: M-93 (10-shot repeater with folding stock, detachable magazine). $4,150.00

MARLIN MODEL 2000L TARGET RIFLE
Caliber: 22 LR, single shot. Barrel: 22" heavy, Micro-Groove® rifling, match chamber, recessed muzzle. Weight: 8 lbs. Length: 41" overall. Stock: Laminated black/gray with ambidextrous pistol grip. Sights: Hooded front with ten aperture inserts, fully adjustable target rear peep. Features: Buttplate adjustable for length of pull, height and angle. Aluminum forend rail with stop and quick-detachable swivel. Two-stage target trigger; red cocking indicator. Five-shot adaptor kit available. Introduced 1991. From Marlin.
Price: $711.00

254 • GUNS ILLUSTRATED

COMPETITION RIFLES — CENTERFIRE & RIMFIRE

Marlin Model 7000T

Savage Model 900TR

Savage Model 112BT

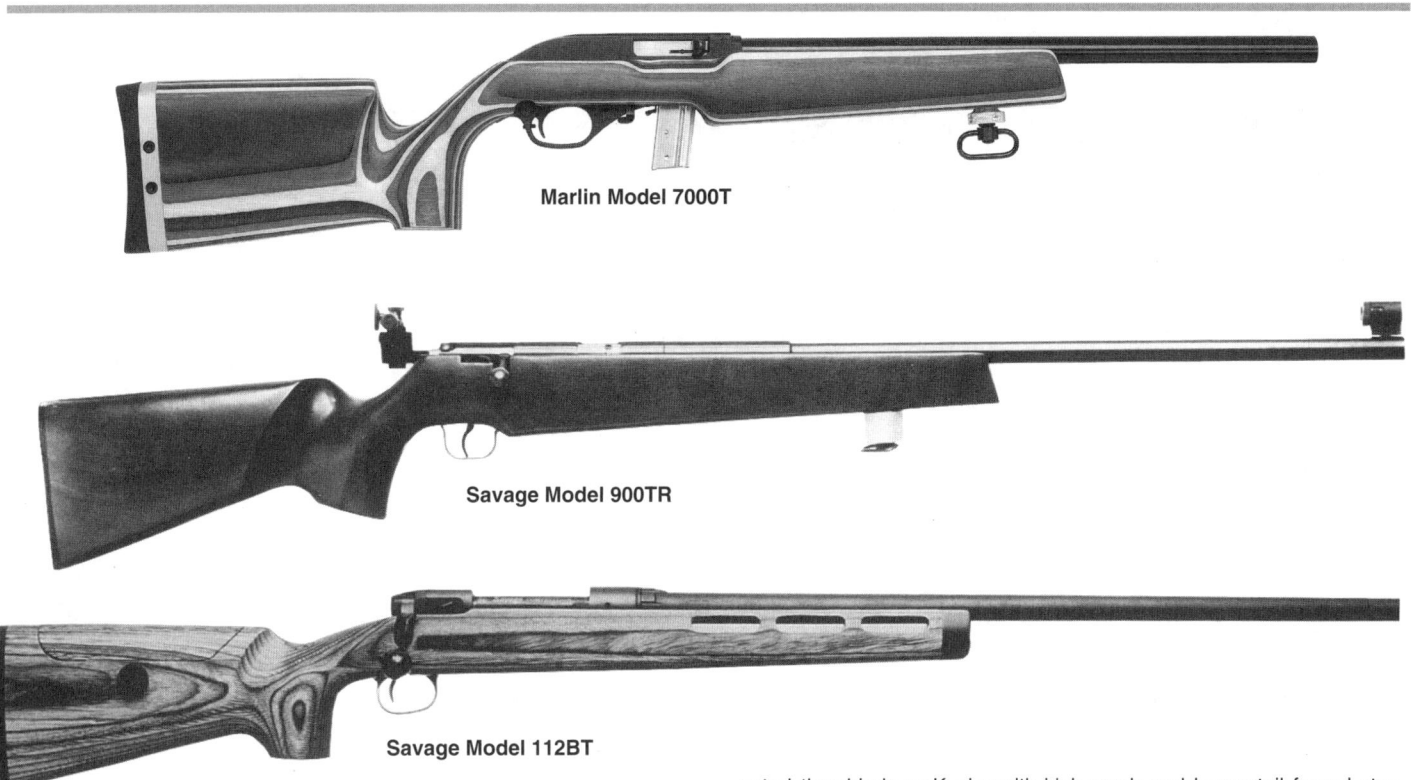

MARLIN MODEL 7000T AUTO RIFLE
Caliber: 22 LR, 10-shot magazine. **Barrel:** 18" heavy target with Micro-Groove® rifling. **Weight:** 7-1/2 lbs. **Length:** 37" overall. **Stock:** Laminated red, white and blue hardwood with ambidextrous pistol grip, adjustable buttplate, aluminum forend rail. **Sights:** None furnished; grooved receiver for scope mounting. **Features:** Trigger stop; last-shot bolt hold-open; blue finish; scope mounts included. Introduced 1999. Made in U.S. by Marlin.
Price: $465.00

OLYMPIC ARMS PCR-SERVICEMATCH RIFLE
Caliber: 223, 10-shot magazine. **Barrel:** 20", broach-cut 416 stainless steel. **Weight:** About 10 lbs. **Length:** 39.5" overall. **Stock:** A2 stowaway grip and trapdoor buttstock. **Sights:** Post front, E2-NM fully adjustable aperture rear. **Features:** Based on the AR-15. Conforms to all DCM standards. Free-floating 1:8.5" or 1:10" barrel; crowned barrel; no bayonet lug. Introduced 1996. Made in U.S. by Olympic Arms, Inc.
Price: $1,062.00

OLYMPIC ARMS PCR-1 RIFLE
Caliber: 223, 10-shot magazine. **Barrel:** 20", 24"; 416 stainless steel. **Weight:** 10 lbs., 3 oz. **Length:** 38.25" overall with 20" barrel. **Stock:** A2 stowaway grip and trapdoor butt. **Sights:** None supplied; flattop upper receiver, cut-down front sight base. **Features:** Based on the AR-15 rifle. Broach-cut, free-floating barrel with 1:8.5" or 1:10" twist. No bayonet lug. Crowned barrel; fluting available. Introduced 1994. Made in U.S. by Olympic Arms, Inc.
Price: $1,038.00

Olympic Arms PCR-2, PCR-3 Rifles
Similar to the PCR-1 except has 16" barrel, weighs 8 lbs., 2 oz.; has post front sight, fully adjustable aperture rear. Model PCR-3 has flattop upper receiver, cut-down front sight base. Introduced 1994. Made in U.S. by Olympic Arms, Inc.
Price: $958.00

REMINGTON 40-XB RANGEMASTER TARGET CENTERFIRE
Caliber: 15 calibers from 220 Swift to 300 Win. Mag. **Barrel:** 27-1/4". **Weight:** 11-1/4 lbs. **Length:** 47" overall. **Stock:** American walnut, laminated thumbhole or Kevlar with high comb and beavertail forend stop. Rubber non-slip buttplate. **Sights:** None. Scope blocks installed. **Features:** Adjustable trigger. Stainless barrel and action. Receiver drilled and tapped for sights.
Price: Standard single shot $1,565.00
Price: Repeater $1,684.00

REMINGTON 40-XBBR KS
Caliber: Five calibers from 22 BR to 308 Win. **Barrel:** 20" (light varmint class), 24" (heavy varmint class). **Weight:** 7-1/4 lbs. (light varmint class); 12 lbs. (heavy varmint class). **Length:** 38" (20" bbl.), 42" (24" bbl.). **Stock:** Kevlar. **Sights:** None. Supplied with scope blocks. **Features:** Unblued stainless steel barrel, trigger adjustable from 1-1/2 lbs. to 3-1/2 lbs. Special 2-oz. trigger at extra cost. Scope and mounts extra.
Price: With Kevlar stock $1,742.00

REMINGTON 40-XC TARGET RIFLE
Caliber: 7.62 NATO, 5-shot. **Barrel:** 24", stainless steel. **Weight:** 11 lbs. without sights. **Length:** 43-1/2" overall. **Stock:** Kevlar, with palm rail. **Sights:** None furnished. **Features:** Designed to meet the needs of competitive shooters. Stainless steel barrel and action.
Price: $1,742.00

SAKO TRG-22 BOLT-ACTION RIFLE
Caliber: 308 Win., 10-shot magazine. **Barrel:** 26". **Weight:** 10-1/4 lbs. **Length:** 45-1/4" overall. **Stock:** Reinforced polyurethane with fully adjustable cheekpiece and buttplate. **Sights:** None furnished. Optional quick-detachable, one-piece scope mount base, 1" or 30mm rings. **Features:** Resistance-free bolt, free-floating heavy stainless barrel, 60-degree bolt lift. Two-stage trigger is adjustable for length, pull, horizontal or vertical pitch. Introduced 2000. Imported from Finland by Beretta USA.
Price: $2,699.00
Price: Model TRG-42, as above except in 338 Lapua Mag or 300 Win. Mag. $3,099.00

SAVAGE MODEL 900TR TARGET RIFLE
Caliber: 22 LR, 5-shot magazine. **Barrel:** 25". **Weight:** 8 lbs. **Length:** 43-5/8" overall. **Stock:** Target-type, walnut-finished hardwood. **Sights:** Target front with inserts, peep rear with 1/4-minute click adjustments. **Features:** Comes with shooting rail and hand stop. Introduced 1991. Made in Canada, from Savage Arms Inc.
Price: Right- or left-hand $440.00

34TH EDITION, 2002 • 255

COMPETITION RIFLES — CENTERFIRE & RIMFIRE

Springfield, Inc. M1A Super Match

Springfield, Inc. M1A/M-21

SAVAGE MODEL 112BT COMPETITION GRADE RIFLE
Caliber: 223, 308, 5-shot magazine, 300 Win. Mag., single shot. **Barrel:** 26", heavy contour stainless with black finish; 1:9" twist (223), 1:10" (308). **Weight:** 10.8 lbs. **Length:** 47.5" overall. **Stock:** Laminated wood with straight comb, adjustable cheek rest, Wundhammer palm swell, ventilated forend. Recoil pad is adjustable for length of pull. **Sights:** None furnished; drilled and tapped for scope mounting and aperture target-style sights. Recessed target-style muzzle has .812" diameter section for universal target sight base. **Features:** Pillar-bedded stock, matte black alloy receiver. Bolt has black titanium nitride coating, large handle ball. Has alloy accessory rail on forend. Comes with safety gun lock, target and ear muffs. Introduced 1994. Made in U.S. by Savage Arms, Inc.
Price: $1,028.00
Price: 300 Win. Mag. (single shot 112BT-S) $1,028.00

SPRINGFIELD, INC. M1A SUPER MATCH
Caliber: 308 Win. **Barrel:** 22", heavy Douglas Premium. **Weight:** About 10 lbs. **Length:** 44.31" overall. **Stock:** Heavy walnut competition stock with longer pistol grip, contoured area behind the rear sight, thicker butt and forend, glass bedded. **Sights:** National Match front and rear. **Features:** Has figure-eight-style operating rod guide. Introduced 1987. From Springfield, Inc.
Price: About $2,479.00

Springfield, Inc. M1A/M-21 Tactical Model Rifle
Similar to the M1A Super Match except has special sniper stock with adjustable cheekpiece and rubber recoil pad. Weighs 11.2 lbs. From Springfield, Inc.
Price: $2,975.00

STONER SR-15 MATCH RIFLE
Caliber: 223. **Barrel:** 20". **Weight:** 7.9 lbs. **Length:** 38" overall. **Stock:** Black synthetic. **Sights:** None furnished; flat-top upper receiver for scope mounting. **Features:** Short Picatinny rail; two-stage match trigger. Introduced 1998. Made in U.S. by Knight's Mfg.Co.
Price: $1,595.00

STONER SR-25 MATCH RIFLE
Caliber: 7.62 NATO, 10-shot steel magazine, 5-shot optional. **Barrel:** 24" heavy match; 1:11.25" twist. **Weight:** 10.75 lbs. **Length:** 44" overall. **Stock:** Black synthetic AR-15A2 design. Full floating forend of Mil-spec synthetic attaches to upper receiver at a single point. **Sights:** None furnished. Has integral Weaver-style rail. Rings and iron sights optional. **Features:** Improved AR-15 trigger; AR-15-style seven-lug rotating bolt. Gas block rail mounts detachable front sight. Introduced 1993. Made in U.S. by Knight's Mfg. Co.
Price: $2,995.00
Price: SR-25 Lightweight Match (20" medium match target contour barrel, 9.5 lbs., 40" overall) $2,995.00

TANNER 50 METER FREE RIFLE
Caliber: 22 LR, single shot. **Barrel:** 27.7". **Weight:** 13.9 lbs. **Length:** 44.4" overall. **Stock:** Seasoned walnut with palm rest, accessory rail, adjustable hook buttplate. **Sights:** Globe front with interchangeable inserts, Tanner micrometer-diopter rear with adjustable aperture. **Features:** Bolt action with externally adjustable set trigger. Supplied with 50-meter test target. Imported from Switzerland by Mandall Shooting Supplies. Introduced 1984.
Price: About $3,900.00

TANNER STANDARD UIT RIFLE
Caliber: 308, 7.5mm Swiss, 10-shot. **Barrel:** 25.9". **Weight:** 10.5 lbs. **Length:** 40.6" overall. **Stock:** Match style of seasoned nutwood with accessory rail; coarsely stippled pistol grip; high cheekpiece; vented forend. **Sights:** Globe front with interchangeable inserts, Tanner micrometer-diopter rear with adjustable aperture. **Features:** Two locking lug revolving bolt encloses case head. Trigger adjustable from 1/2 to 6-1/2 lbs.; match trigger optional. Comes with 300-meter test target. Imported from Switzerland by Mandall Shooting Supplies. Introduced 1984.
Price: About $4,700.00

TANNER 300 METER FREE RIFLE
Caliber: 308 Win., 7.5 Swiss, single shot. **Barrel:** 27.58". **Weight:** 15 lbs. **Length:** 45.3" overall. **Stock:** Seasoned walnut, thumbhole style, with accessory rail, palm rest, adjustable hook butt. **Sights:** Globe front with interchangeable inserts, Tanner-design micrometer-diopter rear with adjustable aperture. **Features:** Three-lug revolving-lock bolt design; adjustable set trigger; short firing pin travel; supplied with 300-meter test target. Imported from Switzerland by Mandall Shooting Supplies. Introduced 1984.
Price: About $4,900.00

TIKKA SPORTER RIFLE
Caliber: 223, 22-250, 308, detachable 5-shot magazine. **Barrel:** 23-1/2" heavy. **Weight:** 9 lbs. **Length:** 43-5/8" overall. **Stock:** European walnut with adjustable comb, adjustable buttplate; stippled grip and forend. **Sights:** None furnished; drilled and tapped for scope mounting. **Features:** Buttplate is adjustable for distance, angle, height and pitch; adjustable trigger; free-floating barrel. Introduced 1998. Imported from Finland by Beretta USA.
Price: $939.00

SHOTGUNS — AUTOLOADERS

Includes a wide variety of sporting guns and guns suitable for various competitions.

Benelli Legacy

Benelli M1 Super 90 Camouflage

Benelli Super Black Eagle

BENELLI LEGACY SHOTGUN
Gauge: 12, 20, 3" chamber. **Barrel:** 26", 28" (Full, Mod., Imp. Cyl., Imp. Mod., Skeet choke tubes). Mid-bead sight. **Weight:** 7.1 to 7.6 lbs. **Length:** 49-5/8" overall (26" barrel). **Stock:** European walnut with high-gloss finish. Special competition stock comes with drop adjustment kit. **Features:** Uses the rotating bolt inertia recoil operating system with a two-piece steel/aluminum etched receiver (bright on lower, blue upper). Drop adjustment kit allows the stock to be custom fitted without modifying the stock. Black lower receiver finish, blued upper. Introduced 1998. Imported from Italy by Heckler & Koch, Inc.
Price: $1,350.00

Benelli Limited Edition Legacy
Similar to the Legacy model except receiver has gold-filled, etched game scenes and limited to 250 12 gauge (28" barrel) and 250 20 gauge (26" barrel) guns to commemorate the year 2000.
Price: $1,600.00

Benelli Sport Shotgun
Similar to the Legacy model except has matte blue receiver, two carbon fiber interchangeable ventilated ribs, adjustable butt pad, adjustable buttstock, and functions with ultra-light target loads. Walnut stock with satin finish. Introduced 1997. Imported from Italy by Benelli U.S.A.
Price: $1,340.00

BENELLI M1 FIELD AUTO SHOTGUN
Gauge: 12, 3" chamber. **Barrel:** 21", 24", 26", 28" (choke tubes). **Weight:** 7 lbs., 4 oz. **Stock:** High impact polymer; wood on 26", 28". **Sights:** Metal bead front. **Features:** Sporting version of the military & police gun. Uses the rotating Montefeltro bolt system. Ventilated rib; blue finish. Comes with set of five choke tubes. Imported from Italy by Benelli U.S.A.
Price: $920.00
Price: Wood stock version $935.00
Price: 24" rifled barrel, polymer stock........ $1,000.00
Price: 24" rifled barrel, camo stock $1,100.00
Price: Synthetic stock, left-hand version (24", 26", 28" brls) $935.00
Price: Camo Stock, left-hand version (24", 26", 28" brls.) $1,025.00

Benelli Montefeltro 90 Shotgun
Similar to the M1 Super 90 except has checkered walnut stock with high-gloss finish. Uses the Montefeltro rotating bolt system with a simple inertia recoil design. Full, Imp. Mod, Mod., Imp. Cyl. choke tubes. Weighs 6.8-7.1 lbs. Finish is matte black. Introduced 1987.
Price: 24", 26", 28" $940.00
Price: Left-hand, 26", 28" $960.00

Benelli Montefeltro 20 gauge Shotgun
Similar to the 12 gauge Montefeltro except chambered for 3" 20 gauge, 24" or 26" barrel (choke tubes), weighs 5-1/2 lbs., has drop-adjustable walnut stock with satin or camo finish, blued receiver. Overall length 47.5". Introduced 1993. Imported from Italy by Benelli U.S.A.
Price: 26" barrels $940.00
Price: 26", camouflage finish $1,040.00
Price: Montefeltro Short Stock, 24" and 26" brls. $975.00

BENELLI SUPER BLACK EAGLE SHOTGUN
Gauge: 12, 3-1/2" chamber. **Barrel:** 24", 26", 28" (Cyl. Imp. Cyl., Mod., Imp. Mod., Full choke tubes). **Weight:** 7 lbs., 5 oz. **Length:** 49-5/8" overall (28" barrel). **Stock:** European walnut with satin finish, or polymer. Adjustable for drop. **Sights:** Bead front. **Features:** Uses Montefeltro inertia recoil bolt system. Fires all 12 gauge shells from 2-3/4" to 3-1/2" magnums. Introduced 1991. Imported from Italy by Benelli U.S.A.
Price: With 26" and 28" barrel, wood stock $1,240.00
Price: With 24", 26" and 28" barrel, polymer stock......... $1,220.00
Price: Left-hand, 24", 26", 28", polymer stock $1,250.00
Price: Left-hand, 24", 26", 28", camo stock $1,330.00

Benelli Super Black Eagle Slug Gun
Similar to the Benelli Super Black Eagle except has 24" rifled barrel with 3" chamber, and drilled and tapped for scope. Uses the inertia recoil bolt system. Matte-finish receiver. Weight is 7.5 lbs., overall length 45.5". Wood or polymer stocks available. Introduced 1992. Imported from Italy by Benelli U.S.A.
Price: With wood stock $1,280.00
Price: With polymer stock $1,270.00
Price: 26" barrels $1,390.00

Benelli Executive Series Shotguns
Similar to the Super Black Eagle except has grayed steel lower receiver, hand-engraved and gold inlaid (Grade III), and has highest grade of walnut stock with drop adjustment kit. Barrel lengths 26" or 28"; 3" chamber. Special order only. Introduced 1995. Imported from Italy by Benelli U.S.A.
Price: Grade I (engraved game scenes) $5,035.00
Price: Grade II (game scenes with scroll engraving) $5,720.00
Price: Grade III (full coverage, gold inlays) $6,670.00

SHOTGUNS — AUTOLOADERS

Beretta Urika Gold Sporting

Beretta Urika Sporting

Beretta Urika Gold Trap

BERETTA AL391 URIKA AUTO SHOTGUNS
Gauge: 12, 20 gauge; 3" chamber. **Barrel:** 22", 24", 26", 28", 30"; five Mobilchoke choke tubes. **Weight:** 5.95 to 7.28 lbs. **Length:** Varies by model. **Stock:** Walnut, black or camo synthetic; shims, spacers and interchangeable recoil pads allow custom fit. **Features:** Self-compensating gas operation handles full range of loads; recoil reducer in receiver; enlarged trigger guard; reduced-weight receiver, barrel and forend; hard-chromed bore. Introduced 2000. Imported from Italy by Beretta USA.
Price: AL391 Urika (12 ga., 26", 28", 30" barrels) $984.00
Price: AL391 Urika (20 ga., 24", 26", 28" barrels) $984.00
Price: AL391 Urika Synthetic (12 ga., 24", 26", 28", 30" barrels) $984.00
Price: AL391 Urika Camo. (12 ga., Realtree Hardwoods
or Advantage Wetlands) $1,083.00

Beretta AL391 Urika Gold and Gold Sporting Auto Shotguns
Similar to AL391 Urika except features deluxe wood, jeweled bolt and carrier, gold-inlaid receiver with black or silver finish. Introduced 2000. Imported from Italy by Beretta USA.
Price: AL391 Urika Gold (12 or 20 ga., black receiver) $1,180.00
Price: AL391 Urika Gold (silver, lightweight receiver). $1,217.00
Price: AL391 Urika Gold Sporting (12 or 20, black receiver, engraving)
. . . . $1,224.00
Price: AL391 Urika Gold Sporting (12 ga., silver receiver, engraving)
. . . . $1,260.00

Beretta AL391 Urika Sporting Auto Shotguns
Similar to AL391 Urika except has competition sporting stock with rounded rubber recoil pad, wide ventilated rib with white front and mid-rib beads, satin-black receiver with silver markings. Available in 12 and 20 gauge. Introduced 2000. Imported from Italy by Beretta USA.
Price: AL391 Urika Sporting. $1,027.00

Beretta AL391 Urika Trap and Gold Trap Auto Shotguns
Similar to AL391 Urika except in 12 ga. only, has wide ventilated rib with white front and mid-rib beads, Monte Carlo stock and special trap recoil pad. Gold Trap features highly figured walnut stock and forend, gold-filled Beretta logo and signature on receiver. Introduced 2000. Imported from Italy by Beretta USA.
Price: AL391 Urika Trap $1,027.00
Price: AL391 Urika Gold Trap $1,224.00

Beretta AL391 Urika Parallel Target RL and SL Auto Shotguns
Similar to AL391 Urika except has parallel-comb, Monte Carlo stock with tighter grip radius to reduce trigger reach and stepped ventilated rib. SL model has same features but with 13.5" length of pull stock. Introduced 2000. Imported from Italy by Beretta USA.
Price: AL391 Urika Parallel Target RL $1,027.00
Price: AL391 Urika Parallel Target SL $1,027.00

Beretta AL391 Urika Youth Shotgun
Similar to AL391 except has a 24" or 26" barrel with 13.5" stock for youth and smaller shooters. Introduced 2000. From Beretta USA.
Price: $960.00

BERETTA ES100 NWTF SPECIAL AUTO SHOTGUN
Gauge: 12, 3" chamber. **Barrel:** 24", MC3 tubes and Briley extended Extra-Full Turkey. **Weight:** 7.3 lbs. **Stock:** Synthetic, checkered. **Sights:** Truglo fiber optic front and rear three-dot system. **Features:** Short recoil inertia operation. Mossy Oak Break-Up camouflage finish on stock and forend, black matte finish on all metal. Comes with camouflage sling. Introduced 1999. Imported from Italy by Beretta U.S.A.
Price: $945.00

Beretta ES 100 Auto Shotguns
Similar to the ES 100 MWTF model except offered with walnut, black synthetic or camouflage stock and fully rifled slug barrel model. Recoil-operated action. Imported from Italy by Beretta U.S.A.
Price: ES 100 Pintail (24", 26" or 28" bbl., black synthetic stock) . $757.00
Price: ES 100 Camouflage (28" bbl., Advantage Wetlands camo stock)
. . . . $757.00
Price: ES 100 Rifled Slug (24" rifled slug barrel, black syn. stock) $899.00
Price: ES 100 Rifled Slug Combo (24" rifled and 28" smoothbore bbls.)
. . . . $1,047.00

BROWNING GOLD HUNTER AUTO SHOTGUN
Gauge: 12, 3" or 3-1/2" chamber; 20, 3" chamber. **Barrel:** 12 ga.—26", 28", 30", Invector Plus choke tubes; 20 ga.—26", 30", Invector choke tubes. **Weight:** 7 lbs., 9 oz. (12 ga.), 6 lbs., 12 oz. (20 ga.). **Length:** 46-1/4" overall (20 ga., 26" barrel). **Stock:** 14"x1-1/2"x2-1/3"; select walnut with gloss finish; palm swell grip. **Features:** Self-regulating, self-cleaning gas system shoots all loads; lightweight receiver with special non-glare deep black finish; large reversible safety button; large rounded trigger guard, gold trigger. The 20 gauge has slightly smaller dimensions; 12 gauge have back-bored barrels, Invector Plus tube system. Introduced 1994. Imported by Browning.
Price: 12 or 20 gauge, 3" chamber. $894.00
Price: 12 ga., 3-1/2" chamber. $1,038.00
Price: Extra barrels. . . . . $336.00 to $415.00

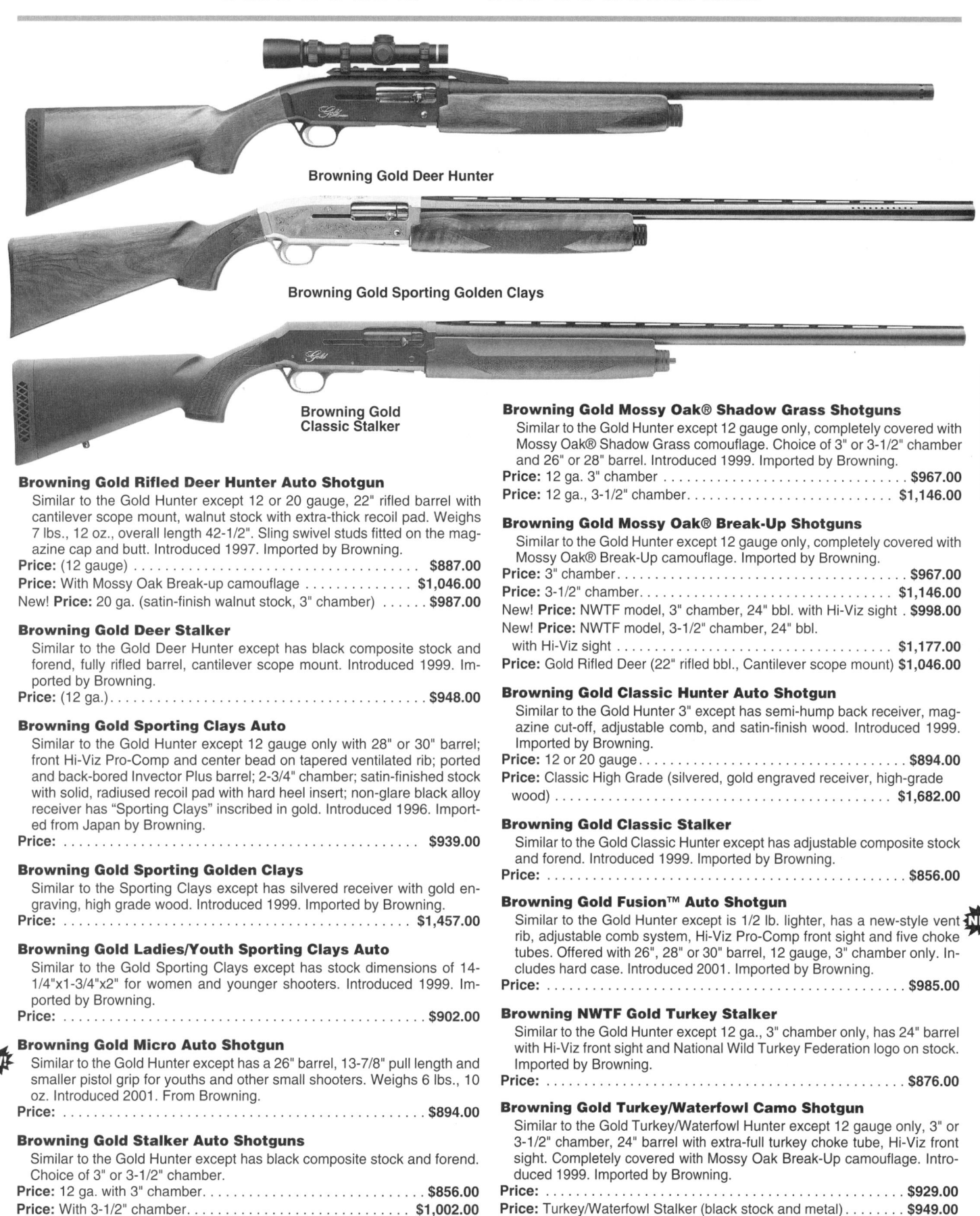

SHOTGUNS — AUTOLOADERS

Browning Gold Deer Hunter

Browning Gold Sporting Golden Clays

Browning Gold Classic Stalker

Browning Gold Rifled Deer Hunter Auto Shotgun
Similar to the Gold Hunter except 12 or 20 gauge, 22" rifled barrel with cantilever scope mount, walnut stock with extra-thick recoil pad. Weighs 7 lbs., 12 oz., overall length 42-1/2". Sling swivel studs fitted on the magazine cap and butt. Introduced 1997. Imported by Browning.
Price: (12 gauge) **$887.00**
Price: With Mossy Oak Break-up camouflage **$1,046.00**
New! Price: 20 ga. (satin-finish walnut stock, 3" chamber) **$987.00**

Browning Gold Deer Stalker
Similar to the Gold Deer Hunter except has black composite stock and forend, fully rifled barrel, cantilever scope mount. Introduced 1999. Imported by Browning.
Price: (12 ga.) **$948.00**

Browning Gold Sporting Clays Auto
Similar to the Gold Hunter except 12 gauge only with 28" or 30" barrel; front Hi-Viz Pro-Comp and center bead on tapered ventilated rib; ported and back-bored Invector Plus barrel; 2-3/4" chamber; satin-finished stock with solid, radiused recoil pad with hard heel insert; non-glare black alloy receiver has "Sporting Clays" inscribed in gold. Introduced 1996. Imported from Japan by Browning.
Price: **$939.00**

Browning Gold Sporting Golden Clays
Similar to the Sporting Clays except has silvered receiver with gold engraving, high grade wood. Introduced 1999. Imported by Browning.
Price: **$1,457.00**

Browning Gold Ladies/Youth Sporting Clays Auto
Similar to the Gold Sporting Clays except has stock dimensions of 14-1/4"x1-3/4"x2" for women and younger shooters. Introduced 1999. Imported by Browning.
Price: **$902.00**

Browning Gold Micro Auto Shotgun
Similar to the Gold Hunter except has a 26" barrel, 13-7/8" pull length and smaller pistol grip for youths and other small shooters. Weighs 6 lbs., 10 oz. Introduced 2001. From Browning.
Price: **$894.00**

Browning Gold Stalker Auto Shotguns
Similar to the Gold Hunter except has black composite stock and forend. Choice of 3" or 3-1/2" chamber.
Price: 12 ga. with 3" chamber **$856.00**
Price: With 3-1/2" chamber **$1,002.00**

Browning Gold Mossy Oak® Shadow Grass Shotguns
Similar to the Gold Hunter except 12 gauge only, completely covered with Mossy Oak® Shadow Grass comouflage. Choice of 3" or 3-1/2" chamber and 26" or 28" barrel. Introduced 1999. Imported by Browning.
Price: 12 ga. 3" chamber **$967.00**
Price: 12 ga., 3-1/2" chamber **$1,146.00**

Browning Gold Mossy Oak® Break-Up Shotguns
Similar to the Gold Hunter except 12 gauge only, completely covered with Mossy Oak® Break-up camouflage. Imported by Browning.
Price: 3" chamber **$967.00**
Price: 3-1/2" chamber **$1,146.00**
New! Price: NWTF model, 3" chamber, 24" bbl. with Hi-Viz sight . **$998.00**
New! Price: NWTF model, 3-1/2" chamber, 24" bbl. with Hi-Viz sight **$1,177.00**
Price: Gold Rifled Deer (22" rifled bbl., Cantilever scope mount) **$1,046.00**

Browning Gold Classic Hunter Auto Shotgun
Similar to the Gold Hunter 3" except has semi-hump back receiver, magazine cut-off, adjustable comb, and satin-finish wood. Introduced 1999. Imported by Browning.
Price: 12 or 20 gauge **$894.00**
Price: Classic High Grade (silvered, gold engraved receiver, high-grade wood) **$1,682.00**

Browning Gold Classic Stalker
Similar to the Gold Classic Hunter except has adjustable composite stock and forend. Introduced 1999. Imported by Browning.
Price: **$856.00**

Browning Gold Fusion™ Auto Shotgun
Similar to the Gold Hunter except is 1/2 lb. lighter, has a new-style vent rib, adjustable comb system, Hi-Viz Pro-Comp front sight and five choke tubes. Offered with 26", 28" or 30" barrel, 12 gauge, 3" chamber only. Includes hard case. Introduced 2001.
Price: **$985.00**

Browning NWTF Gold Turkey Stalker
Similar to the Gold Hunter except 12 ga., 3" chamber only, has 24" barrel with Hi-Viz front sight and National Wild Turkey Federation logo on stock. Imported by Browning.
Price: **$876.00**

Browning Gold Turkey/Waterfowl Camo Shotgun
Similar to the Gold Turkey/Waterfowl Hunter except 12 gauge only, 3" or 3-1/2" chamber, 24" barrel with extra-full turkey choke tube, Hi-Viz front sight. Completely covered with Mossy Oak Break-Up camouflage. Introduced 1999. Imported by Browning.
Price: **$929.00**
Price: Turkey/Waterfowl Stalker (black stock and metal) **$949.00**

SHOTGUNS — AUTOLOADERS

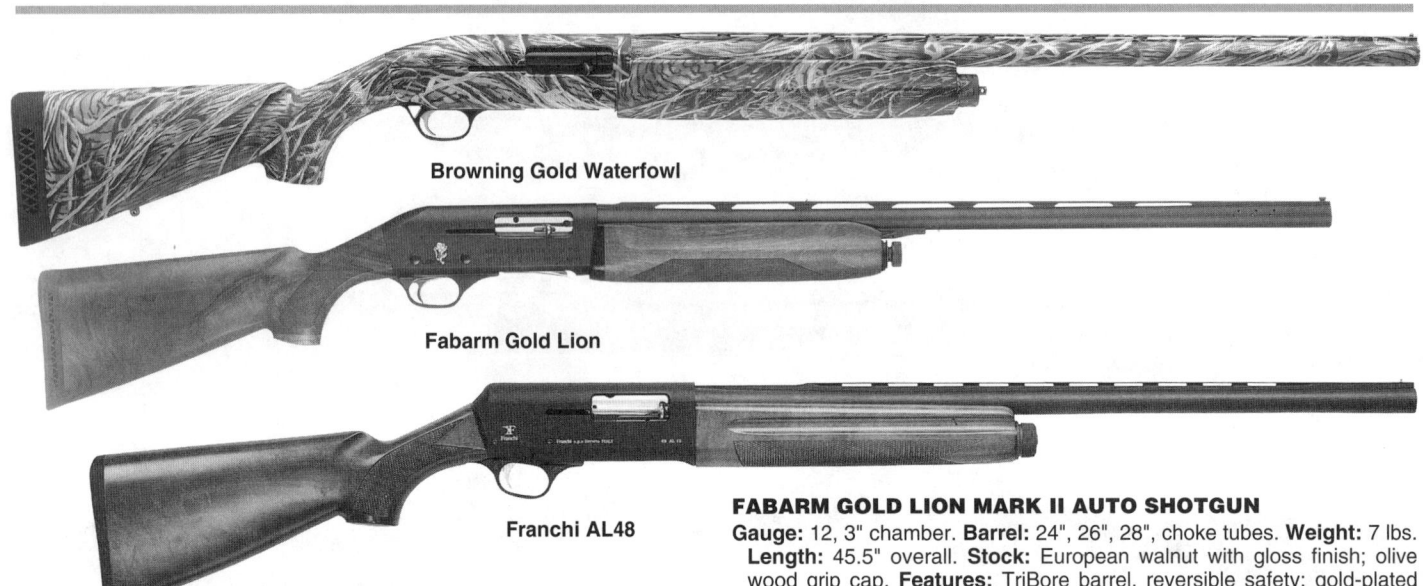

Browning Gold Waterfowl

Fabarm Gold Lion

Franchi AL48

Browning Gold NWTF Turkey Series Camo Shotgun
Similar to the Gold Turkey/Waterfowl model except 10- or 12-gauge (3" or 3-1/2" chamber), 24" barrel with extra-full choke tube, Hi-Viz fiber-optic sights and complete gun coverage in Mossy Oak Break-Up camouflage with National Wild Turkey Federation logo on stock. Introduced 2001. From Browning.
Price: 10 gauge $1,249.00
Price: 12 gauge, 3-1/2" chamber $1,177.00
Price: 12 gauge, 3" chamber $998.00

Browning Gold Upland Special Auto Shotgun
Similar to the Gold Classic Hunter except has straight-grip walnut stock, 12 or 20 gauge, 3" chamber. Introduced 2001. From Browning
Price: 12-gauge model (24" bbl., weighs 7 lbs.) $894.00
Price: 20-gauge model (26" bbl., weighs 6 lbs., 12 oz.) $894.00

BROWNING GOLD 10 AUTO SHOTGUN
Gauge: 10, 3-1/2" chamber, 5-shot magazine. **Barrel:** 26", 28", 30" (Imp. Cyl., Mod., Full standard Invector). **Weight:** 10 lbs. 7 oz. (28" barrel). **Stock:** 14-3/8"x1-1/2"x2-3/8". Select walnut with gloss finish; cut checkering, recoil pad. **Features:** Short-stroke, gas-operated action, cross-bolt safety. Forged steel receiver with polished blue finish. Introduced 1993. Imported by Browning.
Price: $1,007.95
Price: Extra barrel $293.00

Browning Gold 10 Gauge Auto Combo
Similar to the Gold 10 except comes with 24" and 26" barrels with Imp. Cyl., Mod., Full Invector choke tubes. Introduced 1999. Imported by Browning.
Price: $1,059.00

Browning Gold Light 10 Gauge Auto Shotgun
Similar to the Browning Gold 10, except has an alloy receiver that is 1 lb. lighter than standard model. Offered in 26" or 28" bbls. With Mossy Oak Break-Up or Shadow Grass coverage; 5-shot magazine. Weighs 9 lbs., 10 oz. (28" bbl.). Introduced 2001. Imported by Browning.
Price: $1,224.00
Price: Gold Light 10 Stalker (black composite stock and forearm)
.... $1,155.00

EAA/BAIKAL MP-153 AUTO SHOTGUN
Gauge: 12, 3-1/2" chamber. **Barrel:** 18-1/2", 20", 24", 26", 28"; imp., mod. and full choke tubes. **Weight:** 7.8 lbs. **Stock:** Walnut. **Features:** Gas-operated action with automatic gas-adjustment valve allows use of light and heavy loads interchangeably; 4-round magazine; rubber recoil pad. Introduced 2000. Imported by European American Armory.
Price: MP-153 (blued finish, walnut stock and forend) $459.00

FABARM GOLD LION MARK II AUTO SHOTGUN
Gauge: 12, 3" chamber. **Barrel:** 24", 26", 28", choke tubes. **Weight:** 7 lbs. **Length:** 45.5" overall. **Stock:** European walnut with gloss finish; olive wood grip cap. **Features:** TriBore barrel, reversible safety; gold-plated trigger and carrier release button; leather-covered rubber recoil pad. Introduced 1998. Imported from Italy by Heckler & Koch, Inc.
Price: $849.00

Fabarm Camo Lion Auto Shotgun
Similar to the Gold Lion except has 24", 26" or 28" ported TriBore barrel system with five choke tubes, and is completely covered with Wetlands camouflage pattern. Has red front sight bead and mid-rib bead. Introduced 1999. Imported from Italy by Heckler & Koch, Inc.
Price: $979.00

Fabarm Sporting Clays Extra Auto Shotgun
Similar to the Gold Lion except has 28" TriBore ported barrel with interchangeable colored front-sight beads, mid-rib bead, 10mm channeled vent rib, carbon-fiber finish, oil-finished walnut stock and forend with olive wood grip-cap. Stock dimensions are 14.58"x1.58"x2.44". Has distinctive gold-colored receiver logo. Available in 12 gauge only, 3" chamber. Introduced 1999. Imported from Italy by Heckler & Koch, Inc.
Price: $1,249.00

FRANCHI AL 48 SHOTGUN
Gauge: 12, 20 or 28, 2-3/4" chamber. **Barrel:** 24", 26", 28" (Franchoke cyl. imp. cyl., mod., choke tubes). **Weight:** 5.5 lbs. (20 gauge). **Length:** NA **Stock:** 14-1/4"x1-5/8"x2-1/2". Walnut with checkered grip and forend. **Features:** Recoil-operated action. Chrome-lined bore; cross-bolt safety. Imported from Italy by Benelli U.S.A.
Price: 12 ga. $630.00
Price: 20 ga. $613.00
Price: 28 ga. $680.00

Franchi AL 48 Deluxe Shotgun
Similar to AL 48 but with select walnut stock and forend and high-polish blue finish. Introduced 2000.
Price: (20 gauge, 26" barrel) $710.00
Price: (28 gauge, 26" barrel) $680.00

Franchi AL 48 Short Stock Shotgun
Similar to AL 48 but with stock shortened to 12-1/2" length of pull.
Price: (20 gauge, 26" barrel) $594.00

FRANCHI VARIOPRESS 612 SHOTGUN
Gauge: 12, 3" chamber. **Barrel:** 24", 26", 28", Franchoke tubes. **Weight:** 7 lbs., 2 oz. **Length:** 47-1/2" overall. **Stock:** 14-1/4"x1-1/2"x2-1/2". European walnut. **Features:** Alloy frame with matte black finish; gas-operated with Variopress System; four-lug rotating bolt; loaded chamber indicator. Introduced 1996. Imported from Italy by Benelli U.S.A.
Price: $595.00
Price: Camo (Advantage camo) $657.00
Price: Synthetic (black synthetic stock, forend) $579.00
Price: (20 gauge, 24", 26", 28") $595.00
Price: Variopress 620 (Advantage camo) $657.00

260 • GUNS ILLUSTRATED

SHOTGUNS — AUTOLOADERS

Remington Model 11-87 Premier

Remington Model 11-87 SPS Camo

Remington Model 11-87 SPS-T Turkey Camo

Franchi Variopress 612 Defense Shotgun
Similar to Variopress 612 except has 18-1/2 ", cylinder-bore barrel with black, synthetic stock. Available in 12 gauge, 3" chamber only. Weighs 6-1/2 pounds. Introduced 2000.
Price: $520.00

Franchi Variopress 612 Sporting Shotgun
Similar to Variopress 612 except has 30" ported barrel to reduce muzzle jump. Available in 12 gauge, 3" chamber only. Introduced 2000.
Price: $900.00

Franchi Variopress 620 Short Stock Shotgun
Similar to Variopress 620 but with stock shortened to 12-1/2 "length of pull for smaller shooters. Introduced 2000.
Price: (20 gauge, 26" barrel) $605.00

LUGER ULTRA LIGHT SEMI-AUTOMATIC SHOTGUNS
Gauge: 12, 3" and 3-1/2" chambers. **Barrel:** 26", 28"; Imp. cyl., mod. and full choke tubes. **Weight:** 6-1/2 lbs. **Length:** 48" overall (28" barrel) **Stock:** Gloss-finish European walnut, checkered grip and forend. **Features:** Gas-operated action handles 2-3/4" and 3" loads; chrome-line barrel handles steel shot; blued finish. Introduced 2000. From Stoeger Industries.
Price: $479.00

REMINGTON MODEL 11-87 PREMIER SHOTGUN
Gauge: 12, 20, 3" chamber. **Barrel:** 26", 28", 30" Rem Choke tubes. Light Contour barrel. **Weight:** About 7-3/4 lbs. **Length:** 46" overall (26" bbl.). **Stock:** Walnut with satin or high-gloss finish; cut checkering; solid brown buttpad; no white spacers. **Sights:** Bradley-type white-faced front, metal bead middle. **Features:** Pressure compensating gas system allows shooting 2-3/4" or 3" loads interchangeably with no adjustments. Stainless magazine tube; redesigned feed latch, barrel support ring on operating bars; pinned forend. Introduced 1987.
Price: $756.00
Price: Left-hand $809.00
Price: Premier Cantilever Deer Barrel, sling, swivels, Monte Carlo stock $836.00

Remington Model 11-87 Special Purpose Magnum
Similar to the 11-87 Premier except has dull stock finish, Parkerized exposed metal surfaces. Bolt and carrier have dull blackened coloring. Comes with 26" or 28" barrel with Rem Chokes, padded Cordura nylon sling and quick detachable swivels. Introduced 1987.
Price: $756.00
Price: With synthetic stock and forend (SPS). $756.00

Remington Model 11-87 SPS Special Purpose Synthetic Camo
Similar to the 11-87 Special Purpose Magnum except has synthetic stock and all metal (except bolt and trigger guard) and stock covered with Mossy Oak Break-Up camo finish. In 12 gauge only, 26", Rem Choke. Comes with camo sling, swivels. Introduced 1992.
Price: $869.00

Remington Model 11-87 SPS-T Turkey Camo
Similar to the 11-87 Special Purpose Magnum except with synthetic stock, 21" vent. rib barrel with Rem Choke tube. Completely covered with Mossy Oak Break-Up Brown camouflage. Bolt body, trigger guard and recoil pad are non-reflective black.
Price: $869.00
Price: Model 11-87 SPS-T RS/TG (TruGlo fiber optics sights) . . . $808.00
Price: Model 11-87 SPS-T Camo CL/RD (Leupold/Gilmore red dot sight) $1,193.00

Remington Model 11-87 SPS-T Super Magnum Synthetic Camo
Similar to the 11-87 SPS-T Turkey Camo except has 23" vent rib barrel with Rem Choke tube, chambered for 12 ga., 3-1/2". Introduced 2001.
Price: $935.00

Remington Model 11-87 SPS-Deer Shotgun
Similar to the 11-87 Special Purpose Camo except has fully-rifled 21" barrel with rifle sights, black non-reflective, synthetic stock and forend, black carrying sling. Introduced 1993.
Price: $789.00
Price: With wood stock (Model 11-87 SP Deer gun) Rem choke, 21" barrel w/rifle sights $736.00

Remington Model 11-87 SPS Cantilever Shotgun
Similar to the 11-87 SPS except has fully rifled barrel; synthetic stock with Monte Carlo comb; cantilever scope mount deer barrel. Comes with sling and swivels. Introduced 1994.
Price: $836.00

SHOTGUNS — AUTOLOADERS

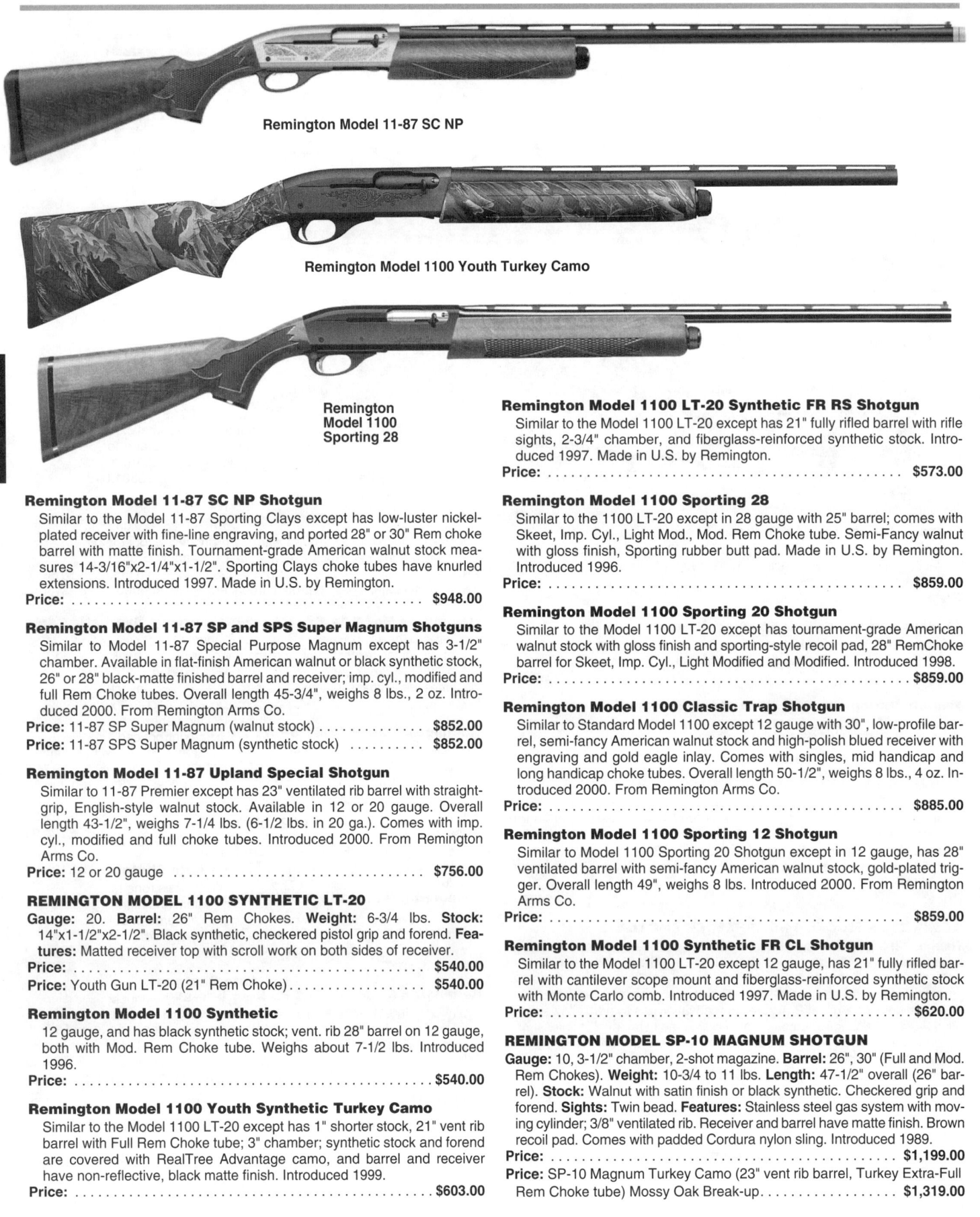

Remington Model 11-87 SC NP

Remington Model 1100 Youth Turkey Camo

Remington Model 1100 Sporting 28

Remington Model 11-87 SC NP Shotgun
Similar to the Model 11-87 Sporting Clays except has low-luster nickel-plated receiver with fine-line engraving, and ported 28" or 30" Rem choke barrel with matte finish. Tournament-grade American walnut stock measures 14-3/16"x2-1/4"x1-1/2". Sporting Clays choke tubes have knurled extensions. Introduced 1997. Made in U.S. by Remington.
Price: $948.00

Remington Model 11-87 SP and SPS Super Magnum Shotguns
Similar to Model 11-87 Special Purpose Magnum except has 3-1/2" chamber. Available in flat-finish American walnut or black synthetic stock, 26" or 28" black-matte finished barrel and receiver; imp. cyl., modified and full Rem Choke tubes. Overall length 45-3/4", weighs 8 lbs., 2 oz. Introduced 2000. From Remington Arms Co.
Price: 11-87 SP Super Magnum (walnut stock) $852.00
Price: 11-87 SPS Super Magnum (synthetic stock) $852.00

Remington Model 11-87 Upland Special Shotgun
Similar to 11-87 Premier except has 23" ventilated rib barrel with straight-grip, English-style walnut stock. Available in 12 or 20 gauge. Overall length 43-1/2", weighs 7-1/4 lbs. (6-1/2 lbs. in 20 ga.). Comes with imp. cyl., modified and full choke tubes. Introduced 2000. From Remington Arms Co.
Price: 12 or 20 gauge $756.00

REMINGTON MODEL 1100 SYNTHETIC LT-20
Gauge: 20. **Barrel:** 26" Rem Chokes. **Weight:** 6-3/4 lbs. **Stock:** 14"x1-1/2"x2-1/2". Black synthetic, checkered pistol grip and forend. **Features:** Matted receiver top with scroll work on both sides of receiver.
Price: $540.00
Price: Youth Gun LT-20 (21" Rem Choke) $540.00

Remington Model 1100 Synthetic
12 gauge, and has black synthetic stock; vent. rib 28" barrel on 12 gauge, both with Mod. Rem Choke tube. Weighs about 7-1/2 lbs. Introduced 1996.
Price: $540.00

Remington Model 1100 Youth Synthetic Turkey Camo
Similar to the Model 1100 LT-20 except has 1" shorter stock, 21" vent rib barrel with Full Rem Choke tube; 3" chamber; synthetic stock and forend are covered with RealTree Advantage camo, and barrel and receiver have non-reflective, black matte finish. Introduced 1999.
Price: $603.00

Remington Model 1100 LT-20 Synthetic FR RS Shotgun
Similar to the Model 1100 LT-20 except has 21" fully rifled barrel with rifle sights, 2-3/4" chamber, and fiberglass-reinforced synthetic stock. Introduced 1997. Made in U.S. by Remington.
Price: $573.00

Remington Model 1100 Sporting 28
Similar to the 1100 LT-20 except in 28 gauge with 25" barrel; comes with Skeet, Imp. Cyl., Light Mod., Mod. Rem Choke tube. Semi-Fancy walnut with gloss finish, Sporting rubber butt pad. Made in U.S. by Remington. Introduced 1996.
Price: $859.00

Remington Model 1100 Sporting 20 Shotgun
Similar to the Model 1100 LT-20 except has tournament-grade American walnut stock with gloss finish and sporting-style recoil pad, 28" RemChoke barrel for Skeet, Imp. Cyl., Light Modified and Modified. Introduced 1998.
Price: $859.00

Remington Model 1100 Classic Trap Shotgun
Similar to Standard Model 1100 except 12 gauge with 30", low-profile barrel, semi-fancy American walnut stock and high-polish blued receiver with engraving and gold eagle inlay. Comes with singles, mid handicap and long handicap choke tubes. Overall length 50-1/2", weighs 8 lbs., 4 oz. Introduced 2000. From Remington Arms Co.
Price: $885.00

Remington Model 1100 Sporting 12 Shotgun
Similar to Model 1100 Sporting 20 Shotgun except in 12 gauge, has 28" ventilated barrel with semi-fancy American walnut stock, gold-plated trigger. Overall length 49", weighs 8 lbs. Introduced 2000. From Remington Arms Co.
Price: $859.00

Remington Model 1100 Synthetic FR CL Shotgun
Similar to the Model 1100 LT-20 except 12 gauge, has 21" fully rifled barrel with cantilever scope mount and fiberglass-reinforced synthetic stock with Monte Carlo comb. Introduced 1997. Made in U.S. by Remington.
Price: $620.00

REMINGTON MODEL SP-10 MAGNUM SHOTGUN
Gauge: 10, 3-1/2" chamber, 2-shot magazine. **Barrel:** 26", 30" (Full and Mod. Rem Chokes). **Weight:** 10-3/4 to 11 lbs. **Length:** 47-1/2" overall (26" barrel). **Stock:** Walnut with satin finish or black synthetic. Checkered grip and forend. **Sights:** Twin bead. **Features:** Stainless steel gas system with moving cylinder; 3/8" ventilated rib. Receiver and barrel have matte finish. Brown recoil pad. Comes with padded Cordura nylon sling. Introduced 1989.
Price: $1,199.00
Price: SP-10 Magnum Turkey Camo (23" vent rib barrel, Turkey Extra-Full Rem Choke tube) Mossy Oak Break-up. $1,319.00

SHOTGUNS — AUTOLOADERS

Remington SP-10 NWTF

Weatherby SAS

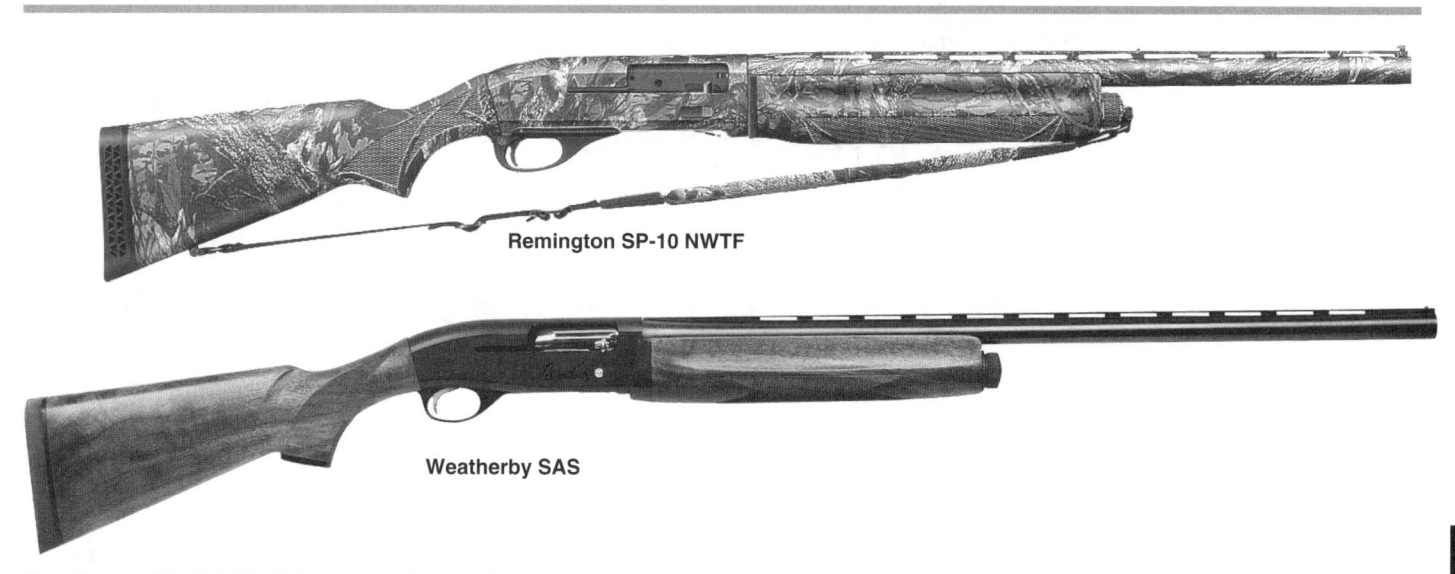

Remington Model SP-10 Magnum Camo Shotgun
Similar to the SP-10 Magnum except buttstock, forend, receiver, barrel and magazine cap are covered with Mossy Oak Break-Up camo finish; bolt body and trigger guard have matte black finish. Rem Choke tube, 26" vent. rib barrel with mid-rib bead and Bradley-style front sight, swivel studs and quick-detachable swivels, and a non-slip Cordura carrying sling in the same camo pattern. Introduced 1993.
Price: $1,319.00
Price: SP-10 Magnum Synthetic. $1,199.00

SARSILMAZ SEMI-AUTOMATIC SHOTGUN
Gauge: 12, 3" chamber. **Barrel:** 26" or 28"; fixed chokes. **Weight:** NA. **Length:** NA. **Stock:** Walnut or synthetic. **Features:** Handles 2-3/4" or 3" magnum loads. Introduced 2000. Imported from Turkey by Armsport Inc.
Price: With walnut stock $969.95
Price: With synthetic stock $919.95

TRADITIONS ALS 2100 SERIES SEMI-AUTOMATIC SHOTGUNS
Gauge: 12, 3" chamber; 20, 3" chamber. **Barrel:** 24", 26", 28" (Imp. Cyl., Mod. and Full choke tubes). **Weight:** 5 lbs., 10 oz. to 6 lbs., 5 oz. **Length:** 44" to 48" overall. **Stock:** Walnut or black composite. **Features:** Gas-operated; vent-rib barrelwith Beretta-style threaded muzzle. Introduced 2001 by Traditions.
Price: (12 or 20 ga., 26" or 28" barrel with walnut stock) $469.00
Price: (12 or 20 ga., 24" barrel Youth Model with walnut stock). . . $469.00
Price: (12 or 20 ga., 26" or 28" barrel with composite stock) $439.00

TRADITIONS ALS 2100 TURKEY SEMI-AUTOMATIC SHOTGUN
Similar to ALS 2100 field models above, except chambered in 12 gauge, 3" only with 21" barrel and Mossy Oak® Break Up™ camo finish. Weighs 6 lbs., 1 oz.; 41" overall.
Price: $509.00

TRADITIONS ALS 2100 WATERFOWL SEMI-AUTOMATIC SHOTGUN
Similar to ALS 2100 field models above, except chambered in 12 gauge, 3" only with 28" barrel and Advantage® Wetlands™ camo finish. Weighs 6 lbs., 5 oz.; 48" overall.
Price: $509.00

TRISTAR PHANTOM AUTO SHOTGUNS
Gauge: 12, 3", 3-1/2" chamber. **Barrel:** 24", 26", 28" (Imp. Cyl., Mod., Full choke tubes). **Stock:** European walnut or black synthetic. **Features:** Gas-operated action; blued barrel; checkered pistol grip and forend; vent rib barrel. Introduced 1999. Imported by Tristar Sporting Arms Ltd.
Price: . . . . $381.00 to $499.00

WEATHERBY SAS AUTO SHOTGUN
Gauge: 12, 20, 2-3/4" or 3" chamber. **Barrel:** 26", 28" (20 ga.); 26", 28", 30" (12 ga.); Briley Multi-Choke tubes. **Weight:** 6-3/4 to 7-3/4 lbs. **Stock:** 14-1/4"x2-1/4"x1-1/2". Claro walnut; black, Shadow Grass or Mossy Oak Break-Up camo synthetic. **Features:** Alloy receiver with matte finish; gold-plated trigger; magazine cut-off. Introduced 1999. Imported by Weatherby.
Price: 12 or 20 ga. (walnut stock). $945.00
Price: 12 or 20 ga. (black synthetic stock) $979.00
Price: 12 ga. (camo stock) $1,115.00

WINCHESTER SUPER X2 AUTO SHOTGUN
Gauge: 12, 3", 3-1/2" chamber. **Barrel:** 24", 26", 28"; Invector Plus choke tubes. **Weight:** 7-1/4 to 7-1/2 lbs. **Stock:** 14-1/4"x1-3/4"x2". Walnut or black synthetic. **Features:** Gas-operated action shoots all loads without adjustment; vent. rib barrels; 4-shot magazine. Introduced 1999. Made in U.S. by U.S. Repeating Arms Co.
Price: Field, walnut or synthetic stock, 3". $819.00
Price: Magnum, 3-1/2", synthetic stock, 26" or 28" bbl. $936.00
Price: Camo Waterfowl, 3-1/2", Mossy Oak Shadow Grass. . . . $1,080.00
New! Price: NWTF Turkey, 3-1/2", black synthetic stock, 24" bbl. . $997.00
New! Price: NWTF Turkey, 3-1/2", Mossy Oak Break-Up camo $1,080.00

Winchester Super X2 Sporting Clays Auto Shotgun
Similar to the Super X2 except has two gas pistons (one for target loads, one for heavy 3" loads), adjustable comb system and high-post rib. Back-bored barrel with Invector Plus choke tubes. Offered in 28" and 30" barrels. Introduced 2001. From U.S. Repeating Arms Co.
Price: Super X2 Sporting Clays $1,206.00

Winchester Super X2 Field 3" Auto Shotgun
Similar to the Super X2 except has a 3" chamber, walnut stock and forearm and high-profile rib. Back-bored barrel and Invector Plus choke tubes. Introduced 2001. From U.S. Repeating Arms Co.
Price: Super X2 Field 3", 26" or 28" bbl.. . . . . $819.00

SHOTGUNS — SLIDE & LEVER ACTIONS

Includes a wide variety of sporting guns and guns suitable for competitive shooting.

Armscor M-30F Field

Benelli Nova Pump

Benelli Nova Pump Rifled Slug

Browning BPS 10 gauge

ARMSCOR M-30F FIELD PUMP SHOTGUN
Gauge: 12, 3" chamber. **Barrel:** 28" fixed Mod., or with Mod. and Full choke tubes. **Weight:** 7.6 lbs. **Stock:** Walnut-finished hardwood. **Features:** Double action slide bars; blued steel receiver; damascened bolt. Introduced 1996. Imported from the Philippines by K.B.I., Inc.
Price: With fixed choke $239.00
Price: With choke tubes $269.00

BENELLI NOVA PUMP SHOTGUN
Gauge: 12, 3-1/2" chamber. **Barrel:** 24", 26", 28"; chrome lined, vent rib; choke tubes. **Weight:** 8 lbs. **Length:** 47.5" overall. **Stock:** Black polymer. **Features:** Montefeltro rotating bolt design with dual action bars; magazine cut-0ff; synthetic trigger assembly. Four-shot magazine Introduced 1999. Imported from Italy by Benelli USA.
Price: With black stock $390.00
Price: With Camo finish $456.00

Benelli Nova Pump Slug Gun
Similar to the Nova except has 18.5" barrel with adjustable rifle-type or ghost ring sights; weighs 7.2 lbs.; black synthetic stock. Introduced 1999. Imported from Italy by Benelli USA.
Price: With rifle sights. $320.00
Price: With ghost-ring sights $355.00

Benelli Nova Pump Rifled Slug Gun
Similar to Nova Pump Slug Gun except has 24" barrel and rifled bore; open rifle sights; synthetic stock; weighs 8.1 pounds.
Price: $544.00

BROWNING BPS PUMP SHOTGUN
Gauge: 10, 12, 3-1/2" chamber; 12 or 20, 3" chamber (2-3/4" in target guns), 28, 2-3/4" chamber, 5-shot magazine, 410 ga., 3" chamber. **Barrel:** 10 ga.— 24" Buck Special, 28", 30", 32" Invector; 12, 20 ga.—22", 24", 26", 28", 30", 32" (Imp. Cyl., mod. or full). 410 ga.—26" barrel. (Imp. Cyl., mod. and full choke tubes.) Also available with Invector choke tubes, 12 or 20 ga.; Upland Special has 22" barrel with Invector tubes. BPS 3" and 3-1/2" have back-bored barrel. **Weight:** 7 lbs., 8 oz. (28" barrel). **Length:** 48-3/4" overall (28" barrel). **Stock:** 14-1/4"x1-1/2"x2-1/2". Select walnut, semi-beavertail forend, full pistol grip stock. **Features:** All 12 gauge 3" guns except Buck Special and game guns have back-bored barrels with Invector Plus choke tubes. Bottom feeding and ejection, receiver top safety, high post vent. rib. Double action bars eliminate binding. Vent. rib barrels only. All 12 and 20 gauge guns with 3" chamber available with fully engraved receiver flats at no extra cost. Each gauge has its own unique game scene. Introduced 1977. Imported from Japan by Browning.
Price: 10 ga., Hunter, Invector $552.00
Price: 12 ga., 3-1/2" Magnum Hunter, Invector Plus $552.00
Price: 12 ga., 3-1/2" Magnum Stalker (black syn. stock) $537.00
Price: 12, 20 ga., Hunter, Invector Plus $464.00
Price: 12 ga. Deer Hunter (22" rifled bbl., cantilever mount) $568.00
Price: 28 ga., Hunter, Invector $495.00
Price: 410 ga., Hunter, Invector $495.00

Browning BPS 10 Gauge Shotguns
Chambered for the 10 gauge, 3-1/2" load. Offered in 24", 26" and 28" barrels. Offered with walnut, black composite (Stalker models) or camouflage stock and forend. Introduced 1999. Imported by Browning.
Price: Hunter (walnut). $552.00
Price: Stalker (composite) $537.00
Price: Mossy Oak® Shadow Grass or Break-Up Camo $617.00

Browning BPS 10 gauge Camo Pump
Similar to the BPS 10 gauge Hunter except completely covered with Mossy Oak Shadow Grass camouflage. Available with 24", 26", 28" barrel. Introduced 1999. Imported by Browning.
Price: $602.00

Browning BPS Waterfowl Camo Pump Shotgun
Similar to the BPS Hunter except completely covered with Mossy Oak Shadow Grass camouflage. Available in 12 gauge, with 24", 26" or 28" barrel, 3" chamber. Introduced 1999. Imported by Browning.
Price: $514.00

SHOTGUNS — SLIDE & LEVER ACTIONS

Fabarm Field Pump

Ithaca Model 37 Turkeyslayer

Browning BPS Game Gun Deer Hunter
Similar to the standard BPS except has newly designed receiver/magazine tube/barrel mounting system to eliminate play, heavy 20.5" barrel with rifle-type sights with adjustable rear, solid receiver scope mount, "rifle" stock dimensions for scope or open sights, sling swivel studs. Gloss or matte finished wood with checkering, polished blue metal. Introduced 1992.
Price: $568.00

Browning BPS Game Gun Turkey Special
Similar to the standard BPS except has satin-finished walnut stock and dull-finished barrel and receiver. Receiver is drilled and tapped for scope mounting. Rifle-style stock dimensions and swivel studs. Has Extra-Full Turkey choke tube. Introduced 1992.
Price: $500.00

Browning BPS Stalker Pump Shotgun
Same gun as the standard BPS except all exposed metal parts have a matte blued finish and the stock has a durable black finish with a black recoil pad. Available in 10 ga. (3-1/2") and 12 ga. with 3" or 3-1/2" chamber, 22", 28", 30" barrel with Invector choke system. Introduced 1987.
Price: 12 ga., 3" chamber, Invector Plus $448.00
Price: 10, 12 ga., 3-1/2" chamber. $537.00

Browning BPS NWTF Turkey Series Pump Shotgun
Similar to the BPS Stalker except has full coverage Mossy Oak® Break-Up camo finish on synthetic stock, forearm and exposed metal parts. Offered in 10 and 12 gauge, 3" or 3-1/2" chamber; 24" bbl. has extra-full choke tube and Hi-Viz fiber optic sights. Introduced 2001. From Browning.
Price: 10 ga., 3-1/2" chamber. $637.00
Price: 12 ga., 3-1/2" chamber. $637.00
Price: 12 ga., 3" chamber. $549.00

Browning BPS Micro Pump Shotgun
Same as BPS Upland Special except 20 ga. only, 22" Invector barrel, stock has pistol grip with recoil pad. Length of pull is 13-1/4"; weighs 6 lbs., 12 oz. Introduced 1986.
Price: $464.00

EAA/BAIKAL MP-133 PUMP SHOTGUN
Gauge: 12, 3-1/2" chamber. Barrel: 18-1/2", 20", 24", 26", 28"; imp., mod. and full choke tubes. Weight: NA. Stock: Walnut; checkered grip and grooved forearm. Features: Hammer-forged, chrome-lined barrel with ventilated rib; machined steel parts; dual action bars; trigger-block safety; 4-shot magazine tube; handles 2-3/4" through 3-1/2" shells. Introduced 2000. Imported by European American Armory.
Price: MP-133 (blued finish, walnut stock and forend). $279.00

FABARM FIELD PUMP SHOTGUN
Gauge: 12, 3" chamber. Barrel: 28" (24" rifled slug barrel available). Weight: 6.6 lbs. Length: 48.25" overall. Stock: Polymer. Features: Similar to Fabarm FP6 Pump Shotgun. Alloy receiver; twin action bars; available in black or Mossy Oak Break-Up™ camo finish. Includes cyl., mod. and full choke tubes. Introduced 2001. Imported from Italy by Heckler & Koch Inc.
Price: Matte black finish $399.00
Price: Mossy Oak Break-Up™ finish $469.00

ITHACA MODEL 37 DELUXE PUMP SHOTGUN
Gauge: 12, 16, 20, 3" chamber. Barrel: 26", 28", 30" (12 gauge), 26", 28" (16 and 20 gauge), choke tubes. Weight: 7 lbs. Stock: Walnut with cut-checkered grip and forend. Features: Steel receiver; bottom ejection; brushed blue finish, vent rib barrels. Reintroduced 1996. Made in U.S. by Ithaca Gun Co.
Price: $545.95
Price: With straight English-style stock $545.95
Price: Model 37 New Classic (ringtail forend, sunburst recoil pad, hand-finished walnut stock, 26" or 28" barrel) $695.95

Ithaca Model 37 Waterfowler
Similar to the Model 37 Deluxe except in 12 gauge only with 28" barrel, special extended steel shot choke tube system. Complete coverage of Advantage Wetlands couflage. Introduced 1999. Made in U.S. by Ithaca Gun Co.
Price: $595.00

Ithaca Model 37 Turkeyslayer Pump Shotgun
Similar to the Model 37 Deluxe except has 22" barrel with rifle sights, extended ported choke tube and full-coverage, Realtree Advantage, Realtree All-Purpose Brown, All-Purpose Grey, or Xtra Brown camouflage finish. Introduced 1996. Made in U.S. by Ithaca Gun Co.
Price: 12 ga. only $569.95
Price: Youth Turkeyslayer (20 gauge, 6.5 lbs., shorter stock) $569.95

ITHACA MODEL 37 DEERSLAYER II PUMP SHOTGUN
Gauge: 12, 20, 3" chamber. Barrel: 20", 25", fully rifled. Weight: 7 lbs. Stock: Cut-checkered American walnut with Monte Carlo comb. Sights: Rifle-type. Features: Integral barrel and receiver. Bottom ejection. Brushed blue finish. Reintroduced 1997. Made in U.S. by Ithaca Gun Co.
Price: $565.95
Price: Smooth Bore Deluxe $515.95
Price: Rifled Deluxe $515.95

Ithaca Model 37 Hardwoods 20/2000 Deerslayer
Similar to the Model 37 Deerslayer II except has synthetic stock and forend, and has the Truglo Fibre Optic sight system. Drilled and tapped for scope mounting. Complete coverage of RealTree 20/2000 Hardwoods camouflage. Introduced 1999. Made in U.S. by Ithaca Gun Co.
Price: $565.95

Ithaca Model 37 Hardwoods 20/2000 Turkeyslayer
Similar to the Model 37 Turkeyslayer except has synthetic stock and forend, Extra-Full extended and ported choke tube, long forcing cone, and Truglo Fibre Optic sight system. Complete coverage of RealTree Hardwoods 20/2000 camouflage. Introduced 1999. Made in U.S. by Ithaca Gun Co.
Price: $565.95

MOSSBERG MODEL 835 ULTI-MAG PUMP
Gauge: 12, 3-1/2" chamber. Barrel: Ported 24" rifled bore, 24", 28", Accu-Mag choke tubes for steel or lead shot. Weight: 7-3/4 lbs. Length: 48-1/2" overall. Stock: 14"x1-1/2"x2-1/2". Dual Comb. Cut-checkered hardwood or camo synthetic; both have recoil pad. Sights: White bead front, brass mid-bead; Fiber Optic. Features: Shoots 2-3/4", 3" or 3-1/2" shells. Back-bored and ported barrel to reduce recoil, improve patterns. Ambidextrous thumb safety, twin extractors, dual slide bars. Mossberg Cablelock included. Introduced 1988.

Shotguns — Slide & Lever Actions

Mossberg Model 835 Shadowgrass

Mossberg Model 500 Sporting

Mossberg Model 500 Trophy Slugster

Price: 28" vent. rib, hardwood stock $370.00
Price: Combo, 24" rifled bore, rifle sights, 24" vent. rib, Accu-Mag choke tube, Woodlands camo finish $572.00
Price: RealTree Camo Turkey, 24" vent. rib, Accu-Mag Extra-Full tube, synthetic stock $525.00
Price: Mossy Oak Camo, 28" vent. rib, Accu-Mag tubes, synthetic stock $583.00
Price: OFM Camo, 28" vent. rib, Accu-Mag Mod. tube, synthetic stock $407.00

Mossberg Model 835 Synthetic Stock
Similar to the Model 835, except with 28" ported barrel with Accu-Mag Mod. choke tube, Parkerized finish, black synthetic stock and forend. Introduced 1998. Made in U.S. by Mossberg.
Price: $370.00

MOSSBERG MODEL 500 SPORTING PUMP
Gauge: 12, 20, 410, 3" chamber. **Barrel:** 18-1/2" to 28" with fixed or Accu-Choke, plain or vent. rib. **Weight:** 6-1/4 lbs. (410), 7-1/4 lbs. (12). **Length:** 48" overall (28" barrel). **Stock:** 14"x1-1/2"x2-1/2". Walnut-stained hardwood. Cut-checkered grip and forend. **Sights:** White bead front, brass mid-bead; Fiber Optic. **Features:** Ambidextrous thumb safety, twin extractors, disconnecting safety, dual action bars. Quiet Carry forend. Many barrels are ported. Mossberg Cablelock included. From Mossberg.
Price: From about $301.00
Price: Sporting Combos (field barrel and Slugster barrel), from . . $403.00

Mossberg Model 500 Bantam Pump
Same as the Model 500 Sporting Pump except 12 (new for 2001) or 20 gauge, 22" vent. rib Accu-Choke barrel with choke tube set; has 1" shorter stock, reduced length from pistol grip to trigger, reduced forend reach. Introduced 1992.
Price: $301.00
Price: With full Woodlands camouflage finish (20 ga. only) $384.00

Mossberg Model 500 Camo Pump
Same as the Model 500 Sporting Pump except 12 gauge only and entire gun is covered with special camouflage finish. Receiver drilled and tapped for scope mounting. Comes with quick detachable swivel studs, swivels, camouflage sling, Mossberg Cablelock.
Price: From about $370.00

Mossberg Model 500 Persuader/Cruiser Shotguns
Similar to Mossberg Model 500 except has 18-1/2" or 20" barrel with cylinder bore choke, synthetic stock and blue or parkerized finish. Available in 12, 20 and 410 gauge with bead or ghost ring sights, 6- or 8-shot magazines. From Mossberg.
Price: 12 gauge, 20" barrel, 8-shot, bead sight. $308.00
Price: 20 or 410 gauge, 18-1/2" barrel, 6-shot, bead sight $329.00
Price: 12 gauge, parkerized finish, 6-shot, 18-1/2" barrel, ghost ring sights $437.00
Price: Home Security 410 (410 gauge, 18-1/2" barrel with spreader choke) $335.00

Mossberg Model 590 Special Purpose Shotguns
Similar to Model 500 except has parkerized or Marinecote finish, 9-shot magazine and black synthetic stock (some models feature Speed Feed. Available in 12 gauge only with 20", cylinder bore barrel. Weighs 7-1/4 lbs. From Mossberg.
Price: Bead sight, heat shield over barrel $389.00
Price: Ghost ring sight, Speed Feed stock. $546.00

MOSSBERG MODEL 500 SLUGSTER
Gauge: 12, 20, 3" chamber. **Barrel:** 24", ported rifled bore. Integral scope mount. **Weight:** 7-1/4 lbs. **Length:** 44" overall. **Stock:** 14" pull, 1-3/8" drop at heel. Walnut; Dual Comb design for proper eye positioning with or without scoped barrels. Recoil pad and swivel studs. **Features:** Ambidextrous thumb safety, twin extractors, dual slide bars. Comes with scope mount. Mossberg Cablelock included. Introduced 1988.
Price: Rifled bore, with integral scope mount, Dual-Comb stock, 12 or 20 . . . . $398.00
Price: Fiber Optic, rifle sights $398.00
Price: Rifled bore, rifle sights $367.00
Price: 20 ga., Standard or Bantam, from $367.00

REMINGTON MODEL 870 WINGMASTER
Gauge: 12, 3" chamber. **Barrel:** 26", 28", 30" (Rem Chokes). Light Contour barrel. **Weight:** 7-1/4 lbs. **Length:** 46-1/2" overall (26" bbl.). **Stock:** 14"x2-1/2"x1". American walnut with satin or high-gloss finish, cut-checkered pistol grip and forend. Rubber butt pad. **Sights:** Ivory bead front, metal mid-bead. **Features:** Double action bars; cross-bolt safety; blue finish. Introduced 1986.
Price: $569.00
Price: 870 Wingmaster Super Magnum $649.00

Shotguns — Slide & Lever Actions

Remington 870 Wingmaster

Remington Model 870 Express Super Magnum

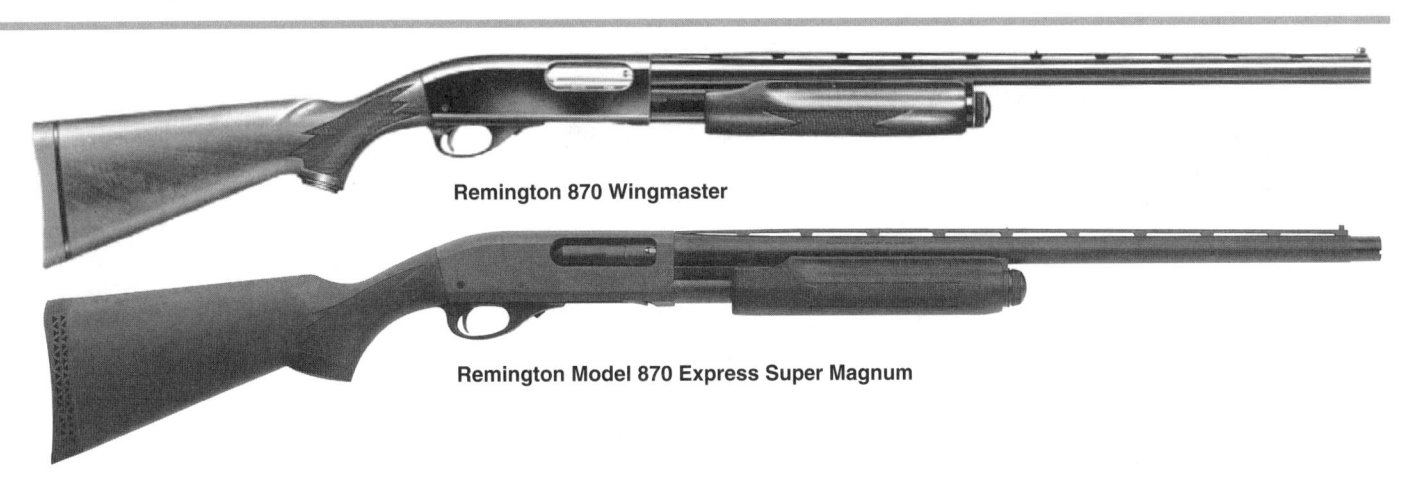

Remington Model 870 50th Anniversary Classic Trap Shotgun
Similar to Model 870 TC Wingmaster except has 30" ventilated rib with singles, mid handicap and long handicap choke tubes, semi-fancy American walnut stock and high-polish blued receiver with engraving and gold shield inlay. From Remington Arms Co.
Price: $775.00

Remington Model 870 Marine Magnum
Similar to the 870 Wingmaster except all metal is plated with electroless nickel and has black synthetic stock and forend. Has 18" plain barrel (Cyl.), bead front sight, 7-shot magazine. Introduced 1992.
Price: $545.00

Remington Model 870 Wingmaster LW 20 ga.
Similar to the Model 870 Wingmaster except in 28 gauge and 410-bore only, 25" vent rib barrel with Rem Choke tubes, high-gloss wood finish. 26" & 28" barrels-20 ga.
Price: 20 gauge $569.00
Price: 410-bore $596.00
Price: 28 gauge $649.00

Remington Model 870 Express
Similar to the 870 Wingmaster except has a walnut-toned hardwood stock with solid, black recoil pad and pressed checkering on grip and forend. Outside metal surfaces have a black oxide finish. Comes with 26" or 28" vent. rib barrel with a Mod. Rem Choke tube. Introduced 1987.
Price: 12 or 20 .... $329.00
Price: Express Combo, 12 ga., 26" vent rib with Mod. Rem Choke and 20" fully rifled barrel with rifle sights $436.00
Price: Express 20 ga., 26" or 28" with Mod. Rem Choke tubes .. $329.00
Price: Express L-H (left-hand), 12 ga., 28" vent rib with Mod. Rem Choke tube $356.00
Price: Express Synthetic, 12-ga, 26" or 28" $329.00
Price: Express Combo (20 ga.) with extra Deer rifled barrel $436.00

Remington Model 870 Express Super Magnum
Similar to the 870 Express except has 28" vent. rib barrel with 3-1/2" chamber, vented recoil pad. Introduced 1998.
Price: $369.00
Price: Super Magnum Synthetic $376.00
Price: Super Magnum Turkey Camo (Turkey Extra Full Rem Choke, full-coverage RealTree Advantage camo) $500.00
Price: Super Magnum Combo (26" with Mod. Rem Choke and 20" fully rifled deer barrel with 3" chamber and rifle sights; wood stock) $516.00
Price: Super Magnum Synthetic Turkey (black) $389.00

Remington Model 870 Wingmaster Super Magnum Shotgun
Similar to Model 870 Express Super Magnum except has high-polish blued finish, 28" ventilated barrel with imp. cyl., modified and full choke tubes, checkered high-gloss walnut stock. Overall length 48", weighs 7-1/2 lbs. Introduced 2000.
Price: $649.00

Remington Model 870 Express Youth Gun
Same as the Model 870 Express except comes with 13" length of pull, 21" barrel with Mod. Rem Choke tube. Hardwood stock with low-luster finish. Introduced 1991.
Price: 20 ga. Express Youth (1" shorter stock), from $329.00
Price: 20 ga. Youth Deer 20" FR/RS $363.00

Remington Model 870 Express Rifle-Sighted Deer Gun
Same as the Model 870 Express except comes with 20" barrel with fixed Imp. Cyl. choke, open iron sights, Monte Carlo stock. Introduced 1991.
Price: $329.00
Price: With fully rifled barrel $363.00
Price: Express Synthetic Deer (black synthetic stock, black matte metal) $369.00

Remington Model 870 Express Turkey
Same as the Model 870 Express except comes with 3" chamber, 21" vent. rib turkey barrel and Extra-Full Rem Choke Turkey tube; 12 ga. only. Introduced 1991.
Price: $343.00
Price: Express Turkey Camo stock has RealTree Advantage camo, matte black metal $396.00
Price: Express Youth Turkey camo (as above with 1" shorter length of pull) $396.00

Remington Model 870 Express Synthetic HD Home Defense
Similar to the 870 Express with 18" barrel except has synthetic stock and forend. Introduced 1994.
Price: $316.00

Remington Model 870 SPS Super Slug Deer Gun
Similar to the Model 870 Express Synthetic except has 23" rifled, modified contour barrel with cantilever scope mount. Comes with black synthetic stock and forend with swivel studs, black Cordura nylon sling. Introduced 1999. Fully rifled centilever barrel.
Price: $555.00

Remington Model 870 SPS-T Synthetic Camo Shotgun
Chambered for 12 ga., 3" shells, has Mossy Oak Break-Up® synthetic stock and metal treatment, Tru-Glo fiber optic sights. Introduced 2001.
Price: $569.00

Remington Model 870 SPS Super Magnum Camo
Has synthetic stock and all metal (except bolt and trigger guard) and stock covered with Mossy Oak Break-Up camo finish In 12 gauge 3-1/2", 26" vent. rib, Rem Choke. Comes with camo sling, swivels.
Price: $569.00
Price: Model 870 SPS-T Super Magnum Camo (3-1/2" chamber) . $569.00
Price: Model 870 SPS-T RS/TG (TruGlo fiber optics sights) $544.00
New! Price: Model 870 SPS-T Super Magnum Synthetic Camo (3-1/2" chamber, cantilever mount) $895.00
Price: Model 870 SPS-T Super Mag Camo CL/RD (Leupold/Gilmore dot sight) $889.00

SHOTGUNS — SLIDE & LEVER ACTIONS

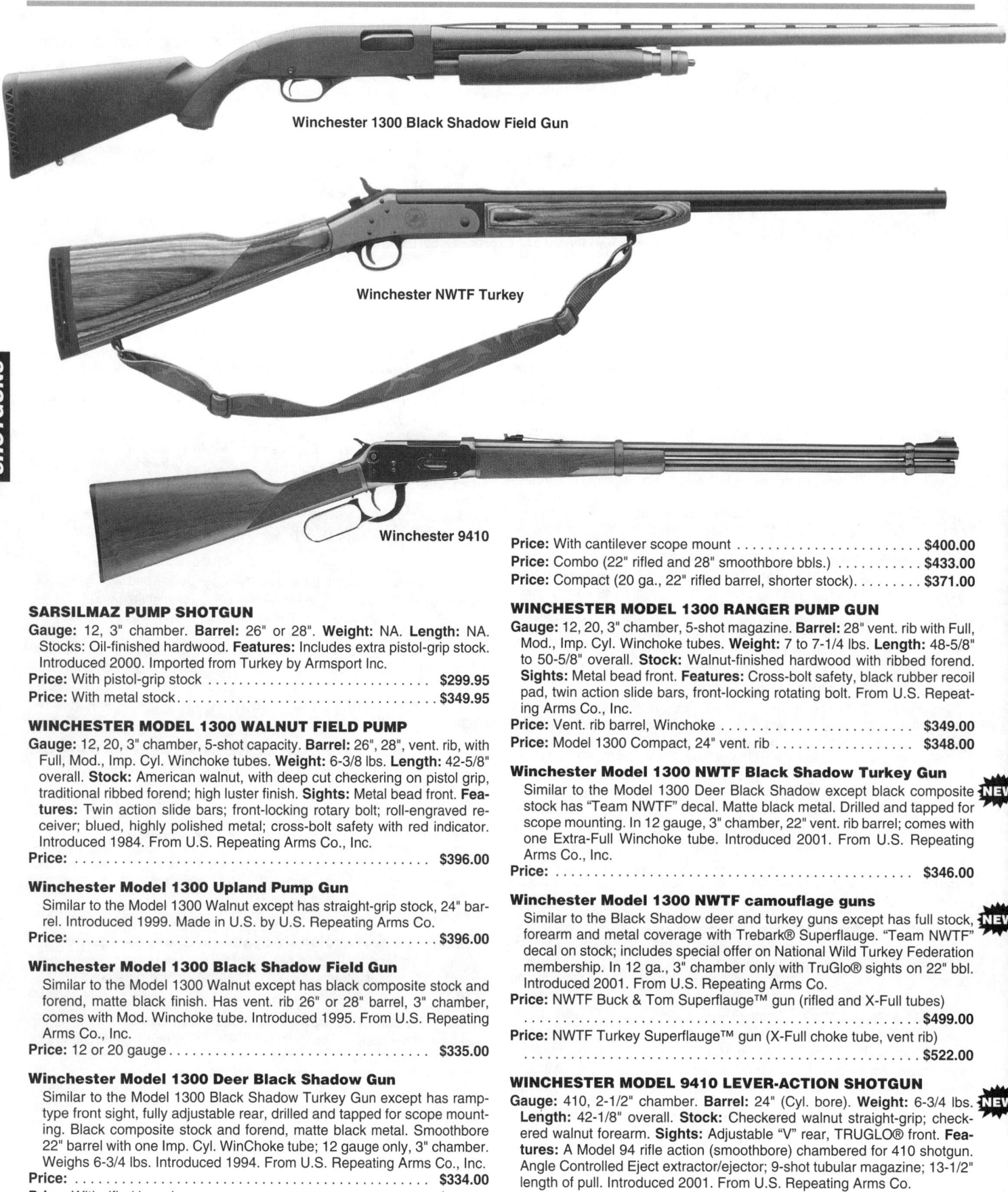

Winchester 1300 Black Shadow Field Gun

Winchester NWTF Turkey

Winchester 9410

SARSILMAZ PUMP SHOTGUN
Gauge: 12, 3" chamber. **Barrel:** 26" or 28". **Weight:** NA. **Length:** NA. **Stocks:** Oil-finished hardwood. **Features:** Includes extra pistol-grip stock. Introduced 2000. Imported from Turkey by Armsport Inc.
Price: With pistol-grip stock $299.95
Price: With metal stock $349.95

WINCHESTER MODEL 1300 WALNUT FIELD PUMP
Gauge: 12, 20, 3" chamber, 5-shot capacity. **Barrel:** 26", 28", vent. rib, with Full, Mod., Imp. Cyl. Winchoke tubes. **Weight:** 6-3/8 lbs. **Length:** 42-5/8" overall. **Stock:** American walnut, with deep cut checkering on pistol grip, traditional ribbed forend; high luster finish. **Sights:** Metal bead front. **Features:** Twin action slide bars; front-locking rotary bolt; roll-engraved receiver; blued, highly polished metal; cross-bolt safety with red indicator. Introduced 1984. From U.S. Repeating Arms Co., Inc.
Price: $396.00

Winchester Model 1300 Upland Pump Gun
Similar to the Model 1300 Walnut except has straight-grip stock, 24" barrel. Introduced 1999. Made in U.S. by U.S. Repeating Arms Co.
Price: $396.00

Winchester Model 1300 Black Shadow Field Gun
Similar to the Model 1300 Walnut except has black composite stock and forend, matte black finish. Has vent. rib 26" or 28" barrel, 3" chamber, comes with Mod. Winchoke tube. Introduced 1995. From U.S. Repeating Arms Co., Inc.
Price: 12 or 20 gauge $335.00

Winchester Model 1300 Deer Black Shadow Gun
Similar to the Model 1300 Black Shadow Turkey Gun except has ramp-type front sight, fully adjustable rear, drilled and tapped for scope mounting. Black composite stock and forend, matte black metal. Smoothbore 22" barrel with one Imp. Cyl. WinChoke tube; 12 gauge only, 3" chamber. Weighs 6-3/4 lbs. Introduced 1994. From U.S. Repeating Arms Co., Inc.
Price: $334.00
Price: With rifled barrel $359.00

Price: With cantilever scope mount $400.00
Price: Combo (22" rifled and 28" smoothbore bbls.) $433.00
Price: Compact (20 ga., 22" rifled barrel, shorter stock) $371.00

WINCHESTER MODEL 1300 RANGER PUMP GUN
Gauge: 12, 20, 3" chamber, 5-shot magazine. **Barrel:** 28" vent. rib with Full, Mod., Imp. Cyl. Winchoke tubes. **Weight:** 7 to 7-1/4 lbs. **Length:** 48-5/8" to 50-5/8" overall. **Stock:** Walnut-finished hardwood with ribbed forend. **Sights:** Metal bead front. **Features:** Cross-bolt safety, black rubber recoil pad, twin action slide bars, front-locking rotating bolt. From U.S. Repeating Arms Co., Inc.
Price: Vent. rib barrel, Winchoke $349.00
Price: Model 1300 Compact, 24" vent. rib $348.00

Winchester Model 1300 NWTF Black Shadow Turkey Gun
Similar to the Model 1300 Deer Black Shadow except black composite stock has "Team NWTF" decal. Matte black metal. Drilled and tapped for scope mounting. In 12 gauge, 3" chamber, 22" vent. rib barrel; comes with one Extra-Full Winchoke tube. Introduced 2001. From U.S. Repeating Arms Co., Inc.
Price: $346.00

Winchester Model 1300 NWTF camouflage guns
Similar to the Black Shadow deer and turkey guns except has full stock, forearm and metal coverage with Trebark® Superflauge. "Team NWTF" decal on stock; includes special offer on National Wild Turkey Federation membership. In 12 ga., 3" chamber only with TruGlo® sights on 22" bbl. Introduced 2001. From U.S. Repeating Arms Co.
Price: NWTF Buck & Tom Superflauge™ gun (rifled and X-Full tubes)
. . . . $499.00
Price: NWTF Turkey Superflauge™ gun (X-Full choke tube, vent rib)
. . . . $522.00

WINCHESTER MODEL 9410 LEVER-ACTION SHOTGUN
Gauge: 410, 2-1/2" chamber. **Barrel:** 24" (Cyl. bore). **Weight:** 6-3/4 lbs. **Length:** 42-1/8" overall. **Stock:** Checkered walnut straight-grip; checkered walnut forearm. **Sights:** Adjustable "V" rear, TRUGLO® front. **Features:** A Model 94 rifle action (smoothbore) chambered for 410 shotgun. Angle Controlled Eject extractor/ejector; 9-shot tubular magazine; 13-1/2" length of pull. Introduced 2001. From U.S. Repeating Arms Co.
Price: 9410 Lever-Action Shotgun $531.00

268 • GUNS ILLUSTRATED

SHOTGUNS — OVER/UNDERS

Includes a variety of game guns and guns for competitive shooting.

Beretta 682 Gold Skeet

Beretta 682 Gold Sporting

APOLLO TR AND TT SHOTGUNS
Gauge: 12, 20, 410, 3" chambers; 28 2-3/4" chambers. **Barrel:** 26", 28", 30", 32". **Weight:** 6 to 7-1/4 lbs. **Length:** NA. **Stock:** Oil-finished European walnut. **Features:** Boxlock action; hard-chromed bores; automatic ejectors; single selective trigger; choke tubes (12 and 20 ga. only). Introduced 2000. From Sigarms.
Price: Apollo TR 30 Field (color casehardened side plates)....$2,240.00
Price: Apollo TR 40 Gold (gold overlays on game scenes)....$2,675.00
Price: Apollo TT 25 Competition (wide vent. rib with mid-bead)....$1,995.00

BERETTA DT 10 TRIDENT SHOTGUNS
Gauge: 12, 2-3/4", 3" chambers. **Barrel:** 28", 30", 32", 34"; competition-style vent rib; fixed or Optima Choke tubes. **Weight:** 7.9 to 9 lbs. **Length:** NA. **Stock:** High-grade walnut stock with oil finish; hand-checkered grip and forend; adjustable stocks available. **Features:** Detachable, adjustable trigger group; raised and thickened receiver; forend iron has replaceable nut to guarantee wood-to-metal fit; Optima Bore to improve shot pattern and reduce felt recoil. Introduced 2000. Imported from Italy by Beretta USA.
Price: DT 10 Trident Trap (selective, lockable single trigger; adjustable stock)....$9,450.00
Price: DT 10 Trident Trap Combo (single and o/u barrels)...$11,995.00
New! Price: DT 10 Trident Trap Bottom Single Combo (adj. point of impact rib on single bbl.)....$12,270.00
Price: DT 10 Trident Skeet (skeet stock with rounded recoil pad, tapered rib)....$9,450.00
Price: DT 10 Trident Sporting (sporting clays stock with rounded recoil pad)....$9,240.00

BERETTA SERIES S682 GOLD SKEET, TRAP OVER/UNDERS
Gauge: 12, 2-3/4" chambers. **Barrel:** Skeet—28"; trap—30" and 32", Imp. Mod. & Full and Mobilchoke; trap mono shotguns—32" and 34" Mobilchoke; trap top single guns—32" and 34" Full and Mobilchoke; trap combo sets—from 30" O/U, to 32" O/U, 34" top single. **Stock:** Close-grained walnut, hand checkered. **Sights:** White Bradley bead front sight and center bead. **Features:** Receiver has Greystone gunmetal gray finish with gold accents. Trap Monte Carlo stock has deluxe trap recoil pad. Various grades available; contact Beretta USA for details. Imported from Italy by Beretta USA
Price: S682 Gold Skeet....$2,850.00
Price: S682 Gold Skeet, adjustable stock....$3,515.00
Price: S682 Gold Trap....$3,100.00
Price: S682 Gold Trap Top Combo....$4,085.00
Price: S682 Gold Trap with adjustable stock....$3,625.00
Price: S686 Silver Pigeon Trap....$1,850.00
Price: S686 Silver Pigeon Trap Top Mono....$1,850.00
Price: S686 Silver Pigeon Skeet (28")....$1,760.00
Price: S687 EELL Diamond Pigeon Trap....$4,815.00
Price: S687 EELL Diamond Pigeon Skeet....$4,790.00
Price: S687 EELL Diamond Pigeon Skeet, adjustable stock...$5,810.00
Price: S687 EELL Diamond Pigeon Trap Top Mono....$5,055.00 to $5,105.00
Price: ASE Gold Skeet....$12,060.00
Price: ASE Gold Trap....$12,145.00
Price: ASE Gold Trap Combo....$16,055.00

Beretta S682 Gold E Trap O/U
Similar to other S682 Gold models except has a select walnut stock in International style with interchangeable rubber recoil pad and beavertail forend, flat top rib with white front sight, gold non-selective single trigger. Introduced 2001. Imported from Italy by Beretta U.S.A.
Price: Gold E Trap, adj. stock....$4,320.00
Price: Gold E Skeet, adj. stock....$4,320.00
Price: Gold E Trap Combo Top (O/U and single bbls.)....$5,305.00

BERETTA MODEL S686 WHITEWING O/U
Gauge: 12, 3" chambers. **Barrel:** 26", 28", Mobilchoke tubes (Imp. Cyl., Mod., Full). **Weight:** 6.7 lbs. **Length:** 45.7" overall (28" barrels). **Stock:** 14.5"x2.2"x1.4". American walnut; radiused black buttplate. **Features:** Matte chrome finish on receiver, matte blue barrels; hard-chrome bores; low-profile receiver with dual conical locking lugs; single selective trigger; ejectors. Introduced 1999. Imported from Italy by Beretta U.S.A.
Price: $1,295.00

BERETTA S686 ONYX SPORTING O/U SHOTGUN
Gauge: 12, 3" chambers. **Barrel:** 28", 30" (Mobilchoke tubes). **Weight:** 7.7 lbs. **Stock:** Checkered American walnut. **Features:** Intended for the beginning Sporting Clays shooter. Has wide, vented 12.5mm target rib, radiused recoil pad. Polished black finish on receiver and barrels. Introduced 1993. Imported from Italy by Beretta U.S.A.
Price: $1,583.00
New! Price: With X-Tra Wood (highly figured)....$1,737.00

BERETTA ULTRALIGHT OVER/UNDER
Gauge: 12, 2-3/4" chambers. **Barrel:** 26", 28", Mobilchoke choke tubes. **Weight:** About 5 lbs., 13 oz. **Stock:** Select American walnut with checkered grip and forend. **Features:** Low-profile aluminum alloy receiver with titanium breech face insert. Electroless nickel receiver with game scene engraving. Single selective trigger; automatic safety. Introduced 1992. Imported from Italy by Beretta U.S.A.
Price: $1,795.00

Beretta Ultralight Deluxe Over/Under Shotgun
Similar to the Ultralight except has matte electroless nickel finish receiver with gold game scene engraving; matte oil-finished, select walnut stock and forend. Introduced 1999. Imported from Italy by Beretta U.S.A.
Price: $1,985.00

Shotguns — Over/Unders

Beretta Over/Under Field Shotgun

Browning Citori White Lightning

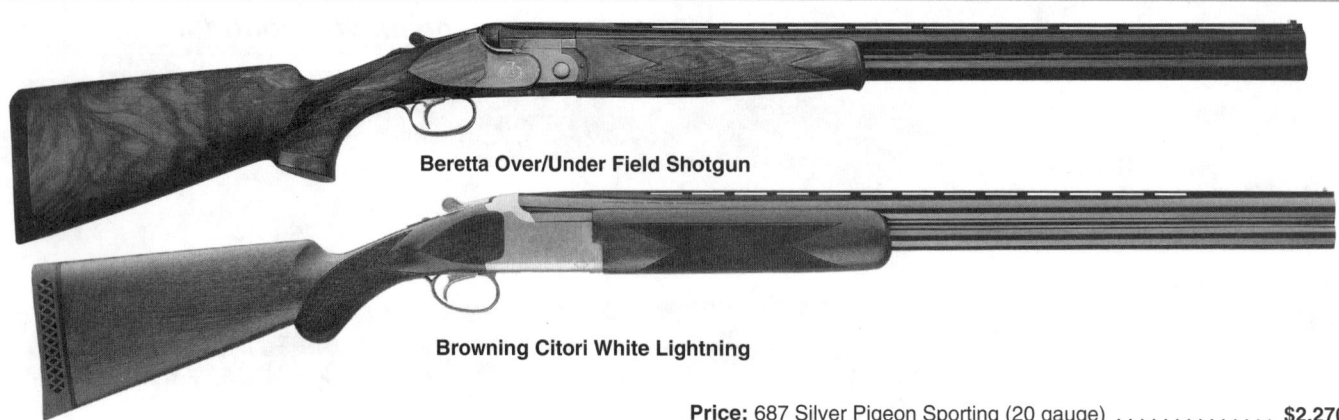

BERETTA OVER/UNDER FIELD SHOTGUNS
Gauge: 12, 20, 28, and 410 bore, 2-3/4", 3" and 3-1/2" chambers. **Barrel:** 26" and 28" (Mobilchoke tubes). **Stock:** Close-grained walnut. **Features:** Highly-figured, American walnut stocks and forends, and a unique, weather-resistant finish on barrels. The S686 Onyx bears a gold P. Beretta signature on each side of the receiver. Silver designates standard 686, 687 models with silver receivers; 686 Silver Pigeon has enhanced engraving pattern, Schnabel forend; 686 Silver Essential has matte chrome finish; Gold indicates higher grade 686EL, 687EL models with full sideplates; Diamond is for 687EELL models with highest grade wood, engraving. Case provided with Gold and Diamond grades. Silver Gold, Diamond grades introduced 1994. Imported from Italy by Beretta U.S.A.
Price: S686 Onyx $1,565.00
Price: S686 Silver Pigeon two-bbl. set $2,560.00
Price: S686 Silver Pigeon $1,869.00
Price: S687 Silver Pigeon $2,255.00
Price: S687 Silver Pigeon II (deep relief game scene engraving, oil finish wood, 12 ga. only) $2,134.00
Price: S687EL Gold Pigeon (gold inlays, sideplates) $4,099.00
Price: S687EL Gold Pigeon, 410, 26"; 28 ga., 28" $4,273.00
New! **Price:** S687 EL Gold Pigeon II (deep relief engraving) . . . $4,513.00
New! **Price:** S687 EL Gold Pigeon II Sporting (d.r. engraving) . . . $4,554.00
Price: S687EELL Diamond Pigeon (engraved sideplates) $5,540.00
Price: S687EELL Diamond Pigeon Combo, 20 and 28 ga., 26". $6,180.00

BERETTA MODEL SO5, SO6, SO9 SHOTGUNS
Gauge: 12, 2-3/4" chambers. **Barrel:** To customer specs. **Stock:** To customer specs. **Features:** SO5—Trap, Skeet and Sporting Clays models SO5; SO6—SO6 and SO6 EELL are field models. SO6 has a case-hardened or silver receiver with contour hand engraving. SO6 EELL has hand-engraved receiver in a fine floral or "fine English" pattern or game scene, with bas-relief chisel work and gold inlays. SO6 and SO6 EELL are available with sidelocks removable by hand. Imported from Italy by Beretta U.S.A.
Price: SO5 Trap, Skeet, Sporting $13,000.00
Price: SO6 Trap, Skeet, Sporting $17,500.00
Price: SO6 EELL Field, custom specs $28,000.00
Price: SO9 (12, 20, 28, 410, 26", 28", 30", any choke) $31,000.00

BERETTA SPORTING CLAYS SHOTGUNS
Gauge: 12 and 20, 2-3/4" and 3" chambers. **Barrel:** 28", 30", 32" Mobilchoke. **Stock:** Close-grained walnut. **Features:** Equipped with Beretta Mobilchoke flush-mounted screw-in choke tube system. Dual-purpose O/U for hunting and Sporting Clays.12 or 20 gauge, 28", 30" Mobilchoke tubes (four, Skeet, Imp. Cyl., Mod., Full). Wide 12.5mm top rib with 2.5mm center groove; 686 Silver Pigeon has silver receiver with scroll engraving; 687 Silver Pigeon Sporting has silver receiver, highly figured walnut; 687 EL Pigeon Sporting has game scene engraving with gold inlaid animals on full sideplate. Introduced 1994. Imported from Italy by Beretta USA.
Price: 682 Gold Sporting, 28", 30", 31" (with case) $3,100.00
Price: 682 Gold Sporting, 28", 30", ported, adj. l.o.p. $3,230.00
Price: 686 Silver Pigeon Sporting $1,931.00
Price: 686 Silver Pigeon Sporting (20 gauge) $1,931.00
New! **Price:** 686 E Sporting (enhanced styling, 5 choke tubes) . . $2,008.00
687 Silver Pigeon Sporting $2,270.00
Price: 687 Silver Pigeon Sporting (20 gauge) $2,270.00
Price: 687 Diamond Pigeon EELL Sporter (hand engraved sideplates, deluxe wood) $5,515.00
Price: ASE Gold Sporting Clay $12,145.00

Beretta S687EL Gold Pigeon Sporting O/U
Similar to the S687 Silver Pigeon Sporting except has sideplates with gold inlay game scene, vent. side and top ribs, bright orange front sight. Stock and forend are of high grade walnut with fine-line checkering. Available in 12 gauge only with 28" or 30" barrels and Mobilchoke tubes. Weight is 6 lbs., 13 oz. Introduced 1993. Imported from Italy by Beretta USA.
Price: $4,015.00

BRNO ZH 300 OVER/UNDER SHOTGUN
Gauge: 12, 2-3/4" chambers. **Barrel:** 26", 27-1/2", 29" (Skeet, Imp. Cyl., Mod., Full). **Weight:** 7 lbs. **Length:** 44.4" overall. **Stock:** European walnut. **Features:** Double triggers; automatic safety; polished blue finish engraved receiver. Announced 1998. Imported from the Czech Republic by Euro-Imports.
Price: ZH 301, field $594.00
Price: ZH 302, Skeet $608.00
Price: ZH 303, 12 ga. trap $608.00
Price: ZH 321, 16 ga. $595.00

BRNO 501.2 OVER/UNDER SHOTGUN
Gauge: 12, 2-3/4" chambers. **Barrel:** 27.5" (Full & Mod.). **Weight:** 7 lbs. **Length:** 44" overall. **Stock:** European walnut. **Features:** Boxlock action with double triggers, ejectors; automatic safety; hand-cut checkering. Announced 1998. Imported from The Czech Republic by Euro-Imports.
Price: $850.00

BROWNING CITORI O/U SHOTGUNS
Gauge: 12, 20, 28 and 410. **Barrel:** 26", 28" in 28 and 410. Offered with Invector choke tubes. All 12 and 20 gauge models have back-bored barrels and Invector Plus choke system. **Weight:** 6 lbs., 8 oz. (26" 410) to 7 lbs., 13 oz. (30" 12 ga.). **Length:** 43" overall (26" bbl.). **Stock:** Dense walnut, hand checkered, full pistol grip, beavertail forend. Field-type recoil pad on 12 ga. field guns and trap and Skeet models. **Sights:** Medium raised beads, German nickel silver. **Features:** Barrel selector integral with safety, automatic ejectors, three-piece takedown. Imported from Japan by Browning. Contact Browning for complete list of models and prices.
Price: Grade I, Hunter, Invector, 12 and 20 . . . . $1,486.00
Price: Grade I, Lightning, 28 and 410, Invector $1,594.00
Price: Grade III, Lightning, 28 and 410, Invector $2,570.00
Price: Grade VI, 28 and 410 Lightning, Invector $3,780.00
Price: Grade I, Lightning, Invector Plus, 12, 20 . . . . $1,534.00
Price: Grade I, Hunting, 28", 30" only, 3-1/2", Invector Plus . . . $1,489.00
Price: Grade III, Lightning, Invector, 12, 20 . . . . $2,300.00
Price: Grade VI, Lightning, Invector, 12, 20 . . . . $3,510.00
Price: Gran Lightning, 26", 28", Invector, 12, 20 . . . . $2,184.00
Price: Gran Lightning, 28, 410 . . . . $2,302.00
Price: Micro Lightning, 20 ga., 24" bbl., 6 lbs., 4 oz. $1,591.00
Price: White Lightning (silver nitride receiver w/engraving, 12 or 20 ga., 26", 28") $1,583.00
Price: White Lightning, 28 or 410 gauge $1,654.00
Price: Citori Satin Hunter (12 ga., satin-finished wood, matte-finished barrels and receiver) 3-1/2" chambers $1,535.00

SHOTGUNS — OVER/UNDERS

Browning Citori Ultra Sporter

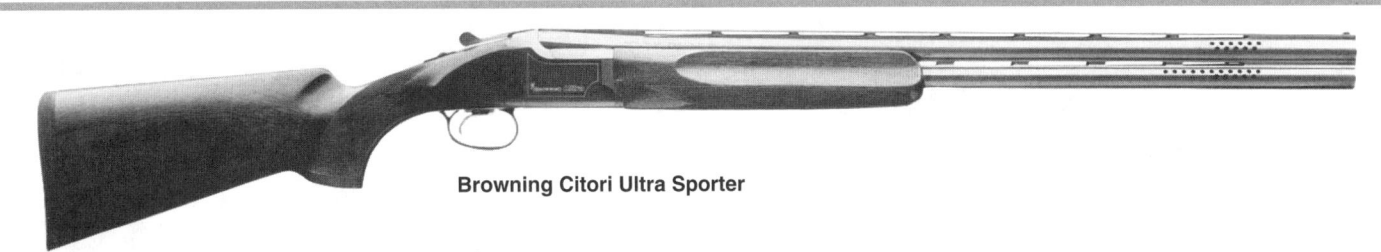

Browning Superlight Citori Over/Under
Similar to the standard Citori except available in 12, 20 with 24", 26" or 28" Invector barrels, 28 or 410 with 26" barrels choked Imp. Cyl. & Mod. or 28" choked Mod. & Full. Has straight grip stock, Schnabel forend tip. Superlight 12 weighs 6 lbs., 9 oz. (26" barrels); Superlight 20, 5 lbs., 12 oz. (26" barrels). Introduced 1982.
Price: Grade I, 28 or 410, Invector $1,666.00
Price: Grade III, Invector, 12. . . . . $2,300.00
Price: Grade VI, Invector, 12 or 20, gray or blue $3,510.00
Price: Grade VI, 28 or 410, Invector, gray or blue $3,780.00
Price: Grade I Invector, 12 or 20 . . . . $1,580.00
Price: Grade I Invector, White Upland Special (24" bbls.), 12 or 20 . . . . $1,583.00
Price: Citori Superlight Feather (12 ga., alloy receiver, 6 lbs. 4 oz.) $1,756.00

Browning Citori XT Trap Over/Under
Similar to the Citori Special Trap except has engraved silver nitride receiver with gold highlights, vented side barrel rib. Available in 12 gauge with 30" or 32" barrels, Invector-Plus choke tubes. Introduced 1999. Imported by Browning.
Price: $1,834.00
Price: With adjustable-comb stock $2,054.00

Browning Micro Citori Lightning
Similar to the standard Citori 20 ga. Lightning except scaled down for smaller shooter. Comes with 24" Invector Plus back-bored barrels, 13-3/4" length of pull. Weighs about 6 lbs., 3 oz. Introduced 1991.
Price: Grade I $1,486.00

Browning Citori Lightning Feather O/U
Similar to the 12 gauge Citori Grade I except has 2-3/4" chambers, rounded pistol grip, Lightning-style forend, and lighweight alloy receiver. Weighs 6 lbs. 15 oz. with 26" barrels (12 ga.); 6 lbs., 2 oz. (20 ga., 26" bbl.). Silvered, engraved receiver. Introduced 1999. Imported by Browning.
Price: 12 or 20 ga., 26" or 28" barrels $1,693.00
Price: Lightning Feather Combo (20 and 28 ga. bbls., 27" each) $2,751.00

Browning Citori Sporting Hunter
Similar to the Citori Hunting I except has Sporting Clays stock dimensions, a Superposed-style forend, and Sporting Clays butt pad. Available in 12 gauge with 3" chambers, back-bored 26", 28" and 30", all with Invector Plus choke tube system. Introduced 1998. Imported from Japan by Browning.
Price: 12 gauge, 3-1/2" $1,709.00
Price: 12, 20 gauge, 3" $1,607.00

Browning Citori Ultra XS Skeet
Similar to other Citori Ultra models except features a semi-beavertail forearm with deep finger grooves, ported barrels and triple system. Adjustable comb is optional. Introduced 2000.
Price: 12 ga., 28" or 30" barrel $2,162.00
New! Price: 20 ga., 28" or 30" barrel $2,162.00
Price: Adjustable comb model, 12 or 20 ga. $2,380.00

Browning Citori Ultra XS Trap
Similar to other Citori Ultra models except offered in 12 ga. only with 30" or 32" ported barrel, high-post rib, ventilated side ribs, Triple Trigger System™ and silver nitride receiver. Includes full, modified and imp. cyl. choke tubes. From Browning.
Price: 30" or 32" barrel $2,022.00
Price: Adjustable-comb model $2,265.00

Browning Citori Ultra XS Sporting
Similar to other Citori Ultra XS models except offered in 12, 20, 28 and 410 gauge. Silver nitride receiver, Schnabel forearm, ventilated side rib. Imported by Browning.
Price: 410 or 28 ga. $2,268.00
Price: 12 or 20 ga. $2,196.00

Browning Citori Feather XS Shotguns
Similar to the standard Citori except has lightweight alloy receiver, silver nitrade Nitex receiver, Schnabel forearm, ventilated side rib and Hi-Viz Comp fiber optics sight. Available in 12, 20, 28 and 410 gauges. Introduced 2000.
Price: 28" or 30" barrel . . . . $2,266.00 to $2,338.00

Browning Citori High Grade Shotguns
Similar to standard Citori except has full sideplates with engraved hunting scenes and gold inlays, high-grade, hand-oiled walnut stock and forearm. Introduced 2000. From Browning.
Price: Citori Privilege (fully embellished sideplates), 12 or 20 ga. $5,376.00
Price: Citori BG VI Lightning (gold inlays of ducks and pheasants) . . . . from $3,340.00
Price: Citori BG III Superlight (scroll engraving on grayed receiver, gold inlays) $2,190.00
Price: Citori 425 Golden Clays (engraving of game bird-clay bird transition, gold accents), 12 or 20 ga. $3,977.00

Browning Nitra Citori XS Sporting Clays
Similar to the Citori Grade I except has silver nitride receiver with gold accents, stock dimensions of 14-3/4"x1-1/2"x2-1/4" with satin finish, right-hand palm swell, Schnabel forend. Comes with Modified, Imp. Cyl. and Skeet Invector-Plus choke tubes. Back-bored barrels; vented side ribs. Introduced 1999. Imported by Browning.
Price: 12, 20 ga. $2,011.00
Price: 28 ga., 410-bore $2,077.00

Browning Special Sporting Clays
Similar to the Citori Ultra Sporter except has full pistol grip stock with palm swell, gloss finish, 28", 30" or 32" barrels with back-bored Invector Plus chokes (ported or non-ported); high post tapered rib. Also available as 28" and 30" two-barrel set. Introduced 1989.
Price: With ported barrels. $1,636.00
Price: As above, adjustable comb $1,856.00

Browning Lightning Sporting Clays
Similar to the Citori Lightning with rounded pistol grip and classic forend. Has high post tapered rib or lower hunting-style rib with 30" back-bored Invector Plus barrels, ported or non-ported, 3" chambers. Gloss stock finish, radiused recoil pad. Has "Lightning Sporting Clays Edition" engraved and gold filled on receiver. Introduced 1989.
Price: Low-rib, ported $1,691.00
Price: High-rib, ported $1,770.00

BROWNING LIGHT SPORTING 802 ES O/U
Gauge: 12, 2-3/4" chambers. **Barrel:** 28", back-bored Invector Plus. Comes with flush-mounted Imp. Cyl. and Skeet; 2" extended Imp. Cyl. and Mod.; and 4" extended Imp. Cyl. and Mod. tubes. **Weight:** 7 lbs., 5 oz. **Length:** 45" overall. **Stock:** 14-3/8" x 1/8" x 1-9/16" x 1-3/4". Select walnut with radiused solid recoil pad, Schnabel-type forend. **Features:** Trigger adjustable for length of pull; narrow 6.2mm ventilated rib; ventilated barrel side rib; blued receiver. Introduced 1996. Imported from Japan from Browning.
Price: $2,063.00

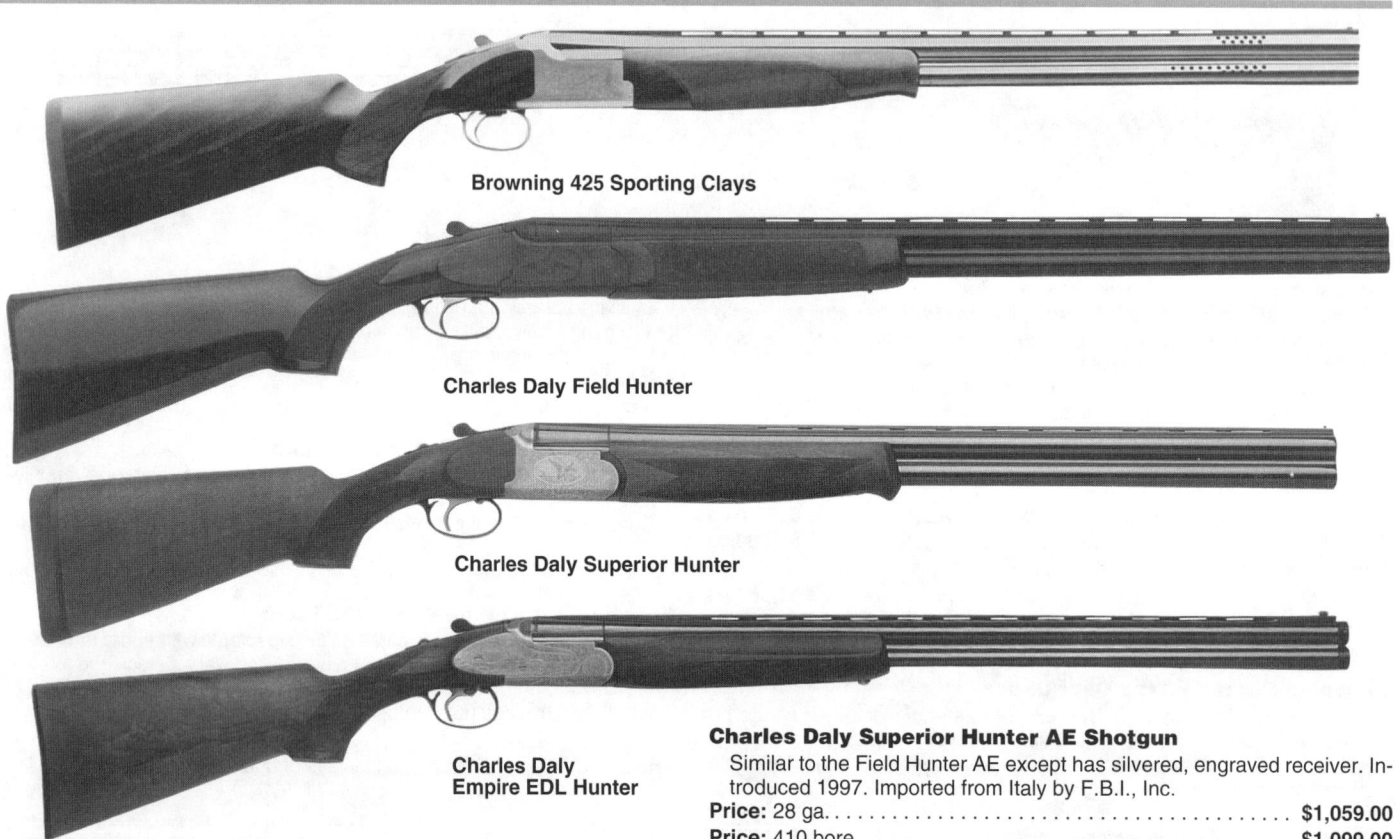

SHOTGUNS — OVER/UNDERS

Browning 425 Sporting Clays

Charles Daly Field Hunter

Charles Daly Superior Hunter

Charles Daly Empire EDL Hunter

BROWNING 425 SPORTING CLAYS
Gauge: 12, 20, 2-3/4" chambers. **Barrel:** 12 ga.—28", 30", 32" (Invector Plus tubes), back-bored; 20 ga.—28", 30" (Invector Plus tubes). **Weight:** 7 lbs., 13 oz. (12 ga., 28"). **Stock:** 14-13/16" (1/8")x1-7/16"x2-3/16" (12 ga.). Select walnut with gloss finish, cut checkering, Schnabel forend. **Features:** Grayed receiver with engraving, blued barrels. Barrels are ported on 12 gauge guns. Has low 10mm wide vent rib. Comes with three interchangeable trigger shoes to adjust length of pull. Introduced in U.S. 1993. Imported by Browning.
Price: Grade I, 12, 20 ga., Invector Plus............ $2,006.00
Price: Golden Clays, 12, 20 ga., Invector Plus............ $3,977.00

CHARLES DALY SUPERIOR TRAP AE MC
Gauge: 12, 2-3/4" chambers. **Barrel:** 30" choke tubes. **Weight:** About 7 lbs. **Stock:** Checkered walnut; pistol grip, semi-beavertail forend. **Features:** Silver engraved receiver, chrome moly steel barrels; gold single selective trigger; automatic safety, automatic ejectors; red bead front sight, metal bead center; recoil pad. Introduced 1997. Imported from Italy by K.B.I., Inc.
Price: $1,219.00

CHARLES DALY FIELD HUNTER OVER/UNDER SHOTGUN
Gauge: 12, 20, 28 and 410 bore (3" chambers, 28 ga. has 2-3/4"). **Barrel:** 28" Mod & Full, 26" Imp. Cyl. & Mod (410 is Full & Full). **Weight:** About 7 lbs. **Length:** NA. **Stock:** Checkered walnut pistol grip and forend. **Features:** Blued engraved receiver, chrome moly steel barrels; gold single selective trigger; automatic safety; extractors; gold bead front sight. Introduced 1997. Imported from Italy by K.B.I., Inc.
Price: 12 or 20 ga............ $749.00
Price: 28 ga............ $809.00
Price: 410 bore............ $849.00

Charles Daly Field Hunter AE Shotgun
Similar to the Field Hunter except 28 gauge and 410-bore only; 26" (Imp. Cyl. & Mod., 28 gauge), 26" (Full & Full, 410); automatic; ejectors. Introduced 1997. Imported from Italy by K.B.I., Inc.
Price: 28............ $889.00
Price: 410............ $929.00

Charles Daly Superior Hunter AE Shotgun
Similar to the Field Hunter AE except has silvered, engraved receiver. Introduced 1997. Imported from Italy by F.B.I., Inc.
Price: 28 ga............ $1,059.00
Price: 410 bore............ $1,099.00

Charles Daly Field Hunter AE-MC
Similar to the Field Hunter except in 12 or 20 only, 26" or 28" barrels with five multichoke tubes; automatic ejectors. Introduced 1997. Imported from Italy by K.B.I., Inc.
Price: 12 or 20............ $979.95

Charles Daly Superior Sporting O/U
Similar to the Field Hunter AE-MC except 28" or 30" barrels; silvered, engraved receiver; five choke tubes; ported barrels; red bead front sight. Introduced 1997. Imported from Italy by K.B.I., Inc.
Price: $1,259.95

CHARLES DALY EMPIRE TRAP AE MC
Gauge: 12, 2-3/4" chambers. **Barrel:** 30" choke tubes. **Weight:** About 7 lbs. **Stock:** Checkered walnut; pistol grip, semi-beavertail forend. **Features:** Silvered, engraved, reinforced receiver; chrome moly steel barrels; gold single selective trigger; automatic safety, automatic ejector; red bead front sight, metal bead center; recoil pad. Introduced 1997. Imported from Italy by K.B.I., Inc.
Price: $1,539.95

CHARLES DALY DIAMOND REGENT GTX DL HUNTER O/U
Gauge: 12, 20, 410, 3" chambers, 28, 2-3/4" chambers. **Barrel:** 26", 28", 30" (choke tubes), 26" (Imp. Cyl. & Mod. in 28, 26" (Full & Full) in 410. **Weight:** About 7 lbs. **Stock:** Extra select fancy European walnut with 24" hand checkering, hand rubbed oil finish. **Features:** Boss-type action with internal side lumps. Deep cut hand-engraved scrollwork and game scene set in full sideplates. GTX detachable single selective trigger system with coil springs; chrome moly steel barrels; automatic safety; automatic ejectors, white bead front sight, metal bead center sight. Introduced 1997. Imported from Italy by K.B.I., Inc.
Price: 12 or 20............ $22,299.00
Price: 28............ $22,369.00
Price: 410............ $22,419.00
Price: Diamond Regent GTX EDL Hunter (as above with engraved scroll and birds, 10 gold inlays), 12 or 20............ $26,249.00
Price: As above, 28............ $26,499.00
Price: As above, 410............ $26,549.00

SHOTGUNS — OVER/UNDERS

CZ 581 Solo

Fabarm Max Lion

CHARLES DALY EMPIRE EDL HUNTER O/U
Gauge: 12, 20, 410, 3" chambers, 28 ga., 2-3/4". **Barrel:** 26", 28" (12, 20, choke tubes), 26" (Imp. Cyl. & Mod., 28 ga.), 26" (Full & Full, 410). **Weight:** About 7 lbs. Stocks: Checkered walnut pistol grip buttstock, semi-beavertail forend; recoil pad. **Features:** Silvered, engraved receiver; chrome moly barrels; gold single selective trigger; automatic safety; automatic ejectors; red bead front sight, metal bead middle sight. Introduced 1997. Imported from Italy by K.B.I., Inc.
Price: Empire EDL (dummy sideplates) 12 or 20 . . . . $1,559.95
Price: Empire EDL, 28 . . . . $1,559.95
Price: Empire EDL, 410 . . . . $1,599.95

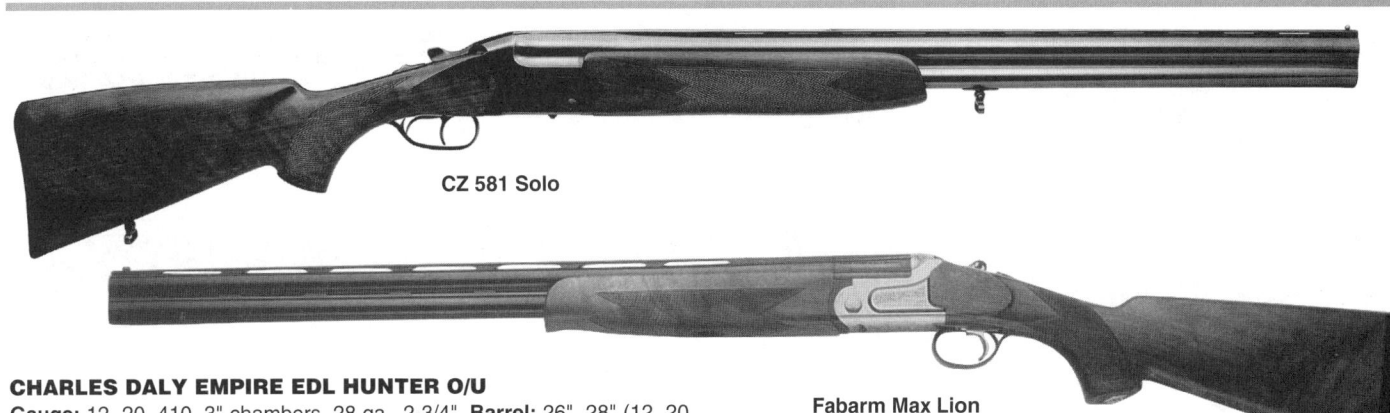

Charles Daly Empire Sporting O/U
Similar to the Empire EDL Hunter except 12 or 20 gauge only, 28", 30" barrels with choke tubes; ported barrels; special stock dimensions. Introduced 1997. Imported from Italy by K.B.I., Inc.
Price: $1,499.95

CHARLES DALY DIAMOND GTX SPORTING O/U SHOTGUN
Gauge: 12, 20, 3" chambers. **Barrel:** 28", 30" with choke tubes. **Weight:** About 8.5 lbs. **Stock:** Checkered deluxe walnut; Sporting clays dimensions. Pistol grip; semi-beavertail forend; hand rubbed oil finish. **Features:** Chromed, hand-engraved receiver; chrome moly steel barrels; GTX detachable single selective trigger system with coil springs, automatic safety; automatic ejectors; red bead front sight; ported barrels. Introduced 1997. Imported from Italy by K.B.I., Inc.
Price: $5,804.95

CHARLES DALY DIAMOND GTX TRAP AE-MC O/U SHOTGUN
Gauge: 12, 2-3/4" chambers. **Barrel:** 30" (Full & Full). **Weight:** About 8.5 lbs. **Stock:** Checkered deluxe walnut; pistol grip; trap dimensions; semi-beavertail forend; hand-rubbed oil finish. **Features:** Silvered, hand-engraved receiver; chrome moly steel barrels; GTX detachable single selective trigger system with coil springs, automatic safety, automatic-ejectors, red bead front sight, metal bead middle; recoil pad. Introduced 1997. Imported from Italy by K.B.I., Inc.
Price: $5,804.95

CHARLES DALY DIAMOND GTX DL HUNTER O/U
Gauge: 12, 20, 410, 3" chambers, 28, 2-3/4" chambers. **Barrel:** 26, 28", choke tubes in 12 and 20 ga., 26" (Imp. Cyl. & Mod.), 26" (Full & Full) in 410-bore. **Weight:** About 8.5 lbs. **Stock:** Select fancy European walnut stock, with 24 lpi hand checkering; hand-rubbed oil finish. **Features:** Boss-type action with internal side lugs, hand-engraved scrollwork and game scene. GTX detachable single selective trigger system with coil springs; chrome moly steel barrels; automatic safety, automatic ejectors, red bead front sight, recoil pad. Introduced 1997. Imported from Italy by K.B.I., Inc.
Price: 12 or 20 . . . . $12,399.00
Price: 28 . . . . $12,489.00
Price: 410 . . . . $12,529.00
Price: GTX EDL Hunter (with gold inlays), 12, 20 . . . . $15,999.00
Price: As above, 28 . . . . $16,179.00
Price: As above, 410 . . . . $16,219.00

CZ 581 SOLO OVER/UNDER SHOTGUN
Gauge: 12, 2-3/4" chambers. **Barrel:** 27.6" (Mod. & Full). **Weight:** 7.37 lbs. **Length:** 44.5" overall. **Stock:** Circassian walnut. **Features:** Automatic ejectors; double triggers; Kersten-style double lump locking system. Imported from the Czech Republic by CZ-USA.
Price: $799.00

EAA/BAIKAL MP-233 OVER/UNDER SHOTGUN
Gauge: 12, 3" chambers. **Barrel:** 26", 28", 30"; imp., mod. and full choke tubes. **Weight:** 7.28 lbs. **Stock:** Walnut; checkered forearm and grip. **Features:** Hammer-forged barrels; chrome-lined bores; removable trigger assembly (optional single selective trigger or double trigger); ejectors. Introduced 2000. Imported by European American Armory.
Price: MP-233. . . . . $879.00

EAA/BAIKAL IZH-27 OVER/UNDER SHOTGUN
Gauge: 12 (3" chambers), 16 (2-3/4" chambers), 20 (3" chambers), 28 (2-3/4" chambers), 410 (3"). **Barrel:** 26-1/2", 28-1/2" (imp., mod. and full choke tubes for 12 and 20 gauges; improved cylinder and modified for 16 and 28 gauges; improved modified and full for 410; 16 also offered in mod. and full). **Weight:** NA. **Stock:** Walnut, checkered forearm and grip. Imported by European American Armory.
Price: IZH-27 (12, 16 and 20 gauge) $459.00
Price: IZH-27 (28 and 410 gauge) $499.00

FABARM MAX LION OVER/UNDER SHOTGUNS
Gauge: 12, 3" chambers, 20, 3" chambers. **Barrel:** 26", 28", 30" (12 ga.); 26", 28" (20 ga.), choke tubes. **Weight:** 7.4 lbs. **Length:** 47.5" overall (26" barrel). **Stock:** European walnut; leather-covered recoil pad. **Features:** TriBore barrel, boxlock action with single selective trigger, manual safety, automatic ejectors; chrome-lined barrels; adjustable trigger. Silvered, engraved receiver. Comes with locking, fitted luggage case. Introduced 1998. Imported from Italy by Heckler & Koch, Inc.
Price: 12 or 20 . . . . $1,899.00

FABARM ULTRA MAG LION O/U SHOTGUN
Gauge: 12, 3-1/2" chambers. **Barrel:** 28" (Cyl., Imp. Cyl., Mod., Imp. Mod., Full, SS-Mod., SS-Full choke tubes). **Weight:** 7.9 lbs. **Length:** 50" overall. **Stock:** Black-colored walnut. **Features:** TriBore barrel, matte finished metal surfaces; single selective trigger; non-auto ejectors; leather-covered recoil pad. Comes with locking hard plastic case. Introduced 1998. Imported from Italy by Heckler & Koch, Inc.
Price: $1,229.00

Fabarm Ultra Camo Mag Lion O/U Shotgun
Similar to the Ultra Mag Lion except completely covered with Wetlands camouflage pattern, has the ported TriBore barrel system, and a mid-rib bead. Chambered for 3-1/2" shells. Stock and forend are walnut. Introduced 1999. Imported from Italy by Heckler & Koch, Inc.
Price: $1,299.00

FABARM SILVER LION OVER/UNDER SHOTGUNS
Gauge: 12, 3" chambers, 20, 3" chambers. **Barrel:** 26", 28", 30" (12 ga.); 26", 28" (20 ga.), choke tubes. **Weight:** 7.2 lbs. **Length:** 47.5" overall (26" barrels). **Stock:** Walnut; leather-covered recoil pad. **Features:** TriBore barrel, boxlock action with single selective trigger; silvered receiver with engraving; automatic ejectors. Comes with locking hard plastic case. Introduced 1998. Imported from Italy by Heckler & Koch, Inc.
Price: 12 or 20 . . . . $1,299.00

SHOTGUNS — OVER/UNDERS

Franchi Alcione

Kolar Sporting Clays

Krieghoff K-80 Sporting Clays

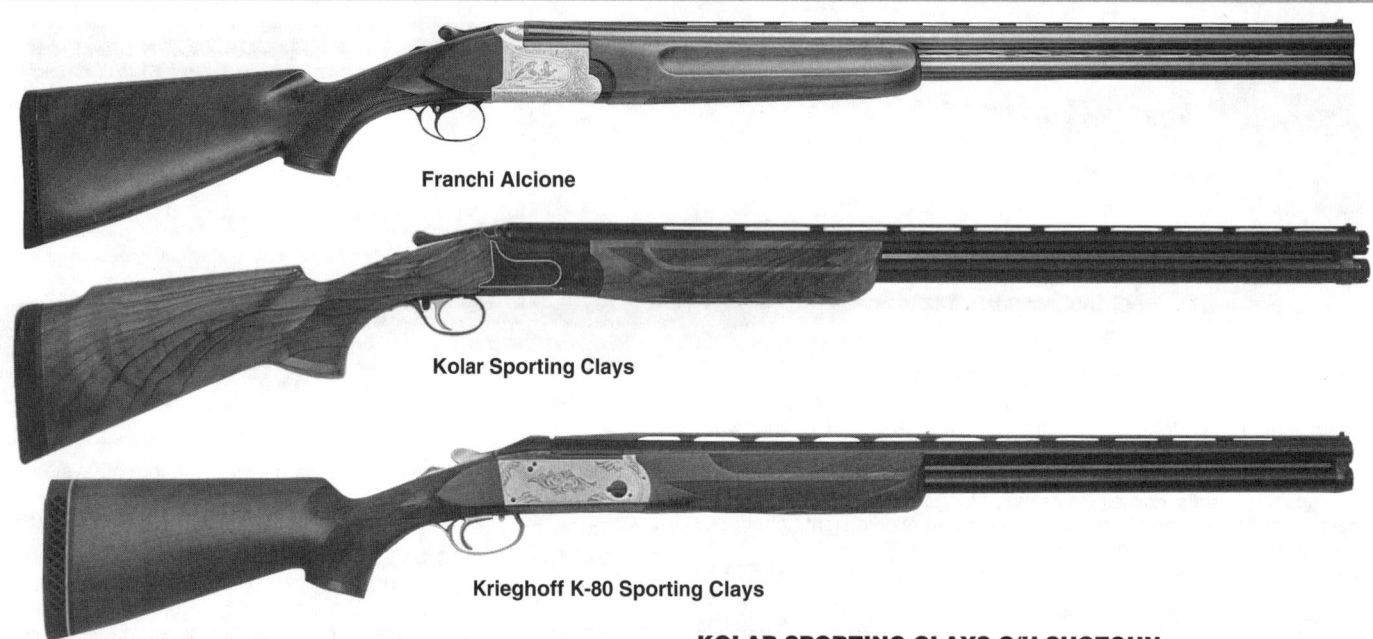

Fabarm Silver Lion Cub Model O/U
Similar to the Silver Lion except has 12.5" length of pull, is in 20 gauge only (3-1/2" chambers), and comes with 24" TriBore barrel system. Weight is 6 lbs. Introduced 1999. Imported from Italy by Heckler & Koch, Inc.
Price: $1,299.00

FABARM CAMO TURKEY MAG O/U SHOTGUN
Gauge: 12, 3-1/2" chambers. **Barrel:** 20" TriBore (Ultra-Full ported tubes). **Weight:** 7.5 lbs. **Length:** 46" overall. **Stock:** 14.5"x1.5"x2.29". Walnut. **Sights:** Front bar, Picatinny rail scope base. **Features:** Completely covered with Xtra Brown camouflage finish. Unported barrels. Introduced 1999. Imported from Italy by Heckler & Koch, Inc.
Price: $1,339.00

FABARM SPORTING CLAYS COMPETITION EXTRA O/U
Gauge: 12, 20, 3" chambers. **Barrel:** 12 ga. has 30", 20 ga. has 28"; ported TriBore barrel system with five tubes. **Weight:** 7 to 7.8 lbs. **Length:** 49.6" overall (20 ga.). **Stock:** 14.50"x1.38"x2.17" (20 ga.); deluxe walnut; leather-covered recoil pad. **Features:** Single selective trigger, auto ejectors; 10mm channeled rib; carbon fiber finish. Introduced 1999. Imported from Italy by Heckler & Koch, Inc.
Price: $1,749.00

FRANCHI ALCIONE FIELD OVER/UNDER SHOTGUN
Gauge: 12, 3" chambers. **Barrel:** 26", 28"; Franchoke tubes. **Weight:** 7.5 lbs. **Length:** 43" overall with 26" barrels. **Stock:** European walnut. **Features:** Boxlock action with ejectors; barrel selector is mounted on the trigger; silvered, engraved receiver; vent center rib; automatic safety. Imported from Italy by Benelli USA. Hard case included.
Price: $993.00
Price: (20 gauge barrel set) $336.00

Franchi Alcione Sport O/U Shotgun
Similar to the Alcione except has 2-3/4" chambers, elongated forcing cones and porting for Sporting Clays shooting. 10mm vent rib, tightly curved pistol grip, manual safety, removeable sideplates. Imported from Italy by Benelli USA.
Price: $1,300.00

Franchi Alcione Light Field (LF) Shotgun
Similar to Alcione Field except features alloy frame, weighs 6.8 pounds (12 gauge) or 6.7 pounds (20 gauge). Both frames accept either the 2-3/4"-chamber 12 gauge or 3"-chamber 20 gauge barrel sets.
Price: $1,100.00

KOLAR SPORTING CLAYS O/U SHOTGUN
Gauge: 12, 2-3/4" chambers. **Barrel:** 28", 30", 32"; extended choke tubes. **Stock:** 14-5/8"x2-1/2"x1-7/8"x1-3/8". French walnut. **Features:** Single selective trigger, detachable, adjustable for length; overbored barrels with long forcing cones; flat tramline rib; matte blue finish. Made in U.S. by Kolar.
Price: Standard. $7,250.00
Price: Elite $10,050.00
Price: Elite Gold $11,545.00
Price: Legend $13,045.00
Price: Custom Gold $24,750.00

Kolar AAA Competition Trap Over/Under Shotgun
Similar to the Sporting Clays gun except has 32" O/U /34" Unsingle or 30" O/U /34" Unsingle barrels as an over/under, unsingle, or combination set. Stock dimensions are 14-1/2"x2-1/2"x1-1/2"; American or French walnut; step parallel rib standard. Contact maker for full listings. Made in U.S. by Kolar.
Price: Over/under, choke tubes, Standard $7,025.00
Price: Unsingle, choke tubes, Standard $7,775.00
Price: Combo (30"/34", 32"/34"), Standard. $10,170.00

Kolar AAA Competition Skeet Over/Under Shotgun
Similar to the Sporting Clays gun except has 28" or 30" barrels with Kolarite AAA sub gauge tubes; stock of American or French walnut with matte finish; flat tramline rib; under barrel adjustable for point of impact. Many options available. Contact maker for complete listing. Made in U.S. by Kolar.
Price: Standard, choke tubes $8,645.00
Price: Standard, choke tubes, two-barrel set $10,710.00

KRIEGHOFF K-80 SPORTING CLAYS O/U
Gauge: 12. **Barrel:** 28", 30" or 32" with choke tubes. **Weight:** About 8 lbs. **Stock:** #3 Sporting stock designed for gun-down shooting. **Features:** Choice of standard or lightweight receiver with satin nickel finish and classic scroll engraving. Selective mechanical trigger adjustable for position. Choice of tapered flat or 8mm parallel flat barrel rib. Free-floating barrels. Aluminum case. Imported from Germany by Krieghoff International, Inc.
Price: Standard grade with five choke tubes, from $8,150.00

KRIEGHOFF K-80 SKEET SHOTGUN
Gauge: 12, 2-3/4" chambers. **Barrel:** 28" (Skeet & Skeet, optional Tula or choke tubes). **Weight:** About 7-3/4 lbs. **Stock:** American Skeet or straight Skeet stocks, with palm-swell grips. Walnut. **Features:** Satin gray receiver finish. Selective mechanical trigger adjustable for position. Choice of ventilated 8mm parallel flat rib or ventilated 8-12mm tapered flat rib. Introduced 1980. Imported from Germany by Krieghoff International, Inc.

Shotguns — Over/Unders

Ljutic LM-6 Super Deluxe

Marocchi Conquista Sporting Clay

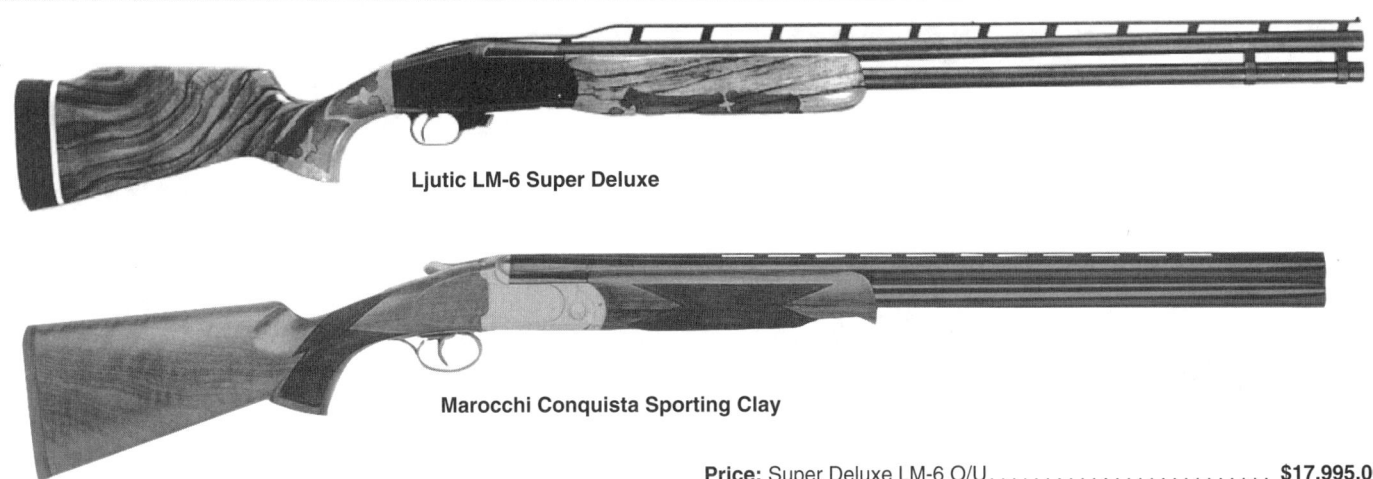

Price: Standard, Skeet chokes $6,900.00
Price: As above, Tula chokes $7,825.00
Price: Lightweight model (weighs 7 lbs.), Standard $6,900.00
Price: Two-Barrel Set (tube concept), 12 ga., Standard. $11,840.00
Price: Skeet Special (28", tapered flat rib, Skeet & Skeet choke tubes) $7,575.00

Krieghoff K-80 Four-Barrel Skeet Set
Similar to the Standard Skeet except comes with barrels for 12, 20, 28, 410. Comes with fitted aluminum case.
Price: Standard grade. $16,950.00

Krieghoff K-80 International Skeet
Similar to the Standard Skeet except has 1/2" ventilated Broadway-style rib, special Tula chokes with gas release holes at muzzle. International Skeet stock. Comes in fitted aluminum case.
Price: Standard grade. $7,825.00

KRIEGHOFF K-80 O/U TRAP SHOTGUN
Gauge: 12, 2-3/4" chambers. **Barrel:** 30", 32" (Imp. Mod. & Full or choke tubes). **Weight:** About 8-1/2 lbs. **Stock:** Four stock dimensions or adjustable stock available; all have palm swell grips. Checkered European walnut. **Features:** Satin nickel receiver. Selective mechanical trigger, adjustable for position. Ventilated step rib. Introduced 1980. Imported from Germany by Krieghoff International, Inc.
Price: K-80 O/U (30", 32", Imp. Mod. & Full), from $7,375.00
Price: K-80 Unsingle (32", 34", Full), Standard, from $7,950.00
Price: K-80 Combo (two-barrel set), Standard, from $10,475.00

Krieghoff K-20 O/U Shotguns
Similar to the K-80 except built on a 20-gauge frame. Designed for skeet, sporting clays and field use. Offered in 20, 28 and 410 gauge, 28" and 30" barrels. Imported from Germany by Krieghoff International Inc.
Price: K-20, 20 gauge, from $8,150.00
Price: K-20, 28 gauge, from $8,425.00
Price: K-20, 410 gauge, from $8,425.00

LEBEAU - COURALLY BOSS-VEREES O/U
Gauge: 12, 20, 2-3/4" chambers. **Barrel:** 25" to 32". **Weight:** To customer specifications. **Stock:** Exhibition-quality French walnut. **Features:** Boss-type sidelock with automatic ejectors; single or double triggers; chopper lump barrels. A custom gun built to customer specifications. Imported from Belgium by Wm. Larkin Moore.
Price: From $65,000.00

LJUTIC LM-6 SUPER DELUXE O/U SHOTGUN
Gauge: 12. **Barrel:** 28" to 34", choked to customer specs for live birds, trap, International Trap. **Weight:** To customer specs. **Stock:** To customer specs. Oil finish, hand checkered. **Features:** Custom-made gun. Hollow-milled rib, pull or release trigger, pushbutton opener in front of trigger guard. From Ljutic Industries.

Price: Super Deluxe LM-6 O/U. $17,995.00
Price: Over/Under Combo (interchangeable single barrel, two trigger guards, one for single trigger, one for doubles) $24,995.00
Price: Extra over/under barrel sets, 29"-32" $5,995.00

LUGER CLASSIC O/U SHOTGUNS
Gauge: 12, 3" and 3-1/2" chambers. **Barrel:** 26", 28", 30"; imp. cyl. mod. and full choke tubes. **Weight:** 7-1/2 lbs. **Length:** 45" overall (28" barrel) **Stock:** Select-grade European walnut, hand-checkered grip and forend. **Features:** Gold, single selective trigger; automatic ejectors. Introduced 2000. From Stoeger Industries.
Price: Classic (26", 28" or 30" barrel; 3-1/2" chambers). $919.00
Price: Classic Sporting (30" barrel; 3" chambers) $964.00

MAROCCHI CONQUISTA SPORTING CLAYS O/U SHOTGUNS
Gauge: 12, 2-3/4" chambers. **Barrel:** 28", 30", 32" (ContreChoke tubes); 10mm concave vent. rib. **Weight:** About 8 lbs. **Stock:** 14-1/2"-14-7/8"x2-3/16"x1-7/16"; American walnut with checkered grip and forend; Sporting Clays butt pad. **Sights:** 16mm luminescent front. **Features:** Has lower monoblock and frame profile. Fast lock time. Ergonomically-shaped trigger is adjustable for pull length. Automatic selective ejectors. Coin-finished receiver, blued barrels. Comes with five choke tubes, hard case. Also available as true left-hand model—opening lever operates from left to right; stock has left-hand cast. Introduced 1994. Imported from Italy by Precision Sales International.
Price: Grade I, right-hand. $1,995.00
Price: Grade I, left-hand $2,120.00
Price: Grade II, right-hand $2,330.00
Price: Grade II, left-hand $2,685.00
Price: Grade III, right-hand, from $3,599.00
Price: Grade III, left-hand, from $3,995.00

Marocchi Lady Sport O/U Shotgun
Ergonomically designed specifically for women shooters. Similar to the Conquista Sporting Clays model except has 28" or 30" barrels with five Contrechoke tubes, stock dimensions of 13-7/8"-14-1/4"x1-11/32"x2-9/32"; weighs about 7-1/2 lbs. Also available as left-hand model—opening lever operates from left to right; stock has left-hand cast. Also available with colored graphics finish on frame and opening lever. Introduced 1995. Imported from Italy by Precision Sales International.
Price: Grade I, right-hand. $2,120.00
Price: Left-hand, add (all grades) $101.00
Price: Lady Sport Spectrum (colored receiver panel) $2,199.00
Price: Lady Sport Spectrum, left-hand $2,300.00

Marocchi Conquista Trap Over/Under Shotgun
Similar to the Conquista Sporting Clays model except has 30" or 32" barrels choked Full & Full, stock dimensions of 14-1/2"-14-7/8"x1-11/16"x1-9/32"; weighs about 8-1/4 lbs. Introduced 1994. Imported from Italy by Precision Sales International.
Price: Grade I, right-hand $1,995.00
Price: Grade II, right-hand $2,330.00
Price: Grade III, right-hand, from $3,599.00

SHOTGUNS — OVER/UNDERS

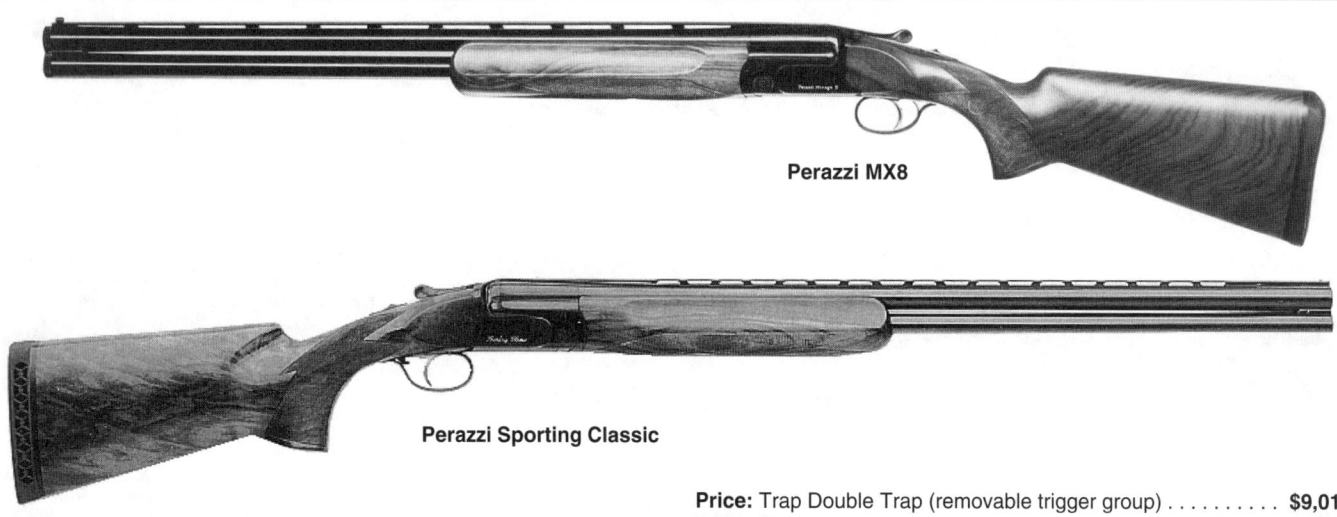

Perazzi MX8

Perazzi Sporting Classic

Marocchi Conquista Skeet Over/Under Shotgun
Similar to the Conquista Sporting Clays except has 28" (Skeet & Skeet) barrels, stock dimensions of 14-3/8"-14-3/4"x2-3/16"x1-1/2". Weighs about 7-3/4 lbs. Introduced 1994. Imported from Italy by Precision Sales International.
Price: Grade I, right-hand............................ $1,995.00
Price: Grade II, right-hand $2,330.00
Price: Grade III, right-hand, from $3,599.00

MAROCCHI CLASSIC DOUBLES
MODEL 92 SPORTING CLAYS O/U SHOTGUN
Gauge: 12, 3" chambers. **Barrel:** 30"; back-bored, ported (ContreChoke Plus tubes); 10 mm concave ventilated top rib, ventilated middle rib. **Weight:** 8 lbs. 2 oz. **Stock:** 14-1/4"-14-5/8"x 2-1/8"x1-3/8"; American walnut with checkered grip and forend; Sporting Clays butt pad. **Features:** Low profile frame; fast lock time; automatic selective ejectors; blued receiver and barrels. Comes with three choke tubes. Ergonomically shaped trigger adjustable for pull length without tools. Barrels are back-bored and ported. Introduced 1996. Imported from Italy by Precision Sales International.
Price: $1,598.00

MERKEL MODEL 2001EL O/U SHOTGUN
Gauge: 12, 20, 3" chambers, 28, 2-3/4" chambers. **Barrel:** 12—28"; 20, 28 ga.—26-3/4". **Weight:** About 7 lbs. (12 ga.). **Stock:** Oil-finished walnut; English or pistol grip. **Features:** Self-cocking Blitz boxlock action with cocking indicators; Kersten double cross-bolt lock; silver-grayed receiver with engraved hunting scenes; coil spring ejectors; single selective or double triggers. Imported from Germany by GSI, Inc.
Price: 12, 20 .... $6,495.00
Price: 28 ga....................................... $6,495.00
Price: Model 2000EL (scroll engraving, 12 or 20) $5,195.00

Merkel Model 303EL O/U Shotgun
Similar to the Model 2001 EL except has Holland & Holland-style sidelock action with cocking indicators; English-style Arabesque engraving. Available in 12, 20 gauge. Imported from Germany by GSI, Inc.
Price: $19,995.00

Merkel Model 2002 EL O/U Shotgun
Similar to the Model 2001 EL except has dummy sideplates, Arabesque engraving with hunting scenes; 12, 20 gauge. Imported from Germany by GSI, Inc.
Price: $9,995.00

PERAZZI MX8 OVER/UNDER SHOTGUNS
Gauge: 12, 2-3/4" chambers. **Barrel:** 28-3/8" (Imp. Mod. & Extra Full), 29-1/2" (choke tubes). **Weight:** 7 lbs., 12 oz. **Stock:** Special specifications. **Features:** Has single selective trigger; flat 7/16"x5/16" vent. rib. Many options available. Imported from Italy by Perazzi U.S.A., Inc.
Price: Sporting $9,980.00
Price: Trap Double Trap (removable trigger group) $9,010.00
Price: Skeet $9,010.00
Price: SC3 grade (variety of engraving patterns) ..... Starting at $15,300
Price: SCO grade (more intricate engraving, gold inlays)
.... Starting at $26,000

PERAZZI MX12 HUNTING OVER/UNDER
Gauge: 12, 2-3/4" chambers. **Barrel:** 26-3/4", 27-1/2", 28-3/8", 29-1/2" (Mod. & Full); choke tubes available in 27-5/8", 29-1/2" only (MX12C). **Weight:** 7 lbs., 4 oz. **Stock:** To customer specs; Interchangeable. **Features:** Single selective trigger; coil springs used in action; Schnabel forend tip. Imported from Italy by Perazzi U.S.A., Inc.
Price: From $9,010.00
Price: MX12C (with choke tubes), from $9,460.00

Perazzi MX20 Hunting Over/Under
Similar to the MX12 except 20 ga. frame size. Non-removable trigger group. Available in 20, 28, 410 with 2-3/4" or 3" chambers. 26" standard, and choked Mod. & Full. Weight is 6 lbs., 6 oz.
Price: From $9,010.00
Price: MX20C (as above, 20 ga. only, choke tubes), from..... $9,460.00

PERAZZI MX8/MX8 SPECIAL TRAP, SKEET
Gauge: 12, 2-3/4" chambers. **Barrel:** Trap—29-1/2" (Imp. Mod. & Extra Full), 31-1/2" (Full & Extra Full). Choke tubes optional. Skeet—27-5/8" (Skeet & Skeet). **Weight:** About 8-1/2 lbs. (Trap); 7 lbs., 15 oz. (Skeet). **Stock:** Interchangeable and custom made to customer specs. **Features:** Has detachable and interchangeable trigger group with flat V springs. Flat 7/16" ventilated rib. Many options available. Imported from Italy by Perazzi U.S.A., Inc.
Price: From....................................... $8,840.00
Price: MX8 Special (adj. four-position trigger), from $9,350.00
Price: MX8 Special Combo (o/u and single barrel sets), from . $12,340.00

Perazzi MX8 Special Skeet Over/Under
Similar to the MX8 Skeet except has adjustable four-position trigger, Skeet stock dimensions.
Price: From....................................... $9,350.00

Perazzi MX8/20 Over/Under Shotgun
Similar to the MX8 except has smaller frame and has a removable trigger mechanism. Available in trap, Skeet, sporting or game models with fixed chokes or choke tubes. Stock is made to customer specifications. Introduced 1993.
Price: From....................................... $9,790.00

PERAZZI MX10 OVER/UNDER SHOTGUN
Gauge: 12, 2-3/4" chambers. **Barrel:** 29.5", 31.5" (fixed chokes). **Weight:** NA. **Stock:** Walnut; cheekpiece adjustable for elevation and cast. **Features:** Adjustable rib; vent. side rib. Externally selective trigger. Available in single barrel, combo, over/under trap, Skeet, pigeon and sporting models. Introduced 1993. Imported from Italy by Perazzi U.S.A., Inc.
Price: From $11,030.00

SHOTGUNS — OVER/UNDERS

Perazzi MX8 Special Combo Single Barrel

Perazzi MX28

Piotti Boss

Rizzini S790 Emel

PERAZZI MX28, MX410 GAME O/U SHOTGUNS
Gauge: 28, 2-3/4" chambers, 410, 3" chambers. **Barrel:** 26" (Imp. Cyl. & Full). **Weight:** NA. **Stock:** To customer specifications. **Features:** Made on scaled-down frames proportioned to the gauge. Introduced 1993. Imported from Italy by Perazzi U.S.A., Inc.
Price: From $17,670.00

PIOTTI BOSS OVER/UNDER SHOTGUN
Gauge: 12, 20. **Barrel:** 26" to 32", chokes as specified. **Weight:** 6.5 to 8 lbs. **Stock:** Dimensions to customer specs. Best quality figured walnut. **Features:** Essentially a custom-made gun with many options. Introduced 1993. Imported from Italy by Wm. Larkin Moore.
Price: From $34,000.00

REMINGTON MODEL 300 IDEAL O/U SHOTGUN
Gauge: 12, 3" chambers. **Barrel:** 26", 28", 30" (imp. cyl., mod. and full Rem Choke tubes). **Weight:** 7 lbs. 6 oz. to 7 lbs. 14 oz. **Length:** 42-3/4" overall (26" brl.) **Stock:** Satin-finished American walnut; checkered forearm and grip; rubber recoil pad. **Features:** Low-profile rib; mid-bead and ivory front bead; fine-line engraved receiver with high-polish blued finish; automatic ejectors. Introduced 2000. From Remington Arms Co.
Price: $1,999.00

RIZZINI S790 EMEL OVER/UNDER SHOTGUN
Gauge: 20, 28, 410. **Barrel:** 26", 27.5" (Imp. Cyl. & Imp. Mod.). **Weight:** About 6 lbs. **Stock:** 14"x1-1/2"x2-1/8". Extra-fancy select walnut. **Features:** Boxlock action with profuse engraving; automatic ejectors; single selective trigger; silvered receiver. Comes with Nizzoli leather case. Introduced 1996. Imported from Italy by Wm. Larkin Moore & Co.
Price: From $7,800.00

Rizzini S792 EMEL Over/Under Shotgun
Similar to the S790 EMEL except has dummy sideplates with extensive engraving coverage. Comes with Nizzoli leather case. Introduced 1996. Imported from Italy by Wm. Larkin Moore & Co.
Price: From $7,300.00

RIZZINI UPLAND EL OVER/UNDER SHOTGUN
Gauge: 12, 16, 20, 28, 410. **Barrel:** 26", 27-1/2", Mod. & Full, Imp. Cyl. & Imp. Mod. choke tubes. **Weight:** About 6.6 lbs. **Stock:** 14-1/2"x1-1/2"x2-1/4". **Features:** Boxlock action; single selective trigger; ejectors; profuse engraving on silvered receiver. Comes with fitted case. Introduced 1996. Imported from Italy by Wm. Larkin Moore & Co.
Price: From $2,800.00

Rizzini Artemis Over/Under Shotgun
Same as the Upland EL model except has dummy sideplates with extensive game scene engraving. Fancy European walnut stock. Comes with fitted case. Introduced 1996. Imported from Italy by Wm. Larkin Moore & Co.
Price: From $1,700.00

RIZZINI S782 EMEL OVER/UNDER SHOTGUN
Gauge: 12, 2-3/4" chambers. **Barrel:** 26", 27.5" (Imp. Cyl. & Imp. Mod.). **Weight:** About 6.75 lbs. **Stock:** 14-1/2"x1-1/2"x2-1/4". Extra fancy select walnut. **Features:** Boxlock action with dummy sideplates; extensive engraving with gold inlaid game birds; silvered receiver; automatic ejectors; single selective trigger. Comes with Nizzoli leather case. Introduced 1996. Imported from Italy by Wm. Larkin Moore & Co.
Price: From $9,200.00

ROTTWEIL PARAGON OVER/UNDER
Gauge: 12, 2-3/4" chambers. **Barrel:** 28", 30", five choke tubes. **Weight:** 7 lbs. **Stock:** 14-1/2"x1-1/2"x2-1/2"; European walnut. **Features:** Boxlock action. Detachable trigger assembly; ejectors can be deactivated; convertible top lever for right- or left-hand use; trigger adjustable for position. Imported from Germany by Dynamit Nobel-RWS, Inc.
Price: $5,995.00

SHOTGUNS — OVER/UNDERS

Ruger Woodside

Sigarms SA5 Field

SKB 785 Sporting Clays

RUGER WOODSIDE OVER/UNDER SHOTGUN
Gauge: 12, 3" chambers. **Barrel:** 26", 28", 30" (Full, Mod., Imp. Cyl. and two Skeet tubes). **Weight:** 7-1/2 to 8 lbs. **Stock:** 14-1/8"x1-1/2"x2-1/2". Select Circassian walnut; pistol grip or straight English grip. **Features:** Has a newly patented Ruger cocking mechanism for easier, smoother opening. Buttstock extends forward into action as two side panels. Single selective mechanical trigger, selective automatic ejectors; serrated free-floating rib; back-bored barrels with stainless steel choke tubes. Blued barrels, stainless steel receiver. Engraved action available. Introduced 1995. Made in U.S. by Sturm, Ruger & Co.
Price: $1,889.00
Price: Woodside Sporting Clays (30" barrels) $1,889.00

RUGER RED LABEL O/U SHOTGUN
Gauge: 12, 20, 3" chambers; 28 2-3/4" chambers. **Barrel:** 26", 28" (Skeet [two], Imp. Cyl., Full, Mod. screw-in choke tubes). Proved for steel shot. **Weight:** About 7 lbs. (20 ga.); 7-1/2 lbs. (12 ga.). **Length:** 43" overall (26" barrels). **Stock:** 14"x1-1/2"x2-1/2". Straight grain American walnut or black synthetic. Checkered pistol grip and forend, rubber butt pad. **Features:** Stainless steel receiver. Single selective mechanical trigger, selective automatic ejectors; serrated free-floating vent. rib. Comes with two Skeet, one Imp. Cyl., one Mod., one Full choke tube and wrench. Made in U.S. by Sturm, Ruger & Co.
Price: Red Label with pistol grip stock $1,399.00
Price: English Field with straight-grip stock $1,399.00
Price: All-Weather Red Label with black synthetic stock $1,399.00
Price: Factory engraved All-Weather models .... $1,575.00 to $1,650.00

Ruger Engraved Red Label O/U Shotguns
Similar to Red Label except has scroll engraved receiver with 24-carat gold game bird (pheasant in 12 gauge, grouse in 20 gauge, woodcock in 28 gauge, duck on All-Weather 12 gauge). Introduced 2000.
Price: Engraved Red Label (12 gauge, 30" barrel) $1,650.00
Price: Engraved Red Label (12, 20 and 28 gauge in 26" and 28" barrels) $1,575.00
Price: Engraved Red Label, All-Weather (synthetic stock, 12 gauge only; 26" and 28" brls.) $1,575.00
Price: Engraved Red Label, All-Weather (synthetic stock, 12 gauge only, 30" barrel) $1,650.00

Ruger Sporting Clays O/U Shotgun
Similar to the Red Label except 30" back-bored barrels, stainless steel choke tubes. Weighs 7.75 lbs., overall length 47". Stock dimensions of 14-1/8"x1-1/2"x2-1/2". Free-floating serrated vent. rib with brass front and mid-rib beads. No barrel side spacers. Comes with two Skeet, one Imp. Cyl., one Mod. + Full choke tubes. 12 ga. introduced 1992, 20 ga. introduced 1994.
Price: 12 or 20 .... $1,475.00
Price: All-Weather with black synthetic stock $1,475.00

SARSILMAZ OVER/UNDER SHOTGUN
Gauge: 12, 3" chambers. **Barrel:** 26", 28"; fixed chokes or choke tubes. **Weight:** NA. **Length:** NA. **Stock:** Oil-finished hardwood. **Features:** Double or single selective trigger; wide ventilated rib; chrome-plated parts; blued finish. Introduced 2000. Imported from Turkey by Armsport Inc.
Price: Double triggers; mod. and full or imp. cyl. and mod. fixed chokes $499.95
Price: Single selective trigger; imp. cyl. and mod. or mod. and full fixed chokes $575.00
Price: Single selective trigger; five choke tubes and wrench $695.00

SIGARMS SA5 OVER/UNDER SHOTGUN
Gauge: 12, 20, 3" chamber. **Barrel:** 26-1/2", 27" (Full, Imp. Mod., Mod., Imp. Cyl., Cyl. choke tubes). **Weight:** 6.9 lbs. (12 gauge), 5.9 lbs. (20 gauge). **Stock:** 14-1/2" x 1-1/2" x 2-1/2". Select grade walnut; checkered 20 l.p.i. at grip and forend. **Features:** Single selective trigger, automatic ejectors; hand-engraved detachable sideplated; matte nickel receiver, rest blued; tapered bolt lock-up. Introduced 1997. Imported by Sigarms, Inc.
Price: Field, 12 gauge $2,670.00
Price: Sporting Clays $2,800.00
Price: Field 20 gauge $2,670.00

SKB Model 505 Shotguns
Similar to the Model 585 except blued receiver, standard bore diameter, standard Inter-Choke system on 12, 20, 28, different receiver engraving. Imported from Japan by G.U. Inc.
Price: Field, 12 (26", 28"), 20 (26", 28") $1,189.00
Price: Sporting Clays, 12 (28", 30") $1,299.00

SKB MODEL 785 OVER/UNDER SHOTGUN
Gauge: 12, 20, 3"; 28, 2-3/4"; 410, 3". **Barrel:** 26", 28", 30", 32" (Inter-Choke tubes). **Weight:** 6 lbs., 10 oz. to 8 lbs. **Stock:** 14-1/8"x1-1/2"x2-3/16" (Field). Hand-checkered American black walnut with high-gloss finish; semi-beavertail forend. Target stocks available in standard or Monte Carlo styles. **Sights:** Metal bead front (Field), target style on Skeet, trap, Sporting Clays models. **Features:** Boxlock action with Greener-style cross bolt; single selective chrome-plated trigger, chrome-plated selective ejectors; manual safety. Chrome-plated, over-size, back-bored barrels with lengthened forcing cones. Introduced 1995. Imported from Japan by G.U. Inc.
Price: Field, 12 or 20 .... $2,119.00
Price: Field, 28 or 410 .... $2,199.00
Price: Field set, 12 and 20 .... $3,079.00
Price: Field set, 20 and 28 or 28 and 410 .... $3,179.00
Price: Sporting Clays, 12 or 20 .... $2,269.00
Price: Sporting Clays, 28 .... $2,349.00
Price: Sporting Clays set, 12 and 20 .... $3,249.00
Price: Skeet, 12 or 20 .... $2,199.00
Price: Skeet, 28 or 410 .... $2,239.00
Price: Skeet, three-barrel set, 20, 28, 410 .... $4,439.00
Price: Trap, standard or Monte Carlo $2,199.00
Price: Trap combo, standard or Monte Carlo $3,079.00

SHOTGUNS — OVER/UNDERS

Tristar-TR-SC

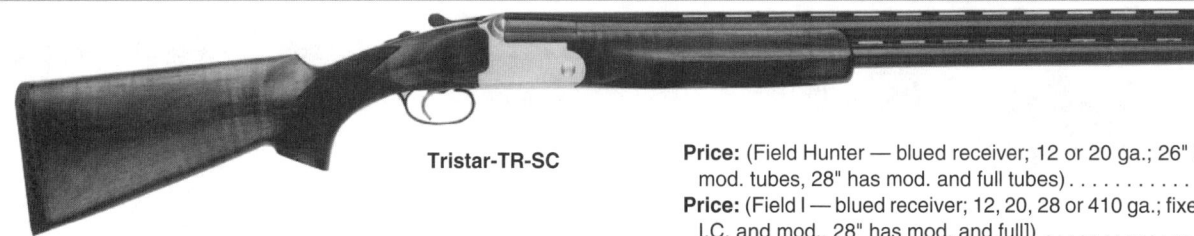

SKB MODEL 585 OVER/UNDER SHOTGUN
Gauge: 12 or 20, 3"; 28, 2-3/4"; 410, 3". **Barrel:** 12 ga.—26", 28", 30", 32", 34" (Inter-Choke tubes); 20 ga.—26", 28" (Inter-Choke tube); 28—26", 28" (Inter-Choke tubes); 410—26", 28" (Inter-Choke tubes). Ventilated side ribs. **Weight:** 6.6 to 8.5 lbs. **Length:** 43" to 51-3/8" overall. **Stock:** 14-1/8"x1-1/2"x2-3/16". Hand checkered walnut with high-gloss finish. Target stocks available in standard and Monte Carlo. **Sights:** Metal bead front (field), target style on Skeet, trap, Sporting Clays. **Features:** Boxlock action; silver nitride finish with Field or Target pattern engraving; manual safety, automatic ejectors, single selective trigger. All 12 gauge barrels are back-bored, have lengthened forcing cones and longer choke tube system. Sporting Clays models in 12 gauge with 28" or 30" barrels available with optional 3/8" step-up target-style rib, matte finish, nickel center bead, white front bead. Introduced 1992. Imported from Japan by G.U., Inc.
Price: Field $1,499.00
Price: Two-barrel Field Set, 12 & 20 . . . . $2,399.00
Price: Two-barrel Field Set, 20 & 28 or 28 & 410 . . . . $2,469.00
Price: Trap, Skeet $1,619.00
Price: Two-barrel trap combo $2,419.00
Price: Sporting Clays model . . . . $1,679.00 to $1,729.00
Price: Skeet Set (20, 28, 410) $3,779.00

SKB Model 585 Gold Package
Similar to the Model 585 Field except has gold-plated trigger, two gold-plated game inlays, and Schnabel forend. Silver or blue receiver. Introduced 1998. Imported from Japan by G.U. Inc.
Price: 12, 20 ga. $1,689.00
Price: 28, 410 . . . . $1,749.00

STOEGER/IGA CONDOR I OVER/UNDER SHOTGUN
Gauge: 12, 20, 3" chambers. **Barrel:** 26" (Imp. Cyl. & Mod. choke tubes), 28" (Mod. & Full choke tubes). **Weight:** 6-3/4 to 7 lbs. **Stock:** 14-1/2"x1-1/2"x2-1/2". Oil-finished hardwood with checkered pistol grip and forend. **Features:** Manual safety, single trigger, extractors only, ventilated top rib. Introduced 1983. Imported from Brazil by Stoeger Industries.
Price: With choke tubes $559.00
Price: Condor Supreme (same as Condor I with single trigger, choke tubes, but with auto. ejectors), 12 or 20 ga., 26", 28" . . . $674.00

Stoeger/IGA Condor Waterfowl O/U
Similar to the Condor I except has Advantage camouflage on the barrels, stock and forend; all other metal has matte black finish. Comes only with 30" choke tube barrels, 3" chambers, automatic ejectors, single trigger and manual safety. Designed for steel shot. Introduced 1997. Imported from Brazil by Stoeger.
Price: $729.00

Stoeger/IGA Turkey Model O/U
Similar to the Condor I model except has Advantage camouflage on the barrels stock and forend. All exposed metal and recoil pad are matte black. Has 26" (Full & Full) barrels, single trigger, manual safety, 3" chambers. Introduced 1997. Imported from Brazil by Stoeger.
Price: $729.00

TRADITIONS CLASSIC SERIES O/U SHOTGUNS
Gauge: 12, 3"; 20, 3"; 16, 2-3/4"; 28, 2-3/4"; 410, 3". **Barrel:** 26" and 28". **Weight:** 6 lbs., 5 oz. to 7 lbs., 6 oz. **Length:** 43" to 45" overall. **Stock:** Walnut. **Features:** Single-selective trigger; chrome-lined barrels with screw-in choke tubes; extractors (Field Hunter and Field I models) or automatic ejectors (Field II and Field III models); rubber butt pad; top tang safety. Imported from Fausti of Italy by Traditions.
Price: (Field Hunter — blued receiver; 12 or 20 ga.; 26" bbl. has I.C. and mod. tubes, 28" has mod. and full tubes) $649.00
Price: (Field I — blued receiver; 12, 20, 28 or 410 ga.; fixed chokes [26" has I.C. and mod., 28" has mod. and full]) $589.00
Price: (Field II — coin-finish receiver; 12, 16, 20, 28 or 410 ga.; gold trigger; choke tubes) . . . . $759.00 ($799.00 for 16 ga.)
Price: (Field III — coin-finish receiver; gold engraving and trigger; 12 ga.; 26" or 28" bbl.; choke tubes) $979.00
Price: (Upland II — blued receiver; 12 or 20 ga.; English-style straight walnut stock; choke tubes) $799.00
Price: (Upland III — blued receiver with gold engraving; 20 ga.; high-grade pistol grip walnut stock; choke tubes) $1,019.00
Price: (Sporting Clay II — silver receiver; 12 ga.; ported barrels with skeet, i.c., mod. and full extended tubes) $919.00

TRADITIONS MAG 350 SERIES O/U SHOTGUNS
Gauge: 12, 3-1/2". **Barrels:** 24", 26" and 28". **Weight:** 7 lbs. to 7 lbs., 4 oz. **Length:** 41" to 45" overall. **Stock:** Walnut or composite with Mossy Oak® Break-Up™ or Advantage® Wetlands™ camouflage. **Features:** Black matte, engraved receiver; vent rib; automatic ejectors; single-selective trigger; three screw-in choke tubes; rubber recoil pad; top tang safety. Imported from Fausti of Italy by Traditions.
Price: (Mag Hunter II — 28" black matte barrels, walnut stock, includes I.C., Mod. and Full tubes) $769.00
Price: (Turkey II — 24" or 26" camo barrels, Break-Up camo stock, includes Mod., Full and X-Full tubes) $849.00
Price: (Waterfowl II — 28" camo barrels, Advantage Wetlands camo stock, includes I.C., Mod. and Full tubes) $849.00

Tristar Silver II Shotgun
Similar to the Silver I except 26" barrel (Imp. Cyl., Mod., Full choke tubes, 12 and 20 ga.), 28" (Imp. Cyl., Mod., Full choke tubes, 12 ga. only), 26" (Imp. Cyl. & Mod. fixed chokes, 28 and 410), automatic selective ejectors. Weight is about 6 lbs., 15 oz. (12 ga., 26").
Price: $566.00

TRISTAR SILVER SPORTING O/U
Gauge: 12, 2-3/4" chambers, 20 3" chambers. **Barrel:** 28", 30" (Skeet, Imp. Cyl., Mod., Full choke tubes). **Weight:** 7-3/8 lbs. **Length:** 45-1/2" overall. **Stock:** 14-3/8"x1-1/2"x2-3/8". Figured walnut, cut checkering; Sporting Clays quick-mount buttpad. **Sights:** Target bead front. **Features:** Boxlock action with single selective mechanical trigger, automatic selective ejectors; special broadway channeled rib; vented barrel rib; chrome bores. Chrome-nickel finish on frame, with engraving. Introduced 1990. Imported from Italy by Tristar Sporting Arms Ltd.
Price: $765.00

TRISTAR-TR-SC "EMILIO RIZZINI" OVER/UNDER
Gauge: 12, 20, 2-3/4" chambers. **Barrel:** 28", 30" (Imp. Cyl., Mod., Full choke tubes). **Weight:** 7-1/2 lbs. **Length:** 46" overall (28" barrel). **Stock:** 1-1/2"x2-3/8"x14-3/8". Semi-fancy walnut; pistol grip with palm swell; semi-beavertail forend; black Sporting Clays recoil pad. **Features:** Silvered boxlock action with Four Locks locking system, auto ejectors, single selective (inertia) trigger, auto safety. Hard chrome bores. Vent. 10mm rib with target-style front and mid-rib beads, vent. spacer rib. Introduced 1998. Imported from Italy by Tristar Sporting Arms, Ltd.
Price: Sporting Clay model $996.00
Price: 20 ga. $1,073.00

Tristar TR-Royal Emillio Rizzini Over/Under
Similar to the TR-SC except has special parallel stock dimensions (1-1/2"x1-5/8"x14-3/8") to give low felt recoil; Rhino ported, extended choke tubes; solid barrel spacer; has "TR-Royal" gold engraved on the silvered receiver. Available in 12 gauge (28", 30") 20 and 28 gauge (28" only). Introduced 1999. Imported from Italy by Tristar Sporting Arms, Ltd.
Price: 12 ga. $1,340.00
Price: 20, 28 ga. $1,258.00

Shotguns — Over/Unders

Weatherby Athena Grade IV

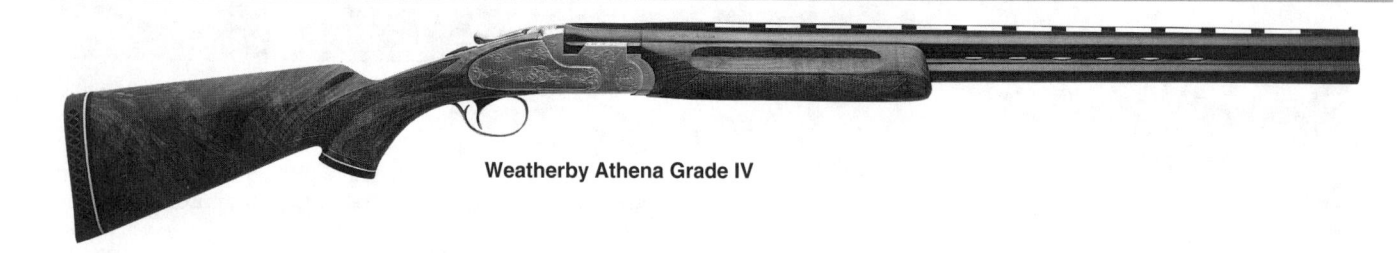

Tristar-TR-L "Emilio Rizzini" Over/Under
Similar to the TR-SC except has stock dimensions designed for female shooters (1-1/2" x 3" x 13-1/2"). Standard grade walnut. Introduced 1998. Imported from Italy by Tristar Sporting Arms, Ltd.
Price: $1,014.00

TRISTAR-TR-I, II "EMILIO RIZZINI" OVER/UNDERS
Gauge: 12, 20, 3" chambers (TR-I); 12, 16, 20, 28, 410 3" chambers (except 28, 2-3/4"). **Barrel:** 12 ga., 26" (Imp. Cyl. & Mod.), 28" (Mod. & Full); 20 ga., 26" (Imp. Cyl. & Mod.), fixed chokes. **Weight:** 7-1/2 lbs. **Stock:** 1-1/2"x2-3/8"x14-3/8". Walnut with palm swell pistol grip, hand checkering, semi-beavertail forend, black recoil pad. **Features:** Boxlock action with blued finish, Four Locks locking system, gold single selective (inertia) trigger system, automatic safety, extractors. Introduced 1998. Imported from Italy by Tristar Sporting Arms, Ltd.
Price: TR-I $687.00
Price: TR-II (automatic ejectors, choke tubes) 12, 16 ga. $879.00
Price: 20, 28 ga., 410 . . . . $924.00

Tristar-TR-MAG "Emilio Rizzini" Over/Under
Similar to the TR-I except 12 gauge, 3-1/2" chambers; choke tubes; 24" or 28" barrels with three choke tubes; extractors; auto safety. Matte blue finish on all metal, non-reflective wood finish. Introduced 1998. Imported from Italy by Tristar Sporting Arms, Ltd.
Price: $764.00
Price: Mossy Oak® Break-Up camo. $942.00
Price: Mossy Oak® Shadow Grass camo $942.00
Price: 10 ga., Mossy Oak® camo patterns $1,132.10

TRISTAR TR-CLASS SL EMILIO RIZZINI O/U
Gauge: 12, 2-3/4" chambers. **Barrel:** 28", 30", (Imp. Cyl., Mod., Full choke tubes). **Weight:** 7-1/2-7-3/4 lbs. **Stock:** 1-1/2"x1-3/8"x14-1/4". Fancy walnut with palm swell, hand checkering, semi-beavertail forend, black recoil pad, gloss finish. **Features:** Boxlock action with silvered, engraved sideplates; Four Lock locking system; automatic ejectors; hard chrome bores; vent tapered 7mm rib with target-style front bead. hand-fitted gun. Introduced 1999. Imported from Italy by Tristar Sporting Arms, Ltd.
Price: $1,775.00

TRISTAR WS/OU 12 SHOTGUN
Gauge: 12, 3-1/2" chambers. **Barrel:** 28" or 30" (Imp. Cyl., Mod., Full choke tubes). **Weight:** 6 lbs., 15 oz. **Length:** 46" overall. **Stock:** 14-1/8"x1-1/8"x2-3/8". European walnut with cut checkering, black vented recoil pad, matte finish. **Features:** Boxlock action with single selective trigger, automatic selective ejectors; chrome bores. Matte metal finish. Imported by Tristar Sporting Arms Ltd.
Price: $610.00

VERONA LX501 HUNTING O/U SHOTGUNS
Gauge: 12, 20, (3" chambers), 28, 410 (2-3/4"). **Barrel:** 28"; 12, 20 ga. have Interchoke tubes, 28 ga. and 410 have fixed Full & Mod. **Weight:** 6-7 lbs. **Stock:** Matte-finished walnut with machine-cut checkering. **Features:** Gold-plated single-selective trigger; ejectors; engraved, blued receiver; non-automatic safety; coil spring-operated firing pins. Introduced 1999. Imported from Italy by B.C. Outdoors.
Price: 12 and 20 ga. $720.00
Price: 28 ga. and 410 . . . . $755.00

Verona LX692 Gold Hunting Over/Under Shotguns
Similar to tthe Verona LX501 except has engraved, silvered receiver with false sideplates showing gold-inlaid bird hunting scenes on three sides; Schnabel forend tip; hand-cut checkering; black rubber butt pad. Available in 12 and 20 gauge only, with five InterChoke tubes. Introduced 1999. Imported from Italy by B.C. Outdoors.
Price: $1,295.00

Verona LX680 Sporting Over/Under Shotguns
Similar to the Verona LX501 except has engraved, silvered receiver; ventilated middle rib; beavertail forend; hand-cut checkering; available in 12 or 20 gauge only with 2-3/4" chambers. Introduced 1999. Imported from Italy by B.C. Outdoors.
Price: $1,020.00

Verona LX680 Skeet/Sporting, Trap O/U Shotguns
Similar to the Verona LX501 except with Skeet or trap stock dimensions; beavertail forend, palm swell on pistol grip; ventilated center barrel rib. Introduced 1999. Imported from Italy by B.C. Outdoors.
Price: $1,130.00
Price: Gold Competition (false sideplates with gold-inlaid hunting scenes) $1,500.00

Verona LX692 Gold Sporting Over/Under Shotguns
Similar to the Verona LX680 except with false sideplates that have gold-inlaid bird hunting scenes on three sides; red high-visibility front sight. Introduced 1999. Imported from Italy by B.C. Outdoors.
Price: $1,365.00

WEATHERBY ATHENA GRADE IV O/U SHOTGUNS
Gauge: 12, 20, 3" chambers. Action: Boxlock (simulated sidelock) top lever break-open. Selective auto ejectors, single selective trigger (selector inside trigger guard). **Barrel:** 26", 28", IMC Multi-Choke tubes. **Weight:** 12 ga., 7-3/8 lbs.; 20 ga. 6-7/8 lbs. **Stock:** American walnut, checkered pistol grip and forend (14-1/4"x1-1/2"x2-1/2"). **Features:** Mechanically operated trigger. Top tang safety, Greener cross bolt, fully engraved receiver, recoil pad installed. IMC models furnished with three interchangeable flush-fitting choke tubes. Imported from Japan by Weatherby. Introduced 1982.
Price: 12 ga., IMC, 26", 28" $2,499.00
Price: 20 ga., IMC, 26", 28" $2,499.00

Weatherby Athena Grade V Classic Field O/U
Similar to the Athena Grade IV except has rounded pistol grip, slender forend, oil-finished Claro walnut stock with fine-line checkering, Old English recoil pad. Sideplate receiver has rose and scroll engraving. Available in 12 gauge, 26", 28", 20 gauge, 26", 28", all with 3" chambers. Introduced 1993.
Price: $2,919.00

Weatherby Athena III Classic Field O/U
Has Grade III Claro walnut with oil finish, rounded pistol grip, slender forend; silver nitride/gray receiver has rose and scroll engraving with gold-overlay upland game scenes. Introduced 1999. Imported from Japan by Weatherby.
Price: 12, 20, 28 ga. $2,089.00

WEATHERBY ORION GRADE III FIELD O/U SHOTGUNS
Gauge: 12, 20, 3" chambers. **Barrel:** 26", 28", IMC Multi-Choke tubes. **Weight:** 6-1/2 to 9 lbs. **Stock:** 14-1/4"x1-1/2"x2-1/2". American walnut, checkered grip and forend. Rubber recoil pad. **Features:** Selective automatic ejectors, single selective inertia trigger. Top tang safety, Greener cross bolt. Has silver-gray receiver with engraving and gold duck/pheasant. Imported from Japan by Weatherby.
Price: Orion III, Field, 12, IMC, 26", 28" $1,879.00
Price: Orion III, Field, 20, IMC, 26", 28" $1,879.00

Shotguns — Over/Unders

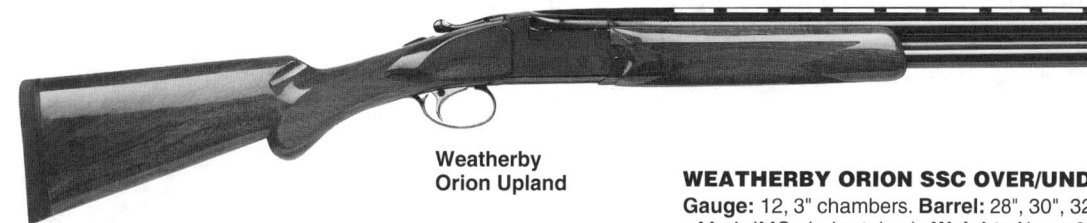

Weatherby Orion Upland

Weatherby Orion Grade III Classic Field O/U
Similar to the Orion III Field except the stock has a rounded pistol grip, satin oil finish, slender forend, Old English recoil pad. Introduced 1993. Imported from Japan by Weatherby.
Price: $1,879.00

Weatherby Orion III English Field O/U
Similar to the Orion III Classic Field except has straight grip English-style stock. Available in 12 gauge (28"), 20 gauge (26", 28") with IMC Multi-Choke tubes. Silver/gray nitride receiver is engraved and has gold-plate overlay. Introduced 1997. Imported from Japan by Weatherby.
Price: $1,959.00

Weatherby Orion Grade II Classic Field O/U
Similar to the Orion III Classic Field except stock has high-gloss finish, and the bird on the receiver is not gold. Available in 12 gauge, 26", 28", 30" barrels, 20 gauge, 26" 28", both with 3" chambers, 28 gauge, 26", 2-3/4" chambers. All have IMC choke tubes. Imported from Japan by Weatherby.
Price: $1,559.00

Weatherby Orion Grade I Field O/U
Similar to the Orion Grade III Field except has blued receiver with engraving, and the bird is not gold. Available in 12 gauge, 26", 28", 30", 20 gauge, 20", 28", both with 3" chambers and IMC choke tubes. Imported from Japan by Weatherby.
Price: $1,509.00

Weatherby Orion Upland O/U
Similar to the Orion Grade I. Plain blued receiver, gold W on the trigger guard; rounded pistol grip, slender forend of Claro walnut with high-gloss finish; black butt pad. Available in 12 and 20 gauge with 26" and 28" barrels. Introduced 1999. Imported from Japan by Weatherby.
Price: $1,249.00

WEATHERBY ORION SSC OVER/UNDER SHOTGUN
Gauge: 12, 3" chambers. **Barrel:** 28", 30", 32" (Skeet, SC1, Imp. Cyl., SC2, Mod. IMC choke tubes). **Weight:** About 8 lbs. **Stock:** 14-3/4"x2-1/4"x1-1/2". Claro walnut with satin oil finish; Schnabel forend tip; Sporter-style pistol grip; Pachmayr Decelerator recoil pad. **Features:** Designed for Sporting Clays competition. Has lengthened forcing cones and back-boring; ported barrels with 12mm grooved rib with mid-bead sight; mechanical trigger is adjustable for length of pull. Introduced 1998. Imported from Japan by Weatherby.
Price: SSC (Super Sporting Clays) $1,979.00

Weatherby Orion Grade II Classic Sporting O/U
Similar to the Orion II Classic Field except in 12 gauge only with (3" chambers), 28", 30" barrels with Skeet, SC1, SC2 Imp. Cyl., Mod. chokes. Weighs 7.5-8 lbs. Competition center vent rib; middle barrel and enlarged front beads. Rounded grip; high gloss stock. Radiused heel recoil pad. Receiver finished in silver nitride with acid-etched, gold-plate clay pigeon monogram. Barrels have lengthened forcing cones. Introduced 1993. Imported by Weatherby.
Price: $1,719.00

Weatherby Orion Grade II Sporting
Similar to the Orion II Classic Sporting except has traditional pistol grip with diamond inlay, and standard full-size forend. Available in 12 gauge only, 28", 30" barrels with Skeet, Imp. Cyl., SC2, Mod. Has lengthened forcing cones, back-boring, stepped competition rib, radius heel recoil pad, hand-engraved, silver/nitride receiver. Introduced 1992. Imported by Weatherby.
Price: $1,719.00

WINCHESTER SUPREME O/U SHOTGUNS
Gauge: 12, 2-3/4", 3" chambers. **Barrel:** 28", 30", Invector Plus choke tubes. **Weight:** 7 lbs. 6 oz. to 7 lbs. 12. oz. **Length:** 45" overall (28" barrel). **Stock:** Checkered walnut stock. **Features:** Chrome-plated chambers; back-bored barrels; tang barrel selector/safety; deep-blued finish. Introduced 2000. From U.S. Repeating Arms. Co.
Price: Supreme Field (26" or 28" barrel, 6mm ventilated rib) . . $1,383.00
Price: Supreme Sporting (28" or 30" barrel, 10mm rib,
 adj. trigger) $1,551.00

SHOTGUNS — SIDE BY SIDES

Variety of models for utility and sporting use, including some competitive shooting.

Beretta Model 470 Silver Hawk

Charles Daly Field Hunter

ARRIETA SIDELOCK DOUBLE SHOTGUNS
Gauge: 12, 16, 20, 28, 410. **Barrel:** Length and chokes to customer specs. **Weight:** To customer specs. **Stock:** 14-1/2"x1-1/2"x2-1/2 (standard dimensions), or to customer specs. Straight English with checkered butt (standard), or pistol grip. Select European walnut with oil finish. **Features:** Essentially a custom gun with myriad options. Holland & Holland-pattern hand-detachable sidelocks, selective automatic ejectors, double triggers (hinged front) standard. Some have self-opening action. Finish and engraving to customer specs. Imported from Spain by Wingshooting Adventures.
Price: Model 557, auto ejectors, from $2,750.00
Price: Model 570, auto ejectors, from $3,380.00
Price: Model 578, auto ejectors, from $3,740.00
Price: Model 600 Imperial, self-opening, from $4,990.00
Price: Model 601 Imperial Tiro, self-opening, from $5,750.00
Price: Model 801, from $7,950.00
Price: Model 802, from $7,950.00
Price: Model 803, from $5,850.00
Price: Model 871, auto ejectors, from $4,290.00
Price: Model 872, self-opening, from $9,790.00
Price: Model 873, self-opening, from $6,850.00
Price: Model 874, self-opening, from $7,950.00
Price: Model 875, self-opening, from $12,950.00

BERETTA MODEL 470 SILVER HAWK SHOTGUN
Gauge: 12, 20, 3" chambers. **Barrel:** 26" (Imp. Cyl. & Imp. Mod.), 28" (Mod. & Full). **Weight:** 5.9 lbs. (20 gauge). **Stock:** Select European walnut, straight English grip. **Features:** Boxlock action with single selective trigger; selector provides automatic ejection or extraction; silver-chrome action and forend iron with fine engraving; top lever highlighted with gold inlaid hawk's head. Comes with ABS case. Introduced 1997. Imported from Italy by Beretta U.S.A.
Price: 12 ga. $3,630.00
Price: 20 ga. $3,755.00

CHARLES DALY SUPERIOR HUNTER DOUBLE SHOTGUN
Gauge: 12, 20, 3" chambers, 28, 2-3/4" chambers. **Barrel:** 28" (Mod. & Full) 26" (Imp. Cyl. & Mod.). **Weight:** About 7 lbs. **Stock:** Checkered walnut pistol grip buttstock, splinter forend. **Features:** Silvered, engraved receiver; chrome-lined barrels; gold single trigger; automatic safety; extractors; gold bead front sight. Introduced 1997. Imported from Italy by K.B.I., Inc.
Price: $1,179.95
Price: 28 ga., 26" $1,094.95

Charles Daly Empire Hunter Double Shotgun
Similar to the Superior Hunter except has deluxe wood, game scene engraving, automatic ejectors. Introduced 1997. Imported from Italy by K.B.I., Inc.
Price: 12 or 20 .... $1,595.95

CHARLES DALY DIAMOND REGENT DL DOUBLE SHOTGUN
Gauge: 12, 20, 410, 3" chambers, 28, 2-3/4" chambers. **Barrel:** 28" (Mod. & Full), 26" (Imp. Cyl. & Mod.), 26" (Full & Full, 410). **Weight:** About 5-7 lbs. **Stock:** Special select fancy European walnut, English-style butt, splinter forend; hand-checkered; hand-rubbed oil finish. **Features:** Drop-forged action with gas escape valves; demiblock barrels of chrome-nickel steel with concave rib; selective automatic-ejectors; hand-detachable, double-safety H&H sidelocks with demi-relief hand engraving; H&H pattern easy-opening feature; hinged trigger; coin finished action. Introduced 1997. Imported from Spain by K.B.I., Inc.
Price: 12 or 20 .... $19,999.00
Price: 28 .... $20,499.00
Price: 410 .... $20,499.00

CHARLES DALY FIELD HUNTER DOUBLE SHOTGUN
Gauge: 10, 12, 20, 28, 410 (3" chambers; 28 has 2-3/4"). **Barrel:** 32" (Mod. & Mod.), 28", 30" (Mod. & Full.), 26" (Imp. Cyl. & Mod.) 410 (Full & Full). **Weight:** 6 lbs. to 11.4 lbs. **Stock:** Checkered walnut pistol grip and forend. **Features:** Silvered, engraved receiver; gold single selective trigger in 10-, 12-, and 20 ga.; double triggers in 28 and 410; automatic safety; extractors; gold bead front sight. Introduced 1997. Imported from Spain by K.B.I., Inc.
Price: 10 ga. $984.95
Price: 12 or 20 ga. $809.95
Price: 28 ga. $854.95
Price: 410-bore $854.95
Price: As above, 12 or 20 AE. MC $939.95

CHARLES DALY DIAMOND DL DOUBLE SHOTGUN
Gauge: 12, 20, 410, 3" chambers, 28, 2-3/4" chambers. **Barrel:** 28" (Mod. & Full), 26" (Imp. Cyl. & Mod.), 26" (Full & Full, 410). **Weight:** About 5-7 lbs. **Stock:** Select fancy European walnut, English-style butt, beavertail forend; hand-checkered, hand-rubbed oil finish. **Features:** Drop-forged action with gas escape valves; demiblock barrels with concave rib; selective automatic ejectors; hand-detachable double safety sidelocks with hand-engraved rose and scrollwork. Hinged front trigger. Color case-hardened receiver. Introduced 1997. Imported from Spain by K.B.I., Inc.
Price: 12 or 20 .... $6,959.95
Price: 28 .... $7,274.95
Price: 410 .... $7,274.95

DAKOTA PREMIER GRADE SHOTGUNS
Gauge: 12, 16, 20, 28, 410. **Barrel:** 27". **Weight:** NA. **Length:** NA. **Stock:** Exhibition-grade English walnut, hand-rubbed oil finish with straight grip and splinter forend. **Features:** French grey finish; 50 percent coverage engraving; double triggers; selective ejectors. Finished to customer specifications. Made in U.S. by Dakota Arms.
Price: 12, 16, 20 gauge $13,950.00
Price: 28 and 410 gauge $15,345.00

Dakota The Dakota Legend Shotguns
Similar to Premier Grade except has special selection English walnut, full-coverage scroll engraving, oak and leather case. Made in U.S. by Dakota Arms.
Price: 12, 16, 20 gauge $18,000.00
Price: 28 and 410 gauge $19,800.00

SHOTGUNS — SIDE BY SIDES

Fabarm Classic Lion

A.H. Fox DE Grade

Garbi Model 100

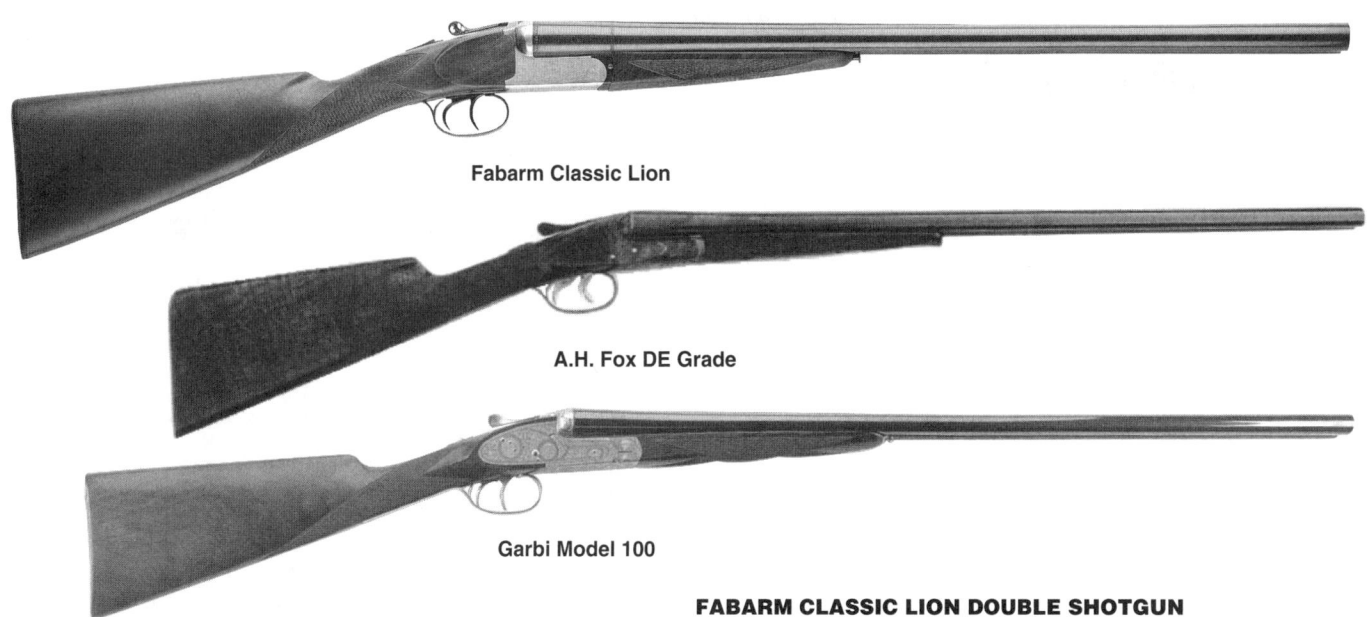

EAA/BAIKAL BOUNTY HUNTER IZH-43K SHOTGUN
Gauge: 12 (2-3/4", 3" chambers), 20 (3" chambers), 28 (2-3/4" chambers), 410 (3" chambers). **Barrel:** 18-1/2", 20", 24", 26", 28", three choke tubes. **Weight:** 7.28 lbs. **Overall length:** NA. **Stock:** Walnut, checkered forearm and grip. **Features:** Machined receiver; hammer-forged barrels with chrome-line bores; external hammers; double triggers (single, selective trigger available); rifle barrel inserts optional. Imported by European American Armory.
Price: IZH-43K (12 gauge) $439.00
Price: IZH-43K (20, 28 and 410 gauge) $469.00

EAA/BAIKAL IZH-43 BOUNTY HUNTER SHOTGUNS
Gauge: 12 (2-3/4", 3" chambers), 16 (2-3/4" chambers), 20 (2-3/4" and 3" chambers). **Barrel:** 20", 24", 26", 28"; imp., mod. and full choke tubes. **Weight:** NA. **Stock:** Hardwood or walnut; checkered forend and grip. **Features:** Hammer forged barrel; internal hammers; extractors; engraved receiver; automatic tang safety; non-glare rib. Imported by European American Armory.
Price: IZH-43 Bounty Hunter (12 gauge, 2-3/4" chambers, 20" brl., dbl. triggers, hardwood stock) $299.00
Price: IZH-43 Bounty Hunter (12 or 20 gauge, 2-3/4" chambers, 20" brl., dbl. triggers, walnut stock) $359.00

EAA/BAIKAL MP-213 SHOTGUN
Gauge: 12, 3" chambers. **Barrel:** 24", 26", 28"; imp., mod. and full choke tubes. **Weight:** 7.28 lbs. **Stock:** Walnut, checkered forearm and grip; rubber butt pad. **Features:** Hammer-forged barrels; chrome-lined bores; machined receiver; double trigger (each trigger fires both barrels independently); ejectors. Introduced 2000. Imported by European American Armory.
Price: IZH-213 . . . . $899.00

EAA/BAIKAL BOUNTY HUNTER MP-213 COACH GUN
Gauge: 12, 2-3/4" chambers. **Barrel:** 20", imp., mod. and full choke tubes. **Weight:** 7 lbs. **Stock:** Walnut, checkered forend and grip. **Features:** Selective double trigger with removable assembly (single trigger and varied pull weights available); ejectors; engraved receiver. Imported by European American Armory.
Price: MP-213 . . . . $899.00

E.M.F. HARTFORD MODEL COWBOY SHOTGUN
Gauge: 12. **Barrel:** 20". **Weight:** NA. **Length:** NA. **Stock:** Checkered walnut. **Sights:** Center bead. **Features:** Exposed hammers; color-case hardened receiver; blued barrel. Introduced 2001. Imported from Spain by E.M.F. Co. Inc.
Price: $625.00

FABARM CLASSIC LION DOUBLE SHOTGUN
Gauge: 12, 3" chambers. **Barrel:** 26" (Cyl., Imp. Cyl., Mod., Imp. Mod., Full choke tubes). **Weight:** 7.2 lbs. **Length:** 47.6" overall. **Stock:** English-style oil-finished European walnut. **Features:** Boxlock action with double triggers, automatic ejectors, automatic safety. Introduced 1998. Imported from Italy by Heckler & Koch, Inc.
Price: Grade I $1,499.00
Price: Grade II $2,249.00

A.H. FOX SIDE-BY-SIDE SHOTGUNS
Gauge: 16, 20, 28, 410. **Barrel:** Length and chokes to customer specifications. Rust-blued Chromox or Krupp steel. **Weight:** 5-1/2 to 6-3/4 lbs. **Stock:** Dimensions to customer specifications. Hand-checkered Turkish Circassian walnut with hand-rubbed oil finish. Straight, semi or full pistol grip; splinter, Schnabel or beavertail forend; traditional pad, hard rubber buttplate or skeleton butt. **Features:** Boxlock action with automatic ejectors; double or Fox single selective trigger. Scalloped, rebated and color case-hardened receiver; hand finished and hand-engraved. Grades differ in engraving, inlays, grade of wood, amount of hand finishing. Add $1,500 for 28 or 410-bore. Introduced 1993. Made in U.S. by Connecticut Shotgun Mfg.
Price: CE Grade $11,000.00
Price: XE Grade $12,500.00
Price: DE Grade $15,000.00
Price: FE Grade $20,000.00
Price: Exhibition Grade $30,000.00
Price: 28/410 CE Grade $12,500.00
Price: 28/410 XE Grade $14,000.00
Price: 28/410 DE Grade $16,500.00
Price: 28/410 FE Grade $21,500.00
Price: 28/410 Exhibition Grade $30,000.00

GARBI MODEL 100 DOUBLE
Gauge: 12, 16, 20, 28. **Barrel:** 26", 28", choked to customer specs. **Weight:** 5-1/2 to 7-1/2 lbs. **Stock:** 14-1/2"x2-1/4"x1-1/2". European walnut. Straight grip, checkered butt, classic forend. **Features:** Sidelock action, automatic ejectors, double triggers standard. Color case-hardened action, coin finish optional. Single trigger; beavertail forend, etc. optional. Five other models are available. Imported from Spain by Wm. Larkin Moore.
Price: From $3,700.00

Garbi Model 200 Side-by-Side
Similar to the Garbi Model 100 except has heavy-duty locks, magnum proofed. Very fine Continental-style floral and scroll engraving, well figured walnut stock. Other mechanical features remain the same. Imported from Spain by Wm. Larkin Moore.
Price: $10,000.00

SHOTGUNS — SIDE BY SIDES

Bill Hanus Birdgun

Merkel Model 47E

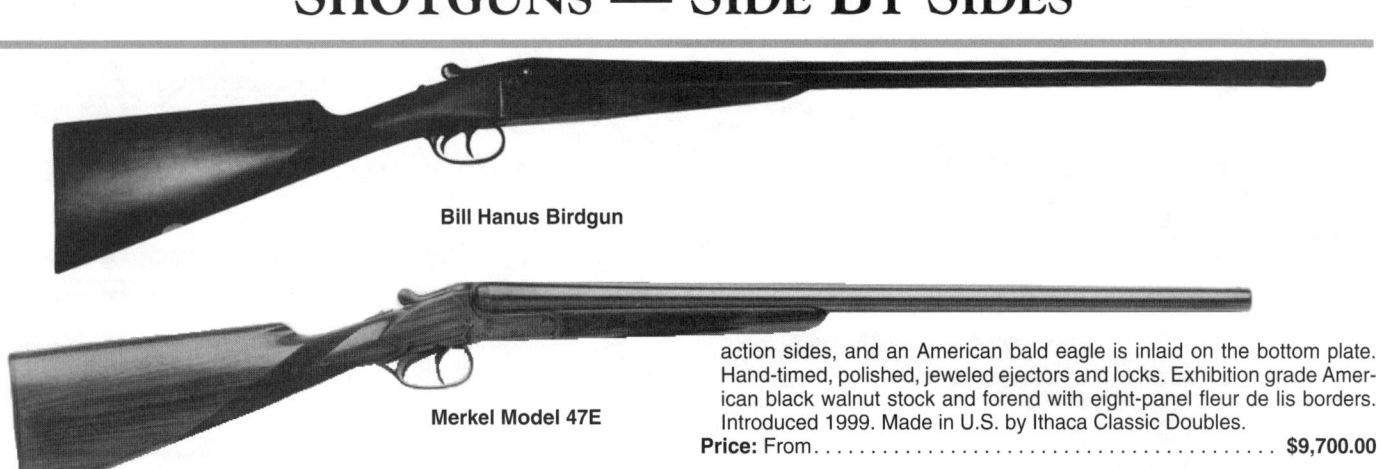

Garbi Model 101 Side-by-Side
Similar to the Garbi Model 100 except is hand engraved with scroll engraving, select walnut stock. Better overall quality than the Model 100. Imported from Spain by Wm. Larkin Moore.
Price: From $4,750.00

Garbi Model 103A, B Side-by-Side
Similar to the Garbi Model 100 except has Purdey-type fine scroll and rosette engraving. Better overall quality than the Model 101. Model 103B has nickel-chrome steel barrels, H&H-type easy opening mechanism; other mechanical details remain the same. Imported from Spain by Wm. Larkin Moore.
Price: Model 103A, from $5,900.00
Price: Model 103B, from $8,200.00

BILL HANUS BIRDGUN
Gauge: 16, 20, 28. **Barrel:** 27", 20 and 28 ga.; 28", 16 ga. (Skeet 1 & Skeet 2). **Weight:** 5 lbs., 4 oz. to 6 lbs., 4 oz. **Stock:** 14-3/8"x1-1/2"x2-3/8", with 1/4" cast-off. Select walnut. **Features:** Boxlock action with ejectors; splinter forend, straight English grip; checkered butt; English leather-covered handguard included. Made by AYA. Introduced 1998. Imported from Spain by Bill Hanus Birdguns.
Price: $2,295.00
Price: Single-selective trigger, add $350.00

IAR COWBOY SHOTGUNS
Gauge: 12. **Barrel:** 20", 28". **Weight:** 7 lbs. (20" barrel). **Length:** 36-7/8" overall (20" barrel). **Stock:** Walnut. **Features:** Exposed hammers; blued or brown barrels; double triggers. Introduced 1997. Imported from Italy by IAR, Inc.
Price: Gentry model, 20" or 28", engraved, bright-finished locks, blue barrels $1,895.00
Price: Cowboy model, 20" or 28", no engraving on color case-hardened locks, brown patina barrels $1,895.00

ITHACA CLASSIC DOUBLES SPECIAL FIELD GRADE SxS
Gauge: 20, 28, 2-3/4" chambers, 410, 3". **Barrel:** 26", 28", 30", fixed chokes. **Weight:** 5 lbs., 14 oz. (20 gauge). **Stock:** 14-1/2"x2-1/4"x1-3/8". High-grade American black walnut, hand-rubbed oil finish; splinter or beavertail forend, straight or pistol grip. **Features:** Double triggers, ejectors; color case-hardened, engraved action body with matted top surfaces. Introduced 1999. Made in U.S. by Ithaca Classic Doubles.
Price: From $3,150.00

Ithaca Classic Doubles Grade 4E Classic SxS Shotgun
Similar to the Special Field Grade except has gold-plated triggers, jeweled barrel flats and hand-turned locks. Feather crotch and flame-grained black walnut is hand-checkered 28 lpi with fleur de lis pattern. Action body is engraved with three game scenes and bank note scroll, and color case-hardened. Introduced 1999. Made in U.S. by Ithaca Classic Doubles.
Price: From $4,900.00

Ithaca Classic Doubles Grade 7E Classic SxS Shotgun
Similar to the Special Field Grade except engraved with bank note scroll and flat 24k gold game scenes: gold setter and gold pointer on opposite action sides, and an American bald eagle is inlaid on the bottom plate. Hand-timed, polished, jeweled ejectors and locks. Exhibition grade American black walnut stock and forend with eight-panel fleur de lis borders. Introduced 1999. Made in U.S. by Ithaca Classic Doubles.
Price: From $9,700.00

Ithaca Classic Doubles Sousa Special Grade SxS Shotgun
Similar to the Special Field Grade except presentation grade American black walnut, hand-carved and checkered; hand-engraving with 24-karat gold inlays; tuned action and hand-applied finishes. Made in U.S. by Ithaca Classic Doubles.
Price: From $14,900.00

LEBEAU - COURALLY BOXLOCK SxS SHOTGUN
Gauge: 12, 16, 20, 28, 410-bore. **Barrel:** 25" to 32". **Weight:** To customer specifications. **Stock:** French walnut. **Features:** Anson & Deely-type action with automatic ejectors; single or double triggers. Essentially a custom gun built to customer specifications. Imported from Belgium by Wm. Larkin Moore.
Price: From $18,500.00

LEBEAU - COURALLY SIDELOCK SxS SHOTGUN
Gauge: 12, 16, 20, 28, 410-bore. **Barrel:** 25" to 32". **Weight:** To customer specifications. **Stock:** Fancy French walnut. **Features:** Holland & Holland-type action with automatic ejectors; single or double triggers. Essentially a custom gun built to customer specifications. Imported from Belgium by Wm. Larkin Moore.
Price: From $37,500.00

MERKEL MODEL 47E, 147E SIDE-BY-SIDE SHOTGUNS
Gauge: 12, 3" chambers, 16, 2-3/4" chambers, 20, 3" chambers. **Barrel:** 12, 16 ga.—28"; 20 ga.—26-3/4" (Imp. Cyl. & Mod., Mod. & Full). **Weight:** About 6-3/4 lbs. (12 ga.). **Stock:** Oil-finished walnut; straight English or pistol grip. **Features:** Anson & Deeley-type boxlock action with single selective or double triggers, automatic safety, cocking indicators. Color case-hardened receiver with standard Arabesque engraving. Imported from Germany by GSI.
Price: Model 47E (H&H ejectors) $2,795.00
Price: Model 147E (as above with ejectors) $3,395.00

Merkel Model 47SL, 147SL Side-by-Sides
Similar to the Model 122 except with Holland & Holland-style sidelock action with cocking indicators, ejectors. Silver-grayed receiver and sideplates have Arabesque engraving, engraved border and screws (Model 47S), or fine hunting scene engraving (Model 147S). Imported from Germany by GSI.
Price: Model 47SL $5,395.00
Price: Model 147SL $6,995.00
Price: Model 247SL (English-style engraving, large scrolls) . . . $6,995.00
Price: Model 447SL (English-style engraving, small scrolls) . . . $8,995.00

Merkel Model 280EL and 360EL Shotguns
Similar to Model 47E except has smaller frame. Greener cross bolt with double under-barrel locking lugs, fine engraved hunting scenes on silver-grayed receiver, luxury-grade wood, Anson and Deely box-lock action. Holland & Holland ejectors, single-selective or double triggers. Introduced 2000. From Merkel.
Price: Model 280EL (28 gauge, 28" barrel, imp. cyl. and mod. chokes) 4 mod. chokes) $4,995.00
Price: Model 360EL (410 gauge, 28" barrel, mod. and full chokes) $4,995.00
Price: Model 280/360EL two-barrel set (28 and 410 gauge as above) $7,495.00

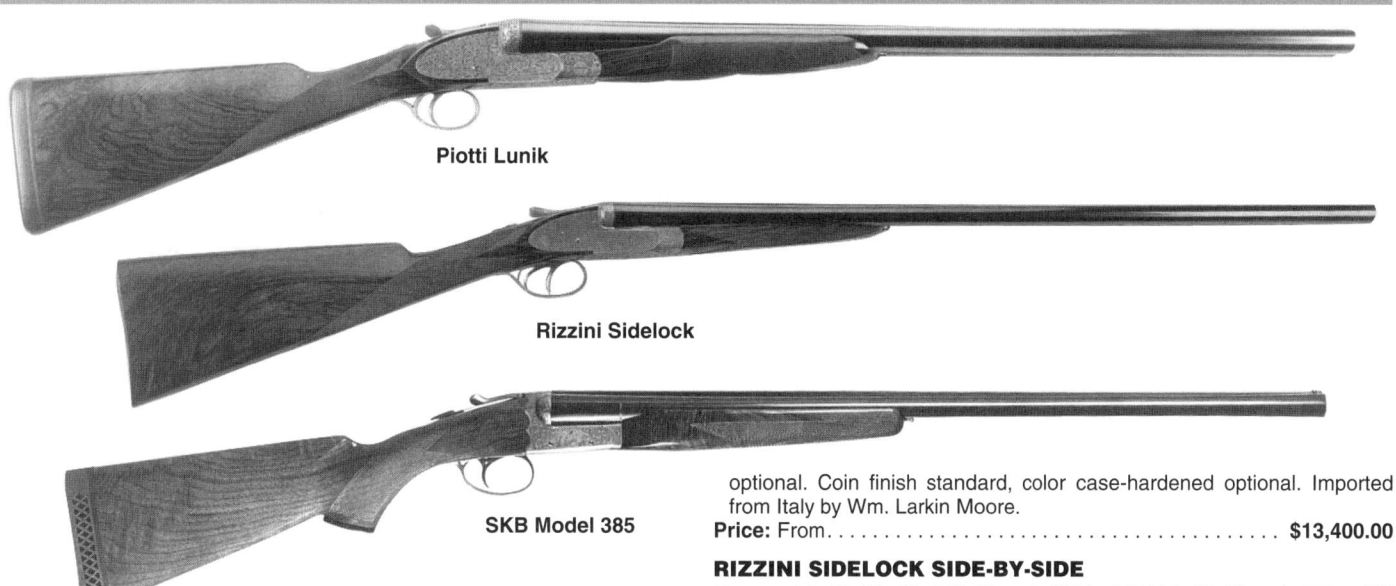

SHOTGUNS — SIDE BY SIDES

Piotti Lunik

Rizzini Sidelock

SKB Model 385

Merkel Model 280SL and 360SL Shotguns
 Similar to Model 280EL and 360EL except has sidelock action, double triggers, English-style Arabesque engraving. Introduced 2000. From Merkel.
Price: Model 280SL (28 gauge, 28" barrel, imp. cyl. and
  mod. chokes) $7,495.00
Price: Model 360SL (410 gauge, 28" barrel, mod. and
  full chokes) $7,495.00
Price: Model 280/360SL two-barrel set $10,995.00

PIOTTI KING NO. 1 SIDE-BY-SIDE
 Gauge: 12, 16, 20, 28, 410. **Barrel:** 25" to 30" (12 ga.), 25" to 28" (16, 20, 28, 410). To customer specs. Chokes as specified. **Weight:** 6-1/2 lbs. to 8 lbs. (12 ga. to customer specs.). **Stock:** Dimensions to customer specs. Finely figured walnut; straight grip with checkered butt with classic splinter forend and hand-rubbed oil finish standard. Pistol grip, beavertail forend. **Features:** Holland & Holland pattern sidelock action, automatic ejectors. Double trigger; non-selective single trigger optional. Coin finish standard; color case-hardened optional. Top rib; level, file-cut; concave, ventilated optional. Very fine, full coverage scroll engraving with small floral bouquets. Imported from Italy by Wm. Larkin Moore.
Price: From. $20,900.00

Piotti King Extra Side-by-Side
 Similar to the Piotti King No. 1 except with upgraded engraving. Choice of any type of engraving, including bulino game scene engraving and game scene engraving with gold inlays. Engraved and signed by a master engraver. Other mechanical specifications remain the same. Imported from Italy by Wm. Larkin Moore.
Price: From. $25,900.00

Piotti Lunik Side-by-Side
 Similar to the Piotti King No. 1 in overall quality. Has Renaissance-style large scroll engraving in relief. Best quality Holland & Holland-pattern sidelock ejector double with chopper lump (demi-bloc) barrels. Other mechanical specifications remain the same. Imported from Italy by Wm. Larkin Moore.
Price: From. $21,900.00

PIOTTI PIUMA SIDE-BY-SIDE
 Gauge: 12, 16, 20, 28, 410. **Barrel:** 25" to 30" (12 ga.), 25" to 28" (16, 20, 28, 410). **Weight:** 5-1/2 to 6-1/4 lbs. (20 ga.). **Stock:** Dimensions to customer specs. Straight grip stock with walnut checkered butt, classic splinter forend, hand-rubbed oil finish are standard; pistol grip, beavertail forend, satin luster finish optional. **Features:** Anson & Deeley boxlock ejector double with chopper lump barrels. Level, file-cut rib, light scroll and rosette engraving, scalloped frame. Double triggers; single non-selective optional. Coin finish standard, color case-hardened optional. Imported from Italy by Wm. Larkin Moore.
Price: From. $13,400.00

RIZZINI SIDELOCK SIDE-BY-SIDE
 Gauge: 12, 16, 20, 28, 410. **Barrel:** 25" to 30" (12, 16, 20 ga.), 25" to 28" (28, 410). To customer specs. Chokes as specified. **Weight:** 6-1/2 lbs. to 8 lbs. (12 ga. to customer specs). **Stock:** Dimensions to customer specs. Finely figured walnut; straight grip with checkered butt with classic splinter forend and hand-rubbed oil finish standard. Pistol grip, beavertail forend. **Features:** Sidelock action, auto ejectors. Double triggers or non-selective single trigger standard. Coin finish standard. Imported from Italy by Wm. Larkin Moore.
Price: 12, 20 ga., from $52,000.00
Price: 28, 410 bore, from $60,000.00

SKB Model 385 Sporting Clays
 Similar to the Field Model 385 except 12 gauge only; 28" barrel with choke tubes; raised ventilated rib with metal middle bead and white front. Stock dimensions 14-1/4"x1-7/16"x1-7/8". Introduced 1998. Imported from Japan by G.U. Inc.
Price: $2,159.00
Price: Sporting Clays set, 20, 28 ga. $3,059.00

SKB MODEL 385 SIDE-BY-SIDE
 Gauge: 12, 20, 3" chambers; 28, 2-3/4" chambers. **Barrel:** 26" (Imp. Cyl., Mod., Skeet choke tubes). **Weight:** 6-3/4 lbs. **Length:** 42-1/2" overall. **Stock:** 14-1/8"x1-1/2"x2-1/2" American walnut with straight or pistol grip stock, semi-beavertail forend. **Features:** Boxlock action. Silver nitrided receiver with engraving; solid barrel rib; single selective trigger, selective automatic ejectors, automatic safety. Introduced 1996. Imported from Japan by G.U. Inc.
Price: $2,049.00
Price: Field Set, 20, 28 ga., 26" or 28", English or pistol grip. . . $2,929.00

SKB Model 485 Side-by-Side
 Similar to the Model 385 except has dummy sideplates, raised ventilated rib with metal middle bead and white front, extensive upland game scene engraving, semi-fancy American walnut English or pistol grip stock. Imported from Japan by G.U. Inc.
Price: $2,769.00
Price: Field set, 20, 28 ga., 26" $2,769.00

STOEGER/IGA UPLANDER SIDE-BY-SIDE SHOTGUN
 Gauge: 12, 20, 28, 2-3/4" chambers; 410, 3" chambers. **Barrel:** 26" (Full & Full, 410 only, Imp. Cyl. & Mod.), 28" (Mod. & Full). **Weight:** 6-3/4 to 7 lbs. **Stock:** 14-1/2"x1-1/2"x2-1/2". Oil-finished hardwood. Checkered pistol grip and forend. **Features:** Automatic safety, extractors only, solid matted barrel rib. Double triggers only. Introduced 1983. Imported from Brazil by Stoeger Industries.
Price: $437.00
Price: With choke tubes $477.00
Price: Coach Gun, 12, 20, 410, 20" bbls. $415.00
Price: Coach Gun, nickel finish, black stock. $464.00
Price: Coach Gun, engraved stock. $479.00

34TH EDITION, 2002

SHOTGUNS — SIDE BY SIDES

Stoeger/IGA Turkey

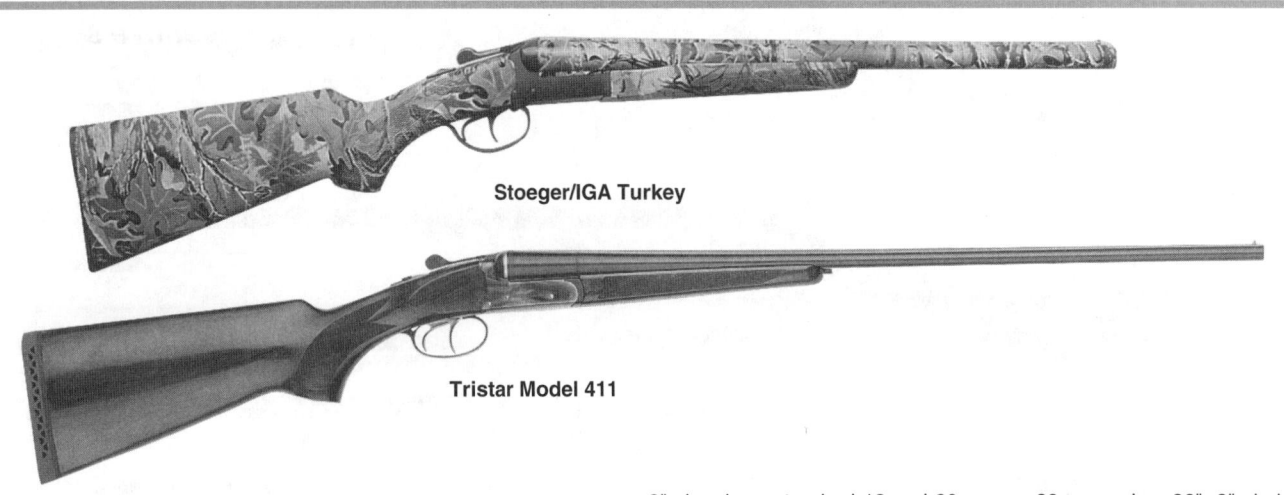

Tristar Model 411

Stoeger/IGA Ladies Side-by-Side
Similar to the Uplander except in 20 ga. only with 24" barrels (Imp. Cyl. & Mod. choke tubes), 13" length of pull, ventilated rubber recoil pad. Has extractors, double triggers, automatic safety. Introduced 1996. Imported from Brazil by Stoeger.
Price: $489.00

Stoeger/IGA Turkey Side-by-Side
Similar to the Uplander Model except has Advantage camouflage on stock, forend and barrels; 12 gauge only with 3" chambers, and has 24" choke tube barrels. Overall length 40". Introduced 1997. Imported from Brazil by Stoeger.
Price: $559.00

Stoeger/IGA English Stock Side-by-Side
Similar to the Uplander except in 410 or 20 ga. only with 24" barrels, straight English stock and beavertail forend. Has automatic safety, extractors, double triggers. Intro 1996. Imported from Brazil by Stoeger.
Price: 410 ga (mod. and mod. chokes)................. $437.00
Price: 20 ga (imp. cyl and mod. choke tubes) $477.00

Stoeger/IGA Youth Side-by-Side
Similar to the Uplander except in 410-bore with 24" barrels (Mod.), or 20 ga. (imp. cyl. and mod.), 13" length of pull, ventilated recoil pad. Has double triggers, extractors, auto safety. Intro 1996. Imported from Brazil by Stoeger.
Price: 410 gauge $449.00
Price: 20 gauge $449.00

Stoeger/IGA Coach and Deluxe Coach Gun
Similar to the Uplander except 12, 20 or 410 gauges, 20" barrels, choked Imp. Cyl. & Mod., 3" chambers; hardwood pistol grip stock with checkering; double triggers; extractors. Introduced 1997. Imported form Brazil by Stoeger.
Price: Coach Gun.. $415.00
Price: Deluxe Coach Gun (engraved stagecoach on stock)..... $415.00

Stoeger/IGA Uplander Shotgun
Gauge: 12, 20, 410 (3" chambers); 28 (2-3/4" chambers). **Barrel:** 24", 26", 28". **Weight:** 6-3/4 lbs. **Length:** 40" to 44" overall. **Stock:** Brazilian hardwood; checkered grip and forearm. **Features:** Automatic safety; extractors; handles steel shot. Introduced 1997. Imported from Brazil by Stoeger.
Price: With chokes tubes $477.00

Stoeger/IGA Deluxe Uplander Supreme Shotgun
Similar to the Uplander except with semi-fancy American walnut with thin black Pachmayr rubber recoil pad, matte lacquer finish. Choke tubes and 3" chambers standard 12 and 20 gauge; 28 gauge has 26", 3" chokes, fixed Mod. & Full. Double gold plated triggers; extractors. Introduced 1997. Imported from Brazil by Stoeger.
Price: 12, 20 .... $599.00

TRADITIONS ELITE SERIES SIDE-BY-SIDE SHOTGUNS
Gauge: 12, 3"; 20, 3"; 28, 2-3/4"; 410, 3". **Barrel:** 26". **Weight:** 5 lbs., 12 oz. to 6-1/2 lbs. **Length:** 43" overall. **Stock:** Walnut. **Features:** Chrome-lined barrels; fixed chokes (Elite Field III ST, Field I DT and Field I ST) or choke tubes (Elite Hunter ST); extractors (Hunter ST and Field I models) or automatic ejectors (Field III ST); top tang safety. Imported from Fausti of Italy by Traditions.
Price: (Elite Field I DT — 12, 20, 28 or 410 ga.; I.C. and Mod. fixed chokes [F and F on 410]; double triggers) .... $759.00 to $819.00
Price: (Elite Field I ST — 12, 20, 28 or 410 ga.; same as DT but with single trigger) .... $889.00 to $949.00
Price: (Elite Field III ST — 28 or 410 ga.; gold-engraved receiver; high-grade walnut stock) $1,999.00
Price: (Elite Hunter ST — 12 or 20 ga.; blued receiver; I.C. and Mod. choke tubes) $949.00

TRISTAR ROTA MODEL 411 SIDE-BY-SIDE
Gauge: 12, 16, 20, 410, 3" chambers; 28, 2-3/4". **Barrel:** 12 ga., 26", 28"; 16, 20, 28 ga., 410-bore, 26"; 12 and 20 ga. have three choke tubes, 16, 28 (Imp. Cyl. & Mod.), 410 (Mod. & Full) fixed chokes. **Weight:** 6-6-3/4 lbs. **Stock:** 14-3/8" l.o.p. Standard walnut with pistol grip, splinter-style forend; hand checkered. **Features:** Engraved, color case-hardened boxlock action; double triggers; extractors; solid barrel rib. Introduced 1998. Imported from Italy by Tristar Sporting Arms, Ltd.
Price: $745.00

Tristar Rota Model 411D Side-by-Side
Similar to the Model 411 except has automatic ejectors, straight English-style stock, single trigger. Solid barrel rib with matted surface; chrome bores; color case-hardened frame; splinter forend. Introduced 1999. Imported from Italy by Tristar Sporting Arms, Ltd.
Price: $1,110.00

Tristar Rota Model 411R Coach Gun Side-by-Side
Similar to the Model 411 except in 12 or 20 gauge only with 20" barrels and fixed chokes (Cyl. & Cyl.). Has double triggers, extractors, choke tubes. Introduced 1999. Imported from Italy by Tristar Sporting Arms, Ltd.
Price: $745.00

Tristar Rota Model 411F Side-by-Side
Similar to the Model 411 except has silver, engraved receiver, ejectors, IC, M and F choke tubes, English-style stock. Imported from Italy by Tristar Sporting Arms Ltd.
Price: $1,602.00

SHOTGUNS — BOLT ACTIONS & SINGLE SHOTS

Variety of designs for utility and sporting purposes, as well as for competitive shooting.

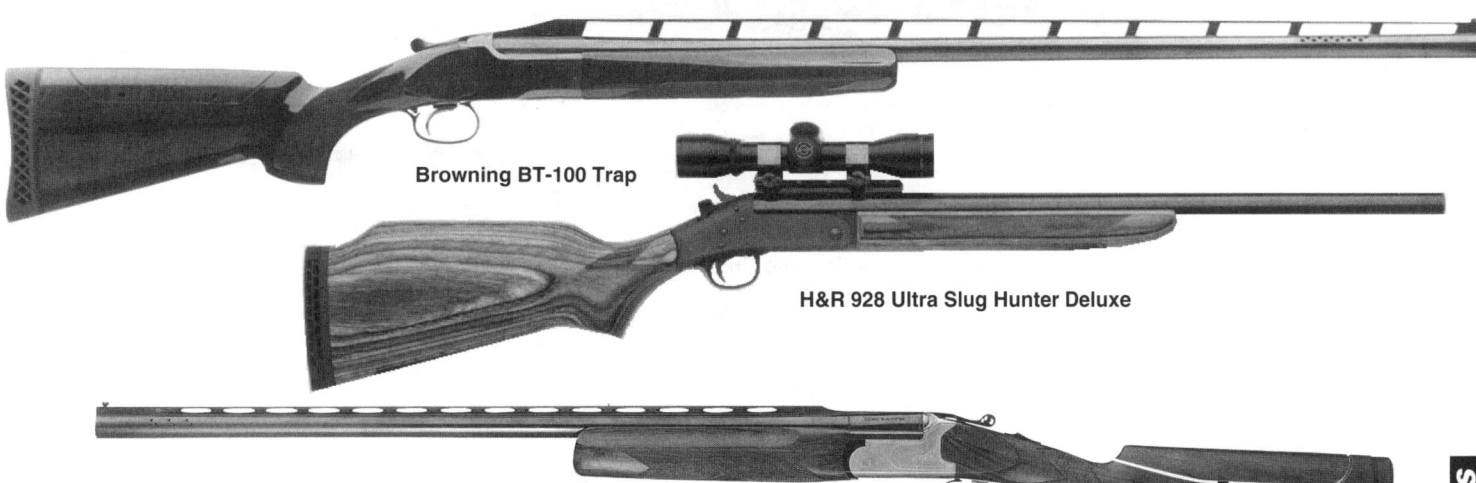

Browning BT-100 Trap

H&R 928 Ultra Slug Hunter Deluxe

Fabarm Monotrap

BERETTA DT 10 TRIDENT TRAP TOP SINGLE SHOTGUN
Gauge: 12, 3" chamber. **Barrel:** 34"; five Optima Choke tubes (full, full, imp. modified, mod. and imp. cyl.). **Weight:** 8.8 lbs. **Length:** NA. **Stock:** High-grade walnut; adjustable. **Features:** Detachable, adjustable trigger group; Optima Bore for improved shot pattern and reduced recoil; slim Optima Choke tubes; raised and thickened receiver for long life. Introduced 2000. Imported from Italy by Beretta USA.
Price: $9,450.00

BRNO ZBK 100 SINGLE BARREL SHOTGUN
Gauge: 12 or 20. **Barrel:** 27.5". **Weight:** 5.5 lbs. **Length:** 44" overall. **Stock:** Beech. **Features:** Polished blue finish; sling swivels. Announced 1998. Imported from The Czech Republic by Euro-Imports.
Price: $185.00

BROWNING BT-99 TRAP SHOTGUN
Gauge: 12, 2-3/4" chamber. **Barrel:** 32" or 34"; Invector choke system (full choke tube only included); High Post Rib; back-bored. **Weight:** 8 lbs., 10 oz. (34" bbl.). **Length:** 50-1/2" overall (34" bbl.). **Stock:** Conventional or adjustable-comb. **Features:** Re-introduction of the BT-99 Trap Shotgun. Full beavertail forearm; checkered walnut stock; ejector; rubber butt pad. Re-introduced 2001. Imported by Browning.
Price: Conventional stock, 32" or 34" barrel............ $1,216.00
Price: Adj.-comb stock, 32" or 34" barrel................ $1,449.00

BROWNING BT-100 TRAP SHOTGUN
Gauge: 12, 2-3/4" chamber. **Barrel:** 32", 34" (Invector Plus); back-bored; also with fixed Full choke. **Weight:** 8 lbs., 10 oz. (34" bbl.). **Length:** 48-1/2" overall (32" barrel). **Stock:** 14-3/8"x1-9/16"x1-7/16x2" (Monte Carlo); 14-3/8"x1-3/4"x1-1/4"x2-1/8" (thumbhole). Walnut with high gloss finish; cut checkering. Wedge-shaped forend with finger groove. **Features:** Available in stainless steel or blue. Has drop-out trigger adjustable for weight of pull from 3-1/2 to 5-1/2 lbs., and for three length positions; Ejector-Selector allows ejection or extraction of shells. Available with adjustable comb stock and thumbhole style. Introduced 1995. Imported from Japan by Browning.
Price: Grade I, blue, Monte Carlo, Invector Plus $2,222.00
Price: Grade I, blue, adj. comb, Invector Plus $2,455.00
Price: Stainless steel, Monte Carlo, Invector Plus $2,688.00
Price: Stainless steel, adj. comb, Invector Plus $2,923.00

EAA/BAIKAL IZH-18 SINGLE BARREL SHOTGUN
Gauge: 12 (2-3/4" and 3" chambers), 20 (2-3/4" and 3"), 16 (2-3/4"), 410 (3"). **Barrel:** 26-1/2", 28-1/2"; modified or full choke (12 and 20 gauge); full only (16 gauge), improved cylinder (20 gauge) and full or improved modified (410). **Weight:** NA. **Stock:** Walnut-stained hardwood; rubber recoil pad. **Features:** Hammer-forged steel barrel; machined receiver; cross-block safety; cocking lever with external cocking indicator; optional automatic ejector, screw-in chokes and rifle barrel. Imported by European American Armory.
Price: IZH-18 (12, 16, 20 or 410) $95.00
Price: IZH-18 (20 gauge with imp. cyl. or 410 with imp. mod.).... $109.00

EAA/BAIKAL IZH-18MAX SINGLE BARREL SHOTGUN
Gauge: 12, 3"; 20, 3"; 410, 3". **Barrel:** 24" (410), 26" (410 or 20 ga.) or 28" (12 ga.). **Weight:** 6.4 to 6.6 lbs. **Length:** NA. **Stock:** Walnut. **Features:** Polished nickel receiver; ventilated rib; I.C., Mod. and Full choke tubes; titanium-coated trigger; internal hammer; selectable ejector/extractor; rubber butt pad; decocking system. Imported by European American Armory.
Price: (12 or 20 ga., choke tubes) $169.00
Price: (410 ga., full choke only) $189.00

FABARM MONOTRAP SHOTGUN
Caliber: 12; 2-3/4" chamber. **Barrel:** 30", 34". **Weight:** 6.7 to 6.9 lbs. **Length:** 48.5" overall (30" bbl.) **Stock:** Walnut; adjustable comb competition-style. **Sights:** Red front sight bar, mid-rib bead. **Features:** Built on 20-gauge receiver for quick handling. Silver receiver with blued barrel; special trap rib (micrometer adjustable); includes three choke tubes (M, IM, F). Introduced 2000.
Price: $1,799.00

HARRINGTON & RICHARDSON NWTF SHOTGUNS
Gauge: 12, 3-1/2" chamber, fixed full choke; 20, 3" chamber, fixed modified choke. **Barrel:** 24" (12 ga.) or 22" (20 ga.) **Weight:** 5 to 6 lbs. **Length:** NA. **Stock:** Straight-grip camo laminate with recoil pad and sling swivel studs. **Sights:** Bead front. **Features:** Break-open single-shot action with side lever release; hand-checkered stock and forearm; includes trigger lock. Purchase supports National Wild Turkey Federation; NWTF logo on receiver.
Price: 12 ga... $176.95
Price: 20 ga. youth gun (12-1/2" length of pull, weighs 5 lbs.) $169.95

HARRINGTON & RICHARDSON SB2-980 ULTRA SLUG
Gauge: 12, 20, 3" chamber. **Barrel:** 22" (20 ga. Youth) 24", fully rifled. **Weight:** 9 lbs. **Length:** NA. **Stock:** Walnut-stained hardwood. **Sights:** None furnished; comes with scope mount. **Features:** Uses the H&R 10 gauge action with heavy-wall barrel. Monte Carlo stock has sling swivels; comes with black nylon sling. Introduced 1995. Made in U.S. by H&R 1871, LLC.
Price: $209.95

Harrington & Richardson Model 928 Ultra Slug Hunter Deluxe
Similar to the SB2-980 Ultra Slug except uses 12 gauge action and 12 gauge barrel blank bored to 20 gauge, then fully rifled with 1:35" twist. Has hand-checkered camo laminate Monte Carlo stock and forend. Comes with Weaver-style scope base, offset hammer extension, ventilated recoil pad, sling swivels and nylon sling. Introduced 1997. Made in U.S. by H&R 1871 LLC.
Price: $255.95

SHOTGUNS — BOLT ACTIONS & SINGLE SHOTS

Krieghoff KS-5 Trap

Ljutic Mono Gun

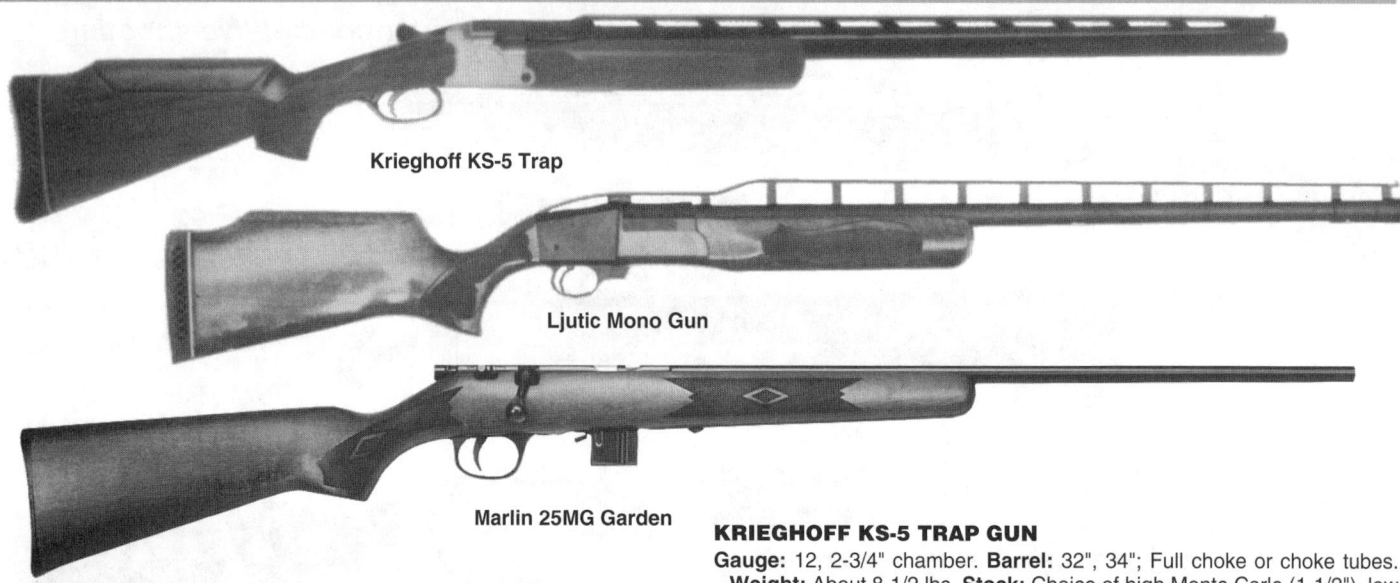

Marlin 25MG Garden

HARRINGTON & RICHARDSON TAMER SHOTGUN
Gauge: 410, 3" chamber. **Barrel:** 20" (Full). **Weight:** 5-6 lbs. **Length:** 33" overall. **Stock:** Thumbhole grip of high density black polymer. **Features:** Uses H&R Topper action with matte electroless nickel finish. Stock holds four spare shotshells. Introduced 1994. From H&R 1871, LLC.
Price: $124.95

HARRINGTON & RICHARDSON TOPPER MODEL 098
Gauge: 12, 16, 20, 28 (2-3/4"), 410, 3" chamber. **Barrel:** 12 ga.—28" (Mod., Full); 16 ga.— 28" (Mod.); 20 ga.—26" (Mod.); 28 ga.—26" (Mod.); 410 bore—26" (Full). **Weight:** 5-6 lbs. **Stock:** Black-finish hardwood with full pistol grip; semi-beavertail forend. **Sights:** Gold bead front. **Features:** Break-open action with side-lever release, automatic ejector. Satin nickel frame, blued barrel. Reintroduced 1992. From H&R 1871, LLC.
Price: $116.95
Price: Topper Junior 098 (as above except 22" barrel, 20 ga. (Mod.), 410-bore (Full), 12-1/2" length of pull) $122.95

Harrington & Richardson Topper Deluxe Model 098
Similar to the standard Topper 098 except 12 gauge only with 3-1/2" chamber, 28" barrel with choke tube (comes with Mod. tube, others optional). Satin nickel frame, blued barrel, black-finished wood. Introduced 1992. From H&R 1871, LLC.
Price: $136.95

Harrington & Richardson Topper Junior Classic Shotgun
Similar to the Topper Junior 098 except available in 20 gauge (3", Mod.), 410-bore (Full) with 3" chamber; 28 gauge, 2-3/4" chamber (Mod.); all have 22" barrel. Stock is American black walnut with cut-checkered pistol grip and forend. Ventilated rubber recoil pad with white line spacers. Blued barrel, blued frame. Introduced 1992. From H&R 1871, LLC.
Price: $150.95

Harrington & Richardson Topper Deluxe Rifled Slug Gun
Similar to the 12 gauge Topper Model 098 except has fully rifled and ported barrel, ramp front sight and fully adjustable rear. Barrel twist is 1:35". Nickel-plated frame, blued barrel, black-finished stock and forend. Introduced 1995. Made in U.S. by H&R 1871, Inc.
Price: $169.95

KRIEGHOFF K-80 SINGLE BARREL TRAP GUN
Gauge: 12, 2-3/4" chamber. **Barrel:** 32" or 34" Unsingle; 34" Top Single. Fixed Full or choke tubes. **Weight:** About 8-3/4 lbs. **Stock:** Four stock dimensions or adjustable stock available. All hand-checkered European walnut. **Features:** Satin nickel finish with K-80 logo. Selective mechanical trigger adjustable for finger position. Tapered step vent. rib. Adjustable point of impact on Unsingle.
Price: Standard grade full Unsingle, from.................. $7,950.00
Price: Standard grade full Top Single combo (special order), from $9,975.00
Price: RT (removable trigger) option, add $1,000.00

KRIEGHOFF KS-5 TRAP GUN
Gauge: 12, 2-3/4" chamber. **Barrel:** 32", 34"; Full choke or choke tubes. **Weight:** About 8-1/2 lbs. **Stock:** Choice of high Monte Carlo (1-1/2"), low Monte Carlo (1-3/8") or factory adjustable stock. European walnut. **Features:** Ventilated tapered step rib. Adjustable trigger or optional release trigger. Satin gray electroless nickel receiver. Comes with fitted aluminum case. Introduced 1988. Imported from Germany by Krieghoff International, Inc.
Price: Fixed choke, cased $3,695.00
Price: With choke tubes $4,120.00

Krieghoff KS-5 Special
Same as the KS-5 except the barrel has a fully adjustable rib and adjustable stock. Rib allows shooter to adjust point of impact from 50%/50% to nearly 90%/10%. Introduced 1990.
Price: $4,695.00

LJUTIC MONO GUN SINGLE BARREL
Gauge: 12 only. **Barrel:** 34", choked to customer specs; hollow-milled rib, 35-1/2" sight plane. **Weight:** Approx. 9 lbs. **Stock:** To customer specs. Oil finish, hand checkered. **Features:** Totally custom made. Pull or release trigger; removable trigger guard contains trigger and hammer mechanism; Ljutic pushbutton opener on front of trigger guard. From Ljutic Industries.
Price: With standard, medium or Olympic rib, custom 32"-34" bbls., and fixed choke. $5,795.00
Price: As above with screw-in choke barrel $6,095.00
Price: Stainless steel mono gun. $6,795.00

Ljutic LTX PRO 3 Deluxe Mono Gun
Deluxe light weight version of the Mono Gun with high quality wood, upgrade checkering, special rib height, screw in chokes, ported and cased.
Price: $8,995.00
Price: Stainless steel model $9,995.00

MARLIN MODEL 25MG GARDEN GUN SHOTGUN
Gauge: 22 WMR shotshell, 7-shot magazine. **Barrel:** 22" smoothbore. **Weight:** 6 lbs. **Length:** 41" overall. **Stock:** Press-checkered hardwood. **Sights:** High-visibility bead front. **Features:** Bolt action; thumb safety; red cocking indicator. Introduced 1999. Made in U.S. by Marlin.
Price: $231.00

MARLIN MODEL 512P SLUGMASTER SHOTGUN
Gauge: 12, 3" chamber; 2-shot detachable box magazine. **Barrel:** 21", rifled (1:28" twist). **Weight:** 8 lbs. **Length:** 41-3/4" overall. **Stock:** Black fiberglass-filled synthetic stock with moulded-in checkering, swivel studs; ventilated recoil pad; padded black nylon sling. **Sights:** Ramp front with brass bead and removable Wide-Scan hood and fiber-optic inserts, adjustable fiber-optic rear. Drilled and tapped for scope mounting. **Features:** Uses Model 55 action with thumb safety. Designed for shooting saboted slugs. Comes with special Weaver scope mount. Introduced 1997. Made in U.S. by Marlin Firearms Co.
Price: $388.00

SHOTGUNS — BOLT ACTIONS & SINGLE SHOTS

Marlin 512P Slugmaster

Mossberg 695

New England Firearms Camo Turkey

MOSSBERG MODEL 695 SLUGSTER
Gauge: 12, 3" chamber. **Barrel:** 22"; fully rifled, ported. **Weight:** 7-1/2 lbs. **Stock:** Black synthetic, with swivel studs and rubber recoil pad. **Sights:** Blade front, folding rifle-style leaf rear; Fiber Optic. Comes with Weaver-style scope bases. **Features:** Matte metal finish; rotating thumb safety; detachable 2-shot magazine. Mossberg Cablelock. Made in U.S. by Mossberg. Introduced 1996.
Price: $345.00
Price: With Fiber Optic rifle sights $367.00
Price: With woodlands camo stock, Fiber Optic sights $397.00

MOSSBERG SSi-ONE 12 GAUGE SLUG SHOTGUN
Gauge: 12, 3" chamber. **Barrel:** 24", fully rifled. **Weight:** 8 pounds. **Length:** 40" overall. **Stock:** Walnut, fluted and cut checkered; sling-swivel studs; drilled and tapped for scope base. **Sights:** None (scope base supplied). **Features:** Frame accepts interchangeable rifle barrels (see Mossberg SSi-One rifle listing); lever-opening, break-action design; ambidextrous, top-tang safety; internal eject/extract selector. Introduced 2000. From Mossberg.
Price: $480.00

Mossberg SSi-One Turkey Shotgun
Similar to SSi-One 12 gauge Slug Shotgun, but chambered for 12 ga., 3-1/2" loads. Includes Accu-Mag Turkey Tube. Introduced 2001. From Mossberg.
Price: $459.00

NEW ENGLAND FIREARMS CAMO TURKEY SHOTGUNS
Gauge: 10, 3-1/2 "; 12, 20, 3" chamber. **Barrel:** 24"; extra-full, screw-in choke tube (10 ga.); fixed full choke (12, 20). **Weight:** NA. **Stock:** American hardwood, green and black camouflage finish with sling swivels and ventilated recoil pad. **Sights:** Bead front. **Features:** Matte metal finish; stock counterweight to reduce recoil; patented transfer bar system for hammer-down safety; includes camo sling and trigger lock. Accepts other factory-fitted barrels. Introduced 2000. From New England Firearms.
Price: 10, 12 ga. $205.95
Price: 20 ga. youth model (22" bbl.) $128.95

NEW ENGLAND FIREARMS TRACKER SLUG GUN
Gauge: 12, 20, 3" chamber. **Barrel:** 24" (Cyl.). **Weight:** 5-1/4 lbs. **Length:** 40" overall. **Stock:** Walnut-finished hardwood with full pistol grip, recoil pad. **Sights:** Blade front, fully adjustable rifle-type rear. **Features:** Break-open action with side-lever release; blued barrel, color case-hardened frame. Introduced 1992. From New England Firearms.
Price: Tracker $142.95
Price: Tracker II (as above except fully rifled bore) $150.95

NEW ENGLAND FIREARMS SPECIAL PURPOSE SHOTGUNS
Gauge: 10, 3-1/2" chamber. **Barrel:** 28" (Full), 32" (Mod.). **Weight:** 9.5 lbs. **Length:** 44" overall (28" barrel). **Stock:** American hardwood with walnut or matte camo finish; ventilated rubber recoil pad. **Sights:** Bead front. **Features:** Break-open action with side-lever release; ejector. Matte finish on metal. Introduced 1992. From New England Firearms.
Price: Walnut-finish wood sling and swivels $168.95
Price: Camo finish, sling and swivels $183.95
Price: Camo finish, 32", sling and swivels $197.95
Price: Black matte finish, 24", Turkey Full choke tube,
  sling and swivels. $199.95

NEW ENGLAND FIREARMS SURVIVOR
Gauge: 12, 20, 410/45 Colt, 3" chamber. **Barrel:** 22" (Mod.); 20" (410/45 Colt, rifled barrel, choke tube). **Weight:** 6 lbs. **Length:** 36 overall. **Stock:** Black polymer with thumbhole/pistol grip, sling swivels; beavertail forend. **Sights:** Bead front. **Features:** Buttplate removes to expose storage for extra ammunition; forend also holds extra ammunition. Black or nickel finish. Introduced 1993. From New England Firearms.
Price: Black $129.95
Price: Nickel $150.95
Price: 410/45 Colt, black $164.95
Price: 410/45 Colt, nickel $178.95

NEW ENGLAND FIREARMS STANDARD PARDNER
Gauge: 12, 20, 410, 3" chamber; 16, 28, 2-3/4" chamber. **Barrel:** 12 ga.—28" (Full, Mod.), 32" (Full); 16 ga.—28" (Full), 32" (Full); 20 ga.—26" (Full, Mod.); 28 ga.—26" (Mod.); 410-bore—26" (Full). **Weight:** 5-6 lbs. **Length:** 43" overall (28" barrel). **Stock:** Walnut-finished hardwood with full pistol grip. **Sights:** Bead front. **Features:** Transfer bar ignition; break-open action with side-lever release. Introduced 1987. From New England Firearms.
Price: $106.95
Price: Youth model (12, 20, 28 ga., 410, 22" barrel, recoil pad). $114.95
Price: 12 ga., 32" (Full) $119.95

34TH EDITION, 2002

SHOTGUNS — BOLT ACTIONS & SINGLE SHOTS

Ruger KTS-1234-BRE

Tar-Hunt Mountaineer

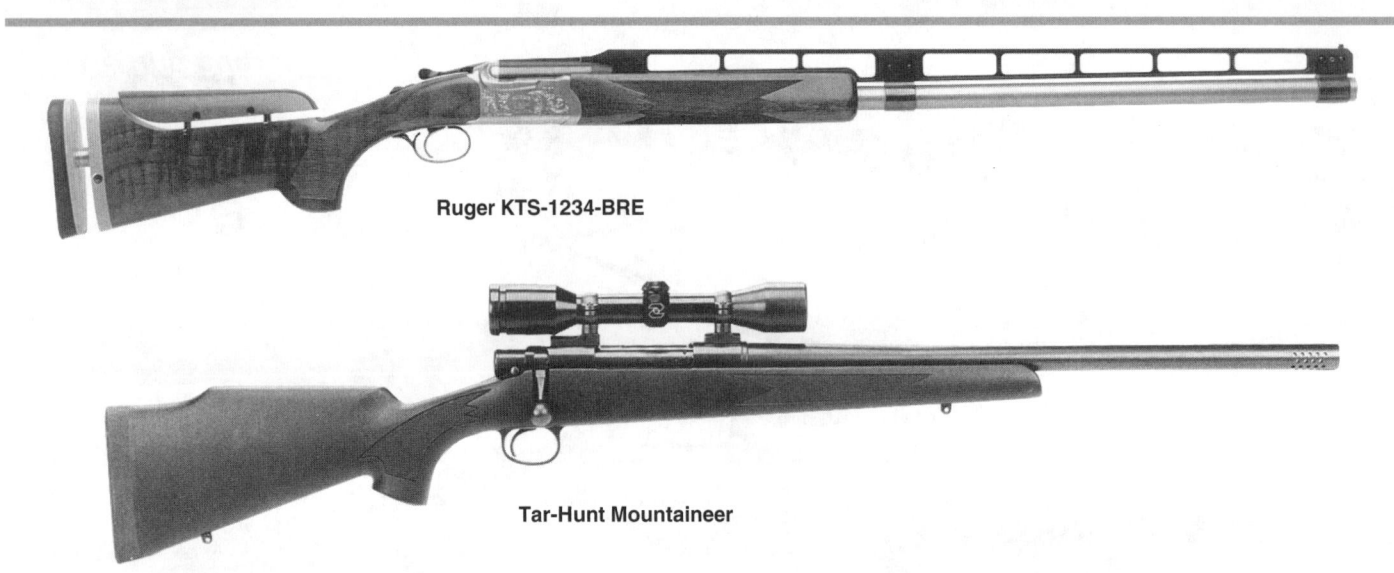

RUGER KTS-1234-BRE TRAP MODEL SINGLE-BARREL SHOTGUN
Gauge: 12, 2-3/4" chamber. **Barrel:** 34". **Weight:** 9 lbs. **Length:** 50 -1/2" overall. **Stock:** Select walnut checkered; adjustable pull length 13 -15". **Features:** Fully adjustable rib for pattern position; adjustable stock comb cast for right- or left-handed shooters; straight grooves the length of barrel to keep wad from rotating for pattern improvement. Full and modified choke tubes supplied. Gold inlaid eagle and Ruger name on receiver. Introduced 2000. From Sturm Ruger & Co.
Price: $2,850.00

ROSSI MODEL 12-G SHOTGUN
Gauge: 12, 20, 2-3/4" chamber; 410, 3" chamber. **Barrel:** 28". **Weight:** 5 lbs. **Length:** NA. **Stock:** Stained hardwood. **Features:** Spur hammer; intregral safety; ejector; spur hammer. Imported from Brazil by BrazTech/Taurus.
Price: $99.00
Price: Youth (shorter stock, 22" barrel) $99.00

ROSSI MATCHED PAIR SINGLE-SHOT SHOTGUN/RIFLE
NEW! **Gauge:** 410, 20 or 12. **Barrel:** 22" (410 or 20 ga.), 28" (12 ga.). **Weight:** NA. **Length:** NA. **Stock:** Hardwood (brown or black finish). **Sights:** bead front. **Features:** Break-open breech with external hammer; transfer-bar manual safety; blued or stainless steel finish; sling-swivel studs; includes matched 22 LR or 22 WMR barrel with fully adjustable rear sight. Introduced 2001. Imported by BrazTech/Taurus.
Price: 22 LR/410-, 20- or 12-gauge, blued finish, brown hardwood stock
.... $140.00
Price: 22 LR/410-gauge, stainless finish, black hardwood stock .. $170.00
Price: 22 WMR/12-gauge, blued finish, brown hardwood stock... $140.00

SAVAGE MODEL 210F MASTER SHOT SLUG GUN
Gauge: 12, 3" chamber; 2-shot magazine. **Barrel:** 24" 1:35" rifling twist. **Weight:** 7-1/2 lbs. **Length:** 43.5" overall. **Stock:** Glass-filled polymer with positive checkering. **Features:** Based on the Savage Model 110 action; 60 bolt lift; controlled round feed; comes with scope mount. Introduced 1996. Made in U.S. by Savage Arms.
Price: $402.00

Savage Model 210FT Master Shot Shotgun
Similar to the Model 210F except has smoothbore barrel threaded for Winchoke-style choke tubes (comes with one Full tube); Advantage camo pattern covers the stock; pillar-bedded synthetic stock; bead front sight, U-notch rear. Introduced 1997. Made in U.S. by Savage Arms, Inc.
Price: $466.00

SNAKE CHARMER II SHOTGUN
Gauge: 410, 3" chamber. **Barrel:** 18-1/4". **Weight:** About 3-1/2 lbs. **Length:** 28-5/8" overall. **Stock:** ABS grade impact resistant plastic. **Features:** Thumbhole-type stock holds four extra rounds. Stainless steel barrel and frame. Reintroduced 1989. From Sporting Arms Mfg., Inc.
Price: $149.00
Price: Snake Charmer II Field Gun (as above except has conventional wood buttstock with 14" length of pull, 24" barrel 410 or 28 ga.) . $160.00
Price: New Generation Snake Charmer (as above except with black carbon steel bbl.) $139.00

TAR-HUNT RSG-12 PROFESSIONAL RIFLED SLUG GUN
Gauge: 12, 2-3/4" chamber, 1-shot magazine. **Barrel:** 21-1/2"; fully rifled, with muzzle brake. **Weight:** 7-3/4 lbs. **Length:** 41-1/2" overall. **Stock:** Matte black McMillan fiberglass with Pachmayr Decelerator pad. **Sights:** None furnished; comes with Leupold windage bases only. **Features:** Uses rifle-style action with two locking lugs; two-position safety; Shaw barrel; single-stage, trigger; muzzle brake. Many options available. Right- and left-hand models at same prices. Introduced 1991. Made in U.S. by Tar-Hunt Custom Rifles, Inc.
Price: Professional model, right- or left-hand $1,695.00
Price: Millennium/10th Anniversary models (limited to 25 guns): NP-3 nickel/Teflon metal finish, black McMillan Fibergrain stock, Jewell adj. trigger $2,300.00

Tar-Hunt RSG-20 Mountaineer Slug Gun
Similar to the RSG-12 Professional except chambered for 20 gauge (2-3/4") shells; 21" Shaw rifled barrel, with muzzle brake; two-lug bolt; one-shot blind magazine; matte black finish; McMillan fiberglass stock with Pachmayr Decelerator pad; receiver drilled and tapped for Rem. 700 bases. Weighs 6-1/2 lbs. Introduced 1997. Made in U.S. by Tar-Hunt Custom Rifles, Inc.
Price: $1,695.00

THOMPSON/CENTER ENCORE RIFLED SLUG GUN
Gauge: 20, 3" chamber. **Barrel:** 26", fully rifled. **Weight:** About 7 pounds. **Length:** 40-1/2" overall. **Stock:** Walnut with walnut forearm. **Sights:** Steel, click-adjustable rear and ramp-style front, both with fiber optics. **Features:** Encore system features a variety of rifle, shotgun and muzzle-loading rifle barrels interchangeable with the same frame. Break-open design operates by pulling up and back on trigger guard spur. Composite stock and forearm available. Introduced 2000.
Price: $612.48

WESSON & HARRINGTON LONG TOM CLASSIC SHOTGUN
Gauge: 12, 3" chamber. **Barrel:** 32", (Full). **Weight:** 7-1/2 lbs. **Length:** 46" overall. **Stock:** 14"x1-3/4"x2-5/8". American black walnut with hand-checkered grip and forend. **Features:** Color case-hardened receiver and crescent steel buttplate, blued barrel. Receiver engraved with the National Wild Turkey Federation logo. Introduced 1998. Made in U.S. by H&R 1871, Inc.
Price: $349.95

Shotguns — Military & Police

Designs for utility, suitable for and adaptable to competitions and other sporting purposes.

Benelli M1 Tactical

Fabarm Tactical

Mossberg M500 Persuader

BENELLI M3 CONVERTIBLE SHOTGUN
Gauge: 12, 3" chamber, 5-shot magazine. **Barrel:** 19-3/4" (Cyl.). **Weight:** 7 lbs., 8 oz. **Length:** 41" overall. **Stock:** High-impact polymer with sling loop in side of butt; rubberized pistol grip on stock. **Sights:** Post front, buckhorn rear adjustable for windage. Ghost ring system available. **Features:** Combination pump/auto action. Alloy receiver with inertia recoil rotating locking lug bolt; matte finish; automatic shell release lever. Introduced 1989. Imported by Benelli USA.
Price: With standard stock, open rifle sights. $1,060.00
Price: With ghost ring sight system, standard stock. $1,100.00
Price: With ghost ring sights, pistol grip stock $1,120.00

BENELLI M1 TACTICAL SHOTGUN
Gauge: 12, 3", 5-shot magazine. **Barrel:** 18.5", choke tubes. **Weight:** 6.5 lbs. **Length:** 39.75" overall. **Stock:** Black polymer. **Sights:** Rifle type with Ghost Ring system, tritium night sights optional. **Features:** Semi-auto inertia recoil action. Cross-bolt safety; bolt release button; matte-finish metal. Introduced 1993. Imported from Italy by Benelli USA.
Price: With rifle sights, standard stock $890.00
Price: With ghost ring rifle sights, standard stock. $960.00
Price: With ghost ring sights, pistol grip stock $970.00
Price: With rifle sights, pistol grip stock $910.00

Benelli M1 Practical
Similar to M1 Field Shotgun, but with Picatinny receiver rail for scope mounting, nine-round magazine, 26" compensated barrel and ghost-ring sights. Designed for IPSC competition.
Price: $1,200.00

BENELLI M4 SUPER 90 JOINT SERVICE COMBAT SHOTGUN
Gauge: 12, 3" chamber. **Barrel:** 18.5". **Weight:** 8.4 pounds. **Length:** 39.8 inches. **Stock:** Synthetic, modular. **Sights:** Ghost-ring style, rear adjustable for windage and elevation using cartridge rim. **Features:** Auto-regulating, gas-operated (ARGO) action. Integral, Picatinny rail on receiver for sight mounting. Black matte finish. Improved cylinder. Can be reconfigured without tools with three buttstocks and two barrels. Introduced 2000. Imported from Italy by Benelli USA.
Price: . . . . NA

BERETTA MODEL 1201FP GHOST RING AUTO SHOTGUN
Gauge: 12, 3" chamber. **Barrel:** 18" (Cyl.). **Weight:** 6.3 lbs. **Stock:** Special strengthened technopolymer, matte black finish. **Stock:** Fixed rifle type. **Features:** Has 5-shot magazine. Adjustable Ghost Ring rear sight, tritium front. Introduced 1988. Imported from Italy by Beretta U.S.A.
Price: $860.00

CROSSFIRE SHOTGUN/RIFLE
Gauge/Caliber: 12, 2-3/4" **Chamber:** 4-shot/223 Rem. (5-shot). **Barrel:** 20" (shotgun), 18" (rifle). **Weight:** About 8.6 lbs. **Length:** 40" overall. **Stock:** Composite. **Sights:** Meprolight night sights. Integral Weaver-style scope rail. **Features:** Combination pump-action shotgun, rifle; single selector, single trigger; dual action bars for both upper and lower actions; ambidextrous selector and safety. Introduced 1997. Made in U.S. From Hesco.
Price: About $1,895.00
Price: With camo finish. $1,995.00

FABARM FP6 PUMP SHOTGUN
Gauge: 12, 3" chamber. **Barrel:** 20" (Cyl.); accepts choke tubes. **Weight:** 6.6 lbs. **Length:** 41.25" overall. **Stock:** Black polymer with textured grip, grooved slide handle. **Sights:** Blade front. **Features:** Twin action bars; anodized finish; free carrier for smooth reloading. Introduced 1998. Imported from Italy by Heckler & Koch, Inc.
Price: (Carbon fiber finish) $499.00
Price: With flip-up front sight, Picatinny rail with rear sight, oversize safety button $499.00

FABARM TACTICAL SEMI-AUTOMATIC SHOTGUN
Gauge: 12, 3" chamber. **Barrel:** 20". **Weight:** 6.6 lbs. **Length:** 41.2" overall. **Stock:** Polymer or folding. **Sights:** Ghost ring (tritium night sights optional). **Features:** Gas operated; matte receiver; twin forged action bars; oversized bolt handle and safety button; Picatinny rail; includes cylinder bore choke tube. Introduced 2001. Imported from Italy by Heckler & Koch Inc.
Price: . . . . NA

MOSSBERG MODEL 500 PERSUADER SECURITY SHOTGUNS
Gauge: 12, 20, 410, 3" chamber. **Barrel:** 18-1/2", 20" (Cyl.). **Weight:** 7 lbs. **Stock:** Walnut-finished hardwood or black synthetic. **Sights:** Metal bead front. **Features:** Available in 6- or 8-shot models. Top-mounted safety, double action slide bars, swivel studs, rubber recoil pad. Blue, Parkerized, Marinecote finishes. Mossberg Cablelock included. From Mossberg.
Price: 12 or 20 ga., 18-1/2", blue, wood or synthetic stock, 6-shot $329.00
Price: Cruiser, 12 or 20 ga., 18-1/2", blue, pistol grip, heat shield $333.00
Price: As above, 410-bore $322.00

SHOTGUNS — MILITARY & POLICE

Tactical Response TR-870

Winchester Model 1300 Defender

Mossberg Model 500, 590 Mariner Pump
Similar to the Model 500 or 590 Security except all metal parts finished with Marinecote metal finish to resist rust and corrosion. Synthetic field stock; pistol grip kit included. Mossberg Cablelock included.
Price: 6-shot, 18-1/2" barrel $468.00
Price: 9-shot, 20" barrel $484.00

Mossberg Model HS410 Shotgun
Similar to the Model 500 Security pump except chambered for 20 gauge or 410 with 3" chamber; has pistol grip forend, thick recoil pad, muzzle brake and has special spreader choke on the 18.5" barrel. Overall length is 37.5", weight is 6.25 lbs. Blue finish; synthetic field stock. Mossberg Cablelock and video included. Introduced 1990.
Price: HS 410 .... $335.00

Mossberg Model 500, 590 Ghost-Ring Shotguns
Similar to the Model 500 Security except has adjustable blade front, adjustable Ghost-Ring rear sight with protective "ears." Model 500 has 18.5" (Cyl.) barrel, 6-shot capacity; Model 590 has 20" (Cyl.) barrel, 9-shot capacity. Both have synthetic field stock. Mossberg Cablelock included. Introduced 1990. From Mossberg.
Price: 500 parkerized $437.00
Price: 590 parkerized $445.00
Price: Parkerized Speedfeed stock .... $546.00 to $634.00

MOSSBERG MODEL 590 SHOTGUN
Gauge: 12, 3" chamber. **Barrel:** 20" (Cyl.). **Weight:** 7-1/4 lbs. **Stock:** Synthetic field or Speedfeed. **Sights:** Metal bead front. **Features:** Top-mounted safety, double slide action bars. Comes with heat shield, bayonet lug, swivel studs, rubber recoil pad. Blue, Parkerized or Marinecote finish. Mossberg Cablelock included. From Mossberg.
Price: Blue, synthetic stock. $389.00
Price: Parkerized, synthetic stock. $445.00
Price: Parkerized, Speedfeed stock $485.00

Mossberg 590DA Double-Action Pump Shotgun
Similar to Model 590 except trigger requires a long stroke for each shot, duplicating the trigger pull of double-action-only pistols and revolvers. Available in 12 gauge only with black synthetic stock and parkerized finish with 14" (law enforcement only), 18-1/2 "and 20" barrels. Six-shot magazine tube (nine-shot for 20" barrel). Front bead or ghost ring sights. Weighs 7 pounds (18 1/2" barrel). Introduced 2000. From Mossberg.
Price: Bead sight, 6-shot magazine $510.00
Price: Ghost ring sights, 6-shot magazine $558.00
Price: Bead sight, 9-shot magazine $541.00
Price: Ghost ring sights, 9-shot magazine $597.00

TACTICAL RESPONSE TR-870 STANDARD MODEL SHOTGUN
Gauge: 12, 3" chamber, 7-shot magazine. **Barrel:** 18" (Cyl.). **Weight:** 9 lbs. **Length:** 38" overall. **Stock:** Fiberglass-filled polypropolene with non-snag recoil absorbing butt pad. Nylon tactical forend houses flashlight. **Sights:** Trak-Lock ghost ring sight system. Front sight has tritium insert. **Features:** Highly modified Remington 870P with Parkerized finish. Comes with nylon three-way adjustable sling, high visibility non-binding follower, high performance magazine spring, Jumbo Head safety, and Side Saddle extended 6-shot shell carrier on left side of receiver. Introduced 1991. From Scattergun Technologies, Inc.
Price: Standard model $815.00
Price: FBI model. $770.00
Price: Patrol model. $595.00
Price: Border Patrol model. $605.00
Price: K-9 model (Rem. 11-87 action) $995.00
Price: Urban Sniper, Rem. 11-87 action. $1,290.00
Price: Louis Awerbuck model. $705.00
Price: Practical Turkey model. $725.00
Price: Expert model $1,350.00
Price: Professional model. $815.00
Price: Entry model $840.00
Price: Compact model $635.00
Price: SWAT model $1,195.00

TRISTAR PHANTOM HP AUTO SHOTGUN
Gauge: 12, 3" chamber. **Barrel:** 19"; threaded for external choke tubes. **Stock:** Black synthetic. **Sights:** Bead front. **Features:** Gas-operated action; blue/black finish; five-shot extended magazine tube. Imported by Tristar Sporting Arms Ltd.
Price: .... NA

WINCHESTER MODEL 1300 DEFENDER PUMP GUNS
Gauge: 12, 20, 3" chamber, 5- or 8-shot capacity. **Barrel:** 18" (Cyl.). **Weight:** 6-3/4 lbs. **Length:** 38-5/8" overall. **Stock:** Walnut-finished hardwood stock and ribbed forend, synthetic or pistol grip. **Sights:** Metal bead front or TRUGLO® fiber-optic. **Features:** Cross-bolt safety, front-locking rotary bolt, twin action slide bars. Black rubber butt pad. From U.S. Repeating Arms Co.
Price: 8-Shot (black synthetic stock, TRUGLO® sight) $326.00
Price: 8-Shot Pistol Grip (pistol grip synthetic stock) $326.00

Winchester Model 1300 Stainless Marine Pump Gun
Same as the Defender 8-Shot except has bright chrome finish, stainless steel barrel, bead front sight. Phosphate coated receiver for corrosion resistance.
Price: $518.00

Winchester Model 1300 Camp Defender®
Same as the Defender 8-Shot except has hardwood stock and forearm, fully adjustable open sights and 22" barrel with WinChoke® choke tube system (cylinder choke tube included). Weighs 6-7/8 lbs. Introduced 2001. From U.S. Repeating Arms Co.
Price: Camp Defender® $373.00

BLACKPOWDER SINGLE SHOT PISTOLS — FLINT & PERCUSSION

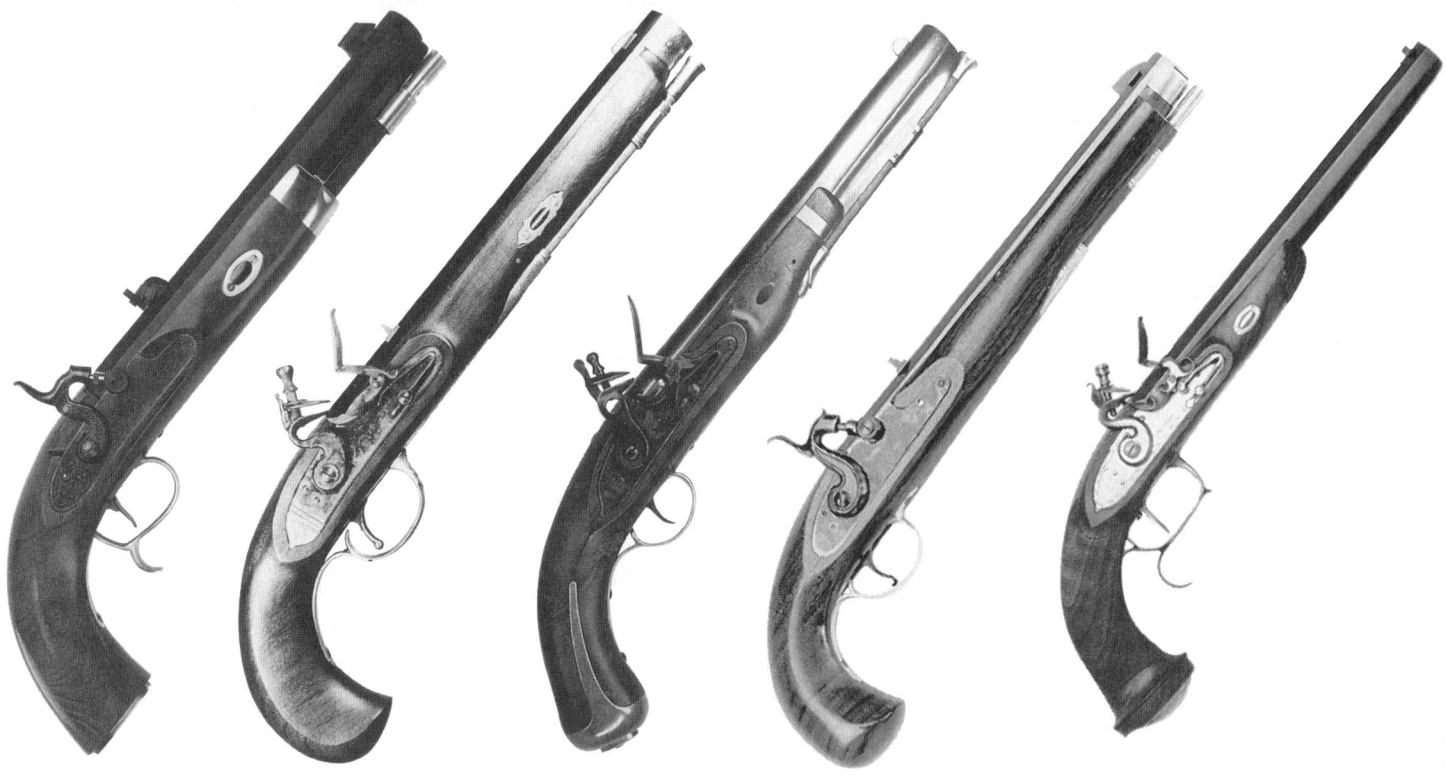

CVA Hawken   Dixie Pennsylvania   Harper's Ferry   Kentucky   Le Page

CVA HAWKEN PISTOL
Caliber: 50. **Barrel:** 9-3/4"; 15/16" flats. **Weight:** 50 oz. **Length:** 16-1/2" overall. **Stocks:** Select hardwood. **Sights:** Beaded blade front, fully adjustable open rear. **Features:** Color case-hardened lock, polished brass wedge plate, instep, ramrod thimble, trigger guard, grip cap. Imported by CVA.
Price: $167.95
Price: Kit $127.95

DIXIE PENNSYLVANIA PISTOL
Caliber: 44 (.430" round ball). **Barrel:** 10", (7/8" octagon). **Weight:** 2-1/2 labs. **Stocks:** Walnut-stained hardwood. **Sights:** Blade front, open rear drift-adjustable for windage; brass. **Features:** Available in flint only. Brass trigger guard, thimbles, instep, wedge plates; high-luster blue barrel. Imported from Italy by Dixie Gun Works.
Price: Finished $195.00
Price: Kit $185.00

FRENCH-STYLE DUELING PISTOL
Caliber: 44. **Barrel:** 10". **Weight:** 35 oz. **Length:** 15-3/4" overall. **Stocks:** Carved walnut. **Sights:** Fixed. **Features:** Comes with velvet-lined case and accessories. Imported by Mandall Shooting Supplies.
Price: $295.00

HARPER'S FERRY 1806 PISTOL
Caliber: 58 (.570" round ball). **Barrel:** 10". **Weight:** 40 oz. **Length:** 16" overall. **Stocks:** Walnut. **Sights:** Fixed. **Features:** Case-hardened lock, brass-mounted browned barrel. Replica of the first U.S. Gov't.-made flintlock pistol. Imported by Navy Arms, Dixie Gun Works.
Price: .... $275.00 to $405.00
Price: Kit (Dixie) $249.00

KENTUCKY FLINTLOCK PISTOL
Caliber: 44, 45. **Barrel:** 10-1/8". **Weight:** 32 oz. **Length:** 15-1/2" overall. **Stocks:** Walnut. **Sights:** Fixed. **Features:** Specifications, including caliber, weight and length may vary with importer. Case-hardened lock, blued barrel; available also as brass barrel flint Model 1821. Imported by Navy Arms, The Armoury.
Price: .... $145.00 to $235.00
Price: In kit form, from .... $90.00 to $112.00
Price: Single cased set (Navy Arms) $360.00
Price: Double cased set (Navy Arms) $590.00

Kentucky Percussion Pistol
Similar to flint version but percussion lock. Imported by The Armoury, Navy Arms, CVA (50-cal.).
Price: .... $129.95 to $225.00
Price: Blued steel barrel (CVA) $167.95
Price: Kit form (CVA) $119.95
Price: Steel barrel (Armoury) $179.00
Price: Single cased set (Navy Arms) $355.00
Price: Double cased set (Navy Arms) $600.00

LE PAGE PERCUSSION DUELING PISTOL
Caliber: 44. **Barrel:** 10", rifled. **Weight:** 40 oz. **Length:** 16" overall. **Stocks:** Walnut, fluted butt. **Sights:** Blade front, notch rear. **Features:** Double-set triggers. Blued barrel; trigger guard and buttcap are polished silver. Imported by Dixie Gun Works.
Price: $259.95

LYMAN PLAINS PISTOL
Caliber: 50 or 54. **Barrel:** 8"; 1:30" twist, both calibers. **Weight:** 50 oz. **Length:** 15" overall. **Stocks:** Walnut half-stock. **Sights:** Blade front, square notch rear adjustable for windage. **Features:** Polished brass trigger guard and ramrod tip, color case-hardened coil spring lock, spring-loaded trigger, stainless steel nipple, blackened iron furniture. Hooked patent breech, detachable belt hook. Introduced 1981. From Lyman Products.
Price: Finished $229.95
Price: Kit $184.95

PEDERSOLI MANG TARGET PISTOL
Caliber: 38. **Barrel:** 10.5", octagonal; 1:15" twist, **Weight:** 2.5 lbs. **Length:** 17.25" overall. **Stocks:** Walnut with fluted grip. **Sights:** Blade front, open rear adjustable for windage. **Features:** Browned barrel, polished breech plug, rest color case-hardened. Imported from Italy by Dixie Gun Works.
Price: $786.00

BLACKPOWDER SINGLE SHOT PISTOLS — FLINT & PERCUSSION

Lyman Plains Pistol **Pedersoli Mang** **Queen Anne** **Traditions Pioneer** **Traditions William Parker**

Traditions Buckhunter Pro

QUEEN ANNE FLINTLOCK PISTOL
Caliber: 50 (.490" round ball). **Barrel:** 7-1/2", smoothbore. **Stocks:** Walnut. **Sights:** None. **Features:** Browned steel barrel, fluted brass trigger guard, brass mask on butt. Lockplate left in the white. Made by Pedersoli in Italy. Introduced 1983. Imported by Dixie Gun Works.
Price: $225.00
Price: Kit $175.00

THOMPSON/CENTER ENCORE 209x50 MAGNUM PISTOL
Caliber: 50. **Barrel:** 15"; 1:20" twist. **Weight:** About 4 lbs. **Grips:** American walnut grip and forend. **Sights:** Click-adjustable, steel rear, ramp front. **Features:** Uses 209 shotgun primer for closed-breech ignition; accepts charges up to 110 grains of FFg black powder or two, 50-grain Pyrodex pellets. Introduced 2000.
Price: $569.47

TRADITIONS BUCKHUNTER PRO IN-LINE PISTOL
Caliber: 50. **Barrel:** 9-1/2", round. **Weight:** 48 oz. **Length:** 14" overall. **Stocks:** Smooth walnut or black epoxy-coated hardwood grip and forend. **Sights:** Beaded blade front, folding adjustable rear. **Features:** Thumb safety; removable stainless steel breech plug; adjustable trigger, barrel drilled and tapped for scope mounting. From Traditions.
Price: With walnut grip $229.00
Price: Nickel with black grip $239.00
Price: With walnut grip and 12-1/2" barrel $239.00
Price: Nickel with black grip, muzzle brake and 14-3/4" fluted barrel. $284.00

TRADITIONS KENTUCKY PISTOL
Caliber: 50. **Barrel:** 10"; octagon with 7/8" flats; 1:20" twist. **Weight:** 40 oz. **Length:** 15" overall. **Stocks:** Stained beech. **Sights:** Blade front, fixed rear. **Features:** Birds-head grip; brass thimbles; color case-hardened lock. Percussion only. Introduced 1995. From Traditions.
Price: Finished $139.00
Price: Kit $109.00

TRADITIONS PIONEER PISTOL
Caliber: 45. **Barrel:** 9-5/8"; 13/16" flats, 1:16" twist. **Weight:** 31 oz. **Length:** 15" overall. **Stocks:** Beech. **Sights:** Blade front, fixed rear. **Features:** V-type mainspring. Single trigger. German silver furniture, blackened hardware. From Traditions.
Price: $139.00
Price: Kit $119.00

TRADITIONS TRAPPER PISTOL
Caliber: 50. **Barrel:** 9-3/4"; 7/8" flats; 1:20" twist. **Weight:** 2-3/4 lbs. **Length:** 16" overall. **Stocks:** Beech. **Sights:** Blade front, adjustable rear. **Features:** Double-set triggers; brass buttcap, trigger guard, wedge plate, forend tip, thimble. From Traditions.
Price: Percussion $189.00
Price: Flintlock $209.00
Price: Kit $149.00

TRADITIONS VEST-POCKET DERRINGER
Caliber: 31. **Barrel:** 2-1/4"; brass. **Weight:** 8 oz. **Length:** 4-3/4" overall. **Stocks:** Simulated ivory. **Sights:** Beed front. **Features:** Replica of riverboat gamblers' derringer; authentic spur trigger. From Traditions.
Price: $109.00

TRADITIONS WILLIAM PARKER PISTOL
Caliber: 50. **Barrel:** 10-3/8"; 15/16" flats; polished steel. **Weight:** 37 oz. **Length:** 17-1/2" overall. **Stocks:** Walnut with checkered grip. **Sights:** Brass blade front, fixed rear. **Features:** Replica dueling pistol with 1:20" twist, hooked breech. Brass wedge plate, trigger guard, cap guard; separate ramrod. Double-set triggers. Polished steel barrel, lock. Imported by Traditions.
Price: $269.00

BLACKPOWDER REVOLVERS

Army 1860

Colt 1860 Army

Baby Dragoon 1848

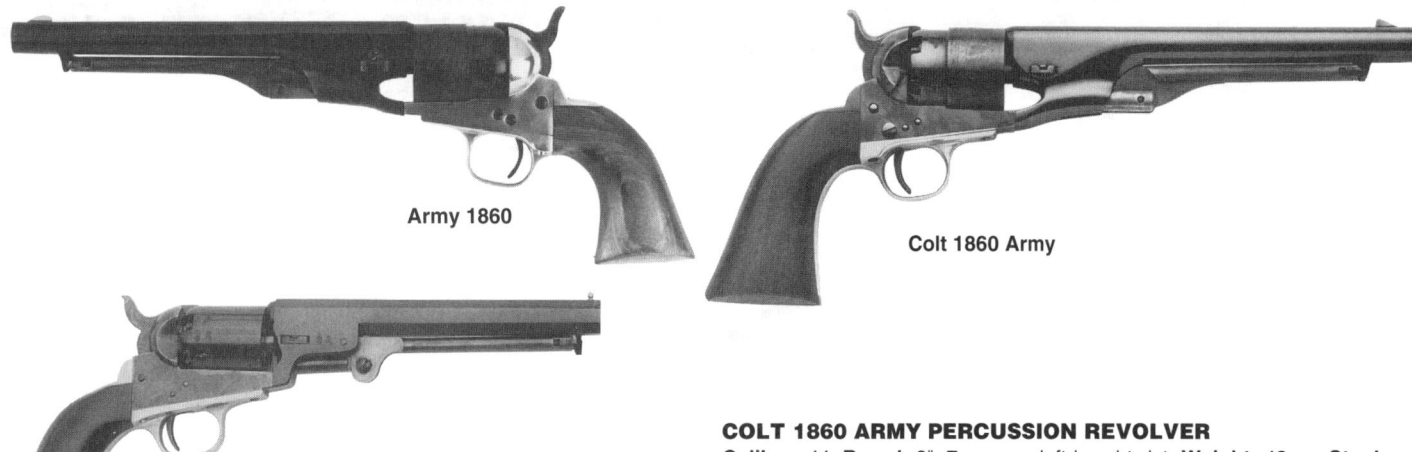

ARMY 1851 PERCUSSION REVOLVER
Caliber: 44, 6-shot. **Barrel:** 7-1/2". **Weight:** 45 oz. **Length:** 13" overall. **Stocks:** Walnut finish. **Sights:** Fixed. **Features:** 44-caliber version of the 1851 Navy. Imported by The Armoury, Armsport.
Price: $129.00

ARMY 1860 PERCUSSION REVOLVER
Caliber: 44, 6-shot. **Barrel:** 8". **Weight:** 40 oz. **Length:** 13-5/8" overall. **Stocks:** Walnut. **Sights:** Fixed. **Features:** Engraved Navy scene on cylinder; brass trigger guard; case-hardened frame, loading lever and hammer. Some importers supply pistol cut for detachable shoulder stock, have accessory stock available. Imported by Cabela's (1860 Lawman), E.M.F., Navy Arms, The Armoury, Cimarron, Dixie Gun Works (half-fluted cylinder, not roll engraved), Euroarms of America (brass or steel model), Armsport, Traditions (brass or steel), Uberti U.S.A. Inc., United States Patent Fire-Arms.
Price: About .... $92.95 to $395.00
Price: Hartford model, steel frame, German silver trim,
cartouches (E.M.F.) $215.00
Price: Single cased set (Navy Arms) $300.00
Price: Double cased set (Navy Arms) $490.00
Price: 1861 Navy: Same as Army except 36-cal., 7-1/2" bbl., weighs 41 oz., cut for shoulder stock; round cylinder (fluted available), from Cabela's, CVA (brass frame, 44-cal.), United States Patent Fire-Arms
.... $99.95 to $385.00
Price: Steel frame kit (E.M.F., Euroarms)......... $125.00 to $216.25
Price: Colt Army Police, fluted cyl., 5-1/2", 36-cal. (Cabela's) ... $124.95
Price: With nickeled frame, barrel and backstrap, gold-tone fluted cylinder, trigger and hammer, simulated ivory grips (Traditions) $199.00

BABY DRAGOON 1848, 1849 POCKET, WELLS FARGO
Caliber: 31. **Barrel:** 3", 4", 5", 6"; seven-groove; RH twist. **Weight:** About 21 oz. **Stocks:** Varnished walnut. **Sights:** Brass pin front, hammer notch rear. **Features:** No loading lever on Baby Dragoon or Wells Fargo models. Unfluted cylinder with stagecoach holdup scene; cupped cylinder pin; no grease grooves; one safety pin on cylinder and slot in hammer face; straight (flat) mainspring. From Armsport, Cimarron F.A. Co., Dixie Gun Works, Uberti U.S.A. Inc.
Price: 6" barrel, with loading lever (Dixie Gun Works) $254.95
Price: 4" (Uberti USA Inc.) $335.00

CABELA'S STARR PERCUSSION REVOLVERS
Caliber: 44. **Barrel:** 6", 8". **Weight:** N/A. **Length:** N/A. **Grips:** Walnut. **Sights:** Blade front. **Features:** Replicas of government-contract revolvers made by Ebenezer T. Starr. Knurled knob allows quick removal and replacement of cylinder. Introduced 2000. From Cabela's.
Price: Starr 1858 Army double action, 6" barrel. $349.99
Price: Starr 1863 Army single action, 8" barrel $349.99

COLT 1860 ARMY PERCUSSION REVOLVER
Caliber: 44. **Barrel:** 8", 7-groove, left-hand twist. **Weight:** 42 oz. **Stocks:** One-piece walnut. **Sights:** German silver front sight, hammer notch rear. **Features:** Steel backstrap cut for shoulder stock; brass trigger guard. Cylinder has Navy scene. Color case-hardened frame, hammer, loading lever. Reproduction of original gun with all original markings. From Colt Blackpowder Arms Co.
Price: $449.95

COLT 1848 BABY DRAGOON REVOLVER
Caliber: 31, 5-shot. **Barrel:** 4". **Weight:** About 21 oz. **Stocks:** Smooth walnut. **Sights:** Brass pin front, hammer notch rear. **Features:** Color case-hardened frame; no loading lever; square-back trigger guard; round bolt cuts; octagonal barrel; engraved cylinder scene. Imported by Colt Blackpowder Arms Co.
Price: $429.95

Colt 1860 "Cavalry Model" Percussion Revolver
Similar to the 1860 Army except has fluted cylinder. Color case-hardened frame, hammer, loading lever and plunger; blued barrel, backstrap and cylinder, brass trigger guard. Has four-screw frame cut for optional shoulder stock. From Colt Blackpowder Arms Co.
Price: $399.95

COLT 1851 NAVY PERCUSSION REVOLVER
Caliber: 36. **Barrel:** 7-1/2", octagonal; 7-groove left-hand twist. **Weight:** 40-1/2 oz. **Stocks:** One-piece oiled American walnut. **Sights:** Brass pin front, hammer notch rear. **Features:** Faithful reproduction of the original gun. Color case-hardened frame, loading lever, plunger, hammer and latch. Blue cylinder, trigger, barrel, screws, wedge. Silver-plated brass backstrap and square-back trigger guard. From Colt Blackpowder Arms Co.
Price: $449.95

COLT 1861 NAVY PERCUSSION REVOLVER
Caliber: 36. **Barrel:** 7-1/2". **Weight:** 42 oz. **Length:** 13-1/8" overall. **Stocks:** One-piece walnut. **Sights:** Blade front, hammer notch rear. **Features:** Color case-hardened frame, loading lever, plunger; blued barrel, backstrap, trigger guard; roll-engraved cylinder and barrel. From Colt Blackpowder Arms Co.
Price: $449.95

COLT 1849 POCKET DRAGOON REVOLVER
Caliber: 31. **Barrel:** 4". **Weight:** 24 oz. **Length:** 9-1/2" overall. **Stocks:** One-piece walnut. **Sights:** Fixed. Brass pin front, hammer notch rear. **Features:** Color case-hardened frame. No loading lever. Unfluted cylinder with engraved scene. Exact reproduction of original. From Colt Blackpowder Arms Co.
Price: $429.95

COLT 1862 POCKET POLICE "TRAPPER MODEL" REVOLVER
Caliber: 36. **Barrel:** 3-1/2". **Weight:** 20 oz. **Length:** 8-1/2" overall. **Stocks:** One-piece walnut. **Sights:** Blade front, hammer notch rear. **Features:** Has separate 4-5/8" brass ramrod. Color case-hardened frame and hammer; silver-plated backstrap and trigger guard; blued semi-fluted cylinder, blued barrel. From Colt Blackpowder Arms Co.
Price: $429.95

BLACKPOWDER REVOLVERS

Colt 1847 Walker

Griswold & Gunnison

Dixie Wyatt Earp

Le Mat Revolver

COLT THIRD MODEL DRAGOON
Caliber: 44. **Barrel:** 7-1/2". **Weight:** 66 oz. **Length:** 13-3/4" overall. **Stocks:** One-piece walnut. **Sights:** Blade front, hammer notch rear. **Features:** Color case-hardened frame, hammer, lever and plunger; round trigger guard; flat mainspring; hammer roller; rectangular bolt cuts. From Colt Blackpowder Arms Co.
Price: Three-screw frame with brass grip straps $499.95
Price: First Dragoon (oval bolt cuts in cylinder, square-back trigger guard) $499.95
Price: Second Dragoon (rectangular bolt cuts in cylinder, square-back trigger guard) $499.95

Colt Walker 150th Anniversary Revolver
Similar to the standard Walker except has original-type "A Company No. 1" markings embellished in gold. Serial numbers begin with 221, a continuation of A Company numbers. Imported by Colt Blackpowder Arms Co.
Price: $699.95

COLT 1847 WALKER PERCUSSION REVOLVER
Caliber: 44. **Barrel:** 9", 7-groove; right-hand twist. **Weight:** 73 oz. **Stocks:** One-piece walnut. **Sights:** German silver front sight, hammer notch rear. **Features:** Made in U.S. Faithful reproduction of the original gun, including markings. Color case-hardened frame, hammer, loading lever and plunger. Blue steel backstrap, brass square-back trigger guard. Blue barrel, cylinder, trigger and wedge. From Colt Blackpowder Arms Co.
Price: $499.95

DIXIE WYATT EARP REVOLVER
Caliber: 44. **Barrel:** 12", octagon. **Weight:** 46 oz. **Length:** 18" overall. **Stocks:** Two-piece walnut. **Sights:** Fixed. **Features:** Highly polished brass frame, backstrap and trigger guard; blued barrel and cylinder; case-hardened hammer, trigger and loading lever. Navy-size shoulder stock ($45) will fit with minor fitting. From Dixie Gun Works.
Price: $150.00

GRISWOLD & GUNNISON PERCUSSION REVOLVER
Caliber: 36 or 44, 6-shot. **Barrel:** 7-1/2". **Weight:** 44 oz. (36-cal.). **Length:** 13" overall. **Stocks:** Walnut. **Sights:** Fixed. **Features:** Replica of famous Confederate pistol. Brass frame, backstrap and trigger guard; case-hardened loading lever; rebated cylinder (44-cal. only). Rounded Dragoon-type barrel. Imported by Navy Arms as Reb Model 1860.
Price: $115.00
Price: Kit $90.00
Price: Single cased set $235.00
Price: Double cased set $365.00

LE MAT REVOLVER
Caliber: 44/65. **Barrel:** 6-3/4" (revolver); 4-7/8" (single shot). **Weight:** 3 lbs., 7 oz. **Stocks:** Hand-checkered walnut. **Sights:** Post front, hammer notch rear. **Features:** Exact reproduction with all-steel construction; 44-cal. 9-shot cylinder, 65-cal. single barrel; color case-hardened hammer with selector; spur trigger guard; ring at butt; lever-type barrel release. From Navy Arms.
Price: Cavalry model (lanyard ring, spur trigger guard) $595.00
Price: Army model (round trigger guard, pin-type barrel release) $595.00
Price: Naval-style (thumb selector on hammer) $595.00
Price: Engraved 18th Georgia cased set $795.00
Price: Engraved Beauregard cased set $1,000.00

NAVY ARMS NEW MODEL POCKET REVOLVER
Caliber: 31, 5-shot. **Barrel:** 3-1/2", octagon. **Weight:** 15 oz. **Length:** 7-3/4". **Stocks:** Two-piece walnut. **Sights:** Fixed. **Features:** Replica of the Remington New Model Pocket. Available with polishd brass frame or nickel plated finish. Introduced 2000. Imported by Navy Arms.
Price: Brass frame $165.00
Price: Nickel plated $175.00

NAVY ARMS DELUXE 1858 REMINGTON-STYLE REVOLVER
Caliber: 44. **Barrel:** 6". **Weight:** 3 lbs. **Length:** 11-3/4". **Stocks:** Smooth walnut. **Sights:** Blade front, notch rear. **Features:** Replica of the famous percussion double action revolver. Polished blue finish. Introduced 1999. Imported by Navy Arms.
Price: $355.00

NAVY ARMS STARR SINGLE ACTION MODEL 1863 ARMY REVOLVER
Caliber: 44. **Barrel:** 8". **Weight:** 3 lbs. **Length:** 13-3/4". **Stocks:** Smooth walnut. **Sights:** Blade front, notch rear. **Features:** Replica of the third most popular revolver used by Union forces during the Civil War. Polished blue finish. Introduced 1999. Imported by Navy Arms.
Price: $355.00

NAVY ARMS STARR DOUBLE ACTION MODEL 1858 ARMY REVOLVER
Caliber: 44. **Barrel:** 8". **Weight:** 2 lbs., 13 oz. **Stocks:** Smooth walnut. **Sights:** Dovetailed blade front. **Features:** First exact reproduction—correct in size and weight to the original, with progressive rifling; highly polished with blue finish. From Navy Arms.
Price: Deluxe model $415.00

BLACKPOWDER REVOLVERS

Uberti 1858

Rogers & Spencer

North American Companion

Ruger Old Army

Pocket Police 1862

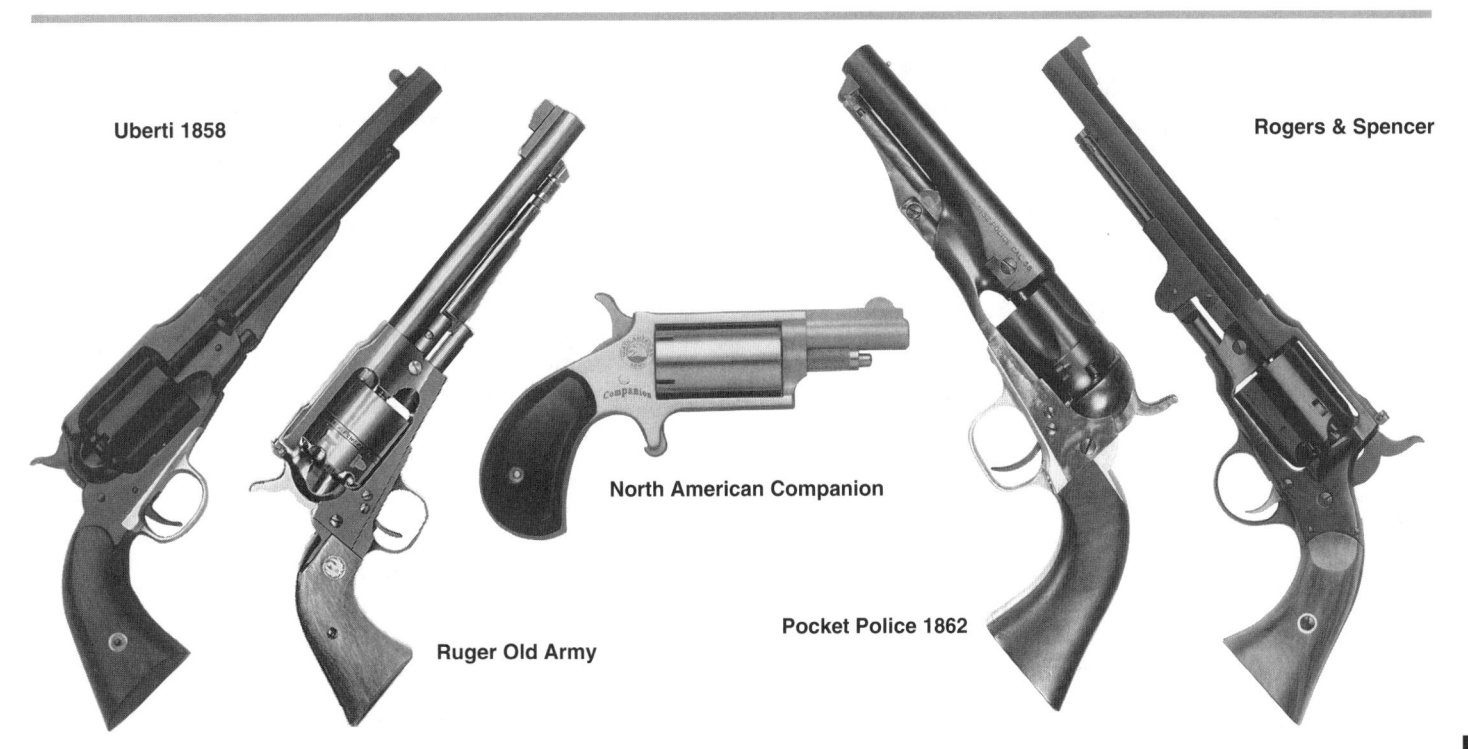

NAVY MODEL 1851 PERCUSSION REVOLVER
Caliber: 36, 44, 6-shot. **Barrel:** 7-1/2". **Weight:** 44 oz. **Length:** 13" overall. **Stocks:** Walnut finish. **Sights:** Post front, hammer notch rear. **Features:** Brass backstrap and trigger guard; some have 1st Model squareback trigger guard, engraved cylinder with navy battle scene; case-hardened frame, hammer, loading lever. Imported by The Armoury, Cabela's, Cimarron F.A. Co., Navy Arms, E.M.F., Dixie Gun Works, Euroarms of America, Armsport, CVA (44-cal. only), Traditions (44 only), Uberti U.S.A. Inc., United States Patent Fire-Arms.

Price: Brass frame	$99.95 to $385.00
Price: Steel frame	$130.00 to $285.00
Price: Kit form	$110.00 to $123.95
Price: Engraved model (Dixie Gun Works)	$159.95
Price: Single cased set, steel frame (Navy Arms)	$280.00
Price: Double cased set, steel frame (Navy Arms)	$455.00
Price: Confederate Navy (Cabela's)	$89.99
Price: Hartford model, steel frame, German silver trim, cartouche (E.M.F.)	$190.00

NEW MODEL 1858 ARMY PERCUSSION REVOLVER
Caliber: 36 or 44, 6-shot. **Barrel:** 6-1/2" or 8". **Weight:** 38 oz. **Length:** 13-1/2" overall. **Stocks:** Walnut. **Sights:** Blade front, groove-in-frame rear. **Features:** Replica of Remington Model 1858. Also available from some importers as Army Model Belt Revolver in 36-cal., a shortened and lightened version of the 44. Target Model (Uberti U.S.A. Inc., Navy Arms) has fully adjustable target rear sight, target front, 36 or 44. Imported by Cabela's, Cimarron F.A. Co., CVA (as 1858 Army, brass frame, 44 only), Dixie Gun Works, Navy Arms, The Armoury, E.M.F., Euroarms of America (engraved, stainless and plain), Armsport, Traditions (44 only), Uberti U.S.A. Inc.

Price: Steel frame, about	$99.95 to $280.00
Price: Steel frame kit (Euroarms, Navy Arms)	$115.95 to $150.00
Price: Single cased set (Navy Arms)	$290.00
Price: Double cased set (Navy Arms)	$480.00
Price: Stainless steel Model 1858 (Euroarms, Uberti U.S.A. Inc., Cabela's, Navy Arms, Armsport, Traditions)	$169.95 to $380.00
Price: Target Model, adjustable rear sight (Cabela's, Euroarms, Uberti U.S.A. Inc., Stone Mountain Arms)	$95.95 to $399.00
Price: Brass frame (CVA, Cabela's, Traditions, Navy Arms)	$79.95 to $159.95
Price: As above, kit (Dixie Gun Works, Navy Arms)	$145.00 to $188.95
Price: Buffalo model, 44-cal. (Cabela's)	$119.99
Price: Hartford model, steel frame, German silver trim, cartouche (E.M.F.)	$215.00

NORTH AMERICAN COMPANION PERCUSSION REVOLVER
Caliber: 22. **Barrel:** 1-1/8". **Weight:** 5.1 oz. **Length:** 4-5/10" overall. **Stocks:** Laminated wood. **Sights:** Blade front, notch fixed rear. **Features:** All stainless steel construction. Uses standard #11 percussion caps. Comes with bullets, powder measure, bullet seater, leather clip holster, gun rug. Long Rifle or Magnum frame size. Introduced 1996. Made in U.S. by North American Arms.

Price: Long Rifle frame	$191.00

North American Magnum Companion Percussion Revolver
Similar to the Companion except has larger frame. Weighs 7.2 oz., has 1-5/8" barrel, measures 5-7/16" overall. Comes with bullets, powder measure, bullet seater, leather clip holster, gun rag. Introduced 1996. Made in U.S. by North American Arms.

Price:	$209.00

POCKET POLICE 1862 PERCUSSION REVOLVER
Caliber: 36, 5-shot. **Barrel:** 4-1/2", 5-1/2", 6-1/2", 7-1/2". **Weight:** 26 oz. **Length:** 12" overall (6-1/2" bbl.). **Stocks:** Walnut. **Sights:** Fixed. **Features:** Round tapered barrel; half-fluted and rebated cylinder; case-hardened frame, loading lever and hammer; silver or brass trigger guard and backstrap. Imported by Dixie Gun Works, Navy Arms (5-1/2" only), Uberti U.S.A. Inc. (5-1/2", 6-1/2" only), United States Patent Fire-Arms and Cimarron F.A. Co.

Price: About	$139.95 to $335.00
Price: Single cased set with accessories (Navy Arms)	$365.00
Price: Hartford model, steel frame, German silver trim, cartouche (E.M.F.)	$215.00

ROGERS & SPENCER PERCUSSION REVOLVER
Caliber: 44. **Barrel:** 7-1/2". **Weight:** 47 oz. **Length:** 13-3/4" overall. **Stocks:** Walnut. **Sights:** Cone front, integral groove in frame for rear. **Features:** Accurate reproduction of a Civil War design. Solid frame; extra large nipple cut-out on rear of cylinder; loading lever and cylinder easily removed for cleaning. From Dixie Gun Works, Euroarms of America (standard blue, engraved, burnished, target models), Navy Arms.

Price:	$160.00 to $299.95
Price: Nickel-plated	$215.00
Price: Engraved (Euroarms)	$287.00

34TH EDITION, 2002 • 297

BLACKPOWDER REVOLVERS

Spiller & Burr

Texas Paterson

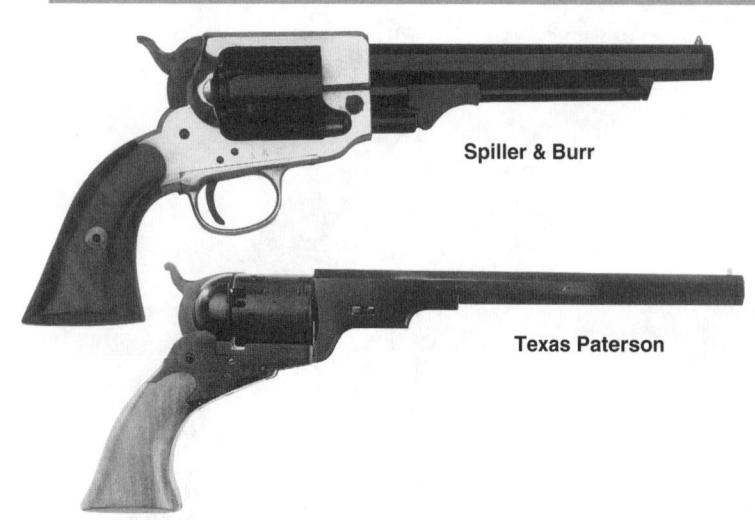

Walker

Price: Kit version. . . . . $245.00 to $252.00
Price: Target version (Euroarms) . . . . $239.00 to $270.00
Price: Burnished London Gray (Euroarms) . . . . $245.00 to $270.00

RUGER OLD ARMY PERCUSSION REVOLVER
Caliber: 45, 6-shot. Uses .457" dia. lead bullets. **Barrel:** 7-1/2" (6-groove; 16" twist). **Weight:** 46 oz. **Length:** 13-3/4" overall. **Stocks:** Smooth walnut. **Sights:** Ramp front, rear adjustable for windage and elevation; or fixed (groove). **Features:** Stainless steel; standard size nipples, chrome-moly steel cylinder and frame, same lockwork as in original Super Blackhawk. Also available in stainless steel. Includes hard case and lock. Made in USA. From Sturm, Ruger & Co.
Price: Stainless steel (Model KBP-7) $510.00
Price: Blued steel (Model BP-7) $478.00
Price: Blued steel, fixed sight (BP-7F) $478.00
Price: Stainless steel, fixed sight (KBP-7F) $510.00

SHERIFF MODEL 1851 PERCUSSION REVOLVER
Caliber: 36, 44, 6-shot. **Barrel:** 5". **Weight:** 40 oz. **Length:** 10-1/2" overall. **Stocks:** Walnut. **Sights:** Fixed. **Features:** Brass backstrap and trigger guard; engraved navy scene; case-hardened frame, hammer, loading lever. Imported by E.M.F.
Price: Steel frame $172.00
Price: Brass frame $140.00

SPILLER & BURR REVOLVER
Caliber: 36 (.375" round ball). **Barrel:** 7", octagon. **Weight:** 2-1/2 lbs. **Length:** 12-1/2" overall. **Stocks:** Two-piece walnut. **Sights:** Fixed. **Features:** Reproduction of the C.S.A. revolver. Brass frame and trigger guard. Also available as a kit. From Dixie Gun Works, Navy Arms.
Price: $145.00
Price: Kit form (Dixie) $149.95
Price: Single cased set (Navy Arms) $270.00
Price: Double cased set (Navy Arms). $430.00

TEXAS PATERSON 1836 REVOLVER
Caliber: 36 (.375" round ball). **Barrel:** 7-1/2". **Weight:** 42 oz. **Stocks:** One-piece walnut. **Sights:** Fixed. **Features:** Copy of Sam Colt's first commercially-made revolving pistol. Has no loading lever but comes with loading tool. From Cimarron F.A. Co., Dixie Gun Works, Navy Arms, Uberti U.S.A. Inc.
Price: About . . . . $310.00 to $395.00
Price: With loading lever (Uberti U.S.A. Inc.) $450.00
Price: Engraved (Navy Arms) $485.00

Uberti 1861 Navy Percussion Revolver
Similar to Colt 1851 Navy except has round 7-1/2" barrel, rounded trigger guard, German silver blade front sight, "creeping" loading lever. Available with fluted or round cylinder. Imported by Uberti U.S.A. Inc.
Price: Steel backstrap, trigger guard, cut for stock. $300.00

1ST U.S. MODEL DRAGOON
Caliber: 44. **Barrel:** 7-1/2", part round, part octagon. **Weight:** 64 oz. **Stocks:** One-piece walnut. **Sights:** German silver blade front, hammer notch rear. **Features:** First model has oval bolt cuts in cylinder, square-back flared trigger guard, V-type mainspring, short trigger. Ranger and Indian scene roll-engraved on cylinder. Color case-hardened frame, loading lever, plunger and hammer; blue barrel, cylinder, trigger and wedge. Available with old-time charcoal blue or standard blue-black finish. Polished brass backstrap and trigger guard. From Cimarron F.A. Co., Uberti U.S.A. Inc., United States Patent Fire-Arms, Navy Arms.
Price: . . . . $325.00 to $435.00

2nd U.S. Model Dragoon Revolver
Similar to the 1st Model except distinguished by rectangular bolt cuts in the cylinder. From Cimarron F.A. Co., Uberti U.S.A. Inc., United States Patent Fire-Arms, Navy Arms.
Price: . . . . $325.00 to $435.00

3rd U.S. Model Dragoon Revolver
Similar to the 2nd Model except for oval trigger guard, long trigger, modifications to the loading lever and latch. Imported by Cimarron F.A. Co., Uberti U.S.A. Inc., United States Patent Fire-Arms.
Price: Military model (frame cut for shoulder stock,
steel backstrap) . . . . $330.00 to $435.00
Price: Civilian (brass backstrap, trigger guard) $325.00

1862 POCKET NAVY PERCUSSION REVOLVER
Caliber: 36, 5-shot. **Barrel:** 5-1/2", 6-1/2", octagonal, 7-groove, LH twist. **Weight:** 27 oz. (5-1/2" barrel). **Length:** 10-1/2" overall (5-1/2" bbl.). **Stocks:** One-piece varnished walnut. **Sights:** Brass pin front, hammer notch rear. **Features:** Rebated cylinder, hinged loading lever, brass or silver-plated backstrap and trigger guard, color-cased frame, hammer, loading lever, plunger and latch, rest blued. Has original-type markings. From Cimarron F.A. Co. and Uberti U.S.A. Inc.
Price: With brass backstrap, trigger guard $310.00

1861 Navy Percussion Revolver
Similar to Colt 1851 Navy except has round 7-1/2" barrel, rounded trigger guard, German silver blade front sight, "creeping" loading lever. Fluted or round cylinder. Imported by Cimarron F.A. Co., Uberti U.S.A. Inc.
Price: Steel backstrap, trigger guard, cut for stock. $300.00

U.S. PATENT FIRE-ARMS 1862 POCKET NAVY
Caliber: 36. **Barrel:** 4-1/2", 5-1/2", 6-1/2". **Weight:** 27 oz. (5-1/2" barrel). **Length:** 10-1/2" overall (5-1/2" barrel). **Stocks:** Smooth walnut. **Sights:** Brass pin front, hammer notch rear. **Features:** Blued barrel and cylinder, color case-hardened frame, hammer, lever; silver-plated backstrap and trigger guard. Imported from Italy; available from United States Patent Fire-Arms Mfg. Co.
Price: $335.00

WALKER 1847 PERCUSSION REVOLVER
Caliber: 44, 6-shot. **Barrel:** 9". **Weight:** 84 oz. **Length:** 15-1/2" overall. **Stocks:** Walnut. **Sights:** Fixed. **Features:** Case-hardened frame, loading lever and hammer; iron backstrap; brass trigger guard; engraved cylinder. Imported by Cabela's, Cimarron F.A. Co., Navy Arms, Dixie Gun Works, Uberti U.S.A. Inc., E.M.F., Cimarron, Traditions, United States Patent Fire-Arms.
Price: About . . . . $225.00 to $445.00
Price: Single cased set (Navy Arms) $405.00
Price: Deluxe Walker with French fitted case (Navy Arms) $540.00
Price: Hartford model, steel frame, German silver trim,
cartouche (E.M.F.) $295.00

298 • GUNS ILLUSTRATED

BLACKPOWDER MUSKETS & RIFLES

Cabela's Blue Ridge

Cabela's Traditional Hawken

Cook & Brother

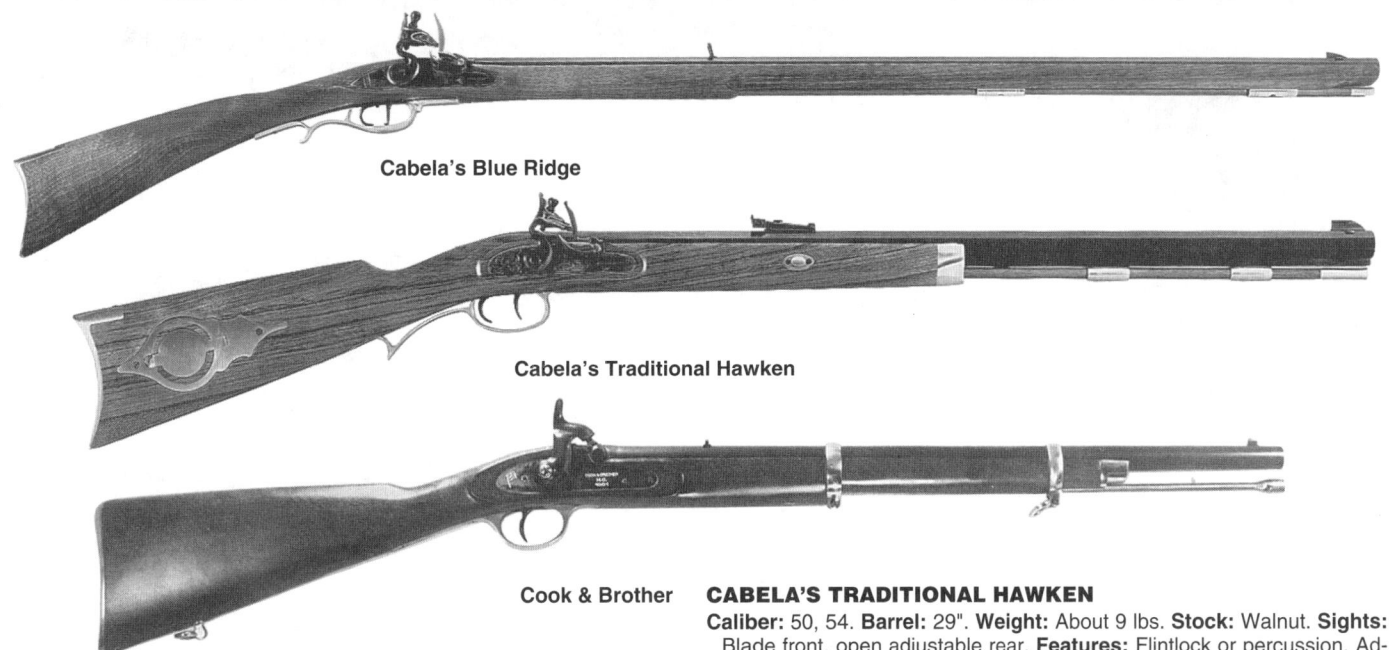

ARMOURY R140 HAWKEN RIFLE
Caliber: 45, 50 or 54. **Barrel:** 29". **Weight:** 8-3/4 to 9 lbs. **Length:** 45-3/4" overall. **Stock:** Walnut, with cheekpiece. **Sights:** Dovetail front, fully adjustable rear. **Features:** Octagon barrel, removable breech plug; double set triggers; blued barrel, brass stock fittings, color case-hardened percussion lock. From Armsport, The Armoury.
Price: .... $225.00 to $245.00

AUSTIN & HALLECK MODEL 420 LR IN-LINE RIFLE
Caliber: 50. **Barrel:** 26", 1" octagon to 3/4" round; 1:28" twist. **Weight:** 7-7/8 lbs. **Length:** 47-1/2" overall. **Stock:** Lightly figured maple in Classic or Monte Carlo style. **Sights:** Ramp front, fully adjustable rear. **Features:** Blue or electroless nickel finish; in-line percussion action with removable weather shroud; Timney adjustable target trigger with sear block safety. Introduced 1998. Made in U.S. by Austin & Halleck.
Price: Blue $459.00
Price: Stainless steel $549.00
Price: Blue, hand-select highly figured stock $775.00
Price: Blue, exhibition-grade Monte Carlo stock. $1,322.00
Price: Stainless steel, exhibition-grade Monte Carlo stock. $1,422.00

Austin & Halleck Model 320 LR In-Line Rifle
Similar to the Model 420 LR except has black resin synthetic stock with checkered grip and forend. Introduced 1998. Made in U.S. by Austin & Halleck.
Price: Blue $380.00
Price: Stainless steel $447.00

AUSTIN & HALLECK MOUNTAIN RIFLE
Caliber: 50. **Barrel:** 32"; 1:28" or 1:66" twist; 1" flats. **Weight:** 7-1/2 lbs. **Length:** 49" overall. **Stock:** Curly maple. **Sights:** Silver blade front, buckhorn rear. **Features:** Available in percussion or flintlock; double throw adjustable set triggers; rust brown finish. Made in U.S. by Austin & Halleck.
Price: Flintlock $539.00
Price: Percussion $578.00
Price: Percussion, fancy wood $592.00
Price: Percussion, select wood. $660.00

BOSTONIAN PERCUSSION RIFLE
Caliber: 45. **Barrel:** 30", octagonal. **Weight:** 7-1/4 lbs. **Length:** 46" overall. **Stock:** Walnut. **Sights:** Blade front, fixed notch rear. **Features:** Color case-hardened lock, brass trigger guard, buttplate, patchbox. Imported from Italy by E.M.F.
Price: $285.00

CABELA'S TRADITIONAL HAWKEN
Caliber: 50, 54. **Barrel:** 29". **Weight:** About 9 lbs. **Stock:** Walnut. **Sights:** Blade front, open adjustable rear. **Features:** Flintlock or percussion. Adjustable double-set triggers. Polished brass furniture, color case-hardened lock. Imported by Cabela's.
Price: Percussion, right-hand $189.99
Price: Percussion, left-hand $199.99
Price: Flintlock, right-hand $224.99

CABELA'S BLUE RIDGE RIFLE
Caliber: 32, 36, 45, 50. **Barrel:** 39", octagonal. **Weight:** About 7-3/4 lbs. **Length:** 55" overall. **Stock:** American black walnut. **Sights:** Blade front, rear drift adjustable for windage. **Features:** Color case-hardened lockplate and cock/hammer, brass trigger guard and buttplate, double set, double-phased triggers. From Cabela's.
Price: Percussion $379.99
Price: Flintlock $399.99

CABELA'S KODIAK EXPRESS DOUBLE RIFLE
Caliber: 50, 54, 58, 72. **Barrel:** Length n/a; 1:48" twist. **Weight:** 9.3 lbs. **Length:** 45-1/4" overall. **Stock:** European walnut, oil finish. **Sights:** Fully adjustable double folding-leaf rear, ramp front. **Features:** Percussion. Barrels regulated to point of aim at 75 yards; polished and engraved lock, top tang and trigger guard. From Cabela's.
Price: 50, 54, 58 calibers $649.99
Price: 72 caliber $679.99

CABELA'S PINE RIDGE LR IN-LINE RIFLE
Caliber: 50. **Barrel:** 26" blued or stainless steel. **Weight:** About 7 lbs. **Length:** N/A. **Stock:** Black synthetic. **Sights:** Fiber-optic blade front, fully adjustable rear. **Features:** No. 209 Flame-Thrower ignition system; adjustable trigger; handles up to 150 grains of blackpowder or Pyrodex. From Cabela's.
Price: (blued barrel) $229.99
Price: (stainless steel barrel) $269.99

Cabela's Sporterized Hawken Hunter Rifle
Similar to the Traditional Hawken except has more modern stock style with rubber recoil pad, blued furniture, sling swivels. Percussion only, in 50- or 54-caliber.
Price: Carbine or rifle, right-hand $219.99

COLT MODEL 1861 MUSKET
Caliber: 58. **Barrel:** 40". **Weight:** 9 lbs., 3 oz. **Length:** 56" overall. **Stock:** Oil-finished walnut. **Sight:** Blade front, adjustable folding leaf rear. **Features:** Made to original specifications and has authentic Civil War Colt markings. Bright-finished metal, blued nipple and rear sight. Bayonet and accessories available. From Colt Blackpowder Arms Co.
Price: $799.95

34TH EDITION, 2002

BLACKPOWDER MUSKETS & RIFLES

CVA Firebolt

CVA St. Louis Hawken

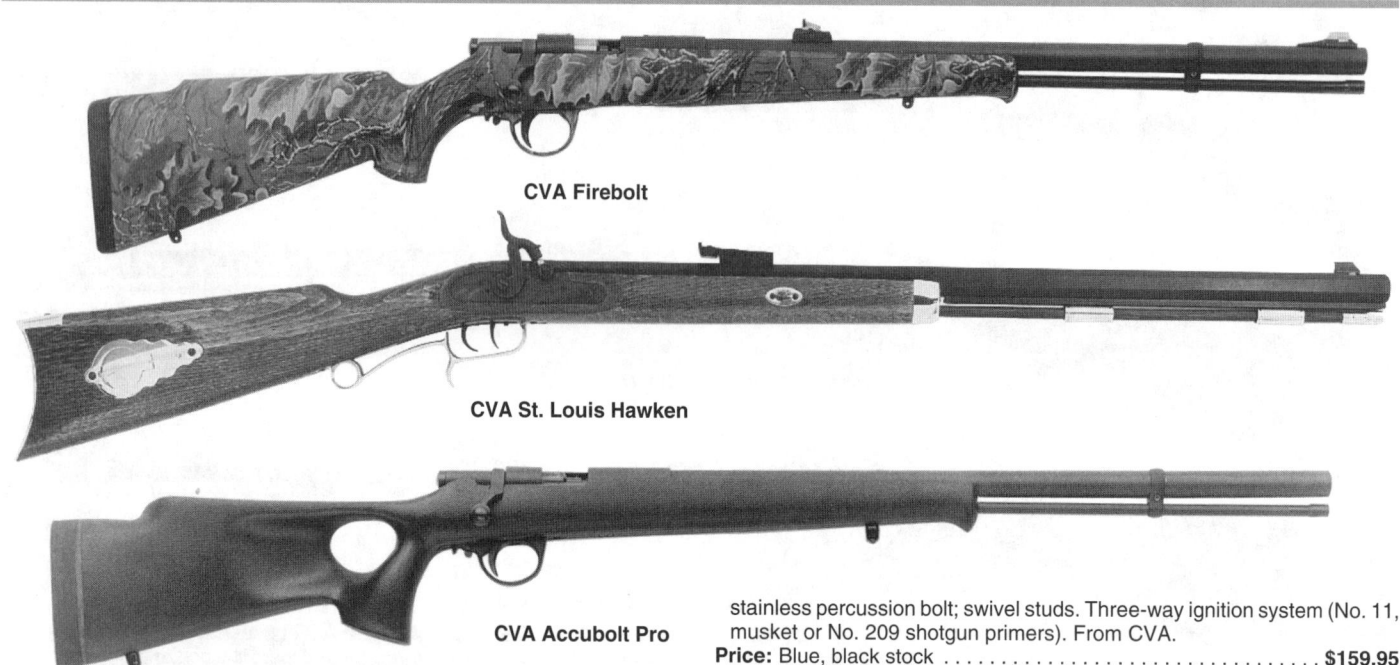

CVA Accubolt Pro

COOK & BROTHER CONFEDERATE CARBINE
Caliber: 58. **Barrel:** 24". **Weight:** 7-1/2 lbs. **Length:** 40-1/2" overall. **Stock:** Select walnut. **Features:** Recreation of the 1861 New Orleans-made artillery carbine. Color case-hardened lock, browned barrel. Buttplate, trigger guard, barrel bands, sling swivels and nosecap of polished brass. From Euroarms of America.
Price: $447.00
Price: Cook & Brother rifle (33" barrel) $480.00

CUMBERLAND MOUNTAIN BLACKPOWDER RIFLE
Caliber: 50. **Barrel:** 26", round. **Weight:** 9-1/2 lbs. **Length:** 43" overall. **Stock:** American walnut. **Sights:** Bead front, open rear adjustable for windage. **Features:** Falling block action fires with shotshell primer. Blued receiver and barrel. Introduced 1993. Made in U.S. by Cumberland Mountain Arms, Inc.
Price: $931.50

CVA COLORADO MUSKET MAG 100 RIFLE
Caliber: 50, 54 **Barrel:** 26"; 1:32" twist. **Weight:** 7-1/2 lbs. **Length:** 42" overall. **Stock:** Synthetic; black, Hardwoods or X-Tra Brown camo. **Sights:** Illuminator front and rear. **Features:** Sidelock action uses musket caps for ignition. Introduced 1999. From CVA.
Price: With black stock $184.95
Price: With camo stock $219.95

CVA YOUTH HUNTER RIFLE
Caliber: 50. **Barrel:** 24"; 1:48" twist, octagonal. **Weight:** 5-1/2 lbs. **Length:** 38" overall. **Stock:** Stained hardwood. **Sights:** Bead front, Williams adjustable rear. **Features:** Oversize trigger guard; wooden ramrod. Introduced 1999. From CVA.
Price: $135.95

CVA BOBCAT RIFLE
Caliber: 50 or 54. **Barrel:** 26"; 1:48" twist. **Weight:** 6-1/2 lbs. **Length:** 42" overall. **Stock:** Dura-Grip synthetic or wood. **Sights:** Blade front, open rear. **Features:** Oversize trigger guard; wood ramrod; matte black finish. Introduced 1995. From CVA.
Price: (wood stock, 50 cal. only) $127.95
Price: (black synthetic stock, 50 or 54 cal.) $104.95

CVA ECLIPSE 209 MAGNUM IN-LINE RIFLE
Caliber: 50. **Barrel:** 24" round; 1:32" rifling. **Weight:** 7 lbs. **Length:** 42" overall. **Stock:** Black or Mossy Oak® Break-Up™ camo synthetic. **Sights:** Illuminator Fiber Optic Sight System; drilled and tapped for scope mounting. **Features:** In-line action uses modern trigger with automatic safety; stainless percussion bolt; swivel studs. Three-way ignition system (No. 11, musket or No. 209 shotgun primers). From CVA.
Price: Blue, black stock $159.95
Price: Blue, Break-Up™ camo stock $189.95

CVA Stag Horn 209 Magnum Rifle
Similar to the Eclipse except has light-gathering Solar Sights, manual safety, black synthetic stock and ramrod. Weighs 6 lbs. From CVA.
Price: 50 cal. $129.95

CVA MOUNTAIN RIFLE
Caliber: 50. **Barrel:** 32"; 1:66" rifling. **Weight:** 8-1/2 lbs. **Length:** NA. **Stock:** American hard maple. **Sights:** Blade front, buckhorn rear. **Features:** Browned steel furniture; German silver wedge plates; patchbox. Made in U.S. From CVA.
Price: $399.95

CVA ST. LOUIS HAWKEN RIFLE
Caliber: 50, 54. **Barrel:** 28", octagon; 15/16" across flats; 1:48" twist. **Weight:** 8 lbs. **Length:** 44" overall. **Stock:** Select hardwood. **Sights:** Beaded blade front, fully adjustable open rear. **Features:** Fully adjustable double-set triggers; synthetic ramrod (kits have wood); brass patchbox, wedge plates, nosecap, thimbles, trigger guard and buttplate; blued barrel; color case-hardened, engraved lockplate. V-type mainspring. Button breech. Introduced 1981. From CVA.
Price: St. Louis Hawken, finished (50-, 54-cal.) $207.95
Price: Left-hand, percussion $264.95
Price: Flintlock, 50-cal. only $264.95
Price: Percussion kit (50-cal., blued, wood ramrod) $191.95

CVA HunterBolt 209 Magnum Rifle
Similar to the Firebolt except has 24" barrel and black or Mossy Oak® Break-Up™ synthetic stock. Three-way ignition system. Weighs 6 lbs. From CVA.
Price: 45 or 50 cal. .... $199.95 to $254.95

CVA FIREBOLT MUSKETMAG BOLT-ACTION IN-LINE RIFLES
Caliber: 45 or 50. **Barrel:** 26". **Weight:** 7 lbs. **Length:** 44". **Stock:** Rubber-coated black or Mossy Oak® Break-Up™ camo synthetic. **Sights:** CVA Illuminator Fiber Optic Sight System. **Features:** Bolt-action, in-line ignition system handles up to 150 grains blackpowder or Pyrodex; Nickel or matte blue barrel; removable breech plug; trigger-block safety. Introduced 1997. Three-way ignition system. From CVA.
Price: Nickel finish, black stock, 50 cal. $279.95
Price: Nickel finish, black stock, 45 cal. $289.95
Price: Nickel finish, Break-Up™ stock, 45 cal. $329.95
Price: Matte blue finish, Break-Up™ camo stock, 50 cal. . $299.95
Price: Matte blue finish, black stock, 50 cal. $259.95
Price: Matte blue finish, Break-Up™ stock, 45 cal. $309.95

BLACKPOWDER MUSKETS & RIFLES

Dixie English Matchlock

Dixie Inline Carbine

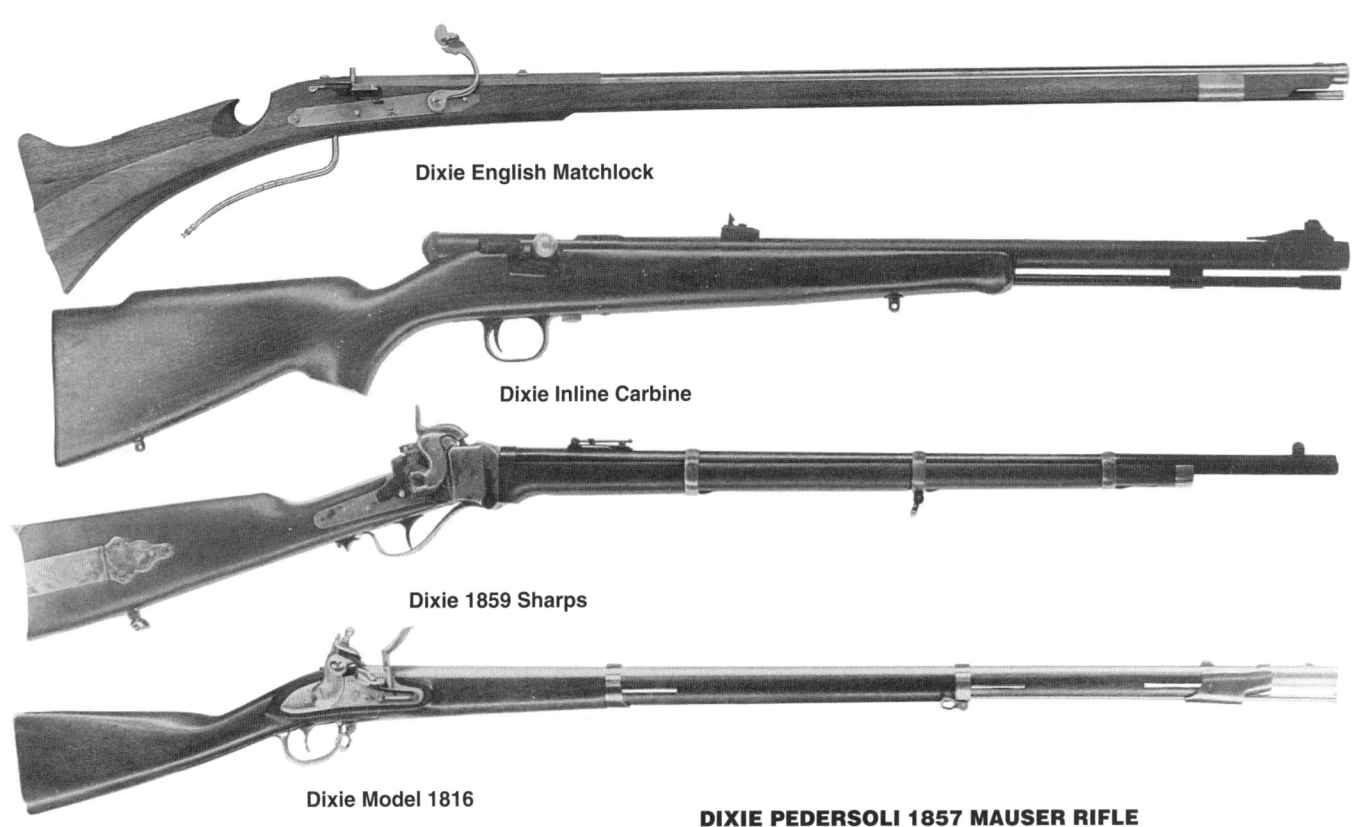

Dixie 1859 Sharps

Dixie Model 1816

DIXIE ENGLISH MATCHLOCK MUSKET
Caliber: 72. **Barrel:** 44". **Weight:** 8 lbs. **Length:** 57.75" overall. **Stock:** Walnut with satin oil finish. **Sights:** Blade front, open rear adjustable for windage. **Features:** Replica of circa 1600-1680 English matchlock. Getz barrel with 11" octagonal area at rear, rest is round with cannon-type muzzle. All steel finished in the white. Imported by Dixie Gun Works.
Price: $895.00

DIXIE EARLY AMERICAN JAEGER RIFLE
Caliber: 54. **Barrel:** 27-1/2" octagonal; 1:24" twist. **Weight:** 8-1/4 lbs. **Length:** 43-1/2" overall. **Stock:** American walnut; sliding wooden patchbox on on butt. **Sights:** Notch rear, blade front. **Features:** Flintlock or percussion. Browned steel furniture. Introduced 2000. Imported from Italy by Dixie Gun Works.
Price: Flintlock or percussion $695.00

DIXIE DELUXE CUB RIFLE
Caliber: 40. **Barrel:** 28". **Weight:** 6-1/2 lbs. **Stock:** Walnut. **Sights:** Fixed. **Features:** Short rifle for small game and beginning shooters. Brass patchbox and furniture. Flint or percussion. From Dixie Gun Works.
Price: Finished $415.00
Price: Kit.. $375.00
Price: Super Cub (50-caliber)........................... $367.00

DIXIE 1863 SPRINGFIELD MUSKET
Caliber: 58 (.570" patched ball or .575" Minie). **Barrel:** 50", rifled. **Stock:** Walnut stained. **Sights:** Blade front, adjustable ladder-type rear. **Features:** Bright-finish lock, barrel, furniture. Reproduction of the last of the regulation muzzleloaders. Imported from Japan by Dixie Gun Works.
Price: Finished $595.00
Price: Kit.. $525.00

DIXIE INLINE CARBINE
Caliber: 50, 54. **Barrel:** 24"; 1:32" twist. **Weight:** 6.5 lbs. **Length:** 41" overall. **Stock:** Walnut-finished hardwood with Monte Carlo comb. **Sights:** Ramp front with red insert, open fully adjustable rear. **Features:** Sliding "bolt" fully encloses cap and nipple. Fully adjustable trigger, automatic safety. Aluminum ramrod. Imported from Italy by Dixie Gun Works.
Price: $349.95

DIXIE PEDERSOLI 1857 MAUSER RIFLE
Caliber: 54. **Barrel:** 39-3/8". **Weight:** N/A. **Length:** 52" overall. **Stock:** European walnut with oil finish, sling swivels. **Sights:** Fully adjustable rear, lug front. **Features:** Percussion (musket caps). Armory bright finish with color case-hardened lock and barrel tang, engraved lockplate, steel ramrod. Introduced 2000. Imported from Italy by Dixie Gun Works.
Price: $895.00

DIXIE PEDERSOLI 1766 CHARLEVILLE MUSKET
Caliber: 69. **Barrel:** 44-3/4". **Weight:** 10-1/2 lbs. **Length:** 57-1/2" overall. **Stock:** European walnut with oil finish. **Sights:** Fixed rear, lug front. **Features:** Smoothbore flintlock. Armory bright finish with steel furniture and ramrod. Introduced 2000. Imported from Italy by Dixie Gun Works.
Price: $795.00

DIXIE SHARPS NEW MODEL 1859 MILITARY RIFLE
Caliber: 54. **Barrel:** 30", 6-groove; 1:48" twist. **Weight:** 9 lbs. **Length:** 45-1/2" overall. **Stock:** Oiled walnut. **Sights:** Blade front, ladder-style rear. **Features:** Blued barrel, color case-hardened barrel bands, receiver, hammer, nosecap, lever, patchbox cover and buttplate. Introduced 1995. Imported from Italy by Dixie Gun Works.
Price: $895.00

DIXIE U.S. MODEL 1816 FLINTLOCK MUSKET
Caliber: 69. **Barrel:** 42", smoothbore. **Weight:** 9.75 lbs. **Length:** 56.5" overall. **Stock:** Walnut with oil finish. **Sights:** Blade front. **Features:** All metal finished "National Armory Bright"; three barrel bands with springs; steel ramrod with button-shaped head. Imported by Dixie Gun Works.
Price: $725.00

DIXIE U.S. MODEL 1861 SPRINGFIELD
Caliber: 58. **Barrel:** 40". **Weight:** About 8 lbs. **Length:** 55-13/16" overall. **Stock:** Oil-finished walnut. **Sights:** Blade front, step adjustable rear. **Features:** Exact recreation of original rifle. Sling swivels attached to trigger guard bow and middle barrel band. Lockplate marked "1861" with eagle motif and "U.S. Springfield" in front of hammer; "U.S." stamped on top of buttplate. From Dixie Gun Works.
Price: $595.00
Price: From Stone Mountain Arms $599.00
Price: Kit.. $525.00

34TH EDITION, 2002 • 301

BLACKPOWDER MUSKETS & RIFLES

Dixie U.S. Model 1861

Euroarms Volunteer

Euroarms 1861

Gonic Model 93 Thumbhole

Harper's Ferry 1803

E.M.F. 1863 SHARPS MILITARY CARBINE
Caliber: 54. **Barrel:** 22", round. **Weight:** 8 lbs. **Length:** 39" overall. **Stock:** Oiled walnut. **Sights:** Blade front, military ladder-type rear. **Features:** Color case-hardened lock, rest blued. Imported by E.M.F.
Price: $600.00

EUROARMS VOLUNTEER TARGET RIFLE
Caliber: .451. **Barrel:** 33" (two-band), 36" (three-band). **Weight:** 11 lbs. (two-band). **Length:** 48.75" overall (two-band). **Stock:** European walnut with checkered wrist and forend. **Sights:** Hooded bead front, adjustable rear with interchangeable leaves. **Features:** Alexander Henry-type rifling with 1:20" twist. Color case-hardened hammer and lockplate, brass trigger guard and nosecap, rest blued. Imported by Euroarms of America.
Price: Two-band $720.00
Price: Three-band $773.00

EUROARMS 1861 SPRINGFIELD RIFLE
Caliber: 58. **Barrel:** 40". **Weight:** About 10 lbs. **Length:** 55.5" overall. **Stock:** European walnut. **Sights:** Blade front, three-leaf military rear. **Features:** Reproduction of the original three-band rifle. Lockplate marked "1861" with eagle and "U.S. Springfield." Metal left in the white. Imported by Euroarms of America.
Price: $530.00

GONIC MODEL 93 M/L RIFLE
Caliber: 45, 50. **Barrel:** 26"; 1:24" twist. **Weight:** 6-1/2 to 7 lbs. **Length:** 43" overall. **Stock:** American hardwood with black finish. **Sights:** Adjustable or aperture rear, hooded post front. **Features:** Adjustable trigger with side safety; unbreakable ram rod; comes with A. Z. scope bases installed. Introduced 1993. Made in U.S. by Gonic Arms, Inc.
Price: Model 93 Standard (blued barrel) $720.00
Price: Model 93 Standard (stainless brl., 50 cal. only) $782.00

Gonic Model 93 Deluxe M/L Rifle
Similar to the Model 93 except has classic-style walnut or gray laminated wood stock. Introduced 1998. Made in U.S. by Gonic Arms, Inc.
Price: Blue barrel, sights, scope base, choice of stock $902.00
Price: Stainless barrel, sights, scope base, choice of stock
(50 cal. only) $964.00

Gonic Model 93 Mountain Thumbhole M/L Rifles
Similar to the Model 93 except has high-grade walnut or gray laminate stock with extensive hand-checkered panels, Monte Carlo cheekpiece and beavertail forend; integral muzzle brake. Introduced 1998. Made in U.S. by Gonic Arms, Inc.
Price: Blue or stainless $2,625.00

HARPER'S FERRY 1803 FLINTLOCK RIFLE
Caliber: 54 or 58. **Barrel:** 35". **Weight:** 9 lbs. **Length:** 59-1/2" overall. **Stock:** Walnut with cheekpiece. **Sights:** Brass blade front, fixed steel rear. **Features:** Brass trigger guard, sideplate, buttplate; steel patchbox. Imported by Euroarms of America, Navy Arms (54-cal. only), Cabela's.
Price: .... $495.95 to $729.00
Price: 54-cal. (Navy Arms) $625.00
Price: 54-caliber (Cabela's) $599.99

BLACKPOWDER MUSKETS & RIFLES

J.P. Murray

Kentucky Flintlock

Knight Bighorn In/Line

HAWKEN RIFLE
Caliber: 45, 50, 54 or 58. **Barrel:** 28", blued, 6-groove rifling. **Weight:** 8-3/4 lbs. **Length:** 44" overall. **Stock:** Walnut with cheekpiece. **Sights:** Blade front, fully adjustable rear. **Features:** Coil mainspring, double-set triggers, polished brass furniture. From Armsport, Navy Arms, E.M.F.
Price: .... $220.00 to $345.00

J.P. MURRAY 1862-1864 CAVALRY CARBINE
Caliber: 58 (.577" Minie). **Barrel:** 23". **Weight:** 7 lbs., 9 oz. **Length:** 39" overall. **Stock:** Walnut. **Sights:** Blade front, rear drift adjustable for windage. **Features:** Browned barrel, color case-hardened lock, blued swivel and band springs, polished brass buttplate, trigger guard, barrel bands. From Navy Arms, Euroarms of America.
Price: .... $405.00 to $453.00

J.P. HENRY TRADE RIFLE
Caliber: 54. **Barrel:** 34"; 1" flats. **Weight:** 8-1/2 lbs. **Length:** 45" overall. **Stock:** Premium curly maple. **Sights:** Silver blade front, fixed buckhorn rear. **Features:** Brass buttplate, side plate, trigger guard and nosecap; browned barrel and lock; L&R Large English percussion lock; single trigger. Made in U.S. by J.P. Gunstocks, Inc.
Price: $965.50

KENTUCKIAN RIFLE
Caliber: 44. **Barrel:** 35". **Weight:** 7 lbs. (Rifle), 5-1/2 lbs. (Carbine). **Length:** 51" overall (Rifle), 43" (Carbine). **Stock:** Walnut stain. **Sights:** Brass blade front, steel V-ramp rear. **Features:** Octagon barrel, case-hardened and engraved lockplates. Brass furniture. Imported by Dixie Gun Works.
Price: Flintlock $269.95
Price: Percussion $259.95

KENTUCKY FLINTLOCK RIFLE
Caliber: 44, 45, or 50. **Barrel:** 35". **Weight:** 7 lbs. **Length:** 50" overall. **Stock:** Walnut stained, brass fittings. **Sights:** Fixed. **Features:** Available in carbine model also, 28" bbl. Some variations in detail, finish. Kits also available from some importers. Imported by Navy Arms, The Armoury.
Price: About .... $217.95 to $345.00
Price: Flintlock, 45 or 50-cal. (Navy Arms) $435.00

Kentucky Percussion Rifle
Similar to flintlock except percussion lock. Finish and features vary with importer. Imported by Navy Arms, The Armoury, CVA.
Price: About $259.95
Price: 45- or 50-cal. (Navy Arms) $425.00
Price: Kit, 50-cal. (CVA) $189.95

KNIGHT 50 CALIBER DISC IN-LINE RIFLE
Caliber: 50. **Barrel:** 24", 26". **Weight:** 7 lbs., 14 oz. **Length:** 43" overall (24" barrel). **Stock:** Checkered synthetic with palm swell grip, rubber recoil pad, swivel studs; black, Advantage or Mossy Oak Break-Up camouflage. **Sights:** Bead on ramp front, fully adjustable open rear. **Features:** Bolt-action in-line system uses #209 shotshell primer for ignition; primer is held in plastic drop-in Primer Disc. Available in blued or stainless steel. Made in U.S. by Knight Rifles (Modern Muzzleloading).
Price: .... $459.95 to $615.95

Knight Master Hunter II DISC In-Line Rifle
Similar to Knight 50 caliber DISC rifle except features premier, wood laminated two-tone stock, gold-plated trigger and engraved trigger guard, jeweled bolt and fluted, air-gauged Green Mountain 26" barrel. Length 45" overall, weighs 7 lbs., 7 oz. Includes black composite thumbhole stock. Introduced 2000. Made in U.S. by Knight Rifles (Modern Muzzleloading).
Price: $1,099.95

Knight 45 Super DISC In-Line Rifle
Similar to the 50 caliber DISC rifle except in 45 caliber to fire saboted bullets and up to 150 grains of blackpowder or equivalent at up to 2,600 fps. Fluted 26" Green Mountain barrel in blue or stainless finish; thumbhole or standard synthetic stock in black, Advantage Timber HD or Mossy Oak Break-Up camouflage. Weighs 8 lbs., 3 oz. Made in U.S. by Knight Rifles (Modern Muzzleloading).

KNIGHT BIGHORN IN-LINE RIFLE
Caliber: 50. **Barrel:** 22", 26"; 1:28" twist. **Weight:** About 7 lbs. **Length:** 41" overall (22" barrel). **Stock:** Synthetic; black Advantage or Mossy Oak Break-Up camouflage. Black rubber recoil pad. **Sights:** Fully adjustable Tru-Glo fiber optic. **Features:** Patented double safety system; adjustable trigger; comes with #11 Red Hot Nipple and 209 shotshell primer conversion kit. Available in blue or stainless steel. Made in U.S. by Knight Rifles.
Price: (right- or left-hand model) .... $349.95 to $478.95

KNIGHT AMERICAN KNIGHT M/L RIFLE
Caliber: 50. **Barrel:** 22"; 1:28" twist. **Weight:** 6 lbs. **Length:** 41" overall. **Stock:** Black composite. **Sights:** Bead on ramp front, open fully adjustable rear. **Features:** Double safety system; one-piece removable hammer assembly; drilled and tapped for scope mounting. Introduced 1998. Made in U.S. by Knight Rifles.
Price: $199.95

BLACKPOWDER MUSKETS & RIFLES

Knight Wolverine II

London Armory 1861

Lyman Cougar In/Line

Lyman Trade

KNIGHT WOLVERINE II RIFLE
Caliber: 50, 54. **Barrel:** 22". **Weight:** 6 lbs., 7 oz. **Stock:** Black, Advantage Timber HD, Mossy Oak Break-Up camo. **Sights:** Fully adjustable Tru-Glo fiber optic. **Features:** Blued or stainless finish; patented double safety system; removable breech plug; Sure-Fire in-line percussion ignition system; can be converted to use 209 shotshell primers. Handles up to 150 grains of blackpowder. Introduced 2000. Made in U.S. by Knight Rifles.
Price: From $277.95
Price: Wolverine II stainless, from $341.95
Price: Wolverine II thumbhole, from $312.95
Price: Youth model value pack, blued, 50-cal. only $299.95

LONDON ARMORY 2-BAND 1858 ENFIELD
Caliber: .577" Minie, .575" round ball. **Barrel:** 33". **Weight:** 10 lbs. **Length:** 49" overall. **Stock:** Walnut. **Sights:** Folding leaf rear adjustable for elevation. **Features:** Blued barrel, color case-hardened lock and hammer, polished brass buttplate, trigger guard, nosecap. From Navy Arms, Euroarms of America, Dixie Gun Works.
Price: . . . . $385.00 to $531.00

LONDON ARMORY 1861 ENFIELD MUSKETOON
Caliber: 58, Minie ball. **Barrel:** 24", round. **Weight:** 7 - 7-1/2 lbs. **Length:** 40-1/2" overall. **Stock:** Walnut, with sling swivels. **Sights:** Blade front, graduated military-leaf rear. **Features:** Brass trigger guard, nosecap, buttplate; blued barrel, bands, lockplate, swivels. Imported by Euroarms of America, Navy Arms.
Price: . . . . $300.00 to $427.00
Price: Kit . . . . $365.00 to $373.00

LONDON ARMORY 3-BAND 1853 ENFIELD
Caliber: 58 (.577" Minie, .575" round ball, .580" maxi ball). **Barrel:** 39". **Weight:** 9-1/2 lbs. **Length:** 54" overall. **Stock:** European walnut. **Sights:** Inverted "V" front, traditional Enfield folding ladder rear. **Features:** Recreation of the famed London Armory Company Pattern 1853 Enfield Musket. One-piece walnut stock, brass buttplate, trigger guard and nosecap. Lockplate marked "London Armoury Co." and with a British crown. Blued Baddeley barrel bands. From Dixie Gun Works, Euroarms of America, Navy Arms.
Price: About . . . . $350.00 to $495.00
Price: Assembled kit (Dixie, Euroarms of America) . . $425.00 to $431.00

LYMAN COUGAR IN-LINE RIFLE
Caliber: 50 or 54. **Barrel:** 22"; 1:24" twist. **Weight:** NA. **Length:** NA. **Stock:** Smooth walnut; swivel studs. **Sights:** Bead on ramp front, folding adjustable rear. Drilled and tapped for Lyman 57WTR receiver sight and Weaver scope bases. **Features:** Blued barrel and receiver. Has bolt safety notch and trigger safety. Rubber recoil pad. Delrin ramrod. Introduced 1996. From Lyman.
Price: $249.95
Price: Stainless steel $299.95

LYMAN TRADE RIFLE
Caliber: 50, 54. **Barrel:** 28" octagon;1:48" twist. **Weight:** 8-3/4 lbs. **Length:** 45" overall. **Stock:** European walnut. **Sights:** Blade front, open rear adjustable for windage or optional fixed sights. **Features:** Fast twist rifling for conical bullets. Polished brass furniture with blue steel parts, stainless steel nipple. Hook breech, single trigger, coil spring percussion lock. Steel barrel rib and ramrod ferrules. Introduced 1980. From Lyman.
Price: Percussion $299.95
Price: Flintlock $324.95

BLACKPOWDER MUSKETS & RIFLES

Lyman Deerstalker

Lyman Great Plains

Markesbery Black Bear

Markesbery KM Colorado

LYMAN DEERSTALKER RIFLE
Caliber: 50, 54. **Barrel:** 24", octagonal; 1:48" rifling. **Weight:** 7-1/2 lbs. **Stock:** Walnut with black rubber buttpad. **Sights:** Lyman #37MA beaded front, fully adjustable fold-down Lyman #16A rear. **Features:** Stock has less drop for quick sighting. All metal parts are blackened, with color case-hardened lock; single trigger. Comes with sling and swivels. Available in flint or percussion. Introduced 1990. From Lyman.
Price: 50- or 54-cal., percussion............................ $304.95
Price: 50- or 54-cal., flintlock............................... $334.95
Price: 50- or 54-cal., percussion, left-hand................. $319.95
Price: 50-cal., flintlock, left-hand.......................... $349.95
Price: Stainless steel.. $384.95

LYMAN GREAT PLAINS RIFLE
Caliber: 50- or 54-cal. **Barrel:** 32"; 1:60" twist. **Weight:** 9 lbs. **Stock:** Walnut. **Sights:** Steel blade front, buckhorn rear adjustable for windage and elevation and fixed notch primitive sight included. **Features:** Blued steel furniture. Stainless steel nipple. Coil spring lock, Hawken-style trigger guard and double-set triggers. Round thimbles recessed and sweated into rib. Steel wedge plates and toe plate. Introduced 1979. From Lyman.
Price: Percussion... $434.95
Price: Flintlock... $459.95
Price: Percussion kit... $349.95
Price: Flintlock kit... $374.95
Price: Left-hand percussion................................. $444.95
Price: Left-hand flintlock.................................... $469.95

Lyman Great Plains Hunter Rifle
Similar to the Great Plains model except has 1:32" twist shallow-groove barrel and comes drilled and tapped for the Lyman 57GPR peep sight.
Price:.. $434.95 to $459.95

MARKESBERY KM BLACK BEAR M/L RIFLE
Caliber: 36, 45, 50, 54. **Barrel:** 24"; 1:26" twist. **Weight:** 6-1/2 lbs. **Length:** 38-1/2" overall. **Stock:** Two-piece American hardwood, walnut, black laminate, green laminate, black composition, X-Tra or Mossy Oak Break-Up camouflage. **Sights:** Bead front, open fully adjustable rear. **Features:** Interchangeable barrels; exposed hammer; Outer-Line Magnum ignition system uses small rifle primer or standard No. 11 cap and nipple. Blue, black matte, or stainless. Made in U.S. by Markesbery Muzzle Loaders.
Price: American hardwood walnut, blue finish................. $536.63
Price: American hardwood walnut, stainless.................. $553.09
Price: Black laminate, blue finish............................ $539.67
Price: Camouflage stock, blue finish......................... $556.46
Price: Black composite, blue finish.......................... $532.65

MARKESBERY KM COLORADO ROCKY MOUNTAIN M/L RIFLE
Caliber: 36, 45, 50, 54. **Barrel:** 24"; 1:26" twist. **Weight:** 6-1/2 lbs. **Length:** 38-1/2" overall. **Stock:** American hardwood walnut, green or black laminate. **Sights:** Firesight bead on ramp front, fully adjustable open rear. **Features:** Replicates Reed/Watson rifle of 1851. Straight grip stock with or without two barrel bands, rubber recoil pad, large-spur hammer. Made in U.S. by Markesbery Muzzle Loaders, Inc.
Price: American hardwood walnut, blue finish................. $545.92
Price: Black or green laminate, blue finish................... $548.30
Price: American hardwood walnut, stainless.................. $563.17
Price: Black or green laminate, stainless..................... $566.34

BLACKPOWDER MUSKETS & RIFLES

Markesbery KM Grizzly Bear

Markesbery KM Brown Bear

Mississippi 1841

Navy Arms 1763

Markesbery KM Brown Bear M/L Rifle
Similar to the KM Black Bear except has one-piece thumbhole stock with Monte Carlo comb. Stock available in Crotch Walnut composite, green or black laminate, black composite or X-Tra or Mossy Oak Break-Up camouflage. Contact maker for complete price listing. Made in U.S. by Markesbery Muzzle Loaders, Inc.
- **Price:** Black composite, blue finish $658.83
- **Price:** Crotch Walnut composite, stainless $676.11
- **Price:** Green laminate, stainless $680.07

Markesbery KM Grizzly Bear M/L Rifle
Similar to the KM Black Bear except has thumbhole buttstock with Monte Carlo comb. Stock available in Crotch Walnut composite, green or black laminate, black composite or X-Tra or Mossy Oak Break-Up camouflage. Contact maker for complete price listing. Made in U.S. by Markesbery Muzzle Loaders, Inc.
- **Price:** Black composite, blue finish $642.96
- **Price:** Crotch Walnut composite, stainless $660.98
- **Price:** Camouflage composite, blue finish $666.67

Markesbery KM Polar Bear M/L Rifle
Similar to the KM Black Bear except has one-piece stock with Monte Carlo comb. Stock available in American Hardwood walnut, green or black laminate, black composite, or X-Tra or Mossy Oak Break-Up camouflage. Has interchangeable barrel system, Outer-Line ignition system, cross-bolt double safety. Available in 36, 45, 50, 54 caliber. Contact maker for full price listing. Made in U.S. by Markesbery Muzzle Loaders, Inc.
- **Price:** American Hardwood walnut, blue finish $539.01
- **Price:** Black composite, blue finish $536.63
- **Price:** Black laminate, blue finish $541.17
- **Price:** Camouflage, stainless $573.94

MDM BUCKWACKA IN-LINE RIFLES
Caliber: 45, 50. **Barrel:** 23", 25". **Weight:** 7 to 7-3/4 lbs. **Length:** N/A. **Stock:** Black, walnut, laminated and camouflage finishes. **Sights:** Williams Fire Sight blade front, Williams fully adjustable rear with ghost-ring peep aperture. **Features:** Break-open action; Incinerating Ignition System incorporates 209 shotshell primer directly into breech plug; 50-caliber models handle up to 150 grains of Pyrodex; synthetic ramrod; transfer bar safety; stainless or blued finish. Made in U.S. by Millennium Designed Muzzleloaders Ltd.
- **Price:** 50 cal., blued finish $309.95
- **Price:** 50 cal., stainless $339.95
- **Price:** Camouflage stock . . . . $359.95 to $389.95

MDM M2K In-Line Rifle
Similar to Buckwacka except has adjustable trigger and double-safety mechanism designed to prevent misfires. Made in U.S. by Millennium Designed Muzzleloaders Ltd.
- **Price:** . . . . $529.00 to $549.00

Mississippi 1841 Percussion Rifle
Similar to Zouave rifle but patterned after U.S. Model 1841. Imported by Dixie Gun Works, Euroarms of America, Navy Arms.
- **Price:** About . . . . $430.00 to $500.00

NAVY ARMS 1763 CHARLEVILLE
Caliber: 69. **Barrel:** 44-5/8". **Weight:** 8 lbs., 12 oz. **Length:** 59-3/8" overall. **Stock:** Walnut. **Sights:** Brass blade front. **Features:** Replica of the French musket used by American troops during the Revolution. Imported by Navy Arms.
- **Price:** $1,020.00

BLACKPOWDER MUSKETS & RIFLES

Navy Arms 1859 Sharps

Navy Arms Berdan

Navy Arms Whitworth

Navy Arms Smith Carbine

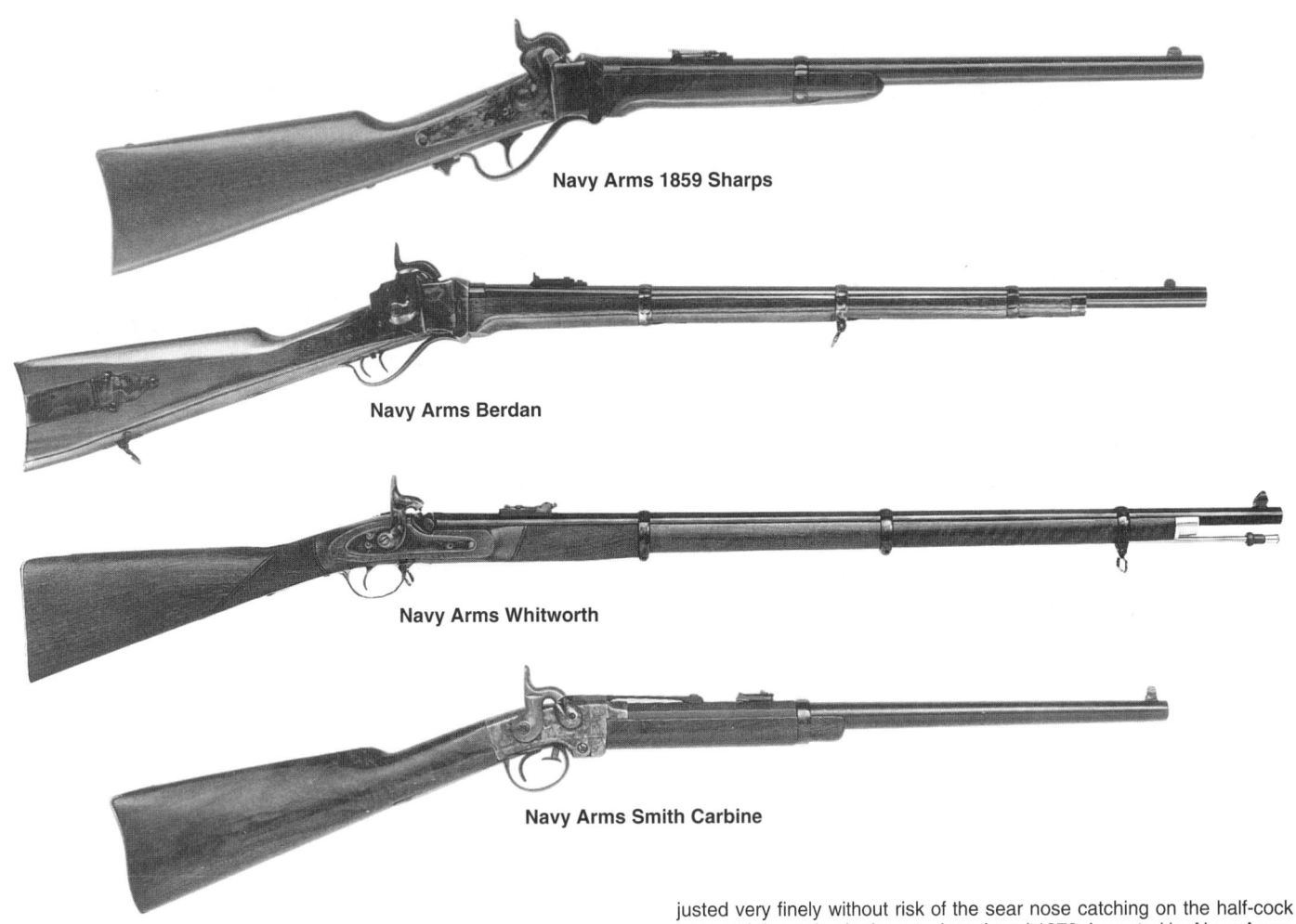

NAVY ARMS PARKER-HALE VOLUNTEER RIFLE

Caliber: .451. **Barrel:** 32". **Weight:** 9-1/2 lbs. **Length:** 49" overall. **Stock:** Walnut, checkered wrist and forend. **Sights:** Globe front, adjustable ladder-type rear. **Features:** Recreation of the type of gun issued to volunteer regiments during the 1860s. Rigby-pattern rifling, patent breech, detented lock. Stock is glass bedded for accuracy. Imported by Navy Arms.
Price: $905.00

NAVY ARMS 1859 SHARPS CAVALRY CARBINE

Caliber: 54. **Barrel:** 22". **Weight:** 7-3/4 lbs. **Length:** 39" overall. **Stock:** Walnut. **Sights:** Blade front, military ladder-type rear. **Features:** Color case-hardened action, blued barrel. Has saddle ring. Introduced 1991. Imported from Navy Arms.
Price: $1,000.00

NAVY ARMS BERDAN 1859 SHARPS RIFLE

Caliber: 54. **Barrel:** 30". **Weight:** 8 lbs., 8 oz. **Length:** 46-3/4" overall. **Stock:** Walnut. **Sights:** Blade front, folding military ladder-type rear. **Features:** Replica of the Union sniper rifle used by Berdan's 1st and 2nd Sharpshooter regiments. Color case-hardened receiver, patchbox, furniture. Double-set triggers. Imported by Navy Arms.
Price: $1,165.00
Price: 1859 Sharps Infantry Rifle (three-band) $1,100.00

NAVY ARMS PARKER-HALE WHITWORTH MILITARY TARGET RIFLE

Caliber: 45. **Barrel:** 36". **Weight:** 9-1/4 lbs. **Length:** 52-1/2" overall. **Stock:** Walnut. Checkered at wrist and forend. **Sights:** Hooded post front, open step-adjustable rear. **Features:** Faithful reproduction of the Whitworth rifle, only bored for 45-cal. Trigger has a detented lock, capable of being ad-

justed very finely without risk of the sear nose catching on the half-cock bent and damaging both parts. Introduced 1978. Imported by Navy Arms.
Price: $930.00

NAVY ARMS SMITH CARBINE

Caliber: 50. **Barrel:** 21-1/2". **Weight:** 7-3/4 lbs. **Length:** 39" overall. **Stock:** American walnut. **Sights:** Brass blade front, folding ladder-type rear. **Features:** Replica of the breech-loading Civil War carbine. Color case-hardened receiver, rest blued. Cavalry model has saddle ring and bar, Artillery model has sling swivels. Imported by Navy Arms.
Price: Cavalry model $635.00
Price: Artillery model $635.00

NAVY ARMS 1863 C.S. RICHMOND RIFLE

Caliber: 58. **Barrel:** 40". **Weight:** 10 lbs. **Length:** NA. **Stocks:** Walnut. **Sights:** Blade front, adjustable rear. **Features:** Copy of the three-band rifle musket made at Richmond Armory for the Confederacy. All steel polished bright. Imported by Navy Arms.
Price: $590.00

NAVY ARMS 1861 SPRINGFIELD RIFLE

Caliber: 58. **Barrel:** 40" **Weight:** 10 lbs., 4 oz. **Length:** 56" overall. **Stock:** Walnut. **Sights:** Blade front, military leaf rear. **Features:** Steel barrel, lock and all furniture have polished bright finish. Has 1855-style hammer. Imported by Navy Arms.
Price: $590.00

NAVY ARMS 1863 SPRINGFIELD

Caliber: 58, uses .575 Minie. **Barrel:** 40", rifled. **Weight:** 9-1/2 lbs. **Length:** 56" overall. **Stock:** Walnut. **Sights:** Open rear adjustable for elevation. **Features:** Full-size, three-band musket. Polished bright metal, including lock. From Navy Arms.
Price: Finished rifle $590.00

BLACKPOWDER MUSKETS & RIFLES

Navy Arms 1863

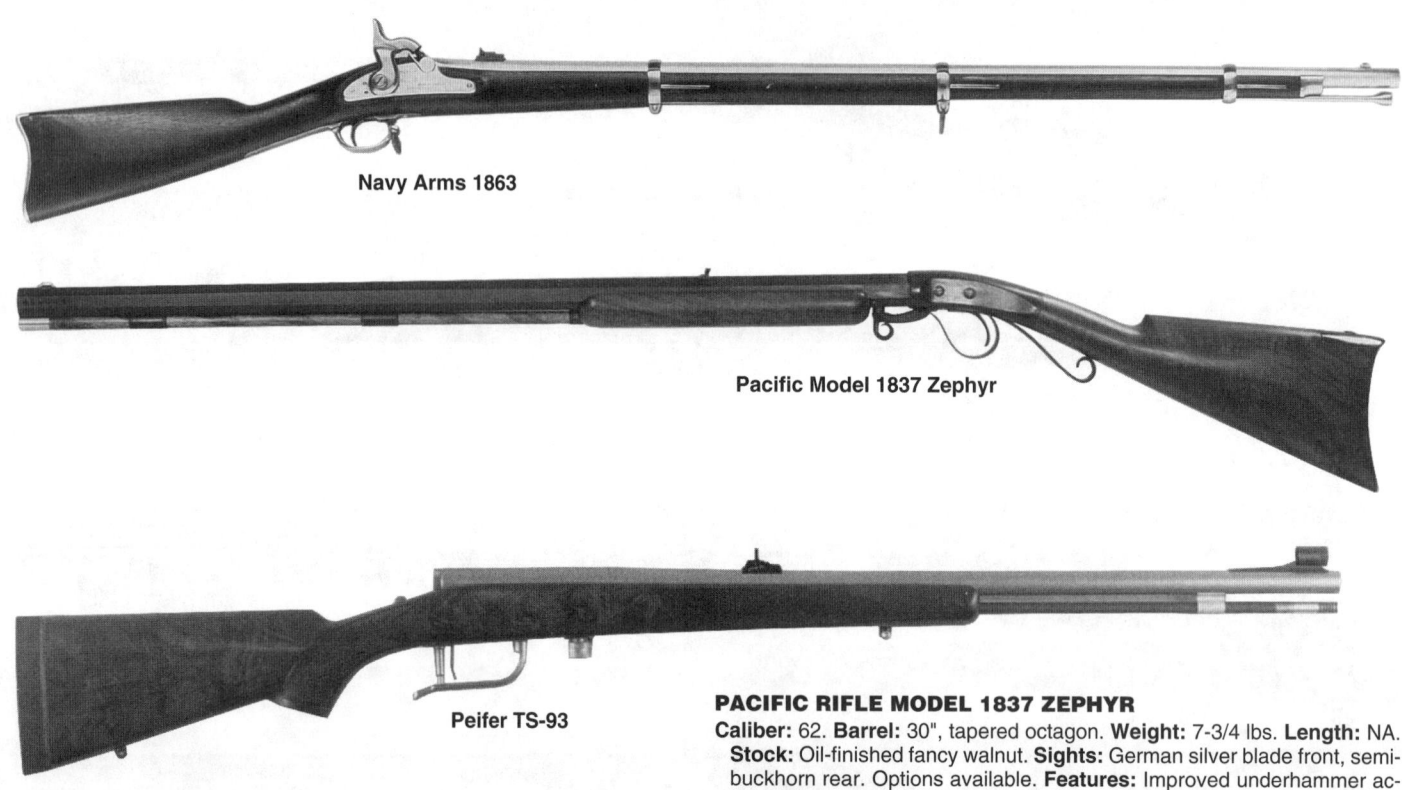

Pacific Model 1837 Zephyr

Peifer TS-93

OCTOBER COUNTRY GREAT AMERICAN SPORTING RIFLE
Caliber: 62, 66, 69, 72. **Barrel:** 28" or 36"; tapered octagon 1-1/4" to 1"; 1:104" twist. **Weight:** 9 lbs. (28" bbl.) **Length:** 48" overall. **Stock:** Walnut (optional maple with ebony nosecap). **Sights:** Silver blade front, adjustable shallow "V" rear (optional three-blade express or A.O. ghost ring). **Features:** Hooked, patent Manton-style breech plug; iron furniture; bedded barrel; blue finish. Made in U.S. by October Country Muzzleloading Inc.
Price: $1,695.00

OCTOBER COUNTRY LIGHT AMERICAN SPORTING RIFLE
Caliber: 62. **Barrel:** 28" or 36"; tapered octagon 1-1/8" to 1"; 1:104" twist. **Weight:** 8 lbs. **Length:** 48" overall. **Stock:** Walnut (optional maple with ebony nosecap). **Sights:** Blade front, adjustable shallow "V" rear (optional three-blade express or A.O. ghost ring). **Features:** English-style hooked breach with side bar; L&R lock; iron furniture; bedded barrel; hot blue finish. Made in U.S. by October Country Muzzleloading Inc.
Price: $1,595.00

OCTOBER COUNTRY HEAVY RIFLE
Caliber: 8 bore or 4 bore. **Barrel:** 30"; tapered octagon 1-1/2" to 1-1/4" (8 bore) or 1-3/4" to 1-1/2" (4 bore); 1:144" twist. **Weight:** 14 lbs. (8 bore) or 18 lbs. (4 bore). **Length:** 50" overall. **Stock:** Checkered English walnut. **Sights:** Blade front, three-blade express rear. **Features:** English-style hooked breech; L&R lock; iron furniture; bedded barrel; hot blue finish. Made in U.S. by October Country Muzzleloading Inc.
Price: $2,995.00

OCTOBER COUNTRY DOUBLE RIFLE
Caliber: 8 bore. **Barrel:** 30" round; 1:144" twist. **Weight:** 14 lbs. **Length:** 50". **Stock:** Checkered English walnut. **Sights:** Blade front, three-blade express rear. **Features:** English-style hooked breech; L & R lock; iron furniture; bedded barrel; hot blue finish. Made in U.S. by October Country Muzzleloaders Inc.
Price: $4,995.00

PACIFIC RIFLE MODEL 1837 ZEPHYR
Caliber: 62. **Barrel:** 30", tapered octagon. **Weight:** 7-3/4 lbs. **Length:** NA. **Stock:** Oil-finished fancy walnut. **Sights:** German silver blade front, semi-buckhorn rear. Options available. **Features:** Improved underhammer action. First production rifle to offer Forsyth rifle, with narrow lands and shallow rifling with 1:144" pitch for high-velocity round balls. Metal finish is slow rust brown with nitre blue accents. Optional sights, finishes and integral muzzle brake available. Introduced 1995. Made in U.S. by Pacific Rifle Co.
Price: From $995.00

Pacific Rifle Big Bore, African Rifles
Similar to the 1837 Zephyr except in 72-caliber and 8-bore. The 72-caliber is available in standard form with 28" barrel, or as the African with flat buttplate, checkered upgraded wood; weight is 9 lbs. The 8-bore African has dual-cap ignition, 24" barrel, weighs 12 lbs., checkered English walnut, engraving, gold inlays. Introduced 1998. Made in U.S. by Pacific Rifle Co.
Price: 72-caliber, from $1,150.00
Price: 8-bore from $2,500.00

PEIFER MODEL TS-93 RIFLE
Caliber: 45, 50. **Barrel:** 24" Douglas premium; 1:20" twist in 45; 1:28" in 50. **Weight:** 7 lbs. **Length:** 43-1/4" overall. **Stock:** Bell & Carlson solid composite, with recoil pad, swivel studs. **Sights:** Williams bead front on ramp, fully adjustable open rear. Drilled and tapped for Weaver scope mounts with dovetail for rear peep. **Features:** In-line ignition uses #209 shotshell primer; extremely fast lock time; fully enclosed breech; adjustable trigger; automatic safety; removable primer holder. Blue or stainless. Made in U.S. by Peifer Rifle Co. Introduced 1996.
Price: Blue, black stock $730.00
Price: Blue, wood or camouflage composite stock, or stainless with black composite stock $803.00
Price: Stainless, wood or camouflage composite stock $876.00

PRAIRIE RIVER ARMS PRA CLASSIC RIFLE
Caliber: 50, 54. **Barrel:** 26"; 1:28" twist. **Weight:** 7-1/2 lbs. **Length:** 40-1/2" overall. **Stock:** Hardwood or black all-weather. **Sights:** Blade front, open adjustable rear. **Features:** Patented internal percussion ignition system. Drilled and tapped for scope mount. Introduced 1995. Made in U.S. by Prairie River Arms, Ltd.
Price: 4140 alloy barrel, hardwood stock $375.00
Price: As above, stainless barrel $425.00
Price: 4140 alloy barrel, black all-weather stock $390.00
Price: As above, stainless barrel $440.00

308 • GUNS ILLUSTRATED

BLACKPOWDER MUSKETS & RIFLES

Remington Model 700 ML

C.S. Richmond 1863

Ruger K77/50RSBBZ

Second Model Brown Bess

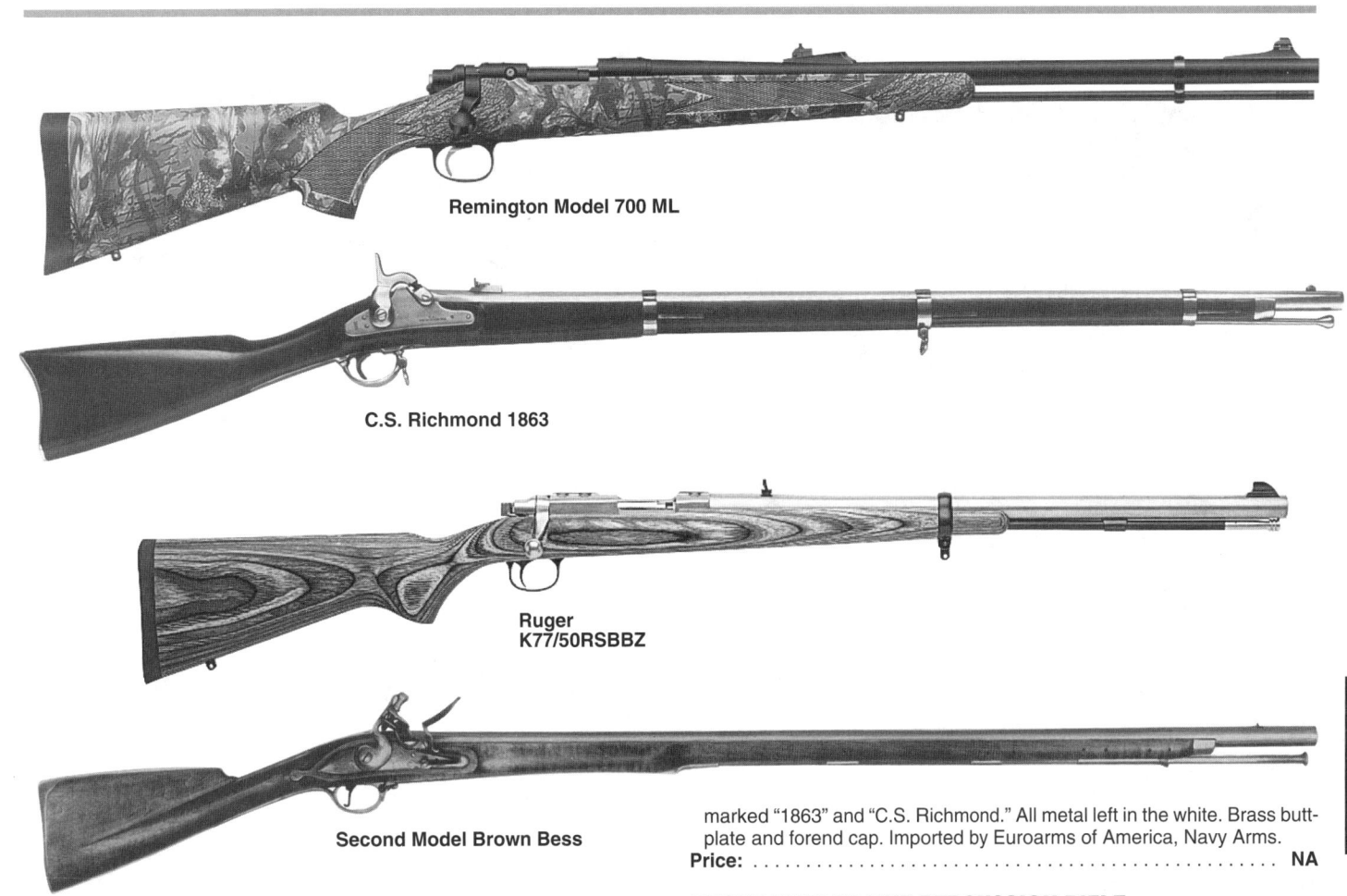

PRAIRIE RIVER ARMS PRA BULLPUP RIFLE
Caliber: 50, 54. **Barrel:** 28"; 1:28" twist. **Weight:** 7-1/2 lbs. **Length:** 31-1/2" overall. **Stock:** Hardwood or black all-weather. **Sights:** Blade front, open adjustable rear. **Features:** Bullpup design thumbhole stock. Patented internal percussion ignition system. Left-hand model available. Dovetailed for scope mount. Introduced 1995. Made in U.S. by Prairie River Arms, Ltd.
Price: 4140 alloy barrel, hardwood stock $375.00
Price: As above, black stock. $390.00
Price: Stainless barrel, hardwood stock $425.00
Price: As above, black stock. $440.00

REMINGTON MODEL 700 ML, MLS RIFLES
Caliber: 50, 54. **Barrel:** 24"; 1:28" twist. **Weight:** 7-3/4 lbs. **Length:** 44-1/2" overall. **Stock:** Black fiberglass-reinforced synthetic with checkered grip and forend; magnum-style buttpad. **Sights:** Ramped bead front, open fully adjustable rear. Drilled and tapped for scope mounts. **Features:** Uses the Remington 700 bolt action, stock design, safety and trigger mechanisms; removable stainelss steel breech plug, No. 11 nipple; solid aluminum ramrod. Comes with cleaning tools and accessories.
Price: ML, blued, 50-caliber only $396.00
Price: MLS, stainless, 50- or 54-caliber $496.00
Price: ML, blued, Mossy Oak Break-Up camo stock $439.00
Price: MLS, stainless, Mossy Oak Break-Up camo stock. $532.00
Price: ML Youth (12-3/8" length of pull, 21" barrel) $396.00

C.S. RICHMOND 1863 MUSKET
Caliber: 58. **Barrel:** 40". **Weight:** 11 lbs. **Length:** 56-1/4" overall. **Stock:** European walnut with oil finish. **Sights:** Blade front, adjustable folding leaf rear. **Features:** Reproduction of the three-band Civil War musket. Sling swivels attached to trigger guard and middle barrel band. Lockplate marked "1863" and "C.S. Richmond." All metal left in the white. Brass buttplate and forend cap. Imported by Euroarms of America, Navy Arms.
Price: . . . . NA

RUGER 77/50 IN-LINE PERCUSSION RIFLE
Caliber: 50. **Barrel:** 22"; 1:28" twist. **Weight:** 6-1/2 lbs. **Length:** 41-1/2" overall. **Stock:** Birch with rubber buttpad and swivel studs. **Sights:** Gold bead front, folding leaf rear. Comes with Ruger scope mounts. **Features:** Shares design features with the Ruger 77/22 rifle. Stainless steel bolt and nipple/breech plug; uses #11 caps; three-position safety; blued steel ramrod. Introduced 1997. Made in U.S. by Sturm, Ruger & Co.
Price: 77/50RS $434.00
Price: 77/50RSO Officer's (straight-grip checkered walnut stock, blued) $555.00
Price: K77/50RSBBZ (stainless steel, black laminated stock) . . . $601.00
Price: K77/50RSP All-Weather (stainless steel, synthetic stock). . $580.00

SECOND MODEL BROWN BESS MUSKET
Caliber: 75, uses .735" round ball. **Barrel:** 42", smoothbore. **Weight:** 9-1/2 lbs. **Length:** 59" overall. **Stock:** Walnut (Navy); walnut-stained hardwood (Dixie). **Sights:** Fixed. **Features:** Polished barrel and lock with brass trigger guard and buttplate. Bayonet and scabbard available. From Navy Arms, Dixie Gun Works, Cabela's.
Price: Finished . . . . $475.00 to $850.00
Price: Kit (Dixie Gun Works, Navy Arms) . . . . $575.00 to $625.00
Price: Carbine (Navy Arms) $835.00

THOMPSON/CENTER BLACK MOUNTAIN MAGNUM RIFLE
Caliber: 50, 54. **Barrel:** 26"; 1:28" twist. **Weight:** 7 lbs. **Length:** 4-3/4" overall. **Stock:** American Walnut or black composite. **Sights:** Ramp front with Tru-Glo fiber optic inseat, click adjustable open rear with Tru-Glo fiber optic inserts. **Features:** Side lock percussion with breeech designed for Pyrodex Pellets, loose blackpowder and Pyrodex. blued steel. Uses QLA muzzle system. Introduced 1999. Made in U.S. by Thompson/Center Arms.
Price: Blue, composite stock, 50-cal. $353.52
Price: Blue, walnut stock, 50- or 54-cal. (westraner) $387.16

BLACKPOWDER MUSKETS & RIFLES

T/C System 1

T/C Encore

T/C Thunderhawk Shadow

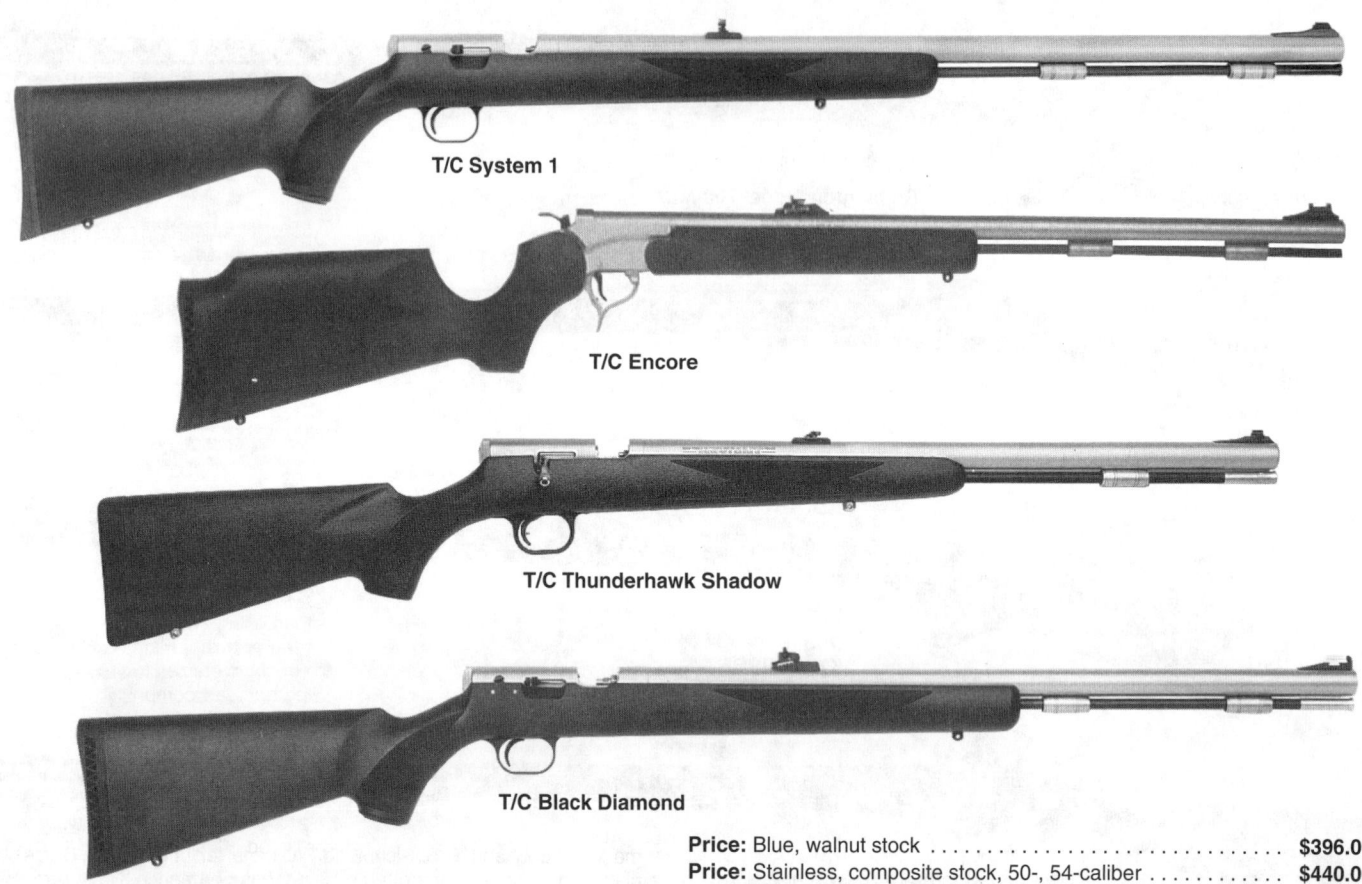

T/C Black Diamond

THOMPSON/CENTER FIRE STORM RIFLE
Caliber: 50. **Barrel:** 26"; 1:28" twist. **Weight:** 7 lbs. **Length:** 41-3/4" overall. **Stock:** Black synthetic with rubber recoil pad, swivel studs. **Sights:** Click-adjustable steel rear and ramp-style front, both with fiber optic inserts. **Features:** Side hammer lock is the first designed for up to three 50-grain Pyrodex pellets; patented Pyrodex Pyramid breech directs ignition fire 360 degrees around base of pellet; uses 209 shotgun primers; Quick Load Accurizor Muzzle System; aluminum ramrod. Introduced 2000. Made in U.S. by Thomson/Center Arms.
Price: Blue finish, percussion model. $391.00
Price: Blue finish, flintlock model with 1:48" twist for round balls, conicals. $391.00

THOMPSON/CENTER PENNSYLVANIA HUNTER RIFLE
Caliber: 50. **Barrel:** 28", octagonal. **Weight:** About 7-1/2 lbs. **Length:** 48" overall. **Stock:** Black walnut. **Sights:** Open, adjustable. **Features:** Rifled 1:66" for round-ball shooting. Available in flintlock only. From Thompson/Center.
Price: $417.00

Thompson/Center Pennsylvania Hunter Carbine
Similar to the Pennsylvania Hunter except has 21" barrel, weighs 6.5 lbs., and has an overall length of 38". Designed for shooting patched round balls. Available in flintlock only. Introduced 1992. From Thompson/Center.
Price: $438.00

THOMPSON/CENTER SYSTEM 1 IN-LINE RIFLE
Caliber: 32, 50, 54, 58; 12-gauge. **Barrel:** 26" round; 1:38" twist. **Weight:** About 7-1/2lbs. **Length:** 44" overall. **Stock:** American black walnut or composite. **Sights:** Ramp front with white bead, adjustable leaf rear. **Features:** In-line ignition. Interchangeable barrels; removable breech plug allows cleaning from the breech; fully adjustable trigger; sliding thumb safety; QLA muzzle system; rubber recoil pad; sling swivel studs. Introduced 1997. Made in U.S. by Thompson/Center Arms.
Price: Blue, walnut stock $396.00
Price: Stainless, composite stock, 50-, 54-caliber $440.00
Price: Stainless, camo composite stock, 50-caliber $479.00
Price: Extra barrels, blue $176.00
Price: Extra barrels, stainless, 50-, 54-caliber $220.00

THOMPSON/CENTER ENCORE 209x50 MAGNUM
Caliber: 50. **Barrel:** 26"; interchangeable with centerfire calibers. **Weight:** 7 lbs. **Length:** 40-1/2" overall. **Stock:** American walnut butt and forend, or black composite. **Sights:** Tru-Glo Fiber Optic front, Tru-Glo Fiber Optic rear. **Features:** Blue or stainless steel. Uses the stock, frame and forend of the Encore centerfire pistol; break-open design using trigger guard spur; stainless steel universal breech plug; uses #209 shotshell primers. Introduced 1998. Made in U.S. by Thompson/Center Arms.
Price: $590.03
Price: Blue, walnut stock and forend $590.03
Price: Blue, composite stock and forend $590.03
Price: Stainless, composite stock and forend. $665.91

THOMPSON/CENTER THUNDERHAWK SHADOW
Caliber: 50, 54. **Barrel:** 24"; 1:38" twist. **Weight:** 7 lbs. **Length:** 41-3/4" overall. **Stock:** American walnut or black composite with rubber recoil pad. **Sights:** Bead on ramp front, adjustable leaf rear. **Features:** Uses modern in-line ignition system, adjustable trigger. Knurled striker handle indicators for Safe and Fire. Black wood ramrod, Drilled and tapped for T/C scope mounts. Introduced 1996. From Thompson/Center Arms.
Price: Blued $294.00

THOMPSON/CENTER BLACK DIAMOND RIFLE
Caliber: 50. **Barrel:** 22-1/2" with QLA; 1:28" twist. **Weight:** 6 lbs., 9 oz. **Length:** 41-1/2" overall. **Stock:** Black Rynite with moulded-in checkering and grip cap, or walnut. **Sights:** Tru-Glo Fiber Optic ramp-style front, Tru-Glo Fiber Optic open rear. **Features:** In-line ignition system for musket cap, No. 11 cap, or 209 shotshell primer; removable universal breech plug; stainless steel construction. Introduced 1998. Made in U.S. by Thompson/Center Arms.
Price: $312.87
Price: With walnut stock $353.32

BLACKPOWDER MUSKETS & RIFLES

T/C Hawken

Traditions Buckhunter Pro In-Line

Traditions Buckhunter

THOMPSON/CENTER HAWKEN RIFLE
Caliber: 45, 50 or 54. **Barrel:** 28" octagon, hooked breech. **Stock:** American walnut. **Sights:** Blade front, rear adjustable for windage and elevation. **Features:** Solid brass furniture, double-set triggers, button rifled barrel, coil-type mainspring. From Thompson/Center Arms.
Price: Percussion model (45-, 50- or 54-cal.) $489.35
Price: Flintlock model (50-cal.) $501.14

TRADITIONS BUCKHUNTER IN-LINE RIFLES
Caliber: 50, 54. **Barrel:** 24", round; 1:32" (50); 1:48" (54) twist. **Weight:** About 7 lbs. **Length:** 41" overall. **Stock:** All-Weather black composite. **Sights:** blade front, click adjustable rear. Drilled and tapped for scope mounting. **Features:** Removable breech plug; PVC ramrod; sling swivels. Introduced 1995. From Traditions.
Price: (blued barrel) $149.00
Price: (C-Nickel barrel, 50 caliber only) $159.00
Price: With RS Redi-Pak (powder measure, powder flask, two fast loaders, 5-in-1 loader, capper, ball starter, ball puller, cleaning jag, nipple wrench, bullets); 50 caliber only. $199.00

TRADITIONS BUCKHUNTER PRO MAGNUM IN-LINE RIFLES
Caliber: 50 (1:32" twist); 54 (1:48" twist). **Barrel:** 24" tapered round. **Weight:** 7 lbs., 4 oz. **Length:** 43" overall. **Stock:** Composite in black or Mossy Oak Break-Up™ camouflage. **Sights:** Fiber-optic ramp front, fully adjustable rear. Drilled and tapped for scope mounting. **Features:** In-line percussion ignition system that allows use of 209 shotgun primers, musket caps or No. 11 percussion caps; adjustable trigger; manual thumb safety; removable stainless steel breech plug. From Traditions.
Price: (24" blued barrel) $169.00
Price (24" C-Nickel barrel). $189.00
Price (24" C-Nickel barrel, Mossy Oak Break-Up™ stock) $219.00

TRADITIONS BUCKSKINNER CARBINE
Caliber: 50. **Barrel:** 21"; 15/16" flats, half octagon, half round; 1:20" or 1:66" twist. **Weight:** 6 lbs. **Length:** 37" overall. **Stock:** Beech or black laminated. **Sights:** Beaded blade front, fiber optic open rear click adjustable for windage and elevation or fiber optics. **Features:** Uses V-type mainspring, single trigger. Non-glare hardware; sling swivels. From Traditions.
Price: Flintlock $219.00
Price: Flintlock, laminated stock $299.00

TRADITIONS DEERHUNTER RIFLE SERIES
Caliber: 32, 50 or 54. **Barrel:** 24", octagonal; 15/16" flats; 1:48" or 1:66" twist. **Weight:** 6 lbs. **Length:** 40" overall. **Stock:** Stained hardwood or All-Weather composite with rubber buttpad, sling swivels. **Sights:** Lite Optic blade front, adjustable rear fiber optics. **Features:** Flint or percussion with color case-hardened lock. Hooked breech, oversized trigger guard, blackened furniture, PVC ramrod. All-Weather has composite stock and C-Nickel barrel. Drilled and tapped for scope mounting. Imported by Traditions, Inc.
Price: Percussion, 50; blued barrel; 1:48" twist $159.00
Price: Flintlock, 50-caliber only; 1:66" twist $189.00
Price: Flintlock, All-Weather, 50-cal. $179.00
New! **Price:** Flintlock, left-handed hardwood, 50-cal. $189.00
Price: Percussion, All-Weather, 50 or 54 cal. $159.00
Price: Percussion; 32 cal. $169.00

TRADITIONS E-BOLT 209 BOLT-ACTION RIFLES
Caliber: 50. **Barrel:** 22" blued or C-Nickel finish; 1:28" twist. **Weight:** 6 lbs., 7 oz. **Length:** 41" overall. **Stock:** Black or Advantage Timber® composite. **Sights:** Lite Optic blade front, adjustable rear. **Features:** Thumb safety; quick-release bolt; covered breech; one-piece breech plug takes 209 shotshell primers; accepts 150 grains of Pyrodex pellets; receiver drilled and tapped for scope; sling swivel studs and rubber butt pad. Introduced 2001. From Traditions.
Price: (Black composite stock with 22" blued barrel) $169.00
Price: (Black composite stock with 22" C-Nickel barrel) $179.00
Price: (Advantage Timber® stock with 22"C-Nickel barrel) $229.00
Price: (Redi-Pak with black stock/blued barrel and powder flask, capper, ball starter, other supplies) $219.00
Price: (Redi-Pak with Advantage Timber® stock/C-Nickel barrel and powder flask, capper, ball starter, other supplies) $279.00

TRADITIONS HAWKEN WOODSMAN RIFLE
Caliber: 50 and 54. **Barrel:** 28"; 15/16" flats. **Weight:** 7 lbs., 11 oz. **Length:** 44-1/2" overall. **Stock:** Walnut-stained hardwood. **Sights:** Beaded blade front, hunting-style open rear adjustable for windage and elevation. **Features:** Percussion only. Brass patchbox and furniture. Double triggers. From Traditions.
Price: 50 or 54 . . . . $249.00
Price: 50-cal., left-hand $239.00
Price: 50-caliber, flintlock $249.00

TRADITIONS KENTUCKY RIFLE
Caliber: 50. **Barrel:** 33-1/2"; 7/8" flats; 1:66" twist. **Weight:** 7 lbs. **Length:** 49" overall. **Stock:** Beech; inletted toe plate. **Sights:** Blade front, fixed rear. **Features:** Full-length, two-piece stock; brass furniture; color case-hardened lock. Introduced 1995. From Traditions.
Price: Finished $229.00
Price: Kit $179.00

34TH EDITION, 2002 • 311

BLACKPOWDER MUSKETS & RIFLES

Traditions Lightning

Traditions Panther

Traditions Pennsylvania

Traditions Shenandoah

TRADITIONS LIGHTNING MAG BOLT-ACTION MUZZLELOADER
Caliber: 50, 54. **Barrel:** 24" round; blued, stainless, C-Nickel or Ultra Coat. **Weight:** 6-1/2 to 7 lbs. 10 oz. **Length:** 43" overall. **Stock:** All-Weather composite, Advantage, or Break-Up camouflage. **Sights:** Fiber Optic blade front, fully adjustable open rear. **Features:** Field-removable stainless steel bolt; silent thumb safety; adjustable trigger; drilled and tapped for scope mounting. Lightning Fire Magnum System allows use of No. 11, musket caps or 209 shotgun primers. Introduced 1997. Imported by Traditions.
Price: All-Weather composite stock, blue finish $199.00
Price: All-Weather composite stock, blue finish, muzzle brake . . . $229.00
Price: All-Weather composite, stainless steel. $279.00
Price: Camouflage composite, stainless steel $309.00
Price: Camouflage composite $229.00
Price: Composite, with muzzle brake, stainless, fluted barrel $329.00

NEW! TRADITIONS LIGHTNING 45 LD BOLT-ACTION RIFLES
Similar to Lightning Mag, but chambered for 45 caliber with a 26" fluted blued or C-Nickel barrel; 1:20" twist. Black or Advantage Timber® stock; fiber optic blade front and adjustable rear sights. Accepts 150 grains of Pyrodex. Weighs 7 lbs., 2 oz. Overall length 45". Introduced 2001. From Traditions.
Price: (black stock with blued barrel) $229.00
Price: (black stock with C-Nickel barrel). $239.00
Price: (Advantage Timber® stock with C-Nickel barrel) $289.00

TRADITIONS LIGHTNING LIGHTWEIGHT MAGNUM BOLT-ACTION RIFLES
Similar to Lightning Mag except features 22" lightweight, fluted barrel and Spider Web-pattern black composite stock. Overall length 41", weighs 6 lb., 5 oz. Introduced 2000. From Traditions.
Price: Blued finish. $239.00
Price: C-Nickel finish. $249.00
Price: Stainless $279.00
Price: Stainless, camo stock $289.00

TRADITIONS MAGNUM PLAINS RIFLE
Similar to Thunder Magnum except has 28" blued, octagonal barrel, double-set triggers and adj. steel fiber optics sights.
Price: $359.00

TRADITIONS PANTHER SIDELOCK RIFLE
Similar to Deerhunter rifle, but has blade front and windage-adjustable-only rear sight, black composite stock.
Price: $119.00

TRADITIONS PENNSYLVANIA RIFLE
Caliber: 50. **Barrel:** 40-1/4"; 7/8" flats; 1:66" twist, octagon. **Weight:** 9 lbs. **Length:** 57-1/2" overall. **Stock:** Walnut. **Sights:** Blade front, adjustable rear. **Features:** Brass patchbox and ornamentation. Double-set triggers. From Traditions.
Price: Flintlock $479.00
Price: Percussion $469.00

TRADITIONS SHENANDOAH RIFLE
Caliber: 50. **Barrel:** 33-1/2" octagon; 1:66" twist. **Weight:** 7 lbs., 3 oz. **Length:** 49-1/2" overall. **Stock:** Walnut. **Sights:** Blade front, buckhorn rear. **Features:** V-type mainspring; double-set trigger; solid brass buttplate, patchbox, nosecap, thimbles, trigger guard. Introduced 1996. From Traditions.
Price: Flintlock $369.00
Price: Percussion $349.00

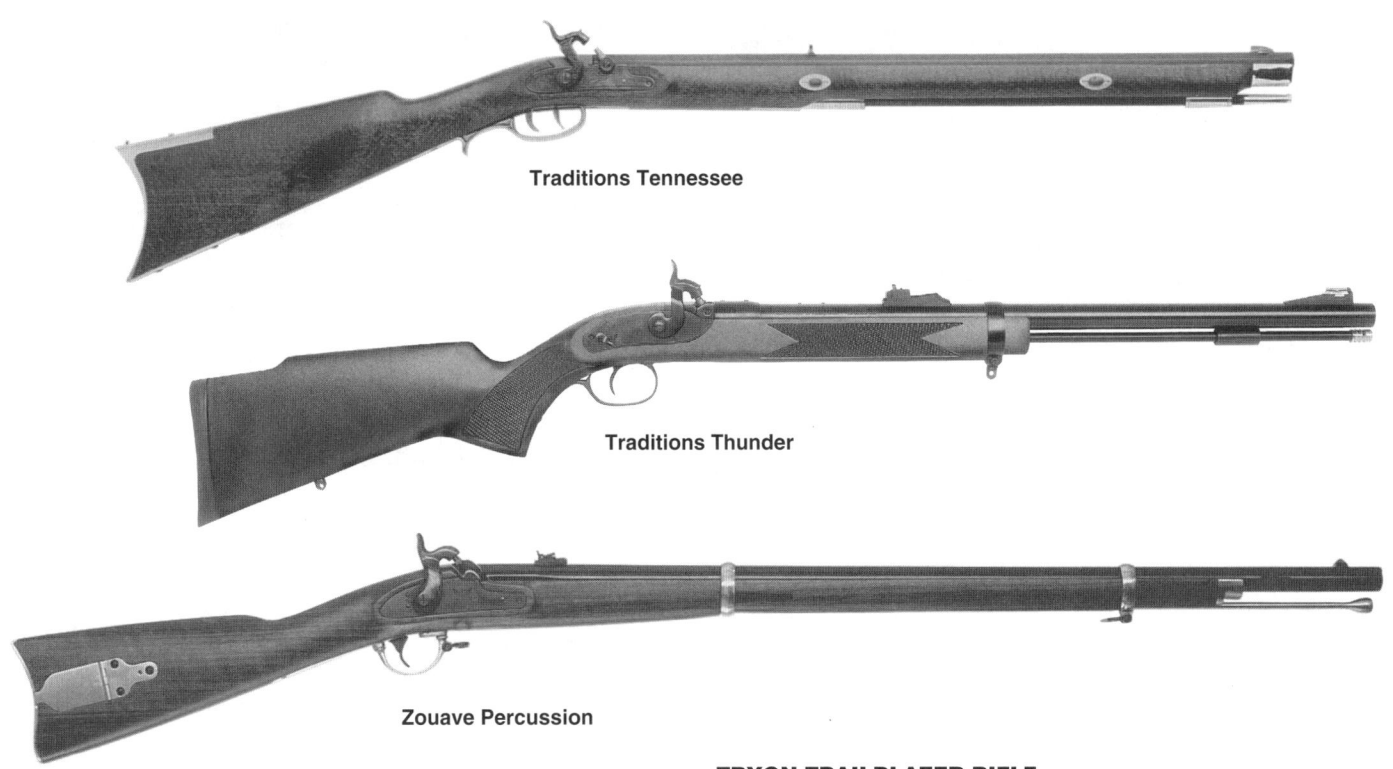

BLACKPOWDER MUSKETS & RIFLES

Traditions Tennessee

Traditions Thunder

Zouave Percussion

TRADITIONS TENNESSEE RIFLE
Caliber: 50. **Barrel:** 24", octagon; 15/16" flats; 1:66" twist. **Weight:** 6 lbs. **Length:** 40-1/2" overall. **Stock:** Stained beech. **Sights:** Blade front, fixed rear. **Features:** One-piece stock has inletted brass furniture, cheekpiece; double-set trigger; V-type mainspring. Flint or percussion. Introduced 1995. From Traditions.
Price: Flintlock $289.00
Price: Percussion $269.00

TRADITIONS THUNDER MAGNUM RIFLE
Caliber: 50. **Barrel:** 24"; 1:32" twist. **Weight:** 7 lbs., 9 oz. **Length:** 42-1/2" overall. **Stock:** Hardwood or composite. **Sights:** Fiber optic front, adjustable rear. **Features:** Sidelock action with thumb-activated safety. Takes 150 grains of Pyrodex pellets and musket caps. Introduced 1999. From Traditions.
Price: Hardwood. $349.00
Price: All-weather hardwood, C-Nickel. $359.00

TRADITIONS TRACKER 209 IN-LINE RIFLES
Caliber: 50. **Barrel:** 22" blued or C-Nickel finish; 1:28" twist. **Weight:** 6 lbs., 4 oz. **Length:** 41" overall. **Stock:** Black or Advantage Timber® composite. **Sights:** Lite Optic blade front, adjustable rear. **Features:** Thumb safety; adjustable trigger; rubber butt pad and sling swivel studs; takes 150 grains of Pyrodex pellets; one-piece breech system takes 209 shotshell primers. Drilled and tapped for scope. Introduced 2001. From Traditions.
Price: (Black composite stock with 22" blued barrel) $119.00
Price: (Black composite stock with 22" C-Nickel barrel). $129.00
Price: (Advantage Timber® stock with 22" C-Nickel barrel) $179.00
Price: (Redi-Pak with black stock and blued barrel, powder flask, capper, ball starter and other access.) $169.00

TRYON TRAILBLAZER RIFLE
Caliber: 50, 54. **Barrel:** 28", 30". **Weight:** 9 lbs. **Length:** 48" overall. **Stock:** European walnut with cheekpiece. **Sights:** Blade front, semi-buckhorn rear. **Features:** Reproduction of a rifle made by George Tryon about 1820. Double-set triggers, back action lock, hooked breech with long tang. From Armsport.
Price: About $825.00

WHITE MODEL 97 WHITETAIL HUNTER RIFLE
Caliber: 45, 50. **Barrel:** 22", 1:24" twist (50 cal.). **Weight:** 7.6 lbs. **Length:** 39-7/8" overall. **Stock:** Black laminated wood or black composite with swivel studs. **Sights:** Marble fully adjustable, steel rear with white diamond; red-bead front with high-visibility inserts. **Features:** In-line ignition with FlashFire one-piece nipple and breech plug that uses standard or magnum No. 11 caps; fully adjustable trigger; double safety system; aluminum ramrod; drilled and tapped for scope. Includes hard gun case. Introduced 2000. Made in U.S. by Muzzleloading Technologies Inc.
Price: Laminated wood stock $549.95
Price: Black composite stock $549.95

White Model 98 Elite Hunter Rifle
Similar to Model 97 but features 24" barrel with longer action for extended sight radius. Overall length 43-5/16", weighs 8.2 lbs. Choice of black laminated or black hardwood stock. From Muzzleloading Technologies Inc.
Price: Black laminated stock (45 or 50 cal.) $699.95
Price: Black hardwood stock (45 or 50 cal.) $699.95

ZOUAVE PERCUSSION RIFLE
Caliber: 58, 59. **Barrel:** 32-1/2". **Weight:** 9-1/2 lbs. **Length:** 48-1/2" overall. **Stock:** Walnut finish, brass patchbox and buttplate. **Sights:** Fixed front, rear adjustable for elevation. **Features:** Color case-hardened lockplate, blued barrel. From Navy Arms, Dixie Gun Works, E.M.F., Cabela's.
Price: About . . . . $325.00 to $465.00

BLACKPOWDER SHOTGUNS

CVA NWTF Gobbler

Dixie Magnum

Knight TK2000

Traditions Buckhunters Pro

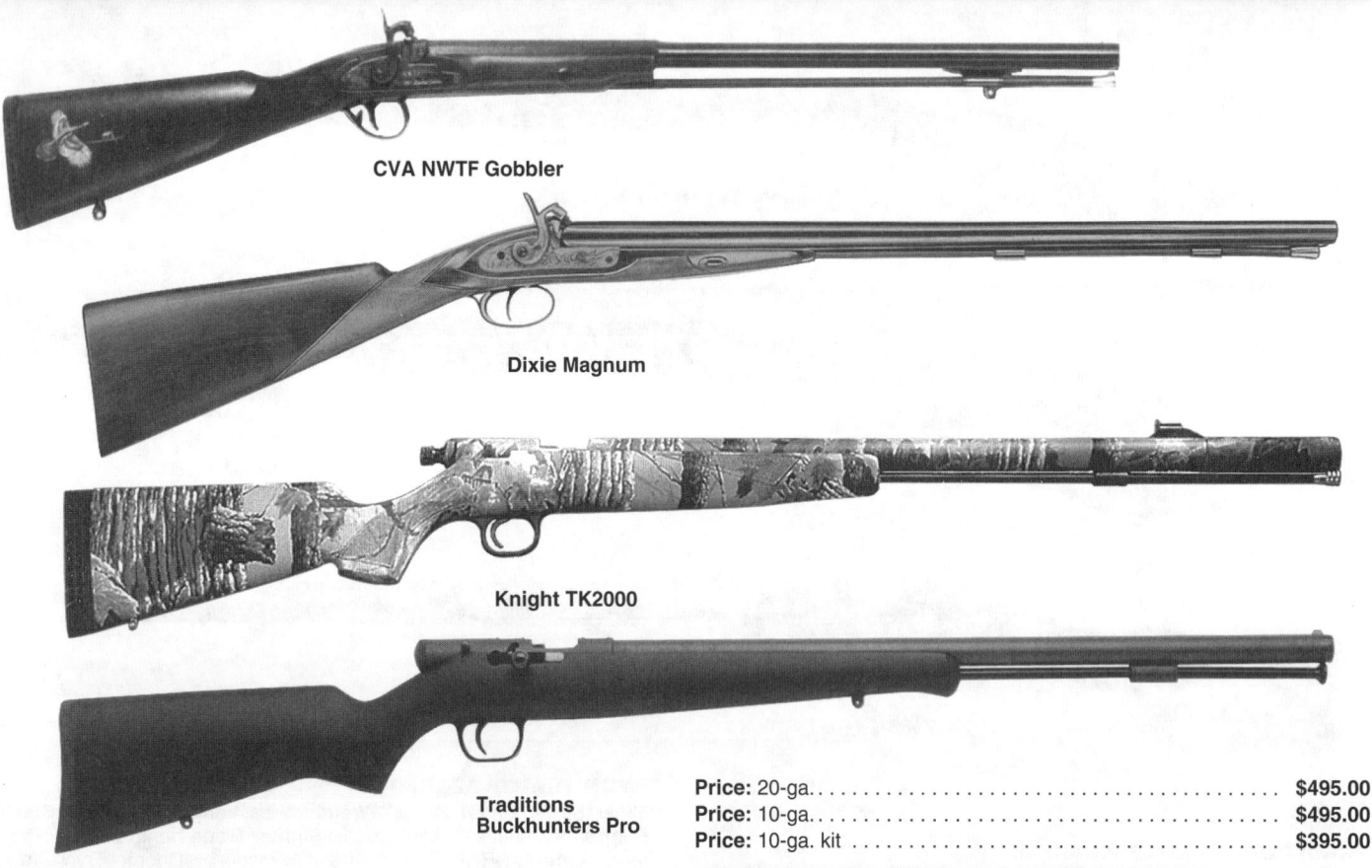

CABELA'S BLACKPOWDER SHOTGUNS
Gauge: 10, 12, 20. **Barrel:** 10-ga., 30"; 12-ga., 28-1/2" (Extra-Full, Mod., Imp. Cyl. choke tubes); 20-ga., 27-1/2" (Imp. Cyl. & Mod. fixed chokes). **Weight:** 6-1/2 to 7 lbs. **Length:** 45" overall (28-1/2" barrel). **Stock:** American walnut with checkered grip; 12- and 20-gauge have straight stock, 10-gauge has pistol grip. **Features:** Blued barrels, engraved, color case-hardened locks and hammers, brass ramrod tip. From Cabela's.
Price: 10-gauge $499.99
Price: 12-gauge $449.99
Price: 20-gauge $429.99

CVA NWTF GOBBLER SERIES SHOTGUN
NEW! **Gauge:** 12. **Barrel:** 28". **Weight:** 6 lbs. **Length:** 46" overall. **Stock:** Hardwood. **Sights:** Bead front. **Features:** National Wild Turkey Federation logo engraved on lock plate; full-color laser engraving of a flying wild turkey on the stock; portion of sales goes to NWTF. Limited edition introduced 2001. From CVA.
Price: $367.95

CVA TRAPPER PERCUSSION SHOTGUN
Gauge: 12. **Barrel:** 28". **Weight:** 6 lbs. **Length:** 46" overall. **Stock:** English-style checkered straight grip of walnut-finished hardwood. **Sights:** Brass bead front. **Features:** Single-blued barrel; color case-hardened lockplate and hammer; screw adjustable sear engagements, V-type mainspring; brass wedge plates; color case-hardened and engraved trigger guard and tang. From CVA.
Price: Finished $287.95

DIXIE MAGNUM PERCUSSION SHOTGUN
Gauge: 10, 12, 20. **Barrel:** 30" (Imp. Cyl. & Mod.) in 10-gauge; 28" in 12-gauge. **Weight:** 6-1/4 lbs. **Length:** 45" overall. **Stock:** Hand-checkered walnut, 14" pull. **Features:** Double triggers; light hand engraving; case-hardened locks in 12-gauge, polished steel in 10-gauge; sling swivels. From Dixie Gun Works.
Price: Upland $449.00
Price: 12-ga. kit $375.00

Price: 20-ga. $495.00
Price: 10-ga. $495.00
Price: 10-ga. kit $395.00

KNIGHT TK2000 MUZZLELOADING SHOTGUN
Gauge: 12. **Barrel:** 26", extra-full choke tube. **Weight:** 7 lbs., 9 oz. **Length:** 45" overall. **Stock:** Synthetic black or Advantage Timber HD; recoil pad; swivel studs. **Sights:** Fully adjustable rear, blade front with fiber optics. **Features:** Receiver drilled and tapped for scope mount; in-line ignition; adjustable trigger; removable breech plug; double safety system; imp. cyl. choke tube available. Introduced 2000. Made in U.S. by Knight Rifles.
Price: .... $349.95 to $399.95

NAVY ARMS STEEL SHOT MAGNUM SHOTGUN
Gauge: 10. **Barrel:** 28" (Cyl. & Cyl.). **Weight:** 7 lbs., 9 oz. **Length:** 45-1/2" overall. **Stock:** Walnut, with cheekpiece. **Features:** Designed specifically for steel shot. Engraved, polished locks; sling swivels; blued barrels. Imported by Navy Arms.
Price: $605.00

NAVY ARMS T&T SHOTGUN
Gauge: 12. **Barrel:** 28" (Full & Full). **Weight:** 7-1/2 lbs. **Stock:** Walnut. **Sights:** Bead front. **Features:** Color case-hardened locks, double triggers, blued steel furniture. From Navy Arms.
Price: $580.00

TRADITIONS BUCKHUNTER PRO SHOTGUN
Gauge: 12. **Barrel:** 24", choke tube. **Weight:** 6 lbs., 4 oz. **Length:** 43" overall. **Stock:** Composite matte black, Break-Up or Advantage camouflage. **Features:** In-line action with removable stainless steel breech plug; thumb safety; adjustable trigger; rubber buttpad. Introduced 1996. From Traditions.
Price: $248.00
Price: With Advantage, Shadow Branch, or Break-Up
  camouflage stock $292.00

THOMPSON/CENTER BLACK MOUNTAIN MAGNUM SHOTGUN
Gauge: 12. **Barrel:** 27" screw-in Turkey choke tube. **Weight:** 7 lbs. **Length:** 41-3/4" overall. **Stock:** Black composite. **Sights:** Bead front. **Features:** Sidelock percussion action. Polished blue finish. Introduced in 1999. Made in U.S. by Thompson/Center Arms.
Price: $387.16

AIRGUNS — HANDGUNS

Beeman P1

Beeman/Feinwerkbau 103

Beeman/FWB P30

Beeman/FWB C55

Benjamin Sheridan CO2

BEEMAN P1 MAGNUM AIR PISTOL
Caliber: 177, 5mm, single shot. **Barrel:** 8.4". **Weight:** 2.5 lbs. **Length:** 11" overall. **Power:** Top lever cocking; spring-piston. **Stocks:** Checkered walnut. **Sights:** Blade front, square notch rear with click micrometer adjustments for windage and elevation. Grooved for scope mounting. **Features:** Dual power for 177 and 20-cal.: low setting gives 350-400 fps; high setting 500-600 fps. Rearward expanding mainspring simulates firearm recoil. All Colt 45 auto grips fit gun. Dry-firing feature for practice. Optional wooden shoulder stock. Introduced 1985. Imported by Beeman.
Price: 177, 5mm $415.00

Beeman P2 Match Air Pistol
Similar to the Beeman P1 Magnum except shoots only 177 pellets; completely recoilless single-stroke pnuematic action. Weighs 2.2 lbs. Choice of thumbrest match grips or standard style. Introduced 1990.
Price: 177, 5mm, standard grip $385.00
Price: 177, match grip $455.00

BEEMAN P3 AIR PISTOL
Caliber: 177 pellet, single shot. **Barrel:** N/A. **Weight:** 1.7 lbs. **Length:** 9.6" overall. **Power:** Single-stroke pneumatic; overlever barrel cocking. **Grips:** Reinforced polymer. **Sights:** Adjustable rear, blade front. **Features:** Velocity 410 fps. Polymer frame; automatic safety; two-stage trigger; built-in muzzle brake. Introduced 1999 by Beeman.
Price: $159.00

BEEMAN/FEINWERKBAU 65 MKII AIR PISTOL
Caliber: 177, single shot. **Barrel:** 6.1", removable bbl. wgt. available. **Weight:** 42 oz. **Length:** 13.3" overall. **Power:** Spring, sidelever cocking. **Stocks:** Walnut, stippled thumbrest; adjustable or fixed. **Sights:** Front, interchangeable post element system, open rear, click adjustable for windage and elevation and for sighting notch width. Scope mount available. **Features:** New shorter barrel for better balance and control. Cocking effort 9 lbs. Two-stage trigger, four adjustments. Quiet firing, 525 fps. Programs instantly for recoil or recoilless operation. Permanently lubricated. Steel piston ring. Imported by Beeman.
Price: Right-hand $1,070.00

BEEMAN/FEINWERKBAU 103 PISTOL
Caliber: 177, single shot. **Barrel:** 10.1", 12-groove rifling. **Weight:** 2.5 lbs. **Length:** 16.5" overall. **Power:** Single-stroke pneumatic, underlever cocking. **Stocks:** Stippled walnut with adjustable palm shelf. **Sights:** Blade front, open rear adjustable for windage and elevation. Notch size adjustable for width. Interchangeable front blades. **Features:** Velocity 510 fps. Fully adjustable trigger. Cocking effort of 2 lbs. Imported by Beeman.
Price: Right-hand $1,195.00
Price: Left-hand $1,235.00

BEEMAN/FWB P30 MATCH AIR PISTOL
Caliber: 177, single shot. **Barrel:** 10-5/16", with muzzlebrake. **Weight:** 2.4 lbs. **Length:** 16.5" overall. **Power:** Pre-charged pneumatic. **Stocks:** Stippled walnut; adjustable match type. **Sights:** Undercut blade front, fully adjustable match rear. **Features:** Velocity to 525 fps; up to 200 shots per CO_2 cartridge. Fully adjustable trigger; built-in muzzlebrake. Introduced 1995. Imported from Germany by Beeman.
Price: Right-hand $1,275.00
Price: Left-hand $1,350.00

BEEMAN/FWB C55 CO_2 RAPID FIRE PISTOL
Caliber: 177, single shot or 5-shot magazine. **Barrel:** 7.3". **Weight:** 2.5 lbs. **Length:** 15" overall. **Power:** Special CO_2 cylinder. **Stocks:** Anatomical, adjustable. **Sights:** Interchangeable front, fully adjustable open micro-click rear with adjustable notch size. **Features:** Velocity 510 fps. Has 11.75" sight radius. Built-in muzzlebrake. Introduced 1993. Imported by Beeman Precision Airguns.
Price: Right-hand $1,460.00
Price: Left-hand $1,520.00

BEEMAN HW70A AIR PISTOL
Caliber: 177, single shot. **Barrel:** 6-1/4", rifled. **Weight:** 38 oz. **Length:** 12-3/4" overall. **Power:** Spring, barrel cocking. **Stocks:** Plastic, with thumbrest. **Sights:** Hooded post front, square notch rear adjustable for windage and elevation. Comes with scope base. **Features:** Adjustable trigger, 31-lb. cocking effort, 440 fps MV; automatic barrel safety. Imported by Beeman.
Price: $185.00
Price: HW70S, black grip, silver finish $210.00

BEEMAN/WEBLEY TEMPEST AIR PISTOL
Caliber: 177, 22, single shot. **Barrel:** 6-7/8". **Weight:** 32 oz. **Length:** 8.9" overall. **Power:** Spring-piston, break barrel. **Stocks:** Checkered black plastic with thumbrest. **Sights:** Blade front, adjustable rear. **Features:** Velocity to 500 fps (177), 400 fps (22). Aluminum frame; black epoxy finish; manual safety. Imported from England by Beeman.
Price: $180.00

Beeman/Webley Hurricane Air Pistol
Similar to the Tempest except has extended frame in the rear for a click-adjustable rear sight; hooded front sight; comes with scope mount. Imported from England by Beeman.
Price: $225.00

BENJAMIN SHERIDAN CO_2 PELLET PISTOLS
Caliber: 177, 20, 22, single shot. **Barrel:** 6-3/8", rifled brass. **Weight:** 29 oz. **Length:** 9.8" overall. **Power:** 12-gram CO_2 cylinder. **Stocks:** Walnut. **Sights:** High ramp front, fully adjustable notch rear. **Features:** Velocity to 500 fps. Turn-bolt action with cross-bolt safety. Gives about 40 shots per CO_2 cylinder. Black or nickel finish. Made in U.S. by Benjamin Sheridan Co.
Price: Black finish, EB17 (177), EB20 (20), about $115.23

34TH EDITION, 2002

AIRGUNS—HANDGUNS

BRNO TAU-7

Crosman Model 1377

Crosman Auto Air II

Crosman Model 1008

BENJAMIN SHERIDAN PNEUMATIC PELLET PISTOLS
Caliber: 177, 20, 22, single shot. **Barrel:** 9-3/8", rifled brass. **Weight:** 38 oz. **Length:** 13-1/8" overall. **Power:** Underlever pnuematic, hand pumped. **Stocks:** Walnut stocks and pump handle. **Sights:** High ramp front, fully adjustable notch rear. **Features:** Velocity to 525 fps (variable). Bolt action with cross-bolt safety. Choice of black or nickel finish. Made in U.S. by Benjamin Sheridan Co.
Price: Black finish, HB17 (177), HB20 (20), HB22 (22), about............ $129.50

BERETTA 92 FS/CO$_2$ AIR PISTOLS
Caliber: 177 pellet, 8-shot magazine. **Barrel:** 4.9". **Weight:** 44.4 oz. **Length:** 8.2" (10.2" with compensator). Power: CO2 cartridge. **Grips:** Plastic or wood. **Sights:** Adjustable rear, blade front. **Features:** Velocity 375 fps. Replica of Beretta 92 FS pistol. Single- and double-action trigger; ambidextrous safety; black or nickel-plated finish. Made by Umarex for Beretta USA.
Price: Starting at $200.00

BRNO TAU-7 CO$_2$ MATCH PISTOL
Caliber: 177. **Barrel:** 10.24". **Weight:** 37 oz. **Length:** 15.75" overall. **Power:** 12.5-gram CO$_2$ cartridge. **Stocks:** Stippled hardwood with adjustable palm rest. **Sights:** Blade front, open fully adjustable rear. **Features:** Comes with extra seals and counterweight. Blue finish. Imported by Great Lakes Airguns.
Price: About $299.50

BSA 240 MAGNUM AIR PISTOL
Caliber: 177, 22, single shot. **Barrel:** 6". **Weight:** 2 lbs. **Length:** 9" overall. **Power:** Spring-air, top-lever cocking. **Stocks:** Walnut. **Sights:** Blade front, micrometer adjustable rear. **Features:** Velocity 510 fps (177), 420 fps (22); crossbolt safety. Combat autoloader styling. Imported from U.K. by Precision Sales International, Inc.
Price: $259.99

COLT GOVERNMENT 1911 A1 AIR PISTOL
Caliber: 177, 8-shot cylinder magazine. **Barrel:** 5", rifled. **Weight:** 38 oz. **Length:** 8-1/2" overall. **Power:** CO$_2$ cylinder. **Stocks:** Checkered black plastic or smooth wood. **Sights:** Post front, adjustable rear. **Features:** Velocity to 393 fps. Quick-loading cylinder magazine; single and double action; black or silver finish. Introduced 1998. Imported by Colt's Mfg. Co., Inc.
Price: Black finish.. $199.00
Price: Silver finish... $209.00

CROSMAN BLACK VENOM PISTOL
Caliber: 177 pellets, BB, 17-shot magazine; darts, single shot. **Barrel:** 4.75" smoothbore. **Weight:** 16 oz. **Length:** 10.8" overall. **Power:** Spring. **Stocks:** Checkered. **Sights:** Blade front, adjustable rear. **Features:** Velocity to 270 fps (BBs), 250 fps (pellets). Spring-fed magazine; cross-bolt safety. Introduced 1996. Made in U.S. by Crosman Corp.
Price: About $20.00

CROSMAN BLACK FANG PISTOL
Caliber: 177 BB, 17-shot magazine. **Barrel:** 4.75" smoothbore. **Weight:** 10 oz. **Length:** 10.8" overall. **Power:** Spring. **Stocks:** Checkered. **Sights:** Blade front, fixed notch rear. **Features:** Velocity to 250 fps. Spring-fed magazine; cross-bolt safety. Introduced 1996. Made in U.S. by Crosman Corp.
Price: About $16.00

CROSMAN MODEL 1322, 1377 AIR PISTOLS
Caliber: 177 (M1377), 22 (M1322), single shot. **Barrel:** 8", rifled steel. **Weight:** 39 oz. **Length:** 13-5/8". **Power:** Hand pumped. **Sights:** Blade front, rear adjustable for windage and elevation. **Features:** Bolt action moulded plastic grip, hand size pump forearm. Cross-bolt safety. From Crosman.
Price: About $60.00

CROSMAN AUTO AIR II PISTOL
Caliber: BB, 17-shot magazine, 177 pellet, single shot. **Barrel:** 8-5/8" steel, smoothbore. **Weight:** 13 oz. **Length:** 10-3/4" overall. **Power:** CO$_2$ Powerlet. **Stocks:** Grooved plastic. **Sights:** Blade front, adjustable rear; highlighted system. **Features:** Velocity to 480 fps (BBs), 430 fps (pellets). Semi-automatic action with BBs, single shot with pellets. Silvered finish. Introduced 1991. From Crosman.
Price: About $38.00

CROSMAN MODEL 357 SERIES AIR PISTOL
Caliber: 177 10-shot pellet clips. **Barrel:** 4" (Model 3574GT), 6" (Model 3576GT). **Weight:** 32 oz. (6"). **Length:** 11-3/8" overall (357-6). **Power:** CO$_2$ Powerlet. **Stocks:** Grip, wrap-around style. **Sights:** Ramp front, fully adjustable rear. **Features:** Average 430 fps (Model 3574GT). Break-open barrel for easy loading. Single or double action. Vent. rib barrel. Wide, smooth trigger. Two cylinders come with each gun. Black finish. From Crosman.
Price: 4" or 6", about $65.00

CROSMAN MODEL 1008 REPEAT AIR
Caliber: 177, 8-shot pellet clip. **Barrel:** 4.25", rifled steel. **Weight:** 17 oz. **Length:** 8.625" overall. **Power:** CO$_2$ Powerlet. **Stocks:** Checkered black plastic. **Sights:** Post front, adjustable rear. **Features:** Velocity about 430 fps. Break-open barrel for easy loading; single or double semi-automatic action; two 8-shot clips included. Optional carrying case available. Introduced 1992. From Crosman.
Price: About $60.00
Price: With case, about $70.00
Price: Model 1008SB (silver and black finish), about.............. $60.00

DAISY MODEL 2003 PELLET PISTOL
Caliber: 177 pellet, 35-shot clip. **Barrel:** Rifled steel. **Weight:** 2.2 lbs. **Length:** 11.7" overall. **Power:** CO$_2$. **Stocks:** Checkered plastic. **Sights:** Blade front, open rear. **Features:** Velocity to 400 fps. Crossbolt trigger-block safety. Made in U.S. by Daisy Mfg. Co.
Price: About $67.95

DAISY MODEL 454 AIR PISTOL
Caliber: 177 BB, 20-shot clip. **Barrel:** Smoothbore steel. **Weight:** 1.6 lbs. **Length:** 10.4" overall. **Power:** CO$_2$. **Stocks:** Moulded black, ribbed composition. **Sights:** Blade front, fixed rear. **Features:** Velocity to 420 fps. Semi-automatic action; cross-bolt safety; black finish. Introduced 1998. Made in U.S. by Dairy Mfg. Co.
Price: $61.95

AIRGUNS—HANDGUNS

Daisy/Power Line 717

Daisy/PowerLine 1270

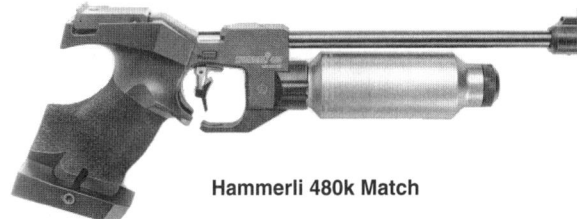

Hammerli 480k Match

Marksman 2005 Laserhawk

DAISY/POWERLINE 717 PELLET PISTOL
Caliber: 177, single shot. **Barrel:** 9.61". **Weight:** 2.25 lbs. **Length:** 13-1/2" overall. **Stocks:** Moulded wood-grain plastic, with thumbrest. **Sights:** Blade and ramp front, micro-adjustable notch rear. **Features:** Single pump pneumatic pistol. Rifled steel barrel. Cross-bolt trigger block. Muzzle velocity 385 fps. From Daisy Mfg. Co. Introduced 1979.
Price: About $71.95

Daisy/PowerLine 747 Pistol
Similar to the 717 pistol except has a 12-groove rifled steel barrel by Lothar Walther, and adjustable trigger pull weight. Velocity of 360 fps. Manual cross-bolt safety.
Price: About $140.00

DAISY/POWERLINE 1140 PELLET PISTOL
Caliber: 177, single shot. **Barrel:** Rifled steel. **Weight:** 1.3 lbs. **Length:** 11.7" overall. **Power:** Single-stroke barrel cocking. **Stocks:** Checkered resin. **Sights:** Hooded post front, open adjustable rear. **Features:** Velocity to 325 fps. Made of black lightweight engineering resin. Introduced 1995. From Daisy.
Price: About $38.95

DAISY/POWERLINE 44 REVOLVER
Caliber: 177 pellets, 6-shot. **Barrel:** 6", rifled steel; interchangeable 4" and 8". **Weight:** 2.7 lbs. **Length:** 13.1" overall. **Power:** CO_2. **Stocks:** Moulded plastic with checkering. **Sights:** Blade on ramp front, fully adjustable notch rear. **Features:** Velocity up to 400 fps. Replica of 44 Magnum revolver. Has swingout cylinder and interchangeable barrels. Introduced 1987. From Daisy Mfg. Co.
Price: $59.95

DAISY/POWERLINE 1270 CO_2 AIR PISTOL
Caliber: BB, 60-shot magazine. **Barrel:** Smoothbore steel. **Weight:** 17 oz. **Length:** 11.1" overall. **Power:** CO_2 pump action. **Stocks:** Moulded black polymer. **Sights:** Blade on ramp front, adjustable rear. **Features:** Velocity to 420 fps. Crossbolt trigger block safety; plated finish. Introduced 1997. Made in U.S. by Daisy Mfg. Co.
Price: About $39.95

EAA/BAIKAL IZH-46 TARGET AIR PISTOL
Caliber: 177, single shot. **Barrel:** 11.02". **Weight:** 2.87 lbs. **Length:** 16.54" overall. **Power:** Underlever single-stroke pneumatic. **Grips:** Adjustable wooden target. **Sights:** Micrometer fully adjustable rear, blade front. **Features:** Velocity about 420 fps. Hammer-forged, rifled barrel. Imported from Russia by European American Armory.
Price: $275.00

EAA/BAIKAL MP-654K AIR PISTOL
Caliber: 177 BB, detachable 13-shot magazine. **Barrel:** 3.75". **Weight:** 1.6 lbs. **Length:** 6.34". **Power:** CO_2 cartridge. **Grips:** Black checkered plastic. **Sights:** Notch rear, blade front. **Features:** Velocity about 380 fps. Double-action trigger; slide safety; metal slide and frame. Replica of Makarov pistol. Imported from Russia by European American Armory.
Price: $110.00

EAA/BAIKAL MP-651K AIR PISTOL/RIFLE
Caliber: 177 pellet (8-shot magazine); 177 BB (23-shot). **Barrel:** 5.9" (17.25" with rifle attachment). **Weight:** 1.54 lbs. (3.3 lbs. with rifle attachment). **Length:** 9.4" (31.3" with rifle attachment) **Power:** CO_2 cartridge, semi-automatic. **Stock:** Plastic. **Sights:** Notch rear/blade front (pistol); periscopic sighting system (rifle). **Features:** Velocity 328 fps. Unique pistol/rifle combination allows the pistol to be inserted into the rifle shell. Imported from Russia by European American Armory.
Price: $95.00

"GAT" AIR PISTOL
Caliber: 177, single shot. **Barrel:** 7-1/2" cocked, 9-1/2" extended. **Weight:** 22 oz. **Power:** Spring-piston. **Stocks:** Cast checkered metal. **Sights:** Fixed. **Features:** Shoots pellets, corks or darts. Matte black finish. Imported from England by Stone Enterprises, Inc.
Price: $24.95

HAMMERLI 480 MATCH AIR PISTOL
Caliber: 177, single shot. **Barrel:** 9.8". **Weight:** 37 oz. **Length:** 16.5" overall. **Power:** Air or CO_2. **Stocks:** Walnut with 7-degree rake adjustment. Stippled grip area. **Sights:** Undercut blade front, fully adjustable open match rear. **Features:** Under-barrel cannister charges with air or CO_2 for power supply; gives 320 shots per filling. Trigger adjustable for position. Introduced 1994. Imported from Switzerland by Hammerli Pistols U.S.A.
Price: $1,325.00

Hammerli 480K2 Match Air Pistol
Similar to the 480 except has a short, detachable aluminum air cylinder for use only with compressed air; can be filled while on the gun or off; special adjustable barrel weights. Muzzle velocity of 470 fps, gives about 180 shots. Has stippled black composition grip with adjustable palm shelf and rake angle. Comes with air pressure gauge. Introduced 1996. Imported from Switzerland by SIGARMS, Inc.
Price: $1,112.50

MARKSMAN 1010 REPEATER PISTOL
Caliber: 177, 18-shot BB repeater. **Barrel:** 2-1/2", smoothbore. **Weight:** 24 oz. **Length:** 8-1/4" overall. **Power:** Spring. **Features:** Velocity to 200 fps. Thumb safety. Black finish. Uses BBs, darts, bolts or pellets. Repeats with BBs only. From Marksman Products.
Price: Matte black finish $26.00
Price: Model 2000 (as above except silver-chrome finish) $27.00

MARKSMAN 2005 LASERHAWK SPECIAL EDITION AIR PISTOL
Caliber: 177, 24-shot magazine. **Barrel:** 3.8", smoothbore. **Weight:** 22 oz. **Length:** 10.3" overall. **Power:** Spring-air. **Stocks:** Checkered. **Sights:** Fixed fiber optic front sight. **Features:** Velocity to 300 fps with Hyper-Velocity pellets. Square trigger guard with skeletonized trigger; extended barrel for greater velocity and accuracy. Shoots BBs, pellets, darts or bolts. Made in the U.S. From Marksman Products.
Price: $32.00

MORINI 162E MATCH AIR PISTOL
Caliber: 177, single shot. **Barrel:** 9.4". **Weight:** 32 oz. **Length:** 16.1" overall. **Power:** Scuba air. **Stocks:** Adjustable match type. **Sights:** Interchangeable blade front, fully adjustable match-type rear. **Features:** Power mechanism shuts down when pressure drops to a pre-set level. Adjustable electronic trigger. Introduced 1995. Imported from Switzerland by Nygord Precision Products.
Price: $995.00

AIRGUNS—HANDGUNS

PARDINI K58 MATCH AIR PISTOL
Caliber: 177, single shot. **Barrel:** 9.0". **Weight:** 37.7 oz. **Length:** 15.5" overall. **Power:** Pre-charged compressed air; single-stroke cocking. **Stocks:** Adjustable match type; stippled walnut. **Sights:** Interchangeable post front, fully adjustable match rear. **Features:** Fully adjustable trigger. Introduced 1995. Imported from Italy by Nygord Precision Products.
Price: $750.00
Price: K2 model, precharged air pistol, introduced in 1998 .... $895.00

RWS 9B/9N AIR PISTOLS *NEW!*
Caliber: 177, single shot. **Barrel:** N/A. **Weight:** N/A. **Length:** N/A. **Grips:** Plastic with thumbrest. **Sights:** Adjustable. **Features:** Spring-piston powered; 550 fps. Black or nickel finish. Introduced 2001. Imported from Germany by Dynamit Nobel-RWS.
Price: .... NA

RWS C-225 AIR PISTOLS
Caliber: 177, 8-shot rotary magazine. **Barrel:** 4", 6". **Weight:** NA. **Length:** NA. **Power:** CO2. **Stocks:** Checkered black plastic. **Sights:** Post front, rear adjustable for windage. **Features:** Velocity to 385 fps. Semi-automatic fire; decocking lever. Imported from Germany by Dynamit Nobel-RWS.
Price: 4", blue.. $210.00
Price: 4", nickel.. $220.00
Price: 6", blue.. $220.00

STEYR LP 5CP MATCH AIR PISTOL
Caliber: 177, 5-shot magazine. **Barrel:** NA. **Weight:** 40.7 oz. **Length:** 15.2" overall. **Power:** Pre-charged air cylinder. **Stocks:** Adjustable match type. **Sights:** Interchangeable blade front, fully adjustable match rear. **Features:** Adjustable sight radius; fully adjustable trigger. Has barrel compensator. Introduced 1995. Imported from Austria by Nygord Precision Products.
Price: $1,150.00

STEYR LP10P MATCH PISTOL
Caliber: 177, single shot. **Barrel:** 9". **Weight:** 38.7 oz. **Length:** 15.3" overall. **Power:** Scuba air. **Stocks:** Fully adjustable Morini match with palm shelf; stippled walnut. **Sights:** Interchangeable blade in 4mm, 4.5mm or 5mm widths, fully adjustable open rear with interchangeable 3.5mm or 4mm leaves. **Features:** Velocity about 500 fps. Adjustable trigger, adjustable sight radius from 12.4" to 13.2". With compensator. Imported from Austria by Nygord Precision Products.
Price: $1,195.00

TECH FORCE SS2 OLYMPIC COMPETITION AIR PISTOL
Caliber: 177 pellet, single shot. **Barrel:** 7.4". **Weight:** 2.8 lbs. **Length:** 16.5" overall. **Power:** Spring piston, sidelever. **Grips:** Hardwood. **Sights:** Extended adjustable rear, blade front accepts inserts. **Features:** Velocity 520 fps. Recoilless design; adjustments allow duplication of a firearm's feel. Match-grade, adjustable trigger; includes carrying case. Imported from China by Compasseco Inc.
Price: $295.00

TECH FORCE 35 AIR PISTOL
Caliber: 177 pellet, single shot. **Barrel:** N/A. **Weight:** 2.86 lbs. **Length:** 14.9" overall. **Power:** Spring piston, underlever. **Grips:** Hardwood. **Sights:** Micrometer adjustable rear, blade front. **Features:** Velocity 400 fps. Grooved for scope mount; trigger safety. Imported from China by Compasseco Inc.
Price: $49.95

Tech Force 8 Air Pistol
Similar to Tech Force 35, but with break-barrel action, ambidextrous polymer grips. From Compasseco Inc.
Price: $59.95

Tech Force S2-1 Air Pistol
Similar to Tech Force 8, but more basic grips and sights for plinking. From Compasseco Inc.
Price: $29.95

Walther CP88

WALTHER CP88 PELLET PISTOL
Caliber: 177, 8-shot rotary magazine. **Barrel:** 4", 6". **Weight:** 37 oz. (4" barrel) **Length:** 7" (4" barrel). **Power:** CO_2. **Stocks:** Checkered plastic. **Sights:** Blade front, fully adjustable rear. **Features:** Faithfully replicates size, weight and trigger pull of the 9mm Walther P88 compact pistol. Has SA/DA trigger mechanism; ambidextrous safety, levers. Comes with two magazines, 500 pellets, one CO2 cartridge. Introduced 1997. Imported from Germany by Interarms.
Price: Blue $179.00
Price: Nickel $189.00

WALTHER LP20I MATCH PISTOL
Caliber: 177, single shot. **Barrel:** 8.66". **Weight:** NA. **Length:** 15.1" overall. **Power:** Scuba air. **Stocks:** Orthopaedic target type. **Sights:** Undercut blade front, open match rear fully adjustable for windage and elevation. **Features:** Adjustable velocity; matte finish. Introduced 1995. Imported from Germany by Nygord Precision Products.
Price: $1,095.00

Walther CP88 Competition Pellet Pistol
Similar to the standard CP88 except has 6" match-grade barrel, muzzle weight, wood or plastic stocks. Weighs 41 oz., has overall length of 9". Introduced 1997. Imported from Germany by Interarms.
Price: Blue, plastic grips....................................... $170.00
Price: Nickel, plastic grips $195.00
Price: Blue, wood grips... $205.00
Price: Nickel, wood grips $232.00

WALTHER CP99 AIR PISTOL
Caliber: 177 pellet, 8-shot rotary magazine. **Barrel:** 3". **Weight:** 26 oz. **Length:** 7.1" overall. **Power:** CO2 cartridge. **Grip:** Polymer. **Sights:** Drift-adjustable rear, blade front. **Features:** Velocity 320 fps. Replica of Walther P99 pistol. Trigger allows single and double action; ambidextrous magazine release; interchangeable backstraps to fit variety of hand sizes. Introduced 2000. From Walther USA.
Price: .... NA

WALTHER PPK/S AIR PISTOL
Caliber: 177 BB. **Barrel:** N/A. **Weight:** 20 oz. **Length:** 6.3" overall. **Power:** CO2 cartridge. **Grip:** Plastic. **Sights:** Fixed rear, blade front. **Features:** Replica of Walther PPK pistol. Blow back system moves slide when fired; trigger allows single and double action. Introduced 2000. From Walther USA.
Price: .... NA

AIRGUNS — LONG GUNS

Airrow A-8S1P

ARS/Career 707

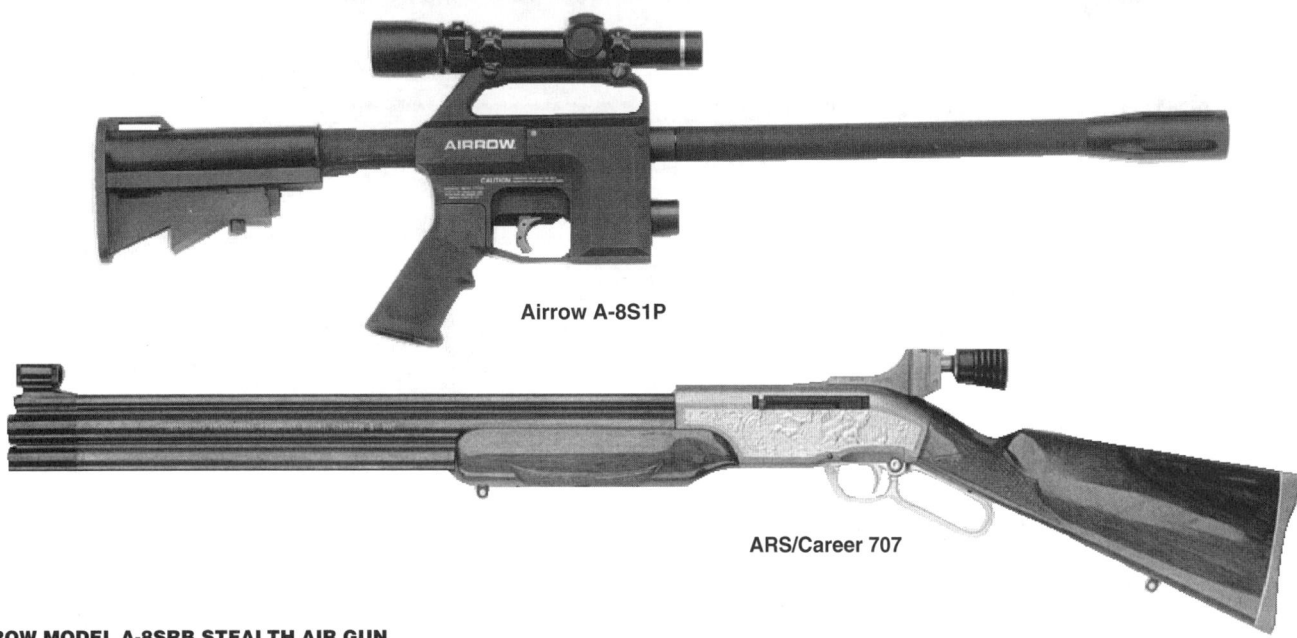

AIRROW MODEL A-8SRB STEALTH AIR GUN
Caliber: 177, 22, 25, 38, 9-shot. **Barrel:** 19.7"; rifled. **Weight:** 6 lbs. **Length:** 34" overall. **Power:** CO2 or compressed air; variable power. **Stock:** Telescoping CAR-15-type. **Sights:** Variable 3.5-10x scope. **Features:** Velocity 1100 fps in all calibers. Pneumatic air trigger. All aircraft aluminum and stainless steel construction. Mil-spec materials and finishes. Introduced 1992. From Swivel Machine Works, Inc.
Price: About **$2,599.00**

AIRROW MODEL A-8S1P STEALTH AIR GUN
Caliber: #2512 16" arrow. **Barrel:** 16". **Weight:** 4.4 lbs. **Length:** 30.1" overall. **Power:** CO2 or compressed air; variable power. **Stock:** Telescoping CAR-15-type. **Sights:** Scope rings only. **Features:** Velocity to 650 fps with 260-grain arrow. Pneumatic air trigger. All aircraft aluminum and stainless steel construction. Mil-spec materials and finishes. Waterproof case. Introduced 1991. From Swivel Machine Works, Inc.
Price: About **$1,699.00**

ARS/KING HUNTING MASTER AIR RIFLE
Caliber: 22, 5-shot repeater. **Barrel:** 22-3/4". **Weight:** 7-3/4 lbs. **Length:** 42" overall. **Power:** Pre-compressed air from 3000 psi diving tank. **Stock:** Indonesian walnut with checkered grip and forend; rubber buttpad. **Sights:** Blade front, fully adjustable open rear. **Features:** Velocity over 1000 fps with 32-grain pellet. High and low power switch for hunting or target velocities. Side lever cocks action and inserts pellet. Rotary magazine. Imported from Korea by Air Rifle Specialists.
Price: **$580.00**
Price: Hunting Master 900 (9mm, limited production) **$1,000.00**

ARS/Magnum 6 Air Rifle
Similar to the King Hunting Master except is 6-shot repeater with 23-3/4" barrel, weighs 8-1/4 lbs. Stock is walnut-stained hardwood with checkered grip and forend; rubber buttpad. Velocity of 1000+ fps with 32-grain pellet. Imported from Korea by Air Rifle Specialists.
Price: **$500.00**

ARS HUNTING MASTER AR6 AIR RIFLE
Caliber: 22, 6-shot repeater. **Barrel:** 25-1/2". **Weight:** 7 lbs. **Length:** 41-1/4" overall. **Power:** Pre-compressed air from 3000 psi diving tank. **Stock:** Indonesian walnut with checkered grip; rubber buttpad. **Sights:** Blade front, adjustable peep rear. **Features:** Velocity over 1000 fps with 32-grain pellet. Receiver grooved for scope mounting. Has 6-shot rotary magazine. Imported by Air Rifle Specialists.
Price: **$580.00**

ARS/CAREER 707 AIR RIFLE
Caliber: 22, 6-shot repeater. **Barrel:** 23". **Weight:** 7.75 lbs. **Length:** 40.5" overall. **Power:** Pre-compressed air; variable power. **Stock:** Indonesian walnut with checkered grip, gloss finish. **Sights:** Hooded post front with interchangeable inserts, fully adjustable diopter rear. **Features:** Velocity to 1000 fps. Lever-action with straight feed magazine; pressure gauge in lower front air reservoir; scope mounting rail included. Introduced 1996. Imported from the Philippines by Air Rifle Specialists.
Price: **$580.00**

ARS/FARCO FP SURVIVAL AIR RIFLE
Caliber: 22, 25, single shot. **Barrel:** 22-3/4". **Weight:** 5-3/4 lbs. **Length:** 42-3/4" overall. **Power:** Multi-pump foot pump. **Stock:** Philippine hardwood. **Sights:** Blade front, fixed rear. **Features:** Velocity to 850 fps (22 or 25). Receiver grooved for scope mounting. Imported from the Philippines by Air Rifle Specialists.
Price: **$295.00**

ARS/FARCO CO2 AIR SHOTGUN
Caliber: 51 (28-gauge). **Barrel:** 30". **Weight:** 7 lbs. **Length:** 48-1/2" overall. **Power:** 10-oz. refillable CO2 tank. **Stock:** Hardwood. **Sights:** Blade front, fixed rear. **Features:** Gives over 100 ft. lbs. energy for taking small game. Imported from the Philippines by Air Rifle Specialists.
Price: **$460.00**

ARS/Farco CO2 Stainless Steel Air Rifle
Similar to the ARS/Farco CO2 shotgun except in 22- or 25-caliber with 21-1/2" barrel; weighs 6-3/4 lbs., 42-1/2" overall; Philippine hardwood stock with stippled grip and forend; blade front sight, adjustable rear, grooved for scope mount. Uses 10-oz. refillable CO2 cylinder. Made of stainless steel. Imported from the Philippines by Air Rifle Specialists.
Price: Including CO2 cylinder **$460.00**

ARS/QB77 DELUXE AIR RIFLE
Caliber: 177, 22, single shot. **Barrel:** 21-1/2". **Weight:** 5-1/2 lbs. **Length:** 40" overall. **Power:** Two 12-oz. CO2 cylinders. **Stock:** Walnut-stained hardwood. **Sights:** Blade front, adjustable rear. **Features:** Velocity to 625 fps (22), 725 fps (177). Receiver grooved for scope mounting. Comes with bulk-fill valve. Imported by Air Rifle Specialists.
Price: **$195.00**

ANSCHUTZ 2002 MATCH AIR RIFLE
Caliber: 177, single shot. **Barrel:** 25.2". **Weight:** 10.4 lbs. **Length:** 44.5" overall. **Stock:** European walnut, blonde hardwood or colored laminated hardwood; stippled grip and forend. Also available with flat-forend walnut stock for benchrest shooting and aluminum. **Sights:** Optional sight set #6834. **Features:** Muzzle velocity 575 fps. Balance, weight match the 1907 ISU smallbore rifle. Uses #5021 match trigger. Recoil and vibration free. Fully adjustable cheekpiece and buttplate; accessory rail under forend. Available in Pneumatic and Compressed Air versions. Introduced 1988. Imported from Germany by Gunsmithing, Inc., Accuracy International, Champion's Choice.
Price: Right-hand, blonde hardwood stock, with sights **$1,275.00**
Price: Right-hand, walnut stock **$1,275.00**
Price: Right-hand, color laminate stock **$1,300.00**
Price: Right-hand, aluminum stock, butt plate **$1,495.00**
Price: Left-hand, color laminate stock **$1,595.00**
Price: Model 2002D-RT Running Target, right-hand, no sights **$1,248.90**
Price: #6834 Sight Set **$227.10**

BEEMAN BEARCUB AIR RIFLE
Caliber: 177, single shot. **Barrel:** 13". **Weight:** 7.2 lbs. **Length:** 37.8" overall. **Power:** Spring-piston, barrel cocking. **Stock:** Stained hardwood. **Sights:** Hooded post front, open fully adjustable rear. **Features:** Velocity to 915 fps. Polished blue finish; receiver dovetailed for scope mounting. Imported from England by Beeman Precision Airguns.
Price: **$325.00**

BEEMAN CROW MAGNUM AIR RIFLE
Caliber: 20, 22, 25, single shot. **Barrel:** 16"; 10-groove rifling. **Weight:** 8.5 lbs. **Length:** 46" overall. **Power:** Gas-spring; adjustable power to 32 foot pounds muzzle energy. Barrel-cocking. **Stock:** Classic-style hardwood; hand checkered. **Sights:** For scope use only; built-in base and 1" rings included. **Features:** Adjustable two-stage trigger. Automatic safety. Also available in 22-caliber on special order. Introduced 1992. Imported by Beeman.
Price: **$1,220.00**

34TH EDITION, 2002 • **319**

AIRGUNS—LONG GUNS

Beeman Kodiak

Beeman Mako

Beeman R1 Rifle

Beeman R1 Laser Mk II

BEEMAN KODIAK AIR RIFLE
Caliber: 25, single shot. **Barrel:** 17.6". **Weight:** 9 lbs. **Length:** 45.6" overall. **Power:** Spring-piston, barrel cocking. **Stock:** Stained hardwood. **Sights:** Blade front, open fully adjustable rear. **Features:** Velocity to 820 fps. Up to 30 foot pounds muzzle energy. Introduced 1993. Imported by Beeman.
Price: $625.00

BEEMAN MAKO AIR RIFLE
Caliber: 177, single shot. **Barrel:** 20", with compensator. **Weight:** 7.3 lbs. **Length:** 38.5" overall. **Power:** Pre-charged pneumatic. **Stock:** Stained beech; Monte Carlo cheekpiece; checkered grip. **Sights:** None furnished. **Features:** Velocity to 930 fps. Gives over 50 shots per charge. Manual safety; brass trigger blade; vented rubber butt pad. Requires scuba tank for air. Introduced 1994. Imported from England by Beeman.
Price: $1,000.00
Price: Mako FT (thumbhole stock) $1,350.00

BEEMAN R1 AIR RIFLE
Caliber: 177, 20 or 22, single shot. **Barrel:** 19.6", 12-groove rifling. **Weight:** 8.5 lbs. **Length:** 45.2" overall. **Power:** Spring-piston, barrel cocking. **Stock:** Walnut-stained beech; cut-checkered pistol grip; Monte Carlo comb and cheekpiece; rubber buttpad. **Sights:** Tunnel front with interchangeable inserts, open rear click-adjustable for windage and elevation. Grooved for scope mounting. **Features:** Velocity of 940-1000 fps (177), 860 fps (20), 800 fps (22). Non-drying nylon piston and breech seals. Adjustable metal trigger. Milled steel safety. Right- or left-hand stock. Available with adjustable cheekpiece and buttplate at extra cost. Custom and Super Laser versions available. Imported by Beeman.
Price: Right-hand, 177, 20, 22 . . . . $540.00
Price: Left-hand, 177, 20, 22 . . . . $575.00

BEEMAN R6 AIR RIFLE
Caliber: 177, single shot. **Barrel:** NA. **Weight:** 7.1 lbs. **Length:** 41.8" overall. **Power:** Spring-piston, barrel cocking. **Stock:** Stained hardwood. **Sights:** Tunnel post front, open fully adjustable rear. **Features:** Velocity to 815 fps. Two-stage Rekord adjustable trigger; receiver dovetailed for scope mounting; automatic safety. Introduced 1996. Imported from Germany by Beeman Precision Airguns.
Price: $285.00

BEEMAN R1 LASER MK II AIR RIFLE
Caliber: 177, 20, 22, 25, single shot. **Barrel:** 16.1" or 19.6". **Weight:** 8.4 lbs. **Length:** 41.7" overall. **Power:** Spring-piston, barrel cocking. **Stock:** Laminated wood with high cheekpiece, ventilated recoil pad. **Sights:** Tunnel front with interchangeable inserts, open adjustable rear; receiver grooved for scope mounting. **Features:** Velocity to 1150 fps (177). Special powerplant components. Built from the Beeman R1 rifle by Beeman.
Price: $895.00

BEEMAN R7 AIR RIFLE
Caliber: 177, 20, single shot. **Barrel:** 17". **Weight:** 6.1 lbs. **Length:** 40.2" overall. **Power:** Spring piston. **Stock:** Stained beech. **Sights:** Hooded front, fully adjustable micrometer click open rear. **Features:** Velocity to 700 fps (177), 620 fps (20). Receiver grooved for scope mounting; double-jointed cocking lever; fully adjustable trigger; checkered grip. Imported by Beeman.
Price: $280.00

BEEMAN R9 AIR RIFLE
Caliber: 177, 20, single shot. **Barrel:** NA. **Weight:** 7.3 lbs. **Length:** 43" overall. **Power:** Spring-piston, barrel cocking. **Stock:** Stained hardwood. **Sights:** Tunnel post front, fully adjustable open rear. **Features:** Velocity to 1000 fps (177), 800 fps (20). Adjustable Rekord trigger; automatic safety; receiver dovetailed for scope mounting. Introduced 1996. Imported from Germany by Beeman Precision Airguns.
Price: $320.00

Beeman R9 Deluxe Air Rifle
Same as the R9 except has an extended forend stock, checkered pistol grip, grip cap, carved Monte Carlo cheekpiece. Globe front sight with inserts. Introduced 1997. Imported by Beeman.
Price: $370.00

BEEMAN R11 AIR RIFLE
Caliber: 177, single shot. **Barrel:** 19.6". **Weight:** 8.8 lbs. **Length:** 47" overall. **Power:** Spring-piston, barrel cocking. **Stock:** Walnut-stained beech; adjustable buttplate and cheekpiece. **Sights:** None furnished. Has dovetail for scope mounting. **Features:** Velocity 910-940 fps. All-steel barrel sleeve. Imported by Beeman.
Price: $530.00

BEEMAN SUPER 12 AIR RIFLE
Caliber: 22, 25, 12-shot magazine. **Barrel:** 19", 12-groove rifling. **Weight:** 7.8 lbs. **Length:** 41.7" overall. **Power:** Pre-charged pneumatic; external air reservoir. **Stock:** European walnut. **Sights:** None furnished; drilled and tapped for scope mounting; scope mount included. **Features:** Velocity to 850 fps (25-caliber). Adjustable power setting gives 30-70 shots per 400 cc air bottle. Requires scuba tank for air. Introduced 1995. Imported by Beeman.
Price: $1,675.00

AIRGUNS—LONG GUNS

Beeman R6 Rifle

Beeman R9 Deluxe

Beeman R11

Beeman Super 12

BEEMAN S1 MAGNUM AIR RIFLE
Caliber: 177, single shot. **Barrel:** 19". **Weight:** 7.1 lbs. **Length:** 45.5" overall. **Power:** Spring-piston, barrel cocking. **Stock:** Stained beech with Monte Carlo cheekpiece; checkered grip. **Sights:** Hooded post front, fully adjustable micrometer click rear. **Features:** Velocity to 900 fps. Automatic safety; receiver grooved for scope mounting; two-stage adjustable trigger; curved rubber buttpad. Introduced 1995. Imported by Beeman.
Price: $210.00

BEEMAN RX-1 GAS-SPRING MAGNUM AIR RIFLE
Caliber: 177, 20, 22, 25, single shot. **Barrel:** 19.6", 12-groove rifling. **Weight:** 8.8 lbs. **Power:** Gas-spring piston air; single stroke barrel cocking. **Stock:** Walnut-finished hardwood, hand checkered, with cheekpiece. Adjustable cheekpiece and buttplate. **Sights:** Tunnel front, click-adjustable rear. **Features:** Velocity adjustable to about 1200 fps. Uses special sealed chamber of air as a mainspring. Gas-spring cannot take a set. Introduced 1990. Imported by Beeman.
Price: 177, 20, 22 or 25 regular, right-hand $590.00
Price: 177, 20, 22, 25, left-hand................................. $625.00

BEEMAN R1 CARBINE
Caliber: 177, 20, 22, 25, single shot. **Barrel:** 16.1". **Weight:** 8.6 lbs. **Length:** 41.7" overall. **Power:** Spring-piston, barrel cocking. **Stock:** Stained beech; Monte Carlo comb and checkpiece; cut checkered pistol grip; rubber buttpad. **Sights:** Tunnel front with interchangeable inserts, open adjustable rear; receiver grooved for scope mounting. **Features:** Velocity up to 1000 fps (177). Non-drying nylon piston and breech seals. Adjustable metal trigger. Machined steel receiver end cap and safety. Right- or left-hand stock. Imported by Beeman.
Price: 177, 20, 22, 25, right-hand............................... $540.00
Price: As above, left-hand $575.00
Price: R1-AW (synthetic stock, nickel plating) $650.00

BEEMAN/FEINWERKBAU 300-S SERIES MATCH RIFLE
Caliber: 177, single shot. **Barrel:** 19.9", fixed solid with receiver. **Weight:** Approx. 10 lbs. with optional bbl. sleeve. **Length:** 42.8" overall. **Power:** Spring-piston, single stroke sidelever. **Stock:** Match model—walnut, deep forend, adjustable buttplate. **Sights:** Globe front with interchangeable inserts. Click micro. adjustable match aperture rear. Front and rear sights move as a single unit. **Features:** Recoilless, vibration free. Five-way adjustable match trigger. Grooved for scope mounts. Permanent lubrication, steel piston ring. Cocking effort 9 lbs. Optional 10-oz. barrel sleeve. Available from Beeman.
Price: Right-hand $1,235.00
Price: Left-hand $1,370.00

BEEMAN/FEINWERKBAU 603 AIR RIFLE
Caliber: 177, single shot. **Barrel:** 16.6". **Weight:** 10.8 lbs. **Length:** 43" overall. **Power:** Single stroke pneumatic. **Stock:** Special laminated hardwoods and hard rubber for stability. Multi-colored stock also available. **Sights:** Tunnel front with interchangeable inserts, click micrometer match aperture rear. **Features:** Velocity to 570 fps. Recoilless action; double supported barrel; special, short rifled area frees pellet form barrel faster so shooter's motion has minimum effect on accuracy. Fully adjustable match trigger with separately adjustable trigger and trigger slack weight. Trigger and sights blocked when loading latch is open. Introduced 1997. Imported by Beeman.
Price: Right-hand $1,625.00
Price: Left-hand $1,775.00

BEEMAN/FEINWERKBAU 300-S MINI-MATCH
Caliber: 177, single shot. **Barrel:** 17-1/8". **Weight:** 8.8 lbs. **Length:** 40" overall. **Power:** Spring-piston, single stroke sidelever cocking. **Stock:** Walnut. Stippled grip, adjustable buttplate. Scaled-down for youthful or slightly built shooters. **Sights:** Globe front with interchangeable inserts, micro. adjustable rear. Front and rear sights move as a single unit. **Features:** Recoilless, vibration free. Grooved for scope mounts. Steel piston ring. Cocking effort about 9-1/2 lbs. Barrel sleeve optional. Left-hand model available. Introduced 1978. Imported by Beeman.
Price: Right-hand $1,270.00
Price: Left-hand $1,370.00

BEEMAN/FEINWERKBAU P70 AIR RIFLE
Caliber: 177, single shot. **Barrel:** 16.6". **Weight:** 10.6 lbs. **Length:** 42.6" overall. **Power:** Precharged pneumatic. **Stock:** Laminated hardwoods and hard rubber for stability. Multi-colored stock also available. **Sights:** Tunnel front with interchangeable inserts, click micrometer match aperture rear. **Features:** Velocity to 570 fps. Recoilless action; double supported barrel; special short rifled area frees pellet from barrel faster so shooter's motion has minimum effect on accuracy. Fully adjustable match trigger with separately adjustable trigger and trigger slack weight. Trigger and sights blocked when loading latch is open. Introduced 1997. Imported by Beeman.
Price: P70, pre-charged, right-hand.............................. $1,545.00
Price: P70, pre-charged, left-hand $1,640.00
Price: P70, pre-charged, right-hand, multi $1,645.00
Price: P70, pre-charged, left-hand, multi $1,745.00

BEEMAN/HW 97 AIR RIFLE
Caliber: 177, 20, single shot. **Barrel:** 17.75". **Weight:** 9.2 lbs. **Length:** 44.1" overall. **Power:** Spring-piston, underlever cocking. **Stock:** Walnut-stained beech; rubber buttpad. **Sights:** None. Receiver grooved for scope mounting. **Features:** Velocity 830 fps (177). Fixed barrel with fully opening, direct loading breech. Adjustable trigger. Introduced 1994. Imported by Beeman Precision Airguns.
Price: Right-hand only $530.00

34TH EDITION, 2002 • 321

AIRGUNS—LONG GUNS

Beeman/Feinwerkbau 300-S

Beeman/Feinwerkbau 603

Benjamin Sheridan Pneumatic

BENJAMIN SHERIDAN PNEUMATIC (PUMP-UP) AIR RIFLES
Caliber: 177 or 22, single shot. **Barrel:** 19-3/8", rifled brass. **Weight:** 5-1/2 lbs. **Length:** 36-1/4" overall. **Power:** Underlever pneumatic, hand pumped. **Stock:** American walnut stock and forend. **Sights:** High ramp front, fully adjustable notch rear. **Features:** Variable velocity to 800 fps. Bolt action with ambidextrous push-pull safety. Black or nickel finish. Introduced 1991. Made in the U.S. by Benjamin Sheridan Co.
Price: Black finish, Model 397 (177), Model 392 (22), about $140.00
Price: Nickel finish, Model S397 (177), Model S392 (22), about $150.00

BENJAMIN SHERIDAN W.F. AIR RIFLE
Caliber: 177 single-shot. **Barrel:** 19-3/8", rifled brass. **Weight:** 5 lbs. **Length:** 36-1/2" overall. Power 12-gram CO2 cylinder. **Stocks:** American walnut with buttplate. **Sights:** High ramp front, fully adjustable notch rear. **Features:** Velocity to 680 fps (177). Bolt action with ambidextrous push-pull safety. Gives about 40 shots per cylinder. Black finish. Introduced 1991. Made in the U.S. by Benjamin Sheridan Co.
Price: Black finish, Model G397 (177) $140.00

BRNO TAU-200 AIR RIFLE
Caliber: 177, single shot. **Barrel:** 19", rifled. **Weight:** 7-1/2 lbs. **Length:** 42" overall. **Power:** 6-oz. CO2 cartridge. **Stock:** Wood match style with adjustable comb and buttplate. **Sights:** Globe front with interchangeable inserts, fully adjustable open rear. **Features:** Adjustable trigger. Comes with extra seals, large CO2 bottle, counterweight. Introduced 1993. Imported by Great Lakes Airguns. Available in Standard Universal, Deluxe Universal, International and Target Sporter versions.
Price: Standard Universal (ambidex. stock with buttstock extender, adj. cheekpiece).. . . . . $349.50
Price: Deluxe Universal (as above but with micro-adj. aperture sight) $449.50
Price: International (like Deluxe Universal but with right- or left-hand stock) $454.50
Price: Target Sporter (like Std. Universal but with 4X scope, no sights) $412.50

BSA MAGNUM SUPERSTAR™ MK2 MAGNUM AIR RIFLE, CARBINE
Caliber: 177, 22, 25, single shot. **Barrel:** 18". **Weight:** 8 lbs., 8 oz. **Length:** 43" overall. **Power:** Spring-air, underlever cocking. **Stock:** Oil-finished hardwood; Monte Carlo with cheekpiece, checkered at grip; recoil pad. **Sights:** Ramp front, micrometer adjustable rear. Maxi-Grip scope rail. **Features:** Velocity 1020 fps (177), 800 fps (22), 675 fps (25). Patented rotating breech design. Maxi-Grip scope rail protects optics from recoil; automatic anti-beartrap plus manual safety. Imported from U.K. by Precision Sales International, Inc.
Price: $479.99
Price: MKII Carbine (14" barrel, 39-1/2" overall) $479.99

BSA MAGNUM SUPERSPORT™ AIR RIFLE
Caliber: 177, 22, 25, single shot. **Barrel:** 18". **Weight:** 6 lbs., 8 oz. **Length:** 41" overall. **Power:** Spring-air, barrel cocking. **Stock:** Oil-finished hardwood; Monte Carlo with cheekpiece, recoil pad. **Sights:** Ramp front, micrometer adjustable rear. Maxi-Grip scope rail. **Features:** Velocity 1020 fps (177), 800 fps (22), 675 fps (25). Patented Maxi-Grip scope rail protects optics from recoil; automatic anti-beartrap plus manual tang safety. Muzzle brake standard. Imported for U.K. by Precision Sales International, Inc.
Price: $279.99
Price: Carbine, 14" barrel, muzzle brake $299.99

BSA MAGNUM GOLDSTAR MAGNUM AIR RIFLE
Caliber: 177, 22, 10-shot repeater. **Barrel:** 18". **Weight:** 8 lbs, 8 oz. **Length:** 42.5" overall. **Power:** Spring-air, underlever cocking. **Stock:** Oil-finished hardwood; Monte Carlo with cheekpiece, checkered at grip; recoil pad. **Sights:** Ramp front, micrometer adjustable rear; comes with Maxi-Grip scope rail. **Features:** Velocity 1020 fps (177), 800 fps (22). Patented 10-shot indexing magazine; Maxi-Grip scope rail protects optics from recoil; automatic anti-beartrap plus manual safety; muzzlebrake standard. Imported from U.K. by Precision Sales International, Inc.
Price: $699.99

BSA MAGNUM SUPERTEN AIR RIFLE
Caliber: 177, 22 10-shot repeater. **Barrel:** 17-1/2". **Weight:** 7 lbs., 8 oz. **Length:** 37" overall. **Power:** Precharged pneumatic via buddy bottle. **Stock:** Oil-finished hardwood; Monte Carlo with cheekpiece, cut checkering at grip; adjustable recoil pad. **Sights:** No sights; intended for scope use. **Features:** Velocity 1300+ fps (177), 1000+ fps (22). Patented 10-shot indexing magazine, bolt-action loading. Left-hand version also available. Imported from U.K. by Precision Sales International, Inc.
Price: $879.99
Price: Left-hand $1,069.00

BSA METEOR MK6 AIR RIFLE
Caliber: 177, 22, single shot. **Barrel:** 18". **Weight:** 6 lbs. **Length:** 41" overall. **Power:** Spring-air, barrel cocking. **Stock:** Oil-finished hardwood. **Sights:** Ramp front, micrometer adjustable rear. **Features:** Velocity 650 fps (177), 500 fps (22). Automatic anti-beartrap; manual tang safety. Receiver grooved for scope mounting. Imported from U.K. by Precision Sales International, Inc.
Price: Rifle $199.99
Price: Carbine $219.99

COPPERHEAD BLACK SERPENT RIFLE
Caliber: 177 pellets, 5-shot, on BB, 195-shot magazine. **Barrel:** 19-1/2" smoothbore steel. **Weight:** 2 lbs., 14 oz. **Length:** 35-7/8" overall. **Power:** Pneumatic, single pump. **Stock:** Textured plastic. **Sights:** Blade front, open adjustable rear. **Features:** Velocity to 405 fps. Introduced 1996. Made in U.S. by Crosman Corp.
Price: About $48.00

CROSMAN CHALLENGER 2000 AIR RIFLE
Caliber: 177, single shot. **Barrel:** N/A. **Weight:** 6.95 lbs. **Power:** CO2 Powerlet. **Length:** 36 1/4" overall. **Stock:** Black synthetic with adjustable buttplate and cheekpiece. **Sights:** Hooded front, micrometer-adjustable aperture rear. **Features:** Up to 485 fps. Two-stage trigger; accessory rail on forearm. Designed for competition shooting. Introduced 2001. Made in U.S. by Crosman Corp.
Price: $299.00

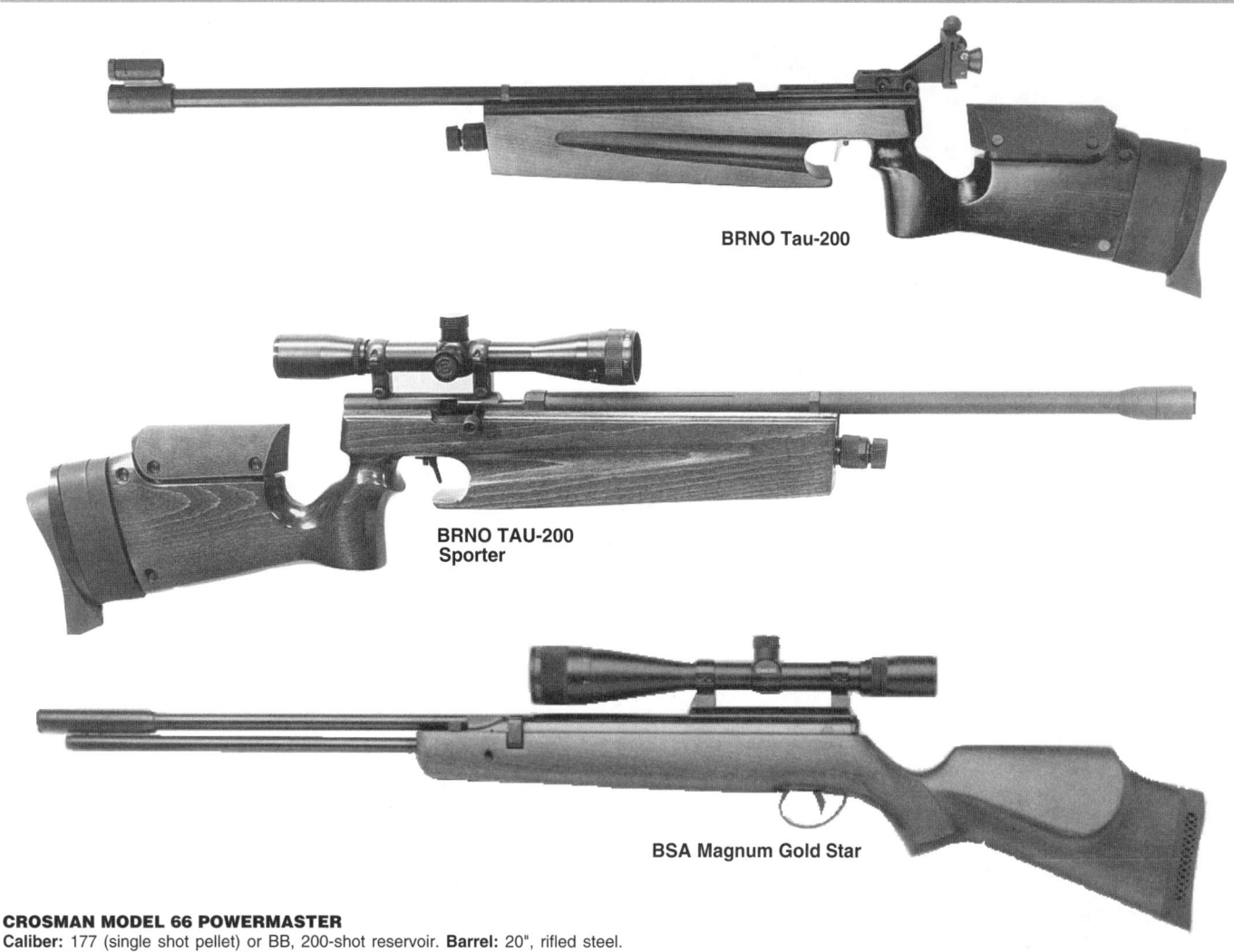

AIRGUNS—LONG GUNS

BRNO Tau-200

BRNO TAU-200 Sporter

BSA Magnum Gold Star

CROSMAN MODEL 66 POWERMASTER
Caliber: 177 (single shot pellet) or BB, 200-shot reservoir. **Barrel:** 20", rifled steel. **Weight:** 3 lbs. **Length:** 38-1/2" overall. **Power:** Pneumatic; hand pumped. **Stock:** Wood-grained ABS plastic; checkered pistol grip and forend. **Sights:** Ramp front, fully adjustable open rear. **Features:** Velocity about 645 fps. Bolt action, cross-bolt safety. Introduced 1983. From Crosman.
Price: About $60.00
Price: Model 664X (as above, with 4x scope) $70.00
Price: Model 664SB (as above with silver and black finish), about $75.00
Price: Model 664GT (black and gold finish, 4x scope) about $73.00

CROSMAN MODEL 760 PUMPMASTER
Caliber: 177 pellets (single shot) or BB (200-shot reservoir). **Barrel:** 19-1/2", rifled steel. **Weight:** 2 lbs., 12 oz. **Length:** 33.5" overall. **Power:** Pneumatic, hand pumped. **Stock:** Walnut-finished ABS plastic stock and forend. **Features:** Velocity to 590 fps (BBs, 10 pumps). Short stroke, power determined by number of strokes. Post front sight and adjustable rear sight. Cross-bolt safety. Introduced 1966. From Crosman.
Price: About $40.00
Price: Model 760SB (silver and black finish), about $55.00

CROSMAN MODEL 782 BLACK DIAMOND AIR RIFLE
Caliber: 177 pellets (5-shot clip) or BB (195-shot reservoir). **Barrel:** 18", rifled steel. **Weight:** 3 lbs. **Power:** CO2 Powerlet. **Stock:** Wood-grained ABS plastic; checkered grip and forend. **Sights:** Blade front, open adjustable rear. **Features:** Velocity up to 595 fps (pellets), 650 fps (BB). Black finish with white diamonds. Introduced 1990. From Crosman.
Price: About $63.00

CROSMAN MODEL 795 SPRING MASTER RIFLE
Caliber: 177, single shot. **Barrel:** Rifled steel. **Weight:** 4 lbs., 8 oz. **Length:** 42" overall. **Power:** Spring-piston. **Stock:** Black synthetic. **Sights:** Hooded front, fully adjustable rear. **Features:** Velocity about 550 fps. Introduced 1995. From Crosman.
Price: About $90.00

CROSMAN MODEL 1077 REPEATAIR RIFLE
Caliber: 177 pellets, 12-shot clip. **Barrel:** 20.3", rifled steel. **Weight:** 3 lbs., 11 oz. **Length:** 38.8" overall. **Power:** CO2 Powerlet. **Stock:** Textured synthetic or American walnut. **Sights:** Blade front, fully adjustable rear. **Features:** Velocity 590 fps. Removable 12-shot clip. True semi-automatic action. Introduced 1993. From Crosman.
Price: About $75.00
Price: 1077W (walnut stock) $110.00

CROSMAN 2264 X AIR RIFLE
Caliber: 22, single shot. **Barrel:** 24". **Weight:** 5 lbs., 12 oz. **Length:** 39.75" overall. **Power:** C02 Powerlet. **Stock:** Hardwood. **Sights:** Blade front, adjustable rear; includes 4x32 scope, rings and base included. **Features:** About 600 fps. Scoped version of 2260 rifle. Introduced 2001. Made in U.S. by Crosman Corp.
Price: $159.95

CROSMAN 2260 AIR RIFLE
Caliber: 22, single shot. **Barrel:** 24". **Weight:** 4 lbs., 12 oz. **Length:** 39.75" overall. **Power:** CO2 Powerlet. **Stock:** Hardwood. **Sights:** Blade front, adjustable rear open or peep. **Features:** About 600 fps. Made in U.S. by Crosman Corp.
Price: . . . . NA

CROSMAN MODEL 2289 RIFLE
Caliber: .22, single shot. **Barrel:** 14.625", rifled steel. **Weight:** 3 lbs 3 oz. **Length:** 31" overall. **Power:** Hand pumped, pneumatic. **Stock:** Composition, skeletal type. **Sights:** Blade front, rear adjustable for windage and elevation. **Features:** Velocity to 575 fps. Detachable stock. Metal parts blued. From Crosman.
Price: About $73.00

CROSMAN MODEL 2100 CLASSIC AIR RIFLE
Caliber: 177 pellets (single shot), or BB (200-shot BB reservoir). **Barrel:** 21", rifled. **Weight:** 4 lbs., 13 oz. **Length:** 39-3/4" overall. **Power:** Pump-up, pneumatic. **Stock:** Wood-grained checkered ABS plastic. **Features:** Three pumps give about 450 fps, 10 pumps about 755 fps (BBs). Cross-bolt safety; concealed reservoir holds over 200 BBs. From Crosman.
Price: About $75.00
Price: Model 2104GT (black and gold finish, 4x scope), about $95.00
Price: Model 2100W (walnut stock, pellets only), about $120.00

AIRGUNS—LONG GUNS

Crosman Model 760

Crosman Model 795

Crosman Model 2289

CROSMAN MODEL 2200 MAGNUM AIR RIFLE
Caliber: 22, single shot. **Barrel:** 19", rifled steel. **Weight:** 4 lbs., 12 oz. **Length:** 39" overall. **Stock:** Full-size, wood-grained ABS plastic with checkered grip and forend or American walnut. **Sights:** Ramp front, open step-adjustable rear. **Features:** Variable pump power—three pumps give 395 fps, six pumps 530 fps, 10 pumps 595 fps (average). Full-size adult air rifle. Has white line spacers at pistol grip and buttplate. Introduced 1978. From Crosman.
Price: About $75.00
Price: 2200W, about. $120.00

DAISY MODEL 840
Caliber: 177 pellet single shot; or BB 350-shot. **Barrel:** 19", smoothbore, steel. **Weight:** 2.7 lbs. **Length:** 36.8" overall. **Power:** Pneumatic, single pump. **Stock:** Moulded wood-grain stock and forend. **Sights:** Ramp front, open, adjustable rear. **Features:** Muzzle velocity 335 fps (BB), 300 fps (pellet). Steel buttplate; straight pull bolt action; cross-bolt safety. Forend forms pump lever. Introduced 1978. From Daisy Mfg. Co.
Price: About $32.95

DAISY/POWERLINE 853
Caliber: 177 pellets. **Barrel:** 20.9"; 12-groove rifling, high-grade solid steel by Lothar Waltherô, precision crowned; bore size for precision match pellets. **Weight:** 5.08 lbs. **Length:** 38.9" overall. **Power:** Single-pump pneumatic. **Stock:** Full-length, select American hardwood, stained and finished; black buttplate with white spacers. **Sights:** Globe front with four aperture inserts; precision micrometer adjustable rear peep sight mounted on a standard 3/8" dovetail receiver mount. **Features:** Single shot. From Daisy Mfg. Co.
Price: About $225.00

DAISY/POWERLINE 856 PUMP-UP AIRGUN
Caliber: 177 pellets (single shot) or BB (100-shot reservoir). **Barrel:** Rifled steel with shroud. **Weight:** 2.7 lbs. **Length:** 37.4" overall. **Power:** Pneumatic pump-up. **Stock:** Moulded wood-grain with Monte Carlo cheekpiece. **Sights:** Ramp and blade front, open rear adjustable for elevation. **Features:** Velocity from 315 fps (two pumps) to 650 fps (10 pumps). Shoots BBs or pellets. Heavy die-cast metal receiver. Cross-bolt trigger-block safety. Introduced 1984. From Daisy Mfg. Co.
Price: About $39.95

DAISY MODEL 990 DUAL-POWER AIR RIFLE
Caliber: 177 pellets (single shot) or BB (100-shot magazine). **Barrel:** Rifled steel. **Weight:** 4.1 lbs. **Length:** 37.4" overall. **Power:** Pneumatic pump-up and 12-gram CO2. **Stock:** Moulded woodgrain. **Sights:** Ramp and blade front, adjustable open rear. **Features:** Velocity to 650 fps (BB), 630 fps (pellet). Choice of pump or CO2 power. Shoots BBs or pellets. Heavy die-cast receiver dovetailed for scope mount. Cross-bolt trigger block safety. Introduced 1993. From Daisy Mfg. Co.
Price: About $58.95

DAISY 1938 RED RYDER 60th ANNIVERSARY CLASSIC
Caliber: BB, 650-shot repeating action. **Barrel:** Smoothbore steel with shroud. **Weight:** 2.2 lbs. **Length:** 35.4" overall. **Stock:** Walnut stock burned with Red Ryder lariat signature. **Sights:** Post front, adjustable V-slot rear. **Features:** Walnut forend. Saddle ring with leather thong. Lever cocking. Gravity feed. Controlled velocity. One of Daisy's most popular guns. From Daisy Mfg. Co.
Price: About $39.95

DAISY/POWERLINE 1170 PELLET RIFLE
Caliber: 177, single shot. **Barrel:** Rifled steel. **Weight:** 5.5 lbs. **Length:** 42.5" overall. **Power:** Spring-air, barrel cocking. **Stock:** Hardwood. **Sights:** Hooded post front, micrometer adjustable open rear. **Features:** Velocity to 800 fps. Monte Carlo comb. Introduced 1995. From Daisy Mfg. Co.
Price: About $129.95
Price: Model 131 (velocity to 600 fps) $117.95
Price: Model 1150 (black copolymer stock, velocity to 600 fps). $77.95

DAISY/POWERLINE EAGLE 7856 PUMP-UP AIRGUN
Caliber: 177 (pellets), BB, 100-shot BB magazine. **Barrel:** Rifled steel with shroud. **Weight:** 3.3 lbs. **Length:** 37.4" overall. **Power:** Pneumatic pump-up. **Stock:** Moulded wood-grain plastic. **Sights:** Ramp and blade front, open rear adjustable for elevation. **Features:** Velocity from 315 fps (two pumps) to 650 fps (10 pumps). Finger grooved forend. Cross-bolt trigger-block safety. Introduced 1985. From Daisy Mfg. Co.
Price: With 4x scope, about $49.95

DAISY/POWERLINE 880
Caliber: 177 pellet or BB, 50-shot BB magazine, single shot for pellets. **Barrel:** Rifled steel. **Weight:** 3.7 lbs. **Length:** 37.6" overall. **Power:** Multi-pump pneumatic. **Stock:** Moulded wood grain; Monte Carlo comb. **Sights:** Hooded front, adjustable rear. **Features:** Velocity to 685 fps. (BB). Variable power (velocity and range) increase with pump strokes; resin receiver with dovetail scope mount. Introduced 1997. Made in U.S. by Daisy Mfg. Co.
Price: About $50.95
Price: Model 4880 with Glo-Point fiber optic sight $57.95

DAISY/POWERLINE 1000 AIR RIFLE
Caliber: 177, single shot. **Barrel:** NA. **Weight:** 6.15 lbs. **Length:** 43" overall. **Power:** Spring-air, barrel cocking. **Stock:** Stained hardwood. **Sights:** Hooded blade front on ramp, fully adjustable micrometer rear. **Features:** Velocity to 1000 fps. Blued finish; trigger block safety. Introduced 1997. From Daisy Mfg. Co.
Price: About $208.95

DAISY/YOUTHLINE MODEL 105 AIR RIFLE
Caliber: BB, 400-shot magazine. **Barrel:** 13-1/2". **Weight:** 1.6 lbs. **Length:** 29.8" overall. **Power:** Spring. **Stock:** Moulded woodgrain. **Sights:** Blade on ramp front, fixed rear. **Features:** Velocity to 275 fps. Blue finish. Cross-bolt trigger block safety. Made in U.S. by Daisy Mfg. Co.
Price: $28.95

AIRGUNS—LONG GUNS

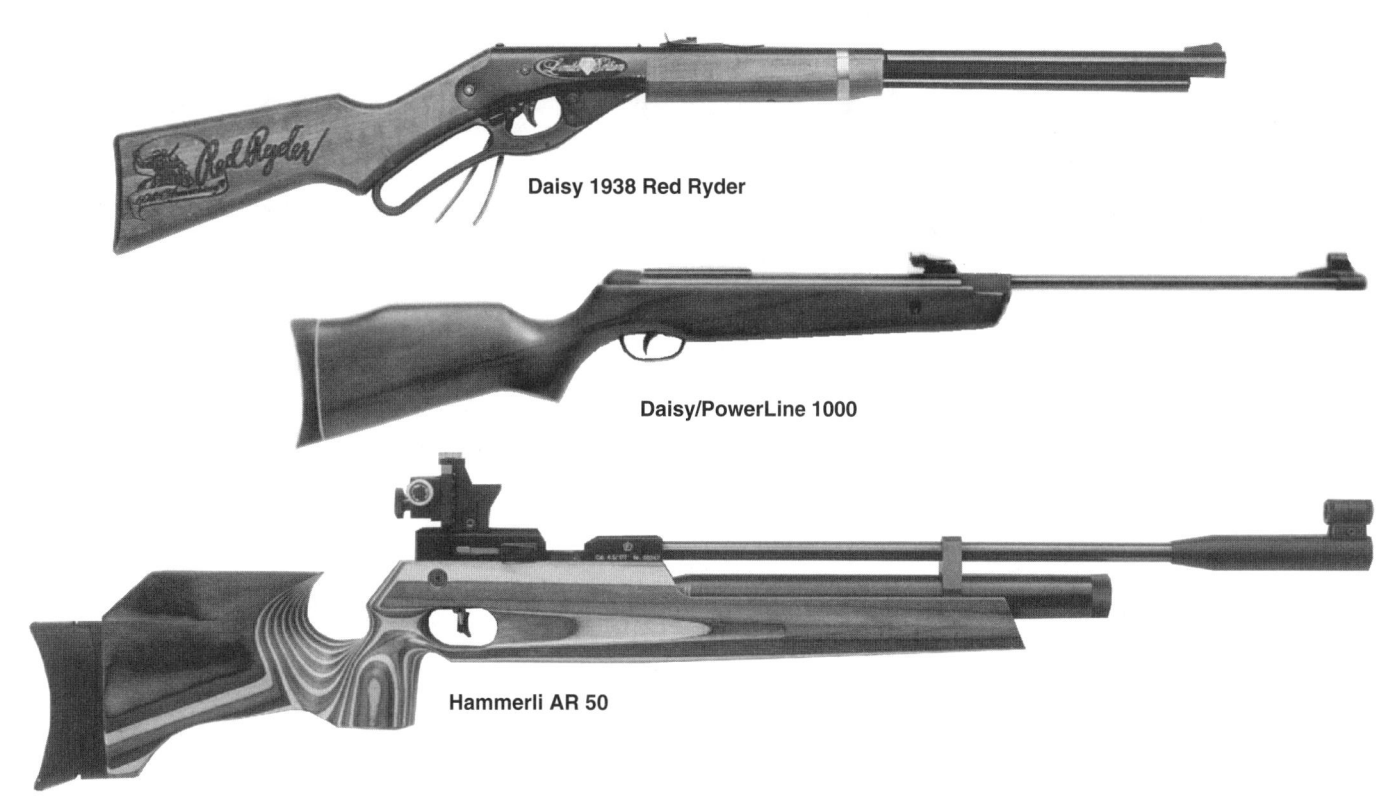

Daisy 1938 Red Ryder

Daisy/PowerLine 1000

Hammerli AR 50

DAISY/YOUTHLINE MODEL 95 AIR RIFLE
Caliber: BB, 700-shot magazine. **Barrel:** 18". **Weight:** 2.4 lbs. **Length:** 35.2" overall. **Power:** Spring. **Stock:** Stained hardwood. **Sights:** Blade on ramp front, open adjustable rear. **Features:** Velocity to 325 fps. Cross-bolt trigger block safety. Made in U.S. by Daisy Mfg. Co.
Price: $38.95

EAA/BAIKAL IZH-32BK AIR RIFLE
Caliber: 177 pellet, single shot. **Barrel:** 11.68". **Weight:** 12.13 lbs. **Length:** 47.24" overall. **Power:** Single-stroke pneumatic. **Stock:** Walnut with full pistol grip, adjustable cheek piece and butt stock. **Sights:** None; integral rail for scope mount. **Features:** Velocity 541 fps. Side-cocking mechanism; hammer-forged, rifled barrel; five-way adjustable trigger. Designed for 10-meter running target competition. Introduced 2000. Imported from Russia by European American Armory.
Price: $1,099.00

EAA/BAIKAL IZH-61 AIR RIFLE
Caliber: 177 pellet, 5-shot magazine. **Barrel:** 17.75". **Weight:** 6.39 lbs. **Length:** 30.98" overall. **Power:** Spring piston, side-cocking lever. **Stock:** Black plastic. **Sights:** Adjustable rear, fully hooded front. **Features:** Velocity 490 fps. Futuristic design with adjustable stock. Imported from Russia by European American Armory.
Price: $99.00

EAA/BAIKAL MP-512 AIR RIFLE
Caliber: 177 or 22 pellet, single shot. **Barrel:** 17.7". **Weight:** 6.17 lbs. **Length:** 41.34" overall. **Power:** Spring-piston, single stroke. **Stock:** Black synthetic. **Sights:** Adjustable rear, hooded front. **Features:** Velocity 490 fps. Hammer-forged, rifled barrel; automatic safety; scope mount rail. Introduced 2000. Imported from Russia by European American Armory.
Price: 177 caliber $50.00
Price: 22 caliber $63.00

EAA/BAIKAL MP-532 AIR RIFLE
Caliber: 177 pellet, single shot. **Barrel:** 15.75". **Weight:** 9.26 lbs. **Length:** 46.06" overall. **Power:** Single-stroke pneumatic. **Stock:** One- or two-piece competition-style stock with adjustable butt pad, pistol grip. **Sights:** Fully adjustable rear, hooded front. **Features:** Velocity 460 fps. Five-way adjustable trigger. Introduced 2000. Imported from Russia by European American Armory.
Price: $599.00

HAMMERLI AR 50 AIR RIFLE
Caliber: 177. **Barrel:** 19.8". **Weight:** 10 lbs. **Length:** 43.2" overall. **Power:** Compressed air. **Stock:** Anatomically-shaped universal and right-hand; match style; multi-colored laminated wood. **Sights:** Interchangeable element tunnel front, fully adjustable Hammerli peep rear. **Features:** Vibration-free firing release; fully adjustable match trigger and trigger stop; stainless air tank, built-in pressure gauge. Gives 270 shots per filling. Introduced 1998. Imported from Switzerland by Sigarms, Inc.
Price: . . . . $1,062.50 to $1,400.00

HAMMERLI MODEL 450 MATCH AIR RIFLE
Caliber: 177, single shot. **Barrel:** 19.5". **Weight:** 9.8 lbs. **Length:** 43.3" overall. **Power:** Pneumatic. **Stock:** Match style with stippled grip, rubber buttpad. Beach or walnut. **Sights:** Match tunnel front, Hammerli diopter rear. **Features:** Velocity about 560 fps. Removable sights; forend sling rail; adjustable trigger; adjustable comb. Introduced 1994. Imported from Switzerland by Sigarms, Inc.
Price: Beech stock $1,355.00
Price: Walnut stock. $1,395.00

MARKSMAN BB BUDDY AIR RIFLE
Caliber: 177, 20-shot magazine. **Barrel:** 10.5" smoothbore. **Weight:** 1.6 lbs. **Length:** 33" overall. **Power:** Spring-air. **Stock:** Moulded composition. **Sights:** Blade on ramp front, adjustable V-slot rear. **Features:** Velocity 275 fps. Positive feed; automatic safety. Youth-sized lightweight design. Introduced 1998. Made in U.S. From Marksman Products.
Price: $27.95

MARKSMAN 1798 COMPETITION TRAINER AIR RIFLE
Caliber: 177, single shot. **Barrel:** 15", rifled. **Weight:** 4.7 lbs. **Power:** Spring-air, barrel cocking. **Stock:** Synthetic. **Sights:** Laserhawk fiber optic front, match-style diopter rear. **Features:** Velocity about 495 fps. Automatic safety. Introduced 1998. Made in U.S. From Marksman Products.
Price: $70.00

MARKSMAN 1745 BB REPEATER AIR RIFLE
Caliber: 177 BB or pellet, 18-shot BB reservoir. **Barrel:** 15-1/2", rifled. **Weight:** 4.75 lbs. **Length:** 36" overall. **Power:** Spring-air. **Stock:** Moulded composition with ambidextrous Monte Carlo cheekpiece and rubber recoil pad. **Sights:** Hooded front, adjustable rear. **Features:** Velocity about 450 fps. Break-barrel action; automatic safety. Uses BBs, pellets, darts or bolts. Introduced 1997. Made in the U.S. From Marksman Products.
Price: $58.00
Price: Model 1745S (same as above except comes with #1804 4x20 scope) . $73.00

MARKSMAN 1790 BIATHLON TRAINER
Caliber: 177, single shot. **Barrel:** 15", rifled. **Weight:** 4.7 lbs. **Power:** Spring-air, barrel cocking. **Stock:** Synthetic. **Sights:** Hooded front, match-style diopter rear. **Features:** Velocity of 450 fps. Endorsed by the U.S. Shooting Team. Introduced 1989. From Marksman Products.
Price: $70.00

MARKSMAN 2015 LASERHAWK™ BB REPEATER AIR RIFLE
Caliber: 177 BB, 20-shot magazine. **Barrel:** 10.5" smoothbore. **Weight:** 1.6 lbs. **Length:** Adjustable to 33", 34" or 35" overall. **Power:** Spring-air. **Stock:** Moulded composition. **Sights:** Fixed fiber optic front sight, adjustable elevation V-slot rear. **Features:** Velocity about 275 fps. Positive feed; automatic safety. Adjustable stock. Introduced 1997. Made in the U.S. From Marksman Products.
Price: $33.00

AIRGUNS—LONG GUNS

Marksman 1790

RWS Model 24C

RWS/DIANA MODEL 24 AIR RIFLE
Caliber: 177, 22, single shot. Barrel: 17", rifled. Weight: 6 lbs. Length: 42" overall. Power: Spring-air, barrel cocking. Stock: Beech. Sights: Hooded front, adjustable rear. Features: Velocity of 700 fps (177). Easy cocking effort; blue finish. Imported from Germany by Dynamit Nobel-RWS, Inc.
Price: $215.00
Price: Model 24C $215.00

RWS/Diana Model 34 Air Rifle
Similar to the Model 24 except has 19" barrel, weighs 7.5 lbs. Gives velocity of 1000 fps (177), 800 fps (22). Adjustable trigger, synthetic seals. Comes with scope rail.
Price: 177 or 22 .... $290.00
Price: Model 34N (nickel-plated metal, black epoxy-coated wood stock) ... $350.00
Price: Model 34BC (matte black metal, black stock, 4x32 scope, mounts) .. $510.00

RWS/DIANA MODEL 36 AIR RIFLE
Caliber: 177, 22, single shot. Barrel: 19", rifled. Weight: 8 lbs. Length: 45" overall. Power: Spring-air, barrel cocking. Stock: Beech. Sights: Hooded front (interchangeable inserts available), adjustable rear. Features: Velocity of 1000 fps (177-cal.). Comes with scope mount; two-stage adjustable trigger. Imported from Germany by Dynamit Nobel-RWS, Inc.
Price: $435.00
Price: Model 36 Carbine (same as Model 36 rifle except has 15" barrel) ... $435.00

RWS/DIANA MODEL 52 AIR RIFLE
Caliber: 177, 22, single shot. Barrel: 17", rifled. Weight: 8-1/2 lbs. Length: 43" overall. Power: Spring-air, sidelever cocking. Stock: Beech, with Monte Carlo, cheekpiece, checkered grip and forend. Sights: Ramp front, adjustable rear. Features: Velocity of 1100 fps (177). Blue finish. Solid rubber buttpad. Imported from Germany by Dynamit Nobel-RWS, Inc.
Price: $565.00
Price: Model 52 Deluxe (select walnut stock, rosewood grip and forend caps, palm swell grip). $810.00
Price: Model 48B (as above except matte black metal, black stock) $535.00
Price: Model 48 (same as Model 52 except no Monte Carlo, cheekpiece or checkering)................................. $510.00

RWS/DIANA MODEL 45 AIR RIFLE
Caliber: 177, single shot. Weight: 8 lbs. Length: 45" overall. Power: Spring-air, barrel cocking. Stock: Walnut-finished hardwood with rubber recoil pad. Sights: Globe front with interchangeable inserts, micro. click open rear with four-way blade. Features: Velocity of 820 fps. Dovetail base for either micrometer peep sight or scope mounting. Automatic safety. Imported from Germany by Dynamit Nobel-RWS, Inc.
Price: $350.00

RWS/DIANA MODEL 46 AIR RIFLE
Caliber: 177, 22, single shot. Barrel: 18". Weight: 8.2 lbs. Length: 45" overall. Stock: Hardwood Monte Carlo. Sights: Blade front, adjustable rear. Features: Underlever cocking spring-air (950 fps in 177, 780 fps in 22); extended scope rail, automatic safety, rubber buttpad, adjustable trigger. Imported from Germany by Dynamit Nobel-RWS Inc.
Price: .... $430.00 to $470.00

RWS/DIANA MODEL 54 AIR RIFLE
Caliber: 177, 22, single shot. Barrel: 17". Weight: 9 lbs. Length: 43" overall. Power: Spring-air, sidelever cocking. Stock: Walnut with Monte Carlo cheekpiece, checkered grip and forend. Sights: Ramp front, fully adjustable rear. Features: Velocity to 1000 fps (177), 900 fps (22). Totally recoilless system; floating action absorbs recoil. Imported from Germany by Dynamit Nobel-RWS, Inc.
Price: $785.00

RWS/DIANA MODEL 93/94 AIR RIFLES
Caliber: 177, 22, single shot. Barrel: N/A. Weight: N/A. Length: N/A. Stock: Beechwood; Monte Carlo. Sights: Hooded front, fully adjustable rear. Features: Break-barrel, spring-air; receiver grooved for scope; adjustable trigger; lifetime warranty. Imported from Spain by Dynamit Nobel-RWS Inc.
Price: Model 93 (manual safety, 850 fps in 177) $180.00
Price: Model 94 (auto safety, 1,000 fps in 177) $225.00

RWS/DIANA MODEL 350 MAGNUM AIR RIFLE
Caliber: 177, single shot. Barrel: 19-1/2". Weight: 8 lbs. Length: 48". Stock: Beechwood; Monte Carlo. Sights: Hooded front, fully adjustable rear. Features: Break-barrel, spring-air; 1,250 fps. Imported from Germany by Dynamit Nobel-RWS Inc.
Price: Model 350 .... $600.00

RWS/DIANA MODEL 707/EXCALIBRE AIR RIFLES
Caliber: 22, 25, 9mm, 8-shot lever-action repeater or side-loading single shot. Barrel: 23". Weight: 7 to 9 1/4 lbs. Length: 40" to 42" overall. Stock: Checkered walnut. Sights: Hooded post front, fully adjustable rear (Excalibre has no sights, integral scope grooves). Features: Pre-charged pneumatic stores compressed air from SCUBA tank or optional hand pump in reservoir for 18 to 30 shots at full power (adjustable power to 1,200 fps in 22 cal.); pressure gauge; adjustable trigger (9mm and Excalibre). Imported from Germany by Dynamit Nobel-RWS Inc.
Price: 707 (22, 25, 9 mm) $730.00
Price: 707 Carbine (22) $730.00
Price: Excalibre (22, 25)................................... $840.00

SAVAGE MODEL 1000G AIR RIFLE
Caliber: 177 pellet, single shot. Barrel: 18". Weight: 7.25 lbs. Length: 45.3" overall. Power: Spring piston, break-barrel action. Stock: Walnut-finished hardwood with recoil pad. Sights: Adjustable rear notch, hooded front post. Features: Velocity 1,000 fps. Also available with 2.5-power scope. Introduced 2000. From Savage Arms.
Price: $181.00

SAVAGE MODEL 600F AIR RIFLE
Caliber: 177 pellet, 25-shot tubular magazine. Barrel: 18" polymer-coated steel. Weight: 6 lbs. Length: 40" overall. Power: spring piston, break-barrel action. Stock: Black polymer stock with lacquer finish. Sights: Adjustable rear notch, hooded front post. Features: Velocity 600 fps. Repeating action. Also available with 2.5-power scope. Introduced 2000. From Savage Arms.
Price: $126.00

SAVAGE MODEL 560F AIR RIFLE
Caliber: 177 pellet, single shot. Barrel: 18" polymer-coated steel. Weight: 5.5 lbs. Length: 39" overall. Power: Spring piston, break-barrel action. Stock: Metallic-black finished polymer stock. Sights: Adjustable notch rear, post front. Features: Velocity 560 fps. Introduced 2000. From Savage Arms.
Price: $92.00

AIRGUNS—LONG GUNS

Savage Model 600F

Savage Model 560F

Whiscombe JW70 FB

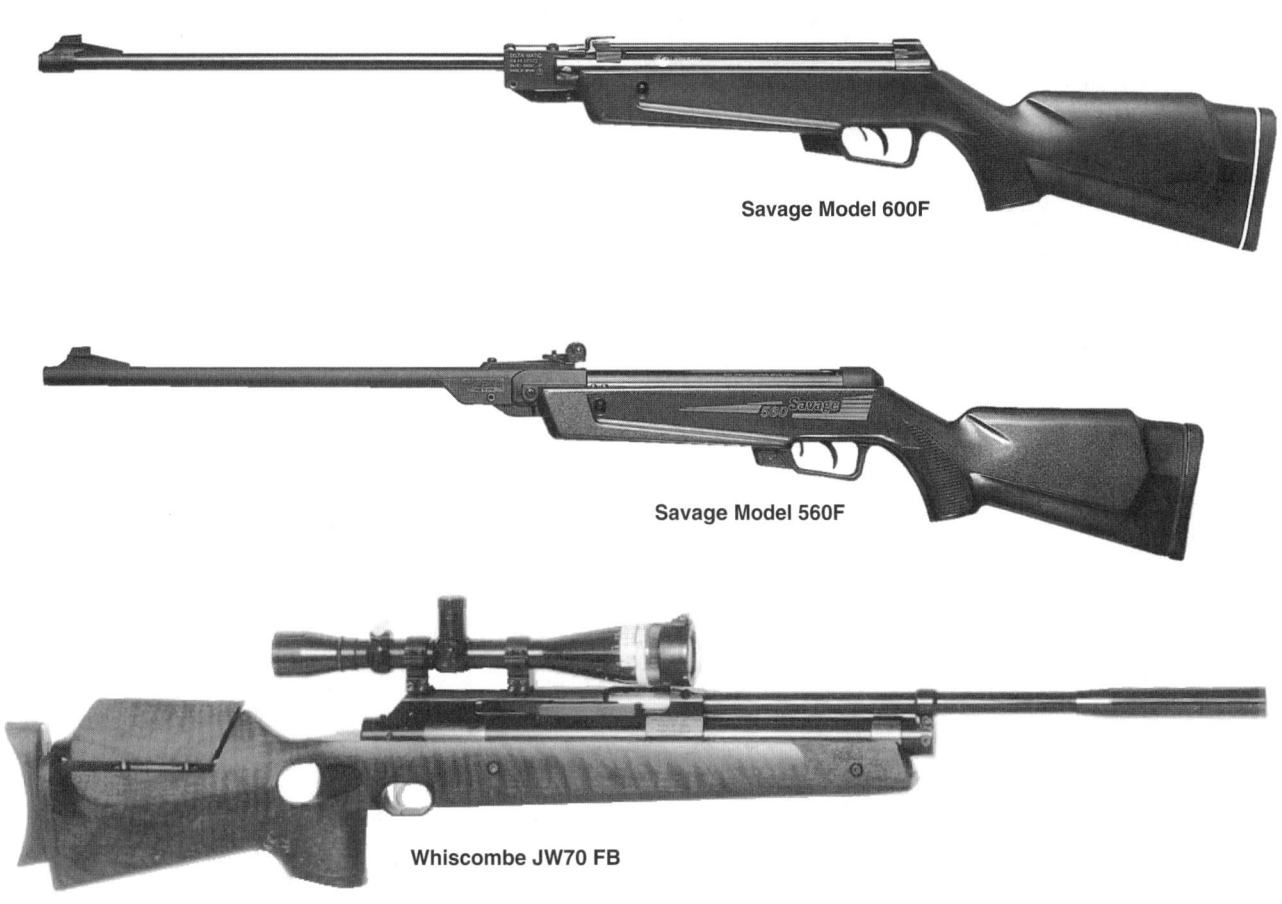

TECH FORCE BS4 OLYMPIC COMPETITION AIR RIFLE
Caliber: 177 pellet, single shot. **Barrel:** N/A. **Weight:** 10.8 lbs. **Length:** 43.3" overall. **Power:** Spring piston, sidelever action. **Stock:** Wood with semi-pistol grip, adjustable butt plate. **Sights:** Micro-adjustable competition rear, hooded front. **Features:** Velocity 640 fps. Recoilless action; adjustable trigger. Includes carrying case. Imported from China by Compasseco Inc.
Price: $595.00
Price: Optional diopter rear sight. $79.95

TECH FORCE 6 AIR RIFLE
Caliber: 177 pellet, single shot. **Barrel:** 14". **Weight:** 6 lbs. **Length:** 35.5" overall. **Power:** Sspring piston, sidelever action. **Stock:** Paratrooper-style folding, full pistol grip. **Sights:** Adjustable rear, hooded front. **Features:** Velocity 800 fps. All-metal construction; grooved for scope mounting. Imported from China by Compasseco Inc.
Price: $69.95

Tech Force 51 Air Rifle
Similar to Tech Force 6, but with break-barrel cocking mechanism and folding stock fitted with recoil pad. Overall length, 36". Weighs 6 lbs. From Compasseco Inc.
Price: $69.95

TECH FORCE 25 AIR RIFLE
Caliber: 177, 22 pellet; single shot. **Barrel:** N/A. **Weight:** 7.5 lbs. **Length:** 46.2" overall. **Power:** Spring piston, break-action barrel. **Stock:** Oil-finished wood; Monte Carlo stock with recoil pad. **Sights:** Adjustable rear, hooded front with insert. **Features:** Velocity 1,000 fps (177); grooved receiver and scope stop for scope mounting; adjustable trigger; trigger safety. Imported from China by Compasseco Inc.
Price: 177 or 22 caliber $125.00
Price: Includes rifle and Tech Force 96 red dot point sight $164.95

TECH FORCE 36 AIR RIFLE
Caliber: 177 pellet, single shot. **Barrel:** N/A. **Weight:** 7.4 lbs. **Length:** 43" overall. **Power:** Spring piston, underlever cocking. **Stock:** Monte Carlo hardwood stock; recoil pad. **Sights:** Adjustable rear, hooded front. **Features:** Velocity 900 fps; grooved receiver and scope stop for scope mounting; auto-reset safety. Imported from China by Compasseco Inc.
Price: $89.95

WHISCOMBE JW SERIES AIR RIFLES
Caliber: 177, 20, 22, 25, single shot. **Barrel:** 15", Lothar Walther. Polygonal rifling. **Weight:** 9 lbs., 8 oz. **Length:** 39" overall. **Power:** Dual spring-piston, multi-stroke; underlever cocking. **Stock:** Walnut with adjustable buttplate and cheekpiece. **Sights:** None furnished; grooved scope rail. **Features:** Velocity 660-1000 (JW80) fps (22-caliber, fixed barrel) depending upon model. Interchangeable barrels; automatic safety; muzzle weight; semi-floating action; twin opposed pistons with counter-wound springs; adjustable trigger. All models include H.O.T. System (Harmonic Optimization Tunable System). Introduced 1995. Imported from England by Pelaire Products.
Price: JW50, MKII fixed barrel only $1,895.00
Price: JW60, MKII fixed barrel only $1,895.00
Price: JW70, MKII fixed barrel only $1,950.00
Price: JW80, MKII. $1,995.00

34TH EDITION, 2002 • **327**

Manufacturers Directory

A

A Zone Bullets, 2039 Walter Rd., Billings, MT 59105 / 800-252-3111; FAX: 406-248-1961
A&B Industries,Inc (See Top-Line USA Inc)
A&M Waterfowl,Inc., P.O. Box 102, Ripley, TN 38063 / 901-635-4003; FAX: 901-635-2320
A&W Repair, 2930 Schneider Dr., Arnold, MO 63010 / 314-287-3725
A-Square Co.,Inc., One Industrial Park, Bedford, KY 40006-9667 / 502-255-7456; FAX: 502-255-7657
A-Tech Corp., P.O. Box 1281, Cottage Grove, OR 97424
A.A. Arms, Inc., 4811 Persimmont Ct., Monroe, NC 28110 / 704-289-5356 or 800-935-1119; FAX: 704-289-5859
A.B.S. III, 9238 St. Morritz Dr., Fern Creek, KY 40291
A.G. Russell Knives,Inc., 1705 Hwy. 71B North, Springdale, AR 72764 / 501-751-7341
A.R.M.S., Inc., 230 W. Center St., West Bridgewater, MA 02379-1620 / 508-584-7816; FAX: 508-588-8045
A.W. Peterson Gun Shop, Inc., 4255 W. Old U.S. 441, Mt. Dora, FL 32757-3299 / 352-383-4258; FAX: 352-735-1001
ABO (USA) Inc, 615 SW 2nd Avenue, Miami, FL 33130 / 305-859-2010 FAX: 305-859-2099
AC Dyna-tite Corp., 155 Kelly St., P.O. Box 0984, Elk Grove Village, IL 60007 / 847-593-5566; FAX: 847-593-1304
Acadian Ballistic Specialties, P.O. Box 787, Folsom, LA 70437 / 504-796-0078 gunsmith@neasolft.com
Accu-Tek, 4510 Carter Ct, Chino, CA 91710
Accupro Gun Care, 15512-109 Ave., Surrey, BC U3R 7E8 CANADA / 604-583-7807
Accura-Site (See All's, The Jim Tembelis Co., Inc.)
Accuracy Innovations, Inc., P.O. Box 376, New Paris, PA 15554 / 814-839-4517; FAX: 814-839-2601
Accuracy Int'l. North America, Inc., PO Box 5267, Oak Ridge, TN 37831 / 423-482-0330; FAX: 423-482-0336
Accuracy International, 9115 Trooper Trail, P.O. Box 2019, Bozeman, MT 59715 / 406-587-7922; FAX: 406-585-9434
Accuracy Internationl Precision Rifles (See U.S. Importer-Gunsite Custom Shop; Gunsite Training Center)
Accuracy Unlimited, 16036 N. 49 Ave., Glendale, AZ 85306 / 602-978-9089; FAX: 602-978-9089
Accuracy Unlimited, 7479 S. DePew St., Littleton, CO 80123
Accurate Arms Co., Inc., 5891 Hwy. 230 West, McEwen, TN 37101 / 800-416-3006 FAX: 931-729-4211
Accuright, RR 2 Box 397, Sebeka, MN 56477 / 218-472-3383
Ace Custom 45's, Inc., 1880 1/2 Upper Turtle Creek Rd., Kerrville, TX 78028 / 830-257-4290; FAX: 830-257-5724
Ace Sportswear, Inc., 700 Quality Rd., Fayetteville, NC 28306 / 919-323-1223; FAX: 919-323-5392
Ackerman & Co., Box 133 US Highway Rt. 7, Pownal, VT 05261 / 802-823-9874 muskets@togsther.net
Ackerman, Bill (See Optical Services Co)
Acra-Bond Laminates, 134 Zimmerman Rd., Kalispell, MT 59901 / 406-257-9003; FAX: 406-257-9003
Action Bullets & Alloy Inc, RR 1, P.O. Box 189, Quinter, KS 67752 / 913-754-3609; FAX: 913-754-3629
Action Direct, Inc., P.O. Box 830760, Miami, FL 33283 / 305-559-4652; FAX: 305-559-4652 action-direct.com
Action Products, Inc., 22 N. Mulberry St., Hagerstown, MD 21740 / 301-797-1414; FAX: 301-733-2073
Action Target, Inc., P.O. Box 636, Provo, UT 84603 / 801-377-8033; FAX: 801-377-8096
Actions by "T" Teddy Jacobson, 16315 Redwood Forest Ct., Sugar Land, TX 77478 / 281-277-4008
AcuSport Corporation, 1 Hunter Place, Bellefontaine, OH 43311-3001 / 513-593-7010 FAX: 513-592-5625
Ad Hominem, 3130 Gun Club Lane, RR, Orillia, ON L3V 6H3 CANADA / 705-689-5303; FAX: 705-689-5303
Adair Custom Shop, Bill, 2886 Westridge, Carrollton, TX 75006
Adams & Son Engravers, John J, 87 Acorn Rd., Dennis, MA 02638 / 508-385-7971
Adams Jr., John J., 87 Acorn Rd., Dennis, MA 02638 / 508-385-7971
ADCO Sales, Inc., 4 Draper St. #A, Woburn, MA 01801 / 781-935-1799; FAX: 781-935-1011
Adkins, Luther, 1292 E. McKay Rd., Shelbyville, IN 46176-8706 / 317-392-3795
Advance Car Mover Co., Rowell Div., P.O. Box 1, 240 N. Depot St., Juneau, WI 53039 / 414-386-4464; FAX: 414-386-4416
Adventure 16, Inc., 4620 Alvarado Canyon Rd., San Diego, CA 92120 / 619-283-6314

Adventure Game Calls, R.D. 1, Leonard Rd., Spencer, NY 14883 / 607-589-4611
Adventurer's Outpost, P.O. Box 547, Cottonwood, AZ 86326-0547 / 800-762-7471; FAX: 602-634-8781
Aero Peltor, 90 Mechanic St, Southbridge, MA 01550 / 508-764-5500; FAX: 508-764-0188
African Import Co., 22 Goodwin Rd, Plymouth, MA 02360 / 508-746-8552 FAX: 508-746-0404
AFSCO Ammunition, 731 W. Third St., P.O. Box L, Owen, WI 54460 / 715-229-2516
Ahlman Guns, 9525 W. 230th St., Morristown, MN 55052 / 507-685-4243; FAX: 507-685-4280
Ahrends, Kim (See Custom Firearms, Inc), Box 203, Clarion, IA 50525 / 515-532-3449; FAX: 515-532-3926
Aimpoint c/o Springfield, Inc., 420 W. Main St, Geneseo, IL 61254 / 309-944-1702
Aimtech Mount Systems, P.O. Box 223, Thomasville, GA 31799-1638 / 912-226-4313; FAX: 912-227-0222 aimtech@surfsouth.com www.aimtech-mounts.com
Air Arms, Hailsham Industrial Park, Diplocks Way, Hailsham, E. Sussex, BN27 3JF ENGLAND / 011-0323-845853
Air Rifle Specialists, P.O. Box 138, 130 Holden Rd., Pine City, NY 14871-0138 / 607-734-7340; FAX: 607-733-3261
Air Venture Airguns, 9752 E. Flower St., Bellflower, CA 90706 / 310-867-6355
Airgun Repair Centre, 3227 Garden Meadows, Lawrenceburg, IN 47025 / 812-637-1463; FAX: 812-637-1463
Airrow, 11 Monitor Hill Rd, Newtown, CT 06470 / 203-270-6343
Aitor-Cuchilleria Del Norte S.A., Izelaieta, 17, 48260, Ermua, S SPAIN / 43-17-08-50
Ajax Custom Grips, Inc., 9130 Viscount Row, Dallas, TX 75247 / 214-630-8893; FAX: 214-630-4942
Aker International, Inc., 2248 Main St., Suite 6, Chula Vista, CA 91911 / 619-423-5182; FAX: 619-423-1363
Al Lind Custom Guns, 7821 76th Ave. SW, Tacoma, WA 98498 / 206-584-6361
Alana Cupp Custom Engraver, P.O. Box 207, Annabella, UT 84711 / 801-896-4834
Alaska Bullet Works, Inc., 9978 Crazy Horse Drive, Juneau, AK 99801 / 907-789-3834; FAX: 907-789-3433
Alco Carrying Cases, 601 W. 26th St., New York, NY 10001 / 212-675-5820; FAX: 212-691-5935
Aldis Gunsmithing & Shooting Supply, 502 S. Montezuma St., Prescott, AZ 86303 / 602-445-6723; FAX: 602-445-6763
Alessi Holsters, Inc., 2465 Niagara Falls Blvd., Amherst, NY 14228-3527 / 716-691-5615
Alex, Inc., Box 3034, Bozeman, MT 59772 / 406-282-7396; FAX: 406-282-7396
Alfano, Sam, 36180 Henry Gaines Rd., Pearl River, LA 70452 / 504-863-3364; FAX: 504-863-7715
All American Lead Shot Corp., P.O. Box 224566, Dallas, TX 75062
All Rite Products, Inc., 5752 N. Silverstone Circle, Mountain Green, UT 84050 / 801-876-3330; FAX: 801-876-2216
All's, The Jim J. Tembelis Co., Inc., 216 Loper Ct., Neenah, WI 54956 / 920-725-5251; FAX: 920-725-5251
Allard, Gary/Creek Side Metal & Woodcrafters, Fishers Hill, VA 22626 / 703-465-3903
Allen Co., Bob, 214 SW Jackson, P.O. Box 477, Des Moines, IA 50315 / 515-283-2191 or 800-685-7020; FAX: 515-283-0779
Allen Co., Inc., 525 Burbank St., Broomfield, CO 80020 / 303-469-1857 or 800-876-8600; FAX: 303-466-7437
Allen Firearm Engraving, 339 Grove Ave., Prescott, AZ 86301 / 520-778-1237
Allen Mfg., 6449 Hodgson Rd., Circle Pines, MN 55014 / 612-429-8231
Allen Sportswear, Bob (See Allen Co., Bob)
Alley Supply Co., P.O. Box 848, Gardnerville, NV 89410 / 702-782-3800
Alliant Techsystems Smokeless Powder Group, 200 Valley Rd., Suite 305, Mt. Arlington, NJ 07856 / 800-276-9337; FAX: 201-770-2528
Allred Bullet Co., 932 Evergreen Drive, Logan, UT 84321 / 435-752-6983; FAX: 435-752-6983
Alpec Team, Inc., 201 Ricken Backer Cir., Livermore, CA 94550 / 510-606-8245; FAX: 510-606-4279
Alpha 1 Drop Zone, 2121 N. Tyler, Wichita, KS 67212 / 316-729-0800
Alpha Gunsmith Division, 1629 Via Monserate, Fallbrook, CA 92028 / 619-723-9279 or 619-728-2663
Alpha LaFranck Enterprises, P.O. Box 81072, Lincoln, NE 68501 / 402-466-3193

Alpha Precision, Inc., 2765-B Preston Rd. NE, Good Hope, GA 30641 / 770-267-6163
Alpine Indoor Shooting Range, 2401 Government Way, Coeur d'Alene, ID 83814 / 208-676-8824 FAX: 208-676-8824
Altamont Co., 901 N. Church St., P.O. Box 309, Thomasboro, IL 61878 / 217-643-3125 or 800-626-5774; FAX: 217-643-7973
Alumna Sport by Dee Zee, 1572 NE 58th Ave., P.O. Box 3090, Des Moines, IA 50316 / 800-798-9899
Amadeo Rossi S.A., Rua: Amadeo Rossi, 143, Sao Leopoldo, RS 93030-220 BRAZIL / 051-592-5566
AmBr Software Group Ltd., P.O. Box 301, Reistertown, MD 21136-0301 / 800-888-1917; FAX: 410-526-7212
American Ammunition, 3545 NW 71st St., Miami, FL 33147 / 305-835-7400; FAX: 305-694-0037
American Arms Inc., 2604 NE Industrial Dr, N. Kansas City, MO 64116 / 816-474-3161; FAX: 816-474-1225
American Bullet, 1512 W Chester Pike #298, West Chester, PA 19382-7754 / 610-399-6584
American Custom Gunmakers Guild, PO Box 812, Burlington, IA 52601 / 319-752-6114; FAX: 319-752-6114 acgg@acgg.org acgg.org
American Derringer Corp., 127 N. Lacy Dr., Waco, TX 76705 / 800-642-7817 or 817-799-9111; FAX: 817-799-7935
American Display Co., 55 Cromwell St., Providence, RI 02907 / 401-331-2464; FAX: 401-421-1264
American Frontier Firearms Mfg., Inc, PO Box 744, Aguanga, CA 92536 / 909-763-0014; FAX: 909-763-0014
American Gas & Chemical Co., Ltd, 220 Pegasus Ave, Northvale, NJ 07647 / 201-767-7300
American Gripcraft, 3230 S Dodge 2, Tucson, AZ 85713 / 602-790-1222
American Gunsmithing Institute, 1325 Imola Ave #504, Napa, CA 94559 / 707-253-0462; FAX: 707-253-7149
American Handgunner Magazine, 591 Camino de la Reina, Ste 200, San Diego, CA 92108 / 619-297-5350; FAX: 619-297-5353
American Pioneer Video, PO Box 50049, Bowling Green, KY 42102-2649 / 800-743-4675
American Products, Inc., 14729 Spring Valley Road, Morrison, IL 61270 / 815-772-3336; FAX: 815-772-8046
American Safe Arms, Inc., 1240 Riverview Dr., Garland, UT 84312 / 801-257-7472; FAX: 801-785-8156
American Sales & Kirkpatrick Mfg. Co., P.O. Box 677, Laredo, TX 78042 / 210-723-6893; FAX: 210-725-0672
American Sales & Mfg. Co., PO Box 677, Laredo, TX 78042 / 956-723-6893; FAX: 956-725-0672 holsters@kirkpatrickleather.com http://kirkpatrickleather.com
American Security Products Co., 11925 Pacific Ave., Fontana, CA 92337 / 909-685-9680 or 800-421-6142; FAX: 909-685-9685
American Small Arms Academy, P.O. Box 12111, Prescott, AZ 86304 / 602-778-5623
American Target, 1328 S. Jason St., Denver, CO 80223 / 303-733-0433; FAX: 303-777-0311
American Target Knives, 1030 Brownwood NW, Grand Rapids, MI 49504 / 616-453-1998
American Western Arms, Inc., 1450 S.W. 10th St., Suite 3B, Delray Beach, FL 33444 / 877-292-4867; FAX: 561-330-0881
American Whitetail Target Systems, P.O. Box 41, 106 S. Church St., Tennyson, IN 47637 / 812-567-4527
Americase, P.O. Box 271, 1610 E. Main, Waxahachie, TX 75165 / 800-880-3629; FAX: 214-937-8373
Ames Metal Products, 4323 S. Western Blvd., Chicago, IL 60609 / 773-523-3230; or 800-255-6937 FAX: 773-523-3854
Amherst Arms, P.O. Box 1457, Englewood, FL 34295 / 941-475-2020; FAX: 941-473-1212
Ammo Load, Inc., 1560 E. Edinger, Suite G, Santa Ana, CA 92705 / 714-558-8858; FAX: 714-569-0319
Amrine's Gun Shop, 937 La Luna, Ojai, CA 93023 / 805-646-2376
Amsec, 11925 Pacific Ave., Fontana, CA 92337
Amtec 2000, Inc., 84 Industrial Rowe, Gardner, MA 01440 / 508-632-9608; FAX: 508-632-2300
Analog Devices, Box 9106, Norwood, MA 02062
Andela Tool & Machine, Inc., RD3, Box 246, Richfield Springs, NY 13439
Anderson Manufacturing Co., Inc., 22602 53rd Ave. SE, Bothell, WA 98021 / 206-481-1858; FAX: 206-481-7839
Andres & Dworsky, Bergstrasse 18, A-3822 Karlstein, Thaya, AUSTRIA / 0 28 44-285
Angel Arms, Inc., 1825 Addison Way, Haywood, CA 94545 / 510-783-7122

328 • GUNS ILLUSTRATED

MANUFACTURERS DIRECTORY

Angelo & Little Custom Gun Stock Blanks, P.O. Box 240046, Dell, MT 59724-0046
Anics Firm Inc3 Commerce Park Square, 23200 Chagrin Blvd., Suite 240, Beechwood, OH 44122 / 800-556-1582; FAX: 216-292-2588
Anschutz GmbH, Postfach 1128, D-89001 Ulm, Donau, GERMANY / 731-40120
Answer Products Co., 1519 Westbury Drive, Davison, MI 48423 / 810-653-2911
Anthony and George Ltd., Rt. 1, P.O. Box 45, Evington, VA 24550 / 804-821-8117
Antique American Firearms, P.O. Box 71035, Dept. GD, Des Moines, IA 50325 / 515-224-6552
Antique Arms Co., 1110 Cleveland Ave., Monett, MO 65708 / 417-235-6501
Apel GmbH, Ernst, Am Kirschberg 3, D-97218, Gerbrunn, GERMANY / 0 (931) 707192
Aplan Antiques & Art, James O., HC 80, Box 793-25, Piedmont, SD 57769 / 605-347-5016
AR-7 Industries, LLC, 998 N. Colony Rd., Meriden, CT 06450 / 203-630-3536; FAX: 203-630-3637
Arco Powder, HC-Rt. 1 P.O. Box 102, County Rd. 357, Mayo, FL 32066 / 904-294-3882; FAX: 904-294-1498
Arizona Ammunition, Inc., 21421 No. 14th Ave., Suite E, Phoenix, AZ 85027 / 623-516-9004; FAX: 623-516-9012 azammo.com
Arkansas Mallard Duck Calls, Rt. Box 182, England, AR 72046 / 501-842-3597
ArmaLite, Inc., P.O. Box 299, Geneseo, IL 61254 / 309-944-6939; FAX: 309-944-6949
Armament Gunsmithing Co., Inc., 525 Rt. 22, Hillside, NJ 07205 / 908-686-0960 FAX: 718-738-5019
Armas Kemen S. A. (See U.S. Importers)
Armas Urki Garbi, 12-14 20.600, Eibar (Guipuzcoa), / 43-11 38 73
Armfield Custom Bullets, 4775 Caroline Drive, San Diego, CA 92115 / 619-582-7188; FAX: 619-287-3238
Armi Perazzi S.p.A., Via Fontanelle 1/3, 1-25080, Botticino Mattina, / 030-2692591; FAX: 030 2692594+
Armi San Marco (See U.S. Importers-Taylor's & Co I
Armi San Paolo, 172-A, I-25062, via Europa, ITALY / 030-2751725
Armi Sport (See U.S. Importers-Cape Outfitters)
Armite Laboratories, 1845 Randolph St., Los Angeles, CA 90001 / 213-587-7768; FAX: 213-587-5075
Armoloy Co. of Ft. Worth, 204 E. Daggett St., Fort Worth, TX 76104 / 817-332-5604; FAX: 817-335-6517
Armor (See Buck Stop Lure Co., Inc.)
Armor Metal Products, P.O. Box 4609, Helena, MT 59604 / 406-442-5560; FAX: 406-442-5650
Armory Publications, 17171 Bothall Way NE, #276, Seattle, WA 98155 / 208-664-5061; FAX: 208-664-9906 armorypub@aol.com www.grocities.com/armorypub
Arms & Armour Press, Wellington House, 125 Strand, London, WC2R 0BB ENGLAND / 0171-420-5555; FAX: 0171-240-7265
Arms Corporation of the Philippines, Bo. Parang Marikina, Metro Manila, PHILIPPINES / 632-941-6243 or 632-941-6244; FAX: 632-942-0682
Arms Craft Gunsmithing, 1106 Linda Dr., Arroyo Grande, CA 93420 / 805-481-2830
Arms Ingenuity Co., P.O. Box 1, 51 Canal St., Weatogue, CT 06089 / 203-658-5624
Arms Software, P.O. Box 1526, Lake Oswego, OR 97035 / 800-366-5559 or 503-697-0533; FAX: 503-697-3337
Arms, Programming Solutions (See Arms Software)
Armscorp USA, Inc., 4424 John Ave., Baltimore, MD 21227 / 410-247-6200; FAX: 410-247-6205 armscorp_md@yahoo.com
Armsport, Inc., 3950 NW 49th St., Miami, FL 33142 / 305-635-7850; FAX: 305-633-2877
Arnold Arms Co., Inc., P.O. Box 1011, Arlington, WA 98223 / 800-371-1011 or 360-435-1011; FAX: 360-435-7304
Aro-Tek Ltd., 206 Frontage Rd. North, Suite C, Pacific, WA 98047 / 206-351-2984; FAX: 206-833-4483
Arratoonian, Andy (See Horseshoe Leather Products)
Arrieta S.L., Morkaiko 5, Elgoibar, SPAIN / 34-43-743150; FAX: 34-43-743154+
Art Jewel Enterprises Ltd., Eagle Business Ctr., 460 Randy Rd., Carol Stream, IL 60188 / 708-260-0400
Art's Gun & Sport Shop, Inc., 6008 Hwy. Y, Hillsboro, MO 63050
Artistry in Wood, 134 Zimmerman Rd., Kalispell, MT 59901 / 406-257-9003
Arundel Arms & Ammunition, Inc., A., 24A Defense St., Annapolis, MD 21401 / 410-224-8683

Arvo Ojala Holsters, P.O. Box 98, N. Hollywood, CA 91603 / 818-222-9700; FAX: 818-222-0401
Ashby Turkey Calls, P.O. Box 1466, Ava, MO 65608-1466 / 417-967-3787
Ashley Outdoors, Inc, 2401 Ludelle St, Fort Worth, TX 76105 / 888-744-4880; FAX: 800-734-7939
Aspen Outfitting Co, Jon Hollinger, 9 Dean St, Aspen, CO 81611 / 970-925-3406
Astra Sport, S.A., Apartado 3, 48300 Guernica, Espagne, SPAIN / 34-4-6250100; FAX: 34-4-6255186+
Atamec-Bretton, 19 rue Victor Grignard, F-42026, St.-Etienne (Cedex 1, / 77-93-54-69; FAX: 33-77-93-57-98+
Atlanta Cutlery Corp., 2143 Gees Mill Rd., Box 839 CIS, Conyers, GA 30207 / 800-883-0300; FAX: 404-388-0246
Atlantic Mills, Inc., 1295 Towbin Ave., Lakewood, NJ 08701-5934 / 800-242-7374
Atlantic Rose, Inc., P.O. Box 10717, Bradenton, FL 34282-0717
Atsko/Sno-Seal, Inc., 2664 Russell St., Orangeburg, SC 29115 / 803-531-1820; FAX: 803-531-2139
Auguste Francotte & Cie S.A., rue du Trois Juin 109, 4400 Herstal-Liege, BELGIUM / 32-4-248-13-18; FAX: 32-4-948-11-79
Austin & Halleck, 1099 Welt, Weston, MO 64098 / 816-386-2176; FAX: 816-386-2177
Austin Sheridan USA, Inc., P.O. Box 577, 36 Haddam Quarter Rd., Durham, CT 06422 / 860-349-1772; FAX: 860-349-1771 swalzer@palm.net
Autauga Arms, Inc., Pratt Plaza Mall No. 13, Prattville, AL 36067 / 800-262-9563; FAX: 334-361-2961
Auto Arms, 738 Clearview, San Antonio, TX 78228 / 512-434-5450
Auto-Ordnance Corp., PO Box 220, Blauvelt, NY 10913 / 914-353-7770
Automatic Equipment Sales, 627 E. Railroad Ave., Salesburg, MD 21801
Autumn Sales, Inc. (Blaser), 1320 Lake St., Fort Worth, TX 76102 / 817-335-1634; FAX: 817-338-0119
Avnda Otaola Norica, 16 Apartado 68, 20600, Eibar,
AWC Systems Technology, P.O. Box 41938, Phoenix, AZ 85080-1938 / 602-780-1050 FAX: 602-780-2967
AYA (See U.S. Importer-New England Custom Gun Service)

B

B & P America, 12321 Brittany Cir, Dallas, TX 75230 / 972-726-9069
B&D Trading Co., Inc., 3935 Fair Hill Rd., Fair Oaks, CA 95628 / 800-334-3790 or 916-967-9366; FAX: 916-967-4873
B-Square Company, Inc., ;, P.O. Box 11281, 2708 St. Louis Ave., Ft. Worth, TX 76110 / 817-923-0964 or 800-433-2909 FAX: 817-926-7012
B-West Imports, Inc., 2425 N. Huachuca Dr., Tucson, AZ 85745-1201 / 602-628-1990; FAX: 602-628-3602
B.B. Walker Co., PO Box 1167, 414 E Dixie Dr, Asheboro, NC 27203 / 910-625-1380; FAX: 910-625-8125
B.C. Outdoors, Larry McGhee, PO Box 61497, Boulder City, NV 89006 / 702-294-0025
B.M.F. Activator, Inc., 12145 Mill Creek Run, Plantersville, TX 77363 / 936-894-2397 or 800-527-2881 FAX: 936-894-2397
Badger Shooters Supply, Inc., P.O. Box 397, Owen, WI 54460 / 800-424-9069; FAX: 715-229-2332
Baekgaard Ltd., 1855 Janke Dr., Northbrook, IL 60062 / 708-498-3040; FAX: 708-493-3106
Baelder, Harry, Alte Goennebeker Strasse 5, 24635, Rickling, GERMANY / 04328-722732; FAX: 04328-722733
Baer Custom, Inc, Les, 29601 34th Ave, Hillsdale, IL 61257 / 309-658-2716; FAX: 309-658-2610
Baer's Hollows, P.O. Box 284, Eads, CO 81036 / 719-438-5718
Bagmaster Mfg., Inc., 2731 Sutton Ave., St. Louis, MO 63143 / 314-781-8002; FAX: 314-781-3363
Bain & Davis, Inc., 307 E. Valley Blvd., San Gabriel, CA 91776-3522 / 818-573-4241 or 213-283-7449 caindavis@aol.com
Baker, Stan, 10000 Lake City Way, Seattle, WA 98125 / 206-522-4575
Baker's Leather Goods, Roy, PO Box 893, Magnolia, AR 71753 / 501-234-0344
Balance Co., 340-39 Ave., S.E., Box 505, Calgary, AB T2G 1X6 CANADA
Bald Eagle Precision Machine Co., 101-A Allison St., Lock Haven, PA 17745 / 570-748-6772; FAX: 570-748-4443

Balickie, Joe, 408 Trelawney Lane, Apex, NC 27502 / 919-362-5185
Ballard Industries, 10271 Lockwood Dr., Suite B, Cupertino, CA 95014 / 408-996-0957; FAX: 408-257-6828
Ballard Rifle & Cartridge Co., LLC, 113 W Yellowstone Ave, Cody, WY 82414 / 307-587-4914; FAX: 307-527-6097
Ballisti-Cast, Inc., 6347 49th St. NW, Plaza, ND 58771 / 701-497-3333; FAX: 701-497-3335
Ballistic Engineering & Software, Inc., 185 N. Park Blvd., Suite 330, Lake Orion, MI 48362 / 313-391-1074
Ballistic Product, Inc., 20015 75th Ave. North, Corcoran, MN 55340-9456 / 612-494-9237; FAX: 612-494-9236 info@ballisticproducts.com www.ballisticproducts.com
Ballistic Research, 1108 W. May Ave., McHenry, IL 60050 / 815-385-0037
Bandcor Industries, Div. of Man-Sew Corp., 6108 Sherwin Dr., Port Richey, FL 34668 / 813-848-0432
Bang-Bang Boutique (See Holster Shop, The)
Banks, Ed, 2762 Hwy. 41 N., Ft. Valley, GA 31030 / 912-987-4665
Bansner's Gunsmithing Specialties, 261 East Main St. Box VH, Adamstown, PA 19501 / 800-368-2379; FAX: 717-484-0523
Bar-Sto Precision Machine, 73377 Sullivan Rd., P.O. Box 1838, Twentynine Palms, CA 92277 / 760-367-2747; FAX: 760-367-2407
Barbour, Inc., 55 Meadowbrook Dr., Milford, NH 03055 / 603-673-1313; FAX: 603-673-6510
Barnes, 110 Borner St S, Prescott, WI 54021-1149 / 608-897-8416
Barnes Bullets, Inc., P.O. Box 215, American Fork, UT 84003 / 801-756-4222 or 800-574-9200; FAX: 801-756-2465 email@barnesbullets.com www.barnesbullets.com
Baron Technology, 62 Spring Hill Rd., Trumbull, CT 06611 / 203-452-0515; FAX: 203-452-0663
Barraclough, John K., 55 Merit Park Dr., Gardena, CA 90247 / 310-324-2574
Barramundi Corp., P.O. Drawer 4259, Homosassa Springs, FL 32687 / 904-628-0200
Barrett Firearms Manufacturer, Inc., P.O. Box 1077, Murfreesboro, TN 37133 / 615-896-2938; FAX: 615-896-7313
Barry Lee Hands Engraving, 26192 E. Shore Route, Bigfork, MT 59911 / 406-837-0035
Barta's Gunsmithing, 10231 US Hwy. 10, Cato, WI 54206 / 920-732-4472
Barteaux Machete, 1916 SE 50th Ave., Portland, OR 97215-3238 / 503-233-5880
Bartlett Engineering, 40 South 200 East, Smithfield, UT 84335-1645 / 801-563-5910
Basics Information Systems, Inc., 1141 Georgia Ave., Suite 515, Wheaton, MD 20902 / 301-949-1070; FAX: 301-949-5326
Bates Engraving, Billy, 2302 Winthrop Dr, Decatur, AL 35603 / 256-355-3690
Bauer, Eddie, 15010 NE 36th St., Redmond, WA 98052
Baumgartner Bullets, 3011 S. Alane St., W. Valley City, UT 84120
Bauska Barrels, 105 9th Ave. W., Kalispell, MT 59901 / 406-752-7706
Bear Archery, RR 4, 4600 Southwest 41st Blvd., Gainesville, FL 32601 / 904-376-2327
Bear Arms, 121 Rhodes St., Jackson, SC 29831 / 803-471-9859
Bear Hug Grip, Inc., P.O. Box 16649, Colorado Springs, CO 80935-6649 / 800-232-7710
Bear Mountain Gun & Tool, 120 N. Plymouth, New Plymouth, ID 83655 / 208-278-5221; FAX: 208-278-5221
Beartooth Bullets, P.O. Box 491, Dept. HLD, Dover, ID 83825-0491 / 208-448-1865 beartooth@trasport.com
Beaver Lodge (See Fellowes, Ted)
Beaver Park Product, Inc., 840 J St., Penrose, CO 81240 / 719-372-6744
BEC, Inc., 1227 W. Valley Blvd., Suite 204, Alhambra, CA 91803 / 626-281-5751; FAX: 626-293-7073
Beeline Custom Bullets Limited, P.O. Box 85, Yarmouth, NS B5A 4B1 CANADA / 902-648-3494; FAX: 902-648-0253
Beeman Precision Airguns, 5454 Argosy Dr., Huntington Beach, CA 92649 / 714-890-4800; FAX: 714-890-4808
Behlert Precision, Inc., P.O. Box 288, 7067 Easton Rd., Pipersville, PA 18947 / 215-766-8681 or 215-766-7301; FAX: 215-766-8681
Beitzinger, George, 116-20 Atlantic Ave, Richmond Hill, NY 11419 / 718-847-7661
Belding's Custom Gun Shop, 10691 Sayers Rd., Munith, MI 49259 / 517-596-2388

34TH EDITION, 2002 • 329

Manufacturers Directory

Bell & Carlson, Inc., Dodge City Industrial Park, 101 Allen Rd., Dodge City, KS 67801 / 800-634-8586 or 316-225-6688; FAX: 316-225-9095

Bell Reloading, Inc., 1725 Harlin Lane Rd., Villa Rica, GA 30180

Bell's Gun & Sport Shop, 3309-19 Mannheim Rd, Franklin Park, IL 60131

Bell's Legendary Country Wear, 22 Circle Dr., Bellmore, NY 11710 / 516-679-1158

Bellm Contenders, P.O. Box 459, Cleveland, UT 84518 / 801-653-2530

Belltown Ltd., 11 Camps Rd., Kent, CT 06757 / 860-354-5750 FAX: 860-354-6764

Ben William's Gun Shop, 1151 S. Cedar Ridge, Duncanville, TX 75137 / 214-780-1807

Ben's Machines, 1151 S. Cedar Ridge, Duncanville, TX 75137 / 214-780-1807 FAX: 214-780-0316

Benchmark Guns, 12593 S. Ave. 5 East, Yuma, AZ 85365

Benchmark Knives (See Gerber Legendary Blades)

Benelli Armi S.p.A., Via della Stazione, 61029, Urbino, ITALY / 39-722-307-1; FAX: 39-722-327427+

Benelli USA Corp, 17603 Indian Head Hwy, Accokeek, MD 20607 / 301-283-6981; FAX: 301-283-6988 benelliusa.com

Bengtson Arms Co., L., 6345-B E. Akron St., Mesa, AZ 85205 / 602-981-6375

Benjamin/Sheridan Co., Crossman, Rts. 5 and 20, E. Bloomfield, NY 14443 / 716-657-6161; FAX: 716-657-5405

Bentley, John, 128-D Watson Dr., Turtle Creek, PA 15145

Beomat of America, Inc., 300 Railway Ave., Campbell, CA 95008 / 408-379-4829

Beretta S.p.A., Pietro, Via Beretta, 18-25063, Gardone V.T., ITALY / 39-30-8341-1 FAX: 39-30-8341-421

Beretta U.S.A. Corp., 17601 Beretta Drive, Accokeek, MD 20607 / 301-283-2191; FAX: 301-283-0435

Berger Bullets Ltd., 5342 W. Camelback Rd., Suite 200, Glendale, AZ 85301 / 602-842-4001; FAX: 602-934-9083

Bernardelli S.p.A., Vincenzo, 125 Via Matteotti, PO Box 74, Brescia, ITALY / 39-30-8912821-2-3; FAX: 39-30-8910249

Berry's Mfg., Inc., 401 North 3050 East St., St. George, UT 84770 / 435-634-1682; FAX: 435-634-1683 sales@berrysmfg.com www.berrysmfg.com

Bersa S.A., Gonzales Castillo 312, 1704, Ramos Mejia, ARGENTINA / 541-656-2377; FAX: 541-656-2093+

Bert Johanssons Vapentillbehor, S-430 20 Veddige, SWEDEN,

Bertuzzi (See U.S. Importer-New England Arms Co)

Better Concepts Co., 663 New Castle Rd., Butler, PA 16001 / 412-285-9000

Beverly, Mary, 3201 Horseshoe Trail, Tallahassee, FL 32312

Bianchi International, Inc., 100 Calle Cortez, Temecula, CA 92590 / 909-676-5621; FAX: 909-676-6777

Biesen, Al, 5021 Rosewood, Spokane, WA 99208 / 509-328-9340

Biesen, Roger, 5021 W. Rosewood, Spokane, WA 99208 / 509-328-9340

Big Bear Arms & Sporting Goods, Inc., 1112 Milam Way, Carrollton, TX 75006 / 972-416-8051 or 800-400-BEAR; FAX: 972-416-0771

Big Bore Bullets of Alaska, P.O. Box 872785, Wasilla, AK 99687 / 907-373-2673; FAX: 907-373-2673 doug@mta-online.net ww.awloo.com/bbb/index.

Big Bore Express, 7154 W. State St., Boise, ID 83703 / 800-376-4010; FAX: 208-376-4020

Big Sky Racks, Inc., P.O. Box 729, Bozeman, MT 59771-0729 / 406-586-9393; FAX: 406-585-7378

Big Spring Enterprises "Bore Stores", P.O. Box 1115, Big Spring Rd., Yellville, AR 72687 / 870-449-5297; FAX: 870-449-4446

Bilal, Mustafa, 908 NW 50th St., Seattle, WA 98107-3634 / 206-782-4164

Bilinski, Bryan. See: FIELDSPORT LTD

Bill Austin's Calls, Box 284, Kaycee, WY 82639 / 307-738-2552

Bill Adair Custom Shop, 2886 Westridge, Carrollton, TX 75006 / 972-418-0950

Bill Hanus Birdguns LLC, P.O. Box 533, Newport, OR 97365 / 541-265-7433; FAX: 541-265-7400

Bill Johns Master Engraver, 7927 Ranch Roach 965, Fredericksburg, TX 78624-9545 / 830-997-6795

Bill Wiseman and Co., P.O. Box 3427, Bryan, TX 77805 / 409-690-3456; FAX: 409-690-0156

Bill's Custom Cases, P.O. Box 2, Dunsmuir, CA 96025 / 530-235-0177; FAX: 530-235-4959

Bill's Gun Repair, 1007 Burlington St., Mendota, IL 61342 / 815-539-5786

Billeb, Stephen L., 1101 N. 7th St., Burlington, IA 52601 / 319-753-2110

Billings Gunsmiths Inc., 1841 Grand Ave., Billings, MT 59102 / 406-256-8390

Billingsley & Brownell, P.O. Box 25, Dayton, WY 82836 / 307-655-9344

Billy Bates Engraving, 2302 Winthrop Dr., Decatur, AL 35603 / 205-355-3690

Birchwood Casey, 7900 Fuller Rd., Eden Prairie, MN 55344 / 800-328-6156 or 612-937-7933; FAX: 612-937-7979

Birdsong & Assoc, W. E., 1435 Monterey Rd, Florence, MS 39073-9748 / 601-366-8270

Bismuth Cartridge Co., 3500 Maple Ave., Suite 1650, Dallas, TX 75219 / 214-521-5880; FAX: 214-521-9035

Bison Studios, 1409 South Commerce St., Las Vegas, NV 89102 / 702-388-2891; FAX: 702-383-9967

Bitterroot Bullet Co., PO Box 412, Lewiston, ID 83501-0412 / 208-743-5635 FAX: 208-743-5635

BKL Technologies, PO Box 5237, Brownsville, TX 78523

Black Belt Bullets (See Big Bore Express)

Black Hills Ammunition, Inc., P.O. Box 3090, Rapid City, SD 57709-3090 / 605-348-5150; FAX: 605-348-9827

Black Hills Shooters Supply, P.O. Box 4220, Rapid City, SD 57709 / 800-289-2506

Black Powder Products, 67 Township Rd. 1411, Chesapeake, OH 45619 / 614-867-8047

Black Sheep Brand, 3220 W. Gentry Parkway, Tyler, TX 75702 / 903-592-3853; FAX: 903-592-0527

Blackhawk East, Box 2274, Loves Park, IL 61131

Blacksmith Corp., PO Box 280, North Hampton, OH 45349 / 800-531-2665; FAX: 937-969-8399 bcbooks@glasscity.net

BlackStar AccuMax Barrels, 11501 Brittmoore Park Drive, Houston, TX 77041 / 281-721-6040; FAX: 281-721-6041

BlackStar Barrel Accurizing (See BlackStar AccuMax Barrels)

Blacktail Mountain Books, 42 First Ave. W., Kalispell, MT 59901 / 406-257-5573

Blair Engraving, J. R., PO Box 64, Glenrock, WY 82637 / 307-436-8115

Blammo Ammo, P.O. Box 1677, Seneca, SC 29679 / 803-882-1768

Blaser Jagdwaffen GmbH, D-88316, Isny Im Allgau, GERMANY

Bleile, C. Roger, 5040 Ralph Ave., Cincinnati, OH 45238 / 513-251-0249

Blount, Inc., Sporting Equipment Div., 2299 Snake River Ave., P.O. Box 856, Lewiston, ID 83501 / 800-627-3640 or 208-746-2351; FAX: 208-799-3904

Blue and Gray Products Inc (See Ox-Yoke Originals, Inc.)

Blue Book Publications, Inc., One Appletree Square, 8009 34th Ave. S. Suite 175, Minneapolis, MN 55425 / 800-877-4867 or 612-854-5229; FAX: 612-853-1486

Blue Mountain Bullets, HCR 77, P.O. Box 231, John Day, OR 97845 / 541-820-4594

Blue Ridge Machinery & Tools, Inc., P.O. Box 536-GD, Hurricane, WV 25526 / 800-872-6500; FAX: 304-562-5311

BMC Supply, Inc., 26051 - 179th Ave. S.E., Kent, WA 98042

Bo-Mar Tool & Mfg. Co., Rt. 8, Box 405, Longview, TX 75604 / 903-759-4784; FAX: 903-759-9141

Bob Allen Co.214 SW Jackson, P.O. Box 477, Des Moines, IA 50315 / 800-685-7020 FAX: 515-283-0779

Bob Rogers Gunsmithing, P.O. Box 305, 344 S. Walnut St., Franklin Grove, IL 61031 / 815-456-2685; FAX: 815-288-7142

Bob Schrimsher's Custom Knifemaker's Supply, P.O. Box 308, Emory, TX 75440 / 903-473-3330; FAX: 903-473-2235

Bob's Gun Shop, P.O. Box 200, Royal, AR 71968 / 501-767-1970; FAX: 501-767-1970

Bob's Tactical Indoor Shooting Range & Gun Shop, 90 Lafayette Rd., Salisbury, MA 01952 / 508-465-5561

Boessler, Erich, Am Vogeltal 3, 97702, Munnerstadt, GERMANY

Bohemia Arms Co., 17101 Los Modelos St., Fountain Valley, CA 92708 / 619-442-7005; FAX: 619-442-7005

Boker USA, Inc., 1550 Balsam Street, Lakewood, CO 80215 / 303-462-0662; FAX: 303-462-0668 bokerusa@world-net.att.net bokerusa.com

Boltin, John M., P.O. Box 644, Estill, SC 29918 / 803-625-2315

Bonanza (See Forster Products), 310 E Lanark Ave, Lanark, IL 61046 / 815-493-6360; FAX: 815-493-2371

Bond Arms, Inc., P.O. Box 1296, Granbury, TX 76048 / 817-573-4445; FAX: 817-573-5636

Bond Custom Firearms, 8954 N. Lewis Ln., Bloomington, IN 47408 / 812-332-4519

Bondini Paolo, Via Sorrento 345, San Carlo di Cesena, ITALY / 0547-663-240; FAX: 0547-663-780

Bone Engraving, Ralph, 718 N Atlanta, Owasso, OK 74055 / 918-272-9745

Boone Trading Co., Inc., P.O. Box BB, Brinnan, WA 98320

Boone's Custom Ivory Grips, Inc., 562 Coyote Rd., Brinnon, WA 98320 / 206-796-4330

Boonie Packer Products, P.O. Box 12204, Salem, OR 97309 / 800-477-3244 or 503-581-3244; FAX: 503-581-3191

Borden Ridges Rimrock Stocks, RR 1 Box 250 BC, Springville, PA 18844 / 570-965-2505 FAX: 570-965-2328

Borden Rifles Inc, RD 1, Box 250BC, Springville, PA 18844 / 717-965-2505; FAX: 717-965-2328

Border Barrels Ltd., Riccarton Farm, Newcastleton, SCOTLAND UK

Borovnik KG, Ludwig, 9170 Ferlach, Bahnhofstrasse 7, AUSTRIA / 042 27 24 42; FAX: 042 26 43 49

Bosis (See U.S. Importer-New England Arms Co.)

Boss Manufacturing Co., 221 W. First St., Kewanee, IL 61443 / 309-852-2131 or 800-447-4581; FAX: 309-852-0848

Bostick Wildlife Calls, Inc., P.O. Box 728, Estill, SC 29918 / 803-625-2210 or 803-625-4512

Bowen Classic Arms Corp., P.O. Box 67, Louisville, TN 37777 / 865-984-3583 bowsarms.com

Bowen Knife Co., Inc., P.O. Box 590, Blackshear, GA 31516 / 912-449-4794

Bowerly, Kent, 710 Golden Pheasant Dr, Redmond, OR 97756 / 541-595-6028

Boyds' Gunstock Industries, Inc., 25376 403RD AVE, MITCHELL, SD 57301 / 605-996-5011; FAX: 605-996-9878

Brace, Larry D., 771 Blackfoot Ave., Eugene, OR 97404 / 541-688-1278; FAX: 541-607-5833

Bradley Gunsight Co., P.O. Box 340, Plymouth, VT 05056 / 860-589-0531; FAX: 860-582-6294

Brass Eagle, Inc., 7050A Bramalea Rd., Unit 19, Mississauga, ON L4Z 1C7 CANADA / 416-848-4844

Bratcher, Dan, 311 Belle Air Pl., Carthage, MO 64836 / 417-358-1518

Brauer Bros. Mfg. Co., 2020 Delman Blvd., St. Louis, MO 63103 / 314-231-2864; FAX: 314-249-4952

Break-Free, Inc., P.O. Box 25020, Santa Ana, CA 92799 / 714-953-1900; FAX: 714-953-0402

Brenneke KG, Wilhelm, Ilmenauweg 2, 30851 Langenhagen, GERMANY / 0511-97262-0; FAX: 0511-97262-62

Brian Perazone-Gunsmith, Cold Spring Rd., Roxbury, NY 12474 / 607-326-4088; FAX: 607-326-3140

Bridgeman Products, Harry Jaffin, 153 B Cross Slope Court, Englishtown, NJ 07726 / 732-536-3604; FAX: 732-972-1004

Bridgers Best, P.O. Box 1410, Berthoud, CO 80513

Briese Bullet Co., Inc., RR1, Box 108, Tappen, ND 58487 / 701-327-4578; FAX: 701-327-4579

Brigade Quartermasters, 1025 Cobb International Blvd., Dept. VH, Kennesaw, GA 30144-4300 / 404-428-1248 or 800-241-3125; FAX: 404-426-7726

Briganti, A.J., 512 Rt. 32, Highland Mills, NY 10930 / 914-928-9573

Briley Mfg. Inc., 1230 Lumpkin, Houston, TX 77043 / 800-331-5718 or 713-932-6995; FAX: 713-932-1043

British Antiques, P.O. Box 35369, Tucson, AZ 85740 / 520-575-9063 britishantiques@hotmail.com

British Sporting Arms, RR1, Box 130, Millbrook, NY 12545 / 914-677-8303

BRNO (See U.S. Importers-Bohemia Arms Co.)

Broad Creek Rifle Works, Ltd., 120 Horsey Ave., Laurel, DE 19956 / 302-875-5446; FAX: 302-875-1449 bcqw4guns@aol.com

Brockman's Custom Gunsmithing, P.O. Box 357, Gooding, ID 83330 / 208-934-5050

Brocock Ltd., 43 River Street, Digbeth, Birmingham, B5 5SA ENGLAND / 011-021-773-1200

Broken Gun Ranch, 10739 126 Rd., Spearville, KS 67876 / 316-385-2587; FAX: 316-385-2597

Brolin Arms, 2755 Thompson Creek Rd., Pomona, CA 91767 / 909-392-7822; FAX: 909-392-7824

Brooker, Dennis, Rt. 1, Box 12A, Derby, IA 50068 / 515-533-2103

Brooks Tactical Systems, 279-C Shorewood Ct., Fox Island, WA 98333 / 253-549-2866 FAX: 253-549-2703 brooks@brookstactical.com www.brookstactical.com

Brown, H. R. (See Silhouette Leathers)

Manufacturers Directory

Brown Co, E. Arthur, 3404 Pawnee Dr, Alexandria, MN 56308 / 320-762-8847
Brown Dog Ent., 2200 Calle Camelia, 1000 Oaks, CA 91360 / 805-497-2318; FAX: 805-497-1618
Brown Manufacturing, P.O. Box 9219, Akron, OH 44305 / 800-837-GUNS
Brown Precision,Inc., 7786 Molinos Ave., Los Molinos, CA 96055 FAX: 916-384-1638
Brown Products, Inc., Ed, 43825 Muldrow Trail, Perry, MO 63462 / 573-565-3261; FAX: 573-565-2791
Brownells, Inc., 200 S. Front St., Montezuma, IA 50171 / 515-623-5401; FAX: 515-623-3896
Browning Arms Co., One Browning Place, Morgan, UT 84050 / 801-876-2711; FAX: 801-876-3331
Browning Arms Co. (Parts & Service), 3005 Arnold Tenbrook Rd., Arnold, MO 63010 / 314-287-6800; FAX: 314-287-9751
BRP, Inc. High Performance Cast Bullets, 1210 Alexander Rd., Colorado Springs, CO 80909 / 719-633-0658
Brunton U.S.A., 620 E. Monroe Ave., Riverton, WY 82501 / 307-856-6559; FAX: 307-856-1840
Bryan & Assoc, R D Sauls, PO Box 5772, Anderson, SC 29623-5772 / 864-261-6810
Brynin, Milton, P.O. Box 383, Yonkers, NY 10710 / 914-779-4333
BSA Guns Ltd., Armoury Rd. Small Heath, Birmingham, ENGLAND / 011-021-772-8543; FAX: 011-021-773-084
BSA Optics, 3911 SW 47th Ave #914, Ft Lauderdale, FL 33314 / 954-581-2144 FAX: 954-581-3165
Bucheimer, J. (See JUMBO SPORTS PRODUCTS)
Bucheimer, J. M. (See Jumbo Sports Products), 721 N 20th St, St Louis, MO 63103 / 314-241-1020
Buck Knives, Inc., 1900 Weld Blvd., P.O. Box 1267, El Cajon, CA 92020 / 619-449-1100 or 800-326-2825; FAX: 619-562-5774 8
Buck Stix--SOS Products Co., Box 3, Neenah, WI 54956
Buck Stop Lure Co., Inc., 3600 Grow Rd. NW, P.O. Box 636, Stanton, MI 48888 / 517-762-5091; FAX: 517-762-5124
Buckeye Custom Bullets, 6490 Stewart Rd., Elida, OH 45807 / 419-641-4463
Buckhorn Gun Works, 8109 Woodland Dr., Black Hawk, SD 57718 / 605-787-6472
Buckskin Bullet Co., P.O. Box 1893, Cedar City, UT 84721 / 435-586-3286
Buckskin Machine Works, A. Hunkeler, 3235 S. 358th St., Auburn, WA 98001 / 206-927-5412
Budin, Dave, Main St., Margaretville, NY 12455 / 914-568-4103; FAX: 914-586-4105
Buenger Enterprises/Goldenrod Dehumidifier, 3600 S. Harbor Blvd., Oxnard, CA 93035 / 800-451-6797 or 805-985-5828; FAX: 805-985-1534
Buffalo Arms Co., 99 Raven Ridge, Samuels, ID 83864 / 208-263-6953; FAX: 208-265-2096
Buffalo Bullet Co., Inc., 12637 Los Nietos Rd., Unit A., Santa Fe Springs, CA 90670 FAX: 562-944-5054
Buffalo Rock Shooters Supply, R.R. 1, Ottawa, IL 61350 / 815-433-2471
Buffer Technologies, P.O. Box 104930, Jefferson City, MO 65110 / 573-634-8529; FAX: 573-634-8522
Bull Mountain Rifle Co., 6327 Golden West Terrace, Billings, MT 59106 / 406-656-0778
Bull-X, Inc., 520 N. Main, Farmer City, IL 61842 / 309-928-2574 or 800-248-3845; FAX: 309-928-2130
Bullberry Barrel Works, Ltd., 2430 W. Bullberry Ln. 67-5, Hurricane, UT 84737 / 435-635-9866; FAX: 435-635-0348
Bullet Metals, P.O. Box 1238, Sierra Vista, AZ 85636 / 520-458-5321; FAX: 520-458-1421 alloymetalsmith@theriver.com
Bullet Swaging Supply Inc., P.O. Box 1056, 303 McMillan Rd, West Monroe, LA 71291 / 318-387-3266; FAX: 318-387-7779
Bullet'n Press, 19 Key St., Eastport, ME 04631 / 207-853-4116 www.nemaine.com/bnpress
Bullet, Inc., 3745 Hiram Alworth Rd., Dallas, GA 30132
Bullseye Bullets, 8100 E Broadway Ave #A, Tampa, FL 33619-2223 / 813-630-9186 bbullets8100@aol.com
Burgess, Byron, PO Box 6853, Los Osos, CA 93412 / 805-528-1005
Burkhart Gunsmithing, Don, P.O. Box 852, Rawlins, WY 82301 / 307-324-6007
Burnham Bros., P.O. Box 1148, Menard, TX 78659 / 915-396-4572; FAX: 915-396-4574
Burris Co., Inc., P.O. Box 1747, 331 E. 8th St., Greeley, CO 80631 / 970-356-1670; FAX: 970-356-8702
Bushmann Hunters & Safaris, P.O. Box 293088, Lewisville, TX 75029 / 214-317-0768
Bushmaster Firearms (See Quality Parts Co/Bushmaster Firearms)
Bushmaster Hunting & Fishing, 451 Alliance Ave., Toronto, ON M6N 2J1 Canada / 416-763-4040; FAX: 416-763-0623
Bushnell Sports Optics Worldwide, 9200 Cody, Overland Park, KS 66214 / 913-752-3400 or 800-423-3537; FAX: 913-752-3550
Bushwacker Backpack & Supply Co (See Counter Assault)
Bustani, Leo, P.O. Box 8125, W. Palm Beach, FL 33410 / 305-622-2710
Buster's Custom Knives, P.O. Box 214, Richfield, UT 84701 / 801-896-5319
Butler Creek Corp., 290 Arden Dr., Belgrade, MT 59714 / 800-423-8327 or 406-388-1356; FAX: 406-388-7204
Butler Enterprises, 834 Oberting Rd., Lawrenceburg, IN 47025 / 812-537-3584
Butterfield & Butterfield, 220 San Bruno Ave., San Francisco, CA 94103 / 415-861-7500
Buzztail Brass (See Grayback Wildcats)
Byron Burgess, P.O. Box 6853, Los Osos, CA 93412 / 805-528-1005

C

C&D Special Products (See Claybuster Wads & Harvester Bullets)
C&H Research, 115 Sunnyside Dr., Box 351, Lewis, KS 67552 / 316-324-5445 www.09.net(chr)
C-More Systems, P.O. Box 1750, 7553 Gary Rd., Manassas, VA 20108 / 703-361-2663; FAX: 703-361-5881
C. Palmer Manufacturing Co., Inc., P.O. Box 220, West Newton, PA 15089 / 412-872-8200; FAX: 412-872-8302
C. Sharps Arms Co. Inc., 100 Centennial, Box 885, Big Timber, MT 59011 / 406-932-4353; FAX: 406-932-4443
C.S. Van Gorden & Son, Inc., 1815 Main St., Bloomer, WI 54724 / 715-568-2612
C.W. Erickson's Mfg. Inc., 530 Garrison Ave NE, PO Box 522, Buffalo, MN 55313 / 612-682-3665; FAX: 612-682-4328
Cabanas (See U.S. Importer-Mandall Shooting Supplies, Inc.)
Cabela's, 812-13th Ave., Sidney, NE 69160 / 308-254-6644 or 800-237-4444; FAX: 308-254-6745
Cabinet Mtn. Outfitters Scents & Lures, P.O. Box 766, Plains, MT 59859 / 406-826-3970
Cache La Poudre Rifleworks, 140 N. College, Ft. Collins, CO 80524 / 303-482-6913
Cali'co Hardwoods, Inc., 3580 Westwind Blvd., Santa Rosa, CA 95403 / 707-546-4045; FAX: 707-546-4027 calicohardwoods@msn.com
Calibre Press, Inc., 666 Dundee Rd., Suite 1607, Northbrook, IL 60062 / 800-323-0037; FAX: 708-498-6869
Calico Light Weapon Systems, 1489 Greg St., Sparks, NV 89431
California Sights (See Fautheree, Andy)
Cambos Outdoorsman, 532 E. Idaho Ave., Ontario, OR 97914 / 541-889-3138 FAX: 541-889-2633
Camdex, Inc., 2330 Alger, Troy, ML 48083 / 810-528-2300; FAX: 810-528-0989
Cameron's, 16690 W. 11th Ave., Golden, CO 80401 / 303-279-7365; FAX: 303-628-5413
Camilli, Lou, 600 Sandtree Dr., Suite 212, Lake Park, FL 33403
Camillus Cutlery Co., 54 Main St., Camillus, NY 13031 / 315-672-8111; FAX: 315-672-8832
Camp-Cap Products, P.O. Box 3805, Chesterfield, MO 63006 / 314-532-4340; FAX: 314-532-4340
Campbell, Dick, 20000 Silver Ranch Rd., Conifer, CO 80433 / 303-697-0150; FAX: 303-697-0150
Cannon, Andy. (See CANNON'S)
Cannon Safe, Inc., 9358 Stephens St., Pico Rivera, CA 90660 / 310-692-0636 or 800-242-1055; FAX: 310-692-7252
Cannon's, Andy Cannon, Box 1026, 320 Main St., Polson, MT 59860 / 406-887-2048
Canons Delcour, Rue J.B. Cools, B-4040, Herstal, BELGIUM / +32.(0)42.40.61.40; FAX: +32(0)42.40.22.88
Canyon Cartridge Corp., P.O. Box 152, Albertson, NY 11507 FAX: 516-294-8946
Cape Outfitters, 599 County Rd. 206, Cape Girardeau, MO 63701 / 573-335-4103; FAX: 573-335-1555
Caraville Manufacturing, P.O. Box 4545, Thousand Oaks, CA 91359 / 805-499-1234
Carbide Checkering Tools (See J&R Engineering)
Carbide Die & Mfg. Co., Inc., 15615 E. Arrow Hwy., Irwindale, CA 91706 / 626-337-2518
Carhartt,Inc., P.O. Box 600, 3 Parklane Blvd., Dearborn, MI 48121 / 800-358-3825 or 313-271-8460; FAX: 313-271-3455
Carl Walther GmbH, B.P. 4325, D-89033, Ulm, GERMANY
Carl Walther USA, PO Box 208, Ten Prince St, Alexandria, VA 22313 / 703-548-1400; FAX: 703-549-7826
Carl Zeiss Inc., 13017 N Kingston Ave, Chester, VA 23836-2743 / 804-861-0033 or 800-388-2984; FAX: 804-733-4024
Carlson, Douglas R, Antique American Firearms, PO Box 71035, Dept GD, Des Moines, IA 50325 / 515-224-6552
Carnahan Bullets, 17645 110th Ave. SE, Renton, WA 98055
Carolina Precision Rifles, 1200 Old Jackson Hwy., Jackson, SC 29831 / 803-827-2069
Carrell's Precision Firearms, 643 Clark Ave., Billings, MT 59101-1614 / 406-962-3593
Carry-Lite, Inc., 5203 W. Clinton Ave., Milwaukee, WI 53223 / 414-355-3520; FAX: 414-355-4775
Carter's Gun Shop, 225 G St., Penrose, CO 81240 / 719-372-6240
Cartridge Transfer Group, Pete de Coux, 235 Oak St., Butler, PA 16001 / 412-282-3426
Cascade Bullet Co., Inc., 2355 South 6th St., Klamath Falls, OR 97601 / 503-884-9316
Cascade Shooters, 2155 N.W. 12th St., Redwood, OR 97756
Case & Sons Cutlery Co., W R, Owens Way, Bradford, PA 16701 / 814-368-4123 or 800-523-6350; FAX: 814-768-5369
Case Sorting System, 12695 Cobblestone Creek Rd., Poway, CA 92064 / 619-486-9340
Cash Mfg. Co., Inc., P.O. Box 130, 201 S. Klein Dr., Waunakee, WI 53597-0130 / 608-849-5664; FAX: 608-849-5664
Caspian Arms, Ltd., 14 North Main St., Hardwick, VT 05843 / 802-472-6454; FAX: 802-472-6709
Cast Performance Bullet Company, 113 Riggs Rd, Shoshoni, WY 82649 / 307-876-4347
Casull Arms Corp., P.O. Box 1629, Afton, WY 83110 / 307-886-0200
Caswell Detroit Armor Companies, 1221 Marshall St. NE, Minneapolis, MN 55413-1055 / 612-379-2000; FAX: 612-379-2367
Catco-Ambush, Inc., P.O.Box 300, Corte Madera, CA 94926
Cathey Enterprises, Inc., P.O. Box 2202, Brownwood, TX 76804 / 915-643-2553; FAX: 915-643-3653
Cation, 2341 Alger St., Troy, MI 48083 / 810-689-0658; FAX: 810-689-7558
Caywood, Shane J., P.O. Box 321, Minocqua, WI 54548 / 715-277-3866
CBC, Avenida Humberto de Campos 3220, 09400-000, Ribeirao Pires, SP, BRAZIL / 55-11-742-7500; FAX: 55-11-459-7385
CBC-BRAZIL, 3 Cuckoo Lane, Honley, Yorkshire HD7 2BR, ENGLAND / 44-1484-661062; FAX: 44-1484-663709
CCG Enterprises, 5217 E. Belknap St., Halton City, TX 76117 / 800-819-7464
CCI Div. of Blount, Inc., Sporting Equipment Div.2299 Sn, P.O. Box 856, Lewiston, ID 83501 / 800-627-3640 or 208-746-2351; FAX: 208-746-2915
CCL Security Products, 199 Whiting St, New Britain, CT 06051 / 800-733-8588
Cedar Hill Game Calls Inc., 238 Vic Allen Rd, Downsville, LA 71234 / 318-982-5632; FAX: 318-368-2245
Celestron International, P.O. Box 3578, 2835 Columbia St., Torrance, CA 90503 / 310-328-9560; FAX: 310-212-5835
Centaur Systems, Inc., 1602 Foothill Rd., Kalispell, MT 59901 / 406-755-8609; FAX: 406-755-8609
Center Lock Scope Rings, 9901 France Ct., Lakeville, MN 55044 / 612-461-2114
Central Specialties Ltd (See Trigger Lock Division/Central Specialties Ltd.,)
Century Gun Dist. Inc., 1467 Jason Rd., Greenfield, IN 46140 / 317-462-4524
Century International Arms, Inc., 1161 Holland Dr, Boca Raton, FL 33487
CFVentures, 509 Harvey Dr., Bloomington, IN 47403-1715
CH Tool & Die Co (See 4-D Custom Die Co), 711 N Sandusky St, PO Box 889, Mt Vernon, OH 43050-0889 / 740-397-7214; FAX: 740-397-6600
Chace Leather Products, 507 Alden St., Fall River, MA 02722 / 508-678-7556; FAX: 508-675-9666
Chadick's Ltd., P.O. Box 100, Terrell, TX 75160 / 214-563-7577
Chambers Flintlocks Ltd., Jim, 116 Sams Branch Rd, Candler, NC 28715 / 828-667-8361 FAX: 828-665-0852

MANUFACTURERS DIRECTORY

Champion Shooters' Supply, P.O. Box 303, New Albany, OH 43054 / 614-855-1603; FAX: 614-855-1209
Champion Target Co., 232 Industrial Parkway, Richmond, IN 47374 / 800-441-4971
Champion's Choice, Inc., 201 International Blvd., LaVergne, TN 37086 / 615-793-4066; FAX: 615-793-4070
Champlin Firearms, Inc., P.O. Box 3191, Woodring Airport, Enid, OK 73701 / 580-237-7388; FAX: 580-242-6922
Chapman Academy of Practical Shooting, 4350 Academy Rd., Hallsville, MO 65255 / 573-696-5544 or 573-696-2266
Chapman, J Ken. (See OLD WEST BULLET MOULDS J ken Champman)
Chapman Manufacturing Co., 471 New Haven Rd., P.O. Box 250, Durham, CT 06422 / 860-349-9228; FAX: 860-349-0084
Chapuis Armes, 21 La Gravoux, BP15, 42380, St. Bonnet-le-Chatea, FRANCE / (33)77.50.06.96+
Chapuis USA, 416 Business Park, Bedford, KY 40006
Charter 2000, 273 Canal St, Shelton, CT 06484 / 203-922-1652
Checkmate Refinishing, 370 Champion Dr., Brooksville, FL 34601 / 352-799-5774 FAX: 352-799-2986
Cheddite France S.A., 99 Route de Lyon, F-26501, Bourg-les-Valence, FRANCE / 33-75-56-4545; FAX: 33-75-56-3587
Chelsea Gun Club of New York City Inc., 237 Ovington Ave., Apt. D53, Brooklyn, NY 11209 / 718-836-9422 or 718-833-2704
Chem-Pak Inc., PO Box 2058, Winchester, VA 22604-1258 / 800-336-9828 or 703-667-1341 FAX: 703-722-3993
Cherry Creek State Park Shooting Center, 12500 E. Belleview Ave., Englewood, CO 80111 / 303-693-1765
Chet Fulmer's Antique Firearms, P.O. Box 792, Rt. 2 Buffalo Lake, Detroit Lakes, MN 56501 / 218-847-7712
CheVron Bullets, RR1, Ottawa, IL 61350 / 815-433-2471
Cheyenne Pioneer Products, PO Box 28425, Kansas City, MO 64188 / 816-413-9196 FAX: 816-455-2859 cheyennepp@aol.com www.cartridgeboxes.com
Chicago Cutlery Co., 1536 Beech St., Terre Haute, IN 47804 / 800-457-2665
Chicasaw Gun Works, 4 Mi. Mkr., Pluto Rd. Box 868, Shady Spring, WV 25918-0868 / 304-763-2848 FAX: 304-763-3725
Chipmunk (See Oregon Arms, Inc.)
Choate Machine & Tool Co., Inc., P.O. Box 218, 116 Lovers Ln., Bald Knob, AR 72010 / 501-724-6193 or 800-972-6390; FAX: 501-724-5873
Chopie Mfg.,Inc., 700 Copeland Ave., LaCrosse, WI 54603 / 608-784-0926
Christensen Arms, 385 N. 3050 E., St. George, UT 84790 / 435-624-9535; FAX: 435-674-9293
Christie's East, 219 E. 67th St., New York, NY 10021 / 212-606-0400
Chu Tani Ind., Inc., P.O. Box 2064, Cody, WY 82414-2064
Chuck's Gun Shop, P.O. Box 597, Waldo, FL 32694 / 904-468-2264
Churchill (See U.S. Importer-Ellett Bros)
Churchill, Winston, Twenty Mile Stream Rd., RFD P.O. Box 29B, Proctorsville, VT 05153 / 802-226-7772
Churchill Glove Co., James, PO Box 298, Centralia, WA 98531 / 360-736-2816 FAX: 360-330-0151
CIDCO, 21480 Pacific Blvd., Sterling, VA 22170 / 703-444-5353
Ciener Inc., Jonathan Arthur, 8700 Commerce St., Cape Canaveral, FL 32920 / 407-868-2200; FAX: 407-868-2201
Cimarron F.A. Co., P.O. Box 906, Fredericksburg, TX 78624-0906 / 210-997-9090; FAX: 210-997-0802
Cincinnati Swaging, 2605 Marlington Ave., Cincinnati, OH 45208
Clark Custom Guns, Inc., 336 Shootout Lane, Princeton, LA 71067 / 318-949-9884; FAX: 318-949-9829
Clark Firearms Engraving, P.O. Box 80746, San Marino, CA 91118 / 818-287-1652
Clarkfield Enterprises, Inc., 1032 10th Ave., Clarkfield, MN 56223 / 612-669-7140
Claro Walnut Gunstock Co., 1235 Stanley Ave., Chico, CA 95928 / 530-342-5188; FAX: 530-342-5199
Classic Arms Company, Rt 1 Box 120F, Burnet, TX 78611 / 512-756-4001
Classic Arms Corp., P.O. Box 106, Dunsmuir, CA 96025-0106 / 530-235-2000
Classic Guns, Inc., Frank S. Wood, 3230 Medlock Bridge Rd., Suite 110, Norcross, GA 30092 / 404-242-7944
Classic Old West Styles, 1060 Doniphan Park Circle C, El Paso, TX 79936 / 915-587-0684

Claybuster Wads & Harvester Bullets, 309 Sequoya Dr., Hopkinsville, KY 42240 / 800-922-6287 or 800-284-1746; FAX: 502-885-8088 50
Clean Shot Technologies, 21218 St. Andrews Blvd. Ste 504, Boca Raton, FL 33433 / 888-866-2532
Clear Creek Outdoors, Pat LaBoone, 2550 Hwy 23, Wrenshall, MN 55797 / 218-384-3670
Clearview Mfg. Co., Inc., 413 S. Oakley St., Fordyce, AR 71742 / 501-352-8557; FAX: 501-352-7120
Clearview Products, 3021 N. Portland, Oklahoma City, OK 73107
Cleland's Outdoor World, Inc, 10306 Airport Hwy, Swanton, OH 43558 / 419-865-4713; FAX: 419-865-5865
Clements' Custom Leathercraft, Chas, 1741 Dallas St., Aurora, CO 80010-2018 / 303-364-0403; FAX: 303-739-9824
Clenzoil Corp., P.O. Box 80226, Sta. C, Canton, OH 44708-0226 / 330-833-9758; FAX: 330-833-4724
Clift Mfg., L. R., 3821 hammonton Rd, Marysville, CA 95901 / 916-755-3390; FAX: 916-755-3393
Clift Welding Supply & Cases, 1332-A Colusa Hwy., Yuba City, CA 95993 / 916-755-3390; FAX: 916-755-3393
Cloward's Gun Shop, 4023 Aurora Ave. N, Seattle, WA 98103 / 206-632-2072
Clymer Manufacturing Co. Inc., 1645 W. Hamlin Rd., Rochester Hills, MI 48309-3312 / 248-853-5555; FAX: 248-853-1530
Cobalt Mfg., Inc., 4020 Mcewen Rd Ste 180, Dallas, TX 75244-5090 / 817-382-8986 FAX: 817-383-4281
Cobra Sport S.r.l., Via Caduti Nei Lager No. 1, 56020 San Romano, Montopoli v/Arno (Pi, ITALY / 0039-571-450490; FAX: 0039-571-450492
Coffin, Charles R., 3719 Scarlet Ave., Odessa, TX 79762 / 915-366-4729 FAX: 915-366-4729
Coffin, Jim (See Working Guns)
Coffin, Jim. See WORKING GUNS
Cogar's Gunsmithing, P.O. Box 755, Houghton Lake, MI 48629 / 517-422-4591
Coghlan's Ltd., 121 Irene St., Winnipeg, MB R3T 4C7 CANADA / 204-284-9550; FAX: 204-475-4127
Cold Steel Inc., 2128-D Knoll Dr., Ventura, CA 93003 / 800-255-4716 or 800-624-2363 FAX: 805-642-9727
Cole's Gun Works, Old Bank Building, Rt. 4 Box 250, Moyock, NC 27958 / 919-435-2345
Cole-Grip, 16135 Cohasset St., Van Nuys, CA 91406 / 818-782-4424
Coleman Co., Inc., 250 N. St. Francis, Wichita, KS 67201
Coleman's Custom Repair, 4035 N. 20th Rd., Arlington, VA 22207 / 703-528-4486
Collectors Firearms Etc, P.O. Box 62, Minnesota City, MN 55959 / 507-689-2925
Collings, Ronald, 1006 Cielta Linda, Vista, CA 92083
Colonial Arms, Inc., P.O. Box 636, Selma, AL 36702-0636 / 334-872-9455; FAX: 334-872-9540 colonialarms@mindspring.com www.colonialarms.com
Colonial Knife Co., Inc., P.O. Box 3327, Providence, RI 02909 / 401-421-1600; FAX: 401-421-2047
Colonial Repair, 47 NAVARRE ST, ROSLINDALE, MA 02131-4725 / 617-469-4951
Colorado Gunsmithing Academy, 27533 Highway 287 South, Lamar, CO 81052 / 719-336-4099 or 800-754-2046; FAX: 719-336-9642
Colorado School of Trades, 1575 Hoyt St., Lakewood, CO 80215 / 800-234-4594; FAX: 303-233-4723
Colorado Sutlers Arsenal (See Cumberland States Arsenal)
Colt Blackpowder Arms Co., 110 8th Street, Brooklyn, NY 11215 / 212-925-2159; FAX: 212-966-4986
Colt's Mfg. Co., Inc., P.O. Box 1868, Hartford, CT 06144-1868 / 800-962-COLT or 860-236-6311; FAX: 860-244-1449
Compass Industries, Inc., 104 East 25th St., New York, NY 10010 / 212-473-2614 or 800-221-9904; FAX: 212-353-0826
Compasseco, Ltd., 151 Atkinson Hill Ave., Bardtown, KY 40004 / 502-349-0910
Competition Electronics, Inc., 3469 Precision Dr., Rockford, IL 61109 / 815-874-8001; FAX: 815-874-8181
Competitor Corp. Inc., Appleton Business Center, 30 Tricnit Road Unit 16, New Ipswich, NH 03071 / 603-878-3891; FAX: 603-878-3950
Component Concepts, Inc., 530 S Springbrook Dr, Newberg, OR 97132-7056 / 503-554-8095 FAX: 503-554-9370
Concept Development Corp., 14715 N. 78th Way, Suite 300, Scottsdale, AZ 85260 / 800-472-4405; FAX: 602-948-7560
Conetrol Scope Mounts, 10225 Hwy. 123 S., Seguin, TX 78155 / 210-379-3030 or 800-CONETROL; FAX: 210-379-3030

CONKKO, P.O. Box 40, Broomall, PA 19008 / 215-356-0711
Connecticut Shotgun Mfg. Co., P.O. Box 1692, 35 Woodland St., New Britain, CT 06051 / 860-225-6581; FAX: 860-832-8707
Connecticut Valley Classics (See CVC)
Conrad, C. A., 3964 Ebert St., Winston-Salem, NC 27127 / 919-788-5469
Cook Engineering Service, 891 Highbury Rd., Vict, 3133 AUSTRALIA
Coonan Arms (JS Worldwide DBA), 1745 Hwy. 36 E., Maplewood, MN 55109 / 612-777-3156; FAX: 612-777-3683
Cooper Arms, P.O. Box 114, Stevensville, MT 59870 / 406-777-5534; FAX: 406-777-5228
Cooper-Woodward, 3800 Pelican Rd., Helena, MT 59602 / 406-458-3800
Cor-Bon Bullet & Ammo Co., 1311 Industry Rd., Sturgis, SD 57785 / 800-626-7266; FAX: 800-923-2666
Corbin Mfg. & Supply, Inc., 600 Industrial Circle, P.O. Box 2659, White City, OR 97503 / 541-826-5211; FAX: 541-826-8669
Corkys Gun Clinic, 4401 Hot Springs Dr., Greeley, CO 80634-9226 / 970-330-0516
Corry, John, 861 Princeton Ct., Neshanic Station, NJ 08853 / 908-369-8019
Cosmi Americo & Figlio s.n.c., Via Flaminia 307, Ancona, ITALY / 071-888208; FAX: 39-071-887008+
Coulston Products, Inc., P.O. Box 30, 201 Ferry St. Suite 212, Easton, PA 18044-0030 / 215-253-0167 or 800-445-9927; FAX: 215-252-1511
Counter Assault, Box 4721, Missoula, MT 59806 / 406-728-6241 FAX: 406-728-8800
Cousin Bob's Mountain Products, 7119 Ohio River Blvd., Ben Avon, PA 15202 / 412-766-5114 FAX: 412-766-5114
Cox, Ed. C., RD 2, Box 192, Prosperity, PA 15329 / 412-228-4984
CP Bullets, 1310 Industrial Hwy #5-6, South Hampton, PA 18966 / 215-953-7264; FAX: 215-953-7275
CQB Training, P.O. Box 1739, Manchester, MO 63011
Craftguard, 3624 Logan Ave., Waterloo, IA 50703 / 319-232-2959 FAX: 319-234-0804
Craig, Spegel, P.O. Box 3108, Bay City, OR 97107 / 503-377-2697
Craig Custom Ltd., Research & Development, 629 E. 10th, Hutchinson, KS 67501 / 316-669-0601
Crandall Tool & Machine Co., 19163 21 Mile Rd., Tustin, MI 49688 / 616-829-4430
Creative Concepts USA, Inc., P.O. Box 1705, Dickson, TN 37056 / 615-446-8346 or 800-874-6965 FAX: 615-446-0646
Creedmoor Sports, Inc., P.O. Box 1040, Oceanside, CA 92051 / 619-757-5529
Creek Side Metal & Woodcrafters, Fishers Hill, VA 22626 / 703-465-3903
Creekside Gun Shop Inc., Main St., Holcomb, NY 14469 / 716-657-6338 FAX: 716-657-7900
Creighton Audette, 19 Highland Circle, Springfield, VT 05156 / 802-885-2331
Crimson Trace Lasers, 1433 N.W. Quimby, Portland, OR 97209 / 503-295-2406; FAX: 503-295-2225
Crit'R Call (See Rocky Mountain Wildlife Products)
Crosman Airguns, Rts. 5 and 20, E. Bloomfield, NY 14443 / 716-657-6161 FAX: 716-657-5405
Crosman Blades (See Coleman Co., Inc.)
Crosman Products of Canada Ltd., 1173 N. Service Rd. West, Oakville, ON L6M 2V9 CANADA / 905-827-1822
Crossfire, L.L.C., 2169 Greenville Rd., La Grange, GA 30241 / 706-882-8070 FAX: 706-882-9050
Crouse's Country Cover, P.O. Box 160, Storrs, CT 06268 / 860-423-8736
CRR, Inc./Marble's Inc., 420 Industrial Park, P.O. Box 111, Gladstone, MI 49837 / 906-428-3710; FAX: 906-428-3711
Crucelegui, Hermanos (See U.S. Importer-Mandall Shooting Supplies Inc.)
Cryo-Accurizing, 2250 N. 1500 West, Ogden, UT 84404 / 801-395-2796 or 888-279-6266
Cubic Shot Shell Co., Inc., 98 Fatima Dr., Campbell, OH 44405 / 330-755-0349
Cullity Restoration, 209 Old Country Rd., East Sandwich, MA 02537 / 508-888-1147
Cumberland Arms, 514 Shafer Road, Manchester, TN 37355 / 800-797-8414
Cumberland Mountain Arms, P.O. Box 710, Winchester, TN 37398 / 615-967-8414; FAX: 615-967-9199
Cumberland States Arsenal, 1124 Palmyra Road, Clarksville, TN 37040

MANUFACTURERS DIRECTORY

Cummings Bullets, 1417 Esperanza Way, Escondido, CA 92027
Cupp, Alana, Custom Engraver, PO Box 207, Annabella, UT 84711 / 801-896-4834
Curly Maple Stock Blanks (See Tiger-Hunt)
Curtis Cast Bullets, 527 W. Babcock St., Bozeman, MT 59715 / 406-587-8117; FAX: 406-587-8117
Curtis Custom Shop, RR1, Box 193A, Wallingford, KY 41093 / 703-659-4265
Curtis Gun Shop (See Curtis Cast Bullets)
Custom Bullets by Hoffman, 2604 Peconic Ave., Seaford, NY 11783
Custom Calls, 607 N. 5th St., Burlington, IA 52601 / 319-752-4465
Custom Checkering Service, Kathy Forster, 2124 SE Yamhill St., Portland, OR 97214 / 503-236-5874
Custom Chronograph, Inc., 5305 Reese Hill Rd., Sumas, WA 98295 / 360-988-7801
Custom Firearms (See Ahrends, Kim)
Custom Gun Products, 5021 W. Rosewood, Spokane, WA 99208 / 509-328-9340
Custom Gun Stocks, 3062 Turners Bend Rd, McMinnville, TN 37110 / 615-668-3912
Custom Products (See Jones Custom Products)
Custom Quality Products, Inc., 345 W. Girard Ave., P.O. Box 71129, Madison Heights, MI 48071 / 810-585-1616; FAX: 810-585-0644
Custom Riflestocks, Inc., Michael M. Kokolus, 7005 Herber Rd., New Tripoli, PA 18066 / 610-298-3013
Custom Tackle and Ammo, P.O. Box 1886, Farmington, NM 87499 / 505-632-3539
Cutco Cutlery, P.O. Box 810, Olean, NY 14760 / 716-372-3111
CVA, 5988 Peachtree Corners East, Norcross, GA 30071 / 800-251-9412; FAX: 404-242-8546
CVC, 5988 Peachtree Crns East, Norcross, GA 30071
Cylinder & Slide, Inc., William R. Laughridge, 245 E. 4th St., Fremont, NE 68025 / 402-721-4277; FAX: 402-721-0263
CZ USA, PO Box 171073, Kansas City, KS 66117 / 913-321-1811; FAX: 913-321-4901

D

D&D Gunsmiths, Ltd., 363 E. Elmwood, Troy, MI 48083 / 810-583-1512; FAX: 810-583-1524
D&G Precision Duplicators (See Greene Precision Du
D&H Precision Tooling, 7522 Barnard Mill Rd., Ringwood, IL 60072 / 815-653-4011
D&H Prods. Co., Inc., 465 Denny Rd., Valencia, PA 16059 / 412-898-2840 or 800-776-0281; FAX: 412-898-2013
D&J Bullet Co. & Custom Gun Shop, Inc., 426 Ferry St., Russell, KY 41169 / 606-836-2663; FAX: 606-836-2663
D&L Industries (See D.J. Marketing)
D&L Sports, P.O. Box 651, Gillette, WY 82717 / 307-686-4008
D&R Distributing, 308 S.E. Valley St., Myrtle Creek, OR 97457 / 503-863-6850
D-Boone Ent., Inc., 5900 Colwyn Dr., Harrisburg, PA 17109
D.C.C. Enterprises, 259 Wynburn Ave., Athens, GA 30601
D.D. Custom Stocks, R.H. "Dick" Devereaux, 5240 Mule Deer Dr., Colorado Springs, CO 80919 / 719-548-8468
D.J. Marketing, 10602 Horton Ave., Downey, CA 90241 / 310-806-0891; FAX: 310-806-6231
Da-Mar Gunsmith's Inc., 102 1st St., Solvay, NY 13209
Dade Screw Machine Products, 2319 NW 7th Ave., Miami, FL 33127 / 305-573-5050
Daewoo Precision Industries Ltd., 34-3 Yeoeuido-Dong, Yeongdeungoo-GU 15th Fl., Seoul, KOREA
Daisy Mfg. Co., PO Box 220, Rogers, AR 72757 / 501-621-4210; FAX: 501-636-0573
Dakota (See U.S. Importer-EMF Co., Inc.)
Dakota Arms, Inc., HC 55, Box 326, Sturgis, SD 57785 / 605-347-4686; FAX: 605-347-4459
Dakota Corp., 77 Wales St., P.O. Box 543, Rutland, VT 05701 / 802-775-6062 or 800-451-4167; FAX: 802-773-3919
DAMASCUS-U.S.A., 149 Deans Farm Rd., Tyner, NC 27980 / 252-221-2010; FAX: 252-221-2009
DAN WESSON FIREARMS, 119 Kemper Lane, Norwich, NY 13815 / 607-336-1174; FAX: 607-336-2730
Dan's Whetstone Co., Inc., 130 Timbs Place, Hot Springs, AR 71913 / 501-767-1616; FAX: 501-767-9598
Danforth, Mikael. (See VEKTOR USA, Mikael Danforth)
Dangler, Homer L., Box 254, Addison, MI 49220 / 517-547-6745

Danner Shoe Mfg. Co., 12722 NE Airport Way, Portland, OR 97230 / 503-251-1100 or 800-345-0430; FAX: 503-251-1119
Danuser Machine Co., 550 E. Third St., P.O. Box 368, Fulton, MO 65251 / 573-642-2246; FAX: 573-642-2240
Dara-Nes, Inc. (See Nesci Enterprises, Inc.)
Darlington Gun Works, Inc., P.O. Box 698, 516 S. 52 Bypass, Darlington, SC 29532 / 803-393-3931
Darwin Hensley Gunmaker, P.O. Box 329, Brightwood, OR 97011 / 503-622-5411
Data Tech Software Systems, 19312 East Eldorado Drive, Aurora, CO 80013
Datumtech Corp., 2275 Wehrle Dr., Buffalo, NY 14221
Dave Norin Schrank's Smoke & Gun, 2010 Washington St., Waukegan, IL 60085 / 708-662-4034
Dave's Gun Shop, 555 Wood Street, Powell, WY 82435 / 307-754-9724
David Clark Co., Inc., PO Box 15054, Worcester, MA 01615-0054 / 508-756-6216; FAX: 508-753-5827
David Condon, Inc., 109 E. Washington St., Middleburg, VA 22117 / 703-687-5642
David Miller Co., 3131 E Greenlee Rd, Tucson, AZ 85716 / 520-326-3117
David R. Chicoine, 19 Key St., Eastport, ME 04631 / 207-853-4116 gnpress@nemaine.com
David W. Schwartz Custom Guns, 2505 Waller St, Eau Claire, WI 54703 / 715-832-1735
Davide Pedersoli and Co., Via Artigiani 57, Gardone VT, Brescia 25063, ITALY / 030-8912402; FAX: 030-8911019
Davidson, Jere, Rt. 1, Box 132, Rustburg, VA 24588 / 804-821-3637
Davis, Don, 1619 Heights, Katy, TX 77493 / 713-391-3090
Davis Industries, 15150 Sierra Bonita Ln., Chino, CA 91710 / 909-597-4726; FAX: 909-393-9771
Davis Products, Mike, 643 Loop Dr., Moses Lake, WA 98837 / 509-765-6178 or 509-766-7281
Daystate Ltd., Birch House Lanee, Cotes Heath Staffs, ST15.022, ENGLAND / 01782-791755; FAX: 01782-791617
Dayton Traister, 4778 N. Monkey Hill Rd., P.O. Box 593, Oak Harbor, WA 98277 / 360-679-4657; FAX: 360-675-1114
DBI Books Division of Krause Publications 700 E State St, Iola, WI 54990-0001 / 630-759-1229
de Coux, Pete (See Cartridge Transfer Group)
Dead Eye's Sport Center, RD 1, 76 Baer Rd, Shickshinny, PA 18655 / 570-256-7432
Decker Shooting Products, 1729 Laguna Ave., Schofield, WI 54476 / 715-359-5873
Deepeeka Exports Pvt. Ltd., D-78, Saket, Meerut-250-006, INDIA / 011-91-121-512889 or 011-91-121-545363; FAX: 011-91-121-542988
Deer Me Products Co., Box 34, 1208 Park St., Anoka, MN 55303 / 612-421-8971; FAX: 612-422-0526
Defense Training International, Inc., 749 S. Lemay, Ste. A3-337, Ft. Collins, CO 80524 / 303-482-2520; FAX: 303-482-0548
Degen Inc. (See Aristocrat Knives)
deHaas Barrels, RR 3, Box 77, Ridgeway, MO 64481 / 816-872-6308
Del Rey Products, P.O. Box 5134, Playa Del Rey, CA 90296-5134 / 213-823-0494
Del-Sports, Inc., Box 685, Main St., Margaretville, NY 12455 / 914-586-4103; FAX: 914-586-4105
Delhi Gun House, 1374 Kashmere Gate, Delhi, 0110 006 INDIA FAX: 91-11-2917344
Delorge, Ed, 6734 W. Main, Houma, LA 70360 / 504-223-0206
Delta Arms Ltd., P.O. Box 1000, Delta, VT 84624-1000
Delta Enterprises, 284 Hagemann Drive, Livermore, CA 94550
Delta Frangible Ammunition LLC, P.O. Box 2350, Stafford, VA 22555-2350 / 540-720-5778 or 800-339-1933; FAX: 540-720-5667
Dem-Bart Checkering Tools, Inc., 6807 Bickford Ave., Old Hwy. 2, Snohomish, WA 98290 / 360-568-7356; FAX: 360-568-1798
Denver Instrument Co., 6542 Fig St., Arvada, CO 80004 / 800-321-1135 or 303-431-7255; FAX: 303-423-4831
DeSantis Holster & Leather Goods, Inc., P.O. Box 2039, 149 Denton Ave., New Hyde Park, NY 11040-0701 / 516-354-8000; FAX: 516-354-7501
Desert Mountain Mfg., P.O. Box 130184, Coram, MT 59913 / 800-477-0762 or 406-387-5361; FAX: 406-387-5361
Detroit-Armor Corp., 720 Industrial Dr. No. 112, Cary, IL 60013 / 708-639-7666; FAX: 708-639-7694

Dever Co, Jack, 8590 NW 90, Oklahoma City, OK 73132 / 405-721-6393
Devereaux, R.H. "Dick" (See D.D. Custom Stocks, R.H. "Dick Devereaux)
Dewey Mfg. Co., Inc., J., P.O. Box 2014, Southbury, CT 06488 / 203-264-3064; FAX: 203-262-6907 deweyrods@worldnet.att.net www.deweyrods.com
DGR Custom Rifles, 4191 37th Ave SE, Tappen, ND 58487 / 701-327-8135
DGS, Inc., Dale A. Storey, 1117 E. 12th, Casper, WY 82601 / 307-237-2414 FAX: 307-237-2414 dalest@trib.com www.dgsrifle.com
DHB Products, P.O. Box 3092, Alexandria, VA 22302 / 703-836-2648
Diamond Machining Technology, Inc. (See DMT)
Diamond Mfg. Co., P.O. Box 174, Wyoming, PA 18644 / 800-233-9601
Diana (See U.S. Importer - Dynamit Nobel-RWS, Inc., 81 Ruckman Rd., Closter, NJ 07624 / 201-767-7971; (FAX: 201-767-1589)
Dibble, Derek A., 555 John Downey Dr., New Britain, CT 06051 / 203-224-2630
Dick Marple & Associates, 21 Dartmouth St, Hooksett, NH 03106 / 603-627-1837; FAX: 603-627-1837
Dietz Gun Shop & Range, Inc., 421 Range Rd., New Braunfels, TX 78132 / 210-885-4662
Dilliott Gunsmithing, Inc., 657 Scarlett Rd., Dandridge, TN 37725 / 865-397-9204 gunsmithd@aol.com dilliottgunsmithing.com
Dillon, Ed, 1035 War Eagle Dr. N., Colorado Springs, CO 80919 / 719-598-4929; FAX: 719-598-4929
Dillon Precision Products, Inc., 8009 East Dillon's Way, Scottsdale, AZ 85260 / 602-948-8009 or 800-762-3845; FAX: 602-998-2786
Dina Arms Corporation, P.O. Box 46, Royersford, PA 19468 / 610-287-0266; FAX: 610-287-0266
Division Lead Co., 7742 W. 61st Pl., Summit, IL 60502
Dixie Gun Works, Inc., Hwy. 51 South, Union City, TN 38261 / order 800-238-6785;
Dixon Muzzleloading Shop, Inc., 9952 Kunkels Mill Rd., Kempton, PA 19529 / 610-756-6271
DKT, Inc., 14623 Vera Drive, Union, MI 49130-9744 / 800-741-7083 orders; FAX: 616-641-2015
DLO Mfg., 10807 SE Foster Ave., Arcadia, FL 33821-7304
DMT--Diamond Machining Technology Inc., 85 Hayes Memorial Dr., Marlborough, MA 01752 FAX: 508-485-3924
Doctor Optic Technologies, Inc., 4685 Boulder Highway, Suite A, Las Vegas, NV 89121 / 800-290-3634 or 702-898-7161; FAX: 702-898-3737
Dohring Bullets, 100 W. 8 Mile Rd., Ferndale, MI 48220
Dolbare, Elizabeth, P.O. Box 222, Sunburst, MT 59482-0222
Domino, PO Box 108, 20019 Settimo Milanese, Milano, ITALY / 1-39-2-33512040; FAX: 1-39-2-33511587
Donnelly, C. P., 405 Kubli Rd., Grants Pass, OR 97527 / 541-846-6604
Doskocil Mfg. Co., Inc., P.O. Box 1246, 4209 Barnett, Arlington, TX 76017 / 817-467-5116; FAX: 817-472-9810
Double A Ltd., P.O. Box 11306, Minneapolis, MN 55411 / 612-522-0306
Douglas Barrels Inc., 5504 Big Tyler Rd., Charleston, WV 25313-1398 / 304-776-1341; FAX: 304-776-8560
Downsizer Corp., P.O. Box 710316, Santee, CA 92072-0316 / 619-448-5510; FAX: 619-448-5780 www.downsizer.com
Dr. O's Products Ltd., P.O. Box 111, Niverville, NY 12130 / 518-784-3333; FAX: 518-784-2800
Drain, Mark, SE 3211 Kamilche Point Rd., Shelton, WA 98584 / 206-426-5452
Dremel Mfg. Co., 4915-21st St., Racine, WI 53406
Dressel Jr., Paul G., 209 N. 92nd Ave., Yakima, WA 98908 / 509-966-9233; FAX: 509-966-3365
Dri-Slide, Inc., 411 N. Darling, Fremont, MI 49412 / 616-924-3950
Dropkick, 1460 Washington Blvd., Williamsport, PA 17701 / 717-326-6561; FAX: 717-326-4950
DTM International, Inc., 40 Joslyn Rd., P.O. Box 5, Lake Orion, MI 48362 / 313-693-6670
Du-Lite Corp., 171 River Rd., Middletown, CT 06457 / 203-347-2505; FAX: 203-347-9404
Duane A Hobbie Gunsmithing, 2412 Pattie Ave, Wichita, KS 67216 / 316-264-8266
Duane's Gun Repair (See DGR Custom Rifles)
Dubber, Michael W., P.O. Box 312, Evansville, IN 47702 / 812-424-9000; FAX: 812-424-6551
Duck Call Specialists, P.O. Box 124, Jerseyville, IL 62052 / 618-498-9855

MANUFACTURERS DIRECTORY

Duffy, Charles E (See Guns Antique & Modern DBA), Williams Lane, PO Box 2, West Hurley, NY 12491 / 914-679-2997
Dumoulin, Ernest, Rue Florent Boclinville 8-10, 13-4041, Votten, BELGIUM / 41 27 78 92
Duncan's Gun Works, Inc., 1619 Grand Ave., San Marcos, CA 92069 / 619-727-0515
Dunham Boots, 1 Keuka business Park #300, Penn Yan, NY 14527-8995 / 802-254-2316
Duofold, Inc., RD 3 Rt. 309, Valley Square Mall, Tamaqua, PA 18252 / 717-386-2666; FAX: 717-386-3652
Dybala Gun Shop, P.O. Box 1024, FM 3156, Bay City, TX 77414 / 409-245-0866
Dykstra, Doug, 411 N. Darling, Fremont, MI 49412 / 616-924-3950
Dynalite Products, Inc., 215 S. Washington St., Greenfield, OH 45123 / 513-981-2124
Dynamit Nobel-RWS, Inc., 81 Ruckman Rd., Closter, NJ 07624 / 201-767-7971; FAX: 201-767-1589

E

E&L Mfg., Inc., 4177 Riddle By Pass Rd., Riddle, OR 97469 / 541-874-2137; FAX: 541-874-3107
E-A-R, Inc., Div. of Cabot Safety Corp., 5457 W. 79th St., Indianapolis, IN 46268 / 800-327-3431; FAX: 800-488-8007
E-Z-Way Systems, P.O. Box 4310, Newark, OH 43058-4310 / 614-345-6645 or 800-848-2072; FAX: 614-345-6600
E. Arthur Brown Co., 3404 Pawnee Dr., Alexandria, MN 56308 / 320-762-8847
E.A.A. Corp., P.O. Box 1299, Sharpes, FL 32959 / 407-639-4842 or 800-536-4442; FAX: 407-639-7006
Eagan, Donald V., P.O. Box 196, Benton, PA 17814 / 717-925-6134
Eagle Arms, Inc. (See ArmaLite, Inc.)
Eagle Grips, Eagle Business Center, 460 Randy Rd., Carol Stream, IL 60188 / 800-323-6144 or 708-260-0400; FAX: 708-260-0486
Eagle Imports, Inc., 1750 Brielle Ave., Unit B1, Wanamassa, NJ 07712 / 908-493-0333
EAW (See U.S. Importer-New England Custom Gun Service)
Echols & Co., D'Arcy, 164 W. 580 S., Providence, UT 84332 / 801-753-2367
Eckelman Gunsmithing, 3125 133rd St. SW, Fort Ripley, MN 56449 / 218-829-3176
Eclectic Technologies, Inc., 45 Grandview Dr., Suite A, Farmington, CT 06034
Ed~ Brown Products, Inc., 43825 Muldrow Trail, Perry, MO 63462 / 573-565-3261; FAX: 573-565-2791
Eddie Salter Calls, Inc., Hwy. 31 South-Brewton Industrial, Park, Brewton, AL 36426 / 205-867-2584; FAX: 206-867-9005
Edenpine, Inc. c/o Six Enterprises, Inc., 320 D Turtle Creek Ct., San Jose, CA 95125 / 408-999-0201; FAX: 408-999-0216
EdgeCraft Corp., S. Weiner, 825 Southwood Road, Avondale, PA 19311 / 610-268-0500 or 800-342-3255; FAX: 610-268-3545 www.chefschoice.com
Edmisten Co., P.O. Box 1293, Boone, NC 28607
Edmund Scientific Co., 101 E. Gloucester Pike, Barrington, NJ 08033 / 609-543-6250
Ednar, Inc., 2-4-8 Kayabacho, Nihonbashi Chuo-ku, Tokyo, JAPAN / 81(Japan)-3-3667-1651; FAX: 81-3-3661-8113
Eezox, Inc., P.O. Box 772, Waterford, CT 06385-0772 / 800-462-3331; FAX: 860-447-3484
Effebi SNC-Dr. Franco Beretta, via Rossa, 4, 25062, ITALY / 030-2751955; FAX: 030-2180414
Efficient Machinery Co, 12878 NE 15th Pl, Bellevue, WA 98005
Eggleston, Jere D., 400 Saluda Ave., Columbia, SC 29205 / 803-799-3402
EGW Evolution Gun Works, 4050 B-8 Skyron Dr., Doylestown, PA 18901 / 215-348-9892; FAX: 215-348-1056
Eichelberger Bullets, Wm, 158 Crossfield Rd., King Of Prussia, PA 19406
Ekol Leather Care, P.O. Box 2652, West Lafayette, IN 47906 / 317-463-2250; FAX: 317-463-7004
El Dorado Leather (c/o Dill), P.O. Box 566, Benson, AZ 85602 / 520-586-4791; FAX: 520-586-4791
El Paso Saddlery Co., P.O. Box 27194, El Paso, TX 79926 / 915-544-2233; FAX: 915-544-2535
Eldorado Cartridge Corp (See PMC/Eldorado Cartridge Corp.)

Electro Prismatic Collimators, Inc., 1441 Manatt St., Lincoln, NE 68521
Electronic Shooters Protection, Inc., 11997 West 85th Place, Arvada, CO 80005 / 800-797-7791; FAX: 303-456-7179
Electronic Trigger Systems, Inc., P.O. Box 13, 230 Main St. S., Hector, MN 55342 / 320-848-2760; FAX: 320-848-2760
Eley Ltd., P.O. Box 705, Witton, Birmingham, B6 7UT ENGLAND / 021-356-8899; FAX: 021-331-4173
Elite Ammunition, P.O. Box 3251, Oakbrook, IL 60522 / 708-366-9006
Elk River, Inc., 1225 Paonia St., Colorado Springs, CO 80915 / 719-574-4407
Elkhorn Bullets, P.O. Box 5293, Central Point, OR 97502 / 541-826-7440
Ellett Bros., 267 Columbia Ave., P.O. Box 128, Chapin, SC 29036 / 803-345-3751 or 800-845-3711; FAX: 803-345-1820
Ellicott Arms, Inc./Woods Pistolsmithing, 3840 Dahlgren Ct., Ellicott City, MD 21042 / 410-465-7979
Elliott Inc., G. W., 514 Burnside Ave, East Hartford, CT 06108 / 203-289-5741; FAX: 203-289-3137
Elsen Inc., Pete, 1523 S 113th St, West Allis, WI 53214
Emerging Technologies, Inc. (See Laseraim Technologies, Inc.)
Emap USA, 6420 Wilshire Blvd., Los Angeles, CA 90048 / 213-782-2000; FAX: 213-782-2867
EMF Co., Inc., 1900 E. Warner Ave., Suite 1-D, Santa Ana, CA 92705 / 714-261-6611; FAX: 714-756-0133
Empire Cutlery Corp., 12 Kruger Ct., Clifton, NJ 07013 / 201-472-5155; FAX: 201-779-0759
English, Inc., A.G., 708 S. 12th St., Broken Arrow, OK 74012 / 918-251-3399
Engraving Artistry, 36 Alto Rd., RFD 2, Burlington, CT 06013 / 203-673-6837
Enguix Import-Export, Alpujarras 58, Alzira, Valencia, SPAIN / (96) 241 43 95; FAX: (96) (241 43 95
Enhanced Presentations, Inc., 5929 Market St., Wilmington, NC 28405 / 910-799-1622; FAX: 910-799-5004
Enlow, Charles, 895 Box, Beaver, OK 73932 / 405-625-4487
Entre'prise Arms, Inc., 15861 Business Center Dr., Irwindale, CA 91706
EPC, 1441 Manatt St., Lincoln, NE 68521 / 402-476-3946
Epps, Ellwood (See "Gramps" Antique, Box 341, Washago, ON L0K 2B0 CANADA / 705-689-5348
Erhardt, Dennis, 3280 Green Meadow Dr., Helena, MT 59601 / 406-442-4533
Erma Werke GmbH, Johan Ziegler St., 13/15/FeldigISt., D-8060 Dachau, GERMANY
Eskridge Rifles, Steven Eskridge, 218 N. Emerson, Mart, TX 76664 / 817-876-3544
Eskridge, Steven. (See ESKRIDGE RIFLES)
Essex Arms, P.O. Box 363, Island Pond, VT 05846 / 802-723-6203 FAX: 802-723-6203
Essex Metals, 1000 Brighton St., Union, NJ 07083 / 800-282-8369
Estate Cartridge, Inc., 12161 FM 830, Willis, TX 77378 / 409-856-7277; FAX: 409-856-5486
Euber Bullets, No. Orwell Rd., Orwell, VT 05760 / 802-948-2621
Euro-Imports, 905 West Main St Ste E, El Cajon, CA 92020 / 619-442-7005; FAX: 619-442-7005
Euroarms of America, Inc., P.O. Box 3277, Winchester, VA 22604 / 540-662-1863; FAX: 540-662-4464
European American Armory Corp (See E.A.A. Corp)
Evans, Andrew, 2325 NW Squire St., Albany, OR 97321 / 541-928-3190; FAX: 541-928-4128
Evans Engraving, Robert, 332 Vine St, Oregon City, OR 97045 / 503-656-5693
Evans Gunsmithing (See Evans, Andrew)
Eversull Co., Inc., K., 1 Tracemont, Boyce, LA 71409 / 318-793-8728; FAX: 318-793-5483
Excalibur Electro Optics Inc., P.O. Box 400, Fogelsville, PA 18051-0400 / 610-391-9105; FAX: 610-391-9220
Excel Industries Inc., 4510 Carter Ct., Chino, CA 91710 / 909-627-2404; FAX: 909-627-7817
Executive Protection Institute, PO Box 802, Berryville, VA 22611 / 540-955-1128
Eyster Heritage Gunsmiths, Inc., Ken, 6441 Bishop Rd., Centerburg, OH 43011 / 614-625-6131
Eze-Lap Diamond Prods., P.O. Box 2229, 15164 West State St., Westminster, CA 92683 / 714-847-1555; FAX: 714-897-0280

F

F&A Inc. (See ShurKatch Corporation)
F.A.I.R. Techni-Mec s.n.c. di Isidoro Rizzini & C., Via Gitti, 41 Zona Industrial, 25060 Marcheno (Bres, ITALY / 030/861162-8610344; FAX: 030/8610179
Fabarm S.p.A., Via Averolda 31, 25039 Travagliato, Brescia, ITALY / 030-6863629; FAX: 030-6863684
Fagan & Co.Inc, 22952 15 Mile Rd., Clinton Township, MI 48035 / 810-465-4637; FAX: 810-792-6996
Fair Game International, P.O. Box 77234-34053, Houston, TX 77234 / 713-941-6269
Faith Associates, Inc., PO Box 549, Flat Rock, NC 28731-0549 / 828-692-1916; FAX: 828-697-6827
Fanzoj GmbH, Griesgasse 1, 9170 Ferlach, 9170 AUSTRIA / (43) 04227-2283; FAX: (43) 04227-2867
Far North Outfitters, Box 1252, Bethel, AK 99559
Farm Form Decoys, Inc., 1602 Biovu, P.O. Box 748, Galveston, TX 77553 / 409-744-0762 or 409-765-6361; FAX: 409-765-8513
Farmer-Dressel, Sharon, 209 N. 92nd Ave., Yakima, WA 98908 / 509-966-9233; FAX: 509-966-3365
Farr Studio,Inc., 1231 Robinhood Rd., Greeneville, TN 37743 / 615-638-8825
Farrar Tool Co., Inc., 12150 Bloomfield Ave., Suite E, Santa Fe Springs, CA 90670 / 310-863-4367; FAX: 310-863-5123
Faulhaber Wildlocker, Dipl.-Ing. Norbert Wittasek, Seilergasse 2, A-1010 Wien, AUSTRIA / OM-43-1-5137001; FAX: OM-43-1-5137001
Faulk's Game Call Co., Inc., 616 18th St., Lake Charles, LA 70601 / 318-436-9726 FAX: 318-494-7205
Faust Inc., T. G., 544 minor St, Reading, PA 19602 / 610-375-8549; FAX: 610-375-4488
Fausti Cav. Stefano & Figlie snc, Via Martiri Dell Indipendenza, 70, Marcheno, 25060 ITALY
Fautheree, Andy, P.O. Box 4607, Pagosa Springs, CO 81157 / 970-731-5003; FAX: 970-731-5009
Feather, Flex Decoys, 1655 Swan Lake Rd., Bossier City, LA 71111 / 318-746-8596; FAX: 318-742-4815
Federal Arms Corp. of America, 7928 University Ave, Fridley, MN 55432 / 612-780-8780; FAX: 612-780-8780
Federal Cartridge Co., 900 Ehlen Dr., Anoka, MN 55303 / 612-323-2300; FAX: 612-323-2506
Federal Champion Target Co., 232 Industrial Parkway, Richmond, IN 47374 / 800-441-4971; FAX: 317-966-7747
Federated-Fry (See Fry Metals)
FEG, Budapest, Soroksariut 158, H-1095, HUNGARY
Feken, Dennis, Rt. 2, Box 124, Perry, OK 73077 / 405-336-5611
Felk, Inc., 2121 Castlebridge Rd., Midlothian, VA 23113 / 804-794-3744
Fellowes, Ted, Beaver Lodge, 9245 16th Ave. SW, Seattle, WA 98106 / 206-763-1698
Feminine Protection, Inc., 949 W. Kearney Ste. 100, Mesquite, TX 75149 / 972-289-8997 FAX: 972-289-4410
Ferguson, Bill, P.O. Box 1238, Sierra Vista, AZ 85636 / 520-458-5321; FAX: 520-458-9125
FERLIB, Via Costa 46, 25063, Gardone V.T., ITALY / 30-89-12-586; FAX: 30-89-12-586
Ferris Firearms, 7110 F.M. 1863, Bulverde, TX 78163 / 210-980-4424
Fibron Products, Inc., P.O. Box 430, Buffalo, NY 14209-0430 / 716-886-2378; FAX: 716-886-2394
Fieldsport Ltd, Bryan Bilinski, 3313 W South Airport Rd, Traverse Vity, MI 49684 / 616-933-0767
Fiocchi Munizioni S.p.A. (See U.S. Importer-Fiocchi of America, Inc.,)
Fiocchi of America Inc., 5030 Fremont Rd., Ozark, MO 65721 / 417-725-4118 or 800-721-2666 FAX: 417-725-1039
Firearms Co Ltd/Alpine (See U.S. Importer-Mandall Shooting Supplies, Inc.)
Firearms Engraver's Guild of America, 332 Vine St., Oregon City, OR 97045 / 503-656-5693
Firearms International, 5709 Hartsdale, Houston, TX 77036 / 713-460-2447
First Inc, Jack, 1201 Turbine Dr., Rapid City, SD 57701 / 605-343-9544; FAX: 605-343-9420
Fish Mfg. Gunsmith Sptg. Co., Marshall F, Rd. Box 2439, Rt. 22 N, Westport, NY 12993 / 518-962-4897 FAX: 518-962-4897
Fisher, Jerry A., 553 Crane Mt. Rd., Big Fork, MT 59911 / 406-837-2722
Fisher Custom Firearms, 2199 S. Kittredge Way, Aurora, CO 80013 / 303-755-3710
Fisher Enterprises, Inc., 1071 4th Ave. S., Suite 303, Edmonds, WA 98020-4143 / 206-771-5382

Manufacturers Directory

Fisher, R. Kermit (See Fisher Enterprises, Inc), 1071 4th Ave S Ste 303, Edmonds, WA 98020-4143 / 206-771-5382

Fitz Pistol Grip Co., P.O. Box 744, LEWISTON, CA 96052-0744 / 916-778-0240

Flambeau Products Corp., 15981 Valplast Rd., Middlefield, OH 44062 / 216-632-1631; FAX: 216-632-1581

Flannery Engraving Co., Jeff W, 11034 Riddles Run Rd, Union, KY 41091 / 606-384-3127

Flashette Co., 4725 S. Kolin Ave., Chicago, IL 60632 FAX: 773-927-3083

Flayderman & Co., Inc., PO Box 2446, Ft Lauderdale, FL 33303 / 954-761-8855

Fleming Firearms, 7720 E 126th St. N, Collinsville, OK 74021-7016 / 918-665-3624

Flents Products Co., Inc., P.O. Box 2109, Norwalk, CT 06852 / 203-866-2581; FAX: 203-854-9322

Flintlocks Etc., 160 Rositter Rd, Richmond, MA 01254 / 413-698-3822

Flintlocks, Etc, 160 Rossiter Rd., P.O. Box 181, Richmond, MA 01254 / 413-698-3822; FAX: 413-698-3866 flintetc@vgernet.net pedersoli

Flitz International Ltd., 821 Mohr Ave., Waterford, WI 53185 / 414-534-5898; FAX: 414-534-2991

Flores Publications Inc, J (See Action Direct Inc), PO Box 830760, Miami, FL 33283 / 305-559-4652; FAX: 305-559-4652

Fluoramics, Inc., 18 Industrial Ave., Mahwah, NJ 07430 / 800-922-0075; FAX: 201-825-7035

Flynn's Custom Guns, P.O. Box 7461, Alexandria, LA 71306 / 318-455-7130

FN Herstal, Voie de Liege 33, Herstal, 4040 Belgium / (32)41.40.82.83; FAX: (32)41.40.86.79

Fobus International Ltd., P.O. Box 64, Kfar Hess, 40692 ISRAEL / 972-9-7964170; FAX: 972-9-7964169

Folks, Donald E., 205 W. Lincoln St., Pontiac, IL 61764 / 815-844-7901

Foothills Video Productions, Inc., P.O. Box 651, Spartanburg, SC 29304 / 803-573-7023 or 800-782-5358

Foredom Electric Co., Rt. 6, 16 Stony Hill Rd., Bethel, CT 06801 / 203-792-8622

Forgett Jr., Valmore J., 689 Bergen Blvd., Ridgefield, NJ 07657 / 201-945-2500; FAX: 201-945-6859

Forgreens Tool Mfg., Inc., P.O. Box 990, 723 Austin St., Robert Lee, TX 76945 / 915-453-2800; FAX: 915-453-2460

Forkin, Ben (See Belt MTN Arms)

Forkin Arms, 205 10th Ave SW, White Sulphur Spring, MT 59645 / 406-547-2344; FAX: 406-547-2456

Forrest Inc., Tom, PO Box 326, Lakeside, CA 92040 / 619-561-5800; FAX: 619-561-0227

Forrest Tool Co., P.O. Box 768, 44380 Gordon Lane, Mendocino, CA 95460 / 707-937-2141; FAX: 717-937-1817

Forster, Kathy (See Custom Checkering Service, Kathy Forster)

Forster, Larry L., P.O. Box 212, 220 First St. NE, Gwinner, ND 58040-0212 / 701-678-2475

Forster Products, 310 E Lanark Rd, Lanark, IL 61046 / 815-493-6360; FAX: 815-493-2371

Fort Hill Gunstocks, 12807 Fort Hill Rd., Hillsboro, OH 45133 / 513-466-2763

Fort Knox Security Products, 1051 N. Industrial Park Rd., Orem, UT 84057 / 801-224-7233 or 800-821-5216; FAX: 801-226-5493

Fort Worth Firearms, 2006-B, Martin Luther King Fwy., Ft. Worth, TX 76104-6303 / 817-536-0718; FAX: 817-535-0290

Forthofer's Gunsmithing & Knifemaking, 5535 U.S. Hwy 93S, Whitefish, MT 59937-8411 / 406-862-2674

Fortune Products, Inc., HC04, Box 303, Marble Falls, TX 78654 / 210-693-6111; FAX: 210-693-6394

Forty Five Ranch Enterprises, Box 1080, Miami, OK 74355-1080 / 918-542-5875

Fountain Products, 492 Prospect Ave., West Springfield, MA 01089 / 413-781-4651; FAX: 413-733-8217

4-D Custom Die Co., 711 N. Sandusky St., P.O. Box 889, Mt. Vernon, OH 43050-0889 / 740-397-7214; FAX: 740-397-6600

Fowler Bullets, 806 Dogwood Dr., Gastonia, NC 28054 / 704-867-3259

Fowler, Bob (See Black Powder Products)

Fox River Mills, Inc., P.O. Box 298, 227 Poplar St., Osage, IA 50461 / 515-732-3798; FAX: 515-732-5128

Foy Custom Bullets, 104 Wells Ave., Daleville, AL 36322

Francesca, Inc., 3115 Old Ranch Rd., San Antonio, TX 78217 / 512-826-2584; FAX: 512-826-8211

Franchi S.p.A., Via del Serpente 12, 25131, Brescia, ITALY / 030-3581833; FAX: 030-3581554

Francotte & Cie S.A. Auguste, rue de Trois Juin 109, 4400 Herstal-Liege, BELGIUM / 32-4-248-13-18; FAX: 32-4-948-11-79

Frank Custom Classic Arms, Ron, 7131 Richland Rd, Ft Worth, TX 76118 / 817-284-9300; FAX: 817-284-9300

Frank E. Hendricks Master Engravers, Inc., HC03, Box 434, Dripping Springs, TX 78620 / 512-858-7828

Frank Knives, 13868 NW Keleka Pl., Seal Rock, OR 97376 / 541-563-3041; FAX: 541-563-3041

Frank Mittermeier, Inc., P.O. Box 2G, 3577 E. Tremont Ave., Bronx, NY 10465 / 718-828-3843

Frankonia Jagd Hofmann & Co., D-97064 Wurzburg, Wurzburg, GERMANY / 09302-200; FAX: 09302-20200

Franzen International,Inc (U.S. Importer for Peters Stahl GmbH)

Fred F. Wells/Wells Sport Store, 110 N Summit St, Prescott, AZ 86301 / 520-445-3655

Freedom Arms, Inc., P.O. Box 150, Freedom, WY 83120 / 307-883-2468 or 800-833-4432; FAX: 307-883-2005

Freeman Animal Targets, 5519 East County Road, 100 South, Plainsfield, IN 46168 / 317-272-2663; FAX: 317-272-2674

Fremont Tool Works, 1214 Prairie, Ford, KS 67842 / 316-369-2327

French, Artistic Engraving, J. R., 1712 Creek Ridge Ct, Irving, TX 75060 / 214-254-2654

Frielich Police Equipment, 211 East 21st St., New York, NY 10010 / 212-254-3045

Front Sight Firearms Training Institute, P.O. Box 2619, Aptos, CA 95001 / 800-987-7719; FAX: 408-684-2137

Frontier, 2910 San Bernardo, Laredo, TX 78040 / 956-723-5409; FAX: 956-723-1774

Frontier Arms Co.,Inc., 401 W. Rio Santa Cruz, Green Valley, AZ 85614-3932

Frontier Products Co., 2401 Walker Rd., Roswell, NM 88201-8950 / 614-262-9357

Frontier Safe Co., 3201 S. Clinton St., Fort Wayne, IN 46806 / 219-744-7233; FAX: 219-744-6678

Frost Cutlery Co., P.O. Box 22636, Chattanooga, TN 37422 / 615-894-6079; FAX: 615-894-9576

Fry Metals, 4100 6th Ave., Altoona, PA 16602 / 814-946-1611

Fujinon, Inc., 10 High Point Dr., Wayne, NJ 07470 / 201-633-5600; FAX: 201-633-5216

Fullmer, Geo. M., 2499 Mavis St., Oakland, CA 94601 / 510-533-4193

Fulmer's Antique Firearms, Chet, PO Box 792, Rt 2 Buffalo Lake, Detroit Lakes, MN 56501 / 218-847-7712

Fulton Armory, 8725 Bollman Place No. 1, Savage, MD 20763 / 301-490-9485; FAX: 301-490-9547

Furr Arms, 91 N. 970 W., Orem, UT 84057 / 801-226-3877; FAX: 801-226-3877

Fusilier Bullets, 10010 N. 6000 W., Highland, UT 84003 / 801-756-6813

FWB, Neckarstrasse 43, 78727, Oberndorf a. N., GERMANY / 07423-814-0; FAX: 07423-814-89

G

G&H Decoys,Inc., P.O. Box 1208, Hwy. 75 North, Henryetta, OK 74437 / 918-652-3314; FAX: 918-652-3400

G.C.C.T., 4455 Torrance Blvd., Ste. 453, Torrance, CA 90503-4398

G.G. & G., 3602 E. 42nd Stravenue, Tucson, AZ 85713 / 520-748-7167; FAX: 520-748-7583

G.H. Enterprises Ltd., Bag 10, Okotoks, AB T0L 1T0 CANADA / 403-938-6070

G.U. Inc (See U.S. Importer for New SKB Arms Co)

G.W. Elliott, Inc., 514 Burnside Ave., East Hartford, CT 06108 / 203-289-5741; FAX: 203-289-3137

G96 Products Co., Inc., 85 5th Ave, Bldg #6, Paterson, NJ 07544 / 973-684-4050 FAX: 973-684-4050

Gage Manufacturing, 663 W. 7th St., A, San Pedro, CA 90731 / 310-832-3546

Gaillard Barrels, P.O. Box 21, Pathlow, SK S0K 3B0 CANADA / 306-752-3769; FAX: 306-752-5969

Gain Twist Barrel Co. Rifle Works and Armory, 707 12th Street, Cody, WY 82414 / 307-587-4919; FAX: 307-527-6097

Galati International, PO Box 10, Wesco, MO 65586 / 314-257-4837; FAX: 314-257-2268

Galaxy Imports Ltd.,Inc., P.O. Box 3361, Victoria, TX 77903 / 361-573-4867; FAX: 361-576-9622 galaxy@tisd.net

GALCO International Ltd., 2019 W. Quail Ave., Phoenix, AZ 85027 / 602-258-8295 or 800-874-2526; FAX: 602-582-6854

Galena Industries AMT, 3551 Mayer Ave., Sturgis, SD 57785 / 605-423-4105

Gamba S.p.A. Societa Armi Bresciane Srl, Renato, Via Artigiani 93, ITALY / 30-8911640; FAX: 30-8911648

Gamba, USA, P.O. Box 60452, Colorado Springs, CO 80960 / 719-578-1145; FAX: 719-444-0731

Game Haven Gunstocks, 13750 Shire Rd., Wolverine, MI 49799 / 616-525-8257

Game Winner, Inc., 2625 Cumberland Parkway, Suite 220, Atlanta, GA 30339 / 770-434-9210; FAX: 770-434-9215

Gamebore Division, Polywad Inc, PO Box 7916, Macon, GA 31209 / 912-477-0669

Gamo (See U.S. Importers-Arms United Corp, Daisy Mfg. Co.,)

Gamo USA, Inc., 3911 SW 47th Ave., Suite 914, Ft. Lauderdale, FL 33314 / 954-581-5822; FAX: 954-581-3165

Gander Mountain, Inc., 12400 Fox River Rd., Wilmont, WI 53192 / 414-862-6848

GAR, 590 McBride Avenue, West Paterson, NJ 07424 / 973-754-1114; FAX: 973-754-1114

Garbi, Armas Urki, 12-14 20.600 Eibar, Guipuzcoa, SPAIN

Garcia National Gun Traders, Inc., 225 SW 22nd Ave., Miami, FL 33135 / 305-642-2355

Garrett Cartridges Inc., P.O. Box 178, Chehalis, WA 98532 / 360-736-0702

Garthwaite Pistolsmith, Inc., Jim, Rt 2 Box 310, Watsontown, PA 17777 / 570-538-1566; FAX: 570-538-2965

Gary Goudy Classic Stocks, 263 Hedge Rd., Menlo Park, CA 94025-1711 / 415-322-1338

Gary Reeder Custom Guns, 2710 N Steves Blvd. #22, Flagstaff, AZ 86004 / 520-526-3313; FAX: 520-527-0840 gary@reedercustomguns.com www.reedercustomguns.com

Gary Schneider Rifle Barrels Inc., 12202 N. 62nd Pl., Scottsdale, AZ 85254 / 602-948-2525

Gator Guns & Repair, 6255 Spur Hwy., Kenai, AK 99611 / 907-283-7947

Gaucher Armes, S.A., 46 rue Desjoyaux, 42000, Saint-Etienne, FRANCE / 04-77-33-38-92; FAX: 04-77-61-95-72

GDL Enterprises, 409 Le Gardeur, Slidell, LA 70460 / 504-649-0693

Gehmann, Walter (See Huntington Die Specialties)

Genco, P.O. Box 5704, Asheville, NC 28803

Gene's Custom Guns, P.O. Box 10534, White Bear Lake, MN 55110 / 612-429-5105

Genecco Gun Works, K, 10512 Lower Sacramento Rd., Stockton, CA 95210 / 209-951-0706 FAX: 209-931-3872

Gentex Corp., 5 Tinkham Ave., Derry, NH 03038 / 603-434-0311; FAX: 603-434-3002 sales@derry.gentexcorp.com www.derry.gentexcorp.com

Gentner Bullets, 109 Woodlawn Ave., Upper Darby, PA 19082 / 610-352-9396

Gentry Custom Gunmaker, David, 314 N Hoffman, Belgrade, MT 59714 / 406-388-GUNS

George & Roy's, PO Box 2125, Sisters, OR 97759-2125 / 503-228-5424 or 800-553-3022; FAX: 503-225-9409

George, Tim, Rt. 1, P.O. Box 45, Evington, VA 24550 / 804-821-8117

George E. Mathews & Son, Inc., 10224 S. Paramount Blvd., Downey, CA 90241 / 562-862-6719; FAX: 562-862-6719

George Ibberson (Sheffield) Ltd., 25-31 Allen St., Sheffield, S3 7AW ENGLAND / 0114-2766123; FAX: 0114-2738465

Gerald Pettinger Books, see Pettinger Books, G, Rt. 2, Box 125, Russell, IA 50238 / 515-535-2239

Gerber Legendary Blades, 14200 SW 72nd Ave., Portland, OR 97223 / 503-639-6161 or 800-950-6161; FAX: 503-684-7008

Gervais, Mike, 3804 S. Cruise Dr., Salt Lake City, UT 84109 / 801-277-7729

Getz Barrel Co., P.O. Box 88, Beavertown, PA 17813 / 717-658-7263

Giacomo Sporting USA, 6234 Stokes Lee Center Rd., Lee Center, NY 13363

Gibbs Rifle Co., Inc., 211 Lawn St, Martinsburg, WV 25401 / 304-262-1651; FAX: 304-262-1658

Gil Hebard Guns, 125-129 Public Square, Knoxville, IL 61448 / 309-289-2700 FAX: 309-289-2233

Gilbert Equipment Co., Inc., 960 Downtowner Rd., Mobile, AL 36609 / 205-344-3322

Gilkes, Anthony W., 26574 HILLMAN HWY, MEADOWVIEW, VA 24361-3142 / 303-657-1873; FAX: 303-657-1885

Gillmann, Edwin, 33 Valley View Dr., Hanover, PA 17331 / 717-632-1662

Gilman-Mayfield, Inc., 3279 E. Shields, Fresno, CA 93703 / 209-221-9415; FAX: 209-221-9419

34TH EDITION, 2002 • 335

Manufacturers Directory

Gilmore Sports Concepts, 5949 S. Garnett, Tulsa, OK 74146 / 918-250-3810; FAX: 918-250-3845 gilmore@web-zone.net www.gilmoresports.com

Giron, Robert E., 1328 Pocono St., Pittsburgh, PA 15218 / 412-731-6041

Glacier Glove, 4890 Aircenter Circle, Suite 210, Reno, NV 89502 / 702-825-8225; FAX: 702-825-6544

Glaser Safety Slug, Inc., P.O. Box 8223, Foster City, CA 94404 / 800-221-3489; FAX: 510-785-6685 safetyslug.com

Glass, Herb, P.O. Box 25, Bullville, NY 10915 / 914-361-3021

Glimm, Jerome C., 19 S. Maryland, Conrad, MT 59425 / 406-278-3574

Glock GmbH, P.O. Box 50, A-2232, Deutsch Wagram, AUSTRIA

Glock, Inc., PO Box 369, Smyrna, GA 30081 / 770-432-1202; FAX: 770-433-8719

Glynn Scobey Duck & Goose Calls, Rt. 3, Box 37, Newbern, TN 38059 / 901-643-6241

GML Products, Inc., 394 Laredo Dr., Birmingham, AL 35226 / 205-979-4867

Gner's Hard Cast Bullets, 1107 11th St., LaGrande, OR 97850 / 503-963-8796

Goens, Dale W., P.O. Box 224, Cedar Crest, NM 87008 / 505-281-5419

Goergen's Gun Shop, Inc., 17985 538th Ave, Austin, MN 55912 / 507-433-9280 FAX: 507-433-9280

GOEX Inc., PO Box 659, Doyline, LA 71023-0659 / 318-382-9300; FAX: 318-382-9303

Golden Age Arms Co., 115 E. High St., Ashley, OH 43003 / 614-747-2488

Golden Bear Bullets, 3065 Fairfax Ave., San Jose, CA 95148 / 408-238-9515

Gonic Arms/North American Arm, 134 Flagg Rd., Gonic, NH 03839 / 603-332-8456 or 603-332-8457

Gonzalez Guns, Ramon B, PO Box 370, 93 St. Joseph's Hill Rd, Monticello, NY 12701 / 914-794-4515

Goodling's Gunsmithing, R.D. 1, Box 1097, Spring Grove, PA 17362 / 717-225-3350

Goodwin, Fred, Silver Ridge Gun Shop, Sherman Mills, ME 04776 / 207-365-4451

Gordie's Gun Shop, 1401 Fulton St., Streator, IL 61364 / 815-672-7202

Gordon Wm. Davis Leather Co., P.O. Box 2270, Walnut, CA 91788 / 909-598-5620

Gotz Bullets, 7313 Rogers St., Rockford, IL 61111

Gould & Goodrich, 709 E. McNeil, Lillington, NC 27546 / 910-893-2071; FAX: 910-893-4742

Gournet, Geoffroy, 820 Paxinosa Ave., Easton, PA 18042 / 610-559-0710

Gozon Corp. U.S.A., P.O. Box 6278, Folson, CA 95763 / 916-983-2026; FAX: 916-983-9500

Grace, Charles E., 1305 Arizona Ave., Trinidad, CO 81082 / 719-846-9435

Grace Metal Products, P.O. Box 67, Elk Rapids, MI 49629 / 616-264-8133

Graf & Sons, 4050 S Clark St, Mexico, MO 65265 / 573-581-2266 FAX: 573-581-2875

"Gramps" Antique Cartridges, Box 341, Washago, ON L0K 2B0 CANADA / 705-689-5348

Granite Mountain Arms, Inc, 3145 W Hidden Acres Trail, Prescott, AZ 86305 / 520-541-9758; FAX: 520-445-6826

Grant, Howard V., Hiawatha 15, Woodruff, WI 54568 / 715-356-7146

Graphics Direct, P.O. Box 372421, Reseda, CA 91337-2421 / 818-344-9002

Graves Co., 1800 Andrews Ave., Pompano Beach, FL 33069 / 800-327-9103; FAX: 305-960-0301

Grayback Wildcats, 5306 Bryant Ave., Klamath Falls, OR 97603 / 541-884-1072

Graybill's Gun Shop, 1035 Ironville Pike, Columbia, PA 17512 / 717-684-2739

GrE-Tan Rifles, 29742 W.C.R. 50, Kersey, CO 80644 / 970-353-6176; FAX: 970-356-9133

Great American Gunstock Co., 3420 Industrial Drive, Yuba City, CA 95993 / 530-671-4570; FAX: 530-671-3906

Great Lakes Airguns, 6175 S. Park Ave, New York, NY 14075 / 716-648-6666; FAX: 716-648-5279

Green, Arthur S., 485 S. Robertson Blvd., Beverly Hills, CA 90211 / 310-274-1283

Green, Roger M., P.O. Box 984, 435 E. Birch, Glenrock, WY 82637 / 307-436-9804

Green Genie, Box 114, Cusseta, GA 31805

Green Head Game Call Co., RR 1, Box 33, Lacon, IL 61540 / 309-246-2155

Green Mountain Rifle Barrel Co., Inc., P.O. Box 2670, 153 West Main St., Conway, NH 03818 / 603-447-1095; FAX: 603-447-1099

Greenwood Precision, P.O. Box 468, Nixa, MO 65714-0468 / 417-725-2330

Greg Gunsmithing Repair, 3732 26th Ave. North, Robbinsdale, MN 55422 / 612-529-8103

Greg's Superior Products, P.O. Box 46219, Seattle, WA 98146

Greider Precision, 431 Santa Marina Ct., Escondido, CA 92029 / 619-480-8892; FAX: 619-480-9800

Gremmel Enterprises, 2111 Carriage Drive, Eugene, OR 97408-7537 / 541-302-3000

Grier's Hard Cast Bullets, 1107 11th St., LaGrande, OR 97850 / 503-963-8796

Griffin & Howe, Inc., 36 W. 44th St., Suite 1011, New York, NY 10036 / 212-921-0980

Griffin & Howe, Inc., 33 Claremont Rd., Bernardsville, NJ 07924 / 908-766-2287

Grifon, Inc., 58 Guinam St., Waltham, MS 02154

Groenewold, John, P.O. Box 830, Mundelein, IL 60060 / 847-566-2365

GRS Corp., Glendo, P.O. Box 1153, 900 Overlander St., Emporia, KS 66801 / 316-343-1084 or 800-835-3519

Grulla Armes, Apartado 453, Avda Otaloa 12, Eiber, SPAIN

Gruning Precision Inc, 7101 Jurupa Ave., No. 12, Riverside, CA 92504 / 909-689-6692 FAX: 909-689-7791

GSI, Inc., 7661 Commerce Ln., Trussville, AL 35173 / 205-655-8299

GTB, 482 Comerwood Court, San Francisco, CA 94080 / 650-583-1550

Guarasi, Robert. (See WILCOX INDUSTRIES CORP)

Guardsman Products, 411 N. Darling, Fremont, MI 49412 / 616-924-3950

Gun Accessories (See Glaser Safety Slug, Inc.), PO Box 8223, Foster City, CA 94404 / 800-221-3489; FAX: 510-785-6685

Gun City, 212 W. Main Ave., Bismarck, ND 58501 / 701-223-2304

Gun Hunter Books (See Gun Hunter Trading Co), 5075 Heisig St, Beaumont, TX 77705 / 409-835-3006

Gun Hunter Trading Co., 5075 Heisig St., Beaumont, TX 77705 / 409-835-3006

Gun Leather Limited, 116 Lipscomb, Ft. Worth, TX 76104 / 817-334-0225; FAX: 800-247-0609

Gun List (See Krause Publications), 700 E State St, Iola, WI 54945 / 715-445-2214; FAX: 715-445-4087

Gun Locker Div. of Airmold W.R. Grace & Co.-Conn., Becker Farms Ind. Park, P.O. Box 610, Roanoke Rapids, NC 27870 / 800-344-5716; FAX: 919-536-2201

Gun South, Inc. (See GSI, Inc.)

Gun Vault, 7339 E Acoma Dr., Ste. 7, Scottsdale, AZ 85260 / 602-951-6855

Gun-Alert, 1010 N. Maclay Ave., San Fernando, CA 91340 / 818-365-0864; FAX: 818-365-1308

Gun-Ho Sports Cases, 110 E. 10th St., St. Paul, MN 55101 / 612-224-9491

Guncraft Books (See Guncraft Sports Inc), 10737 Dutchtown Rd, Knoxville, TN 37932 / 423-966-4545; FAX: 423-966-4500

Guncraft Sports Inc., 10737 Dutchtown Rd., Knoxville, TN 37932 / 423-966-4545; FAX: 423-966-4500

Gunfitters, P.O. 426, Cambridge, WI 53523-0426 / 608-764-8128 gunfitters@aol.com www.gunfitters.com

Gunline Tools, 2950 Saturn St., "O", Brea, CA 92821 / 714-993-5100; FAX: 714-572-4128

Gunnerman Books, P.O. Box 217, Owosso, MI 48867 / 517-729-7018; FAX: 517-725-9391

Guns, 81 E. Streetsboro St., Hudson, OH 44236 / 330-650-4563

Guns Antique & Modern DBA/Charles E. Duffy, Williams Lane, West Hurley, NY 12491 / 914-679-2997

Guns Div. of D.C. Engineering, Inc., 8633 Southfield Fwy., Detroit, MI 48228 / 313-271-7111 or 800-886-7623; FAX: 313-271-7112

GUNS Magazine, 591 Camino de la Reina, Suite 200, San Diego, CA 92108 / 619-297-5350 FAX: 619-297-5353

Gunsite Custom Shop, P.O. Box 451, Paulden, AZ 86334 / 520-636-4104; FAX: 520-636-1236

Gunsite Gunsmithy (See Gunsite Custom Shop)

Gunsite Training Center, P.O. Box 700, Paulden, AZ 86334 / 520-636-4565; FAX: 520-636-1236

Gunsmithing Ltd., 57 Unquowa Rd., Fairfield, CT 06430 / 203-254-0436; FAX: 203-254-1535

Gunsmithing, Inc., 208 West Buchanan St., Colorado Springs, CO 80907 / 719-632-3795; FAX: 719-632-3493

Gurney, F. R., Box 13, Sooke, BC V0S 1N0 CANADA / 604-642-5282; FAX: 604-642-7859

Gwinnell, Bryson J., P.O. Box 248C, Maple Hill Rd., Rochester, VT 05767 / 802-767-3664

H

H&B Forge Co., Rt. 2, Geisinger Rd., Shiloh, OH 44878 / 419-895-1856

H&P Publishing, 7174 Hoffman Rd., San Angelo, TX 76905 / 915-655-5953

H&R 1871, Inc., 60 Industrial Rowe, Gardner, MA 01440 / 978-632-9393; FAX: 978-632-2300

H&S Liner Service, 515 E. 8th, Odessa, TX 79761 / 915-332-1021

H-S Precision, Inc., 1301 Turbine Dr., Rapid City, SD 57701 / 605-341-3006; FAX: 605-342-8964

H. Krieghoff Gun Co., Boschstrasse 22, D-89079, Ulm, GERMANY / 731-401820; FAX: 731-4018270

H.K.S. Products, 7841 Founion Dr., Florence, KY 41042 / 606-342-7841 or 800-354-9814; FAX: 606-342-5865

H.P. White Laboratory, Inc., 3114 Scarboro Rd., Street, MD 21154 / 410-838-6550; FAX: 410-838-2802

Hafner World Wide, Inc., P.O. Box 1987, Lake City, FL 32055 / 904-755-6481; FAX: 904-755-6595

Hagn Rifles & Actions, Martin, PO Box 444, Cranbrook, BC V1C 4H9 CANADA / 604-489-4861

Hakko Co. Ltd., 1-13-12, Narimasu, Itabashiku Tokyo, JAPAN / 03-5997-7870/2; FAX: 81-3-5997-7840

Hale, Engraver, Peter, 800 E Canyon Rd., Spanish Fork, UT 84660 / 801-798-8215

Half Moon Rifle Shop, 490 Halfmoon Rd., Columbia Falls, MT 59912 / 406-892-4409

Hall Manufacturing, 142 CR 406, Clanton, AL 35045 / 205-755-4094

Hall Plastics, Inc., John, P.O. Box 1526, Alvin, TX 77512 / 713-489-8709

Hallberg Gunsmith, Fritz, 532 E. Idaho Ave., Ontario, OR 97914 / 541-889-3135; FAX: 541-889-2633

Hallowell & Co., PO Box 1445, Livingston, MT 59047 / 406-222-4770 FAX: 406-222-4792 morris@hallowellco.com hallowellco.com

Hally Caller, 443 Wells Rd., Doylestown, PA 18901 / 215-345-6354

Halstead, Rick, 313 TURF ST, CARL JUNCTION, MO 64834-9658 / 918-540-0933

Hamilton, Jim, Rte. 5, Box 278, Guthrie, OK 73044 / 405-282-3634

Hamilton, Alex B (See Ten-Ring Precision, Inc)

Hammans, Charles E., P.O. Box 788, 2022 McCracken, Stuttgart, AR 72106 / 870-673-1388

Hammerli Ltd., Seonerstrasse 37, CH-5600, SWITZERLAND / 064-50 11 44; FAX: 064-51 38 27

Hammerli USA, 19296 Oak Grove Circle, Groveland, CA 95321 FAX: 209-962-5311

Hammets VLD Bullets, P.O. Box 479, Rayville, LA 71269 / 318-728-2019

Hammond Custom Guns Ltd., 619 S. Pandora, Gilbert, AZ 85234 / 602-892-3437

Hammonds Rifles, RD 4, Box 504, Red Lion, PA 17356 / 717-244-7879

HandCrafts Unltd (See Clements' Custom Leathercraft, Chas,), 1741 Dallas St, Aurora, CO 80010-2018 / 303-364-0403; FAX: 303-739-9824

Handgun Press, P.O. Box 406, Glenview, IL 60025 / 847-657-6500; FAX: 847-724-8831 jschroed@inter-access.com

Hands Engraving, Barry Lee, 26192 E Shore Route, Bigfork, MT 59911 / 406-837-0035

Hank's Gun Shop, Box 370, 50 West 100 South, Monroe, UT 84754 / 801-527-4456

Hanned Precision (See Hanned Line, The)

Hansen & Co. (See Hansen Cartridge Co.), 244-246 Old Post Rd, Southport, CT 06490 / 203-259-6222; FAX: 203-254-3832

Hanson's Gun Center, Dick, 233 Everett Dr, Colorado Springs, CO 80911

Hanus Birdguns Bill, PO Box 533, Newport, OR 97365 / 541-265-7433; FAX: 541-265-7400

Hanusin, John, 3306 Commercial, Northbrook, IL 60062 / 708-564-2706

Hardin Specialty Dist., P.O. Box 338, Radcliff, KY 40159-0338 / 502-351-6649

Harford (See U.S. Importer-EMF Co. Inc.)

Harper's Custom Stocks, 928 Lombrano St., San Antonio, TX 78207 / 210-732-5780

336 • GUNS ILLUSTRATED

Manufacturers Directory

Harrell's Precision, 5756 Hickory Dr., Salem, VA 24133 / 703-380-2683
Harrington & Richardson (See H&R 1871, Inc.)
Harris Engineering Inc., Dept GD54, Barlow, KY 42024 / 502-334-3633 FAX: 502-334-3000
Harris Enterprises, P.O. Box 105, Bly, OR 97622 / 503-353-2625
Harris Gunworks, 20813 N. 19th Ave., PO Box 9249, Phoenix, AZ 85027 / 602-582-9627; FAX: 602-582-5178
Harris Hand Engraving, Paul A., 113 Rusty Ln, Boerne, TX 78006-5746 / 512-391-5121
Harris Publications, 1115 Broadway, New York, NY 10010 / 212-807-7100 FAX: 212-627-4678
Harrison Bullets, 6437 E. Hobart St., Mesa, AZ 85205
Harry Lawson Co., 3328 N. Richey Blvd., Tucson, AZ 85716 / 520-326-1117
Hart & Son, Inc., Robert W., 401 Montgomery St, Nescopeck, PA 18635 / 717-752-3655; FAX: 717-752-1088
Hart Rifle Barrels,Inc., P.O. Box 182, 1690 Apulia Rd., Lafayette, NY 13084 / 315-677-9841; FAX: 315-677-9610 hartrb@aol.com hartbarrels.com
Hartford (See U.S. Importer-EMF Co. Inc.)
Hartmann & Weiss GmbH, Rahlstedter Bahnhofstr. 47, 22143, Hamburg, GERMANY / (40) 677 55 85; FAX: (40) 677 55 92
Harvey, Frank, 218 Nightfall, Terrace, NV 89015 / 702-558-6998
Harwood, Jack O., 1191 S. Pendlebury Lane, Blackfoot, ID 83221 / 208-785-5368
Hastings Barrels, 320 Court St., Clay Center, KS 67432 / 913-632-3169; FAX: 913-632-6554
Hatfield Gun, 224 N. 4th St., St. Joseph, MO 64501
Hawk Laboratories, Inc. (See Hawk, Inc.), 849 Hawks Bridge Rd, Salem, NJ 08079 / 609-299-2700; FAX: 609-299-2800
Hawk, Inc., 849 Hawks Bridge Rd., Salem, NJ 08079 / 609-299-2700; FAX: 609-299-2800
Hawken Shop, The (See Dayton Traister)
Haydel's Game Calls, Inc., 5018 Hazel Jones Rd., Bossier City, LA 71111 / 800-HAYDELS; FAX: 318-746-3711
Haydon Shooters Supply, Russ, 15018 Goodrich Dr NW, Gig Harbor, WA 98329-9738 / 253-857-7557; FAX: 253-857-7884
Heatbath Corp., P.O. Box 2978, Springfield, MA 01101 / 413-543-3381
Hebard Guns, Gil, 125-129 Public Square, Knoxville, IL 61448
HEBB Resources, P.O. Box 999, Mead, WA 99021-0999 / 509-466-1292
Hecht, Hubert J, Waffen-Hecht, PO Box 2635, Fair Oaks, CA 95628 / 916-966-1020
Heckler & Koch GmbH, P.O. Box 1329, 78722 Oberndorf, Neckar, GERMANY / 49-7423179-0; FAX: 49-7423179-2406
Heckler & Koch, Inc., 21480 Pacific Blvd., Sterling, VA 20166-8900 / 703-450-1900; FAX: 703-450-8160
Hege Jagd-u. Sporthandels GmbH, P.O. Box 101461, W-7770, Ueberlingen a. Boden, GERMANY
Heidenstrom Bullets, Urdngt 1, 3937 Heroya, NORWAY
Heilmann, Stephen, P.O. Box 657, Grass Valley, CA 95945 / 530-272-8758
Heinie Specialty Products, 301 Oak St., Quincy, IL 62301-2500 / 217-228-9500; FAX: 217-228-9502 rheinie@heinie.com www.heinie.com
Hellweg Ltd., 40356 Oak Park Way, Suite W, Oakhurst, CA 93644 / 209-683-3030; FAX: 209-683-3422
Helwan (See U.S. Importer-Interarms)
Hendricks, Frank E. Inc., Master Engravers, HC 03, Box 434, Dripping Springs, TX 78620 / 512-858-7828
Henigson & Associates, Steve, PO Box 2726, Culver City, CA 90231 / 310-305-8288; FAX: 310-305-1905
Henriksen Tool Co., Inc., 8515 Wagner Creek Rd., Talent, OR 97540 / 541-535-2309 FAX: 541-535-2309
Henry Repeating Arms Co., 110 8th St., Brooklyn, NY 11215 / 718-499-5600
Hensley, Gunmaker, Darwin, PO Box 329, Brightwood, OR 97011 / 503-622-5411
Heppler, Keith. (See KEITH'S CUSTOM GUNSTOCKS)
Heppler's Machining, 2240 Calle Del Mundo, Santa Clara, CA 95054 / 408-748-9166; FAX: 408-988-0711
Heppler, Keith M, Keith's Custom Gunstocks, 540 Banyan Cir, Walnut Creek, CA 94598 / 510-934-3509; FAX: 510-934-3143
Hercules, Inc. (See Alliant Techsystems, Smokeless Powder Group)
Heritage Firearms (See Heritage Mfg., Inc.)

Heritage Manufacturing, Inc., 4600 NW 135th St., Opa Locka, FL 33054 or 305-685-5966; FAX: 305-687-6721
Heritage Wildlife Carvings, 2145 Wagner Hollow Rd., Fort Plain, NY 13339 / 518-993-3983
Heritage/VSP Gun Books, P.O. Box 887, McCall, ID 83638 / 208-634-4104; FAX: 208-634-3101
Herrett's Stocks, Inc., P.O. Box 741, Twin Falls, ID 83303 / 208-733-1498
Hertel & Reuss, Werk fr Optik und Feinmechanik GmbH, Quellhofstrasse 67, 34 127, GERMANY / 0561-83006; FAX: 0561-893308
Herter's Manufacturing, Inc., 111 E. Burnett St., P.O. Box 518, Beaver Dam, WI 53916 / 414-887-1765; FAX: 414-887-8444
Hesco-Meprolight, 2139 Greenville Rd., LaGrange, GA 30241 / 706-884-7967; FAX: 706-882-4683
Heydenberk, Warren R., 1059 W. Sawmill Rd., Quakertown, PA 18951 / 215-538-2682
Hi-Grade Imports, 8655 Monterey Rd., Gilroy, CA 95021 / 408-842-9301; FAX: 408-842-2374
Hi-Performance Ammunition Company, 484 State Route 366, Apollo, PA 15613 / 412-327-8100
Hi-Point Firearms, 5990 Philadelphia Dr., Dayton, OH 45415 / 513-275-4991; FAX: 513-522-8330
Hickman, Jaclyn, Box 1900, Glenrock, WY 82637
Hidalgo, Tony, 12701 SW 9th Pl., Davie, FL 33325 / 954-476-7645
High Bridge Arms, Inc, 3185 Mission St., San Francisco, CA 94110 / 415-282-8358
High North Products, Inc., P.O. Box 2, Antigo, WI 54409 / 715-627-2331 FAX: 715-623-5451
High Performance International, 5734 W. Florist Ave., Milwaukee, WI 53218 / 414-466-9040
High Standard Mfg. Co., Inc., 10606 Hempstead Hwy., Suite 116, Houston, TX 77092 / 713-462-4200, 800-467-2228
High Tech Specialties, Inc., P.O. Box 387R, Adamstown, PA 19501 / 215-484-0405 or 800-231-9385
Highline Machine Co., Randall Thompson, 654 Lela Place, Grand Junction, CO 81504 / 970-434-4971
Hill, Loring F., 304 Cedar Rd., Elkins Park, PA 19027
Hill Speed Leather, Ernie, 4507 N 195th Ave, Litchfield Park, AZ 85340 / 602-853-9222; FAX: 602-853-9235
Hines Co, S C, PO Box 423, Tijeras, NM 87059 / 505-281-3783
Hinman Outfitters, Bob, 107 N Sanderson Ave, Bartonville, IL 61607-1839 / 309-691-8132
HIP-GRIP Barami Corp., 6689 Orchard Lake Rd. No. 148, West Bloomfield, MI 48322 / 248-738-0462; FAX: 248-738-2542
Hiptmayer, Armurier, RR 112 750, P.O. Box 136, Eastman, PQ J0E 1P0 CANADA / 514-297-2492
Hiptmayer, Heidemarie, RR 112 750, P.O. Box 136, Eastman, PQ J0E 1P0 CANADA / 514-297-2492
Hiptmayer, Klaus, RR 112 750, P.O. Box 136, Eastman, PQ J0E 1P0 CANADA / 514-297-2492
Hirtenberger Aktiengesellschaft, Leobersdorferstrasse 31, A-2552, Hirtenberg, / 43(0)2256 81184; FAX: 43(0)2256 81807
HiTek International, 484 El Camino Real, Redwood City, CA 94063 / 415-363-1404 or 800-54-NIGHT FAX: 415-363-1408
Hiti-Schuch, Atelier Wilma, A-8863 Predlitz, Pirming, Y1 AUSTRIA / 0353418278
HJS Arms,Inc., P.O. Box 3711, Brownsville, TX 78523-3711 / 800-453-2767; FAX: 210-542-2767
Hoag, James W., 8523 Canoga Ave., Suite C, Canoga Park, CA 91304 / 818-998-1510
Hobson Precision Mfg. Co., 210 Big Oak Ln, Brent, AL 35034 / 205-926-4662 FAX: 205-926-3193 cahobbob@dbtech.net
Hoch Custom Bullet Moulds (See Colorado Shooter's
Hodgdon Powder Co., 6231 Robinson, Shawnee Mission, KS 66202 / 913-362-9455; FAX: 913-362-1307
Hodgman, Inc., 1750 Orchard Rd., Montgomery, IL 60538 / 708-897-7555; FAX: 708-897-7558
Hodgson, Richard, 9081 Tahoe Lane, Boulder, CO 80301
Hoehn Sales, Inc., 2045 Kohn Road, Wright City, MO 63390 / 636-745-8144; FAX: 636-745-7868 hoehnsal@us-mo.com benchrestcentral.com
Hoelscher, Virgil, 8230 Hillrose St, Sunland, CA 91040-2404 / 310-631-8545
Hoenig & Rodman, 6521 Morton Dr., Boise, ID 83704 / 208-375-1116
Hofer Jagdwaffen, P., Buchsenmachermeister, Kirchgasse 24, A-9170 Ferlach, AUSTRIA

Hoffman New Ideas, 821 Northmoor Rd., Lake Forest, IL 60045 / 312-234-4075
Hogue Grips, P.O. Box 1138, Paso Robles, CA 93447 / 800-438-4747 or 805-239-1440; FAX: 805-239-2553
Holland & Holland Ltd., 33 Bruton St., London, ENGLAND / 44-171-499-4411; FAX: 44-171-408-7962
Holland's Gunsmithing, P.O. Box 69, Powers, OR 97466 / 541-439-5155; FAX: 541-439-5155
Hollinger, Jon. (See ASPEN OUTFITTING CO)
Hollis Gun Shop, 917 Rex St., Carlsbad, NM 88220 / 505-885-3782
Hollywood Engineering, 10642 Arminta St., Sun Valley, CA 91352 / 818-842-8376
Homak, 5151 W. 73rd St., Chicago, IL 60638-6613 / 312-523-3100; FAX: 312-523-9455
Home Shop Machinist The Village Press Publications, P.O. Box 1810, Traverse City, MI 49685 / 800-447-7367; FAX: 616-946-3289
Hondo Ind., 510 S. 52nd St., I04, Tempe, AZ 85281
Hoover, Harvey, 5750 Pearl Dr., Paradise, CA 95969-4829
Hoppe's Div. Penguin Industries, Inc., Airport Industrial Mall, Coatesville, PA 19320 / 610-384-6000
Horizons Unlimited, P.O. Box 426, Warm Springs, GA 31830 / 706-655-3603; FAX: 706-655-3603
Hornady Mfg. Co., P.O. Box 1848, Grand Island, NE 68802 / 800-338-3220 or 308-382-1390; FAX: 308-382-5761
Horseshoe Leather Products, Andy Arratoonian, The Cottage Sharow, Ripon, ENGLAND / 44-1765-605858
Houtz & Barwick, P.O. Box 435, W. Church St., Elizabeth City, NC 27909 / 800-775-0337 or 919-335-4191; FAX: 919-335-1152
Howa Machinery, Ltd., Sukaguchi, Shinkawa-cho Nishikasugai-gun, Aichi 452, JAPAN
Howell Machine, 815 1/2 D St., Lewiston, ID 83501 / 208-743-7418
Hoyt Holster Co., Inc., P.O. Box 69, Coupeville, WA 98239-0069 / 360-678-6640; FAX: 360-678-6549
HT Bullets, 244 Belleville Rd., New Bedford, MA 02745 / 508-999-3338
Hubert J. Hecht Waffen-Hecht, P.O. Box 2635, Fair Oaks, CA 95628 / 916-966-1020
Hubertus Schneidwarenfabrik, P.O. Box 180 106, D-42626, Solingen, GERMANY / 01149-212-59-19-94; FAX: 01149-212-59-19-92
Huebner, Corey O., P.O. Box 2074, Missoula, MT 59806-2074 / 406-721-7168
Huey Gun Cases, P.O. Box 22456, Kansas City, MO 64113 / 816-444-1637; FAX: 816-444-1637
Hugger Hooks Co., 3900 Easley Way, Golden, CO 80403 / 303-279-0600
Hughes, Steven Dodd, P.O. Box 545, Livingston, MT 59047 / 406-222-9377; FAX: 406-222-9377
Hume, Don, P.O. Box 351, Miami, OK 74355 / 800-331-2686 FAX: 918-542-4340
Hungry Horse Books, 4605 Hwy. 93 South, Whitefish, MT 59937 / 406-862-7997
Hunkeler, A (See Buckskin Machine Works, A. Hunkeler) 3235 S 358th St., Auburn, WA 98001 / 206-927-5412
Hunter Co., Inc., 3300 W. 71st Ave., Westminster, CO 80030 / 303-427-4626; FAX: 303-428-3980
Hunter's Specialties Inc., 6000 Huntington Ct. NE, Cedar Rapids, IA 52402-1268 / 319-395-0321; FAX: 319-395-0326
Hunterjohn, P.O. Box 771457, St. Louis, MO 63177 / 314-531-7250
Hunters Supply, Inc., PO Box 313, Tioga, TX 76271 / 940-437-2458; FAX: 940-437-2228 hunterssupply@hotmail.com www.hunterssupply.net
Hunting Classics Ltd., P.O. Box 2089, Gastonia, NC 28053 / 704-867-1307; FAX: 704-867-0491
Huntington Die Specialties, 601 Oro Dam Blvd., Oroville, CA 95965 / 530-534-1210; FAX: 530-534-1212
Hutton Rifle Ranch, P.O. Box 45236, Boise, ID 83711 / 208-345-8781
Hydrosorbent Products, P.O. Box 437, Ashley Falls, MA 01222 / 413-229-2967; or 800-229-8743 FAX: 413-229-8743 orders@dehumidify.com www.dehumidify.com
Hyper-Single, Inc., 520 E. Beaver, Jenks, OK 74037 / 918-299-2391

I

I.A.B. (See U.S. Importer-Taylor's & Co. Inc.)
I.D.S.A. Books, 1324 Stratford Drive, Piqua, OH 45356 / 937-773-4203; FAX: 937-778-1922

MANUFACTURERS DIRECTORY

I.N.C. Inc (See Kick Eez)
I.S.S., P.O. Box 185234, Ft. Worth, TX 76181 / 817-595-2090
I.S.W., 106 E. Cairo Dr., Tempe, AZ 85282
IAR Inc., 33171 Camino Capistrano, San Juan Capistrano, CA 92675 / 949-443-3642; FAX: 949-443-3647
IGA (See U.S. Importer-Stoeger Industries)
Ignacio Ugartechea S.A., Chonta 26, Eibar, 20600 SPAIN / 43-121257; FAX: 43-121669
Illinois Lead Shop, 7742 W. 61st Place, Summit, IL 60501
Image Ind. Inc., 382 Balm Court, Wood Dale, IL 60191 / 630-766-2402; FAX: 630-766-7373
IMI, P.O. Box 1044, Ramat Hasharon, 47100 ISRAEL / 972-3-5485617; FAX: 972-3-5406908
IMI Services USA, Inc., 2 Wisconsin Circle, Suite 420, Chevy Chase, MD 20815 / 301-215-4800; FAX: 301-657-1446
Impact Case Co., P.O. Box 9912, Spokane, WA 99209-0912 / 800-262-3322 or 509-467-3303; FAX: 509-326-5436 kkair.com
Imperial (See E-Z-Way Systems), PO Box 4310, Newark, OH 43058-4310 / 614-345-6645; FAX: 614-345-6600
Imperial Magnum Corp., P.O. Box 249, Oroville, WA 98844 / 604-495-3131; FAX: 604-495-2816
Imperial Miniature Armory, 10547 S. Post Oak, Houston, TX 77035 / 713-729-8428 FAX: 713-729-2274
Imperial Schrade Corp., 7 Schrade Ct., Box 7000, Ellenville, NY 12428 / 914-647-7601; FAX: 914-647-8701
Import Sports Inc., 1750 Brielle Ave., Unit B1, Wanamassa, NJ 07712 / 908-493-0302; FAX: 908-493-0301
IMR Powder Co., 1080 Military Turnpike, Suite 2, Plattsburgh, NY 12901 / 518-563-2253; FAX: 518-563-6916
Info-Arm, P.O. Box 1262, Champlain, NY 12919 / 514-955-0355; FAX: 514-955-0357
Ingle, Ralph W., Engraver, 112 Manchester Ct., Centerville, GA 31028 / 912-953-5824
Innovative Weaponry Inc., 2513 E. Loop 820 N., Fort Worth, TX 76118 / 817-284-0099; or 800-334-3573
Innovision Enterprises, 728 Skinner Dr., Kalamazoo, MI 49001 / 616-382-1681 FAX: 616-382-1830
INTEC International, Inc., P.O. Box 5708, Scottsdale, AZ 85261 / 602-483-1708
Inter Ordnance of America LP, 3305 Westwood Industrial Dr, Monroe, NC 28110-5204 / 704-821-8337; FAX: 704-821-8523
Interarms/Howa, PO Box 208, Ten Prince St, Alexandria, VA 22313 / 703-548-1400; FAX: 703-549-7826
Intercontinental Distributors, Ltd., PO Box 815, Beulah, ND 58523
Intrac Arms International, 5005 Chapman Hwy., Knoxville, TN 37920
Intratec, 12405 SW 130th St., Miami, FL 33186-6224 / 305-232-1821; FAX: 305-253-7207
Ion Industries, Inc, 3508 E Allerton Ave, Cudahy, WI 53110 / 414-486-2007; FAX: 414-486-2017
Iosso Products, 1485 Lively Blvd., Elk Grove Village, IL 60007 / 847-437-8400; FAX: 847-437-8478
Iron Bench, 12619 Bailey Rd., Redding, CA 96003 / 916-241-4623
Ironside International Publishers, Inc., P.O. Box 55, 800 Slaters Lane, Alexandria, VA 22313 / 703-684-6111; FAX: 703-683-5486
Ironsighter Co., P.O. Box 85070, Westland, MI 48185 / 734-326-8731; FAX: 734-326-3378
Irwin, Campbell H., 140 Hartland Blvd., East Hartland, CT 06027 / 203-653-3901
Island Pond Gun Shop, Cross St., Island Pond, VT 05846 / 802-723-4546
Israel Arms International, Inc., 5709 Hartsdale, Houston, TX 77036 / 713-789-0745; FAX: 713-789-7513
Israel Military Industries Ltd. (See IMI), PO Box 1044, Ramat Hasharon, ISRAEL / 972-3-5485617; FAX: 972-3-5406908
Ithaca Classic Doubles, Stephen Lamboy, PO Box 665, Mendon, NY 14506 / 706-569-6760; FAX: 706-561-9248
Ithaca Gun Co. LLC, 891 Route 34-B, King Ferry, NY 13081 / 888-9ITHACA; FAX: 315-364-5134
Ivanoff, Thomas G (See Tom's Gun Repair)

J

J J Roberts Firearm Engraver, 7808 Lake Dr, Manassas, VA 20111 / 703-330-0448 FAX: 703-264-8600
J Martin Inc, PO Drawer AP, Beckley, WV 25802 / 304-255-4073; FAX: 304-255-4077
J&D Components, 75 East 350 North, Orem, UT 84057-4719 / 801-225-7007
J&J Products, Inc., 9240 Whitmore, El Monte, CA 91731 / 818-571-5228; FAX: 800-927-8361
J&J Sales, 1501 21st Ave. S., Great Falls, MT 59405 / 406-453-7549
J&L Superior Bullets (See Huntington Die Specialties)
J&R Engineering, P.O. Box 77, 200 Lyons Hill Rd., Athol, MA 01331 / 508-249-9241
J&R Enterprises, 4550 Scotts Valley Rd., Lakeport, CA 95453
J&S Heat Treat, 803 S. 16th St., Blue Springs, MO 64015 / 816-229-2149; FAX: 816-228-1135
J-4 Inc., 1700 Via Burton, Anaheim, CA 92806 / 714-254-8315; FAX: 714-956-4421
J-Gar Co., 183 Turnpike Rd., Dept. 3, Petersham, MA 01366-9604
J. Dewey Mfg. Co., Inc., P.O. Box 2014, Southbury, CT 06488 / 203-264-3064; FAX: 203-262-6907
J. Korzinek Riflesmith, RD 2, Box 73D, Canton, PA 17724 / 717-673-8512
J.A. Blades, Inc. (See Christopher Firearms Co.)
J.A. Henckels Zwillingswerk Inc., 9 Skyline Dr., Hawthorne, NY 10532 / 914-592-7370
J.G. Dapkus Co., Inc., Commerce Circle, P.O. Box 293, Durham, CT 06422
J.I.T. Ltd., P.O. Box 230, Freedom, WY 83120 / 708-494-0937
J.J. Roberts/Engraver, 7808 Lake Dr., Manassas, VA 22111 / 703-330-0448
J.M. Bucheimer Jumbo Sports Products, 721 N. 20th St., St. Louis, MO 63103 / 314-241-1020
J.P. Enterprises Inc., P.O. Box 26324, Shoreview, MN 55126 / 612-486-9064; FAX: 612-482-0970
J.P. Gunstocks, Inc., 4508 San Miguel Ave., North Las Vegas, NV 89030 / 702-645-0718
J.R. Blair Engraving, P.O. Box 64, Glenrock, WY 82637 / 307-436-8115
J.R. Williams Bullet Co., 2008 Tucker Rd., Perry, GA 31069 / 912-987-0274
J.W. Morrison Custom Rifles, 4015 W. Sharon, Phoenix, AZ 85029 / 602-978-3754
J/B Adventures & Safaris Inc., 2275 E. Arapahoe Rd., Ste. 109, Littleton, CO 80122-1521 / 303-771-0977
Jack Dever Co., 8590 NW 90, Oklahoma City, OK 73132 / 405-721-6393
Jack A. Rosenberg & Sons, 12229 Cox Ln., Dallas, TX 75234 / 214-241-6302
Jack First, Inc., 1201 Turbine Dr., Rapid City, SD 57701 / 605-343-9544; FAX: 605-343-9420
Jackalope Gun Shop, 1048 S. 5th St., Douglas, WY 82633 / 307-358-3441
Jaffin, Harry. (See BRIDGEMAN PRODUCTS)
Jagdwaffen, P. Hofer, Buchsenmachermeister, Kirchgasse 24 A-9170, Ferlach, AUSTRIA / 04227-3683
James Calhoon Varmint Bullets, Shambo Rt., 304, Havre, MT 59501 / 406-395-4079
James Churchill Glove Co., P.O. Box 298, Centralia, WA 98531
James Calhoon Mfg., Rt. 304, Havre, MT 59501 / 406-395-4079
James Wayne Firearms for Collectors and Investors, 2608 N. Laurent, Victoria, TX 77901 / 512-578-1258; FAX: 512-578-3559
Jamison's Forge Works, 4527 Rd. 6.5 NE, Moses Lake, WA 98837 / 509-762-2659
Jantz Supply, P.O. Box 584-GD, Davis, OK 73030-0584 / 580-369-2316; FAX: 580-369-3082
Jarrett Rifles, Inc., 383 Brown Rd., Jackson, SC 29831 / 803-471-3616
Jarvis, Inc., 1123 Cherry Orchard Lane, Hamilton, MT 59840 / 406-961-4392
JAS, Inc., P.O. Box 0, Rosemount, MN 55068 / 612-890-7631
Javelina Lube Products, P.O. Box 337, San Bernardino, CA 92402 / 714-882-5847; FAX: 714-434-6937
JB Custom, P.O. Box 6912, Leawood, KS 66206 / 913-381-2329
Jeff W. Flannery Engraving Co., 11034 Riddles Run Rd., Union, KY 41091 / 606-384-3127
Jeffredo Gunsight, P.O. Box 669, San Marcos, CA 92079 / 619-728-2695
Jena Eur, PO Box 319, Dunmore, PA 18512
Jenco Sales, Inc., P.O. Box 1000, Manchaca, TX 78652 / 800-531-5301 FAX: 800-266-2373
Jenkins Recoil Pads, Inc., 5438 E. Frontage Ln., Olney, IL 62450 / 618-395-3416
Jensen Bullets, 86 North, 400 West, Blackfoot, ID 83221 / 208-785-5590
Jensen's Custom Ammunition, 5146 E. Pima, Tucson, AZ 85712 / 602-325-3346 FAX: 602-322-5704
Jensen's Firearms Academy, 1280 W. Prince, Tucson, AZ 85705 / 602-293-8516
Jericho Tool & Die Co., Inc., RD 3 Box 70, Route 7, Bainbridge, NY 13733-9496 / 607-563-8222; FAX: 607-563-8560
Jerry Phillips Optics, P.O. Box L632, Langhorne, PA 19047 / 215-757-5037 FAX: 215-757-7097
Jesse W. Smith Saddlery, 16909 E. Jackson Road, Elk, WA 99009-9600 / 509-325-0622
Jester Bullets, Rt. 1 Box 27, Orienta, OK 73737
Jewell Triggers, Inc., 3620 Hwy. 123, San Marcos, TX 78666 / 512-353-2999
JGS Precision Tool Mfg., 100 Main Sumner, Coos Bay, OR 97420 / 541-267-4331 FAX: 541-267-5996
Jim Chambers Flintlocks Ltd., Rt. 1, Box 513-A, Candler, NC 28715 / 704-667-8361
Jim Garthwaite Pistolsmith, Inc., Rt. 2 Box 310, Watsontown, PA 17777 / 717-538-1566
Jim Noble Co., 1305 Columbia St, Vancouver, WA 98660 / 360-695-1309; FAX: 360-695-6835 jnobleco@aol.com
Jim Norman Custom Gunstocks, 14281 Cane Rd, Valley Center, CA 92082 / 619-749-6252
Jim's Gun Shop (See Spradlin's)
Jim's Precision, Jim Ketchum, 1725 Moclips Dr., Petaluma, CA 94952 / 707-762-3014
JLK Bullets, 414 Turner Rd., Dover, AR 72837 / 501-331-4194
Johanssons Vapentillbehor, Bert, S-430 20, Veddige, SWEDEN
John Hall Plastics, Inc., Inc., P.O. Box 1526, Alvin, TX 77512 / 713-489-8709
John J. Adams & Son Engravers, PO Box 66, Vershire, VT 05079 / 802-685-0019
John Masen Co. Inc., 1305 Jelmak, Grand Prairie, TX 75050 / 817-430-8732; FAX: 817-430-1715
John Norrell Arms, 2608 Grist Mill Rd, Little Rock, AR 72207 / 501-225-7864
John Partridge Sales Ltd., Trent Meadows Rugeley, Staffordshire, WS15 2HS ENGLAND
John Rigby & Co., 1317 Spring St., Paso Robles, CA 93446 / 805-227-4236; FAX: 805-227-4723
John Unertl Optical Co., Inc., 308-310 Clay Ave., Mars, PA 16046-0818 / 724-625-3810
John's Custom Leather, 523 S. Liberty St., Blairsville, PA 15717 / 412-459-6802
Johnny Stewart Game Calls, Inc., P.O. Box 7954, 5100 Fort Ave., Waco, TX 76714 / 817-772-3261; FAX: 817-772-3670
Johnson Wood Products, 34968 Crystal Road, Strawberry Point, IA 52076 / 319-933-4930
Johnson's Gunsmithing, Inc, Neal, 208 W Buchanan St, Ste B, Colorado Springs, CO 80907 / 800-284-8671; FAX: 719-632-3493
Johnston Bros. (See C&T Corp. TA Johnson Brothers)
Johnston, James (See North Fork Custom Gunsmithing, James Johnston)
Jonad Corp., 2091 Lakeland Ave., Lakewood, OH 44107 / 216-226-3161
Jonathan Arthur Ciener, Inc., 8700 Commerce St., Cape Canaveral, FL 32920 / 407-868-2200; FAX: 407-868-2201
Jones Co., Dale, 680 Hoffman Draw, Kila, MT 59920 / 406-755-4684
Jones Custom Products, Neil A., 17217 Brookhouser Rd., Saegertown, PA 16433 / 814-763-2769; FAX: 814-763-4228
Jones Moulds, Paul, 4901 Telegraph Rd, Los Angeles, CA 90022 / 213-262-1510
Jones, J.D./SSK Industries, 590 Woodvue Ln., Wintersville, OH 43953 / 740-264-0176; FAX: 740-264-2257
JP Sales, Box 307, Anderson, TX 77830
JRP Custom Bullets, RR2 2233 Carlton Rd., Whitehall, NY 12887 / 518-282-0084 or 802-438-5548
JS Worldwide DBA (See Coonan Arms)
JSL Ltd (See U.S. Importer-Specialty Shooters Supply, Inc.)
Juenke, Vern, 25 Bitterbush Rd., Reno, NV 89523 / 702-345-0225
Jumbo Sports Products, J. M. Bucheimer, 721 N. 20th St., St. Louis, MO 63103 / 314-241-1020
Jungkind, Reeves C., 5001 Buckskin Pass, Austin, TX 78745-2841 / 512-442-1094
Jurras, L. E., P.O. Box 680, Washington, IN 47501 / 812-254-7698
Justin Phillippi Custom Bullets, P.O. Box 773, Ligonier, PA 15658 / 412-238-9671

MANUFACTURERS DIRECTORY

K

K&M Industries, Inc., Box 66, 510 S. Main, Troy, ID 83871 / 208-835-2281; FAX: 208-835-5211
K&M Services, 5430 Salmon Run Rd., Dover, PA 17315 / 717-292-3175; FAX: 717-292-3175
K-D, Inc., 636, 585 N. Hwy. 155, Cleveland, UT 84518 / 801-653-2530
K-Sports Imports Inc., 2755 Thompson Creek Rd., Pomona, CA 91767 / 909-392-2345 FAX: 909-392-2354
K. Eversull Co., Inc., 1 Tracemont, Boyce, LA 71409 / 318-793-8728
K.B.I. Inc, PO Box 6625, Harrisburg, PA 17112 / 717-540-8518; FAX: 717-540-8567
K.K. Arms Co., Star Route Box 671, Kerrville, TX 78028 / 210-257-4718 FAX: 210-257-4891
K.L. Null Holsters Ltd., 161 School St. NW, Hill City Station, Resaca, GA 30735 / 706-625-5643; FAX: 706-625-9392
Ka Pu Kapili, P.O. Box 745, Honokaa, HI 96727 / 808-776-1644; FAX: 808-776-1731
KA-BAR Knives, 1116 E. State St., Olean, NY 14760 / 800-282-0130; FAX: 716-373-6245
Kahles A Swarovski Company, 1 Wholesale Way, Cranston, RI 02920-5540 / 401-946-2220; FAX: 401-946-2587
Kahr Arms, P.O. Box 220, 630 Route 303, Blauvelt, NY 10913 / 914-353-5996; FAX: 914-353-7833
Kalispel Case Line, P.O. Box 267, Cusick, WA 99119 / 509-445-1121
Kamik Outdoor Footwear, 554 Montee de Liesse, Montreal, PQ H4T 1P1 CANADA / 514-341-3950; FAX: 514-341-1861
Kamyk Engraving Co., Steve, 9 Grandview Dr, Westfield, MA 01085-1810 / 413-568-0457
Kane, Edward, P.O. Box 385, Ukiah, CA 95482 / 707-462-2937
Kane Products, Inc., 5572 Brecksville Rd., Cleveland, OH 44131 / 216-524-9962
Kapro Mfg.Co. Inc. (See R.E.I.)
Kasenit Co., Inc., 13 Park Ave., Highland Mills, NY 10930 / 914-928-9595; FAX: 914-928-7292
Kasmarsik Bullets, 4016 7th Ave. SW, Puyallup, WA 98373
Kaswer Custom, Inc., 13 Surrey Drive, Brookfield, CT 06804 / 203-775-0564; FAX: 203-775-6872
KDF, Inc., 2485 Hwy. 46 N., Seguin, TX 78155 / 210-379-8141; FAX: 210-379-5420
KeeCo Impressions, Inc., 346 Wood Ave., North Brunswick, NJ 08902 / 800-468-0546
Keeler, R. H., 817 "N" St., Port Angeles, WA 98362 / 206-457-4702
Kehr, Roger, 2131 Agate Ct. SE, Lacy, WA 98503 / 360-456-0831
Keith's Bullets, 942 Twisted Oak, Algonquin, IL 60102 / 708-658-3520
Keith's Custom Gunstocks (See Heppler, Keith M)
Keith's Custom Gunstocks, Keith M Heppler, 540 Banyan Circle, Walnut Creek, CA 94598 / 925-934-3509; FAX: 925-934-3143
Kel-Tec CNC Industries, Inc., P.O. Box 3427, Cocoa, FL 32924 / 407-631-0068; FAX: 407-631-1169
Kelbly, Inc., 7222 Dalton Fox Lake Rd., North Lawrence, OH 44666 / 216-683-4674; FAX: 216-683-7349
Kelley's, P.O. Box 125, Woburn, MA 01801 / 617-935-3389
Kellogg's Professional Products, 325 Pearl St., Sandusky, OH 44870 / 419-625-6551; FAX: 419-625-6167
Kelly, Lance, 1723 Willow Oak Dr., Edgewater, FL 32132 / 904-423-4933
Kemen America, 2550 Hwy. 23, Wrenshall, MN 55797
Ken Eyster Heritage Gunsmiths, Inc., 6441 Bishop Rd., Centerburg, OH 43011 / 614-625-6131
Ken Starnes Gunmaker, 15940 SW Holly Hill Rd, Hillsboro, OR 97123-9033 / 503-628-0705; FAX: 503-628-6005
Ken's Gun Specialties, Rt. 1, Box 147, Lakeview, AR 72642 / 501-431-5606
Ken's Kustom Kartridges, 331 Jacobs Rd., Hubbard, OH 44425 / 216-534-4595
Ken's Rifle Blanks, Ken McCullough, Rt. 2, P.O. Box 85B, Weston, OR 97886 / 503-566-3879
Keng's Firearms Specialty, Inc./US Tactical Systems, 875 Wharton Dr., P.O. Box 44405, Atlanta, GA 30336-1405 / 404-691-7611; FAX: 404-505-8445
Kennebec Journal, 274 Western Ave., Augusta, ME 04330 / 207-622-6288
Kennedy Firearms, 10 N. Market St., Muncy, PA 17756 / 717-546-6695
Kenneth W. Warren Engraver, P.O. Box 2842, Wenatchee, WA 98807 / 509-663-6123 FAX: 509-665-6123
KenPatable Ent., Inc., P.O. Box 19422, Louisville, KY 40259 / 502-239-5447
Kent Cartridge America, Inc, PO Box 849, 1000 Zigor Rd, Kearneysville, WV 25430
Kent Cartridge Mfg. Co. Ltd., Unit 16 Branbridges Industrial Esta, Tonbridge, Kent, ENGLAND / 622-872255; FAX: 622-872645
Keowee Game Calls, 608 Hwy. 25 North, Travelers Rest, SC 29690 / 864-834-7204; FAX: 864-834-7831
Kershaw Knives, 25300 SW Parkway Ave., Wilsonville, OR 97070 / 503-682-1966 or 800-325-2891; FAX: 503-682-7168
Kesselring Gun Shop, 400 Hwy. 99 North, Burlington, WA 98233 / 206-724-3113; FAX: 206-724-7003
Ketchum, Jim (See Jim's Precision)
Kickeez Inc, 301 Industrial Dr, Carl Junction, MO 64834-8806 / 419-649-2100; FAX: 417-649-2200 kickey@ipa.net
Kilham & Co., Main St., P.O. Box 37, Lyme, NH 03768 / 603-795-4112
Kim Ahrends Custom Firearms, Inc., Box 203, Clarion, IA 50525 / 515-532-3449; FAX: 515-532-3926
Kimar (See U.S. Importer-IAR,Inc)
Kimball, Gary, 1526 N. Circle Dr., Colorado Springs, CO 80909 / 719-634-1274
Kimber of America, Inc., 1 Lawton St., Yonkers, NY 10705 / 800-880-2418; FAX: 914-964-9340
King & Co., P.O. Box 1242, Bloomington, IL 61702 / 309-473-2161
King's Gun Works, 1837 W. Glenoaks Blvd., Glendale, CA 91201 / 818-956-6010; FAX: 818-548-8606
Kingyon, Paul L. (See Custom Calls)
Kirkpatrick Leather Co., PO Box 677, Laredo, TX 78040 / 956-723-6631; FAX: 956-725-0672
KK Air International (See Impact Case Co.)
KLA Enterprises, P.O. Box 2028, Eaton Park, FL 33840 / 941-682-2829 FAX: 941-682-2829
Kleen-Bore,Inc., 16 Industrial Pkwy., Easthampton, MA 01027 / 413-527-0300; FAX: 413-527-2522 info@kleen-bore.com www.kleen-bore.com
Klein Custom Guns, Don, 433 Murray Park Dr, Ripon, WI 54971 / 920-748-2931
Kleinendorst, K. W., RR 1, Box 1500, Hop Bottom, PA 18824 / 717-289-4687
Klingler Woodcarving, P.O. Box 141, Thistle Hill, Cabot, VT 05647 / 802-426-3811
Kmount, P.O. Box 19422, Louisville, KY 40259 / 502-239-5447
Kneiper, James, P.O. Box 1516, Basalt, CO 81621-1516 / 303-963-9880
Knife Importers, Inc., P.O. Box 1000, Manchaca, TX 78652 / 512-282-6860
Knight & Hale Game Calls, Box 468, Industrial Park, Cadiz, KY 42211 / 502-924-1755; FAX: 502-924-1763
Knight Rifles, 21852 hwy j46, P.O. Box 130, Centerville, IA 52544 / 515-856-2626; FAX: 515-856-2628
Knight Rifles (See Modern Muzzle Loading, Inc.)
Knight's Mfg. Co., 7750 9th St. SW, Vero Beach, FL 32968 / 561-562-5697; FAX: 561-569-2955
Knippel, Richard, 500 Gayle Ave Apt 213, Modesto, CA 95350-4241 / 209-869-1469
Knock on Wood Antiques, 355 Post Rd., Darien, CT 06820 / 203-655-9031
Knoell, Doug, 9737 McCardle Way, Santee, CA 92071
Koevenig's Engraving Service, Box 55 Rabbit Gulch, Hill City, SD 57745 / 605-574-2239
KOGOT, 410 College, Trinidad, CO 81082 / 719-846-9406 FAX: 719-846-9406
Kokolus, Michael M. (See Custom Riflestocks, Inc., Michael M. Kokolus)
Kolar, 1925 Roosevelt Ave, Racine, WI 53406 / 414-554-0800; FAX: 414-554-9093
Kolpin Mfg., Inc., P.O. Box 107, 205 Depot St., Fox Lake, WI 53933 / 414-928-3118; FAX: 414-928-3687
Korth, Robert-Bosch-Str. 4, P.O. Box 1320, 23909 Ratzeburg, GERMANY / 451-4991497; FAX: 451-4993230
Korzinek Riflesmith, J, RD 2 Box 73D, Canton, PA 17724 / 717-673-8512
Koval Knives, 5819 Zarley St., Suite A, New Albany, OH 43054 / 614-855-0777; FAX: 614-855-0945
Kowa Optimed, Inc., 20001 S. Vermont Ave., Torrance, CA 90502 / 310-327-1913; FAX: 310-327-4177
Kramer Designs, P.O. Box 129, Clancy, MT 59634 / 406-933-8658; FAX: 406-933-8658
Kramer Handgun Leather, P.O. Box 112154, Tacoma, WA 98411 / 206-564-6652; FAX: 206-564-1214
Krause Publications, Inc., 700 E. State St., Iola, WI 54990 / 715-445-2214; FAX: 715-445-4087
Krico Jagd-und Sportwaffen GmbH, Nurnbergerstrasse 6, D-90602, Pyrbaum, GERMANY / 09180-2780; FAX: 09180-2661
Krieger Barrels, Inc., N114 W18697 Clinton Dr., Germantown, WI 53022 / 414-255-9593; FAX: 414-255-9586
Krieghoff Gun Co., H., Boschstrasse 22, D-89079 Elm, GERMANY or 731-4018270
Krieghoff International,Inc., 7528 Easton Rd., Ottsville, PA 18942 / 610-847-5173; FAX: 610-847-8691
Kris Mounts, 108 Lehigh St., Johnstown, PA 15905 / 814-539-9751
KSN Industries Ltd (See U.S. Importer-Israel Arms International, Inc.,)
Kudlas, John M., 622 14th St. SE, Rochester, MN 55904 / 507-288-5579
Kulis Freeze Dry Taxidermy, 725 Broadway Ave., Bedford, OH 44146 / 216-232-8352; FAX: 216-232-7305 jkulis@kastaway.com
KVH Industries, Inc., 110 Enterprise Center, Middletown, RI 02842 / 401-847-3327; FAX: 401-849-0045
Kwik Mount Corp., P.O. Box 19422, Louisville, KY 40259 / 502-239-5447
Kwik-Site Co., 5555 Treadwell, Wayne, MI 48184 / 734-326-1500; FAX: 734-326-4120

L

L&R Lock Co., 1137 Pocalla Rd., Sumter, SC 29150 / 803-775-6127 FAX: 803-775-5171
L&S Technologies Inc (See Aimtech Mount Systems)
L. Bengtson Arms Co., 6345-B E. Akron St., Mesa, AZ 85205 / 602-981-6375
L.A.R. Mfg., Inc., 4133 W. Farm Rd., West Jordan, UT 84088 / 801-280-3505; FAX: 801-280-1972
L.E. Wilson, Inc., Box 324, 404 Pioneer Ave., Cashmere, WA 98815 / 509-782-1328; FAX: 509-782-7200
L.L. Bean, Inc., Freeport, ME 04032 / 207-865-4761; FAX: 207-552-2802
L.P.A. Snc, Via Alfieri 26, Gardone V.T., Brescia, ITALY / 30-891-14-81; FAX: 30-891-09-51
L.R. Clift Mfg., 3821 Hammonton Rd., Marysville, CA 95901 / 916-755-3390; FAX: 916-755-3393
L.S. Starrett Co., 121 Crescent St., Athol, MA 01331 / 617-249-3551
L.W. Seecamp Co., Inc., P.O. Box 255, New Haven, CT 06502 / 203-877-3429
La Clinique du .45, 1432 Rougemont, Chambly,, PQ J3L 2L8 CANADA / 514-658-1144
Labanu, Inc., 2201-F Fifth Ave., Ronkonkoma, NY 11779 / 516-467-6197; FAX: 516-981-4112
LaBoone, Pat. (See CLEAR CREEK OUTDOORS)
LaBounty Precision Reboring, Inc, 7968 Silver Lake Rd., PO Box 186, Maple Falls, WA 98266 / 360-599-2047 FAX: 360-599-3018
LaCrosse Footwear, Inc., P.O. Box 1328, La Crosse, WI 54602 / 608-782-3020 or 800-323-2668; FAX: 800-658-9444
LaFrance Specialties, P.O. Box 87933, San Diego, CA 92138-7933 / 619-293-3373; FAX: 619-293-7087
Lage Uniwad, P.O. Box 2302, Davenport, IA 52809 / 319-388-LAGE; FAX: 319-388-LAGE
Lair, Sam, 520 E. Beaver, Jenks, OK 74037 / 918-299-2391
Lake Center, P.O. Box 38, St. Charles, MO 63302 / 314-946-7500
Lakefield Arms Ltd (See Savage Arms Inc)
Lakewood Products LLC, 275 June St., Berlin, WI 54923 / 800-872-8458; FAX: 920-361-7719
Lamboy, Stephen. (See ITHACA CLASSIC DOUBLES)
Lampert, Ron, Rt. 1, Box 177, Guthrie, MN 56461 / 218-854-7345
Lamson & Goodnow Mfg. Co., 45 Conway St., Shelburne Falls, MA 03170 / 413-625-6564; or 800-872-6564 FAX: 413-625-9816 www.lamsonsharp.com
Lanber Armas, S.A., Zubiaurre 5, Zaldibar, 48250 SPAIN / 34-4-6827702; FAX: 34-4-6827999
Langenberg Hat Co., P.O. Box 1860, Washington, MO 63090 / 800-428-1860; FAX: 314-239-3151
Lanphert, Paul, P.O. Box 1985, Wenatchee, WA 98807
Lansky Levine, Arthur. (See LANSKY SHARPENERS)
Lansky Sharpeners, Arthur Lansky Levine, PO Box 50830, Las Vegas, NV 89016 / 702-361-7511; FAX: 702-896-9511
Lapua Ltd., P.O. Box 5, Lapua, FINLAND / 6-310111; FAX: 6-4388991

MANUFACTURERS DIRECTORY

LaRocca Gun Works, 51 Union Place, Worcester, MA 01608 / 508-754-2887; FAX: 508-754-2887
Larry Lyons Gunworks, 110 Hamilton St., Dowagiac, MI 49047 / 616-782-9478
Laser Devices, Inc., 2 Harris Ct. A-4, Monterey, CA 93940 / 408-373-0701; FAX: 408-373-0903
Laseraim Technologies, Inc., P.O. Box 3548, Little Rock, AR 72203 / 501-375-2227
LaserMax, Inc., 3495 Winton Place, Bldg. B, Rochester, NY 14623-2807 / 800-527-3703 FAX: 716-272-5427
Lassen Community College, Gunsmithing Dept., P.O. Box 3000, Hwy. 139, Susanville, CA 96130 / 916-251-8800; FAX: 916-251-8838
Lathrop's, Inc., Inc., 5146 E. Pima, Tucson, AZ 85712 / 520-881-0266 or 800-875-4867; FAX: 520-322-5704
Laughridge, William R (See Cylinder & Slide Inc)
Laurel Mountain Forge, P.O. Box 52, Crown Point, IN 48065 / 219-548-2950; FAX: 219-548-2950
Laurona Armas Eibar, S.A.L., Avenida de Otaola 25, P.O. Box 260, Eibar 20600, SPAIN / 34-43-700600; FAX: 34-43-700616
Lawrence Brand Shot (See Precision Reloading, Inc.)
Lawrence Leather Co., P.O. Box 1479, Lillington, NC 27546 / 910-893-2071; FAX: 910-893-4742
Lawson Co., Harry, 3328 N Richey Blvd., Tucson, AZ 85716 / 520-326-1117 FAX: 520-326-1117
Lawson, John. (See THE SIGHT SHOP)
Lawson, John G (See Sight Shop, The)
Lazzeroni Arms Co., PO Box 26696, Tucson, AZ 85726 / 888-492-7247; FAX: 520-624-4250
LBT, HCR 62, Box 145, Moyie Springs, ID 83845 / 208-267-3588
Le Clear Industries (See E-Z-Way Systems), PO Box 4310, Newark, OH 43058-4310 / 614-345-6645; FAX: 614-345-6600
Lea Mfg. Co., 237 E. Aurora St., Waterbury, CT 06720 / 203-753-5116
Leapers, Inc., 7675 Five Mile Rd., Northville, MI 48167 / 248-486-1231; FAX: 248-486-1430
Leatherman Tool Group, Inc., 12106 NE Ainsworth Cir., P.O. Box 20595, Portland, OR 97294 / 503-253-7826; FAX: 503-253-7830
Lebeau-Courally, Rue St. Gilles, 386 4000, Liege, BELGIUM / 042-52-48-43; FAX: 32-042-52-20-08
Leckie Professional Gunsmithing, 546 Quarry Rd., Ottsville, PA 18942 / 215-847-8594
Lectro Science, Inc., 6410 W. Ridge Rd., Erie, PA 16506 / 814-833-6487; FAX: 814-833-0447
Ledbetter Airguns, Riley, 1804 E Sprague St, Winston Salem, NC 27107-3521 / 919-784-0676
Lee Co., T. K., 1282 Branchwater Ln, Birmingham, AL 35216 / 205-913-5222
Lee Precision, Inc., 4275 Hwy. U, Hartford, WI 53027 / 414-673-3075; FAX: 414-673-9273 leeprecision.com
Lee Supplies, Mark, 9901 France Ct., Lakeville, MN 55044 / 612-461-2114
Lee's Red Ramps, 4 Kristine Ln., Silver City, NM 88061 / 505-538-8529
LeFever Arms Co., Inc., 6234 Stokes, Lee Center Rd., Lee Center, NY 13363 / 315-337-6722; FAX: 315-337-1543
Legacy Sports International, 10 Prince St., Alexandria, VA 22314
Legend Products Corp., 21218 Saint Andrews Blvd., Boca Raton, FL 33433-2435
Leibowitz, Leonard, 1205 Murrayhill Ave., Pittsburgh, PA 15217 / 412-361-5455
Leica USA, Inc., 156 Ludlow Ave., Northvale, NJ 07647 / 201-767-7500; FAX: 201-767-8666
LEM Gun Specialties Inc. The Lewis Lead Remover, P.O. Box 2855, Peachtree City, GA 30269-2024
Leonard Day, 6 Linseed Rd Box 1, West Hatfield, MA 01088-7505 / 413-337-8369
Les Baer Custom,Inc., 29601 34th Ave., Hillsdale, IL 61257 / 309-658-2716; FAX: 309-658-2610
Lestrom Laboratories, Inc., P.O. Box 628, Mexico, NY 13114-0628 / 315-343-3076; FAX: 315-592-3370
Lethal Force Institute (See Police Bookshelf), PO Box 122, Concord, NH 03301 / 603-224-6814; FAX: 603-226-3554
Lett Custom Grips, 672 Currier Rd., Hopkinton, NH 03229-2652 / 800-421-5388 FAX: 603-226-4580
Leupold & Stevens, Inc., 14400 NW Greenbrier Pky., Beaverton, OR 97006 / 503-646-9171; FAX: 503-526-1455
Lever Arms Service Ltd., 2131 Burrard St., Vancouver, BC V6J 3H7 CANADA / 604-736-2711; FAX: 604-738-3503
Lew Horton Dist. Co., Inc., 15 Walkup Dr., Westboro, MA 01581 / 508-366-7400; FAX: 508-366-5332

Liberty Metals, 2233 East 16th St., Los Angeles, CA 90021 / 213-581-9171; FAX: 213-581-9351
Liberty Safe, 1060 N. Spring Creek Pl., Springville, UT 84663 / 800-247-5625; FAX: 801-489-6409
Liberty Shooting Supplies, P.O. Box 357, Hillsboro, OR 97123 / 503-640-5518; FAX: 503-640-5518
Liberty Trouser Co., 3500 6 Ave S., Birmingham, AL 35222-2406 / 205-251-9143
Lightfield Ammunition Corp. (See Slug Group, Inc.), PO Box 376, New Paris, PA 15554 / 814-839-4517; FAX: 814-839-2601
Lightforce U.S.A. Inc., 19226 66th Ave. So., L-103, Kent, WA 98032 / 206-656-1577; FAX: 206-656-1578
Lightning Performance Innovations, Inc., RD1 Box 555, Mohawk, NY 13407 / 800-242-5873; FAX: 315-866-1578
Lilja Precision Rifle Barrels, P.O. Box 372, Plains, MT 59859 / 406-826-3084; FAX: 406-826-3083 lilja@riflebarrels.com www.riflebarrel.com
Lincoln, Dean, Box 1886, Farmington, NM 87401
Lind Custom Guns, Al, 7821 76th Ave SW, Tacoma, WA 98498 / 253-584-6361 lindcustguns@worldnot.att.net
Linder Solingen Knives, 4401 Sentry Dr., Tucker, GA 30084 / 770-939-6915; FAX: 770-939-6738
Lindsay, Steve, RR 2 Cedar Hills, Kearney, NE 68847 / 308-236-7885
Lindsley Arms Cartridge Co., P.O. Box 757, 20 College Hill Rd., Henniker, NH 03242 / 603-428-3127
Linebaugh Custom Sixguns, Route 2, Box 100, Maryville, MO 64468 / 660-562-3031 sixgunner.com
Lion Country Supply, P.O. Box 480, Port Matilda, PA 16870
List Precision Engineering, Unit 1 Ingley Works, 13 River Road, Barking, ENGLAND / 011-081-594-1686
Lithi Bee Bullet Lube, 1728 Carr Rd., Muskegon, MI 49442 / 616-788-4479
"Little John's" Antique Arms, 1740 W. Laveta, Orange, CA 92668
Little Trees Ramble (See Scott Pilkington, Little
Littler Sales Co., 20815 W. Chicago, Detroit, MI 48228 / 313-273-6888; FAX: 313-273-1099
Littleton, J. F., 275 Pinedale Ave., Oroville, CA 95966 / 916-533-6084
Ljutic Industries, Inc., 732 N. 16th Ave., Suite 22, Yakima, WA 98907 / 509-248-0476; FAX: 509-576-8233
Llama Gabilondo Y Cia, Apartado 290, E-01080, Victoria, spain, SPAIN
Loch Leven Industries, P.O. Box 2751, Santa Rosa, CA 95405 / 707-573-8735; FAX: 707-573-0369
Lock's Philadelphia Gun Exchange, 6700 Rowland Ave., Philadelphia, PA 19149 / 215-332-6225; FAX: 215-332-4800
Lodewick, Walter H., 2816 NE Halsey St., Portland, OR 97232 / 503-284-2554
Log Cabin Sport Shop, 8010 Lafayette Rd., Lodi, OH 44254 / 330-948-1082; FAX: 330-948-4307
Logan, Harry M., Box 745, Honokaa, HI 96727 / 808-776-1644
Lohman Mfg. Co., Inc., 4500 Doniphan Dr., P.O. Box 220, Neosho, MO 64850 / 417-451-4438; FAX: 417-451-2576
Lomont Precision Bullets, RR 1, Box 34, Salmon, ID 83467 / 208-756-6819; FAX: 208-756-6824
London Guns Ltd., Box 3750, Santa Barbara, CA 93130 / 805-683-4141; FAX: 805-683-1712
Lone Star Gunleather, 1301 Brushy Bend Dr., Round Rock, TX 78681 / 512-255-1805
Lone Star Rifle Company, 11231 Rose Road, Conroe, TX 77303 / 409-856-3363
Long, George F., 1500 Rogue River Hwy., Ste. F, Grants Pass, OR 97527 / 541-476-7552
Lortone Inc., 2856 NW Market St., Seattle, WA 98107
Lothar Walther Precision Tool Inc., 3425 Hutchinson Rd., Cumming, GA 30040 / 770-889-9998; FAX: 770-889-4918 lotharwalther@mindspring.com www.lothar-walther.com
Loweth, Richard H.R., 29 Hedgegrow Lane, Kirby Muxloe, Leics, LE9 2BN ENGLAND / (0) 116 238 6295
LPS Laboratories, Inc., 4647 Hugh Howell Rd., P.O. Box 3050, Tucker, GA 30084 / 404-934-7800
Lucas, Edward E, 32 Garfield Ave., East Brunswick, NJ 08816 / 201-251-5526
Lucas, Mike, 1631 Jessamine Rd., Lexington, SC 29073
Lupton, Keith. (See PAWLING MOUNTAIN CLUB)
Lutz Engraving, Ron E., E1998 Smokey Valley Rd, Scandinavia, WI 54977 / 715-467-2674
Lyman Instant Targets, Inc. (See Lyman Products, Corp.)

Lyman Products Corp., 475 Smith Street, Middletown, CT 06457-1541 / 860-632-2020 or 800-22-LYMAN FAX: 860-632-1699
Lyman Products Corporation, 475 Smith Street, Middletown, CT 06457-1529 / 800-22-LYMAN or 860-632-2020; FAX: 860-632-1699
Lyte Optronics (See TracStar Industries Inc)

M

M. Thys (See U.S. Importer-Champlin Firearms Inc)
M.H. Canjar Co., 500 E. 45th Ave., Denver, CO 80216 / 303-295-2638; FAX: 303-295-2638
M.O.A. Corp., 2451 Old Camden Pike, Eaton, OH 45320 / 937-456-3669
MA Systems, P.O. Box 1143, Chouteau, OK 74337 / 918-479-6378
Mac-1 Airgun Distributors, 13974 Van Ness Ave., Gardena, CA 90249 / 310-327-3581; FAX: 310-327-0238 mac1@concentric.net mac1airgun.com
Macbean, Stan, 754 North 1200 West, Orem, UT 84057 / 801-224-6446
Madis, George, P.O. Box 545, Brownsboro, TX 75756 / 903-852-6480
Madis Books, 2453 West Five Mile Pkwy., Dallas, TX 75233 / 214-330-7168
MAG Instrument, Inc., 1635 S. Sacramento Ave., Ontario, CA 91761 / 909-947-1006; FAX: 909-947-3116
Mag-Na-Port International, Inc., 41302 Executive Dr., Harrison Twp., MI 48045-1306 / 810-469-6727; FAX: 810-469-0425
Mag-Pack Corp., P.O. Box 846, Chesterland, OH 44026
Magma Engineering Co., P.O. Box 161, 20955 E. Ocotillo Rd., Queen Creek, AZ 85242 / 602-987-9008 FAX: 602-987-0148
Magnolia Sports,Inc., 211 W. Main, Magnolia, AR 71753 / 501-234-8410 or 800-530-7816; FAX: 501-234-8117
Magnum Power Products, Inc., P.O. Box 17768, Fountain Hills, AZ 85268
Magnum Research, Inc., 7110 University Ave. NE, Minneapolis, MN 55432 / 800-772-6168 or 612-574-1868; FAX: 612-574-0109 magnumresearch.com
Magnus Bullets, P.O. Box 239, Toney, AL 35773 / 256-420-8359; FAX: 256-420-8360
MagSafe Ammo Co., 4700 S US Highway 17/92, Casselberry, FL 32707-3814 / 407-834-9966; FAX: 407-834-8185
Magtech Ammunition Co. Inc., 837 Boston Rd #12, Madison, CT 06443 / 203-245-8983; FAX: 203-245-2883 rfinemtek@aol.com
Mahony, Philip Bruce, 67 White Hollow Rd., Lime Rock, CT 06039-2418 / 203-435-9341
Mahovsky's Metalife, R.D. 1, Box 149a Eureka Road, Grand Valley, PA 16420 / 814-436-7747
Maine Custom Bullets, RFD 1, Box 1755, Brooks, ME 04921
Maionchi-L.M.I., Via Di Coselli-Zona, Industriale Di Guamo 55060, Lucca, ITALY / 011 39-583 94291
Makinson, Nicholas, RR 3, Komoka, ON N0L 1R0 CANADA / 519-471-5462
Malcolm Enterprises, 1023 E. Prien Lake Rd., Lake Charles, LA 70601
Mallardtone Game Calls, 2901 16th St., Moline, IL 61265 / 309-762-8089
Mandall Shooting Supplies Inc., 3616 N. Scottsdale Rd., Scottsdale, AZ 85252 / 480-945-2553; FAX: 480-949-0734
Marathon Rubber Prods. Co., Inc., 1009 3rd St, Wausau, WI 54403-4765 / 715-845-6255
Marble Arms (See CRR, Inc./Marble's Inc.)
Marchmon Bullets, 8191 Woodland Shore Dr., Brighton, MI 48116
Marent, Rudolf, 9711 Tiltree St., Houston, TX 77075 / 713-946-7028
Mark Lee Supplies, 9901 France Ct., Lakeville, MN 55044 / 612-461-2114
Markell,Inc., 422 Larkfield Center 235, Santa Rosa, CA 95403 / 707-573-0792; FAX: 707-573-9867
Markesbery Muzzle Loaders, Inc., 7785 Foundation Dr., Ste. 6, Florence, KY 41042 / 606-342-5553; or 606-342-2380
Marksman Products, 5482 Argosy Dr., Huntington Beach, CA 92649 / 714-898-7535 or 800-822-8005; FAX: 714-891-0782
Marlin Firearms Co., 100 Kenna Dr., North Haven, CT 06473 / 203-239-5621; FAX: 203-234-7991
MarMik, Inc., 2116 S. Woodland Ave., Michigan City, IN 46360 / 219-872-7231; FAX: 219-872-7231

340 • GUNS ILLUSTRATED

MANUFACTURERS DIRECTORY

Marocchi F.lli S.p.A, Via Galileo Galilei 8, I-25068 Zanano, ITALY
Marquart Precision Co., (See Morrison Precision)
Marsh, Johnny, 1007 Drummond Dr., Nashville, TN 37211 / 615-833-3259
Marsh, Mike, Croft Cottage, Main St., Derbyshire, DE4 2BY ENGLAND / 01629 650 669
Marshall Enterprises, 792 Canyon Rd., Redwood City, CA 94062
Marshall F. Fish Mfg. Gunsmith Sptg. Co., Rd. Box 2439, Rt. 22 North, Westport, NY 12993 / 518-962-4897 FAX: 518-962-4897
Martin B. Retting Inc., 11029 Washington, Culver City, CA 90232 / 213-837-2412
Martin Hagn Rifles & Actions, P.O. Box 444, Cranbrook, BC V1C 4H9 CANADA / 604-489-4861
Martin's Gun Shop, 937 S. Sheridan Blvd., Lakewood, CO 80226 / 303-922-2184
Martz, John V., 8060 Lakeview Lane, Lincoln, CA 95648 FAX: 916-645-3815
Marvel, Alan, 3922 Madonna Rd., Jarretsville, MD 21084 / 301-557-6545
Marx, Harry (See U.S. Importer for FERLIB)
Maryland Paintball Supply, 8507 Harford Rd., Parkville, MD 21234 / 410-882-5607
MAST Technology, 4350 S. Arville, Suite 3, Las Vegas, NV 89103 / 702-362-5043; FAX: 702-362-9554
Master Engravers, Inc. (See Hendricks, Frank E)
Master Lock Co., 2600 N. 32nd St., Milwaukee, WI 53245 / 414-444-2800
Match Prep--Doyle Gracey, P.O. Box 155, Tehachapi, CA 93581 / 661-822-5383; FAX: 661-823-8680
Matco, Inc., 1003-2nd St., N. Manchester, IN 46962 / 219-982-8282
Mathews & Son, Inc., George E., 10224 S Paramount Blvd, Downey, CA 90241 / 562-862-6719; FAX: 562-862-6719
Matthews Cutlery, 4401 Sentry Dr., Tucker, GA 30084 / 770-939-6915
Mauser Werke Oberndorf Waffensysteme GmbH, Postfach 1349, 78722, Oberndorf/N., GERMANY
Maverick Arms, Inc., 7 Grasso Ave., P.O. Box 497, North Haven, CT 06473 / 203-230-5300; FAX: 203-230-5420
Maxi-Mount, P.O. Box 291, Willoughby Hills, OH 44094-0291 / 216-944-9456; FAX: 216-944-9456
Maximum Security Corp., 32841 Calle Perfecto, San Juan Capistrano, CA 92675 / 714-493-3684; FAX: 714-496-7733
Mayville Engineering Co. (See MEC, Inc.)
Mazur Restoration, Pete, 13083 Drummer Way, Grass Valley, CA 95949 / 530-268-2412
McBros Rifle Co., P.O. Box 86549, Phoenix, AZ 85080 / 602-582-3713; FAX: 602-581-3825
McCament, Jay, 1730-134th St. Ct. S., Tacoma, WA 98444 / 253-531-8832
McCann Industries, P.O. Box 641, Spanaway, WA 98387 / 253-537-6919; FAX: 253-537-6919 mccann.machine@worldnet.att.net www.mccannindustries.com
McCann's Machine & Gun Shop, P.O. Box 641, Spanaway, WA 98387 / 253-537-6919; FAX: 253-537-6993 mccann.machine@worldnet.att.net www.mccannindustries.com
McCann's Muzzle-Gun Works, 14 Walton Dr., New Hope, PA 18938 / 215-862-2728
McCluskey Precision Rifles, 10502 14th Ave. NW, Seattle, WA 98177 / 206-781-2776
McCombs, Leo, 1862 White Cemetery Rd., Patriot, OH 45658 / 614-256-1714
McCormick Corp., Chip, 1825 Fortview Rd Ste 115, Austin, TX 78704 / 800-328-CHIP; FAX: 512-462-0009
McCullough, Ken. (See KEN'S RIFLE BLANKS)
McDonald, Dennis, 8359 Brady St., Peosta, IA 52068 / 319-556-7940
McFarland, Stan, 2221 Idella Ct., Grand Junction, CO 81505 / 970-243-4704
McGhee, Larry. (See B.C. OUTDOORS)
McGowen Rifle Barrels, 5961 Spruce Lane, St. Anne, IL 60964 / 815-937-9816; FAX: 815-937-4024
McGuire, Bill, 1600 N. Eastmont Ave., East Wenatchee, WA 98802 / 509-884-6021
Mchalik, Gary. (See ROSSI FIREARMS, BRAZTECH)
McKenzie, Lynton, 6940 N. Alvernon Way, Tucson, AZ 85718 / 520-299-5090
McKillen & Heyer, Inc., 35535 Euclid Ave., Suite 11, Willoughby, OH 44094 / 216-942-2044
McKinney, R.P. (See Schuetzen Gun Co.)

McMillan Fiberglass Stocks, Inc., 21421 N. 14th Ave., Suite B, Phoenix, AZ 85027 / 602-582-9635; FAX: 602-581-3825
McMillan Optical Gunsight Co., 28638 N. 42nd St., Cave Creek, AZ 85331 / 602-585-7868; FAX: 602-585-7872
McMillan Rifle Barrels, P.O. Box 3427, Bryan, TX 77805 / 409-690-3456; FAX: 409-690-0156
McMurdo, Lynn (See Specialty Gunsmithing), PO Box 404, Afton, WY 83110 / 307-886-5535
MCRW Associates Shooting Supplies, R.R. 1, Box 1425, Sweet Valley, PA 18656 / 717-864-3967; FAX: 717-864-2669
MCS, Inc., 34 Delmar Dr., Brookfield, CT 06804 / 203-775-1013; FAX: 203-775-9462
McWelco Products, 6730 Santa Fe Ave., Hesperia, CA 92345 / 619-244-8876; FAX: 619-244-9398
MDS, P.O. Box 1441, Brandon, FL 33509-1441 / 813-653-1180; FAX: 813-684-5953
Meadow Industries, 24 Club Lane, Palmyra, VA 22963 / 804-589-7672; FAX: 804-589-7672
Measurement Group Inc., Box 27777, Raleigh, NC 27611
Measures, Leon. (See SHOOT WHERE YOU LOOK)
MEC, Inc., 715 South St., Mayville, WI 53050 / 414-387-4500; FAX: 414-387-5802 reloaders@mayul.com www.mayvl.com
MEC-Gar S.r.l., Via Madonnina 64, Gardone V.T. Brescia, ITALY / 39-30-8912687; FAX: 39-30-8910065
MEC-Gar U.S.A., Inc., Box 112, 500B Monroe Turnpike, Monroe, CT 06468 / 203-635-8662; FAX: 203-635-8662
Mech-Tech Systems, Inc., 1602 Foothill Rd., Kalispell, MT 59901 / 406-755-8055
Meister Bullets (See Gander Mountain)
Mele, Frank, 201 S. Wellow Ave., Cookeville, TN 38501 / 615-526-4860
Melton Shirt Co., Inc., 56 Harvester Ave., Batavia, NY 14020 / 716-343-8750; FAX: 716-343-6887
Men-Metallwerk Elisenhuette GmbH, P.O. Box 1263, Nassau/Lahn, D-56372 GERMANY / 2604-7819
Menck, Gunsmith Inc., T.W., 5703 S 77th St, Ralston, NE 68127
Mendez, John A., P.O. Box 620984, Orlando, FL 32862 / 407-344-2791
Meprolight (See Hesco-Meprolight)
Mercer Custom Stocks, R. M., 216 S Whitewater Ave, Jefferson, WI 53549 / 920-674-3839
Merit Corp., Box 9044, Schenectady, NY 12309 / 518-346-1420
Merkel Freres, Strasse 7 October, 10, Suhl, GERMANY
Merkuria Ltd., Argentinska 38, 17005, Praha 7 CZECH, REPUBLIC / 422-875117; FAX: 422-809152
Metal Merchants, PO Box 186, Walled Lake, MI 48390-0186
Metalife Industries (See Mahovsky's Metalife)
Metaloy, Inc., Rt. 5, Box 595, Berryville, AR 72616 / 501-545-3611
Metals Hand Engraver/European Hand Engraving, Ste. 216, 12 South First St., San Jose, CA 95113 / 408-293-6559
MI-TE Bullets, 1396 Ave. K, Ellsworth, KS 67439 / 785-472-4575; FAX: 785-472-5579
Michael's Antiques, Box 591, Waldoboro, ME 04572
Michaels Of Oregon, 1710 Red Soils Ct., Oregon City, OR 97045
Micro Sight Co., 242 Harbor Blvd., Belmont, CA 94002 / 415-591-0769; FAX: 415-591-7531
Microfusion Alfa S.A., Paseo San Andres N8, P.O. Box 271, Eibar, 20600 SPAIN / 34-43-11-89-16; FAX: 34-43-11-40-38
Mid-America Guns and Ammo, 1205 W. Jefferson, Suite E, Effingham, IL 62401 / 800-820-5177
Mid-America Recreation, Inc., 1328 5th Ave., Moline, IL 61265 / 309-764-5089; FAX: 309-764-2722
Middlebrooks Custom Shop, 7366 Colonial Trail East, Surry, VA 23883 / 757-357-0881; FAX: 757-365-0442
Midway Arms, Inc., 5875 W. Van Horn Tavern Rd., Columbia, MO 65203 / 800-243-3220 or 573-445-6363; FAX: 573-446-1018
Midwest Gun Sport, 1108 Herbert Dr., Zebulon, NC 27597 / 919-269-5570
Midwest Sport Distributors, Box 129, Fayette, MO 65248
Mike Davis Products, 643 Loop Dr., Moses Lake, WA 98837 / 509-765-6178 or 509-766-7281
Milberry House Publishing, PO Box 575, Corydon, IN 47112 / 888-738-1567; FAX: 888-738-1567
Military Armament Corp., P.O. Box 120, Mt. Zion Rd., Lingleville, TX 76461 / 817-965-3253
Millennium Designed Muzzleloaders, PO Box 536, Routes 11 & 25, Limington, ME 04049 / 207-637-2316

Miller Arms, Inc., P.O. Box 260 Purl St., St. Onge, SD 57779 / 605-642-5160; FAX: 605-642-5160
Miller Custom, 210 E. Julia, Clinton, IL 61727 / 217-935-9362
Miller Single Trigger Mfg. Co., Rt. 209, Box 1275, Millersburg, PA 17061 / 717-692-3704
Millett Sights, 7275 Murdy Circle, Adm. Office, Huntington Beach, CA 92647 / 714-842-5575 or 800-645-5388; FAX: 714-843-5707
Mills Jr., Hugh B., 3615 Canterbury Rd., New Bern, NC 28560 / 919-637-4631
Milstor Corp., 80-975 Indio Blvd., Indio, CA 92201 / 760-775-9998; FAX: 760-775-5229 milstor@webtv.net
Miltex, Inc, 700 S Lee St, Alexandria, VA 22314-4332 / 888-642-9123; FAX: 301-645-1430
Minute Man High Tech Industries, 10611 Canyon Rd. E., Suite 151, Puyallup, WA 98373 / 800-233-2734
Mirador Optical Corp., P.O. Box 11614, Marina Del Rey, CA 90295-7614 / 310-821-5587; FAX: 310-305-0386
Miroku, B C/Daly, Charles (See U.S. Importer-Bell's)
Mitchell, Jack, c/o Geoff Gaebe, Addieville East Farm, 200 Pheasant Dr, Mapleville, RI 02839 / 401-568-3185
Mitchell Bullets, R.F., 430 Walnut St, Westernport, MD 21562
Mitchell Optics, Inc., 2072 CR 1100 N, Sidney, IL 61877 / 217-688-2219 or 217-621-3018; FAX: 217-688-2505
Mitchell's Accuracy Shop, 68 Greenridge Dr., Stafford, VA 22554 / 703-659-0165
Mittermeier, Inc., Frank, PO Box 2G, 3577 E Tremont Ave, Bronx, NY 10465 / 718-828-3843
Mixson Corp., 7635 W. 28th Ave., Hialeah, FL 33016 / 305-821-5190 or 800-327-0078; FAX: 305-558-9318
MJK Gunsmithing, Inc, 417 N. Huber Ct., E. Wenatchee, WA 98802 / 509-884-7683
MJM Mfg., 3283 Rocky Water Ln., Suite B, San Jose, CA 95148 / 408-270-4207
MKS Supply, Inc. (See Hi-Point Firearms)
MMC, 2513 East Loop 820 North, Ft. Worth, TX 76118 / 817-595-0404; FAX: 817-595-3074
MMP, Rt. 6, Box 384, Harrison, AR 72601 / 501-741-5019; FAX: 501-741-3104
Mo's Competitor Supplies (See MCS Inc)
Modern Gun Repair School, P.O. Box 92577, Southlake, TX 76092 / 800-493-4114; FAX: 800-556-5112
Modern Muzzleloading, Inc, PO Box 130, Centerville, IA 52544 / 515-856-2626
Moeller, Steve, 1213 4th St., Fulton, IL 61252 / 815-589-2300
Molin Industries, Tru-Nord Division, P.O. Box 365, 204 North 9th St., Brainerd, MN 56401 / 218-829-2870
Monell Custom Guns, 228 Red Mills Rd., Pine Bush, NY 12566 / 914-744-3021
Moneymaker Guncraft Corp., 1420 Military Ave., Omaha, NE 68131 / 402-556-0226
Montana Armory, Inc (See C. Sharps Arms Co. Inc.), 100 Centennial, Box 885, Big Timber, MT 59011 / 406-932-4353
Montana Outfitters, Lewis E. Yearout, 308 Riverview Dr. E., Great Falls, MT 59404 / 406-761-0859
Montana Precision Swaging, P.O. Box 4746, Butte, MT 59702 / 406-782-7502
Montana Vintage Arms, 2354 Bear Canyon Rd., Bozeman, MT 59715
Montgomery Community College, P.O. Box 787-GD, Troy, NC 27371 / 910-576-6222 or 800-839-6222; FAX: 910-576-2176
Morini (See U.S. Importers-Mandall Shooting Supplies, Inc.,)
Morrison Custom Rifles, J. W., 4015 W Sharon, Phoenix, AZ 85029 / 602-978-3754
Morrison Precision, 6719 Calle Mango, Hereford, AZ 85615 / 520-378-6207 / morprec@c2i2.com (e-mail)
Morrow, Bud, 11 Hillside Lane, Sheridan, WY 82801-9729 / 307-674-8360
Morton Booth Co., P.O. Box 123, Joplin, MO 64802 / 417-673-1962; FAX: 417-673-3642
Moss Double Tone, Inc., P.O. Box 1112, 2101 S. Kentucky, Sedalia, MO 65301 / 816-827-0827
Mountain Hollow Game Calls, Box 121, Cascade, MD 21719 / 301-241-3282
Mountain Plains, Inc., 244 Glass Hollow Rd., Alton, VA 22920 / 800-687-3000
Mountain Rifles, Inc., P.O. Box 2789, Palmer, AK 99645 / 907-373-4194; FAX: 907-373-4195
Mountain South, P.O. Box 381, Barnwell, SC 29812 / FAX: 803-259-3227

34TH EDITION, 2002 • 341

Manufacturers Directory

Mountain State Muzzleloading Supplies, Inc., Box 154-1, Rt. 2, Williamstown, WV 26187 / 304-375-7842; FAX: 304-375-3737
Mountain View Sports, Inc., Box 188, Troy, NH 03465 / 603-357-9690; FAX: 603-357-9691
Mowrey Gun Works, P.O. Box 246, Waldron, IN 46182 / 317-525-6181; FAX: 317-525-9595
Mowrey's Guns & Gunsmithing, 119 Fredericks St., Canajoharie, NY 13317 / 518-673-3483
MPC, P.O. Box 450, McMinnville, TN 37110-0450 / 615-473-5513; FAX: 615-473-5516
MPI Stocks, PO Box 83266, Portland, OR 97283 / 503-226-1215; FAX: 503-226-2661
MSC Industrial Supply Co., 151 Sunnyside Blvd., Plainview, NY 11803-9915 / 516-349-0330
MSR Targets, P.O. Box 1042, West Covina, CA 91793 / 818-331-7840
Mt. Alto Outdoor Products, Rt. 735, Howardsville, VA 24562
Mt. Baldy Bullet Co., 12981 Old Hill City Rd., Keystone, SD 57751-6623 / 605-666-4725
MTM Molded Products Co., Inc., 3370 Obco Ct., Dayton, OH 45414 / 937-890-7461; FAX: 937-890-1747
Mulhern, Rick, Rt. 5, Box 152, Rayville, LA 71269 / 318-728-2688
Mullins Ammunition, Rt. 2, Box 304K, Clintwood, VA 24228 / 540-926-6772; FAX: 540-926-6092
Mullis Guncraft, 3523 Lawyers Road E., Monroe, NC 28110 / 704-283-6683
Multi-Scale Charge Ltd., 3269 Niagara Falls Blvd., N. Tonawanda, NY 14120 / 905-566-1255; FAX: 905-276-6295
Multiplex International, 26 S. Main St., Concord, NH 03301 / FAX: 603-796-2223
Multipropulseurs, La Bertrandiere, 42580, FRANCE / 77 74 01 30; FAX: 77 93 19 34
Mundy, Thomas A., 69 Robbins Road, Somerville, NJ 08876 / 201-722-2199
Murmur Corp., 2823 N. Westmoreland Ave., Dallas, TX 75222 / 214-630-5400
Murray State College, 1 Murray Campus St., Tishomingo, OK 73460 / 508-371-2371
Muscle Products Corp., 112 Fennell Dr., Butler, PA 16001 / 800-227-7049 or 412-283-0567; FAX: 412-283-8310
Museum of Historical Arms, Inc., 2750 Coral Way, Suite 204, Miami, FL 33145 / 305-444-9199
Mushroom Express Bullet Co., 601 W. 6th St., Greenfield, IN 46140-1728 / 317-462-6332
Muzzleloaders Etcetera, Inc., 9901 Lyndale Ave. S., Bloomington, MN 55420 / 612-884-1161 muzzleloaders-etcetera.com
Muzzleloading Technologies, Inc, 25 E. Hwy. 40, Suite 330-12, Roosevelt, UT 84066 / 801-722-5996; FAX: 801-722-5909
MWG Co., P.O. Box 971202, Miami, FL 33197 / 800-428-9394 or 305-253-8393; FAX: 305-232-1247

N

N&J Sales, Lime Kiln Rd., Northford, CT 06472 / 203-484-0247
N.B.B., Inc., 24 Elliot Rd., Sterling, MA 01564 / 508-422-7538 or 800-942-9444
N.C. Ordnance Co., P.O. Box 3254, Wilson, NC 27895 / 919-237-2440; FAX: 919-243-9845
Nagel's Custom Bullets, 100 Scott St., Baytown, TX 77520-2849
Nalpak, 1937-C Friendship Drive, El Cajon, CA 92020 / 619-258-1200
Nastoff's 45 Shop, Inc., Steve, 12288 Mahoning Ave, PO Box 446, North Jackson, OH 44451 / 330-538-2977
National Bullet Co., 1585 E. 361 St., Eastlake, OH 44095 / 216-951-1854; FAX: 216-951-1761
National Target Co., 4690 Wyaconda Rd., Rockville, MD 20852 / 800-827-7060 or 301-770-7060; FAX: 301-770-7892
Naval Ordnance Works, Rt. 2, Box 919, Sheperdstown, WV 25443 / 304-876-0998
Navy Arms Co., 689 Bergen Blvd., Ridgefield, NJ 07657 / 201-945-2500; FAX: 201-945-6859
NCP Products, Inc., 3500 12th St. N.W., Canton, OH 44708 / 330-456-5130; FAX: 330-456-5234
Neal Johnson's Gunsmithing, Inc., 208 W. Buchanan St., Suite B, Colorado Springs, CO 80907 / 800-284-8671; FAX: 719-632-3493
Necessary Concepts, Inc., P.O. Box 571, Deer Park, NY 11729 / 516-667-8509; FAX: 516-667-8588
Necromancer Industries, Inc., 14 Communications Way, West Newton, PA 15089 / 412-872-8722
NEI Handtools, Inc., 51583 Columbia River Hwy., Scappoose, OR 97056 / 503-543-6776; FAX: 503-543-6799
Neil A. Jones Custom Products, 17217 Brookhouser Road, Saegertown, PA 16433 / 814-763-2769; FAX: 814-763-4228
Nelson, Gary K., 975 Terrace Dr., Oakdale, CA 95361 / 209-847-4590
Nelson, Stephen, 7365 NW Spring Creek Dr., Corvallis, OR 97330 / 541-745-5232
Nelson/Weather-Rite, Inc., 14760 Santa Fe Trail Dr., Lenexa, KS 66215 / 913-492-3200; FAX: 913-492-8749
Nesci Enterprises Inc., P.O. Box 119, Summit St., East Hampton, CT 06424 / 203-267-2588
Nesika Bay Precision, 22239 Big Valley Rd., Poulsbo, WA 98370 / 206-697-3830
Nettestad Gun Works, RR 1, Box 160, Pelican Rapids, MN 56572 / 218-863-4301
Neumann GmbH, Am Galgenberg 6, 90575, GERMANY / 09101/8258; FAX: 09101/6356
Nevada Pistol Academy, Inc., 4610 Blue Diamond Rd., Las Vegas, NV 89139 / 702-897-1100
New England Ammunition Co., 1771 Post Rd. East, Suite 223, Westport, CT 06880 / 203-254-8048
New England Arms Co., Box 278, Lawrence Lane, Kittery Point, ME 03905 / 207-439-0593; FAX: 207-439-0525 info@newenglandarms.com www.newenglandarms.com
New England Custom Gun Service, 438 Willow Brook Rd., Plainfield, NH 03781 / 603-469-3450; FAX: 603-469-3471
New England Firearms, 60 Industrial Rowe, Gardner, MA 01440 / 508-632-9393; FAX: 508-632-2300
New Orleans Jewelers Supply Co., 206 Charters St., New Orleans, LA 70130 / 504-523-3839; FAX: 504-523-3836
New SKB Arms Co., C.P.O. Box 1401, Tokyo, JAPAN / 81-3-3943-9550; FAX: 81-3-3943-0695
New Win Publishing, Inc., 186 Center St., Clinton, NJ 08809 / 908-735-9701; FAX: 908-735-9703
Newark Electronics, 4801 N. Ravenswood Ave., Chicago, IL 60640
Newell, Robert H., 55 Coyote, Los Alamos, NM 87544 / 505-662-7135
Newman Gunshop, 119 Miller Rd., Agency, IA 52530 / 515-937-5775
Nicholson Custom, 17285 Thornlay Road, Hughesville, MO 65334 / 816-826-8746
Nickels, Paul R., 4789 Summerhill Rd., Las Vegas, NV 89121 / 702-435-5318
Nicklas, Ted, 5504 Hegel Rd., Goodrich, MI 48438 / 810-797-4493
Niemi Engineering, W. B., Box 126 Center Rd, Greensboro, VT 05841 / 802-533-7180; FAX: 802-533-7141
Nightforce (See Lightforce USA Inc)
Nikolai leather, 15451 Electronic In, Huntington Beach, CA 92649 / 714-373-2721 FAX: 714-373-2723
Nikon, Inc., 1300 Walt Whitman Rd., Melville, NY 11747 / 516-547-8623; FAX: 516-547-0309
Nitex, Inc., P.O. Box 1706, Uvalde, TX 78801 / 888-543-8843
No-Sho Mfg. Co., 10727 Glenfield Ct., Houston, TX 77096 / 713-723-5332
Noreen, Peter H., 5075 Buena Vista Dr., Belgrade, MT 59714 / 406-586-7383
Norica, Avnda Otaola, 16 Apartado 68, Eibar, SPAIN
Norinco, 7A Yun Tan N, Beijing, CHINA
Norincoptics (See BEC, Inc.)
Norma Precision AB (See U.S. Importers-Dynamit Nobel-RWS, Inc.,)
Normark Corp., 10395 Yellow Circle Dr., Minnetonka, MN 55343-9101 / 612-933-7060 FAX: 612-933-0046
North American Arms, Inc., 2150 South 950 East, Provo, UT 84606-6285 / 800-821-5783 or 801-374-9990; FAX: 801-374-9998
North American Correspondence Schools The Gun Pro, Oak & Pawney St., Scranton, PA 18515 / 717-342-7701
North American Shooting Systems, P.O. Box 306, Osoyoos, BC V0H 1V0 CANADA / 604-495-3131; FAX: 604-495-2816
North Devon Firearms Services, 3 North St., Braunton, EX33 1AJ ENGLAND / 01271 813624; FAX: 01271 813624
North Fork Custom Gunsmithing, James Johnston, 428 Del Rio Rd., Roseburg, OR 97470 / 503-673-4467
North Mountain Pine Training Center (See Executive Protection Institute)
North Pass, 425 South Bowen St., Ste. 6, Longmount, CO 80501 / 303-682-4315; FAX: 303-678-7109
North Specialty Products, 2664-B Saturn St., Brea, CA 92621 / 714-524-1665
North Star West, P.O. Box 488, Glencoe, CA 95232 / 209-293-7010
North Wind Decoy Co., 1005 N. Tower Rd., Fergus Falls, MN 56537 / 218-736-4378; FAX: 218-736-7060
Northern Precision Custom Swaged Bullets, 329 S. James St., Carthage, NY 13619 / 315-493-1711
Northlake Outdoor Footwear, P.O. Box 10, Franklin, TN 37065-0010 / 615-794-1556; FAX: 615-790-8005
Northside Gun Shop, 2725 NW 109th, Oklahoma City, OK 73120 / 405-840-2353
Northwest Arms, 26884 Pearl Rd., Parma, ID 83660 / 208-722-6771; FAX: 208-722-1062
Nosler, Inc., P.O. Box 671, Bend, OR 97709 / 800-285-3701 or 541-382-3921; FAX: 541-388-4667
Novak's, Inc., 1206 1/2 30th St., P.O. Box 4045, Parkersburg, WV 26101 / 304-485-9295; FAX: 304-428-6722
Now Products, Inc., PO Box 27608, Tempe, AZ 85285 / 800-662-6063; FAX: 480-966-0890
Nowlin Mfg. Co., 20622 S 4092 Rd, Claremore, OK 74017 / 918-342-0689; FAX: 918-342-0624
NRI Gunsmith School, 4401 Connecticut Ave. NW, Washington, DC 20008
Nu-Line Guns,Inc., 1053 Caulks Hill Rd., Harvester, MO 63304 / 314-441-4500 or 314-447-4501; FAX: 314-447-5018
Null Holsters Ltd. K.L., 161 School St NW, Resaca, GA 30735 / 706-625-5643; FAX: 706-625-9392
Numrich Arms Corp., 203 Broadway, W. Hurley, NY 12491
NW Sinker and Tackle, 380 Valley Dr., Myrtle Creek, OR 97457-9717
Nygord Precision Products, P.O. Box 12578, Prescott, AZ 86304 / 520-717-2315; FAX: 520-717-2198

O

O.F. Mossberg & Sons,Inc., 7 Grasso Ave., North Haven, CT 06473 / 203-230-5300; FAX: 203-230-5420
Oakland Custom Arms,Inc., 4690 W. Walton Blvd., Waterford, MI 48329 / 810-674-8261
Oakman Turkey Calls, RD 1, Box 825, Harrisonville, PA 17228 / 717-485-4620
Obermeyer Rifled Barrels, 23122 60th St., Bristol, WI 53104 / 262-843-3537; FAX: 262-843-2129
October Country Muzzleloading, P.O. Box 969, Dept. GD, Hayden, ID 83835 / 208-772-2068; FAX: 208-772-9230 octobercountry.com
Oehler Research,Inc., P.O. Box 9135, Austin, TX 78766 / 512-327-6900 or 800-531-5125; FAX: 512-327-6903
Oil Rod and Gun Shop, 69 Oak St., East Douglas, MA 01516 / 508-476-3687
Ojala Holsters, Arvo, PO Box 98, N Hollywood, CA 91603 / 503-669-1404
OK Weber,Inc., P.O. Box 7485, Eugene, OR 97401 / 541-747-0458; FAX: 541-747-5927
Oker's Engraving, 365 Bell Rd., P.O. Box 126, Shawnee, CO 80475 / 303-838-6042
Oklahoma Ammunition Co., 3701A S. Harvard Ave., No. 367, Tulsa, OK 74135-2265 / 918-396-3187; FAX: 918-396-4270
Oklahoma Leather Products,Inc., 500 26th NW, Miami, OK 74354 / 918-542-6651; FAX: 918-542-6653
Old Wagon Bullets, 32 Old Wagon Rd., Wilton, CT 06897
Old West Bullet Moulds, J Ken Chapman, P.O. Box 519, Flora Vista, NM 87415 / 505-334-6970
Old West Reproductions,Inc. R.M. Bachman, 446 Florence S. Loop, Florence, MT 59833 / 406-273-2615; FAX: 406-273-2615
Old Western Scrounger,Inc., 12924 Hwy. A-12, Montague, CA 96064 / 916-459-5445; FAX: 916-459-3944
Old World Gunsmithing, 2901 SE 122nd St., Portland, OR 97236 / 503-760-7681
Old World Oil Products, 3827 Queen Ave. N., Minneapolis, MN 55412 / 612-522-5037
Ole Frontier Gunsmith Shop, 2617 Hwy. 29 S., Cantonment, FL 32533 / 904-477-8074
Olson, Myron, 989 W. Kemp, Watertown, SD 57201 / 605-886-9787
Olson, Vic, 5002 Countryside Dr., Imperial, MO 63052 / 314-296-8086
Olympic Arms Inc., 620-626 Old Pacific Hwy. SE, Olympia, WA 98513 / 360-491-3447; FAX: 360-491-3447

342 • GUNS ILLUSTRATED

Manufacturers Directory

Olympic Optical Co., P.O. Box 752377, Memphis, TN 38175-2377 / 901-794-3890 or 800-238-7120; FAX: 901-794-0676 80
Omark Industries,Div. of Blount,Inc., 2299 Snake River Ave., P.O. Box 856, Lewiston, ID 83501 / 800-627-3640 or 208-746-2351
Omega Sales, P.O. Box 1066, Mt. Clemens, MI 48043 / 810-469-7323; FAX: 810-469-0425
One Of A Kind, 15610 Purple Sage, San Antonio, TX 78255 / 512-695-3364
Op-Tec, P.O. Box L632, Langhorn, PA 19047 / 215-757-5037
Optical Services Co., P.O. Box 1174, Santa Teresa, NM 88008-1174 / 505-589-3833
Orchard Park Enterprise, P.O. Box 563, Orchard Park, NY 14227 / 616-656-0356
Oregon Arms, Inc. (See Rogue Rifle Co., Inc.)
Oregon Trail Bullet Company, P.O. Box 529, Dept. P, Baker City, OR 97814 / 800-811-0548; FAX: 514-523-1803
Original Box, nc., 700 Linden Ave., York, PA 17404 / 717-854-2897; FAX: 717-845-4276
Original Mink Oil,Inc., 10652 NE Holman, Portland, OR 97220 / 503-255-2814 or 800-547-5895; FAX: 503-255-2487
Orion Rifle Barrel Co., RR2, 137 Cobler Village, Kalispell, MT 59901 / 406-257-5649
Otis Technology, Inc, RR 1 Box 84, Boonville, NY 13309 / 315-942-3320
Ottmar, Maurice, Box 657, 113 E. Fir, Coulee City, WA 99115 / 509-632-5717
Outa-Site Gun Carriers, 219 Market St., Laredo, TX 78040 / 210-722-4678 or 800-880-9715; FAX: 210-726-4858
Outdoor Edge Cutlery Corp., 2888 Bluff St., Suite 130, Boulder, CO 80301 / 303-652-8212; FAX: 303-652-8238
Outdoor Enthusiast, 3784 W. Woodland, Springfield, MO 65807 / 417-883-9841
Outdoor Sports Headquarters,Inc., 967 Watertower Ln., West Carrollton, OH 45449 / 513-865-5855; FAX: 513-865-5962
Outers Laboratories Div. of Blount, Inc.Sporting E, Route 2, P.O. Box 39, Onalaska, WI 54650 / 608-781-5800; FAX: 608-781-0368
Ox-Yoke Originals, Inc., 34 Main St., Milo, ME 04463 / 800-231-8313 or 207-943-7351; FAX: 207-943-2416
Ozark Gun Works, 11830 Cemetery Rd., Rogers, AR 72756 / 501-631-6944; FAX: 501-631-6944 ogw@hotmail.com http://members.tripod.com~ozarkw1

P

P&M Sales and Service, 5724 Gainsborough Pl., Oak Forest, IL 60452 / 708-687-7149
P.A.C.T., Inc., P.O. Box 531525, Grand Prairie, TX 75053 / 214-641-0049
P.M. Enterprises, Inc., 146 Curtis Hill Rd., Chehalis, WA 98532 / 360-748-3743; FAX: 360-748-1802
P.S.M.G. Gun Co., 10 Park Ave., Arlington, MA 02174 / 617-646-8845; FAX: 617-646-2133
Pac-Nor Barreling, 99299 Overlook Rd., P.O. Box 6188, Brookings, OR 97415 / 503-469-7330; FAX: 503-469-7331
Pace Marketing, Inc., P.O. Box 2039, Stuart, FL 34995 / 561-871-9682; FAX: 561-871-6552
Pachmayr Div. Lyman Products, 1875 S. Mountain Ave., Monrovia, CA 91016 / 626-357-7771
Pacific Cartridge, Inc., 2425 Salashan Loop Road, Ferndale, WA 98248 / 360-366-4444; FAX: 360-366-4445
Pacific Research Laboratories, Inc. (See Rimrock R
Pacific Rifle Co., PO Box 1473, Lake Oswego, OR 97035 / 503-538-7437
Paco's (See Small Custom Mould & Bullet Co)
Page Custom Bullets, P.O. Box 25, Port Moresby, NEW GUINEA
Pagel Gun Works, Inc., 1407 4th St. NW, Grand Rapids, MN 55744 / 218-326-3003
Pager Pal, 200 W Pleasantview, Hurst, TX 76054 / 800-561-1603 FAX: 817-285-8769 www.pagerpal.com
Paintball Games International Magazine (Aceville Publications, Castle House) 97 High St., Essex, ENGLAND / 011-44-206-564840
Palmer Security Products, 2930 N. Campbell Ave., Chicago, IL 60618 / 800-788-7725; FAX: 773-267-8080
Palsa Outdoor Products, P.O. Box 81336, Lincoln, NE 68501 / 402-488-5288; FAX: 402-488-2321

Para-Ordnance Mfg., Inc., 980 Tapscott Rd., Scarborough, ON M1X 1E7 CANADA / 416-297-7855; FAX: 416-297-1289
Para-Ordnance, Inc., 1919 NE 45th St., Ste 215, Ft. Lauderdale, FL 33308
Paragon Sales & Services, Inc., 2501 Theodore St, Crest Hill, IL 60435-1613 / 815-725-9212; FAX: 815-725-8974
Pardini Armi Srl, Via Italica 154, 55043, Lido Di Camaiore Lu, ITALY / 584-90121; FAX: 584-90122
Paris, Frank J., 17417 Pershing St., Livonia, MI 48152-3822
Parker & Sons Shooting Supply, 9337 Smoky Row Rd, Straw Plains, TN 97871-1257
Parker Gun Finishes, 9337 Smokey Row Rd., Strawberry Plains, TN 37871 / 423-933-3286
Parker Reproductions, 124 River Rd., Middlesex, NJ 08846 / 908-469-0100 FAX: 908-469-9692
Parsons Optical Mfg. Co., P.O. Box 192, Ross, OH 45061 / 513-867-0820; FAX: 513-867-8380
Partridge Sales Ltd., John, Trent Meadows, Rugeley, ENGLAND
Parts & Surplus, P.O. Box 22074, Memphis, TN 38122 / 901-683-4007
Pasadena Gun Center, 206 E. Shaw, Pasadena, TX 77506 / 713-472-0417; FAX: 713-472-1322
Passive Bullet Traps, Inc. (See Savage Range Systems, Inc.)
PAST Sporting Goods,Inc., P.O. Box 1035, Columbia, MO 65205 / 314-445-9200; FAX: 314-446-6606
Paterson Gunsmithing, 438 Main St., Paterson, NJ 07502 / 201-345-4100
Pathfinder Sports Leather, 2920 E. Chambers St., Phoenix, AZ 85040 / 602-276-0016
Patrick Bullets, P.O. Box 172, Warwick, QSLD, 4370 AUSTRALIA
Patrick W. Price Bullets, 16520 Worthley Drive, San Lorenzo, CA 94580 / 510-278-1547
Pattern Control, 114 N. Third St., P.O. Box 462105, Garland, TX 75046 / 214-494-3551; FAX: 214-272-8447
Paul A. Harris Hand Engraving, 113 Rusty Lane, Boerne, TX 78006-5746 / 512-391-5121
Paul D. Hillmer Custom Gunstocks, 7251 Hudson Heights, Hudson, IA 50643 / 319-988-3941
Paul Jones Moulds, 4901 Telegraph Rd., Los Angeles, CA 90022 / 213-262-1510
Paulsen Gunstocks, Rt. 71, Box 11, Chinook, MT 59523 / 406-357-3403
Pawling Mountain Club, Keith Lupton, PO Box 573, Pawling, NY 12564 / 914-855-3825
Paxton Quigley's Personal Protection Strategies, 9903 Santa Monica Blvd., 300, Beverly Hills, CA 90212 / 310-281-1762 www.defend-net.com/paxton
Payne Photography, Robert, Robert, P.O. Box 141471, Austin, TX 78714 / 512-272-4554
PC Co., 5942 Sector Rd., Toledo, OH 43623 / 419-472-6222
Peacemaker Specialists, P.O. Box 157, Whitmore, CA 96096 / 916-472-3438
Pearce Grip, Inc., P.O. Box 187, Bothell, WA 98041-0187 / 206-485-5488; FAX: 206-488-9497
Pease Accuracy, Bob, P.O. Box 310787, New Braunfels, TX 78131 / 210-625-1342
Pease International, 53 Durham St, Portsmouth, NH 03801 / 603-431-1331; FAX: 603-431-1221
PECAR Herbert Schwarz GmbH, Kreuzbergstrasse 6, 10965, Berlin, GERMANY / 004930-785-7383; FAX: 004930-785-1934
Pecatonica River Longrifle, 5205 Nottingham Dr., Rockford, IL 61111 / 815-968-1995 FAX: 815-968-1996
Pedersen, C. R., 2717 S. Pere Marquette Hwy., Ludington, MI 49431 / 616-843-2061
Pedersen, Rex C., 2717 S. Pere Marquette Hwy., Ludington, MI 49431 / 616-843-2061
Peerless Alloy, Inc., 1445 Osage St., Denver, CO 80204-2439 / 303-825-6394 or 800-253-1278
Peet Shoe Dryer, Inc., 130 S. 5th St., P.O. Box 618, St. Maries, ID 83861 / 208-245-2095 or 800-222-PEET; FAX: 208-245-5441
Peifer Rifle Co., P.O. Box 192, Nokomis, IL 62075-0192 / 217-563-7050; FAX: 217-563-7060
Pejsa Ballistics, 2120 Kenwood Pkwy., Minneapolis, MN 55405 / 612-374-3337; FAX: 612-374-5383
Pelaire Products, 5346 Bonky Ct., W. Palm Beach, FL 33415 / 561-439-0691; FAX: 561-967-0052
Pell, John T. (See KOGOT)
Peltor, Inc. (See Aero Peltor)
PEM's Mfg. Co., 5063 Waterloo Rd., Atwater, OH 44201 / 216-947-3721
Pence Precision Barrels, 7567 E. 900 S., S. Whitley, IN 46787 / 219-839-4745

Pendleton Royal, c/o Swingler Buckland Ltd., 4/7 Highgate St., Birmingham, ENGLAND / 44 121 440 3060 or 44 121 446 5898; FAX: 44 121 446 4165
Pendleton Woolen Mills, P.O. Box 3030, 220 N.W. Broadway, Portland, OR 97208 / 503-226-4801
Penn Bullets, P.O. Box 756, Indianola, PA 15051
Penn's Woods Products, Inc., 19 W. Pittsburgh St., Delmont, PA 15626 / 412-468-8311; FAX: 412-468-8975
Pennsylvania Gun Parts Inc, PO Box 665, 300 Third St, East Berlin, PA 17316-0665 / 717-259-8010; FAX: 717-259-0057
Pennsylvania Gunsmith School, 812 Ohio River Blvd., Avalon, Pittsburgh, PA 15202 / 412-766-1812 FAX: 412-766-0855 pgs@pagunsmith.com www.pagunsmith.com
Penrod Precision, 312 College Ave., P.O. Box 307, N. Manchester, IN 46962 / 219-982-8385
Pentax Corp., 35 Inverness Dr. E., Englewood, CO 80112 / 303-799-8000; FAX: 303-790-1131
Pentheny de Pentheny, 108 Petaluma Ave #202, Sebastopol, CA 95472-4220 / 707-573-1390; FAX: 707-573-1390
Perazone-Gunsmith, Brian, Cold Spring Rd, Roxbury, NY 12474 / 607-326-4088; FAX: 607-326-3140
Perazzi USA, Inc., 1207 S. Shamrock Ave., Monrovia, CA 91016 / 626-303-0068; FAX: 626-303-2081
Performance Specialists, 308 Eanes School Rd., Austin, TX 78746 / 512-327-0119
Perugini Visini & Co. S.r.l., Via Camprelle, 126, 25080 Nuvolera, ITALY / 30-6897535; FAX: 30-6897821
Pete Elsen, Inc., 1529 S. 113th St., West Allis, WI 53214
Pete Mazur Restoration, 13083 Drummer Way, Grass Valley, CA 95949 / 916-268-2412
Pete Rickard, Inc., 115 Roy Walsh Rd, Cobleskill, NY 12043 / 518-234-2731; FAX: 518-234-2454 rickard@telenet.net peterickard.com
Peter Dyson & Son Ltd., 3 Cuckoo Lane, Honley Huddersfield, Yorkshire, HD7 2BR ENGLAND / 44-1484-661062; FAX: 44-1484-663709
Peter Hale/Engraver, 800 E. Canyon Rd., Spanish Fork, UT 84660 / 801-798-8215
Peters Stahl GmbH, Stettiner Strasse 42, D-33106, Paderborn, / 05251-750025; FAX: 05251-75611
Petersen Publishing Co., (See Emap USA)
Peterson Gun Shop, Inc., A.W., 4255 W. Old U.S. 441, Mt. Dora, FL 32757-3299 / 352-383-4258; FAX: 352-735-1001
Petro-Explo Inc., 7650 U.S. Hwy. 287, Suite 100, Arlington, TX 76017 / 817-478-8888
Pettinger Books, Gerald, Rt. 2, Box 125, Russell, IA 50238 / 515-535-2239
Pflumm Mfg. Co., 10662 Widmer Rd., Lenexa, KS 66215 / 800-888-4867; FAX: 913-451-7857
PFRB Co., P.O. Box 1242, Bloomington, IL 61702 / 309-473-3964; FAX: 309-473-2161
Philip S. Olt Co., P.O. Box 550, 12662 Fifth St., Pekin, IL 61554 / 309-348-3633; FAX: 309-348-3300
Phillippi Custom Bullets, Justin, P.O. Box 773, Ligonier, PA 15658 / 724-238-2962; FAX: 724-238-9671 jrp@wpa.net http://www.wpa.net~jrphil
Phillips & Rogers, Inc., 100 Hilbig #C, Conroe, TX 77301 / 409-435-0011
Phoenix Arms, 1420 S. Archibald Ave., Ontario, CA 91761 / 909-947-4843; FAX: 909-947-6798
Photronic Systems Engineering Company, 6731 Via De La Reina, Bonsall, CA 92003 / 619-758-8000
Piedmont Community College, P.O. Box 1197, Roxboro, NC 27573 / 336-599-1181 FAX: 336-597-3817 www.piedmont.cc.nc.us
Pierce Pistols, 55 Sorrellwood Lane, Sharpsburg, GA 30277-9523 / 404-253-8192
Pietta (See U.S. Importers-Navy Arms Co, Taylor's & Co.,)
Pilgrim Pewter,Inc. (See Bell Originals Inc. Sid)
Pilkington, Scott (See Little Trees Ramble)
Pine Technical College, 1100 4th St., Pine City, MN 55063 / 800-521-7463; FAX: 612-629-6766
Pinetree Bullets, 133 Skeena St., Kitimat, BC V8C 1Z1 CANADA / 604-632-3768; FAX: 604-632-3768
Pioneer Arms Co., 355 Lawrence Rd., Broomall, PA 19008 / 215-356-5203
Piotti (See U.S. Importer-Moore & Co, Wm. Larkin)
Piquette, Paul R., 80 Bradford Dr., Feeding Hills, MA 01030 / 413-786-8118; or 413-789-4582
Plaxco, J. Michael, Rt. 1, P.O. Box 203, Roland, AR 72135 / 501-868-9787
Plaza Cutlery, Inc., 3333 Bristol, 161 South Coast Plaza, Costa Mesa, CA 92626 / 714-549-3932

Manufacturers Directory

Plum City Ballistic Range, N2162 80th St., Plum City, WI 54761 / 715-647-2539

PlumFire Press, Inc., 30-A Grove Ave., Patchogue, NY 11772-4112 / 800-695-7246; FAX: 516-758-4071

PMC/Eldorado Cartridge Corp., P.O. Box 62508, 12801 U.S. Hwy. 95 S., Boulder City, NV 89005 / 702-294-0025; FAX: 702-294-0121

Poburka, Philip (See Bison Studios)

Pohl, Henry A. (See Great American Gun Co.

Pointing Dog Journal, Village Press Publications, P.O. Box 968, Dept. PGD, Traverse City, MI 49685 / 800-272-3246; FAX: 616-946-3289

Police Bookshelf, P.O. Box 122, Concord, NH 03301 / 603-224-6814; FAX: 603-226-3554

Polywad, Inc., P.O. Box 7916, Macon, GA 31209 / 912-477-0669 polywadmpb@aol.com www.poly-wad.com

Pomeroy, Robert, RR1, Box 50, E. Corinth, ME 04427 / 207-285-7721

Ponsness/Warren, P.O. Box 8, Rathdrum, ID 83858 / 208-687-2231; FAX: 208-687-2233

Pony Express Reloaders, 608 E. Co. Rd. D, Suite 3, St. Paul, MN 55117 / 612-483-9406; FAX: 612-483-9884

Pony Express Sport Shop, 16606 Schoenborn St., North Hills, CA 91343 / 818-895-1231

Potts, Wayne E., 912 Poplar St., Denver, CO 80220 / 303-355-5462

Powder Horn Antiques, P.O. Box 4196, Ft. Lauderdale, FL 33338 / 305-565-6060

Powell & Son (Gunmakers) Ltd., William, 35-37 Carrs Lane, Birmingham, B4 7SX ENGLAND / 121-643-0689; FAX: 121-631-3504

Powell Agency, William, 22 Circle Dr., Bellmore, NY 11710 / 516-679-1158

Power Custom, Inc., 29739 Hwy. J, Gravois Mills, MO 65037 / 513-372-5684; FAX: 573-372-5799 pwpowers@laurie.net www.powercustom.com

Power Plus Enterprises, Inc., PO Box 38, Warm Springs, GA 31830 / 706-655-2132

Powley Computer (See Hutton Rifle Ranch)

Practical Tools, Inc., 7067 Easton Rd., P.O. Box 133, Pipersville, PA 18947 / 215-766-7301; FAX: 215-766-8681

Prairie Gun Works, 1-761 Marion St., Winnipeq, MB R2J 0K6 Canada / 204-231-2976; FAX: 204-231-8566

Prairie River Arms, 1220 N. Sixth St., Princeton, IL 61356 / 815-875-1616 or 800-445-1541; FAX: 815-875-1402

Pranger, Ed G., 1414 7th St., Anacortes, WA 98221 / 206-293-3488

Pre-Winchester 92-90-62 Parts Co., P.O. Box 8125, W. Palm Beach, FL 33407

Precise Metalsmithing Enterprises, 146 Curtis Hill Rd., Chehalis, WA 98532 / 206-748-3743; FAX: 206-748-8102

Precision Airgun Sales, Inc., 5247 Warrensville Ctr Rd, Maple Hts., OH 44137 / 216-587-5005 FAX: 216-587-5005

Precision Cartridge, 176 Eastside Rd., Deer Lodge, MT 59722 / 800-397-3901 or 406-846-3900

Precision Cast Bullets, 101 Mud Creek Lane, Ronan, MT 59864 / 406-676-5135

Precision Castings & Equipment, P.O. Box 326, Jasper, IN 47547-0135 / 812-634-9167

Precision Components, 3177 Sunrise Lake, Milford, PA 18337 / 570-686-4414

Precision Components and Guns, Rt. 55, P.O. Box 337, Pawling, NY 12564 / 914-855-3040

Precision Delta Corp., P.O. Box 128, Ruleville, MS 38771 / 601-756-2810; FAX: 601-756-2590

Precision Gun Works, 104 Sierra Rd Dept. GD, Kerrville, TX 78028 / 830-367-4587

Precision Munitions, Inc., P.O. Box 326, Jasper, IN 47547

Precision Reloading, Inc., P.O. Box 122, Stafford Springs, CT 06076 / 860-684-5680 FAX: 860-686-6788

Precision Sales International, Inc., P.O. Box 1776, Westfield, MA 01086 / 413-562-5055; FAX: 413-562-5056

Precision Shooting, Inc., 222 McKee St., Manchester, CT 06040 / 860-645-8776; FAX: 860-643-8215

Precision Small Arms, 9777 Wilshire Blvd., Suite 1005, Beverly Hills, CA 90212 / 310-859-4867; FAX: 310-859-2868

Precision Small Arms Inc, 9272 Jeronimo Rd, Ste 121, Irvine, CA 92618 / 800-554-5515; FAX: 949-768-4808 www.tcbebe.com

Precision Specialties, 131 Hendom Dr., Feeding Hills, MA 01030 / 413-786-3365; FAX: 413-786-3365

Precision Sport Optics, 15571 Producer Lane, Unit G, Huntington Beach, CA 92649 / 714-891-1309; FAX: 714-892-6920

Premier Reticles, 920 Breckinridge Lane, Winchester, VA 22601-6707 / 540-722-0601; FAX: 540-722-3522

Prescott Projectile Co., 1808 Meadowbrook Road, Prescott, AZ 86303

Preslik's Gunstocks, 4245 Keith Ln., Chico, CA 95926 / 916-891-8236

Price Bullets, Patrick W., 16520 Worthley Dr., San Lorenzo, CA 94580 / 510-278-1547

Prime Reloading, 30 Chiswick End, Meldreth, ROYSTON UK / 0763-260636

Primos, Inc., P.O. Box 12785, Jackson, MS 39236-2785 / 601-366-1288; FAX: 601-362-3274

PRL Bullets, c/o Blackburn Enterprises, 114 Stuart Rd., Ste. 110, Cleveland, TN 37312 / 423-559-0340

Pro Load Ammunition, Inc., 5180 E. Seltice Way, Post Falls, ID 83854 / 208-773-9444; FAX: 208-773-9441

Pro-Mark Div. of Wells Lamont, 6640 W. Touhy, Chicago, IL 60648 / 312-647-8200

Pro-Port Ltd., 41302 Executive Dr., Harrison Twp., MI 48045-1306 / 810-469-6727 FAX: 810-469-0425

Pro-Shot Products, Inc., P.O. Box 763, Taylorville, IL 62568 / 217-824-9133; FAX: 217-824-8861

Professional Gunsmiths of America,Inc., Route 1, Box 224F, Lexington, MO 64067 / 816-259-2636

Professional Hunter Supplies (See Star Custom Bullets,) PO Box 608, 468 Main St, Ferndale, CA 95536 / 707-786-9140; FAX: 707-786-9117

Professional Ordnance, Inc., 1215 E. Airport Dr., Box 182, Ontario, CA 91761 / 909-923-5559; FAX: 909-923-0899

Prolixrr Lubricants, P.O. Box 1348, Victorville, CA 92393 / 800-248-5823 or 760-243-3129; FAX: 760-241-0148

Proofmark Corp., P.O. Box 610, Burgess, VA 22432 / 804-453-4337; FAX: 804-453-4337 proofmark@riv.net

Protektor Model, 1-11 Bridge St., Galeton, PA 16922 / 814-435-2442

Prototech Industries, Inc., Rt. 1, Box 81, Delia, KS 66418 / 913-771-3571; FAX: 913-771-2531

ProWare, Inc., 15847 NE Hancock St., Portland, OR 97230 / 503-239-0159

PWL Gunleather, P.O. Box 450432, Atlanta, GA 31145 / 770-822-1640; FAX: 770-822-1704 covert@pwlusa.com www.pwlusa.com

Pyromid, Inc., 3292 S. Highway 97, Redmond, OR 97756 / 503-548-1041; FAX: 503-923-1004

Q

Quack Decoy & Sporting Clays, 4 Ann & Hope Way, P.O. Box 98, Cumberland, RI 02864 / 401-723-8202; FAX: 401-722-5910

Quaker Boy, Inc., 5455 Webster Rd., Orchard Parks, NY 14127 / 716-662-3979; FAX: 716-662-9426

Quality Arms, Inc., Box 19477, Dept. GD, Houston, TX 77224 / 281-870-8377; FAX: 281-870-8524 arrieta2@excite.com www.gunshop.com

Quality Firearms of Idaho, Inc., 659 Harmon Way, Middleton, ID 83644-3065 / 208-466-1631

Quality Parts Co./Bushmaster Firearms, 999 Roosevelt Trail Bldg. 3, Windham, ME 04062 / 207-892-2005; FAX: 207-892-8068

Quarton USA, Ltd. Co., 7042 Alamo Downs Pkwy., Suite 370, San Antonio, TX 78238-4518 / 800-520-8435 or 210-520-8430; FAX: 210-520-8433

Que Industries, Inc., P.O. Box 2471, Everett, WA 98203 / 800-769-6930 or 206-347-9843; FAX: 206-514-3266

Queen Cutlery Co., P.O. Box 500, Franklinville, NY 14737 / 800-222-5233; FAX: 800-299-2618

R

R&C Knives & Such, 2136 CANDY CANE WALK, Manteca, CA 95336-9501 / 209-239-3722; FAX: 209-825-6947

R&D Gun Repair, Kenny Howell, RR1 Box 283, Beloit, WI 53511

R&J Gun Shop, 337 S Humbolt St, Canyon City, OR 97820 / 541-575-2130 rjgunshop@highdestertnet.com

R&S Industries Corp., 8255 Brentwood Industrial Dr., St. Louis, MO 63144 / 314-781-5400 polishingcloth.com

R. Murphy Co., Inc., 13 Groton-Harvard Rd., P.O. Box 376, Ayer, MA 01432 / 617-772-3481

R.A. Wells Custom Gunsmith, 3452 1st Ave., Racine, WI 53402 / 414-639-5223

R.E. Seebeck Assoc., P.O. Box 59752, Dallas, TX 75229

R.E.I., P.O. Box 88, Tallevast, FL 34270 / 813-755-0085

R.E.T. Enterprises, 2608 S. Chestnut, Broken Arrow, OK 74012 / 918-251-GUNS; FAX: 918-251-0587

R.F. Mitchell Bullets, 430 Walnut St., Westernport, MD 21562

R.I.S. Co., Inc., 718 Timberlake Circle, Richardson, TX 75080 / 214-235-0933

R.M. Precision, P.O. Box 210, LaVerkin, UT 84745 / 801-635-4656; FAX: 801-635-4430

R.T. Eastman Products, P.O. Box 1531, Jackson, WY 83001 / 307-733-3217 or 800-624-4311

Rabeno, Martin, 92 Spook Hole Rd., Ellenville, NY 12428 / 914-647-4567; FAX: 914-647-2129

Radack Photography, Lauren, 21140 Jib Court L-12, Aventura, FL 33180 / 305-931-3110

Radiator Specialty Co., 1900 Wilkinson Blvd., P.O. Box 34689, Charlotte, NC 28234 / 800-438-6947; FAX: 800-421-9525

Radical Concepts, P.O. Box 1473, Lake Grove, OR 97035 / 503-538-7437

Rainier Ballistics Corp., 4500 15th St. East, Tacoma, WA 98424 / 800-638-8722 or 206-922-7589; FAX: 206-922-7854

Ralph Bone Engraving, 718 N. Atlanta, Owasso, OK 74055 / 918-272-9745

Ram-Line Blount, Inc., P.O. Box 39, Onalaska, WI 54650

Ramon B. Gonzalez Guns, P.O. Box 370, 93 St. Joseph's Hill Road, Monticello, NY 12701 / 914-794-4515

Rampart International, 2781 W. MacArthur Blvd., B-283, Santa Ana, CA 92704 / 800-976-7240 or 714-557-6405

Ranch Products, P.O. Box 145, Malinta, OH 43535 / 313-277-3118; FAX: 313-565-8536

Randall-Made Knives, P.O. Box 1988, Orlando, FL 32802 / 407-855-8075

Randco UK, 286 Gipsy Rd., Welling, DA16 1JJ ENGLAND / 44 81 303 4118

Randolph Engineering, Inc., 26 Thomas Patten Dr., Randolph, MA 02368 / 800-541-1405; FAX: 800-875-4200

Randy Duane Custom Stocks, 110 W. North Ave., Winchester, VA 22601 / 703-667-9461; FAX: 703-722-3993

Range Brass Products Company, P.O. Box 218, Rockport, TX 78381

Ranger Products, 2623 Grand Blvd., Suite 209, Holiday, FL 34609 / 813-942-4652 or 800-407-7007; FAX: 813-942-6221

Ranger Shooting Glasses, 26 Thomas Patten Dr., Randolph, MA 02368 / 800-541-1405; FAX: 617-986-0337

Ranging, Inc., Routes 5 & 20, East Bloomfield, NY 14443 / 716-657-6161; FAX: 716-657-5405

Ransom International Corp., 1027 Spire Dr, Prescott, AZ 86302 / 520-778-7899; FAX: 520-778-7993 ransom@primenet.com www.ransom-intl.com

Rapine Bullet Mould Mfg. Co., 9503 Landis Lane, East Greenville, PA 18041 / 215-679-5413; FAX: 215-679-9795

Raptor Arms Co., Inc., 273 Canal St, #179, Shelton, CT 06484 / 203-924-7618; FAX: 203-924-7624

Ravell Ltd., 289 Diputacion St., 08009, Barcelona, SPAIN / 34(3) 4874486; FAX: 34(3) 4881394

Ray Riling Arms Books Co., 6844 Gorsten St., P.O. Box 18925, Philadelphia, PA 19119 / 215-438-2456; FAX: 215-438-5395

Ray's Gunsmith Shop, 3199 Elm Ave., Grand Junction, CO 81504 / 970-434-6162; FAX: 970-434-6162

Raytech Div. of Lyman Products Corp., 475 Smith Street, Middletown, CT 06457-1541 / 860-632-2020; FAX: 860-632-1699

RCBS Div. of Blount, 605 Oro Dam Blvd., Oroville, CA 95965 / 800-533-5000 or 916-533-5191; FAX: 916-533-1647 www.rcbs.com

Reagent Chemical & Research, Inc. (See Calico Hardwoods, Inc.)

Reardon Products, P.O. Box 126, Morrison, IL 61270 / 815-772-3155

Red Diamond Dist. Co., 1304 Snowdon Dr., Knoxville, TN 37912

Redding Reloading Equipment, 1089 Starr Rd., Cortland, NY 13045 / 607-753-3331; FAX: 607-756-8445

Redfield Media Resource Center, 4607 N.E. Cedar Creek Rd., Woodland, WA 98674 / 360-225-5000 FAX: 360-225-7616

Redfield, Inc, 5800 E Jewell Ave, Denver, CO 80224 / 303-757-6411; FAX: 303-756-2338

Redfield/Blount, PO Box 39, Onalaska, WI 54650 / 800-635-7656

Redman's Rifling & Reboring, 189 Nichols Rd., Omak, WA 98841 / 509-826-5512

MANUFACTURERS DIRECTORY

Redwood Bullet Works, 3559 Bay Rd., Redwood City, CA 94063 / 415-367-6741
Reed, Dave, Rt. 1, Box 374, Minnesota City, MN 55959 / 507-689-2944
Reiswig, Wallace E. (See Claro Walnut Gunstock Co.,)
Reloaders Equipment Co., 4680 High St., Ecorse, ML 48229
Reloading Specialties, Inc., Box 1130, Pine Island, MN 55463 / 507-356-8500; FAX: 507-356-8800
Remington Arms Co., Inc., 870 Remington Drive, P.O. Box 700, Madison, NC 27025-0700 / 800-243-9700; FAX: 910-548-8700
Remington Double Shotguns, 7885 Cyd Dr., Denver, CO 80221 / 303-429-6947
Renato Gamba S.p.A.-Societa Armi Bresciane Srl., Via Artigiani 93, 25063.Gardone, Val Trompia (BS), ITALY / 30-8911640; FAX: 30-8911648
Renegade, P.O. Box 31546, Phoenix, AZ 85046 / 602-482-6777; FAX: 602-482-1952
Renfrew Guns & Supplies, R.R. 4, Renfrew, ON K7V 3Z7 CANADA / 613-432-7080
Reno, Wayne, 2808 Stagestop Rd, Jefferson, CO 80456 / 719-836-3452
Republic Arms, Inc., 15167 Sierra Bonita Lane, Chino, CA 91710 / 909-597-3873; FAX: 909-597-2612
Retting, Inc., Martin B, 11029 Washington, Culver City, CA 90232 / 213-837-2412
RG-G, Inc., PO Box 935, Trinidad, CO 81082 / 719-845-1436
Rhino, P.O. Box 787, Locust, NC 28097 / 704-753-2198
Rhodeside, Inc., 1704 Commerce Dr., Piqua, OH 45356 / 513-773-5781
Rice, Keith (See White Rock Tool & Die)
Richard H.R. Loweth (Firearms), 29 Hedgerow Lane, Kirby Muxloe, Leics. LE9 2BN, ENGLAND
Richards Micro-Fit Stocks, 8331 N. San Fernando Ave., Sun Valley, CA 91352 / 818-767-6097; FAX: 818-767-7121
Rickard, Inc., Pete, RD 1, Box 292, Cobleskill, NY 12043 / 800-282-5663; FAX: 518-234-2454
Ridgeline, Inc, Bruce Sheldon, PO Box 930, Dewey, AZ 86327-0930 / 800-632-5900; FAX: 520-632-5900
Ridgetop Sporting Goods, P.O. Box 306, 42907 Hilligoss Ln. East, Eatonville, WA 98328 / 360-832-6422; FAX: 360-832-6422
Ries, Chuck, 415 Ridgecrest Dr., Grants Pass, OR 97527 / 503-476-5623
Rifles, Inc., 873 W. 5400 N., Cedar City, UT 84720 / 801-586-5996; FAX: 801-586-5996
Rigby & Co., John, 66 Great Suffolk St, London, ENGLAND / 0171-620-0690; FAX: 0171-928-9205
Riggs, Jim, 206 Azalea, Boerne, TX 78006 / 210-249-8567
Riley Ledbetter Airguns, 1804 E. Sprague St., Winston Salem, NC 27107-3521 / 919-784-0676
Riling Arms Books Co., Ray, 6844 Gorsten St, PO Box 18925, Philadelphia, PA 19119 / 215-438-2456; FAX: 215-438-5395
Rim Pac Sports, Inc., 1034 N. Soldano Ave., Azusa, CA 91702-2135
Ringler Custom Leather Co., 31 Shining Mtn. Rd., Powell, WY 82435 / 307-645-3255
Ripley Rifles, 42 Fletcher Street, Ripley, Derbyshire, DE5 3LP ENGLAND / 011-0773-748153
River Road Sporting Clays, Bruce Barsotti, P.O. Box 3016, Gonzales, CA 93926 / 408-675-2473
Rizzini F.lli (See U.S. Importers-Moore & C England)
Rizzini SNC, Via 2 Giugno, 7/7Bis-25060, Marcheno (Brescia), ITALY
RLCM Enterprises, 110 Hill Crest Drive, Burleson, TX 76028
RMS Custom Gunsmithing, 4120 N. Bitterwell, Prescott Valley, AZ 86314 / 520-772-7626
Robert Evans Engraving, 332 Vine St., Oregon City, OR 97045 / 503-656-5693
Robert Valade Engraving, 931 3rd Ave., Seaside, OR 97138 / 503-738-7672
Roberts Products, 25328 SE Iss. Beaver Lk. Rd., Issaquah, WA 98029 / 206-392-8172
Robinett, R. G., P.O. Box 72, Madrid, IA 50156 / 515-795-2906
Robinson, Don, Pennsylvaia Hse, 36 Fairfax Crescent, W Yorkshire, ENGLAND / 0422-364458
Robinson Firearms Mfg. Ltd., 1699 Blondeaux Crescent, Kelowna, B.C. V1Y 4J8 CANADA / 604-868-9596
Robinson H.V. Bullets, 3145 Church St., Zachary, LA 70791 / 504-654-4029
Rochester Lead Works, 76 Anderson Ave., Rochester, NY 14607 / 716-442-8500; FAX: 716-442-4712
Rock River Arms, 101 Noble St., Cleveland, IL 61241

Rockwood Corp., Speedwell Division, 136 Lincoln Blvd., Middlesex, NJ 08846 / 800-243-8274; FAX: 980-560-7475
Rocky Mountain Arms, Inc., 1813 Sunset Pl, Unit D, Longmont, CO 80501 / 800-375-0846; FAX: 303-678-8766
Rocky Mountain High Sports Glasses, 8121 N. Central Park Ave., Skokie, IL 60076 / 847-679-1012 or 800-323-1418; FAX: 847-679-0184
Rocky Mountain Rifle Works Ltd., 1707 14th St., Boulder, CO 80302 / 303-443-9189
Rocky Mountain Target Co., 3 Aloe Way, Leesburg, FL 34788 / 352-365-9598
Rocky Mountain Wildlife Products, P.O. Box 999, La Porte, CO 80535 / 970-484-2768; FAX: 970-484-0807
Rocky Shoes & Boots, 294 Harper St., Nelsonville, OH 45764 / 800-848-9452 or 614-753-1951; FAX: 614-753-4024
Rodgers & Sons Ltd., Joseph (See George Ibberson (Sheffield) Ltd.,)
Rogue Rifle Co., Inc., P.O. Box 20, Prospect, OR 97536 / 541-560-4040; FAX: 541-560-4041
Rogue River Rifleworks, 1317 Spring St., Paso Robles, CA 93446 / 805-227-4706; FAX: FAX:805-227-4723
Rohner, Hans, 1148 Twin Sisters Ranch Rd., Nederland, CO 80466-9600
Rohner, John, 186 Virginia Ave., Asheville, NC 28806 / 303-444-3841
Romain's Custom Guns, Inc., RD 1, Whetstone Rd., Brockport, PA 15823 / 814-265-1948
Ron Frank Custom Classic Arms, 7131 Richland Rd., Ft. Worth, TX 76118 / 817-284-9300; FAX: 817-284-9300
Ron Lutz Engraving, E. 1998 Smokey Valley Rd., Scandinavia, WI 54977 / 715-467-2674
Rooster Laboratories, P.O. Box 412514, Kansas City, MO 64141 / 816-474-1622; FAX: 816-474-1307
Rorschach Precision Products, P.O. Box 151613, Irving, TX 75015 / 214-790-3487
Rosenberg & Son, Jack A, 12229 Cox Ln, Dallas, TX 75234 / 214-241-6302
Rosenthal, Brad and Sallie, 19303 Ossenfort Ct., St. Louis, MO 63038 / 314-273-5159; FAX: 314-273-5149
Ross, Don, 12813 West 83 Terrace, Lenexa, KS 66215 / 913-492-6982
Rosser, Bob, 1824 29th Ave., Suite 214, Birmingham, AL 35209 / 205-870-4422; FAX: 205-870-4421
Rossi Firearms, Braztech, Gary Mchalik, 16175 NW 49th Ave, Miami, FL 33014-6314 / 305-474-0401
Roto Carve, 2754 Garden Ave., Janesville, IA 50647
Rottweil Compe, 1330 Glassell, Orange, CA 92667
Round Edge, Inc., P.O. Box 723, Lansdale, PA 19446 / 215-361-0859
Roy Baker's Leather Goods, P.O. Box 893, Magnolia, AR 71753 / 501-234-0344
Roy's Custom Grips, Rt. 3, Box 174-E, Lynchburg, VA 24504 / 804-993-3470
Royal Arms Gunstocks, 919 8th Ave. NW, Great Falls, MT 59404 / 406-453-1149 FAX: 406-453-1194 royalarms@lmt.net lmt.net/~royalarms
RPM, 15481 N. Twin Lakes Dr., Tucson, AZ 85739 / 520-825-1233; FAX: 520-825-3333
Rubright Bullets, 1008 S. Quince Rd., Walnutport, PA 18088 / 215-767-1339
Rucker Dist. Inc., P.O. Box 479, Terrell, TX 75160 / 214-563-2094
Ruger (See Sturm, Ruger & Co., Inc.)
Rumanya Inc., 11513 Piney Lodge Rd, Gaithersburg, MD 20878-2443 / 281-345-2077; FAX: 281-345-2005
Rundell's Gun Shop, 6198 Frances Rd., Clio, MI 48420 / 313-687-0559
Runge, Robert P., 94 Grove St., Ilion, NY 13357 / 315-894-3036
Rupert's Gun Shop, 2202 Dick Rd., Suite B, Fenwick, MI 48834 / 517-248-3252
Russ Haydon Shooters' Supply, 15018 Goodrich Dr. NW, Gig Harbor, WA 98329 / 253-857-7557; FAX: 253-857-7884
Russ Trading Post, William A. Russ, 23 William St., Addison, NY 14801-1326 / 607-359-3896
Russ, William (See RUSS TRADING POST)
Rusteprufe Laboratories, 1319 Jefferson Ave., Sparta, WI 54656 / 608-269-4144
Rusty Duck Premium Gun Care Products, 7785 Foundation Dr., Suite 6, Florence, KY 41042 / 606-342-5553; FAX: 606-342-5556
Rutgers Book Center, 127 Raritan Ave., Highland Park, NJ 08904 / 732-545-4344 FAX: 732-545-6686
Rutten (See U.S. Importer-Labanu Inc)

RWS (See US Importer-Dynamit Nobel-RWS, Inc.), 81 Ruckman Rd, Closter, NJ 07624 / 201-767-7971; FAX: 201-767-1589
Ryan, Chad L., RR 3, Box 72, Cresco, IA 52136 / 319-547-4384

S

S&B Industries, 11238 McKinley Rd., Montrose, MI 48457 / 810-639-5491
S&K Mfg. Co., P.O. Box 247, Pittsfield, PA 16340 / 814-563-7808; FAX: 814-563-4067
S&S Firearms, 74-11 Myrtle Ave., Glendale, NY 11385 / 718-497-1100; FAX: 718-497-1105
S.A.R.L. G. Granger, 66 cours Fauriel, 42100, Saint Etienne, FRANCE / 04 77 25 14 73; FAX: 04 77 38 66 99
S.C.R.C., P.O. Box 660, Katy, TX 77492-0660 FAX: 713-578-2124
S.D. Meacham, 1070 Angel Ridge, Peck, ID 83545
S.G.S. Sporting Guns Srl., Via Della Resistenza, 37 20090, Buccinasco, ITALY / 2-45702446; FAX: 2-45702464
S.I.A.C.E. (See U.S. Importer-IAR Inc)
S.L.A.P. Industries, P.O. Box 1121, Parklands, 02121 SOUTH AFRICA / 27-11-788-0030; FAX: 27-11-788-0030
Sabatti S.r.l., via Alessandro Volta 90, 25063 Gardone V.T., Brescia, ITALY / 030-8912207-831312; FAX: 030-8912059
SAECO (See Redding Reloading Equipment)
Saf-T-Lok, 5713 Corporate Way, Suite 100, W. Palm Beach, FL 33407
Safari Outfitters Ltd., 71 Ethan Allan Hwy., Ridgefield, CT 06877 / 203-544-9505
Safari Press, Inc., 15621 Chemical Lane B, Huntington Beach, CA 92649 / 714-894-9080; FAX: 714-894-4949
Safariland Ltd., Inc., 3120 E. Mission Blvd., P.O. Box 51478, Ontario, CA 91761 / 909-923-7300; FAX: 909-923-7400
SAFE, P.O. Box 864, Post Falls, ID 83854 / 208-773-3624 FAX: 208-773-6819 staysafe@safe-llc.com www.safe-llc.com
Safety Speed Holster, Inc., 910 S. Vail Ave., Montebello, CA 90640 / 323-723-4140; FAX: 323-726-6973
Sako Ltd (See U.S. Importer-Stoeger Industries)
Samco Global Arms, Inc., 6995 NW 43rd St., Miami, FL 33166 / 305-593-9782 FAX: 305-593-1014
Sampson, Roger, 2316 Mahogany St., Mora, MN 55051 / 612-679-4868
San Francisco Gun Exchange, 124 Second St., San Francisco, CA 94105 / 415-982-6097
San Marco (See U.S. Importers-Cape Outfitters-EMF)
Sanders Custom Gun Service, 2358 Tyler Lane, Louisville, KY 40205 / 502-454-3338; FAX: 502-451-8857
Sanders Gun and Machine Shop, 145 Delhi Road, Manchester, IA 52057
Sandia Die & Cartridge Co., 37 Atancacio Rd. NE, Auquerque, NM 87123 / 505-298-5729
Sarco, Inc., 323 Union St., Stirling, NJ 07980 / 908-647-3800; FAX: 908-647-9413
Sauer (See U.S. Importers-Paul Co., The, Sigarms Inc.,)
Sauls, R. (See BRYAN & ASSOC)
Saunders Gun & Machine Shop, R.R. 2, Delhi Road, Manchester, IA 52057
Savage Arms (Canada), Inc., 248 Water St., P.O. Box 1240, Lakefield, ON K0L 2H0 CANADA / 705-652-8000; FAX: 705-652-8431
Savage Arms, Inc., 100 Springdale Rd., Westfield, MA 01085 / 413-568-7001; FAX: 413-562-7764
Savage Range Systems, Inc., 100 Springdale RD., Westfield, MA 01085 / 413-568-7001; FAX: 413-562-1152
Saville Iron Co. (See Greenwood Precision)
Savino, Barbara J., P.O. Box 51, West Burke, VT 05871-0051
Scanco Environmental Systems, 5000 Highlands Parkway, Suite 180, Atlanta, GA 30082 / 770-431-0025; FAX: 770-431-0028
Scansport, Inc., P.O. Box 700, Enfield, NH 03748 / 603-632-7654
Scattergun Technologies, Inc., 620 8th Ave. South, Nashville, TN 37203 / 615-254-1441; FAX: 615-254-1449
Sceery Game Calls, P.O. Box 6520, Sante Fe, NM 87502 / 505-471-9110; FAX: 505-471-3476
Schaefer Shooting Sports, P.O. Box 1515, Melville, NY 11747-0515 / 516-643-5466 FAX: 516-643-2426 rschaefe@optonline.net www.schaefershooting.com
Scharch Mfg., Inc., 10325 CR 120, Salida, CO 81201 / 719-539-7242 or 800-836-4683; FAX: 719-539-3021

MANUFACTURERS DIRECTORY

Scherer, Box 250, Ewing, VA 24240 / 615-733-2615; FAX: 615-733-2073
Schiffman, Curt, 3017 Kevin Cr., Idaho Falls, ID 83402 / 208-524-4684
Schiffman, Mike, 8233 S. Crystal Springs, McCammon, ID 83250 / 208-254-9114
Schiffman, Norman, 3017 Kevin Cr., Idaho Falls, ID 83402 / 208-524-4684
Schmidt & Bender, Inc., 438 Willow Brook Rd., Meriden, NH 03770 / 800-468-3450 or 800-468-3450; FAX: 603-469-3471
Schmidtke Group, 17050 W. Salentine Dr., New Berlin, WI 53151-7349
Schmidtman Custom Ammunition, 6 Gilbert Court, Cotati, CA 94931
Schneider Bullets, 3655 West 214th St., Fairview Park, OH 44126
Schneider Rifle Barrels, Inc, Gary, 12202 N 62nd Pl, Scottsdale, AZ 85254 / 602-948-2525
Schroeder Bullets, 1421 Thermal Ave., San Diego, CA 92154 / 619-423-3523; FAX: 619-423-8124
Schuetzen Pistol Works, 620-626 Old Pacific Hwy. SE, Olympia, WA 98513 / 360-459-3471; FAX: 360-491-3447
Schulz Industries, 16247 Minnesota Ave., Paramount, CA 90723 / 213-439-5903
Schumakers Gun Shop, 512 Prouty Corner Lp. A, Colville, WA 99114 / 509-684-4848
Scope Control, Inc., 5775 Co. Rd. 23 SE, Alexandria, MN 56308 / 612-762-7295
ScopLevel, 151 Lindbergh Ave., Suite C, Livermore, CA 94550 / 925-449-5052; FAX: 925-373-0861
Score High Gunsmithing, 9812-A, Cochiti SE, Albuquerque, NM 087123 / 800-526-3322 or 505-292-5532; FAX: 505-292-2592
Scot Powder, Rt.1 Box 167, McEwen, TN 37101 / 800-416-3006; FAX: 615-729-4211
Scot Powder Co. of Ohio, Inc., Box GD96, Only, TN 37140 / 615-729-4207 or 800-416-3006; FAX: 615-729-4217
Scott, Dwight, 23089 Englehardt St., Clair Shores, MI 48080 / 313-779-4735
Scott Fine Guns Inc., Thad, PO Box 412, Indianola, MS 38751 / 601-887-5929
Scott McDougall & Associates, 7950 Redwood Dr., Suite 13, Cotati, CA 94931 / 707-546-2264; FAX: 707-795-1911 www.colt380.com
Searcy Enterprises, PO Box 584, Boron, CA 93596 / 760-762-6771 FAX: 760-762-0191
Second Chance Body Armor, P.O. Box 578, Central Lake, MI 49622 / 616-544-5721; FAX: 616-544-9824
Seebeck Assoc., R.E., P. O. Box 59752, Dallas, TX 75229
Seecamp Co. Inc., L. W., PO Box 255, New Haven, CT 06502 / 203-877-3429
Segway Industries, P.O. Box 783, Suffern, NY 10901-0783 / 914-357-5510
Seligman Shooting Products, Box 133, Seligman, AZ 86337 / 602-422-3607
Sellier & Bellot, USA Inc, PO Box 27006, Shawnee Mission, KS 66225 / 913-685-0916; FAX: 913-685-0917
Selsi Co., Inc., P.O. Box 10, Midland Park, NJ 07432-0010 / 201-935-0388; FAX: 201-935-5851
Semmer, Charles (See Remington Double Shotguns), 7885 Cyd Dr, Denver, CO 80221 / 303-429-6947
Sentinel Arms, P.O. Box 57, Detroit, MI 48231 / 313-331-1951; FAX: 313-331-1456
Service Armament, 689 Bergen Blvd., Ridgefield, NJ 07657
Servus Footwear Co., 1136 2nd St., Rock Island, IL 61204 / 309-786-7741; FAX: 309-786-9808
Shappy Bullets, 76 Milldale Ave., Plantsville, CT 06479 / 203-621-3704
Sharp Shooter Supply, 4970 Lehman Road, Delphos, OH 45833 / 419-695-3179
Sharps Arms Co., Inc., C., 100 Centennial, Box 885, Big Timber, MT 59011 / 406-932-4353
Shaw, E. R. (See Small Arms Mfg. Co.)
Shay's Gunsmithing, 931 Marvin Ave., Lebanon, PA 17042
Sheffield Knifemakers Supply, Inc., P.O. Box 741107, Orange City, FL 32774-1107 / 904-775-6453; FAX: 904-774-5754
Sheldon, Bruce. (See RIDGELINE, INC)
Shepherd Enterprises, Inc., Box 189, Waterloo, NE 68069 / 402-779-2424; FAX: 402-779-4010 sshepherd@shepherdscopes.com www.shepherdscopes.com
Sherwood, George, 46 N. River Dr., Roseburg, OR 97470 / 541-672-3159
Shilen, Inc., 205 Metro Park Blvd., Ennis, TX 75119 / 972-875-5318; FAX: 972-875-5402

Shiloh Creek, Box 357, Cottleville, MO 63338 / 314-925-1842; FAX: 314-925-1842
Shiloh Rifle Mfg., 201 Centennial Dr., Big Timber, MT 59011 / 406-932-4454; FAX: 406-932-5627
Shockley, Harold H., 204 E. Farmington Rd., Hanna City, IL 61536 / 309-565-4524
Shoemaker & Sons Inc., Tex, 714 W Cienega Ave, San Dimas, CA 91773 / 909-592-2071; FAX: 909-592-2378
Shoot Where You Look, Leon Measures, Dept GD, 408 Fair, Livingston, TX 77351
Shoot-N-C Targets (See Birchwood Casey)
Shooter's Choice, 16770 Hilltop Park Place, Chagrin Falls, OH 44023 / 216-543-8808; FAX: 216-543-8811
Shooter's Edge Inc., P.O.Box 769, Trinidad, CO 81082
Shooter's World, 3828 N. 28th Ave., Phoenix, AZ 85017 / 602-266-0170
Shooters Supply, 1120 Tieton Dr., Yakima, WA 98902 / 509-452-1181
Shootin' Accessories, Ltd., P.O. Box 6810, Auburn, CA 95604 / 916-889-2220
Shootin' Shack, Inc., 1065 Silver Beach Rd., Riviera Beach, FL 33403 / 561-842-0990
Shooting Chrony, Inc., 3269 Niagara Falls Blvd., N. Tonawanda, NY 14120 / 905-276-6292; FAX: 416-276-6295
Shooting Specialties (See Titus, Daniel)
Shooting Star, 1715 FM 1626 Ste 105, Manchaca, TX 78652 / 512-462-0009
Shotgun Sports, PO Box 6810, Auburn, CA 95604 / 530-889-2220; FAX: 530-889-9106
Shotguns Unlimited, 2307 Fon Du Lac Rd., Richmond, VA 23229 / 804-752-7115
ShurKatch Corporation, PO Box 850, Richfield Springs, NY 13439 / 315-858-1470; FAX: 315-858-2969
Siegrist Gun Shop, 8752 Turtle Road, Whittemore, MI 48770
Sierra Bullets, 1400 W. Henry St., Sedalia, MO 65301 / 816-827-6300; FAX: 816-827-6300
Sierra Specialty Prod. Co., 1344 Oakhurst Ave., Los Altos, CA 94024 FAX: 415-965-1536
SIG, CH-8212 Neuhausen, SWITZERLAND
SIG-Sauer (See U.S. Importer-Sigarms Inc.)
Sigarms, Inc., Corporate Park, Exeter, NH 03833 / 603-772-2302; FAX: 603-772-9082
Sightron, Inc., 1672B Hwy. 96, Franklinton, NC 27525 / 919-528-8783; FAX: 919-528-0995
Signet Metal Corp., 551 Stewart Ave., Brooklyn, NY 11222 / 718-384-5400; FAX: 718-388-7488
Sile Distributors, Inc., 7 Centre Market Pl., New York, NY 10013 / 212-925-4111; FAX: 212-925-3149
Silencio/Safety Direct, 56 Coney Island Dr., Sparks, NV 89431 / 800-648-1812 or 702-354-4451; FAX: 702-359-1074
Silent Hunter, 1100 Newton Ave., W. Collingswood, NJ 08107 / 609-854-3276
Silhouette Leathers, P.O. Box 1161, Gunnison, CO 81230 / 303-641-6639
Silver Eagle Machining, 18007 N. 69th Ave., Glendale, AZ 85308
Silver Ridge Gun Shop (See Goodwin, Fred)
Simmons, Jerry, 715 Middlebury St., Goshen, IN 46526 / 219-533-8546
Simmons Gun Repair, Inc., 700 S. Rogers Rd., Olathe, KS 66062 / 913-782-3131; FAX: 913-782-4189
Simmons Outdoor Corp., PO Box 217, Heflin, AL 36264
Sinclair International, Inc., 2330 Wayne Haven St., Fort Wayne, IN 46803 / 219-493-1858; FAX: 219-493-2530
Singletary, Kent, 2915 W. Ross, Phoenix, AZ 85027 / 602-582-4900
Sipes Gun Shop, 7415 Asher Ave., Little Rock, AR 72204 / 501-565-8480
Siskiyou Gun Works (See Donnelly, C. P.)
Six Enterprises, 320-D Turtle Creek Ct., San Jose, CA 95125 / 408-999-0201; FAX: 408-999-0216
SKAN A.R., 4 St. Catherines Road, Long Melford, Suffolk, 010 9JU ENGLAND / 011-0787-312942
SKB Shotguns, 4325 S. 120th St., Omaha, NE 68137 / 800-752-2767; FAX: 402-330-8029
Skeoch, Brian R., P.O. Box 279, Glenrock, WY 82637 / 307-436-9655 FAX: 307-436-9034
Skip's Machine, 364 29 Road, Grand Junction, CO 81501 / 303-245-5417
Sklany's Machine Shop, 566 Birch Grove Dr., Kalispell, MT 59901 / 406-755-4257
Slezak, Jerome F., 1290 Marlowe, Lakewood (Cleveland), OH 44107 / 216-221-1668
Slug Group, Inc., P.O. Box 376, New Paris, PA 15554 / 814-839-4517; FAX: 814-839-2601

Slug Site, Ozark Wilds, 21300 Hwy. 5, Versailles, MO 65084 / 573-378-6430 john.ebeling.com
Small Arms Mfg. Co., 5312 Thoms Run Rd., Bridgeville, PA 15017 / 412-221-4343; FAX: 412-221-4303
Small Arms Specialists, 443 Firchburg Rd, Mason, NH 03048 / 603-878-0427 FAX: 603-878-3905 miniguns@empire.net miniguns.com
Small Custom Mould & Bullet Co., Box 17211, Tucson, AZ 85731
Smart Parts, 1203 Spring St., Latrobe, PA 15650 / 412-539-2660; FAX: 412-539-2298
Smires, C. L., 5222 Windmill Lane, Columbia, MD 21044-1328
Smith & Wesson, 2100 Roosevelt Ave., Springfield, MA 01104 / 413-781-8300; FAX: 413-731-8980
Smith, Art, 230 Main St. S., Hector, MN 55342 / 320-848-2760; FAX: 320-848-2760
Smith, Mark A., P.O. Box 182, Sinclair, WY 82334 / 307-324-7929
Smith, Michael, 620 Nye Circle, Chattanooga, TN 37405 / 615-267-8341
Smith, Ron, 5869 Straley, Ft. Worth, TX 76114 / 817-732-6768
Smith, Sharmon, 4545 Speas Rd., Fruitland, ID 83619 / 208-452-6329
Smith Abrasives, Inc., 1700 Sleepy Valley Rd., P.O. Box 5095, Hot Springs, AR 71902-5095 / 501-321-2244; FAX: 501-321-9232
Smith Saddlery, Jesse W., 16909 E Jackson Rd, Elk, WA 99009-9600 / 509-325-0622
Smokey Valley Rifles (See Lutz Engraving, Ron E)
Snapp's Gunshop, 6911 E. Washington Rd., Clare, MI 48617 / 517-386-9226
Sno-Seal, Inc. (See Atsko/Sno-Seal)
Societa Armi Bresciane Srl (See U.S. Importer-Cape Outfitters)
SOS Products Co. (See Buck Stix-SOS Products Co.), Box 3, Neenah, WI 54956
Sotheby's, 1334 York Ave. at 72nd St., New York, NY 10021 / 212-606-7260
Sound Technology, Box 391, Pelham, AL 35124 / 205-664-5860 or 907-486-2825
South Bend Replicas, Inc., 61650 Oak Rd.., South Bend, IN 46614 / 219-289-4500
Southeastern Community College, 1015 S. Gear Ave., West Burlington, IA 52655 / 319-752-2731
Southern Ammunition Co., Inc., 4232 Meadow St., Loris, SC 29569-3124 / 803-756-3262; FAX: 803-756-3583
Southern Bloomer Mfg. Co., P.O. Box 1621, Bristol, TN 37620 / 615-878-6660; FAX: 615-878-8761
Southern Security, 1700 Oak Hills Dr., Kingston, TN 37763 / 423-376-6297; FAX: 800-251-9992
Southwind Sanctions, P.O. Box 445, Aledo, TX 76008 / 817-441-8917
Sparks, Milt, 605 E. 44th St. No. 2, Boise, ID 83714-4800
Spartan-Realtree Products, Inc., 1390 Box Circle, Columbus, GA 31907 / 706-569-9101; FAX: 706-569-0042
Specialty Gunsmithing, Lynn McMurdo, P.O. Box 404, Afton, WY 83110 / 307-886-5535
Specialty Shooters Supply, Inc., 3325 Griffin Rd., Suite 9mm, Fort Lauderdale, FL 33317
Speedfeed Inc., PO Box 1146, Rocklin, CA 95677 / 916-630-7720; FAX: 916-630-7719
Speer Products Div. of Blount Inc. Sporting Equipm, P.O. Box 856, Lewiston, ID 83501 / 208-746-2351; FAX: 208-746-2915
Spegel, Craig, PO Box 387, Nehalem, OR 97131 / 503-368-5653
Speiser, Fred D., 2229 Dearborn, Missoula, MT 59801 / 406-549-8133
Spencer Reblue Service, 1820 Tupelo Trail, Holt, MI 48842 / 517-694-7474
Spencer's Custom Guns, 4107 Jacobs Creek Dr, Scottsville, VA 24590 / 804-293-6836 FAX: 804-293-6836
SPG LLC, P.O. Box 1625, Cody, WY 82414 / 307-587-7621; FAX: 307-587-7695
Sphinx Engineering SA, Ch. des Grandex-Vies 2, CH-2900, Porrentruy, SWITZERLAND FAX: 41 66 66 30 90
Spokhandguns, Inc., 1206 Fig St., Benton City, WA 99320 / 509-588-5255
Sport Flite Manufacturing Co., P.O. Box 1082, Bloomfield Hills, MI 48303 / 248-647-3747
Sporting Arms Mfg., Inc., 801 Hall Ave., Littlefield, TX 79339 / 806-385-5665; FAX: 806-385-3394
Sporting Clays Of America, 9257 Bluckeye Rd, Sugar Grove, OH 43155-9632 / 740-746-8334; FAX: 740-746-8605

346 • GUNS ILLUSTRATED

Manufacturers Directory

Sports Innovations Inc., P.O. Box 5181, 8505 Jacksboro Hwy., Wichita Falls, TX 76307 / 817-723-6015

Sportsman Safe Mfg. Co., 6309-6311 Paramount Blvd., Long Beach, CA 90805 / 800-266-7150 or 310-984-5445

Sportsman Supply Co., 714 E. Eastwood, P.O. Box 650, Marshall, MO 65340 / 816-886-9393

Sportsman's Communicators, 588 Radcliffe Ave., Pacific Palisades, CA 90272 / 800-538-3752

Sportsmatch U.K. Ltd., 16 Summer St., Leighton Buzzard, Bedfordshire, LU7 8HT ENGLAND / 01525-381638; FAX: 01525-851236

Sportsmen's Exchange & Western Gun Traders, Inc., 560 S. C St., Oxnard, CA 93030 / 805-483-1917

Spradlin's, 457 Shannon Rd, Texos Creek, CO 81223 / 719-275-7105 FAX: 719-275-3852 spradlins@prodigt.net jimspradlin.com

Springfield Sporters, Inc., RD 1, Penn Run, PA 15765 / 412-254-2626; FAX: 412-254-9173

Springfield, Inc., 420 W. Main St., Geneseo, IL 61254 / 309-944-5631; FAX: 309-944-3676

Spyderco, Inc., 4565 N. Hwy. 93, P.O. Box 800, Golden, CO 80403 / 303-279-8383 or 800-525-7770; FAX: 303-278-2229

SSK Industries, 590 Woodvue Lane, Wintersville, OH 43953 / 740-264-0176; FAX: 740-264-2257

Stackpole Books, 5067 Ritter Rd., Mechanicsburg, PA 17055-6921 / 717-796-0411; FAX: 717-796-0412

Stalker, Inc., P.O. Box 21, Fishermans Wharf Rd., Malakoff, TX 75148 / 903-489-1010

Stalwart Corporation, 76 Imperial, Unit A, Evanston, WY 82930 / 307-789-7687; FAX: 307-789-7688

Stan De Treville & Co., 4129 Normal St., San Diego, CA 92103 / 619-298-3393

Stanley Bullets, 2085 Heatheridge Ln., Reno, NV 89509

Stanley Scruggs' Game Calls, Rt. 1, Hwy. 661, Cullen, VA 23934 / 804-542-4241 or 800-323-4828

Star Ammunition, Inc., 5520 Rock Hampton Ct., Indianapolis, IN 46268 / 800-221-5927; FAX: 317-872-5847

Star Bonifacio Echeverria S.A., Torrekva 3, Eibar, 20600 SPAIN / 43-107340; FAX: 43-101524

Star Custom Bullets, P.O. Box 608, 468 Main St., Ferndale, CA 95536 / 707-786-9140; FAX: 707-786-9117

Star Machine Works, PO Box 1872, Pioneer, CA 95666 / 209-295-5000

Stark's Bullet Mfg., 2580 Monroe St., Eugene, OR 97405

Starke Bullet Company, P.O. Box 400, 605 6th St. NW, Cooperstown, ND 58425 / 888-797-3431

Starkey Labs, 6700 Washington Ave. S., Eden Prairie, MN 55344

Starkey's Gun Shop, 9430 McCombs, El Paso, TX 79924 / 915-751-3030

Starlight Training Center, Inc., Rt. 1, Box 88, Bronaugh, MO 64728 / 417-843-3555

Starline, Inc., 1300 W. Henry St., Sedalia, MO 65301 / 660-827-6640 FAX: 660-827-6650 bjhayden@starlinebra.com http://www.starlinebrass.com

Starr Trading Co., Jedediah, P.O. Box 2007, Farmington Hills, MI 48333 / 810-683-4343; FAX: 810-683-3282

Starrett Co., L. S., 121 Crescent St, Athol, MA 01331 / 978-249-3551 FAX: 978-249-8495

State Arms Gun Co., 815 S. Division St., Waunakee, WI 53597 / 608-849-5800

Steelman's Gun Shop, 10465 Beers Rd., Swartz Creek, MI 48473 / 810-735-4884

Steffens, Ron, 18396 Mariposa Creek Rd., Willits, CA 95490 / 707-485-0873

Stegall, James B., 26 Forest Rd., Wallkill, NY 12589

Steger, James R., 1131 Dorsey Pl., Plainfield, NJ 07062

Steve Henigson & Associates, P.O. Box 2726, Culver City, CA 90231 / 310-305-8288; FAX: 310-305-1905

Steve Kamyk Engraver, 9 Grandview Dr., Westfield, MA 01085-1810 / 413-568-0457

Steve Nastoff's 45 Shop, Inc., 12288 Mahoning Ave., P.O. Box 44, North Jackson, OH 44451 / 330-538-2977

Steves House of Guns, Rt. 1, Minnesota City, MN 55959 / 507-689-2573

Stewart Game Calls, Inc., Johnny, PO Box 7954, 5100 Fort Ave, Waco, TX 76714 / 817-772-3261; FAX: 817-772-3670

Stewart's Gunsmithing, P.O. Box 5854, Pietersburg North 0750, Transvaal, SOUTH AFRICA / 01521-89401

Steyr Mannlicher AG & CO KG, Mannlicherstrasse 1, A-4400, Steyr, AUSTRIA / 0043-7252-78621; FAX: 0043-7252-68621

STI International, 114 Halmar Cove, Georgetown, TX 78628 / 800-959-8201; FAX: 512-819-0465

Stiles Custom Guns, 76 Cherry Run Rd, Box 1605, Homer City, PA 15748 / 712-479-9945

Stillwell, Robert, 421 Judith Ann Dr., Schertz, TX 78154

Stoeger Industries, 5 Mansard Ct., Wayne, NJ 07470 / 201-872-9500 or 800-631-0722; FAX: 201-872-2230

Stoeger Publishing Co. (See Stoeger Industries)

Stone Enterprises Ltd., Rt. 609, P.O. Box 335, Wicomico Church, VA 22579 / 804-580-5114; FAX: 804-580-8421

Stone Mountain Arms, 5988 Peachtree Corners E., Norcross, GA 30071 / 800-251-9412

Stoney Point Products, Inc., PO Box 234, 1822 N Minnesota St, New Ulm, MN 56073-0234 / 507-354-3360; FAX: 507-354-7236 stoney@newulmtel.net www.stoneypoint.com

Storage Tech, 1254 Morris Ave., N. Huntingdon, PA 15642 / 800-437-9393

Storey, Dale A. (See DGS Inc.)

Storm, Gary, P.O. Box 5211, Richardson, TX 75083 / 214-385-0862

Stott's Creek Armory, Inc., 2526 S. 475W, Morgantown, IN 46160 / 317-878-5489; FAX: 317-878-9489 www.sccalendar.com

Stratco, Inc., P.O. Box 2270, Kalispell, MT 59901 / 406-755-1221; FAX: 406-755-1226

Strawbridge, Victor W., 6 Pineview Dr., Dover, NH 03820 / 603-742-0013

Strayer, Sandy. (See STRAYER-VOIGT, INC)

Strayer-Voigt, Inc, Sandy Strayer, 3435 Ray Orr Blvd, Grand Prairie, TX 75050 / 972-513-0575

Streamlight, Inc., 1030 W. Germantown Pike, Norristown, PA 19403 / 215-631-0600; FAX: 610-631-0712

Strong Holster Co., 39 Grove St., Gloucester, MA 01930 / 508-281-3300; FAX: 508-281-6321

Strutz Rifle Barrels, Inc., W. C., PO Box 611, Eagle River, WI 54521 / 715-479-4766

Stuart, V. Pat, Rt.1, Box 447-S, Greenville, VA 24440 / 804-556-3845

Sturgeon Valley Sporters, K. Ide, P.O. Box 283, Vanderbilt, MI 49795 / 517-983-4338

Sturm Ruger & Co. Inc., 200 Ruger Rd., Prescott, AZ 86301 / 520-541-8820; FAX: 520-541-8850

Sullivan, David S .(See Westwind Rifles Inc.)

Summit Specialties, Inc., P.O. Box 786, Decatur, AL 35602 / 205-353-0634; FAX: 205-353-9818

Sun Welding Safe Co., 290 Easy St. No.3, Simi Valley, CA 93065 / 805-584-6678 or 800-729-SAFE FAX: 805-584-6169

Sunny Hill Enterprises, Inc., W1790 Cty. HHH, Malone, WI 53049 / 920-795-4722 FAX: 920-795-4822

"Su-Press-On",Inc., P.O. Box 09161, Detroit, MI 48209 / 313-842-4222

Sure-Shot Game Calls, Inc., P.O. Box 816, 6835 Capitol, Groves, TX 77619 / 409-962-1636; FAX: 409-962-5465

Survival Arms, Inc., 273 Canal St., Shelton, CT 06484-3173 / 203-924-6533; FAX: 203-924-2581

Svon Corp., 280 Eliot St., Ashland, MA 01721 / 508-881-8852

Swann, D. J., 5 Orsova Close, Eltham North Vic., 3095 AUSTRALIA / 03-431-0323

Swanndri New Zealand, 152 Elm Ave., Burlingame, CA 94010 / 415-347-6158

SwaroSports, Inc. (See JagerSport Ltd, One Wholesale Way, Cranston, RI 02920 / 800-962-4867; FAX: 401-946-2587

Swarovski Optik North America Ltd., 2 Slater Rd., Cranston, RI 02920 / 401-946-2220 or 800-426-3089 FAX: 401-946-2587

Sweet Home, Inc., P.O. Box 900, Orrville, OH 44667-0900

Swenson's 45 Shop, A. D., 3839 Ladera Vista Rd, Fallbrook, CA 92028-9431

Swift Bullet Co., P.O. Box 27, 201 Main St., Quinter, KS 67752 / 913-754-3959; FAX: 913-754-2359

Swift Instruments, Inc., 952 Dorchester Ave., Boston, MA 02125 / 617-436-2960; FAX: 617-436-3232

Swift River Gunworks, 450 State St., Belchertown, MA 01007 / 413-323-4052

Szweda, Robert (See RMS Custom Gunsmithing)

T

T&S Industries, Inc., 1027 Skyview Dr., W. Carrollton, OH 45449 / 513-859-8414

T.F.C. S.p.A., Via G. Marconi 118, B, Villa Carcina 25069, ITALY / 030-881271; FAX: 030-881826

T.G. Faust, Inc., 544 Minor St., Reading, PA 19602 / 610-375-8549; FAX: 610-375-4488

T.H.U. Enterprises, Inc., P.O. Box 418, Lederach, PA 19450 / 215-256-1665; FAX: 215-256-9718

T.K. Lee Co., 1282 Branchwater Ln., Birmingham, AL 35216 / 205-913-5222

T.W. Menck Gunsmith Inc., 5703 S. 77th St., Ralston, NE 68127

Tabler Marketing, 2554 Lincoln Blvd., Suite 555, Marina Del Rey, CA 90291 / 818-755-4565; FAX: 818-755-0972

Taconic Firearms Ltd., Perry Lane, PO Box 553, Cambridge, NY 12816 / 518-677-2704; FAX: 518-677-5974

TacStar, PO Box 547, Cottonwood, AZ 86326-0547 / 602-639-0072; FAX: 602-634-8781

TacTell, Inc., P.O. Box 5654, Maryville, TN 37802 / 615-982-7855; FAX: 615-558-8294

Tactical Defense Institute, 574 Miami Bluff Ct., Loveland, OH 45140 / 513-677-8229 FAX: 513-677-0447

Talley, Dave, P.O. Box 821, Glenrock, WY 82637 / 307-436-8724 or 307-436-9315

Talmage, William G., 10208 N. County Rd. 425 W., Brazil, IN 47834 / 812-442-0804

Talon Mfg. Co., Inc., 621 W. King St., Martinsburg, WV 25401 / 304-264-9714; FAX: 304-264-9725

Tamarack Products, Inc., P.O. Box 625, Wauconda, IL 60084 / 708-526-9333; FAX: 708-526-9353

Tanfoglio Fratelli S.r.l., via Valtrompia 39, 41, Brescia, ITALY / 30-8910361; FAX: 30-8910183

Tanglefree Industries, 1261 Heavenly Dr., Martinez, CA 94553 / 800-982-4868; FAX: 510-825-3874

Tank's Rifle Shop, P.O. Box 474, Fremont, NE 68026-0474 / 402-727-1317; FAX: 402-721-2573

Tanner (See U.S. Importer-Mandall Shooting Supplies Inc.,)

Tar-Hunt Custom Rifles, Inc., RR3, P.O. Box 572, Bloomsburg, PA 17815-9351 / 717-784-6368; FAX: 717-784-6368

Taracorp Industries, Inc., 1200 Sixteenth St., Granite City, IL 62040 / 618-451-4400

Target Shooting, Inc., PO Box 773, Watertown, SD 57201 / 605-882-6955; FAX: 605-882-8840

Tarnhelm Supply Co., Inc., 431 High St., Boscawen, NH 03303 / 603-796-2551; FAX: 603-796-2918

Tasco Sales, Inc., 2889 Commerce Pky., Miramar, FL 33025

Taurus International Firearms, Inc., 16175 NW 49th Ave., Miami, FL 33014 / 305-624-1115; FAX: 305-623-7506

Taurus S.A. Forjas, Avenida Do Forte 511, Porto Alegre, RS BRAZIL 91360 / 55-51-347-4050; FAX: 55-51-347-3065

Taylor & Robbins, P.O. Box 164, Rixford, PA 16745 / 814-966-3233

Taylor's & Co., Inc., 304 Lenoir Dr., Winchester, VA 22603 / 540-722-2017; FAX: 540-722-2018

TCCI, P.O. Box 302, Phoenix, AZ 85001 / 602-237-3823; FAX: 602-237-3858

TCSR, 3998 Hoffman Rd., White Bear Lake, MN 55110-4626 / 800-328-5323; FAX: 612-429-0526

TDP Industries, Inc., 606 Airport Blvd., Doylestown, PA 18901 / 215-345-8687; FAX: 215-345-6057

Techno Arms (See U.S. Importer- Auto-Ordnance Corp.)

Tecnolegno S.p.A., Via A. Locatelli, 6 10, 24019 Zogno, I ITALY / 0345-55111; FAX: 0345-55155

Ted Blocker Holsters, Inc., Clackamas Business Park Bldg A, 14787 SE 82nd Dr, Clackamas, OR 97015 / 503-557-7757; FAX: 503-557-3771

Tele-Optics, 630 E. Rockland Rd., PO Box 6313, Libertyville, IL 60048 / 847-362-7757

Ten-Ring Precision, Inc., Alex B. Hamilton, 1449 Blue Crest Lane, San Antonio, TX 78232 / 210-494-3063; FAX: 210-494-3066

TEN-X Products Group, 1905 N Main St, Suite 133, Cleburne, TX 76031-1305 / 972-243-4016 or 800-433-2225; FAX: 972-243-4112

Tennessee Valley Mfg., P.O. Box 1175, Corinth, MS 38834 / 601-286-5014

Tepeco, P.O. Box 342, Friendswood, TX 77546 / 713-482-2702

Terry K. Kopp Professional Gunsmithing, Rt 1 Box 224F, Lexington, MO 64067 / 816-259-2636

Testing Systems, Inc., 220 Pegasus Ave., Northvale, NJ 07647

Teton Arms, Inc., P.O. Box 411, Wilson, WY 83014 / 307-733-3395

Tetra Gun Lubricants (See FTI, Inc.)

Tex Shoemaker & Sons, Inc., 714 W. Cienega Ave., San Dimas, CA 91773 / 909-592-2071; FAX: 909-592-2378

Texas Armory (See Bond Arms, Inc.)

Texas Platers Supply Co., 2453 W. Five Mile Parkway, Dallas, TX 75233 / 214-330-7168

Thad Rybka Custom Leather Equipment, 134 Havilah Hill, Odenville, AL 35120

MANUFACTURERS DIRECTORY

Thad Scott Fine Guns, Inc., P.O. Box 412, Indianola, MS 38751 / 601-887-5929
The Accuracy Den, 25 Bitterbrush Rd., Reno, NV 89523 / 702-345-0225
The Armoury, Inc., Rt. 202, Box 2340, New Preston, CT 06777 / 860-868-0001; FAX: 860-868-2919
The Ballistic Program Co., Inc., 2417 N. Patterson St., Thomasville, GA 31792 / 912-228-5739 or 800-368-0835
The BulletMakers Workshop, RFD 1 Box 1755, Brooks, ME 04921
The Competitive Pistol Shop, 5233 Palmer Dr., Ft. Worth, TX 76117-2433 / 817-834-8479
The Country Armourer, P.O. Box 308, Ashby, MA 01431-0308 / 508-827-6797; FAX: 508-827-4845
The Creative Craftsman, Inc., 95 Highway 29 North, P.O. Box 331, Lawrenceville, GA 30246 / 404-963-2112; FAX: 404-513-9488
The Custom Shop, 890 Cochrane Crescent, Peterborough, ON K9H 5N3 CANADA / 705-742-6693
The Dutchman's Firearms, Inc., 4143 Taylor Blvd., Louisville, KY 40215 / 502-366-0555
The Ensign-Bickford Co., 660 Hopmeadow St., Simsbury, CT 06070
The Eutaw Co., Inc., P.O. Box 608, U.S. Hwy. 176 West, Holly Hill, SC 29059 / 803-496-3341
The Firearm Training Center, 9555 Blandville Rd., West Paducah, KY 42086 / 502-554-5886
The Fouling Shot, 6465 Parfet St., Arvada, CO 80004
The Gun Doctor, 435 East Maple, Roselle, IL 60172 / 708-894-0668
The Gun Doctor, P.O. Box 39242, Downey, CA 90242 / 310-862-3158
The Gun Parts Corp., 226 Williams Lane, West Hurley, NY 12491 / 914-679-2417; FAX: 914-679-5849
The Gun Room, 1121 Burlington, Muncie, IN 47302 / 765-282-9073; FAX: 765-282-5270 bshstleguns@aol.com
The Gun Room Press, 127 Raritan Ave., Highland Park, NJ 08904 / 732-545-4344; FAX: 732-545-4344
The Gun Shop, 62778 Spring Creek Rd., Montrose, CO 81401
The Gun Shop, 5550 S. 900 East, Salt Lake City, UT 84117 / 801-263-3633
The Gun Shop, 716-A South Rogers Road, Olathe, KS 66062
The Gun Works, 247 S. 2nd, Springfield, OR 97477 / 541-741-4118; FAX: 541-988-1097 gunworks@worldnet.att.net www.thegunworks.com
The Gunsight, 1712 North Placentia Ave., Fullerton, CA 92631
The Gunsmith in Elk River, 14021 Victoria Lane, Elk River, MN 55330 / 612-441-7761
The Hanned Line, P.O. Box 2387, Cupertino, CA 95015-2387 smith@hanned.com www.hanned.com
The Holster Shop, 720 N. Flagler Dr., Ft. Lauderdale, FL 33304 / 305-463-7910; FAX: 305-761-1483
The House of Muskets, Inc., P.O. Box 4640, Pagosa Springs, CO 81157 / 970-731-2295
The Keller Co., 4215 McEwen Rd., Dallas, TX 75244 / 214-770-8585
The Lewis Lead Remover (See LEM Gun Specialties Inc.)
The NgraveR Co., 67 Wawecus Hill Rd., Bozrah, CT 06334 / 860-823-1533
The Ordnance Works, 2969 Pidgeon Point Road, Eureka, CA 95501 / 707-443-3252
The Orvis Co., Rt. 7, Manchester, VT 05254 / 802-362-3622; FAX: 802-362-3525
The Outdoor Connection,Inc., 201 Cotton Dr., P.O. Box 7751, Waco, TX 76714-7751 / 800-533-6076 or 817-772-5575; FAX: 817-776-3553
The Outdoorsman's Bookstore, Llangorse, Brecon, LD3 7UE U.K. / 44-1874-658-660; FAX: 44-1874-658-650
The Park Rifle Co., Ltd., Unit 6a Dartford Trade Park, Power Mill Lane, Dartford DA7 7NX, ENGLAND / 011-0322-222512
The Paul Co., 27385 Pressonville Rd., Wellsville, KS 66092 / 785-883-4444; FAX: 785-883-2525
The Powder Horn, Inc., P.O. Box 114 Patty Drive, Cusseta, GA 31805 / 404-989-3257
The Protector Mfg. Co., Inc., 443 Ashwood Place, Boca Raton, FL 33431 / 407-394-6011
The Robar Co.'s, Inc., 21438 N. 7th Ave., Suite B, Phoenix, AZ 85027 / 602-581-2648; FAX: 602-582-0059
The School of Gunsmithing, 6065 Roswell Rd., Atlanta, GA 30328 / 800-223-4542
The Shooting Gallery, 8070 Southern Blvd., Boardman, OH 44512 / 216-726-7788

The Sight Shop, John G. Lawson, 1802 E. Columbia Ave., Tacoma, WA 98404 / 206-474-5465
The Southern Armory, 25 Millstone Road, Woodlawn, VA 24381 / 703-238-1343; FAX: 703-238-1453
The Surecase Co., 233 Wilshire Blvd., Ste. 900, Santa Monica, CA 90401 / 800-92ARMLOC
The Swampfire Shop (See Peterson Gun Shop, Inc.)
The Walnut Factory, 235 West Rd. No. 1, Portsmouth, NH 03801 / 603-436-2225; FAX: 603-433-7003
The Wilson Arms Co., 63 Leetes Island Rd., Branford, CT 06405 / 203-488-7297; FAX: 203-488-0135
Theis, Terry, HC 63 Box 213, Harper, TX 78631 / 830-864-4438
Theoben Engineering, Stephenson Road, St. Ives Huntingdon, Cambs., PE17 4WJ ENGLAND / 011-0480-461718
Thiewes, George W., 14329 W. Parada Dr., Sun City West, AZ 85375
Things Unlimited, 235 N. Kimbau, Casper, WY 82601 / 307-234-5277
Thirion Gun Engraving, Denise, PO Box 408, Graton, CA 95444 / 707-829-1876
Thomas, Charles C., 2600 S. First St., Springfield, IL 62794 / 217-789-8980; FAX: 217-789-9130
Thompson, Norm, 18905 NW Thurman St., Portland, OR 97209
Thompson Bullet Lube Co., P.O. Box 472343, Garland, TX 75047-2343 / 972-271-8063; FAX: 972-840-6743 thomlube@flash.net www.thompsonbulletlube.com
Thompson Precision, 110 Mary St., P.O. Box 251, Warren, IL 61087 / 815-745-3625
Thompson, Randall. (See HIGHLINE MACHINE CO.)
Thompson Target Technology, 618 Roslyn Ave., SW, Canton, OH 44710 / 216-453-7707; FAX: 216-478-4723
Thompson, Randall (See Highline Machine Co.)
Thompson/Center Arms, P.O. Box 5002, Rochester, NH 03867 / 603-332-2394; FAX: 603-332-5133
3-D Ammunition & Bullets, PO Box 433, Doniphan, NE 68832 / 402-845-2285 or 800-255-6712; FAX: 402-845-6546
3-Ten Corp., P.O. Box 269, Feeding Hills, MA 01030 / 413-789-2086; FAX: 413-789-1549
300 Below Services (See Cryo-Accurizing)
Thunden Ranch, HCR 1, Box 53, Mt. Home, TX 78058 / 830-640-3138
Thunder Mountain Arms, P.O. Box 593, Oak Harbor, WA 98277 / 206-679-4657; FAX: 206-675-1114
Thurston Sports, Inc., RD 3 Donovan Rd., Auburn, NY 13021 / 315-253-0966
Tiger-Hunt Gunstocks, Box 379, Beaverdale, PA 15921 / 814-472-5161 tigerhunt4@aol.com www.gunstockwood.com
Tikka (See U.S. Importer-Stoeger Industries)
Timber Heirloom Products, 618 Roslyn Ave. SW, Canton, OH 44710 / 216-453-7707; FAX: 216-478-4723
Time Precision, Inc., 640 Federal Rd., Brookfield, CT 06804 / 203-775-8343
Tink's Safariland Hunting Corp., P.O. Box 244, 1140 Monticello Rd., Madison, GA 30650 / 706-342-4915; FAX: 706-342-7568
Tinks & Ben Lee Hunting Products (See Wellington Outdoors)
Tioga Engineering Co., Inc., P.O. Box 913, 13 Cone St., Wellsboro, PA 16901 / 717-724-3533; FAX: 717-662-3347
Tippman Pneumatics, Inc., 3518 Adams Center Rd., Fort Wayne, IN 46806 / 219-749-6022; FAX: 219-749-6619
Tirelli, Snc Di Tirelli Primo E.C., Via Matteotti No. 359, Gardone V.T. Brescia, I ITALY / 030-8912819; FAX: 030-832240
TM Stockworks, 6355 Maplecrest Rd., Fort Wayne, IN 46835 / 219-485-5389
TMI Products (See Haselbauer Products, Jerry)
Tom Forrest, Inc., P.O. Box 326, Lakeside, CA 92040 / 619-561-5800; FAX: 619-561-0227
Tom's Gun Repair, Thomas G. Ivanoff, 76-6 Rt. Southfork Rd., Cody, WY 82414 / 307-587-6949
Tom's Gunshop, 3601 Central Ave., Hot Springs, AR 71913 / 501-624-3856
Tombstone Smoke'n' Deals, 3218 East Bell Road, Phoenix, AZ 85032 / 602-905-7013; FAX: 602-443-1998
Tonoloway Tack Drives, HCR 81, Box 100, Needmore, PA 17238
Tooley Custom Rifles, 516 Creek Meadow Dr., Gastonia, NC 28054 / 704-864-7525
Top-Line USA, Inc., 7920-28 Hamilton Ave., Cincinnati, OH 45231 / 513-522-2992 or 800-346-6699; FAX: 513-522-0916

Torel, Inc., 1708 N. South St., P.O. Box 592, Yoakum, TX 77995 / 512-293-2341; FAX: 512-293-3413
TOZ (See U.S. Importer-Nygord Precision Products)
Track of the Wolf, Inc., P.O. Box 6, Osseo, MN 55369-0006 / 612-424-2500; FAX: 612-424-9860
TracStar Industries, Inc., 218 Justin Dr., Cottonwood, AZ 86326 / 520-639-0072; FAX: 520-634-8781
Tradewinds, Inc., P.O. Box 1191, 2339-41 Tacoma Ave. S., Tacoma, WA 98401 / 206-272-4887
Traditions Performance Firearms, P.O. Box 776, 1375 Boston Post Rd., Old Saybrook, CT 06475 / 860-388-4656; FAX: 860-388-4657 trad@ctz.nai.net www.traditionsmuzzle.com
Trafalgar Square, P.O. Box 257, N. Pomfret, VT 05053 / 802-457-1911
Traft Gunshop, P.O. Box 1078, Buena Vista, CO 81211
Trail Visions, 5800 N. Ames Terrace, Glendale, WI 53209 / 414-228-1328
Trammco, 839 Gold Run Rd., Boulder, CO 80302
Trax America, Inc., P.O. Box 898, 1150 Eldridge, Forrest City, AR 72335 / 870-633-0410 or 800-232-2327; FAX: 870-633-4788
Treadlok Gun Safe, Inc., 1764 Granby St. NE, Roanoke, VA 24012 / 800-729-8732 or 703-982-6881; FAX: 703-982-1059
Treemaster, P.O. Box 247, Guntersville, AL 35976 / 205-878-3597
Treso, Inc., P.O. Box 4640, Pagosa Springs, CO 81157 / 303-731-2295
Trevallion Gunstocks, 9 Old Mountain Rd., Cape Neddick, ME 03902 / 207-361-1130
Trico Plastics, 590 S. Vincent Ave., Azusa, CA 91702
Trigger Lock Division/Central Specialties Ltd., 1122 Silver Lake Road, Cary, IL 60013 / 847-639-3900; FAX: 847-639-3972
Trijicon, Inc., 49385 Shafer Ave., P.O. Box 930059, Wixom, MI 48393-0059 / 810-960-7700; FAX: 810-960-7725
Trilux, Inc., P.O. Box 24608, Winston-Salem, NC 27114 / 910-659-9438; FAX: 910-768-7720
Trinidad St. Jr Col Gunsmith Dept, 600 Prospect St., Trinidad, CO 81082 / 719-846-5631; FAX: 719-846-5667
Triple-K Mfg. Co., Inc., 2222 Commercial St., San Diego, CA 92113 / 619-232-2066; FAX: 619-232-7675
Tristar Sporting Arms, Ltd., 1814-16 Linn St., P.O. Box 7496, N. Kansas City, MO 64116 / 816-421-1400; FAX: 816-421-4182
Trius Traps, Inc., P.O. Box 471, 221 S. Miami Ave., Cleves, OH 45002 / 513-941-5682; FAX: 513-941-7970
Trooper Walsh, 2393 N Edgewood St, Arlington, VA 22207
Trophy Bonded Bullets, Inc., 900 S. Loop W., Suite 190, Houston, TX 77054 / 713-645-4499 or 888-308-3006; FAX: 713-741-6393
Trotman, Ken, 135 Ditton Walk, Unit 11, Cambridge, CB5 8PY ENGLAND / 01223-211030; FAX: 01223-212317
Tru-Balance Knife Co., P.O. Box 140555, Grand Rapids, MI 49514 / 616-453-3679
Tru-Square Metal Prods., Inc., 640 First St. SW, P.O. Box 585, Auburn, WA 98071 / 206-833-2310; FAX: 206-833-2349
True Flight Bullet Co., 5581 Roosevelt St., Whitehall, PA 18052 / 610-262-7630; FAX: 610-262-7806
Truglo, Inc, PO Box 1612, McKinna, TX 75070 / 972-774-0300 FAX: 972-774-0323 www.truglosights.com
Trulock Tool, Broad St., Whigham, GA 31797 / 912-762-4678
TTM, 1550 Solomon Rd., Santa Maria, CA 93455 / 805-934-1281
Tucker, James C., P.O. Box 1212, Paso Robles, CA 93447-1212
Tucson Mold, Inc., 930 S. Plumer Ave., Tucson, AZ 85719 / 520-792-1075; FAX: 520-792-1075
Turkish Firearms Corp., 522 W. Maple St., Allentown, PA 18101 / 610-821-8660; FAX: 610-821-9049
Turnbull Restoration, Doug, 6680 Rt 58 & 20 Dept. SM 2000, PO Box 471, Bloomfield, NY 14469 / 716-657-6338
Tuttle, Dale, 4046 Russell Rd., Muskegon, MI 49445 / 616-766-2250
Tyler Manufacturing & Distributing, 3804 S. Eastern, Oklahoma City, OK 73129 / 405-677-1487 or 800-654-8415

348 • GUNS ILLUSTRATED

MANUFACTURERS DIRECTORY

U

U.S. Fire-Arms Mfg. Co. Inc., 55 Van Dyke Ave., Hartford, CT 06106 / 877-227-6901; FAX: 860-724-6809 sales @ us-firearms.com; www.usfirearms.com
U.S. Importer-Wm. Larkin Moore, 8430 E. Raintree Ste. B-7, Scottsdale, AZ 85260
U.S. Repeating Arms Co., Inc., 275 Winchester Ave., Morgan, UT 84050-9333 / 801-876-3440; FAX: 801-876-3737
U.S. Tactical Systems (See Keng's Firearms Specialty)
U.S.A. Magazines, Inc., P.O. Box 39115, Downey, CA 90241 / 800-872-2577
Uberti, Aldo, Casella Postale 43, I-25063 Gardone V.T., ITALY
Uberti USA, Inc., P.O. Box 469, Lakeville, CT 06039 / 860-435-8068; FAX: 860-435-8146
UFA, Inc., 6927 E. Grandview Dr., Scottsdale, AZ 85254 / 800-616-2776
Ugartechea S. A., Ignacio, Chonta 26, Eibar, SPAIN / 43-121257; FAX: 43-121669
Ultimate Accuracy, 121 John Shelton Rd., Jacksonville, AR 72076 / 501-985-2530
Ultra Dot Distribution, 2316 N.E. 8th Rd., Ocala, FL 34470
Ultra Light Arms, Inc., P.O. Box 1270, 214 Price St., Granville, WV 26505 / 304-599-5687; FAX: 304-599-5687
Ultralux (See U.S. Importer-Keng's Firearms Specia
UltraSport Arms, Inc., 1955 Norwood Ct., Racine, WI 53403 / 414-554-3237; FAX: 414-554-9731
Uncle Bud's, HCR 81, Box 100, Needmore, PA 17238 / 717-294-6000; FAX: 717-294-6005
Uncle Mike's (See Michaels of Oregon Co)
Unertl Optical Co. Inc., John, 308 Clay Ave, PO Box 818, Mars, PA 16046-0818 / 412-625-3810
Unique/M.A.P.F., 10 Les Allees, 64700, Hendaye, FRANCE / 33-59 20 71 93
UniTec, 1250 Bedford SW, Canton, OH 44710 / 216-452-4017
United Binocular Co., 9043 S. Western Ave., Chicago, IL 60620
United Cutlery Corp., 1425 United Blvd., Sevierville, TN 37876 / 865-428-2532 or 800-548-0835 FAX: 865-428-2267
United States Optics Technologies, Inc., 5900 Dale St., Buena Park, CA 90621 / 714-994-4901; FAX: 714-994-4904
United States Products Co., 518 Melwood Ave., Pittsburgh, PA 15213 / 412-621-2130; FAX: 412-621-8740
Universal Sports, P.O. Box 532, Vincennes, IN 47591 / 812-882-8680; FAX: 812-882-8680
Unmussig Bullets, D. L., 7862 Brentford Dr., Richmond, VA 23225 / 804-320-1165
Upper Missouri Trading Co., 304 Harold St., Crofton, NE 68730 / 402-388-4844
USAC, 4500-15th St. East, Tacoma, WA 98424 / 206-922-7589
Utica Cutlery Co., 820 Noyes St., Utica, NY 13503 / 315-733-4663; FAX: 315-733-6602

V

V.H. Blackinton & Co., Inc., 221 John L. Dietsch, Attleboro Falls, MA 02763-0300 / 508-699-4436; FAX: 508-695-5349
Valade Engraving, Robert, 931 3rd Ave, Seaside, OR 97138 / 503-738-7672
Valor Corp., 5555 NW 36th Ave., Miami, FL 33142 / 305-633-0127; FAX: 305-634-4536
Valtro USA, Inc, 1281 Andersen Dr., San Rafael, CA 94901 / 415-256-2575; FAX: 415-256-2576
VAM Distribution Co LLC, 1141-B Mechanicsburg Rd, Wooster, OH 44691 www.rex10.com
Van Gorden & Son Inc., C. S., 1815 Main St., Bloomer, WI 54724 / 715-568-2612
Van Horn, Gil, P.O. Box 207, Llano, CA 93544
Van Patten, J. W., P.O. Box 145, Foster Hill, Milford, PA 18337 / 717-296-7069
Van's Gunsmith Service, 224 Route 69-A, Parish, NY 13131 / 315-625-7251
Vancini, Carl (See Bestload, Inc.)
Vann Custom Bullets, 330 Grandview Ave., Novato, CA 94947
Varmint Masters, LLC, Rick Vecqueray, PO Box 6724, Bend, OR 97708 / 541-318-7306; FAX: 541-318-7306 varmintmasters@bendnet.com
Vecqueray, Rick. (See VARMINT MASTERS, LLC)
Vega Tool Co., c/o T.R. Ross, 4865 Tanglewood Ct., Boulder, CO 80301 / 303-530-0174
Vektor USA, Mikael Danforth, 5139 Stanart St, Norfolk, VA 23502 / 888-740-0837; or 757-455-8895; FAX: 757-461-9155
Venco Industries, Inc. (See Shooter's Choice)
Venus Industries, P.O. Box 246, Sialkot-1, PAKISTAN FAX: 92 432 85579
Verney-Carron, B.P. 72, 54 Boulevard Thiers, 42002, FRANCE / 33-477791500; FAX: 33-477790702
Vest, John, P.O. Box 1552, Susanville, CA 96130 / 916-257-7228
Vibra-Tek Co., 1844 Arroya Rd., Colorado Springs, CO 80906 / 719-634-8611; FAX: 719-634-6886
VibraShine, Inc., P.O. Box 577, Taylorsville, MS 39168 / 601-785-9854; FAX: 601-785-9874
Vic's Gun Refinishing, 6 Pineview Dr., Dover, NH 03820-6422 / 603-742-0013
Victory Ammunition, PO Box 1022, Milford, PA 18337 / 717-296-5768; FAX: 717-296-9298
Victory USA, P.O. Box 1021, Pine Bush, NY 12566 / 914-744-2060; FAX: 914-744-5181
Vihtavuori Oy, FIN-41330 Vihtavuori, FINLAND, / 358-41-3779211; FAX: 358-41-3771643
Vihtavuori Oy/Kaltron-Pettibone, 1241 Ellis St., Bensenville, IL 60106 / 708-350-1116; FAX: 708-350-1606
Viking Video Productions, P.O. Box 251, Roseburg, OR 97470
Vincent's Shop, 210 Antoinette, Fairbanks, AK 99701
Vincenzo Bernardelli S.p.A., 125 Via Matteotti, P.O. Box 74, Gardone V.T., Bresci, 25063 ITALY / 39-30-8912851-2-3; FAX: 39-30-8910249+
Vintage Arms, Inc., 6003 Saddle Horse, Fairfax, VA 22030 / 703-968-0779; FAX: 703-968-0780
Vintage Industries, Inc., 781 Big Tree Dr., Longwood, FL 32750 / 407-831-8949; FAX: 407-831-5346
Viper Bullet and Brass Works, 11 Brock St., Box 582, Norwich, ON N0J 1P0 CANADA
Viramontez, Ray, 601 Springfield Dr., Albany, GA 31707 / 912-432-9683
Virgin Valley Custom Guns, 450 E 800 N #20, Hurricane, UT 84737 / 435-635-8941; FAX: 435-635-8943 vvc-guns@infowest.com www.virginvalleyguns.com
Visible Impact Targets, Rts. 5 & 20, E. Bloomfield, NY 14443 / 716-657-6161; FAX: 716-657-5405
Vitt/Boos, 2178 Nichols Ave., Stratford, CT 06614 / 203-375-6859
Voere-KGH m.b.H., P.O. Box 416, A-6333 Kufstein, Tirol, AUSTRIA / 0043-5372-62547; FAX: 0043-5372-65752
Volquartsen Custom Ltd., 24276 240th Street, P.O. Box 397, Carroll, IA 51401 / 712-792-4238; FAX: 712-792-2542
Vom Hoffe (See Old Western Scrounger, Inc., The), 12924 Hwy A-12, Montague, CA 96064 / 916-459-5445; FAX: 916-459-3944
Vorhes, David, 3042 Beecham St., Napa, CA 94558 / 707-226-9116
Vortek Products, Inc., P.O. Box 871181, Canton, MI 48187-6181 / 313-397-5656; FAX: 313-397-5656
VSP Publishers (See Heritage/VSP Gun Books), PO Box 887, McCall, ID 83638 / 208-634-4104; FAX: 208-634-3101
Vulpes Ventures, Inc. Fox Cartridge Division, P.O. Box 1363, Bolingbrook, IL 60440-7363 / 630-759-1229; FAX: 815-439-3945

W

W. Square Enterprises, 9826 Sagedale, Houston, TX 77089 / 713-484-0935; FAX: 281-484-0935
W. Square Enterprises, Load From A Disk, 9826 Sagedale, Houston, TX 77089 / 713-484-0935; FAX: 281-484-0935
W. Waller & Son, Inc., 2221 Stoney Brook Rd., Grantham, NH 03753-7706 / 603-863-4177
W.B. Niemi Engineering, Box 126 Center Road, Greensboro, VT 05841 / 802-533-7180 or 802-533-7141
W.C. Strutz Rifle Barrels, Inc., P.O. Box 611, Eagle River, WI 54521 / 715-479-4766
W.C. Wolff Co., PO Box 458, Newtown Square, PA 19073 / 610-359-9600; FAX: 610-359-9496
W.E. Birdsong & Assoc., 1435 Monterey Rd., Florence, MS 39073-9748 / 601-366-8270
W.E. Brownell Checkering Tools, 9390 Twin Mountain Cir, San Diego, CA 92126 / 619-695-2479; FAX: 619-695-2479
W.J. Riebe Co., 3434 Tucker Rd., Boise, ID 83703
W.R. Case & Sons Cutlery Co., Owens Way, Bradford, PA 16701 / 814-368-4123 or 800-523-6350; FAX: 814-768-5369
Wagoner, Vernon G., 2325 E. Encanto, Mesa, AZ 85213 / 602-835-1307
Wakina by Pic, 24813 Alderbrook Dr., Santa Clarita, CA 91321 / 800-295-8194
Waldron, Herman, Box 475, 80 N. 17th St., Pomeroy, WA 99347 / 509-843-1404
Walker Arms Co., Inc., 499 County Rd. 820, Selma, AL 36701 / 334-872-6231; FAX: 334-872-6262
Walker Mfg., Inc., 8296 S. Channel, Harsen's Island, MI 48028
Wallace, Terry, 385 San Marino, Vallejo, CA 94589 / 707-642-7041
Walls Industries, Inc., P.O. Box 98, 1905 N. Main, Cleburne, TX 76031 / 817-645-4366; FAX: 817-645-7946
Walt's Custom Leather, Walt Whinnery, 1947 Meadow Creek Dr., Louisville, KY 40218 / 502-458-4361
Walters, John, 500 N. Avery Dr., Moore, OK 73160 / 405-799-0376
Walters Industries, 6226 Park Lane, Dallas, TX 75225 / 214-691-6973
Walther GmbH, Carl, B.P. 4325, D-89033 Ulm, GERMANY
WAMCO, Inc., Mingo Loop, P.O. Box 337, Oquossoc, ME 04964-0337 / 207-864-3344
WAMCO--New Mexico, P.O. Box 205, Peralta, NM 87042-0205 / 505-869-0826
Ward & Van Valkenburg, 114 32nd Ave. N., Fargo, ND 58102 / 701-232-2351
Ward Machine, 5620 Lexington Rd., Corpus Christi, TX 78412 / 512-992-1221
Wardell Precision Handguns Ltd., 48851 N. Fig Springs Rd., New River, AZ 85027-8513 / 602-465-7995
Warenski, Julie, 590 E. 500 N., Richfield, UT 84701 / 801-896-5319; FAX: 801-896-5319
Warne Manufacturing Co., 9039 SE Jannsen Rd., Clackamas, OR 97015 / 503-657-5590 or 800-683-5590; FAX: 503-657-5695
Warren & Sweat Mfg. Co., P.O. Box 350440, Grand Island, FL 32784 / 904-669-3166; FAX: 904-669-7272
Warren Muzzleloading Co., Inc., Hwy. 21 North, P.O. Box 100, Ozone, AR 72854 / 501-292-3268
Warren, Kenneth W. (See Mountain States Engraving)
Washita Mountain Whetstone Co., P.O. Box 378, Lake Hamilton, AR 71951 / 501-525-3914
Wasmundt, Jim, P.O. Box 511, Fossil, OR 97830
WASP Shooting Systems, Rt. 1, Box 147, Lakeview, AR 72642 / 501-431-5606
Waterfield Sports, Inc., 13611 Country Lane, Burnsville, MN 55337 / 612-435-8339
Watson Bros., 39 Redcross Way, London Bridge, LONDON U.K. FAX: 44-171-403-336
Watson Trophy Match Bullets, 2404 Wade Hampton Blvd., Greenville, SC 29615 / 864-244-7948 or 941-635-7948
Wayne E. Schwartz Custom Guns, 970 E. Britton Rd., Morrice, MI 48857 / 517-625-4079
Wayne Firearms for Collectors and Investors, James, 2608 N. Laurent, Victoria, TX 77901 / 512-578-1258; FAX: 512-578-3559
Wayne Reno, 2808 Stagestop Rd., Jefferson, CO 80456 / 719-836-3452
Wayne Specialty Services, 260 Waterford Drive, Florissant, MO 63033 / 413-831-7083
WD-40 Co., 1061 Cudahy Pl., San Diego, CA 92110 / 619-275-1400; FAX: 619-275-5823
Weatherby, Inc., 3100 El Camino Real, Atascadero, CA 93422 / 805-466-1767 or 800-227-2016; FAX: 805-466-2527
Weaver Arms Corp. Gun Shop, RR 3, P.O. Box 266, Bloomfield, MO 63825-9528
Weaver Products, P.O. Box 39, Onalaska, WI 54650 / 800-648-9624 or 608-781-5800; FAX: 608-781-0368
Weaver Scope Repair Service, 1121 Larry Mahan Dr., Suite B, El Paso, TX 79925 / 915-593-1005
Webb, Bill, 6504 North Bellefontaine, Kansas City, MO 64119 / 816-453-7431
Weber & Markin Custom Gunsmiths, 4-1691 Powick Rd., Kelowna, BC V1X 4L1 CANADA / 250-762-7575; FAX: 250-861-3655
Weber Jr., Rudolf, P.O. Box 160106, D-5650, GERMANY / 0212-592136
Webley and Scott Ltd., Frankley Industrial Park, Tay Rd., Birmingham, B45 0PA ENGLAND / 011-021-453-1864; FAX: 021-457-7846
Webster Scale Mfg. Co., P.O. Box 188, Sebring, FL 33870 / 813-385-6362

MANUFACTURERS DIRECTORY

Weems, Cecil, 510 W Hubbard St, Mineral Wells, TX 76067-4847 / 817-325-1462
Weigand Combat Handguns, Inc., 685 South Main Rd., Mountain Top, PA 18707 / 570-868-8358; FAX: 570-868-5218 sales@jackweigand.com www.jackweigand.com
Weihrauch KG, Hermann, Industriestrasse 11, 8744 Mellrichstadt, Mellrichstadt, GERMANY
Weisz Parts, P.O. Box 20038, Columbus, OH 43220-0038 / 614-45-70-500; FAX: 614-846-8585
Welch, Sam, CVSR 2110, Moab, UT 84532 / 801-259-8131
Wellington Outdoors, P.O. Box 244, 1140 Monticello Rd., Madison, GA 30650 / 706-342-4915; FAX: 706-342-7568
Wells, Rachel, 110 N. Summit St., Prescott, AZ 86301 / 520-445-3655
Wells Creek Knife & Gun Works, 32956 State Hwy. 38, Scottsburg, OR 97473 / 541-587-4202; FAX: 541-587-4223
Welsh, Bud, 80 New Road, E. Amherst, NY 14051 / 716-688-6344
Wenger North America/Precise Int'l, 15 Corporate Dr., Orangeburg, NY 10962 / 800-431-2996 FAX: 914-425-4700
Wenig Custom Gunstocks, 103 N. Market St., P.O. Box 249, Lincoln, MO 65338 / 816-547-3334; FAX: 816-547-2881 gunstock@wenig.com www.wenig.com
Werth, T. W., 1203 Woodlawn Rd., Lincoln, IL 62656 / 217-732-1300
Wescombe, Bill (See North Star West)
Wessinger Custom Guns & Engraving, 268 Limestone Rd., Chapin, SC 29036 / 803-345-5677
West, Jack L., 1220 W. Fifth, P.O. Box 427, Arlington, OR 97812
Western Cutlery (See Camillus Cutlery Co.)
Western Design (See Alpha Gunsmith Division)
Western Gunstock Mfg. Co., 550 Valencia School Rd., Aptos, CA 95003 / 408-688-5884
Western Missouri Shooters Alliance, P.O. Box 11144, Kansas City, MO 64119 / 816-597-3950; FAX: 816-229-7350
Western Nevada West Coast Bullets, PO BOX 2270, DAYTON, NV 89403-2270 / 702-246-3941; FAX: 702-246-0836
Westley Richards & Co., 40 Grange Rd., Birmingham, ENGLAND / 010-214722953
Westley Richards Agency USA (See U.S. Importer for Westley Richards & Co.,)
Westrom, John (See Precision Metal Finishing)
Westwind Rifles, Inc., David S. Sullivan, P.O. Box 261, 640 Briggs St., Erie, CO 80516 / 303-828-3823
Weyer International, 2740 Nebraska Ave., Toledo, OH 43607 / 419-534-2020; FAX: 419-534-2697
Whildin & Sons Ltd, E.H., RR 2 Box 119, Tamaqua, PA 18252 / 717-668-6743; FAX: 717-668-6745
Whinnery, Walt (See Walt's Custom Leather)
Whiscombe (See U.S. Importer-Pelaire Products)
White Barn Workshop, 431 County Road, Broadlands, IL 61816
White Flyer Targets, 124 River Road, Middlesex, NJ 08846 / 908-469-0100 or 602-972-7528 FAX: 908-469-9692
White Owl Enterprises, 2583 Flag Rd., Abilene, KS 67410 / 913-263-2613; FAX: 913-263-2613
White Pine Photographic Services, Hwy. 60, General Delivery, Wilno, ON K0J 2N0 CANADA / 613-756-3452
White Rock Tool & Die, 6400 N. Brighton Ave., Kansas City, MO 64119 / 816-454-0478
White Shooting Systems, Inc. (See White Muzzleloading)
Whitestone Lumber Corp., 148-02 14th Ave., Whitestone, NY 11357 / 718-746-4400; FAX: 718-767-1748
Whitetail Design & Engineering Ltd., 9421 E. Mannsiding Rd., Clare, MI 48617 / 517-386-3932
Wichita Arms, Inc., 923 E. Gilbert, P.O. Box 11371, Wichita, KS 67211 / 316-265-0661; FAX: 316-265-0760
Wick, David E., 1504 Michigan Ave., Columbus, IN 47201 / 812-376-6960
Widener's Reloading & Shooting Supply, Inc., P.O. Box 3009 CRS, Johnson City, TN 37602 / 615-282-6786; FAX: 615-282-6651
Wideview Scope Mount Corp., 13535 S. Hwy. 16, Rapid City, SD 57701 / 605-341-3220; FAX: 605-341-9142 wvdon@rapidnet.com
Wiebe, Duane, 846 Holly WYA, Placerville, CA 95667-3415
Wiest, M. C., 10737 Dutchtown Rd., Knoxville, TN 37932 / 423-966-4545
Wilcox All-Pro Tools & Supply, 4880 147th St., Montezuma, IA 50171 / 515-623-3138; FAX: 515-623-3104
Wilcox Industries Corp, Robert F Guarasi, 53 Durham St, Portsmouth, NH 03801 / 603-431-1331; FAX: 603-431-1221
Wild Bill's Originals, P.O. Box 13037, Burton, WA 98013 / 206-463-5738; FAX: 206-465-5925
Wild West Guns, 7521 Old Seward Hwy, Unit A, Anchorage, AK 99518 / 800-992-4570 or 907-344-4500; FAX: 907-344-4005
Wilderness Sound Products Ltd., 4015 Main St. A, Springfield, OR 97478 / 503-741-0263 or 800-437-0006; FAX: 503-741-7648
Wildey, Inc., 45 Angevine Rd, Warren, CT 06754-1818 / 203-355-9000; FAX: 203-354-7759
Wildlife Research Center, Inc., 1050 McKinley St., Anoka, MN 55303 / 612-427-3350 or 800-USE-LURE; FAX: 612-427-8354
Wilhelm Brenneke KG, Ilmenauweg 2, 30851, Langenhagen, GERMANY / 0511/97262-0; FAX: 0511/97262-62
Will-Burt Co., 169 S. Main, Orrville, OH 44667
William Fagan & Co., 22952 15 Mile Rd., Clinton Township, MI 48035 / 810-465-4637; FAX: 810-792-6996
William Powell & Son (Gunmakers) Ltd., 35-37 Carrs Lane, Birmingham, B4 7SX ENGLAND / 121-643-0689; FAX: 121-631-3504
William Powell Agency, 22 Circle Dr., Bellmore, NY 11710 / 516-679-1158
Williams Gun Sight Co., 7389 Lapeer Rd., Box 329, Davison, MI 48423 / 810-653-2131 or 800-530-9028; FAX: 810-658-2140 williamsgunsight.com
Williams Mfg. of Oregon, 110 East B St., Drain, OR 97435 / 503-836-7461; FAX: 503-836-7245
Williams Shootin' Iron Service, The Lynx-Line, Rt 2 Box 223A, Mountain Grove, MO 65711 / 417-948-0902 FAX: 417-948-0902
Williamson Precision Gunsmithing, 117 W. Pipeline, Hurst, TX 76053 / 817-285-0064; FAX: 817-280-0044
Willow Bend, P.O. Box 203, Chelmsford, MA 01824 / 978-256-8508; FAX: 978-256-8508
Willson Safety Prods. Div., PO Box 622, Reading, PA 19603-0622 / 610-376-6161; FAX: 610-371-7725
Wilson Case, Inc., P.O. Box 1106, Hastings, NE 68902-1106 / 800-322-5493; FAX: 402-463-5276 sales@wilson-case.com www.wilsoncase.com
Wilson Gun Shop, 2234 County Road 719, Berryville, AR 72616 / 870-545-3618; FAX: 870-545-3310
Winchester Div. Olin Corp., 427 N. Shamrock, E. Alton, IL 62024 / 618-258-3566; FAX: 618-258-3599
Winchester Press (See New Win Publishing, Inc.), 186 Center St, Clinton, NJ 08809 / 908-735-9701; FAX: 908-735-9703
Winchester Sutler, Inc., The, 270 Shadow Brook Lane, Winchester, VA 22603 / 540-888-3595; FAX: 540-888-4632
Windish, Jim, 2510 Dawn Dr., Alexandria, VA 22306 / 703-765-1994
Windjammer Tournament Wads Inc., 750 W. Hampden Ave., Suite 170, Englewood, CO 80110 / 303-781-6329
Wingshooting Adventures, 0-1845 W. Leonard, Grand Rapids, MI 49544 / 616-677-1980; FAX: 616-677-1986
Winkle Bullets, R.R. 1, Box 316, Heyworth, IL 61745
Winter, Robert M., P.O. Box 484, 42975-287th St., Menno, SD 57045 / 605-387-5322
Wise Custom Guns, 1402 Blanco Rd, San Antonio, TX 78212-2716 / 210-828-3388
Wise Guns, Dale, 333 W Olmos Dr, San Antonio, TX 78212 / 210-828-3388
Wiseman and Co., Bill, PO Box 3427, Bryan, TX 77805 / 409-690-3456; FAX: 409-690-0156
Wisners Inc/Twin Pine Armory, P.O. Box 58, Hwy. 6, Adna, WA 98522 / 360-748-4590; FAX: 360-748-1802
Wolf (See J.R. Distributing)
Wolf's Western Traders, 40 E. Works, No. 3F, Sheridan, WY 82801 / 307-674-5352 patwolf@wavecom.net
Wolfe Publishing Co., 6471 Airpark Dr., Prescott, AZ 86301 / 520-445-7810 or 800-899-7810; FAX: 520-778-5124
Wolverine Footwear Group, 9341 Courtland Dr. NE, Rockford, MI 49351 / 616-866-5500; FAX: 616-866-5658
Wood, Mel, P.O. Box 1255, Sierra Vista, AZ 85636 / 602-455-5541
Wood, Frank (See Classic Guns, Inc.), 3230 Medlock Bridge Rd, Ste 110, Norcross, GA 30092 / 404-242-7944
Woodleigh (See Huntington Die Specialties)
Woods Wise Products, P.O. Box 681552, 2200 Bowman Rd., Franklin, TN 37068 / 800-735-8182; FAX: 615-726-2637
Woodstream, P.O. Box 327, Lititz, PA 17543 / 717-626-2125 FAX: 717-626-1912
Woodworker's Supply, 1108 North Glenn Rd., Casper, WY 82601 / 307-237-5354
Woolrich, Inc., Mill St., Woolrich, PA 17701 / 800-995-1299; FAX: 717-769-6234/6259
Working Guns, Jim Coffin, 1224 NW Fernwood Cir, Corvallis, OR 97330-2909 / 541-928-4391
World Class Airguns, 2736 Morningstar Dr., Indianapolis, IN 46229 / 317-897-5548
World of Targets (See Birchwood Casey)
World Trek, Inc., 7170 Turkey Creek Rd., Pueblo, CO 81007-1046 / 719-546-2121; FAX: 719-543-6886
Worthy Products, Inc., RR 1, P.O. Box 213, Martville, NY 13111 / 315-324-5298
Wosenitz VHP, Inc., Box 741, Dania, FL 33004 / 305-923-3748; FAX: 305-925-2217
Wostenholm (See Ibberson [Sheffield] Ltd., George)
Wright's Hardwood Gunstock Blanks, 8540 SE Kane Rd., Gresham, OR 97080 / 503-666-1705
WTA Manufacturing, P.O. Box 164, Kit Carson, CO 80825 / 800-700-3054; FAX: 719-962-3570
Wyant Bullets, Gen. Del., Swan Lake, MT 59911
Wyant's Outdoor Products, Inc., P.O. Box 9, Broadway, VA 22815
Wyoming Bonded Bullets, Box 91, Sheridan, WY 82801 / 307-674-8091
Wyoming Custom Bullets, 1626 21st St., Cody, WY 82414
Wyoming Knife Corp., 101 Commerce Dr., Ft. Collins, CO 80524 / 303-224-3454

X

X-Spand Target Systems, 26-10th St. SE, Medicine Hat, AB T1A 1P7 CANADA / 403-526-7997; FAX: 403-528-2362

Y

Yankee Gunsmith, 2901 Deer Flat Dr., Copperas Cove, TX 76522 / 817-547-8433
Yavapai College, 1100 E. Sheldon St., Prescott, AZ 86301 / 520-776-2353 FAX: 520-776-2355
Yavapai Firearms Academy Ltd., P.O. Box 27290, Prescott Valley, AZ 86312 / 520-772-8262
Yearout, Lewis E. (See Montana Outfitters), 308 Riverview Dr E, Great Falls, MT 59404 / 406-761-0859
Yee, Mike, 29927 56 Pl. S., Auburn, WA 98001 / 206-839-3991
Yellowstone Wilderness Supply, P.O. Box 129, W. Yellowstone, MT 59758 / 406-646-7613
Yesteryear Armory & Supply, P.O. Box 408, Carthage, TN 37030
York M-1 Conversions, 803 Mill Creek Run, Plantersville, TX 77363 / 800-527-2881 or 713-477-8442
Young Country Arms, William, 1409 Kuehner Dr #13, Simi Valley, CA 93063-4478
Yukon Arms Classic Ammunition, 1916 Brooks, P.O. Box 223, Missoula, MT 59801 / 406-543-9614

Z

Z's Metal Targets & Frames, P.O. Box 78, South Newbury, NH 03255 / 603-938-2826
Z-M Weapons, 203 South St., Bernardston, MA 01337 / 413-648-9501; FAX: 413-648-0219
Zabala Hermanos S.A., P.O. Box 97, Eibar, 20600 SPAIN / 43-768085 or 43-768076; FAX: 34-43-768201
Zander's Sporting Goods, 7525 Hwy 154 West, Baldwin, IL 62217-9706 / 800-851-4373 FAX: 618-785-2320
Zanoletti, Pietro, Via Monte Gugielpo, 4, I-25063 Gardone V.T., ITALY
Zanotti Armor, Inc., 123 W. Lone Tree Rd., Cedar Falls, IA 50613 / 319-232-9650
ZDF Import Export, Inc., 2975 South 300 West, Salt Lake City, UT 84115 / 801-485-1012; FAX: 801-484-4363
Zeeryp, Russ, 1601 Foard Dr., Lynn Ross Manor, Morristown, TN 37814 / 615-586-2357
Zero Ammunition Co., Inc., 1601 22nd St. SE, P.O. Box 1188, Cullman, AL 35056-1188 / 800-545-9376; FAX: 205-739-4683
Ziegel Engineering, 2108 Lomina Ave., Long Beach, CA 90815 / 562-596-9481; FAX: 562-598-4734 ziegel@aol.com www.ziegelerg.com
Zim's, Inc., 4370 S. 3rd West, Salt Lake City, UT 84107 / 801-268-2505
Zoli, Antonio, Via Zanardelli 39, Casier Postal 21, I-25063 Gardone V.T., ITALY
Zriny's Metal Targets (See Z's Metal Targets & Frames)
Zufall, Joseph F., P.O. Box 304, Golden, CO 80402-0304

Up-To-Date References From DBI Books

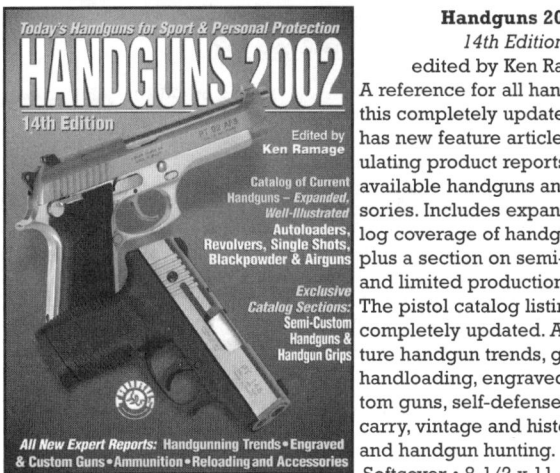

Handguns 2002
14th Edition
edited by Ken Ramage
A reference for all handgun fans, this completely updated edition has new feature articles and stimulating product reports on today's available handguns and accessories. Includes expanded catalog coverage of handgun grips plus a section on semi-custom and limited production handguns. The pistol catalog listings are completely updated. Articles feature handgun trends, gun tests, handloading, engraved and custom guns, self-defense, concealed carry, vintage and historic arms and handgun hunting.
Softcover • 8-1/2 x 11 • 320 pages
500+ b&w photos
Item# H2002 • $22.95

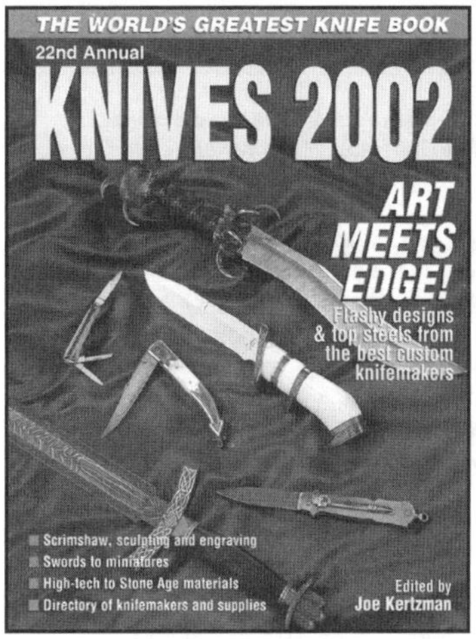

Knives 2002
22nd Edition
edited by Joe Kertzman
This 22nd annual edition is a showcase of stunning photos, completely updated directories and invaluable information regarding trends, state-of-the-art knives, services, supplies, knifemakers and dealers. Only the best knifemakers are found here. Join them as they explain their creative processes for scrimshaw, stonework, damascus blades, sheaths and much more.
Softcover • 8-1/2 x 11 • 304 pages
1,200 b&w photos
Item# KN2002 • $22.95

Gun Digest® 2002
The World's Greatest Gun Book, 56th Annual Edition
edited by Ken Ramage
Keep up-to-date on the latest collecting and accessory information the gun industry offers. This 56th edition showcases a new full-color section on engraved and custom guns, all-new feature articles, fresh new product reports and a completely updated catalog and reference section. Don't miss the expanded and updated Directory of the Arms Trade including directories of products, services and manufacturers.
Softcover • 8-1/2 x 11 • 560 pages
2,000 b&w photos
16-page color section
Item# GD2002 • $27.95

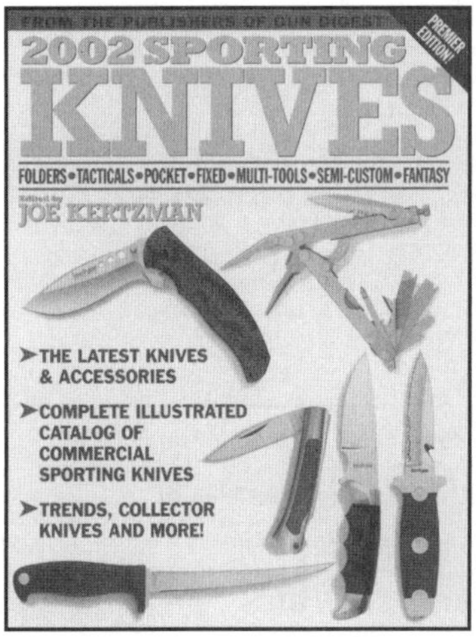

The Gun Digest® Book of Modern Gun Values
11th Edition
edited by Ken Ramage
Identify, evaluate and price any of the commonly encountered firearms made from 1900 to present. This specialized, heavily illustrated, expanded edition helps you easily identify and value older firearms found in gun shops, auctions, advertisements- or that old family gun you've just inherited. More than 7,500 post-1900 models are gathered by type then listed alphabetically. All prices are fully updated to mid-year. Includes more photos, and new sections covering mechanical inspection and (full-color) condition evaluation. New reference section lists books and associations for collectors.
Softcover • 8-1/2 x 11 • 640 pages • 3,000+ b&w photos
Item# MGV11 • $24.95

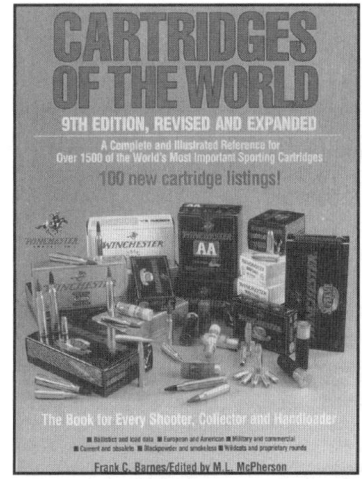

2002 Sporting Knives
edited by Joe Kertzman
This brand-new, heavily illustrated book provides complete coverage of today's sporting cutlery: folders & fixed designs, tactical, semi-custom, multi-tools, swords & fantasy designs and accessories. Read about the latest designs; view the current offerings of the sporting cutlery industry through the heavily illustrated pages of the comprehensive catalog section. Need more information? The reference section includes a complete directory of companies; the Library of Sporting Cutlery & Edged Weapons; periodical publications and a directory of collectors associations.
Softcover • 8-1/2 x 11 • 256 pages
700 b&w photos
Item# DGK01 • $21.95

Cartridges of the World
9th Edition, Revised and Expanded
by Frank C. Barnes,
Edited by M. L. McPherson
Whether you are searching for information on an obsolete cartridge or a new wildcat, a black powder round or a smokeless variety, you will find it here. Tables identify cartridges by measurement and offer ballistics and loading data. Learn the history of 1,500+ American and European cartridges in this single volume.
Softcover • 8-1/2 x 11 • 512 pages
627 b&w photos
Item# COW9 • $27.95

To place a credit card order or for a FREE all-product catalog call
800-258-0929 Offer GNB1

M-F 7am - 8pm • Sat 8am - 2pm, CST

Krause Publications, Offer GNB1
P.O. Box 5009, Iola WI 54945-5009
www.krausebooks.com

DBI BOOKS
a division of Krause Publications, Inc.

Shipping & Handling: $4.00 first book, $2.00 each additional.
Non-US addresses $20.95 first book, $5.95 each additional.
Sales Tax: CA, IA, IL, PA, TN, VA, WI residents please add appropriate sales tax.
Satisfaction Guarantee: If for any reason you are not completely satisfied with your purchase, simply return it within 14 days of receipt and receive a full refund, less shipping charges.

More Superior References from the Leader in Hobby Publishing

2001 Standard Catalog of® Firearms
The Collector's Price & Reference Guide, 11th Edition
by Ned Schwing
80,000 real-world prices on more than 12,000 different firearms and 6,000 photos make this new edition of the *Standard Catalog of® Firearms* the best buy in gun books. Whether you're a hunter, shooter, collector or just a gun enthusiast, you'll be astounded with the wealth of firearms information, history and knowledge that you can find to enjoy your hobby more. Cross-referenced for simple use, you'll be able to find any gun made by any manufacturer from early 1800s to present.
Softcover • 8-1/4 x 10-7/8 • 1,344 pages
6,000 b&w photos • 16-page color section, 40 color photos
Item# GG11 • $32.95

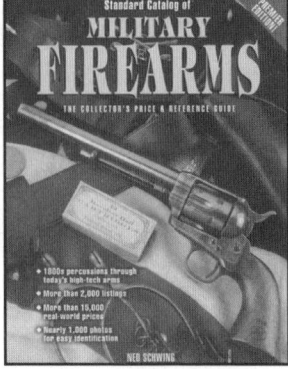

Standard Catalog of® Military Firearms
The Collector's Price & Reference Guide
by Ned Schwing
From the author of the *"Standard Catalog of® Firearms"* comes this completely illustrated catalog of every known military firearm from the 1870s to the latest sniper rifles available to collectors, including handguns, rifles, shotguns, submachine guns, and machine guns up to 55 caliber. You'll be able to place values on your guns and learn about their historical significance. More than 2,000 firearms are evaluated in up to six grades of condition, and up to nine grades for Class 3 firearms.
Softcover • 8-1/2 x 11 • 352 pages
1,000 b&w photos
Item# SMF1 • $24.95

Flayderman's Guide to Antique American Firearms and Their Values
The Complete Handbook of Antique American Gun Collecting, 8th Edition
by Norm Flayderman
Norm Flayderman is today's foremost authority on U.S. antique arms history. His book is the bible for antique American arms and a must-have historical reference and price guide for collectors, shooters, and hunters. Identify and evaluate market prices for more than 4,000 firearms manufactured between 1850 and 1900. This edition includes more expanded histories of individual firearms than the previous edition.
Softcover • 8-1/2 x 11 • 672 pages
1,700+ b&w photos
Item# FLA8 • $34.95

Gunsmithing: Shotguns
by Patrick Sweeney
Have you ever wanted to repair or upgrade your shotgun? Professional gunsmith Patrick Sweeney has all the answers in the third book of his popular gunsmithing series: *Gunsmithing: Shotguns*. You'll be given detailed step-by-step instructions on dozens of projects from repairing a broken stock to restoring an antique gun for Cowboy Action Shooting.
Softcover • 8-1/2 x 11 • 328 pages
750 b&w photos
Item# GSHOT • $24.95

The Gun Digest® Book of Assault Weapons
5th Edition
by Jack Lewis & David E. Steele
Here's the latest information (specifications, applications, etc.) on the world's assault weapons, reported in-depth by retired Marine Jack Lewis. Exclusive, detailed coverage of today's military and police weaponry from France, Germany, Russia, South Africa and the USA. Broad coverage of rifles, submachine guns, crew-served machine guns, combat shotguns - plus an educated look into the 21st century.
Softcover • 8-1/2 x 11 • 256 pages
500 b&w photos
Item# AW5 • $21.95

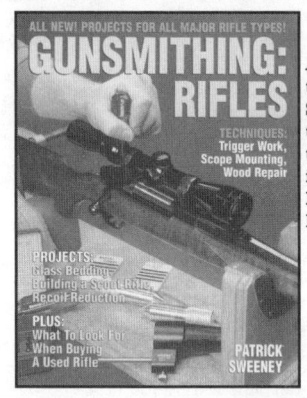

Gunsmithing: Rifles
by Patrick Sweeney
Anyone who owns a rifle will benefit from the information offered on these pages. Step-by-step gunsmithing projects for all types of rifles are presented and fully illustrated with outstanding photography. From improving accuracy to reducing recoil, this book will help every rifle owner put more bullets on target.
Softcover • 8-1/2 x 11 • 352 pages
700 b&w photos
Item# GRIF • $24.95

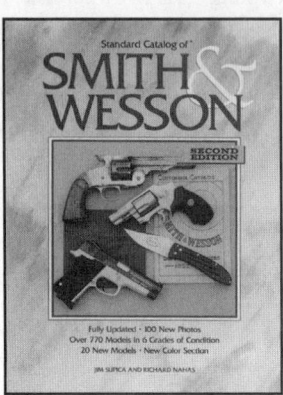

Standard Catalog of® Smith & Wesson
2nd Edition
by Jim Supica & Richard Nahas
This newly updated second edition provides accurate pricing in up to five grades of condition for more than 775 models of guns and variations produced by Smith & Wesson between 1857 and 2001. For easy reference, guns are listed by model and year of manufacture with range of serial numbers by year. Production and historical notes provide important background information for determining rarity.
Hardcover • 8-1/4 x 10-7/8 • 272 pages
350 b&w photos • 16-page color section
Item# FSW02 • $34.95

To place a credit card order or for a FREE all-product catalog call

800-258-0929 Offer GNB1

M-F 7am - 8pm • Sat 8am - 2pm, CST

Krause Publications, Offer GNB1
P.O. Box 5009, Iola WI 54945-5009
www.krausebooks.com

DBI BOOKS
a division of Krause Publications, Inc.

Shipping & Handling: $4.00 first book, $2.00 each additional.
Non-US addresses $20.95 first book, $5.95 each additional.

Sales Tax: CA, IA, IL, PA, TN, VA, WI residents please add appropriate sales tax.

Satisfaction Guarantee: If for any reason you are not completely satisfied with your purchase, simply return it within 14 days of receipt and receive a full refund, less shipping charges.